Are you interested in

a course management system that would

save you time & effort?

If the answer is *yes*, **CourseCompass is for you.**

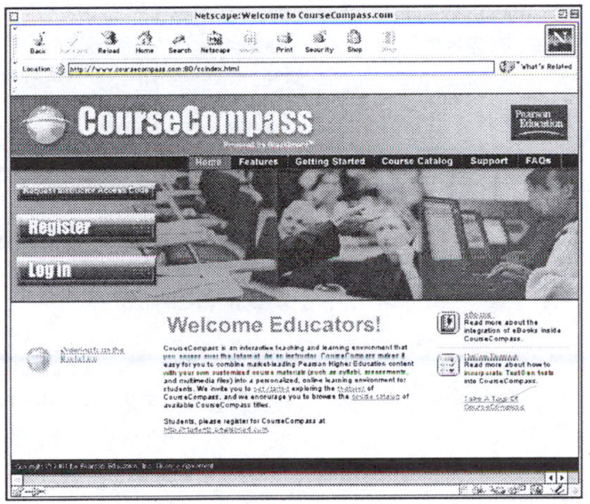

Contact your local Allyn & Bacon/Longman sales representative for a free access code, or visit www.coursecompass.com, and take a tour of this course management system.

Technical support is available for faculty and students:

support@coursecompass.com
1-800-677-6337

CourseCompass is an online course management system designed to help you manage all the aspects of your course – communication, information distribution, testing and grading.

Let it help you:

- **Communicate directly with your students** via email, discussion boards, and announcement pages.
- **Post documents for your course,** eliminating the need for course packs or handouts.
- **Administer online tests,** with automatic grading and analysis.
- **Provide your students with 24/7 access** to key course information, such as syllabus, assignments, and additional resources – as well as check his/her grade instantly.

Demo CourseCompass today! www.coursecompass.com

Best-Selling Professional Resources for College Instructors!

As the world's leader in education, Allyn & Bacon understands your interest in continual professional development. From the latest advancements in technology for the classroom to special insights for adjunct professors, these books were written for you!

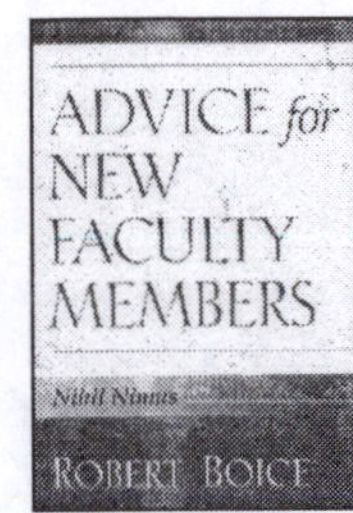

Instructing and Mentoring the African American College Student: Strategies for Success in Higher Education
Louis B. Gallien, Jr., Regent University and
Marshalita Sims Peterson, Ph.D, Spelman College
©2005 / 0-205-38917-1

Grant Writing in Higher Education:
A Step-by-Step Guide
Kenneth Henson, The Citadel
©2004 / 0-205-38919-8

Using Technology in Learner-Centered Education:
Proven Strategies for Teaching and Learning
David G. Brown and Gordon McCray, both of Wake Forest University, Craig Runde, Eckerd College and Heidi Schweizer, Marquette University
©2002 / 0-205-35580-3

Creating Learning-Centered Courses
for the World Wide Web
William B. Sanders, University of Hartford
©2001 / 0-205-31513-5

Success Strategies for Adjunct Faculty
Richard Lyons, Faculty Development Associates
©2004 / 0-205-36017-3

The Effective, Efficient Professor:
Teaching, Scholarship and Service
Philip C. Wankat, Purdue University
©2002 / 0-205-33711-2

Emblems of Quality in Higher Education:
Developing and Sustaining High-Quality Programs
Jennifer Grant Haworth, Loyola University, Chicago and
Clifton F. Conrad, University of Wisconsin, Madison,
©1997 / 0-205-19546-6

Faculty of Color in Academe: Bittersweet Success
Caroline Sotello Viernes Turner, Arizona State University
and Samuel L. Myers Jr., University of Minnesota
©2000 / 0-205-27849-3

An Introduction to Interactive Multimedia
Stephen J. Misovich, Jerome Katrichis, David Demers, William B. Sanders, all of the University of Hartford
©2003 / 0-205-34373-2

Learner-Centered Assessment on College Campuses:
Shifting the Focus from Teaching to Learning
Mary E. Huba, Iowa State University and Jann E. Freed,
Central College
©2000 / 0-205-28738-7

The Online Teaching Guide: A Handbook of Attitudes, Strategies, and Techniques for the Virtual Classroom
Ken W. White and Bob H. Weight, both of University of Phoenix Online Faculty
©2000 / 0-205-29531-2

The Adjunct Professor's Guide to Success:
Surviving and Thriving in the College Classroom
Richard Lyons, Faculty Development Associates, Marcella L. Kysilka, and George E. Pawlas, both of University of Central Florida
©1999 / 0-205-28774-3

Teaching Tips for College and University
Instructors: A Practical Guide
David Royse, University of Kentucky
©2001 / 0-205-29839-7

Advice for New Faculty Members
Robert Boice, Emeritus, SUNY Stony Brook
©2000 / 0-205-28159-1

Writing for Professional Publication:
Keys to Academic and Business Success
Kenneth Henson, The Citadel
©1999 / 0-205-28313-6

Teaching College in an Age of Accountability
Richard Lyons, Faculty Development Associates, Meggin McIntosh, University of Nevada - Reno, and Marcella L. Kysilka, University of Central Florida
©2003 / 0-205-35315-0

Instructor's Manual and Test Bank

for

Schmalleger and Bartollas

Juvenile Delinquency

prepared by

Tom McAninch
Scott Community College

Boston New York San Francisco
Mexico City Montreal Toronto London Madrid Munich Paris
Hong Kong Singapore Tokyo Cape Town Sydney

ISBN-13: 978-0-205-53701-3
ISBN-10: 0-205-53701-4

Printed in the United States of America

10 9 8 7 6 5 4 3 2 1 11 10 09 08 07

Table of Contents

TO THE INSTRUCTOR:

This manual has been prepared to facilitate the effective use of *Juvenile Delinquency*, first edition text for use in the classroom and to enhance the scope of its teachability. This manual is not meant to tell you how to teach, nor is it meant to be exhaustive. Instead, it seeks to provide the user with pedagogical ideas and examples to facilitate the best use of Juvenile Delinquency.

ORGANIZATION OF THE MANUAL

Learning Objectives: This section consists of various statements that students should learn in each chapter.

Chapter Summary: The chapter summary narrates the essential topics contained in each chapter.

Lecture Outline: This section annotates a sequence of major and minor points covered in each chapter under relevant headings and sub-headings.

Key Terms: This section lists and defines various terms used throughout each chapter.

Classroom Activities and Assignments: Assigments are suggested depending on criteria such as available time, relevance, instructor/student interest, and level of class (lower-level or upper-level).

Voices of Delinquency Assignments: Assignments are tailored for use with Voices of Delinquency to increase critical thinking skills of students and dependent upon issues of time, relevance, interest, and level of classroom instruction.

Video and Internet Resources: This section is designed to supplement classroom instruction with specific illustrative video and Internet pedagogical aids strategically selected for use with each chapter.

Test Bank Questions: Four types of evaluation questions are included in the TestGen files: (1) multiple choice, (2) true and false, (3) short-answer essay, and (4) essay questions. The questions are designed to examine issues and conceptualization of ideas throughout each chapter. The wording of each question is carefully chosen as to avoid questions based on gimmicks, nit-picking, or mere guess.

It is my sincere intention that instructors find this manual a valuable classroom supplement in the teaching of juvenile delinquency and related courses. Much time and care has gone into the design of this project to provide instructors with a quality product and I hope I have succeeded. I encourage your feedback and comments. Please direct any comments to drmack716@MSN.com. I want to thank Clemons Bartollas and Frank Schmalleger for allowing me the opportunity to work with them on this project.

CHAPTER 1: ADOLESCENCE AND DELINQUENCY

Learning Objectives

After reading this chapter you should be able to answer the following questions:

1. What does it mean to be an adolescent in American Society today?

2. Are adolescents treated the same now as in the past?

3. What are the problem behaviors that characterize adolescence?

4. How can delinquency be defined?

5. What is a status offense?

6. How have delinquents been handled throughout history?

7. What are the major themes of this text?

CHAPTER SUMMARY

This chapter places delinquent behavior within the wider context of adolescent problem behaviors. Adolescents most likely to become delinquent are high-risk youths who are involved in multiple problem behaviors. Problem behaviors include school failure and dropout, teenage pregnancy and fatherhood, drug use, and delinquency. About one in every four adolescents is at high risk of engaging in multiple problem behaviors.

Bartollas uses a social focus to help understand juvenile delinquency in America. The history of dealing with juvenile misbehavior in the United States has been one of taking authority away from the family and at the same time becoming increasingly dissatisfied with the state's means of handling juvenile crime.

Parens patriae is the legal context and philosophy for dealing with juvenile delinquency, through which the juvenile court becomes a substitute parent for wayward children. The task of juvenile court is to reconcile the best interest of the child with the protection of society. Additionally, juveniles are arrested for *status offenses*, which would not be defined as criminal if adults committed them.

Delinquency in the United States occurs in a social context that has become more and more child oriented. Lower-class youth are often viewed differently by the juvenile system and receive more punitive sanctions. Conversely, middle-and upper-class youth traditionally receive less restrictive sanctions.

However, there is increased concern that society needs to "get tough" on juvenile crime. The present focus is on serious and repeat juvenile offenders. Both the public and its policymakers attempt to hold juvenile offenders accountable for violent crimes through tough sanctions.

Bartollas purports a major goal of this text is to reduce the social cost of letting vast numbers of young people grow up without realizing their potential. Equally, Bartollas proposes the means by with youngsters in our society can realize their potential and lead productive and satisfying lives.

LECTURE OUTLINE

I. Introduction

- A term used to define the life interval between childhood and adulthood.
- Lengthening of adolescence in U.S. culture increases crisis and struggles.
- Unmet childhood needs fester into socially unacceptable behaviors.

II. The Changing Treatment of Adolescents

- The end of child labor (1914) was a watershed in the development of modern adolescence.
- Compulsory education laws held that adolescents needed guidance and control.
- Legal protections in the 1960s and 1970s highlighted special attention and support.
- Erickson suggested childhood repression due to lack of young people's rights.
- Influence of economic, social and political forces.

III. Youth at Risk

- Nanette J. Davis suggests *"structural arrangements"* of racial discrimination, poverty, violence, and drugs/alcohol leads to invisible youth crisis. American institutions contribute to crisis.
- Warehousing approach for juvenile delinquents.

A. High-Risk Behaviors

- High-risk youths experience multiple difficulties such as economically stressed families, physical/sexual abuse, educational/vocational deficits, and drug/alcohol abuse.
- Gottfredson and Hirschi suggest lack of self-control as a common factor for high-risk behavior.
- One in four adolescence is at high risk of engaging in multiple problem behaviors.
- Delinquency is a legal term from Illinois 1899 law.
- Juveniles are five times more likely to be arrested for property crimes than violent crimes.
- *Status offenses* are acts related to age, meaning they would not be defined criminal if committed by adults.
- Three times as many youths are arrested for committing status offenses as violent crime.

IV. Juvenile Court Codes and Definitions of delinquency

- Rehabilitative laws based on the philosophy of *Parens Patriae* were enacted to eliminate arbitrary treatment of juveniles.
- Court has jurisdiction in delinquency, dependency, and neglect cases.
- Diverse definitions of delinquency have developed.
- Controversy surrounds the issue of how long juveniles should remain under control of the court.

V. What is a Status Offense?

- Various definitions of delinquency in juvenile codes (see Box 1.2)
- Delinquency in America: Rise in Income Improves Children's Behavior

A. Explanations For Status Offense Behavior

- Many come from single-parent homes.
- Parents view status offenders as defiant, demanding, and obnoxious, leading to struggles.
- Status offenders often are hyperactive and treated with Ritalin.
- Chesney-Lind suggests a double standard for female status offenders.

B. Offense Behavior of Status Offenders and Delinquents

- Charles W. Thomas contends status offender's progress to delinquent offenses.
- National study of status offenders identified three groups: "heavies", "lightweights" and "conforming youths." This study disputes a linkage between status and delinquent offenses.
- In sum, status offenders are *not* likely to escalate to more serious behaviors.

C. Social Control and the Status Offender

- Confining of status offenders comes under attack in the 1970s. Offenders stayed longer in training schools than delinquents and institutionalization became destructive.
- 1974 Juvenile Justice and Delinquency Act was an impetus for *deinstitutionalization*.
- *Deinstitutionalization of Status Offenders Project (DSO)* revealed little change in the processing of status offenders. In fact, detention of African-American status offenders increased.
- Redefining status offenders as "delinquent" allows for *invisible institutionalization*.
- Some states have decriminalized status offenses.

VI. The Handling of Juvenile Delinquents

A. The Colonial Period (1636-1823)

- Family is the primary source for social control of children. Young chronic offenders were disciplined in public view, such as whippings, dunkings, the stocks and expulsion from the community.

B. The Houses of Refuge Period (1824-1898)

- Disillusioned with family, *houses of refuge* were proposed. Intended to protect children from weak and criminal parents.
- Discipline was firm and harsh. Family authority is superseded by that of the State.

C. The Juvenile Court Period (1899-1966)

- First juvenile court in Cook County, Illinois 1899 is based on the legal concept of *parens patriae*.
- Wayward children were considered "wards of the state" and less responsible for their actions.
- Poverty, ills of city life, inadequate families, schools, and neighborhoods are contributing factors.

D. The Juvenile Rights Period (1967-1975)

- The courts are accused of capricious and arbitrary justice. Supreme Court hands down several landmark cases to ensure children will have *due process*.
- Community based programs receive enthusiastic responses. Some believed training schools would eventually be phased out.

E. The Reform Agenda of the Late 1970s

- The major purpose is to divert status offenses from a criminal to a noncriminal setting.
- Discourage the practice of jailing juveniles and encouraged community-based services.

- Liberal blunder of failing to pay attention to serious juvenile crime became an Achilles' heel.

F. Social Control and Juvenile Crime in the 1980s

- Public demands for something to be done about serious juvenile crime.
- 1984 National Advisory Committee for *Juvenile Justice and Delinquency Prevention* (NAC) leads to a focus on serious, violent, and chronic offenders. Rejects deinstitutionalization.
- Teen pregnancies, drug/alcohol abuse, and teen suicides fueled a time of "*getting tough.*"
- Growing acceptance of parents needing to be stricter with their children.
- Reagan administration encourages five trends: (1) preventative detention; (2) transfer violent juveniles to adult court; (3) mandatory/determinate sentencing; (4) increased confinement; and (5) enforcement of the death penalty.

G. Contemporary Delinquency and U.S. Society

- The "crack epidemic" becomes a major impetus for the spread of drug trafficking street gangs.
- Use of guns and drugs contribute to increased murder rates among young people.
- States pass legislation leading to nine initiatives in juvenile justice: (1) curfews; (2) parental responsibility laws; (3) combating street gangs; (4) the movement toward graduated sanctions; (5) juvenile boot camps; (6) youth and guns; (7) juvenile proceedings; (8) juvenile transfer to criminal courts, and (9) expanded sentencing authority.

VII. Themes in the Study of Delinquency

A. Focus on Social Context

- Historical context influences current perceptions.
- Legal context establishes the definition of delinquent behavior.
- Sociocultural context examines the relationship between social institutions and delinquency.
- Economic context examines conditions and factors in which delinquents live.
- Political context shapes local and national policy decisions on youth crime.
- A contextual analysis reminds students of delinquency that a variety of forces on several levels affect youth crime.

B. Delinquency International

- Young killers at heart of capital punishment fight in Japan

C. Delinquency Across the Life Course

- Glen H. Elder Jr. identified four key factors that determine life course: 1) location in time and place, 2) linked lives, 3) human agency, and 4) timing of lives.
- All levels of social action interact and mutually influence each other as a result of contact with other individuals sharing similar experiences.

D. Policy Oriented Analysis

- Designing of recommendations that provide helpful directions for dealing effectively with adolescents in general and particularly those rendered delinquent.

Key Terms

Adolescence: The life interval between childhood and adulthood, usually the period between the ages of twelve and eighteen years.

Deinstitutionalization of Status Offender Project (DSO): A project that evaluated the effects of deinstitutionalization of status offenders in eight states and prompter a national evaluation.

Houses of Refuge: Institutions that were designed by eighteenth-a and nineteenth-century reformers to provide an orderly disciplined environment similar to that of the "ideal" Puritan family.

Human Agency: The active role juveniles take in their lives; the fact that juveniles are not merely subject to social and structural constraints but make choices and decisions based on the alternatives that they see before them.

Juvenile: A youth at or below the upper age of juvenile court jurisdiction in a particular state.

Juvenile Delinquency: An act committed by a minor that violates the penal code of the government with authority over the area in which the act occurs.

Juvenile Justice and Delinquency Prevention Act of 1974: A federal law that established a juvenile justice office within the Law Enforcement Assistance Administration to provide funds for the prevention and control of youth crime.

Life Course Perspective: A sociological framework suggesting that four key factors determine the shape of the life course: location in time and place, linked lives, human agency, and timing of lives.

***Parens Patriae*:** A Medieval English doctrine that sanctioned the right of the Crown to intervene in natural family relations whenever a child's welfare was threatened. The philosophy of the juvenile court is based on this legal concept.

Status Offender: A juvenile who commits a minor act that is considered illegal only because he or she is underrate. Various terms used to refer to status offenders in clued MINS (minors I need of supervision), CHINS (children in need of supervision), CHINA (children in need of assistance), PINS (persons in need of supervision), FINS (families in need of supervision), and JINS (juveniles in need of supervision).

Status Offense: A nondelinquent/noncriminal offense; an offense that is illegal for underage persons, but not for adults. Status offenses include curfew violations, incorrigibility, running away, truancy, and underage drinking.

CLASSROOM ACTIVITIES AND ASSIGNMENTS

1. Ask students to compare the adolescence period in the United States with that of other nations. Have them compare and contrast any ritualistic (rites of passage) behavior used by both Americans and foreign children.

2. Ask students as a group or individually to research the use of the death penalty in America in regard to juvenile offenders. Students can investigate how many states have executed juveniles and what offenses are subject to the death penalty in each state.

3. Have students list the pros and cons of anti-smoking laws in America. Students can use this concept to help them understand policy formation of laws regarding status offenses.

4. Ask students to discuss or write an essay on how elimination of the juvenile justice system in America would affect their lives.

5. Have students discuss whether they believe parent(s) should be criminally and civilly liable for a child's criminal behavior.

6. Have students discuss or write about the pros and cons of curfew laws. Students can relate to their own experiences for this assignment.

7. Have students compare and contrast modern day punishment of juvenile offenders with that of the colonial period. How would they feel if they were placed in stocks in the center of campus for cheating on an exam?

8. Ask students to research juvenile boot camps to ascertain their success or failure rate in America. Why do they think boot camps may or may not be useful in today's society?

VOICES OF DELINQUENCY ASSIGNMENTS

Have students read article 2 titled: *A Naïve Offender* and answer the following discussion questions.

1. List the multiple problem behaviors this individual reports becoming involved in. How many of those behaviors are actually considered as criminal or delinquent? Conversely, how many of those behaviors are actually status offenses?

2. Ask students to define a *naïve offender*. Is this person justifying their own lack of self-responsibility at the expense of others?

3. Have students prepare a mock-probation report on this person in which they can choose either treatment or punishment. What course of action would they take with this offender?

VIDEO AND INTERNET RESOURCES

Catching Them Early: In Richmond, California gang violence, drug abuse, and teen pregnancy are daily realities for at-risk youth. But this cycle of despair is being broken by a coalition of community agencies.
The methods used by various agencies are revealed to teach children life skills, love, and how to provide emotional support. Early intervention is the core message of this video. (58 minutes) *Films for the Humanities and Sciences*.

Young, Armed and Dangerous: Fort Worth, Texas is trying to deter young offenders from a life of crime and a lifetime of prison by focusing on the social, economic, and psychological causes of violence. (58 minutes) *Films for the Humanities and Sciences*.

Fatherless in America: Increasingly, fathers are not present much beyond the act of procreation. This video examines the problem, its causes, and its effects from poverty to violence. It also looks at reversing the growing trend of fatherlessness in America. (26 minutes) *Films for the Humanities and Sciences*.

Talk 16 and Talk 19 Adolescent Girls: Two videos of five different girls were interviewed when they were 16 and then again when they turned 19. They were interviewed at home, school, work, and with peers. The girls openly share their inner most thoughts about boys, drugs, peer pressure and self-esteem. (48/116 minutes) *Filmakers Library*.

WEBSITES

Visit the Office of Juvenile Justice and Delinquency Prevention (OJJDP) Web site via www. justicestudies.com/WebPlaces

Visit the Youth Risk Behavior Surveillance System (YRBSS) Web site, part of the Centers for Disease Control and Prevention, via www.justicestudeies.com/ WebPlaces

Visit the Child Trends databank, with the latest national trends and research on over 100 key indicators of child and youth well-being, via www.justicestudies.com/WebPlaces.

Visit the U.S. department of health and Human Services (HHS) Child Welfare Information gateway via justicestudies.com/WebPlaces

View the OJJDP PowerPoint presentation " Juvenile Population Characteristics," at justicestudies.com/WebPlaces

www.barefootsworld.net/parensp.html

www.ncjrs.org

CHAPTER 2: THE MEASUREMENT AND NATURE OF DELINQUENCY

LEARNING OBJECTIVES

After reading this chapter you should be able to answer the following questions:

1. What do official and unofficial statistics tell us about the extent of juvenile delinquency?
2. Is juvenile violent crime increasing in the United States?
3. How do such social factors as gender, racial and ethnic backgrounds, and social class relate to juvenile delinquency?
4. What other dimensions of offending appear to be important in delinquent behavior?
5. Why do the majority of juvenile offenders exit from delinquent activity by the end of their adolescent years?

CHAPTER SUMMARY

This chapter discusses the various official and unofficial methods used to measure juvenile delinquency. Official methods of measure include *Uniform Crime Reports, Juvenile Court Statistics, self-report and victimization studies (NCVS).* All of which have contributed to a number of important findings about youth crime in the United States. Measurement methods are commonly affected by *validity* and *reliability* problems.

The various forms of statistics on juvenile delinquency have far more agreement than disagreement and seek to answer pressing questions about juvenile delinquency. The studies have suggested that rates of delinquency in the United States have either leveled off or are declining. Homicide rates have declined rather dramatically since 1993 and the resurgence of a violent crime wave is unlikely to materialize in the near future. There is little evidence to support that there are more juvenile "monsters" than in the past. However, gang members and other serious offenders continue to commit brutal crimes.

Research indicates juveniles commit a disproportionate number of property and violent offenses, carry more guns than in the past, and youth crime is primarily focused in the lower-class youths. Additionally, males commit more delinquent acts than females, nonwhites more frequent and serious acts than whites, and urban youths commit more serious acts than rural youths do.

Intervention strategies by the juvenile justice system frequently make behaviors worse rather than better. Some evidence exits that youthful offenders progress to increasingly serious forms of delinquent behaviors. Youths who begin offending early tend to have long delinquent careers. Delinquents generally show a great deal of versatility, rather than specialization, in committing offenses.

Life Course criminology is concerned with explaining individual changes in offending throughout life. *Desistance*, or terminating delinquent behavior, is strongly related to the maturation process. In the midst of the continuity of childhood antisocial behavior, some adults experience *turning points*, or change, usually related to such matters as stable jobs, or a satisfying marriage or family life.

LECTURE OUTLINE

I. Introduction

- *Prevalence of delinquency* related to proportion of cohort and specific age.
- *Incidence of delinquency* refers to the frequency of offending or number of events.

II. Measuring Delinquency

- 1870 Congress created Department of Justice for federal record keeping.
- Creation of *Uniform Crime Reports* and the FBI to serve as clearinghouse for data.
- UCR's only measure reported crime, not hidden delinquency.
- Problems of UCR's include underestimating crime and police manipulation.
- Amnesty Program Takes Ai at UK's "knife Culture"

A. Crime by Age Groups

- Juveniles ages ten to seventeen are 29.8 percent of all arrests in U.S.
- Juveniles account for 33 percent of all burglary arrests, 25 percent of all robbery arrests, 24 percent of weapon arrests, 14 percent of aggravated assault and 9 percent of murder arrests.
- Between 1993 and 2003 juvenile arrests for murder declined about one-fourth.
- Juveniles were 13.8 percent of all drug arrests in 2002.
- Nonwhites are arrested in higher proportions for violent crimes than whites. Amnesty Program takes Aim at UK's "Knife Culture".

B. Youth Crime Trends

- Per UCR's Part I juvenile arrests declined from 45 percent to 27.5 percent between 1971 and 2005. Property crimes declined from 51 percent to 32 percent
- Alfred Blumstein predicts more guns will lead to crime wave in ten to fifteen years.
- James Alan Fox predicts juvenile violence will increase by 2005.
- Reduction in violent crime related to more effective gun policies, increased incarceration, more effective policing, more services, and maturation of crime-prone age groups.

III. Juvenile Court Statistics

- Inaugurated in 1926 by Children's Bureau of the Department of Labor for the general nature and extent of problems brought before the juvenile court.
- Statistical problems include time lag, small percentage of total offenses, and represent only an estimate of actual crimes before the court.
- Drug offenses showed a dramatic increase between 1987 and 1999.

IV. Cohort Studies

- *Cohort* is a group who has something in common such as age, high school, arrest dates and are studied over time.
- Findings indicate that most serious offenses are committed by lower-class minority males.
- Punishment by the system tends to encourage future criminality.
- Males commit more serious offenses than females.

V. Self-Reports and Official Statistics Compared

A. Reliability and Validity of Self Report Studies

- *Validity* is questionable in self-report studies
- *Reliability* refers to consistency of a questionnaire or interview responses.

B. Findings of Self-Report Studies

- Porterfield's first study of hidden delinquency concluded delinquency is widespread and that no relationship exists between social class and delinquency.
- Recent self-report studies suggest a large portion of juveniles commit violent acts.
- The Denver study suggests a smaller percentage of serious delinquents are using harder drugs.
- The Pittsburgh study reports that African-American boys committed more serious acts of delinquency than white boys (51 percent compared to 28 percent).
- The Rochester study reports levels of attachment and involvement are related to delinquency.

C. Youth Crime Trends

- Illicit drug use peaked around 1979 and declined into the 1990s.
- Marijuana use increases from 1992-1996.

VI. Victimization Surveys

- Began in 1972 in conjunction with the Census Bureau.
- Respondents are asked about perception of crime, extent of fear, and attitudes about crime.
- Limitations include no information on status offenses, victimless crimes, and inaccurate accounts.
- Per the NCVS violent crime fell 54 percent and property crime declined 50 percent between 1993 and 2002.
- African-American males more likely than whites to be victims of violent crime.
- Being victimized increases ones likelihood of offending.
- Victimization findings include more crime is committed than reported. Where one lives will increase/decrease the probability of being victimized. Theft crimes of less than $250 is the most frequently committed crime. Juveniles are more likely to commit crimes than other age groups. African-Americans and females are more likely to report crime.

VII. Social Factors related to Delinquency

A. Gender and Delinquent Behavior

- According to the Per UCR males are arrested more than females.

- Males are likely to be arrested for stolen property, vandalism, weapon offenses, and assaults. Seven times more likely for drug offenses and five times more likely for violent offenses than females.
- Females are likely to be arrested for running away, and prostitution.
- Gender, race, and class create a "*multiple marginality*" per Meda Chesney-Lind.

B. Racial/Ethnic Background and Delinquent Behavior

- African-Americans are arrested more frequently than whites, however self-report measures indicate little difference in involvement exists between African-Americans and whites, per two national studies.
- African-American females are more likely than white females to be victimized by violent crime.

C. Social Class and Delinquency

- Studies suggest that upper-and middle-class juveniles are as delinquent as their lower-class peers.
- Hirschi's survey states that little association exits between income, education, and occupation with delinquency.
- The data provides no firm evidence that social class is a salient factor in delinquency.

VIII. Dimensions of Delinquent Behavior

A. Age of Onset

- Early–onset delinquents tend to persist in offending behavior and are more likely to be arrested.
  The Social World of the delinquent

B. Escalation of Offenses

- Mixed findings reveal that early intervention by the juvenile system may lead to increased delinquency.
- Farrington contends males peak at age seventeen for nonviolent crimes and eighteen for violent crimes.
- Loeber suggests developmental interconnected pathways lead to a delinquent career.

C. Specialization of Offenses

- Most specialized offenses include running away, burglary, motor vehicle theft, drinking liquor, incorrigibility, violating curfew, truancy, and using drugs.
- *Specialization* tends to increase with successive number of referrals.
- Females tend to specialize in running away (status offenses) more than males.
- Recent data suggests early life course offenders are more versatile in their offending than those who begin offending at a later age.

D. Chronic Offending

- *Chronic offenders* constitute the majority of active offenders.
- Chronic offenders are more involved in violent crime and come from ever-growing minority underclass that finds itself trapped.

- Predicting of chronic offending is controversial.

IX. Delinquency the Life Course

- Life course criminology is concerned with explaining individual changes in offending throughout life.
- Relationship of anti-social behavior clusters to delinquency.
- Sampson and Laub contend *turning points* may lead to modifications in behavior.

A. Desistance from Crime

- *Desistance* is the age of termination from crime.
- Maturation towards pursing a conventional lifestyle (Glueck).
- Grove suggests biological and psychological factors play a major role in desistance
- Moffitt contends adolescent limiteds are situational will desist from crime over time compared to persisters who experienced early and long term antisocial behaviors.

KEY TERMS

age of onset The age at which a youth performs their first criminal offense.

chronic youthful offenders Youth involved in serious and repetitive offenses

cohort A group of individuals having one or more statistical factors in common in a demographic study.

cohort study Individuals who are usually born in a particular year in a particular city or county and studied by researchers throughout part or all of their lives.

desistance The age at which an offender is no longer performing delinquent acts.

escalation of offenses Offenses increase in severity from one age to the next.

hidden delinquency Unobserved or unreported delinquency.

incidence of delinquency Frequency of offending or the number of delinquent events.

juvenile court statistics Records the number of children appearing before the court each year.

prevalence of delinquency Refers to the number of young people involved in delinquent behavior.

reliability The extent to which a questionnaire or interview yields the same results two or more times.

self-report studies Studies that ask people to tell about crimes they may have committed in an earlier period of time.

specialization Examines whether youths are involved in one or several types of delinquency.

turning point Displays that some delinquents have a gradual or dramatic change to non-delinquent acts as they move into adulthood.

Uniform Crime Reports The FBI's annual report of crimes committed in the United States.

Validity Issue involving the accuracy of research data concerning self-report truthfulness.

victimization studies (NCVS) Surveys used to determine the extent of criminal victimization in the U.S. by asking people the nature of crimes perpetrated against them.

CLASSROOM ACTIVITIES AND ASSIGNMENTS

1. Ask students to compare and contrast the relative strengths and weaknesses of the various measures of juvenile delinquency.

2. Ask students to anonymously participate in a *victimization study* of minor offenses to illustrate how victimization surveys are conducted.

3. Have students discuss whether they believe early intervention by the juvenile justice system should encourage or discourage youthful offenders in committing delinquent acts.

4. Ask students to anonymously participate in a *self-report study* of status or petty offenses to illustrate how self-report studies can reveal hidden delinquency.

5. Have students discuss the positive and negative effects of *peer relations* on juvenile behavior.

6. Ask students to log onto www.ojp.usdoj.gov/bjs/ and compare victimization statistics for various juvenile crimes.

7. Have students correlate a famous adult offender with the notion of *age of onset,* and ask them to discuss the relevance of offending beginning at an early age.

8. Ask students to discuss *prevalence of delinquency* as it relates to modern gang activities.

VOICES OF DELINQUENCY ASSIGNMENTS

Have students read article 21 titled: Forgotten Children and answer the following questions.

1. Discuss how the juvenile system may have failed this individual.

2. How instrumental were peer relations in creating delinquency within this person?

3. What treatments or actions may have helped prevent this person's criminal career?

VIDEO AND INTERNET RESOURCES

Little Criminals: In California, a six-year old boy entered the home of a neighbor to steal a tricycle and savagely beat a 30-day-old infant. He became the youngest person in the United States to be charged with attempted murder. This PBS video examines violent crimes by young offenders. (60 minutes) *Insight Media.*

Juvenile Justice in the United States: This video presents a history of progress in the American juvenile justice system over the past 200 years. It examines children's welfare, constitutional rights, and treatment focused on reform. (24 minutes) *Insight Media.*

Boys and Guns: ABC News anchor Diane Sawyer investigates the dangerous fascination kids have with guns. A judge, a neuropsychiatrist, and an NRA spokesman comment from different perspectives to help parents understand this behavior. (22 minutes) *Films for the Humanities and Sciences.*

Old Enough to Do Time: This documentary concludes that by locking up juveniles we gain some short relief from crime, but in the long run we may be giving up on children who could have been turned around. (55 minutes) *Filmakers Library.*

WEBSITES

View the OJJDP PowerPoint presentation "Juvenile Offender" by going to www.justicestudies.com/WebPlaces

www.fbi.gov/ucr/ucr95prs.htm

www.icpsr.umich.edu/NACJD/SDA/ncvs.html

CHAPTER 3: INDIVIDUAL CAUSES OF DELINQUENCY

LEARNING OBJECTIVES

After reading this chapter, you should be able to answer the following questions:

1. What role does free will have in the classical school's understanding of criminal or delinquent behavior?

2. What are the main forms of positivism? How does each form explain delinquent behavior?

3. How does rational choice theory differ from positivism?

4. What type of delinquencies are more likely to be brought about by biological factors?

5. Which type of delinquents are more likely to be held responsible for their actions?

CHAPTER SUMMARY

In *biological* and *psychological positivism* the question of what causes delinquency is answered by focusing on biological and psychological factors within the individual. This micro-perspective view suggests that all behavior, including delinquency, is seen as having an organic or psychological basis. This view is *deterministic*, in that the delinquent is perceived as being controlled by such factors in which they have no control.

Biological and psychological factors are sometimes elusive. For example, an *autonomic nervous system* that is difficult to condition, or an inadequately developed *superego*. Yet, others are more easily discerned, such as inappropriate interpersonal relationships. Both early biological and psychological positivism theories have developed into more complex explanations of delinquent behavior. Early biological positivism was replaced by *sociobiology*. *Psychoanalysis* was replaced by modes that are less intrapsychic and more oriented to the interactions between the individual and environment.

The punishment model of old has regained popularity in dealing with juvenile crime and serious delinquent acts. Policymakers are concluding that increasing the costs associated with serious youth crime is the only way to reduce youth crime in the United States. To justify the punishment of juveniles, some theorists have returned to the classical school of criminology and its modern version of rational choice theory. Both make the assertion that individuals have *free will* and therefore are responsible for their behavior. Thus, delinquent behavior is viewed as purposeful and a result of rational decision-making.

LECTURE OUTLINE

I. The Classical School and Delinquency

- Montesquieu began the debate of government's role in punishment of criminals
- Beccaria viewed the legitimacy of criminal sanctions based on the *social contract*.
- Bentham viewed contended punishment would deter persons from crime based on rationality.
- Punishment should: (1) prevent all offenses, (2) persuade those committing offenses to commit less serious ones, (3) do no more mischief than necessary, and (4) prevent crime at a cheap cost.
- The doctrine of *free will* and *utilitarianism* of punishment.
- *Felicific calculus* of balancing pleasure and pain.

II. The Rationality of Crime

- Ecological research and selection of suitable crime targets by rational offenders.
- Economic analysis and responses to incentives and deterrents by rational decision making.

A. Rational Choice Theory

- Cook's *criminal opportunity theory*; targets that offer the highest payoff with smallest amount of risk.
- Cohen/Felson's routine activity approach; increase in suitable targets and decrease in guardians, presence of motivated offenders.
- Association of rationality and free will.
- Some studies suggest delinquent behavior is largely not planned, but spur-of-the-moment.
- Youngsters appear not to be able to control emotions as exemplified in compulsive behaviors.
- Influence of peer groups may lead youngsters to bypass a rational process.

B. Is Delinquent Behavior Rational?

- Antisocial behavior often appears purposeful and rational.
- Persistent offenders often desist from crime as they mature.
- Many youth do not exhibit signs of having free will to commit crime, especially when many delinquent acts are impulsive in nature.
- Robert Agnew suggests freedom of choice varies from one individual to another depending on biological, psychological, and sociological factors.

III. Positivism and Delinquency

A. Development of Positivism

- The causes of human behavior can be modified to eliminate societal problems.
- *Positivism* dominant philosophy at beginning of twentieth century (Progressive era).
- Three assumptions: (1) backgrounds of individuals explain behaviors, (2) behavior is determined by prior causes, and (3) the delinquent is fundamentally different.

B. Early Theories of Biological Positivism

- Nature v. nurture debate.
- Lombroso and the *born criminal* (atavistic).
- Theory could not stand test of scientific investigation (Ferri and Goring).
- Lombroso's contributions include studying individuals and using control groups.
- Goddard's genealogical study of *feebleminded boys* and "badstock."
- Sheldon and body types; *endomorphic, mesomorphic, ectomorphic*.
- Mesomorphic more likely to be delinquent (most aggressive of the types)
- Sheldon's work cited for numerous flaws, too subjective and inaccurate.

C. Sociobiology and Contemporary Biological Positivism

- Stresses interaction between biological factors and influence of environments.
- Relationship of identical twins and adoption studies to delinquency.
- West/Farrington and IQ studies characterize criminals as having low IQ's.
- Wilson/Herrnstein suggested an inverse relationship between school and IQ.
- Eysenck and *autonomic nervous system*, suggesting that *extroverts* are more difficult to condition than *introverts*. Extroverts more likely to be involved with delinquency.
- Moffit's developmental theory: (1) develops lifelong paths at early age (LCP), and (2) develops during adolescent years (AL) delinquents.
- Kandel/Mednick and study of Danish birth cohort suggest pregnancy/delivery events predicted adult violent offending.
- Difficulty of children staying on task and hyperactivity due to attention deficit disorder with hyperactivity (ADHD).
- Learning disabilities (LD) impede learning and may be linked to delinquency.
- Orthomolecular deficits and excesses may contribute to delinquency.

D. Psychological Positivism

- Freud; (1) personality has three components, (2) three psychosexual stages of development, and (3) personality traits developed in early childhood.
- The *id* (primitive drives), *ego* and *superego* (controlling agents of the id)
- Freud's four constructs; (1) delinquent behavior is related to neurotic personality development, (2) defective superego, (3) overdeveloped superego, and (4) fixation in early stages lead to lifelong searches for gratification.
- Hindelang suggests delinquents are pleasure-seekers more than nondelinquents and willing to take a risk for the sake of such experiences.
- Katz's Seduction of Crime purports an emotional process of seduction and compulsion.
- According to Katz, crimes are sensually compelling for some delinquents.
- Glueck's personality of delinquents are defiant, ambivalent about authority, extroverted, fearful of failure, resentful, hostile, suspicious, and defensive.
- Psychopaths (*sociopaths*) are undomesticated children with no sense of trust in adults.
- Wilson/Herrnstein's *reinforcement theory*; rewards of crime are found in material gain, revenge against an enemy, peer approval, and sexual gratification. Critics of Wilson/Herrnstein say they factor society out of their consideration of crime.
- Developmental Theories of delinquency
- Moffit's Trajectories of Offending
- Tremblay's Trajectories of Offending
- The Cambridge Study of delinquent Development

KEY TERMS

attention deficit disorder Disorder of children that can include inattention, distractibility, excessive activity, restlessness, noisiness, and impulsiveness.

autonomic nervous system Hans Eysenks's theory that holds that there is a relationship between delinquency and both biological and environmental factors, affecting extroverts and introverts differently.

biological positivism The belief that biological limitations may lead juveniles to delinquency.

born criminal Lombroso claimed some criminals are atavistic or a reversion to an earlier evolutionary level.

criminal opportunity theory Phillip J. Cook suggests that criminals tend to be attracted to targets that offer high payoffs with little risk of legal consequences.

determinism A view that an individual's acts are determined by a preexisting biological, psychological, or sociological condition beyond the individual's control.

emotionality An aspect of temperament; can range from near absence of emotional response to intense, out-of-control emotions.

felicific calculus A notion that holds that human beings are oriented toward obtaining a favorable balance of pleasure and pain.

free will A belief purported by the *Classical School of Criminology* which holds that juveniles are rational creatures who are free to choose their own actions and therefore should be held responsible for their behavior.

learning disabilities Disorders in one or more of the basic psychological processes involved in understand or using spoken or written language. Some support exists for a theorized link between juvenile delinquency and learning disabilities.

orthomolecular imbalances Chemical imbalances in the body, resulting from poor nutrition, allergies, and exposure to lead and certain other substances, which are said to lead to delinquency.

positivism The view that once human behavior can be understood in a scientific sense, that behavior can be modified to eliminate many of society's problems, such as delinquency.

Progressive Era The period from around 1890 to 1920 , when a wave of optimism swept through American society and led to the acceptance of positivism. The emerging social sciences assured reformers that through positivism society's problems could be solved.

progressivism The belief that through positivism society can be improved.

psychoanalysis Techniques developed by psychologists for examining the subconscious and how it relates to human behavior.

psychoanalytic theory Sigmund Freud's insights. Which have helped shape the handling of juvenile delinquents. They include these axioms: (1) the personality is made up of three components-id, ego, and superego; (2) all normal children pass through three psychosexual stages of development-oral, anal, and phallic; and (3) a person's personality traits are developed in early childhood.

reinforcement theory Wilson and Herrnstein's theory that suggests that behavior is governed by its consequences of rewards and punishments.

routine activity approach Lawrence E. Cohen and Marcus Felson contend that crime rate trends and cycles are affected by the routine activity structure of American society.

social contract A view that purports humans are rational creatures willing to surrender enough liberty to the state, so that society can establish sanctions for the preservation of social order.

sociobiology An expression of biological positivism that stresses interaction between biological factors within an individual and the influence of a particular environment.

sociopath Emotionally deprived children with little or no sense of remorse who frequently become delinquent. Also referred to as psychopaths within the discipline of psychology.

trait-based personality models Theories that attribute delinquent behavior to an individual's basic, inborn personal characteristics.

utilitarianism A doctrine which holds that the useful is the good, and that the aim of social or political action should be the greatest good for the greatest number.

CLASSROOM ACTIVITIES AND ASSIGNMENTS

1. Ask students to list any bizarre behaviors they did in the past few months and have them assess how much rational choice went into their decisions.

2. Have students research any legal defenses used by criminal offenders based on biological or psychological factors which imply legal intent was mitigated by compulsion or mental defect.

3. Ask students to discuss whether the death penalty should be used for youthful offenders based on the notion of biological or psychological inferiority and the assumption one may not get well.

4. Have students research any government sponsored treatment programs (past and current) that were based on the notion of biological or psychological defects.

5. Ask students to debate addiction to drugs/alcohol from a psychological (medical model) point of view and the sociological (ritualism) point of view and whether courts should consider either view when sentencing juvenile offenders.

6. Ask students to discuss the pro and cons of medicating hyperactive children with medications such as Ritalin.
7. Have students conduct a survey of parents or adults in regard to whether they believe that "sugar highs" are real in children or just an imagined cause of hyperactivity.

8. Have students research the topic of "serial murder" to ascertain if the FBI purports that most serial murderers possess any physical defects much like Lombroso once purposed.

VOICES OF DELINQUENCY ASSIGNMENTS

Have students read article 1 titled: What Would I Say to Urban Kids and answer the following questions.

1. Ask students to discuss how this individual made a rational choice not to get involved in crime.

2. Ask students to define what this person means by the term "mental slavery," and does it only exist for urban kids?

3. Ask students to discuss the interaction of environmental and biological factors (sociobiology) that may have been instrumental in keeping this individual law-abiding.

VIDEO AND INTERNET RESOURCES

He Killed His Father: He was only 14 years old, but Elec Trubilla was old enough to take part in a plan to kill his father. Was he really a cold-blooded murderer, or was he a confused kid caught up amidst tragic circumstance? (46 minutes) *Films for the Humanities and Sciences.*

The Mind of a Killer: What compels a seemingly normal person to disregard a fundamental societal principle and commit murder? This video reports on recent scientific research including neurological testing, brain scans, and laboratory studies on animal aggression to shed light on motivation to kill. (46 minutes) *Films for the Humanities and Sciences*

Is Criminal Behavior Genetic?: Are some people born evil? Steve Jones addresses this question by examining the genetic and social factors that contribute to antisocial behavior. Hans Brunner's discovery of the "crime gene" is discussed. (50 minutes) *Films for the Humanities and Sciences.*

Project X: The Castration Experiment: Since 1996 six American states have voted in legislation to castrate sex offenders. Is it treatment or punishment? This video displays how social policy follows timely theories on crime, regardless how weak or poor the theory may be. (51 minutes) *Filmakers Library.*

WEBSITES

www.aecr.org To learn more about the Annie E. Casey Foundation.

www.wholechild.net

www.utilitarinaism.com/mill1.htm To learn more about utilitarianism.

www.pbs.org/wgbh/pages/frontline/angel To learn more about Ernest van den Haag.

CHAPTER 4: SOCIAL STRUCTURAL CAUSES OF DELINQUENCY

LEARNING OBJECTIVES

After reading this chapter, you should be able to answer the following questions:

1. How is cultural deviance theory related to lower-class delinquency?
2. What is the relationship between socially disorganized communities and delinquent behavior?
3. How does strain propel juveniles into delinquency behavior?
4. What delinquent behavior explains homelessness among youth?

CHAPTER SUMMARY

This chapter describes the importance of ecological theories in explaining delinquency. Shaw and McKay, members of the *Chicago School*, showed an association of where a young person lives as having an impact on delinquency. The closer youths live to the inner city, the more likely they are to become involved in delinquency (*social disorganization*). The explanation for the delinquency in these areas goes beyond that of social disorganization, for a cultural tradition passes these criminogenic norms from one generation to the next.

Merton's social structure and anomie theory states that the social structure of a society influences the behavior that occurs within the society. Youths who are caught in *anomie* or normlessness are more likely to become delinquent. Albert Cohen's theory of lower-class gang cultures (*status frustration*), was influenced by the work of Merton. Cohen suggested that lower-class youth aspire to middle-class values, but their inability to attain them causes an inversion of values in which youths engage in delinquent behavior. Similarly, Cloward and Ohlin argue that youths become involved in delinquent behavior when unable to attain legitimate pursuits and are therefore forced to pursue illegitimate avenues. Conversely, Miller suggests that lower-class youths do not aspire to middle-class values, rather they develop their own set of *focal concerns* which encourage delinquent behavior.

The context of all these theories relates to the structure of society. The structural theories view delinquency as a response to social inequalities. They vary in the mechanisms they describe as mediating the impact of inequalities, but their focus is still to identify an explanation to help one understand delinquent behavior. Social structural theories propose that structural and cultural disorder results in high rates of crime, unsafe and disruptive living conditions, and the breeding ground for unsocialized individuals who strike out against society.

LECTURE OUTLINE

Introduction:

- Four Harlem teenagers accused of murder.

I. Social Disorganization Theory

- Durkheim *anomie/normlessness* resulting from society's failure to regulate its member's attitudes and behaviors.

A. Shaw and McKay

- Shaw and McKay focused on social characteristic of the community.
- Delinquency results from breakdown of social control among primary groups.
- Influences of rapid industrialization, urbanization, and immigration.
- Burgess/Park and *The Chicago School* focus on ecology.
- Burgess and *concentric zones* and relationship to delinquency.
- Shaw/McKay find economic and occupational structure influences delinquency and class position in society.
- *Cultural transmission* of delinquent values from generation to the next.
- The theory lost vitality in the late 1960s, but resurfaced in the 1980s.
- Shaw/McKay influenced multiple levels of analysis and shifted focus on delinquency away from individual and to the larger community.
- *Chicago Area Projects* aimed at reducing delinquency.

B. Evaluation of Shaw and McKay's Disorganization Theory

- The theory provided insight into how people and institutions adapt to their environment
- Critics charge delinquency is viewed as both an example and cause of disorganization
- Delinquency in America: Cities Grapple with Crime by Kids
- Social Policy 4.2 Project on Human Development in Chicago Neighborhoods

II. Cultural Deviance Theory and Delinquency

- View delinquency as an expression of conformity to opposing values and norms.

A. Miller's Lower-Class Culture and Delinquent Values

- *Focal concerns* of the lower-class: trouble, toughness, smartness, excitement, fate, and autonomy.
- Physical prowess is demonstrated by strength and endurance.
- Smartness is necessary to achieve material goods and personal status.
- Search for excitement and thrill typically from alcohol and gambling.
- Social forces over which individuals have little control leads to their destiny.
- Miller contends the lower-class have a distinctive culture of their own.
- One-sex peer groups are a significant structural form in the lower-class community.

B. Evaluation of Miller's Thesis

- Critics charge not all youths are affected by the same subculture values.

- Some youth hold the values and norms of the dominant culture.

III. Strain and Delinquency

- Views delinquency as a consequence of frustration when persons are unable to achieve the goals they desire.

A. Merton's Theory of Anomie

- *Culturally defined goals* as legitimate objectives for society.
- *Institutional means* to achieve the goals are acceptable.
- When culture lacks integration, a state of normlessness/*anomie* occurs.
- Typologies of adaptation; conformity, innovation, ritualism, retreatism, and rebellion.

B. Evaluation of Merton's Theory

- Recent research suggests the predictive power of strain theory has been underestimated

C. Strain Theory and the Individual Level of Analysis

- Research has suggested strain is a better predictor of delinquency than financial goals
- Agnew's revised *general strain theory* with three sources of strain: 1) failure to achieve valued goals, 2) removal of positive stimuli, and 3) presentation of negative stimuli.

D. Cohen's Theory of Delinquent Subcultures

- Lower-class youths are protesting against middle-class goals.
- Experience *status frustration* when unable to achieve the goals.
- *Reaction formation* is used to cope with status frustration.
- Delinquent subculture offers status to lower-class males.
- Nonutilitarian crimes are committed "for the hell of it."
- Subculture characterized by "short-run hedonism."

E. Evaluation of Cohens' Theory

- Cohen's theory views delinquency as a process of interaction.
- Critics charge most delinquent boys become law abiding even though their lower-class status does not change.

F. Cloward and Ohlin's Opportunity Theory

- Conceptualized success and status as separate strivings operating independently of each other.
- Type I and Type II boys are striving to increase their status and values are consistent with the middle-class.
- Type IV tend to avoid conflicts with middle-class institutions and authorities.
- Type III experience greatest conflict and are most likely to be delinquent.
- Criminal subculture based on illegal acts of extortion/fraud/theft for success.
- Conflict subculture consists of violence, force/threats to gain status or "rep."
- Retreatist subculture is concerned with drugs for gaining the "kick."

G. Evaluation of Cloward and Ohlin's Theory

- Critics suggest lower class delinquents may not be talented people with lack of legitimate opportunities, rather delinquents may have limited social and intellectual abilities with low expectations and low aspirations.

IV. Social Stratification and Delinquency

- A youth may become delinquent because they live in a disorganized community.
- Class is a significant variable, however some challenge that association.
- Coleman's *social capital theory* suggests lower-class individuals lack the social resources such as social norms, social networks, and interpersonal relationships that contribute to child growth.

V. Explanations of Delinquency Across the Life Course

A. Reduced Social Capital

- Lower-class forced to struggle to meet their basic survival needs.
- The inability to meet goals encourages adolescents to pursue illegitimate means.

B. Disorganized Communities

- Lower-class must deal with cultural patterns conducive to delinquent behavior.
- *Collective efficacy* relates to informal social control, cohesion and mutual trust.

C. Agency and Structure

- Recent evidence supports a relationship between agency and structure.
- Critics contend structural and cultural theories do not explain some youths not becoming delinquent when in the same social setting and economic situations.

KEY TERMS

blocked opportunity Limitation of legitimate opportunities to improve one's economic position which may result in a person turning to delinquent behavior.

Chicago Area Projects A community organization project developed by Shaw and McKay in the 1930s to reduce the incidence of delinquency.

cultural deviance theory View that delinquent behavior is an expression of conformity to cultural values that conflict with dominant values of the larger society.

cultural transmission theories These theories contend that delinquent values are transmitted within a culture over time and from one generation to the next.

culturally defined goals Merton's concept of goals that people feel are worth striving for and are held out as legitimate objectives for all members of society.

differential opportunity structure Shaw/McKay's analysis that economic and social disorganization within a community are influential to delinquency.

focal concerns Miller contends that lower-class youths have different value subsets from those of the middle-class values (toughness, smartness, excitement, fate, and autonomy).

institutional means Merton's concept of acceptable methods which people achieve the culturally defined goals of society.

opportunity theory Cloward and Ohlin's theory which purports that individuals will pursue illegitimate pathways if legitimate opportunities are not available to them within society.

reaction formation A defense mechanism used to handle status frustration where the delinquent directs irrational hostility toward the middle-class.

social capital Coleman's theoretical construct that lower-class individuals have higher rates of delinquency due to lack of norms, social networks, and interpersonal relationships that contribute to a child's growth.

social disorganization Shaw and McKay's view that delinquency results from the breakdown of social control among traditional primary groups, such as family, neighborhood, and the social disorganization of the community.

social structure The relatively stable formal and informal arrangements that characterize society-including its economic arrangements, social institutions and its values and norms.

status frustration Cohen's theoretical construct that lower-class youths protest middle-class values and feel social strain when they are unable to achieve those values.

strain theory A theory that proposes that the pressure of social structure pushes youths into nonconforming behavior when they are unable to attain the cultural goal of success.

CLASSROOM ACTIVITIES AND ASSIGNMENTS

1. Ask students to make a list of various crimes or delinquent acts that they reason could be attributed to cultural strain causation, and discuss if punishment for those crimes should be less than crimes committed by rational choice.

2. Have students research various subculture groups in America such as the Amish or Quakers, and discuss why their differing value systems tend not to be criminal.

3. Have students research crimes committed by "gypsy" subculture groups in America, and discuss why their crimes typically aimed at Americans are related to their cultural beliefs.

4. Ask students to imagine living in a family where children aspire toward going to prison, rather than college (due to security of shelter and food), and discuss their reactions.

5. Ask students to share their own experience in which they used one or more of Merton's modes of adaptation. Have other students vocalize why they conformed.

6. Poll students to find out how many have recently moved into a new home or apartment, and likewise how many have left a new home for a dormitory room. Then have students discuss any changes in their behavior due to environmental factors.

7. Have students bring to class various magazine advertisements and discuss how many of them contain status symbols directed toward upper-middle-and lower-class audiences.

8. Ask students to recollect five fairy-tales from their childhood and discuss the messages of success an happiness contained in each.

VOICES OF DELINQUENCY ASSIGNMENTS

Have students read article 6 titled: Growing up in the Hood and answer the following questions.

1. Have students discuss how the culture of the "hood" has influenced this person's life.

2. Ask students which of the theoretical perspectives in chapter 4 best explains why this person decided to turn their life around?

3. Have students respond to this question: Do you think this person has really reformed or just saying that they have?

VIDEO AND INTERNET RESOURCES

Gangsta Girls*:* This video infiltrates the world of tough young women in their world of drive-by shootings, robberies, and drug violations. It examines the reasons young women join gangs. (50 minutes) *Insight Media.*

I Wanna Be Adored*:* This video documents the alternative social structure of the 90s, showing statistics that establish alternative youth as the most criminalized on record.
(48 minutes) *Insight Media.*

Gang Terror: This video describes the lethal struggle between Crips and Bloods and the plight of residents living in Chicago's gang infested projects. (46 minutes) *Films for the Humanities and Sciences.*

Beyond The Mirage: A documentary video on the cult phenomenon. This video introduces two cult members who explain why they joined, the experiences they had, and why they eventually broke away. (22 minutes) *Filmakers Library.*

WEBSITES

Read the article, *Robert Agnew's Strain Theory Approach,* at www.justicestudies.com/weblibrary

Read the NIJ publication, *National Evaluation of the "I Have a Dream" Program, at* www.justicestudies.com/weblibrary

Visit the Project on Human Development in Chicago Neighborhoods (HDNC) Web site via www.justicestudies.com/webplaces

www.hewett.norfolk.sch.uk

www.criminology.fsu.edu/jjclearinghouse/jj13.html

CHAPTER 5: SOCIAL PROCESS THEORIES OF DELINQUENCY

LEARNING OBJECTIVES

After reading this chapter, you should be able to answer the following questions:

1. Do delinquents learn crime from others?
2. Why is it that some young people routinely go from delinquent to non-delinquent acts and then back to delinquent behavior?
3. What control mechanisms insulate teenagers from delinquent behavior?
4. What role does a teen's self concept play in delinquency?
5. Does considering more than one theory increase our ability to explain delinquency?

CHAPTER SUMMARY

Each of the social process theories in this chapter contributes to understanding how adolescents become delinquent. Sutherland's *differential association* theory suggests that individuals learn delinquent behavior from various interactions with antisocial groups. Thus, if they are involved with antisocial groups, they are more likely to accept antisocial conduct norms and definitions. Matza's *drift theory* attempts to explain why juveniles may choose to drift between conventional and delinquent behavior through a process of neutralizing responsibility of their actions. Reckless's *containment theory* states that positive experiences in the home, school and community will lead to good self-concepts and insulate individuals from crime and delinquency. Hirschi's *social control theory* suggests that the more strongly attached adolescents are to various social bonds, the more likely it is they will refrain from becoming involved in delinquent behavior.

Social process theories explain delinquency on the individual level, which is the strength of their analysis. The process of bonding to significant others, drifting in and out of delinquent behavior, and developing strong self-concepts are key conceptual constructs of these theories. Several of these theories suggest a decision-making process by the juvenile.

Although the strength of these theories is found in their mircroanalysis of the behavior and interactions of the individual delinquent, their significant weakness is ignoring the macroanalysis. These theories fail to place adequate emphasis in regard to the impact of political and economic systems on the delinquent. The paradox that emerges between social structural and social process theories is, while one is preoccupied with structural causes, the other fails to include it. Thus, *integrated theory* attempts to combine two or more existing theories to eradicate any deficiencies created by strictly social process and social structural theories.

Gottfredson and Hirschi, Elliot, Thornberry, and Hawkins and Weiss, all have contributed significantly to understanding delinquency.

LECTURE OUTLINE

Introduction:

- The story of the Bogle Family.

I. Differential Association Theory

- Sutherland purposes delinquents learn crime from others as part of social interaction.
- Individuals internalize definitions that favor law violations when learning delinquency.
- Learning criminal behavior occurs within intimate personal groups.
- Excess contact with those who favor violations of the law leads to delinquency.
- Differential associations may vary in frequency, duration, priority, and intensity.
- Assumes those who are not delinquent have been socialized to conventional values.
- Difficult to reject the notion of learning and the appeal of the theory is positive.
- Glaser's modification applied the *interactionist* concept of *self* in his theory of *differential identification theory*. Glaser suggests a delinquent identifies themselves with real or imaginary persons who find criminal behavior acceptable.
- Burgess and Aker's *social learning theory* contends that learned behavior comprises the individual's main source of reinforcements and behavior can be imitated or modeled.

A. Evaluation of Differential Association

- Impact of Sutherland's theory on differential identification theory (Glaser) and differential reinforcement theory (Burgess and Akers).
- Critics charge the conceptual terms are vague and does not explain why do some youths do not succumb to delinquency. The delinquent is viewed as a passive vessel with no room for purpose or meaning.

II. Drift Theory and Delinquency

- Delinquency occurs when a juvenile neutralizes himself or herself from the moral bounds.
- The delinquent transiently exists in limbo between convention and crime.
- Delinquency is permissible when responsibility is neutralized; denial of responsibility, denial of injury, denial of victim, condemnation of the condemners, and appeal to higher loyalty.
- Subcultural delinquents are filled with injustice and depend on a memory file of inconsistency.
- Demonstration of valor is related to assertion of a harmful wrong tort instead of crime.
- Not all breaking of the moral bind of law will result in a delinquent act.
- Drift theory can be useful to account for those who commit occasional delinquent acts.

A. Evaluation of Drift Theory

- Drift theory builds on a learning process approach and challenges the notion that delinquents are "constrained" to engage in delinquency.

- J. Hagan integrated drift theory into a life course conceptualization with social control theory.

III. Social Control and Delinquent Behavior

- The core notion of control theory suggests an absence or defective controlling force.
- Delinquency in America: Cyberdelinquents—Bot Herders and Cybercrooks

A. Containment Theory

- Reckless's *containment theory* has two reinforcing elements of inner/outer control.
- Assumes strong *inner* and *outer containment* provides insulation against deviant behavior.
- Inner containment includes; self-control, positive self-image, well-developed superego, high frustration tolerance, high resistance to diversions, high sense of responsibility, ability to find substitute satisfactions, goal orientations and tension-reducing rationalizations.
- Outer containment represents structural buffers which include; norms, goals, expectations, effective supervision/discipline, provision for reasonable activity, opportunity for acceptance, identity, and belongingness.
- Internal *pushes* consists of drives, motives, frustrations, restlessness, disappointments, rebellion, hostility, and feelings of inferiority that encourage a person to engage in unacceptable behavior.
- Societal *pulls* consists of distractions, attractions, temptations, patterns of deviancy, carriers of delinquent patterns, and criminogenic advertising and propaganda in society.
- Reckless theorized if a youth has weak inner and outer containment and the pushes and pulls of society are strong enough, then delinquency is likely to result. Conversely, if the insulation qualities of inner and outer containment are strong enough, then delinquency will likely be diverted.
- Reckless suggests that a "good self-concept" is a precondition of law-abiding behavior.
- Critics charge the concepts are difficult to define and measuring self-concept is questionable.

B. Social Control Theory

- Hirschi's *social control theory* states delinquent acts result when one's bond to society is weak or broken.
- Humans are basically antisocial and naturally capable of committing crime.
- Hirschi suggested people tightly bonded to social groups such as family, the school, and peers are less likely to commit delinquent acts.
- Four main elements; *attachment*, *commitment, involvement*, and *belief.*
- Attachment includes ties to parents, teachers and friends.
- Commitment includes the degree of commitment to conventional activities such as educational goals, property, and reputation.
- Involvement consists of the amount of time one devotes to conventional activities.
- Belief includes respect for the law and social norms.

C. Evaluation of Social Control Theory

- Provides valuable insights into intrafamily relationships.
- Great amount of empirical data exists to support social control theory.
- Critics charge the questionnaire used by Hirschi to measure delinquency was limited and only measured a few relatively minor acts.
- Social control theory fails to describe the chain of events that weaken social bonds.

IV. Integrated Theories of Delinquency

- Implies the combination of two or more existing theories on the basis of their perceived commonalities.
- Hirschi identified three types; side by side, end to end, up and down integration.
- End to end integration is the most widely used and refers to placing variables in a temporal order so variables of some theories can be operationalized into integrated theory.

A. Issues and Concerns of Integrated Theory

- Concerns of integrated theory include which propositions of a particular theory should be used and some theories tend to explain only certain types of delinquent behavior.
- Additional concerns include generalizations of theories and different assumptions various theories may make in respect to motivations, attitudes and contributing factors to delinquency.

B. Gottfredson and Hirschi's General Theory of Crime

- People who lack self-control will tend to be impulsive, insensitive, physical, risk-taking, shortsighted, and nonverbal, and will tend to engage in criminal acts.
- Self-control is the degree to which an individual is vulnerable to temptation.
- Ineffective or incomplete socialization causes low self-esteem.
- Critics charge a lack of conceptual clarity and key elements remain to be tested.

C. Elliott's Integrated Social Process Theory

- Synthesizes strain, social control, and social learning theory in a single paradigm.
- Contends that living in socially disorganized areas lead youths to develop weak bonds with conventional groups, activities, and norms. Antisocial peer groups provide both positive reinforcement for delinquent behavior and role models for this behavior.
- This theory represents a pure type of integrated theory. Examinations are largely positive.
- Questions have been raised about its power and utility in regard to certain behaviors.

D. Thornberry's Interactional Theory

- Impetus toward delinquency comes from a weakening bond to conventional society.
- Associations with delinquent peers make up the social setting in which delinquency is learned and reinforced.
- The process develops over the person's life cycle.
- Views delinquency as a result of events that occur in the development process.
- Fails to address the presence of middle-class delinquency and ignores race and gender

issues.

E. Hawkins and Weis's Social Development Model

- Weis and Hawkins integrate social control and cultural learning theory.
- Developments of attachments to parents will lead to attachments to school and a commitment to education, as well as a belief in conventional behavior and the law.
- Youth not receiving support from families and school are vulnerable to delinquency.
- Interventions that seek to increase the likelihood of social bonding are appropriate.

V. Social Process and Delinquency Across the Life Course

A. Lack of Competence in Adolescence

- Competence and social influence at the end of adolescence shapes evolving life course.
- Choice of attractive opportunities permits the most competent to take advantages.

B. Cumulative Disadvantages

- Personal deficits lead to cumulative disadvantages.
- Each negative event in life tends to limit the positive options available to some people.

C. Turning Point

- Sampson and Laub found four turning points in the desistance process (marriage, reform school, military, and neighborhood change).
- Desistance requires positive attitudes, prosocial behaviors, and reinforcing transitions.

KEY TERMS

commitment to delinquency David Matza's term for the attachment that juvenile may have to delinquent identify and values.

commitment to social bond The attachment that a juvenile has to conventional institutions and activities.

containment theory Walter C. Reckless's theory that contends that strong inner and outer containment provide an insulation against the pushes and pulls of delinquent behavior in society.

control theory This theory suggests humans must be controlled to repress delinquent tendencies.

differential association theory Sutherland's theory that suggests that individuals internalize definitions that favor violating the law to a higher degree, than definitions that favor law abiding behaviors.

differential identification theory Daniel Glaser's modification of differential association that applied the interactionist concept of self.

drift theory Matza's theory which contends juveniles may drift from conventional to criminal behavior when neutralizing themselves from the moral bounds of the law.

neutralization theory This theory suggests youngsters justify their actions by neutralizing responsibility through denial of responsibility, injury, and victim, and condemnation of the condemners, and by appealing to a higher loyalty.

social control theory Theory that criminal behavior is controlled by the social bond or processes of socialization, in which delinquent acts will likely occur when an individual's bond to society is weak or broken.

social development model Theory that integrates two or more existing theories on the basis of perceived commonalities. Includes side-to-side, end-to-end, and up and down integrations.

social process theories Theories of delinquency that examine the interactions between individuals and their environments that influence them to become involved in delinquency.

soft determinism David Matza's view that delinquents are neither wholly free or constrained but somewhere in between.

CLASSROOM ACTIVITIES AND ASSIGNMENTS

1. Ask students to identify and describe a personal behavior or mannerism they adopted from observing their parents, siblings, or close friends.

2. Have students research the Internet or library looking for materials that teach a person how to commit a crime, such as recipes for illegal drugs or bomb building, and discuss how social learning affects delinquent behavior.

3. Ask students to identify a situation in which they may have passed on information to another person and later learned the information was incorrect, such as describing the facts-of-life to a younger person.

4. Have students bring to class any magazine or newspaper articles that contain evidence that delinquent behavior is learned.

5. Ask students to describe any situations in which they may have committed a dishonest or delinquent act and have never performed it since, and discuss the influence of drift theory.

6. Have students search for evidence of famous persons that have used a technique of neutralization to justify or account for their behavior, such as Oliver North and the Iran Contra Affair.

7. Ask students to describe any personal experience in which they felt drawn or compelled to action and discuss the elements of containment theory which may have led to or restricted the action.
8. Ask students to describe a situation in which they refrained from violating a rule because of strong bonds they may have with parent, teachers, and friends.

VOICES OF DELINQUENCY ASSIGNMENTS

Have students read article 11 titled: Walking Away From Drugs and answer the following questions.

1. Ask students to discuss what impact parental lifestyle may have had on this person. Do you think social learning created or discouraged the delinquency in this family?

2. What impact does peer pressure have in creating delinquency within this family?

3. Have students apply the concepts of social control theory to the varieties of behaviors contained in this article. How have the behaviors been restricted or how have they been encouraged, according to elements of social control theory?

VIDEO AND INTERNET RESOURCES

Youth Crime: Who's to Blame? This video poses provocative questions about the causes of crime. The program investigates the various motivations of youth offenders. It stimulates discussion of the role of law in society and the causes and consequences of criminal behavior. (22 minutes) *Insight Media.*

How Does a Nation Rot Inside? In the wake of the Littleton, Colorado school shootings, this video features a panel of experts who analyze violence, trace its roots, and debate strategies for the prevention of future such crises. (30 minutes) *Insight Media.*

Violence in Our Schools: This video addresses incidences of school violence and examines factors that may contribute to violence in American schools. It considers the accessibility of guns, violence in the media, and changes in the nature and structure of the American family. (14 minutes) *Insight Media.*

It's Not Okay: Speaking Out Against Youth Violence: This video features high school students that offer a teen perspective on violence and its day-to-day impact at school, at home and in the community. They speak their minds on the causes of delinquency, effects of dysfunctional families, bullying and the mob-mentality, and fear of being killed. (40 minutes) *Films for the Humanities and Sciences*.

WEBSITES

Read the NIJ-sponsored research publication, *Trajectories of Violent Offending and risk Status in Adolescence and Early Adulthood,* at www.justicestudies.com/weblibrary

Read the article, *Social Learning and Structural Factors in Adolescent Substance Use,* at www.justicestudies.com/weblibrary

Read the OJJDP publication, *Causes and Correlates: Findings nad Implications,* at www.justicestudies.com/weblibrary

Read the testimony of Mr. John Wilson, Acting Administrator of the Office of Juvenile Justice and Delinquency Prevention, before the U.S. House of Representatives, Committee on the Judiciary on October 2, 2000, at www.justicestudies.com/weblibrary

Read the OJJDP Fact Sheet, *Highlights of Findings from the Denver Youth Survey,* at www.justicestudies.com/weblibrary

Visit the Serious, Violent, and/or Habitual Offenders section of the Juvenile Justice Evaluation Center's Web site via www.justicestudies.com/webplaces

Visit the National Youth Violence Prevention Resource Center's Web site via www.justicestudies.com/weblibrary

www.criminolgy.fsu.edu/crimtheory/sutherland.html

http://www.cnn.com/SPECIALS/1998/schools/

CHAPTER 6: SOCIAL INTERACTIONIST THEORIES OF DELINQUENCY

LEARNING OBJECTIVES

After reading this chapter you should be able to answer the following questions:

1. How important is the concept of labeling as a cause of future behavior?

2. What kinds of youngsters become more determined to succeed because they have been labeled?

3. Does peer evaluation affect some young people more than others?

4. How does social class affect the system's response to a troublesome youth?

CHAPTER SUMMARY

This chapter examines three explanations used to understand juvenile delinquency. Social reaction is the key concept used to evaluate *labeling* and *symbolic interactionist theories* of delinquency, and the *conflict approach* to delinquency. All three of these theories focus on the role that social and economic groups, and institutions have in producing delinquent behavior.

Social reaction takes place in a particular context that will vary within certain individuals, and groups, such as family, groups, school settings, the justice system and society's political decision makers. Social reaction also takes place during the process of interaction. The process will vary from the formation of the social self, to how one responds to given labels for what is perceived as unacceptable behavior, and to the reaction of what is interpreted as economic exploitation by the larger society. Oppression is instrumental when evaluating what takes place during the labeling process and to understanding exploitation of the lower-class youth.

Variations in conflict theory include the dimensions of *socioeconomic*, *power* and *authority*, and *group* and *cultural conflict*. Marxist theorists relate delinquency to issues of alienation and powerlessness among lower-class youth. The dominant classes, in an attempt to control the subordinate groups, create definitions of delinquency traditionally for economic gain. Thus, the lack of social justice in America becomes a constant class struggle and conflict approach between upper and lower classes. Weber discussed social stratification in terms of "life chances" and argued that they were differentially related to social class. From this perspective, delinquency is a result of political struggles among different groups attempting to promote or enhance their own life chances. Sellins defined conflict as a result of divergent rules of conduct for a specific life situation that conflicts with opposing *conduct norms* held by other groups or individuals. Thus, the more complex a culture becomes, the more likely it is that the number of normative groups, which affect a person, will be large. *Peacemaking* criminologists argue that we need to deescalate violence through conciliation, mediation and dispute settlement.

LECTURE OUTLINE

Introduction

- The story of Patrick V. and Christopher Conley.

I. Labeling Theory

- *Social reaction theory* focuses on the role social groups and institutions have in producing delinquent behavior.

A. Frank Tannenbaum: The Dramatization of Evil

- Frank Tannenbaum in 1938 developed early *labeling theory*, suggesting juveniles are labeled as different when coming to the attention of authorities, and theorized the process produced a change in how individuals are handled by the system, and how they view themselves.
- Tannenbaum referred to the process as the *dramatization of evil*

B. Edwin Lemert: Primary and Secondary Deviation

- Lemert focused on the interaction between social control agents and rule violators, which results in the transformation of a person's identity.
- *Primary deviation* consists of an individual's behavior.
- *Secondary deviation* is society's response to the behavior.
- *Sequence of interaction* is: Primary deviation, social penalties, further primary deviation, stronger rejection, further deviation (perhaps with hostility and resentment), community stigmatization, strengthening of deviance as a reaction to stigmatization, and the ultimate acceptance of deviant social status by the person.

C. Howard Becker: Deviant Careers

- Becker conceptualized the process of being labeled an *outsider.*
- Once caught and labeled, a person gains a new social status with consequences for the person's self-image and his or her public identity.
- The individual is assigned a status within a social structure.

D. The Juvenile Justice Process and Labeling

- Edwin Schur contends radical nonintervention is needed to avoid counterproductive labeling.

E. New Developments in Labeling Theory

- Early labeling theory came under attack for implying labeling is responsible for persistent deviance and increasing the likelihood of subsequent rule breaking.
- Resurgence of labeling theory includes separating labels into: *formal* and *informal* labels. Formal labels result from reactions by official agents and informal labels result from reactions by parents, neighbors and friends(Triplett).
- John Braithwaite *shaming* in the family is good example of informal labels.
- Sampson and Laub contend labeling leads to cumulative disadvantage.

F. Evaluation of Labeling Theory

- Labeling theory explains perpetuation of delinquency until the end of adolescent years.
- Strengths include: importance of rule making and power in the creation of deviance, individuals do take on roles and self-concepts are expected of them (self-fulfilling prophecies), labeling perspective has moved from the unidirectional basis to examining multi-contingencies of labeling effects.
- Critics charge: Whose label really counts?
- Why do youths mature away from official labels if they are so important.

II. Symbolic Interactionist Theory

- Of central importance is the process by which shared meanings, behavioral expectations, and reflected appraisals are constructed in interaction and applied to behavior.

A. Role Taking and Delinquency

- Unit of analysis as the transaction that takes place in interaction between two or more individuals.
- Transaction is built up through *reciprocal role taking* and can lead to delinquent behavior.
- Matsueda's risk-taking includes four features; (1) self is formed by how an individual perceives that others view him or her, (2) the self is an object that arises partly endogenously within situations and partly from prior situational self being carried over from previous experience, (3) the self as an object becomes a process that has been determined by the self at a previous point in time, and (4) delinquent behavior takes place partly because of the formation of habits, and partly because the stable perception of oneself is shaped by others.

B. Evaluation of Symbolic Interactionist Theory

- Builds on the tradition of symbolic interactionist theory and adds further insights into labeling theory.
- Insightful about how delinquent youths form conceptions of themselves.

III. Conflict Theory

- Development related to *"dialectics*" (art of conducting a dispute).
- Simmel argued unity and discord are intertwined and social unity does not exist.
- Functionalism presents a utopian society that does not exist and never will.
- Conflict perspective views social control as an outcome of differential distribution of economic and political power in society.
- Quinney argued that law is a control instrument to serve the interests of the *capitalist* ruling class.

A. Dimensions of Conflict Criminology

- Importance of socioeconomics, power and authority, group and cultural conflict.
- Marx viewed crime as a result of class struggles.
- Capitalist society divided into *bourgeoisie* and *proletariat* with increased strain.
- Ownership class is guilty of the brutal exploiting of the working class.
- Weber focused on *power-authority-prestige* to study social stratification in society.

- Weber discussed *"life chances"* are differentially related to social class.
- Turk constructed an analysis based on conflict and domination between authorities and subjects. Authorities create, interpret, and enforce right-wrong standards.
- Hagen linked power and control to gender and nonserious delinquency suggesting that the greater control of girls explains why boys are frequently more delinquent.
- Regoli and Hewitt's theory of *differential oppression* based on authority is unjustly used against children. Theory employs biological ideas, sociological and psychological theories about behavior: (1) children are easy targets for adults due to size differences, (2) oppression of children falls along a continuum of benign to malignant abuse, 3) oppression leads to adaptive reactions by children, and 4) children's adaptations to oppression create and reinforce the view of children as inferior subordinate beings.
- Sellins and Vold advocated conflict criminology from *group and cultural perspective*.
- Sellins discussed *"conduct norms"* as the ways members of a group should act meaning the more complex a culture becomes, the more likely the number of normative groups will affect a person's behavior.
- Sellins also developed *primary* and *secondary culture conflict* concepts.
- Vold states, as groups move into each others territory competition is inevitable and results in a winner and loser unless compromise is reached. Minority groups are at odds with police maintained by society.
- Delinquency International: Juvenile Crime Rises in Russia

B. Marxist Criminology and Explanations of Delinquent Behavior

- *Alienation* and *powerlessness* among youth who remain in holding until they enter the workforce.
- Limited voting power, lack of organized lobbies, and hold few positions of power.
- Quinney stated violent gang activity might be a collective response of adolescents.
- Marxists purport lengthening of the rites of passage contributes to alienation of youths.
- Certain acts are termed delinquent because it is in the interest of the ruling class.
- *"Haves"* exploit the *"have-nots"* and children become a marginal class.
- *Instrumental theory* suggests that status is relative to delinquency.
- Social injustice linked to; poor youth, sexist treatment of female offenders, and racism.
- Chambliss and *"The Saints and the Roughnecks"* study suggests inequality in justice.

C. Alienation and Delinquency

- Structural and integrated Marxist theory contends that power relations subjected to most lower-class workers are coercive (Colvin).
- Juveniles are alienated from parental bonds and likely to be placed in coercive school control situations.

D. Evaluation of Conflict Theory

- All call attention to nation's macrostructural flaws.
- Radical humanism is rooted in structural inequalities of the social order.

KEY TERMS

capitalism An economic system of private capital that are determined by private decision, prices, production, and the distribution of goods that are determined by competition in a free market.

conduct norms Description for rules of a group in regard to how its members should act.

conflict theory Theory that delinquency is explained by socioeconomic class, power and authority relationships, and by group and cultural differences.

cultural conflict Sellins's perspective that suggests delinquency or crime arises because of conflicts that individuals experience as member of a subculture that has its own particular conduct norms that differ from the dominant groups.

instrumental Marxists Group members who view the entire apparatus of crime control as the tool or instrument of the ruling class.

instrumental theory Schwendinger's theory that states the most important variable in identifying delinquency potential for adolescents is their relative status position among other adolescents.

labeling perspective Assumes society creates deviance by negatively labeling those who are apprehended as different from others, and any subsequent interactions are influenced by the meaning and perception derived from the label.

Marxist criminology View that crime and delinquency in capitalist society emerges due to the efforts of the powerful to maintain their power at all costs.

power control thesis John Hagan and colleagues view the relationship between gender and delinquency as being linked to power and control.

primary deviation Lemert's theoretical concept that deviance committed in the initial act leads to a negative reaction by the social audience and may lead to the attaching of a negative label.

process of becoming delinquent Lemert's labeling theory contends the process of acquiring a delinquent identity occurs through a sequence of interaction leading to secondary deviation.

Radical criminology A perspective that holds that the causes of crime are rooted in social conditions that empower the wealthy and the politically well organized but disenfranchise the less fortunate.

radical nonintervention Schur's purposed policy of delinquency, which advised authorities to not intervene whenever possible.

secondary deviation Lemert's theoretical concept that deviance committed in the initial act leads to a negative reaction by the social audience and may lead to the attaching of a negative label.

social reaction theories Theories that focus on the role that social and economic groups and institutions have on producing delinquent behavior.

symbolic interactionist theory Theory in social psychology that stresses the process of interaction among human beings at the symbolic level.

theory of differential oppression Regoli and Hewitt's theory based on combinations of biological ideas, and sociological and psychological theories that authority is unjustly used against children.

CLASSROOM ACTIVITIES AND ASSIGNMENTS

1. Have students search for crimes or acts of delinquency which illustrate the labeling perspective, and discuss the labeling process.

2. Ask students to report any personal experiences, which may have stigmatized their lives and discuss the issues from a labeling perspective.

3. Have students interview or survey primary educational teachers to discern how labeling children as learning or behavioral disabled may affect their interactions with the labeled students.

4. Ask students to discuss how college students that have been stigmatized as "cheaters" or as "A" students are perceived by, and interacted with differently by the other students.

5. Have students search for recent rule changes or legislation that suggests that they, as students, have been exploited by the upper or ruling classes in control.

6. Ask students to discuss if their choice of a college or university was made with regard to money, and why they may have been forced to choose a less expensive alternative.

7. Have students list practices in the educational process that they think may discriminate against lower-class individuals. Such as jobs that require college degrees, grading practices, testing procedures, school vocational counselors, and others, and use the conflict approach to develop a better understanding of the issues.

8. Ask students to recall famous court cases in which those with money, power, and influence were able to negotiate a better fate than those without the same elements.

VOICES OF DELINQUENCY ASSIGNMENTS

Have students read article 22 titled: A Small Town Boy and answer the following questions.

1. Ask students to discuss how labeling may have affected this person's life in regard to his early years in particular.

2. Have students analyze how the theft crimes of this person could be related to the family's socioeconomic position in life, and would it have been different for him had the family been wealthy?

3. Ask students to discuss how the stigmatization of this person's life will undoubtedly affect him for the rest of his life, in essence what will his "life chances" be.

VIDEO AND INTERNET RESOURCES

Michael Harrington and Today's Other America: Corporate Power and Inequality: This video captures the new American poverty which still existed despite a booming economy. Includes a brief history of socialism in America and raises questions concerning the merits and relevance of labor unions today. (84 minutes) *Filmakers Library.*

Making Welfare Work: This video explores the successes as well as the controversy surrounding welfare reform experiments and cautions us not to further shortchange disadvantaged families in our rush to overhaul a failing welfare system. (58 minutes) *Filmakers Library.*

Male Violence: A Room Full of Men: The video examines male violence toward women. It follows two women from different socioeconomic backgrounds in which they describe their experiences in abusive relationship. (49 minutes) *Films for the Humanities and Sciences.*

Hate.com: Extremists on the Internet: This video narrated by Morris Dees of the Southern Poverty Law Center provides a chilling account of how the Internet is used to spread messages of hate and violence. Contains inflammatory language and imagery. (42 minutes) *Films for the Humanities and Sciences.*

WEBSITES

Read the OJJDP publication, *Report of the Comprehensive Strategy task Force on Serious, Violent and Chronic Juvenile Offenders – Part 1,* at www.justicestudies.com/weblibrary

Read the OJJDP publication, *Report of the Comprehensive strategy Task Force on Serious, Violent, Chronic Juvenile Offenders – Part 2,* at www.justicestudies.com/weblibrary

Learn about OJJDP's Juvenile Mentoring Program (JUMP) at www.justicestudies.com/weblibrary

Learn about labeling theory from CrimeTheory.com via www.justicestudies.com/webplaces

www.criminolgy.fsu.edu/crimtheory/becker.htm

www.capitalism.org

CHAPTER 7: GENDER AND DELINQUENCY

LEARNING OBJECTIVES

After you read this chapter, you should be able to answer the following questions:

1. How is gender important to an understanding of delinquency?

2. How are the categories of gender, class, and race helpful in understanding the issues faced by female delinquent and status offenders?

3. What strides towards gender equality have been made in the past few years? What led to these changes?

CHAPTER SUMMARY

This chapter examines the nature of female delinquency. *Feminist theory* purports that females are positioned in society to become victimized by their male counterparts. Females situated in a patriarchal society, appear to be controlled in greater amounts at home, school, and in the community. The acceptance and rejection of their expected social norms is explored from a contextual analysis.

The basic notion among feminists and nonfeminists is that delinquency theories are preoccupied with why males commit delinquent acts. Some feminists suggest that separate theories are needed to explain female delinquency, while others disagree saying that existing theories are adequate to explain female and male delinquency alike. Considerable evidence supports that female delinquency operates through the same sociological factors as male delinquency. This position also infers that reductionism occurs by assuming women are universal and distinct from men in their delinquency. However, certain evidence exists that suggests new approaches are needed to examine the multiple marginality of adolescent females. Criminologists have generally ignored problems of oppression through sexism, racism, and class, and feminists attempted to examine the relationship of these factors to female delinquency.

Female delinquency studies reveal females receive harsher treatment than males by the juvenile justice system. Some evidence shows that girls are treated punitively for status offenses. However, they receive the benefits of chivalry when committing delinquent offenses. Little evidence supports that female delinquency is more abnormal and pathological than male delinquency. Additionally, the *women's liberation movement* has not been instrumental in influencing delinquency as once speculated by some researchers.

LECTURE OUTLINE

Introduction

- Meda Chesney-Lind claims the study of delinquency is gender biased toward males.
- Females are more controlled than males, they enjoy more social support, and are less disposed to commit crime with fewer opportunities.
- Chesney-Lind suggests a need for a *feminist model of delinquency.*
- The case of Noemi and her sister.

I. Gender and Delinquency

- Gender is a social construction in which children are socialized into gender arrangements.
- Girls are more focused on relationships than boys and tend to have more negative body images.
- Disruptions in family, community, and school affect females more negatively than males.
- Abuses within the juvenile system include; foul/demanding language by staff, inappropriate touching, pushing and hitting by staff, placement in isolation, deprivation of clean clothing.
- Two-thirds of the females in the juvenile justice system are minorities.
- Few gender specific programs (need for intensive family-based programs)

II. Gender Neutral Perspectives on Explanations of Female Delinquency

- Biological and psychological explanations view adolescent females through *sexism.*
- Some criminologists challenge the need for distinct and separate theories.

A. Biological and Constitutional Explanations

- Lombroso: women are primitive, less intelligent, unable to feel pain, lack moral refinement, passive, and predisposed to live dull/unimaginative lives. Women criminals inherit male characteristic, excessive body hair, moles, wrinkles, crow's feet, and abnormal craniums.
- Cowie noted physical overdevelopment results in sexual promiscuity and menstruation is a reminder females will never be males.

B. Psychological Explanations

- Thomas suggests females are *anabolic* (motionless, lethargic, and conservative). He argues girls are driven by four wishes; (1) desire for new experience, (2) desire for security, (3) desire for response, and (4) desire for recognition. Thomas suggested prostitution was a result of the girl's need for love, recognition and ambition.
- Freud suggested that women's sex organs make them inferior to men. Mothers replace the "lost penis" with a baby, and her drive of accomplishment is her longing for a "penis." He also suggested they have little social sense.
- Pollak suggested the crimes of women largely go unreported or are hidden. Women are inherently deceitful.
- The *chivalry factor* is advanced as root cause of hidden crime. Pollak also suggests that early development is related to immoral/delinquent behavior.
- Psychologists suggest a relationship between psychological impairment and delinquency such as sexual abuse and prostitution are due to poor self-esteem.

- Sexism thrives in psychological theories as in the biological explanations.

C. Sociological Explanations

- Datesman found the perception of limited opportunity is more related to female delinquency than male delinquency.
- *Blocked opportunity theory* is more predictive than other variables, however the notion is more applicable to whites than nonwhites.
- Adler argues the rise in female delinquency is related to *women's liberation movement*. Females become more competitive and aggressive.
- Critics charge that minority women were not part of the liberation movement, and changes began prior to the movement. Weis contends female criminality is more of a social invention.
- Hirschi's *social control theory* contends sex-role socialization is greater for females and they are supervised more closely by parents.
- The general theory of crime (GTC) contends females have more self-contol and less access to delinquency compared to males.
- Differential association theory suggests boys are more impacted by differential associations than females.
- The *masculinity hypothesis* purports as females become more male-like they become more delinquent.
- Peer group influence observes that females are more likely to be delinquent in mixed-sex groups.
- Hagan's *power control theory* suggests when daughters are freed from patriarchal influence they are more likely to become delinquent.
- *Labeling* and *interactionist theory* suggest that delinquency is determined in part by the self as conceived by symbolic interactions, which in turn is determined by the process of labeling by significant others. Parents are more likely to falsely accuse male delinquents.

D. Evaluating Explanations of Delinquency

- *Gender* is a strong correlate of delinquency. Biological theories are the least predictive. Personal maladjustment is overemphasized as well.
- Some feminists are satisfied that sociological studies conclude males and females are differentially exposed by the same criminogenic factors.

III. Types of Feminist Theories

- Five expressions; liberal, phenomenological, socialist, Marxist, and radical feminism.

A. Liberal Feminism

- Theory calls for women's equality of opportunity and freedom choice.
- Seeks to *androgynize* gender roles and eliminate discriminatory practices.
- Suggests delinquent women imitate males.

B. Phenomenological Feminism

- Concerned with the impact of chivalrous treatment for female offenders

- Some suggest females have been treated more harshly than males by the justice system.

C. Socialist Feminism

- Views class and gender relations as equal in the interactions with each other.
- Low female crime rates correlated to women's powerless position in society.

D. Marxist Feminism

- Males dominate the private property structure in society.
- Sexism is a result of capitalist relations that structure women, juvenile power and crime.

E. Radical Feminism

- Masculine power is the root cause of all social relations and inequality.
- Focus on sexual violence directed toward women.

IV. A Feminist Theory of Delinquency

- An expression of radical feminism contends that girl's victimization and relationship to crime has been systematically ignored. Chesney-Lind suggests that girls are often in juvenile court at the insistence of their parents.
- Chesney-Lind proposed; (1) girls are frequently victims of violence and sexual abuse, (2) their victimizers have the ability to invoke official agencies of social control, (3) as girls runaway from oppressive environments, they are perceived as escaped convicts, and (4) it is not by accident that impoverished girls become involved in criminal activities.
- Third-Wave Feminism

V. Gender Bias and the Processing Of Female Delinquents

A. Gender Relations

- Females tend to receive discriminatory treatment by agents of the system.
- Female status offenders are more likely to be referred to authorities than males. Younger females receive harsher punishment than older females. Police tend to act paternalistic with young female offenders.
- Adolescent girls engaged in sexual activity are more likely to be placed into confinement.
- Females are commonly confined longer than males for technical probation violations.
- On balance, the *Juvenile Justice and Delinquency Prevention Act of 1974*, may be preventing some discrimination of female status offenders.

B. The Influence of Class

- Problems of adolescence related to poverty sets the stage for homelessness, unemployment, drug use, survival sex, and other more serious delinquent acts.
- Lower-class females are more likely to have unsatisfactory experiences at school, be victims of sexual abuse, deal with pregnancy and motherhood issues, and be involved in drugs/alcohol.

C. **Racial Discrimination**
   - Racism and poverty go hand-in-hand. Coping with same type of problems; abuse, drugs, violence and gang membership.
   - Girls of color receive less chivalry then middle-class white girls.
   - Minority girls are viewed as more dangerous to society than whites.

D. **The Total is Greater Than The Sum Of Its Parts**
   - *Multiple oppression* which suggests that gender, class and race are interlocking forms of oppression and the whole is greater than the parts.

VI. **Gender Across The Life Course**
- Females are more likely to desist from crime faster than males due to conventional life patterns such as marriage, parenting, and work.
- Chronic offending appears to be lower for females compared to males.

KEY TERMS

chivalry factor Purports that males treat offending females more leniently due to their gender.

feminist theory of delinquency Expression of radical feminism which contends that girl's victimization and the relationship between the experience and girl's crime have been systematically ignored.

gender The culturally defined ways of acting as a male or a female that become part of an individual's personal sense of self.

gender roles societal expectations of what is masculine and what is feminine behavior.

masculinity hypothesis Proposition in which girls become more boy-like and acquire more masculine traits as they become more delinquent.

peer group influence Notion that delinquency is influenced in a greater degree by peer group associations and is commonly applied to male delinquency patterns.

sex-role socialization Social learning process in which persons are taught behaviors appropriate only for their gender.

CLASSROOM ACTIVITIES AND ASSIGNMENTS

1. Ask working students to report their hourly wage income to see how female's wages compare with that of males for similar types of employment.

2. Have students research children's books at elementary schools and report on how the roles of females are depicted in accordance with those of males.

3. Ask students to relate any of their childhood experiences in which they perceived that discipline was directed differentially for them due to their gender.

4. Have students watch old re-runs of television shows such as; *Father Knows Best* or *Leave it to Beaver,* and have them report on their interpretations of the overall messages offered in the shows.

5. Ask students to list occupations in which females are discouraged from entering and discuss the effects of institutionalized discrimination.

6. Have students conduct a survey of the salaries of college professors on campus to ascertain if females are being paid equally to that of their male counterparts.

7. Ask students to interview a female and male police officer to compare how each officer reports their views on female offenders, compared to male offenders.

8. Have students search for magazine advertisements that are sexist in nature toward both females and males, and discuss socialization of gender roles.

VOICES OF DELINQUENCY ASSIGNMENTS

Have students read article 8 titled: *She's Just a Party Animal* and answer the following questions.

1. Ask students to list the various behaviors associated with this girl and discuss any effects of status offenses on her life.

2. Ask students to respond to her claim that she had a "normal childhood" and whether they think she really did.

3. Why do you think this person suggests, she "would not trade her experiences for the world?"

VIDEO AND INTERNET ASSIGNMENTS

Some Spirit in Me: This video looks at the feminist movement from the view of women from various racial backgrounds. They discuss how they negotiated, benefited and sometimes, could not benefit from even when changing gender. (58 minutes) *Filmakers Library.*
Motherhood on Trial: This video portrays a variety of notable persons suggesting why Susan Smith drowned her sons in South Carolina. The views range from Newt Gingrich blaming a liberal congress, to Pat Robertson blaming abortion activists. (26 minutes) *Filmakers Library*

Date Violence: A Young Women's Guide: This video describes what happens when relationships turn violent. Preventative information is offered which makes for a good classroom discussion on the impact of theories and policy.(22 minutes) *Films for the Humanities and Sciences.*

Safe: Inside a Battered Women's Shelter: This video provides an insider view of three women who sought to break the cycle of violence by seeking refuge. Portrays how female victims often feel betrayed by those who supposedly love them. (50 minutes) *Films for the Humanities and Sciences.*

WEBSITES

Read the OJJDP publication, *Juvenile Female Offenders: A Status of the States Report,* at www.justicestudies.com/weblibrary

Read the OJJDP publication, *Guiding Principles for Promising Female Programming: An Inventory of Best Practices,* at www.justicestudies.com/weblibrary

Visit the Center on Juvenile and Criminal Justice, and learn about girls in the criminal justice system via www.justicestudies.com/webplaces

www.academicinfo.net/uswomenrights.html

www.criminolgy.fsu.edu/crimtheory/tedeschi/criminological.htm

CHAPTER 8: THE FAMILY AND DELINQUENCY

LEARNING OBJECTIVES

After reading this chapter, you should be able to answer the following questions:

1. How do problems in the family affect adolescents?

2. What factors in the family are most likely to affect the likelihood of delinquent behavior?

3. What are the main forms of child abuse and neglect?

4. What is the relationship of child abuse and neglect to delinquency and status offenses?

CHAPTER SUMMARY

American families are filled with multiple problems that include divorce, single-parent families, blended families, out-of-wedlock births, alcohol and drug abuse, poverty and violence. The more family related problems an adolescent faces the more likely their chances of becoming delinquent.

Studies on the relationship between family and delinquency generally conclude that quality of life at home is more important than whether or not the home is intact. Parental rejection and inconsistent, lax, or severe discipline are associated with increased delinquency. Accumulation of unfavorable factors within the family increases the propensity of delinquent behavior among children.

The concept of parental supremacy rights has perpetuated the mistreatment of children by their parents. The state has been reluctant to interfere in families unless severe injuries or situations have occurred. Additionally, the acceptability of violence in society and social isolation, especially of lower-class families, has further contributed to the mistreatment of children.

Mandatory reporting measures and funding of treatment programs are aimed at reducing family violence, and creating public awareness to the nature and extent of the abuse problem. Research findings have consistently linked child abuse and neglect to delinquent behavior and status offenses. Abused children runaway from home and become involved in truancy, disruptive school behaviors, drug and alcohol abuse, deviant sexual behaviors, and aggressive acts toward others.

A number of strategies are called for to reduce the extent of child abuse and neglect in the United States. Among those strategies, Cathy Spitz Widom recommends six principles that are needed to tailor the effective treatment of child abuse; (1) earlier interventions, (2) not neglecting children, (3) what works with one child may not work with another, (4) sensitivity to differential treatment on the basis of race or ethnic backgrounds, (5) interventions must be continual, and (6) resources should be accessible.

LECTURE OUTLINE

Introduction:

- Eleven year old sells heroin.

I. The Family and Delinquency

- The importance of family as a contributing factor has varied: (1900-1932) role of the family was emphasized, (1933-1950) the role of family was minimized and the focus shifted to school, social class, and influence of peers, and (1950-1972) there was revised interest in the family.

A. The Broken Home

- Debate rages; however studies indicate delinquency is 10 to 15 percent higher in broken homes. The type of family breakup affects delinquency (divorce is the highest, death is the lowest). Broken homes are not related to gender or age differences, and there is no consistent relationship to the negative impact of Stepparents as often cited.

B. Birth Order

- Some evidence supports that middle children are more likely to be delinquent, in that parents guard the first child more closely and are more experienced with the last child.

C. Family Size

- The larger the family, the more likely the delinquency. Parents are unable to effectively supervise larger families (often delegating older children to help) and they typically have fewer finances.

D. Delinquent Siblings or Criminal Parents

- Siblings seem to learn delinquency from other siblings and significant others. Children of fathers with criminal records are more likely to be poor and have an increased risk for an early first conviction.

E. Quality of Home Life

- Good marital relationships are consistent with strong family cohesiveness.
- Happiness of marriage is key to whether children engage in delinquency.

F. Family Rejection

- Parental rejection is related to delinquency. Rejection by the father appears to be more significant than mother's rejection.

G. Discipline in the Home

- Inadequate supervision is related to delinquency. Discipline that is too strict, too lax, and inconsistent were all associated with increased delinquency.

H. Family Factors and Delinquency

- Overall broken homes, birth order, family size, delinquent siblings, quality of life, family rejection, and home discipline appear to be instrumental in rates of delinquency for juvenile offenders.

II. Child Abuse and Neglect

- Child abuse and neglect is in the form of: (1) physical, (2) sexual, (3) verbal, and (4) psychological. One form of maltreatment often leads to another form.
- Being abused increased the likelihood of juvenile arrest by 59 percent, adult arrest by 29 percent, and arrest for violent crime by 30 percent.
- Maltreated children were younger at time of their arrest and committed twice as many offenses.
- Physically abused and neglected children were most likely to arrested for violent crime.
- Abused and neglected females were also an increased risk.
- The rate for African-American children is more affected by abuse than for white children.

A. Extent and Nature of Child Abuse and Neglect

- Passing of legislation in the 1960s focused national attention on the issue.
- Child Abuse and Prevention Act and the National Center on Child Abuse 1974 focused further attention on abuse problems.
- Neglect is the most common form of Maltreatment.
- Mothers are more likely to neglect children than fathers alone.
- Neglectful mothers include; apathetic-futile, impulse-ridden, mentally retarded, reaction depression, and psychotic.
- Neglectful mother is likely to have been neglected as a child.

1. Physical and Emotional Abuse

- Most common forms include; slapping, spanking, hitting with objects, grabbing, and shoving. Mothers hit children more than fathers do.
- Parents who were hit as children are more likely to hit as parents.
- Corporal punishment legitimizes violence (Straus).
- Emotional abuse involves a disregard for the psychological needs. May include a steady diet of put downs, humiliation, labeling, name-calling, scapegoating, lying, demanding excessive responsibility, seductive behavior, ignoring, fear-inducing techniques, unrealistic expectations, and extreme inconsistency.

2. Nature of Abuse

- Five explanations; (1) structural factors, (2) mental illness of parents, (3) history of abuse as a child, (4) transitory situational factors and (5) a particularly demanding or problematic child.
- Incidence of abuse increases with the child's age, however the more serious cases occur with infants and young children.

- More prevalent in urban areas than rural areas, which may be linked to better reporting methods.
- Often one parent is aggressive, while the other is passive.

3. **Sexual Abuse**
   - Any sexual activity that involves physical contact or sexual arousal between nonmarried members of a family. Includes; oral-genital contact, fondling, masturbation, and intercourse.
   - Gordon's examination revealed 98 percent of the cases were father-daughter incest in which girl victims became second wives.
   - The average incestuous relationship last three to four years.
   - Mother-son incest is less common and rarely reported. Father-son is also rare.
   - Justice and Justice study suggests that; fathers with symbiotic personalities make up 70 to 80 percent of incestuous fathers. They have a strong need for warmth and a sense of belonging, use rationalizations to justify their actions. With the psychopathic father sex is simply a vehicle to express hostility. Pedophilic personalities have erotic cravings and do not want rejection. Psychotic fathers come from a subculture that permits incest.

B. Abuse, Neglect and Delinquency

- Abused and neglected children are more likely to become involved in status offenses of truancy, disruptive school behaviors, running away and drugs/alcohol offenses.

1. **Emotional Trauma of Child Abuse and Neglect**
   - Characterized as having low self-esteem, considerable guilt, high anxiety, mild to serious depression, and high internal conflict.
   - Experience sleep disturbances, weight loss or gain, poor social relationships.

2. **Runaways**
   - Abused teens frequently escape their situation by running away. The pattern of escaping often continues even when placed into foster care.

3. **Disruptive and Truant Behavior in School**
   - Abused children have more difficulty in school and tend to become academic and social failures. Suffer deficiencies in language, concentrating and often destructive of property.

4. **Drug and Alcohol Abuse**
   - Many abused children turn to drug and alcohol abuse to blot out pain. Often feel they have nothing to lose and only want to forget their insecurities.

5. **Sexual Behavior**
   - One study revealed 66 percent of pregnant teens had been sexually abused. Victims tend to be sexually promiscuous and favor prostitution, especially male prostitutes.

6. **Violence and Abuse**
   - Male victims tend express outward acts of violence, while female victims tend to engage in self-destructive behaviors.
   - Those that were abused as children also tend to abuse as adults.

III. The Family and the Life Course

- Parental support and control are intertwined for parental efficacy (Wright/Cullen).
- Ineffective parents fail to monitor children and fail to punish deviance.
- Coercive discipline may teach children that force and violence are appropriate tactics.

IV. Child Abuse and the Juvenile Justice System

- Child protective services differ in procedures. Typically includes: identification, reporting, intake and investigation, assessment, case planning, treatment, evaluation of family progress, case closure, and prosecution.
- Reporting often required by law. Service staff required to determine how urgent the response is needed. Police are frequently involved to protect workers and gather evidence. If imminent risk is determined, a temporary removal hearing will occur. Case planning will design a treatment plan and will close a case for successful treatment of the family or refusal of the family to cooperate (in mild cases).
- Adjudication is held in which the charge of abuse or neglect is either substantiated or disposed of. Supremacy of parental rights has widespread support among juvenile judges. Prosecution depends on the severity of the abuse.
- Abuse and neglect cases are more likely to be reported among lower-class families.
- Delinquency in America: A Parent's Right to Know

KEY TERMS

birth order A notion that middle children are more prone to delinquency than the first or last-born.

broken home Early view, which holds that homes broken by divorce, separation, and death are more likely to produce delinquency than intact homes.

brother-sister incest Suggested to be the most frequently occurring type of incest, and believed to be less damaging than father-daughter incest.

child abuse Encompasses many dimensions with the general focus being variations of physical, sexual, emotional, and verbal abuse typically perpetrated by adults against children.

delinquent siblings The notion that having delinquent sisters and brothers will increase the propensity of delinquency within the home by influencing the other sibling(s).

emotional abuse Any action that reduces the self-esteem and psychological well-being of a child normally inflicted by parents and adults, and directed toward children.

family size The number of children in a family; a possible risk factor for delinquency.

father-daughter incest The most devastating form of incest in which the father frequently views the daughter as a second wife.

father-son incest Sexual activity between father and son.

mother-son incest Sexual activity that occurs between mother and son.

neglect A disregard for the physical, emotional, or moral needs of children. Child neglect involves the failure of the parent of caregiver to provide nutritious food, adequate clothing and sleeping arrangements, essential medical care, sufficient supervision, access to education, and normal experiences that produce feelings of being loved, wanted secure, and worthy.

rejection by parents Disapproval, repudiation, or other uncaring behavior directed by parents toward children; it can be a factor in delinquency.

sexual abuse Intentional and wrongful physical contact with a person, with or without his or her consent, that entails a sexual purpose or component. In the study of adolescence, the term generally refers to any sexual activity that involves physical contact or sexual contact between members of a family who are not married to one another, and especially to such contact between a parent and his or her children; also know as incest.

socialization The process by which individuals come to internalize their culture; through this process an individual learns the norms, sanctions, and expectations of being a member of a particular society.

supervision and discipline The parental monitoring, guidance, and control of children's activities and behavior. Unfair and inconsistent supervision and discipline often are associated with delinquency.

CLASSROOM ACTIVITES AND ASSIGNMENTS

1. Ask students to list any minor childhood situations that onlookers may have constituted as emotional abuse, and discuss their reaction to the incident(s) today.

2. Have students compare and contrast family life today with that of the 1900s, and discuss how family life may or may not be all that different.

3. Ask students to list various recent inventions and technologies that may reduce quality time within families, and discuss both the positives and negatives associated with them.

4. Have students discuss the pros and cons of rural family life compared to urban living and which lifestyle would they encourage over the other.

5. Ask students to express their views on corporal punishment, and guide their responses into those for and against its use.

6. Have students observe child-parent interactions in a local store, and report the number of observations, which they would consider abusive versus correctional in nature.
7. Ask students to discuss the pros and cons of using time-outs for minor problematic behaviors and whether they would consider using this approach as a parent.

8. Have students research your local community and ascertain how many social programs are available to work with or provide services for situational families. As part of this exercise have them ascertain what the cost of the services are and if the amount is considered affordable to the average family.

VOICES OF DELINQUENCY ASSIGNMENTS

Have students read article 16 titled: A Sixteen-Year Old Sexual Predator and answer the following questions.

1. Ask students to discuss what family situations may have led to this criminal behavior.

2. Have students write a probationary treatment plan for this case and discuss the various type of treatments suggested.

3. Ask students to predict what will ultimately be the fate of this young man and discuss why society my have failed this person.

VIDEO AND INTERNET RESOURCES

Portrait of a Dysfunctional Family: This ABC video documents a mother's desperation to seek help for her incorrigible teenage twins and ends up with her arrest for parental abuse of the twins. (44 minutes) *Films for the Humanities and Sciences.*

Domestic Violence and Children: This video examines the effects of children who witness the abusive relationships of parents. (14 minutes) *Films for the Humanities and Sciences.*

They Hit Me: When Children are Abused: This video examines the work of social workers and the fine line they walk between intrusion and intervention. (43 minutes) *Films for the Humanities and Sciences).*

Self Esteem Begins in the Family: This video recommends that parents not punish themselves for mistakes, rather treat their children with love and respect. (30 minutes) *Filmakers Library.*

WEBSITES:

Read the NIJ-sponsored publication, *Communitywide Strategies to Reduce child abuse and Neglect: Lessons from the Safe Kids/Safe Streets Program,* at www.justicestudies.com/weblibrary

Read the NIJ-sponsored publication, *Co-Occurring Intimate Partner Violence and Child Maltreatment* , at www.justicestudies.com/weblibrary

Visit the Center on Child Abuse and Neglect's Web site via www.justicestudies.com/webplaces

Visit the Child Welfare League of America's Web site via www.justicestudies.com/webplaces

Visit the National Center for Missing and Exploited Children's Web site via www.justicestudies.com/webplaces

Visit the National Clearinghouse on Child Neglect Information via www.justicestudies.com/webplaces

Visit the Child Exploitation and Obscenity Section of the U.S. Department of Justice's Criminal Division via www.justicestudies.com/webplaces

Visit the Family Violence and Sexual Assault Institute's Web site via www.justicestudies.com/webplaces

Visit the National Center for Children Exposed to Violence via www.justicestudies.com/webplaces

www.childabuse.org

www.angelfire.com/ar/jotsntitles

CHAPTER 9: THE SCHOOL AND DELINQUENCY

LEARNING OBJECTIVES

After reading this chapter, you should be able to answer the following questions:

1. How has education evolved over time in the United States?
2. What is the relationship between delinquency and school failure?
3. What theoretical perspectives related to the school experience best explain delinquency?
4. What rights do school students have?
5. How has the partnership between the school and the justice system changed?
6. Which intervention strategies seem to be the most promising in the school setting?

CHAPTER SUMMARY

The chapter examines the relationship between school and delinquency. School has long been acknowledged as an important socializing agent in the lives of children, but public education is under sharp criticism for contributing to the delinquency of children. Public schools are accused of failing in their task of educating and properly socializing youth in the United States. The baby boom of the 1950s brought large numbers of school-aged children into the educational systems during the 1960s and 1970s.

The pervasiveness of *vandalism* and *violence* in public education came to public attention by the mid 1970s. Assaults on students increased, and crime costs associated with vandalism and violence soared. The 1980s brought to public attention a new form of school violence in which teachers and school officials were now part of the victimization group. Open locker searches revealed students bringing a variety of destructive paraphernalia to schools including, drugs, knives, guns, and dynamite. By the 1990s students are regularly reporting high fear levels. Metal detectors are commonplace and the incidences of school violence are perpetuated by national stories on school shootings, which are claiming the lives of unsuspecting students and teachers. Gang intimidation and other fear factors are now motivating students to report to school with armaments for their own sense of protection.

Various theoretical perspectives offer explanations to help understand the impact of school on delinquent behavior. For schools in the United States to improve, a number of changes involving complex socialization processes must take place. These changes include evaluating the quality of the school experience, providing more *alternative schools* for *disruptive students*, finding ways to renew urban schools, developing more positive social-community relationships, and making schools safe havens from violence.

LECTURE OUTLINE

Introduction

- The story of Jess Weise: Murder on an Indian Reservation

I. A History of American Education

- By 1918 nearly every state has compulsory education laws.
- John Dewey advocated reform in classroom methods/curriculum in early 1900s.
- The impact of the 1954 U.S. Court decision on school segregation issues.
- The baby boom of the 1950s increased school enrollments in 1960s and 1970s.

II. School Crime

A. Vandalism and Violence

- Schools lodged in unsafe neighborhoods are in the center of gang communities and drug infested areas.
- Repressive methods of education fail to work with learning disabled children. Conventional education leads to boredom, frustration and alienation with LD students.
- Authoritarian schools have taught some lower functioning students to loose themselves in the crowd (like inmates).
- Added security in schools make them appear more like prisons.
- Ruled unconstitutional in Boston for every student to be drug tested.
- Vandalism and violence in schools comes to public attention in 1970s. Senate subcommittee investigates with report published in 1978. 36 percent of all assaults on 12 to 19 year olds occurred in school. Total crime cost $200 million per year.
- 1980s adds a new dimension of violence directed against teachers and school officials. Acts include threats of murder, rape, physical assault, arson and destruction of personal property. 1988 NASHS survey reported that; over one-third of students had been threatened at school, one-seventh of students were robbed, one-half of males and one-quarter of females had been in at least one fist-fight at school, a weapon was involved in one-third of the crimes.
- NCVS in 1989 reveals similar type of victimization statistics.
- 1993 CDC survey reveals students missed a day a school for their own safety, and 22 percent carried some type of weapon for safety.
- 2002 annual report on school safety by the Department of Justice and Education provided the following profile: chance of suffering a school-associated death is low, students aged 12 to 18 suffer violent victimization at a rate of 5 per 1000 students.
- Social policy: Indicators of School Crime and Safety 2005

III. Delinquency and School Failure

- Lack of achievement, low social status, and high dropout rate are the factors most frequently cited as related to delinquents failing at school.

A. Achievement in School

- Poor academic performance is related to both male and female delinquency.
- Good relationships with teachers, students, and administrators may reduce vandalism and increase achievement in school.

B. Social Status

- A. Cohen's study with working-class boys reveals that lower-class youth may rebel against middle-class values when frustrated over inability to achieve.
- Some studies suggest association between status and school failure may not be as strong as once thought.
- Delinquency in America: Black Youths Learn to Make the Right Moves

C. The School Dropout

- Poor grades are predictors for dropping out of school.
- Males are more likely than females. Minorities are more likely than whites.
- Dropouts have higher rates of police contact.
- Relationship is multidimensional. Dropouts make less money and have fewer job prospects, are prone to delinquency, more welfare dependent, experience more unstable marriages.
- Delinquency may be caused by school dropout or nonschool reasons such as, personal, environmental, and economic conditions.

IV. Theoretical Perspectives on School and Delinquency

- *Cultural deviance theories* argue children learn deviance through social exposure to others and modeling.
- *Strain theory* contends lower-class students are denied legitimate means to achieve society's goals. Students in turn compensate for feelings of failure and low self-esteem.
- *Social control theorists* suggest delinquency varies according to the strength of the juvenile's bonds to the social order, thus delinquency will result if the bonds do not develop.
- *Labeling theorists* state that as negative labels are assigned to students, that students react accordingly with aggression for differential treatment by school authorities.
- *Marxists* view school as a means in which the privileged classes maintain control over the lower classes. Lower-class children are taught to accept menial roles.

V. Student Rights

- Concept of *loco parentis* in which school authority stands in the place of parents.
- Courts have become involved in areas of: procedural due process, freedom of expression, hair/dress codes, and safety.

A. Procedural Due Process

- *Dixon v. Alabama State Board of Education* results in requirement for due process notification before a student is expelled for misconduct.
- *Goss v. Lopez* case holds that fair fact-finding must precede suspension notices. The *Wood v. Strickland* case found school officials are subject to civil suit for deliberately depriving students of constitutional rights.

B. Freedom of Expression

- *Tinker V. Des Moines* Independent School District holds students have the right to express themselves (black armbands in Vietnam era).
- *W. Virginia State Board of Education v. Barnette* states students could not be compelled to salute the flag.

C. Hair and Dress Codes

- *Yoo v. Moynihan* holds that students have the right to style their hair.
- *Richards v. Thurston* states the right to wear long hair. Other similar cases have prohibited schools from disallowing of slacks, dungarees, etc.

D. School Searches

- *New Jersey v. TLO* in 1985 allowed searches of students lockers and paved the way for random drug testing in schools (*Vernonia School District 47 v. Acton*).
- In 2002, the Court extended the drug testing of students in extracurricular activities.

E. Safety

- School officials have become reluctant to suspend youths for acting insubordinate and creating classroom disturbances that only a few decades earlier would have drawn quick suspension or expulsion.
- In sum, judicial intervention has had both positive and negative impacts.

VI. School and Justice System Partnerships

- Police sponsored programs such as DARE and PAL, along with gang education and training are aimed at crime prevention today rather than education.
- Per U.S. Department of Education's report in 1997: 97 percent of schools use some form of security measures. Shift in language: officers are brought in to *fight campus crime, zero tolerance, combat victimization* etc.
- Focus on investigation, drug sweeps, surveillances and crowd control. (STAR program)

VII. Promising Intervention Strategies

- Education must be oriented toward the individual and progress not compared to that of others in the class, particularly for low achievers.
- Tracking systems should be abolished.
- Students need to feel safe to become involved in the school experience.
- Good teaching is the first line of defense against misbehavior.

A. Improving the Quality of the School Experience

- The need to orient education toward the individual.

- Tracking systems need abolished as they tend to establish class systems within school.
- The need for quality instruction and flexible schedules.

B. Alternative Schools

- Disadvantaged students require special curriculum materials, smaller classes and individualized tutoring to master presented material.
- Ultimate goal of *alternative schools* is to return students to mainstream education after dealing with disruptive behaviors.
- Effectiveness of schools is mixed. Some of the larger schools such as St. Louis and Chicago are very successful.

C. Positive School-Community Relationships

- Legendary *"blackboard jungle"* an investment in hardware and preventative technology.
- Development of multi-component approaches involving home, school, and other institutions that are involved in students' lives.
- Activities arranged around community involvement with educational systems.

D. School-Based Violence Prevention Programs

- Federal grants needed to implement violence and drug prevention programs.
- Interconnectedness of family, peer group, school, and neighborhood.
- Dynamic interactions between individuals and social contexts.
- Prevention efforts require collaboration.
- Need for public health approach to violence prevention.
- Effective programs and strategies for preventing violence.

E. From Correctional Contexts to School Settings

- New priority of transitioning juvenile offenders back to school and life in the community (Franklin Transitional High School).

KEY TERMS

academic performance Achievement in schoolwork as rated by grades and other assessment measures. Poor academic performance is a factor in delinquency.

alternative schools Schools designed to provide alternative educational experiences for youths who are not reaching their academic and behavioral potentials in a traditional school setting.

bullying Hurtful, frightening or menacing actions undertaken by one person to intimidate another (generally weaker) person, to gain that person's unwilling compliance, and/or to put him in fear.

disruptive behavior Includes behaviors, which detract from the educational experience such as unwillingness to follow rules, manipulation of teachers, and defiance of authority.

dropout A public or private school student that chooses no longer to attend school and increases their likelihood of becoming delinquent.

due process rights Constitutional rights that are guaranteed to citizens-whether adult or juvenile- during their contacts with the people, their proceedings in court, and their interactions with the public school.

in loco parentis Legal requirement that schools act in place of the parents in providing educational services for children.

school searches The process of searching students and their lockers to determine whether drugs, weapons or other contraband are present.

vandalism An act in which person(s) cause damage and destruction to property typically associated with schools or other authority venues, in which the perpetrators may find to be oppressive or repressive.

violence An act aimed at serious injury of another, and often perpetrated against students and school officials thereby reducing the quality of the educational experience.

CLASSROOM ACTIVITIES AND ASSIGNMENTS

1. Ask students to relate any school experiences or activities in which disruptive students may have interrupted their learning experiences.

2. Have students in the class list various discipline measures that were used when they attended school to see how they are similar or dissimilar and discuss them.

3. Ask students to engage in a discussion of school athletics and academic performance, and discuss social control theory in terms of the strengths and weaknesses.

4. Have students design and conduct a survey of local school students to determine if a correlation exists between positive and negative grade reinforcement ("A's to F's") and any school activities or involvement.

5. Ask students to list school courses or activities that might be considered cost prohibitive to lower-class students and discuss Marxist theory.

6. Have students search for course offerings that are typically aimed at lower-class student populations such as vocational training classes and discuss the reactions.

7. Ask students to debate the consequences of student dress and conduct codes for secondary educational systems.

8. Have students search for collegiate policies that might be considered as oppressive or repressive by some and discuss the strengths and weaknesses of the debate.

VOICES OF DELINQUENCY ASSIGNMENTS

Have students read article 7 titled: From Gang Member to College Football Star and answer the following questions.

1. Ask students to discuss the effects of school environments on this person life.

2. Have students apply a variety of theoretical applications to this person's situation.

3. Ask students to discuss what central issues they feel contributed the most to changing this person, and if they feel the change will last.

VIDEO AND INTERNET RESOURCES

The Jonesboro Schoolyard Ambush: This video provides commentary of educators, family members, and law enforcement on the 1998 school shooting tragedy. (50 minutes). *Insight Media.*

The Lessons of Littleton: This video features commentary of William Glasser in the exploration of the Columbine High School massacre. (2 volumes 45 minutes each) *Insight Media.*

Sounding the Alarm: This video promotes a proactive approach to fighting school crime. It examines the roles of dysfunctional families, drugs, alcohol, and violence in the media. In addition gangs and efforts by police to control gangs is examined. (23 minutes) *Films for the Humanities and Sciences.*

Campus Combat Zone: This video highlights the work of school administrators, students, and members of the community to prevent school crime in collaboration with law enforcement. The concepts are multicomponent interventional in nature. (23 minutes) *Films for the Humanities and Sciences.*

WEBSITES

Read the OJJDP Fact Sheet, *Overcoming Barriers to school Reentry,* at www.justicestudies.com/weblibrary

Read the Bureau of Justice Statistics (BJS) publication, *Indicators of School Crime and Safety,* at www.justicestudies.com/weblibrary

Read the NIJ-sponsored publication, *Effectiveness of School-Based Violence Prevention Programs for Reducing Disruptive and aggressive Behavior,* at www.justicestudies.com/weblibrary

Read the Office of Community Oriented Policing Services (COPS) publication, *Bullying in Schools,* at www.justicestudies.com/weblibrary

Read the OJJDP Fact Sheer, *Addressing the Problem of Juvenile Bullying,* at www.justicestudies.com/weblibrary

Read the OJJDP publication, *Juvenile Mentoring Program: A Progress Review,* at www.justicestudies.com/weblibrary

Visit the Anti-Bullying Network via www.justicestudies.com/webplaces

Visit Bullying.org via www.justicestudies.com/webplaces

Visit the School Safety sections of the National Education Association's web site via www.justicestudies.com/webplaces

Learn about bullying and what can be done to prevent it from national Youth Violence Prevention Resource Center's web site via www.justicestudies.com/webplaces

www.dropoutprevention.org

www.incacs.org

CHAPTER 10: GANGS AND DELINQUENCY

LEARNING OBJECTIVES

After reading this chapter, you should be able to answer the following questions:

1. What is the relationship between peer groups and gang activity?
2. How have gangs evolved in the United States?
3. What is the relationship between urban-based gangs and emerging gangs and emerging gangs in smaller cities and communities?
4. How extensive is gang activity in this country?
5. How does gang activity affect communities?
6. Why do youths join gangs?
7. How can gangs be prevented and controlled?

CHAPTER SUMMARY

This chapter examines *gangs* and their relationship to delinquent behaviors and other criminal acts. Youngsters derive meaning from social contacts with family members, peers, teachers, and leaders and participants in churches, community organizations and school activities. The socialization of societal values and norms occurs in large part due to both intentional and unintentional agents of our society. As a result of the socialization process, some youngsters find little reason to become involved in law-violating activities. Yet, others with needs often frustrated and nowhere else left to find hope, become attracted to street gangs to fill the physical and emotional voids created by a variety of situations and explanations. In short, gangs become quasi-families and offer acceptance, status, and esteem to children when the soil is fertile for the planting of such seeds.

Youth gangs are proliferating across the United States. Even small towns and rural areas are experiencing a rise in youth gangs and their criminal activities. The advent of gangs in society is not new, however the severity of violence and the methods of inflicting it have changed, especially the use of automatic and semi-automatic weapons by gang members. Drug trafficking has also changed in stature with gangs. What once was a peripheral activity is now a main source of income for many street gangs. Youth gangs have further become street gangs, particularly in urban areas. Juveniles tend to stay with the gang into adulthood and assume more control of gang operations as they age.

Children of the underclass are often susceptible to gang membership due to poverty and conditions associated with urban neighborhoods. Integrated and multidimensional efforts are needed to have any long-term effect on preventing and controlling gangs and their criminal actions.

LECTURE OUTLINE

Introduction

- The case of Walter Simon: Eight shots from a rival gang.
- Social World of the Delinquent: Mara Salvatrucha MS-13

I. Peer Groups and Gangs

A. Peer Groups and Delinquent Behavior

- Conflicting findings within the research, however most agree that delinquency occurs in groups. Shaw and McKay suggested 82 percent. Jensen states juveniles follow *herd instincts* when they violate the law.
- Hirschi refers to peer relations as *cold and brittle*.
- Giordano/Cernkovich found delinquents have *friendship patterns*.
- Warr states delinquent friends tend to be *sticky* friends.
- Debate is largely causal ordered or what comes first, delinquency or peers.

II. The Development of Gangs in the United States

- Gangs have existed since the Revolutionary war. Wild West era with the James/Younger gangs.
- Youth gangs flourished in Chicago and other large cities in nineteenth century.

A. Gangs and Play Activity: The 1920s through 1940s.

- Thrasher viewed gangs as a normal part of ethnic neighborhoods. Largely transitory, organized and protective of turf. Bonded with each other without any sense of particular purpose or goal.

B. West Side Story Era: The 1950s

- Teenage gangs are more established in urban areas. They were violent, but did not have the same weapons of today's gangs.
- Millions of dollars spent to prevent and control the gangs with little or no reduction occurring.

C. Development of the Modern Gang: The 1960s

- Drugs influence gangs for the first time in the midst of rapid social changes. Drugs actually reduced gang activity in some areas due to members being self-absorbed into drugs (out of sight out of mind).
- The emergence also of super-gangs such as Crips, Vice Lords, and Disciples. (see insert 10.1).

- Super-gangs were involved in social and political activism (Operation Bootstrap). After working against Daley's campaign in Chicago, many were sent to prison due to gang crackdowns by law enforcement.

D. Expansion, Violence, and Criminal Operations: the 1970s to the Present

- 1970s and 1980s as gang leadership is assumed by adults, they become more responsible for criminal activities. Some are regarded by law enforcement as organized crime.
- Miller contends that gangs were committing one-third of all violent juvenile crime.
- 1980s crack cocaine was turning point for gangs, some established link to Columbian drug smugglers.
- Gangs are now becoming a worldwide focus in many different countries.

III. The Nature and Extent of Gang Activity

- By 2002 estimated 21,500 gangs are in the United States. This is a decline from 1996.
- 2002 National Youth Gang Survey reveals: Gang activity is down, largest drop in gang membership is suburban areas, most gang members are adult, and most are Hispanic followed by African-American then white and Asian.

A. Definitions of Gangs

- Thrasher's definition in 1927 and Miller's definition in 1970s, suggest a gang is bonded together with mutual interests, identifiable leadership, and other organizational features, to conduct illegal activity and control over territory.
- Esbensen includes ages of 12 to 24, use of colors and a sense of permanence.

B. Profiles of Gang Members

- The smaller the community more likely gang members will be juveniles. Urban gangs tend to have a majority of adult members.
- Younger members tend to run errands and serve as drug runners due to their age.
- *Regulars* are strongly attached to the gang, *peripherals* participate less than regulars and have other interests, *temporaries* are marginally committed, *situational* members participate only in certain activities.
- Reiner identifies; *at-risk* as pre-gang members, *wannabes* are recruits in pre-teen years, *associates* are the lowest level, *hard-core* are regular members, and *veteranos* are the older members.
- Klein and Maxson: traditional gang (20 year existence), neotraditional gang (10 year existence, compressed gang (50 members), collective gang (less developed), and specialty gang (small with narrow focus of activities.
- *People (5 point star) and Folks (6 point star)*: Chicago area beginnings.

C. Gangs in Schools

- School is fertile soil for youth gangs. Members bring guns to school, recruit new members from school, conflict arises at school between rival gangs.
- Schools have an economic base for drug dealing. Drug distribution was so extensive in Dallas, students were required to wear picture ID's.

D. Urban Street Gangs

- Gangs are *quasi-institutionalized.* Students seek protection in gangs.
- Dysfunctional nature of families raises the appeal for gangs. Some gangs take control of schools.
- Vertical/hierarchal gangs (Chicago based gangs).
- Horizontal/commission gangs (Bloods/Crips).
- Influential model gangs (No duties or titles of leadership).
- Gang life can look glamorous to younger recruits.
- Clothing, colors, signing are held as sacred by most gang members (tagging).
- Prayers are rituals in many gangs.
- Loyalty is a chief value in gangs.
- Hispanic gangs and *locura (craziness)* due to presence of fear.
- Gang *migration* occurs three ways: 1) satellite gangs, 2) relocation, and 3) expansion of drug markets (relocation is the most typical pattern).
- Changing structure of economy encourages teen members to continue with gangs into their adult years (loss of jobs).
- Core members are more involved with serious delinquent acts than fringe members. Gang boys persisted nearly three years longer than non-gang boys.
- Rochester study says gangs commit 7 times more delinquency than nongang offenders.
- Studies suggest that gang membership is more influential on youth violence than influence of other delinquent peers.
- Youth gang homicides might be increasing since 1998, according to 2002 NYGS.
- Peaks and valleys of gang violence is related to several factors, gun ownership, and extent of organization into crime groups.

E. Gangs in Small Communities

- No gangs are entirely alike. Expansion began in late 1980s and appeared to be fueled in four ways; expansion of the *crack-cocaine* market into smaller areas, some gang members operating on their own, gang member families that moved to new communities, and independent formation by youths free of outside interventions and constraints.
- Stages include: 1) Implementation, 2) expansion and conflict, 3) organization and consolidation, 4) Gang intimidation and community reaction, 5) expansion of drug markets, 6) gang takeover, and 7) community deterioration.

F. Racial and Ethnic Gangs

- Hispanic and African-American gangs are more numerous, but Asian gangs are rapidly increasing.
- Hispanic gangs are divided into categories with Chicano being most prevalent with codes of *Movidas.* Chicano gangs are very loyal.
- African-American gangs have established drug networks across the nation.
- Asian gangs are largely in California and tend to be more organized than others. Heroin trafficking is characteristic of their economic base.
- White gangs have a propensity to satanic worship and *stoners.* Metal music and outlandish apparel are common. Neo-Nazi groups are involved in hate crimes.

- Native American gangs have centered around Navajo groups involved in drinking.

G. Female Delinquent Gangs

- Female gangs may be independent or have connections to male gangs.
- Most studies suggest female gang activity is lower than males.
- Females are more likely to be involved in property crimes and status offenses.
- Gangs may provide girls with ways to survive in a harsh environment.

IV. Theories of Gang Formation

- Bloch and Niederhoffer suggest joining gangs is part of the male experience to grow up. Gangs provide puberty rites found in other cultures.
- Cloward and Ohlin contend gangs pursue illegitimate means due to being restricted from opportunities to legitimate means to achieve societal goals.
- Miller suggests that gang membership is an expression of lower-class subculture.
- Yablonsky states gangs are created from conditions of urban slums.
- *Underclass theory* states gangs are a natural response to an abnormal social setting.
- Call for an *integrated approach* to understand gang involvement.

A. Gangs Across the Life Course

- Gangs membership is a trajectory for some. Gangs may serve as a turning point.
- Gang membership has an impact on ones' life-course development.

V. Preventing and Controling Youth Gangs

- Communities have a tendency to deny a gang problem, until a dramatic episode occurs.
- Spergel and colleagues suggest five strategies for gang intervention; *(1) community organization, (2) social intervention, (3) opportunities provision, (4) suppression, and (5) creation of special organizational units.*
- Mobilization of school officials, employers, street workers, police, judges, prosecutors, and probation/parole/correctional officers. Community-wide approach.
- Integrated, multidimensional, community oriented effort is likely to have long-term effects in preventing and controlling gangs.

KEY TERMS

cold and brittle Hirschi's term to describe interpersonal relationships between delinquents.

crack Controlled substance derived from cocaine that is usually smoked and is cheaper to produce than conventional cocaine, therefore becoming attractive to gangs for marketing.

emerging gangs Gang formation occurring within smaller communities, which began in the 1980s with the expansions of drug trafficking into smaller cities and promises of satellite operations connected to larger urban gangs.

friendship patterns The nature of the peer relationships that exist within a teenage culture.

gang A group of youths who are bound together by mutual interests, have identifiable leadership, and act in concert to achieve a specific purpose that generally includes the conduct of illegal activity.

locura State of mind associated with Mexican-American street gangs denoting craziness or wildness.

movidas Codes of moral honor and conduct followed by Chicano gangs.

People and Folks During the 1970's the gangs within the Illinois prison system divided themselves up into two categories: the People and the Folks. Some of the gangs were identified as "people" gangs and other gangs were identified as "folk" gangs.

representing Displays by gang affiliates in which a hand sign, colors, articles of clothing, or other objects are used to represent and symbolize affiliation with particular gang membership.

CLASSROOM ACTIVITIES AND ASSIGNMENTS

1. Ask students to list stereotypes associated with gangs, and discuss any misconceptions in an effort to debunk any myths about gangs.

2. Have students research the Internet for gang websites, and report on their findings.

3. Ask students to relate any life experiences in which they interacted with gang members and discuss the accuracy of those portrayals by society.

4. Have students search for gang related graffiti within the community and attempt to identify gang affiliations

5. Ask students to list civic organizations within the community, and report on their codes of conduct, and discuss similarities to any urban gangs.

6. Have students research any sports attire and paraphernalia that gangs often adopt for their own usage and discuss.

7. Ask students to discuss why law enforcement strategies concerned with issues of identify and incarcerate to control gangs, have largely failed.

8. Have students search for recent magazine and newspaper articles that contain proactive measures for curbing gang violence, and discuss whey the number or articles were low.

VOICES OF DELINQUENCY ASSIGNMENTS

Have students read article 14 titled: The Life and Times of Herron Lewiel, Jr. and answer the following questions.

1. Ask students to discuss the impact of gang life on Herron's life.

2. Have students discuss how releasing Herron into an unchanged social environment may have resulted in his failure to stay out of prison.

3. Ask students to discuss whether they think Herron will ever be free from gang life influences.

VIDEO AND INTERNET RESOURCES

Gang Violence in America: This video tours the front lines of contemporary street gangs warfare and reviews the evolution of street gangs. It contains interviews with former gang members and suggests means for keeping children out of gangs. (50 minutes) *Insight Media.*

Gangs it's Your Life: This video examines the frequently tragic consequences of gang activity. Included are peer pressure and a need to belong as motivations to join. (60 minutes) *Insight Media.*

Skinheads USA: The Pathology of Hate: This video examines white gangs and supremacy groups in the U.S. The video does contain footage of violence and brutality. An HBO production.
(54 minutes) *Films for the Humanities and Sciences.*

Prison Gangs and Racism Behind Bars: This video examines ethnic groups struggle for supremacy within the walls of a supermax prison. Ted Koppel narrates this ABC video.
(40 minutes) *Films for the Humanities and Sciences.*

WEBSITES

Read the OJJDP publication, *Co-Offending and Patterns of Juvenile Crime,* at www.justicestudies.com/weblibrary

Read the OJJDP Fact Sheet, *Highlights of the 2002-2003 National Gang Surveys.* at www.justicestudies.com/weblibrary

Read the COPS publication, *Solutions to Address Gang Crime,* at www.justicestudies.com/weblibrary

Visit the National Youth Gang Center's Web site via www.justicestudies.com/webplaces

Visit the National Gang Crime Research Center's Web site via
www.justicestudies.com/webplaces

Read Mike Carlie's, *Into the Abyss: A Personal Journey Into the World of Street Gangs* at
www.justicestudies.com/webplaces

www.streetgangs.com

www.criminology.fsu.edu/jjclearinghouse/jj13.html

CHAPTER 11: DRUGS AND DELINQUENCY

LEARNING OBJECTIVES

After you read this chapter, you should be able to answer the following questions:

1. How are social attitudes related to drug use?

2. How much drug use is there among adolescents in American society?

3. What are the main types of drugs used by adolescents?

4. What is the relationship between drug abuse and delinquency?

5. What theoretical explanations best explain the onset of drug use?

6. What can be done to prevent and control drug use among adolescents?

CHAPTER SUMMARY

This chapter examines the use of drugs and alcohol among adolescents in the United States and its relationship to delinquency. A number of theories have been proposed for the onset and escalation of adolescent drug use. Economic situation, peer influence, addict prone personality, high or peak experience, and sociological origins have all been used to explain the appeal of substance abuse. Bartollas contends that integrated approaches make to most sense in developing an understanding of both drug use and abuse.

Trends in drug use have shown a significant decline from the late 1970s, with perhaps only slight increases occurring since the early 1990s with certain types of drugs. Alcohol continues to be the most abused substance by adolescents, followed by cigarettes, and marijuana topping the list of illicit drugs. The rate of illicit drug use is higher among those using cigarettes and alcohol. While the rate of marijuana use has gone up sharply since 1997, it still has not topped the levels reached in 1979. Studies indicate that fewer adolescents are experimenting with drugs and the heavy drug users tend to be white males. Illicit drug usage is more common on the East and West coasts and less common in the South. Low achievers in school are more susceptible to drug usage than high achievers. Ecstasy (MDMA) became widely used in the 1990s along with Crank (methamphetamine) which some had predicted would set off a new drug epidemic in the 1990s. Bartollas suggests it never fully materialized and federal efforts to control drug usage by declaring war have largely failed.

While the rate of drug usage is still considered high in this nation, it is especially high among high-risk children. Early prevention efforts in school, as well as in other social contexts, appear to be making headway with low-risk children. However, prevention, treatment, or punishment does not appear to be reducing the amount or seriousness of substance abuse with high-risk children. Research contends that social influence and peer interventions were found to have the most lasting effect on prevention and reduction of drug usage in the United States.

LECTURE OUTLINE

Introduction

- Simon Curtis: The story of a graffiti artist.

I. Drug Use Among Adolescents

- Alcohol remains the substance of choice for most adolescents.
- Drug use peaked in1979 and has declined significantly since 2001.
- Marijuana and cocaine use declined since 1999.
- Cigarette use peaked in 1974 and Inhalant use peaked in 1985.
- High school females are more likely to smoke than high school males.
- Males are more likely to be involved in heavy binge drinking than females.
- Substance abuse is higher on the East and West coasts and lowest in the South.

II. Types of Drugs

A. What's in a Name?

- Brand Name
- Generic Name
- Street Name
- Psychoactive Category

B. Alcohol and Tobacco

- Reaction to *Prohibition* fostered the view that alcohol is acceptable.
- Tobacco is often neglected in discussions on drugs, however more deaths are attributed to tobacco than alcohol and illicit drugs combined.

C. Marijuana

- Most frequently used illicit drug. Research indicates more ill effects of long-term use than believed in the past.

D. Cocaine

- Derivative of the coca plant, once believed to be less addicting than other hard drugs.
- Snorting is most common, however *freebasing* (smoking) was popular in 1980s. Intravenous use (*speedballing*) is dangerous and killed John Belushi in 1982.
- *Crack* is a more potent, less expensive refinement of cocaine (usually smoked) that arrived in the inner-cities in the early 1980s.
- *Crack* addicted *babies* are the consequences of adolescent addiction.

E. Methamphetamine

- Synthetic drug (crank, ice, chalk, glass, and crystal).
- The use of methamphetamine is growing.

F. **Inhalants**
- *Butyl nitrite* commonly called *RUSH,* is probably most frequently used. Others include vapors from gasoline, paint thinners, glue, and aerosol cans.

G. **Sedatives**
- Barbiturates used to depress the nervous system. Includes *Quaaludes*, *Amytals*, and *Tuinals*, *Valium*, *Librium*, *Equanil* (*Benzodiazepines*).

H. **Amphetamines**
- Used in WWII by Americans (*Benzedrine, Dexedrine*) used by truckers and people wanting to lose weight.
- 1990s *Ecstasy* (MDMA) became popular. Normally tablets are ingested, but it can be snorted and smoked. Originally used by psychiatrists until outlawed in 1986.

I. **Hallucinogens**
- Mind altering drugs popular in the 1960s include LSD, PCP and 1970s. Popularity dropped after 1980 to a low of less than 3 percent by 1990 after public hysteria over dangers of hallucinogens.

K. **Heroin**
- Derivative of opium introduced at turn of the twentieth century. Known as: horse, shit, smack, H, harry, henry, boy, and brown.

L **Anabolic Steroids**
- There are 100 different types of anabolic steroids. Street names include “Arnolds”, Gym Candy”, “Juice”, “Pampers”, “Stackers”, and “Weight Trainers”.

M **Delinquency in America**
- Prescription drugs find a place in teen culture.

III. Drug Use and Delinquency
- Issue under debate is whether drugs cause delinquency or does delinquency lead to drug use.
- Considered an overlapping and interrelated problem. (Jessor’s Model) Three variables: the personality system, environment system, and the behavior system.
- Abuse is related to delinquency in youth (Denver, Pittsburgh, Rochester studies).
- Widespread support for a sequential pattern of involvement in drug use during adolescence. Alcohol, to marijuana, to other drugs. Some youths experiment then discontinue, others continue into adulthood (without major interference) and some become addicted to the point their lives revolve around drugs.
- Family history, early antisocial behavior and academic failure contribute to drug use.
- Nearly 50 percent of serious juvenile offenders are multiple drug users, alcohol usage is four to nine times greater than for nonoffenders, and marijuana use is fourteen times more likely by serious offenders compared to nonoffenders.

A. Drug-Trafficking Juveniles

- Some researchers have suggested that *crack* distribution is not a street gang phenomenon. Suburbs and schools are generally serviced by independent juveniles.
- Urban settings are largely serviced by adults, not juveniles. Chicago study revealed most juveniles barely make survival income from drug deals.

B. Drug Use Through the Life Course

- Two basic pathways, (1) abusers may not be involved with delinquency, and (2) abusers participating in other delinquent acts.
- About two-thirds of abusers continue to abuse drugs into adulthood but about half desist from other forms of criminality.
- Alcohol and drug use increases the risk of youth pregnancies, early parenthood, dropping out of school, and premature independent living from parents.
- Substance abuse affects adolescent development.
- *Relapse* is attributed to those who do not find the straight life fulfilling.
- Principle Reports that drug testing students works.

IV. Explaining the Onset of Drug Abuse

- Determining whether it is the onset of drug abuse.
- No single comprehensive picture of what causes adolescents' use of drugs
- Cognitive-Affective Theories
- Addictive Personality Theories
- Stress Relief Theories
- Social Learning Theories
- Social Control Theories
- Social Disorganization Theories
- Integrated Theories

V. Solving the Drug Problem

A. Prevention

- Tobler's meta-analysis of prevention programs; (1) knowledge oriented (education), (2) affective strategies (psychological) only, (3) social influence and life skills (peer pressure), (4) knowledge plus affective (attitude and values altered), and (5) alternative strategies (school).
- Tobler concluded that social influence and peer interventions have the most lasting effects.
- Effective programs include: early childhood and family interventions, school-based interventions, and comprehensive community-wide efforts.

B. Treatment Intervention

- Treatment takes place in hospitals for those who can afford it. Others utilize privately administered placements, which vary greatly. Serious delinquents will likely be placed in state facilities whose basic goals are security-oriented.
- No real evidence that juvenile treatment is any more successful than adults.
- Willingness to change may be related to success of some intervention programs.

KEY TERMS

alcohol Considered the most abused substance by adolescents due to the perception that it is not socially unacceptable compared to illicit drugs. Perceptions of alcohol were largely affected by historical significance of Prohibition.

amphetamines A controlled substance largely used by Americans after WWII. Normally ingested in pill or capsule form and known as *uppers* such as Benzedrine and Dexedrine. Ecstasy and methamphetamine are newer forms of amphetamine that were popularized in the 1990s.

club drug A synthetic psychoactive substance often found at nightclubs, bars, "raves", and dance parties. Club drugs include MDMA (Ecstasy), ketamine, methamphetamine (meth), GBL, PCP, GHB, and Rohpnol.

cocaine Derived from coca plants and originally used as a painkiller. Typically snorted, and decreased in popularity after the 1980s due to the high cost, and the advent of cocaine's alternative derivative of *crack,* which is cheaper and more potent.

heroin Derivative of morphine which is extracted from the opiate base of poppies. Normally injected intravenously. Highly addictive and experienced resurgence in the 1990s with juveniles.

inhalants Variety of substances that are *huffed* or snorted which produce disorientation and perceived euphoria. Substances inhaled include glue, paint thinners, aerosol cans, and butyl nitrite.

marijuana The most abused illicit drug by juveniles. Plant material, which contains natural chemical amounts of THC producing mild euphoria and is usually smoked. Sometimes referred to as the *gateway* drug meaning it will lead to harder forms of drug abuse.

sedatives Barbiturates drugs intended to reduce the metabolic rate and commonly known as *downers*, such as Quaaludes. Frequently used in combination with *uppers* to establish a dosage baseline.

CLASSROOM ACTIVITIES AND ASSGINMENTS

1. Ask students to discuss any effects that recent prohibitions on teen smoking may have toward increasing usage of other illicit substances.

2. Have students conduct a survey of persons who smoke cigarettes, to ascertain if the greatest percentage of them also use alcohol.

3. Ask students who have resisted using drugs, to discuss why they think they were able to resist where others have failed.

4. Have students collect alcohol and cigarette advertising and discuss what age group is typically targeted by the various corporations.

5. Ask students to debate legalizing illicit drugs and discuss the various strengths and weaknesses of their arguments.

6. Have students research America's various *wars on drugs* and debate the failures or successes of our efforts.

7. Ask students to watch older television shows or movies in which smoking was prevalent and glamorized, and have them discuss what turned around our social attitude to one of deviance.

8. Have students conduct a self-report study on campus to see what substances are currently being abused and how they match up with the national figures.

VOICES OF DELINQUENCY ASSIGNMENTS

Have students read article 24 titled: Selling Drugs Was My Downfall and answer the following questions.

1. Ask students to discuss how peer pressure may have influenced this person's drug dealing.

2. Have students list all the delinquent/criminal behaviors this person was involved in and discuss the connection between drugs and delinquency.

3. Ask students to discuss *turning-points* and whether this person may or may not have reached it.

VIDEO AND INTERNET RESOURCES

Drugs in Black and White: This video portrays the true racial picture of drug use between black and white drug offenders in the United States. (40 minutes) Insight Media.

The War on Drugs: Winners and Losers: This video suggests the war on drugs is causing greater societal harm than the problem of drug abuse. (90 minutes) Films for the Humanities and Sciences.

Hooked on Heroin: From Hollywood to Main Street: This ABC news program examines some of the most unlikely junkies. The video discusses the rise of heroin usage in America and conducts interviews with several noted celebrities. (44 minutes). Films for the Humanities and Sciences.

A Passion for Pot: An American Obsession: This video portrays the eradication efforts by police to destroy the most widely abused illegal drug in America. (46 minutes) Films for the Humanities and Sciences.

WEBSITES

Read the COPS publication, *Underage Drinking,* at www.justicestudies.com/weblibrary

Read the OJJDP Fact Sheet, *Substance Abuse: The Nation's Number One Health Problem,* at www.justicestudies.com/weblibrary

Read the OJJDP Fact Sheet, *Assessing Alcohol, Drug, and Mental Disorders in Juvenile Detainees,* at www.justicestudies.com/weblibrary

Read the National Drug Intelligence Center *National Drug Threat Assessment* at www.justicestudies.com/weblibrary

Read the federal *General Counterdrug Intelligence Plan* at www.justicestudies.com/weblibrary

Read Key Findings from the National Institute on Drug Abuse's Monitoring the Future Survey at www.justicestudies.com/weblibrary

Read the Office of National Drug Control Policy's *National Drug Control Strategy 2006* at www.justicestudies.com/weblibrary

Visit the Mothers Against Drunk Driving's Web site via www.justicestudies.com/webplaces

Visit the National Clearinghouse for Alcohol and Drub Information's Web site via www.justicestudies.com/webplaces

Visit the Office of National Drub Control Policy's Web site via www.justicestudies.com/webplaces

Visit the Underage Drinking Enforcement Training Center's Web site via www.justicestudies.com/webplaces

Visit Clubdrugs.org via www.justicestudies.com/webplaces

Visit the drub Enforcement Administration's (DEA) Web site via www.justicestudies.com/webplaces

Visit the National Drug Intelligence Center's Web site via www.justicestudies.com/webplaces

www.lec.org/DrugSearch/Documents/Amphetamines.html

www.virlib.ncjrs.org/DrugsAndCrime.asp

CHAPTER 12: PREVENTION, DIVERSION, AND TREATMENT

LEARNING OBJECTIVES

After reading this chapter your should be able to answer the following questions:

1. What type of prevention programs are likely to work with high-risk youngsters?
2. What ate the advantages and disadvantages of the diversionary programs?
3. What treatment modalities are most widely used with juvenile delinquents?
4. What are the common characteristics of effective programs?

CHAPTER SUMMARY

Delinquency prevention programs have generally fallen short of controlling youth crime. Grass-roots community groups appear to offer the most promising approach of the various prevention programs of the twentieth century in preventing delinquency. For delinquency prevention programs to have significant success in preventing youth crime, it will be necessary to modify the social, economic, and political conditions of American society. *Primary* and *secondary prevention* programs have been barely adequate at delinquency prevention to date.

Diversion programs have evolved mainly from programs initiated by police, probation officers, the juvenile court, and other outside the system agencies. Most of the programs of the 1960s and 1970s were viewed as panaceas for reducing youth crime. The main criticism of diversion programs has been the charge of *net-widening*, in that youths are brought into the system that might not have been otherwise.
Additionally, critics charge that youth prevention programs are considered too expensive. Newly developed *drug* and *teen courts* are recent attempts in the prevention of delinquency. However, it is too soon to analyze their effectiveness.

Much of the research in juvenile delinquency contends that violent and inhumane training schools are among the least promising places for treatment and prevention to occur. Community-based programs traditionally lack resources, which probably helped result in more failures than successes. The 60 Minutes revelation by Robert Martinson, led to a premature and mostly inaccurate perceptions of community-based treatment modalities. Later, meta-analysis revealed reduction in recidivism rates of 10 to 12 percent.

Guided group interaction and *reality therapy* have been used more than most other treatment modalities in treating youth offenders. Both are aimed at making the offender responsible for their actions and teaching a more positive pro-social stance. The *errors in thinking approach*, is a cognitive restructuring strategy that was widely adopted in the 1990s throughout the nation. Program designs have often relied on a single cure for complex problems, lacked integrity, and been inadequate. However, as Bartollas indicates, correctional treatment could work if amenable offenders were offered appropriate treatments.

LECTURE OUTLINE

I. Delinquency Prevention

- Emphasis on prevention was incorporated into several federal laws in the 1970s and 1980s.
- Prevention still has largely been ignored.
- *Primary prevention* is focused on modifying physical and social environments.
- *Secondary prevention* refers to intervention programs and is diversionary.
- *Tertiary prevention* is directed at prevention of recidivism (traditional rehabilitation).

A. A History of Well Meant Intentions

- *Panaceas* stem from tendency to seek easy answers and divert attentions away from long-term comprehensive help.
- Panaceas have ranged from biological, psychological, group therapy, gang intervention, recreational activities, job training/employment, and community organization.
- Studies have suggested the effectiveness of these programs is weak.
- Criticized for widening the nets of social control over children, being too expensive, providing piecemeal solutions, and compromising the rights of children.
- In 1990 the Office of Juvenile Justice and Delinquency Prevention began to target the prevention of serious delinquency through reducing chronic delinquency.

B. Comprehensive Strategy for Delinquency Prevention

- First developed in 1980s, a comprehensive framework is made up of typologies of cause focused strategies and awareness of components of programs that work.
- The National Center for the Assessment of Delinquent Behavior and its Prevention suggest three principles: (1) *focus on the causes of delinquency*, (2) *there are multiple causes and correlates of delinquency*, and (3) *experiences during social development.*

C. Promising Prevention Programs

- Public Health Model of Crime Prevention
- The Office of Juvenile Justice and Delinquency Prevention guide (MPG)
- Big Brothers Big Sisters of America (mentoring programs)
- Bully Prevention Program (school programs)
- Functional Family Therapy (intervention program)
- Incredible Years (parent and teacher program to treat conduct problems)
- Life Skills Training (intervention curriculum)
- Midwestern Prevention Project (school-based intervention)
- Multidimensional Treatment Foster Care (short term therapeutic care)
- Multisystematic Therapy (community-based clinical treatment for chronic offenders)
- Nurse-Family Partner ship (prenatal care)
- Project Towards No Drug Abuse (targets high-school youth)
- Promoting Alternative Thinking Strategies (PATH) (teachers and counselors)

D. Programs That Work

- Dryfoos identified; individual counseling and mentoring for high-risk children, multiagency collaborative approach, early identification and intervention, programs located outside of the school, training of staff, providing of coping skills, and using older peer influence for learning.

E. Comprehensive Delinquency Prevention

- Research indicates that high-risk youth can be impacted by well-equipped prevention and treatment programs.
- The comprehensive or multi-systematic: builds on the youth's strengths, operate outside the formal justice system and combines accountability with intensive rehabilitation.

II. How Diversion Works

- Began in 1967 after President's Commission on Law Enforcement, recommended alternatives to the juvenile system based on labeling perspective and differential association theories.

A. Traditional Forms of Diversion

- Belief that diversion would lead to more effective and humane justice.
- Diversion can come from police, courts or agencies outside of the justice system.

B. New Forms of Diversion

- 1990s brought *community courts* with emphasis on restoration, *alternative dispute resolution*(family and victim meetings), *gun courts*(intense intervention related to weapons), *teen courts* (Adult judge-Youth judge-Tribunal-Peer Jury), and drug courts (deferred prosecution for drug treatment).
- Most teen courts receive less than 100 referrals per year. Handle first time offenders and rarely or never accept youths with prior arrest records.
- *Drug courts* established by Title V of the Violent Crime Control and Law Enforcement Act of 1994. More comprehensive intake assessments, focus on the family, coordination of school, community and the juvenile, continual supervision, and application of immediate sanctions.
- Recent studies suggest effects of drug courts may be more stigmatizing than conventional courts for teens.

III. The Treatment Debate

- Correctional treatment came under increased criticism in the late 1960s and 1970s.
- Robert Martinson's 1974 statement was translated as *"nothing works"* by media.
- General mood in the 1980s was one of pessimism and discouragement.
- *Meta-analysis* of treatment programs reveals treatment leads to reduction in recidivism rates.

IV. Most Frequently Used Treatment Modalities

- Modalities used in community-based corrections and training schools include; *psychotherapy*, *transactional analysis, reality therapy, behavior modification, family therapy, guided group interaction*, and *positive peer culture.*

A. Psychotherapy

- Adaptations of Freudian theory in which offenders are encouraged to talk about past conflicts in individual or group settings. The modality is used more with upper- and middle-class youths and most psychotherapies are conducted in outside agencies.

B. Transactional Analysis

- Focuses on interpreting interpersonal relationships by teaching offenders to relate to problems in a mature manner. Meaning is attached to *"tapes"* of the past and the goal is for offenders to negotiate their own treatment contract.

C. Reality Therapy

- Modality assumes irresponsible behavior occurs when unmet basic needs occur. Uses the three R's; *reality, responsibility, right-and-wrong.*

D. Behavior Modification

- Based on assumption of learning and that behavior is under the control of external environment. Positive reinforcement should encourage good behavior. Some charge the treatment is not long lasting.

E. Guided Group Interaction

- Residential treatment oriented. Assumes confrontation by peers will cause offenders to face the reality of their behaviors. Decision-making is done by the group. Urges the group to be open and honest with each other.

F. Positive Peer Culture

- Teaches group members to care for one another and mobilize the group in positive ways. When caring becomes fashionable, hurting goes out of style.

G. Rational Emotive Therapy

- Rationale is to identify the errors of an offenders thinking such as blaming others, manipulation, and failure to accept obligations. *Cognitive restructuring* of dysfunctional patterns. Widely adopted during the 1990s throughout the nation.

H. Drug and Alcohol Abuse Interventions

- Offenders may be placed in special cottages with specialized staff to lead groups. Outside groups, such as AA or NA make presentations to the group.
- Drug/alcohol problems represent one of the greatest challenges for juvenile justice.

V. What Works for Whom and in What Context

- Some treatment programs have actually made rehabilitation worse. Program designs may have failed to consider what realistically can be accomplished.
- Frequently programs try to apply a single cure for complex problems and lack integrity.

- Correctional treatment could work if amenable offenders are offered appropriate treatments, such as *template-matching* techniques.

KEY TERMS

behavior modification This modality rewards appropriate behavior positively, immediately, and systematically, and it assumes that rewards increase the occurrence of desired behaviors.

diversion programs Programs designed outside the formal juvenile justice system to provide alternatives for disposition of juvenile offenders. Programs are aimed at prevention and treatment of youthful offenders.

drug and alcohol abuse interventions Juvenile offenders may be housed in special cottages with adult team leaders. Outside groups such as Alcoholics Anonymous and Narcotics Anonymous may make presentations to the cottage group.

guided group interaction Places youthful offenders in a group setting under the direction of adult leaders. Groups often make decisions when an offender will be released or furloughed.

juvenile drug courts Community court model established by Title V of the 1994 Violent Crime Control and Law Enforcement Act, in which more focus is placed on the family, school and the juvenile offender with immediate sanctions. Typically offers deferred prosecutions in exchange for drug treatment.

panaceas Quick and generally inadequate remedies for complex problems. Typically panaceas take a piecemeal approach to satisfy public perceptions about juvenile justice problems and solutions.

positive peer culture Derived from guided group interaction, this approach utilizes positive measures to teach caring principles on the assumption that when caring becomes fashionable, hurting will go out of style.

primary prevention Prevention strategies based on the modification of an offender's physical and social environments in order to enact changes in his or her behavior and assumingly create rehabilitation.

psychotherapy Developed by Freud and assumes that talking about one's behavior and feelings of past conflicts will lead to release of emotions. Sessions are conducted in group or individually and are typically reserved more for the upper-and middle-class offenders.

rational emotive therapy Yochelson and Samenow's perception that criminals have certain personality characteristics that lead to some fifty-two errors in thinking. The modality teaches children to accept responsibility for their behaviors.

reality therapy Modality encourages the three R's; realistic, responsibility and right-and-wrong. Assumes that meeting the basic needs of children will encourage responsible behavior.

secondary prevention Prevention strategies aimed at trying to change the attitudes and behavior of a specific offender to become more compliant and law abiding.

teen courts Community court model that utilizes nonjudical members to adjudicate minor offenses. Four types are, Adult Judge (most common), Youth Judge, Tribunal, and Peer Jury.

tertiary prevention Prevention strategies aimed at reducing recidivism by discouraging the offender from repeating their offenses.

transactional analysis Modality of therapy that is based on interpreting and evaluating personal relationships. Meaning is attached to "tape" of the past and offender ultimately will negotiate his or her own treatment.

youth service bureaus Diversionary agencies that offered a variety of alternatives for youth to minimize youthful offending. Programs ranged from drop-in recreational centers to twenty-four hours crisis centers. Lack of funding closed many YSB's in the 1980's.

CLASSROOM ACTIVITIES AND ASSIGNMENTS

1. Ask students to discuss the recent national focus on *faith-based* treatment programs, and based on past history of juvenile treatment strategies; discuss why they may be doomed for failure before they begin. When tax money is being used, are these programs constitutional?

2. Have students research the organizations of Alcoholic and Narcotic Anonymous and discuss why their treatment modalities may have failed for some substance abusers.

3. Ask students to contact local counseling agencies to ascertain what type of services are available within the community, and discuss how they fit with the modalities suggested by Bartollas.

4. Have students conduct a mock teen court trial in the classroom and discuss the advantages and disadvantages of such a modality.

5. Ask students to search for teen recreational programs available within the community and discuss the strengths and weaknesses of those programs.

6. Have students research national drug abuse treatment programs and identify which treatment modalities are being used, and compare and discuss the statistical successes that each organization/program claim.

7. Ask students to list any panaceas or *quick-fixes* that their parents or teachers may have used to correct their behavior and discuss why today they (students) think it worked or failed.

8. Have students list as many preventative measures used by society in areas other than delinquency (preventative medicine or birth control), and discuss why as a society we may fail to connect prevention with delinquency.

VOICES OF DELINQUENCY ASSIGNMENTS

Have students read article 21 titled: Forgotten Children and answer the following questions.

1. Have students find evidence of the effects of institutionalization on this person and discuss possible alternatives that might have been used earlier in this person's life.

2. Ask students to discuss what this person means when suggesting the *wonderment of childhood* had been erased in his life.

3. Have students find the various treatment modalities that were tried with this person and discuss why one could predict why they may or may not have been successful.

VIDEO AND INTERNET RESOURCES

Violence Prevention: This video views violence through the lens of a public health policy and suggests using the same tools to fight violence as we use to fight cigarette smoking and other societal vices. (25 minutes) *Insight Media.*

Stemming Violence and Abuse: This video offers insights and suggestions that can stop dangerous incidents before they start. It covers issues of date rape, domestic assaults and victim precipitation factors. (29 minutes) *Films for the Humanities and Sciences.*

Street Crime: Community Efforts to Stop Crime: This video explores the uptown area of Chicago and Kansas City where ordinary residents organized themselves into grass-root heroes to drive out drug dealers. (57 minutes) *Films for the Humanities and Sciences.*

Exploring Alternatives to Prison and Probation: This video examines a range of alternative sentencing programs being tried around the country. It discusses the risks and costs of programs, and some of the arguments for and against alternatives. (22 minutes) *Filmakers Library.*

WEBSITES

Read the OJJDP publication, *Blueprints for Violence Prevention,* at www.justicestudies.com/weblibrary

Read the OJJDP publication, *YouthBuild U.S.A.,* at www.justicestudies.com/weblibrary

Read the OJJDP publication, *Juvenile Drug Court Programs,* at www.justicestudies.com/weblibrary

Visit AfterSchool.gov via www.justicestudies.com/webplaces

Visit the National Mentoring Partnership Web site via www.justicestudies.com/webplaces

Visit the National Youth Prevention Resource Center's Center's Web site via www.justicestudies.com/webplaces

Visit the National Center for Mental Health and Juvenile Justice Web's site via www.justicestudies.com/webplaces

Visit the National Youth Court Center's Web site via www.justicestudies.com/webplaces

www.grandviewyouthcourt.com/

www.brunswick.oh.us/police/index.htm

CHAPTER 13: THE JUVENILE JUSTICE PROCESS

LEARNING OBJECTIVES

After reading this chapter, you should be able to answer the following questions:

1. What is the juvenile justice process?
2. What are the stages in the juvenile justice process?
3. In what ways are the juvenile and adult justice systems the same?
4. Why is understanding the violent juvenile the key to effective interventions with juvenile offenders?
5. Why is minority over-representation such a serious issue for the juvenile justice system?
6. What will the juvenile justice system look like in the future?

CHAPTER SUMMARY

This chapter examines the organizational context of correcting and controlling juvenile delinquency, and crime in the United States. The *subsystems* of the juvenile justice system are the *police, juvenile courts*, and *corrections*. The functions of each subsystem vary in size and organization. However, most entities of juvenile justice are concerned with maintaining an equilibrium and survival. Most improvements in the juvenile justice system hardly seem to have scratched the surface in effectively dealing with the basic problem of youth crime in America.

Lack of cooperation and communication between the subsystems of juvenile justice, have helped to create a fragmented system of justice for youthful offenders. Lack of common goals, and local biases, help formulate a negative impact on juvenile offenders. The traditional correctional models may all seek a common goal to correct delinquent behavior, but they are not in agreement over what and when they should be used. The basic four discussed are, (1) the *Rehabilitation Model*, (2) the *Justice Model*, (3) the *Balanced and Restorative Model*, and (4) the *Crime Control Model*. The Crime Control Model is probably the most favored model and has wide support. Between 1992 and 1997, state legislatures in 47 states passed laws making the juvenile justice system more punitive. Recently, a trend toward a balanced approach is seen even more in the late 1990s.

The Juvenile Justice and Delinquency Prevention Act of 1974 required the *deinstitutionalization* of *status offenders* and the separation of juvenile delinquents from adult offenders. Amendments in 1980 and additionally, in 1992 required that juveniles be removed from adult jails and states must demonstrate efforts to reduce disparity in minority confinements. Today, jurisdictions still violate these requirements on the contention they have no alternatives available to them.

The return of *graduated sanctions* (indeterminate sentencing) is experiencing a new resurgence in adult corrections and the same movement is beginning to gain momentum in juvenile justice as well. Literature on correctional programs for juveniles, suggest that more effective interventions for at-risk-youth are warranted if certain key areas are addressed. Bartollas offers trend predictions for the future to help those understand which direction the system needs to move toward.

LECTURE OUTLINE

Introduction

An Interview with Marty Beyer

I. Development of the Juvenile Justice System: The Origins of the Juvenile Court

A. Sociocultural Context

- Threes social conditions; (1) jailing children with adults, (2) Chicago's population tripled between 1880 and 1890 which brought filth, corruption, poverty and widespread disenchantment, and (3) higher status given to middle-class women led to child-saving avocation outside the home.

B. Legal Context

- Juvenile court founded in Cook County (Chicago) in 1899 based on the parens patriae doctrine.

C. Political Context

- The juvenile court satisfied the middle-class child-saving movement for offenders.

D. Economic Context

- Large scale immigration and class favoritism toward the middle classes.
- Child-savers were viewed as rescuing immigrant children to protect them from their families.

E. Emergence of Community Based Corrections.

- Expansion and Retrenchment in the Twentieth Century
- The development of Juvenile Institutions
- Twentieth-Century Changes

II. The Juvenile Justice System Today

A. Structures and Functions

- Justice system is comprised of *three subsystems, police, juvenile courts* and *corrections*.

- Equilibrium is a concern, changes in one causes consequences elsewhere.
- Police systems are oriented to law enforcement and order maintenance.
- Juvenile court is responsible for disposing of cases, parens patriae charges the court with treating rather than punishing youngsters.
- Corrections is responsible for care of the offenders. *Probation* is the most widely used disposition. Day treatment and residential programs are charged with preparing youths for their return to the community and humane care. Long term holding facilities are responsible for ensuring residents receive their constitutional rights.

B. Stages in the Juvenile Justice Process

- *Intake* process occurs in which a juvenile might remain in the community or be placed in detention or shelter facilities. More serious cases typically receive a petition, rather than informal adjustments.
- Transfer to adult court must occur prior to any juvenile proceedings or an *adjudicatory hearing* takes place to determine guilt or innocence.
- Disposition hearings occur after *adjudication* has found a juvenile delinquent. Most codes now require that disposition and adjudication occur at different times.
- Juveniles can be placed in public or privately administered day treatment or residential programs. Larger states with several facilities may use diagnostic centers to aid in determining proper institutional placement.
- *Aftercare* normally follows release from the institution.

C. Recidivism in the Juvenile Justice System

- Early cohort studies suggested that housing juveniles with adults increased the probability of juveniles becoming adult offenders.
- A recent Maricopa County cohort study contends that juvenile justice system contact by offenders reduced their propensity to recidivate (54 percent of males and 73 percent of females never returned). Recidivism is higher for males.

F. Comparison of the Juvenile and Adult Justice Systems

- Both systems are made up of three subsystems.
- Vocabulary is different for juvenile systems, yet the intent is the same.
- Both systems are under fire to get *tough* on crime. Most deal with overloads, and overcrowding, face funding problems and burnout.

III. Basic Correctional Models

A. Four basic correctional models: (1) *Rehabilitative*, (2) *Justice*, (3) *Balanced and Restorative Justice* and (4) *Crime Control.*

- The rehabilitative modality seeks to change an offender's character, attitude, or behavior patterns. The *medical, adjustment*, and *reintegration* models are all expressions of the rehabilitative philosophy.
- The medical model contends delinquency is caused by factors that can be cured and punishment should be avoided as it only reinforces negative self-image.

- The adjustment model purports that delinquents need treatment that will demonstrate responsible behavior.
- The basic assumption of the reintegration model is that delinquent's problems must be solved in the community where the problems originated
- The justice model (just deserts) holds that punishment is the basic purpose of juvenile justice.
- The balanced and restorative model is an integrated model and seeks to reconcile the interests of victims, offenders, and the community through supervision programs.
- The crime control model is based on classical school criminology, which emphasizes punishment and that life and property of the innocent should be protected.

B. Emerging Approach to Handling Youthful Offenders

- The crime control model has the largest support for serious and violent offenders. States between 1992 and 1997 enacted laws to make the juvenile system more punitive.
- The trend in the late 1990s was a movement toward a balanced approach.

IV. The Juvenile Justice and Delinquency Prevention Act of 1974

- The Act recommends that status offenses be handled outside the court system and there be separation of juvenile and adult offenders.
- In 1980 an amendment to the Act required that juveniles be removed from adult jails and lockup facilities.
- In 1992 another amendment to the 1974 Act required that states determine the extent of disproportionate confinement of minorities and reduce the disparities.

A. Race and Juvenile Justice

B. Deinstitutionalization of Status Offenders

- More attempts are made to separate status offenders from delinquents.

C. Removal of Juveniles for Jails and Lockups

- Several states have enacted legislation prohibiting the jailing of juveniles with adults.

D. Disproportionate Minority Confinement

- Mounting evidence of unfair evidence of minority confinement.

V. Graduated Sanctions

- Increased attention given to indeterminate sanctions to reduce delinquency.

A. Core Principles of Graduated Sanctions

- A model system combines the treatment and rehabilitation of youth with fair, humane, reasonable, and appropriate sanctions.
- General characteristics include, key areas of risk in a youth's life, strengthen the personal and institutional factors contributing to healthy adolescent development.

VI. Trends for the Future

- It is like that the adult system will become more involved with older offenders.
- There is concerned that with a projected increased juvenile population the juvenile justice system will have greater demands on it.
- Many of these juveniles will come from impoverished homes headed by single mothers, and concern exists that this may mean more minorities in the juvenile justice system.
- With the increase population of poor juveniles the rate of juvenile violence, including homicides may again grow.
- The widespread feeling among many in the American population today is that there are more troubled teenagers than in the past.
- The field of adolescent psychiatry will be more frequently called upon to treat troubled youths.
- Some argue that stiffer penalties could be a deterrent to juveniles who might otherwise kill.
- Gangs are perceived as a serious social problem, but there is a lack of agreement about what to do to reduce the treat of gang violence.
- The use of drugs by adolescents remains an issue in American society.
- Many adolescents consume alcohol to excess.
- Debate has focused for some time on the disparity of juvenile court sentencing.
- State legislatures are increasingly passing laws intended to deter juvenile crime.

KEY TERMS

adjudicatory hearing The juvenile trial stage in which evidence is presented to reach a finding as to the level of guilt or innocence of a juvenile offender.

adjustment model A model of juvenile rehabilitation that focuses on teaching offenders to be accountable for their actions.

aftercare Supervision of juveniles that is designed to make an optimal resocialization and adjustment back into community living, after they have been released from correctional institutions.

balanced and restorative model An integrative correctional model that seeks to reconcile the interests of victims, offenders, and the community through programs and supervision ractices.

child savers The name given to an organized group of progressive social reformers of the late nineteenth and early twentieth centuries who promoted numerous laws aimed at protecting children and institutionalizing an idealized image of childhood innocence.

commitment The sentence of confinement given to a juvenile offender at the disposition stage of the juvenile court proceedings.

cottage system A widely used treatment practice that places small groups of training school residents into cottages. (shall housing units)

detention The holding of a juvenile offender in jail.

dispositional hearing The sentencing stage of a juvenile proceeding in which the judge decides what an appropriate sanction should be given for a particular offense(s).

disproportionate minority confinement The court-ordered confinement, in juvenile institutions, of members of minority groups in numbers disproportionate to their representation in the general population

intake The first stage of the juvenile justice process in which the decision is made to divert the offender or file a juvenile court petition. Typically completed by juvenile probation or police officers.

juvenile court officer A person who typically processes juveniles entering the juvenile court system.

justice model A model of juvenile justice that holds that punishment is pivotal in deterring delinquency and that violators deserved to be punished.

medical model A model of rehabilitation that suggests that delinquency is caused by factors that can be identified, isolated, treated and cured.

petition The indictment document filed into juvenile court alleging the offense(s) committed by a juvenile offender.

probation officer Juvenile officer who supervises offenders assigned to their case list. Typically include formation of social histories, case files, and related enforcement duties of probation conditions.

reintegration model Community-based model of rehabilitation that focuses on restoring the offender back into the community and addresses the social responsibility of both the offender and community.

rehabilitative philosophy The basic tenets of the medical model, the adjustment model and the reintegration model which seeks to change an offender's character, attitude, or behavior.

residential programs Programs conducted for the rehabilitation of youth within community-based and institutional settings.

taking into custody The arrest process of physically taking a juvenile offender into custody.

training school A correctional facility for long-term placement of juvenile delinquents; may be public (ran by a state department of corrections or youth commission) or private.

CLASSROOM ACTIVITIES AND ASSIGNMENTS

1. Ask students to attend an adult trial and discuss the similarities and differences between the adult trial process and typical juvenile court matters.

2. Have students interview a juvenile probation officer to develop a better comprehension of their duties, workload, and general orientation toward the juvenile justice system.

3. Ask students to interview a local law enforcement agency to ascertain their level of cooperation with the juvenile probation authorities and the juvenile court. Discuss whether the views of the agency are proactive or reactive in nature.

4. Have students inquire of local law enforcement agencies as to their policies on housing juveniles with adult offenders, and discuss in class the agency's compliance with JJDPA.

5. Ask students to search for articles and stories that highlight the fragmentation of the juvenile justice system and discuss their findings in class.

6. Have students research where control of the juvenile system in your state is centered (county or state) and discuss the issue of fragmentation and duplication of services.

7. Ask a local juvenile officer to attend your class and make a presentation on their job duties and other related areas.

8. Have students research President Bush's recent legislation of juvenile treatment for drug offenders (war on drugs) and identify which treatment model it follows.

VOICES OF DELINQUENCY ASSIGNMENTS

Have students read article 10 titled: <u>I Have Come A Long Way</u> and answer the following questions:

1. Ask students to discuss which models of rehabilitation have been used in this person's life story and if they had any positive or negative effects on his behavior.

2. Have students discuss the college disciplinary trial process and whether the outcome had a positive or negative effect on this person.

3. Ask students to find indicators within the article that would assist them in preparing a mock social history report, in order to predict the future success or failure of this person in staying straight.

VIDEO AND INTERNET RESOURCES

Juvenile Justice: In the Child's Best Interest: This video sheds light on the juvenile justice system. Courtroom footage reveals the intense proceedings in which judges shape the future of children and parents. (60 minutes) *Films for the Humanities and Sciences.*

Kids in Court: This video examines the promising efforts of rehabilitation facilities and the urgent need for locked juvenile mental health facilities. An ABC three segment program. (59 minutes) *Films for the Humanities and Sciences.*

Juveniles and the Death Penalty: This video visits death row inmates who committed murder as juvenile offenders. The convicted murderers articulate a wide range of attitudes . (58 minutes) *Films for the Humanities and Sciences.*

Order in the Court: This video points out the differences in juvenile proceedings and the adult processes in terms of trial and pre-trial procedures. Various legal experts explain the procedures and process along the way. (30 minutes) *Films for the Humanities and Sciences.*

WEBSITES

Read Chapter 4 of the OJJDP publication, *Juvenile Offenders and Victims: 2006 National Report,* at www.justicestudies.com/weblibrary

Read the OJJDP publication, *How the Justice System Responds to Juvenile Victims: A Comprehensive Model*, at www.justicestudies.com/weblibrary

Read the OJJDP publication, *Juveniles Facing Criminal Sanctions: Three States That Changed the Rules,* at www.justicestudies.com/weblibrary

Read the OJJDP Juvenile Justice Bulletin, *Restorative Justice Conferences as an early Response to Young Offenders,* at www.justicestudies.com/weblibrary

Read the NIJ article, *Brick by Brick: Dismantling the Border Between Juvenile and Adult Justice,* at www.justicestudies.com/weblibrary

Learn more about Disproportionate Minority Contact (DMC) from the Juvenile Justice Evaluation Center Online via www.justicestudies.com/webplaces

Visit the American Bar Association's Juvenile Justice Committee online via www.justicestudies.com/webplaces

Visit the Coalition for Juvenile Justice's Web site via www.justicestudies.com/webplaces

View the OJJDP PowerPoint presentation "Juvenile Justice System Structure and Process", at www.justicestudies.com/webplaces

www.ncjrs.org/txtfiles/ojjjact.txt

www.criminology.fsu.edu/jjclearinghouse/jj19.html

CHAPTER 14: THE POLICE AND THE JUVENILE

LEARNING OBJECTIVES

After reading this chapter you should be able to answer the following questions:

1. What has been the history of police-juvenile relations?
2. How have the attitudes of juveniles changed toward the police?
3. How are juvenile offenders processed?
4. What are the legal rights of juveniles in encounters with police?
5. What kinds of efforts do police make to deter delinquency?
6. How does community police impact juveniles?

CHAPTER SUMMARY

In the late 1800s and early 1900s, the policing of juveniles was viewed differently from the policing of adults. The progressive movement encouraged many social reforms and policing was affected as well. The main focus was on prevention of juvenile delinquency and the development of specialized units to work with juveniles. By the late 1970s and early 1980s, police involvement tended to decline in delinquency prevention and police diversionary programs. Budgetary constraints and specialization encouraged police departments to move away from intensive involvement in juvenile relations. However, by the late 1980s and early 1990s, police once again were encouraged to refocus their efforts on prevention. The latest emphasis of police intervention has been attributed to the rise of juvenile violence and proliferation of youth gangs.

The importance of police-juvenile relations cannot be minimized because the police are generally the first contact juveniles have with the justice system. Today, juveniles have better attitudes toward police than in the past. Police have wide *discretion* in regard to juvenile law violations. Studies reveal that police divert 80 percent to 90 percent of juvenile encounters away from the juvenile justice system. The seriousness of the offense is the key element influencing police-juvenile discretion.

Juveniles have won due process rights in several legal procedural areas. In *State v. Lowry* (1967), the Fourth Amendment protection against unreasonable searches was granted to juveniles. The application of *Miranda rights* has affected police excesses in regard to *police interrogations* of juveniles. The *Gault* case (1967) was instrumental in awarding juveniles most due process rights, with the exclusion of jury trials, which is still applied on a state-by-state basis.

Police have concentrated recent efforts on reduction of violent youth crime. Their role in reducing juvenile availability to handguns is credited in playing a major role in reducing juvenile homicides in urban settings. Police continue to combat drug and gang problems along with the recent frustrations of hate crimes.

LECTURE OUTLINE

I. The History of Police-Juvenile Relations

- Seventeenth and eighteenth centuries use informal methods of control by family, church and community (mutual pledge and watch/ward systems).
- Organized police were largely uneducated, poorly paid and ill-treated (political corruption).
- NY police department began a program in 1914 to prevent juvenile delinquency, by 1924, 90 percent of the nation's cities had established juvenile programs (PAL in 1920).
- August Vollmer introduced the concept of *youth bureau* in 1930 at Berkeley, CA.

A. Contemporary Developments in Juvenile-Police Relations

- The role of juvenile officer developed after WW II with the Central States Juvenile Officers Association (1955) and International Juvenile Officers Association (1957) developing standards (the goal is to be helpful and not punitive).
- In the 1960s police became involved in truancy and drug prevention programs and actual supervision of youthful offenders.
- By the 1970s and 1980s the trend was for police to move away from deep involvement in juvenile work. Detective divisions assumed responsibilities in many departments.
- The 1990s proliferation of substance abuse resulted in police moving back into schools and providing security for gun-free zones and various other programs.

II. Juvenile's Attitudes Toward the Police

- Most attention to attitudes given in the 1970s.
- Whites have a more favorable opinion of police than African-Americans. Females have a more favorable opinion of police than males. Students from middle-and upper-class families have a better attitude toward police than lower class students.
- Juveniles with no police contact have more favorable views than juveniles with police contact.
- Sociocultural context shapes youth attitude toward police. Most youths today have a positive attitude toward police.

III. The Processing of Juvenile Offenders

- Influence of individual factors, sociocultural factors, and organizational factors affecting the processing of juvenile offenders.

A. Factors That Influence Police Discretion

- Police discretion if not used would increase the number of youths two to three times and make the system unmanageable.
- Nature of the offense (seriousness) is the most important factor.
- The number complaints and the presence of a citizen.

- Gender of the offender, girls are less likely to be referred than boys.
- Race of the offender, police are more likely to arrest minority juveniles.
- Socioeconomic status, more "saving" is performed with middle-and upper-class juveniles.
- Individual factors of prior arrest, age, peers and family situation and conduct.
- Nature of police-juvenile interaction and departmental policy.
- Media pressures and the socioeconomic status of the victim creating external pressure.

B. Informal and Formal Dispositions

- Warning and releasing youth back into the community (25 percent of cases in 1997).
- Station adjustment (official contact recorded)
- Referring to a diversion agency (1 percent in 1997)
- Issuing a citation and referral to court. In 1997, two-thirds of juvenile arrests were referred to court by intake officers.
- Detention centers where an intake worker can release offenders or leave them in detention if they pose a danger to themselves or others.

C. Police Attitudes toward Youth Crime

- Leniency of juvenile cases makes police feel the system is too permissive.
- Police know juveniles can be unpredictable and dangerous.
- Juveniles challenge police authority and police are reluctant to engage in encounters.

IV. The Legal Rights of Juveniles

A. Search and Seizure

- Search and seizure rights affirmed for juveniles with the State v. Lowry (1967) case.

B. Interrogation Practices

- Haley v. Ohio is an early case involving excesses in police interrogation of juveniles.
- Miranda v. Arizona (1967) entitles individuals to remain silent during interrogations, and the *In re Gault* case applied due process principles and right to counsel.
- Fare v. Michael C. (1979) decision applied the *totality of circumstances* to juveniles.
- Waiving of Miranda rights is regulated through state-by-state requirements.

C. Fingerprinting

- Some juvenile courts require that judicial approval is required to fingerprint juveniles.
- Police policy dictates the fingerprinting practice in some jurisdictions.

D. Pretrial Identification Practices

- The Juvenile Justice and Delinquency Prevention Act of 1974 recommended that photographs, lineups and media releases be prohibited.
- By 1997 45 states permitted photographing of juveniles for record purposes and 42 states allowed restricted media releases of juvenile crimes.

V. Prevention and Deterrence of Delinquency

- Community-based, school-based, and gang-based interventions are all part of police strategies used to prevent and deter youth crime.
- Community policing moves police from reactive policing to proactive policing, increases police accountability, and encourages police to view citizens as partners.

A. Community-Based Interventions

- Focuses on relations with school, community agencies, youth organizations, and youths themselves. (Curfew arrests increased dramatically to keep youths off the street).
- Drug arrests increased and efforts to get guns out of juvenile hands.
- AMBER Alert

B. School-Based Interventions

- Officer Friendly and McGruff programs were developed to improve relations between police and younger children.
- Gang Resistance Education and Training (GREAT) and Law-Related Education (LRE).
- LRE is designed to teach principles and skills to become responsible citizens. One study suggested juveniles were less likely to associate with delinquent peers after LRE training.
- DARE has been criticized for being ineffective in the long term.
- Officers (SROs) employed full-time in schools for a variety of preventative measures.

C. Gang-Based Interventions

- Three intervention strategies; youth service bureaus, gang details, and gang units.
- 85 percent of specialized gang units have been established since 1990.

KEY TERMS

arrest The process of taking a juvenile into custody for an alleged violation of the law.

citation Legal notification issued by police for a person(s) to appear in court to answer to a specific charge(s)

gang unit A specialized unit found in some police agencies that is responsible for the prevention and intervention of gangs to reduce related crime.

juvenile officer Specialized assignment found in many police department and juvenile agencies for the sole prevention and reduction of juvenile related crime.

Miranda v. Arizona Landmark case that allows citizens to exercise their Fifth Amendment protection against self-incrimination by remaining silent when interrogated by law enforcement officers. The Gault (1967) case reaffirmed the application of the Miranda case to juveniles.

New Jersey v. T.L.O. 1985 Supreme Court ruling which allows police and school authorities to search student lockers and property without a search warrant based upon reasonableness of the search.

police discretion The use of personal judgment by a representative of the justice system during arrest, processing, or sentencing phases of the justice process.

police interrogation Process of questioning a person suspected to be involved in a criminal matter. Some states require juveniles to have parents or legal guardians present and do not allow juveniles to voluntarily waive their Miranda protection.

pretrial identification practices Process and practices include fingerprinting, photographing, and appearing in lineups. Some states require judicial approval for any pretrial process to occur. Recently, more states are allowing such practices without court approval.

search and seizure The Constitution requires police to obtain a lawful search warrant to search a person or property under their control. However, recent efforts to control drug and gang related crimes have led to Supreme Court rulings that have relaxed the requirements of warrant and warrantless searches.

station adjustment Disposition option whereby a juvenile is taken to the police station and then released after an official reprimand and contact is recorded.

CLASSROOM ACTIVITIES AND ASSIGNMENTS

1. Ask students to share their perceptions about police as they were growing up.

2. Have students conduct a survey of persons in regard to their opinions about police and try to isolate how their perceptions may be related to first contact with police experiences.

3. Ask students to discuss how *getting tough* on juvenile offenders may erode police-juvenile relations.

4. Have students divide into two groups; those who were physically punished (spanking) at home, and those who were not (time-outs), and discuss any differences in perceptions toward their parents.

5. Ask students who were graduates of DARE to discuss how well it worked or failed in their own personal experiences.

6. Have students inquire of the local school system or police agencies about the level of police cooperation in juvenile prevention programs.

7. Ask students to design a cooperative juvenile prevention program that they think would work to reduce juvenile delinquency.

8. Have students examine local schools for evidence of crime related prevention (metal detectors, warning signs, etc) and discuss the shifting philosophical nature of police in schools.

VOICES OF DELINQUENCY ASSIGNMENTS

Have students read article 3 titled: The Athlete and answer the following questions.

1. Ask students to discuss how police intervention programs may have been able to change this person's life.

2. Have students discuss why they think she became involved in drug use.

3. Ask students to discuss the merits of random drug testing in schools and would it have prevented the situations this person has faced.

VIDEO AND INTERNET RESOURCES

To a Different Beat: This video addresses the task of changing perceptions in the operations of police. It shows how community-policing initiatives are regaining the trust of the public in selected cities. (48 minutes) *Insight Media.*

Understanding the Juvenile Justice System: This video provides an overview of the juvenile justice system and investigates the elements of a typical judicial proceeding and describes juvenile disposition options. (3 volumes-20 minutes each) *Insight Media.*

Establishing Communication: This video examines programs, which school administrators, students, and members of the community use to work with law enforcement to prevent school crime. The focus is on intervention techniques used to promote community involvement and awareness. (23 minutes). *Films for the Humanities and Sciences.*

Living With The Gun: This video examines the prevalence of guns in America. This thought provoking program weighs in on all sides of this emotional topic. (56 minutes) *Filmakers Library.*

WEBSITES

www.fsu.edu/~crimdo/fagan.html

Read more about police interrogation at the FindLaw site.

http://caselaw.lp.findlaw.com/data/constitution/ammendment05/09.html

Learn more about community policing at the community policing consortium site.
www.communitypolicing.org

To get more information on the Police Athletic League in New York, visit this site.
www.palnyc.org

Read the OLLDP Juvenile Justice Bulletin, *Effective Intervention for Serious Juvenile Offenders*, at www.justicestudies.com/WebLibrary.

Read the NIJ-sponsored publication, *Children in an Adult World: Prosecuting Adolescents in Criminal and Juvenile Jurisdictions*, at www.justicestudies.com/WebLibrary.

CHAPTER 15: THE JUVENILE COURT

After reading this chapter you should be able to answer the following questions:

1. How did the juvenile court begin?
2. What pretrial procedures are involved in juvenile court proceedings?
3. How is a trial conducted in the juvenile court?
4. What are the various forms of sentencing?
5. What can be done to improve the juvenile court?

CHAPTER SUMMARY

The first juvenile court was founded in Cook County, Illinois (Chicago) in 1899. *Parens patriae* was the doctrine that provided the legal catalyst for its creation. The court was an expression of middle class values, which began as a movement to humanize the lives of adolescents. The *child-saving* movement believed that social progress depended on efficient law enforcement, strict supervision and regulation of illicit pleasures. Lower-class children became the children to be saved as they were engaged in behaviors that challenged the social good. The sociocultural conditions also contributed to founding of the court since many citizens were incensed by the treatment of children during the last thirty years of the nineteenth century. Disenchantment with urban dwellers and the tripling of Chicago populations between 1880 and 1890 helped to give rise to the child-saving philosophy.

A series of decisions by the U.S. Supreme Court in the 1960s and 1970s demonstrated the influence of the constitutionalists on juvenile justice. The five most important cases were: *Kent v. United States* (1966), *In re Gault* (1967), *In re Winship*, (1970), *McKeiver v. Pennsylvania* (1971), and *Breed v. Jones* (1975). The Court attempted to balance the juvenile system similar to the adult justice system, but as some point out the abuses of the juvenile court are *Kadi*-like in that decisions are handed down based on the merits of each case.

The trial stage of juvenile court is divided into the *adjudicatory hearing*, the disposition hearing, and various judicial alternatives. Most states allow juveniles the right to appeal by statute, however juveniles do not yet have a constitutional right to appeal. Transfer of juvenile cases into adult court occurs either through *judicial waiver* or *legislative waiver*. Judicial waiver is the most common and takes place after a judicial hearing on a juvenile's amenability to treatment. The numbers of juveniles who are waived to adult court are likely to increase in the future.

Determinate sentencing is a new form of sentencing in juvenile justice and is replacing indeterminate sentencing in some jurisdictions. Additionally, increasing numbers of juvenile courts are using *blended sentencing* forms.

LECTURE OUTLINE

I. The Changing Juvenile Court

- Delinquency in America: In Family Court child defendant's welfare takes priority.
- Juvenile courts throughout the nation were patterned after the Chicago court. Records were sealed. Hearings were not open to the public and children were separately detained from adults.
- The court was founded on the premise it should act as a social clinic to serve the best interests of the children and not treat children as criminals.

A. Changes in Legal Norms

- Constitutionalists were concerned that children have procedural rights was well as rights to shelter, protection, and guardianship. A series of Supreme Court decisions in the 60s and 70s demonstrated the influence of the constitutionalists.
- Kent v. United States (1966) was concerned with the matter of transfer. The court held that Kent was essentially a denial of counsel, and that youths charged with felonies have the right to a hearing and essentials of due process.
- In re Gault (1967) affirmed that a juvenile has the right to due process safeguards in proceedings in which a finding of delinquency can lead to institutional confinement. The decision established that a juvenile has the right to notice of charges, right to counsel, right to confrontation and cross-examination of witnesses, and privilege against self-incrimination.
- In re Winship (1970) held that juveniles are entitled to the legal standard of proof beyond a reasonable doubt and not the former preponderance of evidence standard.
- McKeiver v. Pennsylvania (1971) denied the right of juveniles to jury trials. The Court stated not all constitutional rights are to be given juveniles, jury trials will put an end to the informal nature of adjudication proceedings, jury trials are not necessary for every criminal process, jury trials will bring unnecessary delays, and there is nothing to prevent states from adopting jury trials.
- Breed v. Jones (1975) held that a juvenile is entitled to double jeopardy protection in that a juvenile court cannot adjudicate a case and then transfer the case to adult court for processing for the same offense.

III. Juvenile Court Actors

- Judges, referees, prosecutors, and defense attorneys are the main participants in the juvenile court process and their roles have changed significantly in recent years.

A. Judges

- Judges are responsible for; setting standards, ensuring juveniles receive constitutional rights, ensuring the system is working fairly and efficiently, making certain adequate attorneys represent juveniles, monitoring of cases and progress of the child, being an advocate within the community, and in some jurisdictions serve as administrator of probation departments.

- David Matza refers to the justice of some judges like *Kadi justice* meaning judges make decisions based on the merit of each case and without apparent regard to rules or norms.

B. Referees

- Many courts employ the services of referees. Known as a *commissioner* in Washington state and a *master* in Maryland. They may or may not be members of the bar, but their responsibility is to assist the judge in processing youths through the courts.

C. Prosecutors

- Considered as the petitioner, the prosecutor is expected to protect society and at the same time ensure the children are provided their basic constitutional rights. Prosecutors may have to interpret juvenile law and procedure and some critics charge they have come to dominate the juvenile court proceedings.

D. Defense Attorneys

- The number of juveniles represented by defense counsel has been growing since the 1960s. Barry C. Feld found that many of the juveniles put into placement outside the home did not have counsel.
- Public defenders often do a better job of representing youth than do private attorneys.
- Juveniles with counsel were more likely to receive an institutional disposition.

IV. The Pretrial Procedures

A. The Detention Hearing

- Usually held within forty-eight to seventy-two hours.
- In some states intake officers conduct detention hearings, rather than judges.
- Juveniles may be assigned to four placement options: (1) detention home, (2) shelter care, (3) jail or police lockup, and (4) in-home detention.
- Schall v. Martin (1984) case may encourage the use of *preventative detention* of juveniles and some suggest it is intended solely for punitive punishment only.

B. The Intake Process

- Preliminary screening process to determine whether a court should take action and what type of action would be appropriate for the particular situation. Typically performed by probation officers.
- Intake units have up to five options; (1) dismissal, (2) *informal adjustment* or warning with requirement of restitution, (3) informal probation or casual supervision, (4) *consent decree* or formal agreement between child and court without a formal finding, and (5) filing of a juvenile petition.

C. The Transfer Procedure

- Every state has some provision for transferring juvenile offenders to adult courts.
- *Judicial waiver*, the most common, takes place after a judicial hearing on a juvenile's amenability to treatment and contains procedural safeguards. Criteria typically used

include age/maturity of child, seriousness of offense, past record, and relationship of the offender with parents, school and community.

- *Legislative waiver* is accomplished in five ways; (1) laws excluding certain offenses from juvenile jurisdiction, (2) lowering the jurisdictional age, (3) specifying age to specific offenses, (4) laws regulating specific offenses, and (5) concurrent jurisdiction.
- Legislative waivers are criticized as being inconsistent with rehabilitative philosophy.
- More and more juveniles are being transferred to adult court, however they are not necessarily the most serious or intractable cases.
- Juveniles who have previously been waived are likely to bc waived again in the future.
- Studies conflict on the merits of transferring cases, some suggest transferring does not indicate more severe penalties, while others contend juveniles transferred to adult court receive longer sentences than their adult counterparts (by 2 years and 5 months).
- Reverse waiver and blended sentencing

V. The Juvenile Trial

A. The Adjudicatory Hearing

- Fact finding stage usually includes: the child's plea, presentation of evidence, cross examination of witnesses, and the judge's findings. Ten states allow jury trials, but they are seldom requested.
- The prosecutor has become the dominant force at these proceedings.

B. The Disposition Hearing

- Present trend is bifurcate the adjudicatory hearing into a separate dispositional hearing to allow probation officers to prepare a social history report for sentencing.
- Factors of school attendance and performance, family structure, degree of maturity, attitude, and sense of responsibility are all considered in determining a remedy for the adjudicated offense.
- In 1999, 24 percent of adjudicated youth were court ordered to out-of-home placement.
- The seriousness of the act has the greatest impact on judicial judgments.
- Informal factors of social and racial background of the youth and demeanor in the courtroom also affect a judges handling of juvenile delinquents.

C. Judicial Alternatives

- Depending on the size of the court, most alternatives consist of: dismissal, restitution, psychiatric therapy, probation, foster home placements, day treatment programs, community-based residential programs, institutionalization in mental hospitals, county or city institutions, state or private training schools, and adult facilities.

D. The Right to Appeal

- Juveniles do not have a constitutional right to appeal, however most states grant them the right to appeal by statute.

VI. Juvenile Sentencing Structures

- Determinate sentencing is a new form of sentencing in juvenile justice, replacing the former indeterminate form.
- Blended sentences are increasing in which juvenile and adult sentences are imposed in combination to hold juvenile accountable for their actions.
- The Juvenile Justice Standards Project developed guidelines to base sentences on the seriousness of the crime rather than on the needs of the youth. The belief was that disparity in juvenile sentencing must end and attempts were made to limit the discretion of judges.
- Judges perceive the standards as attacking the underlying philosophy of the juvenile court.
- The get-tough changes are exemplified in both New York and Texas reforms.
- In 1995, Texas enacted legislation that a fourteen-year-old could receive the death penalty.

VII. The Death Penalty and Juveniles

- The United States has executed about 366 juveniles since the seventeenth century.
- The first case was for sodomizing a horse and cow.
- Georgia leads all states with 41 executions, followed by North Carolina and Ohio with 19.
- Twenty-five of thirty-eight states allow capital punishment for those under the age of eighteen when they committed their crimes.
- The cases of Stanford v. Kentucky and Wilkins v. Missouri in 1989 upheld the constitutionality of using the death penalty for juveniles.
- As of 2004 seventy-two individuals were on death row for crimes committed as juveniles with Texas holding the most.

KEY TERMS

adjudicatory hearing The juvenile trial stage that typically consists of the child's plea, presentation of prosecutorial and defense evidence, cross-examination of witnesses, and the finding of the judge.

bail The secured monetary sum an offender(s) uses to gain release from pretrial detention.

bifurcated hearing Present trend of the juvenile court in which the adjudication and disposition hearings are separated.

child-savers A movement of middle-class women at the turn of the twentieth century to rescue children from the filth, corruption and urban disenchantment caused by immigration.

consent decree Formal agreement between the court and the juvenile in which the child is placed under supervision without a formal finding of delinquency.

constitutionalists Justice reform movement, which maintains that children within the juvenile system deserve the same constitutional rights as adults.

detention hearing The hearing in which an intake officer decides whether a juvenile should be detained in detention or released to their parents.

determinate sentencing A form of sentencing that provides fixed sentences for offenses. The terms of the sentences are generally set by legislatures.

indeterminate sentencing Sentencing in which a judge has wide discretion to commit a juvenile to the department of corrections or youth authority until correctional staff make a decision to release the juvenile.

informal adjustment An agreement between a juvenile and the court that allows restitution to be made without a formal petition being filed.

informal probation Youth aggress to supervised probation conditions without being formally adjudicated by the court.

intake The first stage of the juvenile court proceedings in which the decision is made to divert the youth to alternative treatment or to file a juvenile petition.

judicial waiver Occurs after a judicial hearing on the amenability of treatment for the juvenile offender and is the most common form of juvenile to adult court transfer.

jury trial Regulated by state statutes and not permitted by constitutional rights for juveniles.

kadi justice David Matza's description of juvenile court judges that act on the merits of each case and without regard to rules and norms, much like a Moslem market-place judge.

legislative waiver Juvenile to adult court transfer that is determined by prescribed factors established through legislative acts, such as type of offense and age specific offenses.

referee Juvenile court assistants that help judges process cases through the court. They may or may not be members of the bar and are known as both commissioners and masters in some states.

reverse waiver In some states youths who are over the maximum age of jurisdiction may be sent back to the juvenile court if the adult court believes the case is more appropriate for juvenile court jurisdiction.

shelter care Facilities used primarily for short-term holding of juvenile status offenders or neglected children.

transfer The movement of a juvenile case into adult court for disposition.

CLASSROOM ACTIVITIES AND ASSIGNMENTS

1. Ask students to debate the necessity of the juvenile court.

2. Have students observe an adult court proceeding and report how their observations are similar or different to that of juvenile court proceedings.

3. Ask students to form two debate groups, one in favor of maintaining the juvenile court and the other in favor of its abolishment, and discuss the merits of their arguments.

4. Have students interview a juvenile court judge to learn their view on juvenile rights, and discuss the issues in class.

5. Ask students to survey college students to ascertain if the juvenile system is perceived as being too soft on crime, and discuss how those perceptions were probably formed.

6. Have students research the transfer of juvenile cases to adult court, and discuss whether the get-tough approach is really working to reduce crime.

7. Ask students to debate the issues of informal adjustment and informal probation, and discuss whether they believe probation officers violate the due process rights of children.

8. Have students search for recent juvenile cases that have sensationalized and reinforced the get-tough approach on juvenile crime, and discuss the findings in class.

VOICES OF DELINQUENCY ASSIGNMENTS

Have students read article 15 titled: My Experiences as a Juvenile Delinquent and answer the following questions.

1. Ask students to find evidence that psychotherapy intervention may or may not have failed this person.

2. Have students discuss whether this person was really "elated" to leave home or just rationalizing what he could not control.

3. Ask students to debate whether sending this person to adult jail would have helped or hurt this particular case. What if he had not chosen to turn his life around on his own?

VIDEO AND INTERNET RESOURCES

Our Legal System: This video provides a view of the American legal system, which includes ethics, constitutional rights, criminal and civil law as applied to consumers and juveniles. (20 minutes) Insight Media.

Kids Behind Bars: This video examines youth who commit serious crimes and are often themselves the victims of a justice system that sends them to adult prisons. This video investigates the changes taking place in juvenile justice. (50 minutes) Insight Media.

Juvies: This video is an in-depth focus of four young men in Baltimore's juvenile justice system. Each account is of different social circumstance and outcome. (100 minutes) Insight Media.

Young Criminals, Adult Punishment: This ABC news video examines the issue of transferring juvenile cases to adult courts. (23 minutes) Films for the Humanities and Sciences.

WEBSITES

Visit the OJJDP PowerPoint presentation " Juvenile Offenders in Court" at www.justicestudies.com/WebPlaces

Learn about the Juvenile Detention Alternatives Initiative from the Annie E. Casey Foundation via www.justicestudies.com/WebPlaces

Visit the National Institute of Mental Health's Child and Adolescent Mental Health Center's Web Site via www.justicestudies.com/WebPlaces

www.juvenilenet.org

www.sgc.wa.gov/JUVSTD.htm

CHAPTER 16: JUVENILE CORRECTIONS

LEARNING OBJECTIVES

After reading this chapter you should be able to answer the following questions:

1. What types of experience do juveniles have in various institutional placements?
2. Why do some juveniles benefit more from institutionalization than others? How effective are institutions at correcting juvenile crime?
3. What rights do juveniles have while confined?
4. What can be done to improve juvenile correctional institutions in the United States?

CHAPTER SUMMARY

Community-based corrections is comprised of *probation*, *residential* and *day treatment* programs, and *aftercare*. Development of community-based corrections was encouraged in large part at the turn of the twentieth century and again in the 1960s. Support for community-based programs dwindled in the 1970s due to the pressure from hardliners persuading the public as to the danger of youth crime. The get-tough approach remained in place into the 1990s, as the public became more concerned about the threat to public safety of gun carrying, drug-using, and gang involved juveniles.

Early training schools were established as a means to protect children from the harsh treatment of adult facilities. During the 1970s, deinstitutionalization of status offenders and the elimination of staff brutality were the main reform issues. Reception and diagnostic centers do a relatively good job of evaluating the problems of institutionalized juveniles, however the programs are frequently not implemented when youths are transferred to a training school or camp-like facilities. Some ranches and camp programs provide good staff support for offenders but opponents argue that most of these youths could function well in community-based programs. Boot camps offer a disciplined and regimented setting that is generally accompanied by little programming.

Community-based corrections responded to critics through innovative developments such as intensive probation and more accountable means of juvenile probation. The costs of community-based corrections are still less than institutionalization and the fact still remains that more delinquents are treated in the community than are adjudicated to training schools.

The early years of the twenty-first century should be a time of expansion for community-based corrections. The prohibitive expense of long-term institutions may likely mean increased use of alternatives to institutions. Reformers of the 1970s may not see the level of decarceration attained that was once hoped for but economics will in all likelihood reserve institutions only for the hard-core and violent juvenile offenders.

LECTURE OUTLINE

I. Introduction

- Governor Rell
- Is the system broken?

II. Probation

- Probation has several connotations in juvenile justice. Probation is a legal system, an alternative to institutionalization, a subsystem of the juvenile justice system, and it includes the activities, functions, and services of transactions with the juvenile court, the delinquent, and community.

A. The Operation of Probation Services

- *Intake, investigation, and supervision* are the basic functions of probation services.
- The intake officer is generally a probation officer that must decide what to do with a case and whether to detain the juvenile. Ordinarily the child is released to the parents.
- Investigation requires probation officers to prepare social history reports usually within thirty to sixty days. Officers review arrest records, psychiatric or psychological evaluations, and any information from social agencies.
- Supervision is divided into casework management, treatment, and surveillance. The length of time one spends on probation is normally until the sixteenth or eighteenth birthday.
- Casework is typically divided up in categories depending on the juvenile's needs.
- *Surveillance* is required to make sure probationers comply with conditions of probation and they do not break the law. This may include parent visitations. *Revocation of probation* underscored the importance of surveillance with probationers.

B. Risk Control and Crime Reduction

- Current emphasis in juvenile probation is on *risk control and crime reduction*.
- The Office of Juvenile Justice and Delinquency Prevention has spent more than $30 million promoting restitution throughout the nation.
- Goals include; holding juveniles accountable, providing reparations, treating and rehabilitating juveniles, and punishing juveniles.
- A 1991 survey indicated that most juveniles referred to juvenile programs are diverted from the juvenile justice system.
- Intensive supervision programs responded to the criticisms of the 1980s and 1990s that probation was too lenient of punishment. Widely used in adult corrections, they are praised for keeping high-risk offenders out of long-term confinement.
- Recent developments of *Integrated Social Control* (ISC) model of intensive supervision integrates components of social strain, control and social learning theories.
- *Electronic monitoring* (inspired by a comic strip) is used for house arrest sentences, whereby youths remain confined in their own homes. They may be allowed to leave for certain purposes such as religious services, school, or medical reasons.

- Two types of electronic monitors include continuously signaling and programmed contact devices.

C. The Community Volunteer

- Probation began with the using of *volunteers*. Today over two-thousand programs assist in juvenile operations.
- Volunteer programs assist in helping offenders adjust to community life by providing one-to-one support, child advocate with teachers, employers and police, serve as role models, and in general help youth develop realistic responses to the environment.
- Criticism of using volunteers include: they create more work than they return. They are unable to handle serious problems and sometimes cause harm to clients.
- Parents may resist volunteers as an untrained worker.

III. Residential and Day Treatment Programs

- Typically reserved for those having difficulty dealing with the looseness of probation supervision.
- *Day treatment* programs are attended in the morning or afternoons with the juvenile returning home at night.
- *Residential* programs are usually *group home* or *foster care* placements where the juvenile is taken away from the supervision of parents.

A. The Types of Residential and Day Treatment Programs

- *Group homes* or *halfway houses* provide alternatives to institutionalization. They serve as short-term placement and are known as halfway-in or halfway-out.
- A well-developed group home model is the teaching-family group model used in the *Achievement Place* in Lawrence, Kansas. Also the *Criswell House* in Florida.
- The *House of Umoja* in Philadelphia (Sister Fattah) works almost exclusively with gang delinquents.
- *Day treatment* programs are more economical because they do not provide living or sleeping quarters. They generally serve males. Some examples are *STAY* and *AMI* but with the decline of federal funding many day treatment programs have closed their doors.
- *Wilderness* programs seek to help gain self-reliance. *Outward Bound* first established in Colorado in 1962 is the most widely used. *VisionQuest* began in 1973 in Tucson.

IV. Types of Institutional Placements for Juveniles

- *Training schools, reception centers, ranches and forestry camps, and boot camps* are the main forms of juvenile correctional institutions.
- *Adult prisons* are increasingly being used for juvenile corrections in the late twentieth century.
- There are twice as many private juvenile facilities as there are public facilities, yet private facilities hold less than half of the confined offenders.
- Newest information on juveniles in custody is drawn from Census of Juveniles in Residential Placement *(CJRP).*

A. Reception and Diagnostic Centers

- Centers determine the best *placement* and *treatment plan* for each adjudicated youth.
- Average length of stay is thirty-four days. Physical and dental exams are typically given at this time. Psychologists, social workers, and staff evaluate each youth.
- A *diagnostic report* is sent with the youth when transferred, however they are frequently ignored by the receiving facility.

B. Ranches and Forestry Camps

- *Minimum-security* and reserved for youths who have committed *minor offenses.*
- Most forestry camps are located in Florida (16) and New York (14).
- Residents normally do conservation work in state parks.
- Escapes are common due to the *nonsecure nature* of the facilities.
- Private ranches are widely used in California. The average length of stay is 6.5 months.
- Residents are generally more positive about placement in a forestry camp or ranch than institutional placement. However, those that cannot handle these settings will repeatedly run away until placed in institutional settings.
- *Hennepin County Home School* is an innovative *coeducational* facility. The *Alpha* and *Beta* programs are treatment oriented with the Beta program for less serious offenders.

C. Boot Camps

- Emphasize military discipline and regimented training for a period of 30 to 120 days.
- The intent is to *shock the delinquent* into not committing more crimes.
- Boot camps are generally reserved for mid-range offenders and those that have failed lesser sanctions, yet not hardened violent offenders or sex offenders.
- In 1999, ten states had implemented about 50 boot camps for 4,500 offenders.
- Evaluations of boot camps suggest they experience *considerable instability* and are unable to implement well-developed aftercare services.
- Some studies have suggested their *recidivism rates are higher* than traditional facilities.
- *Death cases* such as the dehydration of a 14-year-old girl in South Dakota and the death of a 14 year-old (Anthony Haynes) in Phoenix tarnishes the image of boot camps.
- Critics often charge that boot camps are *abusive* in nature and no long-term rehabilitation effects are found.

D. Public and Private Training Schools

- Some training schools resemble prisons, while others look like college campuses.
- They are used more today than in the 1970s and 1980s.
- Training schools are a very expensive way to treat delinquent youths.
- Gangs are becoming a serious problem in some training schools.
- Massachusetts and Vermont have no training schools.
- Security is higher for public facilities verses private facilities and both medical and dental services are very good.

- Educational programs are usually accredited by the state and range from GED to vocational and academic programming.
- *Treatment modalities* range from transactional analysis and guided group interaction to drug and alcohol treatments.
- Treatment for females is often neglected in lieu of programs for males.
- Recreational activities are popular with residents and religious services are provided, however they tend not to be very popular with residents.
- Punishments vary and the time spent in solitary confinement is less than a decade ago.
- The use of force and mechanical restraints in training schools has recently increased.
- Bartollas suggests there are relatively few differences between private and public placements in terms of their effectiveness in reducing delinquency. Private facilities tend to be more flexible.

E. Adult Prisons

- Life on the inside is extremely austere, crowded and dangerous.
- Juveniles are subject to sexual and physical assaults.
- In October of 2000, Indiana stopped sending juveniles into the general prison population.
- Thirteen states permit the transfer of juveniles to adult facilities.

V. Training School Life

- Many studies present a frightening picture of what juveniles experience in confinement.

A. Training Schools for Boys

- Most studies support that training schools are a society of the strong victimizing the weak.
- Sethard Fisher defined *victimization* as a predatory practice, and *patronage* as building protective relationships for more advantageous situations on the prestige ladder.
- Bartollas suggests that dominant youths exploit submissive ones.

B. Training Schools for Girls and Coeducational Institutions

- Early studies suggested varying degrees of lesbian alliances.
- Propper found that homosexuality and make-believe families was just a prevalent in coeducational facilities as single-sex institutions.
- Bartollas found that females adhered more strongly to inmate groups and peer relations than did males. Females felt more victimized and did not harass or manipulate staff as much as males.

VI. Rights of Confined Juveniles

A. The Courts

- Courts pay more attention to adult prisons than juvenile institutions.

- Several courts have held juveniles have the right to treatment. *Morales v. Thurman* (1973) is the most extensive order ever issued in which several standards were established.
- *CRIPA* (Civil Rights of Institutionalized Persons Act) gives the Department of Justice the power to enforce civil rights violations of institutionalized persons.
- A consent decree in Puerto Rico addressed life-threatening situations and issues such as juveniles having to drink from toilet bowls.
- Access to the courts.

VII. Juvenile Aftercare

- The average length of stay in institutional care for juveniles is 9.8 months. *Aftercare* seeks to make an optimal adjustment to community living upon release from institutional care.
- Cottage staff consider performance in school, recreation, attitude, peer relations, and personality conflicts when reviewing a juvenile for release.

A. The Administration and Operation of Aftercare Services

- *Aftercare* is the responsibility of the state in forty-four states.
- Recidivism rates are lower than for traditional training schools (30 percent v. 50 to 70 percent).
- *Interstate compacts* are used to place children out of state when no acceptable home placement is within his or her state.
- Probation officers frequently carry the load of aftercare along with their other duties.
- Problems include sending youths back to same communities and families to expose them to the same problems they encountered originally.

B. Risk Control and Crime Reduction

- The current emphasis in aftercare is short-term behavior control.
- Intensive aftercare programs are increasingly being used much like supervision models. "*Lifeskills 95*" in California is designed for high-risk offenders.
- Aftercare frequently emphasizes drug and alcohol urinalysis.
- Revocation of aftercare may result in the youth returning to training school.

KEY TERMS

boot camp Regimented facility consisting of military style discipline and training for mid-range juvenile offenders. The goal is to shock the offender into not committing delinquent offenses.

community-based corrections Corrections programs that include probation, residential and day treatment programs, and aftercare which are linked between community programs and their social environment.

day treatment programs Court mandated community based programs that juveniles normally attend in the morning and afternoon, and return home in the evening.

foster home placements The foster home provides a temporary setting for juveniles who must be removed from their natural homes.

forestry camp Minimum security facility for juvenile committing minor offenses. Residents normally perform clean-up work in state parks and other conservation related duties.

group home model A placement for youths who have been adjudicated by the court. Called halfway houses and attention homes and serve a group of about thirteen to twenty-five youths as an alternative to institutionalization.

interstate compact Procedures for transferring a youth on probation or aftercare/parole from one state to another.

Outward Bound A wilderness-type survival program that is popular in many states as an alternative to institutionalization.

ranch Public and private juvenile correctional institution that is usually less secure than training schools. Escapes are common and they typically provide a more normalizing experience for minor offenders

reception and diagnostic center Juveniles are frequently sent to these centers for diagnosis of individualized treatment plans before their placement into a training school.

remote location monitoring A type of house arrest where the juvenile is observed by a remote control device that transmit a signal or information concerning the location of the probationer.

residential programs Placements for juveniles who are having difficulty with the looseness of probation supervision. Consists mainly of group homes or foster care placements.

restitution Reparations offenders pay to victims and/or community as part of their disposition for a delinquent or criminal act they committed.

revocation of aftercare Occurs when a probationer/parolee fails to meet the conditions of his or her aftercare agreement or commits another delinquent or criminal offense, and may lead to their return to training school.

social history report A written report of a juvenile's social background that probation officers prepare for a juvenile judge to assist the court in making a disposition of a youth who has been ruled delinquent.

surveillance A method probation officers use to ensure that probationers are meeting the conditions of their probation. Typically involves parental visitations and underscores revocation of probation.

teaching-family group home model A well-developed group home model with specialized treatment programs to treat the more severe delinquency problems. Currently used in twelve states with Achievement Place, Criswell House, and House of Umoja being the most well known.

training school A juvenile correctional facility for long-term placement of juvenile delinquents.

volunteer programs Probation officers use volunteers for assistance of casework and helping offenders adjust to community life. They often serve as child advocates with teachers, employers and police.

CLASSROOM ACTIVITIES AND ASSIGNMENTS

1. Ask students to share any mentoring experiences they may have had with younger children and discuss the utility of such services.

2. Have students volunteer to be a child advocate worker with a local juvenile service agency and discuss their experiences in class.

3. Ask students to interview a counselor with a local day treatment or group home agency and discuss the interview in class.

4. Invite a former inmate of a correctional institution to class and discuss how their life was changed by the incarceration experience.

5. Have students visit a local jail or prison facility to observe the operations and discuss the humanizing or dehumanizing experiences of the residents that students observed.

6. Have students obtain a copy of a juvenile probation agreement from a local juvenile agency and discuss the harshness or leniency of the conditions in class.

7. Ask a local juvenile probation officer to speak to the class and discuss the typical duties required of them.

8. Have students research the various wilderness programs and discuss why they may or may not be as successful as organizers tend to claim.

VOICES OF DELINQUENCY ASSIGNMENTS

Have students read article 19 titled: <u>*A Sad Story*</u> and answer the following questions.

1. Ask students to discuss what type of intervention treatment may have prevented this person's criminal behavior.

2. Have students prepare a social history report on this person and discuss if they would have agreed with the recommendations the probation officer made to the court.

3. Ask students to discuss what this person means by being a "captive of the system" and his critical view of programs such as Boy Scouts and Upward Bound.

VIDEO AND INTERNET RESOURCES

Community Corrections: This video examines the structure and efficacy of the halfway house. (15 minutes). Insight Media

Electronic Home Monitoring: This video explains the practice of at-home monitoring to reduce overcrowding and for the stretching of budgets. (25 minutes) Insight Media

Exploring Alternatives to Prison and Probation: This video examines restitution programs and five alternatives to prison. (22 minutes) Insight media

Kids Behind Bars: This informative video discusses a variety of issues involving the incarceration of juveniles. At issue is, does the punishment fit the crime (30 minutes) *Films for the Humanities and Sciences.*

Teens in Maximum Security Prisons: This ABC News video examines the issues of juveniles in maximum-security confinement. (24 minutes) *Films for the Humanities and Sciences.*

WEBSITES

Visit www.mycjspace.com , the Web site community for criminal justice professionals, students, and instructors. My CJ space allows you to create your own profile, communicate with others with similar interests, check out employment options in the justice field, and search the Web for criminal justice specific information and sites.

Learn move about John Augustus at the American Probation and Parole Association site.
www.appa-net.org/the_early_years.htm

Learn more about the Outward bound program by visiting the Outward Bound Home page.
www.outwardbound.org

Learn more about Glen Mills School at their home page.
www.glenmillsschool.org/leftnar.html

www.iowacbc.org

http://virlib.ncjrs.org/corr.asp?category=44&subcategory=3

www.cjcj.org/

VIDEO RESOURCE DIRECTORY

***NOTE TO INSTRUCTORS and Students*:** This information is provided for your convenience. Your university or college audiovisual/media services department may have access to the videos listed in this manual.

Filmakers Library
124 East 40th Street
New York, NY 10016

Phone 212 808 4980

Fax 212 808 4983

e-mail: info@filmakers.com

Films for the Humanities and Sciences
PO Box 2053
Princeton, NJ 08543-2053

Phone 800 257 5126

www.films.com

Insight Media
2162 Broadway
New York, NY 10024-0621

Phone 212 721 6316

Fax 212 799 5309

www.insight-media.com

e-mail: cs@insight-media.com

Chapter 1 Adolescence and Delinquency

Multiple Choice Questions

1) Each chapter begins with a particular vignette to introduce the issues in the chapter. This chapter starts with a story about ___________________.
A) The World Trade Center
B) Winslow Township High School
C) The Vice Lords
D) Guns in schools in the south
E) Assaults of young women by football players

Answer: B

2) The Chicago Area Projects are associated with _________________.
A) James Q. Wilson and O.W. Wilson
B) Richard Cloward and Lloyd Ohlin
C) Frank Schmalleger and Thomas McAninch
D) Edwin Sutherland and Donald Cressey
E) Clifford Shaw and Henry McKay

Answer: E

3) An example of a crime that a juvenile can be arrested for but an adult cannot be arrest for is ______________.
A) truancy
B) incorrigibility
C) curfew violations
D) runaway behavior
E) all of the above

Answer: E

4) The Journal of the American Medical Association noted that as incomes of families with children increase deviant behaviors _______________.
A) increased at the same rate
B) increased at a much higher rate
C) decreased
D) remained the same, there was no relationship between income and deviance

Answer: C

5) A Medieval English doctrine that sanctioned the right of the Crown to intervene in natural family relations whenever a child's welfare was threatened. The philosophy of the juvenile court is based on this legal concept.
A) *parens patriae*
B) The Power of the King
C) The Divine Right of Kings
D) in loco parentis
E) none of the above

Answer: A

6) The first juvenile court was created in ________________.
A) New York City
B) Boston
C) Chicago (Cook County)
D) Denver
E) Los Angeles

Answer: C

7) The term defining the life interval between childhood and adulthood is called _____________.
A) delinquency.
B) puberty.
C) adolescence.
D) socialization.

Answer: C

8) By 1914, almost every state had passed laws prohibiting the industrial employment of children under the age of _______.
A) 16.
B) 14.
C) 12.
D) 10.

Answer: B

9) Psychologist Eric Erickson observed that "childhood" is the model of all _______________.
A) guidance.
B) special attention.
C) development.
D) oppression and enslavement.

Answer: D

10) Nanette J. Davis contends that much of the youth crisis today is ________.
A) invisible.
B) arranged.
C) political.
D) inflated.

Answer: A

11) John E. Donovan and Richard Jessor suggested the interrelationships among high-risk behaviors share a common factor of ___________.
A) tolerance.
B) drug use.
C) unconventionality.
D) victimization.

Answer: C

12) Travis Hirschi suggests a common factor underlying problem behaviors is ______________.
A) lack of self-control.
B) racial profiling.
C) inadequate juvenile justice.
D) majority variance.
Answer: A

13) The legal term delinquency first originated in 1899 in the State of
A) Iowa.
B) Illinois.
C) Ohio.
D) Indiana.

Answer: B

14) Actions or behaviors that would NOT be defined as criminal if adults committed them are called ____________.
A) uniform offenses.
B) misdemeanors.
C) petty offenses.
D) status offenses.

Answer: D

15) The rehabilitative philosophy of the juvenile court is referred to as ___________.
A) tempus fugit.
B) parens patriae.
C) duces tecum.
D) Certiorari.

Answer: B

16) Psychological testing of many status offenders has suggested they suffer from ______________.
A) attention deficit disorder.
B) depression.
C) post traumatic stress disorder.
D) multiple-personality disorder.

Answer: A

17) Meda Chesney-Lind contends the juvenile justice system discriminates against girls, because society believes it must protect adolescent girls from consequences of _____________.
A) victimization.
B) power struggles.
C) sexual desires.
D) social inequality.

Answer: C

18) According to data from a national study, which of the following identified groups were more likely to commit misdemeanors along with status offenses?
A) heavies
B) lightweights
C) conforming youths
D) middleweights

Answer: B

19) Most studies generally conclude that status offenders escalating to more serious behaviors is _____________.
A) highly probable.
B) proven to be true.
C) proven to be false.
D) not likely.

Answer: D

20) Which of the following actually increased after the implementation of The Deinstitutionalization of Status Offenders Project (DSO)?
A) detention of African-Americans
B) status offenses
C) juvenile adjudications
D) recidivism rates

Answer: A

21) Invisible institutionalization refers to courts that redefine status offenders as _____________.
A) incorrigible.
B) delinquent.
C) adult cases.
D) neglect cases.

Answer: B

22) The colonists believed the primary source of social control of children was ________________.
A) school.
B) police.
C) religion.
D) family.

Answer: D

23) The intent of the Supreme Court decisions of 1967-1975 was to ensure the children would have ________________.
A) jury trials.
B) supportive parents.
C) educational alternatives.
D) due process rights.

Answer: D

24) In 1988 and 1989, what became a major impetus for the development and spread of drug-trafficking street gangs?
A) crack epidemic
B) deinstitutionalization

C) America's war on drugs
D) decreasing murder rates

Answer: A

25) In 1995, a criminal case involving Susan and Anthony Provenzano of St. Clair Shores, Michigan captured national attention to the growing trend of what type of laws?
A) habitual offender
B) domestic abuse
C) parental responsibility
D) drug

Answer: C

26) Allowing criminal and juvenile courts to impose either juvenile and/or adult sentences is referred to as what type of sentencing?
A) indeterminate
B) creative
C) graduated
D) expanded

Answer: D

27) The social context that examines the relationship between social institutions and delinquency _______________.
is called
A) historical.
B) sociocultural.
C) political.
D) legal.

Answer: B

28) Studies that view delinquent behavior as being affected by a variety of forces on several levels ____________.
is referred to as
A) micro perspective.
B) process analysis.
C) contextual analysis.
D) poly analysis.

Answer: C

29) Which term refers to recognizing that juveniles are acted upon by social influences, structural constraints, and choices made available to them?
A) human agency
B) contextual
C) analytical
D) political

Answer: A

30) Life course theory contends one's cultural background such as location in time and __________ is an element of shaping a person's life course in delinquency.
A) theory
B) mainstream
C) place

D) crime

Answer: C

True/False Questions

1) The lengthening of adolescence in U.S. culture has further increased youth crises and life struggles.

Answer: TRUE

2) According to Bartollas, child labor laws had little impact of defining adolescence.

Answer: FALSE

3) According to Eric Erickson, the lack of rights given to young people is a chief reason for repression.

Answer: TRUE

4) Nanette Davis believes that America's social institutions have little impact on the youth crisis.

Answer: FALSE

5) High-risk youth are more likely to experience multiple problem behaviors that will likely lead to socially undesirable behaviors.

Answer: TRUE

6) Travis Hirschi believes that the relationship between drug abuse and delinquency are manifestations of one common factor, criminality.

Answer: TRUE

7) The average delinquent today is far more likely to commit serious crimes, rather than petty crimes of theft.

Answer: FALSE

Page Ref: 10

8) Juvenile courts typically hear only delinquency cases, while social work agencies have jurisdiction over neglect cases.

Answer: FALSE

9) Status offenders frequently come from single-parent homes and often times engage in verbal and physical abuse directed toward the parent(s).

Answer: TRUE

10) Status offenders tend to resist authority and are frequently prescribed Ritalin to control hyperactivity.

Answer: TRUE

11) Charles W. Thomas contends that status offenders and delinquents differ very little in their behaviors, and status offenders tend to progress to delinquent behaviors.

Answer: TRUE

12)A national study suggested that status offenders are more likely to be white than nonwhite.

Answer: TRUE

13) According to Bartollas, most studies conclude that status offenders are NOT likely to progress into delinquency.

Answer: TRUE

14) Chronic status offenders are the most amenable to community-based intervention strategies.

Answer: FALSE

15) Public whippings and dunkings were common punishments for chronic offenders during the colonial period.

Answer: TRUE

16) The use of training schools flourished during the late 1960s and early 1970s.

Answer: FALSE

17) The main purpose of the reform agenda of the 1970s was to divert status offenses from a criminal to a noncriminal setting.

Answer: TRUE

18) The use of curfew laws to control delinquent behavior decreased during the 1990s.

Answer: FALSE

19) During the 1990s, repressive methods to control gang behaviors were far more typical than intervention strategies.

Answer: TRUE

20)In the 1990s, several states actually decreased legislation efforts for prosecution of juveniles in adult court.

Answer: FALSE

Short Answer Questions

1) __________ __________ of early childhood fester into socially unacceptable behavior in later years.

Answer: Unmet needs

2) Youth in crisis are involved in __________ arrangements such as discrimination and humiliation of racism, deprivations of poverty, the culture of violence, and the ever-present temptation of drugs and alcohol.

Answer: structural

3) Of the twenty-five million adolescents in the United States, approximately one in four is at __________ __________ for engaging in multiple problem behaviors.

Answer: high risk

4) The __________ __________ __________ reveals that in 2000 three times as many youths were arrested for committing status offenses as violent crimes.

Answer: uniform crime reports

5) According to Meda Chesney-Lind, a __________ __________ exists between male and female adolescents.

Answer: double standard

6) The 1974 Juvenile Justice and Delinquency Prevention Act served as an impetus for __________ of status offenders.

Answer: deinstitutionalization

7) Juvenile courts can institutionalize status offenders by simply __________ them as delinquent.

Answer: redefining

8) The period of 1824-1898 is known as the __________ __________ __________ period in which reformers became disillusioned with family control of delinquents.

Answer: house of refuge

9) The medieval English doctrine that sanctions the right of the crown to intervene in family relations is termed __________ __________.

Answer: parens patriae

10) Glen H. Elder and associates have done much to stimulate the use of __________ theory as an appropriate research base in the study of individuals and groups associated with juvenile delinquency.

Answer: life-course

11) The life interval between childhood and adulthood; usually the period between the ages of twelve and eighteen years is called _______.

Answer: adolescence

12) A project that evaluates the effects of deinstitutionalization of status offenders in eight states and prompted a national evaluation is called the ________________.

Answer: Deinstitutionalization of Status Offenders Project (DSO)

13) Institutions that were designed by eighteenth and nineteenth century reformers to provide an orderly disciplined environment similar to the "ideal" Puritan family is called ________________.

Answer: houses of refuge

14) An act committed by a minor that violates the penal code of the government with the authority over the area in which the act occurs is called _____________.

Answer: juvenile delinquency

15) A federal law that established a juvenile justice office within the Law Enforcement Assistance Administration to provide funds for the prevention and control of youth crime was called the _________________.

Answer: Juvenile Justice and Delinquency Prevention Act of 1974

16) A sociological framework suggesting that four key factors determine the shape of the life course: location in time and place, linked lives, human agency, and timing of lives is called the ________________.

Answer: life course perspective

17) A Medieval English doctrine that sanctioned the right of the Crown to intervene in natural family relations whenever a child's welfare was threatened was called ____________. The philosophy of the juvenile court is based on this legal concept.

Answer: parens patriae

18) A juvenile who commits a minor act that is considered illegal only because he or she is underage is called a ____________.

Answer: status offender

19) Offenses like curfew violations, incorrigibility, running away, truancy, and underage drinking are called ______________.

Answer: status offense

Essay Questions

1) Describe how the adolescence period in America is affected by various social factors related to our culture.

2) Discuss the three categories of juvenile behavior in which the juvenile court has jurisdiction.

3) Describe the affects that the Deinstitutionalization of Status Offenders Project (DSO) had on status offenders.

4) Compare and contrast the juvenile control strategies of the 1960s with that of the 1980s.

5) Define the elements of a "social context" focus as described by Bartollas.

Chapter 2 The Measurement and Nature of Delinquency

Multiple Choice Questions

1) Juveniles are more likely to be held for adult trial if they are arrested for ______________.
A) status offenses.
B) Part II property offenses.
C) violent Part I offenses.
D) less serious offenses.

Answer: C

2)A problem associated with Uniform Crime Reports is
A) data is only sent in yearly by police.
B) manipulation of statistics by police.
C) they do not measure clearance by arrest.
D) they are not made public.

Answer: B

3) According to UCRs, which of the following best accounts for the percent of arrests for violent crimes by juveniles between the ages of ten and seventeen?
A) 16
B) 25
C) 36
D) 42

Answer: A

4) The UCRs indicate that between 1971 and 2003, the percentage of Part I arrests involving juveniles under the age of eighteen _______.
A) increased in both violent and property crimes.
B) decreased in violent crime and increased in property crimes.
C) increased in violent crime and decreased in property crimes.
D) decreased in both violent and property crimes.

Answer: D

5) According to A. Blumstein, juvenile crime by 2010 makes for a "chilling picture" largely due to ____________.
A) poverty and single mothers.
B) poor education.
C) pornography.
D) superpredators.

Answer: A

6) According to A. Blumstein, the entire increase in homicides in the mid-1980s can be attributed to __________.
A) urban life.
B) handgun use.
C) lenient courts.
D) single parents.

Answer: B

7) Zimmering, Cook, and Laub all suggest that __________ is not the best predictor of future violence in juvenile delinquency.
A) school problems
B) rural and urban poverty
C) demographic shifts
D) law enforcement arrests

Answer: C

8) Juvenile Court Statistics are often criticized, much like UCRs, for only measuring crimes that ___________.
A) come to the attention of the court.
B) are considered as status offenses.
C) are committed by minorities.
D) typically are referred back to juvenile authorities.

Answer: A

9) Which of the following is a good example of a longitudinal method of research study?
A) survey data
B) content analysis
C) cohort group
D) experiment data

Answer: C

10) Which of the following is a major problem typically suffered by cohort studies?
A) The findings cannot be confidently generalized beyond those in the cohort.
B) Cohort participants frequently report false information.
C) The study time is too short.
D) Studies are inexpensive and not thorough enough.

Answer: A

11) Most cohort studies agree that the juvenile justice system tends to __________.
A) punish middle-class youth more than lower-class offenders.
B) indicate that most crime is committed by first-time offenders.
C) arrest lower-class females more than males.
D) encourage rather than discourage future criminality.

Answer: D

12) Respondents not telling the truth when filling out self-report questionnaires, typically refers to problems associated with ______.
A) validity.
B) reliability.
C) spurious association.
D) ecological fallacy.

Answer: A

13) The consistency of a questionnaire or an interview to measure a variable is referred to as ____________.
A) validity.
B) reliability.
C) spurious association.

D) ecological fallacy.

Answer: B

14) Recent self-report studies indicate that juveniles committed a surprisingly large proportion of ____________.
A) status offenses.
B) property crimes.
C) violent acts.
D) drug related crimes.

Answer: C

15) Recent self-report studies indicate that drug use among juveniles
A) increased by 50 percent.
B) began a dramatic increase in 1992.
C) increased by 10 percent.
D) decreased only slightly.

Answer: B

16) According to the Rochester study, what is significantly related to delinquency?
A) attachment to and involvement with parents
B) bi-directional drug use
C) maturation from peer groups
D) increased dependency on moral turpitude

Answer: A

17) Which of the following methods of measuring crime is conducted by the Census Bureau?
A) self-report surveys
B) victimization surveys
C) Uniform Crime Reports
D) Juvenile Court Statistics

Answer: B

18) Victimization studies reveal that the experience of being victimized increases the likelihood of __________.
A) decreased association with peers.
B) status offenses.
C) dropping out of school.
D) participation in delinquency.

Answer: D

19) Which of the following is the most frequent crime reported by victims?
A) rape
B) theft of property
C) burglary
D) robbery

Answer: B

20) According to self-report studies, who is more likely to be officially delinquent?
A) white males

B) black males
C) Asian males
D) Hispanic males

Answer: B

21) According to P. Tolan, what determines an offender's likelihood to persist in offending?
A) early-onset
B) calculated risks
C) specialization
D) social backgrounds

Answer: A

22) Which of the following offenses do juvenile females tend to specialize in?
A) prostitution
B) drug crimes
C) running away
D) theft crimes

Answer: C

23) What does the research on chronic offenders suggest is very difficult to do?
A) document their social-class
B) investigate sociopathic attitudes
C) measure violent crimes
D) predict their chronic offending

Answer: D

24) Which of the following is the best predictor of severe antisocial behavior among mildly antisocial children?
A) birth-order
B) family economic situation
C) presence of an antisocial father
D) school performance
Answer: C

25) According to Gottfredson and Hirschi, the best predictor of crime is ___________.
A) poverty.
B) prior criminal behavior.
C) peer relations.
D) poor education.

Answer: B

26) The chapter begins with an interesting story involving the death of a _______________.
A) 12 year old girl stolen from her bed room
B) 19 year old college women attacked on campus
C) college student working at a grocery store who was shot in a robbery
D) police officer in a large city
E) 3 year old boy

Answer: E

27) The term incidence of delinquency refers to _______________.
A) the person who committed the crime
B) the frequency of offending or the number of delinquent events.
C) the place where the crime occurred
D) the time of the crime
E) all of the above

Answer: B

28) The term prevalence of delinquency refers to _______________.
A) the person who committed the crime
B) the place where the crime occurred
C) the number of young people involved in delinquent behavior
D) the time of the crime
E) all of the above

Answer: C

29) The most common form of murder in Britain is _______________.
A) shootings with handguns
B) stabbings
C) poison
D) bludgeoning

Answer: B

30) Firearms account for _______________ of all murders in Britain.
A) 9%
B) 19%
C) 29%
D) 39%
E) 49%

Answer: A

31) Most victims of violent crime are between the ages of __________.
A) 55-70
B) 40-44
C) 30-34
D) 16-19

Answer: E

True/False Questions

1) The Federal Bureau of Investigation serves as the clearinghouse for the Uniform Crime Reports program.

Answer: TRUE

2) Uniform Crime Reports are very reliable measures of crime data.

Answer: FALSE

3) According to UCRs, Juvenile murder rates increased greatly between 1993 and 2003.

Answer: FALSE

4) According to UCRs, juveniles were involved in 12 percent of all drug arrests in 2002.

Answer: TRUE

5) According to A. Blumstein, a decline in homicide rates by young people will depend on getting drugs out of their hands and socializing them into lower-risk settings.

Answer: FALSE

6) William Bennett, John DiIulio Jr., and John Walters argue that a new generation of juvenile criminals will be known as "superpredators."

Answer: TRUE

7) One of the most important objectives of compiling juvenile court statistics was to furnish an index of the general nature and extent of the problems brought before the juvenile court.

Answer: TRUE

8) The number of children appearing before the juvenile court significantly decreased from the late 1950s until the mid 1970s.

Answer: FALSE

9) Cohort studies are not only time consuming, but costly as well.

Answer: TRUE

10) Self-report studies are generally considered to be helpful tools in measuring and understanding delinquent behavior.

Answer: TRUE

11) Self-report studies are often challenged in regard to questionable validity and reliability.

Answer: TRUE

12) The first study of hidden delinquency suggested a strong association between social-class and delinquency.

Answer: FALSE

13) According to the Pittsburgh study, prevalence of serious delinquency is greater for African-American boys.

Answer: TRUE

14) According to the Rochester study, the impact of family variables fade as adolescents become older and more independent from their parents.

Answer: TRUE

15) According to the National Household Survey on Drug Abuse, marijuana use decreased in 1992 and continued to decrease until 1996.

Answer: FALSE

16) According to the NCVS, the greatest annual decline in violent crime rates occurred in 2003.

Answer: TRUE

17) According to the NCVS, whites are more likely to be victims of crime than African-Americans.

Answer: FALSE

18) Running away from home accounts for nearly one-fifth of all female arrests.

Answer: TRUE

19) African-American females are more likely to be victimized by violent crime than white females.

Answer: TRUE

20) Self-report studies suggest that middle-and upper-class juveniles are as delinquent as their lower class peers.

Answer: TRUE

Short Answer Questions

1) Federal record keeping was first authorized in 1870 when Congress created the __________ __________ __________.

Answer: Department of Justice

2) __________ __________ __________ indicates that a person is arrested because he or she confesses to an offense or is implicated by other criminal evidence.

Answer: Clearance by arrest

3) According to Juvenile Court Statistics, __________ __________ showed a dramatic increase between 1990 and 1999, especially for nonwhites.

Answer: drug offenses

4) A large amount of __________ __________ is not contained in official arrest statistics.

Answer: hidden delinquency

5) The Census Bureau began __________ __________ in 1972 to determine the extent of crime.

Answer: victimization studies

6) Uniform Crime Reports documented in 2002 that males are arrested __________ times more for drug violations than females.

Answer: seven

7) The __________ __________ __________ refers to when delinquent behavior started.

Answer: age of onset

8)It is perceived that __________ __________ offenders constitute a majority of the active juvenile offenders.

Answer: chronic youthful

9) __________, or the age of termination, is related to the maturation process.

Answer: Desistance

10) A __________ __________ involves a gradual or dramatic change and may lead to a modification, reshaping, or transition from one state, condition, or phase to another.

Answer: turning point

11). The age at which a child begins to commit delinquent acts called __________

Answer: age of onset

12) A juvenile who engages repeatedly in delinquent behavior is called _____.

Answer: chronic youthful offender

13) The solution of a crime by arrest of a perpetrator who has confessed or who has been implicated by witnesses or evidence is called_________.

Answer: clearance by arrest

14) A generational group as defined in demographics, statistics, or for the purpose of social research is called a ___________.

Answer: cohort

15) Research that usually includes all individuals who were born in a particular year in a particular city or county and follows them through part or all of their lives is called a _______________.

Answer: cohort study

16) The termination of a delinquent career or behavior is called __________.

Answer: desistance

17) An increase in the frequency and severity of an individual's offenses; an important dimension of delinquency is sometimes referred to as an ________.

Answer: escalation of offenses

18) Unobserved or unreported delinquency.

Answer: hidden delinquency

19) The frequency with which delinquent behavior takes place.

Answer: incidence of delinquency

20) The most serious offenses reported by the FBI in the *Uniform Crime Reports,* including murder and nonnegligent manslaughter, forcible rape, robbery, aggravated assault, burglary, larceny-theft, motor vehicle theft, and arson are called the ___________.

Answer: index offenses

Essay Questions

1) Discuss the various weaknesses attributed to the Uniform Crime Reports as measures of crime.

2) Describe how some researchers in the 1980s predicted that juvenile crime would reach epidemic proportions. What were they basing their predictions on?

3) Describe what a cohort study is, and what are the most significant findings.

4) Discuss the findings of various studies on racial/ethnic background and delinquent behavior.

5) Discuss the various factors that may lead to juvenile offenders continuing on into adult criminal behavior.

Chapter 3 Individual Causes of Delinquency

Multiple Choice Questions

1) Cesare Beccaria viewed punishment as _____________.
A) evil
B) a necessary evil
C) immoral.
D) moral weaklings.

Answer: B

2) Jeremy Bentham purported that criminal behavior is a result of _______.
A) biological causes.
B) psychological inferiority.
C) utilitarianism.
D) rational choice.

Answer: D

3) Which of the following origins of delinquency became the more widely accepted with positivists?
A) psychological
B) biological
C) environmental
D) structural

Answer: A

4) Positivists believe that once causes of human behavior are discovered, they can be _______________.
A) punished unequally.
B) replicated scientifically.
C) modified.
D) uncontrollable.

Answer: C

5) The first factor early progressives looked at as a major cause of crime was ____________.
A) demons.
B) poverty.
C) rational choice.
D) utilitarianism.

Answer: B

6) Which of the following views are rejected by positivism in regard to causes of delinquency?
A) biological
B) psychological
C) rational choice
D) environmental

Answer: C

7) Lombroso referred to a born criminal as ____________.
A) atavistic.
B) endomorphic.
C) notorious.
D) feebleminded.

Answer: A

8) Goddard concluded that the cause of criminality was due primarily to _________.
A) atavism.
B) low IQ.
C) bad stock.
D) social aggressiveness.

Answer: C

9) According to Sheldon, which of the following are more likely to be delinquent?
A) endomorphic
B) ectomorphic
C) mesomorphic
D) alphamorphic

Answer: C

10) According to twin and adoption studies, which of the following should have higher concordance rates?
A) fraternal twins
B) adopted twins
C) dizygotic twins
D) identical twins

Answer: D

11) West and Farrington suggested that delinquency could be explained by ___________.
A) body types.
B) environmental influences.
C) low IQ's.
D) feeblemindedness.

Answer: C

12) According to Eysenck, delinquency results from the ____________.
A) autonomic nervous system.
B) hypothalamus.
C) subconscious.
D) central atavistic tendency.

Answer: A

13) Moffit's developmental theory refers to a child developing a trajectory of delinquency at age three or younger as __________.
A) adolescent-limited (AL).
B) life-course-persistent (LCP).
C) attention-deficit (AD).
D) developmentally-limited (DL).

Answer: B

14) Kandel and Mednick contend that violent criminal behavior may result from ______________.
A) feeblemindedness.
B) low IQ's.
C) pregnancy and birth complications.
D) sugar-highs.

Answer: C

15) A child that is easily distracted, does not want to listen, and is impulsive, probably suffers from _____________.
A) LCP (life-course persistent).
B) ADHD (attention deficit hyperactivity disorder).
C) PTSD (post-traumatic stress disorder).
D) MPD (multiple-personality disorder).

Answer: B

16) Which of the following did Freud believe was the primitive drive leading to delinquency?
A) ego
B) superego
C) id
D) psychosexual

Answer: C

17) What do Freudians attribute delinquent behavior to?
A) defective superego
B) environment
C) underdeveloped id
D) temperament

Answer: A

18) Some have suggested that delinquency is related to sensation-seekers, meaning a person ____________.
A) wants to be touched.
B) is negatively affected by climate and temperature.
C) seeks positive praise for thrills.
D) is willing to take physical and social risks.

Answer: D

19) What did the Gluecks use to assess the personality traits of juvenile delinquents?
A) SAT scores
B) MMP intelligence tests
C) Rorschach tests
D) ACT scores

Answer: C

20)A person that is intelligent and charming, but lacks remorse and shame, typically describes a ________________.
A) delusional delinquent.
B) sociopath.
C) schizophrenic.
D) manic-depressant.

Answer: B

21) Wilson/Herrnstein's reinforcement theory suggests that offenders find the rewards of crime to be ________________.
A) immediate and pleasurable.
B) harsh and painful.
C) slow and petty.
D) risky and favorable.

Answer: A

22) What do the critics of reinforcement theory believe that Wilson/Herrnstein have factored out of their theory?
A) cost
B) genetics
C) society
D) psychology

Answer: C

23) Ecological researchers infer that offenders choose burglary targets close to them due to ________________.

A) knowing the area better.
B) knowing where to sell stolen items.
C) less expense is involved in committing the crime.
D) escape being easier.

Answer: D

24) The presence of motivated offenders, absence of guardians, and availability of suitable targets is the mainstay of which approach?
A) determinism
B) routine activity
C) sensation-seeking
D) Freudian

Answer: B

25) Which of the following offenders does rational choice theory tend to ignore?
A) thieves
B) burglars
C) kleptomaniacs
D) robbers

Answer: C

26) The vignette at the beginning of the chapter is about __________.
a. infanticide
b. homicide
c. suicide
d. a murder at a grocery store
e. drug sells

Answer: C

27) Who's the author of the 1764 book entitled *On Crime and Punishments*?
a. Charles de Secondat
b. Baron de Montesquieu
c. Cesare Beccaria
d. Jeremy Bentham
e. Cesare Lombroso

Answer: c

28) A doctrine that holds that the useful is the good, and that the aim of social or political action should be the greatest good for the greatest number is called ______________.
a. utilitarianism
b. positivism
c. determinism
d. free-will
e. free-choice

Answer: a

29) Which of the following writers would most likely believe that crime is a rational choice?
a. Ernest van den Haag
b. Cesare Lombroso
c. Emile Durkheim
d. Robert Merton
e. All of the above

Answer: a

30) According to the text, why is it that in youth gangs they sometimes allow the youngest member to do the beatings during a mugging?
a. he is the toughest gang member
b. since he is small, it is harder to hit him
c. since he is under 15, the gang members know he'll be back on the streets in no time
d. since he is small, he is able to sneak up on the person

Answer: c

True/False Questions

1) Baron de Montesquieu is credited with beginning the classical school debate on crime.

Answer: TRUE

2) According to the classical school, offenders deserve treatment and not punishment.

Answer: FALSE

3) Positivism purports that human behaviors can be modified once the causes are discovered.

Answer: TRUE

4) Positivism views a delinquent as fundamentally different from the nondelinquent.

Answer: TRUE

5) Lombroso's theory has been able to stand the test of scientific investigation.

Answer: FALSE

6) Goddard's study of training school boys suggested delinquents are feebleminded.

Answer: TRUE

7) Sheldon postulated that somatotypes had temperamental correlates leading to delinquency.

Answer: TRUE

8) Most twin-adoption studies have suggested that delinquency is related to environment.

Answer: FALSE

9) West/Farrington studies suggest there is a meaningful correlation between IQ and delinquency.

Answer: TRUE

10) According to Moffitt, children develop a lifelong path of delinquency as early as ages three to six.

Answer: TRUE

11) According to Freud, the id has the express purpose of controlling the ego and superego.

Answer: FALSE

12) Hindelang found that delinquents are more pleasure seeking than are nondelinquents.

Answer: TRUE

13) Jack Katz contends that delinquents find crimes sensually compelling and research should focus on situational factors and NOT background factors.

Answer: TRUE

14) The Gluecks found that delinquents were NOT any more defiant or hostile than nondelinquents.

Answer: FALSE

15) The term psychopath and sociopath are interchangeable, meaning they are really one of the same.

Answer: TRUE

16) Cook's criminal opportunity theory emphasizes individual choice guided by the perceived costs and benefits of criminal activity.

Answer: TRUE

17) Most studies of delinquency have reported that delinquency is carefully planned in advance.

Answer: FALSE

18) The concept of rationality assumes that individuals have free will and are not controlled by emotions.

Answer: TRUE

19) Robert Agnew concludes that freedom of choice varies from one individual to another.

Answer: TRUE

20) Youths experiencing intense emotions of reaction to a situation my lead to youths bypassing any rational process, according to critics of rational choice theory.

Answer: TRUE

Short Answer Questions

1) Becarria based the legitimacy of criminal sanctions on the __________ __________.

Answer: social contract

2) __________ became the dominant philosophical perspective of juvenile justice at the beginning of the twentieth century.

Answer: Positivism

3) According to Lombroso, the __________ person was a reversion to an earlier evolutionary form.

Answer: atavistic

4) __________ stresses the interaction between biological and environmental factors within an individual.

Answer: Sociobiology

5) According to Eysenks, __________ are much more likely to welcome involvement in delinquent acts.

Answer: extroverts

6) Children with an inordinate amount of activity are sometimes labeled as having __________ __________ __________.

Answer: attention deficit disorder

7) Jack Katz contends when children commit crime, they become involved in an __________ __________ of seductions and compulsions that have special dynamics.

Answer: emotional process

8) The Gluecks studied delinquent children to determine an association between __________ and crime.

Answer: personality

9) Reinforcement theory suggests behavior is governed by its consequent rewards and __________.

Answer: punishments

10) Phillip J. Cook developed what he calls __________ __________ theory, claiming criminals choose attractive targets with little risk of consequence.

Answer: criminal opportunity

11) A cognitive disorder of childhood that can include inattention, distractibility excessive activity, restlessness, noisiness, impulsiveness, and so on is called ____________.

Answer: Attention Deficit Hyperactivity Disorder (ADHD)

12) The system of nerves that govern reflexes, glands, the iris of the eye, and activities of inferior organs that are not subject to voluntary control is called the ___________.

Answer: automatic nervous system

13) The belief that juveniles' biological characteristics and limitations drive them to delinquent behavior is sometimes called ______________.

Answer: biological positivism

14) According to Cesare Lombroso, an individual who is atavistic, or reverts to an earlier evolutionary level and is unable to conform his or her behavior to the requirements of modern society is called a _________________

Answer: born criminal

15) A theory claiming that criminals tend to be attracted to targets that offer a high payoff with little risk of legal consequences is _________________.

Answer: criminal opportunity theory

16) ____________ is a philosophical position that suggests that individuals are driven into delinquent or criminal behavior by biological or psychological traits that are beyond their control.

Answer: Determinism

17) An aspect of temperament' that can range from a near absence of emotional response to intense, out-of-control emotional reactions is called ___________.

Answer: emotionality

18) A method for determining the sum total of pleasure and pain produced by an act, Also, the assumption that human beings strive to obtain a favorable balance of pleasure and pain is called _________________.

Answer: felicific calculus

19) The ability to make rational choices among possible actions, and to select one over the others is called _______________.

Answer: free will

20) Chemical imbalances in the body, resulting from poor nutrition, allergies, and exposure to lead and certain other substances, which are said to lead to delinquency are referred to as ______________

Answer: Orthomolecular imbalances

Essay Questions

1) Discuss the impact that Cesare Becarria and Jeremy Bentham had on the development of rational choice theory.

2) In regard to the study of juvenile delinquency, identify two significant contributions that Lombroso's theory made.

3) Describe the process in which Freud theorized how a person could become delinquent. Be sure to identify all the concepts and elements.

4) Describe Cook's criminal opportunity theory as it relates to delinquency.

5) Discuss the strengths and weaknesses of rational choice theory. Be sure to cite some of the studies listed in the text.

6) What are the basic theoretical constructs of the classical school of criminology?

7) Jeremy Bentham stated that punishment has 4 objectives. What are those 4 objectives?

8) John Conrad tells the sad story of Billy in this chapter. Write an essay about Billy's sad world.

9) Freud's followers have identified four ways in which emotional problems that develop in childhood might lead to delinquent behavior. What are those four methods?

Chapter 4 Social Structural Causes of Delinquency

Multiple Choice Questions

1) What term did Durkheim use to describe normlessness, which resulted from society's failure to provide adequate regulation of its members?
A) disorganization
B) anomie
C) differential association
D) social capital

Answer: B

2) Shaw and McKay viewed delinquency as resulting from a breakdown in social control among ____________.
A) family and neighborhood.
B) governmental agents.
C) political institutions.
D) religious institutions.

Answer: A

3) Burgess suggested that cities grow in patterns from the ________.
A) edges moving inward.
B) center moving outward.
C) edges moving outward.
D) center moving inward.

Answer: B

4) What was Robert Park's profession before becoming a sociology professor at the University of Chicago in 1914?
A) doctor
B) lawyer
C) newspaper reporter
D) police chief

Answer: C

5) Where did Clifford Shaw report that crimes rates were the highest in Chicago in 1929?
A) rural areas
B) suburbs
C) concentric circles
D) center of the city

Answer: D

6) Burgess's hypothesis of urban growth is referred to as ________.
A) concentric zone.
B) progressive circles.

C) target zone.
D) urban zone.

Answer: A

7) Who did Shaw and McKay report were attracted to inner-city areas?
A) whites
B) Hispanics
C) native Americans
D) African Americans and foreigners

Answer: D

8) Why did Shaw and McKay's theory lose vitality in the 1960s and 1970s?
A) It was speculated they "forged" the data.
B) The research was discovered to be empirically flawed.
C) Theory and research was more interested in focusing of individuals.
D) There was insurgence of street gangs.

Answer: C

9) Cultural deviance theories view delinquency and crime as an expression of _________ to cultural values and norms that are in opposition to those of the larger society
A) conformity
B) deviation
C) anger
D) hostility

Answer: A

10) Walter Miller characterized the value system of the lower class as
A) critical dimensions.
B) focal concerns.
C) urban utilities.
D) endemic entities.

Answer: B

11) What types of behavior did Miller say individuals engage in when searching for excitement?
A) drugs and shoplifting
B) vandalism and curfew violations
C) assaults and theft
D) alcohol and gambling

Answer: D

12) What did Miller reason attracted lower-class boys to one-sex groups?
A) lack of opportunity
B) desire to prove masculinity
C) sexual attraction

D) desire for a delinquent label

Answer: B

13) Critics of Miller's subculture theory charge that ___________.
A) lower-class youths hold the same values as those of the larger culture.
B) the theory has too many concepts.
C) middle-class youths are more delinquent than lower-class youths.
D) the theory is sexist in nature.

Answer: A

14) What term did Robert K. Merton use to describe lack of social integration?
A) disorganization
B) institutionalized
C) anomie
D) conformity

Answer: C

15) According to Merton, when adolescents accept the cultural goal but reject the institutional means of attaining it, they may pursue other illegitimate paths in a stage of adaptation called ____________.
A) conformity.
B) innovation.
C) ritualism.
D) retreatism.

Answer: B

16) What stage of adaptation did Merton refer to when individuals have rejected both the goals of the culture and the institutional means of attaining them?
A) conformity
B) innovation
C) ritualism
D) retreatism

Answer: D

17) What term did Albert K. Cohen use to describe lower-class youths that were unable to attain middle-class goals?
A) status frustration
B) social rebellion
C) aspiration avoidance
D) ascetic hostility

Answer: A

18) What term did Cohen use to characterize the delinquent activities of the lower-class subculture?
A) focal solidarity
B) violent virtues

C) short-run hedonism
D) deliberate duping

Answer: C

19) Bartollas indicates that the importance of Cohen's theory is that it views delinquency as __________.
A) environmentally charged.
B) a process of interaction.
C) genetically based.
D) a result of psychologically inferiority.

Answer: B

20) Which type of delinquents did Cloward and Ohlin contend were the most serious?
A) Type I
B) Type II
C) Type III
D) Type IV

Answer: C

21) What does Cloward and Ohlin assume that delinquent youths do NOT have to improve their economic positions?
A) education
B) materialism
C) working parents
D) legitimate opportunities

Answer: D

22) According to Cloward and Ohlin's opportunity theory, the retreatist subculture generates a new order of goals and criteria for __________.
A) achievement
B) failure
C) satisfaction
D) materialism

Answer: A

23) Social structure theories contend a youth may become delinquent because he or she __________.
A) is biologically predisposed.
B) lacks sufficient education.
C) lives in a disorganized community.
D) lacks will power to resist crime.

Answer: C

24) James S. Coleman suggests that individuals commit delinquent acts because they lack __________.
A) strong resistance.
B) social capital.

C) discipline.
D) beneficial rewards.

Answer: B

25) A weakness of social structure theory is that many youths in the same cultural setting _____________.
A) do not become delinquent.
B) belong to gangs.
C) are of the middle-class.
D) commit only the most serious crimes.

Answer: A

26) In the vignette at the beginning of this chapter, four Harlem teenagers were accused of __________.
A) a murder
B) a rape
C) a suicide
D) a car accident
E) possessing drugs

Answer: A

27) The relatively stable formal and informal arrangements that characterize society-including its economic arrangements, social institutions and its values and norms is called ______________.
A) strain theory
B) social disorganization theory
C) social structure
D) blocked opportunity
E) reaction formation

Answer: C

28) Which of the following is a characteristic of efficacy?
A) residents have mutual trust
B) residents have shared values
C) residents have a disposition to intervene for the public good.
D) all of the above

Answer: D

29) Walter B. Miller said that physical prowess as demonstrated as strength and endurance is valued in lower class culture. Miller called this characteristic __________________.
A) trouble
B) toughness
C) smartness
D) excitement
E) fate

Answer: B

30) _________________ proposes that delinquency results from the frustration individuals feel when they are unable to achieve the goals they desire.
A) strain theory
B) conflict theory

C) functional theory
D) symbolic interaction theory
E) economic theory

Answer: A

True/False Questions

1) Durkheim suggested that regulation of society would deregulate with rapid social change.

Answer: TRUE

2) According to Shaw and McKay, industrialization, urbanization, and immigration all contributed to the disorganization of the community.

Answer: TRUE

3) Burgess theorized that the zone farthest from a city's center would likely be the highest in delinquency.

Answer: FALSE

4) Shaw and McKay reported that as cities industrialized, populations decreased in the center as a result of anticipated displacement.

Answer: TRUE

5) Shaw and McKay assumed that juvenile and adult gangs accounted for the transmission of delinquency within the inner city.

Answer: TRUE

6) Miller argued that the motivation to become delinquent is endemic to the middle-class culture.

Answer: FALSE

7) According to Miller, smartness is necessary to achieve material goods and personal status without physical effort.

Answer: TRUE

8) Miller contends crime permits one to show personal independence from controls placed on him or her.

Answer: TRUE

9) Strain theorists view delinquency as a consequence of community disorganization.

Answer: FALSE

10) According to Merton, a conformist is well integrated and absent of anomie.

Answer: TRUE

11) According to Merton, rebellion consists of rejecting the dominant culture values and substituting them for a new set of values.

Answer: TRUE

12) Strain theory was popular in the 1960s because it required a broad rejection of the social order.

Answer: FALSE

13) Cohen reasoned that American culture defines the middle-class values and norms that children are expected to aspire toward and to achieve.

Answer: TRUE

14) Cohen suggested that most delinquency is for particular reason and purpose.

Answer: FALSE

15) Critics charge that Cohen's theory of delinquent subculture is flawed because most delinquent boys eventually become law-abiding.

Answer: TRUE

16) Cloward and Ohlin claimed that boys of the Type I have values consistent with the middle-class.

Answer: TRUE

17) According to Cloward and Ohlin, within the retreatist subculture the main activity is crimes of extortion, fraud, and theft.

Answer: FALSE

18) Coleman describes resources that reside in the social structure of society itself as social capital.

Answer: TRUE

19) Implications of structural explanations of delinquency is first felt at home and the squalor of the street is what drives many youths to the streets.

Answer: TRUE

20) Recent evidence appears to support a relationship among class, the economic structures of society, and delinquency.

Answer: TRUE

Short Answer Questions

1) Shaw and McKay extended __________ __________ theory by focusing on the social characteristics of the community as a cause of delinquency.

Answer: social disorganization

2) Social disorganization theory argues that delinquent behavior becomes an alternative mode of __________ through which youth are apart of disorganized communities.

Answer: socialization

3) Shaw and McKay's studies addresses the problem of crime in terms of __________ level of analysis.

Answer: multiple

4) Walter B. Miller argued that a set of __________ __________ of the lower class characterizes this socioeconomic group.

Answer: focal concerns

5) Merton defined the purposes and interests held as legitimate objectives for all diversely located members of society as __________ __________ __________.

Answer: culturally defined goals

6) According to Merton, the acceptable method to attain culturally defined goals is the __________ __________.

Answer: institutional means

7) According to Merton, a __________ may go through the motions of attending classes and studying, but abandon the goal of success.

Answer: ritualist

8) Cohen purports that when status frustration occurs, the mechanism of __________ __________ is used to deal with it.

Answer: reaction formation

9) According to Cloward and Ohlin, __________ is the key ingredient in the conflict subculture.

Answer: violence

10) Laub and Sampson emphasize the importance of __________ __________ in the desistance process.

Answer: human agency

11) According to strain theory, limited or nonexistent chances of success are called ________________.

Answer: blocked opportunity

12) A theory promoted by Clifford R. Shaw, Henry D. McKay, and Walter B. Miller, who view delinquent behavior as an expression of conformity to cultural values and norms that are in opposition to those of the larger U.S. society is called

____________________.

Answer: cultural deviance theory

13) The is an approach which holds that areas of concentrated crime maintain their high rates over a long period, even when the composition of the population changes rapidly, because delinquent "values" become cultural norms and are passed from one generation to the next is called ________________.

Answer: cultural transmission theory

14) In Robert K. Merton's version of strain theory, the set of purposes and interests a culture defines as legitimate objectives for individuals are called ________________.

Answer: culturally defined goals

15) Differences in economic and occupational opportunities open to members of different socioeconomic classes are called ________________.

Answer: differential opportunity structure

16) As proposed by Walter B. Miller, values or focal concerns (toughness, smartness, excitement, fate, and autonomy) of lower-class youths that differ from those of middle-class youths are called ________________.

Answer: focal concerns of the lower class

17) In Robert K. Merton's theory, culturally sanctioned methods of attaining individual goals are called

________________.

Answer: institutionalized means

18) Richard A. Cloward and Lloyd E. Ohlin's perspective which holds that gang members turn to delinquency because of a sense of injustice about the lack of legitimate opportunities open to them is called

________________.

Answer: opportunity theory

19) Psychological strategy for dealing with frustrating by becoming hostile towards an unattainable object is called ____________________.

Answer: reaction formation

20) James S. Coleman's perspective which holds that lower-class youth may become delinquent because they lack "social capital," or resources that reside in the social structure, including norms, networks, and relationships are called ____________________.

Answer: social capital theory

Essay Questions

1) Discuss the elements of a recent revival of Shaw and McKay's social disorganization theory to the field of criminology.

2) Describe the framework of the Chicago Area Projects and the strengths and weaknesses of the program.

3) Define the various focal concerns, as described by Walter B. Miller's theory, on lower-class culture.

4) Discuss how Robert Agnew revised strain theory. How is it similar to Merton's and how is it different?

5) Discuss how social policy is affected by structural explanations of delinquency.

6) Explain the reasons why social disorganization has been so influential in the development of criminological theory.

7) What are the main criticisms of social disorganization theory as presented by Robert J. Burisk Jr.

Chapter 5 Social Process Theories of Delinquency

Multiple Choice Questions

1) What is the premise of Sutherland's theory of differential association?
A) People are naturally evil.
B) People learn crime from others.
C) Psychological impressions affect crime.
D) People make rational choices.

Answer: B

2) What interactionist concept did Glaser use to modify differential association theory?
A) self
B) control
C) drift
D) anomie

Answer: A

3) Social learning theory suggests that delinquent behavior can be acquired through ___________.
A) punishment.
B) consequences.
C) imitation and modeling.
D) alternative behaviors.

Answer: C

4) Critics of differential association theory charge that it tends to ignore ____________.
A) social learning from a variety of sources.
B) peer group influence and the commission of crime.
C) parental influence on delinquency.
D) why one may NOT succumb to delinquent definitions

Answer: D

5) What does Matza believe begins or starts the process of becoming delinquent?
A) convention
B) neutralization
C) drifting
D) discrimination

Answer: B

6) What does drift theory emphasize far greater than differential association theory?
A) social learning
B) biological causes
C) choice
D) economics

Answer: C

7) What does Matza claim juveniles use to collect examples of inconsistency that fill them with a sense of injustice?
A) memory file
B) passive vessel
C) legal norms
D) loyal allegiance

Answer: A

8) According to Matza, assertion of tort refers to delinquents demonstrating __________.
A) relative kinship.
B) theft and betrayal.
C) love and friendship.
D) valor and loyalty.

Answer: D

9) Drift theory examines the process in which juveniles release themselves from ___________.
A) the moral binds of the law.
B) parental control.
C) school authority.
D) situational offenses and defenses.

Answer: A

10) Drift theory suggest many teenage delinquent acts decline as adolescents approach adulthood because ___________.
A) drug use stops.
B) the thrill reduces.
C) they were not committed to delinquent norms.
D) policing becomes more intense in their lives.

Answer: C

11) According to John E. Hamlin, what theory occupies a central role in explaining delinquency by combining learning theory and control theory?
A) differential association
B) neutralization
C) bonding
D) containment

Answer: B

12) Matza and Sykes's neutralization theory has been criticized by some because it seems to apply more to ____________.
A) lower-class delinquency.
B) some delinquent behaviors more than others.

C) biological crimes more than sociological crimes.
D) younger delinquents and less to older ones.

Answer: B

13) What did Reckless contend that persons use to insulate themselves from deviant behaviors?
A) strong pushes and pulls
B) weak moral temptations
C) strong inner and outer containments
D) strong techniques of neutralization

Answer: C

14) What did Reckless contend encourages persons to engage in deviant behaviors?
A) strong pushes and pulls
B) weak moral temptations
C) strong inner and outer containments
D) weak techniques of neutralization

Answer: A

15) According to containment theory, what would most delinquent youths have?
A) strong external and internal controls
B) weak external and internal controls
C) weak external and strong internal controls
D) weak internal pushes and strong external controls

Answer: B

16) What does containment theory suggest is a precondition of law-abiding behavior?
A) punishment
B) attachment
C) stale education
D) good self-concept

Answer: D

17) Containment theory has been criticized by some due to the difficulty of measuring the variable of __________.
A) delinquency.
B) self-concept.
C) criminal intent.
D) social drift.

Answer: B

18) What did Travis Hirschi link to delinquent behavior in his social control theory?
A) quality of bonds
B) inadequate law enforcement
C) conventional behavior
D) psychological inadequacies

Answer: A

19) What did Hirschi believe was the most important variable insulating a child against _______________. delinquent behavior?
A) involvement with school
B) commitment to work
C) attachment to parents
D) belief

Answer: C

20) What term did Hirschi use to describe respect for the law and social norms?
A) commitment
B) attachment
C) involvement
D) belief

Answer: D

21) Hirschi's social control theory has been criticized for applying to
A) his theoretical constructs.
B) only relatively minor acts of delinquency.
C) adult crimes.
D) select geographical areas.

Answer: B

22) Gottfredson and Hirschi suggested, in A General Theory of Crime, that delinquency results from _______________.
A) the lack of self-control.
B) poverty.
C) neurological disorders.
D) disorganized communities.

Answer: A

23) What theories did Delbert Elliot integrate to form integrated social process theory?
A) strain, social control, and social learning
B) drift, anomie, and differential association
C) anomie, social control, and psychological
D) biological, social disorganization, and strain

Answer: A

24) According to Thornberry's interactional theory, what factor is the most influential in the adolescent years?
A) money
B) school
C) family
D) peers

Answer: C

25) What elements has interactional theory been criticized for ignoring?

A) upper-class delinquency
B) race and gender
C) lower-class delinquency
D) age and delinquency

Answer: B

26) The story of the Bogel family illustrates ____________.
A) mental illness creates a fertile ground for crime
B) race affects crime rates
C) how criminal behavior came be passed from one generation to the next
D) how income is the main predictor of criminal activity
E) geographic regions have different crime rates

Answer: A

27) Jeanson James Ancheta is famous for ____________?
A) armed bank robberies
B) selling cocaine
C) internet hacking
D) serial murder
E) political bribes

Answer: C

28) The theorist who is most closely identified with social control theory is __________?
A) Travis Hirschi
B) Thomas Hobbs
C) Max Weber
D) Emile Durkheim
E) Edwin Sutherland

Answer: A

29) Another name for social control theory is __________.
A) differential association
B) bonding
C) conflict theory
D) societal reaction theory
E) drift theory

Answer: B

30) Which of the following writers believed that humans are basically antisocial and sinful?
A) Thomas Hobbs
B) Puritan theologians
C) Sigmund Freud
D) all of the above

Answer: D

True/False Questions

1) Edwin Sutherland contends that delinquency results from disorganized social structure.

Answer: FALSE

2) Differential association theory suggests that a person becomes delinquent from exposure to excessive definitions that favor violations of the law.

Answer: TRUE

3)A criticism of differential association theory is that it tends to be viewed as negative.

Answer: FALSE

4) Some criticize differential association theory for treating delinquents as a passive vessel.

Answer: TRUE

5) Matza believes a person can violate legal norms and not surrender allegiance to them.

Answer: TRUE

6) Matza contends that breaking the moral bind to law will always result in delinquency.

Answer: FALSE

7) Drift theory was developed in large part to account for the majority of adolescents who engage in delinquent behavior on a part-time basis.

Answer: TRUE

8) Matza's drift theory views the delinquent as one who is pressured by situational context.

Answer: TRUE

9) Robert Agnew's analysis of drift theory contends that eutralization is more likely to occur with minor offenses than violent behaviors.

Answer: FALSE

10) According to containment theory, juveniles who have both strong external and internal containment are much less likely to become delinquent.

Answer: TRUE

11) Containment theory fails to account for self-esteem when explaining delinquent behavior.

Answer: FALSE

12) The follow-up data to Reckless's four-year intervention project indicated that special classes to improve the self-concept of adolescents had no appreciable effects.

Answer: TRUE

13) Hirschi believes that most humans are basically good and only need social instruction to stay law-abiding.

Answer: FALSE

14) Hirschi's social control theory suggests that if juveniles are committed to conventional values and activities, they will refrain from delinquent behavior.

Answer: TRUE

15) Hirschi contends that absence of effective beliefs will result in delinquency.

Answer: TRUE

16) Social control theory has less empirical support today than most other delinquency explanations.

Answer: FALSE

17) Gottfredson and Hirschi suggested that people who lack self-control would tend to be impulsive, insensitive, physical, and nonverbal.

Answer: TRUE

18)A strength of Gottfredson and Hirschi's general theory of crime is the conceptual clarity.

Answer: FALSE

19) Thornberry's interactional theory views delinquency as leading to the formation of delinquent values that disconnect social bonds.

Answer: TRUE

20) The social development model implies that intervention into juveniles lives will likely lead to increased delinquency.

Answer: FALSE

Short Answer Questions

1) Sutherland's __________ __________ theory suggests delinquency is a learned behavior.

Answer: differential association

2) According to differential association theory, __________ will vary in frequency, duration, priority, and intensity.

Answer: association

3) Glaser's __________ __________ theory is a modification of differential association theory.

Answer: differential identification

4) Matza's __________ __________ places more importance on juveniles to exercise choices than differential association theory.

Answer: drift theory

5) Drift theory contends delinquency becomes permissible when responsibility is __________.

Answer: neutralized

6) Walter C. Reckless developed __________ theory to explain both crime and delinquency.

Answer: containment

7) Hirschi theorized that the __________ __________ is made up of four main elements; attachment, commitment, involvement, and belief.

Answer: social bond

8) The most widely used integrated theory type is __________-__________-__________ integration.

Answer: end-to-end

9) Thornberry's __________ theory contends delinquency comes from a weakening of a person's bond to conventional society.

Answer: interactional

10) John Clausen found that competence and social influence at the end of adolescence gave shape to the evolving __________.

Answer: life course

11) David Matza's term for the attachment that a delinquent juvenile has to a deviant identity and value is called ____________________.

Answer: commitment to delinquency

12) In Travis Hirschi's theory of social control, the attachment that a juvenile has to conventional institutions and activities is called ____________________.

Answer: commitment to the social bond

13) Walter C. Reckless's theoretical perspective that strong inner containment and reinforcing external containment provide insulation against delinquent and criminal behavior is called ____________________.

Answer: containment theory

14) Any of several theoretical approaches that maintain human beings must be held in check, or somehow be controlled, if delinquent tendencies are to be repressed are called ____________________.

Answer: control theory

15) Edward H. Sutherland's view that delinquency is learned from others; and that delinquent behavior is t be expected of individuals who have internalized a preponderance of definitions that are favorable to law violations is called ____________________.

Answer: differential association theory

16) A modification of differential association theory offered by Daniel Glaser is called ____________________.

Answer: differential identification theory

17) David Matza's theoretical perspective that juveniles neutralize the moral hold of society and drift into delinquent behavior is called ____________________.

Answer: drift theory

18) Gresham M. Sykes and David Matza's theory examining how youngsters attempt to justify or rationalize their responsibility for delinquent acts is called ____________________.

Answer: neutralization theory

19) A perspective advocated by Travis Hirschi and others, who propose that delinquent acts result when a juvenile's bond to society is weak or broken is called ____________________.

Answer: social control theory

20) A perspective based on the integration of social control and cultural learning theories which proposes the development of attachments to parents will lead to attachments to school and a commitment to education as well as a belief in and commitment to conventional behavior and the law is called ____________________.

Answer: social development model

Essay Questions

1) List the 9 propositions of Differential Association.

2) According to Matza's drift theory, describe the process that a person would neutralize responsibility. Include the five techniques of neutralization.

3) Describe the process of Reckless's containment theory. Be sure to discuss the importance of pushes, pulls, and external and internal control.

4) Describe the process of becoming delinquent according to Gottfredson and Hirschi's General Theory of Crime.

5) Discuss social policy implications of social process theories. How could public policy be changed to prevent delinquency following the social process paradigms.

6) According to Hirschi, Containment Theory is made-up of 4 main elements. Explain each of these elements.

7) Explain the criminal career of Jeanson James Ancheta.

Chapter 6 Social Interactionist Theories of Delinquency

Multiple Choice Questions

1) What is the basic theoretical premise of labeling theory?
A) Criminals are inherently evil.
B) Society creates deviants.
C) The social structure of society is unequal.
D) Individuals will violate laws regardless of prohibitions.

Answer: B

2) Who is credited with developing an early form of labeling theory?
A) Tannenbaum
B) Marx
C) Sellins
D) Weber

Answer: A

3) What term did Lemert use to refer to society's response to deviant behavior?
A) status deviation
B) primary deviation
C) secondary deviation
D) informal deviation

Answer: C

4) What did Lemert purport would force a change in an individual's status or role?
A) deviation
B) rationalization
C) systematic rewards
D) social reactions

Answer: D

5) Becker argued that once a person is caught and labeled, they become
A) an outsider.
B) justified.
C) compliant.
D) structurally flawed.

Answer: A

170

6) Triplett and Jarjoura referred to reactions by official agents of the justice system to illegal behaviors as ________________.
A) informal labels.
B) formal labels.
C) subjective tags.

D) objective tags.

Answer: B

7) Sampson and Laub claim labeling on one factor leading to ________.
A) cumulative disadvantage.
B) formal labels.
C) subjective tags.
D) objective tags.

Answer: A

8) According to studies, who is more likely to be affected by the attachment of official labels of delinquency?
A) Hispanics
B) Asians
C) whites
D) African-Americans

Answer: C

9) Which of the following theoretical propositions uses reciprocal role taking as part of its theoretical construction?
A) conflict
B) social structural
C) symbolic interactionist
D) psychological

Answer: C

10) According to Bartollas, what ideology is Marx's conflict theory based on?
A) dialectical materialism
B) intertwined discord
C) criminal factions
D) functionalism

Answer: A

11) What did Quinney argue is a social control instrument of the state to serve the interest of the dominant capitalist ruling class?
A) government banks
B) civil courts
C) criminal laws
D) radical criminology

Answer: C

12) Which sociological perspective is Rolf Dahrendorf especially critical of?
A) functionalism
B) peacemaking
C) conflict
D) mediation

Answer: A

13) What variable did Marx suggest was the cause of crime?
A) poverty
B) culture
C) class struggles
D) racial bias

Answer: C

14) What term did Marx use to refer to working class persons?
A) egocentrics
B) proletariat
C) bourgeoisie
D) capitalist

Answer: B

15) The Marxist perspective suggests the ownership class is guilty of the worst crime: __________.
A) crimes of accommodation
B) brutal exploitation
C) crimes of resistance
D) crimes of spiritual malaise

Answer: B

16) Marxists contend poverty and demoralization caused by a capitalist system cause __________ crime.
A) elite
B) corporate
C) conventional
D) public order
Answer: C

17) What concepts did Weber add to Marx's theory to explain social stratification?
A) power and prestige
B) economy and restraint
C) disorganization and culture
D) status and wealth

Answer: A

18) What did Weber say was differentially related to social class?
A) work opportunities
B) life chances
C) urban blight
D) exploitation

Answer: B

19) Hagan suggested that a relationship between power and control would explain why __________.
A) boys commit less delinquency than girls.
B) mothers tend to be more dominant than fathers.
C) girls commit less delinquency than boys.
D) fathers tend to control boys more than girls.

Answer: C

20) What did Regoli and Hewitt suggest causes delinquency?
A) power
B) inadequate wealth
C) broken homes
D) oppression

Answer: D

21) What did Sellins suggest is NOT compatible between cultures that causes conflict and may lead to delinquency?
A) primary conflict
B) secondary conflict
C) dynamic equilibrium
D) conduct norms

Answer: D

22) According to Bartollas, what have Marxist criminologists concluded that leads to powerlessness and alienation among youth?
A) juveniles not having enough money to meet their needs
B) school authorities that unfairly discriminate against lower-class youths
C) lengthening of time before youths assume adult roles
D) lowering of self-concept issues related to deviant labeling

Answer: C

23) What term do Marxists criminologists use to refer to "children of the have-nots?"

A) bourgeoisie
B) marginal class
C) urban survivalists
D) incidental victims

Answer: B

24) What is the name of the upper-middle class delinquents in the social injustice study performed by William J. Chambliss?
A) Saints
B) Wild Ones
C) Roughnecks
D) Outsiders

Answer: A

25) What did Colvin and Pauly suggest that parents experience in the workplace that leads them to become repressive in dealing with children?
A) coerciveness
B) alienation

C) disorganization
D) violence

Answer: A

26) The vignette at the beginning of the chapter involved a crime committed against __________.
A) Tom Cruise
B) Taren Burris
C) President George Bush Sr.
D) President Bill Clinton
E) Michael Jordan

Answer: C

27) The ___________ assumes society creates deviance by negatively labeling those who are apprehended as different from others, and any subsequent interactions are influenced by the meaning and perception derived from the label.
A) conflict theory
B) economic theory
C) heredity theory
D) labeling perspective
E) feeble-mindedness theory

Answer: D

28) The central medium through which symbolic interaction occurs is ______________.
A) language
B) financial advantage
C) education
D) race
E) sex

Answer: A

29) What type of theorists view laws as tools created by the powerful for their own benefit?
A) symbolic interactionists
B) conflict
C) functionalists
D) social biologists
E) anthropologists

Answer: B

30) A prevailing idea, or "thesis", according to Hegel, would eventually be challenged by an opposing idea, or "antithesis". This is called _________.
A) positivism
B) sociobiology theories
C) dialectics
D) hypothesizing
E) the scientific method

Answer: C

True/False Questions

1) Tannenbaum examined the process whereby a juvenile came to the attention of authorities and was labeled as different from other juveniles.

Answer: TRUE

2) Tannenbaum proposed that the less evil is dramatized, the more likely youths are to become involved in deviant careers.

Answer: FALSE

3) Becker referred to delinquents that have been labeled as insiders.

Answer: FALSE

4)A criticism of labeling theory is that it implies that labeling always increases the likelihood of subsequent rule breaking.

Answer: TRUE

5) Triplett concluded that informal labels of significant others have no direct effect on delinquent behaviors for nonwhites.

Answer: TRUE

6) Labeling theory emphasizes the importance of rule making and power in the creation of deviance.

Answer: TRUE

7) The more sophisticated applications of labeling theory developed in 1990 and have become more unidimensional

Answer: FALSE

8) Symbolic interactionists define the unit of analysis as the transaction that takes place in interaction between two or more individuals.

Answer: TRUE

9) Charles Cooley referred to one's reflective self-appraisal as the "mirrored view."

Answer: FALSE

10) Conflict theorists focus on the importance of socioeconomic class, power and authority, and group and cultural conflicts.

Answer: TRUE

11) Marx wrote extensively on crime, which led to the formation of conflict theory.

Answer: FALSE

12) Marx said that murderous theft was the worst crime the ownership class is guilty of.

Answer: FALSE

13) Marxists view the state and the law as the ultimate tools of the ownership class.

Answer: TRUE

14) Weber did not believe that a unidimensional approach could explain social stratification.

Answer: TRUE

15) Turk theorized that social order of society is based on relationships of right and wrong between authorities and subjects.

Answer: FALSE

16) Hagan contends that the relationship between gender and non-serious delinquency is liked to power and control.

Answer: TRUE

17) Sellins stated that the more complex a culture becomes, the more likely it is that the number of normative groups will fail to agree.

Answer: TRUE

18) Vold contends that the outcome of group conflict results in a winner and loser, unless a compromise is reached.

Answer: TRUE

19) Marxist criminologists suggest that it is in the best interest of the working class to define certain acts as delinquent.

Answer: FALSE

20) Marxist criminologists contend the juvenile justice system is racist because minority youths are more likely than whites to be adjudicated and sent to training schools.

Answer: TRUE

Short Answer Questions

1) Tannenbaum referred to the process of labeling as the __________ __________ __________.

Answer: dramatization of evil

2) According to Lemert, __________ __________ consists of the individual's behavior.

Answer: primary deviation

3) The development of the conflict model is indebted to the concept of "__________."

Answer: dialectics

4) Marx contended that __________ is splitting up society into two great classes.

Answer: capitalism

5) Hagan's __________-__________ __________ contends sons are socialized to take risks, but daughters are taught to avoid risks.

Answer: power-control thesis

6) Regoli and Hewitt's theory of __________ __________ is based on the assumption that authority is unjustly used against children.

Answer: differential oppression

7) Sellins argued that to understand the cause of crime, it is necessary to understand the concepts of __________ __________.

Answer: conduct norms

8) The Schwendinger's __________ __________ states that the most important variable in identifying delinquency potential for teenagers is their relative status position among other adolescents.

Answer: instrumental theory

9) William Chambliss analyzed the issue of social injustice in his study titled "__________ __________ __________ __________ __________."

Answer: The Saints and the Roughnecks

10) Colvin and Pauly contend that the power relations subjected to most lower-class workers are __________.

Answer: coercive

11) An economic system in which private individuals or corporations own and control capital (wealth and means of production) and in which competitive free markets control prices, production, and the distribution of goods is called __________________.

Answer: capitalism

12) The rules of a group governing the way its members should act under particular conditions and the violation of these rules that arouses a group reaction is called __________________.

Answer: conduct norms

13) A perspective which holds that delinquency can be explained by socioeconomic class, by power and authority relationships, and by group and cultural differences is called __________________.

Answer: conflict theory

14) Social scientific thinkers who combine Marxist theory with the insights of later theorists, such as Sigmund Freud are called __________________.

Answer: critical criminologists

15) A perspective proposed by Thorsten Sellin and others which includes the idea that delinquency or crime arises because individuals are members of a subculture who have conduct norms which are in conflict with those of the wider society is called __________________.

Answer: culture conflict theory

16) A group whose members view the entire apparatus of crime control as a tool or instrument of the ruling class is called __________________.

Answer: instrumentalist Marxists

17) A perspective developed by Herman Schwendinger and Julia Siegel Schwendinger, which holds that the most important t variable predicting delinquency in teenagers is their status position relative to that of their peers is called __________________.

Answer: instrumental theory

18) The view that society creates the delinquent by labeling those who are apprehended as "different" from other youth, when in reality they are different primarily because they have been "tagged" with a deviant label is called __________________.

Answer: labeling theory

19) The view of John Hagan and his associates that the relationship between gender and delinquency is linked to issues of power and control is called ____________________.

Answer: power-control thesis

20) According to labeling theory, the initial act of deviance that causes a person to be labeled a deviant is called ________ ________.

Answer: primary deviation

Essay Questions

1) Discuss the process of labeling theory as it relates to delinquency. Be sure to include the sequence stages of interaction as defined by Lemert.

2) Identify the various criticisms of labeling theory, and why it experienced resurgence in the 1980s and 1990s.

3) Explain symbolic interactionist theory and include Matsueda's four features of the self and delinquent behavior.

4) Discuss Regoli and Hewitt's theory of differential oppression and how it relates to child abuse.

5) Explain the concept of primary and secondary deviation.

6) Explain the concept of labeling theory and "The Dramatization of Evil".

7) What are the strengths of labeling theory?

8) The theory of differential oppression is organized around 4 principles. What are those 4 principles?

9) Explain the term "dramatization of evil". What does it mean and how does it create delinquency?

10) Describe what evidence Marxist criminologists use to explain economic exploitation, alienation, and powerlessness among youth.

Chapter 7 Gender and Delinquency

Multiple Choice Questions

1) Meda Chesney-Lind claims that the study of delinquency is _________.
A) concentrated strongly in female delinquency.
B) gender biased.
C) racially biased toward nonminorities.
D) centered in violent crimes.

Answer: B

2) According to Funk, the majority of female offenders are more likely to be affected by __________ than male offenders.
A) psychological problems
B) police interaction
C) social relationships
D) academic failure

Answer: C

3) According to a 1998 multidimensional study, most female youthful offenders are between the ages of ________________.
A) 16-18 years.
B) 14-16 years.
C) 12-14 years.
D) 12 and under.

Answer: B

4) According to a 1998 multidimensional study, which ages are female victims most likely to be beaten, raped, stabbed, or shot?
A) 16-17 years
B) 15-16 years
C) 14-15 years
D) 13-14 years

Answer: D

5) According to the NCCD study, females represent one of the _________.
A) least serviced juvenile justice populations.
B) most violent juvenile offenders.
C) most studied areas of delinquency.
D) least preventative victims in juvenile populations.

Answer: A

6) What did Lombroso suggest about female offenders?
A) They haves more mental capacities than men.
B) They are higher on the evolutionary scale.

C) They feel pain more than men.
D) They lack moral refinement.

Answer: D

7) What did Cowie's study suggest leads females into sexual promiscuity?
A) physical overdevelopment
B) menstruation
C) influence of television and movies
D) society's obsession with sex

Answer: A

8) W. I. Thomas assumed that problems with female delinquency are not criminal, but __________.
A) authority linked.
B) immoral.
C) educational.
D) fantasies.

Answer: B

9) What did Freud say makes women anatomically inferior to men?
A) small muscle mass
B) menstruation
C) sex organs
D) small frames

Answer: C

10) What is a common factor shared by biological and psychological theories in explaining female ___________. delinquency?
A) evolution
B) male victims
C) sexism
D) minority focus

Answer: C

11) Which of the following factors is more predictive of delinquency?
A) blocked opportunity
B) hormonal imbalances
C) strain theory
D) feminism

Answer: A

12) Studies have suggested that limited opportunities appears to be more reliable for predicting delinquency among ___________.
A) minority males.
B) minority females.

C) white males and females.
D) both white and minority males.

Answer: C

13) According to Freda Adler, what type of offenses are today's female offenders most likely to commit?
A) incorrigibility
B) running away
C) promiscuity
D) violent acts

Answer: D

14) Hirschi contends that females are less delinquent then males due to _____________.
A) the women's liberation movement.
B) harsh punishment.
C) greater social bonds.
D) physical weakness.

Answer: C

15) Cullen suggests that female delinquency increases as females become ___________.
A) more male-like.
B) independent.
C) sexual.
D) more complex.

Answer: A

16) Studies in peer group influence suggest that females are more likely to commit delinquent acts when in the company of __________.
A) siblings.
B) same-sex groups.
C) male groups.
D) mixed-sex groups.

Answer: D

17) Hagan suggested female delinquency increases as females are freed from ____________.
A) patriarchal relations.
B) school authority.
C) matriarchal families.
D) social bonds.

Answer: A

18) What does liberal feminism contend would eliminate discriminatory practices?
A) eliminate choice
B) systematic opportunity
C) androgynize gender roles

D) public awareness

Answer: C

19) What does phenomenological feminism argue may not exist for adolescent females?
A) harsh punishments
B) chivalrous treatment
C) balanced inequality
D) formal adjudications

Answer: B

20) What type of crime has been the main focus of radical feminists?
A) property crimes
B) simple assaults
C) petty thefts
D) sexual violence

Answer: D

21) Studies in gender relations and delinquency suggest that younger females receive discriminatory treatment because of society's disapproval of _____________.
A) racial minorities.
B) unwed mothers.
C) sexual activity.
D) chivalrous acts.

Answer: C

22) Which Constitutional Amendment does C. Sarri suggest is being violated when juvenile authorities confine females offenders for longer periods of time than males?
A) First
B) Fifth
C) Eighth
D) Fourteenth

Answer: D

23) According to Bartollas, what may have helped reduce some discriminatory treatment of female offenders?
A) Civil Rights Bill of 1964
B) Omnibus Crime Bill of 1968
C) Juvenile Justice and Delinquency Prevention Act of 1974
D) Family Leave Act of 1993

Answer: C

24) What often goes hand-in-hand with racism that forces minority females to engage in problems of abuse, drugs, and violence?
A) discrimination
B) poverty

C) low self-esteem
D) chivalry

Answer: B

25) Diane Lewis noted that black women tend to see racism as a more powerful cause of their subordinate position and they view feminism ________.
A) with mistrust.
B) as their salvation.
C) high regard.
D) as instrumental in their cause.

Answer: A

26) In the vignette at the beginning of this chapter, Noemi was arrested for "armed" robbery using a ___________.
A) gun
B) knife
C) screwdriver
D) baseball bat
E) night stick

Answer: C

27) The ___________ proposes that the gender gap in crime decreases and females account for a greater proportion of crime when women's economic well-being declines.
A) feminists theory
B) economic marginalization thesis
C) the buck stops here thesis
D) economic disparity thesis

Answer: B

28) Anabolic means all but one of the following.
A) motionless
B) lethargic
C) aggressive
D) conservative

Answer: C

29) According to W.I. Thomas, the major cause of prostitution rest in the girls need for _______.
A) sex
B) money
C) attention
D) love
E) power

Answer: D

30) The social learning process in which persons are taught behaviors appropriate only for their sex is called ____________.
A) sex-role socialization
B) stereotyping
C) sex norm socialization
D) training of sex

Answer: A

True/False Questions

1) Some feminist theorists suggest that feminist research should be presented in textbooks as a seamless whole, rather than a separate chapter.

Answer: TRUE

2) Girls tend to dislike themselves more than boys because of the negative body image girls often hold.

Answer: TRUE

3) According to Marty Beyer, boys are more focused on relationships than girls.

Answer: FALSE

4) Jody Miller and Scott Decker suggest that patterns of male dominance are increasingly apparent during adolescence.

Answer: TRUE

5) Inappropriate touching, pushing and hitting by staff, and deprivation of clean clothing are typical of abuses experienced by females placed in detention.

Answer: TRUE

6) Optimum environments for at-risk females would be intensive individual counseling programs tailored to needs of adolescent females.

Answer: FALSE

7) Lombroso contended that female criminals inherent male characteristics such as excess body hair, moles, wrinkles, crow's feet, and abnormal craniums.

Answer: TRUE

8) According to W. I. Thomas, the major cause of prostitution rested in the girl's need for money and the need to build her self-esteem.

Answer: FALSE

9) Freud believed that women had babies to replace the lost penis.

Answer: TRUE

10) Pollack suggested women act as instigators of criminal activity because they are inherently deceitful.

Answer: TRUE

11) Susan Datesman found that social control was more strongly related to female delinquency than it was to male delinquents.

Answer: FALSE

12) Strain theory has been applied almost solely to female delinquency, therefore it may be more strongly related to female involvement in delinquency than male involvement.

Answer: FALSE

13) Adler contended that the rise in official rates of female crime reflects the changes brought about by the liberation of women.

Answer: TRUE

14) Hirschi purported that adolescent females are more dependent on others, which reduces their opportunity to engage in delinquent behaviors.

Answer: TRUE

15) Austin Turk argued that females are more likely to abide by legal norms than males, because their patterns of activity are more restricted than those of males.

Answer: TRUE

16) The majority of female delinquent acts occur in same-sex groups.

Answer: FALSE

17) Parents are more likely to falsely accuse males than females for delinquent acts.

Answer: FALSE

18) Gender is one of the strongest correlates of delinquent behavior, while biological explanations are the least predictable.

Answer: TRUE

19) Liberal feminism suggests that discrimination is systematic in nature.

Answer: FALSE

20) Socialist feminism contends that low female crime rates are related to women's powerless position in the United States.

Answer: TRUE

Short Answer Questions

1) According to the NCCD study, most adolescent girls first enter the juvenile system as __________.

Answer: runaways

2) Lombroso characterized women as __________ and conservative within their approach to life.

Answer: passive

3)W. I. Thomas referred to female release of energy as __________, meaning motionless, lethargic, and conservative.

Answer: anabolic

4) Freud said the female drive to accomplishment is the expression of her longing for a __________.

Answer: penis

5) Pollak states that the __________ __________ is further advanced as a root cause of hidden crime; that is, the police and the court forgive a girl for the same act they would convict a boy.

Answer: chivalry factor

6) Freda Adler traced the increase in female crime figures to the __________ __________ __________.

Answer: women's liberation movement

7) According to Hirschi, __________-__________ __________ results in greater belief in the legitimacy of social rules by girls than by boys.

Answer: sex-role socialization

8)A __________ __________ purposes that females become more male -like to become delinquent.

Answer: masculinity hypothesis

9) __________ feminist theory pays more attention to the regulator than the regulated.

Answer: Phenomenological

10) The ________ ________ ________ ________ is an expression of radical feminism that contends girl's victimization and the relationship between that experience and girl's crime have been systematically ignored.

Answer: feminist theory of delinquency

11) The idea that the justice system treated adolescent females and women more leniently because of their gender is called the __________________.

Answer: chivalry factor

12) An argument made by Meda Chesney-Lind and others that adolescent females' victimization at home causes them to become delinquent is called the __________________.

Answer: feminist theory of delinquency

13) The personal traits, social positions, and values and beliefs that members of a society attach to being male or female are called __________________.

Answer: gender

14) Societal definitions of what constitutes masculine and feminine behavior is known as __________________.

Answer: gender roles

15) The idea that as girls become more boy-like and acquire more "masculine" traits they become more delinquent is called the __________________.

Answer: masculinity hypothesis

16) The impact of the values and behaviors of fellow age-group members on teenagers' involvement in delinquency is called __________________.

Answer: peer group influence

17) The process by which boys and girls internalize their culture's norms, sanctions, and expectations for members of their gender is called __________________.

Answer: sex-role socialization

Essay Questions

1) Discuss the recent profile of a female delinquent and describe how it may or may not have changed over the last ten to twenty years.

2) Discuss the early feminist perspectives on female delinquency and evaluate their usefulness in explaining delinquency.

3) Describe the four feminist theories and discuss how they can be applied to understanding female criminality.

4) Discuss the feminist theory on delinquency as advocated by Meda Chesney-Lind.

5) Discuss how gender bias affects the processing of female juvenile offenders.

6) Explain the key features that distinguish feminist theories from other perspectives.

7) What are the four wishes or ambitions that W.I. Thomas suggested girls were driven by.

8) Konopka identified four key factors contributing to female delinquency. What are those four factors?

Chapter 8 The Family and Delinquency

Multiple Choice Questions

1) What percentage of African-American children will likely experience divorce or family separation by their sixteenth birthday?
A) 85 percent
B) 75 percent
C) 65 percent
D) 35 percent

Answer: B

2) According to the Rochester, Denver, and Pittsburgh studies, what reveals a consistent relationship with families in transition?
A) physical abuse
B) drug use
C) violent crime
D) property crime

Answer: B

3) What percentage of American female-headed households live in poverty?
A) 86 percent
B) 66 percent
C) 40 percent
D) 26 percent

Answer: C

4) Which of the following experienced the highest unemployment rates between 1994 and 2004?
A) young African-American women
B) young white women
C) young African-American men
D) young white men

Answer: C

5) Domestic violence is estimated to affect what portion of the married population?
A) one-fifth
B) two-fifths
C) one-third
D) two-thirds

Answer: C

6) According to studies, which child is more likely to become delinquent?
A) first born
B) middle born
C) last born

D) All are of equal chance.

Answer: B

7) According to studies, children who are rejected by their parents are more likely to exhibit what kind of behaviors?
A) regressive
B) submissive
C) aggressive
D) oppressive

Answer: C

8) Hirschi found that the rate of delinquency increased with the incidence of mothers ________________.
A) hitting their children.
B) arguing with fathers.
C) inconsistent discipline.
D) employed outside the home.

Answer: D

9) Widom's study on child abuse and neglect revealed that being abused or neglected increased the likelihood of __________.
A) juvenile arrest and violent crime.
B) school related problems.
C) psychological depression.
D) parental separation and divorce.

Answer: A

10) What created a need for society to focus on child abuse and neglect in the 1960s?
A) rousing speech by John F. Kennedy
B) state and federal legislation
C) several high profile child abuse cases
D) public education

Answer: B

11) A 1994 report by the NCCA revealed that children harmed by maltreatment mostly were victims of what type of abuse?
A) physical
B) emotional
C) neglect
D) sexual

Answer: C

12) Replication of the Application Study by Polansky and colleagues suggested that a high degree of infantilism was the strongest predictor of ________________.
A) maternal neglect.
B) sexual abuse.

C) child violence.
D) marital failure.

Answer: A

13) According to Straus's study on corporal punishment, who hits children the most?
A) fathers
B) mothers
C) older siblings
D) grandparents

Answer: B

14) Which of the following is NOT considered a myth of corporal punishment by spanking?
A) Spanking is harmless to the child.
B) Spanking is necessary.
C) Spanking works.
D) Spanking legitimizes violence in children.

Answer: D

15) What type of population areas is child abuse more prevalent in?
A) suburbs
B) rural settings
C) urban
D) suburban fringes

Answer: C

16) What did Gordon's study of incest reveal about father-daughter incest relationships?
A) Most daughter victims ran away.
B) Fathers were mentally ill.
C) Daughter victims were made into second wives.
D) Daughters would abuse their sons later in life.

Answer: C

17) How long does the average incestuous relationship last between father and daughter?
A) three to four years
B) two to three years
C) less than one year
D) most of the child's life at home

Answer: A

18) Which of the following types of incest relations is the least common?
A) father-daughter
B) stepfather-stepdaughter
C) brother-sister
D) mother-son

Answer: D

19) According to the Justice's study, what type of personalities make up 70 to 80 percent of incestuous fathers?
A) symbiotic
B) psychopathic
C) pedophilic
D) psychotic

Answer: A

20) According to the Justice's study, what type of personality commits the least amount of incestuous relations?
A) symbiotic
B) psychopathic
C) pedophilic
D) psychotic

Answer: D

21) What is NOT considered a typical consequence of emotional child abuse and neglect?
A) sleep disturbances
B) low internal conflict
C) low self-esteem
D) high anxiety

Answer: B

22) According to the Kempe's study, children who are labeled and assigned to special learning classes in public school are often ______.
A) set up for failure.
B) more intelligent than originally believed.
C) performing better in a short time.
D) aggressive.

Answer: A

23) Studies on sexually abused victims suggest that prostitution is a way for victims to ___________.
A) reduce the shame.
B) take control of others by making them pay.
C) increase their livelihood.
D) leave the home environment.

Answer: B

24) There is considerable support to show that female victims of violence react differently than males by expressing anger through
A) violent crime.
B) aggressive crime.
C) self-destructive behavior.
D) minor crime.

Answer: C

25) A fact-finding hearing of a child welfare case by juvenile authorities is referred to as _________.
A) investigation.
B) adjudication.
C) probative discovery.
D) disposition.

Answer: B

26) In the vignette, at the beginning of the chapter, the authorities were considering charging an eleven year old girl with the crime of ______________.
A) murder
B) rape
C) selling heroin
D) shop lifting
E) prostitution

Answer: c

27. Between 1980 and 1994, the rate of childbearing by unmarried women rose sharply for women of all ages.
A) rose sharply
B) declined sharply
C) rose for older women but declined for younger women
D) remained about the same

Answer: A

28. Gangsta Rap was pioneered by ______________.
A) The Four Tops
B) Michael Jackson
C) Janet Jackson
D) Ice Tea
E) Will Smith

Answer: D

29. A form of Hip Hop music that some believe negatively influences young people by devaluing human life, the family, religious institutions, schools, and the justice system is called ________.
a. Gangsta Rap
b. Rock and Roll
c. Hard Rock
d. Alterative Rock
e. all of the above

Answer: A

30. Which of the following groups have the highest rate of maltreatment of children?
a. African Americans
b. whites
c. Hispanic

d. Asian
e. American Indian

Answer: A

True/False Questions

1) The number of children who live with both parents has increased in America since 1980.

Answer: FALSE

2) Forty percent of the children living in female-headed households experience poverty compared to nine percent of children who live with both parents.

Answer: TRUE

3) The sons of adolescent mothers are more likely to be incarcerated than sons of older mothers.

Answer: TRUE

4) Family break-ups due to parental death has the strongest impact on delinquency.

Answer: FALSE

5) Generally, the smaller the family size, the less likely delinquency will occur.

Answer: TRUE

6) There is virtually no evidence to support that delinquency is more likely in families where children are being raised with criminal parents or siblings.

Answer: FALSE

7) Happiness in marriage is NOT considered a crucial element in family and delinquency.

Answer: FALSE

8) Consistency in discipline within the family is important in deterring delinquent behavior.

Answer: TRUE

9) The rate of delinquency appears to increase with the number of unfavorable factors in the home.

Answer: TRUE

10)In 2002, nearly 900,000 children were determined to be victims of abuse or neglect.

Answer: FALSE

11) According to the Straus study, fathers hit children more than mothers do.

Answer: FALSE

12) Straus suggests that most spanking is a legitimate form of parental punishment.

Answer: FALSE

13) According to the NCCA, the older a child becomes, the more likely they will experience physical abuse.

Answer: TRUE

14) In most abusive situations, both parents are actively involved in aggression in some form or another.

Answer: FALSE

15) Stepfathers are more likely than natural fathers to abuse female children.

Answer: FALSE

16) Father-son incest is rarely reported because it violates both moral codes of incest and homosexuality prohibitions.

Answer: TRUE

17) Abused children are more likely to be involved with status offenses than non-abused children.

Answer: TRUE

18) Placing children in foster homes may not stop their running away behaviors.

Answer: TRUE

19) Drug and alcohol abuse is actually quite rare for abused children.

Answer: FALSE

20) Children that have been abused are likely to abuse their own children later in life.

Answer: TRUE

Short Answer Questions

1) __________, regardless of a child's age, exposes him or her to settings in which there is a high prevalence of substance abuse, promiscuous sex, prostitution, and crime.

Answer: Homelessness

2) The term __________ __________ refers to intentional behavior directed toward a child by the parents or caretaker to cause pain, injury, or death.

Answer: physical abuse

3) __________ __________ is more difficult to define than physical abuse because it involves a disregard for the psychological needs of a child.

Answer: Emotional abuse

4) The term __________ __________ refers to any sexual activity for arousal between nonmarried members of a family.

Answer: sexual abuse

5) __________ personalities make up the largest percentage of incestuous fathers.

Answer: Symbiotic

6) According to the Justices's study, __________ personalities seek stimulation and excitement through incestuous relationships.

Answer: psychopathic

7) __________ __________ becomes a way children cope with the pain of neglect, physical abuse, and sexual abuse, and try to rid themselves of the abusive family.

Answer: Running away

8) The term __________ __________ __________ usually refers to services that are provided by an agency authorized to act on behalf of a child when parents no longer can do so.

Answer: child protective services

9) An __________, or fact-finding hearing, is held if a petition of abuse has been filed by the department of social services.

Answer: adjudication

10) The concept of ___________ ___________ ___________ ___________ refers to a strong presumption of parental autonomy in child rearing.

Answer: supremacy of parental rights

11) A notion that middle children are more prone to delinquency than the first or last-born is because of their _______________.

Answer: birth order

12) An early view, which holds that homes broken by divorce, separation, and death are more likely to produce delinquency than intact homes is called _______________.

Answer: broken homes

13) Suggested to be the most frequently occurring type of incest, and believed to be less damaging than father-daughter incest is _______________.

Answer: brother-sister incest

14) _______________ encompasses many dimensions with the general focus being variations of physical, sexual, emotional, and verbal abuse typically perpetrated by adults against children.

Answer: child abuse

15) The notion that having delinquent sisters and brothers will increase the propensity of delinquency within the home by influencing the other sibling(s) is the idea of _______________.

Answer: delinquent siblings

16) Any action that reduces the self-esteem and psychological well-being of a child normally inflicted by parents and adults, and directed toward children is _______________.

Answer: emotional abuse

17) The number of children in a family sometimes called _______________, is a possible risk factor for delinquency.

Answer: family size

18) The most devastating form of incest in which the father frequently views the daughter as a second wife is called _______________.

Answer: father-daughter incest

19) Sexual activity between father and son is called _______________.

Answer: father-son incest

20) Sexual activity that occurs between mother and son is called __________.

Answer: mother-son incest

Essay Questions

1) Discuss how families are typically affected by divorce, and explain how divorce may affect delinquent behavior in children.

2) Identify and discuss the variety of family factors that may influence delinquency.

3) Identify the various types and forms of child neglect, and discuss how they may influence delinquent behaviors in children.

4) Discuss the relationship of child abuse and neglect to status offenses.

5) Identify and describe the various stages of processing child abuse and neglect complaints by social service departments. What determines if a prosecution may or may not occur.

6) The Child Maltreatment 2004 survey identified several factor that influenced the determination that a child would officially be found to a victim of maltreatment. What are those factors?

7) Norman A. Polansky and colleagues' studies of neglect in Georgia and North Carolina identified five types of mothers who are frequently guilty of child neglect. Explain each of those five types of mothers.

8) Some theorists argue that child abuse has five basic explanations: What are those five basic explanations?

9) David G. Gill, in developing a classification of abusive families, found that seven situations accounted for 97.3 percent of the reported abuse cases. What are those seven classifications?

10) Justice and Justice have developed a classification that is helpful in understanding the behavior of fathers who commit incest. They divide incestuous fathers into four groups. Explain each of those four groups.

Chapter 9 The School and Delinquency

Multiple Choice Questions

1) What educational concept was more widely accepted by private schools, rather than public schools during the 1960s?
A) dress codes
B) athletic programs
C) open-classrooms
D) computer instruction

Answer: C

2) What primarily explains the difference between vandalism rates in large and small schools?
A) police
B) community context
C) time of year
D) education programs

Answer: B

3) Haney and Zimbardo characterized public high schools as being similar to ___________________.
A) prisons.
B) boot camps.
C) zoos.
D) dictatorships.

Answer: A

4) What did a Boston high school require students to do until it was ruled unconstitutional?
A) submit to strip searches
B) pray in school
C) submit to a drug test
D) participate in athletic activities

Answer: C

5) According to Bartollas, what was different about violence in public schools during the 1980s that created a new dimension of school violence?
A) Murders were directed against students.
B) Property damage of schools increased.
C) Acts were directed against teachers.
D) Acts were committed in the presence of police.

Answer: C

6) What did the National School Safety Center indicate about school violence in 1992?
A) Crime actually decreased in schools.

B) Violent crimes had risen markedly since 1987.
C) Violent crimes went down while property crimes escalated.
D) Acts of vandalism makes students feel unsafe.

Answer: B

7) A 1993 study by the Center for Disease Control and Prevention found that ________________.
A) twenty-two percent of students carry weapons for protection.
B) most students are not fearful of crime.
C) the incidence of blood related diseases is related to crime.
D) drug abuse declined from 1990 to 1993.

Answer: A

8) What did a 1995-1996 survey of Los Angeles schools reveal that 49 percent of students had seen at school?
A) sexual crimes
B) murders
C) weapons
D) thefts

Answer: C

9) The 1967 report by the task force on juvenile delinquency concluded that boys who fail in school were __________ times more likely to become delinquent than those who did not fail in school.

A) twenty four
B) fifteen
C) ten
D) seven

Answer: D

10) What does Sampson and Laub suggest high school can be for individuals?
A) a prison
B) a turning point
C) a social happy hour
D) a depressive episode

Answer: B

11) What did Albert Cohen believe encourages school delinquency?
A) status deprivation
B) inadequate parents
C) harsh rules
D) incompetent teachers

Answer: A

12) According to Joy Dryfoos, what can be predicted from student's having poor grades and having to repeat grades?

A) risk-assessment
B) dropping out
C) vandalism
D) low self-esteem

Answer: B

13) What did Elliot and Voss suggest would decrease after students drop out of school?
A) employment
B) drug and alcohol abuse
C) sexually promiscuous behaviors
D) police contact and delinquency

Answer: D

14) According to cultural deviance theory, what may affect the factor of school influencing delinquency?
A) schools located in high-crime areas
B) small rural schools
C) impartial instruction
D) imbalanced selection of courses

Answer: A

15) What does Marxist theory contend that school experiences trains lower-class students to accept in society?
A) crime
B) menial roles
C) rebellion
D) fantasy

Answer: B

16) Which of the following terms is associated with the legal rationale for public schools?
A) tempus fugit
B) parens patriae
C) loco parentis
D) e pluribus unum

Answer: C

17) Which of the following cases held that students are entitled to receive notice and some opportunity for a hearing before being expelled for misconduct?
A) Baker v. Owen
B) Tinker v. Des Moines
C) Yoo v. Moynihan
D) Dixon v. Alabama State Board of Education

Answer: D

18) Which of the following cases held that students had freedom of expression by allowing the wearing of black armbands?
A) Baker v. Owen
B) Tinker v. Des Moines
C) Yoo v. Moynihan
D) Dixon v. Alabama State Board of Education

Answer: B

19) What did the West Virginia State Board of Education v. Barnette hold that students could NOT be compelled to do?
A) salute the flag
B) attend school
C) pray
D) wear uniforms
Answer: A

20) What did the New Jersey v. TLO case allow police to do at schools?
A) arrest students while in class
B) interrogate students only in the company of their parents
C) search student lockers
D) perform drug tests

Answer: C

21) What is different about police programs in schools today, compared to traditional types of programming, such as Drug Abuse and Resistance Education (DARE)?
A) Police are ineffective due to time constraints.
B) States are becoming reluctant to let police teach educational curriculum.
C) Programs over-emphasize educational measures.
D) Programs are structured for student control and crime prevention.

Answer: D

22) What does Bartollas suggest that education must be more directed to in order to improve the quality of education?
A) individuals
B) groups
C) computer assisted instruction
D) more classroom involvement

Answer: A

23) What does Bartollas suggest is the first line of defense against misbehavior?
A) early police intervention
B) more authoritative administrators
C) quality teaching
D) increased school activities

Answer: C

24) What does Bartollas contend that schools should adopt so students can become oriented to the world of work?
A) more vocational courses
B) more flexible hours and schedules
C) less academic courses
D) global diversity

Answer: B

25) According to Bartollas, what is the ultimate long-range goal of alternative schools?
A) create turnovers
B) return students to the public school setting
C) teach a different curriculum to control disruption
D) to socialize lower-class students into menial occupations

Answer: B

26) In the vignette at the beginning of the chapter, 16 year old Jess Weise killed his _________.
A) teacher
B) mother
C) grandfather
D) girlfriend
E) neighbor

Answer: C

27) Eric Harris and Dylan Klebold are best know for _______________.
A) the shooting at Columbine High School
B) the shootings at Red Lake Indian Reservation
C) the shootings at Santana High School
D) the shootings at Westside Middle School, Jonesboro, Arkansas
E) Wheeling High School. Wheeling, WV

Answer: A

28) A student chances of being a homicide victim at school is __________.
A) 1 in a 100
B) 1 in a 1,000
C) 1 in a 10,000
D) 1 in a 100,000
E) 1 in a 1,000,000

Answer: E

29) Annually, from 1999 through 2003, ___________ were more likely to be attacked than other teachers.
A) elementary teachers
B) middle school teachers
C) senior high school teachers
D) community college teachers
E) college professors

Answer: C

30. According to a 2001 report on high school graduation conducted b the Education Policy Center of the Urban Institute, the national graduation rate was ___________.
A) 93%
B) 88%
C) 83%
D) 78%
E) 68%

Answer: E

True/False Questions

1) Public education arose largely from the growing need to socialize immigrant groups coming to America.

Answer: TRUE

2) The Vietnam war in the 1960s and early 1970s reduced enrollments in pubic schools.

Answer: FALSE

3) The repressive methods of education make school one of the most difficult experiences for adolescent children.

Answer: TRUE

4) Presence of police and added security features make schools appear more like prisons.

Answer: TRUE

5) A 1988 study on school violence by the National Adolescent Student Health Survey suggested that violence in schools had gone down in the 1980s.

Answer: FALSE

6) A 1993 survey by the Centers for Disease Control and Prevention contended that fear among students was unfounded.

Answer: FALSE

7) According to the 2002 Annual Report on School Safety, students 12-18 years old are more likely to become serious crime victims away from school, than at school.

Answer: TRUE

8) According to the 2002 Annual Report on School Safety, students carrying weapons and physical fighting have been increasing in recent years.

Answer: FALSE

9) Lack of achievement, low social status, and high dropout rates are most frequently cited as to why delinquents fail in school.

Answer: TRUE

10) There is little evidence to correlate poor academic performance with delinquency among both males and females.

Answer: FALSE

11) Studies have suggested that most delinquents want to succeed in school.

Answer: TRUE

12) School dropouts have fewer job prospects, make lower salaries, and experience more unstable marriages later in life.

Answer: TRUE

13) According to strain theory, youths turn to delinquency to compensate for feelings of status frustration, failure, and low self-esteem.

Answer: TRUE

14) According to labeling theory, students labeled as slow-learners normally stay on the slow track in school for 2 to 3 years.

Answer: FALSE

15) In the 1986, Bethel School District No. 403 v.Fraser case, the Court held that lewd and offensive speech undermined the basic educational mission of the school.

Answer: TRUE

16) The Court has held that schools can enforce policies prohibiting the wearing of slacks, dungarees, or hair falling loosely about the shoulders.

Answer: FALSE

17) Principals have become reluctant to suspend students for wearing outlandish clothing, loitering in the halls, and creating classroom disturbances, which only a few decades earlier would have drawn a quick suspension notice.

Answer: TRUE

18) Bartollas suggests that to improve the quality of education, students should be compared with other classmates to measure their performance.

Answer: FALSE

19) According to Bartollas, tracking systems, which classify students according to their abilities, has wide acceptance and should be maintained.

Answer: FALSE

20) Schools that open-up their facilities to community events and activities are more likely to achieve better school-community relations.

Answer: TRUE

Short Answer Questions

1) __________ __________ advocated reform in classroom methods and curriculum during the progressive period.

Answer: John Dewey

2) The pervasiveness of __________ and __________ in public schools came to public attention in the early to mid 1970s.

Answer: vandalism/violence

3) Numerous researchers have pointed out that delinquents' lack of __________ in school is related to other factors beside academic skills.

Answer: achievement

4) Social control theorists argue that delinquency varies according to the strength of a __________ __________ to the social order.

Answer: juvenile's bond

5) __________ theorists argue that once students are defined as deviant, they adopt a deviant role in response to their lowered status.

Answer: Labeling

6) Marxist theorists view the school as means by which the privileged classes maintain their power over the __________ __________.

Answer: lower classes

7)In the Richards v. Thurston case, the Court ruled that a student's right to wear __________ __________ derived from his interest in personal liberty.

Answer: long hair

8) The changing nature of the partnership between law enforcement agencies and the school is evident by the indicator of the shift of __________ used by schools.

Answer: language

9) The impetus for __________ in Texas grew out of the rise of disruptive behavior on school campuses.

Answer: STAR

10) According to Stanley Cohen, the legendary vision of the __________ __________ has dominated social control policy in schools.

Answer: blackboard jungle

11) Academic achievement in schoolwork as rated by grades and other assessment measures is known as __________________.

Answer: academic performance

12) A facility that provides an alternative educational experience, usually in a different location, for youths who are not doing satisfactory work in the public school setting is know as a/an __________________.

Answer: alternative school

13) Hurtful, frightening, or menacing actions undertaken by one person to intimidate another (generally weaker) person, to gain that person's unwilling compliance, and /or to put him in fear is known as __________________.

Answer: bullying

14) Unacceptable conduct at school; which may include defiance of authority, manipulation of teachers, inability or refusal to follow rules, fights with peers, destruction of property, use of drug, and physical or verbal altercations with teachers is known as __________________.

Answer: disruptive behavior

15) A young person of school age who of his or her own volition no longer attends school is known as a __________________.

Answer: dropout

16) Constitutional rights that are guaranteed to citizens, whether adult or juvenile, during their contacts with the police and during court proceedings are known as __________________.

Answer: due process rights

17) The principle according to which a guardian or an agency is given the rights, duties, and responsibilities of a parent in relation to a particular child or children is know as ________________.

Answer: In loco parentis

18) The process of searching students and their lockers to determine whether drugs, weapons or other contraband are present is know as a ______________.

Answer: school search

19) Destroying or attempting to destroy, (except by burning) public property or the property of another, without the owner's consent is known as __________________.

Answer: vandalism

20) Forceful physical assault, with or without weapons, which includes fighting, rape, gang warfare, or other attacks is termed __________________.

Answer: violence

Essay Questions

1) Describe the evolution of education and the American educational system, and how delinquency may have evolved along with it.

2) Discuss how acts of criminal school violence have changed today from what they were in the 1960s.

3) Identify and discuss the issues of school failure and how it relates to delinquency. Be sure to address why the association between school failure and delinquency is difficult to assess.

4) Discuss the various theoretical perspectives addressed in chapter nine as they apply to explaining any relationship between school and delinquency.

5) Discuss how student rights may have helped to decrease school related delinquency, and conversely helped to increase school related delinquency.

6) Write a brief statement explaining why Craig Haney and Philip Zimbardo compare high schools to prisons.

7) Explain in detail the case of New Jersey v. T.L.O..

8) What can schools do to control bullying in the school system?

9) The text gives 40 examples of school related shootings. Please briefly describe 5 of those examples.

10) Describe the report entitled *Indicators of School Crime and Safety: 2005*. How many students actually become victims of crime at school?

Chapter 10 Gangs and Delinquency

Multiple Choice Questions

1) By the 1980s, most theories of delinquency had virtually ignored what aspect of delinquent behavior?
A) group
B) individual
C) violent
D) school related

Answer: A

2) What instinct did Erickson and Jensen report that juveniles follow when violating the law?
A) primary
B) secondary
C) herd
D) gang-like

Answer: C

3) Which type of pattern did Giordano and Cernkovich suggest is found in both delinquents and nondelinquents?
A) cold and brittle
B) friendship
C) sticky
D) violent

Answer: B

4) Thrasher suggested that ethnic gangs evolve from playgroups without any particular ________________.
A) goal.
B) organization.
C) race.
D) parental supervision.

Answer: A

5) Which type of gang does Bartollas suggest emerged in the political climate of the 1960s?
A) peewee gangs
B) super-gangs
C) violent hoodlums
D) West Side Story gangs

Answer: B

6) According to Bartollas, what helped enable super-gangs to host economic and social ventures in the late 1960s?
A) colleges
B) Rockefeller Foundation grant
C) drug sales
D) political kickbacks

Answer: B

7) What type of crimes did Mayor Richard Daley crackdown on after 1968 that sent many gang members to Illinois prisons?
A) gang related violent crimes
B) fraud crimes
C) political crimes
D) spree murder crimes

Answer: A

8) According to the 2002 National Youth Gang Survey, the largest drop in gang membership occurred in ________________.
A) rural counties.
B) urban areas.
C) suburban counties.
D) small cities.

Answer: C

9) The smaller the community, the more likely the gang membership will be ______________.
A) adults over the age of 30.
B) adults between ages 20 and 30.
C) 18-to 20-year-olds.
D) juveniles.

Answer: D

10) Urban gang members are more likely to be ____________.
A) young whites.
B) females.
C) juveniles.
D) adults.

Answer: D

11) Who does gang members frequently use to deal drugs?
A) experienced veterans
B) younger and smaller members of the gang
C) females
D) adults in the process of "jumping in"

Answer: B

12) Youth gang demographics suggest that most gang members are of which average ages?
A) 10 to 12 years
B) 13 to 14 years
C) 15 to 16 years
D) 17 to 18 years

Answer: D

13) According to Bartollas, what activities are typically given to the youngest members of street gangs?
A) solicitation
B) shoplifting
C) running errands
D) acting as lookouts

Answer: C

14) According to I. Reiner, preteen gang recruits are referred to as ____.
A) at-risk.
B) wannabes.
C) associates.
D) veteranos.

Answer: B

15) According to I. Reiner, older members who often serve as teachers for younger gang members are referred to as ______________.
A) veteranos.
B) associates.
C) homies.
D) hardcore.

Answer: A

16) According to Bartollas, what has become fertile soil for the violence of youth gangs?
A) schools
B) money
C) race/ethnicity
D) guns

Answer: A

17) The terms "people and folks" refers to _________________.
A) fringe gang members.
B) Southwestern gangs.
C) Los Angeles peewee gangs.
D) Chicago-based gangs.

Answer: D

18) Bartollas describes gangs as quasi-institutionalized, meaning they often provide what type of service to students?
A) academic tutoring
B) source of income
C) protection
D) independence

Answer: C

19) What behavior became so extensive at a Dallas high school that it led to students having to wear ID's?
A) drug distributions
B) truancy
C) assaults
D) thefts

Answer: A

20) Which of the following is an example of a vertical/hierarchical type of gang?
A) Bloods
B) Crips
C) Gangster Disciples
D) Locura

Answer: C

21) According to Bartollas, which of the following is considered a ritual with many street gangs?
A) drinking
B) prayer
C) drive-bys
D) drug use

Answer: B

22) How many states did the Drug Enforcement Administration claim that Los Angeles street gangs were selling drugs in by 1988?
A) 16
B) 26
C) 36
D) 46

Answer: D

23) According to Bartollas, large street gangs expanded into smaller cities by deceptively promising local youths ___________.
A) money.
B) satellite operations.
C) drugs.
D) guns.

Answer: B

24) Moore and Hagedorns' 2001 summary of female gangs suggests female gang members are involved in delinquent and criminal behaviors ______.
A) less than male gangs.
B) more than males gangs.
C) equal to male gangs.

D) less than nongang females.
Answer: A

25) According to Bartollas, what typically occurs when communities first begin to pay attention to gangs?
A) graffiti displays
B) police announcements
C) observance by community citizens
D) a dramatic incident

Answer: D

26) The vignette at the beginning of the chapter began with a story about Walter Simon. He is mentioned in the text because ______________.
A) he was murdered by gang members
B) as a gang member he murdered 3 people
C) he started the Gangster Disciples
D) he was shot 8 times in San Francisco
E) he was a San Francisco police officer who was murdered by a Latino Gang.

Answer: D

27) Over the last 30 years, urban street gangs have armed themselves with ___________.
A) Israeli made Uzis
B) Soviet AK-47's
C) American M-16's
D) All of the above

Answer: D

28) *Mara* is a Salvadorian word for ___________.
A) criminal
B) crime
C) gang
D) man
E) macho

Answer: C

29) The gang Mara Salvatrucha is from _________.
A) El Salvador
B) Mexico
C) Nicaragua
D) Costa Rica
E) Columbia

Answer: A

30) Mara Salvatrucha is also known as ______________.
A) Mara Salvatrucha 13
B) MS-13
C) MS XIII
D) All of the above

Answer: d

31) In gang language the number 13 refers to ____________.
A) the original 13 leaders of the Gangster Disciples
B) the unluckiness of gang members
C) 13th letter of the alphabet which is M
D) the age at which a juvenile becomes eligible to join a gang
E) All of the above

Answer: C

True/False Questions

1) Research by Shaw/McKay showed that less than 52 percent of offenders committed their offenses in groups.

Answer: FALSE

2) The debate over a causal linkage between delinquency and peers is centered in whether delinquents merely seek friends like themselves, or do youths become delinquent because they associate with delinquent friends.

Answer: TRUE

3) Morash reported that since females belong to less delinquent groups than males, they are less likely to commit as many delinquent acts as males.

Answer: TRUE

4) Youth gangs began to flourish in Chicago and other large cities in the 1800s due to immigration and population shifts.

Answer: TRUE

5) Gangs of the 1950s may have actually used more lethal weapons than the gangs of today.

Answer: FALSE

6) The detached workers program, funded by tax money of the 1950s, was very successful in reducing rates of juvenile delinquency.

Answer: FALSE

7) Gangs of the early 1970s and 1980s may have been more violent than gangs of the 1950s, but they were also less systematic and less organized.

Answer: FALSE

8) According to Walter B. Miller, there is little or no consensus as to what a gang actually is.

Answer: TRUE

9) The number of gangs in the United States actually declined between 1996 and 2002.

Answer: TRUE

10) Approximately 85 percent of gang members in 2002 came from rural areas.

Answer: FALSE

11) The smaller the community, the more likely gang members will be juveniles.

Answer: TRUE

12) The greatest increase of gang membership has come from the older adult groups.

Answer: TRUE

13) According to Taylor, scavenger gangs focus mainly on illegal moneymaking ventures.

Answer: FALSE

14) The changing structure of the economy has resulted in older gang members remaining with urban gangs.

Answer: TRUE

15) Fringe gang members commit more criminal acts than core members, and they are less likely to be detected.

Answer: FALSE

16) White youths commit fewer delinquent acts after they leave the gang.

Answer: TRUE

17) A juvenile's propensity for gun ownership and violence are known to be closely related.

Answer: TRUE

18) According to the 2002 National Youth Gang Survey, white youths make up nearly 40 percent of the gang population in the U.S.

Answer: FALSE

19) Female gangs concentrate most of their criminal activities in crimes of theft.

Answer: FALSE

20) According to Bloch and Niederhoffer, joining a gang is part of the experience some male adolescents need to transform themselves into adults.

Answer: TRUE

Short Answer Questions

1) Hirschi argues that __________ __________ __________ relationships lead delinquents to be less likely to be attached to each other.

Answer: cold and brittle

2) In the 1960s, the __________ began as a small clique in a section of Los Angeles.

Answer: Crips

3) In the summer of 1967, __________ __________ leaders attended meetings in Chicago, which resulted in the emergence of Operation Bootstrap.

Answer: Vice Lords

4) A street gang's clothing, colors, and hand signs are held __________ by gang members.

Answer: sacred

5) With Hispanic gangs, the desired state of __________ denotes a type of craziness or wildness.

Answer: locura

6) __________ __________ and __________ stand out among the cities with the highest rates of gang homicides.

Answer: Los Angeles/Chicago

7) Chicano street gangs have unwritten codes of conduct referred to as __________.

Answer: Movidas

8) West Coast lower-and middle-class white youths have solidified into groups known as __________.

Answer: stoners

9) More recently, __________ theory has been widely used to explain the origins of gangs in the midst of big-city ghettos and barrios filled with poverty and deprivation.

Answer: underclass

10) According to Bartollas, communities have a tendency to __________ gangs, even when they are causing considerable problems.

Answer: deny

11) In your book, the way Hirschi's described interpersonal relationships between delinquents was _______________.

Answer: cold and brittle

12) A controlled substance derived from cocaine that is usually smoked, cheaper to produce than conventional cocaine, and attractive for gangs to marketing is known as _______________.

Answer: crack

13) _______________ was a problem that occurred within smaller communities beginning in the 1980s with the expansions of drug trafficking and the promise of satellite connections to larger urban gangs.

Answer: Emerging gangs

14) The nature of the peer relationships that exist within a teenage culture is called _______________.

Answer: friendship patterns

15) A group of youths who are bound together by mutual interests, identifiable leadership, and act in concert to achieve a specific illegal activity are commonly called a _______________.

Answer: gang

16) A state of mind associated with Mexican-American street gangs denoting craziness or wildness is called _______________.

Answer: locura

17) The codes of moral honor and conduct followed by Chicano gangs is called _______________

Answer: movidas

18) During the 1970's the gangs within the Illinois prison system divided themselves into two categories, the _______________.

Answer: People and Folks

19) Displays by gang affiliates, or _______________, where hand signs, colors, clothing, or other objects are used to represent and symbolize affiliation with particular gang membership.

Answer: representing

Essay Questions

1) Discuss the controversy surrounding the relationship of peer groups and delinquent behavior.

2) Discuss the evolution of gangs in America and describe how they have changed or remained similar throughout the evolutionary transition.

3) Describe a typical urban street gang of today. Include any features the gang may have and what types of activities they would be involved in.

4) Discuss the various ways the street gangs have emerged into smaller cities and communities. Be sure to discuss what Bartollas meant by some gangs using a carrot.

5) Discuss female gangs and how they are both similar and different to their male counterparts.

6) What are the six major elements most frequently cited in the definition of a gang?

7) Frederick Thrasher, in 1927, was one of the first to attempt to define a youth gang. State clearly and completely his definition of a youth gang.

8) Finn-Aage Esbensan concluded that there had to be five elements present for a group to be classified as a youth gang. What are those five elements?

9) J.D. Vigil and J.M. Long identified four basic types of gang involvement explain each of these types.

10) Ira Reiner identified five different types of gang members based on their commitment to the gang. Explain those different types of gang members.

11) In probably the most comprehensive classification of gangs, Malcolm W. Cline and Sheryl l. Maxson distinguished among 5 types of street gangs. Explain each of those types.

12) Martin Jankowski points out that there are 3 basic recruitment strategies used by the gangs. Briefly explain each of these strategies.

13) What are the different methods of initiation into a gang?

Chapter 11 Drugs and Delinquency

Multiple Choice Questions

1) Who developed and patented an early form of medicinal opium in 1709?
A) Benjamin Franklin
B) Thomas Dover
C) Francisco Pizarro
D) Rachel Carson

Answer: B

2) When did the overall rates of illicit drug use reach its highest peak in the United States?
A) 1965
B) 1969
C) 1979
D) 1990

Answer: C

3) When did the downward trend for marijuana usage end due to a dramatic increase in its usage?
A) 1965
B) 1969
C) 1979
D) 1990
Answer: D

4) According to the 2002 National Survey on Drug Use and Health, __________ percent of juveniles ages 12-17 years use illicit drugs?
A) 11.6
B) 18.2
C) 24.9
D) 31

Answer: A

5) The highest rate for inhalant drug use was recorded in
A) 1965.
B) 1974.
C) 1985.
D) 1992.

Answer: D

6) According to the 2002 National Drug Survey, __________ is the most abused illicit drug for twelve to eighteen years olds.
A) amphetamines
B) marijuana
C) heroin
D) cocaine

Answer: B

7) Which substance/drug are females more likely to use in higher amounts than males?
A) cigarettes
B) alcohol
C) marijuana
D) inhalants

Answer: A

8) Which race/ethnicity appears to be experiencing the greatest rise in drug usage rates?
A) African-Americans
B) Asians
C) American Indians
D) Hispanics

Answer: C

9) Substance abuse is more common for persons living _______________.
A) on the East and West coasts.
B) in the Midwest.
C) in the South.
D) in the North and Northeast.

Answer: A

10) Which is often neglected in discussions of drugs because it is NOT considered by most persons as a mind altering drug?
A) alcohol
B) tobacco
C) marijuana
D) cocaine

Answer: B

11) The most common method for using cocaine is reported as being
A) speedballing.
B) swallowing.
C) intravenously.
D) snorting.

Answer: D

12) Butyl nitrite, gasoline, and paint thinners can typically produce feelings of excitement followed by disorientation when they are
A) ingested.
B) inhaled.
C) injected.
D) absorbed.

Answer: B

13) Quaaludes or methaqualone, as a barbiturate, are considered a form of _______________.
A) sedatives.
B) stimulants.
C) inhalants.
D) opiates.

Answer: A

14) Valium, Librium, and Equanil are commonly prescribed for both anxiety and sleep disorders, and are associated with
A) amphetamines.
B) stimulants.
C) opiates.
D) benzodiazepines.

Answer: D

15) __________ gained popularity in the late 1980s after being produced in California and marketed to other states.
A) Heroin
B) Ecstasy
C) Crank
D) Inhalants

Answer: C

16) Which point in history did Americans first begin to use amphetamines to relieve fatigue and anxiety problems?
A) Prohibition
B) World War I
C) World War II
D) Vietnam War

Answer: C

17) Which drug is considered a hallucinogen and dropped in popularity during the 1990s?
A) heroin
B) crank
C) PCP
D) cocaine

Answer: C

18) Which opiate derived drug gained popularity in 1997 and reached its highest usage level in thirty years for first time users?
A) LSD
B) crank
C) marijuana
D) heroin

Answer: D

19) The basic theoretical structure comprised of a comprehensive framework of antecedent variables to explain drug use and problem behaviors is known as ____________________.

A) the Jessor's model.
B) the behavior system.
C) an addicted model.
D) Wiley's sophisticated paradigm.

Answer: A

20) Kandel and colleagues suggest that youths who become addicted to or dependent on drugs, are more likely to ____________________.

A) cause injury to themselves to steal drugs from medical facilities.
B) commit crimes to maintain their drug supply.
C) raid their parent's drug supplies.
D) reach a turning-point and stop using.

Answer: B

21) According to Bartollas, who controls drug trafficking in urban settings?

A) peewee gangs
B) younger super-gang members
C) adults
D) young female gang members

Answer: C

22) According to Monti's examination of gangs, girls involvement in dealing drugs primarily consists of ________________.

A) holding drugs for boys.
B) luring potential buyers.
C) selling the drugs.
D) fronting the money through prostitution.

Answer: A

23) How many drug-abusing youths continue to use drugs after reaching adulthood?

A) less than one-third
B) slightly more than one-third
C) about half
D) about two-thirds

Answer: D

24) What did Kandel and colleagues report is correlated to with the cessation of marijuana smoking with persons in their mid to late twenties?

A) arrest for drug related crimes
B) significant status change
C) intensive probation sentences

D) time in jail

Answer: B

25) Which explanation is the strongest predictor of an individuals involvement in drug use?
A) drug use by peers
B) addiction prone personality
C) high peak experience
D) bleak economic situation

Answer: A

26) The vignette at the beginning of the chapter involved the IRAK crew who were known for ______________.
A) selling drugs
B) committing a murder
C) being graffiti artists
D) stealing computers from their school
E) terrorism

Answer: C

27) The name that a manufacture gives a chemical substance is its _________________.
A) brand name
B) generic name
C) street name
D) psychoactive category

Answer: A

28) This particular type of drug can be rubbed on the skin in the form of creams or gels.
A) anabolic steroids
B) cocaine
C) heroin
D) amphetamines

Answer: A

29) One of the newest patterns of drug usage is called a "pharm party'.
A "pharm party" is ____________.
A) a keg party on a farm
B) a party where a pig is roasted
C) a fraternity party
D) a party where teens exchange pharmaceutical drugs

Answer: D

30) In 2005, what percentage of U.S. teenagers said they had used prescription pain killers such as Vicodin or stimulants such as Ritalin to get high?
A) 9%
B) 19%
C) 29%
D) 39%

Answer: B

True/False Questions

1) The rise of Satanism in the 1980s is often linked to a drug revolution in America.

Answer: FALSE

2) Alcohol remains the most frequently abused substance by adolescents.

Answer: TRUE

3) The highest rate for adolescent use of inhalants was reported in 1979.

Answer: FALSE

4) Recent studies have suggested that teenagers have increased their usage of marijuana.

Answer: FALSE

5) Illicit drug use took a significant downturn in 2001.

Answer: TRUE

6) Marijuana use rose dramatically in the early 1990s before declining in 1999.

Answer: TRUE

7) Studies indicate that fewer adolescents appear to be experimenting with drugs.
Answer: TRUE

8) Most studies suggest that African-American youth have increased their drug usage above that of white teens.

Answer: FALSE

9) Recent research indicates the effects of marijuana are lesser than previously believed.

Answer: FALSE

10) Amphetamines, such as Benzedrine have been widely abused by truck drivers who had to stay alert for extended periods of times.

Answer: TRUE

11) Heroin is refined from morphine and was introduced in the 1960s by the counterculture.

Answer: FALSE

12) A current debate over drugs is whether delinquency leads to drug use or does drug use lead to delinquency.

Answer: TRUE

13) Recent longitudinal studies have suggested evidence of an overlap of drug abuse with other problem behaviors.

Answer: TRUE

352

14) Elliot and Huizinga found that nearly 10 percent of serious juvenile offenders were also multiple drug users.

Answer: FALSE

15) The less risk-factors a child has, the more likely it is they will become involved in drug abuse.

Answer: FALSE

16) Youths who sell drugs, whether they are users or not, are chronic offenders.

Answer: TRUE

17) Monti suggested the effect of the so-called war on drugs has been making drug trafficking highly profitable.

Answer: TRUE

18) Drug addicts will often relapse in spite of finding straight life exciting and fulfilling.

Answer: FALSE

19) Prevention and treatment are the most effective means to control drug use in America.

Answer: TRUE

20) There is abundant evidence that the various federal wars on drugs have been ineffective with both juveniles and adults.

Answer: TRUE

Short Answer Questions

1) __________ was launched in 1980 in response to a 13 year old youth who was struck down and killed by a drunk driver.

Answer: MADD

2) __________ is the least frequently used illicit drug in America.

Answer: Heroin

3) __________ of cocaine is derived from a chemical process in which the cocaine is crystallized.

Answer: Freebasing

4) The intravenous use of cocaine along with another drug is known as __________.

Answer: speedballing

5) A less expensive, more potent, version of cocaine is referred to as __________.

Answer: crack

6) Secondary smoke exhaled from crack user into the mouth of another is known as a __________.

Answer: shotgun

7) One frequently used __________ is butyl nitrite, commonly called RUSH.

Answer: inhalant

8) The common name for MDMA, which became popular in the 1990s, is called __________.

Answer: Ecstasy

9) Psychedelic substances, such as PCP and LSD, are known as __________.

Answer: hallucinogens

10) __________, a refined form of morphine, was introduced at the turn of the twentieth century.

Answer: Heroin

11) A drug made through a fermentation process that relaxes inhibitions and causes adolescents to participate in risky behavior while under its influence is called __________.

Answer: alcohol

12) Stimulant drugs that occur in various forms and are frequently used by adolescents are called ___________.

Answer: amphetamines

13) A synthetic psychoactive substance often found at nightclubs, bars, "raves," and dance parties is called _____________.

Answer: club drugs

14) A coca extract that creates mood elevation, elation, grandiose feelings, and feelings of heightened physical prowess is ____________.

Answer: cocaine

15) The excessive use of a drug, which is frequently characterized by physical and/or psychological dependence is called ______________.

Answer: drug addition

16) A form of amphetamine that began to be used by adolescents (for sexual enhancement) in the United States in the 1980s and 1990s and is now rather widespread is _______________.

Answer: ecstasy

17) A refined form of morphine that was introduced around the beginning of the twentieth century is ______________.

Answer: heroin

18) Volatile liquids that give off a vapor, which is inhaled, producing short-term excitement and euphoria followed by a period of disorientation is called a _____________

Answer: inhalants

19) The most frequently used illicit drug is _______________. It is usually smoked and consists of dried hemp leaves and buds.

Answer: marijuana

20) Drugs that are taken orally and affect the user by depressing the nervous system causing drowsiness are called ________________.

Answer: sedatives

Essay Questions

1) Discuss the prevalence and incidence of drug use among adolescents in America. Be sure to include the historical evolution and its impact on drug trends in the U.S.

2) Identify and describe the main types of drugs used in America. Include how each type is commonly consumed by its user (ingestion, injection, smoking, etc.).

3) Discuss the research on drug use through life course. Identify the various pathways what may affect one's propensity to desist from using drugs.

4) Identify and discuss the various theoretical explanations for the onset of drug use.

5) Discuss the elements of drug prevention and treatment in the United States. Be sure to discuss the strengths and weaknesses of various programs, such as Elan.

6) Explain the cognitive-affective theory of drug usage.

7) Explain the addictive personality theory of drug usage.

8) Explain the stress relief theory of drug usage.

9) What is the social learning theory of drug usage?

10) Explain Travis Hirschi's social control theory and its relationship to explaining drug usage.

11) Explain how drug courts work.

Chapter 12 Prevention, Diversion, and Treatment

Multiple Choice Questions

1) Which of the following terms refers to intervention methods being used to prevent delinquency?
A) primary prevention
B) secondary prevention
C) tertiary prevention
D) traditional prevention

Answer: B

2) Which of the following terms refers to prevention methods aimed at recidivism?
A) primary prevention
B) secondary prevention
C) tertiary prevention
D) traditional prevention

Answer: C

3) What does Bartollas suggest that society traditionally uses to seek answers to complex problems in delinquency?
A) panaceas
B) futile attempts
C) comprehensive efforts
D) periodic diversion

Answer: A

4) Prevention programs are often criticized for ___________.
A) not investing enough money.
B) putting the rights of children ahead of common sense.
C) targeting chronic offenders.
D) net-widening.

Answer: D

5) What did the Office of Juvenile Justice and Delinquency Prevention begin to target in 1990?
A) drunk driving offenses
B) serious and violent offending
C) parental responsibility
D) first-time offenders

Answer: B

6) How does the "Bully Prevention Program aim to reduce delinquency in schools?
A) isolating the causes
B) increasing student education programs
C) zero tolerance
D) providing few opportunities and reducing peer approval

Answer: D

7) Why does increased literature on diversion programs suggest interventions into the lives of serious offenders is needed?
A) Because the juvenile crime rate is the highest it has ever been.
B) The juvenile justice system does not see them until its too late.
C) High-risk offenders are typically placed on juvenile probation and not punished.
D) They are often the only children worth rehabilitating.

Answer: B

8) Effective programs to prevent delinquency among chronic offenders must be ________________.
A) multi-systematic.
B) unidirectional.
C) exclusively nonprofit.
D) focus on deficiencies.

Answer: A

9) Diversion programs began in 1967 and were based on the theoretical perspectives of differential association and ________________.
A) social control theory.
B) psychotherapy.
C) labeling theory.
D) drift theory.

Answer: C

10) The most positive characteristics of traditional diversionary programs is that they commonly ________________.
A) reduce the complaints by police
B) engulf more students into the "nets" of juvenile justice.
C) reduce crime.
D) minimize the penetration of youthful offenders into the justice system.

Answer: D

11) Generally, what can community courts offer in dealing with juveniles that the juvenile justice system cannot?
A) more bureaucracy
B) more timely responses
C) less conflict resolution
D) victim restitution

Answer: B

12) Which diversion form utilizes restorative justice conferences involving offenders, victims, their families, and other members of the community?
A) community
B) teen court
C) drug court

D) alternative dispute resolution

Answer: D

13) Which of the following teen court models is used the most in the United States?
A) adult judge
B) youth judge
C) tribunal
D) peer jury

Answer: A

14) What will the teen courts rarely or never accept?
A) first-time alcohol offenders
B) theft cases
C) juveniles with prior arrest records
D) assault cases

Answer: C

15) What did Title V of the Violent Crime Control and Law Enforcement Act of 1994 authorize?
A) juvenile death penalties
B) educational programs for inmates
C) the formation of drug courts
D) youth service bureaus

Answer: C

16) Robert Martinson's 1975 public statement about prevention programs on 60 Minutes largely resulted in the media adopting what type of attitude about diversion?
A) optimistic
B) hedonistic
C) opportunistic
D) pessimistic

Answer: D

17) Gendreau and Ross's studies on correctional treatment have disputed the claims of "__________" as predicted by Robert Martinson.
A) kids are evil
B) nothing works
C) all is lost
D) all is well

Answer: B

18) Which of the following treatment modalities has been used more exclusively with upper-and middle-class offenders than with lower-class youthful offenders?
A) psychotherapy

B) transactional analysis
C) reality therapy
D) guided group interaction

Answer: A

19) Which of the following treatment modalities attempts to understand how tapes of the past are influencing the present behavior of juvenile offenders?
A) psychotherapy
B) transactional analysis
C) reality therapy
D) guided group interaction

Answer: B

20) Which of the following treatment modalities assumes that unmet basic needs may lead to delinquent behaviors?
A) psychotherapy
B) transactional analysis
C) reality therapy
D) guided group interaction

Answer: C

21) Which of the following treatment modalities is based on the notion that all behavior is under the control of its consequences in the external environment?
A) behavior modification
B) psychotherapy
C) errors in thinking approach
D) abuse interventions

Answer: A

22) Which of the following treatment modalities has probably been used the most?
A) psychotherapy
B) transactional analysis
C) reality therapy
D) guided group interaction

Answer: D

23) Which of the following treatment modalities suggests that offenders blame others, attempt to manipulate, and lie as part of their rationale for committing delinquent acts?
A) behavior modification
B) psychotherapy
C) rational emotive therapy
D) abuse interventions

Answer: C

24) According to Bartollas, what have program designs frequently relied on to cure a variety of complex problems associated with delinquency?
A) single cures
B) multiple-aspect theories
C) meta-analysis
D) comprehensive strategies

Answer: A

25) What type of technique creates a set of descriptors of the kinds of people that would most likely benefit from a particular treatment?
A) drift-decisions
B) categorical-choosing
C) template-matching
D) survival-strategies

Answer: C

26) The vignette at the beginning of the chapter involved a crime committed by Karl, a 15 year old dropout. His crime was __________.
A) possession of marijuana
B) robbery
C) prostitution
D) stealing computers from the school
E) murder

Answer: A

27) The public health model of dealing with juvenile crime focuses on ___________.
A) psychological counseling
B) group home counseling
C) reducing risk and increasing resiliency
D) punishing the offender
E) getting the delinquent off of the street with some type of incarceration

Answer: C

28) The Model Programs Guide is designed to _________________.
A) assist law enforcement in the apprehension of delinquents
B) assist counselors in guide group interaction with delinquents
C) assist practitioners and communities in implementing evidence-based prevention and intervention programs that can make a difference in the lives of children and communities.
D) assist educators in improving academic test scores for children

Answer: C

29) On the mean streets from East L.A. to South-Central L.A., gang members are leaving the thug life and trying to make in a 60-person business called _______________.
A) Ghetto Boys
B) Alternative Living
C) Homeboy Industries
D) Opportunities
E) The Hip-Hop Shoppe

Answer: C

30) A modality of therapy that is based on interpreting and evaluating personal relationships is called _____________. Meaning is attached to the "tape" of the past and the offender ultimately will negotiate his or her own treatment.
A) guided group interaction
B) behavior modification
C) reality therapy
D) transactional analysis
E) positive peer culture

Answer: D

True/False Questions

1) The areas of prevention have largely been the main focus in the studies of delinquency.

Answer: FALSE

2) The effectiveness of prevention programs has largely been unsuccessful.

Answer: TRUE

3) Providing individual attention to high-risk offenders and developing community-wide interventions are the main two components of prevention programs with the widest application.

Answer: TRUE

4) Recent research suggests that prevention and treatment programs will NOT impact high-risk offenders.

Answer: FALSE

5) Diversion programs are exclusive only to courts and agencies outside the juvenile justice system.

Answer: FALSE

6) Possibly the only positive aspect of traditional diversion programs is that they minimize the penetration of youthful offenders into the justice system.

Answer: TRUE

7) Reducing orientation to weapons and increasing awareness to weapon injuries is the major premise of teen courts.

Answer: FALSE

8) Teen courts generally only handle first-time offenders charged with minor offenses.

Answer: TRUE

9) Correctional treatment for youthful offenders came under increased public attack in the late 1960s and early 1970s.

Answer: TRUE

10) Transactional analysis encourages offenders to negotiate a treatment contract.

Answer: TRUE

11) The term three R's is associated with guided group interaction prevention.

Answer: FALSE

12) Negative reinforcers have been shown to be longer lasting and more effective than positive reinforcers.

Answer: FALSE

13) Behavior modification appears to have more significant impact on sociopathic offenders than other treatment modalities.

Answer: TRUE

14) Behavior modification is frequently criticized for any behavior changes not lasting.

Answer: TRUE

15) Guided group interaction requires adults to make decisions for juvenile offenders until they can become responsible.

Answer: FALSE

16) Guided group interaction is often praised for comprehensive and positive pro-social stance.

Answer: TRUE

17)A mainstay of positive peer culture treatment modality is teaching members to care for one another.

Answer: TRUE

18) The rational emotive therapy approach assumes that offenders have functional cognitive patterns that cannot be restructured.

Answer: FALSE

19) According to Bartollas, drug and alcohol interventions have been one of the more successful program areas for juvenile offenders.

Answer: FALSE

20) Enforced offender rehabilitation has sometimes resulted in making delinquents worse rather than better through treatment.

Answer: TRUE

Short Answer Questions

1) __________ prevention is focused on modifying conditions in the physical and social environments.

Answer: Primary

2) Society's seeking of __________ stem from the tendency to seek easy answers to complex problems.

Answer: panaceas

3) Critics often charge that prevention programs sweep more children into the justice system and they are far too __________.

Answer: expensive

4) Peer juries or youth courts are mainly referred to as ______ ______.

Answer: teen courts

5) __________ courts offer legal incentives such as deferred prosecution in exchange for substance treatment.

Answer: Drug

6) Various adaptations of Freudian __________ have been used by psychiatrists, clinical psychologists, and social workers.

Answer: psychotherapy

7) __________ __________ focuses on interpreting and evaluating interpersonal relationships.

Answer: Transactional analysis

8) __________ __________ was developed by William Glasser and G.L. Harrington, and assumes that unmet basic needs may lead to delinquency.

Answer: Reality therapy

9) __________ __________ refers to the application of instrumental learning theory to problems of human behavior.

Answer: Behavior modification

10) __________ __________ __________ assumes that peers could confront other peers and force them to face the reality of their behavior.

Answer: Guided group interaction

11) A psychological treatment method that rewards appropriate behavior positively, immediately, and systematically and assumes that rewards increase the occurrence of desired behavior is called ______________.

Answer: behavior modification

12) Organized efforts to forestall or prevent the development of delinquent behaviors is called ____________.

Answer: delinquency prevention

13) Dispositional alternatives for youthful offenders that exist outside of the formal juvenile justice system is known as ______________.

Answer: diversion programs

14) Treatment modalities in which drug-abusing juveniles are usually treated in a group context is referred to as ____________.

Answer: drug and alcohol abuse interventions

15) A counseling technique that involves treating all members of a family and a widely used method of dealing with a delinquent's socially unacceptable behavior is know as ____________.

Answer: family therapy

16) Interaction that places youthful offenders in an intensive group environment under the direction of an adult leader who substitutes a whole new structure of beliefs, values, and behaviors of the delinquent is called ____________.

Answer: guided group interaction (GGI)

17) Special courts designed for nonviolent youthful offenders with substance abuse problems who require integrated sanctions and services such as mandatory drug testing, substance abuse treatment, supervised release, and aftercare are known as ______________.

Answer: juvenile drug courts

18) The claim made by Robert Martinson and his colleagues in the mid-1970s that correctional treatment is ineffective in reducing recidivism of correctional clients is know as ______________.

Answer: “nothing works”

19) A group treatment modality that aims to build a positive youth subculture and encompasses a strategy that extends to all aspects of daily life is known as ______________.

Answer: positive peer culture

20) Efforts to reduce delinquency by modifying conditions in the physical and social environments that lead to juvenile crime is called ______________.

Answer: primary prevention

Essay Questions

1) Discuss the various assessments of traditional diversionary prevention programs. Be sure to include any strengths that have led to recent resurgence of interests in diversion.

2) Discuss the common components of diversionary programs that have been shown to work, according to Joy Dryfoos.

3) Discuss the negatives aspects of diversion programs and what reformers have done to change these programs.

4) Discuss what advantages drug courts have over traditional juvenile justice courts in providing services to juvenile substance abusers.

5) Discuss the overall quality of drug and alcohol abuse treatment programs in treating youthful abusers in the United States.

6) What are the three different levels of delinquency prevention?

7) The public health model employs a four step procedure to identify issues that need attention and to develop solutions. Explain each of these four steps.

8) Joy Dryfoos’s 1990s analysis of the 100 most successful delinquency prevention programs tried through the 1980s identified seven common program components. Explain each of those seven components.

9) There are four possible case-processing models that can be used by teen court. Explain each of those four models.

10) Briefly explain transactional analysis.

11) Briefly explain reality therapy.

12) Briefly explain behavior modification.

13) Briefly explain guided group interaction.

14) Briefly explain positive peer culture.

Chapter 13 The Juvenile Justice Process

Multiple Choice Questions

1) What does the parens patriae philosophy of juvenile court charge that the court must do in regard to juvenile offenders?
A) punish their sins
B) provide treatment
C) separate them from their peers
D) initiate victim restitution

Answer: B

2) Which of the following persons is most likely to make the decision whether a juvenile should remain in the community or be placed in a shelter or detention facility?
A) probation officer
B) police officer
C) parents
D) legal guardian

Answer: A

3) Which document does a juvenile generally receive to appear before the court, after the commission of a serious offense?
A) retainer
B) indictment
C) affidavit
D) petition

Answer: D

4) The trial stage of the juvenile justice process to determine whether the juvenile is guilty is referred to as
A) detention proceedings.
B) disposition hearing.
C) an adjudicatory hearing.
D) intake proceedings.

Answer: C

5) Which of the following juvenile court terms is equal to the adult trial sentencing stage?
A) detention proceedings
B) disposition hearing
C) an adjudicatory hearing
D) intake proceedings

Answer: B

6) Where are juveniles commonly sent to determine proper institutional placement, especially in states that have several juvenile facilities?
A) diagnostic centers
B) shelter homes
C) youth service bureaus

D) mental health clinics

Answer: A

7) What did the early cohort studies suggest would probably cause juveniles to continue with crime into their adult years?
A) genetic predisposition
B) parental treatment
C) institutionalizing juveniles
D) a fractured juvenile system

Answer: C

8) Which of the following cohort studies suggested that early intervention by the justice system reduces juvenile recidivism rates?
A) Racine
B) Columbus
C) Philadelphia
D) Maricopa County

Answer: D

9) How does Bartollas describe the relationships between the juvenile justice subsystems?
A) united
B) fragmented
C) cooperative and communicative
D) corrupt

Answer: B

10) According to Bartollas, fragmentation is so great among juvenile and adult systems, that both are frequently referred to as _______.
A) alien systems.
B) predisposed.
C) nonsystems.
D) bureaucratic wastelands.

Answer: C

11) The first factor Bartollas cites among the reasons for juvenile justice systems being fragmented is _______________.
A) lack of a common goal.
B) negative impact.
C) untrained juvenile workers.
D) lack of funding.

Answer: A

12) Fragmentation of the juvenile justice system occurs in part because local government control often leads to _______________.

A) competition.
B) costly programs.
C) unprofessional ideas.
D) local biases.

Answer: D

13) Which model of juvenile justice seeks to change an offender's character, attitude, or behavior to diminish his or her propensities for youth crime through medical or adjustment treatment?
A) rehabilitative model
B) justice model
C) balanced and restorative model
D) crime control model

Answer: A

14) Which model of juvenile justice places an emphasis on the delinquent's current responsibility and encourages them to stop using excuses for past problems?
A) medical model
B) adjustment model
C) reintegration model
D) justice model

Answer: B

15) Which model assumes that delinquent's problems must be solved in the community where they began?
A) medical model
B) adjustment model
C) reintegration model
D) justice model

Answer: C

16) Which model holds to the belief that punishment should be the basic purpose of the juvenile justice system?
A) medical model
B) adjustment model
C) reintegration model
D) justice model

Answer: D

17) Which model of juvenile justice seeks to reconcile the interests of victims, offenders, and the community through programs and supervision practices?
A) rehabilitative model
B) justice model
C) balanced and restorative model
D) crime control model

Answer: C

18) Which model of juvenile justice is based on the classical school of criminology?
A) rehabilitative model
B) justice model
C) balanced and restorative model
D) crime control model

Answer: D

19) Proof that most states adopted the crime control model of juvenile justice in the early 1990s can be found in the various state laws that have made juvenile systems more
A) lenient.
B) punitive.
C) treatment oriented.
D) community-based.

Answer: B

20) According to Bartollas, which model began to gain momentum in the late 1990s?
A) rehabilitative model
B) justice model
C) balanced and restorative model
D) crime control model

Answer: C

21) What type of offenses were the main target of the 1974 Juvenile Justice and Delinquency Prevention Act?
A) violent crimes
B) drug crimes
C) gang related
D) status offenses

Answer: D

22) What did the 1980 amendment to the 1974 Juvenile Justice and Delinquency Prevention Act require?
A) juveniles be removed from adult jails
B) treatment for drug offenders
C) reduce disproportionate confinement of minority youth
D) longer jail sentences for serious offenders

Answer: A

23) What did the 1992 amendment to the 1974 Juvenile Justice and Delinquency Prevention Act require?
A) juveniles be removed from adult jails
B) treatment for drug offenders
C) reduce disproportionate confinement of minority youth
D) longer jail sentences for serious offenders

Answer: C

24) Which state passed a law making it a misdemeanor to lockup a juvenile in jail?

A) New York
B) Oregon
C) Kansas
D) Utah

Answer: D

25) What does Bartollas suggest for juvenile justice trends in the twenty-first century?
A) Legislatures are likely to become less involved with the juvenile process.
B) More children's cases will likely be transferred to adult courts.
C) The use of the death penalty for juveniles will increase.
D) More and more juvenile offenders will come from the middle-class families.

Answer: B

26) The vignette at the beginning of the chapter involved Lionel Tate, who was famous for being ____________.
A) a gang leader in Miami, Florida
B) an abandoned and abuse child found living under an interstate
C) murdered at his grade school
D) the youngest drug dealer in Miami
E) the youngest child in modern times to be sentenced to life imprisonment

Answer: E

27) How old was Lionel Tate?
A) 6
B) 8
C) 10
D) 12
E) 17

Answer: D

28) Lee Boyd Malvo was know for ____________________.
A) being a juvenile serial rapists
B) being the juvenile at Columbine who shot 13 other students
C) being one of the Beltway Killers
D) starting the Vice Lords
E) starting the Gangster Disciples

Answer: C

29) An integrated model that seeks to reconcile the interests of victims, offenders, and the community through programs and supervision practices is called the ______________. This model seeks to ensure accountability to crime victims and to enhance community safety.
A) crime control model
B) balance or restorative model
C) rehabilitation model
D) justice model
E) the education model

Answer: B

30) An indictment in juvenile court language is called ______________.
A) a warrant
B) a charge
C) a petition
D) an information
E) an accusation

Answer: C

True/False Questions

1) Among the variety of agents that refer juveniles to court, it is probably more common for police to make that decision.

Answer: TRUE

2) Juveniles are commonly transferred to adult court after they have been adjudicated as delinquent by the juvenile court for committing the same offense.

Answer: FALSE

3) Most juvenile court codes permit adjudication and disposition hearings to occur together.

Answer: FALSE

4) Juvenile judges are restricted in using only public residential placements for young offenders.

Answer: FALSE

5) Most training school residents currently are not confined as long as they were in the past.

Answer: TRUE

6) The Maricopa County cohort study suggested that females are more positively affected by institutionalization when compared to males, in regard to recidivism rates.

Answer: TRUE

7) The adult justice system is more fragmented than that of the juvenile system.

Answer: FALSE

8) The juvenile term commitment is synonymous with the adult system's term of sentence.

Answer: TRUE

9) According to juvenile terminology, a juvenile that is said to be arrested has actually been taken into custody and not arrested.

Answer: TRUE

10) The adjustment model of rehabilitation contends that offenders must avoid using past problems as an excuse and demonstrate responsible behavior in the present.

Answer: TRUE

11) The "just deserts" philosophy argues that offenders should NOT be punished and deserve to be treated leniently as their behaviors are not their fault.

Answer: FALSE

12) The public has become increasingly intolerant of crime and is more and more receptive to the crime control model of juvenile justice.

Answer: TRUE

13) Bartollas suggests that many youths remain confined in county jails and police lockups since many juvenile jurisdictions simply have no alternatives available to them.

Answer: TRUE

14) The popularity of indeterminate sentences for juveniles has been losing public support similar to the adult system, due to the unexacting nature of their application.

Answer: FALSE

15) Bartollas predicts that the United States will probably combine the adult and juvenile justice systems in the very near future.

Answer: FALSE

16) Predictions for the twenty-first century include that legislatures are likely to become more involved with juvenile court law.

Answer: TRUE

17)It is predicted that in the near future, the death penalty will be used more frequently for juvenile offenders.

Answer: FALSE

18) The issue of gun control may be acknowledged as the most serious problem facing juvenile justice in the twenty-first century.

Answer: TRUE

19) Bartollas predicts upper-and middle-class juvenile offenders will be arrested more frequently in the future than at the present.

Answer: FALSE

20) Bartollas predicts that there will be an increased focus on the medicalization of delinquents in the near future that will mark a return to the 1960s.

Answer: TRUE

Short Answer Questions

1) The juvenile justice system is made up of three basic __________.

Answer: subsystems

2) Juvenile __________ is the most widely used judicial disposition in the United States.

Answer: probation

3) Early __________ studies did NOT present a favorable picture of the juvenile justice process on juvenile delinquents.

Answer: cohort

4) According to Bartollas, both the juvenile and adult systems are under fire to get __________ on crime, especially violent crime.

Answer: tough

5) The __________ model contends that delinquency is caused by factors that can be identified, isolated, treated, and cured.

Answer: medical

6) The __________ model is more concerned that juvenile delinquents receive therapy than institutionalizing them.

Answer: rehabilitation

7) The concept of "__________ __________" is the pivotal philosophical basis of the justice model.

Answer: just deserts

8) The __________ model recommends community-based corrections for all but the hard core offenders and those offenders who must be institutionalized a wide variety of reentry programs.

Answer: reintegration

9) The __________ model strongly advocates that procedural safeguards and fairness be granted to juveniles who have broken the law.

Answer: justice

10) Prior to the 1974 Juvenile Justice and Delinquency Prevention Act, noncriminal youths and __________ __________ frequently stayed longer in institutions because they had more difficulty complying with the rules than most delinquent youths.

Answer: status offenders

11) The stage of juvenile court proceedings that usually includes the child's plea, presentation of evidence by the prosecution and defense, cross-examination of witnesses, and a finding by the judge as to whether the allegations in the petition can be sustained is known as a ________________.

Answer: adjudicatory hearing

12) A rehabilitative correctional approach that emphasizes helping delinquents demonstrate responsible behavior is a(n) ________________.

Answer: adjustment model

13) The supervision of juveniles who are released from correctional institutions so they can make an optimal adjustment to community living; or the status of a juvenile conditionally released from a treatment or confinement facility and placed under supervision in the community is called ________________.

Answer: aftercare

14) An integrative correctional model that seeks to reconcile the interests of victims, offenders, and the community through programs and supervised practices is known as a ________________.

Answer: balanced and restorative model

15) A name given to an organized group of progressive social reformers of the late nineteenth and early twentieth centuries who promoted numerous laws aimed at protecting children and institutionalizing an idealized image of childhood innocence is called ________________.

Answer: child savers

16) A determination made by a juvenile judge at the disposition stage of a juvenile court proceeding that a juvenile is to be sent to a juvenile correctional institution is called a ________________.

Answer: commitment

17) A correctional model supported by James Q. Wilson, Ernest van den Haag, and others, who believe that discipline and punishment are the most effective means of deterring youth crime is know as the ________________.

Answer: crime control model

18) The temporary restraint of a juvenile in a secure facility, usually because he or she is acknowledged to be dangerous either to self or others is called ________________.

Answer: detention

19) The stage of the juvenile court proceedings in which the juvenile judge decides the most appropriate placement for a juvenile who has been adjudicated a delinquent, a status offender, or a dependent child is called a ________________.

Answer: dispositional hearing

20) A philosophical underpinning of the justice model which holds that juveniles deserve to be punished if they violated the law, and the punishment must be proportionate to the seriousness of the offense is known as ________________.

Answer: just deserts

Essay Questions

1) Identify and describe the various structures and functions of the juvenile justice system.

2) Discuss the various factors that fragment the juvenile justice system and describe the consequences of the fragmentation on juvenile offenders brought into the justice system.

3) Define the Juvenile Justice and Delinquency Prevention Act of 1974 and discuss what affects it has had on juvenile justice. Be sure to include the amendments of 1980 and 1992 in your discussion.

4) Using Anthony Platt's *The Childs Savers* describe Platt's position on the origins and purposes of the juvenile court.

5) To correct the behavior of the juvenile delinquent, there have traditionally been four basic correctional models. Explain in detail each of those four models.

6) What evidence does Janet Lauritsen present to support the differential offending hypothesis.

7) The text lists fifteen trends facing the juvenile justice system. Describe at least ten of those fifteen trends.

8) Explain the rehabilitative model of juvenile justice with its three subsystem.

9) Explain the justice model of juvenile justice.

10) Explain the crime control model of juvenile justice.

11) Explain the balanced and restorative model of juvenile justice.

Chapter 14 The Police and the Juvenile

Multiple Choice Questions

1) What percentage of the nation's cities had instituted some type of juvenile program by 1924?
A) 90 percent
B) 70 percent
C) 50 percent
D) 30 percent

Answer: A

2) Who is credited with introducing the concept of youth bureaus in the United States?
A) August Vollmer
B) Lt. Ed Flynn
C) J. Edgar Hoover
D) Orlando Wilson

Answer: A

3) Which of the following best describes the trend for police departments in the late 1970s, in regard to their involvement with juvenile programs?
A) established even more expensive juvenile programs trying to reduce crime
B) concentrated heavily on drug abuse programs only
C) moved away from involvement and many departments dropped juvenile divisions
D) dropped abuse and neglect programs in exchange for specializations

Answer: C

4) According to Bartollas, who generally assumed responsibility for investigating juvenile crime in the early 1980s?
A) specialized juvenile officers
B) detective divisions
C) social work agencies
D) school administrators

Answer: B

5) Where did police become more involved due to the proliferation of drug abuse in the 1990s?
A) schools
B) suburban neighborhoods
C) community watch programs
D) inner-city recreational programs

Answer: A

6) Who is most likely to have the more favorable attitude toward police?
A) African-American boys
B) white boys
C) African-American girls
D) white girls

Answer: D

7) According to Bartollas, what would happen if police were to increase the current number of youths referred to the system by two to three times?
A) The system would be unmanageable.
B) Crime would ultimately reduce.
C) Crime would likely remain constant.
D) The cost of justice would likely reduce.

Answer: A

8) Which factor is considered the most influential in determining police discretion in juvenile cases?
A) age of the offender
B) race of the offender
C) seriousness of the offense
D) socioeconomic class of the offender

Answer: C

9) Which study strongly supports that police are inclined to arrest minority youths in higher numbers than nonminority youths?
A) Kansas City Study
B) Rochester Study
C) Berkeley Study
D) Philadelphia Cohort Study

Answer: D

10) What do patrol and probation officers generally agree about when dealing with upper and middle-class juveniles?
A) There is more concern about saving upper-and middle-class offenders, than the lower class.
B) They frequently commit more drug related crimes.
C) They are always polite compared to lower-class offenders.
D) They rarely commit serious offenses.

Answer: A

11) What percentage of juvenile offenders were handled informally by police departments in 1997?
A) 15 percent
B) 25 percent
C) 35 percent
D) 45 percent

Answer: B

12) What percentage of juvenile offenders were diverted to diversion agencies in 1997?
A) 1 percent
B) 5 percent

C) 9 percent
D) 13 percent

Answer: A

13)In 2000 the majority of delinquency cases handled by the juvenile court were ___________.
A) public order cases.
B) assault cases.
C) property cases.
D) drug cases.

Answer: C

14) Which legal precedent case applied the prohibition of illegal search and seizure cases to juveniles?
A) *Veronia School District 47J v. Acton*
B) *State v. Lowry*
C) *Miranda v. Arizona*
D) *Brown v. Mississippi*

Answer: B

15) Which legal precedent case is an example of police using excessive interrogation tactics directed toward juvenile offenders?
A) *Haley v. Ohio*
B) *New Jersey v. TLO*
C) *Miranda v. Arizona*
D) *Brown v. Mississippi*

Answer: A

16) Which Amendment of the Constitution affirms the standards of fairness and due process toward interrogations?
A) First
B) Fourth
C) Ninth
D) Fourteenth

Answer: D

17) What did the Gault decision fail to clarify in regard to juveniles and the Miranda decision?
A) if juveniles were entitled to counsel
B) if juveniles were entitled to remain silent
C) if juvenile could waive protection of the Miranda rules
D) whether juveniles could be interrogated by police

Answer: C

18) What is a main goal of community policing in regard to police operations?
A) It seeks to make police more proactive in crime prevention.
B) It attempts to centralize police operations.
C) It allows police to become more reactive in emergency situations.

D) Police are encouraged to have trained administrators make decisions about community issues.

Answer: A

19) What happened to juvenile arrests for curfew violations between 1993 and 1996?
A) They decreased by 50 percent.
B) Police barely had time to enforce them.
C) They increased dramatically.
D) More youths were violating curfew laws.

Answer: C

20) According to Bartollas, what age group typically commits the most hate crimes due to them being a primary audience of a culture of hate?
A) twenty to twenty-five year olds
B) twenty years of age and under
C) twenty-five to thirty year olds
D) persons over thirty

Answer: B

21) Which type of offenders is the main concentration of the SHODI community-based program?
A) major property offenders
B) school crime offenders
C) public order offenders
D) chronic drug offenders

Answer: D

22) According to a 2000 Department of Justice report, what do juveniles age 12 and older use in 3 out of four homicides?
A) blunt objects
B) fists
C) knives
D) firearms

Answer: D

23) What was the main reason for the establishment of the Officer Friendly and the McGruff programs in schools?
A) improve police-juvenile relations
B) reduce drug use
C) teach law related education
D) reduce gang membership

Answer: A

24) Which program was designed to teach children skills to resist peer pressure in using tobacco, alcohol, and drugs?
A) LRE
B) GREAT

C) DARE
D) S.H.O.D.I.

Answer: C

25) Which of the following police intervention strategies are typically considered as permanently assigned specialists to deal with gang problems?
A) youth service bureaus
B) juvenile specialist
C) gang detail
D) gang unit

Answer: D

26) The vignette at the beginning of the chapter is about ___________.
A) drug smuggling in Miami
B) the Latin Kings in New York
C) 18 young African-Americans being shot
D) police corruption and juveniles
E) police abuse of juveniles

Answer: C

27) The Supreme Court applied the ban against unreasonable search and seizure to juveniles in _____________
A) *Mapp v. Ohio*
B) *State v. Lowry*
C) *Gideon v. Wainwright*
D) *Miranda v. Arizona*
E) *Haley v. Ohio*

Answer: B

28) The national program to find missing children is called _________.
A) D.A.R.E.
B) N.G.C.R.C.
C) G.R.A.C.E.
D) The Center for Missing Children
E) AMBER Alert

Answer: E

29) The D.A.R.E. program is designed to _________________.
a. reduce the use of drugs
b. reduce the participation in gangs
c. reduce the amount of guns in our society
d. help find missing children
e. none of the above

Answer: A

30) Which case gave adults the right to remain silent, the right to have an attorney present during questioning, and the right to be assigned an attorney?
A) *Mapp v. Ohio*
B) *Miranda v. Arizona*
C) *Gideon v. Wainwright*
D) *In re Gault*
E) *Haley v. Ohio*

Answer: B

True/False Questions

1) Early police were often drawn from the best educated segments of society, and were fairly well paid for the times.

Answer: FALSE

2) Chicago began one of the first juvenile prevention programs in 1914 to help juveniles develop relationships with local police.

Answer: FALSE

3) The basic responsibility of early juvenile officers was to be helpful, rather than punitive.

Answer: TRUE

4) The main duty of police in schools in the 1990s was to provide security and safety, rather than focusing on preventative educational programs.

Answer: TRUE

5) Several studies have revealed that juveniles, who have had contacts with police, react more negatively toward police than juveniles who have not had any police contact.

Answer: TRUE

6) Most juveniles have a negative attitude toward police.

Answer: FALSE

7) Citizen complaints have little impact as a discretionary factor in the disposition of a juvenile incident.

Answer: FALSE

8) There is evidence of the erosion of police chivalry, yet girls are still less likely to be referred to the juvenile court for criminal offenses by police.

Answer: TRUE

9) The older the juvenile, the more likely they will be referred to juvenile court.

Answer: TRUE

10) External pressures from the public and press will negatively affect the discretionary decisions made by police in juvenile matters.

Answer: TRUE

11) Police are not commonly required to contact a juvenile's parents when giving an official reprimand.

Answer: FALSE

12) In 2000, more than four-fifths of the delinquency cases handled by the juvenile courts were referred by law enforcement officers.

Answer: TRUE

13) A juvenile committing a minor violation is more likely to represent the greatest danger to a police officer making an arrest.

Answer: FALSE

14) Most jurisdictions require a parent, legal guardian, or counsel to be present during a police interrogation.

Answer: TRUE

15) The Juvenile Justice and Delinquency Prevention Act of 1974 eliminated the judicial requirement for taking the fingerprints of arrested juveniles.

Answer: FALSE

16)In 1992, seventy-eight percent of the largest police departments in the nation reported practicing community-policing programs.

Answer: TRUE

17) Juvenile drug abuse arrest rates dropped by almost 50 percent between 1992 and 1996.

Answer: FALSE

18) During the Kansas City Gun Experiment, special gun-intercept teams proved to be ten times more effective than regular police patrols.

Answer: TRUE

19) Students of LRE programs were less likely to use violence as a way of resolving conflict and less likely to associate with delinquent peers.

Answer: TRUE

20) DARE programs have been very successful in reducing drug abuse among juveniles in the long-term evaluations.

Answer: FALSE

Short Answer Questions

1)In the seventeenth and eighteenth centuries, American colonists used __________ methods of control, such as the mutual pledge and the watch-and-ward system.

Answer: informal

2) The role of the __________ __________ developed after WWII and was formalized in 1955 and 1957.

Answer: juvenile officer

3) Police __________ can be defined as the choice between two or more possible means of handling a situation.

Answer: discretion

4) The police officer can issue a __________ and refer the youth to the juvenile court.

Answer: citation

5)In the __________ case, the Supreme Court applied the Fourth Amendment ban against unreasonable searches and seizures to juveniles.

Answer: *State v. Lowry*

6) The Supreme Court decision in *Haley v. Ohio* is an early example to the excesses of __________ __________.

Answer: police interrogation

7) The most popular and controversial program aimed at chronic drug offenders initiated by the Office of Juvenile Justice and Delinquency Prevention is known as __________.

Answer: S.H.O.D.I.

8) The __________ __________ Gun Experiment is one of the most innovative efforts that communities have used to get guns out of the hands of juveniles.

Answer: Kansas City

9) Herman Goldstein defines __________ __________ as the "misuse of authority by police to provide personal gain for the officers or for others."

Answer: police corruption

10) __________ is a program designed to teach fundamental skills needed to become responsible citizens in a constitutional democracy.

Answer: LRE

11) The process of taking a person into custody for an alleged violation of the law is called __________.

Answer: arrest

12) A summons to appear in juvenile court is a __________.

Answer: citation

13) A pretrial identification procedure used with both juveniles and adults following arrest: __________.

Answer: fingerprinting

14) A specialized unit established by some police departments to address the problem of gangs is called a __________.

Answer: gang unit

15) A police officer who has received specialized training to work effectively with juveniles in known as a __________.

Answer: juvenile officer

16) The U.S. Supreme Court ruled that before any questioning can take place, suspects taken into custody must be informed they have the right to remain silent, anything they say may be used against them, and they have the right to legal counsel, is the famous 1966 case __________.

Answer: Miranda v. Arizona

17) A police officers ability to choose from among a number of alternative dispositions when handling a situation is known as __________.

Answer: police discretion

18) Procedures such as fingerprinting, photographing, and placing juveniles in lineups for the purpose of identification prior to formal court appearance is known as ________________.

Answer: pretrial identification practices

19) The constitution requires a warrant for the authorized gathering of evidence by the police. This safeguard protects individuals against unlawful ________________.

Answer: search and seizure

20) A disposition option available to a police officer whereby a juvenile is taken to the police station following a complaint, recorded, given an official reprimand, and then released to his or her parents or guardians is known as a(n) ________________.

Answer: station adjustment

Essay Questions

1) Describe the evolution of police-juvenile relations from the seventeenth century through modern day and include the type of prevention programs developed along with way.

2) Discuss the various factors that influence discretionary practices used by police in regard to their handling of juvenile matters.

3) Discuss how legal rights of juveniles have impact police-juvenile relations. Be sure to discuss the significance of the landmark juvenile justice cases.

4) Describe the various interventions used by police to prevent juvenile crime. Be sure to discuss how successful the various programs have or have not been.

5) Discuss recent school and gang related programs being used by police to prevent and control delinquency.

6) What are the nine factors that can influence police discretion?

7) A patrol officer or juvenile officer has at least five options when investigating a complaint against a juvenile or arriving at the scene of law-violating behavior. What are those five options?

8) How does community-oriented policing help in dealing with juveniles?

9) One of the most important challenges the police face today is finding missing children. What is the AMBER alert program? What does it stand for? How did it get started and how does it work?

Chapter 15 The Juvenile Court

Multiple Choice Questions

1) Where was the first juvenile court founded in 1899?
A) Ohio
B) New York
C) Massachusetts
D) Illinois

Answer: D

2) What did Platt suggest was reflected in juvenile justice from its inception?
A) class favoritism
B) prohibitionism
C) rational excuses
D) social progress

Answer: A

3) Which group's influence led to a series of Supreme Court decisions in the 1960s and 1970s?
A) prohibitionists
B) just deserts
C) constitutionalists
D) fundamentalists

Answer: C

4) What concern did the Kent v. United States (1966) case resolve in juvenile justice?
A) double jeopardy
B) self-incrimination
C) jury trials
D) transfer

Answer: D

5) Which right was affirmed for juveniles in the In re Gault case (1967)?
A) jury trials
B) due process
C) double jeopardy
D) transfer

Answer: B

6) Which juvenile justice evidentiary standard was changed due to the Winship case (1970)?
A) direct evidence
B) beyond a shadow of doubt
C) preponderance of evidence
D) circumstantial evidence

Answer: C

7) Which right was denied to juveniles as indicted in the McKeiver v. Pennsylvania (1971) case?
A) jury trials
B) due process
C) double jeopardy
D) transfer

Answer: A

8) Which juvenile protection was affirmed through the Breed v. Jones (1975) case?
A) jury trials
B) due process
C) double jeopardy
D) transfer

Answer: C

9) What type of justice did David Matza refer to as an abuse of power in juvenile court?
A) Kadi
B) informal
C) traditional
D) Gestapo

Answer: A

10) According to Bartollas, which of the following are employed by the court to assist in juvenile cases and are known as the arm of the court?
A) police
B) referees
C) bailiffs
D) clerks

Answer: B

11) What did Barry C. Feld find in his study of the juvenile justice system?
A) Most juvenile offenders are innocent.
B) Nearly half of juvenile offenders were not represented by attorneys.
C) Private attorneys provide better representation than public defenders.
D) Most children placed outside the home were adequately represented.

Answer: B

12) What is the typical time period for a decision to detain a juvenile?
A) eight to twelve hours
B) twenty-four to thirty-six hours
C) forty-eight to seventy-two hours
D) seventy-two to ninety-six hours

Answer: C

13) Which case held that preventative detention of juveniles was constitutional?
A) Kent v. United States
B) Winship case
C) McKeiver v. Pennsylvania
D) Schall v. Martin

Answer: D

14) Which of the following is a typical method used by legislative waivers in juvenile cases?
A) Statues that state that anyone committing a specific crime may be tried as an adult.
B) The decision to transfer is made after a judicial hearing.
C) The child's amenability to treatment will decide the transfer.
D) The child's maturity level coupled with age.

Answer: A

15) What did the Maricopa County Juvenile Court study suggest was the most important factor influencing the waiver decision?
A) race of the offender
B) previous waiver
C) gender of the offender
D) age of the offender
Answer: B

16) What advantage does a bifurcated hearing give a probation officer?
A) time to collect incriminating evidence of guilt
B) reduces the time they spend in court
C) time to prepare a social history investigation
D) opportunity to convince the family treatment is essential to rehabilitation

Answer: C

17) What percentage of adjudicated youth were court ordered to out-of-home placements in 1999?
A) 24 percent
B) 35 percent
C) 45 percent
D) 55 percent
Answer: A

18) Which constitutional right do juveniles not have?
A) right to appeal
B) right to counsel
C) right to due process
D) Miranda rights

Answer: A

19) What traditional form of sentencing is being replaced by determinate sentencing in some juvenile jurisdictions?
A) blended sentences
B) indeterminate sentences
C) retributive sentences
D) restitution sentences

Answer: B

20) What type of reform was the Juvenile Justice Standards Project directed at?
A) prosecutorial
B) treatment methods
C) sentencing
D) institutional

Answer: C

21) Which state was the first to adopt the new standards established through the Juvenile Justice Standards Project?
A) Ohio
B) New York
C) Massachusetts
D) Illinois

Answer: B

22) Approximately how many juveniles has the United States put to death since the seventeenth century?
A) 150
B) 250
C) 366
D) 450

Answer: C

23) What crime was the first juvenile executed for in the United States?
A) horse theft
B) murder
C) drunkenness
D) sodomy of animals

Answer: D

24) Which state has executed the most juveniles in the United States?
A) Ohio
B) Georgia
C) North Carolina
D) Texas

Answer: B

25) According to your text, what do opponents against the use of the death penalty for juveniles contend?
A) It conflicts with the state's duty of parens patriae.

B) It is inhumane to kill children.
C) It is socially too costly.
D) It actually encourages crime rather than deterring it.

Answer: A

26) The vignette at the beginning of the chapter involved ___________.
A) a crime committed against a police officer
B) O. J. Simpson
C) President George Bush Sr.
D) the issue of capital punishment
E) the death of Michael Jordan's father

Answer: D

27. In the *Roper v. Simmons* case, Christopher Simmons committed the crime of __________.
A) murder
B) rape
C) selling drugs to juveniles
D) arson
E) all of the above

Answer: A

28) The juvenile court trial is not called a trial but a ___________.
A) disposition
B) fact finding
C) counseling session
D) mediation
E) juvenile trial

Answer: B

29) When a juvenile court judge imposes both an adult and a juvenile sentence concurrently it is called ___________.
A) unconstitutional
B) excessive
C) a blended sentence
D) an extended sentence
E) a follow-up sentence

Answer: C

30) Justice Abe Fortas said "There is evidence, in fact, that there may be grounds for concern that the child receives the worst of both worlds; that he gets neither the protection accorded to adults not the solicitous care and regenerative treatment postulated for children." In which case?
A) *In re Gault*
B) *Kent v. United States*
C) *In re Winship*
D) *McKeiver V. Pensylavania*
E) *Breed v. Jones*

Answer: B

True/False Questions

1) The child-savers were prohibitionists who believed that social progress depended on efficient law enforcement.

Answer: TRUE

2) Child-saving became an avocation for lower-class women to do outside the home.

Answer: FALSE

3) Juvenile courts throughout the nation were patterned after the first juvenile court of New York.

Answer: FALSE

4) The juvenile court was founded on the premise that it should function as a social clinic designed to serve the best interests of children in trouble.

Answer: TRUE

5)In the Kent v. United States case, the Court decided that withholding Kent's record essentially meant a denial of counsel.

Answer: TRUE

6) The In re Gault case meant that no longer could due process and procedural safeguards be kept out of the adjudication proceedings.

Answer: TRUE

7) The In re Winship case established preponderance of evidence as a new evidentiary standard.

Answer: FALSE

8) The McKeiver v. Pennsylvania case provided double jeopardy protection for juveniles.

Answer: FALSE

9) The Court ruled that juveniles do not have the right to jury trials because not all rights are constitutionally assured for juveniles.

Answer: TRUE

10) The Breed v. Jones case insured a juveniles right to bail.

Answer: FALSE

11) Juvenile court referees are required to be members of the bar.

Answer: FALSE

12) Public defenders frequently do a better job of representing youth than do private and court-appointed attorneys.

Answer: TRUE

13) Juveniles who secure counsel are less likely to receive istitutional time than those without counsel.

Answer: FALSE

14) A judicial waiver is the most common method used to transfer juvenile cases to adult court.

Answer: TRUE

15) According to Bartollas, juveniles who are waived to adult court are the most serious offenders and intractable.

Answer: FALSE

16) Juveniles who are transferred to adult court frequently receive longer prison sentences than their adult counterparts.

Answer: TRUE

17) According to Bartollas, jury trials for juvenile cases are actually quite common.

Answer: FALSE

18) The main thrust of the Juvenile Justice Standards Project was to end juvenile sentence disparity.

Answer: TRUE

19) Blended sentences allow criminal and juvenile courts to impose either juvenile and/or adult sentences.

Answer: TRUE

20) All thirty-eight states allow capital punishment for those under the age of eighteen when they committed the crime.

Answer: FALSE

Short Answer Questions

1) The pressure for social change took place in the midst of a wave of optimism during the __________ period from 1890 to 1920.

Answer: progressive

2) The __________ decision was the first case in which the U.S. Supreme Court dealt with a juvenile court case concerning the matter of transfer.

Answer: Kent

3) __________ __________ means that the intake officer requires restitution from the youth, warns him or her, and then dismisses or diverts the youth to a social agency.

Answer: Informal adjustment

4) The casual supervision of a youth by a probation officer who reserves judgment on the need for filing a petition until the intake officer sees how the youth fares is known as __________ __________.

Answer: informal probation

5) A __________ __________ is a formal agreement between the child and the court in which the child is placed under the court's supervision without a formal finding of delinquency.

Answer: consent decree

6) Transfer of juvenile cases to adult court due to exclusion of certain offenses from juvenile court is referred to as _______ waiver.

Answer: legislative

7) The term "adjudication" refers to the ________ __________ stage of a juvenile proceedings.

Answer: fact finding

8) Ten states provide for __________ __________ for juveniles, but they are seldom demanded.

Answer: jury trials

9) A bifurcated hearing is a split between the adjudicatory and __________ hearings.

Answer: dispositional

10) The Court upheld the constitutionality of the death penalty for juveniles in the case of Stanford v. __________.

Answer: Kentucky

11) The court process wherein a judge determines if the juvenile appearing before the court committed the act with which he or she is charged is known as __________________.

Answer: adjudication

12) A criminal court, also called a(n) __________________ that hears adult or juvenile cases. Juveniles may be waived (transferred) to this court system if they are accused of committing a serious offense.

Answer: adult court

13) The review of a juvenile court proceedings by a higher court is known as a(n) __________________.

Answer: appeal

14) The review of the decision of a juvenile court proceeding by a higher court is referred to as a(n) __________________.

Answer: appellate review

15) An innovative form of detention facility, found in several locations across the nation, that is characterized by an open setting is a(n) __________________.

Answer: attention home

16) The money or property pledged to the court or actually deposited with the court to effect the release of a person from legal custody is referred to as __________________.

Answer: bail

17) A legal standard of __________________ establishes the degree of proof needed for a juvenile to be adjudicated a delinquent by the juvenile court during the adjudicatory stage of the court's proceedings.

Answer: beyond a reasonable doubt

18) Split adjudication and disposition hearings, also known as __________________, are the present trend of juvenile courts.

Answer: bifurcated hearings

19) The process of transferring (certifying) juveniles to adult criminal court is referred to as __________________.

Answer: binding over

20) A 1975 double jeopardy case, __________________ in which the U.S. Supreme Court ruled that a juvenile court cannot adjudicate a case and then transfer it over to the criminal court for adult processing of the same offense.

Answer: Breed v. Jones

Essay Questions

1) Discuss the various contexts that led to the origination of the juvenile court in America.

2) Describe how the juvenile court has been changed by the landmark precedent cases of the 1960s and 1970s.

3) Describe the roles of the various actors within the juvenile court and discuss the various criticisms that some have made of their performances.

4) Describe the various juvenile pretrial procedures used in the juvenile justice process. Be sure to include the transfer of juvenile cases to adult court.

5) Describe the stages of a juvenile trial and discuss the judicial alternatives available to certain juvenile jurisdictions.

6) Today , three different positions have emerged concerning the role of the juvenile court. What are those three different positions? Explain each.

7) What was the case of *Kent v. United States* about and how was it decided?

8) What was the rights granted to juveniles in the case of *In re Gault*?

9) Explain, in detail, the famous case of *In re Gault.*

10) What are the 8 role responsibilities of the juvenile court judge?

11) What are the three roles of a defense counsel in a juvenile court?

12) The intake unit, especially in larger urban courts, may have up to five options for the disposal of cases. List and explain those five options.

13) What are the five methods to accomplish a legislative waiver?

Chapter 16 Juvenile Corrections

Multiple Choice Questions

1) The first community-based corrections for juveniles grew out of juvenile
A) detention.
B) probation.
C) aftercare.
D) diversion.

Answer: C

2) Where did Zebulon Brockway first initiate parole in the late 1870s?
A) Ohio
B) Illinois
C) Massachusetts
D) New York

Answer: D

3) John Augustus is often called the "father of ____________."
A) probation.
B) aftercare.
C) child-savers.
D) law enforcement.

Answer: A

4) What type of activity did the students of the Highfield Projects perform during the day?
A) school
B) recreational
C) work
D) spiritual

Answer: C

5) Which operation of juvenile probation occurs first in the juvenile justice process?
A) investigation
B) surveillance
C) supervision
D) intake

Answer: D

6) Which operation of juvenile probation would likely review a youth's arrest records and psychological evaluations for the purpose of preparing a social history report?
A) investigation
B) surveillance
C) supervision

D) intake

Answer: A

7) Which operation of juvenile probation makes certain that probationers comply with the conditions of probation and try to ensure that they do not break the law?
A) investigation
B) surveillance
C) supervision
D) intake

Answer: B

8) What did the Office of Juvenile and Delinquency Prevention spend more than $30 million promoting the use of in nearly 85 courts throughout the nation?
A) reduction in drug abuse
B) mandatory sentences
C) restitution
D) gang violence

Answer: C

9) Which of the following supervision models integrates components of strain, control, and social learning theory into its prevention strategy?
A) ISC
B) ISP
C) AMA
D) EFI

Answer: A

10) Which of the following is generally used in conjunction with house arrest?
A) weekend jail sentences
B) electronic monitoring
C) implantation of microchips
D) conjugal visits

Answer: B

11) What is the main criticism of using volunteer juvenile workers by parents?
A) invasion of privacy
B) violations of confidence
C) their ages
D) lack of training

Answer: D

12) The House of Umoja and the Achievement Place are examples of what type of juvenile facility?
A) detention lockup
B) foster home

C) teaching-family group home
D) intensive high security home

Answer: C

13) The House of Umoja deals almost exclusively with what type of delinquent offender?
A) abuse cases
B) neglect cases
C) adopted children
D) gang cases

Answer: D

14) What is the average length of stay for a juvenile in a diagnostic or reception center?
A) 14 days
B) 34 days
C) 64 days
D) 94 days

Answer: B

15) According to Bartollas, what generally happens to the diagnostic report when juveniles are transferred to the receiving institution from the diagnostics center?
A) The court places it in record.
B) It is given to various social agencies.
C) It is commonly ignored.
D) Workers use the reports for orientation purposes.

Answer: B

16)In which states are the majority of forestry camps located in the United States?
A) Florida and New York
B) South and North Carolina
C) California and Alabama
D) Maryland and Oregon

Answer: A

17) According to Bartollas, what is the main intent of boot camps?
A) shock juveniles from committing more crime
B) break juveniles afflicted with authority issues
C) provide token reinforcement
D) encourage children to join the military services

Answer: A

18) Which type of offenders are typically excluded from boot camps?
A) drug offenders
B) shoplifters
C) minor offenders

D) sex offenders

Answer: D

19) What did a 14 year-old girl die from in 1999 after being confined to a South Dakota boot camp?
A) exhaustion
B) murder
C) dehydration
D) drowning

Answer: C

20) What is the most expensive way for a state to treat delinquent behavior?
A) training schools
B) boot camps
C) forestry camps
D) community services

Answer: A

21) What did Bartollas's fifteen year follow-up study conclude about institutionalized juveniles?
A) Staff were less disillusioned.
B) The strong victimize the weak.
C) Drug abuse is the cause of most delinquency problems.
D) There is a positive youth culture developing in institutions.

Answer: B

22) Which of the following is used to secure juvenile treatment in another state when a youth has no acceptable placement within his or her own state?
A) warrant
B) extradition
C) interstate compact
D) petition

Answer: C

23) According to Bartollas, what is part of the problem with failed aftercare programs?
A) lack of trained personnel
B) youthful offenders are sent back to the same unchanged environment
C) the time is too short for a person to adequately change
D) the emphasis is on long-term behaviors

Answer: B

24) Which of the following programs is considered as an intensive aftercare treatment program?
A) Project New Pride
B) STAY
C) Lifeskills 95
D) VisionQuest

Answer: C

25) What does Bartollas suggest is the international philosophy of juvenile institutions in most other nations?
A) lowering of crime rates
B) parental accountability
C) rehabilitation
D) confinement

Answer: C

26) The vignette at the beginning of the chapter involved ________.
A) Governor Rell from Connecticut
B) Former President Bill Clinton
C) Governor Velsack from Iowa
D) Senator Baruch Obama
E) Senator George Allen from Virginia

Answer: A

27) A device which uses a transmitter attached to the probationer that emits a continuous radio signal is called a ________.
A) continuous signaling device
B) programmed contact device
C) global position system
D) 24/7 security device
E) supermax security

Answer: A

28) A device which calls the juvenile probationer by phone at scheduled or random times and uses various technologies to determine the identity of the person is called ________.
A) continuous signaling device
B) the phone security device
C) global position system
D) 24/7 security device
E) programmed contact device

Answer: E

29) A device in which the juvenile probationer wears a transmitter that communicates signals to a satellite and back to a computer monitor, pinpointing the offender's whereabouts is called a ________.
A) continuous signaling device
B) programmed contact device
C) global position system
D) 24/7 security device
E) supermax security

Answer: C

30. The Federal Courts have mandated two major rights for juveniles in institutions, the right to ________ and ________.
A) private rooms and clean water
B) a good education and private rooms
C) treatment and to be free from cruel and unusual punishment
D) appeal and good food

E) all of the above

Answer: C

True/False Questions

1) Early juvenile aftercare programs that spread throughout the United States in the early decade of the twentieth century took on many of the features of adult parole.

Answer: TRUE

2)A probation officer commonly has thirty to sixty days to write social history reports.

Answer: TRUE

3)A juvenile will generally remain on probation until he or she reaches the age to twenty-one in most states.

Answer: FALSE

4) According to Bartollas, a probation officer must file a notice of violation with a judge in order to revoke a youth's probation sentence.

Answer: TRUE

5) The current emphasis on juvenile probation is on risk control and crime reduction.

Answer: TRUE

6) Intensive supervision programs are used more for juvenile offenders and rarely used in adult corrections since they are largely perceived as ineffective with high-risk offenders.

Answer: FALSE

7) Probationers sentenced to house arrest are never allowed to leave their homes for any reason unless escorted by law enforcement officers.

Answer: FALSE

8) Programmed contact electronic monitoring devices constantly monitor an offender's presence at a particular location.

Answer: FALSE

9) Volunteer program workers for juveniles are frequently criticized for creating more work for a service agency and causing harm to their clients.

Answer: TRUE

10) Day treatment programs are more economical than residential programs because they do not provide living and sleeping quarters for offenders.

Answer: TRUE

11) Generally, physical and dental exams are given to youths during they stay at a reception center before they enter a placement institution.

Answer: TRUE

12) Forestry camps and ranches are commonly considered as medium-security facilities for juveniles.

Answer: FALSE

13) Youths commonly runaway from forestry camps and ranch settings in hopes of being relocated to an institution.

Answer: TRUE

14) Boot camps are commonly reserved for first-time minimum-security offenders.

Answer: FALSE

15) The recidivism rates of boot camps tend to be slightly greater than those of traditional juvenile facilities.

Answer: TRUE

16) The costs of operating public juvenile facilities increased dramatically over the operating costs of private juvenile facilities.

Answer: FALSE

17) Juveniles tend to respond very favorably toward religious services in juvenile institutions.

Answer: FALSE

18) The amount of time juvenile residents spend in solitary confinement is generally greater today than is was a decade ago.

Answer: FALSE

19) The use of force and mechanical restraints in training schools has recently declined due to the filing of civil law suits.

Answer: FALSE

20) Most studies agree that there is relatively few differences between juveniles sent to private and public placement.

Answer: TRUE

Short Answer Questions

1) Juvenile __________ was influenced by the development of adult parole in the late 1870s.

Answer: aftercare

2) __________, as an alternative to institutional placements, arose from the efforts of John Augustus.

Answer: Probation

3) __________ programs had their origins in the Highfield Projects of New Jersey.

Answer: Residential

4) The investigation operation of juvenile probation requires a probation officer to prepare a __________ __________ report on a youth ruled delinquent.

Answer: social history report

5) __________ __________ equipment receives information about offenders and transmits to a computer at a particular law enforcement agency.

Answer: Electronic monitoring

6) Juveniles attend programs in the morning and afternoon, and then return home in the evening in most __________ __________ programs.

Answer: day treatment

7) The House of __________ in Philadelphia is recognized as one of the most impressive group homes in the nation.

Answer: Umoja

8) Residents of __________ __________ typically do conservation work in state parks including the cutting of weeds and doing general maintenance.

Answer: forestry camps

9) __________ __________ emphasize military discipline and regimented activity geared toward youthful offenders.

Answer: Boot camps

10) In October of 2000, Indiana stopped sending juveniles convicted of __________ crimes into the general prison population.

Answer: adult

11) A military-style facility used as an alternative to prison in order to deal with prison crowding and public demands for severe punishment is called a ________________.

Answer: boot camp

12) A correction program that links community programs with the social environment which includes probation, residential and day treatment programs, or parole is called ________________.

Answer: community-based corrections

13) Court-required restitution in which a juvenile spends a certain number of hours working in a community project is called a ________________.

Answer: community service project

14) An individual who donates his or her time to work with delinquents in the community is a ________________.

Answer: community volunteer

15) A guarantee provided by the Eighth Amendment to the U.S. Constitution against inhumane punishments is the right against is referred to as ________________.

Answer: cruel and unusual punishment

16) Court-mandated, community-based corrections program that juveniles attend in the morning and afternoon, then return home in the evening are the ________________.

Answer: day treatment programs

17) Correctional facilities, or ________________, where residents usually do conservation work in state parks, including cleaning up, cutting grass and weeds, and general maintenance.

Answer: forestry camps

18) A home setting for juveniles who are lawfully removed form their birth parents' home is called

________________.

Answer: foster care

19) A placement for youth who have been adjudicated by the court-called a *group residence, halfway house, or attention home*- that serves a group of about thirteen to twenty-five youths as an alternative to institutionalization: ________________.

Answer: group home

20) A form of community-based residential program that had some success with youthful offenders is a ________________.

Answer: group home model

Essay Questions

1) Describe the evolution of community-based corrections in the United States. Be sure to include the names and contributions made by the pioneers of probation and parole.

2) Describe the various operations of probation and what each operation requires of probation officers to perform as part of their duties.

3) Describe the various types of juvenile institutions and discuss the goals associated with each type.

4) Discuss the differences between residential and day treatment programs. Be sure to include any administrative and operational issues associated with each.

5) List all the people a probation might interview in a social history investigation of a adjudicated juvenile.

6) List ten common probation rules as presented in your text. (The text listed twenty).

7) To make the decision of whether to revoke probation, modify the conditions of probation, or place a juvenile outside the home, what questions should a probation officer consider?

8) List and explain each of the three broad types of restitution.

9) When it comes to making restitution and community service work, probation officers are key players, and in many jurisdictions it is up to a juvenile probation officer to do many things. What are those things as listed in your text.

10) How can community volunteers work effectively with juvenile offenders? What services can they provide?

11) What are some of the advantages of a nonresidential day treatment program?

NOTES

NOTES

NOTES

NOTES

NOTES

NOTES

NOTES

NOTES

NOTES

NOTES

NOTES

Interactive Student Edition

Reveal ALGEBRA 2™

Volume 1

Mc Graw Hill Education

www.my.mheducation.com

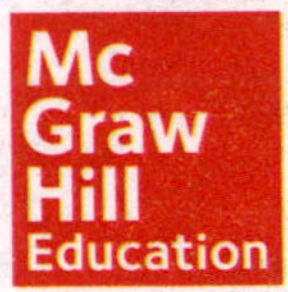

Cover: (t to b, l to r) Kelley Miller/National Geographic/Getty Images; Westend61/Getty Images; skodonnell/E+/Getty Images;

Daniel Viñé Garcia/Moment/Getty Images; Aksonov/E+/Getty Images

Send all inquiries to:
McGraw-Hill Education
8787 Orion Place
Columbus, OH 43240

ISBN: 978-0-07-662600-7 (*Interactive Student Edition*, Volume 1)
MHID: 0-07-662600-8 (*Interactive Student Edition*, Volume 1)
ISBN: 978-0-07-899754-9 (*Interactive Student Edition*, Volume 2)
MHID: 0-07-899754-2 (*Interactive Student Edition*, Volume 2)

Printed in the United States of America.

1 2 3 4 5 6 7 8 9 10 QVS 26 25 24 23 22 21 20 19 18

Contents in Brief

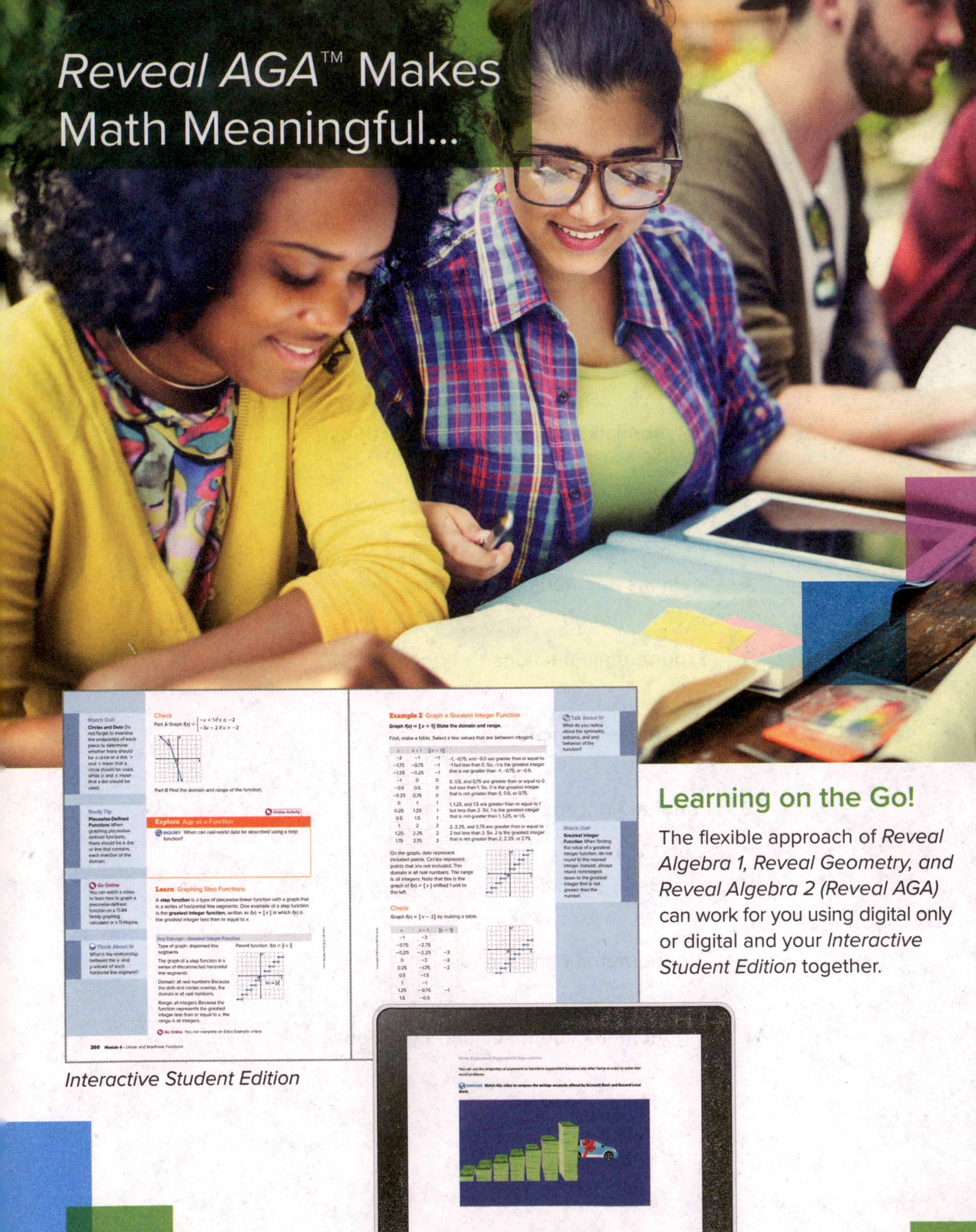
Reveal AGA™ Makes Math Meaningful...
Learning on the Go!
The flexible approach of Reveal Algebra 1, Reveal Geometry, and Reveal Algebra 2 (Reveal AGA) can work for you using digital only or digital and your Interactive Student Edition together.

Interactive Student Edition

Student Digital Center

...to Reveal YOUR Full Potential!

Reveal AGA™ Brings Math to Life in Every Lesson

Reveal AGA is a blended print and digital program that supports access on the go. You'll find the *Interactive Student Edition* mirrors the Student Digital Center, so you can record your digital observations in class and reference your notes later, or access just the digital center, or a combination of both! The Student Digital Center provides access to the interactive lessons, interactive content, animations, videos and technology-enhanced practice questions.

Write down your username and password here

Username: ______________________

Password: ______________________

Go Online! my.mheducation.com

WebSketchpad® Powered by The Geometer's Sketchpad®- Dynamic, exploratory, visual activities embedded at point of use within the lesson.

Animations and Videos – Learn by seeing mathematics in action.

Interactive Tools – Get involved in the content by dragging and dropping, selecting, highlighting, and completing tables.

Personal Tutors – See and hear a teacher explain how to solve problems.

eTools – Math tools are available to help you solve problems and develop concepts.

TABLE OF CONTENTS

Module 1

Relations and Functions

Module 2

Linear Equations, Inequalities, and Systems

TABLE OF CONTENTS

Module 3

Quadratic Functions

Module 4

Polynomials and Polynomial Functions

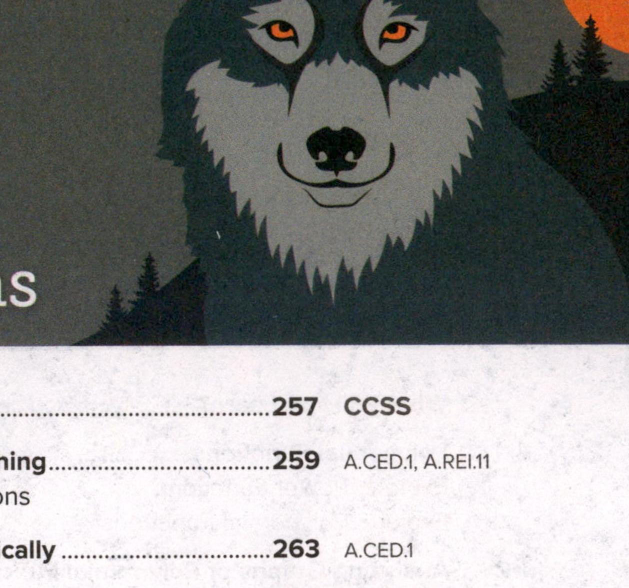

Module 5

Polynomial Equations

Module 6

Inverses and Radical Functions

TABLE OF CONTENTS

Module 7

Exponential Functions

Module 8

Logarithmic Functions

Module 9

Rational Functions

Module 10

Inferential Statistics

Module 11

Trigonometric Functions

Module 12

Trigonometric Identities and Equations

Common Core State Standards for Mathematics, Algebra 2

Number and Quantity

The Complex Number System N-CN

N.CN.1 Perform arithmetic operations with complex numbers.
Know there is a complex number i such that $i^2 = -1$, and every complex number has the form $a + bi$ with a and b real.

N.CN.2 Use the relation $i^2 = -1$ and the commutative, associative, and distributive properties to add, subtract, and multiply complex numbers.

N.CN.7 Use complex numbers in polynomial identities and equations.

Solve quadratic equations with real coefficients that have complex solutions.

N.CN.8 (+) Extend polynomial identities to the complex numbers.

N.CN.9 (+) Know the Fundamental Theorem of Algebra; show that it is true for quadratic polynomials.

Algebra

Seeing Structure in Expressions A-SSE

A.SSE.1 Interpret the structure of expressions.
Interpret expressions that represent a quantity in terms of its context. ★

a. Interpret parts of an expression, such as terms, factors, and coefficients.

b. Interpret complicated expressions by viewing one or more of their parts as a single entity.

A.SSE.2 Use the structure of an expression to identify ways to rewrite it.

A.SSE.4 Write expressions in equivalent forms to solve problems.
Derive the formula for the sum of a finite geometric series (when the common ratio is not 1), and use the formula to solve problems. ★

Arithmetic with Polynomials and Rational Expressions A-APR

A.APR.1 Perform arithmetic operations on polynomials.
Understand that polynomials form a system analogous to the integers, namely, they are closed under the operations of addition, subtraction, and multiplication; add, subtract, and multiply polynomials.

A.APR.2 Understand the relationship between zeros and factors of polynomials.
Know and apply the Remainder Theorem: For a polynomial $p(x)$ and a number a, the remainder on division by $x - a$ is $p(a)$, so $p(a) = 0$ if and only if $(x - a)$ is a factor of $p(x)$.

A.APR.3 Identify zeros of polynomials when suitable factorizations are available, and use the zeros to construct a rough graph of the function defined by the polynomial.

A.APR.4 Use polynomial identities to solve problems.

Prove polynomial identities and use them to describe numerical relationships.

A.APR.5 (+) Know and apply the Binomial Theorem for the expansion of $(x + y)^n$ in powers of x and y for a positive integer n, where x and y are any numbers, with coefficients determined for example by Pascal's Triangle.

A.APR.6 Rewrite rational expressions.

Rewrite simple rational expressions in different forms; write $\frac{a(x)}{b(x)}$ in the form $q(x) + \frac{r(x)}{b(x)}$, where $a(x)$, $b(x)$, $q(x)$, and $r(x)$ are polynomials with the degree of $r(x)$ less than the degree of $b(x)$, using inspection, long division, or, for the more complicated examples, a computer algebra system.

A.APR.7 (+) Understand that rational expressions form a system analogous to the rational numbers, closed under addition, subtraction, multiplication, and division by a nonzero rational expression; add, subtract, multiply, and divide rational expressions.

Creating Equations ★ A-CED

A.CED.1 Create equations that describe numbers or relationships.
Create equations and inequalities in one variable and use them to solve problems.

A.CED.2 Create equations in two or more variables to represent relationships between quantities; graph equations on coordinate axes with labels and scales.

A.CED.3 Represent constraints by equations or inequalities, and by systems of equations and/or inequalities, and interpret solutions as viable or non-viable options in a modeling context.

A.CED.4 Rearrange formulas to highlight a quantity of interest, using the same reasoning as in solving equations.

★ Mathematical Modeling Standards

Common Core State Standards for Mathematics, Algebra 2

Reasoning with Equations and Inequalities A-REI

A.REI.2 Understand solving equations as a process of reasoning and explain the reasoning.
Solve simple rational and radical equations in one variable, and give examples showing how extraneous solutions may arise.

A.REI.11 Represent and solve equations and inequalities graphically.
Explain why the *x*-coordinates of the points where the graphs of the equations $y = f(x)$ and $y = g(x)$ intersect are the solutions of the equation $f(x) = g(x)$; find the solutions approximately, e.g., using technology to graph the functions, make tables of values, or find successive approximations. Include cases where $f(x)$ and/or $g(x)$ are linear, polynomial, rational, absolute value, exponential, and logarithmic functions. ★

Functions

Interpreting Functions F-IF

F.IF.4 Interpret functions that arise in applications in terms of the context.
For a function that models a relationship between two quantities, interpret key features of graphs and tables in terms of the quantities, and sketch graphs showing key features given a verbal description of the relationship. ★

F.IF.5 Relate the domain of a function to its graph and, where applicable, to the quantitative relationship it describes.

F.IF.6 Calculate and interpret the average rate of change of a function (presented symbolically or as a table) over a specified interval. Estimate the rate of change from a graph.

F.IF.7 Analyze functions using different representations.
Graph functions expressed symbolically and show key features of the graph, by hand in simple cases and using technology for more complicated cases. ★

b. Graph square root, cube root, and piecewise-defined functions, including step functions and absolute value functions.

c. Graph polynomial functions, identifying zeros when suitable factorizations are available, and showing end behavior.

e. Graph exponential and logarithmic functions, showing intercepts and end behavior, and trigonometric functions, showing period, midline, and amplitude.

F.IF.8 Write a function defined by an expression in different but equivalent forms to reveal and explain different properties of the function.

a. Use the process of factoring and completing the square in a quadratic function to show zeros, extreme values, and symmetry of the graph, and interpret these in terms of a context.

b. Use the properties of exponents to interpret expressions for exponential functions.

F.IF.9 Compare properties of two functions each represented in a different way (algebraically, graphically, numerically in tables, or by verbal descriptions).

Building Functions F-BF

F.BF.1 Build a function that models a relationship between two quantities.

b. Combine standard function types using arithmetic operations.

F.BF.3 Build new functions from existing functions.
Identify the effect on the graph of replacing $f(x)$ by $f(x) + k$, $k\,f(x)$, $f(kx)$, and $f(x + k)$ for specific values of k (both positive and negative); find the value of k given the graphs. Experiment with cases and illustrate an explanation of the effects on the graph using technology.

F.BF.4 Find inverse functions.
Solve an equation of the form $f(x) = c$ for a simple function f that has an inverse and write an expression for the inverse.

Linear, Quadratic, and Exponential Models F-LE

F.LE.4 Construct and compare linear and exponential models and solve problems.
For exponential models, express as a logarithm the solution to $ab^{ct} = d$ where a, c, and d are numbers and the base b is 2, 10, or e; evaluate the logarithm using technology.

Trigonometric Functions F-TF

F.TF.1 Extend the domain of trigonometric functions using the unit circle.
Understand radian measure of an angle as the length of the arc on the unit circle subtended by the angle.

★ **Mathematical Modeling Standards**

Common Core State Standards for Mathematics, Algebra 2

F.TF.2 Explain how the unit circle in the coordinate plane enables the extension of trigonometric functions to all real numbers, interpreted as radian measures of angles traversed counterclockwise around the unit circle.

F.TF.5 Model periodic phenomena with trigonometric functions.
Choose trigonometric functions to model periodic phenomena with specified amplitude, frequency, and midline. ★

F.TF.8 Prove and apply trigonometric identities.
Prove the Pythagorean identity $\sin^2(\theta) + \cos^2(\theta) = 1$ and use it to calculate trigonometric ratios.

Statistics and Probability

Interpreting Categorical and Quantitative Data S-ID

S.ID.4 Summarize, represent, and interpret data on a single count or measurement variable.
Use the mean and standard deviation of a data set to fit it to a normal distribution and to estimate population percentages. Recognize that there are data sets for which such a procedure is not appropriate. Use calculators, spreadsheets, and tables to estimate areas under the normal curve.

Making Inferences and Justifying Conclusions S-IC

S.IC.1 Understand and evaluate random processes underlying statistical experiments
Understand statistics as a process for making inferences about population parameters based on a random sample from that population.

S.IC.2 Decide if a specified model is consistent with results from a given data-generating process, e.g., using simulation.

S.IC.3 Make inferences and justify conclusions from sample surveys, experiments, and observational studies
Recognize the purposes of and differences among sample surveys, experiments, and observational studies; explain how randomization relates to each.

S.IC.4 Use data from a sample survey to estimate a population mean or proportion; develop a margin of error through the use of simulation models for random sampling.

S.IC.5 Use data from a randomized experiment to compare two treatments; use simulations to decide if differences between parameters are significant.

S.IC.6 Evaluate reports based on data.

Using Probability to Make Decisions S-MD

S.MD.6 (+) Use probabilities to make fair decisions (e.g., drawing by lots, using a random number generator).

S.MD.7 (+) Analyze decisions and strategies using probability concepts (e.g., product testing, medical testing, pulling a hockey goalie at the end of a game).

★ Mathematical Modeling Standards

Module 1

Relations and Functions

Essential Question

How can analyzing a function help you understand the situation it models?

F.IF.4; F.IF.5; F.IF.7b; F.IF.7c; F.IF.9; A.CED.3; F.BF.3
Mathematical Practices: MP1, MP2, MP3, MP4, MP5, MP6, MP7, MP8

What will you learn?

Place a checkmark (✓) in each row that corresponds with how much you already know about each topic **before** starting this module.

KEY
👎 — I don't know. 👉 — I've heard of it. 👍 — I know it!

	Before			After		
	👎	👉	👍	👎	👉	👍
identify one-to-one and onto functions						
identify discrete and continuous functions						
identify intercepts of graphs of functions						
identify linear and nonlinear functions						
identify extrema of graphs and functions						
identify end behavior of graphs of functions						
identify graphs that display line or point symmetry						
sketch and compare graphs of functions						
graph linear functions						
graph linear inequalities in two variables						
graph piecewise, step, and absolute value functions						
translate, dilate & reflect the graphs of functions						

Foldables Make this Foldable to help you organize your notes about relations and functions. Begin with four sheets of notebook paper.

1. **Fold** each sheet of paper in half from top to bottom.
2. **Cut** along the fold. Staple the eight half-sheets together to form a booklet.
3. **Cut** tabs into the margin. The top tab is 2 lines deep, the next tab is 6 lines deep, and so on.
4. **Label** each of the tabs with a lesson number, and the final tab *vocabulary*.

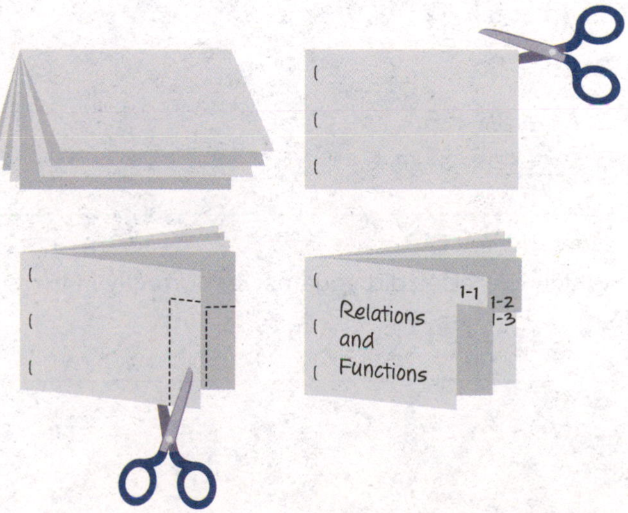

What Vocabulary Will You Learn?

Check the box next to each vocabulary term that you may already know.

- ☐ absolute value function
- ☐ algebraic notation
- ☐ boundary
- ☐ closed half-plane
- ☐ codomain
- ☐ constant function
- ☐ constraint
- ☐ continuous function
- ☐ dilation
- ☐ discontinuous function
- ☐ discrete function
- ☐ domain
- ☐ end behavior
- ☐ even functions
- ☐ extrema
- ☐ family of graphs
- ☐ greatest integer function
- ☐ identity function
- ☐ intercept
- ☐ interval notation
- ☐ line of reflection
- ☐ line of symmetry
- ☐ line symmetry
- ☐ linear equation
- ☐ linear function
- ☐ linear inequality
- ☐ maximum
- ☐ minimum
- ☐ nonlinear function
- ☐ odd functions
- ☐ one-to-one function
- ☐ onto function
- ☐ open half-plane
- ☐ parabola
- ☐ parent function
- ☐ piecewise-defined function
- ☐ point of symmetry
- ☐ point symmetry
- ☐ range
- ☐ reflection
- ☐ relative maximum
- ☐ relative minimum
- ☐ set-builder notation
- ☐ step function
- ☐ symmetry
- ☐ translation
- ☐ transformation
- ☐ *x*-intercept
- ☐ *y*-intercept

Are You Ready?

Complete the Quick Review to see if you are ready to start this module. Then complete the Quick Check.

Quick Review

Example 1

Evaluate $3a^2 - 2ab + b^2$ if $a = 4$ and $b = -3$.

$$\begin{aligned} 3a^2 - 2ab + b^2 &= 3(4^2) - 2(4)(-3) + (-3)^2 \\ &= 3(16) - 2(4)(-3) + 9 \\ &= 48 - (-24) + 9 \\ &= 48 + 24 + 9 \\ &= 81 \end{aligned}$$

Example 2

Solve $3x + 6y = 24$ for y.

$3x + 6y = 24$	Original equation
$3x + 6y - 3x = 24 - 3x$	Subtract $3x$ from each side.
$6y = 24 - 3x$	Simplify.
$\frac{6y}{6} = \frac{24}{6} - \frac{3x}{6}$	Divide each side by 6.
$y = 4 - \frac{1}{2}x$	Simplify.

Quick Check

Evaluate each expression if $a = -3$, $b = 4$, and $c = -2$.

1. $4a - 3$

2. $2b - 5c$

3. $b^2 - 3b + 6$

4. $\frac{2a + 4b}{c}$

Solve each equation for the given variable.

5. $a = 3b + 9$ for b

6. $15w - 10 = 5v$ for v

7. $3x - 4y = 8$ for x

8. $\frac{d}{6} + \frac{f}{3} = 4$ for d

How Did You Do?

Which exercises did you answer correctly in the Quick Check? Shade those exercise numbers below.

① ② ③ ④ ⑤ ⑥ ⑦ ⑧

Functions and Continuity

Explore Analyzing Functions Graphically

Online Activity Use graphing technology to complete the Explore.

INQUIRY How can you use a graph to analyze the relationship between the domain and range of a function?

Explore Defining and Analyzing Variables

Online Activity Use a real-world situation to complete the Explore.

INQUIRY How can you define variables to effectively model a situation?

Learn Functions

A function describes a relationship between input and output values. The **domain** is the set of x-values to be evaluated by a function. The **codomain** is the set of all the y-values that could possibly result from the evaluation of the function. The codomain of a function is assumed to be all real numbers unless otherwise stated. The **range** is the set of y-values that actually result from the evaluation of the function. The range is contained within the codomain.

If each element of a function's range is paired with exactly one element of the domain, then the function is a **one-to-one function**. If a function's codomain is the same as its range, then the function is an **onto function**.

Example 1 Domains, Codomains, and Ranges

Part A Identify the domain, range, and codomain of the graph.

Domain	Range	Codomain
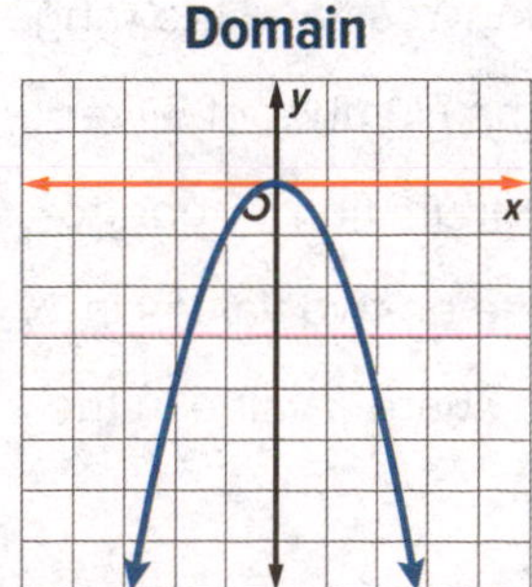	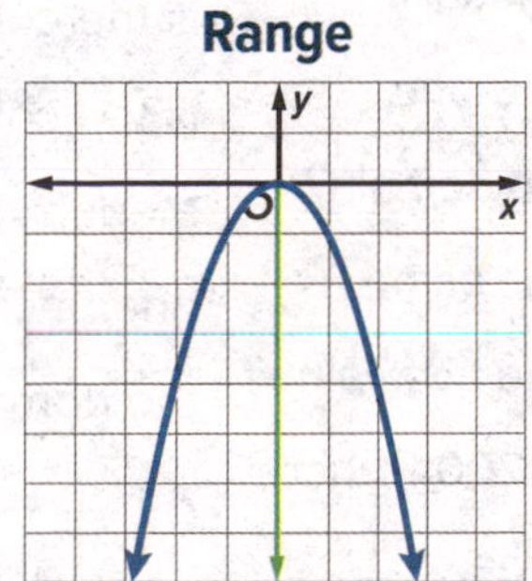	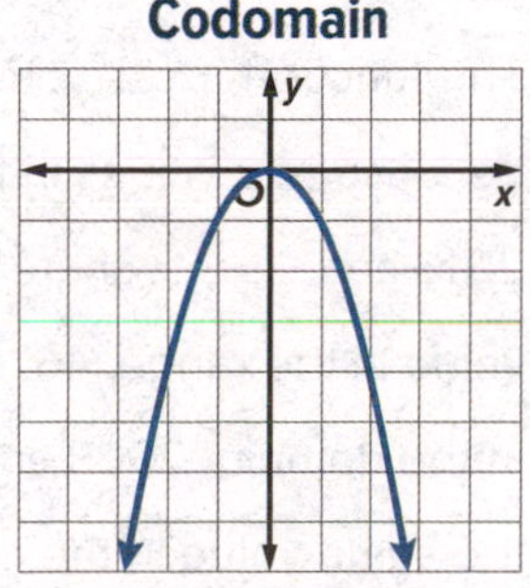
Because there are no restrictions on the x-values, the domain is ________________.	Because the maximum y-value is 0, the range is $y \leq$ ____.	Because it is not stated otherwise, the codomain is ________________.

(continued on the next page)

Today's Standards
F.IF.4; F.IF.5
MP1, MP7

Today's Vocabulary
domain
codomain
range
one-to-one function
onto function
continuous function
discontinuous function
discrete function
algebraic notation
set-builder notation
interval notation

Study Tip

Horizontal Line Test Performing the horizontal line test can help you examine a function. Place a pencil at the top of the graph and slowly move it down the graph to represent a horizontal line. If there are places where pencil intersects the graph at more than one point at a time, then it is not one-to-one. If there are places where the pencil does not intersect the graph at all, then it is not onto. Consider these two results to determine if the function is one-to-one, onto, both, or neither.

Your Notes

Part B Use these values to determine whether the function is onto.

The range is not the same as the codomain because it does not include the ________ real numbers. Therefore, the function ______ onto.

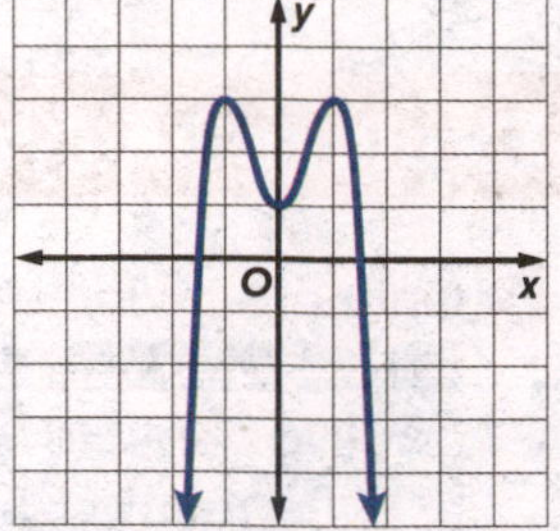

Check

For what codomain is $f(x)$ an onto function? ____

A. $y \leq 3$

B. $y \geq 3$

C. all real numbers

D. $x \leq 3$

Example 2 Identify One-to-One and Onto Functions from Tables

OLYMPICS **The table shows the number of medals the United States won at five Summer Olympic Games.**

Year	Number of Gold Medals	Number of Silver Medals	Number of Bronze Medals
2016	46	37	38
2012	46	29	29
2008	36	38	36
2004	36	39	26
2000	37	24	32

Use a Source

Choose another country and research the number of medals they won in the Summer Olympic Games from 2000–2016. Are the functions that give the number of each type of medal won in a particular year *one-to-one, onto, both,* or *neither*?

Analyze the functions that give the number of gold and silver medals won in a particular year. Define the domain and range of each function and state whether it is *one-to-one, onto, both* or *neither*.

Gold Medals	Silver Medals
Let $f(x)$ be the function that gives the number of gold medals won in a particular year. The domain is in the column Year, and the range is in the column Number of Gold Medals. The function ______ one-to-one because two values in the domain, 2016 and ______, share the same value in the range, 46, and two values in the domain, 2008 and 2004, share the same value in the range, ______.	Let $g(x)$ be the function that gives the number of silver medals won in a particular year. The domain is the column Year, and the range is the column Number of Silver Medals. The function ___ one-to-one because no two values in the domain share a value in the ________.
The function is not onto because the range does not include every whole number.	The function is not onto because the range does not include every whole number.

Go Online You can complete an Extra Example online.

Example 3 Identify One-to-One and Onto Functions from Graphs

Determine whether each function is *one-to-one, onto, both,* or *neither.*

$f(x)$ 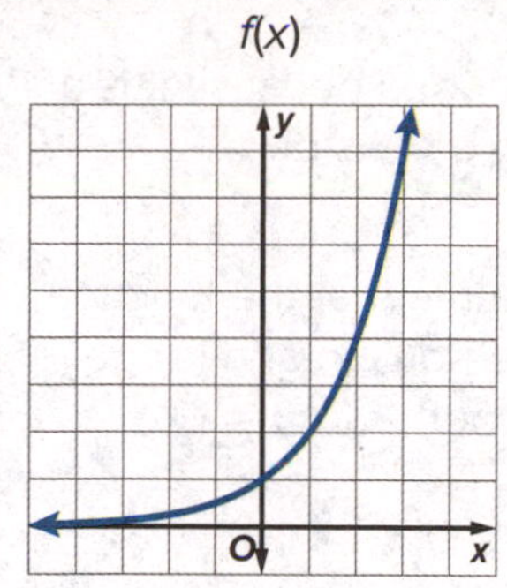	The codomain is all real numbers. The graph indicates that the domain is all real numbers and the range is all positive real numbers. Every x-value is paired with exactly one unique y-value, so the function is one-to-one. If the codomain is all real numbers, then the range is not equal to the codomain. So, the function is not onto.
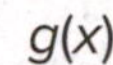 $g(x)$ 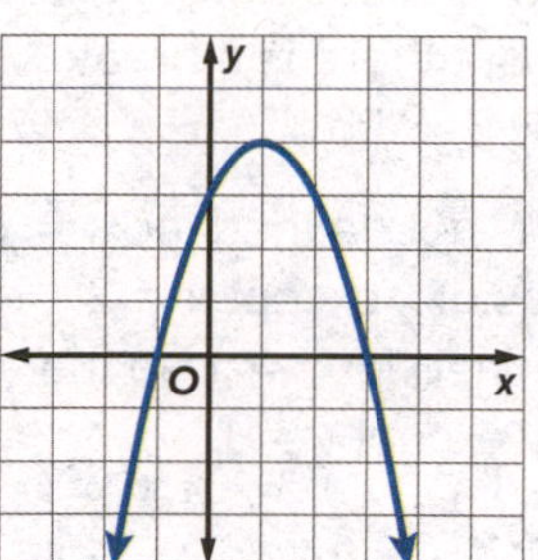	The codomain is $\{y \mid y \leq 4\}$. The graph indicates that the domain is all real numbers, and the range is $y \leq 4$. Each x-value is not paired with a unique y-value; for example, both $x = 0$ and $x = 2$ are paired with $y = 3$. So the function is not one-to one. The codomain and range are equal, so the function is onto.
 $h(x)$ 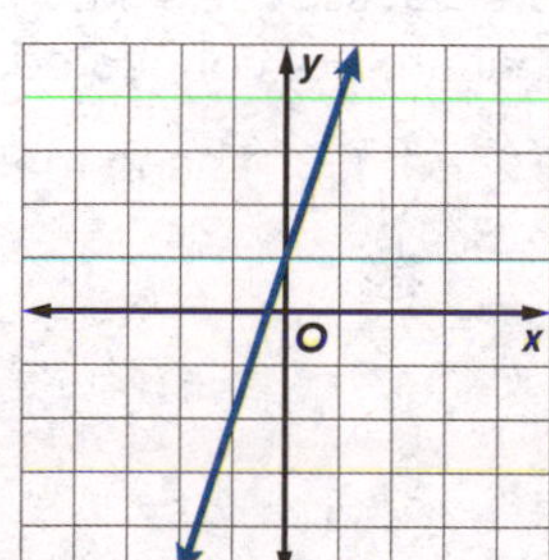	The codomain is all real numbers. The graph indicates that the domain and range are both all real numbers. Every x-value is paired with exactly one unique y-value, so the function is one-to-one. The codomain are equal, so the function is onto.

Learn Discrete and Continuous Functions

Functions can be discrete, continuous, or neither. Real-world situations where only some numbers are reasonable are modeled by discrete functions. Situations where all real numbers are reasonable are modeled by continuous functions.

A **continuous function** is graphed with a line or smooth curve. A function that is not continuous is a **discontinuous function**. A **discrete function** is a discontinuous function in which the points are not connected. A function is neither discrete nor continuous may have a graph in which some points are connected, but it is not continuous everywhere.

Study Tip

Intervals An interval is the set of all real numbers between two given numbers. For example, the interval $-2 < x < 5$ includes all values of x greater than -2 but less than 5. Intervals can also continue on infinitely in a direction. For example, the interval $y \geq 1$ includes all values of y greater than or equal to 1. You can use intervals to describe the values of x or y for which a function exists.

Go Online You can complete an Extra Example online.

Talk About It

Does the range of the function need to be all real numbers for a function to be continuous? Justify your argument.

Problem-Solving Tip

Use a Graph If you are having trouble determining the continuity of a function, you can graph the function to help visualize the situation.

Study Tip

Accuracy When calculating cost, the result can be any fraction of a dollar or cent, and is therefore continuous. However, because the smallest unit of currency is $0.01, the price you actually pay is rounded to the nearest cent. Therefore, the price you pay is discrete.

Example 4 Determine Continuity from Graphs

Examine the functions. Determine whether each function is *discrete, continuous,* or *neither* discrete nor continuous. Then state the domain and range of each function.

a. $f(x)$

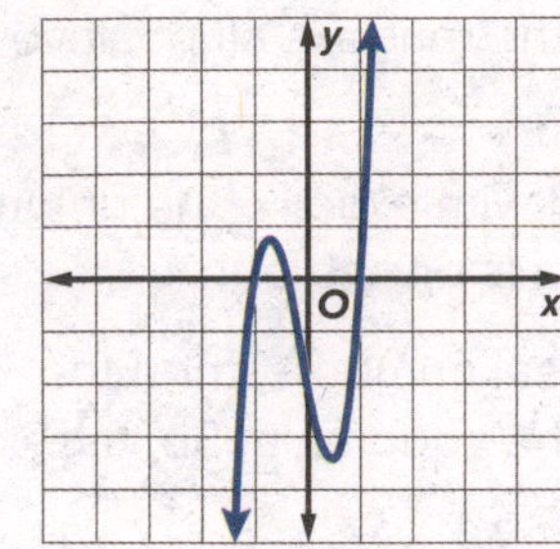

The function is continuous because it is a smooth curve with no breaks or discontinuities.

Because you can assume that the function continues forever, the domain and range are both all real numbers.

b. $g(x)$

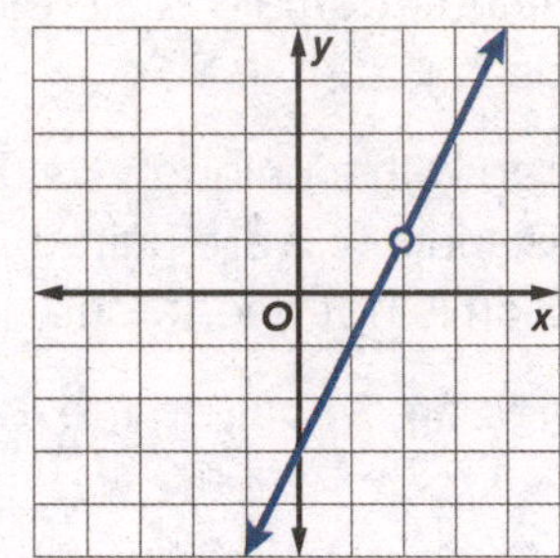

The function is neither because there are continuous sections, but there is a break at (2, 1).

Because the function is not defined for $x = 2$, the domain is all values of x except $x = 2$. The function is not defined for $y = 1$, so the range is all values of y except $y = 1$.

c. $h(x)$

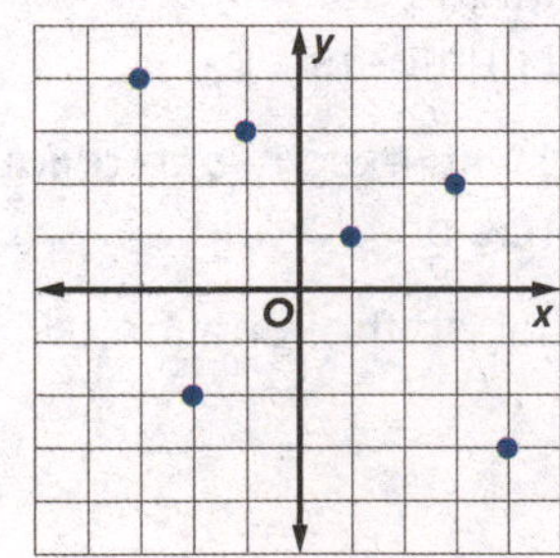

The function is discrete because it is made up of distinct points that are not connected.

The domain is $\{-3, -2, -1, 1, 3, 4\}$ and the range is $\{-3, -2, 1, 2, 3, 4\}$.

Example 5 Determine Continuity

BUSINESS **Determine whether the function that models the cost of coffee beans is *discrete, continuous,* or *neither* discrete nor continuous. Then state the domain and range of the function.**

COFFEE

Weight	Price
Up to 2 lbs	$8/lb
2.5 lbs	$20
3 lbs	$22
5 lbs	$35

Because customers can purchase any amount of coffee up to 2 pounds, the function is continuous over the interval $0 \leq x \leq$ ______.

(continued on the next page)

 **Go Online** You can complete an Extra Example online.

For larger quantities, the coffee is sold by distinct amounts. This part of the function is ________.

Since the domain and range are made up of neither a single interval nor individual points, the function is ________________________.

The domain of the function is $0 \le x \le 2$ or $x = 2.5$, ____, ____. This represents the possible ________ of coffee beans that customers could purchase. The range of the function is $0 \le y \le$ ____ or $y = 20$, ____, 35. This represents the possible ________ of coffee beans.

> **Think About It!**
> Why does the range include values from 0 to 16 instead of 0 to 8?

Learn Set-Builder and Interval Notation

Sets of numbers like the domain and range of a function can be described by using various notations. Set-builder notation, interval notation, and algebraic notation are all concise ways of writing a set of values. Consider the set of values represented by the graph.

- In **algebraic notation**, sets are described using algebraic expressions. Example: $x < 2$
- **Set-builder notation** is similar to algebraic notation. Braces indicate the set. The symbol | is read *as such that*. The symbol ∈ *is read is an element of*. Example: $\{x|x < 2\}$.
- In **interval notation** sets are described using endpoints with parentheses or brackets. A parenthesis, (or), indicates that an endpoint *is not* included in the interval. A bracket, [or], indicates that an endpoint is included in the interval. Example: $(-\infty, 2)$

Example 6 Set-Builder and Interval Notation for Continuous Intervals

Write the domain and range of the graph in set-builder and interval notation.

Domain

The graph will extend to include ____ x-values.

The domain is all real numbers.

$\{x \mid$ ____ ∈ ____$\}$

$(-\infty,$ ____ $)$

Range

The least y-value for this function is ____.

The range is all real numbers ________ than or ________ −6.

$\{x \mid$ ________$\}$

$[-6, \infty)$

Go Online You can complete an Extra Example online.

Check

State the domain and range of each graph in set-builder and interval notation.

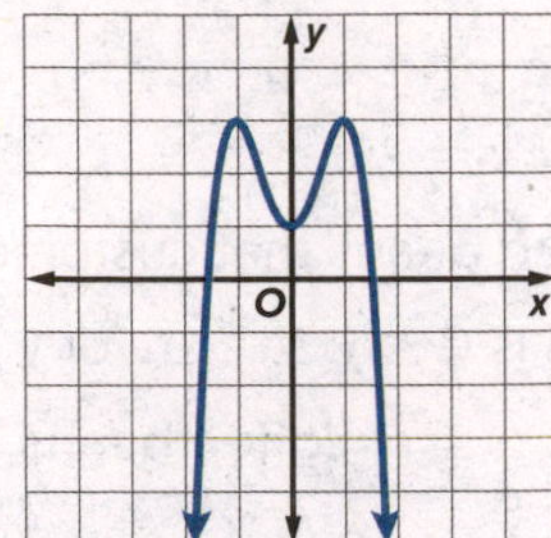

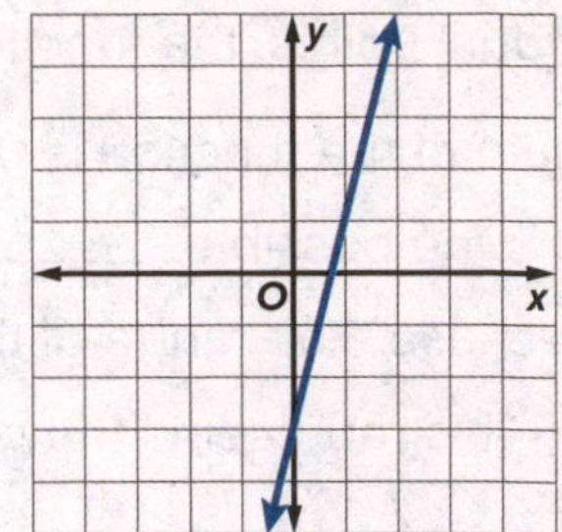

______________________ ______________________

______________________ ______________________

Example 7 Set-Builder and Interval Notation for Discontinuous Intervals

Write the domain and range of the graph in set-builder and interval notation.

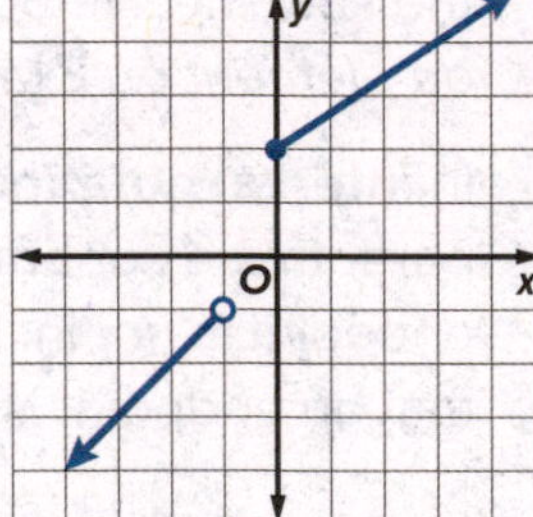

Domain

The domain is all real numbers __________ −1

or ______________________ 0.

$\{x \mid x$ _____ -1 or x _____ $0\}$

$(-\infty, -1$_____ $\cup [0, \infty$_____

Range

The range is all real numbers __________ −1 or

______________________ 2.

$\{y \mid y$ _____ -1 or y _____ 2_____

$(-\infty, -1$_____ $\cup [2, \infty)$

Check

State the domain and range of the graph in set-builder and interval notation.

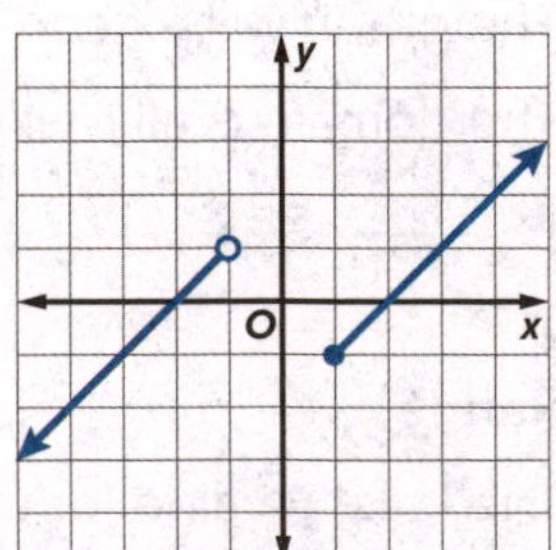

____

____

 **Go Online** You can complete an Extra Example online.

Name ______________________ Period __________ Date __________

Practice

Go Online You can complete your homework online.

Example 1

Identify the domain, range, and codomain in each graph. Then use the codomain and range to determine whether the function is onto.

1.

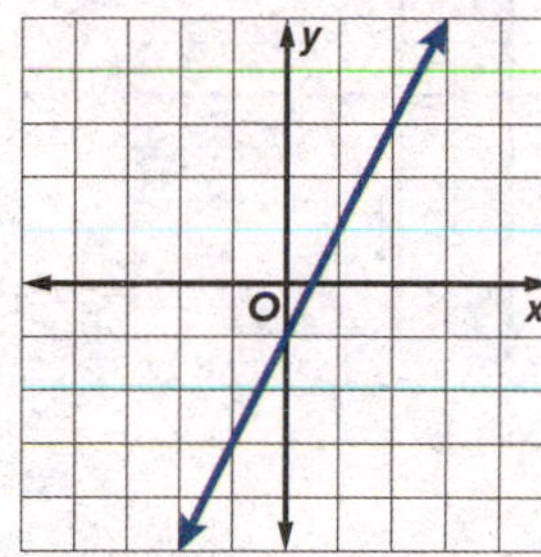

2.

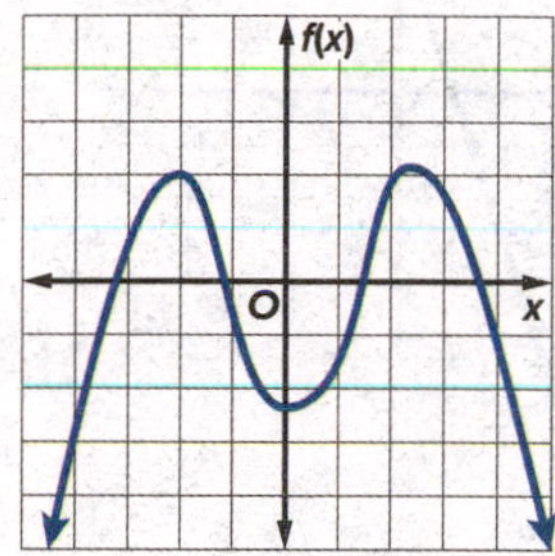

3.

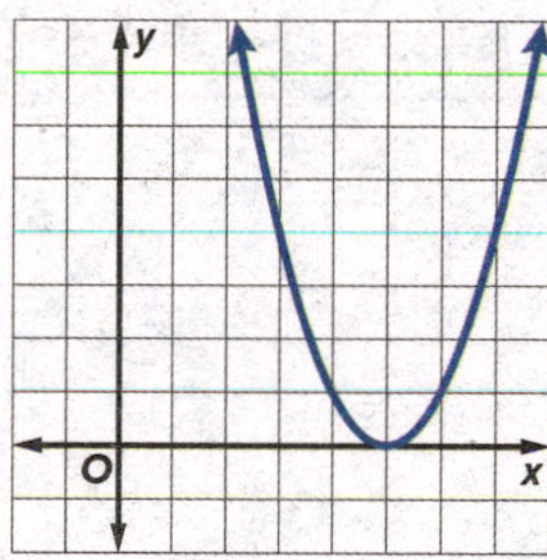

Example 2

4. **SALES** Cool Athletics introduced the new Power Sneaker in one of their stores. The table shows the sales for the first 6 weeks. Define the domain and range of the function and state whether it is *one-to-one, onto, both* or *neither.*

Week	1	2	3	4	5	6
Pairs Sold	8	10	15	22	15	44

5. **TEMPERATURES** The table shows the low temperatures in degrees Fahrenheit for the past week in Sioux Falls, Idaho. Define the domain and range of the function and state whether it is *one-to-one, onto, both,* or *neither.*

Day	1	2	3	4	5	6	7
Low Temp.	56	52	44	41	43	46	53

6. **PLANETS** The table shows the orbital period of the eight major planets in our Solar System given their mean distance from the Sun. Define the domain and range of the function and state whether it is *one-to-one, onto, both* or *neither.*

Planet	Mean Distance from Sun (AU)	Orbital Period (years)
Mercury	0.4	0.241
Venus	0.7	0.615
Earth	1.0	1.0
Mars	1.5	1.881
Jupiter	5.2	11.75
Saturn	9.5	29.5
Uranus	19.2	84
Neptune	30	164.8

Example 3

Determine whether each function is *one-to-one, onto, both,* or *neither.*

7.

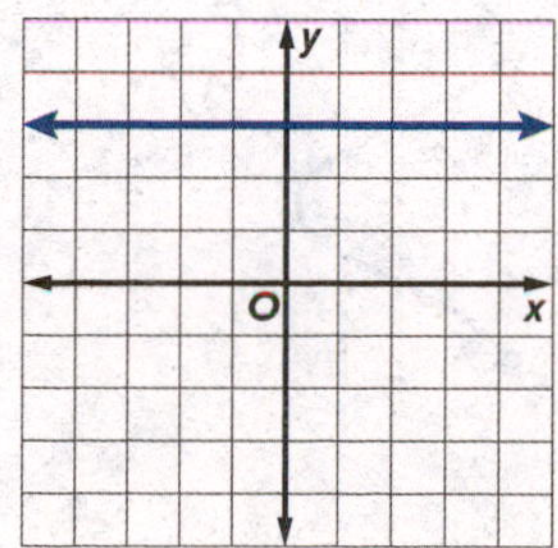

8.

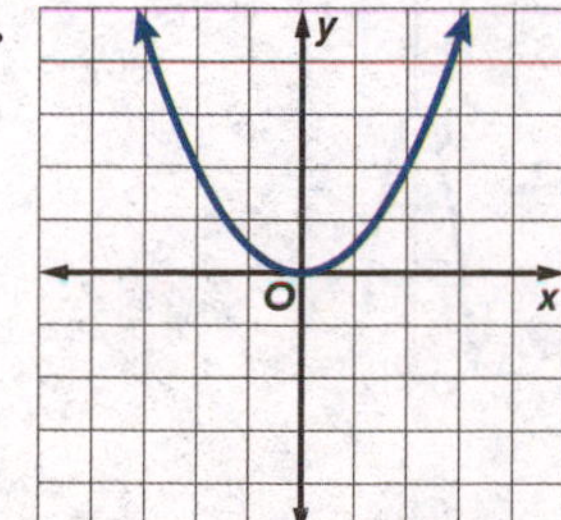

9.

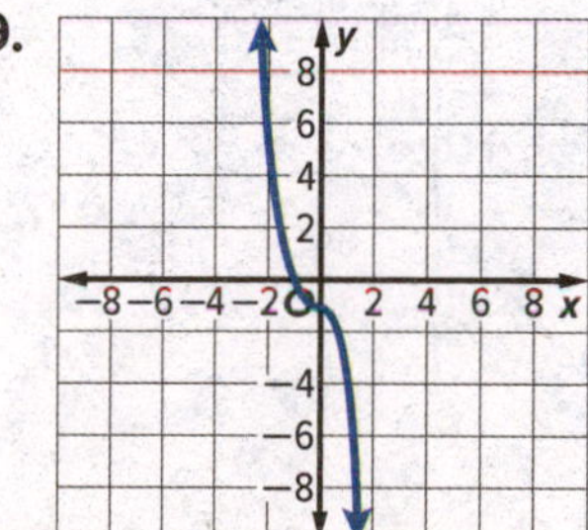

Example 4

Examine the graphs. Determine whether each function is *discrete, continuous*, or *neither* discrete nor continuous. Then state the domain and range of each function.

10.

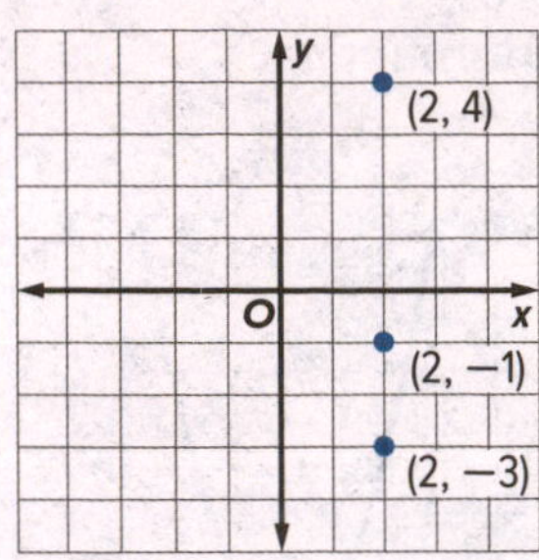

11.

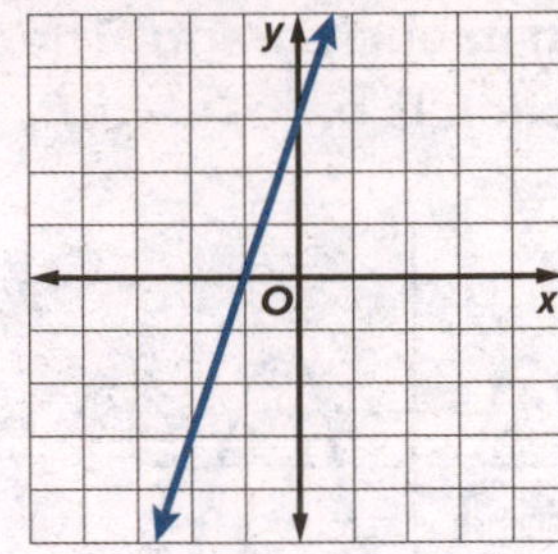

12.

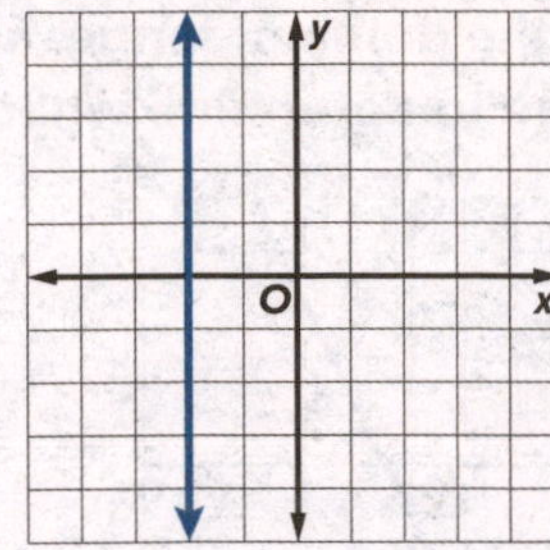

Example 5

13. PROBABILITY The table shows the outcome of rolling a number cube. Determine whether the function that models the outcome of each roll is *discrete, continuous,* or *neither* discrete nor continuous. Then state the domain and range of the function.

Roll	Outcome
1	4
2	3
3	6
4	3
5	5
6	4

14. AMUSEMENT PARK The table shows the price of tickets to an amusement park based on the number of people in the group. Determine whether the function that models the price of tickets is *discrete, continuous,* or *neither* discrete nor continuous. Then state the domain and range of the function.

Group Size	Price
up to 15 people	$45
15–50 people	$38
50–100 people	$30
100 or more people	$26

15. GROCERIES A local grocery store sells grapes for $1.99 per pound. Determine whether the function that models the cost of grapes is *discrete, continuous,* or *neither* discrete nor continuous. Then state the domain and range of the function.

Examples 6 and 7

Write the domain and range of the graph in set-builder and interval notation.

16.

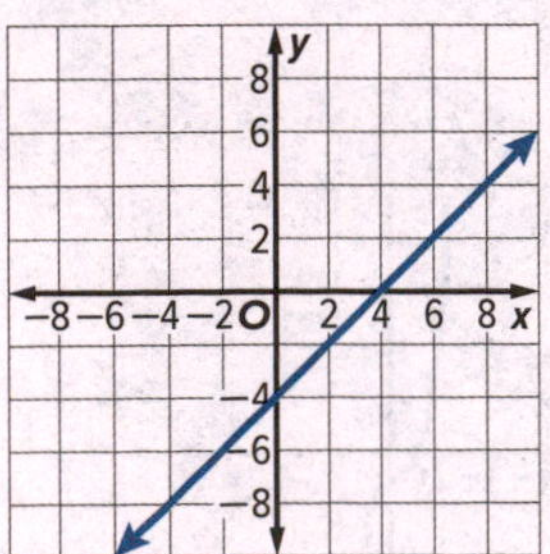

17.

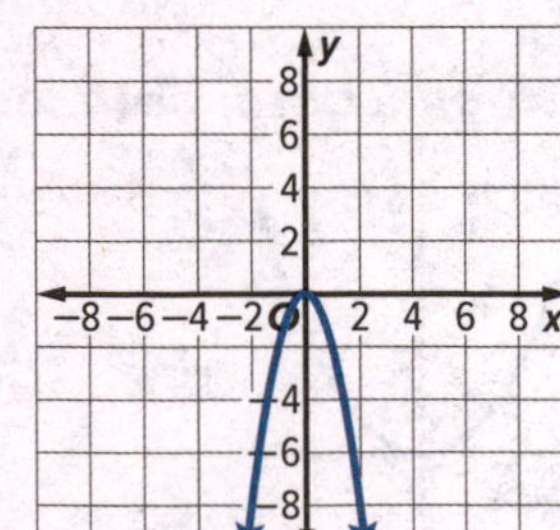

18.

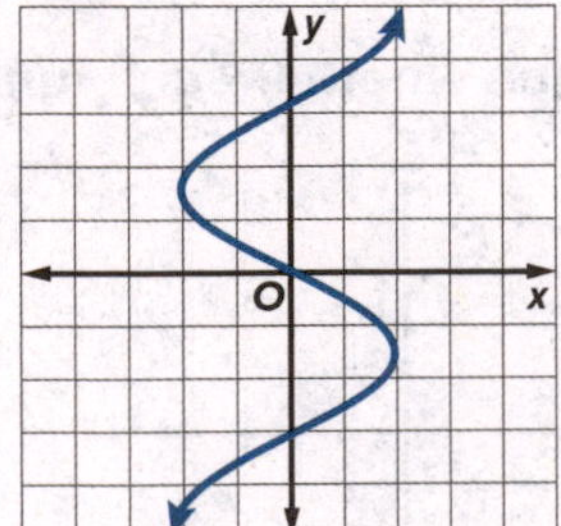

Name ______________________ Period ________ Date ________

Write the domain and range of the graph in set-builder and interval notation.

19.

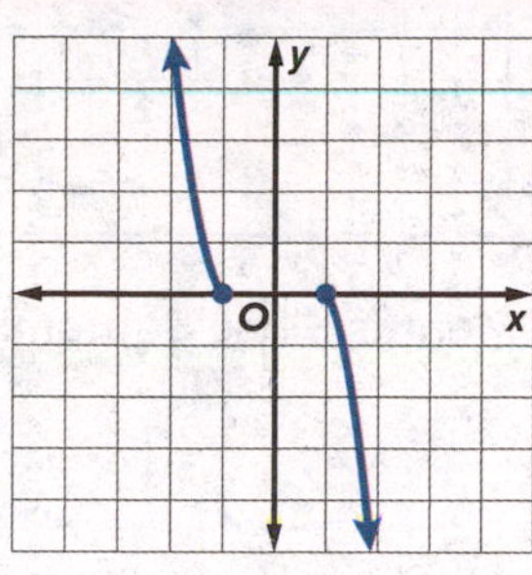

20.

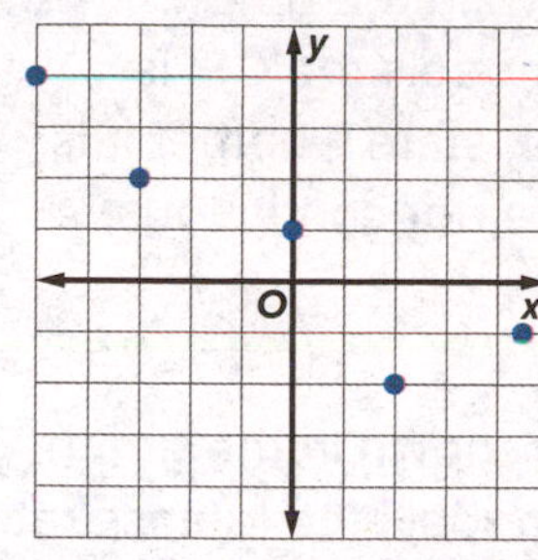

21.

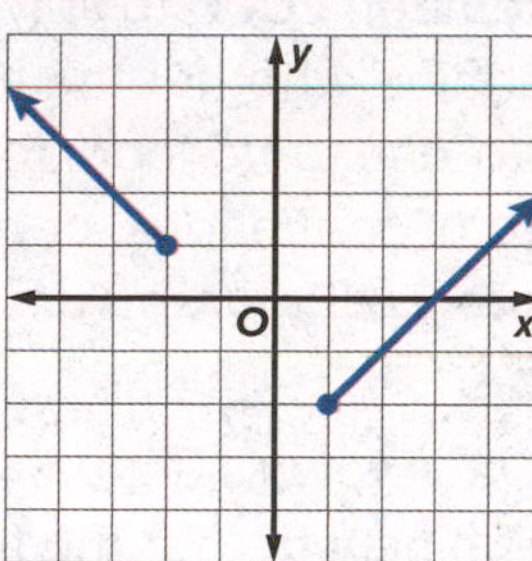

Mixed Exercises

STRUCTURE Write the domain and range of each function in set-builder and interval notation. Determine whether each function is *one-to-one, onto, both,* or *neither*. Then state whether it is *discrete, continuous,* or *neither* discrete nor continuous.

22.

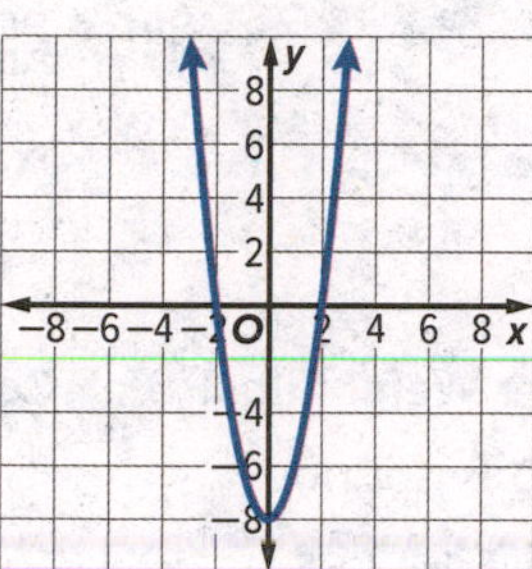

23.

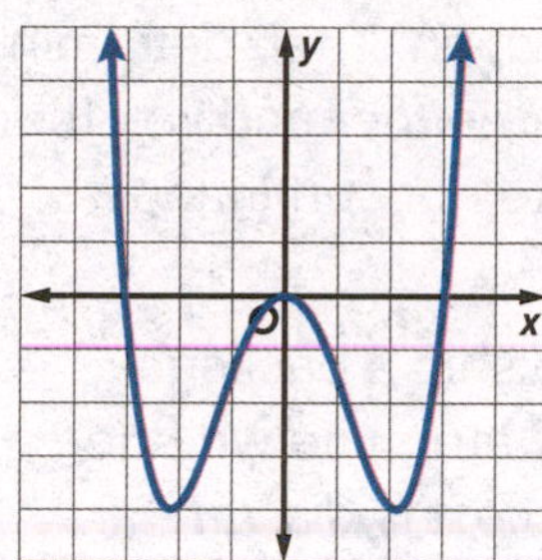

24.

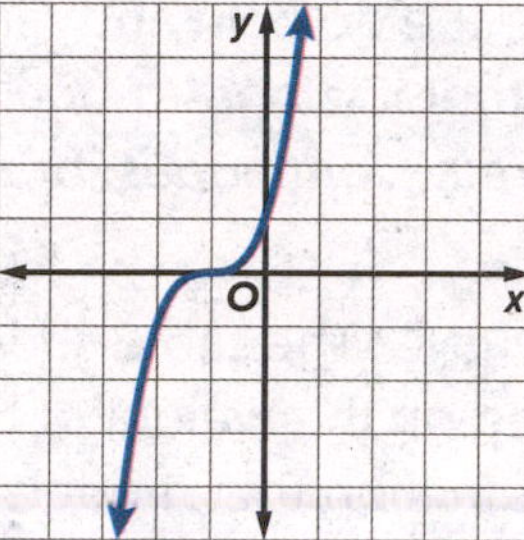

25.

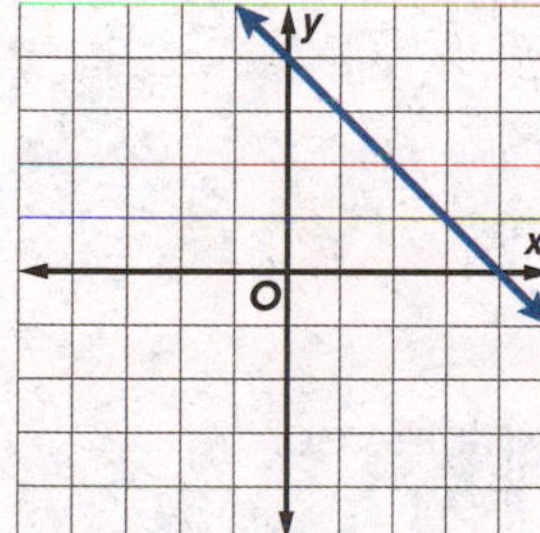

26.

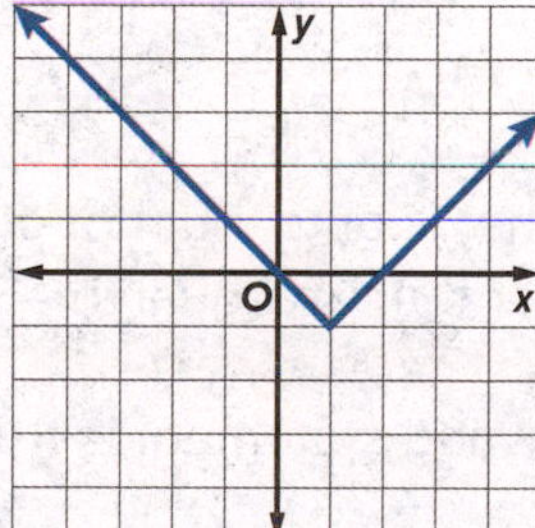

27.

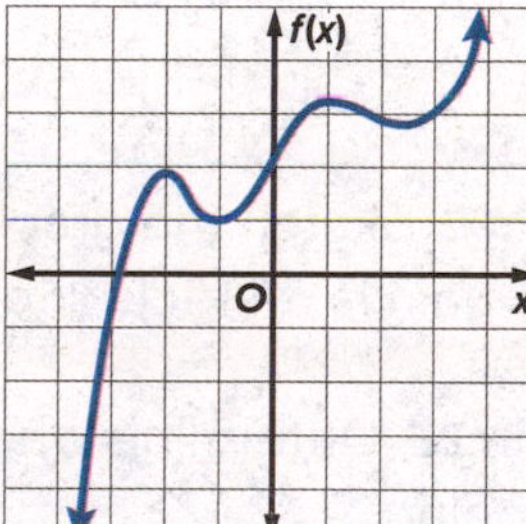

28. **USE A SOURCE** Research the total number of games won by a professional baseball team each season from 2012 to 2016. Determine the domain, range, and continuity of the function that models the number of wins.

29. **SPRINGS** When a weight up to 15 pounds is attached to a 4-inch spring, the length L, in inches, that the spring stretches it is represented by the function $L(w) = \frac{1}{2}w + 4$, where w is the weight, in pounds, of the object. State the domain and range of the function. Then determine whether it is *one-to-one, onto, both,* or *neither* and whether it is *discrete, continuous,* or *neither* discrete nor continuous.

30. **CASHEWS** An airport snack stands sells whole cashews for $12.79 per pound. Determine whether the function that models the cost of cashews is *discrete, continuous,* or *neither* discrete nor continuous. Then state the domain and range of the function.

31. **PRICES** The Consumer Price Index (CPI) gives the relative price for a fixed set of goods and services. The CPI from September, 2000 to July, 2001 is shown in the graph. Determine whether the function that models the CPI is *one-to-one, onto, both,* or *neither.* Then state whether it is *discrete, continuous,* or *neither* discrete nor continuous.
Source: *U. S. Bureau of Labor Statistics*

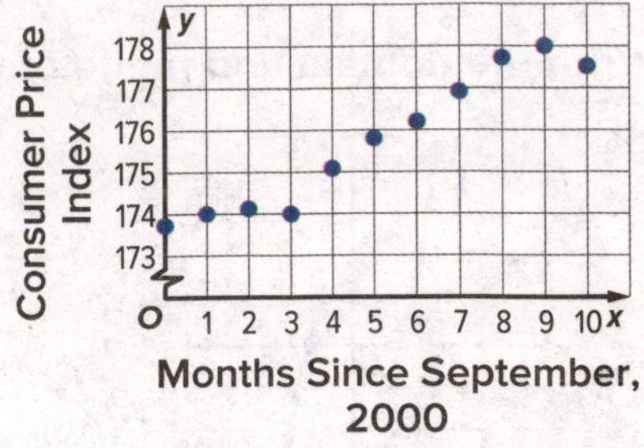

32. **LABOR** A town's annual jobless rate is shown in the graph. Determine whether the function that models the jobless rate is *one-to-one, onto, both,* or *neither.* Then state whether it is *discrete, continuous,* or *neither* discrete nor continuous.

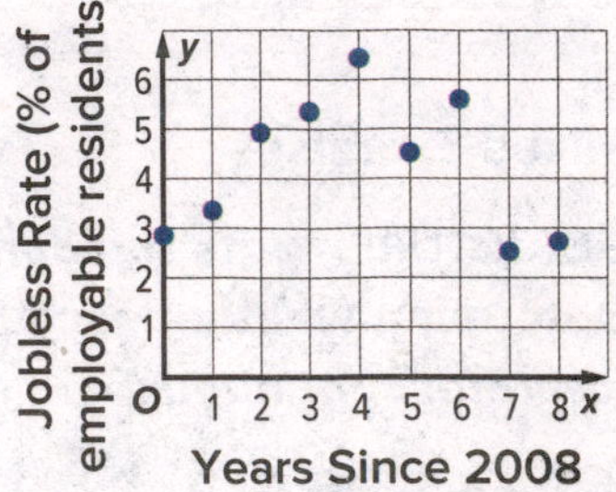

33. **COMPUTERS** If a computer can do one calculation in 0.0000000015 second, then the function $T(n) = 0.0000000015n$ gives the time required for the computer to do n calculations. State the domain and range of the function. Then determine whether it is *one-to-one, onto, both,* or *neither* and whether it is *discrete, continuous,* or *neither* discrete nor continuous.

34. **SHIPPING** The table shows the cost to ship a package based on the weight of the package. Determine whether the function that models the shipping cost is *discrete, continuous,* or *neither* discrete nor continuous. Then state the domain and range of the function.

Package Weight (lbs)	Cost
up to 5 pounds	$4
5–10 pounds	$6
exceeds 10 pounds	$0.65/lb

35. **CREATE** Sketch the graph a function that is onto, but not one-to-one, if the codomain is restricted to values greater than or equal to –3.

36. **ANALYZE** Determine whether the following statement is true or false. Explain your reasoning.

If a function is onto, then it must be one-to-one as well.

37. **USE TOOLS** Use a calculator to graph the function $f(x) = \frac{1}{x}$. State the domain and the range of the function. Determine whether the function is *one-to-one, onto, both,* or *neither.* Determine whether the function is *discrete, continuous,* or *neither* discrete nor continuous.

38. Terrence rents a kayak for an hourly rate of $15, plus an additional deposit of $50. The function $c(h)$ gives the total cost of renting a kayak for h hours.

   a. **WRITE** Write and graph the function described. State the domain and range of the function. Determine whether the function is *one-to one, both,* or *neither.* Then determine whether the function is *discrete, continuous,* or *neither* discrete nor continuous.

   b. **STATE YOUR ASSUMPTION** What assumption did you make in part **a**?

39. **WRITE** Compare and contrast the vertical and horizontal line tests.

Linearity, Intercepts, and Symmetry

Explore Symmetry and Functions

Online Activity Use graphing technology to complete the Explore.

INQUIRY How can you tell whether the graph of a function is symmetric?

Learn Linear and Nonlinear Functions

In a **linear function**, no variable is raised to a power other than 1. Any linear function can be written in the form $f(x) = mx + b$, where m and b are real numbers. Linear functions can be modeled by **linear equations**, which can be written in the form $Ax + By = C$. The graph of a linear equation is a straight line.

A function that is not linear is called a **nonlinear function**. The graph of a nonlinear function includes a set of points that cannot all lie on the same line. A nonlinear function cannot be written in the form $f(x) = mx + b$. A **parabola** is a type of nonlinear function.

Example 1 Identify Linear Functions from Equations

Determine whether each function is a linear function. Justify your answer.

a. $f(x) = \frac{6x - 5}{3}$

$f(x) = \frac{6x - 5}{3}$ Original equation

$f(x) = \frac{6}{3}x - \frac{5}{3}$ Distribute the denominator of 3.

$f(x) = 2x - \frac{5}{3}$ Simplify.

The function _____ be written in the form $f(x) = mx + b$, so it _____ a linear function.

b. $5y = 4 + 3x^3$

$5y = 4 + 3x^3$ Original equation

$5y =$ _____ $+ 4$ Commutative Property

The function _________ be written in the form $f(x) = mx + b$ because the independent variable x is raised to a whole number power

_______________ 1. So, it is a _______________ function.

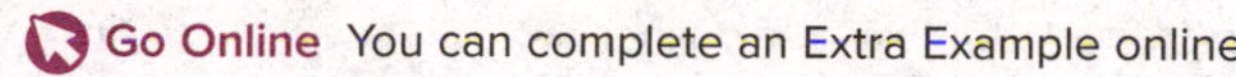

Go Online You can complete an Extra Example online.

Today's Standards
F.IF.4; F.IF.5
MP3, MP4

Today's Vocabulary
linear function
linear equation
nonlinear function
parabola
intercept
x-intercept
y-intercept
symmetry
line symmetry
line of symmetry
point symmetry
point of symmetry
even functions
odd functions

Think About It!
Does every linear equation represent a linear function? Justify your argument.

Study Tip
Linear Functions To write any linear equation in function form, solve the equation for y and replace the variable y with $f(x)$.

Your Notes

Example 2 Identify Linear Functions from Graphs

Determine whether each graph represents a *linear* or *nonlinear* function.

a.

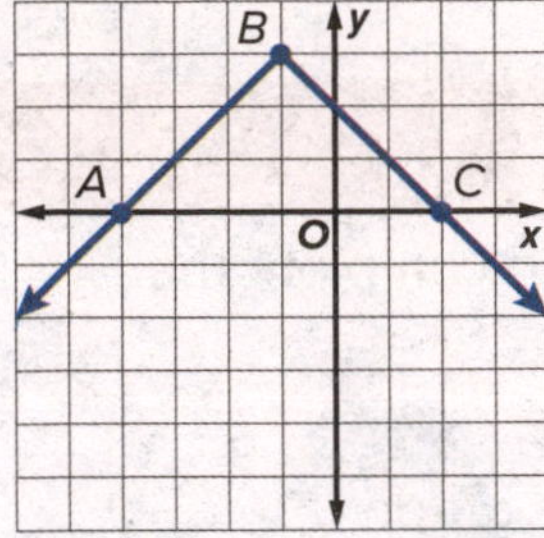

There is no straight line that will contain the chosen points *A*, *B*, and *C*, so this graph represents a ________ function.

b.

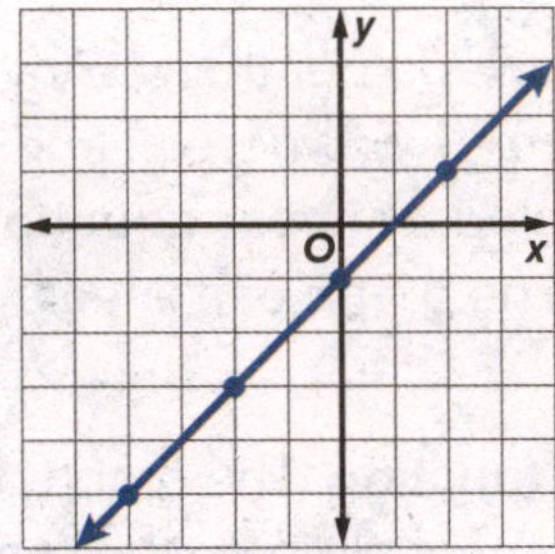

The points on this graph all lie on the same line, so this graph represents a _____ function.

Think About It!

Are negative *x*- or *y*-values possible in the context of the situation?

Example 3 Identify Linear Functions from Tables

EARNINGS **Makayla has started working part-time at the local hardware store. Her time at work steadily increases for the first five weeks. The table shows her total earnings each of those weeks. Are her weekly earnings modeled by a *linear* or *nonlinear* function?**

Week	1	2	3	4	5
Earnings ($)	85	119	153	187	221

Graph the points that represent the week and total earnings and try to draw a line that contains all the points.

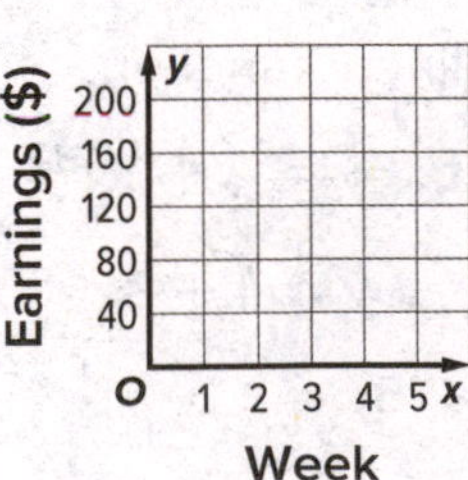

Since there is a line that contains all the points, Makaya's earning can be modeled by a _____ function.

Go Online You can complete an Extra Example online.

Learn Intercepts of Graphs of Functions

A point at which the graph of a function intersects an axis is called an **intercept**. An ***x*-intercept** is the *x*-coordinate of a point where the graph crosses the *x*-axis, and a ***y*-intercept** is the *y*-coordinate of a point where the graph crosses the *y*-axis.

A linear function has at most one *x*-intercept while a nonlinear function may have more than one *x*-intercept.

Example 4 Find Intercepts of a Linear Function

Use the graph to estimate the *x*- and *y*-intercepts.

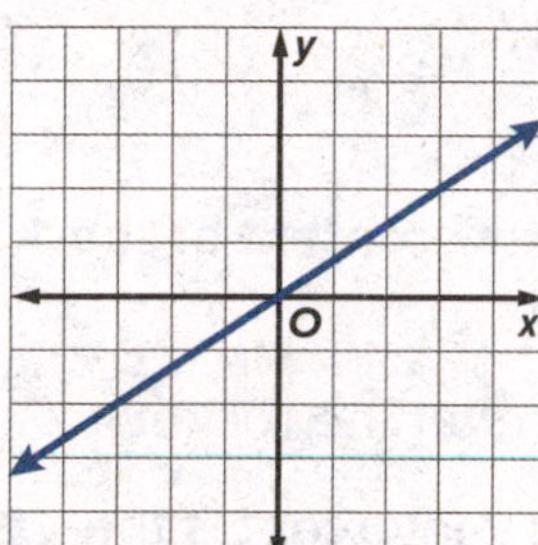

The graph intersects the *x*-axis at

(____, ____), so the *x*-intercept is ____.

The graph intersects the *y*-axis at

(____, ____), so the *y*-intercept is ____.

Example 5 Find Intercepts of a Nonlinear Function

Use the graph to estimate the *x*- and *y*-intercepts.

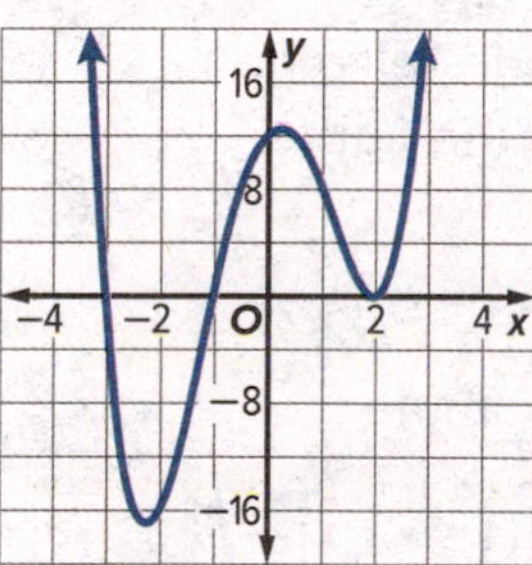

The graph appears to intersect the *x*-axis at (−3, 0), (−1, 0), and (2, 0), so the functions has *x*-intercepts of ____, ____, and ____.

The graph appears to intersect the *y*-axis at (____, ____), so the function has a *y*-intercept of ____.

Check

Estimate the *x*- and *y*-intercepts of each graph.

a.

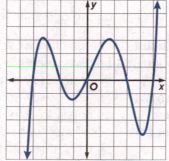

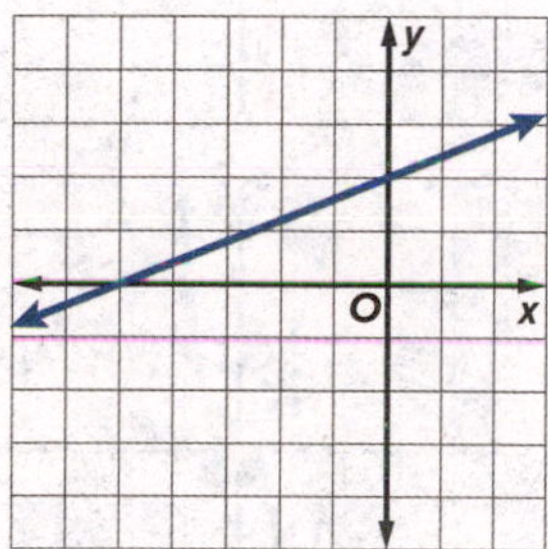

x-intercept(s): ____

y-intercept(s): ____

b.

x-intercept(s): ________

y-intercept(s): ____

Go Online You can complete an Extra Example online.

Study Tip

Point or Coordinate *Intercept* may refer to the point or one of its coordinates. The context of the situation will often dictate which form to use.

Think About It!

Describe a line that does not have two distinct intercepts.

Think About It!

The graph of the nonlinear functions has three *x*-intercepts. Can the graph have more than one *y*-intercept? Explain your reasoning.

Think About It!

Describe the domain of the function that models the rocket's height over time.

Watch Out!

Switching Coordinates A common mistake is to switch the coordinates for the intercepts. Remember that for the x-intercept, the y-coordinate is 0, and for the y-intercept, the x-coordinate is 0.

Talk About It

Can the graph of a function be symmetric in a horizontal line? Justify your answer.

Example 6 Interpret the Meaning of Intercepts

MODEL ROCKETS **Ricardo launches a rocket from a balcony. The table shows the height of the rocket after each second of its flight.**

Time (s)	Height (ft)
0	15
1	60
2	130
3	180
4	210
5	170
6	110
7	55
8	0

Part A Identify the *x*- and *y*-intercepts of the function that models the flight of the rocket.

In the table, the x-coordinate when $y = 0$ is _____. Thus, the x-intercept is _____.

In the table, the y-coordinate when $x = 0$ is _____. Thus, the y-intercept is _____.

Part B What is the meaning of the intercepts in the context of the rocket's flight?

The x-intercept is the ______________ after the rocket is launched that it returns to the ground. The y-intercept is the ______________ from which the rocket is launched.

Learn Symmetry of Graphs of Functions

A figure has **symmetry** if there exists a rigid motion—reflection, translation, rotation, or glide reflection—that maps the figure onto itself.

Key Concept • Symmetry

Type of Symmetry	Description	Example
A graph has **line symmetry** if each half of the graph maps exactly to the other half.	The line dividing the graph into matching halves is called the **line of symmetry**. Each point on one side is reflected in the line to a point equidistant from the line on the opposite side.	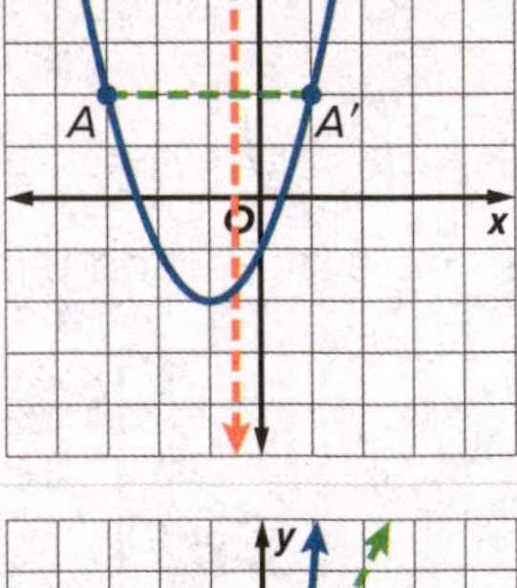
A graph has **point symmetry** when a figure is rotated 180° about a point and maps exactly onto the other part.	The point about which the graph is rotated is called the **point of symmetry**. The image of each point on one side of the point of symmetry can be found on a line through the point of symmetry equidistant from the point of symmetry.	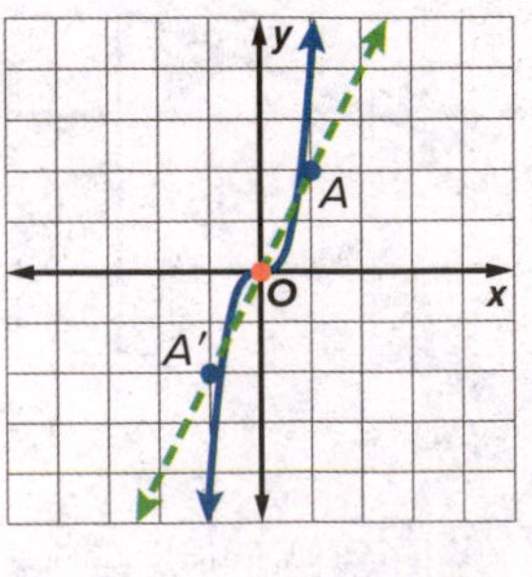

Key Concept • Even and Odd Functions		
Type of Function	**Algebraic Test**	**Example**
Functions that are symmetric in the y-axis are called **even functions.**	For every x in the domain of f, $f(-x) = f(x)$.	
Functions that are symmetric about the origin are called **odd functions.**	For every x in the domain of f, $f(-x) = -f(x)$.	

Example 7 Identify Types of Symmetry

Identify the type of symmetry in the graph of each function. Explain.

a. $f(x) = 3x + 1$

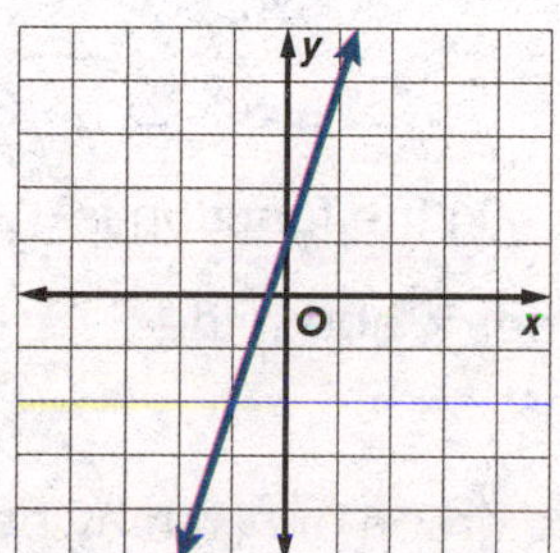

point symmetry: a 180° rotation about ________ on graph is the original graph.

b. $g(x) = -x^2 - 4x - 2$

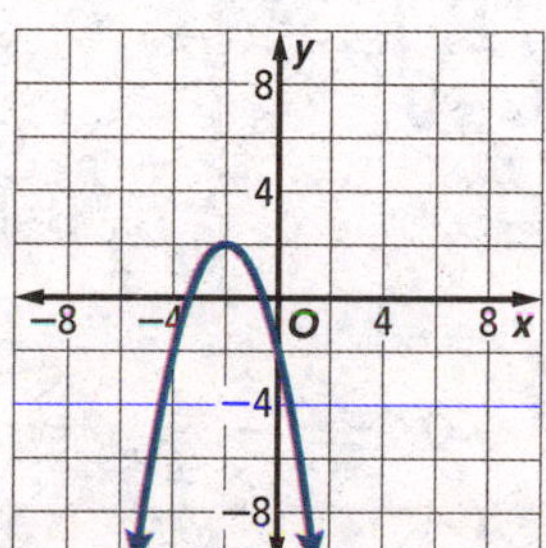

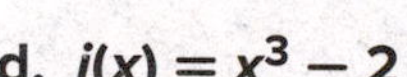 : the reflection in the line $x = -2$ coincides with the original graph.

c. $h(x) = 3x^4 + 4x^3 - 12x^2 + 13$

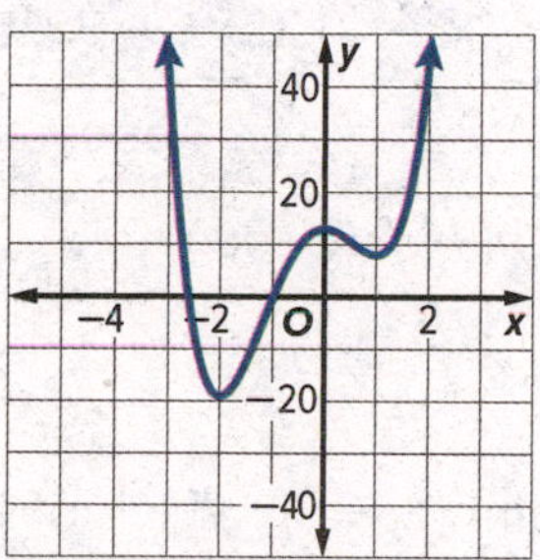

____________: there is no line or point of symmetry.

d. $j(x) = x^3 - 2$

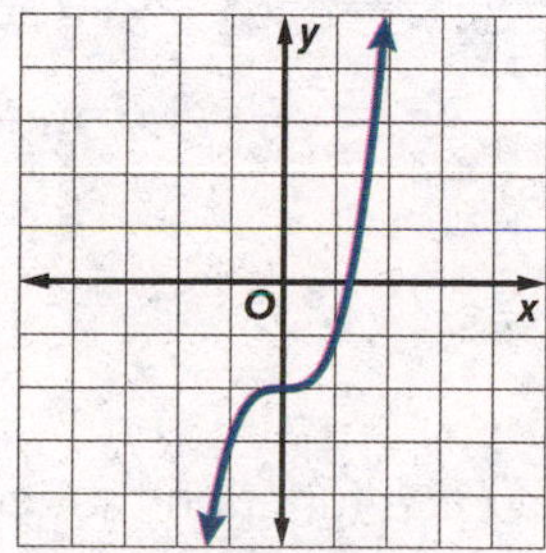

point symmetry: a 180° rotation about the point ________ is the original graph.

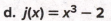

Go Online You can complete an Extra Example online.

Think About It!

How would knowing the type of symmetry help you graph a function?

Example 8 Identify Even and Odd Functions

Determine whether each function is *even*, *odd*, or *neither*. Confirm algebraically. If the function is odd or even, describe the symmetry.

a. $f(x) = x^3 - 4x$

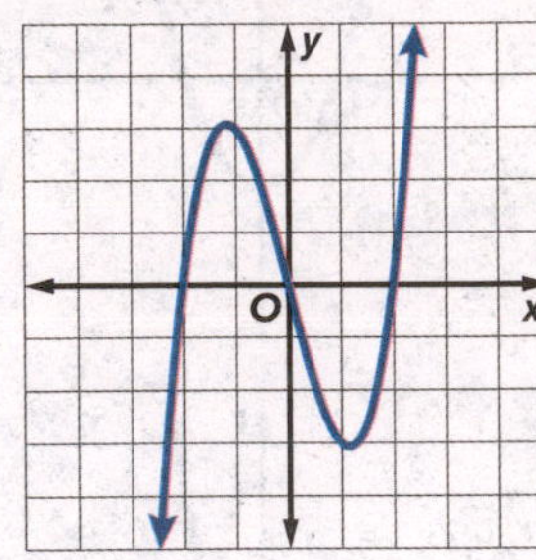

It appears that the graph of $f(x)$ is symmetric about the origin. Substitute $-x$ for x to test this algebraically.

$f(-x) = (\_\_\_)^3 - 4(\_\_\_)$

$= -x^3 + \_\_\_$ Simplify.

$= -(x^3 - 4x)$ Distribute.

$= \_\_\_$ $f(x) = x^3 - 4x$

Because $f(-x) = -f(x)$ the function is ____ and is symmetric about the ________.

b. $g(x) = 2x^4 - 6x^2$

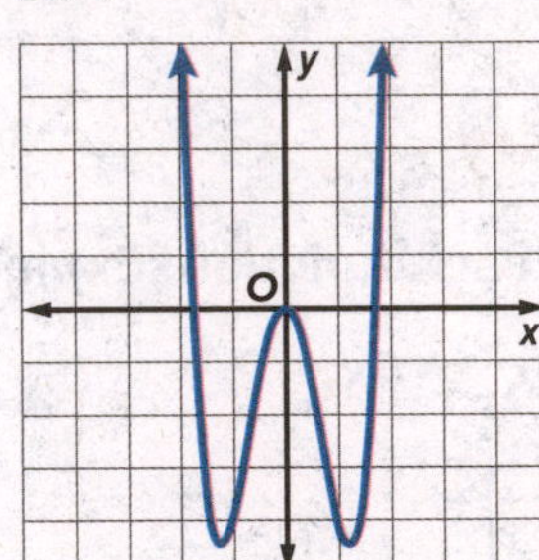

It appears that the graph of $g(x)$ is symmetric about the y-axis. Substitute $-x$ for x to test this algebraically.

$g(-x) = 2(\_\_\_)^4 - 6(\_\_\_)^2$

$= 2x^4 - \_\_\_$ Simplify.

$= g(x)$ $g(x) = 2x^4 - 6x^2$

Because $g(-x) = g(x)$ the function is ____ and is symmetric about the ________.

c. $h(x) = x^3 + 0.25x^2 - 3x$

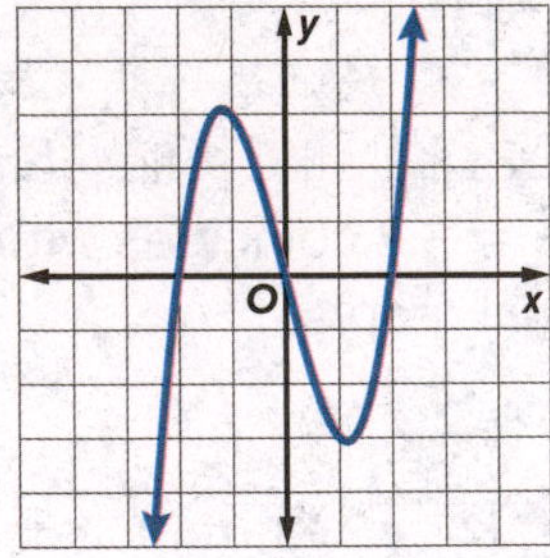

It appears that the graph of $h(x)$ may be symmetric about the origin. Substitute $-x$ for x to test this algebraically.

$h(-x) = (\_\_\_)^3 + 0.25(\_\_\_)^2 - 3(\_\_\_)$

$= \_\_\_ + 0.25x^2 + \_\_\_$ Simplify.

Because $-h(x) = -x^3 - 0.25x^2 + 3x$, the function is ____________ because $h(-x) \neq h(x)$ and $h(-x) \neq -h(x)$

Watch Out!

Even and Odd Functions Always confirm symmetry algebraically. Graphs that appear to be symmetric may not actually be.

Check

Assume that f is a function that contains the point $(2, -5)$. Which of the given points must be included in the function if f is:

even? ________ odd? ________

$(-2, -5)$ $(-2, 5)$ $(2, 5)$ $(-5, -2)$ $(-5, 2)$

Go Online You can complete an Extra Example online.

Name ________________ Period ________ Date ________

Practice

Go Online You can complete your homework online.

Example 1

Determine whether each function is a linear function. Justify your answer.

1. $y = 3x$

2. $y = -2 + 5x$

3. $2x + y = 10$

4. $y = 4x^2$

Example 2

Determine whether each graph represents a *linear* or *nonlinear* function.

5.

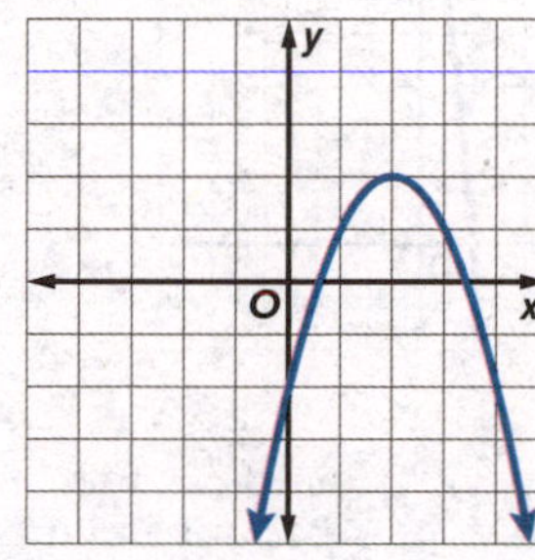

6.

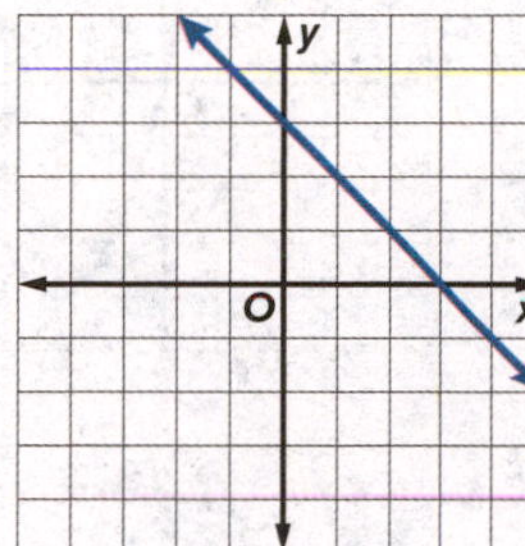

7.

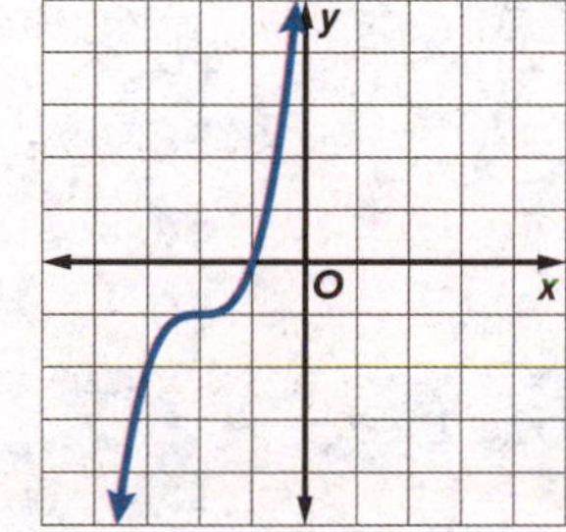

8.

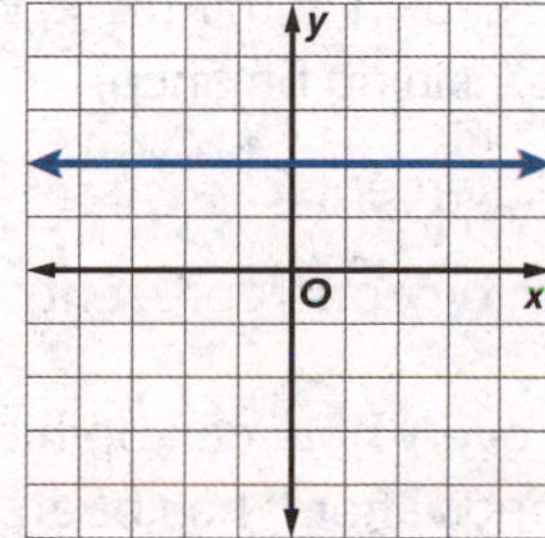

Example 3

9. **MEASUREMENT** The table shows a function modeling the number of inches and feet. Can the table be modeled by a *linear* or *nonlinear* function? Explain.

Inches	0	1	2	3	4
Feet	0	12	24	36	48

10. **ASTRONOMY** The table shows the velocity of *Cassini 2*, a space probe, as it passes Saturn. Is the velocity modeled by a *linear* or *nonlinear* function? Explain.

Cassini 2 Velocity					
Time (s)	5	10	15	20	25
Velocity (mph)	50,000	60,000	70,000	60,000	50,000

Examples 4 and 5

Use the graph to estimate the *x*- and *y*-intercepts.

11. 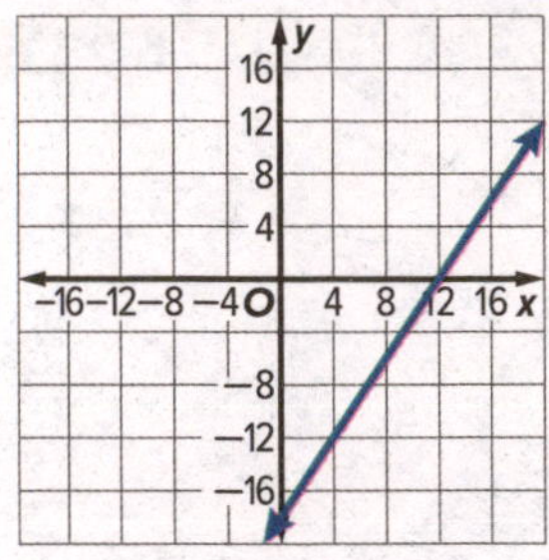

12. 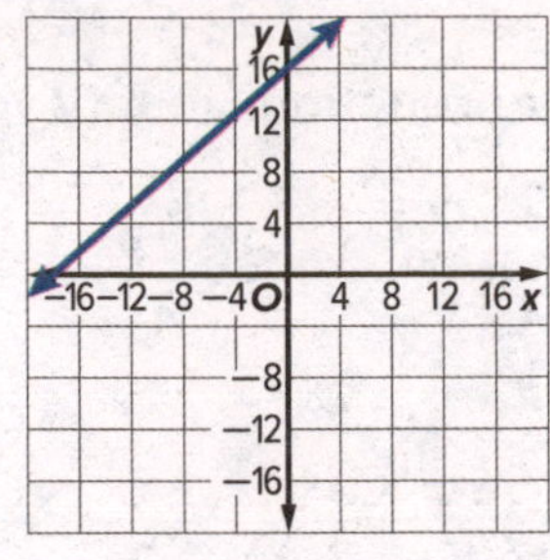

13. 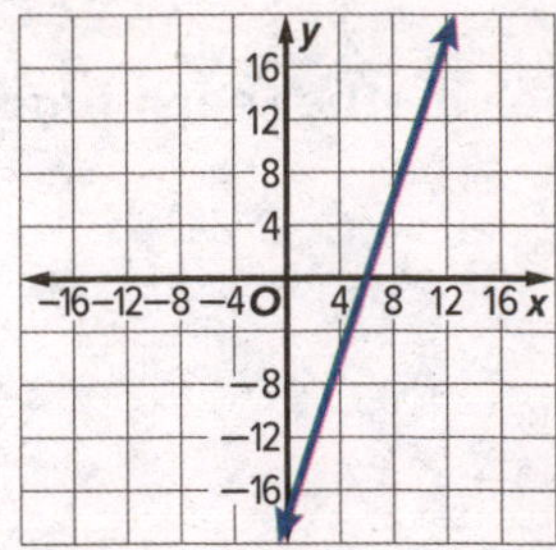

14. 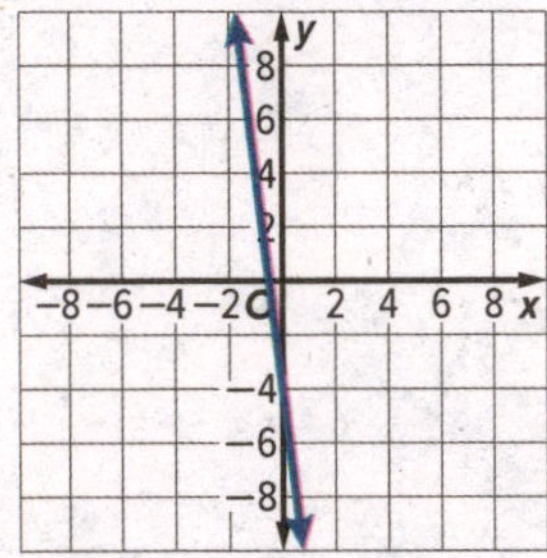

15. 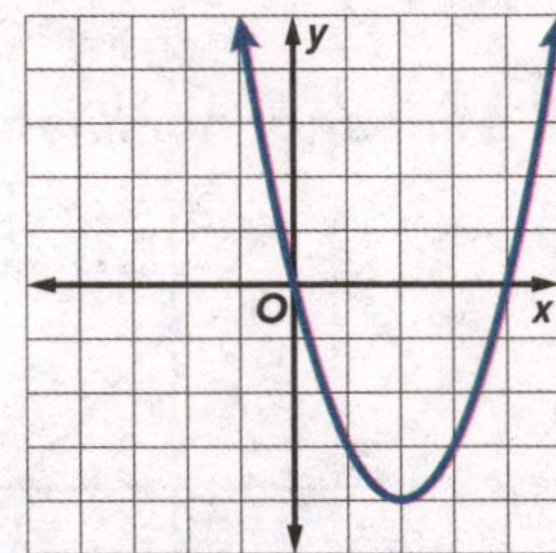

16. 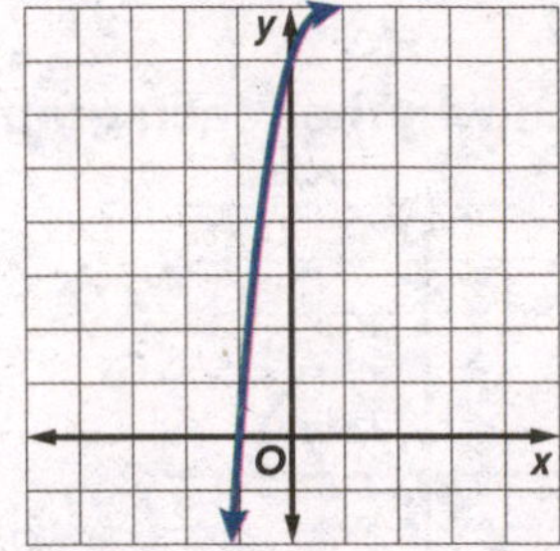

Example 6

17. LUNCH ACCOUNT At the beginning of the week, Aksa's parents deposited \$20 into Aksa's lunch account. The amount of money Aksa had left after each day is shown in the table, where *x* is the number of days and *y* is the remaining balance.

Days	Account Balance
0	\$20
1	\$16
2	\$12
3	\$8
4	\$4
5	\$0

Part A What are the *x*- and *y*-intercepts?

Part B What do the x- and *y*-intercepts represent?

18. GOLF In golf, the first shot on every hole can be hit off a tee. The table shows the height *y* of the golf ball *x* seconds after it has been hit off the tee.

Time (sec)	0	1	3	5	7
Height (in.)	3	20	36	28	0

Part A What are the *x*- and *y*-intercepts?

Part B What do the *x*- and *y*-intercepts represent?

Example 7

Identify the type of symmetry for the graph of each function.

19. 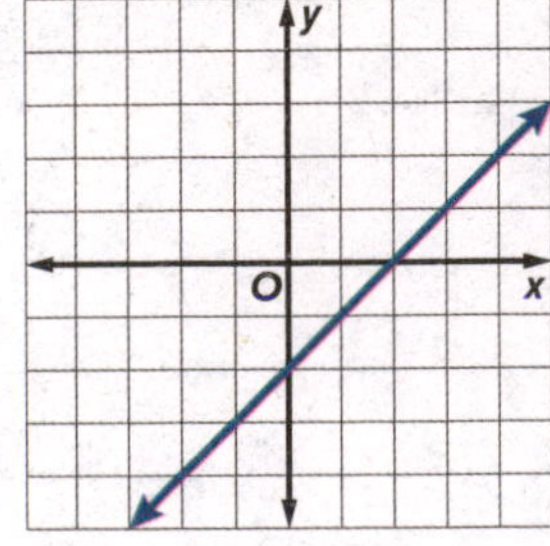

20. 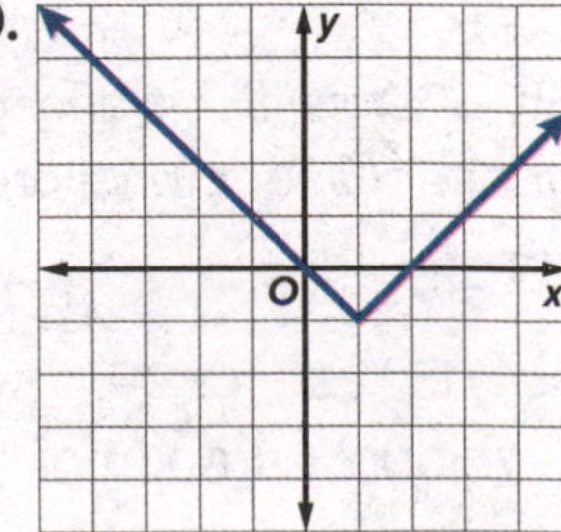

21. 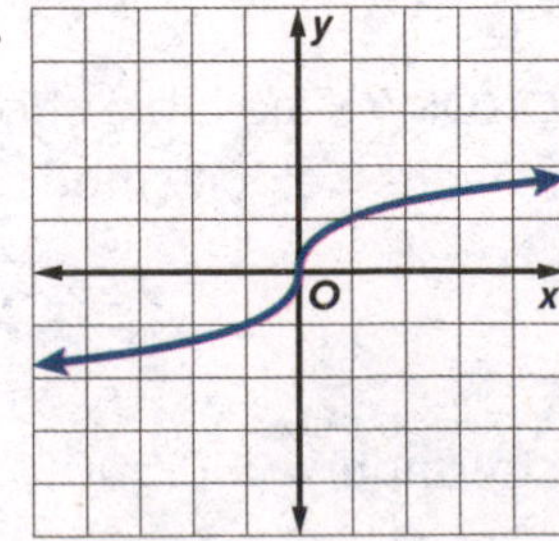

Name ______________________ Period ____________ Date ______________

Example 8

Determine whether each function is *even*, *odd*, or *neither*. Confirm algebraically. If the function is odd or even, describe the symmetry.

22. $f(x) = 2x^3 - 8x$

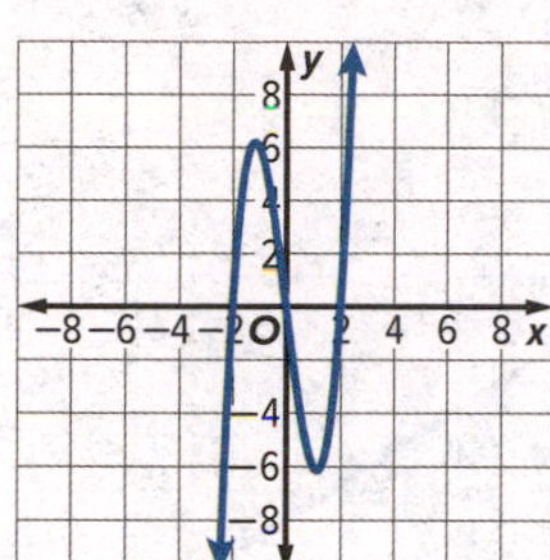

23. $f(x) = x^3 + x^2$

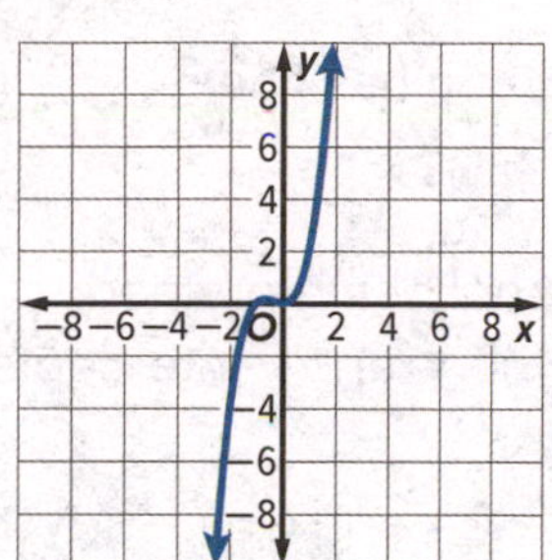

24. $f(x) = x^2 + 2$

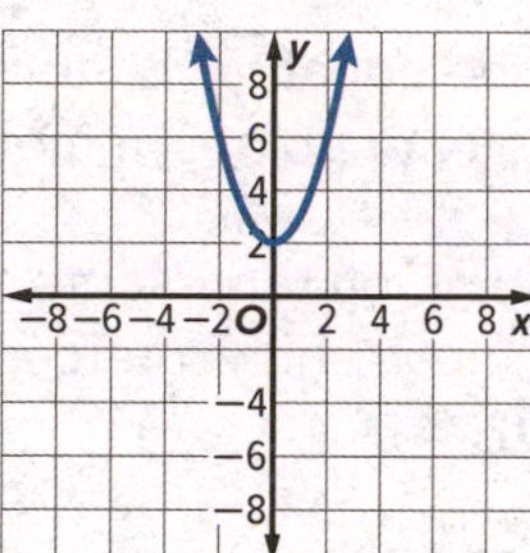

Mixed Exercises

Determine whether each equation represents a linear function. Justify your answer. Algebraically determine whether each equation is even, odd, or neither.

25. $-\frac{3}{x} + y = 15$

26. $x = y + 8$

27. $y = 8$

28. $y = \sqrt{x} + 3$

29. $y = 3x^2 - 1$

30. $y = 2x^3 + x + 1$

Determine whether each graph represents a *linear* or *nonlinear* function. Use the graph to estimate the *x*- and *y*-intercepts. Identify the type of symmetry in each graph.

31.

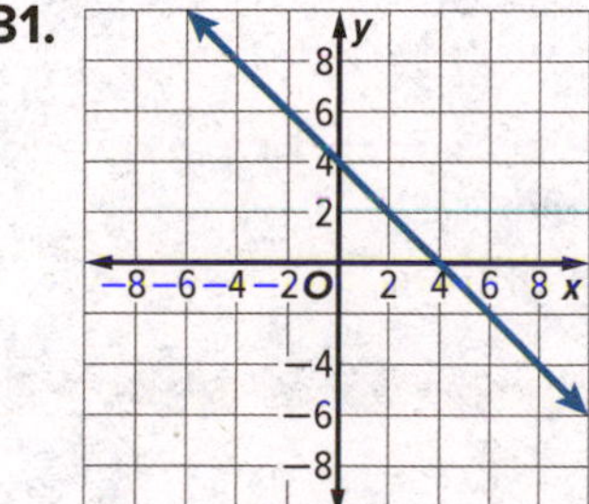

32.

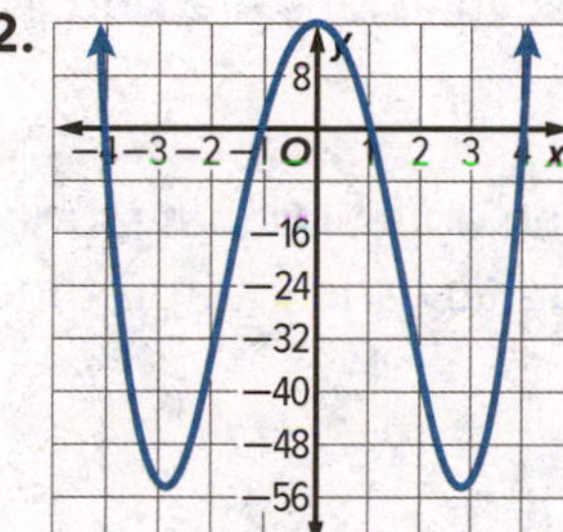

33.

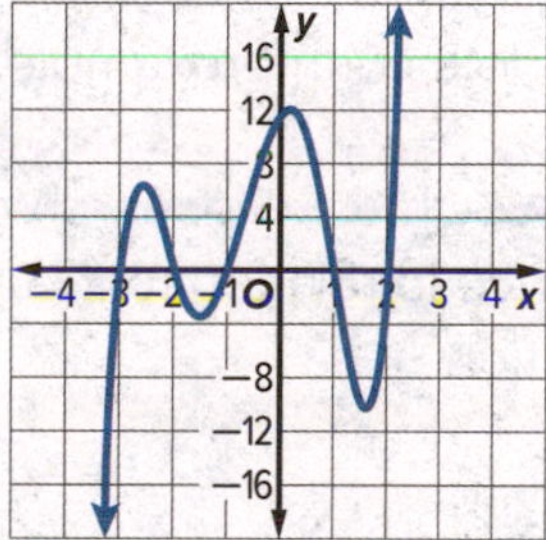

34. GAMES Pedro decided to measure how close he and his friends could throw a football to a target. They counted 1 point for each foot away from the target that the football landed. The graph of points versus distance thrown is shown here. State whether the graph has line symmetry or point symmetry, and identify any lines of symmetry or points of symmetry.

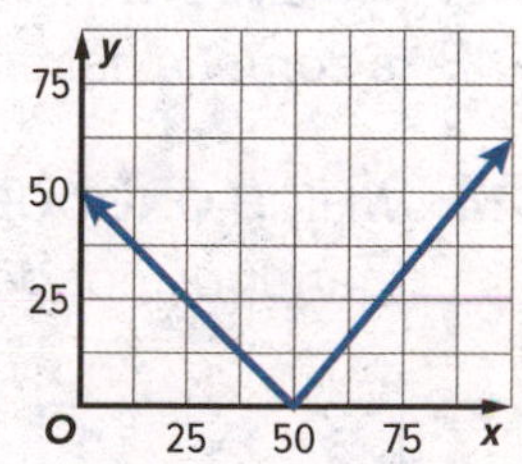

35. BASKETBALL Tiana tossed a basketball. The graph shows the height of the basketball as a function of time. State whether the graph has line symmetry or point symmetry, and identify any lines of symmetry or points of symmetry.

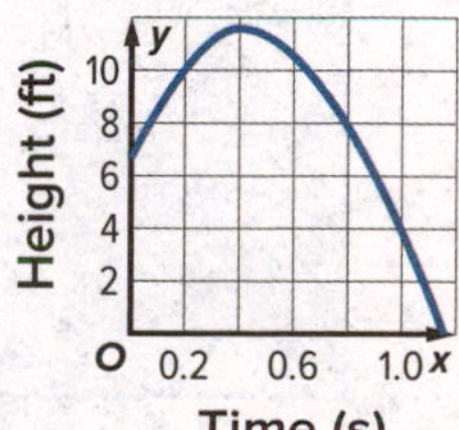

36. PROFIT Stefon charges people $25 to test the air quality in their homes. The device he uses to test air quality cost him $500. The function $y = 25x - 500$ describes Stefon's net profit, y, as a function of the number of clients he gets, x. State whether the function is a linear function. Write *yes* or *no*. Explain.

37. PLAYGROUND A playground is shaped as shown. The total perimeter is 500 feet.

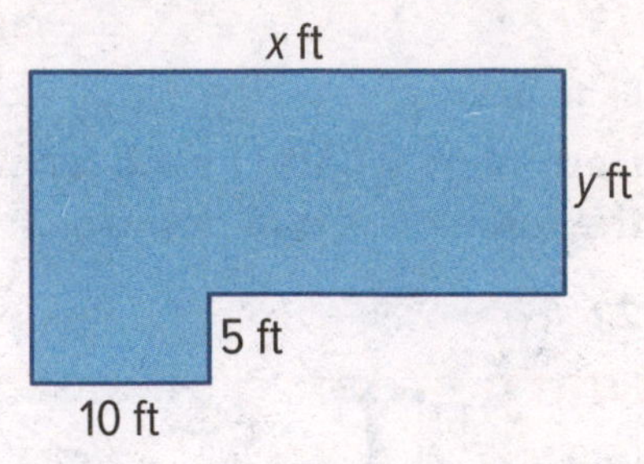

a. **REASONING** Write an equation that relates x and y.

b. Is the equation that relates x and y linear? Explain.

c. Graph the equation. State whether the graph has line symmetry or point symmetry.

38. POOL The graph represents a 720-gallon pool being drained. What are the x- and y-intercepts? What do the x- and y-intercepts represent?

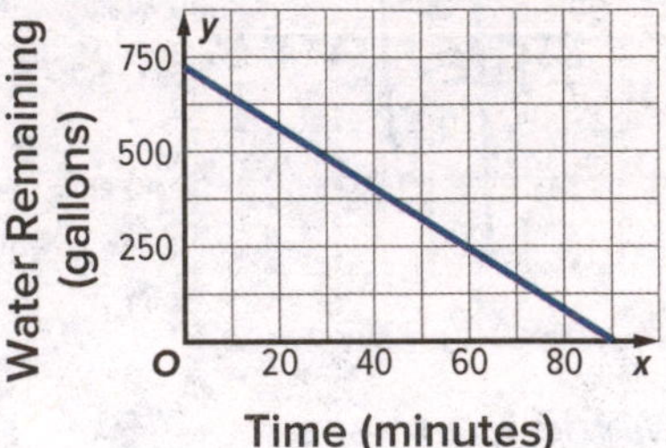

39. VOLUME The function, $f(r) = \frac{4}{3}\pi r^3$ describes the relationship between the volume $f(x)$ and radius r of a sphere. Determine whether the function is odd, even, or neither. Explain your reasoning.

40. STRUCTURE The table shows a function modeling the number of gifts **y** Cornell can wrap if he spends **x** hours wrapping. Can the table be modeled by a *linear* or *nonlinear* function? Explain.

Hours	0	1	2	3	4
Gifts	0	12	24	36	48

41. ARGUMENTS Javier claimed that all cubic functions are odd. Is he correct? If not, provide a counterexample.

42. USE A SOURCE Research online to find an equation that models a car's braking distance in relation to its speed. Then identify and interpret the y-intercept of the equation.

43. ANALYZE Determine whether an equation of the form $x = a$, where a is a constant, is *sometimes*, *always*, or *never* a linear function. Explain your reasoning.

44. WHICH ONE DOESN'T BELONG? Of the four equations shown, identify the one that does not belong. Explain your reasoning.

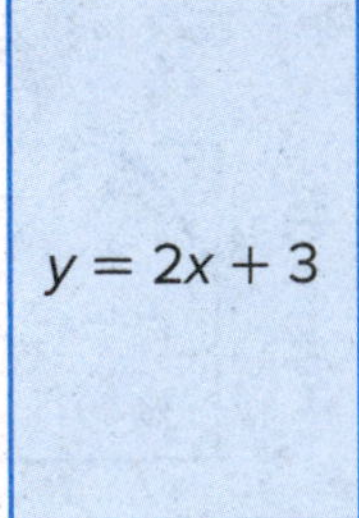

x	y
0	4
1	2
2	0
3	−2

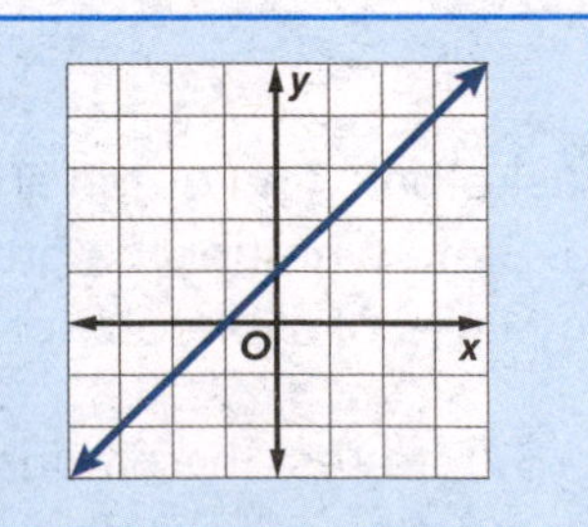

$y = 2xy$

Extrema and End Behavior

Learn Extrema of Functions

Graph of functions can have high and low points where they reach a maximum or minimum value. The maximum and minimum values of a function are called **extrema.** The **maximum** is at the highest point on the graph of a function. The **minimum** is at the lowest point on the graph of a function. The **relative maximum** is located at a point on the graph of a function where no other nearby points have a greater *y*-coordinate. The **relative minimum** is located at a point on the graph of a function where no other nearby points have a lesser *y*-coordinate.

Example 1 Find Extrema from Graphs

Identify and estimate the *x*- and *y*-values of the extrema. Round to the nearest tenth if necessary.

***f*(*x*)**

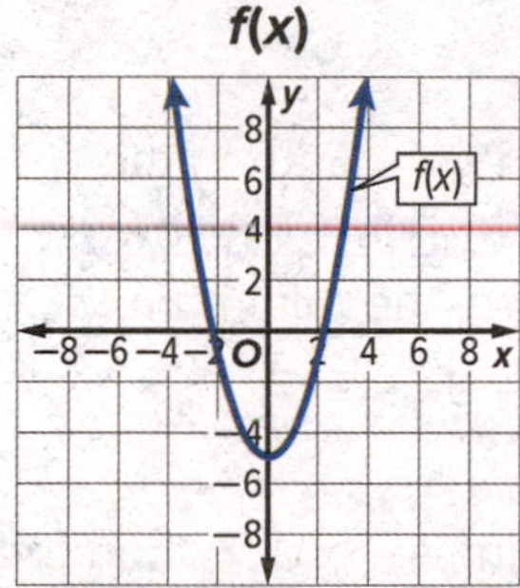

***g*(*x*)**

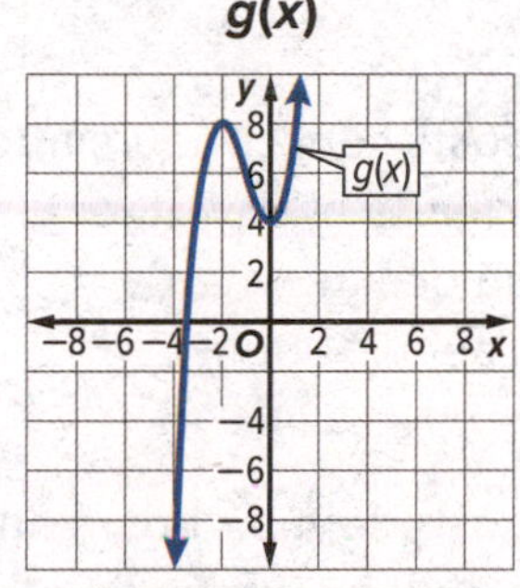

***f*(*x*):** The function $f(x)$ is ________ as it approaches $x = 0$ from the left and ________ as it moves away from $x = 0$. Further, (0, −5) is the lowest point on the graph, so (0, −5) is a ________ .

***g*(*x*)**: The function $g(x)$ is ________ as it approaches $x = -2$ from the left and ________ as it moves away from $x = -2$. Further, there are no greater *y*-coordinates surrounding (−2, 8). However, (−2, 8) is ____ the highest point on the graph, so (−2, 8) is a ________ relative maximum.

The function $g(x)$ is ________ as it approaches $x = 0$ from the left and ________ as it moves away from $x = 0$. Further, there are no ______ *y*-coordinates surrounding (0, 4). However, (0, 4) is not the ______ point on the graph, so (0, 4) is a ______ minimum.

Go Online You can complete an Extra Example online.

Today's Standards
F.IF.4; F.IF.7c
MP2, MP5

Today's Vocabulary
extrema
maximum
minimum
relative maximum
relative minimum
end behavior

Watch Out!

No Extrema Some functions, like $f(x) = x^3$, have no extrema.

Study Tip

Reading in Math In this context, *extrema* is the plural form of *extreme point*. The plural of *maximum* and *minimum* are *maxima* and *minima*, respectively.

Think About It!

Why are the extrema identified on the graph of g(x) relative maxima and minima instead of maxima and minima?

Your Notes

Example 2 Find and Interpret Extrema

SOCIAL MEDIA Use the table and graph to estimate the extrema of the function that models the number of posts on a social media site in hundred thousands *x* given the number hours since midnight *y*. Describe the meaning of the extrema in the context of the situation.

x	*y*
0	2.8
4	1.8
8	3.1
12	11.5
14	9.1
16	10.2
20	5.8
24	2.8

maxima

The number of posts sent ___ hours after midnight is ______ than the number of posts made at any other time during the day. The highest point at the graph occurs when $x =$ ___. Therefore, the maximum number of posts sent is about ________ at _____ noon.

minima

The number of posts sent __ hours after midnight is ____ than the number of posts made at any other time during the day. The lowest point at the graph occurs when $x =$ __. Therefore, the minimum number of posts sent is about ________ at ________.

relative maxima

The number of posts sent ___ hours after midnight is ______ than the number of posts during surrounding times, but is not the greatest number sent during the day. The graph has a relative peak when $x =$ ___. Therefore, there is a relative peak in number of posts sent, or relative maximum, at ________ of about ________ posts.

relative maxima

The number of posts sent ___ hours after midnight is ____ than the number of posts during surrounding times, but is not the least number sent during the day. The graph dips when $x =$ ___. Therefore, there is a relative low in number of posts sent, or relative minimum, at ________ of about ________ posts.

Explore End Behavior of Linear and Quadratic Functions

Online Activity Use graphing technology to complete the Explore.

INQUIRY Given the behavior of a linear or quadratic function as *x* increases towards infinity, how can you find the behavior as *x* decreases toward negative infinity or vice versa?

Go Online You can complete an Extra Example online.

Learn End Behavior of Graphs of Functions

End behavior is the behavior of a graph as x approaches positive or negative infinity. As you move right along the graph, the values of x are increasing toward infinity. This is denoted as $x \to \infty$. At the left end, the values of x are decreasing toward negative infinity, denoted as $x \to -\infty$.

Example 3 End Behavior of Linear Functions

Use the graphs to describe the end behavior of each linear function.

a. *f(x)*

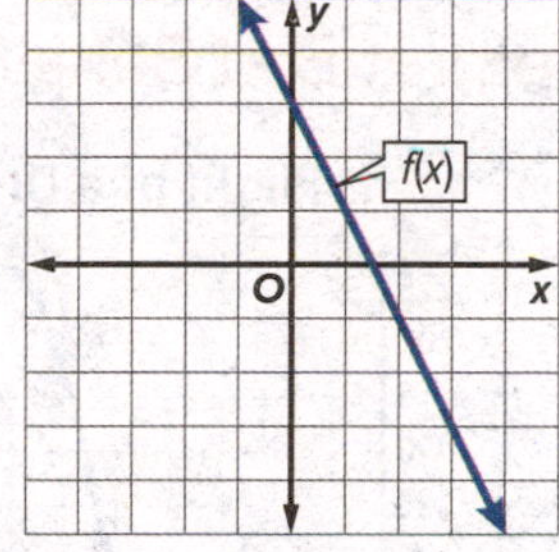

As x decreases, $f(x)$ ________, and as x increases $f(x)$ ________. Thus, as $x \to -\infty$, $f(x) \to$ ___ and as $x \to \infty$, $f(x) \to$ ____.

b. *g(x)*

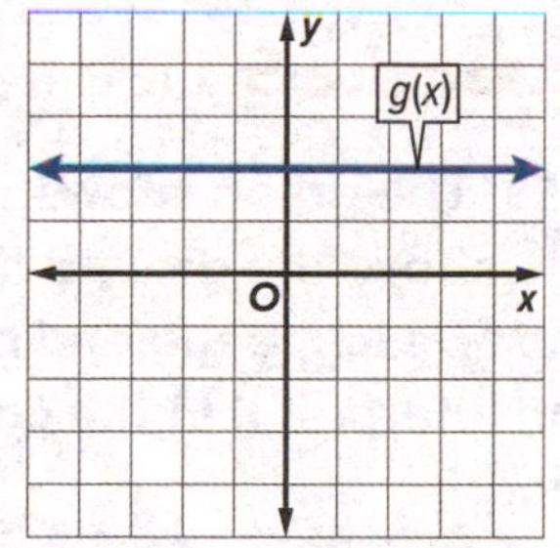

As x decreases or increases, $g(x) = 2$. Thus, as $x \to -\infty$, $g(x) =$ __ , and as $x \to \infty$, $g(x) =$ __ .

Check

Use the graph to describe the end behavior of the function.

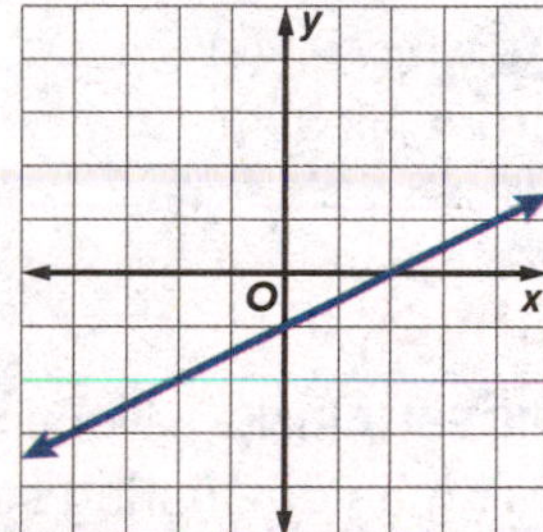

Example 4 End Behavior of Nonlinear Functions

Use the graphs to describe the end behavior of each nonlinear function.

a. *f(x)*

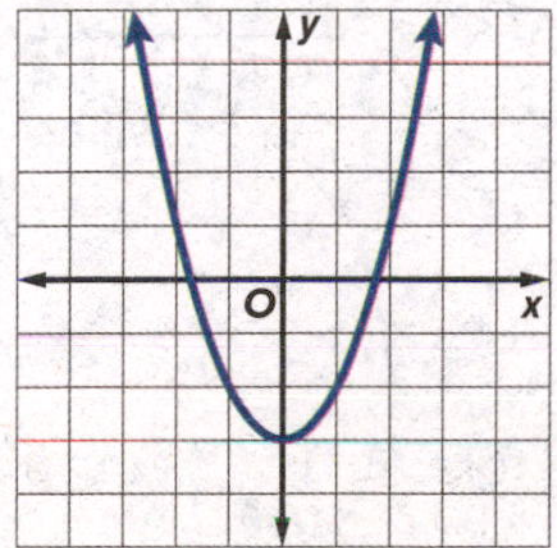

As you move left or right on the graph, $f(x)$ ________. Thus as $x \to -\infty$, $f(x) \to$ ___, and as $x \to \infty$, $f(x) \to$ ___.

b. *g(x)*

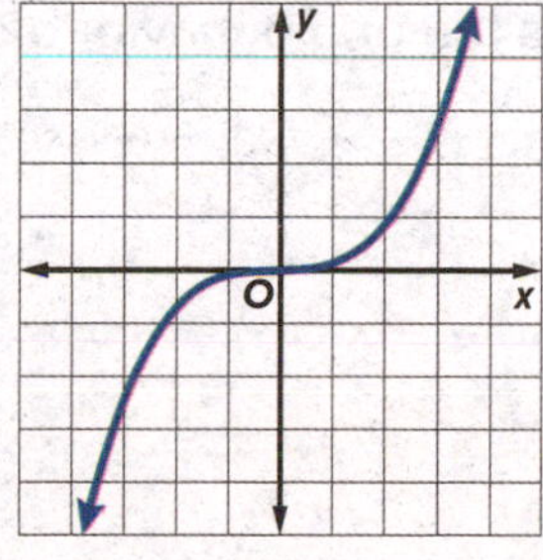

As $x \to -\infty$, $g(x) \to$ _____, and as $x \to \infty$, $g(x) \to$ ___ .

Go Online You can complete an Extra Example online.

Think About It!

For $f(x) = a$, where a is a real number, describe the end behavior of $f(x)$ as $x \to \infty$ and as $x \to -\infty$.

Talk About It!

In part **a**, the function's end behavior as $x \to -\infty$ is the opposite of the end behavior as $x \to \infty$. Do you think this is true for all linear functions where $m \neq 0$? Explain your reasoning.

Math History Minute

Júlio César de Mello e Souza (1895–1974) was a Brazilian mathematician who is known for his books on recreational mathematics. His most famous book, The Man Who Counted, includes problems, puzzles, and curiosities about math. The State Legislature of Rio de Janeiro declared that his birthday, May 6, be Mathematician's Day.

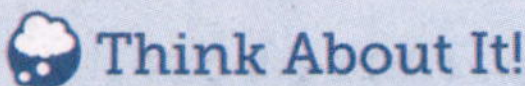

Think About It!

If the graph of a function is symmetric about a vertical line, what do you think is true about the end behavior of $f(x)$ as $x \to -\infty$ and as $x \to \infty$?

Check

Use the graphs to describe the end behavior of each function.

____

____

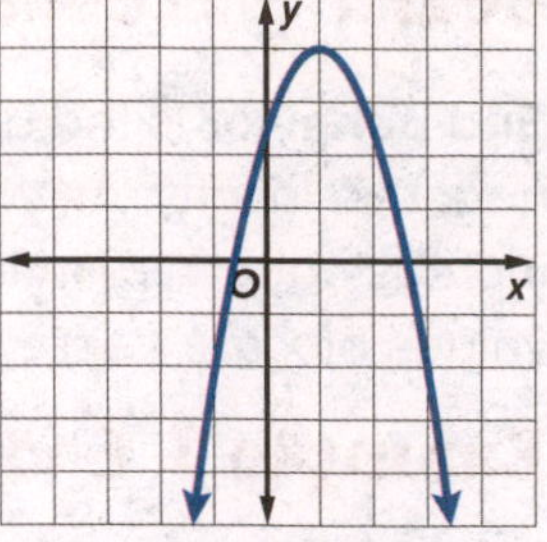

Example 5 Determine and Interpret End Behavior

DRONES **The graph shows the altitude of a drone above the ground $f(x)$ after x minutes. Describe the end behavior of $f(x)$ and interpret it in the context of the situation.**

Flight of a Drone

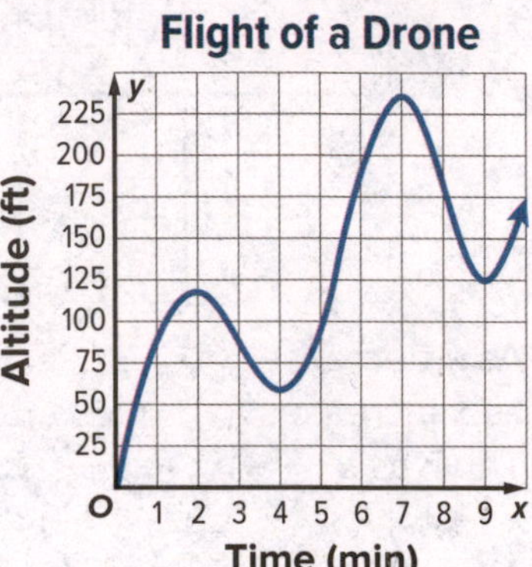

Since the drone cannot travel for a negative amount of time, the function is not defined for $x <$ ___. So, there is ___ end behavior as $x \to$ ___.

As $x \to \infty$, $f(x) \to$ ___. The longer the drone flies, the ___ it goes.

Study Tip:

Assumptions Assuming that the drone can continue to fly for an infinite amount of time and to an infinite altitude lets us analyze the end behavior as $x \to \infty$. While there are maximum legal altitudes that a drone can fly as well as limited battery life, assuming that the time and altitude will continue to increase allows us to describe the end behavior.

Check

RIDESHARING Mika and her friends are using a ride-sharing service to take them to a concert. The function models the cost of the ride $f(x)$ after x miles. Describe the end behavior of $f(x)$ and interpret it in the context of the situation.

Ridesharing

Part A

What is the end behavior of the function? ___

A. as $x \to -\infty$, $f(x) \to -\infty$; as $x \to \infty$, $f(x) \to -\infty$

B. as $x \to -\infty$, $f(x) \to \infty$; as $x \to \infty$, $f(x) \to \infty$

C. as $x \to \infty$, $f(x) \to -\infty$; $f(x)$ is not defined for $x < 0$

D. as $x \to \infty$, $f(x) \to \infty$; $f(x)$ is not defined for $x < 0$

Part B

What does the end behavior represents in the context of the situation?

Go Online to practice what you've learned in Lessons 1-1 through 1-3.

Go Online You can complete an Extra Example online.

Name ______________________ Period ____________ Date ____________

Practice

Go Online You can complete your homework online.

Examples 1 and 2

Identify and estimate the *x*- and *y*-values of the extrema. Round to the nearest tenth if necessary.

1.

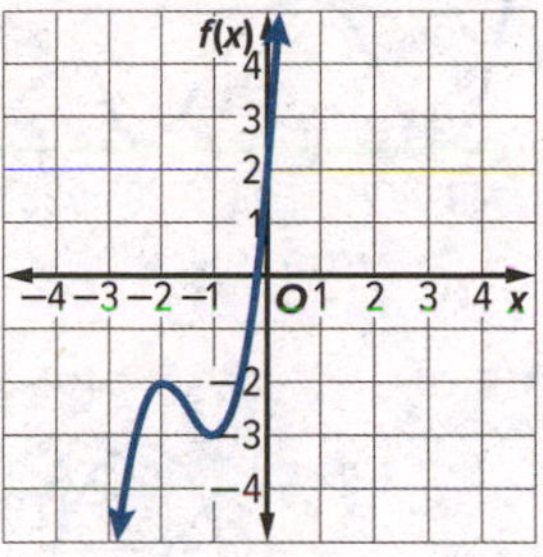

2.

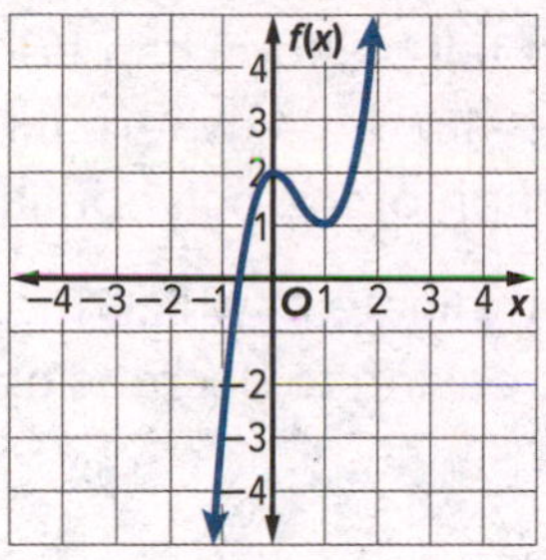

3.

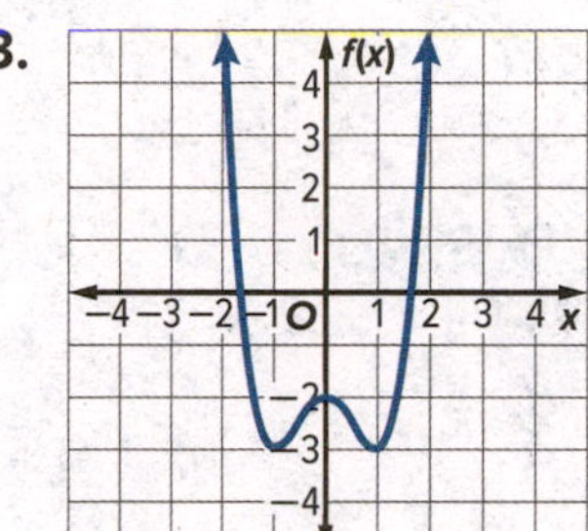

4.

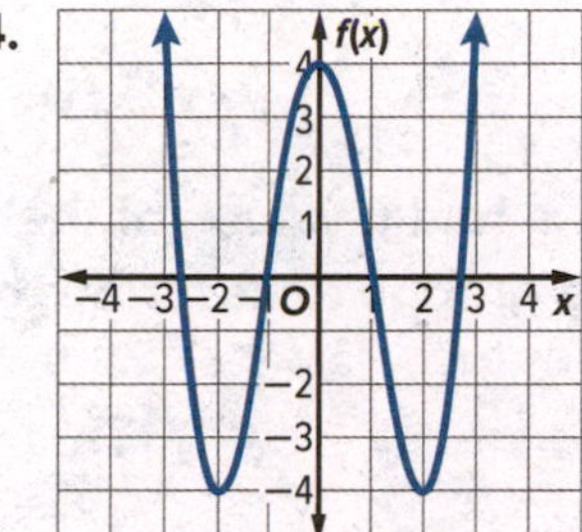

5. LANDSCAPES Jalen uses a graph of a function to model the shape of two hills in the background of a videogame that he is writing. Estimate the *x*-coordinates at which the relative maxima and relative minima occur. Describe the meaning of the extrema in the context of the situation.

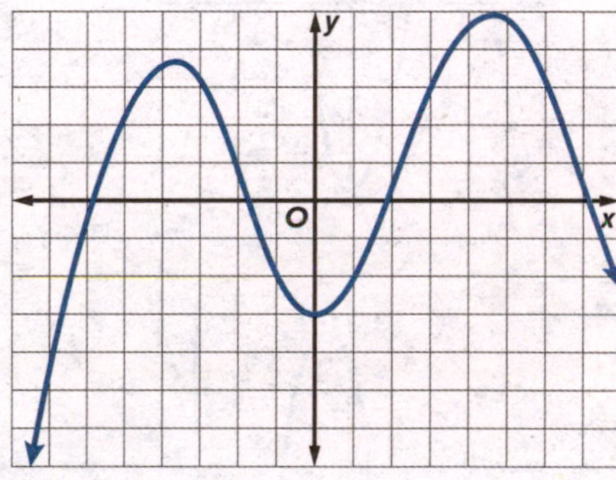

Example 3–5

Use the graphs to describe the end behavior of each function.

6.

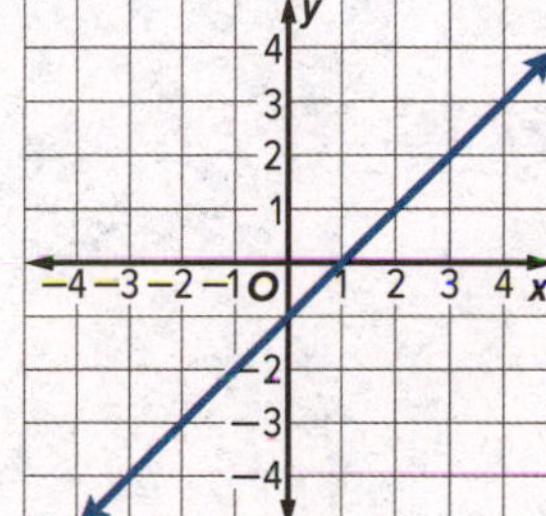

7.

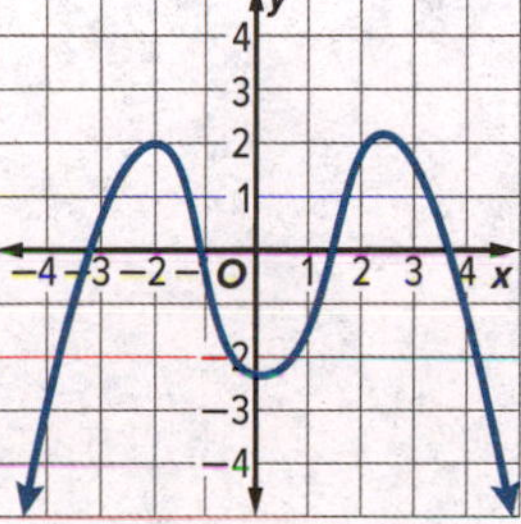

8.

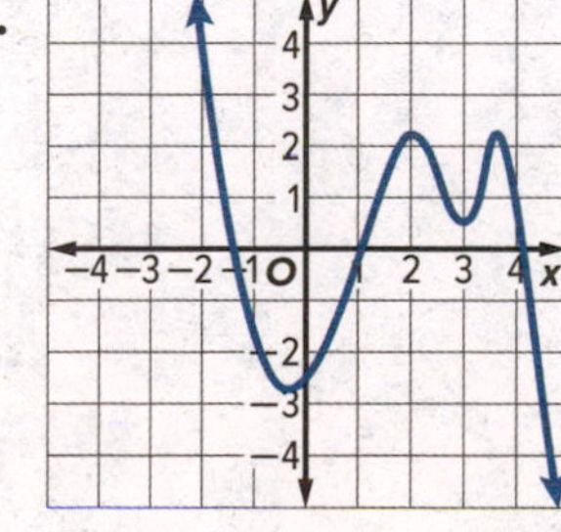

9.

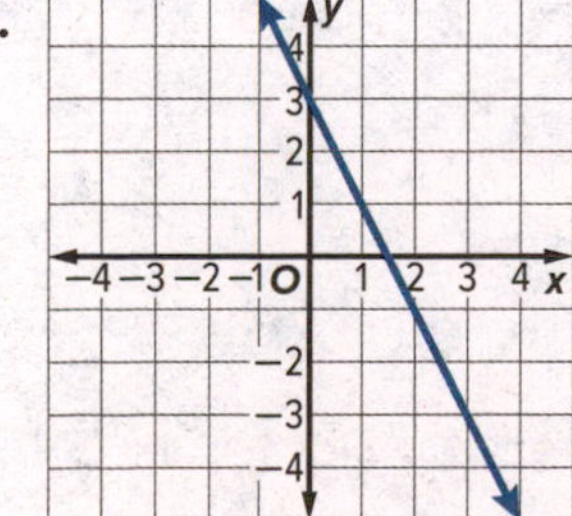

10. **ROLLERCOASTER** The graph shows the height of a rollercoaster in terms of its distance away from the starting point. Describe the end behavior and interpret the end behavior in the context of the situation.

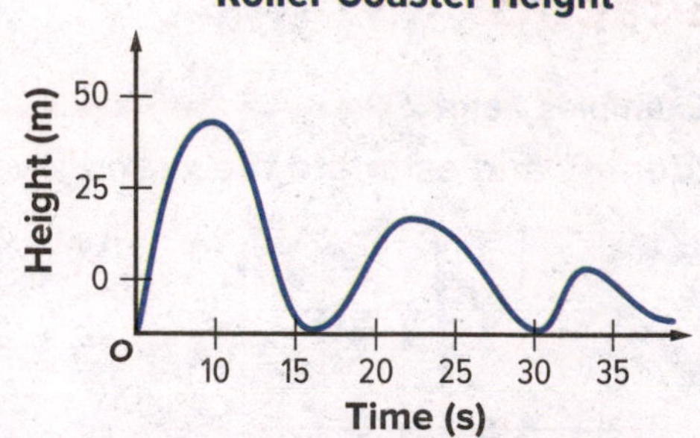

11. **MODEL** The height of a fish t seconds after it is thrown to a dolphin from a 64-foot-tall platform can be modeled by the equation $h(t) = -6t^2 + 48t + 64$, where $h(t)$ is the height of the fish in feet. The graph of the polynomial is shown.

a. Estimate the x-coordinate at which the height of the fish changes from increasing to decreasing. Describe the meaning in terms of the context of the situation.

b. Describe the end behavior of $h(t)$ and interpret the end behavior of $h(t)$ in the context of the situation.

Mixed Exercises

Identify and estimate the x- and y-values of the extrema. Round to the nearest tenth if necessary. Then use the graphs to describe the end behavior of each function.

12.

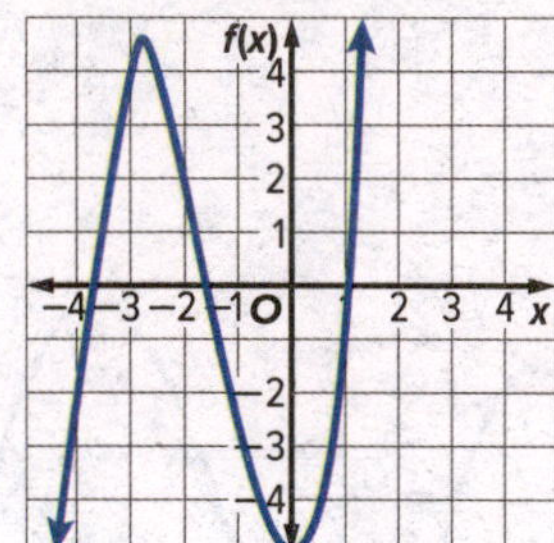

13.

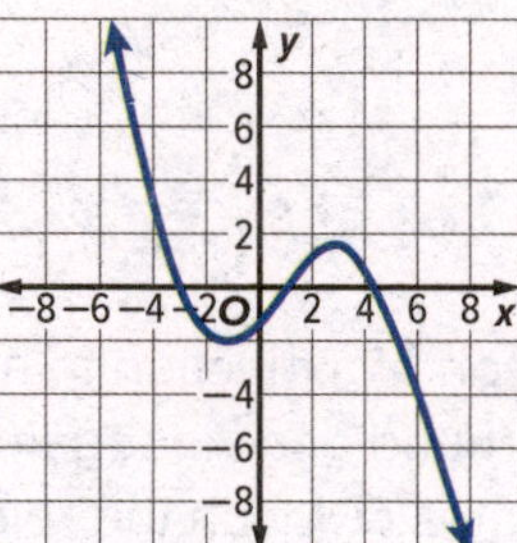

14.

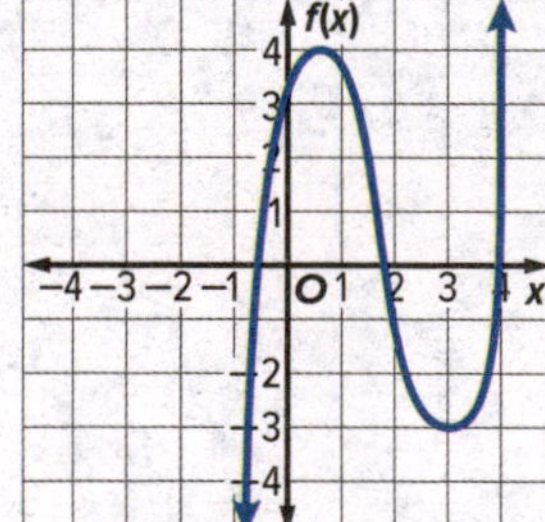

15.

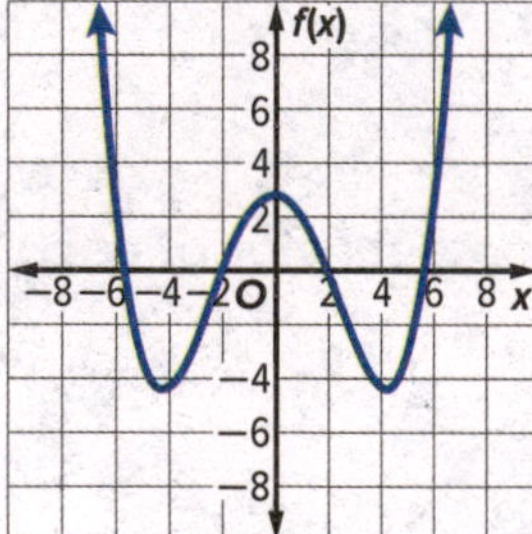

16.

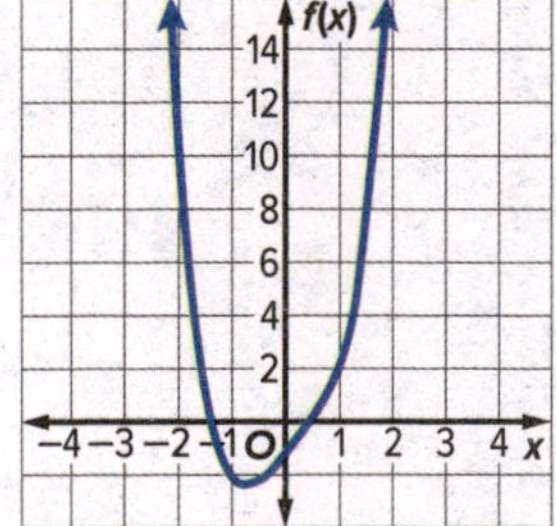

17.

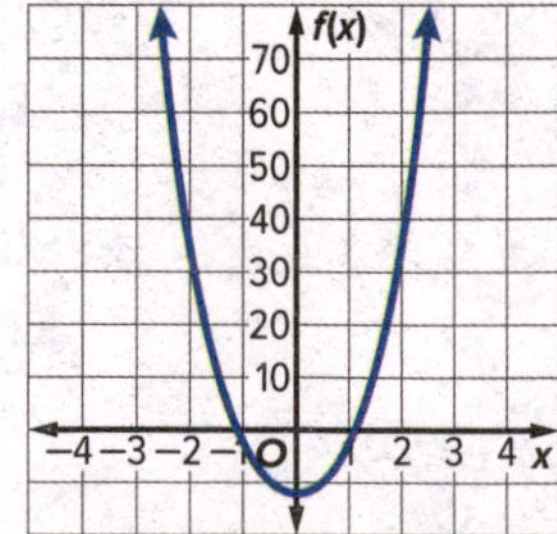

Name ________________ Period ________ Date ________

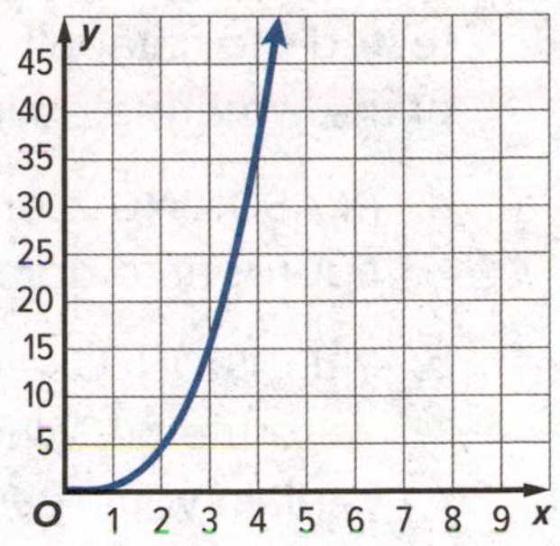

18. **SHAVED ICE** The volume of a conical shaved ice cone can be estimated by the formula $V = \frac{1}{3}\pi hr^2$, where h is the height of the cone and r is its radius. For a cone with a height of $\frac{\sqrt{3}}{3}r$, the volume is estimated as $\frac{\sqrt{3}}{9}\pi r^3$. The graph shows the function of the cone's volume. Describe the end behavior of the graph.

19. **STRUCTURE** Sketch a graph with the following characteristics:

- 2 relative maxima
- 2 relative minima
- end behavior: $x \to \infty$, $f(x) \to \infty$ and as $x \to -\infty$, $f(x) \to -\infty$.

Identify and estimate the *x*- and *y*-values of the extrema. Round to the nearest tenth if necessary. Then use the graphs to describe the end behavior of each function.

20.

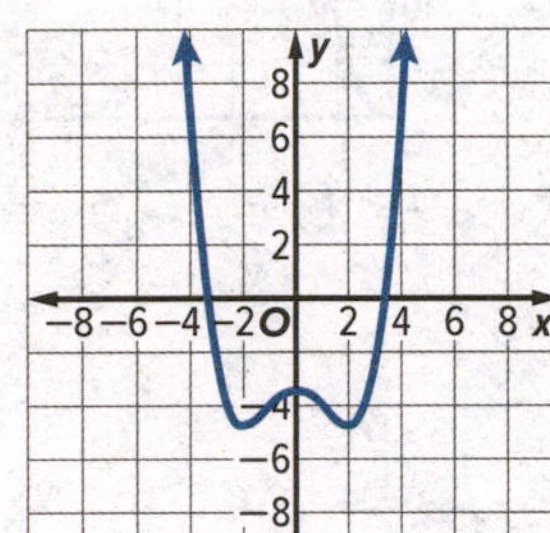

21.

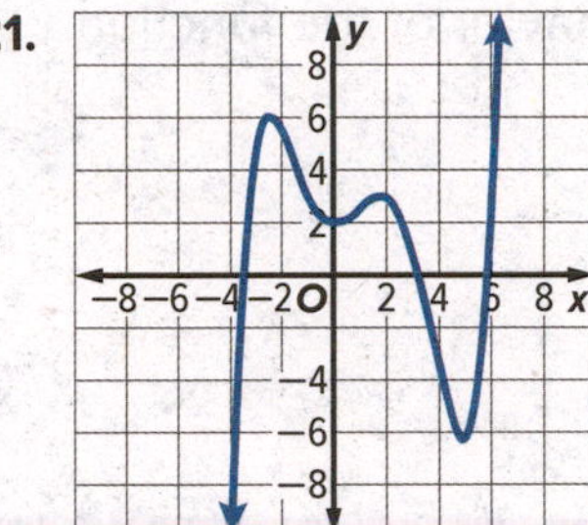

USE TOOLS (ESTIMATION) **Use a graphing calculator to estimate the *x*-coordinates at which the maxima and minima occur for each function. Round to the nearest hundredth.**

22. $f(x) = x^3 + 3x^2 - 6x - 6$

23. $f(x) = -2x^3 + 8$

24. $f(x) = -2x^4 + 5x^3 - 4x^2 + 3x - 7$

25. $f(x) = x^5 - 4x^3 + 3x^2 - 8x - 6$

26. **ARGUMENTS** Sheena says that in the graph of $f(x)$ shown at the right, the graph has relative maxima at B and G, and a relative minimum at A. Is she correct? Explain.

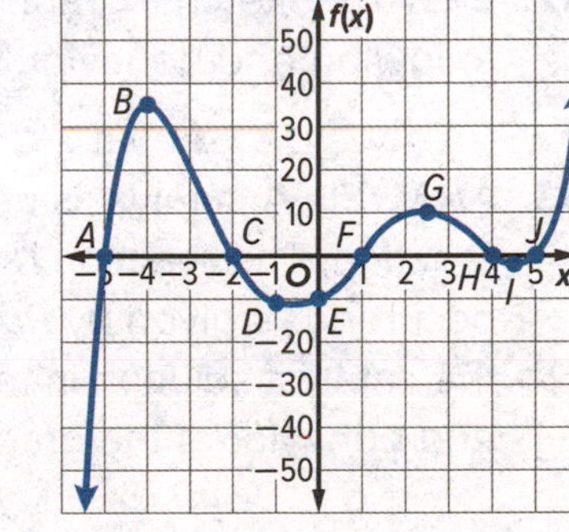

27. **STRUCTURE** Dynamic pressure is the pressure generated by the velocity of the moving fluid and is given by $q(v) = \frac{1}{2}pv^2$, where p is the density of the fluid and v is the velocity of the fluid. Water has a density of 1 g/cm^3. What happens to the dynamic pressure of water when the velocity continuously increases?

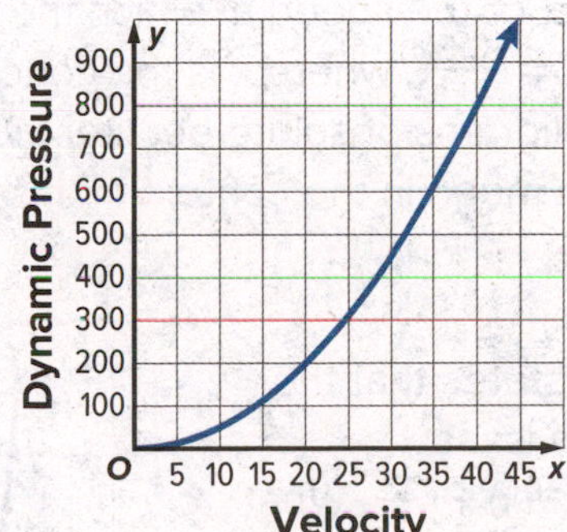

28. Several engineering students built a catapult for a class project. They tested the catapult by launching a watermelon and modeled the height h of the watermelon in feet over time t in seconds.

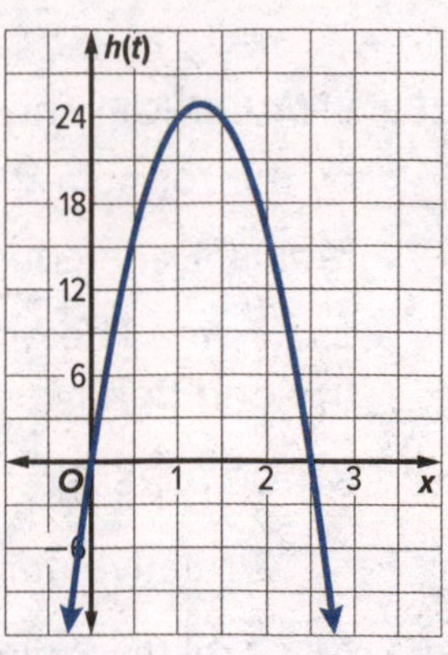

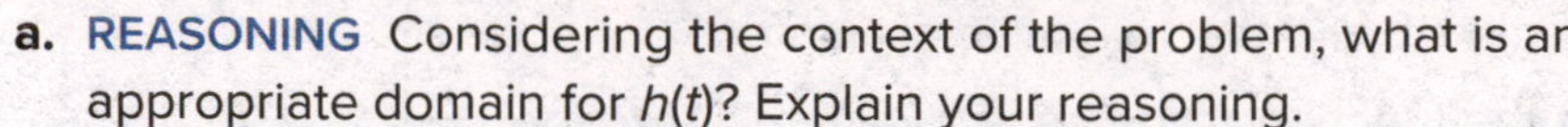

a. **REASONING** Considering the context of the problem, what is an appropriate domain for $h(t)$? Explain your reasoning.

b. **PRECISION** Use the graph of $h(t)$ to find the maximum height of the watermelon. When does the watermelon reach the maximum height? Explain your reasoning.

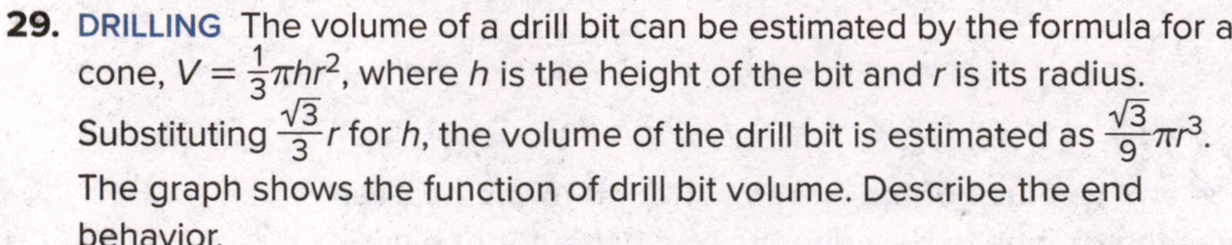

29. **DRILLING** The volume of a drill bit can be estimated by the formula for a cone, $V = \frac{1}{3}\pi hr^2$, where h is the height of the bit and r is its radius. Substituting $\frac{\sqrt{3}}{3}r$ for h, the volume of the drill bit is estimated as $\frac{\sqrt{3}}{9}\pi r^3$. The graph shows the function of drill bit volume. Describe the end behavior.

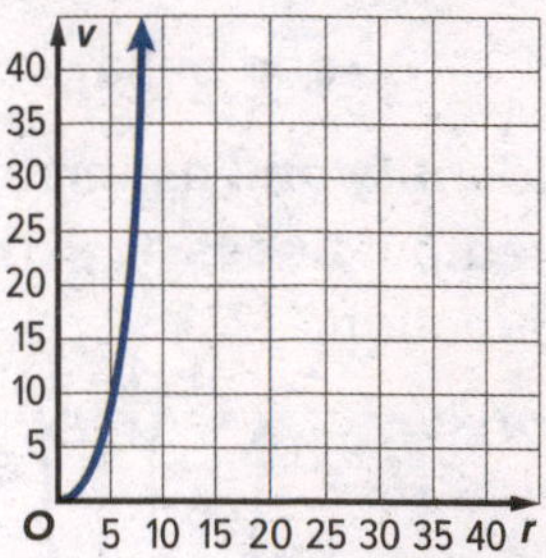

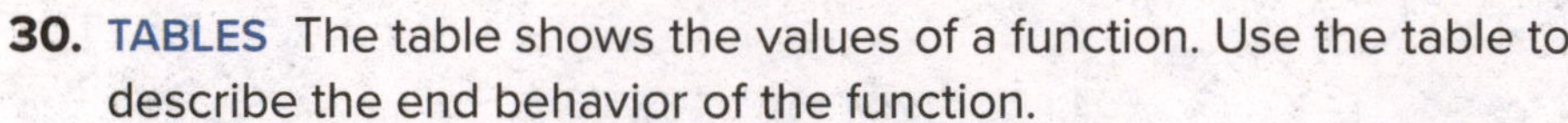

30. **TABLES** The table shows the values of a function. Use the table to describe the end behavior of the function.

x	y
−1000	−1,001,000,000
−100	−1,010,000
−10	−1100
−1	−2
1	0
10	900
100	990,000
1000	999,000,000

31. **WRITE** Describe what the end behavior of a graph is and how it is determined.

32. **CREATE** Sketch a graphs of linear function and nonlinear function with the following end behavior: as $x \to -\infty$, $f(x) \to \infty$ and as $x \to \infty$, $f(x) \to -\infty$.

33. **ANALYZE** A catalyst is used to increase the rate of a chemical reaction. The reaction rate, or the speed at which the reaction is occurring, is given by $R(x) = \frac{0.5x}{x+10}$, where x is the concentration of the catalyst solution in milligrams of solute per liter. What does the end behavior of the graph mean in the context of this experiment?

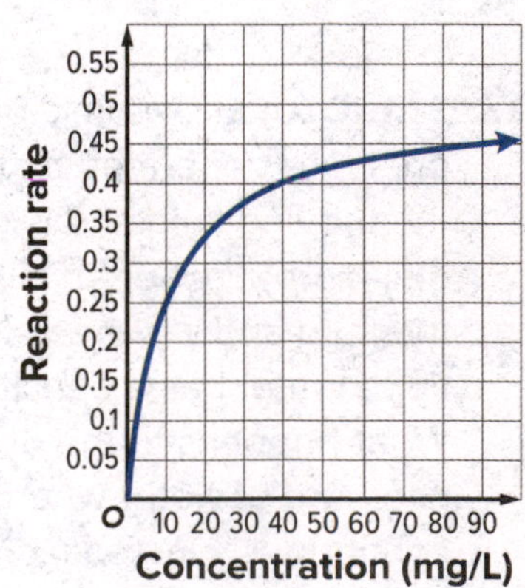

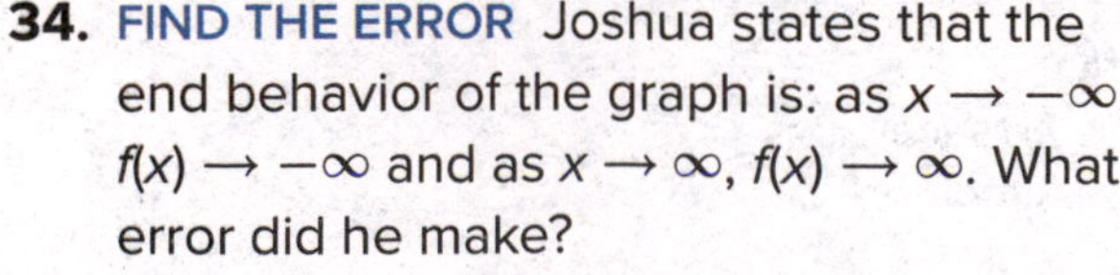

34. **FIND THE ERROR** Joshua states that the end behavior of the graph is: as $x \to -\infty$, $f(x) \to -\infty$ and as $x \to \infty$, $f(x) \to \infty$. What error did he make?

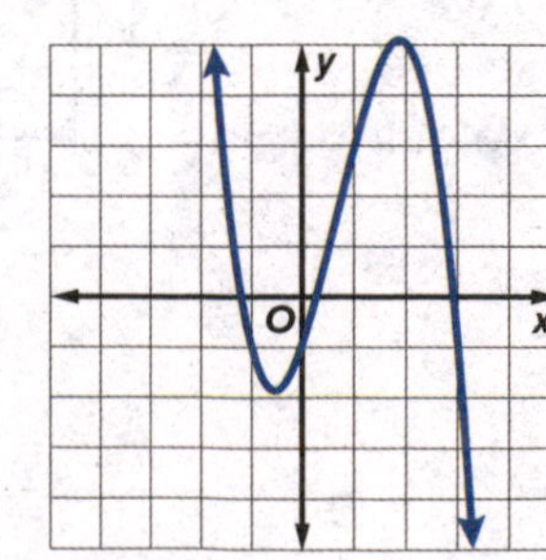

Sketching Graphs and Comparing Functions

Explore Using Technology to Examine Key Features of Graphs

Online Activity Use graphing technology to complete the Explore.

INQUIRY What can key features of a function tell you about its graph?

Learn Sketching Graphs of Functions

You can use key features of a function to sketch its graph.

Key Concept • Using Key Features

Key Feature	What it tells you about the graph
Domain	which values of x are defined for the function
Range	which values of y are defined for the function
Intercepts	where the graph crosses the x- or y axes
Symmetry	where one side of the graph is a reflection or rotation of the other side
End Behavior	what the graph is doing at the right and left sides as x approaches infinity or negative infinity
Extrema	high or low points where the graph changes from increasing to decreasing or vice versa
Increasing/ Decreasing	where the graph is going up or down as x increases
Positive/Negative	where the graph is above or below the x-axis

Example 1 Sketch a Linear Function

Use the key features of the function to sketch its graph.

y-intercept: (0, −70)

Linearity: linear

Positive: for values of x such that $x < -30$

Decreasing: for all values of x

End Behavior: As $x \to \infty$, $f(x) \to -\infty$.
As $x \to -\infty$, $f(x) \to \infty$.

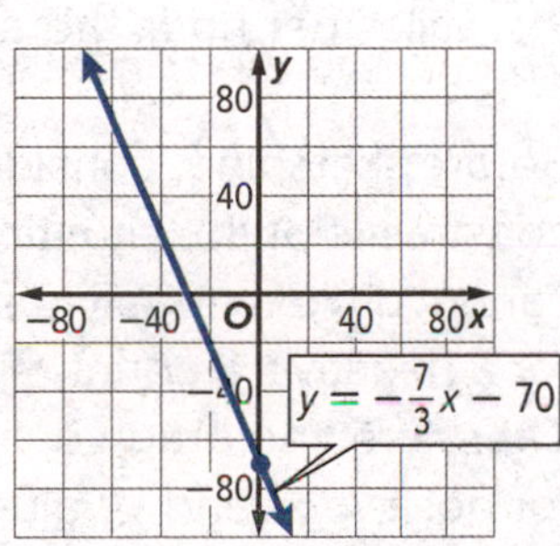

Go Online You can complete an Extra Example online.

Today's Standards
F.IF.4; F.IF.9
MP1, MP6

Study Tip

Scales and Axes Before you sketch a function, consider the scales or axes that best fit the situation. You want to capture as much information as possible, so you want the scales to be big enough to easily see the extrema and x- and y intercepts, but not so big that you cannot determine the values.

Talk About It!

Given the y-intercept and for what values of x the function is positive, what other information do you need to sketch a linear function? Explain your reasoning.

Your Notes

Study Tip

Assumptions When sketching the function using the given key features, assumptions must be made. As in this example, the same key features could describe many different graphs. The key features could also be represented by a parabola, a curve that is narrower or wider, or an absolute value function.

Think About It!

Explain why the end behavior is not defined in the context of this situation.

Think About It!

Based on the graph, the speed of the car at 10 seconds is 40 miles per hour. Is it appropriate to assume that the car is traveling that exact speed at a specific time? Explain.

Example 2 Sketch a Nonlinear Function

Use the key features of the function to sketch its graph.

y-intercept: (0, 3)

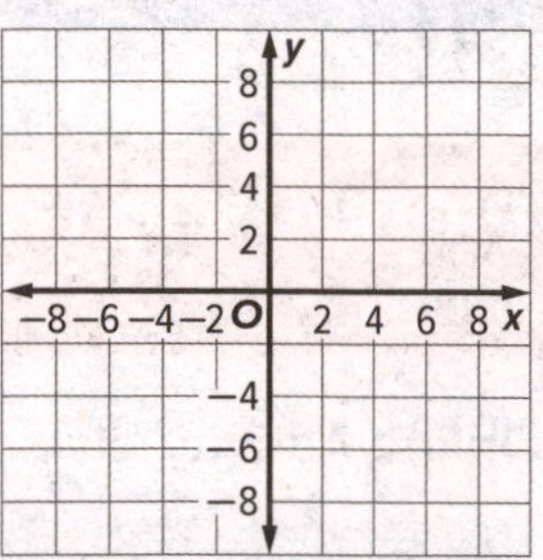

Linearity: nonlinear

Continuity: continuous

Positive: for values of x

Decreasing: for all values of x such that $x < 0$

Extrema: relative minimum at (0, 3)

End Behavior: As $x \to \infty$, $f(x) \to \infty$.
As $x \to -\infty$, $f(x) \to \infty$.

Example 3 Sketch a Real-World Function

TEST DRIVE **Hae is test driving a car she is thinking of buying. She decides to accelerate to 60 miles per hour and then decelerate to a stop to test its acceleration and brakes. It takes her 15 seconds to reach her maximum speed and 15 additional seconds to come to a stop. Use the key features to sketch a graph that shows the speed y as a function of time x.**

***y*-intercept:** Hae starts her test drive at a speed of 0 miles per hour.

Linear or Nonlinear: The function that models the situation is nonlinear.

Extrema: Hae's maximum speed is 60 miles per hour, which she reaches 15 seconds into her test drive.

Increasing: Hae ________ the speed at a uniform rate for the first 15 seconds.

Decreasing: Hae decreases the speed at a ________ rate for the next 15 seconds until she reaches a ________.

End Behavior: Because Hae starts at ____ miles per hour and ends at ____ miles per hour, there is ____ end behavior.

Before sketching, consider the constraints of the situation. Hae cannot drive a negative speed or for a negative amount of time. Therefore, the graph only exists for positive x- and y-values.

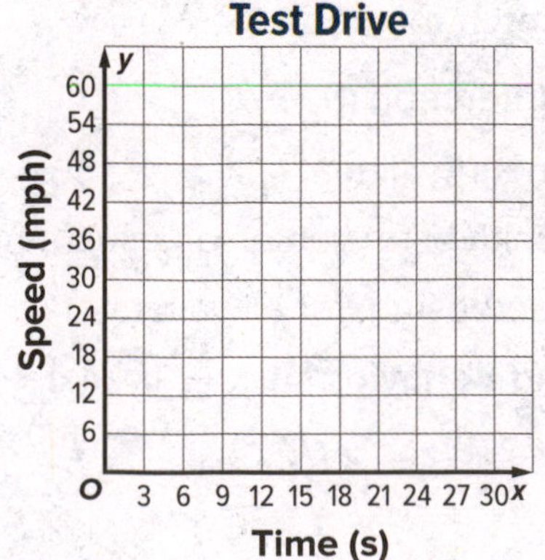

Go Online You can complete an Extra Example online.

Example 4 Compare Properties of Linear Functions

Functions can be represented with a graph, a table, or by a verbal description. You can compare the properties and key features of functions represented in these different ways.

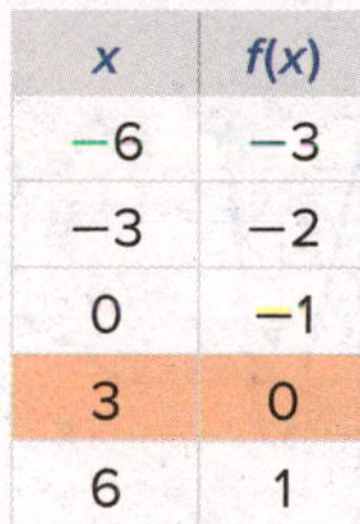

x	$f(x)$
−6	−3
−3	−2
0	−1
3	0
6	1

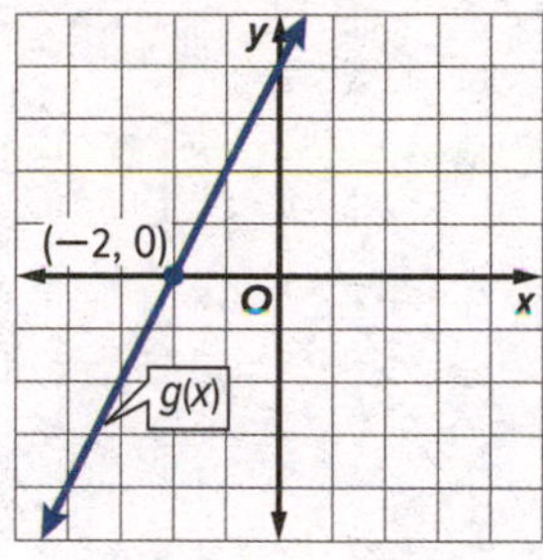

The x-intercept of $f(x)$ is ____, and the x-intercept of $g(x)$ is ____. The x-intercept of $f(x)$ is ______ than the x-intercept of $g(x)$.

So, $f(x)$ intersects the x-axis at a point farther to the ______ than $g(x)$.

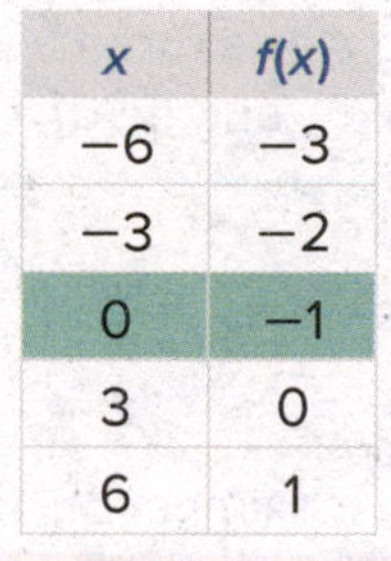

x	$f(x)$
−6	−3
−3	−2
0	−1
3	0
6	1

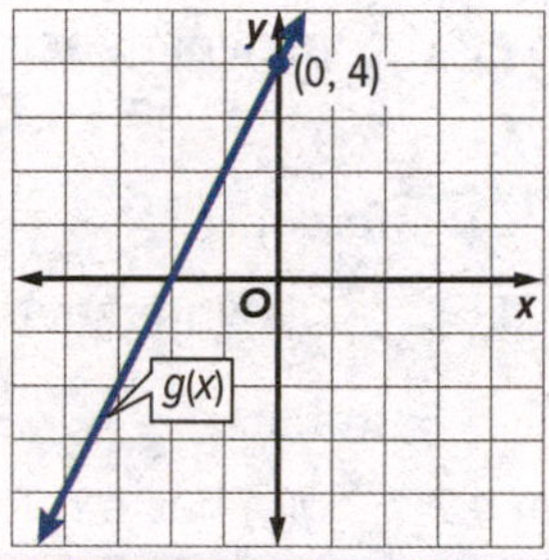

The y-intercept of $f(x)$ is ____, and the y-intercept of $g(x)$ is ____. The y-intercept of $g(x)$ is ______ than the y-intercept of $f(x)$.

So, $g(x)$ intersects the y-axis at a ______ point than $f(x)$.

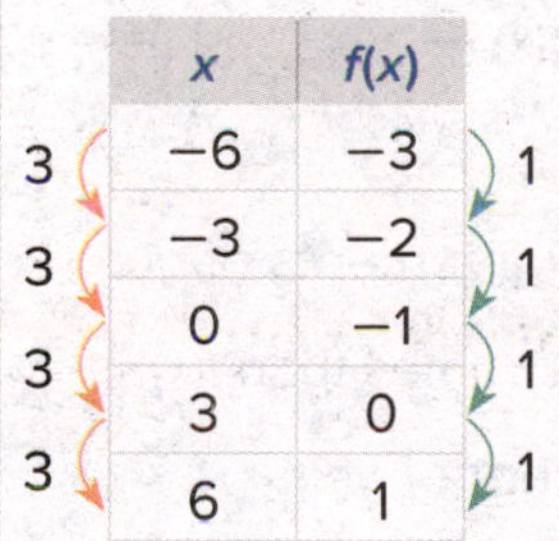

	x	$f(x)$	
3	−6	−3	1
3	−3	−2	1
3	0	−1	1
3	3	0	1
	6	1	

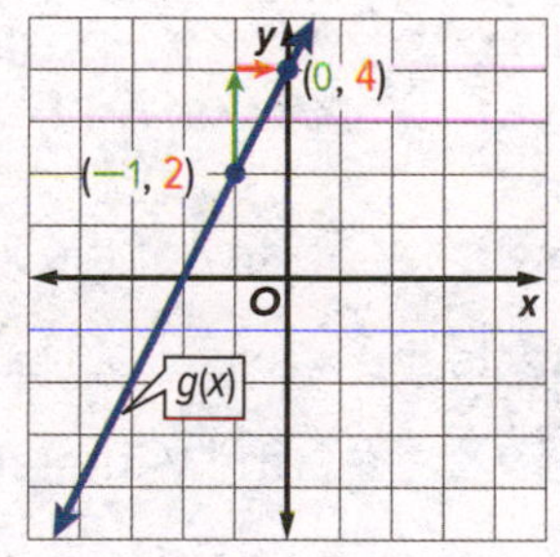

The slope of $f(x)$ is $\frac{1}{3}$ and the slope of $g(x)$ is 2. Each function is increasing, but the slope of $g(x)$ is greater than the slope of $f(x)$.

So, $g(x)$ increases faster than $f(x)$.

Think About It!

How would a function that passes through (1, 0) with a slope of −4 compare to $f(x)$ and $g(x)$?

Pause and Reflect

Did you struggle with anything in this lesson? If so, how did you deal with it?

Go Online You can complete an Extra Example online.

Example 5 Compare Properties of Nonlinear Functions

Examine the categories to see how to use the description and the graph to identify key features of each function. Then complete the statements to compare the two functions.

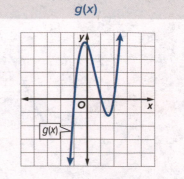

$f(x)$	$g(x)$
x-intercept: $(-3.4, 0)$ y-intercept: $(0, 1.5)$ relative maximum: $(-2.3, 4.7)$ relative minimum: $(-0.4, 1.1)$ end behavior: as $x \to -\infty$, $f(x) \to -\infty$ and as $x \to \infty$, $f(x) \to \infty$	
***x*-intercepts**	
$f(x)$ intersects the x-axis once at $(-3.4, 0)$.	$g(x)$ intersects the x-axis three times at $(-1, 0)$, $(1, 0)$, and $(2, 0)$.
***y*-intercept**	
$f(x)$ intersects the y-axis at $(0, 1.5)$.	$g(x)$ intersects the y-axis at $(0, 4)$.
Extrema	
$f(x)$ has a relative maximum of 4.7 and a relative minimum of 1.1.	$g(x)$ has a relative maximum of about 4.2 and a relative minimum of about -1.2.
End Behavior	
As $x \to -\infty$, $f(x) \to -\infty$, and as $x \to \infty$, $f(x) \to \infty$,	As $x \to -\infty$, $g(x) \to -\infty$, and as $x \to \infty$, $f(x) \to \infty$,

- The x-intercept of $f(x)$ is _______ any of the x-intercepts of $g(x)$.
- The graph of $g(x)$ intersects the x-axis _______ times than $f(x)$.
- The y-intercept of $f(x)$ is _______ the y-intercept of $g(x)$.
- So, $g(x)$ intersects the y-axis at a _______ point than $f(x)$.
- The relative maximum of $f(x)$ is _______ the relative maximum of $g(x)$. The relative minimum of $f(x)$ is _______ the relative minimum of $g(x)$.
- The two functions have _______ end behavior.

Go Online You can complete an Extra Example online.

Name ____________________ Period __________ Date __________

Practice

Go Online You can complete your homework online.

Examples 1 and 2

Use the key features of each function to sketch its graph.

1. ***x*-intercept:** (2, 0)
   ***y*-intercept:** (0, −6)
   Linearity: linear
   Continuity: continuous
   Positive: for values $x > 2$
   Increasing: for all values of x
   End Behavior: As $x \to \infty$, $f(x) \to \infty$ and as $x \to -\infty$, $f(x) \to -\infty$.

2. ***x*-intercept:** (0, 0)
   ***y*-intercept:** (0, 0)
   Linearity: linear
   Continuity: continuous
   Positive: for values $x < 0$
   Negative: for values of $x > 0$
   Decreasing: for all values of x
   End Behavior: As $x \to \infty$, $f(x) \to -\infty$ and as $x \to -\infty$, $f(x) \to \infty$.

3. ***x*-intercept:** (5, 0)
   ***y*-intercept:** (0, 5)
   Linearity: linear
   Continuity: continuous
   Positive: for values $x < 5$
   Decreasing: for all values of x
   End Behavior: As $x \to \infty$, $f(x) \to -\infty$ and as $x \to -\infty$, $f(x) \to \infty$.

4. ***x*-intercept:** (5, 0)
   ***y*-intercept:** (0, 2)
   Linearity: linear
   Continuity: continuous
   Positive: for values $x < 5$
   Decreasing: for all values of x
   End Behavior: As $x \to \infty$, $f(x) \to -\infty$ and as $x \to -\infty$, $f(x) \to \infty$.

5. ***x*-intercept:** (−1, 0) and (1, 0)
   ***y*-intercept:** (0, 1)
   Linearity: nonlinear
   Continuity: continuous
   Symmetry: symmetric about the line $x = 0$
   Positive: for values $-1 < x < 1$
   Negative: for values of $x < -1$ and $x > 1$
   Increasing: for all values of $x < 0$
   Decreasing: for all values of $x > 0$
   Extrema: maximum at (0, 1)
   End Behavior: As $x \to \infty$, $f(x) \to -\infty$ and as $x \to -\infty$, $f(x) \to \infty$.

6. ***x*-intercept:** (−3, 0) and (2, 0)
   ***y*-intercept:** (0, −4)
   Linearity: nonlinear
   Continuity: continuous
   Positive: for values $x < -3$ and $x > 2$
   Negative: for values of $-3 < x < 2$
   Increasing: for all values of $x > 0$
   Decreasing: for all values of $x < 0$
   Extrema: relative minimum at (−2, −3)
   End Behavior: As $x \to \infty$, $f(x) \to \infty$ and as $x \to -\infty$, $f(x) \to \infty$.

Example 3

7. **PELICANS** A pelican descended to the ground. The pelican starts at a height of 6 feet. The pelican reaches the ground, at a height of 0 feet, after 3 seconds. The function that models the situation is linear. Use the key features to sketch a graph.

8. **SCOOTERS** Greg rides his motorized scooter for 20 minutes. Greg starts riding at 0 mph. Greg's maximum speed is 35 mph, which he reaches 5 minutes after he starts riding. Greg's speed increases steadily for 5 minutes. At the 10-minute mark, Greg decreases his speed for 2.5 minutes, then he stays at 20 mph for 5 minutes. At the 17.5-minute mark, he again decreases his speed for 2.5 minutes until he stops. Use the key features to sketch a graph.

Examples 4 and 5

9. Compare the key features of the functions represented with a graph and a table.

$f(x)$

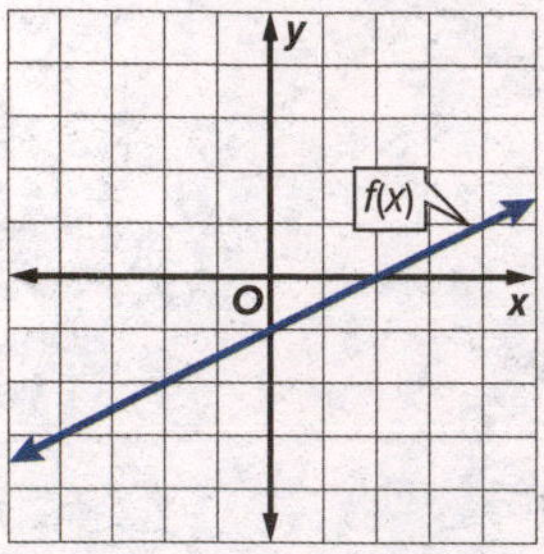

$g(x)$

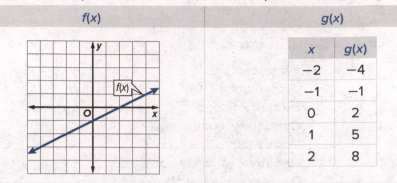

x	$g(x)$
−2	−4
−1	−1
0	2
1	5
2	8

10. Compare the key features of the functions represented with a graph and a verbal description.

$f(x)$

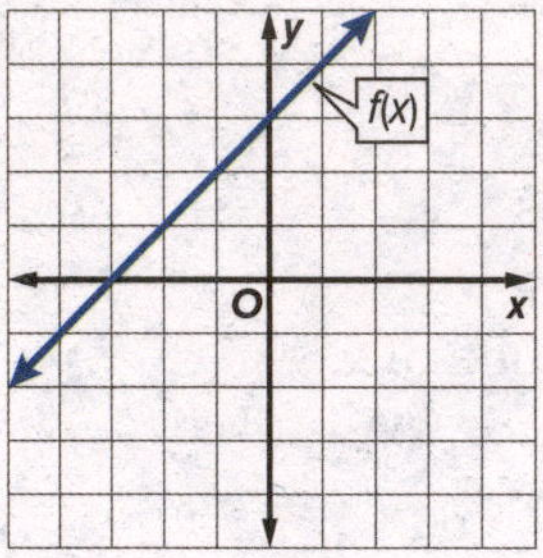

$g(x)$

x-intercept: (−2, 0)

y-intercept: (0, −2)

slope: −1

11. Compare the key features of the functions represented with a table and a verbal description.

$f(x)$

x	$f(x)$
−4	0
−3	−3
−2	−4
−1	−3
0	0

$g(x)$

x-intercept: (1, 0)

y-intercept: (0, −7)

relative maximum: none

relative minimum: none

end behavior: as $x \to -\infty$, $g(x) \to -\infty$ and as $x \to \infty$, $g(x) \to \infty$

12. Compare the key features of the functions represented with a table and a verbal description.

$f(x)$

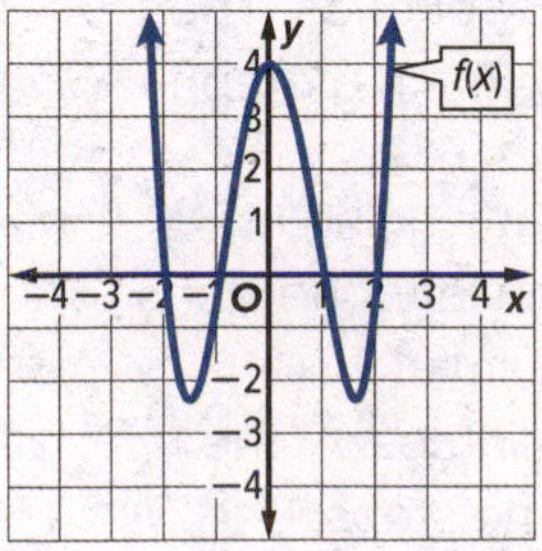

$g(x)$

x-intercept: (−1, 0), (1, 0), (2, 0)

y-intercept: (0, −4)

relative maximum: (1.37, 0.35)

relative minimum: (−0.37, −4.85), (2, 0)

end behavior: as $x \to -\infty$, $g(x) \to \infty$ and as $x \to \infty$, $g(x) \to \infty$

Name ________________ Period ________ Date ________

Mixed Exercises

Use the key features of each function to sketch its graph.

13. ***x*-intercept:** (1, 0)
y-intercept: (0, −1)
Linearity: linear
Continuity: continuous
Positive: for values $x > 1$
Increasing: for all values of x
End Behavior: As $x \to -\infty$, $f(x) \to -\infty$ and as $x \to \infty$, $f(x) \to \infty$

14. ***x*-intercept:** (−2, 0) and (2, 0)
y-intercept: (0, −1)
Linearity: nonlinear
Continuity: continuous
Symmetry: symmetric about the line $x = 0$
Positive: for values $x < -2$ and $x > 2$
Negative: for values of $-2 < x < 2$
Increasing: for all values of $x > 0$
Decreasing: for all values of $x < 0$
Extrema: minimum at (0, −1)
End Behavior: As $x \to -\infty$, $f(x) \to \infty$ and as $x \to \infty$, $f(x) \to \infty$

15. Compare the key features of the functions represented with a table and a verbal description.

f(x)

x	$f(x)$
$-\frac{2}{3}$	1
$-\frac{1}{3}$	$\frac{3}{4}$
0	$\frac{1}{2}$
$\frac{1}{3}$	$\frac{1}{4}$
$\frac{2}{3}$	0

g(x)

x-intercept: $\left(\frac{3}{8}, 0\right)$
y-intercept: $\left(0, \frac{1}{2}\right)$
slope: $-\frac{4}{3}$

16. Compare the key features of the functions represented with a graph and a table.

f(x)

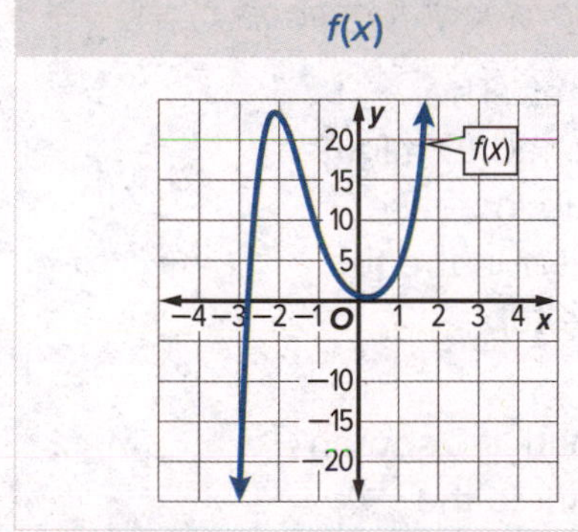

g(x)

x	$g(x)$
−1	7
−0.56	0
0	−3
1.89	0
2	1

17. **MODELING** Sketch the graph of a linear function with the following key features. The *x*-intercept is 2. The *y*-intercept is 2. The function is decreasing for all values of *x*. The function is positive for $x < 2$. As $x \to -\infty$, $f(x) \to \infty$ and as $x \to \infty$, $f(x) \to -\infty$.

18. **WATER** Sia filled a pitcher with water. The pitcher started with 0 ounces of water. After 8 seconds the pitcher contains 64 ounces of water. The function that models the situation is linear.

   a. Use the key features to sketch a graph.

   b. **REASONING** What is the end behavior of the graph? Explain.

19. **USE TOOLS** Monica walks for 60 minutes. She starts walking from her house. The maximum distance Monica is from her house is 2 miles, which she reaches 30 minutes after she starts walking. At the 30-minute mark, Monica starts waking back to her house for 30 minutes until she reaches her house. Use the key features to sketch a graph.

20. **USE A SOURCE** Research the value of a new car after it is purchased. Use the information you collect to describe key features of a graph that represents the value of a new car x years after it is purchased. Then use the key features to sketch a graph.

21. **SKI LIFT** A ski lift descends at a steady pace down a mountainside from a height of 1800 feet to ground level. If it makes no stops along the way to load or unload passengers, then the time it takes to complete its descension is 4 minutes.
    - **a.** Is the graph that relates the lift's height as a function of time linear or nonlinear? Explain.
    - **b.** Use the key features to sketch a graph.

22. **ARGUMENTS** Keisha babysits for her aunt for an hourly rate of \$9. The graph shows Keisha's earnings y as a function of hours spent babysitting x. Explain why the graph only exists for positive x- and y-values.

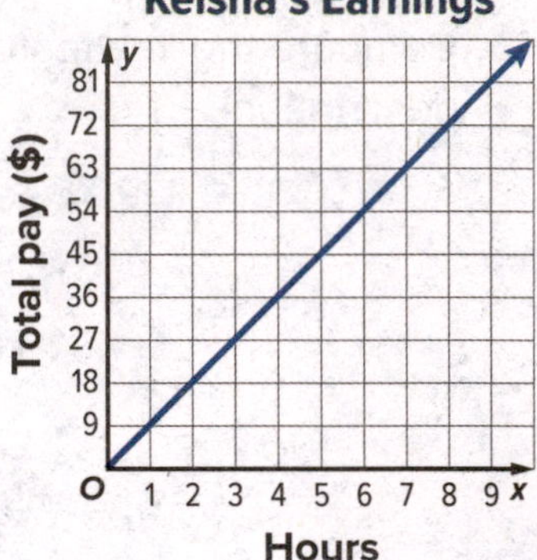

23. **CREATE** Choose a function and create a list key features to describe the function. Then sketch the function.

24. **WRITE** Describe the relationship between the slope of a linear function and when the function is increasing or decreasing.

25. **ANALYZE** Determine whether the statement is always, sometimes, or never true.

    A graph that has more than one x-intercept is represented by a nonlinear function.

26. **PERSEVERE** Deborah filled an empty tub with water for 30 minutes. The maximum amount of water in the tub is 50 gallons, which is reached 10 minutes after Deborah starts filling the tub. The amount of water in the tub increases steadily for 10 minutes. At the 10-minute mark, the amount of water in the tub starts decreasing for 20 minutes until there is no water left in the tub.
    - **a.** Use the key features to sketch a graph.
    - **b.** Describe an event that could have occurred at the 10-minute mark if Deborah continues filling the tub at the same rate from the 10-minute mark to the 30-minute mark as the rate from the 0-minute mark to the 10-minute mark.

27. **FIND THE ERROR** Linda and Rubio sketched a graph with the following key features. The x-intercept is 2. The y-intercept is -9. The function is positive for $x > 2$. As $x \to -\infty$, $f(x) \to -\infty$ and as $x \to \infty$, $f(x) \to \infty$. Is either graph correct based on the key features? Explain your reasoning.

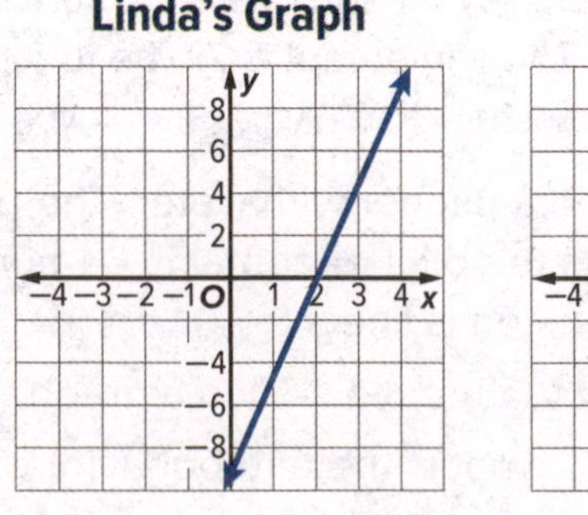

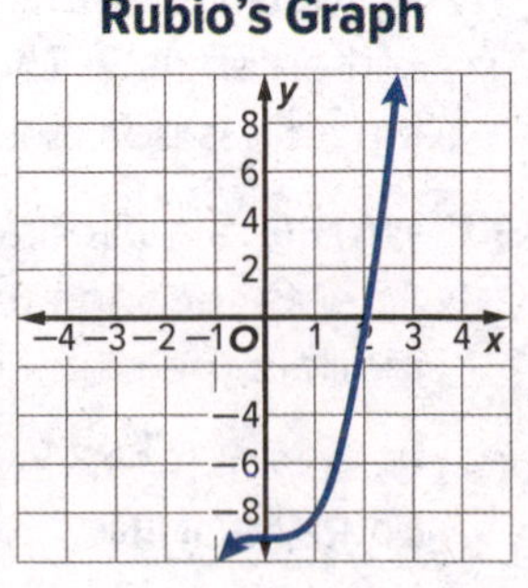

Graphing Linear Functions and Inequalities

Learn Graphing Linear Functions

The graph of a linear function represents all ordered pairs that are true for the function. You can use various methods to graph a linear function.

Example 1 Graph by Using a Table

Graph $x + 3y - 6 = 0$ by using a table.

Solve the equation for y.

$x + 3y - 6 = 0$	Original function
$3y - 6 =$ ______	Subtract x from each side.
$3y = -x$ ______	Add 6 to each side.
$y =$ ______	Divide each side by 3.

Substitute each x-value into the equation to find the corresponding y-value.

Graph the ordered pairs in the table and draw a line through the points.

x	$-\frac{1}{3}x + 2$	y
−6	$-\frac{1}{3}(-6) + 2$	4
−3	$-\frac{1}{3}$ ______ $+ 2$	3
0	$-\frac{1}{3}(0) + 2$	______
3	$-\frac{1}{3}(3) + 2$	______
6	$-\frac{1}{3}$ ______ $+ 2$	0

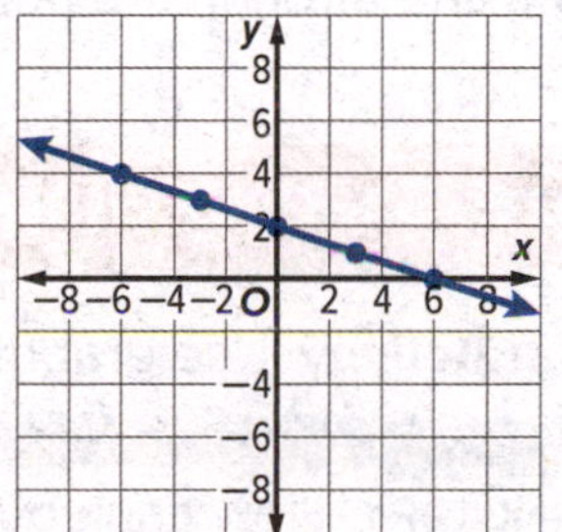

Example 2 Graph by Using Intercepts

Graph $3x - 2y = -12$ by using the x- and y-intercepts.

To find the x-intercept, let $y = 0$.

To find the y-intercept, let $x = 0$.

Case 1		Case 2
$3x - 2y = -12$	Original function	$3x - 2y = -12$
$3x - 2($____$) = -12$	Replace with 0.	$3($____$) - 2y = -12$
______ $= -12$	Simplify.	______ $= -12$
$x =$ ______	Divide.	$y =$ ______

(continued on the next page)

Go Online You can complete an Extra Example online.

Today's Standards
A.CED.3; F.IF.4
MP5, MP6

Today's Vocabulary
linear inequality
boundary
closed half-plane
open half-plane
constraint

Watch the video online.

Study Tip

Recall that **slope** is the ratio of the change in the y-coordinates (rise) to the corresponding change in the x-coordinates (run) as you move from one point to another along a line.

Think About It!

Explain why −6, −3, 0, 3, and 6 were selected for the x-values in the table.

Your Notes

Think About It!
How can you check that the graph is correct?

The x-intercept is -4, and the y-intercept is 6. This means that the graph passes through (____, ____) and (____, ____).

Plot the two intercepts.

Draw a line through the points.

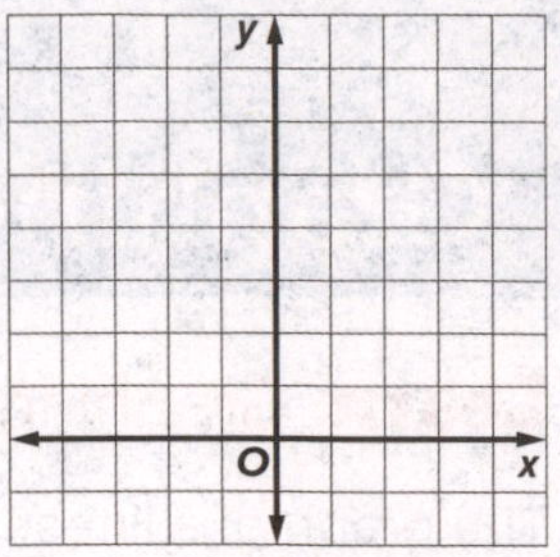

Example 3 Graph by Using the Slope and y-intercept

Graph $y = \frac{3}{2}x - 4$ by using m and b.

Follow these steps

- Begin by identifying the slope m and y-intercept b of the function.

  $m =$ ____ $b =$ ____
- Use the value of b to plot the y-intercept (____, ____).
- Use the slope of the line $m = \frac{3}{2}$ to plot more points. From the y-intercept, move up ____ units and ____ 2 units. Plot a point at (____, ____).
- From the point $(2, -1)$, move ____ 3 units and right ____ units. Plot a point at (____, ____).
- Draw a line through the points.

y
O
x

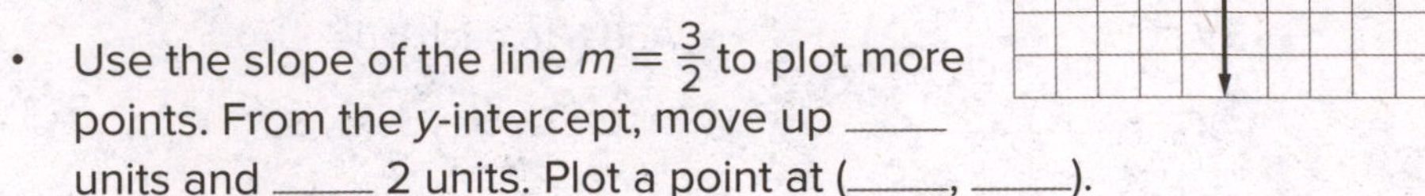

Explore Shading Graphs of Linear Inequalities

Online Activity Use graphing technology to complete the Explore.

INQUIRY How can you use a point to test the graph of an inequality?

Learn Graphing Linear Inequalities in Two Variables

The graph of a **linear inequality** is a half-plane with a boundary that is a straight line. The half-plane is shaded to indicate that all points contained in the region are solutions of the inequality. A **boundary** is a line or curve that separates the coordinate plane into two half-planes. The boundary is solid when the inequality contains $\leq$ or $\geq$ to indicate that the

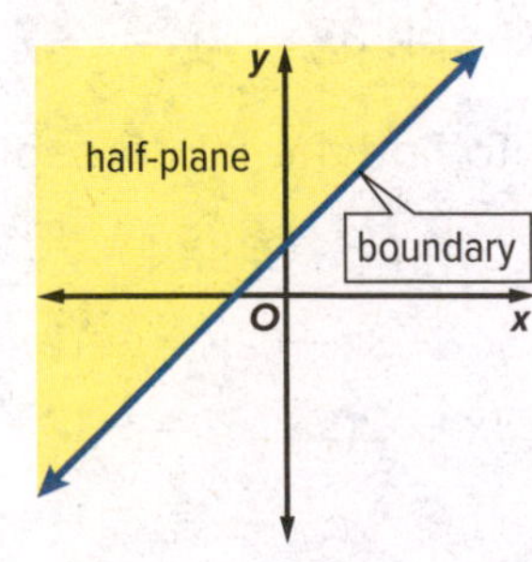

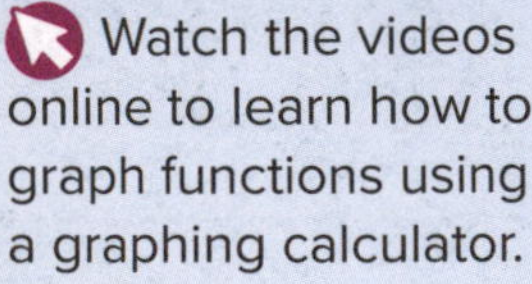

Watch the videos online to learn how to graph functions using a graphing calculator.

Go Online You can complete an Extra Example online.

points on the boundary are included in the solution, creating a **closed half-plane**. The boundary is dashed when the inequality contains $<$ or $>$ because the points on the boundary do not satisfy the inequality. This results in an **open half-plane**.

A **constraint** is a condition that a solution must satisfy. Each solution of the inequality represents a viable, or possible, option that satisfies the constraint.

Example 4 Graph an Inequality with an Open Half-Plane

Graph $x + 4y < 12$.

Step 1 Graph the boundary.

$x + 4y < 12$	Original inequality
$x < \underline{\quad\quad} + 12$	Subtract $4y$ from each side.
$x \underline{\quad\quad} < -4y$	Subtract 12 from each side.
$\underline{\quad\quad} x + \underline{\quad\quad} > y$	Divide each side by -4, and reverse the inequality symbol.

The boundary of the graph is $y \underline{\quad\quad} -\frac{1}{4}x + 3$. Because the inequality symbol is $<$, the boundary is $\underline{\quad\quad\quad\quad}$.

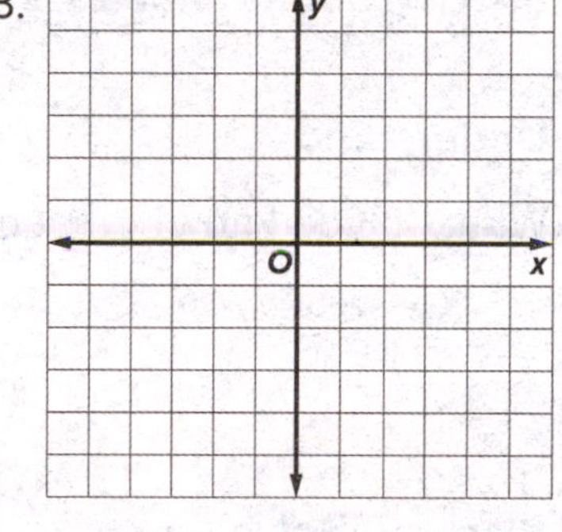

Step 2 Use a test point and shade.

Test (0, 0).

$x + 4y < 12$	Original inequality
$\underline{\quad\quad} + 4(\underline{\quad\quad}) \stackrel{?}{<} 12$	Substitute values of test point (0, 0).
$0 < 12$	True.

Because (0, 0) is a solution of the inequality, shade the half-plane that contains the test point.

Check

You can check by selecting another point in the shaded region to test.

Example 5 Graph an Inequality with a Closed Half-Plane

Graph $9 + 3y \leq 8x$.

Step 1 Graph the boundary.

Solve for y in terms of x and graph the related function.

$9 + 3y \leq 8x$	Original inequality
$3y \leq 8x \underline{\quad\quad}$	Subtract 9 from each side.
$y \leq \underline{\quad\quad} x - \underline{\quad\quad}$	Divide each side by 3.

(continued on the next page)

Go Online You can complete an Extra Example online.

Watch the video online to see how to graph a linear inequality in two variables.

Study Tip

Above or Below Usually the shaded half-plane of a linear inequality is said to be *above* or *below* the line of the related equation. However, if the equation of the boundary is $x = c$ for some constant c, then the function is a vertical line. In this case, the shading is considered to be *to the left* or *to the right* of the boundary.

Talk About It!

Can a linear inequality ever be a function? Explain your reasoning.

Think About It!

Why should you not test a point that is on the boundary?

The related equation of $y \leq \frac{8}{3}x - 3$ is $y = \frac{8}{3}x - 3$, and the boundary is solid.

Step 2 Use a test point and shade.

Select a test point, such as (0, 0).

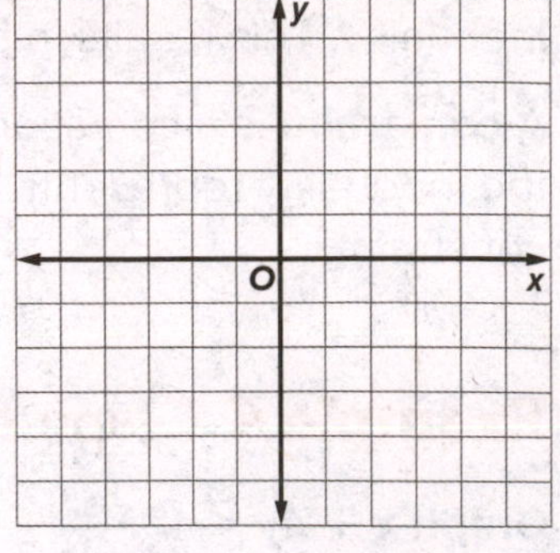

$9 + 3y \leq 8x$	Original inequality
$\_\_ + 3(\_\_) \overset{?}{\leq} 8(\_\_)$	$(x, y) = (0, 0)$.
$9 \nleq 2$	False.

Shade the side of the graph that does not contain the test point.

Think About It!

Is (3, 5) a solution of the inequality? Explain.

Watch the video online to learn how to graph an inequality using agraphing calculator.

Example 6 Linear Inequalities

GRADES **Malik's algebra teacher determines semester grades by finding the sum of 70% of a student's test grade average and 30% of a student's homework grade average. If Malik wants a semester grade of 90% or better, write and graph the inequality that represents the constraints for Malik's test grade *x* and homework grade *y*.**

Understand

What do you know? What do you need to find?

Plan and Solve

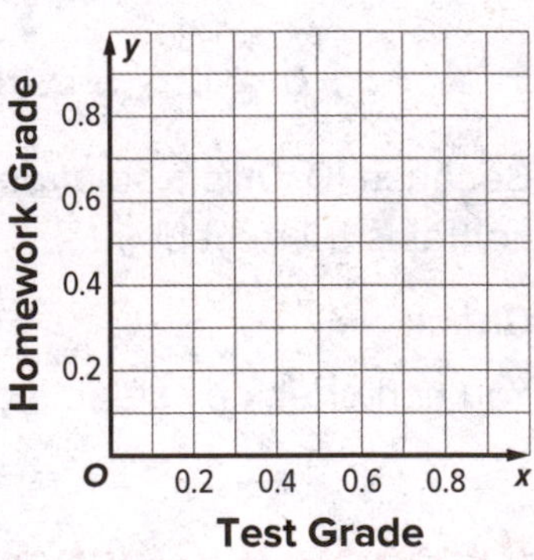

Step 1 Write an inequality that represents the situation. ____________

Step 2 Rearrange the inequality to solve for *y*. $y \geq$ __________

Step 3 Graph the related linear function as the boundary.

Step 4 Shade the half-plane. Use (0, 0) as a test point.

Step 5 Determine viable solutions for the inequality. Viable solutions that will result in Malik receiving an overall grade of at least 90% lie in the shaded region.

Check

How do you know that the shaded region is correct?

Go Online You can complete an Extra Example online.

Name ______________________ Period ________ Date ________

Practice

Go Online You can complete your homework online.

Example 1

Graph each equation by using a table.

1. $4x - 1 = y$
2. $-3 = 5x - y$
3. $y - 4 = -2x$
4. $y + x = 1$
5. $y + 3x = 1$
6. $y + 4x - 1 = 4x + 2$

Example 2

Graph each equation by using the *x*- and *y*-intercepts.

7. $3y - x = 6$
8. $2x - 3y = 6$
9. $y - x = -3$
10. $-2x + y = 4$
11. $y - 2x = -3$
12. $\frac{1}{2}x + y = 2$

Example 3

Graph each equation by using *m* and *b*.

13. $y = -\frac{5}{3}x + 12$
14. $y = \frac{2}{3}x + 6$
15. $y = 4x - 15$
16. $y - 2x = -1$
17. $y - x = -4$
18. $4 = 3x - y$

Examples 4 and 5

Graph each inequality.

19. $y > 1$
20. $y \leq x + 2$
21. $x + y \leq 4$
22. $x + 3 < y$
23. $2 - y < x$
24. $y \geq -x$
25. $x - y > -2$
26. $9x + 3y - 6 \leq 0$
27. $y + 1 \geq 2x$
28. $y - 7 \leq -9$
29. $x > -5$
30. $y + x > 1$

Example 6

31. **FLEA MARKETS** Kylie is going to try to sell two of her oil paintings at the local flea market. She is hoping to earn at least $400.

Part A Write the inequality that represents the constraint of the situation, where x is the price of the first oil painting, and y is the price of the second.

Part B Graph the inequality that represents the constraint on the sale.

32. **BUILDING CODE** A city has a building code that limits the height of buildings around the central park. The code says that the height of a building must be less than $0.1x$, where x is the distance in hundreds of feet of the building from the center of the park. Assume that the park center is located at $x = 0$. Graph the inequality that represents the building code.

33. **WEIGHT** A delivery crew is going to load a truck with tables and chairs. The trucks weight limitations are represented by the inequality $200t + 60c < 1200$, where t is the number of tables and c is the number of chairs. Graph this inequality.

34. **ART** An artist can sell each drawing for \$100 and each watercolor for \$400. He hopes to make at least \$2000 every month.

    a. Write an inequality that expresses how many drawings and/or watercolors the artist needs to sell each month to reach his goal.

    b. Graph the inequality.

    c. If the artist sells three watercolors one month, how many drawings would he have to sell in the same month to reach \$2000?

Mixed Exercises

Graph each equation.

35. $x + y = 1$

36. $2x - y = 1$

37. $y = -2x + 3$

38. $y + 2 = 3x + 3$

39. $y + 3 = 0$

40. $y + 2 = -x + 1$

41. $x + y = 3$

42. $2y - x = 2$

43. $4x + 3y = 12$

44. $\frac{1}{2}x + \frac{1}{4}y = 8$

45. $-\frac{1}{2}x + y = -2$

46. $-2x + 5y = 2$

Graph each inequality.

47. $x + 2y > 6$

48. $y \geq -3x - 2$

49. $2y + 3 \leq 11$

50. $4x - 3y > 12$

51. $6x + 4y \leq -24$

52. $y \geq \frac{3}{4}x + 6$

53. **REASONING** Name the x- and y-intercept for the linear equation given by $6x - 2y = 12$. Use the intercepts to graph the equation and describe the graph as *increasing*, *decreasing*, or *constant*.

54. **LIVESTOCK** During the winter, a horse requires about 36 liters of water per day and a sheep requires about 3.6 liters per day. A farmer is able to supply his horses and sheep with a total of 300 liters of water each day.

    a. **REASONING** Write an inequality that represents the possible number of each type of animal that the farmer can keep.

    b. **PRECISION** Graph the inequality.

55. **COMPUTERS** A school system is buying new computers. They will buy desktop computers costing \$1000 per unit, and notebook computers costing \$1200 per unit. The total cost of the computers cannot exceed \$80,000.

a. **REASONING** Write an inequality that describes this situation.

b. **MODELING** Graph the inequality.

c. If the school wants to buy 50 desktop computers and 25 notebook computers, will they have enough money? Explain.

56. **BAKED GOODS** Mary sells giant chocolate chip and peanut butter cookies for \$1.25 and \$1.00, respectively, at a local bake shop. She wants to make at least \$25 a day.

a. Write and graph an inequality that represents the number of cookies Mary needs to sell each day.

b. **ARGUMENTS** If Mary decides to charge \$1.50 for chocolate chip cookies rather than \$1.25, what impact will this have on the graph of the solution set? Give an (x, y) pair that is not in the original solution set, but is in the solution set of the new revised scenario.

c. HOW does the graph of the inequality change if Mary wants to make at least \$50 a day? How does the graph of the inequality change if Mary wants to make no more than \$25 a day?

57. **FUNDRAISING** The school drama club is putting on a play to raise money. Suppose it will cost \$400 to put on the play and that 300 students and 150 adults will attend.

a. **MODELING** Write an equation to represent revenue from ticket sales if the club wants to raise \$1400 after expenses.

b. **ARGUMENTS** Graph your equation. Then determine four possible prices that could be charged for student and adult tickets to earn \$1400 in profit.

58. **SANDBOX** You want to make a rectangular sandbox area in your backyard. You plan to use no more than 20 linear feet of lumber to make the sides of the sandbox.

a. **MODELING** Write and graph a linear inequality to describe this situation.

b. **REASONING** What are two possible sizes for the sandbox?

c. **ARGUMENTS** Can you make a sandbox that is 7 feet by 6 feet? Justify your answer.

d. **STATE YOUR ASSUMPTION** What can you conclude about the intercepts of your graph?

59. **SPIRITWEAR** A company makes long-sleeved and short-sleeved shirts. The profit on a long-sleeved shirt is \$7 and the profit on a short-sleeved shirt is \$4. How many shirts must the company sell to make a profit of at least \$280?

a. **MODELING** Write and graph a linear inequality to describe this situation.

b. **REASONING** Write two possible solutions to the problem.

c. **ARGUMENTS** Which values are reasonable for the domain and for the range? Explain.

d. **ARGUMENTS** The point $(-10, 90)$ is in the shaded region. Is it a solution of the problem? Explain your reasoning.

60. ONLINE PURCHASING Gemma wants to purchase some scented candles and hand soaps from a website that sells these products. The scented candles cost \$9, and the hand soaps cost \$4. In order for her purchase to qualify for free shipping, Gemma will need to spend at least \$50.

a. Write an inequality that represents the constraints on the number of scented candles x and the number of hand soaps y that Gemma must purchase in order to qualify for free shipping.

b. Graph the inequality.

USE TOOLS Use your graph to answer parts c-e.

c. Suppose Gemma decides not to purchase any hand soaps. Determine the number of candles she will need to purchase in order to qualify for free shipping. Explain.

d. Suppose Gemma decides not to purchase any candles. Determine the number of hand soaps she will need to purchase in order to qualify for free shipping. Explain.

e. Will Gemma qualify for free shipping if she purchases 2 candles and 8 hand soaps? Explain how you can be sure?

61. FIND THE ERROR Paulo and Janette are graphing $x - y \geq 2$. Is either of them correct? Explain your reasoning.

Paulo

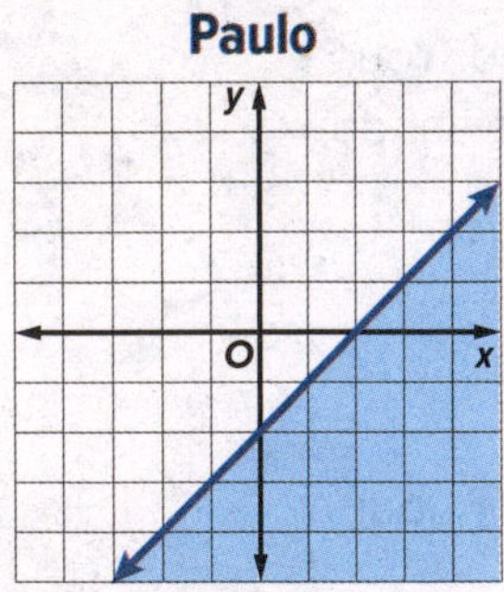

Janette

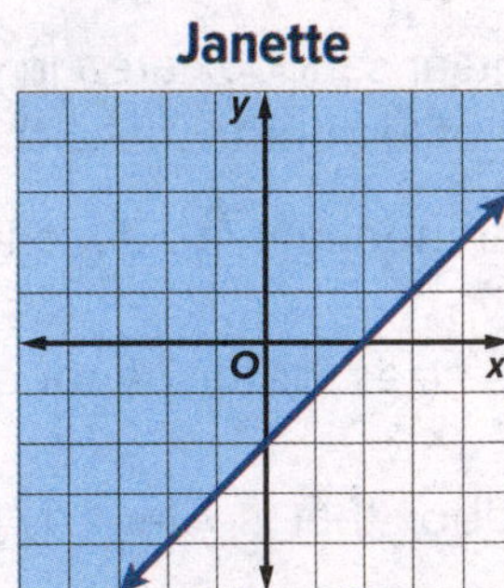

62. CREATE Write an inequality whose graph has a dashed boundary line. Then graph the inequality.

63. WRITE You can graph a line by making a table, using the x- and y- intercepts, or by using m and b. Which method do you prefer? Explain your reasoning.

64. ANALYZE Write a counterexample to show that the following statement is false. *Every point in the first quadrant is a solution for* $3y > -x + 6$.

65. PERSEVERE Write an equation of the line that has the same slope as $2x - 8y = 7$ and the same y-intercept as $4x + 3y = 15$.

Special Functions

Explore Using Tables to Graph Piecewise Functions

Online Activity Use a table and graphing technology to complete the Explore.

INQUIRY How can you write a piecewise function when given a table of values?

Today's Standards
F.IF.4, F.IF.7b
MP4, MP6

Today's Vocabulary
piecewise-defined function
step function
greatest integer function
absolute value function
parent function

Learn Piecewise-Defined Functions

A function that is written using two or more expressions is called a **piecewise-defined function**. Each of the expressions is defined for a distinct interval of the domain.

A dot is used if a point is included in the graph. A circle is used for a point that is not included in the graph.

Example 1 Graph a Piecewise-Defined Function

Graph $f(x) = \begin{cases} x - 3 \text{ if } x \leq 1 \\ 2x \text{ if } x > 1 \end{cases}$**. Then, analyze the key features.**

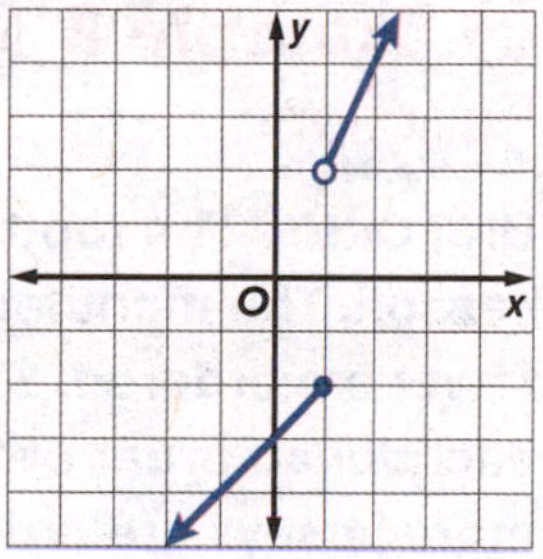

Step 1 Graph $f(x) = x - 3$ for $x \leq 1$.

Find $f(x)$ for the endpoint of the domain interval, $x = 1$.

$f(x) = x - 3$

$= \_\_\_\_ - 3$ or $\_\_\_\_$

Since 1 satisfies the inequality, place a ____ at (1, −2). Because $x - 3$ is defined for values of x ______ or equal to 1, graph the linear function with a slope of ____ to the ____ of the dot.

Step 2 Graph $f(x) = 2x$ for $x > 1$.

Find $f(x)$ for the endpoint of the domain interval, $x = 1$.

$f(x) = 2x$

$= 2(\_\_\_\_)$ or $\_\_\_\_$

Since 1 is not included in the inequality, place a ____ at (1, 2). Because $2x$ is defined for values ________ 1, graph the linear function with a slope of ____ to the ____ of the circle.

(continued on the next page)

Talk About It!
Can the piecewise-defined function in the example have $x \geq 1$ instead of $x > 1$ after the second expression? Explain.

You can learn how to graph a piecewise-defined function on a calculator by watching the video online.

Go Online You can complete an Extra Example online.

Your Notes

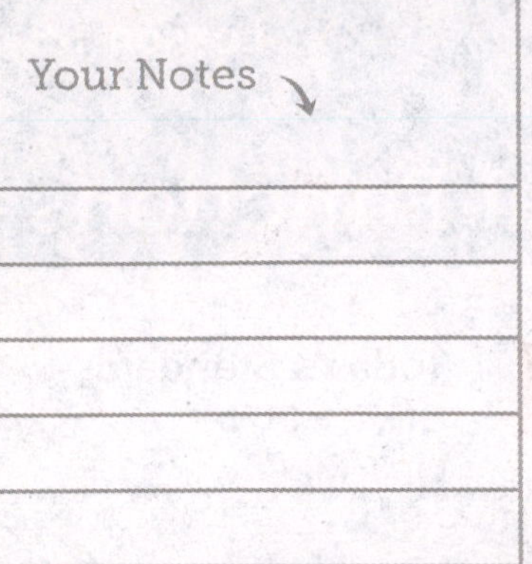

Step 3 Analyze key features.

The function is defined for all values of x, so the domain is all real numbers.

The range is all real numbers less than or equal to -2 and all real numbers greater than 2. This can be represented symbolically as $\{f(x) \mid f(x) \leq -2 \text{ or } f(x) > 2\}$.

The y-intercept is -3, and there is no x-intercept.

The function is increasing for all values of x.

Check

Graph $f(x) = \begin{cases} \frac{2}{3}x \text{ if } x \leq 0 \\ 3 \text{ if } 1 \leq x \leq 3 \\ -2x + 5 \text{ if } x \geq 4 \end{cases}$. Then, analyze the key features.

The domain is __________.

The range is __________.

The x-intercepts is _____.

The y-intercept is _____.

For $\{x \mid x \leq 0\}$, the function is __________.

For $\{x \mid 1 \leq x \leq 3\}$, the function is __________.

For $\{x \mid x \geq 4\}$, the function is __________.

y

O x

Think About It!

What do the domain and range represent in the context of this situation?

Example 2 Model by Using a Piecewise-Defined Function

UNIFORMS **The football coach is ordering new jerseys for the new season. The manufacturer charges \$88 for each jersey when five or fewer are ordered, \$75 each for an order of six to 11 jerseys, \$65 each for an order of 12 to 29 jerseys, and \$56 each when thirty or more jerseys are ordered.**

Part A Write a piece-wise defined function describing the cost of the jerseys.

$$f(x) = \begin{cases} 88x & \text{if } 0 < x \leq 5 \\ 75x & \text{if } \_\_\_\_\_\_ \\ 65x & \text{if } \_\_\_\_\_\_ \\ 56x & \text{if } x > 29 \end{cases}$$

Part B Evaluate the function.

What would it cost to purchase 11 jerseys?

\$_____

What would it cost to purchase 25 jerseys?

\$_____

Evaluate $f(29)$.

$f(29) = \$$_____

Go Online You can complete an Extra Example online.

Watch Out!

Evaluating Endpoints of Intervals When evaluating a piecewise-defined function for a value of x that is an endpoint for two consecutive intervals, be careful to evaluate the function that contains that point.

Learn Graphing Step Functions

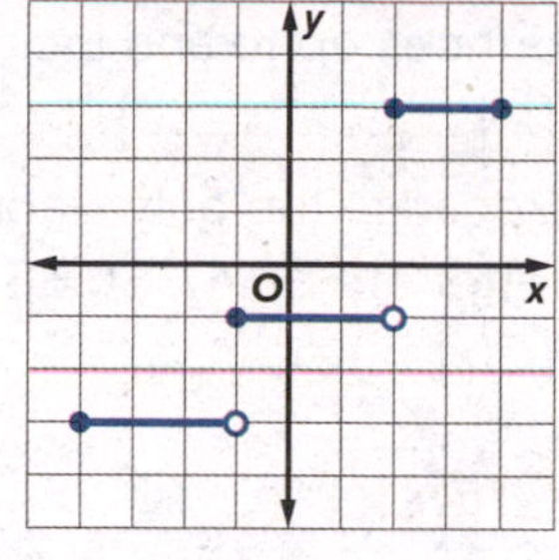

A common type of piecewise-linear function is a step function. A **step function** has a graph that is a series of horizontal line segments that may resemble a staircase.

A step function is defined by a set of constant functions. The domain of a step function is an interval of real numbers. The range of a step function is a subset of the set of integers. The graph of a step function is discontinuous because it cannot be drawn without lifting your pencil.

The **greatest integer function**, written $f(x) = [\![x]\!]$, is one kind of step function in which $f(x)$ is the greatest integer less than or equal to x. For example, $[\![10.7]\!] = 10$, $[\![-6.35]\!] = -7$, and $[\![5]\!] = 5$.

> **Think About It!**
> Why is the range of the function not expressed as $\{y \mid -3 \le y \le 3\}$?

Example 3 Graph a Step Function

POSTAL RATES **The cost of mailing a first-class letter is determined by rates adopted by the U.S. Postal Service. The rates adopted in 2016 charge \$0.47 for letters not over 1 ounce, \$0.68 if not over 2 ounces, \$0.89 if not over 3 ounces, and \$1.10 if not over 3.54 ounces. Complete the table and draw a graph that represents the charges. State the domain and range.**

> **Think About It!**
> Explain why the value of $[\![4.3]\!]$ is 4, but the value of $[\![-4.3]\!]$ is -5.

Step 1 Make a table.

Let x be the weight of a first-class letter and $C(x)$ represent the cost for mailing it. Use the given rates to make a table.

x	$C(x)$
$0 < x \le 1$	\$0.47
$1 < x \le 2$	\$0.68
$2 < x \le 3$	\$0.89
$3 < x \le 3.54$	\$1.10

Step 2 Make a graph.

Graph the first step of the function. Place a circle at (0, 0.47) since there is no charge for not mailing a letter. Place a dot at (1, 0.47) since a letter weighing one ounce will cost \$0.47 to mail. Draw a segment that connects the points.

Graph the remaining steps.

Place a circle on the left end of each segment as that point is included with the segment below it.

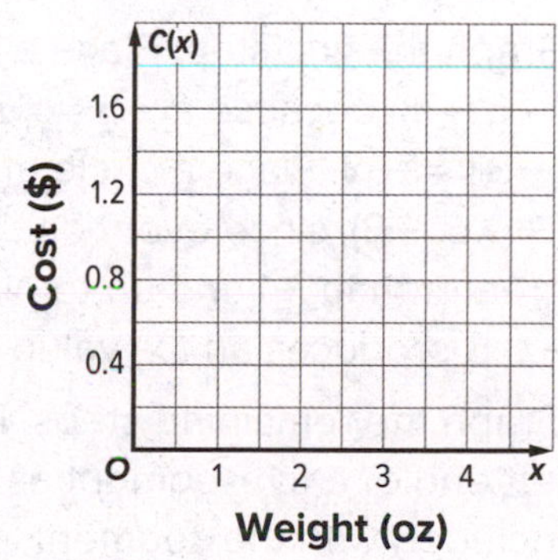

(continued on the next page)

Step 3 State the domain and range.

The constraints for the weight of a first-class letter are more than 0 ounces up to and including 3.54 ounces. Therefore, the domain is $\{x \mid$ ________ $\}$.

Because the only viable solutions for the cost of mailing a first-class letter are \$0.47, \$0.68, \$0.89, and \$1.10, the range is $\{C(x) =$ ________ $\}$.

Check

FIGURINES Chris and Joaquin design figurines for board game and toy companies. The rate they charge $R(x)$ depends on the number of hours x they spend creating the figurines. Draw a graph that represents the charges. State the domain and range.

x	$R(x)$
$0 < x \leq 5$	500
$5 < x \leq 15$	1400
$15 < x \leq 30$	2500
$30 < x \leq 50$	4000

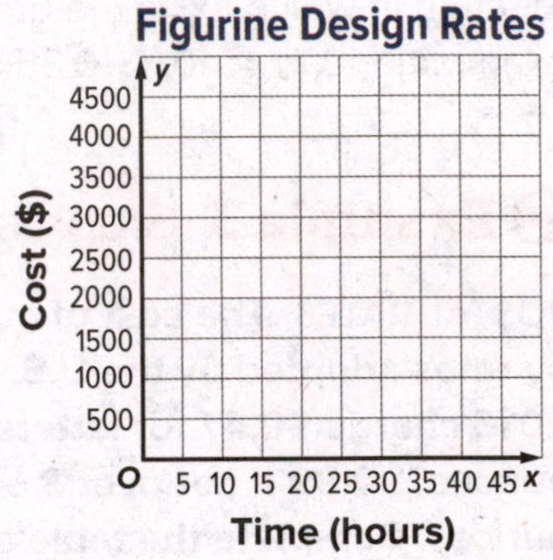

> **Think About It!**
> Would $C(x)$ still be a function if the open points at (0, 0.47), (1, 0.68), (2, 0.89), and (3, 1.10) were closed points? Justify your argument.

Example 4 Graph a Greatest Integer Function

Complete the table and graph $f(x) = [\![2x - 1]\!]$ State the domain and range.

Step 1 Make a table.

Make a table of the intervals of x and associated values of $f(x)$.

x	$f(x)$
$-1 \leq x < 0.5$	-3
$-0.5 \leq x < 0$	
$0 \leq x < 0.5$	
$0.5 \leq x < 1$	
$1 \leq x < 1.5$	
$1.5 \leq x < 2$	

Step 2 Make a graph.

Graph the first step. Place a dot at $(-1, -3)$, because $f(-1) = [\![2(-1) - 1]\!] = [\![-3]\!] = -3$. Place a circle at $(-0.5, -3)$, since every decimal value greater than -1 and up to but not including -0.5 produces an $f(x)$ value of -3.

Graph the remaining steps. Place a dot on the left end of each segment as that point is included with the segment, and place a circle on the right end because that point is included with the segment above it.

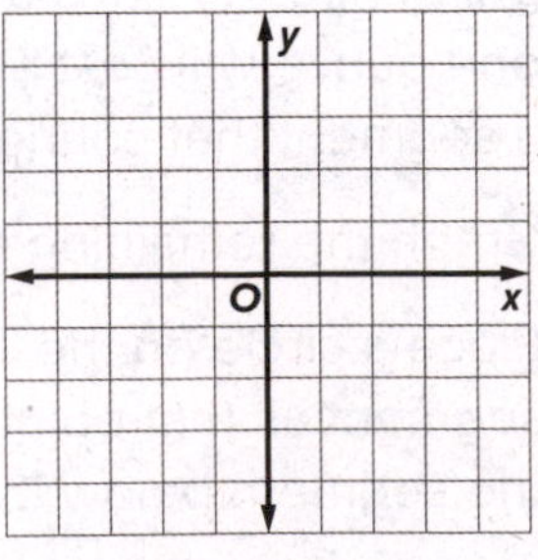

Step 3 State the domain and range.

The domain of $f(x) = [\![2x - 1]\!]$ is all ________. The range is all ________.

> **Think About It!**
> Will the range of a greatest integer function always be all integers? If not, provide a counter example.

> Watch the video online to see how to graph a step function.

Go Online You can complete an Extra Example online.

Learn Graphing Absolute Value Functions

An **absolute value function** is a function that contains an algebraic expression within absolute value symbols. It can be defined and graphed as a piecewise function.

For an absolute value function, $f(x) = |x|$ is the **parent function**, which is the simplest of the functions in a family.

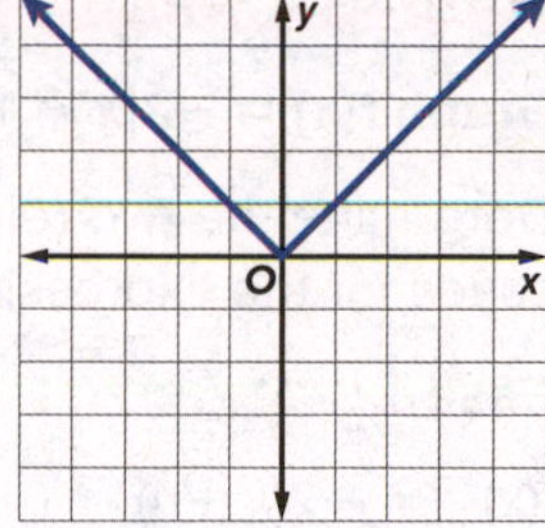

Key Concept • Parent Function of Absolute Value Functions	
parent function	$f(x) = |x|$ or $f(x) = \begin{cases} x \text{ if } x \geq 0 \\ -x \text{ if } x < 0 \end{cases}$
domain	all real numbers
range	all nonnegative real numbers
intercepts	$x = 0, f(x) = 0$

> **Think About It!**
> Describe the line of symmetry of any absolute value function and compare it with the line of symmetry of the parent function.

Example 5 Graph an Absolute Value Function, Positive Coefficient

Graph $f(x) = \left|\frac{3}{4}x\right| + 3$. State the domain and range.

Create a table of values. Choose several values of x and find $f(x)$.

x	$f(x) = \left\|\frac{3}{4}x\right\| + 3$
−4	$\left\|\frac{3}{4}(\_\_\_)\right\| + 3 =$ ____
−2	$\left\|\frac{3}{4}(\_\_\_)\right\| + 3 =$ ____
0	$\left\|\frac{3}{4}(\_\_\_)\right\| + 3 =$ ____
2	$\left\|\frac{3}{4}(\_\_\_)\right\| + 3 =$ ____
4	$\left\|\frac{3}{4}(\_\_\_)\right\| + 3 =$ ____

Plot the point and connect them with two rays.

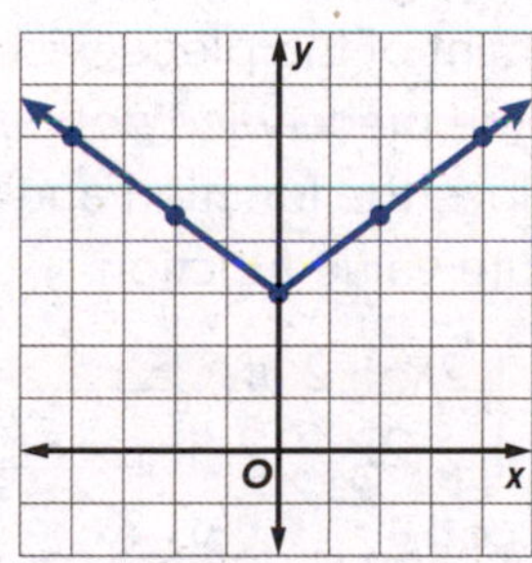

The function is defined for all values of x, so the domain is ____________. The function is defined only for values of $f(x)$ such that $f(x) \geq 3$, so the range is $\{f(x) | f(x) \geq$ ____$\}$.

Check

Graph $f(x) = |x - 1| + 3$. State the domain and range.

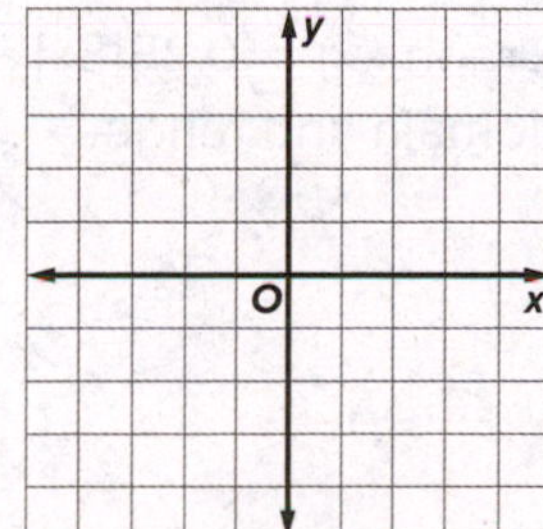

> **Go Online** A second method, *graph by cases*, is available for this example.

Go Online You can complete an Extra Example online.

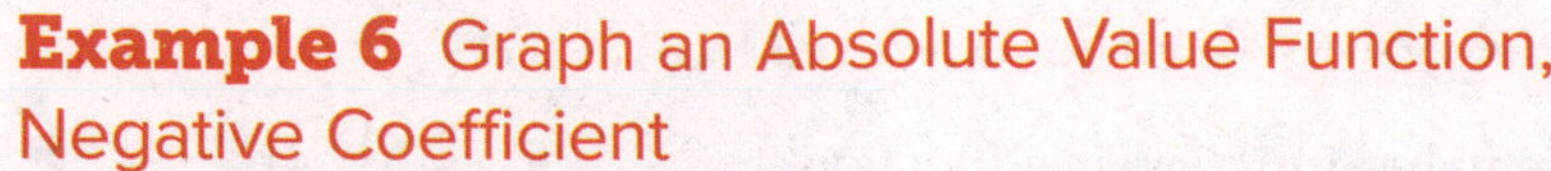

Example 6 Graph an Absolute Value Function, Negative Coefficient

Graph $f(x) = -2|x + 1|$. State the domain and range.

Determine the two related linear equations using the two possible cases for the expression inside of the absolute value.

Case 1

$f(x) = -2(x + 1)$	$x + 1$ is positive, so $|x + 1| = x + 1$.
$= -2x - 2$	Simplify.

Case 2

$f(x) = -2[-(x + 1)]$	$x + 1$ is negative, so $|x + 1| = -(x + 1)$.
$= -2(-x - 1)$	Distributive Property
$= 2x + 2$	Simplify.

The x-coordinate of the vertex is the value of x where the two cases of the absolute value are equal.

$-2x - 2 = 2x + 2$	Set Case 1 equal to Case 2.
$-2x = 2x + 4$	Add 2 to each side.
$-4x = 4$	Subtract $2x$ from each side.
$x = -1$	Divide each side by -4.

> **Think About It!**
> How does multiplying the absolute value by a negative number affect the shape of the graph? the range?

The x-coordinate of the vertex represents the constraint of the piece-wise defined function. Write the piece-wise defined function that describes the function and use it to graph the absolute value function.

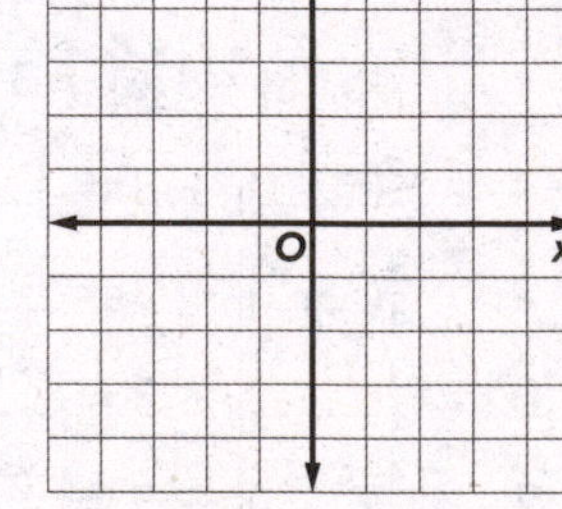

$$f(x) = \begin{cases} 2x + 2 & \text{if } \_\_\_\_\_\_ \\ -2x - 2 & \text{if } \_\_\_\_\_\_ \end{cases}$$

The function is defined for all values of x, so the domain is __________. The function is defined only for values of y such that $f(x) \leq 0$, so the range is $\{f(x) |$ ______$\}$.

Check

Graph $f(x) = 0.25|8x| - 3$. State the domain and range.

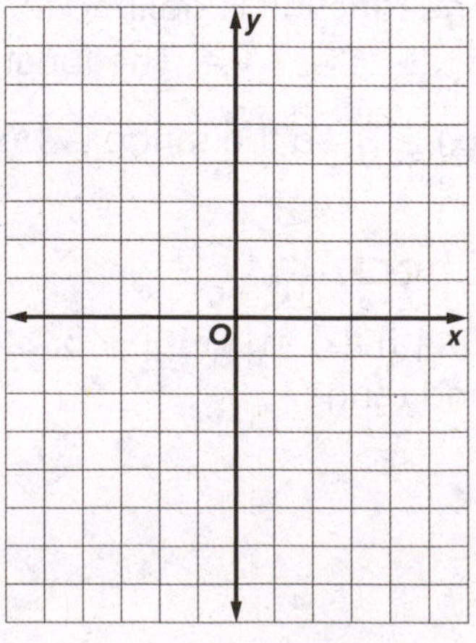

 **Go Online** You can complete an Extra Example online.

Name ______ Period ______ Date ______

Practice

Go Online You can complete your homework online.

Examples 1 and 2

Graph each function. Then, analyze the key features.

1. $f(x) = \begin{cases} -1 & \text{if } x \leq 0 \\ 2x & \text{if } 0 < x \leq 3 \\ 6 & \text{if } x > 3 \end{cases}$

2. $f(x) = \begin{cases} -x & \text{if } x < -1 \\ 0 & \text{if } -1 \leq x \leq 1 \\ x & \text{if } x > 1 \end{cases}$

3. $f(x) = \begin{cases} x & \text{if } x < 0 \\ 2 & \text{if } x \geq 0 \end{cases}$

4. $h(x) = \begin{cases} 3 & \text{if } x < -1 \\ x + 1 & \text{if } x > 1 \end{cases}$

5. **TILE** Mark is purchasing new tile for his bathrooms. The home improvement store charges $48 for each box of tiles when three or fewer boxes are purchased, $45 for each box when 4 to 8 boxes are purchased, $42 for each box when 9 to 19 boxes are purchased, and $38 for each box when more than nineteen boxes are purchased.

PART A Write a piecewise-defined function describing the cost of the boxes of tile.

PART B What it is the cost of purchasing 5 boxes of tile? What it is the cost of purchasing 19 boxes of tile?

6. **BOOKLETS** A digital media company is ordering booklets to promote their business. The manufacturer charges $0.50 for each booklet when 50 or fewer are ordered, $0.45 for each booklet when 51 to 100 booklets are ordered, $0.40 for each booklet when 101 to 250 booklets are ordered, and $0.35 for each booklet when 251 or more booklets are ordered. Each order consists of a $10 shipping charge, no matter the size of the order.

PART A Write a piecewise-defined function describing the cost of ordering booklets.

PART B What is the cost of purchasing 132 booklets? What it is the cost of purchasing 518 booklets?

Examples 3 and 4

Graph each function. State the domain and range.

7. $f(x) = [\![x]\!] - 6$

8. $h(x) = [\![3x]\!] - 8$

9. $f(x) = [\![x + 1]\!]$

10. $f(x) = [\![x - 3]\!]$

11. **PARKING GARAGE** The rates at a short-term parking garage are $5.00 for 2 hours or less, $10.00 for 4 hours or less, $15.00 for 6 hours or less, and $20.00 for 8 hours or less. Draw a graph that represents the charges. State the domain and range.

12. **BOWLING** The bowling alley offers special team rates. They charge $30 for one hour or less of team bowling, $45 for 2 hours or less, and $60 for unlimited bowling after 2 hours of play. Draw a graph that represents the charges. State the domain and range.

Examples 5 and 6

Graph each function. State the domain and range.

13. $f(x) = |x - 5|$

14. $g(x) = |x + 2|$

15. $h(x) = |2x| - 8$

16. $k(x) = |-3x| + 3$

17. $f(x) = 2|x - 4| + 6$

18. $h(x) = -3|0.5x + 1| - 2$

19. $g(x) = 2|x|$

20. $f(x) = |x| + 1$

Mixed Exercises

Graph each function. State the domain and range.

21. $f(x) = \begin{cases} -3x & \text{if } x \leq -4 \\ x & \text{if } 0 < x \leq 3 \\ 8 & \text{if } x > 3 \end{cases}$

22. $f(x) = \begin{cases} 2x & \text{if } x \leq -6 \\ 5 & \text{if } -6 < x \leq 2 \\ -2x + 1 & \text{if } x > 4 \end{cases}$

23. $g(x) = \begin{cases} 2x + 2 & \text{if } x < -6 \\ x & \text{if } -6 \leq x \leq 2 \\ -3 & \text{if } x > 2 \end{cases}$

24. $g(x) = \begin{cases} -2 & \text{if } x < -4 \\ x - 3 & \text{if } -1 \leq x \leq 5 \\ 2x - 15 & \text{if } x > 7 \end{cases}$

25. $f(x) = \begin{cases} -0.5x + 1.5 & \text{if } x \leq 1 \\ -x - 4 & \text{if } x > 1 \end{cases}$

26. $f(x) = |x - 2|$

27. $f(x) = [\![3x + 2]\!]$

28. $g(x) = 2\,[\![0.5x + 4]\!]$

29. $f(x) = [\![|0.5x|]\!]$

30. $g(x) = |[\![2x]\!]|$

31. $g(x) = \begin{cases} [\![x]\!] & \text{if } x < -4 \\ x + 1 & \text{if } -4 \leq x \leq 5 \\ -[\![x]\!] & \text{if } x > 3 \end{cases}$

32. $h(x) = \begin{cases} -|x| & \text{if } x < -6 \\ |x| & \text{if } -6 \leq x \leq 2 \\ |-x| & \text{if } x > 2 \end{cases}$

33. Identify the domain and range of the absolute value function $h(x) = |X + 4| + 2$.

34. FINANCE A financial advisor handles the transactions for a customer. For every transaction, a certain financial advisor gets a 5% commission, regardless of whether the transaction is a deposit or withdrawal. Write a formula using the absolute value function for the advisor's commission C. Let D represent the value of one transaction.

35. GAMING An online gaming company charges players a monthly fee based on the amount of time per day they spend playing online games. The graph shows the monthly charge based on the average number of hours spent online per day. Write the step function represented by the graph.

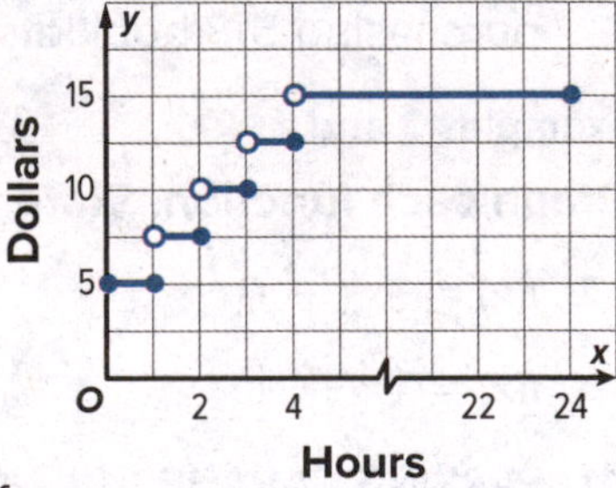

36. ROUNDING A science teacher instructs students to round their measurements as follows: If a measurement is less than 0.5 mm, students are instructed to round down to the nearest whole millimeter. If a measurement is exactly 0.5 or greater, students are told to round up to the next whole millimeter. Write a formula to represent the rounded measurements.

37. REUNIONS For a family reunion, the Cramers have reserved a banquet hall and intend to hire a caterer. The cost to reserve the hall is a flat fee of \$500. The catering cost per guest is \$17.50 for the first 40 guests and \$14.75 per guest beyond the first 40.

a. Write a piece-wise defined function describing the cost C of the reunion.

b. USE TOOLS Use a graphing calculator to graph the piece-wise function.

c. If the Cramers can spend up to \$900 on the event, what is the largest number of guests that can attend? Explain.

Name ______________________ Period ____________ Date ____________

38. **SAVINGS** Nathan puts \$200 into a checking account when he gets his paycheck each month. The value of his checking account is modeled by $200[\![m]\!]$, where m is the number of months that Nathan has been working. After 105 days, how much money is in the account?

39. The approval rating $R(t)$, measured as a percent, of a class officer during her 9-month term starting in September is described by the graph, where t is her time in office.

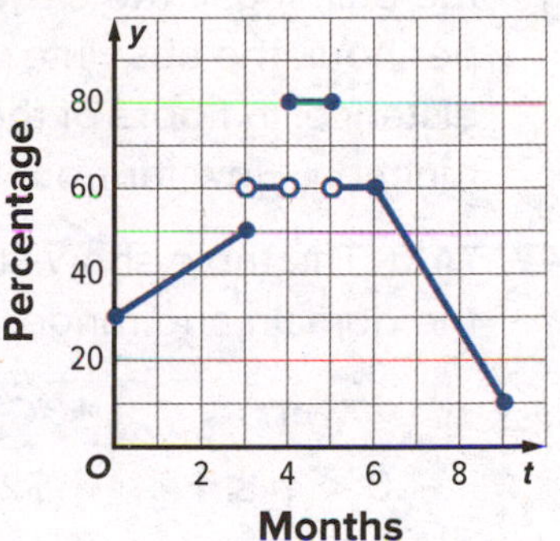

a. **MODELING** Formulate a piecewise-defined function $R(t)$ describing the approval rating of this class officer. Then, identify the range.

b. **REASONING** During which months is the approval rating increasing?

40. Consider the functions $f(x) = 3[\![x]\!]$ and $g(x) = [\![3x]\!]$ for $0 \leq x \leq 2$.

a. **MODELING** Graph each function.

b. **STUCTURE** What effect does this 3 appear to have on the graphs?

c. **MODELING** Consider the functions $f(x) = 4[\![x]\!]$ and $g(x) = [\![4x]\!]$ for $0 \leq x \leq 2$. Graph each function.

d. **STUCTURE** What effect does this 4 appear to have on the graphs?

e. **REGULARITY** Generalize your findings from **parts a through d** to explain the differences between $f(x) = n[\![x]\!]$ and $g(x) = [\![nx]\!]$ for $0 \leq x \leq 2$, where n is any positive integer greater than or equal to 2.

41. **USE TOOLS** Use a graphing calculator to graph the absolute value of the greatest integer of x, or $f(x) = |[\![x]\!]|$. Is the graph what you expected? Explain.

MODELING **Write a piece-wise defined function for each graph.**

42.

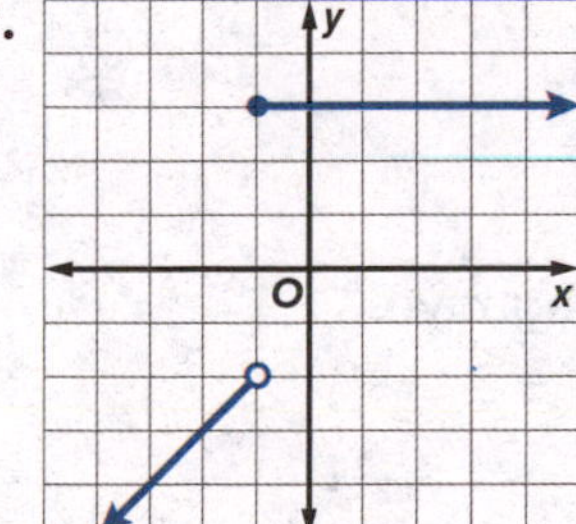

43.

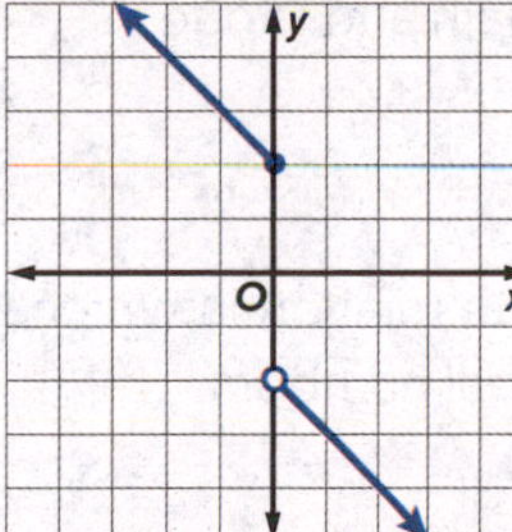

44.

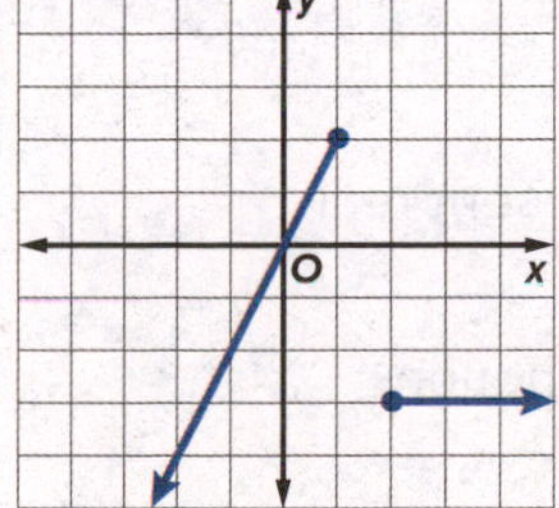

45.

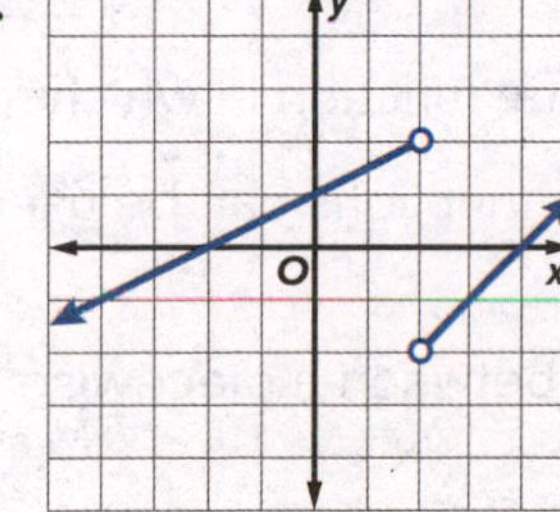

46. **SKYSCRAPERS** To clean windows of skyscrapers, some companies use a carriage. A carriage is mounted on a railing on the roof of a skyscraper and can move up and down using cables, which allows crews to clean the outside windows. The crew plans to start at the 12th floor and clean the west side of the building. Once they reach ground level, they will begin cleaning the east side of the building. If the crew members clean windows at a constant rate of 0.75 floor per hour, the absolute value function $f(t) = |0.75t - 12|$ represents the carriage's distance, in floors of the skyscraper, from the 12th floor after t hours. Graph the function. How far from the 12th floor is the carriage after 4 hours?

47. **TAXI** The table shows the cost C of an m-mile taxi ride. Graph the function. State the domain and range.

m	$C(m)$
$0 < m \leq 1$	\$2.00
$1 < m \leq 2$	\$4.00
$2 < m \leq 3$	\$6.00
$3 < m \leq 4$	\$8.00
$4 < m \leq 5$	\$10.00
$5 < m \leq 6$	\$12.00

48. **WALKING** Jackson left his house and walked at a constant rate. After 20 minutes, he was 2 miles from his house. Jackson then walked back towards his house at a constant rate. After another 30 minutes he arrived at his house.

a. **REASONING** Jackson wants to write a function to model the distance from his house d as after t minutes. Should Jackson write an absolute value function or a piece-wise defined function? Explain your reasoning.

b. **MODELING** Write an appropriate function to model the distance from his house d as after t minutes.

c. **MODELING** Graph the function.

d. **STRUCTURE** State the domain and range.

49. **CREATE** Write an absolute value relation in which the domain is all nonnegative numbers and the range is all real numbers.

50. **PERSEVERE** Graph $|y| = 2|x + 3| - 5$.

51. **ANALYZE** Find a counterexample to the statement and explain your reasoning.

In order to find the greatest integer function of x when x is not an integer, round x to the nearest integer.

52. **CREATE** Write an absolute value function in which $f(5) = -3$.

53. **WRITE** Explain how piecewise functions can be used to accurately represent real-world problems.

54. **WRITE** Explain the difference between a piecewise function and step function.

Transformations of Functions

Explore Using Technology to Transform Functions

Online Activity Use graphing technology to complete the Explore.

INQUIRY How does performing an operation on a function change its graph?

Learn Translations of Functions

A **family of graphs** includes graphs and equations of graphs that have at least one characteristic in common. The parent graph is transformed to create other members in a family of graphs.

Key Concept • Parent Functions

Constant Function	Identity Function
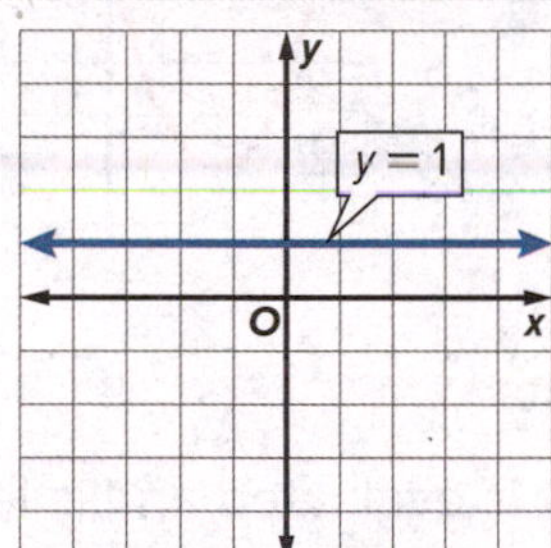	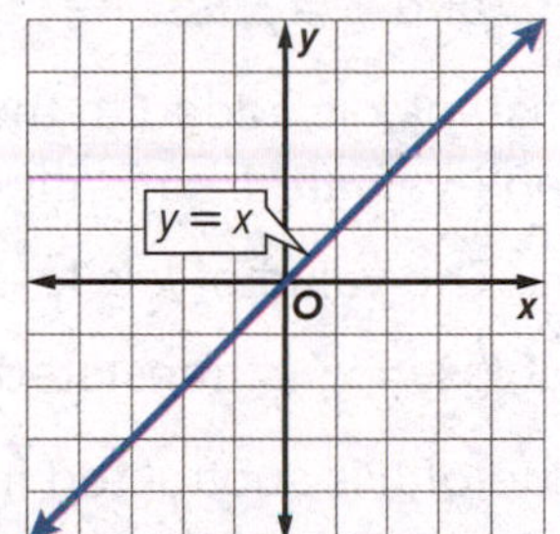
The general equation of a **constant function** is $f(x) = a$, where a is any number. Domain: all real numbers Range: $\{f(x) \mid f(x) = a\}$	The **identity function** $f(x) = x$ includes all points with coordinates (a, a). It is the parent function of most linear functions. Domain: all real numbers Range: all real numbers
Absolute Value Function	**Quadratic Function**
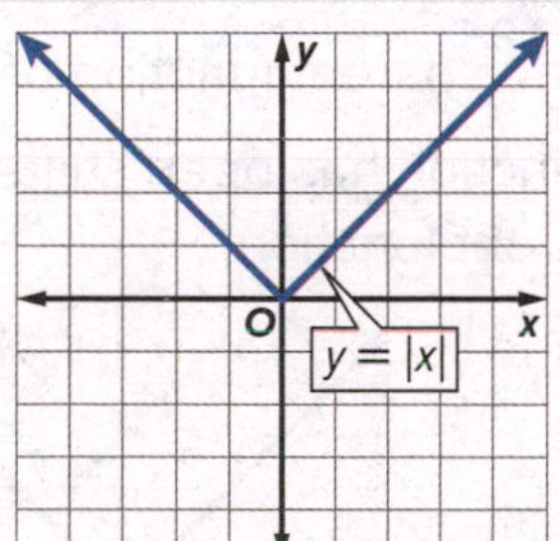	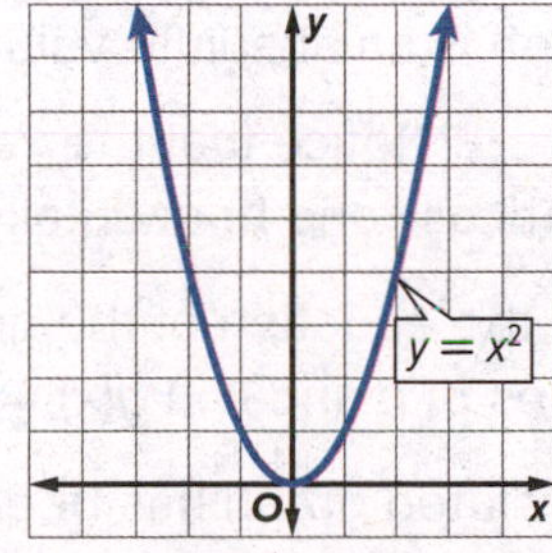
The parent function of absolute value functions is $f(x) = \|x\|$. Domain: all real numbers Range: $\{f(x) \mid f(x) \geq 0\}$	The parent function of quadratic functions is $f(x) = x^2$. Domain: all real numbers Range: $\{f(x) \mid f(x) \geq 0\}$

Today's Standards
F.IF.4; F.BF.3
MP2, MP7

Today's Vocabulary
family of graphs
constant function
identity function
transformations
translation
dilation
reflection
line of reflection

You may want to complete the Concept Check to check your understanding.

Think About It!
How does the graph of $f(x + 2)$ compare to the graph of $f(x)$? Justify your answer.

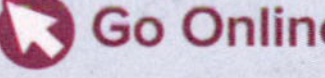

Go Online
You can watch a video to see how to describe translations of functions.

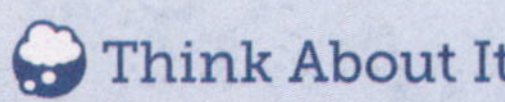

Think About It!

Describe the vertex and axis of symmetry of a translated quadratic function in terms of h and k.

Study Tip

Signs Although the translated function uses subtraction, the translation is in the form $f(x) + k$ because a constant is being added to the parent function. The value of k is negative because adding a negative number is the same as subtracting the positive opposite of that number. The translation $p(x) = (x - 3)^2$ would be in the form $f(x - h)$, because the constant is being subtracted from the variable before evaluating.

Problem-Solving Tip

Use a Graph When writing the equation of a graph, use the key features of the graph to determine transformations. Notice how the maximum, minimum, intercepts, and axis of symmetry have changed from the parent function in order to determine which transformations have been applied.

Transformations on parent graphs occur when the graph is slid, reflected in an axis, stretched, or compressed. A **translation** is a transformation in which a figure is slid from one position to another without being turned.

Key Concept • Translations

Translation	Change to Parent Graph
$f(x) + k$; $k > 0$	The graph is translated k units up.
$f(x) + k$; $k < 0$	The graph is translated $\lvert k \rvert$ units down.
$f(x - h)$; $h > 0$	The graph is translated h units right.
$f(x - h)$; $h < 0$	The graph is translated $\lvert h \rvert$ units left.

Example 1 Translations

Describe the translation in $g(x) = (x + 2)^2 - 4$ as it relates to the graph of the parent function.

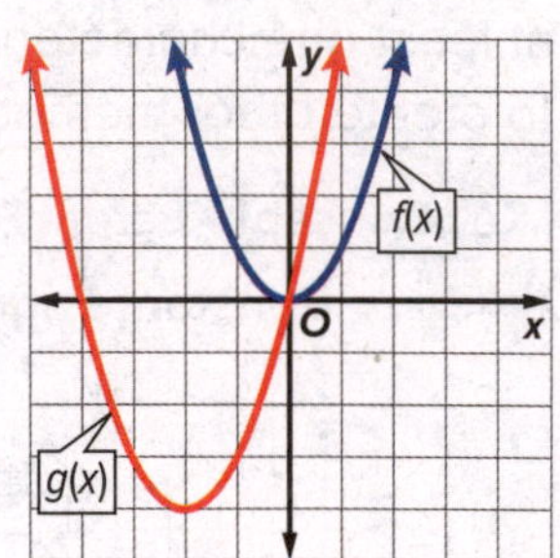

Since $g(x)$ is quadratic, the parent function is $f(x) =$ _____.

Since $f(x) = x^2$, $g(x) = f(x - h) + k$, where $h =$ _____ and $k =$ _____.

The constant k is added to the function after it has been evaluated, so k affects the output, or y-values. The value of k is less than 0, so the graph of $f(x) = x^2$ is translated _______ 4 units.

The value of h is subtracted from x before it is evaluated and is less than 0, so the graph of $f(x) = x^2$ is also translated 2 units _______.

The graph of $g(x) = (x + 2)^2 - 4$ is the translation of the graph of the parent function _____ units left and 4 units _______.

Example 2 Identify Translated Functions from Graphs

Use the graph of the function to write its equation.

The graph is an absolute value function with a parent function of __________. Notice that the vertex of the function has been shifted both vertically and horizontally from the parent function.

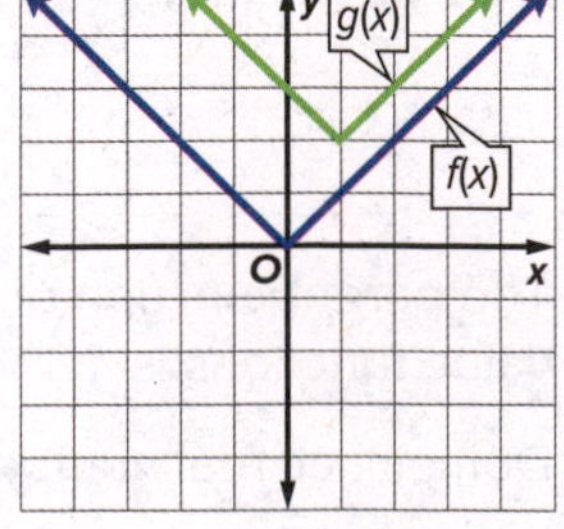

To write the equation of the graph, determine the values of h and k in $g(x) = \lvert x - h \rvert + k$.

The translated graph has been shifted 2 units up and 1 unit right.

So, $h =$ _____ and $k =$ _____. Thus, $g(x) =$ ____________.

Go Online You can complete an Extra Example online.

Learn Dilations and Reflection of Functions

A **dilation** is a transformation that stretches or compresses the graph of a function. Multiplying a function by a constant dilates the graph with respect to the x- or y-axis.

Key Concept • Dilations

Dilation	Change to Parent Graph
$af(x)$, $\lvert a\rvert > 1$	Stretches graph vertically.
$af(x)$, $0 < \lvert a\rvert < 1$	Compresses graph vertically.
$f(ax)$, $\lvert a\rvert > 1$	Compresses graph horizontally.
$f(ax)$, $0 < \lvert a\rvert < 1$	Stretches graph horizontally

You may want to complete the Concept Check to check your understanding.

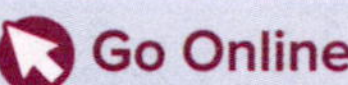

Go Online You can watch a video to see how to describe dilations of functions.

A **reflection** is a transformation where a figure, line, or curve, is flipped in a line. The **line of reflection** divides the figure in such a way that one side of the figure looks like the mirror image of another side. Often the reflection is in the x- or y-axis.

When a parent function $f(x)$ is multiplied by -1, the result $-f(x)$ is a reflection of the graph in the x-axis. When only the variable is multiplied by -1, the result $f(-x)$ is a reflection of the graph in the y-axis.

Key Concept • Reflections

Reflection	Change to Parent Graph
$-f(x)$	Reflection in the x-axis
$f(-x)$	Reflection in the y-axis

Example 3 Vertical Dilations

Describe the dilation and reflection in $g(x) = -\frac{2}{5}x$ as it relates to the parent function.

Since $g(x)$ is a linear function, the parent function is $f(x) =$ ______.

Since $f(x) = x$, $g(x) = -1 \cdot a \cdot f(x)$ where $a =$ ______.

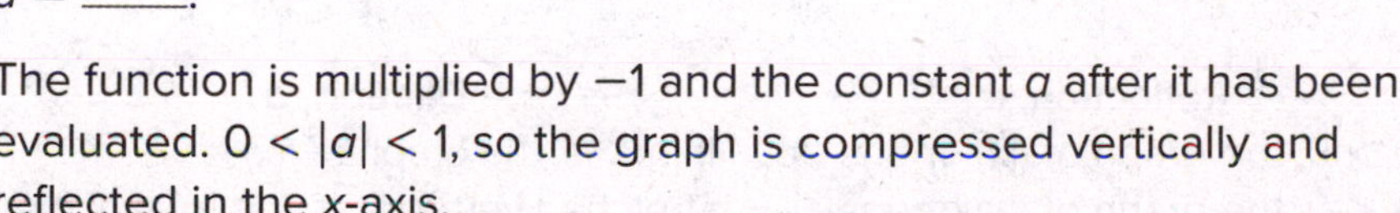

The function is multiplied by -1 and the constant a after it has been evaluated. $0 < \lvert a\rvert < 1$, so the graph is compressed vertically and reflected in the x-axis.

The graph of $g(x) = -\frac{2}{5}x$ is the graph of the parent function ____________ vertically and reflected in the ________.

Think About It! Describe the effect of multiplying the same value of a, $-\frac{2}{5}$, by a different parent function such as $f(x) = \lvert x\rvert$.

Go Online You can complete an Extra Example online.

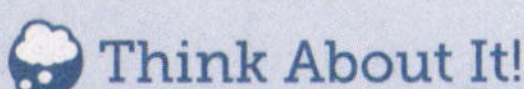

Think About It!

Why does the graph of $g(x) = (-2.5x)^2$ appear the same as $j(x) = (2.5x)^2$?

Example 4 Horizontal Dilations

Describe the dilation and reflection in $g(x) = (-2.5x)^2$ as it relates to the parent function.

Since $g(x)$ is a quadratic function, the parent function is $f(x) =$ ____. Since $f(x) = x^2$, $g(x) = f(-1 \cdot a \cdot x)$, where $a =$ ____.

x is multiplied by ____ and the constant a before the function is performed and $|a|$ is greater than 1, so the graph of $f(x) = x^2$ is compressed ________ and reflected in the ____.

The graph of $g(x) = (-2.5x)^2$ is the graph of the parent function ________ horizontally and ________ in the y-axis.

Learn Transformations of Functions

The general form of a function is $g(x) = a \cdot f(x - h) + k$, where $f(x)$ is the parent function. Each constant in the equation affects the parent graph.

- The value of $|a|$ stretches or compresses (dilates) the parent graph.
- When the value of a is negative, the graph is reflected across the x-axis.
- The value of k shifts (translates) the parent graph up or down.
- The value of h shifts (translates) the parent graph left or right.

Think About It!

Do the values of a, h, and k affect various parent functions in different ways?

Key Concept • Transformations of Functions

Horizontal Translation, h

If $h > 0$, the graph of $f(x)$ is translated h units right. If $h < 0$, the graph of $f(x)$ is translated $|h|$ units left.

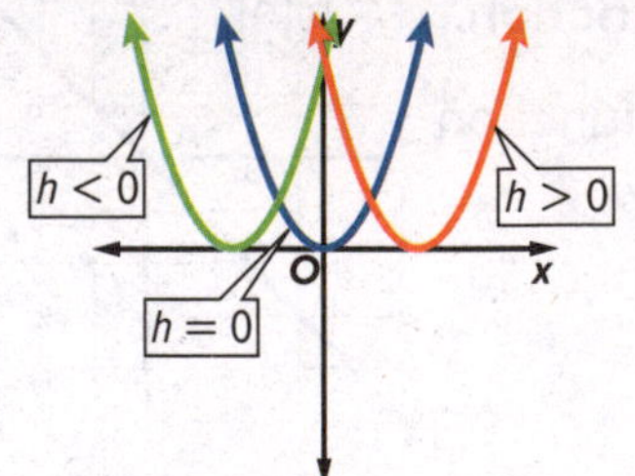

Vertical Translation, k

If $k > 0$, the graph of $f(x)$ is translated k units up. If $k < 0$, the graph of $f(x)$ is translated $|k|$ units down.

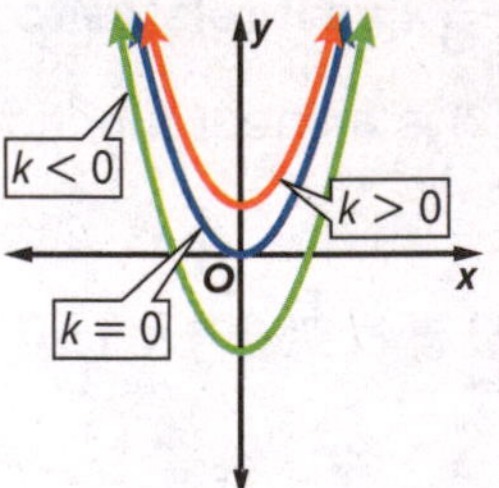

Reflection, a

If $a > 0$, the graph of $f(x)$ opens up. If $a < 0$, the graph of $f(x)$ opens down.

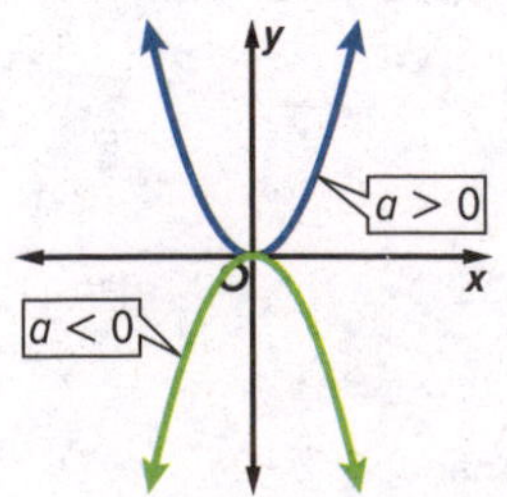

Dilation, a

If $|a| > 1$, the graph of $f(x)$ is stretched vertically. If $0 < |a| < 1$, the graph of $f(x)$ is compressed vertically.

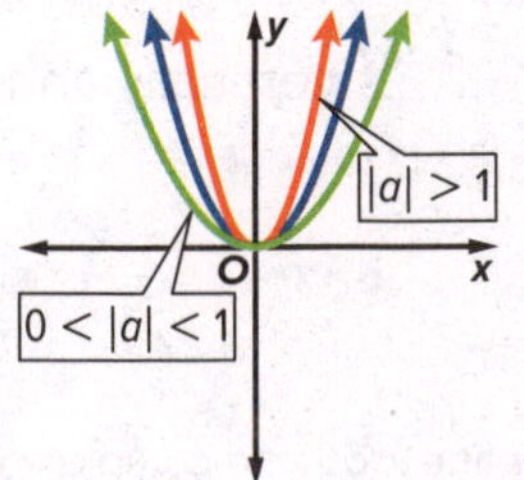

You can learn how to graph transformations of functions on a calculator by watching the video online.

Example 5 Multiple Transformations of Functions

Describe how the graph of $g(x) = -\frac{2}{3}|x + 3| + 1$ is related to the graph of the parent function.

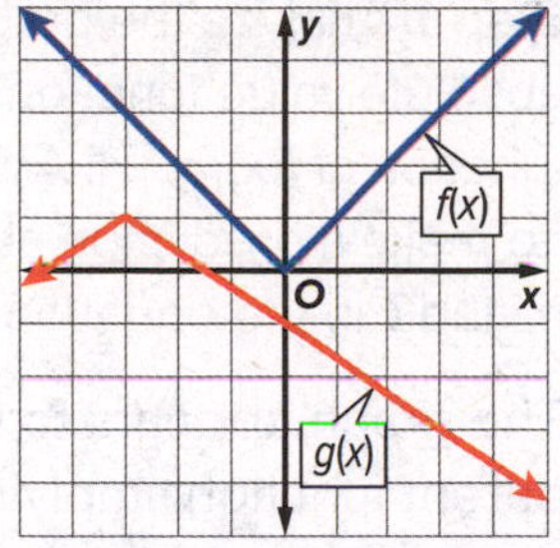

The parent function is $f(x) = |x|$.

Since $f(x) = |x|$, $g(x) = af(x - h) + k$ where $a = -\frac{2}{3}$, $h = -3$ and $k = 1$.

The graph of $g(x) = -\frac{2}{3}|x + 3| + 1$ is the graph of the parent function ____________ vertically, reflected in the ________, and translated 3 units ________ and 1 unit ________.

Check

Describe how $g(x) = -(0.4x + 2)$ is related to the graph of the parent function. ____

____

Example 6 Apply Transformations of Functions

DOLPHINS **Suppose the path of a dolphin during a jump is modeled by $g(x) = -0.125(x - 12)^2 + 18$, where x is the horizontal distance traveled by the dolphin and $g(x)$ is its height above the surface of the water. Describe how $g(x)$ is related to its parent function and interpret the function in the context of the situation.**

Since $f(x) = x^2$ is the parent function, $g(x) = af(x - h) + k$, where $a =$ ________, $h =$ ________, and $k =$ ________.

Translations

$12 > 0$, so the graph of $f(x) = x^2$ is translated 12 units ________.

$18 > 0$, so the graph of $f(x) = x^2$ is translated 18 units ________.

Dilation and Reflection

$0 < |-0.125| < 1$, so the graph of $f(x) = x^2$ is ____________ vertically.

$a < 0$, so the graph of $f(x) = x^2$ is a reflection in the ________.

Interpret the Function

Because a is negative, the path of the dolphin is modeled by a parabola that opens ________. This means that the vertex of the parabola (h, k) represents the ________________ of the dolphin, 18 feet, at 12 feet from the starting point of the jump.

Go Online You can complete an Extra Example online.

You can learn how to use transformations to graph an absolute value function by watching the animation online.

Think About It!

Write an equation for a quadratic function that opens down, has been stretched vertically by a factor of 4, and is translated 2 units right and 5 units down.

Study Tip

Interpretations When interpreting transformations, analyze how each value influences the function and alters the graph. Then determine what you think each value might mean in the context of the situation.

Example 7 Identify an Equation from a Graph

Write an equation for the function.

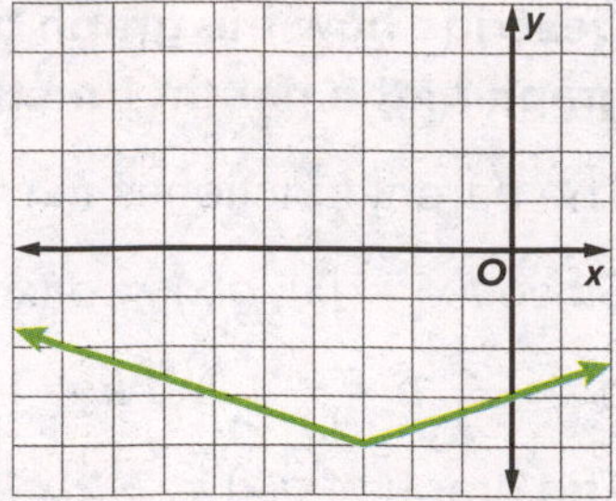

Step 1 Analyze the graph. The graph is an absolute value function with a parent function of $f(x) = |x|$. Analyze the graph to make a prediction about the values of a, h, and k in the equation $y = a|x - h| + k$.

The graph appears to be wider than the parent function, implying a vertical __________, and is not reflected. So, a is __________ and $0 < |a| < 1$.

The graph has also been shifted left and down from the parent graph. So, h ____ 0 and k ____ 0.

Step 2 Identify the translation(s).

Identify the horizontal and vertical translations to find the values of h and k.

The vertex is shifted 3 units left, so $h =$ ____.

It is also shifted 4 units down, so $k =$ ____.

$y = a\|x - h\| + k$	Vertex form of a quadratic equation
$y = a\|x -$ ____ $\| +$ ____	$h = -3$ and $k = -4$
$y = a\|x$ ____ $\|$ ____	Simplify.

Watch Out!

Choosing a Point When substituting for x and y in the equation, use a point other than the vertex.

Step 3 Identify the dilation and/or reflection.

Use the general form of the graph from step 2 and a point on the graph to find the value of a.

The point $(0, -3)$ lies on the graph. Substitute the coordinates in for x and y to solve for a.

$y = a\|x + 3\| - 4$	Vertex form of the graph
____ $= a\|$ ____ $+ 3\| - 4$	$(0, -3) = (x, y)$
$-3 = a\|$ ____ $\| - 4$	Add.
$-3 =$ ____ $a - 4$	Evaluate the absolute value.
____ $= a$	Solve.

Think About It!

How does the equation you found compare to the prediction you made in step 1?

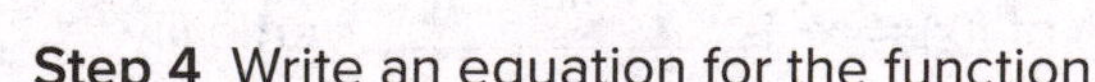

Step 4 Write an equation for the function.

Since $a = \frac{1}{3}$, $h = -3$ and $k = -4$, the equation is $g(x) =$ __________.

Check

Use the graph to write an equation for $g(x)$.

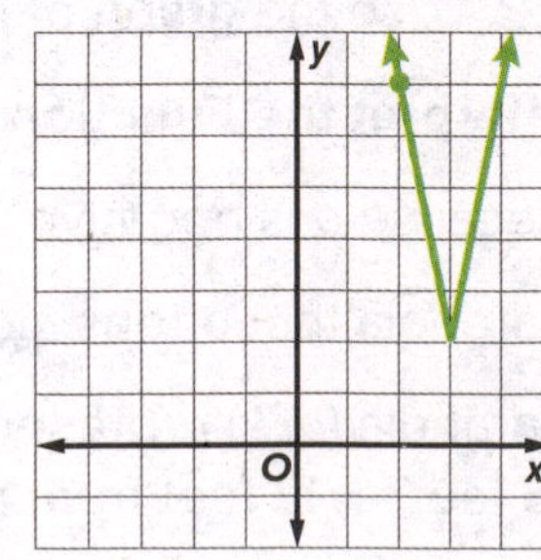

____

 **Go Online** You can complete an Extra Example online.

Name ______________________ Period __________ Date __________

Practice

Go Online You can complete your homework online.

Example 1

Describe each translation as it relates to the graph of the parent function.

1. $y = x^2 + 4$

2. $y = |x| - 3$

3. $y = x - 1$

4. $y = x + 2$

5. $y = (x - 5)^2$

6. $y = |x + 6|$

Example 2

Use the graph of each translated parent function to write its equation.

7.

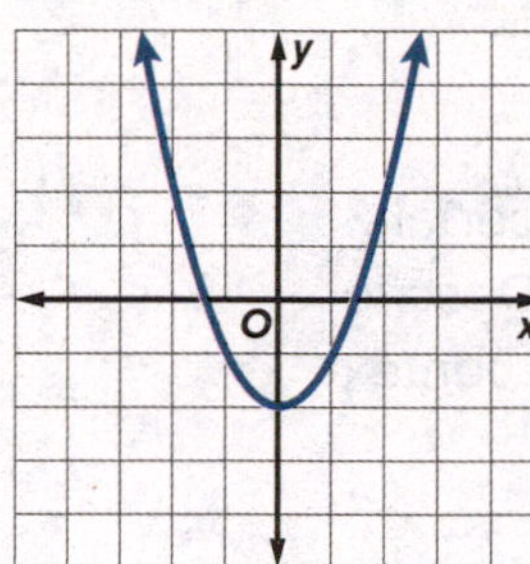

8.

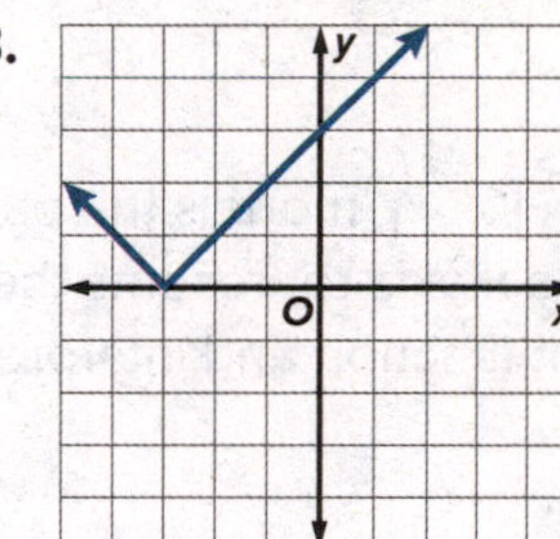

9.

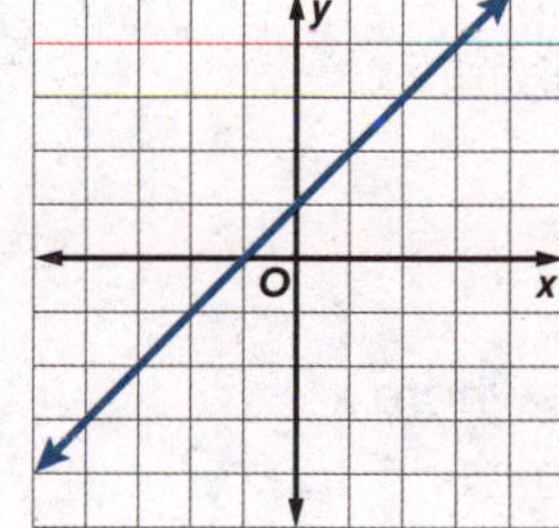

10.

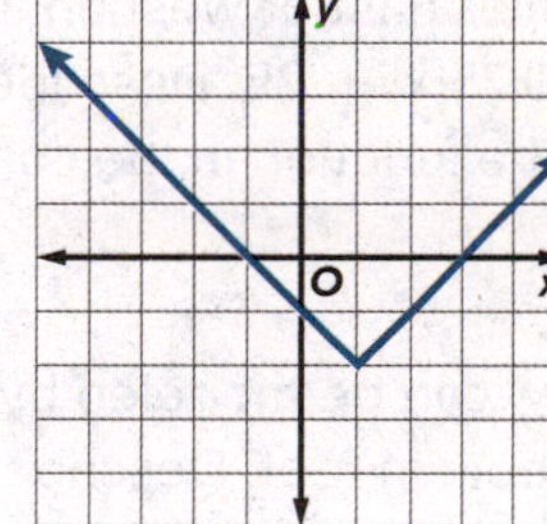

11.

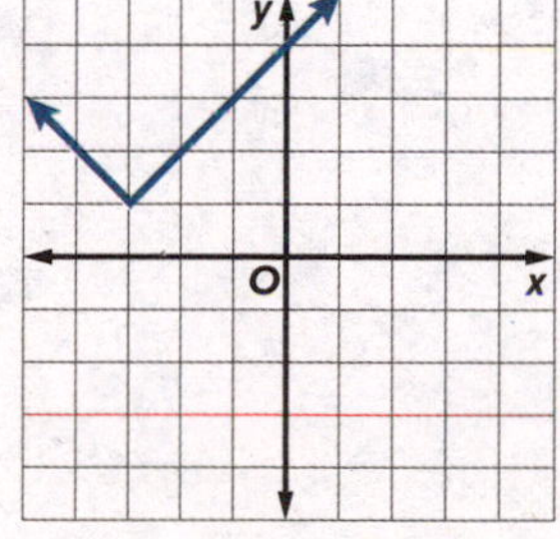

12.

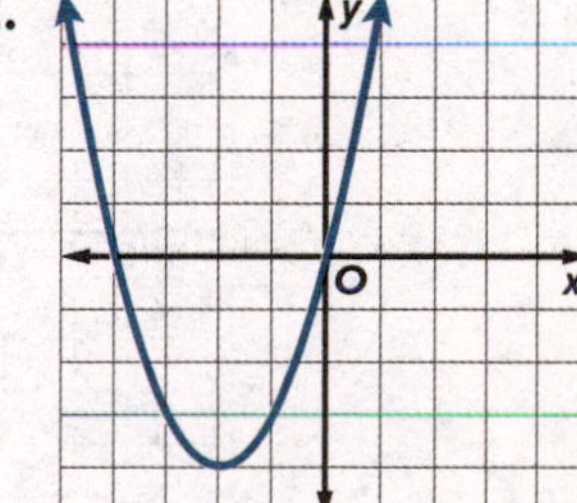

Examples 3 and 4

Describe each dilation and reflection as it relates to the parent function.

13. $y = (-3x)^2$

14. $y = -6x$

15. $y = -4|x|$

16. $y = |-2x|$

17. $y = -\frac{2}{3}x$

18. $y = -\frac{1}{2}x^2$

19. $y = |-\frac{1}{3}x|$

20. $y = \left(-\frac{3}{4}x\right)^2$

Example 5

Describe each transformation as it relates to the graph of the parent function.

21. $y = -6|x| - 4$

22. $y = 3x + 11$

23. $y = \frac{1}{3}x^2 - 2$

24. $y = \frac{1}{2}|x - 1| + 14$

25. $y = -0.8(x + 3)$

26. $y = (1.5x)^2 + 22$

Example 6

27. BILLARDS The function, $g(x) = |0.5x|$, models the path of a cue ball in a certain shot on a pool table, where the x-axis represents the edge of the table. Describe how $g(x)$ is related to its parent function and interpret the function in the context of the situation.

28. SALAD The cost for a salad depends on its weight, x, in ounces, and is described by $c(x) = 4.5 + 0.32x$. Describe how $c(x)$ is related to its parent function and interpret the function in the context of the situation.

29. TRAVEL The cost to travel x miles east or west on a train is the same. The function for the cost is $c(x) = 0.75|x| + 25$. Describe how $c(x)$ is related to its parent function and interpret the function in the context of the situation.

30. ARCHERY The path of an arrow can be modeled by $h(x) = -0.03x^2 + 6$, where x is distance and $h(x)$ is height, both in feet. Describe how $h(x)$ is related to its parent function and interpret the function in the context of the situation.

Example 7

Write an equation for each function.

31.

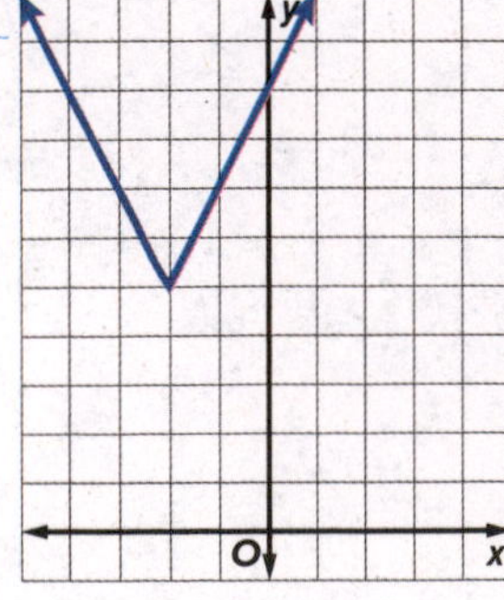

32.

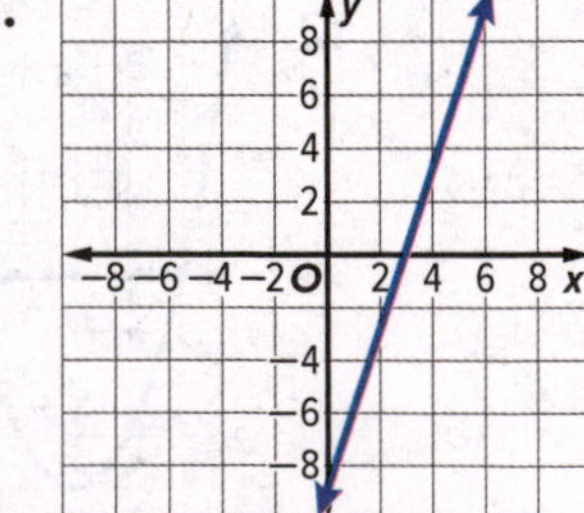

Name ______________________ Period __________ Date __________

Write an equation for each function.

33.

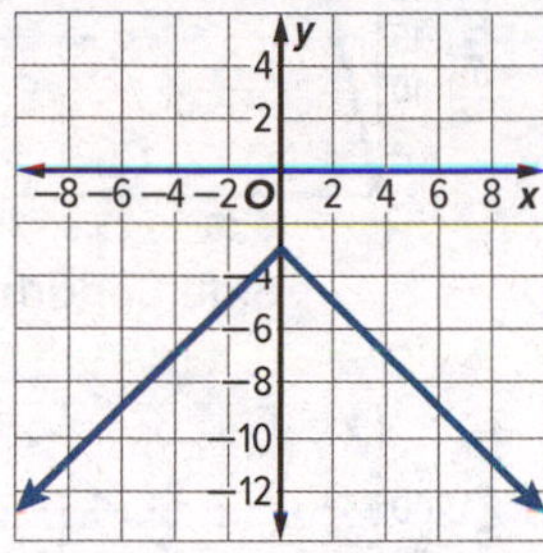

34.

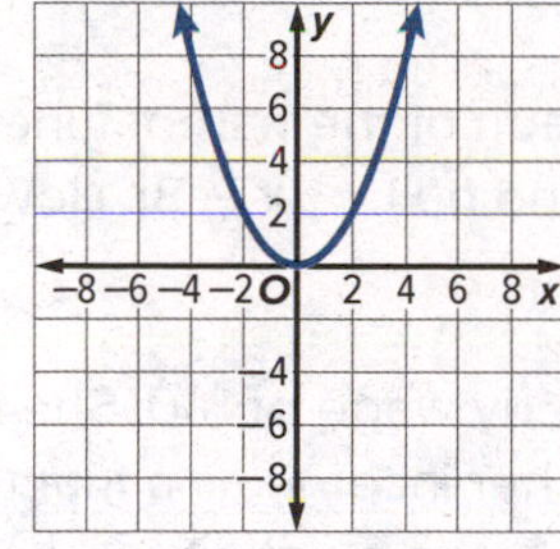

35.

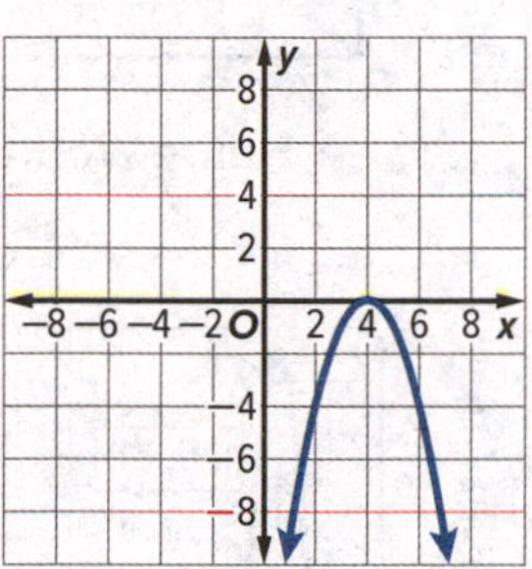

36.

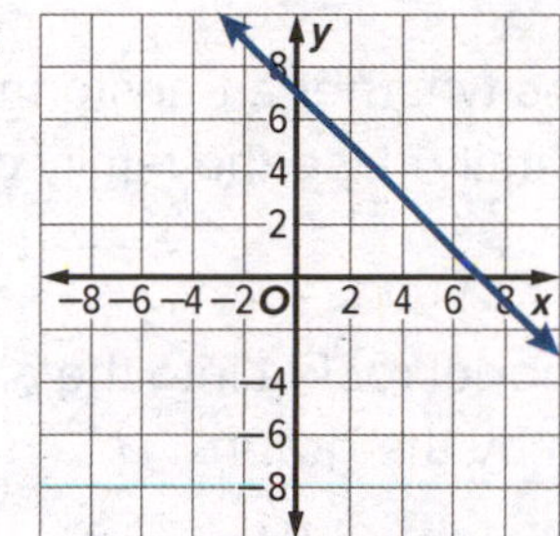

Mixed Exercises

Describe each transformation as it relates to the graph of the parent function. Then graph the function.

37. $y = |x| - 2$

38. $y = (x + 1)^2$

39. $y = -x$

40. $y = -|x|$

41. $y = 5x$

42. $y = 2x^2$

43. Describe the translation in $y = x^2 - 4$ as it relates to the parent function.

44. Describe the reflection in $y = -x^3$ as it relates to the parent function.

45. Describe the type of transformation in the function $f(x) = (5x)^2$.

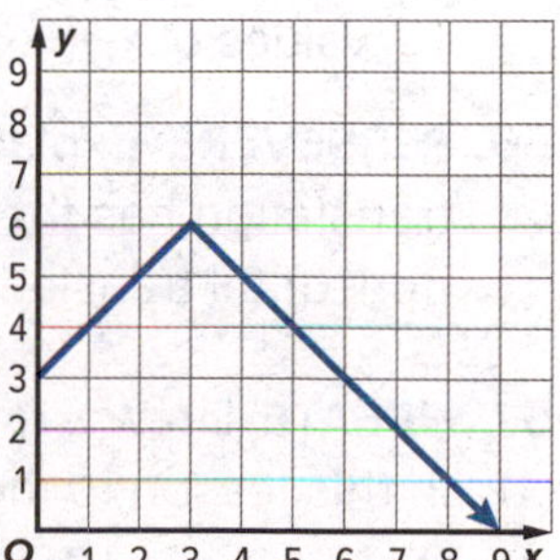

46. **ARCHITECTURE** The cross-section of a roof is shown in the figure. Write an absolute value function that models the shape of the roof.

47. **DARTS** Henry decided to measure how close to the bullseye he could throw a dart at different distances away from the dart board. He counted 1 point for each centimeter away from the bullseye. The function $y = |x - 8|$ represents the number of points y in relation distance thrown x. Describe the translation. Then graph the function.

48. **TILING** Kassie uses the function, $f(x) = -1.25(x - 1)^2 + 18.75$, where x is the size of the tile in square feet, to represent the area of her kitchen floor. Describe the transformations she applied to the parent function in creating her function.

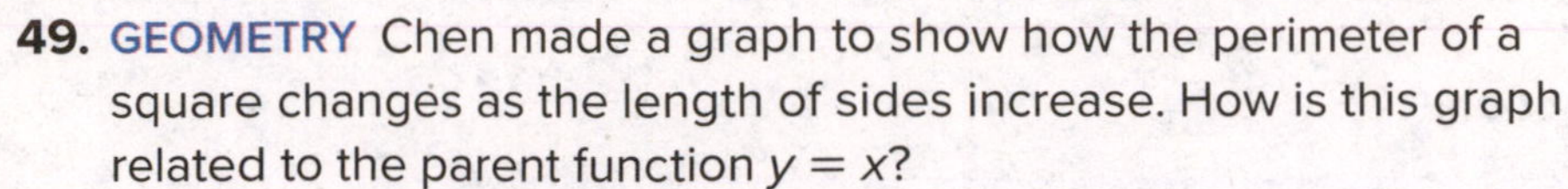

49. GEOMETRY Chen made a graph to show how the perimeter of a square changes as the length of sides increase. How is this graph related to the parent function $y = x$?

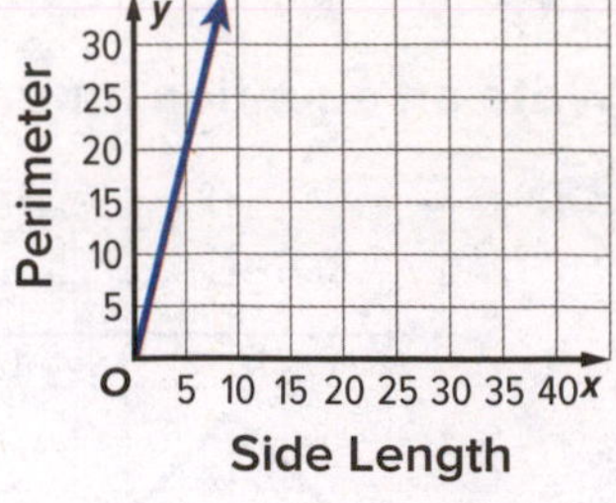

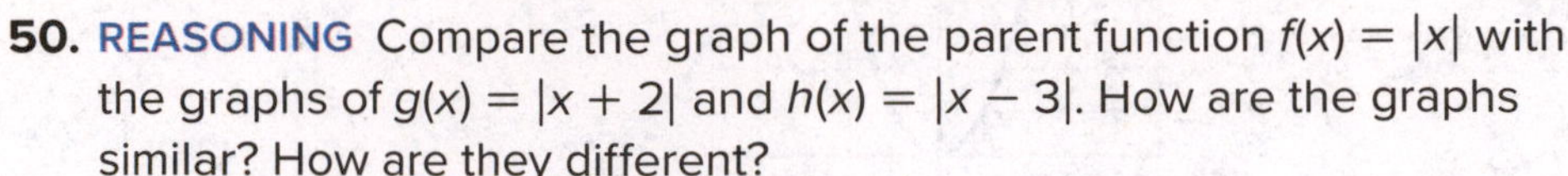

50. REASONING Compare the graph of the parent function $f(x) = |x|$ with the graphs of $g(x) = |x + 2|$ and $h(x) = |x - 3|$. How are the graphs similar? How are they different?

51. BUSINESS Maria earns an hourly wage of $10. She drew the following graph to show the relation of her income as a function of the hours she works. How did she modify the function $y = x$ to create her graph?

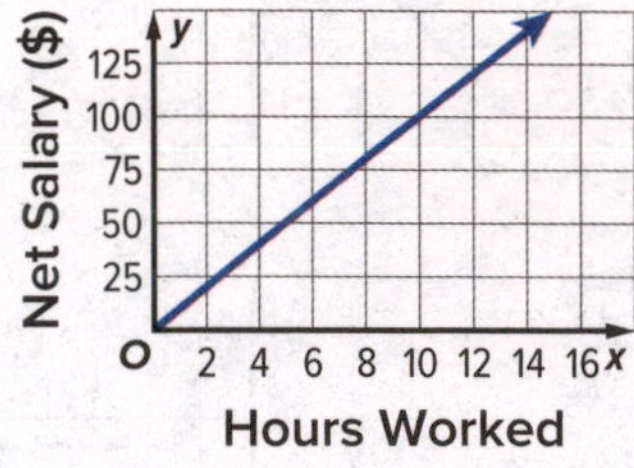

52. REGULARITY What determines whether a transformation will affect the graph vertically or horizontally? Use the family of quadratic functions as an example.

53. HOBBIES Laura launched a model rocket into the air. The height of her rocket over time is shown by the graph.

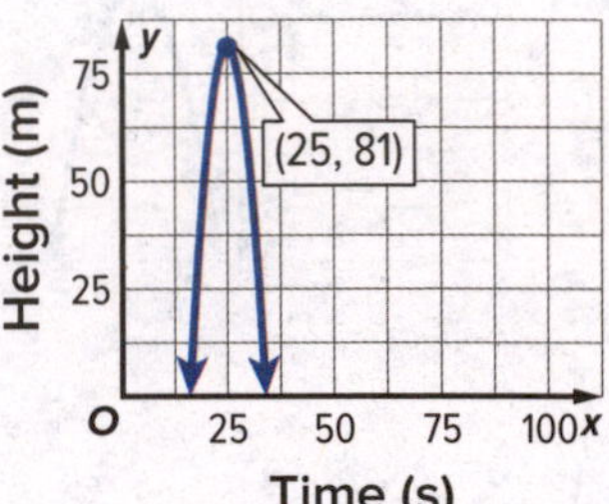

a. What type of function does the graph show?

b. In which axis has the function been reflected?

c. Which directions has the graph been translated? How many units? Assume that the function has not been dilated.

d. What is the equation for the curve shown on the graph?

54. PRECISION Graph $g(x) = -3|x + 5| - 1$. Describe the transformation of the parent function $f(x) = |x|$ that produces the graph of $g(x)$. What are the domain and range?

55. Consider the functions $f(x) = |2x|$, $g(x) = x + 2$, $h(x) = 2x^2$, and $k(x) = 2x^3$.

a. Graph each function and its reflection in the y-axis.

b. Analyze the functions and the graphs. Determine whether each function is *odd*, *even*, or *neither*.

c. Recall that if for all values of x, $f(-x) = f(x)$ the function $f(x)$ is an even function. If for all values of x, $f(-x) = -f(x)$ the function $f(x)$ is an odd function. Explain why this is true.

56. PERSEVERE Explain why performing a horizontal translation followed by a vertical translation has the same results as performing a vertical translation followed by a horizontal translation.

57. CREATE Draw a graph in Quadrant II. Use any of the transformations you learned in this lesson to move your figure to Quadrant IV. Describe your transformation.

58. ANALYZE Study the parent graphs at the beginning of this lesson. Select a parent graph with positive y-values when $x \to -\infty$ and positive y-values when $x \to \infty$.

59. WRITE Explain why the graph of $g(x) = (-x)^2$ appears the same as the graph of $f(x) = x^2$. Is this true for all reflections of quadratic functions? If not, describe a case when it is false.

Review

 Essential Question

How can analyzing a function help you understand the situation it models?

Module Summary

Lesson 1-1 through 1-3

Function Behavior

- The graph of a continuous function is a line or curve. The domain of a continuous function is a single interval of all real numbers.
- A linear function is a function in which no independent variable is raised to a whole number power greater than 1.
- If a vertical line intersects the graph of a relation more than once, then the relation is not a function.
- An *x*-intercept occurs when the graph intersects the *x*-axis, and a *y*-intercept occurs when the graph intersects the *y*-axis.
- A graph has line symmetry if each half of the graph on either side of a line matches the other side exactly.
- A graph has point symmetry when a figure is rotated 180° about a point and maps exactly onto the other part.
- A point is a relative maximum if there are no other nearby points with a greater *y*-coordinate. A point is a relative minimum if there are no other nearby points with a lesser *y*-coordinate.
- End behavior is the behavior of the graph at its ends. At the right end, the values of *x* are increasing toward infinity. This is denoted as $x \rightarrow \infty$. At the left end, the values of *x* are decreasing toward negative infinity, denoted as $x \rightarrow -\infty$.

Lessons 1-4 through 1-7

Graphs of Functions

- You can use key features of a function to sketch its graph. Features such as intercepts, symmetry, end behavior, extrema, and intervals where the function is increasing, decreasing, positive, or negative provide information for sketching the graph.
- A function that is written using two or more expressions is a piecewise-defined function.
- A step function has a graph that is a series of horizontal line segments.
- An absolute value function is a function that contains an algebraic expression within absolute value symbols.
- A translation moves a figure up, down, left, or right.
- A dilation shrinks or enlarges a figure proportionally. Multiplying a function by a constant dilates the graph with respect to the *x*- or *y*-axis.
- A reflection is a transformation that flips a figure in a line of reflection.

Study Organizer

 Foldables

Use your Foldable to review this module. Working with a partner can be helpful. Ask for clarification of concepts as needed.

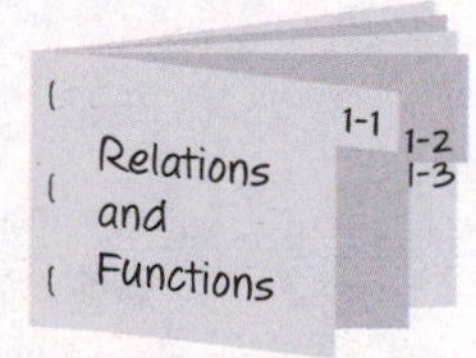

Name ______________________ Period __________ Date __________

Test Practice

1. **MULTIPLE CHOICE** If the codomain is all real numbers, which of the following describes the function shown? (Lesson 1-1)

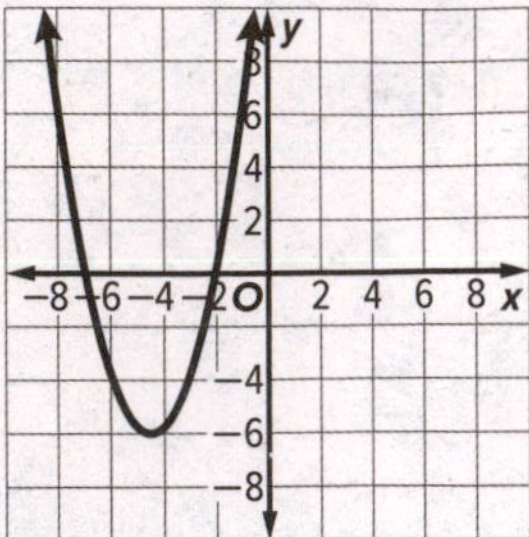

Ⓐ onto

Ⓑ one-to-one

Ⓒ neither

Ⓓ both

2. **MULTIPLE CHOICE** Salvatore is a plumber. He charges \$100 for all work that is completed in less than 2 hours. He charges \$250 for work that requires 2 to 5 hours, and he charges \$400 for work that takes between 5 and 8 hours.

Which best describes the graph of the function that models Salvatore's price scale? (Lesson 1-1)

Ⓐ Continuous; range: $\{y \mid y = 100, 250, 400\}$

Ⓑ Continuous; domain: $\{x \mid 0 < x \le 8\}$

Ⓒ Discontinuous; range: $\{y \mid y = 100, 250, 400\}$

Ⓓ Discontinuous; domain: $\{x \mid x = 2, 5, 8\}$

3. **MULTI-SELECT** Select all functions that are linear. (Lesson 1-2)

Ⓐ $f(x) = 3x^2 + 11$

Ⓑ $y = 9x$

Ⓒ $2x - 11y = 8$

Ⓓ $g(x) = |3x - 4|$

Ⓔ $yx = 5$

4. **OPEN RESPONSE** The table shows the amount of money Tia owed her friend over time after borrowing the money to go to a theme park. (Lesson 1-2)

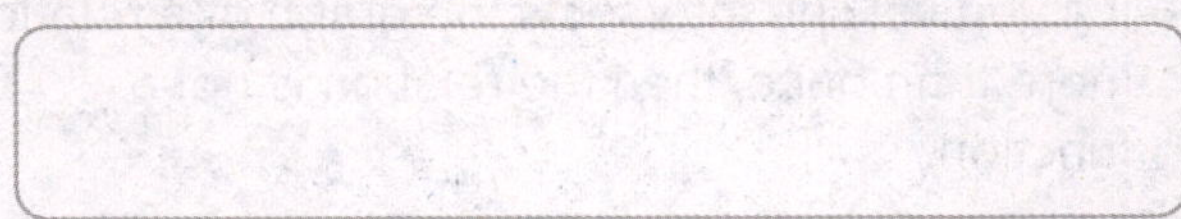

Week	0	1	2	3	4	5	6
Amount	\$80	\$68	\$52	\$39	\$21	\$10	\$0

What are the coordinates of the x-intercept and the coordinates of the y-intercept?

5. **MULTIPLE CHOICE** What type of symmetry is shown? (Lesson 1-2)

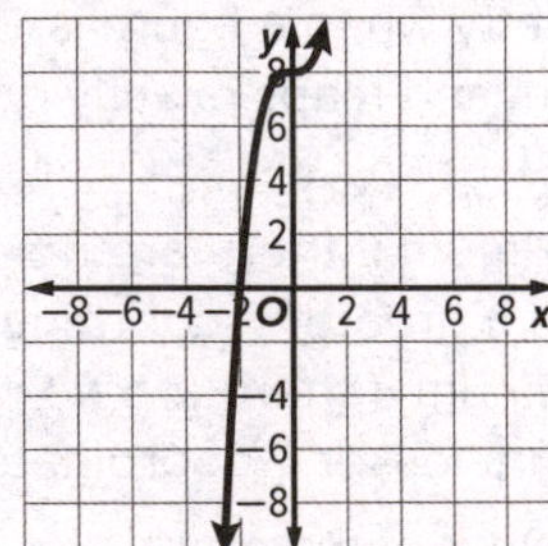

Ⓐ line symmetry

Ⓑ point symmetry

Ⓒ both line and point symmetry

Ⓓ no symmetry

Name ________ Period ________ Date ________

6. TABLE ITEM Indicate whether each of the following x-values is a *relative maximum*, *relative minimum* or *neither*. (Lesson 1-3)

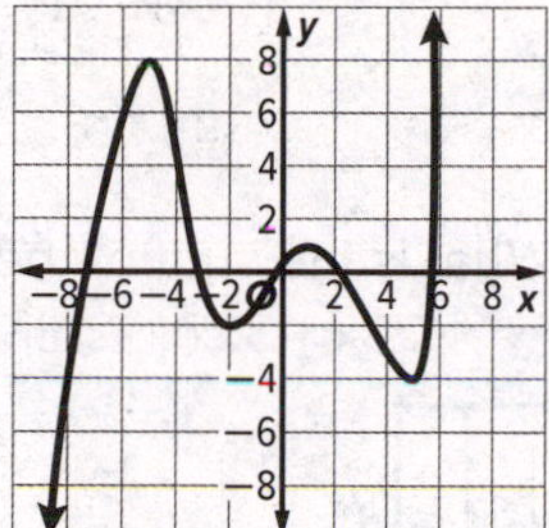

x-coordinate	Relative Maximum	Relative Minimum	Neither
−5			
−4			
−2			
0			
1			
5			

7. OPEN RESPONSE The graph shows the height of a ball after being thrown from a height of 1 foot.

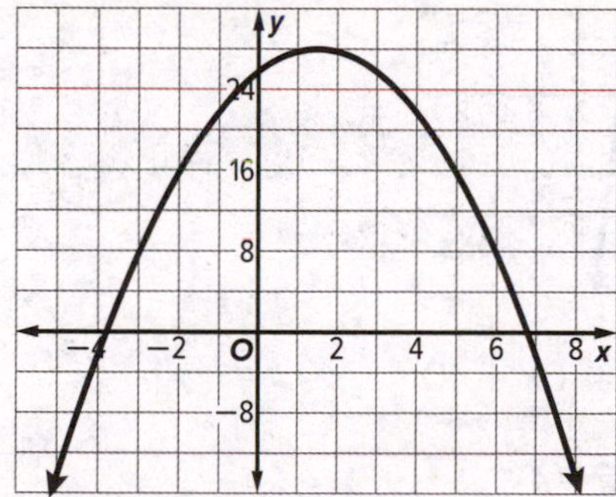

Explain why the end behavior does or does not make sense in this context. (Lesson 1-3)

8. MULTI-SELECT Select the function(s) that could be graphed from these features:

- Has a point located at (0, 0);
- Increasing when $x \geq 0$. (Lesson 1-4)

(A) $f(x) = -x$

(B) $g(x) = x^2$

(C) $h(x) = |x|$

(D) $j(x) = -x^3$

9. MULTIPLE CHOICE Sofia is sketching the graph of a function. She knows that as $x \to \infty$, $y \to -\infty$ and that the function has a y-intercept at (0, 7). Which other feature fits the sketch of the graph? (Lesson 1-4)

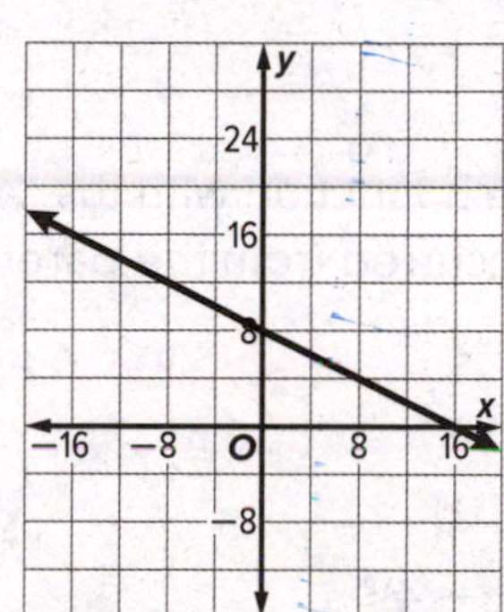

(A) as $x \to -\infty$, $y \to -\infty$

(B) x-intercept at (−14, 0)

(C) increases for y in the interval $7 < x < 14$

(D) decreases for y in the interval $-16 < x < 8$

10. OPEN RESPONSE What are the domain and range of $f(x)$? (Lesson 1-5)

$$f(x) = \begin{cases} \frac{1}{2}x + 5 & \text{if } x > 2 \\ x^2 & \text{if } x < 2 \end{cases}$$

Name ______________________ Period __________ Date __________

11. MULTIPLE CHOICE What is the range of this step function? (Lesson 1-5)

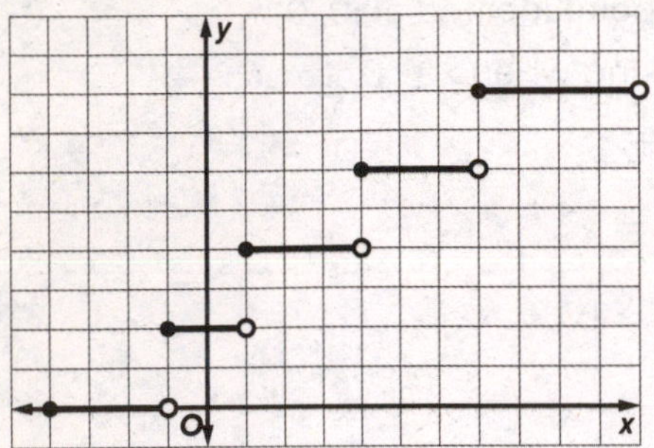

Ⓐ $\{y \mid y = 0, 2, 4, 6, 8\}$

Ⓑ $\{y \mid 0 \leq y \leq 8\}$

Ⓒ $\{y \mid y = -4, 1, 4, 7, 11\}$

Ⓓ $\{y \mid -4 \leq y \leq 11\}$

12. TABLE ITEM Match each function with the transformation that occurred from the parent function $f(x) = x^2$. (Lesson 1-6)

$g(x) = -x^2$

$h(x) = (3x)^2$

$j(x) = (x - 4)^2$

Function	Translation	Reflection	Dilation
$g(x)$			
$h(x)$			
$j(x)$			

13. OPEN RESPONSE Describe the transformation(s) from the parent function to $f(x) = 3(x - 2)^2 + 9$. (Lesson 1-6)

14. OPEN RESPONSE If $g(x) = f(0.75x)$ then how is the graph of $g(x)$ related to the graph of $f(x)$? (Lesson 1-6)

15. GRIDDED RESPONSE What is the sum of the solutions to $10x - 4 = x^2 + 23x + 32$? (Lesson 1-7)

16. MULTIPLE CHOICE Which equation can be solved using the graph? (Lesson 1-7)

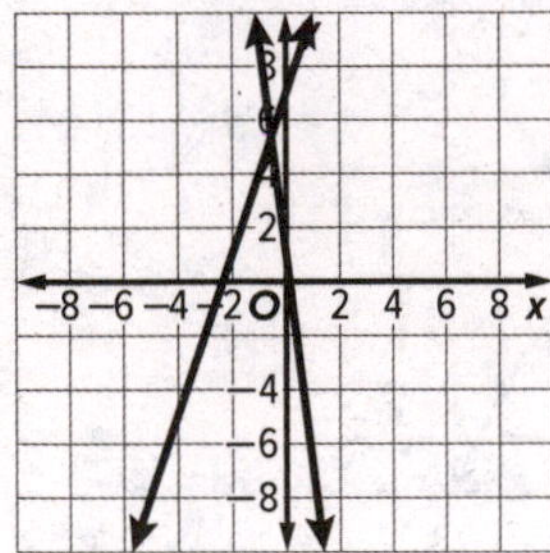

Ⓐ $11x + 2 = 6x + 10$

Ⓑ $2x - 9 = 7x - 1$

Ⓒ $-8x + 1 = 3x + 7$

Ⓓ $-13x = 8x - 8$

Module 2

Linear Equations, Inequalities, and Systems

Essential Question

How are equations, inequalities, and systems of equations or inequalities best used to model to real-world situations?

A.CED.1, A.CED.2, A.CED.3, F.IF.6, A.REI.11
Mathematical Practices: MP1, MP2, MP3, MP4, MP5, MP6, MP7, MP8

What will you learn?

Place a checkmark (✓) in each row that corresponds with how much you already know about each topic **before** starting this module.

KEY

👎 — I don't know. 👉 — I've heard of it. 👍 — I know it!

	Before			After		
	👎	👉	👍	👎	👉	👍
solve linear equations						
solve linear inequalities						
solve absolute value equations and inequalities						
write equations of linear functions in standard, slope-intercept, and point-slope form						
solve systems of equations by graphing, by substitution, and by elimination						
solve systems of inequalities in two variables						
use linear programming to find maximum and minimum values of a function						
solve systems of equations in three variables						

Foldables Make this Foldable to help you organize your notes about equations and inequalities. Begin with one sheet of paper.

1. **Fold** 2-inch tabs on each of the short sides.
2. **Fold** in half in both directions.
3. **Open** and cut as shown.
4. **Refold** along the width. Staple each pocket. Label pockets as *Solving Equations and Inequalities*, *Writing Equations for Functions*, *Systems of Equations and Inequalities*, and *Solve and Graph Inequalities*. Place index cards for notes in each pocket.

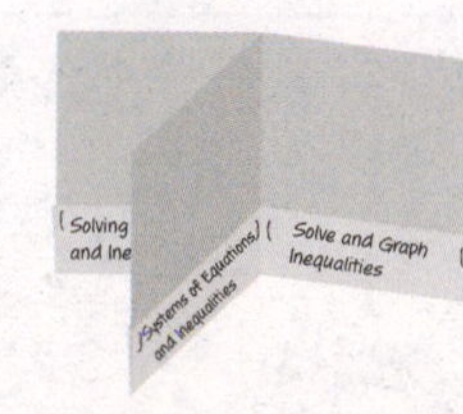

What Vocabulary Will You Learn?

Check the box next to each vocabulary term that you may already know.

- ☐ absolute value
- ☐ bounded
- ☐ consistent
- ☐ dependent
- ☐ elimination
- ☐ empty set
- ☐ equation
- ☐ extraneous solution
- ☐ feasible region
- ☐ inconsistent
- ☐ independent
- ☐ inequality
- ☐ linear programming
- ☐ optimization
- ☐ ordered triple
- ☐ point-slope form
- ☐ root
- ☐ slope-intercept form
- ☐ solution
- ☐ standard form of a linear equation
- ☐ substitution
- ☐ system of equations
- ☐ system of inequalities
- ☐ unbounded
- ☐ zeros

Are You Ready?

Complete the Quick Review to see if you are ready to start this module. Then complete the Quick Check.

Quick Review

Example 1

Graph $2y + 5x = -10$.

Find the x- and y-intercepts.

$$2(0) + 5x = -10 \qquad 2y + 5(0) = -10$$
$$5x = -10 \qquad 2y = -10$$
$$x = -2 \qquad y = -5$$

The graph crosses the x-axis at $(-2, 0)$ and the y-axis at $(0, -5)$. Use these ordered pairs to graph the equation.

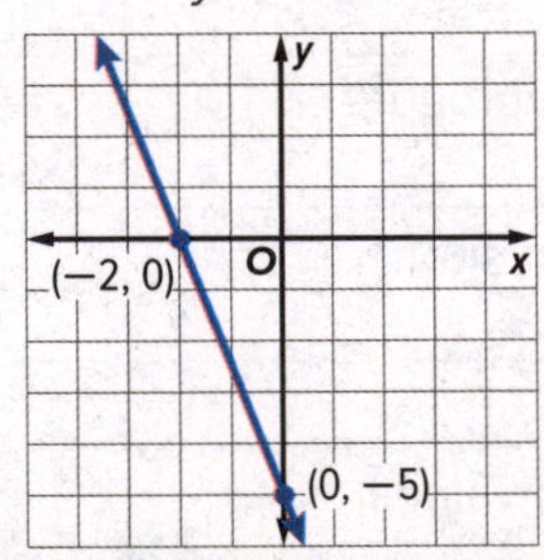

Example 2

Graph $y \geq 3x - 2$.

The boundary is the graph of $y = 3x - 2$. Since the inequality symbol is $\geq$, the boundary will be solid.

Test the point (0, 0).

$0 \geq 3(0) - 2$ $(x, y) = (0, 0)$

$0 \geq -2$

Shade the region that includes (0, 0).

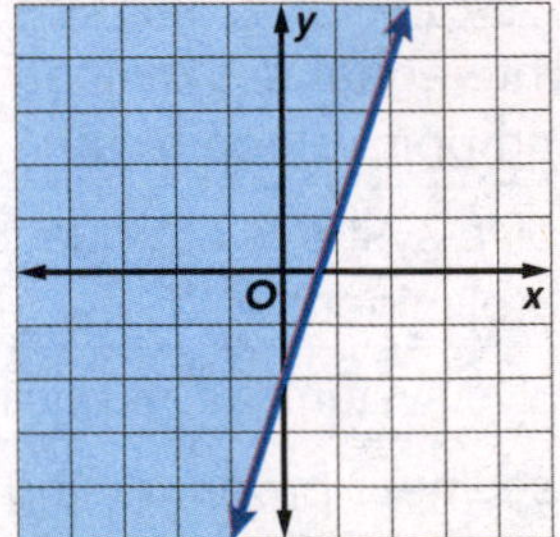

Quick Check

Graph each equation.

1. $x + 2y = 4$
2. $y = -x + 6$
3. $3x + 5y = 15$
4. $3y - 2x = -12$

Graph each inequality.

5. $y < 3$
6. $x + y \geq 1$
7. $3x - y > 6$
8. $x + 2y \leq 5$

How Did You Do?

Which exercises did you answer correctly in the Quick Check? Shade those exercise numbers below.

Solving Linear Equations and Inequalities

Explore Comparing Linear Equations and Inequalities

Online Activity Use a comparison to complete the Explore.

INQUIRY How do the solution methods and the solutions of linear equations and inequalities in one variable compare?

Today's Standards
A.CED.1, A.CED.2
MP1, MP2

Today's Vocabulary
equation
solution
root
zero
inequality

Learn Solving Linear Equations

An **equation** is a mathematical sentence stating that two mathematical expressions are equal. The **solution** of an equation is a value that makes the equation true. To solve equations, use the properties of equality to isolate the variable on one side.

Property of Equality	Symbols
Addition Property of Equality	For any real numbers a, b, and c, if $a = b$, then $a + c = b + c$.
Subtraction Property of Equality	For any real numbers a, b, and c, if $a = b$, then $a - c = b - c$.
Multiplication Property of Equality	For any real numbers a, b, and c, $c \neq 0$, if $a = b$, then $ac = bc$.
Division Property of Equality	For any real numbers a, b, and c, $c \neq 0$, if $a = b$, then $\frac{a}{b} = \frac{b}{c}$.

Study Tip

Justifications The properties of equality are used as justifications above. However, in most future solutions, the justifications for steps will read as "Subtract c from each side," or "Divide each side by c."

Example 1 Solve a Linear Equation

Solve $\frac{1}{3}(2x - 57) + \frac{1}{3}(6 - x) = -4$.

$\frac{1}{3}(2x - 57) + \frac{1}{3}(6 - x) = -4$ Original equation

$\frac{2}{3}x - \_\_ + \_\_ - \frac{1}{3}x = -4$ Distributive Property

$\_\_ - \_\_ = -4$ Combine like terms.

$\frac{1}{3}x = \_\_$ Add 17 to each side and simplify.

$x = \_\_$ Multiply each side by 3 and simplify.

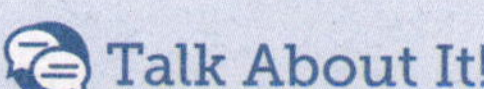

Talk About It!

In the last step, why is each side of the equation multiplied by 3? How is this related to the Division Property of Equality?

Check

Solve $-2(-4n + 1) + 5(\frac{2}{5}n - 8) = -62$.

$n = \_\_$

Go Online You can complete an Extra Example online.

Go Online

You can learn how to use algebra tiles to solve equations in one variable by watching the video online.

Your Notes

Think About It!
What does it mean to solve for a variable?

Example 2 Write and Solve an Equation

SPACE The diameter of Earth is 828 kilometers less than twice the diameter of Mars. If Earth has a diameter of 12,756 kilometers, what is the diameter of Mars?

Part A Write an equation that represents the situation.

Words	The diameter of Earth	is	823 less than twice the diameter of Mars.
Variable	Let m = ____		
Equation	____	=	2m − ____

Part B Solve the equation.

$$12{,}756 = 2m - 288 \qquad \text{Original equation}$$
$$12{,}756 + \_\_\_\_ = 2m - 288 + 888 \qquad \text{Add 828 to each side.}$$
$$\_\_\_\_ = 2m \qquad \text{Simplify.}$$
$$\frac{13{,}584}{} = \frac{2m}{} \qquad \text{Divide each side by 2.}$$
$$\_\_\_\_ = m \qquad \text{Simplify.}$$

The diameter of Mars is ____ kilometers. This is a reasonable solution because 12,756 is a little less than 6792 • 2 = 13,584, as indicated in the problem.

Check

BASKETBALL In 1962, Wilt Chamberlain set the record for the most points scored in a single NBA game. He scored 28 points from free throws and made x field goals, worth two points each. If Wilt Chamberlain scored 100 points, how many field goals did he make? Which equation represents the number of field goals that Chamberlain scored? ____

A. $100 = 28 + 2x$ B. $100 = 2x$ C. $28 = 2x$ D. $100 = 2x$

How many field goals did Chamberlain score? ____ field goals

Example 3 Solve for a Variable

GEOMETRY The formula for the perimeter of a parallelogram is $P = 2a + 2b$ where a and b represent the measures of the bases. Solve the equation for b.

$$P = 2a + 2b \qquad \text{Original equation}$$
$$P - \_\_\_\_ = 2a + 2b - \_\_\_\_ \qquad \text{Subtract } 2a \text{ from each side.}$$
$$P - 2a = \_\_\_\_ \qquad \text{Simplify.}$$
$$\frac{P}{} - \frac{2a}{} = \frac{2b}{} \qquad \text{Divide each side by 2.}$$
$$\frac{P}{} - \_\_\_\_ = b \qquad \text{Simplify.}$$

Go Online You can complete an Extra Example online.

Check

GEOMETRY The formula for the area A of a trapezoid is solved for h. Fill in the missing justification.

$A = \frac{1}{2}h(a + b)$ Original equation.

$2A = 2 \cdot \frac{1}{2}h(a + b)$ Multiplication Property of Equality

$2A = h(a + b)$ Simplify.

$\frac{2A}{(a + b)} = \frac{h(a + b)}{(a + b)}$ ______________________________

$\frac{2A}{(a + b)} = h$ Simplify.

Learn Solving Linear Equations by Graphing

Equation	Related Function
$2x + 13 = 9$	$f(x) = 2x + 4$ or $y = 2x + 4$

The solution of an equation is called a **root**. You can find the root of an equation by examining the graph of its related function $f(x)$. Values of x for which $f(x) = 0$ are called **zeros** of the function f. The zero of a function is the x-intercept of its graph. The solution and root of a linear equation are the same as the zero and x-intercept of its related function.

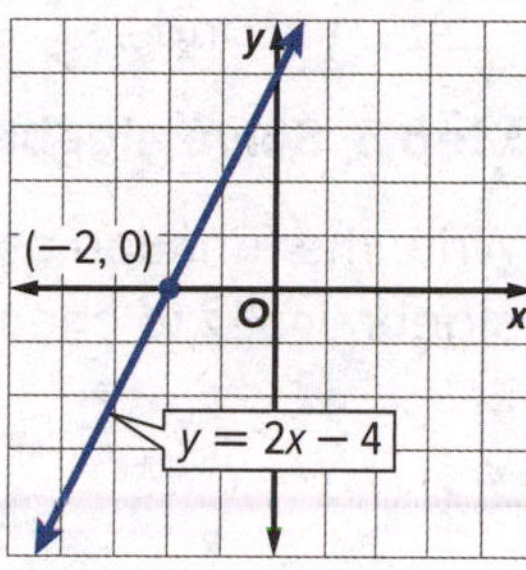

Example 4 Solve a Linear Equation by Graphing

Step 1 Find a related function.

Rewrite the equation with 0 on the right side.

$\frac{1}{2}x - 11 = -8$ Original equation.

$\frac{1}{2}x - 11 + 8 = -8 + 8$ Add 8 to each side.

__________ $= 0$ Simplify.

Replacing 0 with $f(x)$ gives the related function ___________________________

Step 2 Graph the related function.

Since the graph of $f(x) = \frac{1}{2}x - 3$ intersects the x-axis at ___, the solution of the equation is ___.

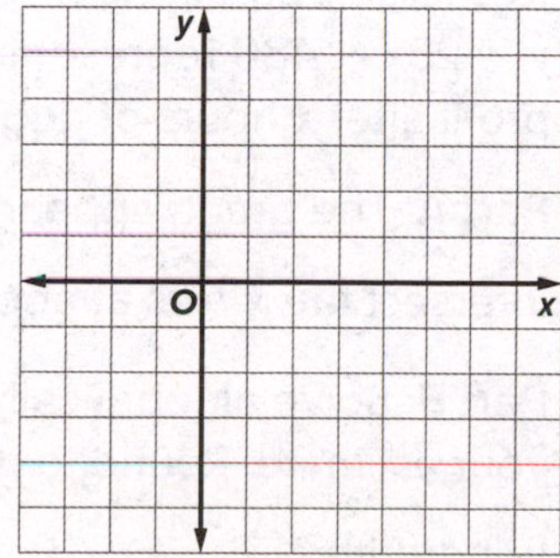

Go Online You can complete an Extra Example online.

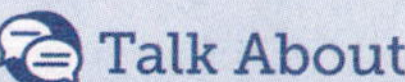

Talk About It!

Because there is typically more than one way to solve an equation for 0, there may be more than one related function for an equation. What is another possible related function of $2x + 13 = 9$? How does the zero of this function compare to the zero of $f(x) = 2x + 4$?

Think About It!

Explain why −3 is *not* a zero of the function.

Watch Out!

Intercepts Be careful not to mistake y-intercepts for zeros of functions. The y-intercept on a graph occurs when $x = 0$. The x-intercepts are the zeros of a function because they are where $f(x) = 0$.

Use a Source

Use available resources to find Paul Crake's actual time. How does this compare to your solution?

Example 5 Estimate Solutions by Graphing

TOWER RACE The Empire State Building Run-Up is a race in which athletes run up the building's 1576 stairs. In 2003, Paul Crake set the record for the fastest time, running up an average of about 165 stairs per minute. The function $c = 1576 - 165m$ represents the number of steps Crake had left to climb c after m minutes. Find the zero of the function and interpret its meaning in the context of the situation.

Step 1 Graph the function.

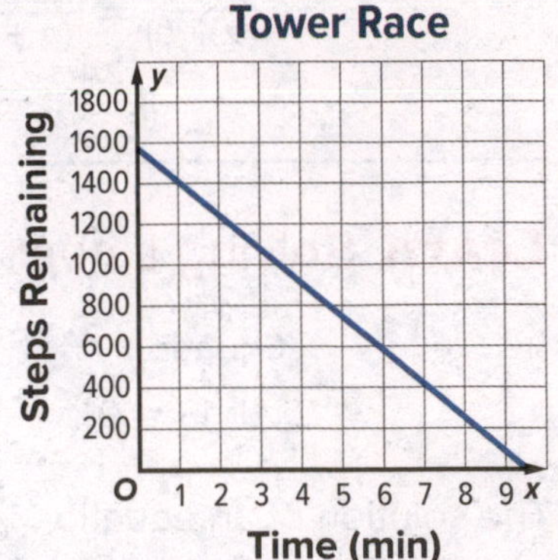

Step 2 Estimate the zero.

The graph appears to intersect the x-axis at about _____. This means that Paul Crake finished the race in about 9.5 minutes, or _____ minutes and _____ seconds.

Step 3 Solve algebraically.

Write the function as an equation set equal to 0, and solve algebraically to check your solution.

$c = 1576 - 165m$		Original equation
$0 = 1576 - 165m$		Replace c with 0.
_____ = _____		Add $165m$ to each side.
$m \approx$ _____		Divide each side by 165.

The solution is about _____. So, Paul Crake completed the Empire State Building Run-Up in about 9.55 minutes, or ___ minutes and ___ seconds. This is close to the estimated time of 9.5 minutes.

Study Tip

Assumptions

Assuming that the rate at which Paul Crake climbed the stairs was constant allows us to represent the situation with a linear equation. While the rate at which he climbed likely varied throughout the race, using constant rates allows for reasonable graphs and solutions.

Check

DOG WALKING Bethany spends \$480 on supplies to start a dog walking service for which she plans to charge \$23 per hour. The function $y = 23x - 480$ represents Bethany's profit after x hours of dog walking.

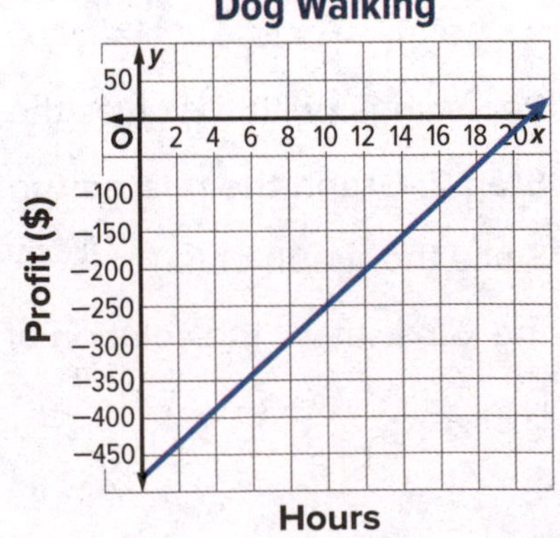

Part A The graph appears to intersect the x-axis at about _____.

Part B Solve algebraically to verify your estimate. Round to the nearest hundredth. _____

Go Online You can complete an Extra Example online.

Learn Solving Linear Inequalities

An **inequality** is an open sentence that contains the symbol $<$, $\leq$, $>$, $\geq$. Properties of inequalities allow you to perform operations on each side of an inequality without changing the truth of the inequality.

Key Concept • Addition and Subtraction Properties of Inequality		
Symbols	For any real numbers, a, b, and c: If $a > b$, then $a + c > b + c$. If $a > b$, then $a - c > b - c$. If $a < b$, then $a + c < b + c$. If $a < b$, then $a - c < b - c$.	
Examples	$2 > 0$ $2 + 1 > 0 + 1$ $3 > 1$	$9 > 6$ $9 - 4 > 6 - 4$ $5 > 2$

Key Concept • Multiplication and Division Properties of Inequality		
Symbols	For any real numbers, a, b, and c: where c is positive: If $a > b$, then $ac > bc$. If $a > b$, then $\frac{a}{c} > \frac{b}{c}$. If $a < b$, then $ac < bc$. If $a < b$, then $\frac{a}{c} < \frac{b}{c}$. where c is negative: If $a > b$, then $ac < bc$. If $a > b$, then $\frac{a}{c} > \frac{b}{c}$. If $a < b$, then $ac > bc$. If $a < b$, then $\frac{a}{c} < \frac{b}{c}$.	
Examples	$8 > -2$ $8(3) > -2(3)$ $24 > -6$	$-4 < -2$ $-4(-8) < -2(-8)$ $32 > 16$
	$-3 > -7$ $\frac{-3}{2} > \frac{-7}{2}$ $-1.5 > -3.5$	$12 > -4$ $\frac{12}{-2} > \frac{-4}{-2}$ $-6 < 2$

The solution sets of inequalities can be expressed by using set-builder notation. For example, $\{x \mid x > 1\}$ represents the set of all numbers x such that x is greater than 1. The solution sets can also be graphed on number lines. Circles and dots are used to indicate whether an endpoint is included in the solution. The circle at 1 means that this point is *not* included in the solution set.

−5 −4 −3 −2 −1 0 1 2 3 4 5

Go Online

You may want to complete the Concept Check to check your understanding.

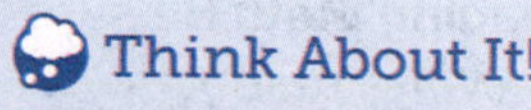

Think About It!

What does the arrow on the graph of a solution set represent?

Think About It!

What does the dot on the graph of a solution set indicate?

Study Tip

Reversing the Inequality Symbol Adding the same number to, or subtracting the same number from, each side of an inequality does not change the truth of the inequality. Multiplying or dividing each side of an inequality by a positive number does not change the truth of the inequality. However, multiplying or dividing each side of an inequality by a negative number requires that the order of the inequality be reversed. In this problem, $\geq$ was replaced with $\leq$.

Watch Out!

Reading Math Be sure to always read problems carefully. The term *at least* is used here, and can be confusing since it actually means *greater than or equal to*, and is represented by $\geq$. In this instance, Jake should intake at least 1300 mg, which means he must intake an amount greater than or equal to 1300 mg.

Example 6 Solve a Linear Inequality

Solve $-5.6n + 12.9 \geq -71.1$. Graph the solution set on a number line.

$-5.6n + 12.9 \geq -71.1$	Original inequality.
$-5.6n + 12.9$ ______ ≥ -71.1 ______	Subtract 12.9 from each side.
$-5.6n \geq -84.4$	Simplify.
$\frac{-5.6n}{\quad} \leq \frac{-84}{\quad}$	Divide each side by -5.6, reversing the inequality symbol.
$n \leq$ ______	Simplify.

The solution set is $\{n \mid n \leq$ ______$\}$. Graph the solution set.

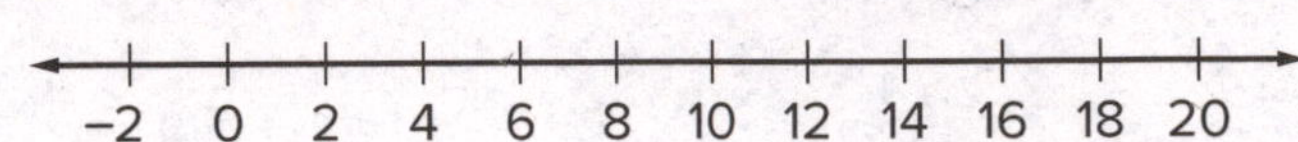

Check

What is the solution of $-p - 3 \geq -4(p + 6)$? ______ Graph the solution set.

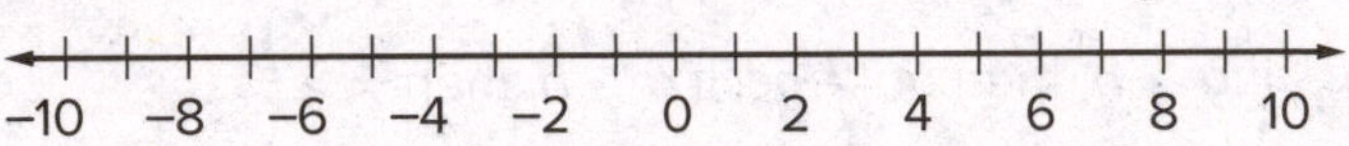

Example 7 Write and Solve an Inequality

NUTRITION **The recommended daily intake of calcium for teens is 1300 mg. Jake gets 237 mg of calcium from a multivitamin he takes each morning and 302 mg from each glass of skim milk that he drinks. How many glasses of milk would Jake need to drink to meet the recommendation?**

Step 1 Write an inequality to represent the situation.

Let g = the number of ______ Jake needs.

______ + 302______ 1300

Step 2 Solve the inequality.

$237 + 302g \geq 1300$	Original inequality.
$302g \geq$ ______	Subtract 237 from each side.
$g \geq$ ______	Simplify.

Step 3 Interpret the solution in the context of the situation.

Jake will need to drink slightly ______ glasses of milk to intake at least the recommended daily amount of calcium. This is a viable solution because Jake can pour part of a full glass of milk.

Go Online You can complete an Extra Example online.

Name ______________________ Period __________ Date __________

Practice

Go Online You can complete your homework online.

Example 1

Solve each equation. Check your solution.

1. $9 + 4n = -59$
2. $14 = 8 - 6r$
3. $\frac{3}{4} - \frac{1}{2}n = \frac{5}{8}$
4. $\frac{5}{6}c + \frac{3}{4} = \frac{11}{12}$
5. $6x - 5 = 7 - 9x$
6. $-1.6r + 5 = -7.8$
7. $2.2n + 0.8n + 5 = 4n$
8. $6y - 5 = -3(2y + 1)$
9. $5(6 - 4v) = v + 21$

Example 2

Solve each problem.

10. **GEOMETRY** The length of a rectangle is twice the width. Find the width if the perimeter is 60 centimeters. Define a variable, write an equation, and solve the problem.

11. **GOLF** Luis and three friends went golfing. Two of the friends rented clubs for \$6 each. The total cost of the rented clubs and the green fees was \$76. What was the cost of the green fees for each person? Define a variable, write an equation, and solve the problem.

12. **AIRPLANES** The Citation Sovereign is a type of small jet that can carry up to 2650 pounds. The number of passengers p and the number of suitcases c that the airplane can carry are estimated by the equation $180p + 60c = 2650$. If 10 people board the aircraft, how many suitcases can the airplane carry?

13. **DOMINOES** Layla is setting up a train of dominos from her front door and straight down the hall to her kitchen entrance. The thickness of each domino is t. Layla places the dominoes so that the space separating consecutive dominoes is $3t$. The total distance that n dominoes takes is given by $d = t(4n + 1)$.

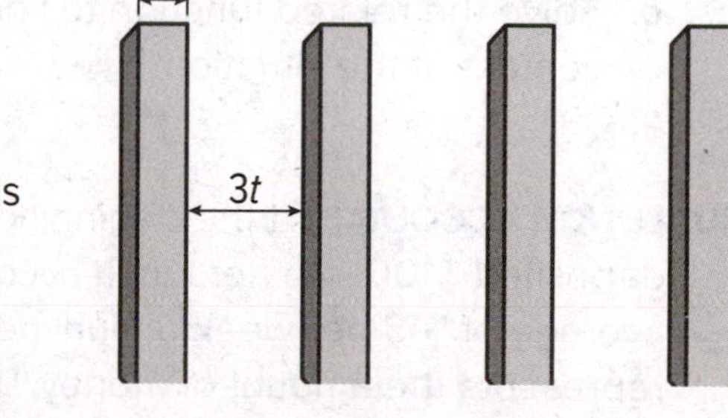

   a. Layla measures her dominoes and finds that $t = 1$ centimeter. She measures the distance of her hallway and finds that $d = 321$ centimeters.

   Rewrite the equation that relates d, t, and n with the given values substituted for t and d.

   b. How many dominoes did Layla have in her hallway?

Example 3

Solve each equation or formula for the specified variable.

14. $I = prt$, for p

15. $y = \frac{1}{4}x - 12$, for x

16. $A = \frac{x + y}{2}$, for y

17. $A = 2\pi r^2 + 2\pi rh$, for h

18. $E = mc^2$, for m

19. $c = \frac{2d + 1}{3}$, for d

20. $h = vt - gt^2$, for $v = 0$

21. $E = \frac{1}{2}Iw^2 + U$, for I

22. $wx + yz = bc$, for z

Example 4

Find the related function for each equation. Then graph the related function. Use the graph to solve the equation.

23. $2x + 5 = -7$

24. $-x + 3 = 6$

25. $\frac{1}{2}x + 4 = 10$

26. $\frac{1}{3}x + 1 = -5$

27. $-3x - 1 = 1$

28. $-\frac{1}{4}x + 1 = -2$

Example 5

Solve each problem.

29. SUMMER READING Mario has a 500-page novel which he is required to read during the summer for his upcoming language arts class.

a. MODELING If Mario reads 24 pages each day, write and graph a function to represent the number of pages that Mario has left to read p after d days.

b. USE TOOLS Estimate the zero of the function. Justify your response.

c. Solve the related function to find the zero and interpret its meaning in the context of the situation.

30. LUNCH ACCOUNT At the beginning of the quarter, Tiffany deposited $100 into her lunch account. If Tiffany spends an average of $18 per week on lunches, then $m = 100 - 18w$ represents the amount of money Tiffany has left in her lunch account m after w weeks of school.

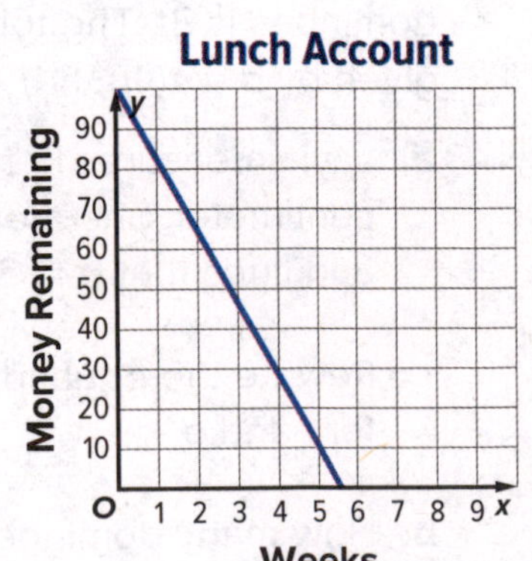

Part A Use the graph to estimate to the nearest tenth the number of weeks that Tiffany can purchase school lunches with the money she deposited at the beginning of the quarter.

Part B Solve algebraically to verify your estimate. Round to the nearest hundredth.

Name ______________________ Period ____________ Date ______________

Example 6

Solve each inequality. Graph the solution set on a number line.

31. $\frac{z}{-4} \geq 2$ **32.** $3a + 7 \leq 16$ **33.** $20 - 3n > 7n$

34. $7f - 9 > 3f - 1$ **35.** $0.7m + 0.3m \geq 2m - 4$ **36.** $4(5x + 7) \leq 13$

Example 7

Solve each problem.

37. **INCOME** Manuel takes a job translating English instruction manuals to Spanish. He will receive $15 per page plus $100 per month. Manuel plans to work for 3 months during the summer and wants to make at least $1500. Write and solve an inequality to find the minimum number of pages Manuel must translate in order to reach his goal.

38. **SHIPPING** On a conveyor belt, there can only be two boxes moving at a time. The two boxes together cannot weigh more than 300 pounds. Let x and y be the weights of the boxes.

a. Write an inequality that describes the weight limitation in terms of x and y.

b. Write an inequality that describes the limit on the average weight a of the two boxes.

c. Two boxes are to be placed on the conveyor below. The first box weighs 175 pounds. What is the maximum weight of the second box?

Mixed Exercises

Solve each equation. Check your solution.

39. $-3b + 7 = -15 + 2b$ **40.** $a - \frac{2a}{5} = 3$ **41.** $2.2n + 0.8n + 5 = 4n$

Solve each inequality. Graph the solution set on a number line.

42. $\frac{4x - 3}{2} \geq -3.5$ **43.** $1 + 5(x - 8) \leq 2 - (x + 5)$ **44.** $-36 - 2(w + 77) > -4(2w + 52)$

45. **REASOINING** An ice rink offers open skating several times a week. An annual membership to the skating rink costs $60. The table shows the cost of one session for members and non-members.

Open Ice Skating Sessions	
members	$6
non-members	$10

Maria plans to spend no more than $90 on skating this year. Define a variable then write and solve inequalities to find the number of sessions she can attend with and without buying a membership. Should Maria buy a membership?

46. **TEMPERATURE** The formula to convert temperature in degrees Fahrenheit to degrees Celsius is $\frac{5}{9}(F - 32) = C$.

a. Solve the equation for F.

b. Use your result from part *a* to determine the temperature in degrees Fahrenheit when the Celsius temperature is 30.

c. If a temperature has the same measure in degrees Fahrenheit and degrees Celsius, write and solve an equation for the temperature in degrees Fahrenheit.

47. **FIND THE ERROR** Steven and Jade are solving $A = \frac{1}{2}h(b_1 + b_2)$ for b_2. Is either of them correct? Explain your reasoning.

Steven	**Jade**
$A = \frac{1}{2}h(b_1 + b_2)$	$A = \frac{1}{2}h(b_1 + b_2)$
$\frac{2A}{h} = (b_1 + b_2)$	$\frac{2A}{h} = (b_1 + b_2)$
$\frac{2A - b_1}{h} = b_2$	$\frac{2A}{h} - b_1 = b_2$

48. **CREATE** Write an equation involving the Distributive Property that has no solution and another example that has infinitely many solutions.

49. **PERSEVERE** Solve $d = \sqrt{(x_2 - x_1)^2 + (y_2 - y_1)^2}$ for y_1.

50. **ANALYZE** Vivek's teacher made the statement, "Four times a number is less than three times a number." Vivek quickly responded that the answer is *no solution*. Do you agree with Vivek? Write and solve an inequality to justify your answer.

51. **WRITE** Why does the inequality symbol need to be reversed when multiplying or dividing by a negative number?

52. **PERSEVERE** Given ABC with sides $AB = 3x + 4$, $BC = 2x + 5$, and $AC = 4x$, determine the values of x such that ΔABC exists.

Lesson 2-2

Solving Absolute Value Equations and Inequalities

Today's Standards
A.CED.1, A.CED.3
MP4, MP7

Today's Vocabulary
absolute value
extraneous solution
empty set

Learn Solving Absolute Value Equations Algebraically

The **absolute value** of a number is its distance from zero on the number line. The definition of absolute value can be used to solve equations that contain absolute value expressions by constructing two cases. For any real numbers a and b, if $|a| = b$ and $b \geq 0$, then $a = b$ or $a = -b$.

Step 1 Isolate the absolute value expression on one side of the equation.

Step 2 Write the two cases.

Step 3 Use the properties of equality to solve each case.

Step 4 Check your solutions.

Absolute value equations may have one, two, or no solutions.

- An absolute value equation has one solution if one of the answers does not meet the constraints of the problem. Such an answer is called an **extraneous solution**.
- An absolute value equation has no solution if there is no answer that meets the constraints of the problem. The solution set of this type of equation is called the **empty set**, symbolized by {} or Ø.

Example 1 Solve an Absolute Value Equation

Solve $2|5x + 1| - 9 = 4x + 17$. Check your solutions. Then graph the solution set.

$2|5x + 1| - 9 = 4x + 17$ Original equation

$2|5x + 1| = 4x +$ ___ Add 9 to each side.

$|5x + 1| =$ ___ $+$ ___ Divide each side by 2.

Case 1	Case 2
$5x + 1 =$ ______	$5x + 1 = -$____ $-$ ___
$3x + 1 =$ ______	$7x + 1 =$ ______
$x =$ ______	$x =$ ______

CHECK Substitute each value in the original equation.

$2\|5(4) + 1\| - 9$	$\stackrel{?}{=} 4(4) + 17$		$2\|5(-2) + 1\| - 9$	$\stackrel{?}{=} 4(-2) + 17$
33	= 33 True		9	= 9 True

Both solutions make the equation true. Thus, the solution set is {4, −2}. The solution set can be graphed by graphing each solution on a number line.

−5 −4 −3 −2 −1 0 1 2 3 4 5

Watch Out!

Distribute the Negative For Case 2, remember to use the Distributive Property to multiply the entire expression on the right side of the equation by −1.

Go Online You can complete an Extra Example online.

Your Notes 

Think About It!

What would the graph of the solution set of an absolute value equation with only one solution look like?

Talk About It!

Is the following statement *always*, *sometimes*, or *never* true? Justify your argument. For real numbers a, b, and c, $|ax + b| = -c$ has no solution.

Check

Graph the solution set of $|5x - 3| - 6 = -2x + 12$.

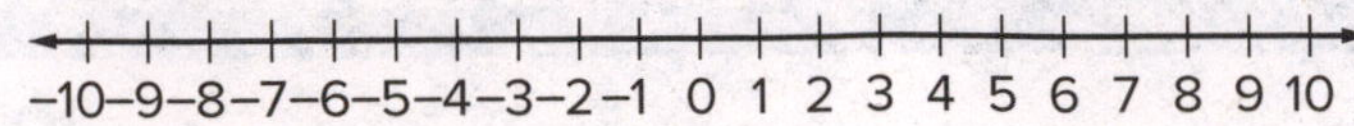

Example 2 Extraneous Solution

Solve $2|x + 1| - x = 3x - 4$. Check your solutions.

$2\|x + 1\| - x$	=	$3x - 4$	Original equation
$2\|x + 1\|$	=	$4x - 4$	Add x to each side.
$\|x + 1\|$	=	___ − ___	Divide each side by 2.

Case 1	Case 2
$x + 1 =$ ______	$x + 1 = -$ ______
$1 = x$ ___	$x + 1 =$ ______
$3 = x$	$3x + 1 = 2$
	$3x =$ ___

There appear to be two solutions, ___ and ___.

CHECK Substitute each value in the original equation.

$2\|3 + 1\| - 3$	$\stackrel{?}{=} 3(3) - 4$		$2\left\|\frac{1}{3} + 1\right\| - \left(\frac{1}{3}\right)$	$\stackrel{?}{=} 3\left(\frac{1}{3}\right) - 4$
5	= 5 True		$\frac{7}{3}$	$\neq -3$ False

Because $\frac{7}{3} \neq -3$, the only solution is 3. Thus, the solution set is ___.

Example 3 The Empty Set

Solve $|4x - 7| + 10 = 2$.

$\|4x - 7\| + 10$	=	2	Original equation
$\|4x - 7\|$	=	___	Subtract 10 from each side.

Because the absolute value of a number is always positive or zero, this sentence is ______ true. The solution is ___.

Check

Solve each absolute value equation.

a. $|x + 10| = 4x - 8$ ______

b. $3|4x - 11| + 1 = 9x + 13$ ______

c. $|2x + 5| - 18 = -3$ ______

d. $-5|7x - 2| + 3x = 3x + 10$ ______

Go Online You can complete an Extra Example online.

Example 4 Write and Solve an Absolute Value Equation

FOOTBALL **The NFL regulates the inflation, or air pressure, of footballs used during games. It requires that footballs have an air pressure of 13 pounds per square inch (PSI), plus or minus 0.5 PSI. What is the greatest and least acceptable air pressure of a regulation NFL football? Write and solve an equation, and graph the solution set.**

UNDERSTAND

What do you know?

footballs have an air pressure of ____ pounds per square inch (PSI),

plus or minus ____ PSI

What do you need to find?

the ________ and _____ acceptable air pressure of a regulation NFL football

PLAN AND SOLVE

Step 1 Write an absolute value equation to represent the situation.

The difference between the air pressure and 13 is 0.5.

$|x - \_\_\_| = \_\_\_$

Step 2 Solve the equation, and graph the solution(s).

Case 1	Case 2
$x - 13 =$	$x - 13 =$
$x =$	$x =$

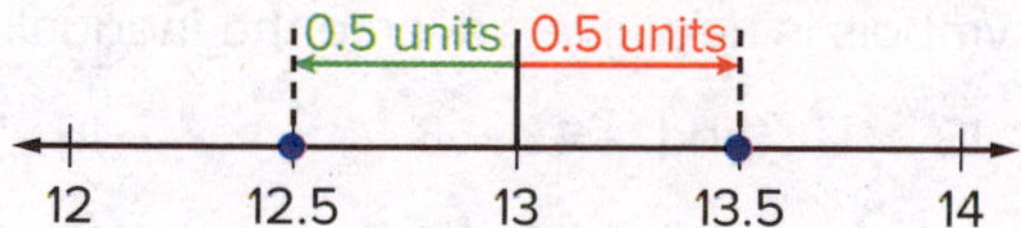

Step 3 Interpret the solution(s) in the context of the situation.

The solutions are _____ and _____. Since the distance between 13 and each solution is 0.5, both solutions satisfy the constraints of the equation. The greatest air pressure an NFL football can have is _____ PSI and the least is _____ PSI.

Check

How do you know that your solutions are correct?

I can ________ each solution back into the original equation and make sure that the value makes the equation ________.

Go Online You can complete an Extra Example online.

Learn Solving Absolute Value Inequalities

When solving absolute value inequalities, there are two cases to consider. These two cases can be rewritten as a compound inequality.

Key Concept • Absolute Value Inequalities

For all real numbers a, b, c and x, $c > 0$, the following statements are true.

Absolute Value Inequality	Case 1	Case 2	Compound Inequality
$\lvert ax + b\rvert < c$	$ax + b < c$	$-(ax + b) < c$ $\frac{-(ax+b)}{-1} > \frac{c}{-1}$ $ax + b > -c$	$ax + b < c$ and $ax + b > -c$ OR $-c < ax + b < c$
$\lvert ax + b\rvert > c$	$ax + b > c$	$-(ax + b) > c$ $\frac{-(ax+b)}{-1} < \frac{c}{-1}$ $ax + b < -c$	$ax + b > c$ or $ax + b < -c$

These statements are also true for $\leq$ and $\geq$, respectively.

Think About It!

Describe a shortcut you could use to write case 2.

Example 5 Solve an Absolute Value Inequality ($<$ or $\leq$)

Solve $\lvert 4x - 8\rvert - 5 < 11$. Then graph the solution set.

$\lvert 4x - 8\rvert - 5 < 11$ Original inequality

$\lvert 4x - 8\rvert <$ ___ Add 5 to each side.

Since the inequality uses $<$, rewrite it as a compound inequality joined by the word *and*. For the case where the expression inside the absolute value symbols is negative, reverse the inequality symbol.

$4x - 8 < 16$ and $4x - 8 > -16$

$4x <$ ___ $\quad 4x >$ ___

$x <$ ___ $\quad x >$ ___

So, x ___ 6 and x ___ -2. The solution set is $\{x \mid$ ___ $< x <$ ___$\}$. All values of x between -2 and 6 satisfy the constraints of the original inequality.

The solution set represents the interval between two numbers. Since the $<$ symbols indicate that -2 and 6 are not solutions, graph the endpoints of the interval on a number line using circles. Then, shade the interval from -2 to 6.

−10 −8 −6 −4 −2 0 2 4 6 8 10

Study Tip

Check Your Solutions Remember to substitute your solutions back into the original inequality to check that they make that inequality true.

Check

Solve $6\lvert x + 4\rvert - 3 \geq 15$. Then graph the solution set.

$x <$ ___ or $x >$ ___

−10 −9 −8 −7 −6 −5 −4 −3 −2 −1 0 1

Go Online You can complete an Extra Example online.

Example 6 Solve an Absolute Value Inequality (> and ≥)

Solve the inequality $\frac{|6x+3|}{2} + 5 \geq 14$. Then graph the solution set.

$\frac{|6x+3|}{2} + 5 \geq 14$ Original inequality.

$\frac{|6x+3|}{2} \geq$ ___ Subtract 5 from each side.

$|6x+3| \geq$ ___ Multiply each side by 2.

Since the inequality uses ≥, rewrite it as a compound inequality joined by the word *or*. For the case where the expression inside the absolute value symbols is negative, reverse the inequality symbol.

$6x + 3 \geq$ ___	or	$6x + 3 \leq$ ___
$6x \geq$ ___		$6x \leq$ ___
$x \geq$ ___		$x \leq$ ___

So, $x \geq$ ___ and $x \leq$ ___. The solution set is $\{x \mid x \leq -\frac{7}{2}$ ___ $x \geq \frac{5}{2}\}$.

All values of x less than or equal to ___ as well as values of x greater than ___ satisfy the constraints of the original inequality.

The solution set represents the union of two intervals. Since the ≤ and ≥ symbols indicate that $-\frac{7}{2}$ and $\frac{5}{2}$ are solutions, graph the endpoints of the interval on a number line using dots. Then, shade all points less than $-\frac{7}{2}$ and all points greater than $\frac{5}{2}$.

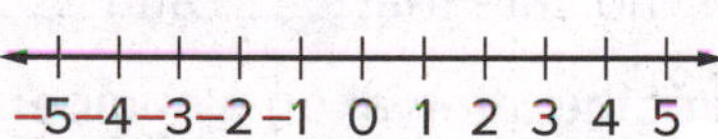

Check

Match each solution set with the appropriate absolute value inequality.

$-8\|x+14\| + 7 \geq -17$	
$\frac{\|2x-8\|}{3} - 10 < 6$	
$5\|2x+28\| + 6 \geq -24$	
$\frac{\|3x-12\|}{4} - 13 > 5$	

$\{x \mid x \leq -17 \text{ or } x \geq -11\}$ $\{x \mid 28 < x < -20\}$ $\{x \mid x < -20 \text{ or } x > 28\}$

$\{x \mid x \leq -11 \text{ or } x \geq -17\}$ $\{x \mid -20 < x < 28\}$ $\{x \mid -17 \leq x \leq -11\}$

Go Online You can complete an Extra Example online.

Watch Out!

Isolate the Expression Remember to isolate the absolute value expression on one side of the inequality symbol before determining whether to rewrite an absolute value inequality using *and* or *or*. When transforming the inequality, you might divide or multiply by a negative number, causing the inequality symbol to be reversed.

Example 7 Write and Solve an Absolute Value Inequality

SLEEP **You can find how much sleep you need by going to sleep without turning on an alarm. Once your sleep pattern has stabilized, record the amount of time you spend sleeping each night. The amount of time you sleep plus or minus 15 minutes is your sleep need. Suppose you sleep 8.5 hours per night. Write and solve an inequality to represent your sleep need, and graph the solution on a number line.**

Part A Write an absolute value inequality to represent the situation.

The difference between your actual sleep need and the amount of time you sleep is less than or equal to _____ minutes. So, _____ hours is the central value and _____ minutes, or _____ hour, is the acceptable range.

The difference between your actual sleep need and 8.5 hours is 0.25 hour.

$|n - \_\_\_\_| = \_\_\_\_$

Part B Solve the inequality and graph the solution set.

Rewrite $|n - 8.5| = 0.25$ as a compound inequality.

$n - 8.5 \leq \_\_\_\_$ and $n - 8.5 \geq \_\_\_\_$

$n \leq \_\_\_\_$ $\quad$ $n \geq \_\_\_\_$

The solution set represents the interval between two numbers. Since the ≤ and ≥ symbols indicate that _____ and _____ are solutions, graph the endpoints of the interval on a number line using dots. Then, shade the interval from _____ to _____.

7 7.25 7.5 7.75 8 8.25 8.5 8.75 9

This means that you need between 8.25 and 8.75 hours of sleep per night, inclusive.

Check

FOOD A survey found that 58% of American adults eat at a restaurant at least once a week. The margin of error was within 3 percentage points.

Part A Write an absolute value inequality to represent the range of the percent of American adults who eat at a restaurant once a week, where x is the actual percent. __________

Part B Use your inequality from Part A to find the range of the percent of American adults who eat at a restaurant once a week.

The actual percent of American adults who eat out at least once a week is __________

Go Online You can complete an Extra Example online.

Name ______________________ Period __________ Date __________

Practice

Examples 1–3

Solve each equation. Check your solutions.

1. $|8 + p| = 2p - 3$

2. $|4w - 1| = 5w + 37$

3. $4|2y - 7| + 5 = 9$

4. $-2|7 - 3y| - 6 = -14$

5. $2|4 - n| = -3n$

6. $5 - 3|2 + 2w| = -7$

7. $5|2r + 3| - 5 = 0$

8. $3 - 5|2d - 3| = 4$

Example 4

Solve each problem.

9. **WEATHER** A thermometer comes with a guarantee that the stated temperature differs from the actual temperature by no more than 1.5 degrees Fahrenheit. Write and solve an equation to find the minimum and maximum actual temperatures when the thermometer states that the temperature is 87.4 degrees Fahrenheit.

10. **OPINION POLLS** Public opinion polls reported in newspapers are usually given with a margin of error. For example, a poll with a margin of error of ±5% is considered accurate to within plus or minus 5% of the actual value. A poll with a stated margin of error of ±3% predicts that candidate Towne will receive 51% of an upcoming vote. Write and solve an equation describing the minimum and maximum percent of the vote that candidate Towne is expected to receive.

11. **LOCATIONS** Identical vacation cottages, equally spaced along a street, are numbered consecutively beginning with 10. Maria is staying in Cottage 17. Joshua lives 4 cottages away from Maria. If n represents Joshua's cottage number, then $|n - 17| = 4$. What are the possible numbers of Joshua's cottage?

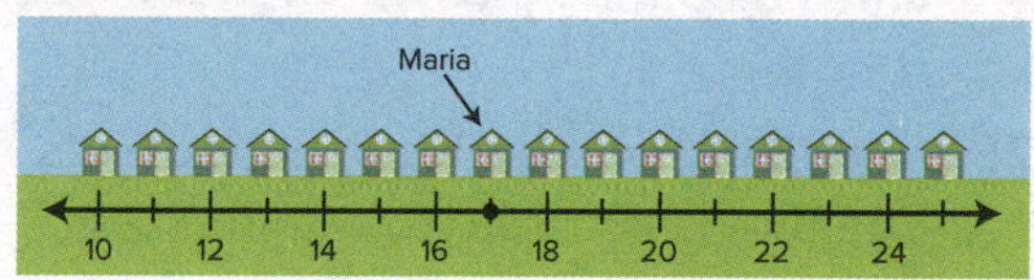

Examples 5 and 6

Solve each inequality. Graph the solution set on a number line.

12. $\left|\frac{x}{2} - 5\right| + 2 > 10$

13. $|2x + 2| - 7 \leq -5$

14. $|x| > x - 1$

15. $|3b + 5| \leq -2$

16. $|3n - 2| - 2 < 1$

17. $|4 - 5x| < 13$

18. $|2x - 1| < 5 + 0.5x$

19. $|3x + 1| > 2$

Example 7

Solve each problem.

20. RAINFALL In 90% of the last 30 years, the rainfall at Shell Beach has varied no more than 6.5 inches from its mean value of 24 inches. Write and solve an absolute value inequality to describe the rainfall in the other 10% of the last 30 years.

21. MANUFACTURING A food manufacturer's guidelines call for each can of soup produced not to vary from its stated volume of 14.5 fluid ounces by more than 0.08 ounces. Write and solve an absolute value inequality to describe acceptable can volumes.

Mixed Exercises

Solve each equation. Check your solutions.

22. $8x = 2|6x - 2|$

23. $-6y + 4 = |4y + 12|$

24. $8z + 20 > -|2z + 4|$

25. $-3y - 2 \leq |6y + 25|$

REASONING **Write an absolute value equation to represent each situation. Then solve the equation and discuss the reasonableness of your solution given the constraints of the absolute value equation.**

26. The absolute value of the difference between 3 times a number and 2 is 7.

27. The absolute value of the sum of 4 times a number and 7 is the sum of 2 times a number and 3.

28. The sum of 7 and the absolute value of the difference of a number and 8 is −2 times a number plus 4.

29. MODELING A woodworking tool cuts rods for stairway banisters to 36 inches. The tool is accurate to within 0.12 in.

a. Write an equation to represent the situation. Explain your reasoning.

b. Solve the equation. Then state the maximum and minimum length for the rods.

30. SAND A toy store sells bags of play sand that are labeled as weighing 35 pounds. The equipment used to package the sand produces bags with a weight that is within 8 ounces of the label weight.

a. Write and solve an absolute value equation to determine the maximum and minimum weight for the bags of play sand.

b. Solve the equation. Then state the maximum and minimum weight for the bags of play sand.

Name ______________________ Period ____________ Date ____________

31. **PRECISION** A quality control inspector at a bolt factory examines a sample of bolts with a diameter of 6.5 mm. All bolts being made must be within a tolerance of 0.04 mm. Write and solve an absolute value equation to find the maximum and minimum diameters of bolts that will pass his inspection.

32. **GEOMETRY** Yonas makes a rectangle that is 12 inches by 30 inches. Kimiko wants to make a rectangle having a length of 8 inches longer than its width. If Kimiko wants the perimeter of her rectangle to be within 20 inches of the perimeter of Yonas's rectangle, what are the minimum and maximum values for the width of her rectangle? What are the corresponding length and perimeter?

33. **ARGUMENTS** Megan and Yuki have been asked to solve the equation $|x - 9| = |5x + 6|$. Megan says that there are 4 cases to consider because there are two possible values for each absolute value expression. Yuki says that they only need to consider 2 cases. With which person, do you agree? Will both girls get the same solution(s)?

Solve each inequality. Graph the solution set on a number line.

34. $3|2z - 4| - 6 > 12$

35. $6|4p + 2| - 8 < 34$

36. $\frac{|5f - 2|}{6} > 4$

37. $\frac{|2w + 8|}{5} \geq 3$

38. **TIRES** The recommended inflation of a car tire is no more than 35 psi (pounds per square inch). Depending on weather conditions, the actual reading of the tire pressure could fluctuate up to 3.4 psi. Write and solve an absolute value inequality to find the maximum and minimum recommended actual tire pressure.

39. **TRAVEL** Gerard has found that in 95% of his highway trips, his cars gas mileage has varied no more than 3 mpg from its mean value of 28 mpg.

a. Write an absolute value inequality to describe the gas mileage in the other 5% of his trips.

b. Solve the inequality. Explain what the solution represents.

40. **PROJECTILE** An object is launched into the air and then falls to the ground. Its velocity is modeled by the equation $v = 200 - 32t$, where the velocity v is measured in feet per second and time t is measured in seconds. The object's speed is the absolute value of its velocity. Write and solve a compound inequality to determine the time intervals in which the speed of the object will be between 40 and 88 feet per second.

41. **ARGUMENTS** Roberto claims that the solution to $|3c - 4| > -4.5$ is the same as the solution to $|3c - 4| \geq 0$, since an absolute value is always greater than or equal to zero. Is he correct? Explain your reasoning.

42. **TOLERANCE** Martin makes exercise weights. For his 10-pound dumbbells, he guarantees that the actual weight of his dumbbells is within 0.1 pound of 10 pounds. Write and solve an equation that describes the minimum and maximum weight of his 10-pound dumbbells.

43. **WHICH ONE DOESN'T BELONG?** Identify the compound inequality that is not the same as the other three. Explain your reasoning.

$-3 < x < 5$	$x > 2$ and $x < 3$	$x > 5$ and $x < 1$	$x > -4$ and $x > -2$

44. **FIND THE ERROR** Ana and Ling are solving $|3x + 14| = -6x$. Is either of them correct? Explain your reasoning.

Ana	*Ling*
$|3x + 14| = -6x$	$|3x + 14| = -6x$
$3x + 14 = -6x$ *or* $3x + 14 = 6x$	$3x + 14 = -6x$ *or* $3x + 14 = 6x$
$9x = -14$ $14 = 3x$	$9x = -14$ $14 = 3x$
$x = -\frac{14}{9}$ $x = \frac{14}{3}$	$x = -\frac{14}{9}$ $x = \frac{14}{3}$

45. **PERSEVERE** Solve $|2x - 1| + 3 = |5 - x|$. List all cases and resulting equations.

ANALYZE **If *a*, *x*, and *y* are real numbers, determine whether each statement is *sometimes*, *always*, or *never* true. Explain your reasoning.**

46. If $|a| > 7$, then $|a + 3| > 10$.

47. If $|x| < 3$, then $|x| + 3 > 0$.

48. If y is between 1 and 5, then $|y - 3| \leq 2$.

49. **CREATE** Write an absolute value inequality with a solution of $a \leq x \leq b$.

50. **WRITE** Summarize the difference between *and* compound inequalities and *or* compound inequalities.

Equations of Linear Functions

Today's Standards
A.CED.2, F.IF.6
MP1, MP2, MP4

Today's Vocabulary
standard form of a linear equation
slope-intercept form
point-slope form

Explore Arithmetic Sequences

Online Activity Use a real-world situation to complete the Explore.

INQUIRY How can you write formulas that relate to the numbers in an arithmetic sequence?

Learn Linear Equations in Standard Form

Any linear equation can be written in **standard form**, $Ax + By = C$, where $A \geq 0$, A and B are not both 0, and A, B, and C are integers with a greatest common factor of 1.

Think About It!
Is $-2x + 2y = 2$ written in standard form? Why or why not?

Example 1 Write Linear Equations in Standard Form

Write $y = \frac{2}{5}x + 14$ in standard form. Identify A, B, and C.

$y = \frac{2}{5}x + 14$ Original equation

$-\frac{2}{5}x + y = 14$ Subtract $\frac{2}{5}x$ from each side.

___x − ___y = ___ Multiply each side by −5.

A = ___ B = ___ C = ___

Learn Linear Equations in Slope-Intercept Form

Any linear equation can be written in **slope-intercept form,** $y = mx + b$ where m is the slope and b is the y-intercept.

The slope is $\frac{\text{rise}}{\text{run}} = \frac{2}{3}$. This value can be substituted for m in the slope-intercept form.

The line intersects the y-axis at 1. This value can be substituted for b in the slope-intercept form.

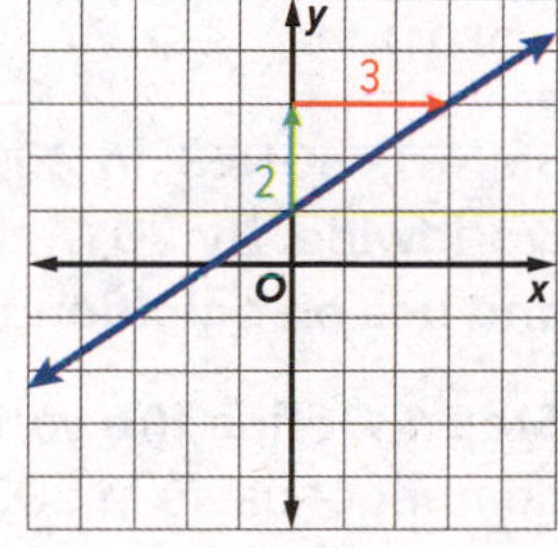

Think About It!
Is the b in slope-intercept form equivalent to the B in standard form, $Ax + By = C$? If yes, explain your reasoning. If no, provide a counterexample.

Go Online You can complete an Extra Example online.

Your Notes

Example 2 Write Linear Equations in Slope-Intercept Form

Write $12x - 4y = 24$ in slope-intercept form. Identify the slope m and y-intercept b.

$12x - 4y = 24$ Original equation

$-4y = -12x + 24$ Subtract $12x$ from each side.

$y = \_\_\_x - \_\_\_$ Divide each side by -4.

$m = \_\_\_$ $b = \_\_\_$

Check

Write $4x = -2y + 22$ in slope-intercept form. $y = -\_\_\_x + \_\_\_$

> **Think About It!**
> When using the equation to estimate the number of smartphone users in the future, what constraint does the world's population place on the possible number of users?

Example 3 Interpret an Equation in Slope-Intercept Form

SHOES **The equation $3246x - 2y = -152{,}722$ can be used to estimate shoes sales in Europe from 2010 to 2015, where x is the number of years after 2010 and y is the revenue in millions of dollars.**

Part A Write the equation in slope-intercept form.

$3246x - 2y = -152{,}722$ Original equation

$-2y = -3246x - 152{,}722$ Subtract $3246x$ from each side.

$y = \_\_\_\_\_x + \_\_\_\_\_$ Divide each side by -2.

Part B Interpret the parameters in the context of the situation.

1623 represents that sales increased by $______ each year.

76,361 represents that in year 0, or in _____, sales were $______.

> **Study Tip**
> **Assumptions**
> Assuming that the rate at which the number of smartphone users increases is constant allows us to represent the situation using a linear equation. While the rate at which the number of smartphone users increases may vary each year, using a constant rate allows for a reasonable equation that can be used to estimate future data.

Example 4 Use a Linear Equation in Slope-Intercept Form

SMARTPHONES **In 2013, there were 1.31 billion smartphone users worldwide. By 2017, there were 2.38 billion smartphone users. Write and use an equation to estimate the number of users in 2025.**

Step 1 Define the variables. Because you want to estimate the number of users in 2025, write an equation that represents the number of smartphone users y after x years. Let x be the number of years after 2013 and let y be the number of billions of smartphone users.

Go Online You can complete an Extra Example online.

Step 2 Find the slope. Since x is the years after 2013, (0, 1.31) and (4, 2.38) represent the number of smartphone users in 2013 and 2017, respectively. Round to the nearest hundredth.

$$m = \frac{2.38 - \_\_\_}{\_\_\_} = \_\_\_\_$$

So, the number of users is increasing at a rate of _____ billion per year.

Step 3 Find the *y*-intercept. The y-intercept represents the number of smartphone users when $x = 0$, or in 2013. So, $b =$ _____

Step 4 Write an equation. Use $m = 0.27$ and $b = 1.31$ to write the equation.

$y =$ _____$x +$ _____ $\quad m = 0.27, b = 1.31$

Step 5 Estimate. Since 2025 is 12 years after 2013, substitute 12 for x.

$y = 0.27(12) + 1.31; y = 4.55$

If the trend continues, there will be about 4.55 billion users in 2025.

Think About It!

Suppose the data spanned 2 years instead of 4 years. That is, there were 1.31 billion smartphone users in 2013 and 2.38 billions users in 2015. How would this affect the rate of change abnd your estimate in **Step 5**?

Learn Linear Equations in Point-Slope Form

Any linear equation can be written in **point-slope form**, $y - y_1 = m(x - x_1)$, where m is the slope and (x_1, y_1) are the coordinates of a point on the line.

Example 5 Point-Slope Form Given Slope and One Point

Write the equation of a line that passes through (3, −5) and has a slope of 11 in point-slope form.

$y - y_1 = m(x - x_1)$	Point-slope form
$y - (-5) = 11(x - 3)$	$m = 11$; $(x_1, y_1) = (3, -5)$
$y + 5 = 11(x - 3)$	Simplify.

Talk About It

What other values would you need to write the equation of this line in slope-intercept form? Could you determine those values given the information above?

Example 6 Point-Slope Form Given Two Points

Write an equation of a line that passes through (1, 1) and (7, 13) in point-slope form.

Step 1 Find the slope.

$m = \frac{y_2 - y_1}{x_2 - x_1}$	Point-slope form
$= \frac{13 - \_\_}{\_\_}$	$(x_1, y_1) = (1, 1)$; $(x_2, y_2) = (7, 13)$
$= \frac{12}{\_\_}$	Simplify.
$=$ _____	Simplify.

(continued on the next page)

 **Go Online** You can complete an Extra Example online.

Step 2 Write an equation.

Substitute the slope for m and the coordinates of either of the given points for (x_1, y_1) in the point-slope form.

$y - y_1 = m(x - x_1)$ Point-slope form

$y - 1 = 2(x - 1)$ $m = 2$; $(x_1, y_1) = (1, 1)$

Check ____, ____

Select all the equations with lines that pass through (–1, 1) and (–2, 13).

A. $x - 1 = -12(y + 1)$ **B.** $y - 1 = -12(x + 1)$

C. $x + 1 = -12(y - 1)$ **D.** $y + 1 = -12(x - 1)$

E. $y - 2 = -12(x + 13)$ **F.** $x - 2 = -12(y + 13)$

G. $x + 2 = -12(y - 13)$ **H.** $y + 2 = -12(x - 13)$

Example 7 Write and Interpret a Linear Equation in Point-Slope Form

Think About It!

Could this equation be used to estimate the lean of the Tower of Pisa for any year? Explain your reasoning.

ARCHITECTURE **The Tower of Pisa leaned 5.4 meters in 1993 compared to a lean of just 1.4 meters in 1350. Write an equation in point-slope form that represents the lean *y* of the Tower of Pisa *x* years after its construction in 1178.**

Step 1 Find the slope. Round to the nearest hundredth.

The tower was leaning 1.4 meters in 1350, ______ years after 1178.

The tower was leaning 5.4 meters in 1993, ______ years after 1178.

$m = \frac{5.4 - \_\_}{\_\_ - \_\_} = \_\_\_\_$ meter per year

Step 2 Write an equation.

Substitute the slope for m and the coordinates of either of the given points for (x_1, y_1) in the point-slope form.

$y - y_1 = m(x - x_1)$ Point-slope form

$y - \_\_\_ = \_\_\_\_ (x - \_\_\_\_)$ $m = 0.006$; $(x_1, y_1) = (172, 1.4)$

Check

SOCIAL MEDIA In 2011, the Miami Marlins had about 11,000 followers on a social media site. In 2016, they had about 240,000 followers. Which equation represents the number of followers *y* the Miami Marlin's had *x* years after they joined the site in 2009? ____

A. $y - 11{,}000 = 45{,}800\ (x - 2)$

B. $y - 45{,}800 = 11{,}000\ (x - 2)$

C. $y - 11{,}000 = 45{,}800\ (x - 2011)$

D. $y - 2 = 45{,}800\ (x - 11{,}000)$

Go Online You can complete an Extra Example online.

Name ______ Period ______ Date ______

Practice

Go Online You can complete your homework online.

Example 1

Write each equation in standard from. Identify *A*, *B*, and *C*.

1. $-7x - 5y = 35$

2. $8x + 3y + 6 = 0$

3. $10y - 3x + 6 = 11$

4. $-6x - 3y - 12 = 21$

5. $3y = 9x - 12$

6. $2.4y = -14.4x$

7. $\frac{2}{3}y - \frac{3}{4}x + \frac{1}{6} = 0$

8. $\frac{4}{5}y + \frac{1}{8}x = 4$

9. $-0.08x = 1.24y - 3.12$

Example 2

Write each equation in slope-intercept form. Identify the slope *m* and the *y*-intercept *b*.

10. $6x + 3y = 12$

11. $14x - 7y = 21$

12. $\frac{2}{3}x + \frac{1}{6}y = 2$

13. $5x + 10y = 20$

14. $6x + 9y = 15$

15. $\frac{1}{5}x + \frac{1}{2}y = 4$

16. $0.4x + 0.2y = 1.8$

17. $-3y = 48 + 18x$

18. $45x - 9y = 27$

Example 3

19. **CHARITY** The linear equation $n = 20h + 83$ relates the number of shirts collected during a charity drive, where h is the number of hours since noon and n is the total number of shirts collected. Interpret the parameters of the equation in the context of the situation.

20. **PHYSICS** The equation $y = -13x + 65$ represents the distance and time it takes an object traveling at a constant speed to come to a complete stop, where x is time, in seconds, and y is distance in meters. Interpret the parameters of the equation in the context of the situation.

Example 4

21. **PLUMBER** A plumber charges a flat rate of \$60 to make a service call and an additional \$40 per hour for labor.

Part A Define variables to represent the situation.

Part B Write an equation that represents the total cost for the plumber's services for a given number of hours working at the job site.

Part C How much would it cost to hire the plumber for 5 hours of work?

22. **HIKING** Tim began a hike near Big Bear Lake, California at the base of the mountain that is 7000 feet above sea level. He is hiking at a steady rate of 5 more feet above sea level per minute.

Part A Define variables to represent the situation.

Part B Write an equation in slope-intercept form that represents how many feet above sea level Tim has hiked.

Part C What will Tim's altitude be after 2 hours of hiking?

Example 5

Write an equation in point-slope form for the line that satisfies each set of conditions.

23. slope of -5, passes through $(-3, -8)$

24. slope of $\frac{4}{5}$, passes through $(10, -3)$

25. slope of $-\frac{2}{3}$, passes through $(6, -8)$

26. slope of 0, passes through $(0, -10)$

27. slope of 3, y-intercept at -4

28. slope of -1, passes through the origin

Example 6

Write an equation in point-slope form for a line that passes through each set of points.

29. $(2, -3)$ and $(1, 5)$

30. $(3, 5)$ and $(-6, -4)$

31. $(-1, -2)$ and $(-3, 1)$

32. $(-2, -4)$ and $(1, 8)$

Example 7

Solve each problem.

33. **MODELING** In 2000, Americans purchased 17.35 million new automobiles. In 2015, the number of new automobiles purchased by Americans was 17.47 million.

Part A Define variables to represent the situation.

Part B Write an equation in point-slope form that represents the number of automobiles purchased by Americans.

Part C **STATE YOUR ASSUMPTION** What assumption is made when writing an equation to represent the number of new autos purchased by Americans?

34. **REASONING** In 2006, there were 4500 participating restaurants in an online reservation service. In 2014, there were 31,000 restaurants participating in the reservation service. Write an equation in point-slope form that represents the number of participating restaurants after x years. Let x be the number of years since the 1998 release of the reservation service.

Name ______________________ Period __________ Date __________

Mixed Exercises

35. Write the equation $-4x - 2y - 8 = 0$ in standard form. Identify A, B, and C.

36. Write $\frac{1}{3}x + \frac{5}{6}y = -4$ in slope-intercept form. Identify the slope m and the y-intercept b.

37. Write an equation in point-slope form of the line that has an x-intercept of -4 and a slope of $\frac{1}{2}$.

REGULARITY **Write an equation in point-slope form for the line that passes through each set of points.**

38. (5.5, 0.6) and (1.1, 2.8)

39. (−25, −16) and (−29, 12)

40. RESERVOIRS The surface of Grand Lake is at an elevation of 648 feet. During the current drought, the water level is dropping at a rate of 3 inches per day. If this trend continues, write an equation in slope-intercept form that gives the elevation in feet y of the surface of Grand Lake after x days.

41. MAPS The post office and city hall are marked on a coordinate plane. Write the equation of the line in point-slope form that passes through these two points.

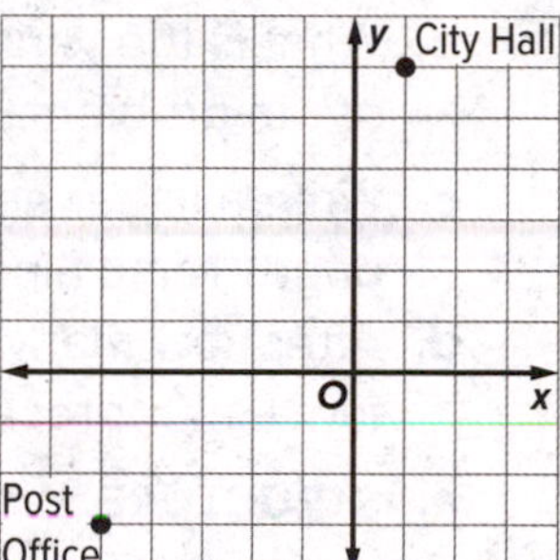

42. USE A SOURCE Go online to find an example of a linear relationship in a real-world situation.

43. SAVINGS ACCOUNT Each week, Jacalyn deposits money weekly into her savings account. The table shows the account balance after various weeks. Write a linear equation in slope-intercept form that relates the balance of her savings account y and the number of weeks she has been saving x.

Week	0	3	6	9	12
Balance ($)	350	440	530	620	710

44. GYM MEMBERSHIP The equation $y = 15x + 75$ represents the cost of a gym membership, where y is the cost, in dollars, including the startup fee and x is the number of months of membership.

a. Interpret the parameters in the context of the situation.

b. A special promotion states that if you sign up today the startup fee will be waived. How does the equation change?

45. ARGUMENTS Consider the points (3, 1) and (0, 7).

Part A Explain why either the point-slope form or the slope-intercept form can be used to find the equation of a line that passes through the given points.

Part B Use both methods to find the equation and verify that the two are equivalent.

46. FUNDRAISING For a math club fund raiser, three club members sell 20 mugs each. Their sales are described as follows. Reiko sold all of her mugs in 5 days and sold the same number each day. The number of mugs Cosmin had left after x days is given by the equation $y = -2x + 20$. The number of mugs that Sheena had left after each day are shown in the table. Write linear equations in the form $f(x) = mx + b$ for the functions that model the number of mugs remaining for Reiko and Sheena after x days.

Sheena's Mug Sales	
Days	Mugs Left
0	20
1	15
2	10
3	5
4	0

47. BOOK REPORTS Joe and Alisha are reading novels for book reports. Joe records the number of pages he has remaining to read after each day in the table below. Alisha records the number of pages she has remaining each day on the graph at the right.

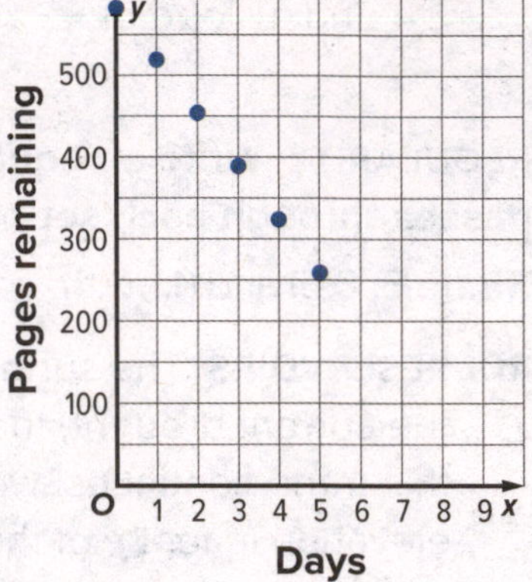

Joe

Days	0	1	2	3	4	5
Pages	585	520	455	390	325	262

a. Describe the function that models the number of pages remaining for each girl.

b. What is the y-intercept for each function? Interpret its meaning in the context of the problem.

c. Write a linear equation in slope-intercept for the function that models the pages remaining for each girl. Then write each equation in standard form.

d. After how many days will each finish with their reading? What feature of the function represents this event? Explain your answer.

e. **STRUCTURE** Who is reading faster and by how many pages per day? Support your answer.

48. PERSEVERE Write an equation in point-slope form of a line that passes through $(a, 0)$ and $(0, b)$.

49. CREATE Write an equation in point-slope form of a line with an x-intercept of 3.

50. WRITE Consider the relationship between hours worked and earnings. When would this situation represent a linear relationship? Explain your reasoning.

51. FIND THE ERROR Dan claims that since $y = x + 1$ and $y = 3x + 2$ are both linear functions, the function $y = (x + 1)(3x + 2)$ must also be linear. Is he correct? Justify your response.

52. PERSEVERE Write $y = ax + b$ in point-slope form.

53. WRITE Why do we represent linear equations in more than one form?

Solving Systems of Equations Graphically

Explore Solutions of Systems of Equations

Online Activity Use graphing technology to complete the Explore.

INQUIRY How is the solution of a system of equations represented on a graph?

Today's Standards
A.CED.3, A.REI.11
MP1, MP5

Today's Vocabulary
system of equations
consistent
inconsistent
independent
dependent

Learn Solving Systems of Equations in Two Variables by Graphing

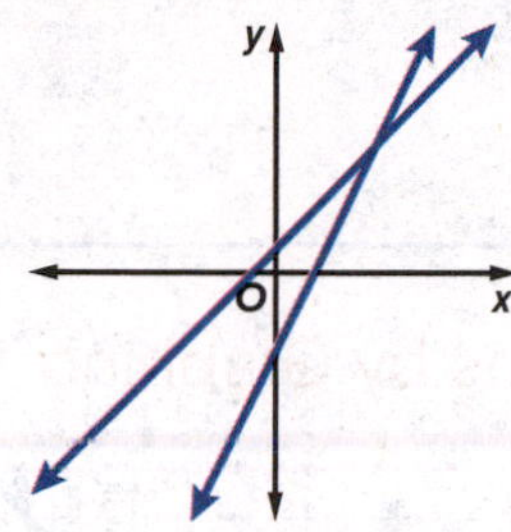	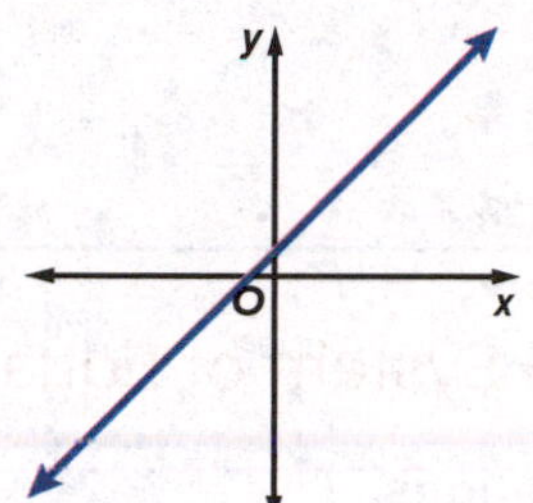	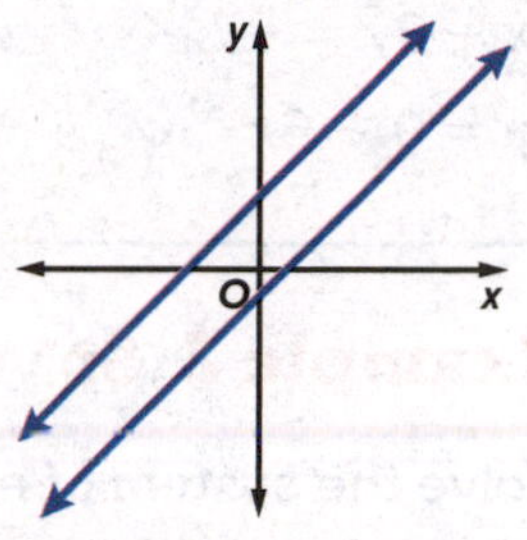
Types of Graphs		
The lines intersect at one point. The equations have different slopes.	The lines are identical. The equations have the same slope and *y*-intercept.	The lines are parallel. The equations have the same slope and different *y*-intercepts.
Solutions		
one solution	infinitely many solutions	no solutions
Classifications		
The system is **consistent** because there is at least one solution. It is **independent** because it has exactly one solution.	The system is **consistent** and **dependent** because there are infinitely many solutions.	The system is **inconsistent** because there is no solution.

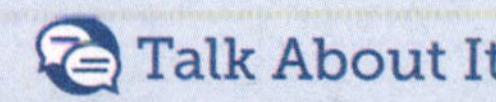

Talk About It!
Explain why the intersection of the two graphs is the solution of the system of equations.

Your Notes

Study Tip

Number of Solutions
By first determining the number of solutions a system has, you can make decisions about whether further steps need to be taken to solve the system. If a system has one solution, you can graph to find it. If a system has infinitely many solutions or no solution, no further steps are necessary. However, you can graph the system to confirm.

Example 1 Classify Systems of Equations

Determine the number of solutions each system has. Then state whether the system of equations is *consistent* or *inconsistent* and whether it is *independent* or *dependent*.

Solve each equation for y.

$2y = 6x - 14 \quad \rightarrow \quad y = 3x - 7$

$3x - y = 7 \quad \rightarrow \quad y = \_\_\_x - \_\_\_$

The equations have the same slope and y-intercept. Thus, both equations represent the same line and the system has ____________ ____________. The system is ____________ and ____________.

Check

Determine the number of solutions and classify the system of equations.

$3x - 2y = -7$

$4y = 9 - 6x$

Example 2 Solve a System of Equations by Graphing

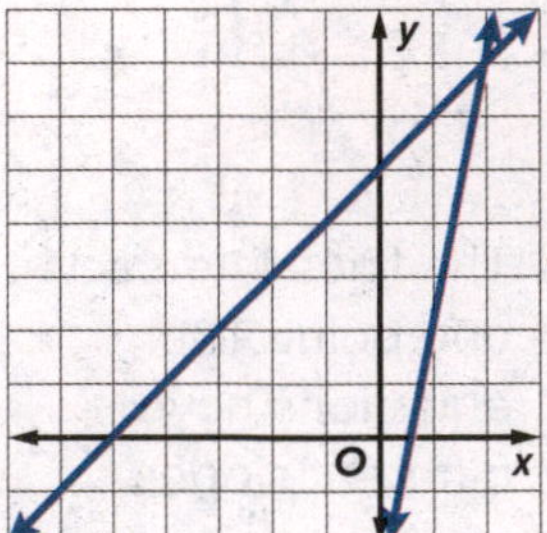

Solve the system of equations.

$5x - y = 3$

$-x + y = 5$

Solve each equation for y. The equations have different slopes, so there is one solution. Graph the system.

$5x - y = 7 \quad \rightarrow \quad \_\_\_\_\_\_\_\_\_\_$

$-x + y = 5 \quad \rightarrow \quad \_\_\_\_\_\_\_\_\_\_$

The lines appear to intersect at one point, (___, ___).

CHECK Substitute the coordinates into each original equation.

$5x - y = 3$	Original equation	$-x + y = 5$
$5(2) - 7 = 3$	$x = 2$ and $y = 7$	$-(2) + 7 = 5$
$3 = 3$	True	$5 = 5$

The solution is (2, 7).

Check

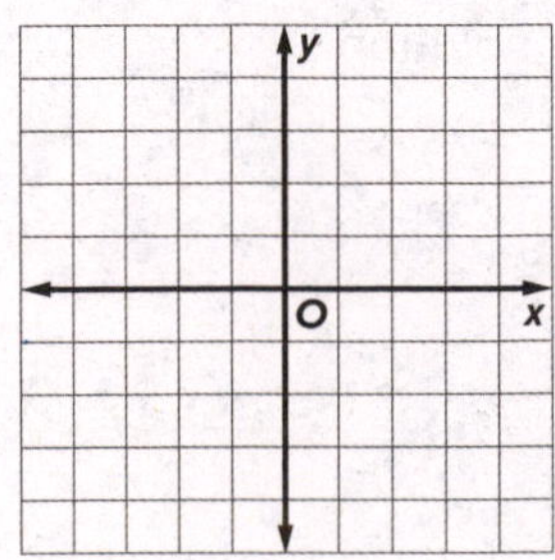

Solve the system of equations by graphing.

$2y + 14x = -6$

$8x = 4y = -24$

The solution is (________).

Example 3 Solve a System of Equations

Solve the system of equations.

$7x + 2y = 16$

$-21x - 6y = 24$

Solve each equation for y to determine the number of solutions the system has.

$7x + 2y = 16 \rightarrow y =$ ____$x +$ ____

$-21x - 6y = 24 \rightarrow y =$ ____$x +$ ____

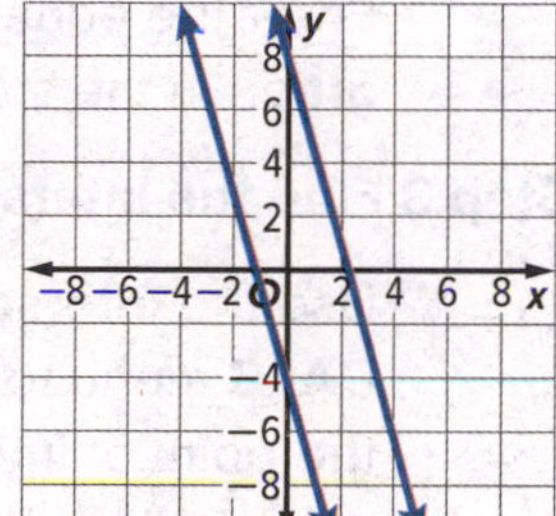

The equations have the ____________

slope and ____________ y-intercepts. So,

these equations represent ____________

____________, and there is ____________.

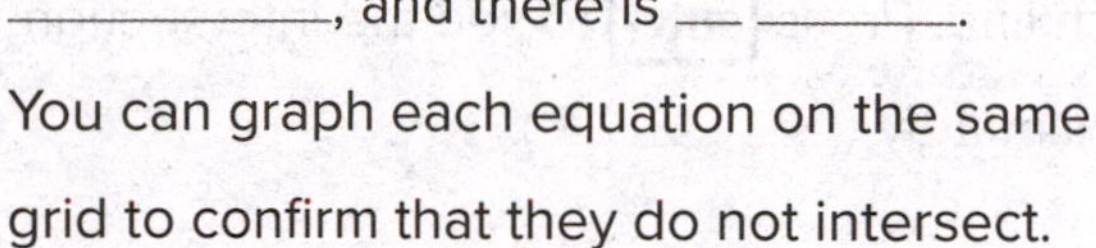

You can graph each equation on the same grid to confirm that they do not intersect.

> **Study Tip**
>
> **Parallel Lines** Graphs of lines with the same slope and different intercepts are, by definition, parallel.

> **Think About It!**
>
> What would the graph of a system with infinitely many solutions look like? Explain your reasoning.

Example 4 Write and Solve a System of Equations by Graphing

CARS **Suppose an electric car costs $29,000 to purchase and $0.036 per mile to drive, and a gasoline-powered car costs $19,000 to purchase and $0.08 per mile to drive. Estimate after how many miles of driving the total cost of each car will be the same.**

Part A Write equations for the total cost of owning each type of car.

Let $y =$ the total cost of owning the car and $x =$ the number of miles driven.

So, the equation is $y =$ ____$x +$ ____ for the electric car and

$y =$ ____$x +$ ____ for the gasoline car.

Part B Examine the graph to estimate the number of miles you would have to drive before the cost of owning each type of car would be same.

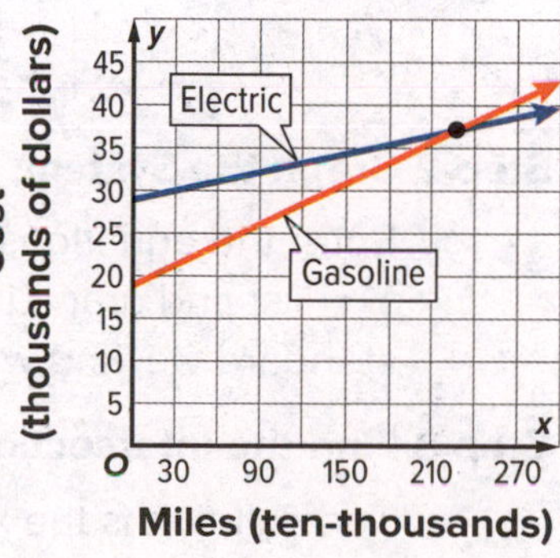

The graphs appear to intersect at approximately (________, ________).

This means that after driving about ________ miles, the cost of owning each car will be the same.

> **Think About It!**
>
> Explain what the two equations represent in the context of the situation.

Watch Out!

Solving by Graphing Solving a system of equations by graphing does not usually give an exact solution. Remember to substitute the solution into both of the original equations to verify the solution or use algebraic method to find the exact solution.

Study Tip

Window Dimensions If the point of intersection is not visible in the standard viewing window, zoom out or adjust the window settings manually until it is visible. If the lines appear to be parallel, zoom out to verify that they do not intersect.

Example 5 Solve a System by Using Technology

Use a graphing calculator to solve the system of equations.

Step 1 Solve for *y*

$3.5y - 5.6x = 18.2 \quad \rightarrow \quad y = \_\_\_\_ x + \_\_\_\_$

$-0.7x - y = -2.4 \quad \rightarrow \quad y = \_\_\_\_ x + \_\_\_\_$

Step 2 Graph the System.

Enter the equations in the ***Y*** = list and graph in the standard viewing window.

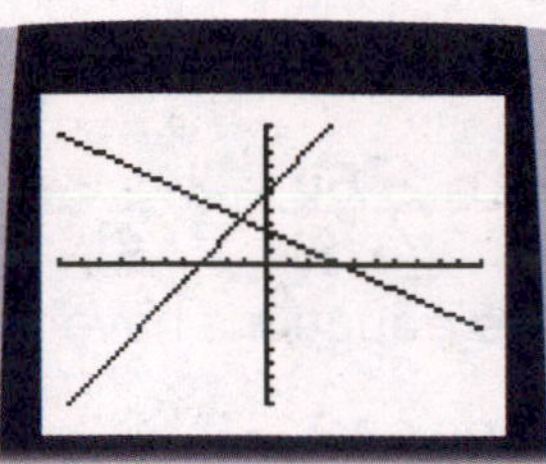

[−10, 10] scl: 1 by [−10, 10] scl: 1

Step 3 Find the Intersection.

Use the **intersect** feature from the **CALC** menu to find the coordinates of the point of intersection. When prompted, select each line. Press **enter** to see the intersection.

The solution is approximately (________).

Check

Use a graphing calculator to solve the system of equations. Round to the nearest hundredth, if necessary.

$-4.55x = 1.25y + 7.15$

$y - 1.08x = -2$

(____, ____)

Example 6 Solve a Linear Equation by Using a System

Use a graphing calculator to solve $4.5x - 3.9 = 6.5 - 2x$ by using a system of equations.

Step 1 Write a system.

Set each side of $4.5x - 3.9 = 6.5 - 2x$ equal to y to create a system of equations.

$y = \_\_\_\_\_\_\_\_$

$y = \_\_\_\_\_\_\_\_$

Step 2 Graph the System.

Enter the equations in the ***Y*** = list and graph in the standard viewing window.

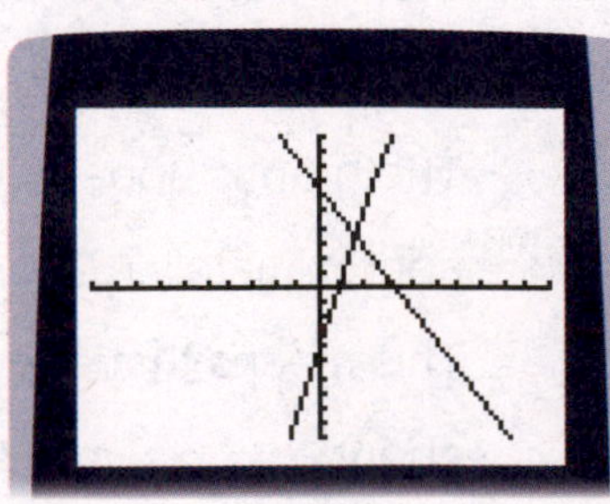

[−10, 10] scl: 1 by [−10, 10] scl: 1

Step 3 Find the Intersection.

The solution is the x-coordinate of the intersection, which is ___.

 **Go Online** You can complete an Extra Example online.

Name ______________________ Period __________ Date __________

Practice

Go Online You can complete your homework online.

Example 1

Determine the number of solutions for each system. Then state whether the system of equations is *consistent* or *inconsistent* and whether it is *independent* or *dependent*.

1. $y = 3x$
$y = -3x + 2$

2. $y = x - 5$
$-2x + 2y = -10$

3. $2x - 5y = 10$
$3x + y = 15$

4. $3x + y = -2$
$6x + 2y = 10$

5. $x + 2y = 5$
$3x - 15 = -6y$

6. $3x - y = 2$
$x + y = 6$

Examples 2 and 3

Solve the system of equations by graphing.

7. $x - 2y = 0$
$y = 2x - 3$

8. $x + 2y = 4$
$2x - 3y = 1$

9. $2x + y = 3$
$y = \frac{1}{2}x - \frac{9}{2}$

10. $y - x = 3$
$y = 1$

11. $2x - 3y = 0$
$4x - 6y = 3$

12. $5x - y = 4$
$-2x + 6y = 4$

Example 4

Solve each problem.

13. MODELING Last year the volleyball team spent \$315 for socks, which cost \$5 per pair, and shorts, which cost \$17. This year they spent \$342 to buy the same number of pairs of socks and shorts because the price of socks is now cost \$6 per pair and shorts cost \$18.

a. Write a system of two equations that represents the number of pairs of socks and shorts bought each year.

b. How many pairs of socks and shorts did the team buy each year?

14. PRICES At a store, toothbrushes cost x dollars and bars of soap cost y dollars. One customer bought 2 toothbrushes and 1 bar of soap for \$11 before sales tax. Another customer bought 6 toothbrushes and 5 bars of soap for \$38 before sales tax. Write and solve a system of equations to find the cost of toothbrushes and bars of soap.

Examples 5 and 6

USE TOOLS **Use a graphing calculator to solve each system of equations. Round the coordinates to the nearest hundredth, if necessary.**

15. $12y = 5x - 15$
$4.2y + 6.1x = 11$

16. $-3.8x + 2.9y = 19$
$6.6x - 5.4y = -23$

17. $5.8x - 6.3y = 18$
$-4.3x + 8.8y = 32$

Mixed Exercises

Solve each system of equations by graphing.

18. $x - 3y = 6$
$2x - y = -3$

19. $2x - y = 3$
$x + 2y = 4$

20. $4x + y = -2$
$2x + \frac{y}{2} = -1$

21. LASERS A machine heats a single point by shining several lasers at it. The equations $y = x + 1$ and $y = -x + 7$ describe the path of the two of the laser beams. Graph both of these lines to find the coordinates of the heated point.

22. SPOTLIGHTS Ship A has coordinates $(-1, -2)$ and Ship B has coordinates $(-4, 1)$. Both ships have their spotlights fixated on the same lifeboat. The light beam from Ship A travels along the line $y = 2x$. The light beam from Ship B travels along the line $y = x + 5$. What are the coordinates of the lifeboat?

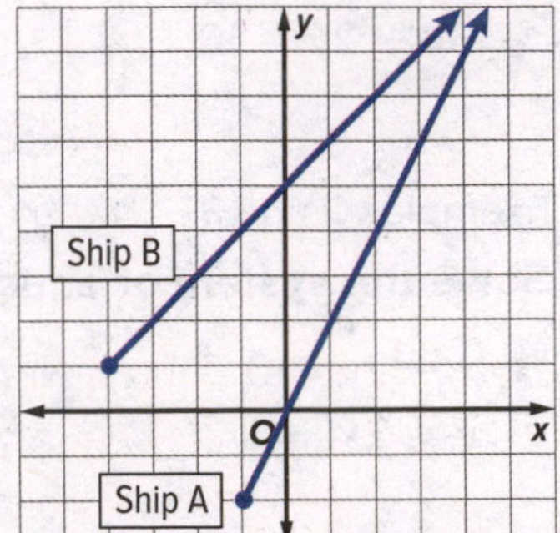

23. REASONING A high school band was selling ride tickets for the school fair. On the first day, 200 child tickets and 100 adult tickets were sold for a total of $400. On the second day, 40 child tickets and 10 adult tickets were sold for a total of $60. What is the price for each child ticket and each adult ticket?

a. Write a system of equations to represent this situation.

b. Graph the system of equations to find the solution.

c. What does the point of intersection represent?

24. ANALYZE If *a* is consistent and dependent with *b*, *b* is inconsistent with *c*, and *c* is consistent and independent with *d*, then *a* will *sometimes*, *always*, or *never* be consistent and independent with *d*. Explain your reasoning.

25. PERSEVERE Classify a system of equations that are perpendicular lines. Explain your reasoning.

26. WRITE Explain how to find the solution to a system of linear equations by graphing.

27. ANALYZE Determine if the following statement is *sometimes*, *always*, or *never* true. Explain your reasoning.

A system of linear equations in two variables can have exactly two solutions.

28. CREATE Write a system of equations that has no solution.

29. WHICH ONE DOESN'T BELONG? Which system of equations does not belong in a group with the other three systems of equations? Explain your reasoning.

$y = 3x - 4$	$y = \frac{1}{2}x - 9$	$y = 0.25x - 9.5$	$y = \frac{1}{2}x + 11$
$y = -2x - 14$	$y = -x - 12$	$y = 2x - 6$	$y = 4x + 2$

Solving Systems of Equations Algebraically

Learn Solving Systems of Equations in Two Variables by Substitution

Key Concept • Substitution Method

Step 1 When necessary, solve at least one equation for one of the variables.

Step 2 Substitute the resulting expression from Step 1 into the other equation to replace the variable. Then solve the equation.

Step 3 Substitute the value from Step 2 into either equation to solve for the other variable. Write the solution as an ordered pair.

Example 1 Substitution When There Is One Solution

Use substitution to solve the system of equations.

$8x - 3y = -1$ Equation 1
$x + 2y = -12$ Equation 2

Step 1 Solve one equation for one of the variables.

Because the coefficient of x in Equation 2 is 1, solve for x in that equation.

$x + 2y = -12$ Equation 2
$x =$ ____$y -$ ____ Subtract $2y$ from each side.

Step 2 Substitute the expression.

Substitute for x in Equation 1. Then solve for y.

$8x - 3y = -1$ Equation 1
$8($________$) - 3y = -1$ $x = -2y - 12$
____$y -$ ____ $- 3y = -1$ Distributive Property
____$y - 96 = -1$ Simplify.
$-19y =$ ____ Add 96 to each side.
$y =$ ____ Divide each side by -19.

Step 3 Substitute to solve.

Substitute the value of y into one of the original equations to solve for x.

$x + 2y = -12$ Equation 2
$x + 2($____$) = -12$ $y = -5$
$x -$ ____ $= -12$ Multiply.
$x =$ ____

Go Online You can complete an Extra Example online.

Today's Standards
A.CED.3
MP1, MP6

Today's Vocabulary
substitution
elimination

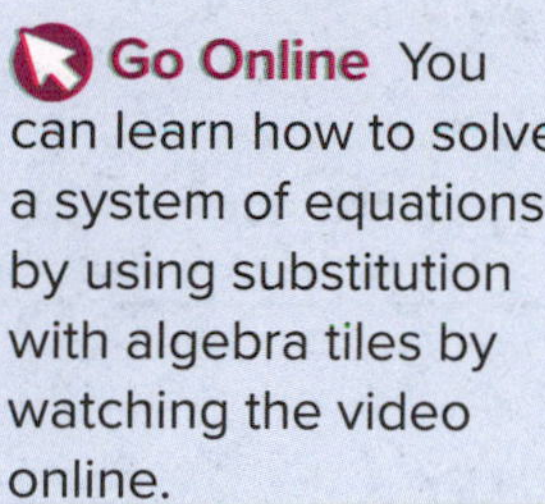

Go Online You can learn how to solve a system of equations by using substitution with algebra tiles by watching the video online.

Talk About It!
Describe the benefit of solving a system of equations by substitution instead of graphing when the coefficients are not integers.

Your Notes

 **Think About It!**

What can you conclude about the slopes and y-intercepts of the equations when a system of equations has no solution? when a system of equations has infinitely many solutions?

Check

Use substitution to solve the system of equations.

$-5x + y = -3$

$3x - 8y = 24$ ________

Example 2 Substitution When There Is Not Exactly One Solution

Use substitution to solve the system of equations.

$\mathbf{-5x + 2.5y = -15}$	Equation 1
$\mathbf{y = 2x - 11}$	Equation 2

Equation 2 is already solved for y, so substitute $2x - 11$ for y in Equation 1.

$-5x + 2.5y = -15$	Equation 1
$-5x + 2.5(\_\_\_\_\_\_) = -15$	$y = 2x - 11$
$-5x + \_\_x - \_\_\_\_ = -15$	Distributive Property
$\_\_\_\_\_\_ = -15$	False

This system has ________ because $-27.5 = -15$ is not true.

Example 3 Apply the Substitution Method

CHEMISTRY **Ms. Washington will need 300 milliliters of a 5% HCl solution for her class to use during a lab. If she has a 3.5% HCl solution and a 7% HCl solution, how much of each solution should she use in order to make the solution needed?**

 **Think About It!**

Explain what approximations were made while solving this problem and how they affect the solution.

Step 1 Write two equations in two variables.

Let x be the amount of 3.5% solution and y be the amount of 7% solution.

$x + y = 300$	Equation 1
$0.035x + 0.07y = 0.05(300)$	Equation 2

Step 2 Solve one equation for one of the variables.

$x + y = 300$	Equation 1
$x = \_\_\_ + 300$	Subtract y from each side.

Step 3 Substitute the resulting expression and solve.

$0.035x + 0.07y = 15$	Equation 2
$0.035\ \_\_\_\_\_\_ + 0.07y = 15$	$x = -y + 300$
$\_\_\_\_\_y + \_\_\_\_ + 0.07y = 15$	Distributive Property
$0.035y = 4.5$	Simplify.
$y \approx \_\_\_\_\_\_$	Divide each side by 0.035.

 **Go Online** You can complete an Extra Example online.

(continued on the next page)

Step 4 Substitute to solve for the other variable.

$x + y = 300$	Equation 1
$x + 128.57 \approx 300$	$y \approx 128.57$
$x \approx 171.43$	Simplify.

The solution of the system is (171.43, 128.57). Ms. Washington should use 171.43 mL of the 3.5% solution and 128.57 mL of the 7% solution.

Learn Solving Systems of Equations in Two Variables by Elimination

Key Concept • Elimination Method

Step 1 Multiply one or both of the equations by a number to result in two equations that contain opposite or equal terms.

Step 2 Add or subtract the equations, eliminating one variable. Then solve the equation.

Step 3 Substitute the value from Step 2 into either equation, and solve for the other variable. Write the solution as an ordered pair.

Example 4 Elimination When There Is One Solution

Use elimination to solve the system of equations.

$-2x - 9y = -25$	Equation 1
$-4x - 9y = -23$	Equation 2

Step 1 Multiply the equations.

Multiply Equation 2 by −1 to get opposite terms $-9y$ and $9y$.

$-4x - 9y = -23$ **Multiply by −1.** → $\underline{\quad}x + \underline{\quad}y = \underline{\quad}$

Step 2 Add the equations.

Add the equations to eliminate the y-term and solve for x.

$-2x - 93 = -25$	Equation 1
$(+)\ 4x + 9y = 23$	Equation 2 × (−1)
$\underline{\quad}x = \underline{\quad}$	Add the equations.
$x = \underline{\quad}$	Divide each side by 2.

Step 3 Substitute and solve.

$-4x - 9y = -23$	Substitute −1 for x in Equation 2.
$-4(\underline{\quad}) - 9y = -23$	$x = -1$
$4 - 9y = -23$	Multiply.
$\underline{\quad}y = \underline{\quad}$	Subtract 4 from each side.
$y = 3$	Divide each side by −9.

The solution of the system is ($\underline{\quad}$, $\underline{\quad}$)

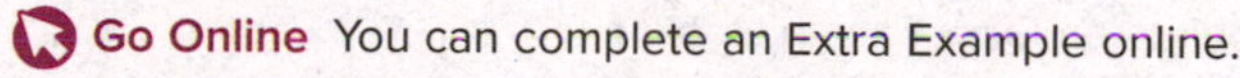

Go Online You can complete an Extra Example online.

Think About It!

When using elimination, when should you add the equations, and when should you subtract the equations?

Think About It!

Describe the benefit of using elimination instead of substitution of this problem.

Example 5 Multiply Both Equations Before Using Elimination

Use elimination to solve the system of equations.

$2x + 5y = 1$ Equation 1
$3x - 4y = -10$ Equation 2

Step 1 Multiply one or both equations.

Multiply Equation 1 by 3 and Equation 2 by 2.

$2x + 5y = 1$	Equation 1	$3x - 4y = -10$	Equation 2
$3(2x + 5y) = 3(1)$	Mult. by 3.	$2(3x - 4y) = 2(-10)$	Mult. by 2.
$\_\_x + \_\_y = \_\_$	Simplify.	$\_\_x + \_\_y = \_\_$	Simplify.

Step 2 Eliminate one variable and solve.

In order to eliminate the x-terms, subtract the equations. Then, solve for y.

$6x + 15y = 3$	Equation 1 × 3
$(-)\ 6x - 8y = -20$	Equation 2 × 2
$\_\_y = \_\_$	Subtract the equations.
$y = \_\_$	Divide each side by 23.

Step 3 Substitute and solve.

Substitute $y = 1$ in either of the original equations and solve for x.

$2x + 5y = 1$	Equation 1
$2x + 5(1) = 1$	$y = 1$
$2x + 5 = 1$	Multiply.
$x = \_\_$	Solve for x.

The solution of the system is (__, __).

Think About It!

Describe the graph of this system of equations.

Example 6 Elimination Where There is Not Exactly One Solution

Use elimination to solve the system of equations.

$18x + 21y = 14$ Equation 1
$6x + 7y = 2$ Equation 2

Steps 1 and 2 Multiply one or both equations and add them.

Multiply Equation 2 by −3. Then add the equations.

$18x + 21y = 14$
$6x + 7y = 2$

Multiply by −3.

$$18x + 21y = 14$$
$$(+)\ -18x - 21x = -6$$
$$0 \neq 8$$

Because $0 \neq 8$, this system has no solution.

Go Online You can complete an Extra Example online.

Go Online to practice what you've learned in Lessons 2-4 and 2-5.

Name ______________________ Period __________ Date __________

Practice

Go Online You can complete your homework online.

Examples 1 and 2

Use substitution to solve each system of equations.

1. $2x - y = 9$
   $x + 3y = -6$

2. $3x + y = 7$
   $4x + 2y = 16$

3. $2x + y = 5$
   $3x - 3y = 3$

4. $2x - y = 7$
   $6x - 3y = 14$

5. $4x - y = 6$
   $2x - \frac{y}{2} = 4$

6. $2x + y = 8$
   $3x + \frac{3}{2}y = 12$

Example 3

Solve each problem.

7. **BAKE SALE** Cassandra and Alberto are selling pies for a fundraiser. Cassandra sold 3 small pies and 14 large pies for a total of $203. Alberto sold 11 small pies and 11 large pies for a total of $220. Determine the cost of each pie.
   - **a.** Write a system of equations and solve using substitution.
   - **b.** What does the solution represent in terms of this situation?
   - **c.** How can you verify that the solution is correct?

8. **STOCKS** Ms. Patel invested in two stocks. She purchased shares of a stock priced at $12 each and shares of a stock priced at $15 each. She purchased a total of 400 shares for $5250.
   - **a.** Write a system of equations and solve by substitution.
   - **b.** How many shares of each stock did Ms. Patel buy? How much did she invest in each of the two stocks?

Examples 4–6

Use elimination to solve each system of equations.

9. $3x - 2y = 4$
   $5x + 3y = -25$

10. $5x + 2y = 12$
    $-6x - 2y = -14$

11. $7x + 2y = -1$
    $4x - 3y = -13$

12. $2x - y = -5$
    $4x + y = 2$

13. $x - 3y = -12$
    $2x + y = 11$

14. $6w - 8z = 16$
    $3w - 4z = 8$

Mixed Exercises

Use either substitution or elimination to solve each system of equations.

15. $0.5x + 2y = 5$
$x - 2y = -8$

16. $h - z = 3$
$-3h + 3z = 6$

17. $-r + t = 5$
$-2r + t = 4$

18. $3r - 2t = 1$
$2r - 3t = 9$

19. $5g + 4k = 10$
$-3g - 5k = 7$

20. $4m - 2p = 0$
$-3m + 9p = 5$

21. The sum of two numbers is 12. The difference of the same two numbers is −4. Find the two numbers.

22. Twice a number minus a second number is −1. Twice the second number added to three times the first number is 9. Find the two numbers.

23. **REASONING** Josh paid for admission to the high school football game. He purchased 3 adult tickets and 2 student tickets for a total of \$36. His friend purchased 6 adult tickets and 2 student tickets for a total of \$60. What is the cost of each adult ticket and each student ticket?

24. **ENTERTAINMENT** At a video game resale shop, Jasmine bought 3 PC games and 2 console games for \$58. Javier bought 1 PC game and 4 console games for \$46.

a. Determine the price for each PC game and each console game.

b. **STATE YOUR ASSUMPTION** Explain what assumption you have to make when solving this problem?

25. **FIND THE ERROR** Gloria and Syreeta are solving the system $6x - 4y = 26$ and $-3x + 4y = -17$. Is either of them correct? Explain your reasoning.

Gloria

$$\begin{array}{r} 6x - 4y = 26 \\ -5x + 4y = -17 \\ \hline 3x = 9 \\ x = 3 \end{array} \qquad \begin{array}{r} 6(3) - 4y = 26 \\ 18 - 4y = 26 \\ -4y = 8 \\ y = -2 \end{array}$$

The solution is (3, −2).

Syreeta

$$\begin{array}{r} 6x - 4y = 26 \\ -3x + 4y = -17 \\ \hline 3x = -9 \\ x = -3 \end{array} \qquad \begin{array}{r} 6(-3) - 4y = 26 \\ -18 - 4y = 26 \\ -4y = 44 \\ y = -11 \end{array}$$

The solution is (−3, −11).

26. **CREATE** Write a system of equations in which one equation should be multiplied by 3 and the other should be multiplied by 4 in order to solve the system with elimination. Then solve your system.

27. **WRITE** Why is substitution sometimes more helpful than elimination?

Solving Systems of Inequalities

Explore Solutions of Systems of Inequalities

Online Activity Use a graph to complete the Explore.

> **INQUIRY** How is a graph used to determine viable solutions of a system of inequalities?

Learn Solving Systems of Inequalities in Two Variables

A **system of inequalities** is a set of two or more inequalities with the same variables. The **feasible region** is the intersection of the graphs. Ordered pairs within the feasible region are viable solutions. The feasible region may be **bounded**, if the graph of the system is a polygonal region, or **unbounded** if it forms a region that is open.

Key Concept • Solving Systems of Inequalities

Step 1 Graph each inequality by graphing the related equation and shading the correct region.

Step 2 Identify the feasible region that is shaded for all of the inequalities. This represents the solution set of the system.

Example 1 Unbounded Region

Solve the system of inequalities.

$y \leq 4x - 3$ Inequality 1

$-2y > x$ Inequality 2

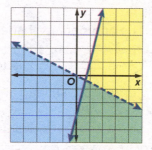

Use a ________ line to graph the first boundary $y = 4x - 3$. The appropriate half plane is shaded yellow. Use a ________ line to graph the second boundary $y = -0.5x$. The appropriate half plane is shaded blue.

The solution of the system is the set of ordered pairs in the intersection of the graphs shaded in green. The feasible region is ____________.

(continued on the next page)

Go Online You can complete an Extra Example online.

Today's Standards
A.CED.3
MP3, MP4

Today's Vocabulary
system of inequalities
feasible region
bounded
unbounded

Study Tip

Related Equation A related equation of the inequality $y \leq mx + b$ is $y = mx + b$. The inequalities $y < mx + b$, $y \geq mx + b$, and $y > mx + b$ all share this same related equation.

Go Online

You can watch a video to see how to graph a system of linear inequalities on a graphing calculator.

Study Tip

Boundaries The boundaries of inequalities with symbols < and > are graphed using dashed lines, indicating that the ordered pairs on the boundary are not included in the feasible region.

CHECK

Test the solution by substituting the coordinate of a point in the unbounded region, such as (2, −3), into the system of inequalities. If the point is viable for both inequalities, it is a solution of the system.

$y \leq 4x - 3$	Original inequality	$-2(y) > x$
$-3 \stackrel{?}{\leq} 4(2) - 3$	$x = 2$ and $y = -3$	$-2(-3) \stackrel{?}{>} 2$
$-3 \leq 5$	True	$6 > 2$

Check

Graph the solution of the system of inequalities.

$y \leq \frac{1}{3}x + 2$

$y > x$

$y \leq 1$

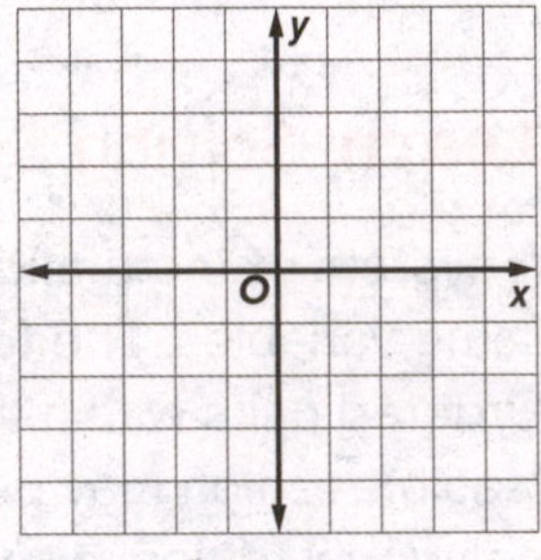

Example 2 Bounded Region

Solve the system of inequalities

$y < -\frac{4}{3}x + 5$ Inequality 1

$y \geq x - 2$ Inequality 2

$x > 1$ Inequality 3

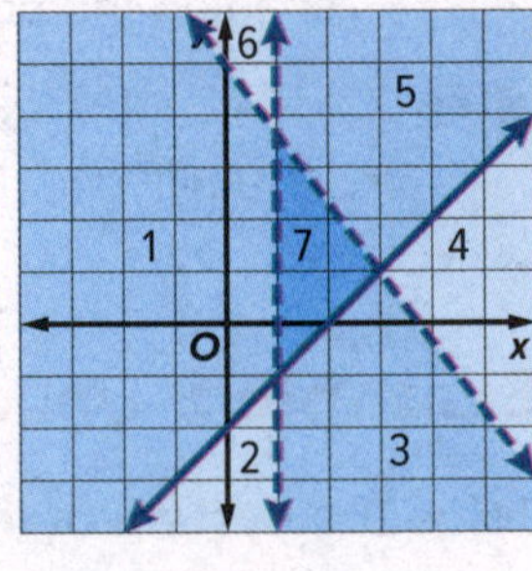

Use a ________ line to graph the first boundary $y = -\frac{4}{3}x + 5$.

The appropriate shaded area contains regions ________.

Use a ________ line to graph the second boundary $y = x - 2$. The appropriate shaded area contains regions ________.

Use a ________ line to graph the third boundary $x = 1$. The appropriate shaded area contains regions ________.

The solution of the system is the set of ordered pairs in the intersection of the graphs, represented by region ___. The feasible region is ________.

 **Go Online** You can complete an Extra Example online.

Check

Graph the solution of the system of inequalities.

$y \geq \frac{4}{5}x - 3$

$y < -\frac{2}{3}x + 2$

$x \geq 0$

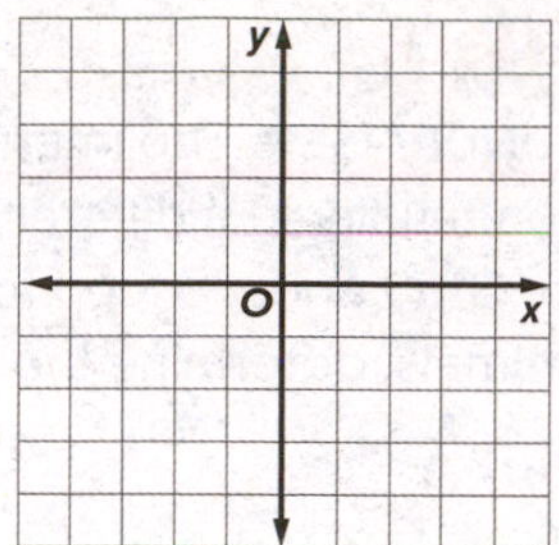

Example 3 Use Systems of Inequalities

TOURS A Niagara Falls boat tour company charges $19.50 for adult tickets and $11 for children's tickets. Each boat has a capacity of 600 passengers, including 8 boat crew members. Suppose the company's operating cost for one boat tour is $2750. Write and graph a system of inequalities to represent the situation so the touring company will make a profit on each tour. Then, identify some viable solutions.

Part A Write the system of inequalities.

Let a represent the number of adult tickets and c represent the number of children's tickets.

Inequality 1: $a + c + 8 \leq$ ____ Inequality 2: ____a + ____$c > 2750$

Part B Graph the system of inequalities.

Graph both inequalities.

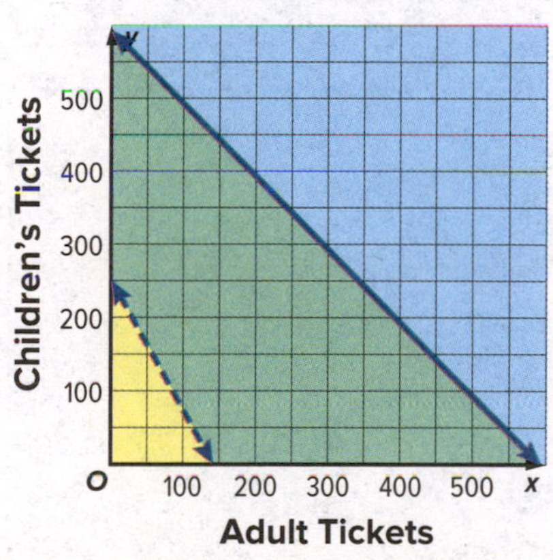

Graph the solution region.

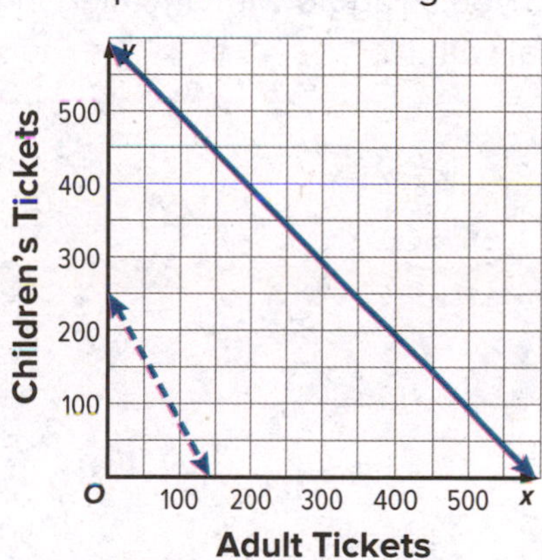

Part C Identify some viable solutions

Passengers	Viable	Nonviable
60 adults, 100 children	☐	☐
210 adults, 350 children	☐	☐
415 adults, 200 children	☐	☐
390 adults, 240 children	☐	☐
550 adults, 0 children	☐	☐

Go Online You can complete an Extra Example online.

Your Notes

Study Tip:

Consider the Context While the feasible region represents the viable solutions, the solution may be limited to only integers or only positive numbers. In this case, the touring company cannot sell a fraction of a ticket. So the solution must be given as whole numbers.

Talk About It!

Why is it important to label the axes given the context of this problem? Explain.

Check

FUNDRAISER The international club raised $1200 to buy livestock for a community in a different part of the world. The club can buy an alpaca for $160 and a sheep for $120. If the club wants to donate at least 8 animals, determine the system of inequalities to represent the situation.

Part A

Graph of the system of inequalities that represents the possible combinations of animals the club can donate.

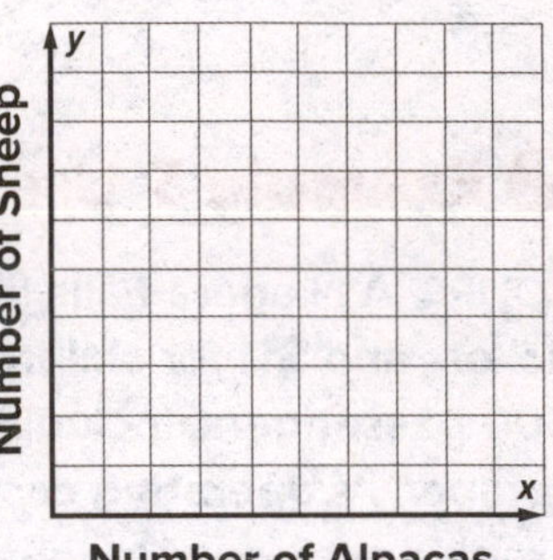

Part B

Select all of the viable solutions given the constraints of the club's funds.

A. 0 alpacas, 10 sheep

B. 1 alpaca, 8 sheep

C. 3 alpacas, 6 sheep

D. 6 alpacas, 3 sheep

E. 8 alpacas, 0 sheep

Pause and Reflect

Did you struggle with anything in this lesson? If so, how did you deal with it?

 **Go Online** You can complete an Extra Example online.

Name ____________________ Period __________ Date __________

Practice

Go Online You can complete your homework online.

Example 1

Solve each system of inequalities by graphing.

1. $x - y \leq 2$
   $x + 2y \geq 1$

2. $3x - 2y \leq -1$
   $x + 4y \geq -12$

3. $y \geq \frac{x}{2} - 3$
   $y < 2x$

4. $y < \frac{x}{3} + 2$
   $y < -2x + 1$

5. $x + y \geq 4$
   $2x - y > 2$

6. $x + 3y < 3$
   $x - 2y \geq 4$

Example 2

Solve each system of inequalities by graphing.

7. $y \geq -3x + 7$
   $y > \frac{1}{2}x$
   $y < 2$

8. $x > -3$
   $y < -\frac{1}{3}x + 3$
   $y > x - 1$

9. $y < -\frac{1}{2}x + 3$
   $y > \frac{1}{2}x + 1$
   $y < 3x + 10$

10. $y \leq 0$
    $x \leq 0$
    $y \geq -x - 1$

11. $y \leq 3 - x$
    $y \geq 3$
    $x \geq -5$

12. $x \geq -2$
    $y \geq x - 2$
    $x + y \leq 2$

Example 3

13. **TICKETS** The high school auditorium has 800 seats. Suppose that the drama club has a goal of making \$3400 each night of their spring play to raise money for the club. Adult tickets are \$7 and student tickets are \$4.

    a. Write a system of inequalities for the number of seats and the money raised by the drama club.

    b. Graph the system of inequalities. In the context of the situation, in which quadrant is the feasible solution?

    c. Could the club meet its goal by selling 200 adult and 475 student tickets? Explain.

14. **MODELING** Anthony charges \$15 an hour for tutoring and \$10 an hour for babysitting. He can work no more than 14 hours a week. How many hours should Anthony spend on each job if he wants to earn at least \$125 each week?

    a. Write a system of inequalities to represent this situation.

    b. Graph the system of inequalities and highlight the solution.

    c. Are the points (4, 5), (7, 6), or (5, 10) solutions to the system? Explain.

Mixed Exercises

Solve each system of inequalities by graphing.

15. $x - 2y > 6$
$x + 4y < -4$

16. $x < 1$
$y \geq -1$

17. $x \leq 2$
$x > 4$

18. **REASONING** The Junior class is selling T-shirts to students to raise money for prom. There are 600 students in the school. Suppose that the Junior class has a goal of making \$5000. Short sleeve T-shirts are \$10 and long sleeve T-shirts are \$15.

a. Write and graph a system of inequalities that describe how many of each type of T-shirt the Junior class must sell to meet its goal.

b. List three different combinations of t-shirts sold that satisfy the inequalities.

19. **TIME MANAGEMENT** On Sheila's off day from work, she plans to run some errands and then spend time with friends. She needs to balance the length of her errands x with the length of time she spends with her friends y. She has a total of 6 hours of free time and thinks that her errands will take between $\frac{1}{2}$ hour and 2 hours, inclusively.

a. Write and graph a system of inequalities that represents this situation.

b. **STRUCTURE** Explain why your graph for this situation is restricted to Quadrant I.

20. **BIRD BATH** Michael wants to put a bird bath in his yard at point (x, y), and wants it to be inside the enclosed shaded area shown in the graph. First, he checks that $x \geq -3$ and $y \geq -2$. What linear inequality must he check to conclude that (x, y) is inside the shaded region?

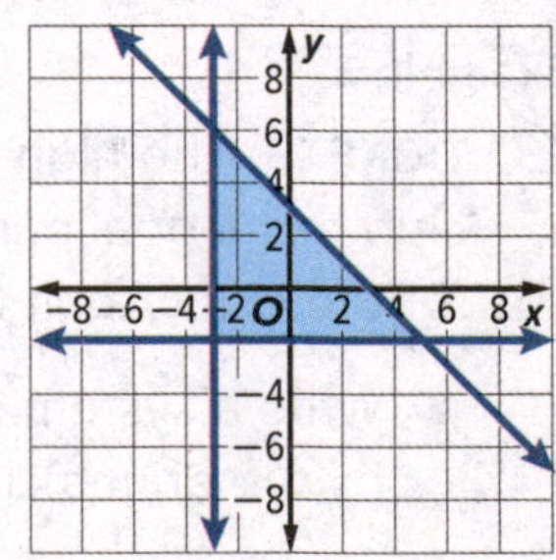

21. **PERSEVERE** Find the area of the region defined by the following inequalities.

$y \geq -4x - 16$ $\quad$ $4y \leq 26 - x$ $\quad$ $3y + 6x \leq 30$ $\quad$ $4y - 2x \geq -10$

22. **CREATE** Write a system of two inequalities in which the solution:

a. lies only in the third quadrant.

b. does not exist.

c. lies only on a line.

23. **ANALYZE** Determine whether the statement is *true* or *false*. If false, give a counter example.

A system of two linear inequalities has either no points or infinitely many points in its solution.

24. **WRITE** Explain how you would determine whether $(-4, 6)$ is a solution of a system of inequalities.

Optimization with Linear Programming

Explore Using Technology with Linear Programming

Online Activity Use graphing technology to complete the Explore.

INQUIRY How can you use technology to find the maximum or minimum values of a function over a given region?

Today's Standards
A.CED.3
MP4, MP5

Today's Vocabulary
linear programming
optimization

Learn Finding Maximum and Minimum Values

Linear programming is the process of finding the maximum or minimum values of a function for a region defined by a system of inequalities.

Key Concept • Linear Programming

Step 1 Graph the inequalities.

Step 2 Determine the coordinates of the vertices.

Step 3 Evaluate the function at each vertex.

Step 4 For a bounded region, determine the maximum and minimum. For an unbounded region, test other points within the feasible region to determine which vertex represents the maximum or minimum.

Study Tip
An unbounded feasible region does not necessarily contain a maximum or minimum. If it does, then it has either a maximum or a minimum, but not both.

Example 1 Maximum and Minimum Values for a Bounded Region

Graph the system of inequalities. Name the coordinates of the vertices of the feasible region. Find the maximum and minimum values of the function for this region.

$-2 \leq x \leq 4$

$y \leq x + 2$

$y \geq -0.5x - 3$

$f(x, y) = -2x + 6y$

Steps 1 and 2 Graph the inequalities and determine the vertices.

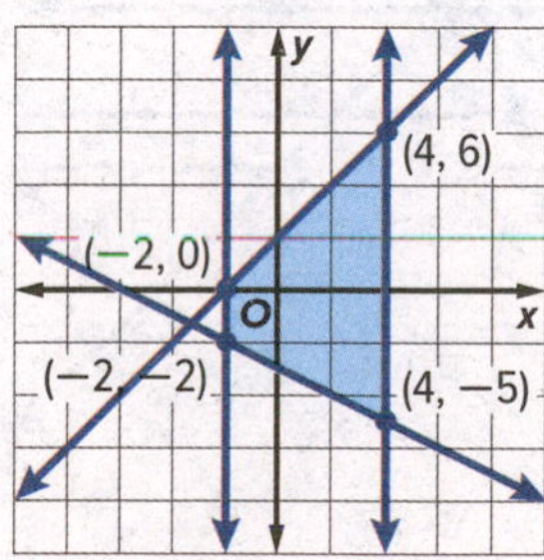

The vertices of the feasible region are

(___, −2), (−2, ___), (___, 6) and (4, ___).

(continued on the next page)

Study Tip
Feasible Region To determine the feasible region, you can shade the solution set of each inequality individually, and then find where they all overlap. Shading each inequality using a different color or shading style can help you easily determine the feasible region.

Your Notes

Step 3 Evaluate the function at each vertex.

(x, y)	$-2x + 6y$	$f(x, y)$
$(-2, -2)$	$-2(-2) + 6(-2)$	
$(-2, -2)$	$-2(-2) + 6(0)$	
$(4, -5)$	$-2(4) + 6(-5)$	
$(4, 6)$	$-2(4) + 6(6)$	

Step 4 The maximum value is ____ at (4, 6). The minimum value is ____ at (4, –5).

Example 2 Maximum and Minimum Values for an Unbounded Region

Graph the system of inequalities. Name the coordinates of the vertices of the feasible region. Find the maximum and minimum values of the function for this region.

$1 \leq y \leq 4$

$y \leq -x$

$y \geq 0.5x + 3$

$f(x, y) = -x + y$

Steps 1 and 2 Graph the inequalities and determine the vertices.

The vertices of the feasible region are

(____, 3), (–2, ____), (–____, 1).

Notice that the region is ____________. This may indicate that there is no minimum or maximum value.

Step 3 Evaluate the function at each vertex and a point in the feasible region.

(x, y)	$-x + y$	$f(x, y)$
$(-3, 3)$	$-(-3) + 3$	
$(-2, 2)$	$-(-2) + 2$	
$(-4, 1)$	$-(-4) + 1$	
$(-10, 2)$	$-(-10) + 2$	

Step 4 The minimum value is ____ at (–2, 2). There is ____ maximum value, because (–10, 2) is a point in the feasible region and yields a greater $f(x, y)$ value than any of the vertices.

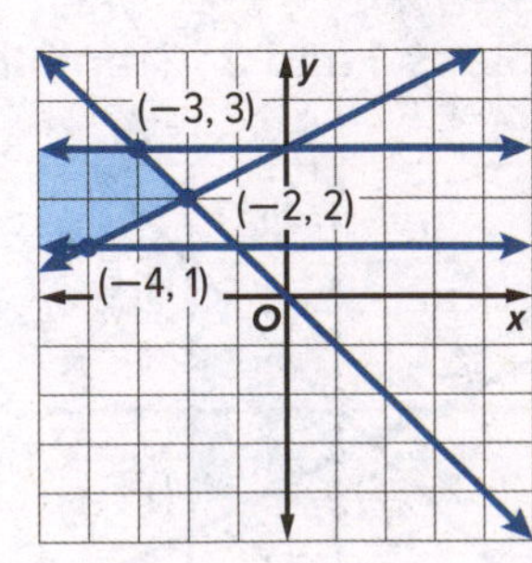

Go Online You can complete an Extra Example online.

Study Tip

Feasible Region To determine whether an unbounded region has a maximum or minimum for the function $f(x, y)$, you need to test several points in the feasible region to see if any values of $f(x, y)$ are greater than or less than the values of $f(x, y)$ for the vertices.

Talk About It!

Why is it not possible for an unbounded feasible region to have both a maximum and a minimum?

Learn Linear Programming

Optimization is the process of seeking the optimal price or amount that is desired to minimize costs or maximize profits.

Key Concept • Optimization

Step 1 Define the variables.

Step 2 Write a system of inequalities.

Step 3 Graph the system of inequalities.

Step 4 Find the coordinates of the vertices of the feasible region.

Step 5 Write a linear function to be maximized or minimized.

Step 6 Evaluate the function at each vertex by substituting the coordinates into the function.

Step 7 Interpret the results.

Math History Minute

In the 1960s, **Christine Darden (1942–)** became one of the "human computers" who crunched numbers for engineers at NASA's Langley Research Center. After earning a doctorate degree in mechanical engineering, Darden became one of few female aerospace engineers at NASA Langley. For most of her career, her focus was sonic boom minimization.

Example 3 Optimizing with Linear Programming

GARDENING **Avoree has a 30-square-foot plot in the school greenhouse and wants to plant lettuce and cucumbers while minimizing the amount of water she uses for them. Each cucumber requires 2.25 square feet of space and uses 25 gallons of water over the lifetime of the plant. Each lettuce plant requires 1.5 square feet of space and uses 17 gallons of water. She wants to grow at least 4 of each type of plant and at least 15 plants in total. Determine how many of each plant Avoree should plot in order to minimize her water usage.**

Complete the table.

Vegetable	Minimum	Maximum	Water per Plant (gal)
cucumber			
lettuce			

Step 1 Define the variables.

Because the number of plants of different types determine the water usage, the independent variables should be the numbers of plants. The dependent variable in the function to be minimized should be total water used. Let _____ represent the number of cucumber plants and _____ represent the number of lettuce plants.

Step 2 Write a system of inequalities.

Determine the maximum number of each type of plant, given a 30-square-foot constraint and the space requirement for each plant.

Cucumber		Lettuce
$2.25c \leq 30$	space required for each plant	$1.5t \leq 30$
$c \leq$ _______	Divide	$t \leq$ _____

(continued on the next page)

Problem Solving Tip

Make a Table You may find it helpful to organize the information in a table before writing the inequalities.

Go Online You can complete an Extra Example online.

Because it is not possible to plant $13\frac{1}{3}$ cucumber plants, it is more appropriate to limit the number of cucumber plants to 13.

Avoree also wants to have at least 4 of each type of plant, so 4 must be included as minimums in the inequalities. The total number of plants must be at least 20.

$4 \leq c \leq$ ____

____ $\leq t \leq 20$

$c + t \leq$ ____

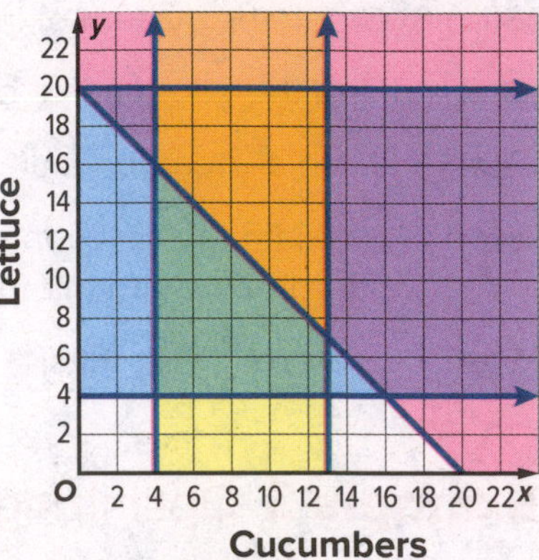

Step 3 Graph the system of inequalities.

Step 4 Find the coordinates of the vertices of the feasible region.

(____, 16), (4, ____), (13, ____), and

(____, 7)

Step 5 Write a linear function to be minimized.

Because Avoree wants to minimize her water usage, the linear function will be the sum of the water usage for each plant.

$f(c, t) =$ ____$c +$ ____t

Think About It!

Does this solution seem reasonable? Explain.

Step 6 Evaluate the function at each vertex.

(c, t)	$25c + 17t$	$f(c, t)$
(4, 16)	25(4) + 17(16)	
(4, 20)	25(4) + 17(20)	
(13, 20)	25(13) + 17(20)	
(13, 7)	25(13) + 17(7)	

Step 7 Interpret the results.

Avoree should plant ____ cucumber plants and ____ lettuce plants to minimize her water usage.

Check

SOCCER A new soccer team needs to hire players. They need at least 10 defenders and forwards, and they want to minimize the amount they spend on player salaries. Determine the number of forwards f and defenders d they should hire to minimize the cost.

Position	Minimum	Maximum	Salary per Player ($)
forward f	5	8	120,000
defender d	7	10	100,000

The least amount of money that the team can spend is $ ____________

by hiring ____ forwards and ____ defenders.

Go Online You can complete an Extra Example online.

Name ______________________ Period ____________ Date ______________

Practice

Go Online You can complete your homework online.

Example 1

Graph the system of inequalities. Name the coordinates of the vertices of the feasible region. Find the maximum and minimum values of the function for this region.

1. $y \geq 2$
$1 \leq x \leq 5$
$y \leq x + 3$
$f(x, y) = 3x - 2y$

2. $y \geq -2$
$y \geq 2x - 4$
$x - 2y \geq -1$
$f(x, y) = 4x - y$

3. $x + y \geq 2$
$4y \leq x + 8$
$y \geq 2x - 5$
$f(x, y) = 4x + 3y$

4. $x \geq 2$
$x \leq 5$
$y \geq 1$
$y \leq 4$
$f(x, y) = x + y$

5. $x \geq 1$
$y \leq 6$
$y \geq x - 2$
$f(x, y) = x - y$

6. $x \geq 0$
$y \geq 0$
$y \leq 7 - x$
$f(x, y) = 3x + y$

Example 2

Graph the system of inequalities. Name the coordinates of the vertices of the feasible region. Find the maximum and minimum values of the function for this region.

7. $x \geq -1$
$x + y \leq 6$
$f(x, y) = x + 2y$

8. $y \leq 2x$
$y \geq 6 - x$
$y \leq 6$
$f(x, y) = 4x + 3y$

9. $y \leq 3x + 6$
$4y + 3x \leq 3$
$x \geq -2$
$f(x, y) = -x + 3y$

Example 3

10. **MODELING** A painter has exactly 32 units of yellow dye and 54 units of green dye. He plans to mix as many gallons as possible of color A and color B. Each gallon of color A requires 4 units of yellow dye and 1 unit of green dye. Each gallon of color B requires 1 unit of yellow dye and 6 units of green dye. Find the maximum number of gallons he can mix.

a. Define the variables and write a system of inequalities.

b. Graph the system of inequalities and find the coordinates of the vertices of the feasible region.

c. Find the maximum number of gallons that he can make.

11. **REASONING** The Jewelry Company makes and sells necklaces. For one type of necklace, the company uses clay beads and glass beads. Each necklace has no more than 10 clay beads and at least 4 glass beads. For every necklace, four times the number of glass beads is less than or equal to 8 more than twice the number of clay beads. Each clay bead costs \$0.20 and each glass bead costs \$0.40. Find the minimum cost to make a necklace with clay and glass beads and find the combination of clay and glass beads in a necklace that costs the least to make.

a. Define the variables and write a system of inequalities. Then write an equation for the cost *C*.

b. Graph the system of inequalities and find the coordinates of the vertices of the feasible region.

c. Find the number of clay beads and glass beads in a necklace that costs the least to make.

Mixed Exercises

12. CERAMICS Juan has 8 days to make pots and plates to sell at a local fair. Each pot weighs 2 pounds and each plate weighs 1 pound. Juan cannot carry more than 50 pounds to the fair. Each day, he can make at most 5 plates and 3 pots. He will make \$12 profit for every plate and \$25 profit for every pot that he sells.

a. Write linear inequalities to represent the number of pots p and plates a Juan may bring to the fair.

b. List the coordinates of the vertices of the feasible region.

c. How many pots and how many plates should Josh make to maximize his potential profit?

13. ELEVATION A trapezoidal park is built on a slight incline. The ground elevation above sea level is given by $f(x, y) = x - 3y + 20$ feet. What are the coordinates of the highest point in the park?

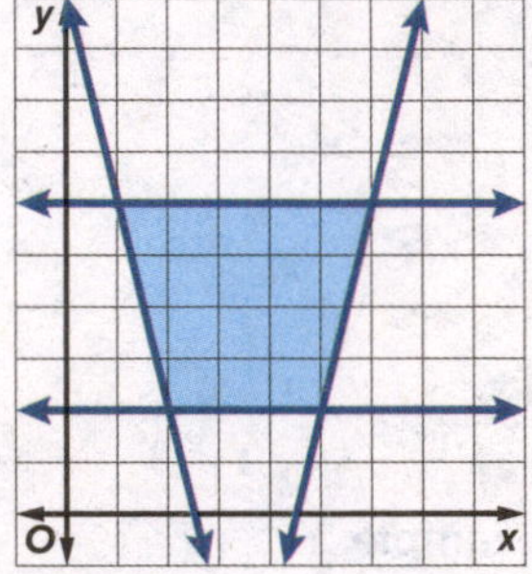

14. FOOD A zoo is mixing two types of food for the animals. Each serving is required to have at least 60 grams of protein and 30 grams of fat. Custom Foods has 15 grams of protein and 10 grams of fat and costs 80 cents per unit. Zookeeper's Best contains 20 grams of protein and 5 grams of fat and costs 50 cents per unit.

a. The zoo wants to minimize their costs. Define the variables and write the inequalities that represent the constraints of the situation.

b. Graph the inequalities. Find how much of each type of food should be used to minimize costs. What does the unbound region represent?

15. ANALYZE Determine whether the following statement is *sometimes*, *always*, or *never* true. Explain your reasoning.

An unbounded region will not have both a maximum and minimum value.

16. WHICH ONE DOESN'T BELONG? Identify the system of inequalities that is not the same as the other three. Explain your reasoning.

a.

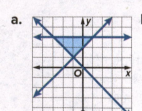

b.

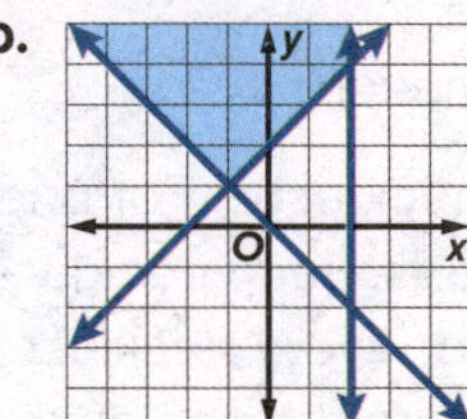

c.

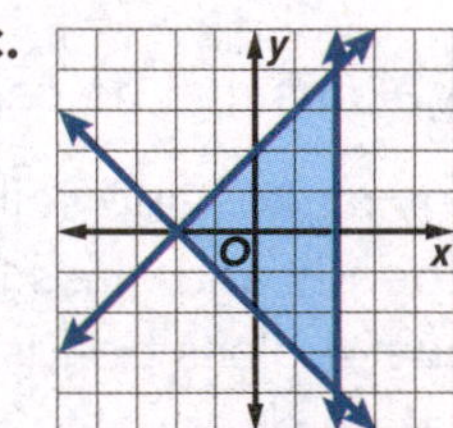

d.

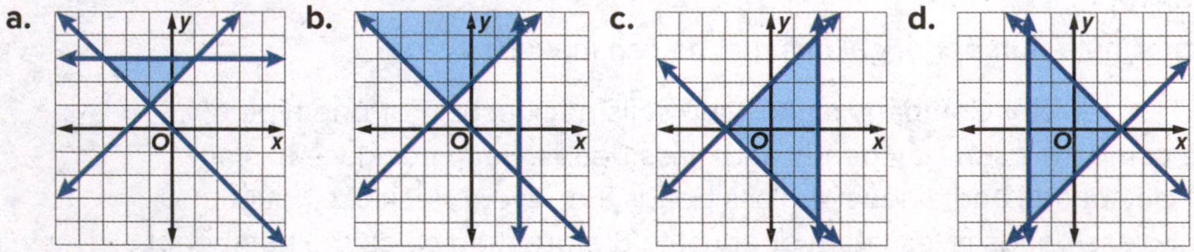

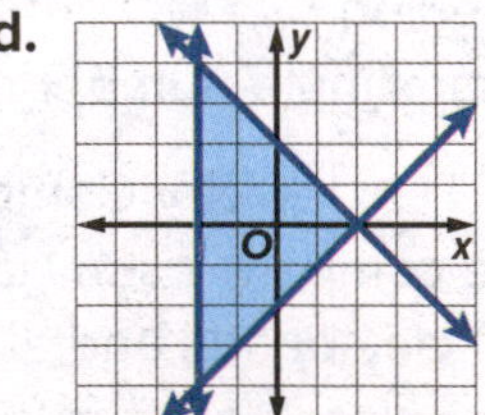

17. WRITE Upon determining a bounded feasible region, Kelvin noticed that vertices $A(-3, 4)$ and $B(5, 2)$ yielded the same maximum value for $f(x, y) = 16y + 4x$. Kelvin confirmed that his constraints were graphed correctly and his vertices were correct. Then he said that those two points were not the only maximum values in the feasible region. Explain how this could have happened.

18. CREATE Create a set of inequalities that forms a bounded region with an area of 20 units^2 and lies only in the fourth quadrant.

Systems of Equations in Three Variables

Today's Standards
A.CED.3
MP1, MP8

Today's Vocabulary
ordered triple

Explore Systems of Equations Represented as Lines and Planes

Online Activity Use concrete models to complete the Explore.

INQUIRY How does the way that lines or planes intersect affect the solution of a system of equations?

Learn Systems of Equations in Three Variables

The graph of an equation in three variables is a plane. The graph of a system of equations in three variables is an intersection of planes.

- If the three individual planes intersect at a specific point, then there is one solution given as an ordered triple (x, y, z). An **ordered triple** is three numbers given in a specific order to locate points in space.
- If the planes intersect in a line, every point on the line represents a solution of the system. If they intersect in the same plane, every equation is equivalent and every coordinate in the plane represents a solution of the system.
- If there are no points in common with all three planes, then there is no solution.

Talk About It!
Is it possible for a system of equations in three variables to have exactly three solutions? Justify your argument.

Example 1 Solve a System with One Solution

Solve the system of equations.

$4x + y + 6z = 12$ Equation 1

$3x - 10y - 2z = 12$ Equation 2

$3x + 8y + 19z = 38$ Equation 3

Step 1 Eliminate one variable.

Select two of the equations and eliminate one of the variables.

$4x + y + 6z = 12$ Equation 1 $3x - 10y - 2z = 12$ Equation 2

Multiply Equation 1 by 10 to eliminate y.

$4x + y + 6z = 12$ 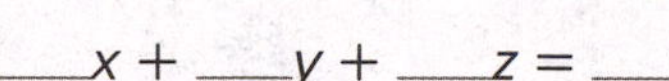

$\_\_\_x + \_\_\_y + \_\_\_z = \_\_\_$

Add the equations to eliminate y.

$40x + 10y + 60z = 120$ Equation 1 × 10

$(+)\quad 3x - 10y - 2z = 12$ Equation 2

$\_\_\_x + \_\_\_z = \_\_\_$ Add the equations.

Your Notes

Study Tip

Identify Subgoals Before you begin solving a system of equations in 3 variables, try to identify which variable would be easiest to eliminate in Step 1. Be sure that it makes sense to select that variable to eliminate from the set of equations. As you work through the problem, check your work after each step. Check for reasonableness before moving on to the next subgoal.

Think About It!

Suppose you initially eliminated x in Step 1. How would that affect the solution? Explain your reasoning.

Use a different combination of the original equations to create another equation in two variables. Eliminate y again.

$4x + y + 6z = 12$ Equation 1 $\quad$ $3x + 8y + 19z = 38$ Equation 3

Multiply Equation 1 by -8 and add the equations to eliminate y.

$4x + y + 6z = 12$ **Multiply by −8.** → $-32x - \_\_\_y - 48z = \_\_\_$

Add the equations to eliminate y.

	$-32x - 8y - 48z = -96$	Equation 1 × (−8).
(+)	$3x + 8y + 19z = 38$	Equation 3
	$\_\_\_x \quad \_\_\_z = \_\_\_$	Add the equations.

Step 2 Solve the system of two equations.

Multiply the second equation by 2 and add the equations to eliminate z.

$42x + 58z = 132$ $\qquad\qquad$ $42x + 58z = 132$

$-29x - 29z = -58$ **Multiply by 2.** → (+) $-58x - 58z = -116$

$= 16x = 16$

$x = -1$

Use substitution to solve for z.

$42x + 58z = 132$	Equation in two variables
$42(\_\_\_) + 58z = 132$	$x = -1$
$\_\_\_ + 58z = 132$	Multiply.
$58z = \_\_\_$	Add 42 to each side.
$z = \_\_\_$	Divide each side by 58.

The result is $x = \_\_\_$ and $z = \_\_\_$.

Step 3 Solve for *y*.

Substitute the two values into one of the original equations to find y.

$4x + y + 6z = 12$	Equation 1
$4(\_\_\_) + y + 6(\_\_\_) = 12$	$x = -1, z = 3$
$\_\_\_ + y + \_\_\_ = 12$	Multiply.
$y = \_\_\_$	Subtract 14 from each side.

The ordered triple is (___, ___, ___).

Go Online You can complete an Extra Example online.

Example 2 Solve a System with Infinitely Many Solutions

Solve the system of equations.

$-x + 5y - 4z = -2$	Equation 1
$4x - 20y + 16z = 8$	Equation 2
$-x - y - z = -1$	Equation 3

Step 1 Eliminate one variable.

Select two of the equations and eliminate one of the variables.

Multiply Equation 1 by 4 and add the equations to eliminate *y*.

$-x + 5y - 4z = -2$ **Multiply by 4.** → $-\_\_\_x + \_\_\_y - \_\_\_z = \_\_\_$

Add the equations to eliminate *x*.

$-4x + 20y - 16z = -8$	Equation 1 × 4.
(+) $4x - 20y + 16z = 8$	Equation 2
$\_\_\_ = \_\_\_$	Add the equations.

The equation $0 = 0$ is always ________. This indicates that the first two equations represent the same plane.

Step 2 Check the third plane.

Multiply Equation 1 by −1 and add the equations to eliminate *x*.

$-x + 5y - 4z = -2$ **Multiply by −1.** → $x - \_\_\_y + \_\_\_z = \_\_\_$

Add the equations to eliminate *x*.

$x - 5y + 4z = 2$	Equation 1 × (−1).
(+) $-x - y - z = -1$	Equation 3
$-6\_\_\_ + 3\_\_\_ = 1$	Add the equations.

The planes intersect in a ________, because the resultant equation is two variables. So, there are an __________ number of solutions.

Check

Determine solution to each system of equations.

$3x - 18y + 6z = 7$ $7x - 2y + z = 1$ $-x + 6y - 2z = -2$	⟶	
$3x - y - z = 2$ $-4x - 2y + 3z = 19$ $5x + 3y + z = 8$	⟶	

Go Online to see Example 3.

 Go Online You can complete an Extra Example online.

Example 4 Write and Solve a System of Equations

MUSEUM MEMBERSHIPS In 2016, Dali Museum in St. Petersburg, Florida offered three types of basic membership, individual, dual, and family, which cost \$60, \$80, and \$100, respectively. Suppose in one month the museum sells a total of 81 new memberships, for a total of \$6420. The number of dual memberships purchased is twice that of individual memberships. Write and solve a system of equations to determine the number of new individual members *x*, dual members *y*, and family members *z*.

Step 1 Write the system of equations.

a total of 81 new memberships: ____________

The number of dual memberships purchased is twice that of individual memberships: ____________

basic membership, individual, dual, and family, which cost \$60, \$80, and \$100, respectively for a total of \$6420 earned: ____________

Step 2 Eliminate one variable.

Substitute $y = 2x$ into Equation 1 and Equation 3 to eliminate y.

$x + y + z = 81$	Equation 1
$x +$ ____ $+ z = 81$	$y = 2x$
____ $x + z = 81$	Add.
$60x + 80y + 100z = 6420$	Equation 3
$60x + 80($____$) + 100z = 6420$	$y = 2x$
____ $x +$ ____ $z = 6420$	Simplify.

Step 3 Solve the resulting system of two equations.

$-300x - 100z = -8100$	Multiply new Equation 1 by -100.
$(+)\ 200x + 100z = 6420$	
$80x = 1680$	Add to eliminate z.
$x = 21$	Solve for x.

Step 4 Substitute to find *z*.

$3x + z = 81$	Remaining equation in two variables
$3($____$) + z = 81$	$x = 21$
____ $+ z = 81$	Multiply.
$z = 18$	Subtract 63 from each side.

Step 5 Substitute to find *y*.

$y = 2x$	Remaining equation in two variables.
$y = 2($____$)$	$x = 21$
$y =$ ____	Multiply.

The solution is (21, 42, 18).

Go Online You can complete an Extra Example online.

Think About It!

Is the solution reasonable? Explain.

Name ______________________ Period __________ Date __________

Practice

Go Online You can complete your homework online.

Examples 1–3

Solve each system of equations.

1. $2x + 3y - z = 0$
$x - 2y - 4z = 14$
$3x + y - 8z = 17$

2. $2p - q + 4r = 11$
$p + 2q - 6r = -11$
$3p - 2q - 10r = 11$

3. $a - 2b + c = 8$
$2a + b - c = 0$
$3a - 6b + 3c = 24$

4. $3s - t - u = 5$
$3s + 2t - u = 11$
$6s - 3t + 2u = -12$

5. $2x - 4y - z = 10$
$4x - 8y - 2z = 16$
$3x + y + z = 12$

6. $p - 6q + 4r = 2$
$2p + 4q - 8r = 16$
$p - 2q = 5$

7. $2a + c = -10$
$b - c = 15$
$a - 2b + c = -5$

8. $x + y + z = 3$
$13x + 2z = 2$
$-x - 5z = -5$

9. $2m + 5n + 2p = 6$
$5m - 7n = -29$
$p = 1$

10. $f + 4g - h = 1$
$3f - g + 8h = 0$
$f + 4g - h = 10$

11. $-2c = -6$
$2a + 3b - c = -2$
$a + 2b + 3c = 9$

12. $3x - 2y + 2z = -2$
$x + 6y - 2z = -2$
$x + 2y = 0$

Example 4

13. **MODELING** The Laredo Sports Shop sold 10 balls, 3 bats, and 2 bases for $99 on Monday. On Tuesday they sold 4 balls, 8 bats, and 2 bases for $78. On Wednesday they sold 2 balls, 3 bats, and 1 base for $33.60. What are the prices of 1 ball, 1 bat, and 1 base?

14. **ENTERTAINMENT** At the arcade, Marcos, Sara, and Tim played video racing games, pinball, and air hockey. Marcos spent $6 for 6 racing games, 2 pinball games, and 1 game of air hockey. Sara spent $12 for 3 racing games, 4 pinball games, and 5 games of air hockey. Tim spent $12.25 for 2 racing games, 7 pinball games, and 4 games of air hockey. How much did each of the games cost?

15. **FOOD** A natural food store makes its own brand of trail mix from dried apples, raisins, and peanuts. A one-pound bag of the trail mix costs $3.18. It contains twice as much peanuts by weight as apples. If a pound of dried apples costs $4.48, a pound of raisins is $2.40, and a pound of peanuts is $3.44, how many ounces of each ingredient are contained in 1 pound of the trail mix?

16. **SIBLINGS** Aniyah, Karen, and Nolan are siblings. Their ages in years can be represented by the variables A, K, and N, respectively. Their combined age is 22 years. Karen is twice as old as Aniyah, and Nolan is 6 years older than Aniyah. Use the equations $A + K + N = 22$, $K = 2A$, and $N = A + 6$ to find the age of each sibling.

17. **NUMBER THEORY** The sum of three numbers is 18. The sum of the first and second numbers is 15, and the first number is 3 times the third number. Find the numbers.

Mixed Exercises

Solve each system of equations.

18. $-x - 5z = -5$

$y - 3x = 0$

$13x + 2z = 2$

19. $-3x + 2z = 1$

$4x + y - 2z = -6$

$x + y + 4z = 3$

20. $x - y + 3z = 3$

$-2x + 2y - 6z = 6$

$y - 5z = -3$

21. FITNESS TRAINING Tiana is training for a triathlon. In her training routine each week, she runs 7 times as far as she swims, and she bikes 3 times as far as she runs. One week she trained a total of 232 miles. How far did Tiana run that week?

22. HOCKEY A hockey player scored G goals, A assists, and P points in his NHL career. By definition, $P = G + A$. He scored 50 more goals than assists. Had he scored 15 more goals and 15 more assists, he would have scored 1200 points. How many goals, assists, and points did this hockey player score?

23. USE A SOURCE A shop is having a sale on pool accessories and offers the following combination deals to entice customers to purchase them. Research the sales tax in your area to determine whether a customer who has $200 could buy 1 chlorine filter, 1 raft, and 1 large lounge chair after sales tax is applied. Justify your response.

Combo	Price Before Tax
1 Raft and 2 Chlorine Filters	$220
1 Chlorine Filter and 2 Large Lounge Chairs	$245
1 Raft and 4 Large Lounge Chairs	$315

24. TICKETS Three kinds of tickets are available for a concert: orchestra seating, mezzanine seating, and balcony seating. The orchestra tickets cost $2 more than the mezzanine tickets, while the mezzanine tickets cost $1 more than the balcony tickets. Twice the cost of an orchestra ticket is $1 less than 3 times the cost of a balcony ticket. Determine the price of each kind of ticket.

25. ARGUMENTS Consider the following system and prove that if $b = c = -a$, then $ty = a$.

$$rx + ty + vz = a$$

$$rx - ty + vz = b$$

$$rx + ty - vz = c$$

26. PERSEVERE The general form of an equation for a parabola is $y = ax^2 + bx + c$, where (x, y) is a point on the parabola. If three points on a parabola are $(2, -10)$, $(-5, -101)$, and $(6, -90)$, determine the values of a, b, and c and write the general form of the equation.

27. CREATE Write a system of three linear equations that has a solution of $(-5, -2, 6)$. Show that the ordered triple satisfies all three equations.

28. WRITE Use your knowledge of solving a system of three linear equations with three variables to explain how to solve a system of four equations with four variables.

Solving Absolute Value Equations and Inequalities by Graphing

Today's Standards
A.CED.1
MP1, MP5

Learn Solving Absolute Value Equations by Graphing

The graph of a related function can be used to solve an absolute value equation. The graph of an absolute value function may intersect the *x*-axis once or twice, or it may not intersect it at all. The number of times the graph intersects the *x*-axis corresponds to the number of solutions of the equation.

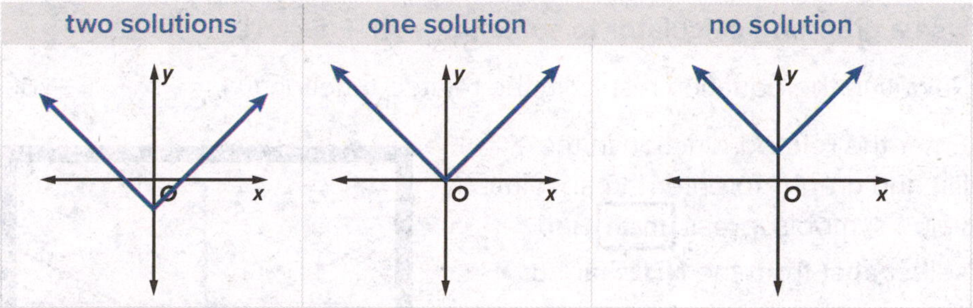

Example 1 Solve an Absolute Value Equation by Graphing

Solve $5 + |2x + 6| = 5$ by graphing.

Step 1 Find the related function.

Rewrite the equation with 0 on the right side.

$5 + \|2x + 6\| = 5$	Original equation
$\|2x + 6\| = 0$	Subtract 5 from each side.

Replacing 0 with $f(x)$ gives the related function $f(x) =$ __________.

Step 2 Graph the related function.

Make a table of values for $f(x) = |2x + 6|$. Then graph the ordered pairs and connect them.

x	$f(x)$
−6	
−5	4
−4	
−3	0
−2	
−1	4
0	

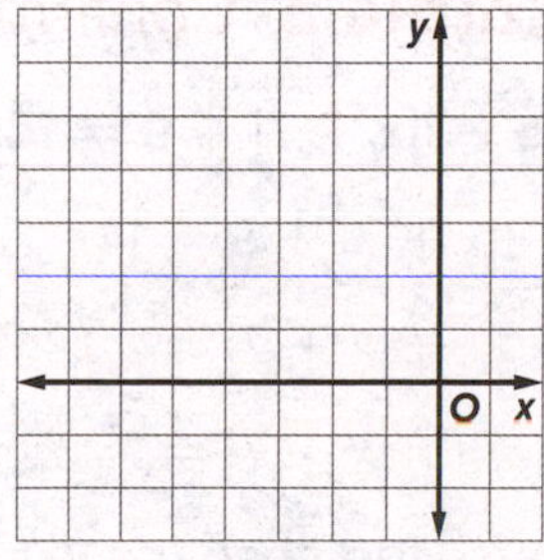

Since the graph of $f(x) = |2x + 6|$ only intersects the *x*-axis at −3, the equation has one solution. The solution set of the equation is {−3}.

Think About It!
How could you use the table of values to find the solutions of the equation?

Go Online You can complete an Extra Example online.

Your Notes

Check

Solve $|x + 1| + 9 = 13$ by graphing.

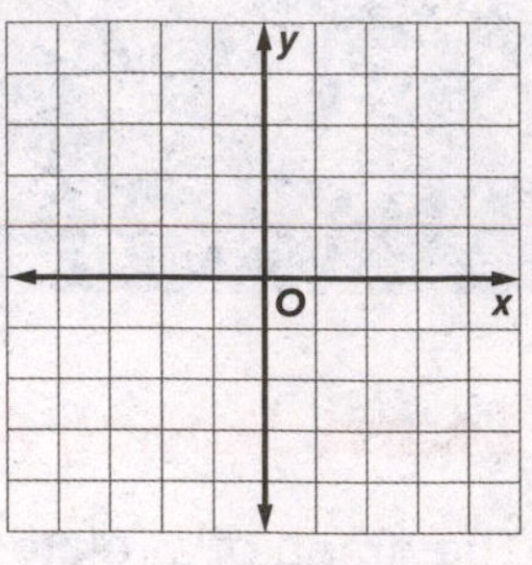

Part A Graph the related function.

Part B What is the solution set of the equation?

____

Example 2 Solve an Absolute Value Equation by Using Technology

Use a graphing calculator to solve $\frac{4}{5}|x - 1| + 8 = 11$.

Rewriting the equation results in the related function $f(x) = \frac{4}{5}|x - 1| - 3$.

Enter the related function in the **Y** = list and graph. To enter the absolute value symbols, press **math** and select **abs(** from the **NUM** menu.

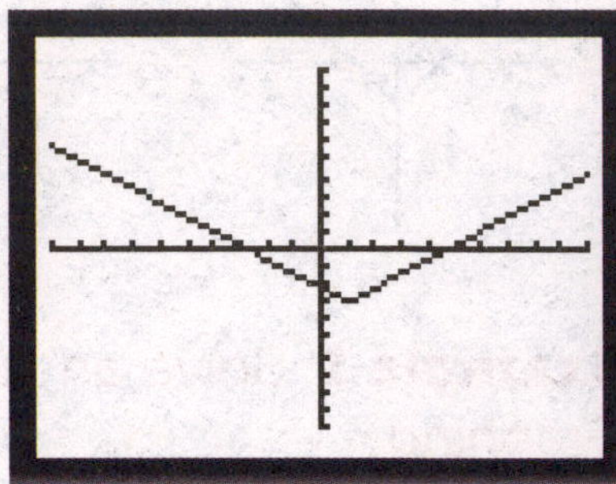

[−10, 10] scl: 1 by [−10, 10] scl: 1

Use the **zero** feature from the **CALC** menu to find the zeros, or *x*-intercepts. When prompted, use the arrow keys to move the cursor to the left and right of each *x*-intercept to select the left and right bounds, and then press **enter** again.

The zeros are located at $x =$ ________ and $x =$ ________. So, the solution set of the equation is {__________}.

Check

Use a graphing calculator to solve $\left|-\frac{2}{3}x + 5\right| - 16 = -10$. _____

Example 3 Confirm Solutions by Using Technology

Solve $-3|x + 7| + 9 = 14$. Check your solutions graphically.

$-3\|x + 7\| + 9 = 14$	Original equation
$-3\|x + 7\| =$ _____	Subtract 9 from each side.
$\|x + 7\| =$ _____	Divide each side by −3.

Because the absolute value of a number is always ________ or zero, this sentence is *never* true. The solution is _____.

 **Go Online** You can complete an Extra Example online.

Step 1 Find and graph the related function.

Rewriting the equation results in the related function $f(x) = -3|x + 7| - $ ______.

Enter the related function in the **Y** = list and graph.

Step 2 Find the zeros.

The graph does not appear to intersect the x-axis. Use the **ZOOM** feature or adjust the window manually to see this more clearly. Since the related function never intersects the x-axis, there are ____________ . This confirms that the equation has no solution.

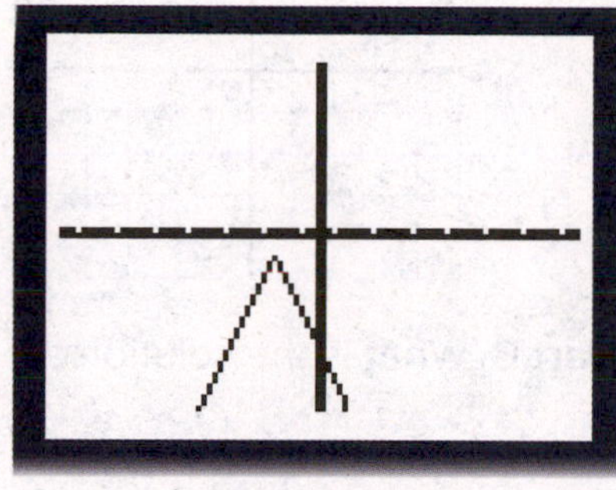

[−40, 40] scl: 1 by [−40, 40] scl: 1

Learn Solving Absolute Value Inequalities by Graphing

The related functions of absolute value inequalities are found by solving the inequality for 0, replacing the inequality symbol with an equals sign, and replacing 0 with $f(x)$.

For $<$ and $\leq$, identify the x-values for which the graph of the related function lies below the x-axis. For $\leq$, include the x-intercepts in the solution. For $>$ and $\geq$, identify the x-values for which the graph of the related function lies *above* the x-axis. For $\geq$, include the x-intercepts in the solution.

Example 4 Solve an Absolute Value Inequality by Graphing

Solve $|3x - 9| - 6 \leq 0$ by graphing.

The solution set consists of x-values for which the graph of the related function lies *below* the x-axis, including the x-intercepts. The related function is $f(x) = |3x - 9| - 6$. Graph $f(x)$ by making a table.

x	$f(x)$
0	
1	4
2	
3	0
4	
5	4
6	

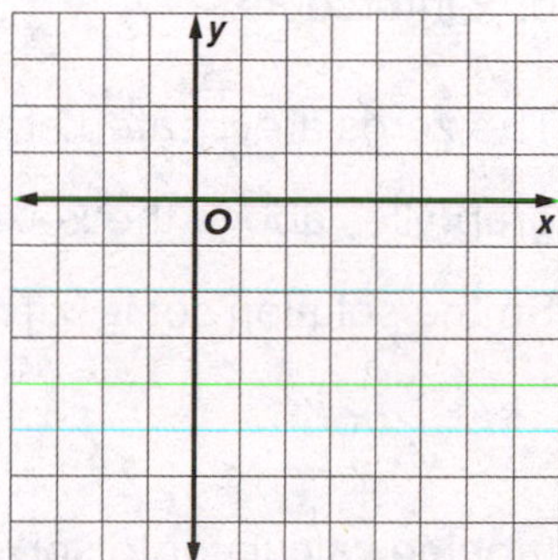

The graph lies below the x-axis between $x =$ _____ and $x =$ _____. Thus, the solution set is $\{x \mid$ _____ $\leq x \leq$ _____$\}$ or [_____, _____]. All values of x between 1 and 5 satisfy the constraints of the original inequality.

Go Online You can complete an Extra Example online.

Think About It!

How could you use a calculator to confirm the solutions of an equation with one or two real solutions?

Talk About It!

Would the solution change if the inequality symbol was changed from $\leq$ to $\geq$? Explain your reasoning.

Check

Solve $|x - 2| - 3 \leq 0$ by graphing.

Part A Graph the related function.

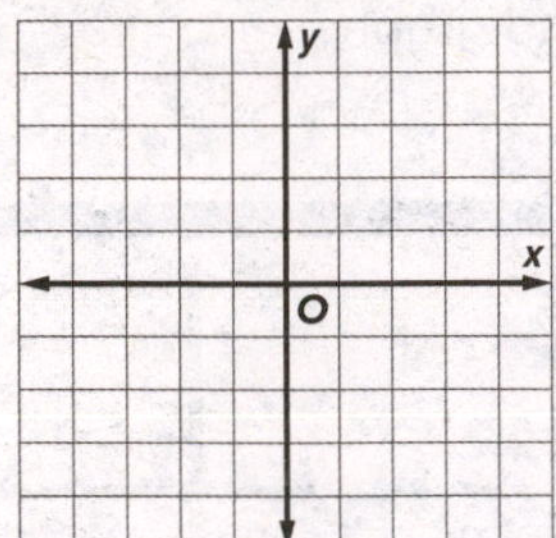

Part B What is the solution set of $|x - 2| - 3 \leq 0$?

____

> **Think About It!**
> The inequality in the example is solved for 0. What additional step(s) would you need to take if the given inequality had a nonzero term on the right side of the inequality symbol?

Example 5 Solve an Absolute Value Equation by Using Technology

Use a graphing calculator to solve $\left|\frac{5}{7}x + 2\right| - 3 > 0$.

Step 1 Graph the related function.

Rewriting the inequality results in the related function $f(x) = \left|\frac{5}{7}x + 2\right| - 3$.

Step 2 Find the zeros.

The $>$ symbol indicates that the solution set consists of x-values for which the graph of the related function lies *above* the x-axis, not including the x-intercepts.

Use the **zero** feature from the **CALC** menu to find the zeros, or x-intercepts.

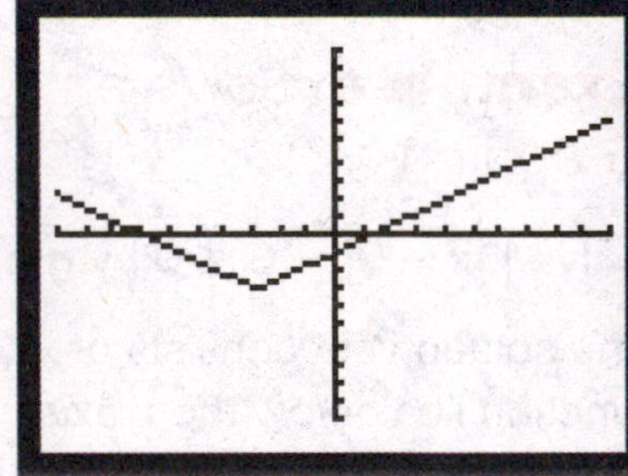

[−10, 10] scl: 1 by [−10, 10] scl: 1

The zeros are located at $x =$ _______ and $x =$ _______. The graph lies above the x-axis when $x <$ _______ and $x >$ _______.

So the solution set is $\{x \mid x <$ _______ _______ $x >$ _______$\}$.

Check

Use a graphing calculator to solve $\frac{1}{2}|4x + 1| - 5 > 0$.

____

Go Online You can complete an Extra Example online.

Name _______________ Period _______ Date _______

Practice

Go Online You can complete your homework online.

Example 1

Solve each equation by graphing.

1. $|x - 4| = 5$
2. $|2x - 3| = 17$
3. $3 + |2x + 1| = 3$
4. $|x - 1| + 6 = 4$
5. $7 + |3x - 1| = 7$
6. $|x + 2| + 5 = 13$

Example 2

USE TOOLS Use a graphing calculator to solve each equation.

7. $\frac{1}{2}|x - 1| + 5 = 9$
8. $\frac{3}{4}|x + 1| + 1 = 7$
9. $\frac{2}{3}|x - 2| - 4 = 4$
10. $2|x + 2| = 10$
11. $\frac{1}{5}|x + 6| - 1 = 9$
12. $3|x + 5| - 1 = 11$

Example 3

Solve each equation algebraically. Use a graphing calculator to check your solutions.

13. $|3x - 6| = 42$
14. $7|x + 3| = 42$
15. $-3|4x - 9| = 24$
16. $-6|5 - 2x| = -9$
17. $5|2x + 3| - 5 = 0$
18. $|15 - 2x| = 45$

Example 4

Solve each inequality by graphing.

19. $|2x - 6| - 4 \leq 0$
20. $|x - 1| - 3 \leq 0$
21. $|2x - 1| \geq 4$
22. $|3x + 2| \geq 6$
23. $2|x + 2| < 8$
24. $3|x - 1| < 12$

Example 5

Use a graphing calculator to solve each inequality.

25. $\left|\frac{1}{4}x + 4\right| - 1 > 0$
26. $\frac{2}{5}|x - 5| + 1 > 0$
27. $|3x - 1| < 2$
28. $|4x + 1| \leq 1$
29. $\frac{1}{6}|x - 1| + 1 \leq 0$
30. $\frac{1}{4}|x + 5| - 1 \leq 1$

Mixed Exercises

Solve by graphing.

31. $0.4|x - 1| = 0.2$

32. $0.16|x + 1| = 4.8$

33. $0.78|2x + 0.1| + 2.3 = 0$

34. $\left|\frac{1}{3}x + 3\right| + 1 = 0$

35. $\frac{1}{2}|6 - 2x| \leq 1$

36. $|3x - 2| < \frac{1}{2}$

STRUCTURE Solve each equation or inequality algebraically. Use a graphing calculator to check your solutions.

37. $\left|\frac{5}{9}x + 1\right| - 5 > 0$

38. $\frac{2}{7}\left|\frac{1}{2}x - 1\right| < 1$

39. $0.28|0.4x - 2| = 10.08$

40. DOG FOOD A pet store sells bags of dog food that are labeled as weighing 50 pounds. The equipment used to package the dog food produces bags with a weight that is within 0.75 lbs of the advertised weight. Write and solve an absolute value equation to determine the maximum and minimum weight for the bags of dog food.

41. SLEEP The recommended ideal sleeping temperature for an adult is 63.5°. Allowing a margin of error of no more than 3.5°, this recommendation is accurate for 98% of the population. Write and solve an absolute value inequality to determine the range of temperatures that are comfortable for 98% of the population.

Write an equation or inequality for each graph.

42.

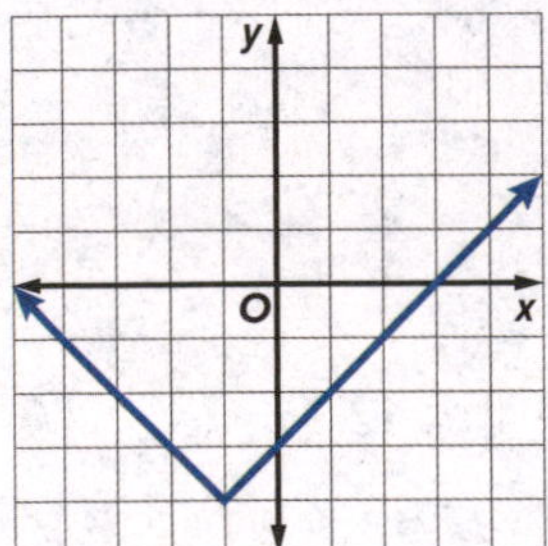

43.

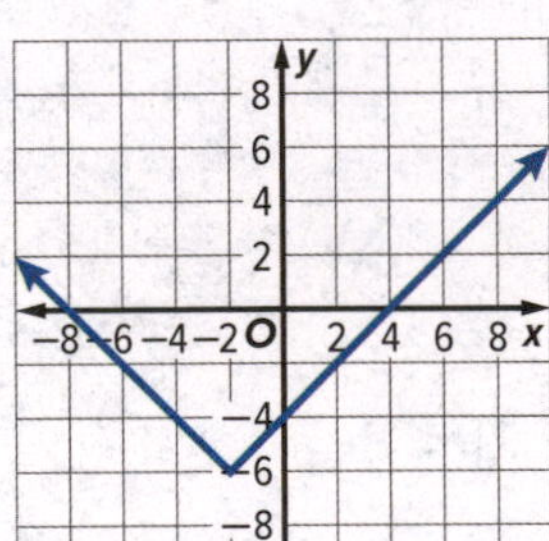

44.

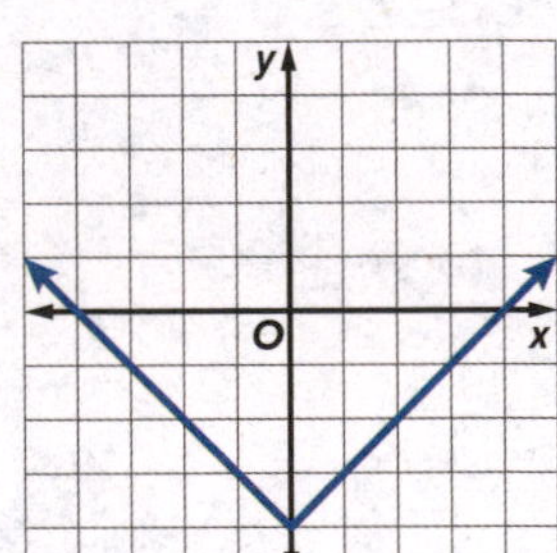

45. WRITE Explain the similarities and differences between solving absolute value equations and absolute values inequalities by graphing.

46. ANALYZE How can you tell that an absolute value equation has no solutions without graphing or completely solving it algebraically?

47. CREATE Create an absolute value equation for which the solution set is {9, 11}.

Review

 Essential Question

How are equations, inequalities, and systems of equations or inequalities best used to model to real-world situations?

Module Summary

Lessons 2-1 and 2-2

Linear and Absolute Value Equations and Inequalities

- The solution of an equation or an inequality is any value that, when substituted into the equation, results in a true statement.
- If both sides of a true inequality are multiplied or divided by a negative number, the direction of the inequality sign must be reversed to make the resulting inequality true.

Lesson 2-3

Equations of Linear Functions

- Standard form: $Ax + By = C$, where A, B, and C are integers with a greatest common factor of 1, $A \geq 0$, and A and B are not both 0
- Slope-intercept form: $y = mx + b$, where m is the slope and b is the y-intercept
- Point-slope form: $y - y_1 = m(x - x_1)$, where m is the slope and (x_1, y_1) are the coordinates of a point on the line

Lessons 2-4 through 2-9

Systems of Equations and Inequalities

- The point of intersection of the two graphs a system of equations represents the solution.
- In the substitution method, one equation is solved for one of the two variables. Then the resulting expression is substituted for that variable in the other equation.
- In the elimination method, the equations are rewritten so that adding or subtracting the equations results in the elimination of one of the variables.
- To solve a system of inequalities, graph each inequality. Then identify the region that is shaded for all of the inequalities.
- Linear programming is a method for finding the maximum or minimum values of a function over a given system of inequalities with each inequality representing a constraint. After the system is graphed and the vertices of the solution set, called the feasible region, are substituted into the function, you can determine the maximum or minimum value.
- Systems of equations in three variables can have one solution, infinite solutions, or no solution. A solution of such a system is an ordered triple (x, y, z).
- For systems with one solution, the ordered triple can be determined through a process of elimination and substitution similar to the process for solving a system of equations in two variables.

Study Organizer

 Foldables

Use your Foldable to review this module. Working with a partner can be helpful. Ask for clarification of concepts as needed.

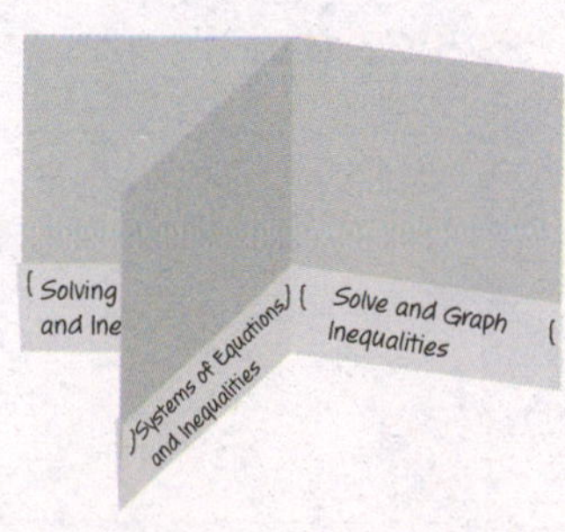

Name ______________________ Period ____________ Date ______________

Test Practice

1. GRIDDED RESPONSE Solve $3(2x + 9) + \frac{1}{2}(4x - 8) = 55$. (Lesson 2-1)

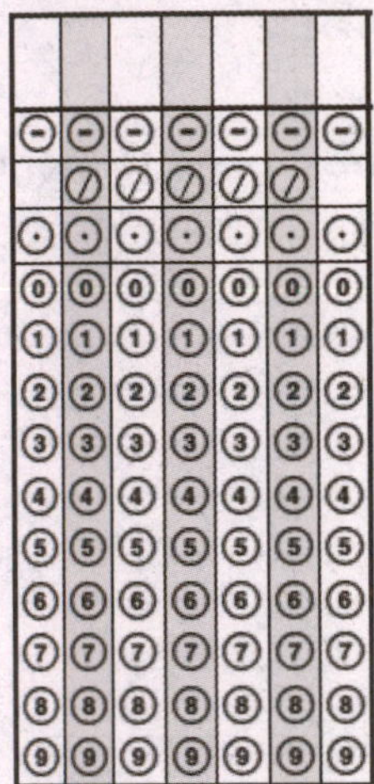

2. MULTIPLE CHOICE Which of the following graphs represents the inequality $2(1 - x) < 4$? (Lesson 2-1)

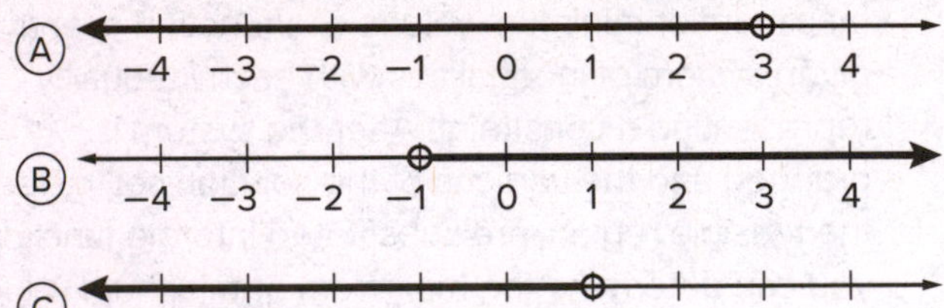

Ⓓ none of the above

3. OPEN RESPONSE The formula for converting temperature between the Fahrenheit and Celsius scales is $C = \frac{5}{9}(F - 32)$, where C is the temperature in degrees Celsius and F is the temperature in degrees Fahrenheit. What Fahrenheit temperature is equivalent to 25°C? (Lesson 2-1)

4. MULTIPLE CHOICE Which equation in standard form is equivalent to $y = -\frac{3}{4}x + 2$? (Lesson 2-2)

Ⓐ $3x + 4y = 8$

Ⓑ $3x - 4y = 8$

Ⓒ $3x + 4y = 2$

Ⓓ $3x - 4y = -2$

5. OPEN RESPONSE Write the equation $5x - 4y = 10$ in slope-intercept form. Write your answer in decimals. (Lesson 2-2)

6. MULTIPLE CHOICE Thomas is driving his truck at a constant speed. The table below gives the distance remaining to his destination y in miles x minutes after he starts driving.

x	15	30	45
y	186.5	173	159.5

Which equation models the distance remaining after any number of minutes? (Lesson 2-2)

Ⓐ $y = \frac{9}{10}x - 200$

Ⓑ $y = -\frac{10}{9}x + 200$

Ⓒ $y = \frac{10}{9}x - 200$

Ⓓ $y = -\frac{9}{10}x + 200$

Name ______________________ Period __________ Date __________

7. MULTIPLE CHOICE Which graph represents the inequality $x - 3y < 4$? (Lesson 2-3)

Ⓐ 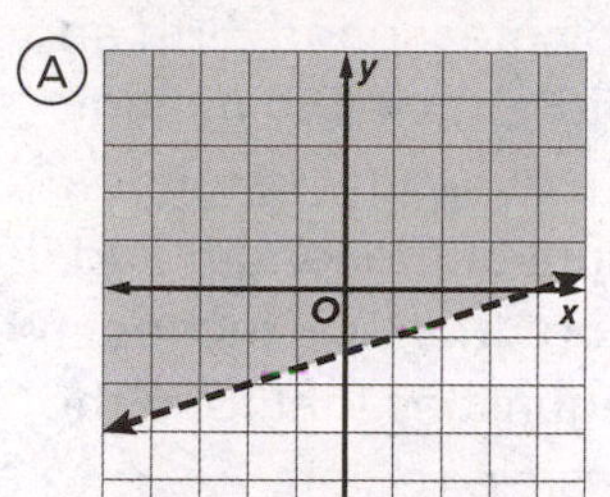

Ⓑ 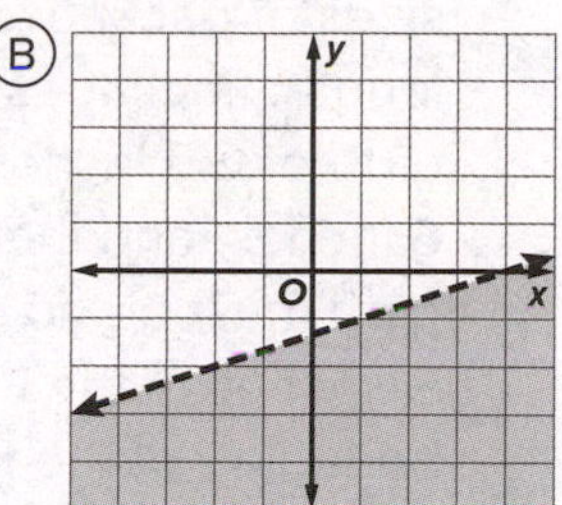

Ⓒ 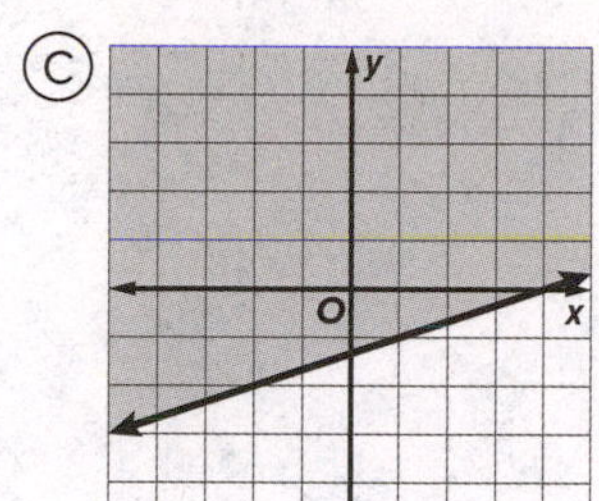

Ⓓ 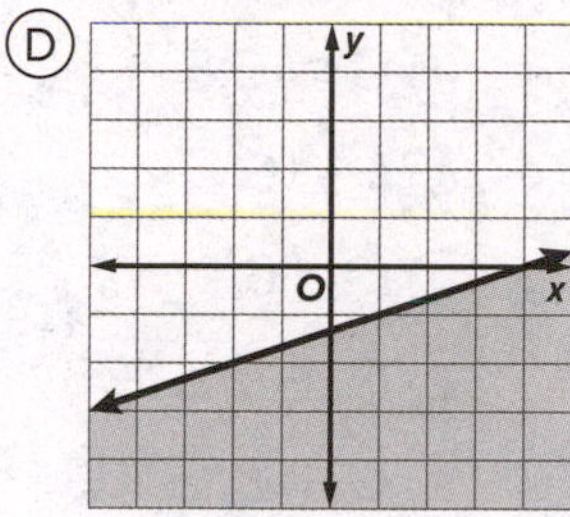

8. OPEN RESPONSE Write an inequality to represent the graph. (Lesson 2-3)

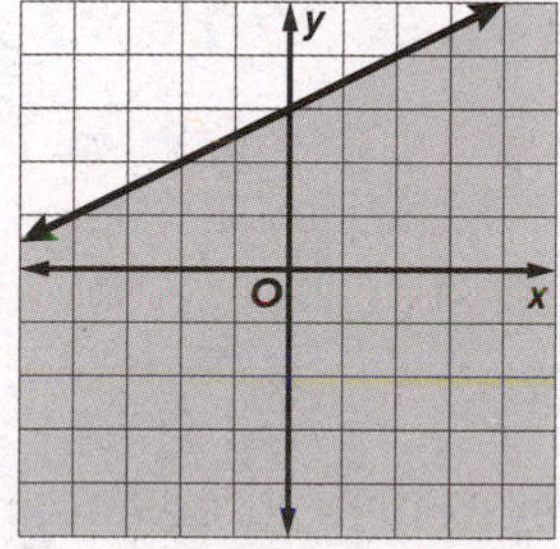

9. OPEN RESPONSE Solve this system of equations.

$5x - 2y = 1$
$2x + 8y = 7$

Round to the nearest hundredth, if necessary. (Lesson 2-4)

10. GRIDDED RESPONSE Solve this system of equations.

$5a - 3b = 7$
$b = 2a - 4$

What is the value of a? (Lesson 2-4)

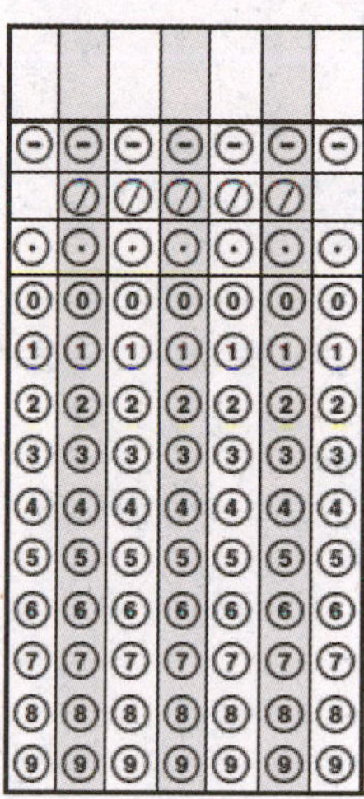

11. MULTIPLE CHOICE Which statement about the system of equations represented by the graph is true? (Lesson 2-4)

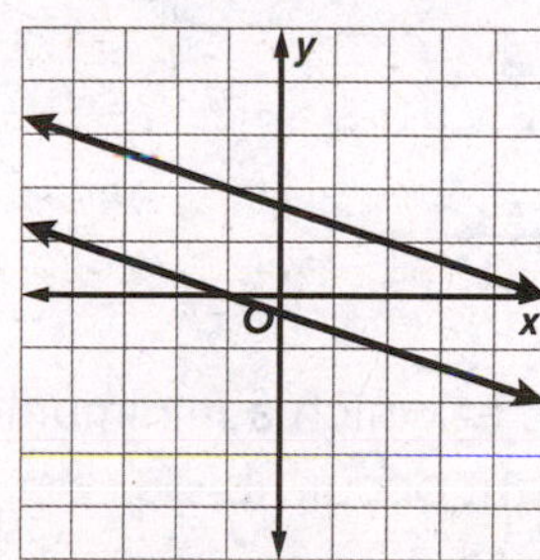

Ⓐ It has no solution, and is consistent and dependent.

Ⓑ It has no solution, and is inconsistent.

Ⓒ It has infinitely many solutions, and is consistent and dependent.

Ⓓ It has infinitely many solutions, and is inconsistent.

12. MULTIPLE CHOICE Which system of inequalities represents the graph shown? (Lesson 2-5)

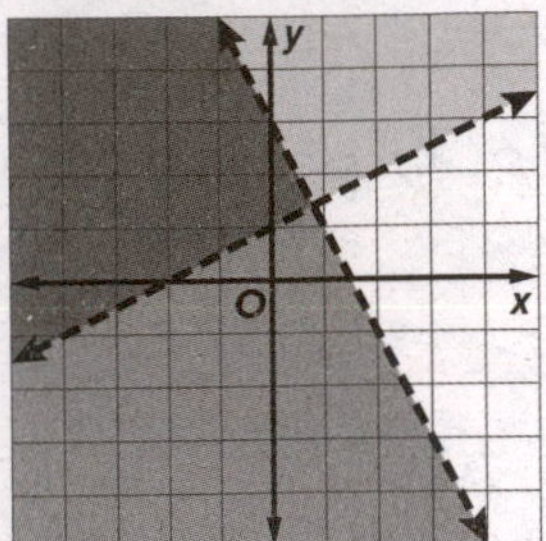

Ⓐ $x - 2y < -2$
$2x + y < 3$

Ⓑ $x - 2y < -2$
$2x + y > 3$

Ⓒ $x - 2y > -2$
$2x + y < 3$

Ⓓ $x - 2y > -2$
$2x + y > 3$

13. MULTI-SELECT The shaded region represents the feasible region for a linear programming problem.

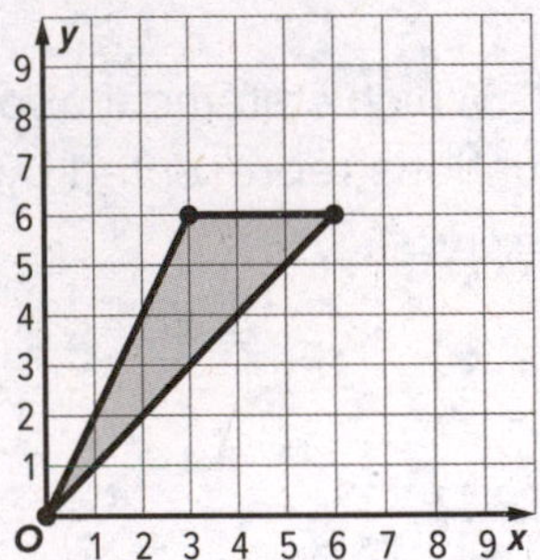

Select all the points at which a minimum or maximum value might occur. (Lesson 2-6)

Ⓐ (0, 0)
Ⓑ (1, 5)
Ⓒ (2, 4)
Ⓓ (3, 6)
Ⓔ (4, 5)
Ⓕ (5, 3)
Ⓖ (6, 6)

14. MULTI-SELECT A shipping company determines the maximum and minimum sizes of packages by measuring girth and length. Packages must have a minimum girth of 6.5 inches, a minimum length of 6 inches, and the sum of the length and the girth must be no more than 108 inches. Select all of the inequalities that form the boundary of the feasible region. (Lesson 2-6)

Ⓐ $G \leq 6.5$
Ⓑ $G \geq 6.5$
Ⓒ $L \leq 6$
Ⓓ $L \geq 6$
Ⓔ $G + L \leq 108$
Ⓕ $G + L \geq 108$

15. OPEN RESPONSE Solve this system of equations. (Lesson 2-7)

$2x + 4y - z = 9$

$-3x + y + z = 14$

$5x + 2y + z = -6$

16. OPEN RESPONSE A system of three linear equations in three variables can be graphed as a system of planes. How many solutions does the system with the graph shown have?. (Lesson 2-7)

Module 3

Quadratic Functions

Essential Question

What characteristics of quadratic functions are important when analyzing real-world situations that are modeled by quadratic functions?

A.SSE.1b; A.CED.1; A.CED.2; A.CED.3; A.REI.11; F.IF.4; F.IF.6; F.IF.8a; N.CN.1; N.CN.2; N.CN.7; N.CN.8
Mathematical Practices: MP1, MP2, MP3, MP4, MP5, MP6, MP7, MP8

What will you learn?

Place a check (✓) in each row that corresponds with how much you already know about each topic **before** starting this module.

KEY

— I don't know. — I've heard of it. — I know it!

	Before			After		
	I don't know	I've heard of it	I know it!	I don't know	I've heard of it	I know it!
find and interpret average rate of change of a quadratic function						
estimate solutions of quadratic equations by graphing						
perform operations with complex numbers						
solve quadratic equations by factoring						
solve quadratic equations by completing the square						
use the discriminant to determine the number and type of roots of a quadratic equation						
solve quadratic inequalities in two variables by graphing						
solve systems of two quadratic equations						
solve systems of nonlinear relations						

Foldables Make this Foldable to help you organize your notes about quadratic functions. Begin with one sheet of 11" by 17" paper.

1. **Fold** in half lengthwise.
2. **Fold** in fifths crosswise.
3. **Cut** along the middle fold from the edge to the last crease as shown.
4. **Refold** along the lengthwise fold and tape the uncut section at the top. Label each section with a lesson number. Close to form a booklet.

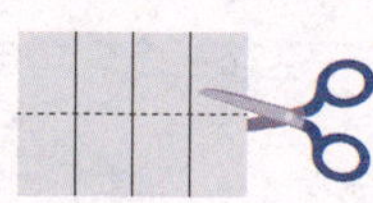

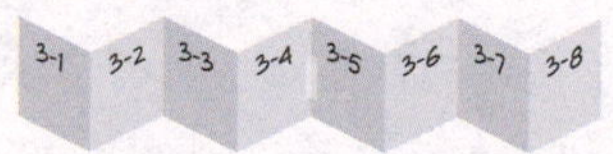

What Vocabulary Will You Learn?

Check the box next to each vocabulary term that you may already know.

- ☐ average rate of change
- ☐ axis of symmetry
- ☐ completing the square
- ☐ complex conjugates
- ☐ complex number
- ☐ difference of squares
- ☐ discriminant
- ☐ factored form
- ☐ imaginary unit *i*
- ☐ maximum
- ☐ minimum
- ☐ perfect square trinomials
- ☐ projectile motion problems
- ☐ pure imaginary number
- ☐ quadratic function
- ☐ quadratic relations
- ☐ rate of change
- ☐ rationalizing the denominator
- ☐ standard form of a quadratic equation
- ☐ vertex
- ☐ vertex form

Are You Ready?

Complete the Quick Review to see if you are ready to start this module. Then complete the Quick Check.

Quick Review

Example 1

Given $f(x) = -2x^2 + 3x - 1$ and $g(x) = 3x^2 - 5$, find each value.

a. $f(2)$

$f(x) = -2x^2 + 3x - 1.$	Original function
$f(2) = -2(2)^2 + 3(2) - 1$	Substitute 2 for *x*.
$= -8 + 6 - 1$ or -3	Simplify.

b. $g(-2)$

$g(x) = 3x^2 - 5.$	Original function
$g(-2) = 3(-2)^2 - 5$	Substitute −2 for *x*.
$= 12 - 5$ or 7	Simplify.

Example 2

Factor $2x^2 - x - 3$ completely. If the polynomial is not factorable, write *prime*.

To find the coefficients of the *x*-terms, you must find two numbers whose product is $2(-3)$ or -6, and whose sum is -1. The two coefficients must be 2 and -3 since $2(-3) = -6$ and $2 + (-3) = -1$. Rewrite the expression and factor by grouping.

$2x^2 - x - 3$	
$= 2x^2 + 2x - 3x - 3$	Substitute $2x - 3x$ for $-x$.
$= (2x^2 + 2x) + (-3x - 3)$	Associative Property
$= 2x(x + 1) + -3(x + 1)$	Factor out the GCF.
$= (2x - 3)(x + 1)$	Distributive Property

Quick Check

Given $f(x) = 2x^2 + 4$ and $g(x) = -x^2 - 2x + 3$, find each value.

1. $f(3)$

2. $f(0)$

3. $g(4)$

4. $g(-3)$

Factor completely. If the polynomial is not factorable, write *prime*.

5. $x^2 - 10x + 21$

6. $2x^2 + 7x - 4$

7. $2x^2 - 7x - 15$

8. $x^2 - 11x + 15$

How Did You Do?

Which exercises did you answer correctly in the Quick Check? Shade those exercise numbers below.

1 2 3 4 5 6 7 8

Graphing Quadratic Functions

Explore Transforming Quadratic Functions

Online Activity Use graphing technology to complete the Explore.

INQUIRY How does changing the values of a, b, and c in a quadratic function affect the shape of the graph?

Learn Graphing Quadratic Functions

A **quadratic function** has a graph that is a parabola. The general form of a quadratic function is shown.

$$f(x) = ax^2 + bx + c, \text{ where } a \neq 0$$

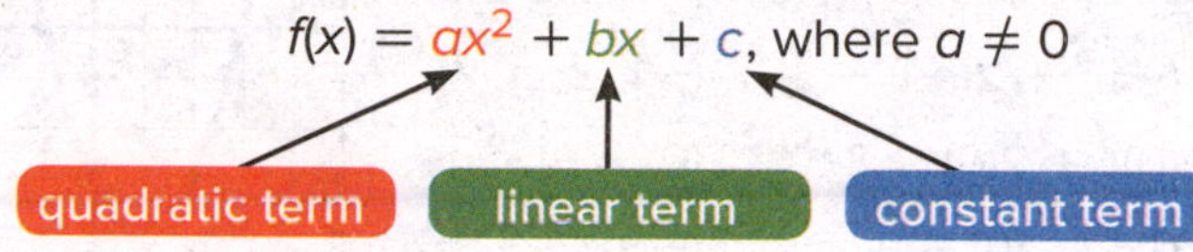

Key Concept • Graph of a Quadratic Function

Consider the graph of $y = ax^2 + bx + c$, where $a \neq 0$.

The y-intercept is $y = a(0)^2 + b(0) + c$ or c.

The equation of the axis of symmetry is $x = -\frac{b}{2a}$.

The x-coordinate of the vertex is $-\frac{b}{2a}$.

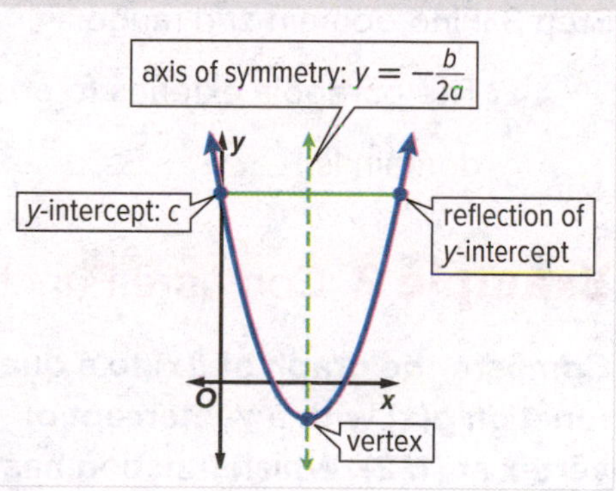

Key Concept • Maximum or Minimum Values of Quadratic Graphs

The graph of $y = ax^2 + bx + c$, where $a \neq 0$, opens up and has a minimum value when $a > 0$, and opens down and has a maximum value when $a < 0$.

a is positive.

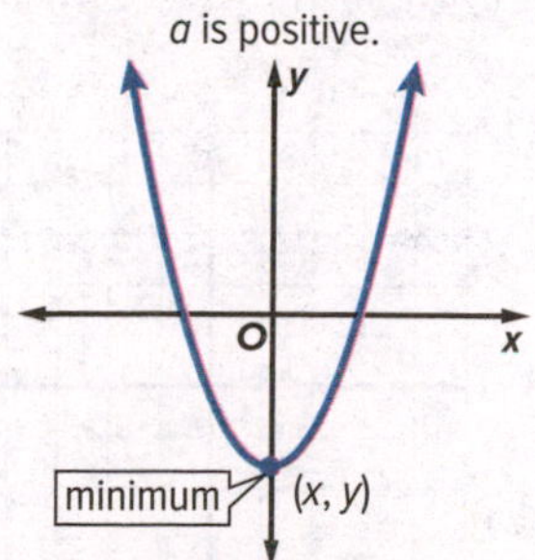

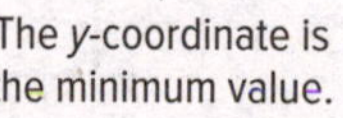

The y-coordinate is the minimum value.

a is negative.

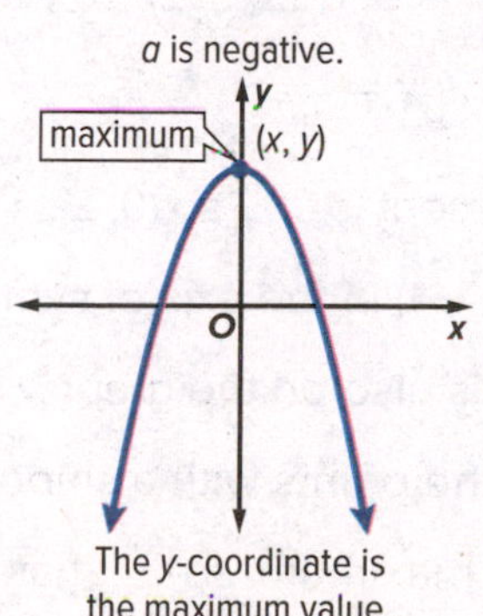

The y-coordinate is the maximum value.

Today's Standards
F.IF.4, F.IF.6
MP1, MP2

Today's Vocabulary
quadratic function
axis of symmetry
vertex
maximum
minimum
rate of change
average rate of change

Think About It!
Why is it important to know whether the vertex is a maximum or minimum when graphing a quadratic function?

Watch Out!

Maxima and Minima Just because a vertex is a maximum does not mean it will be located above the x-axis, and just because a vertex is a minimum does not mean it will be located below the x-axis.

Your Notes

Go Online You can watch videos to see how to graph quadratic functions by using a table or its key features.

Think About It!

If you know that $f(-4) = 5$, find $f(2)$ without substituting 2 for x in the function. Justify your argument.

Think About It!

Compare the end behavior of $f(x)$ and $g(x)$.

Example 1 Graph Quadratic Functions by Using a Table

Graph $f(x) = x^2 + 2x - 3$. State the domain and range.

Step 1 Analyze the function.

For $f(x) = x^2 + 2x - 3$. $a =$ ____, $b =$ ____, and $c =$ ____.

c is the y-intercept, so the y-intercept is ____.

Find the axis of symmetry.

$x = -\frac{b}{2a}$ Equation of the axis of symmetry

$= -\frac{\quad}{2(\ )}$ $a = 1, b = 2$

$=$ ____ Simplify.

The equation of the axis of symmetry is $x = -1$, so the x-coordinate of the vertex is ____. Because $a > 0$, the vertex is a ______.

Step 2 Graph the function.

x	$x^2 + 2x - 3$	$(x, f(x))$
-3	$(-3)^2 + 2(-3) - 3$	$(-3,$ ____$)$
-2	$(-2)^2 + 2(-2) - 3$	$(-2,$ ____$)$
-1	$(-1)^2 + 2(-1) - 3$	$(-1,$ ____$)$
0	$(0)^2 + 2(0) - 3$	$(0,$ ____$)$
1	$(1)^2 + 2(1) - 3$	$(-3,$ ____$)$

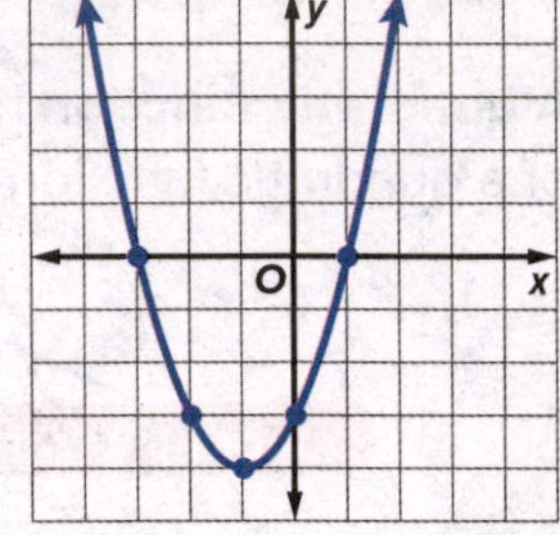

Step 3 Find domain and range.

The parabola extends to positive and negative infinity, so the domain is ________. The range is $\{y \mid y \geq$ ____$\}$.

Example 2 Compare Functions

Compare the graph of $f(x)$ to a quadratic function $g(x)$ with a y-intercept of -1 and a vertex at (1, 2). Which function has a greater maximum?

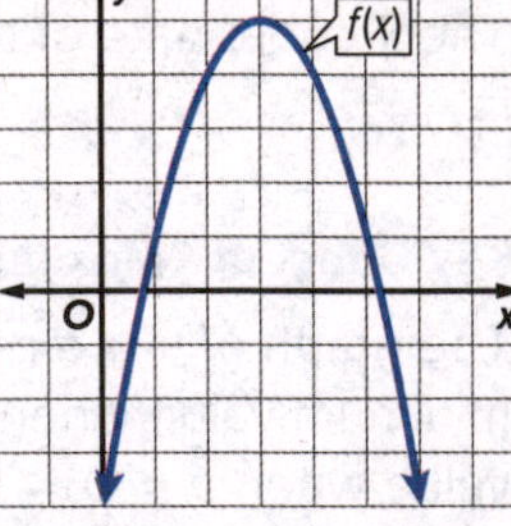

From the graph, $f(x)$ appears to have a maximum of 5. Graph $g(x)$ using the given information.

The vertex is at (____, ____), so the axis of symmetry is $x =$ ____.

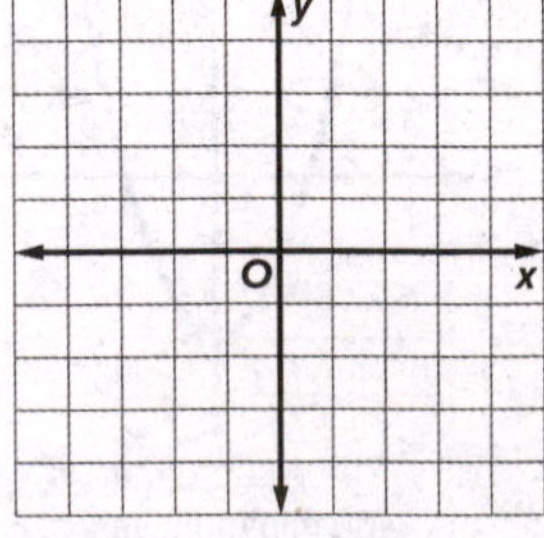

The y-intercept is ____, so (0, ____) is on the graph.

Reflect $(0, -1)$ in the axis of symmetry. So, (____, ____) is also on the graph.

Connect the points with a smooth curve.

____ is the maximum, so ____ has the greater maximum.

Example 3 Use Quadratic Functions

SKIING A ski resort has extended hours on one holiday weekend per year. Last year, the resort sold 680 ski passes at $120 per holiday weekend pass. This year, the resort is considering a price increase. They estimate that for each $5 increase, they will sell 20 fewer holiday weekend passes.

Part A How much should they charge in order to maximize profit?

Step 1 Define the variables.

Let x represent the number of price increases, and let $P(x)$ represent the total amount of money generated. $P(x)$ is equal to the price of each pass (120 + ____) times the total number of passes sold (____ − 20x).

Step 2 Write an equation.

$P(x) = (120 + 5x)(680 - 20x)$ Original equation

$= \_\_\_\_ - 24000x + \_\_\_\_x - 100x^2$ Multiply.

$= -100x^2 + \_\_\_\_x + 81{,}600$ Simplify.

Step 3 Find the axis of symmetry.

$x = -\frac{b}{2a}$ Formula for the axis of symmetry

$= -\frac{\_\_\_\_}{2(\_\_\_\_)}$ $a = 1000, b = -100$

$= \_\_\_\_$ Simplify.

Step 4 Interpret the results.

The ski resort will make the most money with ___ price increases, so they should charge 120 + 5(___) or $____ for each holiday weekend pass.

Part B Find the domain and range in the context of the situation.

The domain is $\{x \mid x \geq \_\_\}$ because the number of price increases cannot be negative. The range is $\{y \mid \_\_ \leq y \leq \_\_\_\_\}$ because the amount of money generated cannot be negative, and the maximum amount of money generated is $P(5) = -100(5)^2 + 1000(5) + 81{,}600$ or ____.

Check

CONCERTS Last year, a ticket provider sold 1350 lawn seats for a concert at $70 per ticket. This year, the store is considering increasing the price. They estimate that for each $2 increase, they will sell 30 fewer tickets.

Part A How much should the ticket provider charge in order to maximize profit? $____

Part B Find the domain and range in the context of the situation.

D = ________ R = ____________

Go Online You can complete an Extra Example online.

Think About It!

Why is the maximum amount of money generated from holiday weekend passes $P(5)$?

Study Tip:

Assumptions You assumed that the ski resort has the ability to increase the price indefinitely and that every price increase of will be $5 and will cause the resort to lose sales from exactly 20 holiday weekend passes.

Learn Finding and Interpreting Average Rate of Change

A function's **rate of change** is how a quantity is changing with respect to a change in another quantity. For nonlinear functions, the rate of change is not the same over the entire function. You can calculate the **average rate of change** of a nonlinear function over an interval.

Key Concept • Average Rate of Change

The average rate of change of a function $f(x)$ is equal to the change in the value of the dependent variable $f(b) - f(a)$ divided by the change in the value of the independent variable $b - a$ over the interval $[b, a]$.

$$\frac{f(b) - f(a)}{b - a}$$

Think About It!

Find the average rate of change of the function over the interval $[-3, 1]$. Compare it to your results from the interval $[-4, 4]$.

Example 4 Find Average Rate of Change from an Equation

Determine the average rate of change of $f(x) = -x^2 + 2x - 1$ over the interval $[-4, 4]$.

The average rate of change is equal to $\frac{f(4) - f(-4)}{4 - (-4)}$.

First find $f(-4)$ and $f(4)$.

$f(4) = -(4)^2 + 2(4) - 1$ or ____

$f(-4) = -(-4)^2 + 2(-4) - 1$ or ____

$\frac{f(4) - f(-4)}{4 - (-4)} = \frac{-9 - (-25)}{4 - (-4)} =$ ____

The average rate of change of the function over the interval $[-4, 4]$ is ____.

Talk About It!

Without graphing, how can you tell that this function is nonlinear? Justify your argument.

Check

Find the average rate of change of $f(x) = -2x^2 - 5x + 7$ over the interval $[-5, 5]$.

average rate of change = ____

Example 5 Find Average Rate of Change from a Table

Determine the average rate of change of $f(x)$ over the interval $[-3, 3]$.

x	$f(x)$
−3	48
−2	21
−1	0
0	−15
1	−24
2	−27
3	−24

The average rate of change is equal to $\frac{f(3) - f(-3)}{3 - (-3)}$.

First find $f(3)$ and $f(-3)$ from the table.

$f(3) =$ ____ $f(-3) =$ ____

$\frac{f(3) - f(-3)}{3 - (-3)} = \frac{-24 - 48}{3 - (-3)} =$ ____

The average rate of change of the function over the interval $[-3, 3]$ is ____.

 **Go Online** You can complete an Extra Example online.

Check

TESTING The table shows the number of students who took the ACT between 2011 and 2015.

Year	Number of Students
2011	1,623,112
2012	1,666,017
2013	1,799,243
2014	1,845,787
2015	1,924,436

Part A

Find the average rate of change in the number of students taking the ACT from 2011 to 2015.

average rate of change = ______

Part B

Interpret your results in the context of the situation.

From 2011 to _____, the number of students taking the ACT

__________ by an average of ______ students per year.

Example 6 Find Average Rate of Change from a Graph

FOOTWEAR **The graph shows the amount of money the United States has spent on sports footwear since 2005.**

Part A

Use the graph to estimate the average rate of change of spending on sports footwear from 2005 to 2015. Then check your results algebraically.

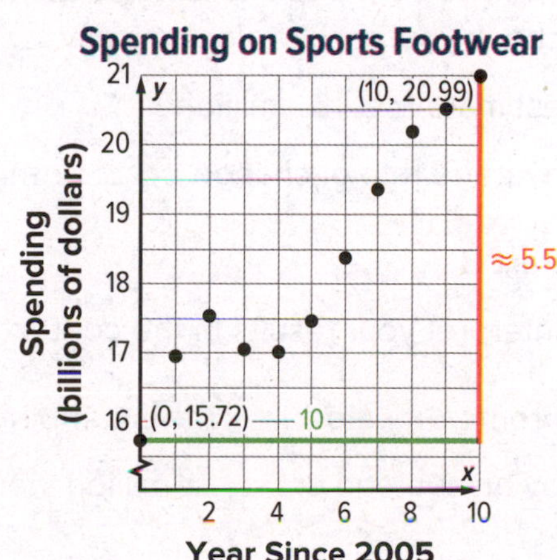

Estimate

From the graph, the change in the y-values is approximately 5.5, and the change in the x-values is ____.

So, the rate of change is approximately $\frac{5.5}{10}$ or _____.

(*continued on the next page*)

Use a Source

Research the sales of another industry over a ten year period. Then find the average rate of change during that time.

Algebraically

The average rate of change is equation to $\frac{f(10) - f(0)}{10 - 0}$.

$\frac{f(10) - f(0)}{10 - 0} = \frac{\_\_\_\_ - \_\_\_\_}{10 - 0}$ or _____.

Part B

Interpret your results in the context of the situation.

From _____ to 2015, the amount of money spent on sports footwear in the United States _______ by an average of _________ per year.

Check

SUPER BOWL The graph shows the number of television viewers of the Super Bowl since 2006.

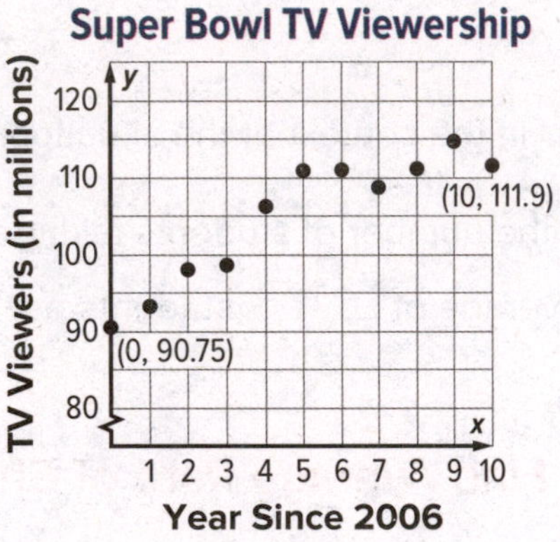

Super Bowl TV Viewership

Part A

Use the graph to estimate the average rate of change in Super Bowl viewers from 2006 to 2016 to the nearest hundredth of a million. Then check your results algebraically.

estimate = _____ million

average rate of change = _____ million

Part B

Interpret your results in the context of the situation.

From _____ to _____, the number of Super Bowl viewers ________ by an average of _____ million viewers per year.

Go Online You can complete an Extra Example online.

Name ______________________ Period ________ Date ________

Practice

Go Online You can complete your homework online.

Example 1

Graph each function. Then state the domain and range.

1. $f(x) = x^2 + 6x + 8$

2. $f(x) = -x^2 - 2x + 2$

3. $f(x) = 2x^2 - 4x + 3$

4. $f(x) = 2x^2$

5. $f(x) = x^2 - 4x + 4$

6. $f(x) = x^2 - 6x + 8$

Example 2

7. Compare the graph of $f(x)$ to a quadratic function $g(x)$ with a y-intercept of 1 and a vertex at (1, 3). Which function has a greater maximum? Explain.

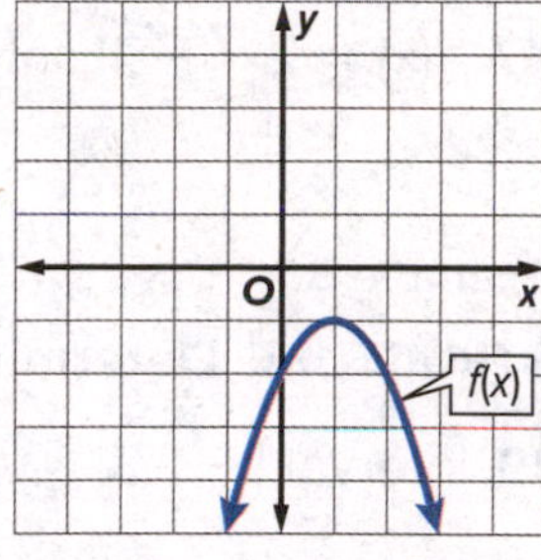

8. Compare the graph of $f(x)$ to a quadratic function $g(x)$ with a y-intercept of 0.5 and a vertex at (−1, −5). Which function has a lesser minimum? Explain.

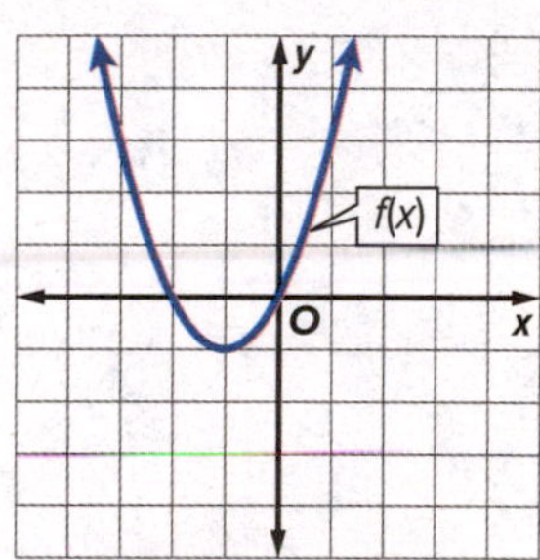

9. Compare $f(x) = x^2 - 10x + 5$ to the quadratic function $g(x)$ shown in the table. Which function has the lesser minimum? Explain.

x	$g(x)$
−10	170
−5	70
0	10
5	−10
10	10

10. Compare $f(x) = -x^2 + 6x - 15$ to the quadratic function $g(x)$ shown in the table. Which function has the greater maximum? Explain.

x	$g(x)$
−6	−26
−3	−11
0	−2
3	1
6	−2

Example 3

11. **FISHING** A county park sells annual permits to its fishing lake. Last year, the county sold 480 fishing permits at \$80. This year, the park is considering a price increase. They estimate that for each \$4 increase, they will sell 16 fewer annual fishing permits.

a. How much would the park have to charge in order to maximize its profits?

b. Find the domain and range in the context of this situation.

12. **SALES** Last month, a candle retailer sold 120 jar candles at $30 per candle. This month the retailer is considering putting the candles on sale. They estimate that for each $2 decrease in price, they will sell 10 additional candles.

a. How much should the retailer charge in order to maximize its profit?

b. Find the domain and the range in the context of this situation.

Example 4

REGULARITY Determine the average rate of change of $f(x)$ over the specified interval.

13. $f(x) = x^2 - 10x + 5$; interval $[-4, 4]$

14. $f(x) = 2x^2 + 4x - 6$; interval $[-3, 3]$

15. $f(x) = 3x^2 - 3x + 1$; interval $[-5, 5]$

16. $f(x) = 4x^2 + x + 3$; interval $[-2, 2]$

17. $f(x) = 2x^2 - 11$; interval $[-3, 3]$

18. $f(x) = -2x^2 + 8x + 7$; interval $[-4, 4]$

Example 5

STRUCTURE Determine the average rate of change of $f(x)$ over the specified interval.

19. interval $[-3, 3]$

x	f(x)
−3	0
−2	3
−1	−4
0	−3
1	0
2	5
3	12

20. interval $[-4, 4]$

x	f(x)
−4	−27
−2	−3
0	5
2	−3
4	−27

21. interval $[-2, 2]$

x	f(x)
−2	−3
−1	−3
0	−1
1	3
2	9

22. interval $[-5, 5]$

x	f(x)
−5	−39
−3	−15
−1	1
0	6
1	9
3	9
5	1

23. interval $[-3, 3]$

x	f(x)
−3	27
−2	12
−1	3
0	0
1	3
2	12
3	27

24. interval $[-2, 2]$

x	f(x)
−2	12
−1	5
0	0
1	−3
2	−4

Example 6

25. **FOOD** The graph shows the number of people in the U.S. who consumed between 8 and 11 bags of potato chips in a year since 2011.

a. Use the graph to estimate the average rate of change of consumption from 2011 to 2016. Then check your results algebraically.

b. Interpret your results in the context of the situation.

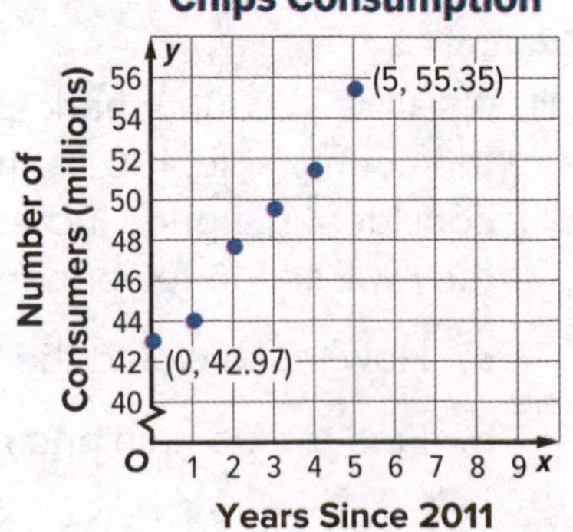

Name ______________________ Period ____________ Date ____________

26. **EARNINGS** The graph shows the amount of money Sheila earned each year since 2008.

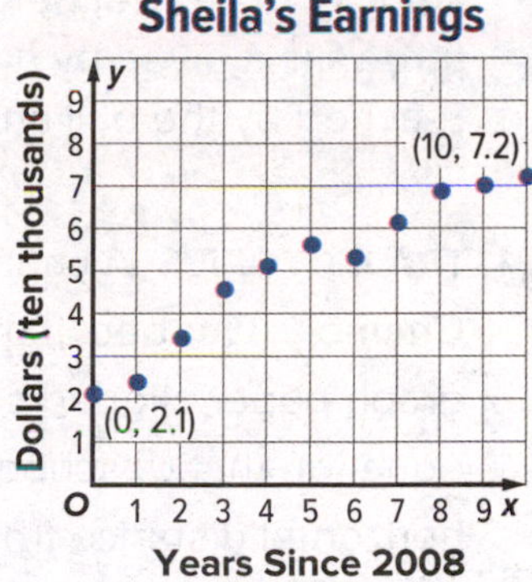

Part A Use the graph to estimate the average rate of change of Sheila's earnings from 2005 to 2015. Then check your results algebraically.

Part B Interpret your results in the context of the situation.

Mixed Exercises

Complete parts a-c for each quadratic function.

a. Find the y-intercept, the equation of the axis of symmetry, and the x-coordinate of the vertex.

b. Make a table of values that includes the vertex.

c. Use this information to graph the function.

27. $f(x) = 2x^2 - 6x - 9$

28. $f(x) = -3x^2 - 9x + 2$

29. $f(x) = -4x^2 + 5x$

30. $f(x) = 2x^2 + 11x$

31. $f(x) = 0.25x^2 + 3x + 4$

32. $f(x) = -0.75x^2 + 4x + 6$

33. Graph $f(x) = \begin{cases} -0.5x + 3 & \text{if } x < -4 \\ 0.5x^2 + 2x + 5 & \text{if } x \geq -4 \end{cases}$. Identify the domain and range.

USE TOOLS Use a calculator to find the maximum or minimum of each function. Round to the nearest hundredth, if necessary.

34. $f(x) = -9x^2 - 12x + 19$

35. $f(x) = 12x^2 - 21x + 8$

36. $f(x) = -8.3x^2 + 14x - 6$

37. $f(x) = 9.7x^2 - 13x - 9$

38. $f(x) = 28x - 15 - 18x^2$

39. $f(x) = -16 - 14x - 12x^2$

40. **HEALTH CLUBS** Last year, the Sports Time Athletic Club charged $20 to participate in an aerobics class. Seventy people attended the classes. The club wants to increase the class price this year. They expect to lose one customer for each $1 increase in the price.

a. What price should the club charge to maximize the income from the aerobics classes?

b. What is the maximum income the Sports Time Athletic Club can expect to make?

41. **TICKETS** The manager of a symphony estimates that the symphony will earn $-40P^2 + 1100P$ dollars per concert if they charge P dollars for tickets. What ticket price should the symphony charge in order to maximize its profits?

42. **REASONING** On Friday nights, the local cinema typically sells 200 tickets at $6.00 each. The manager estimates that for each $0.50 increase in the ticket price, 10 fewer people will go to the cinema.

a. Write and graph a function to represent the expected revenue, and determine the domain of the function for the situation.

b. What price should the manager set for a ticket in order to maximize the revenue? Justify your reasoning.

c. Explain why the graph decreases from $x = 4$ to $x = 20$, and interpret the meaning of the x-intercept of the graph.

43. MODELING From 4 feet above a swimming pool, Sofia throws a ball upward with a velocity of 32 feet per second. The height $h(t)$ of the ball t seconds after Sofia throws it is given by $h(t) = -16t^2 + 32t + 4$. For $t \geq 0$, find the maximum height reached by the ball and the time that this height is reached.

44. TRAJECTORIES A cannonball is launched from a cannon on the wall of Fort Chambly, Quebec. If the path of the cannonball is traced on a piece of graph paper aligned so that the cannon is situated on the y-axis, the equation that describes the path is $y = -\frac{1}{1600}x^2 + \frac{1}{2}x + 20$, where x is the horizontal distance from the cliff and y is the vertical distance above the ground in feet. How high above the ground is the cannon?

45. ARGUMENTS Which function has a greater maximum: $f(x) = -2x^2 + 6x - 7$ or the function shown in the graph at the right? Explain your reasoning using a graph.

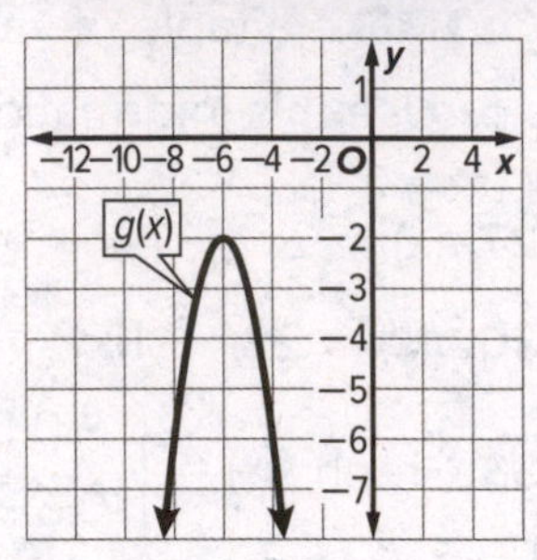

46. FIND THE ERROR Clara thinks that the function $f(x)$ graphed at the right, and the function $g(x)$ described below the graph the same maximum. Madison thinks that $g(x)$ has a greater maximum. Is either of them correct? Explain your reasoning.

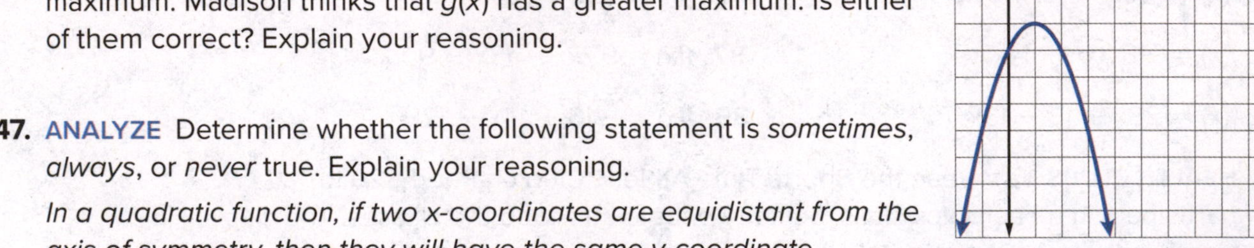

$g(x)$ is a quadratic function with roots of 4 and 2 and a y-intercept of −8.

47. ANALYZE Determine whether the following statement is *sometimes*, *always*, or *never* true. Explain your reasoning.

In a quadratic function, if two x-coordinates are equidistant from the axis of symmetry, then they will have the same y-coordinate.

48. PERSEVERE The table at the right represents some points on the graph of a quadratic function.

a. Find the values of a, b, c, and d.

b. What is the x-coordinate of the vertex of the function?

c. Does the function have a maximum or a minimum?

x	y
−20	−377
c	−13
−5	−2
−1	22
$d - 1$	a
5	$a - 24$
7	$-b$
15	−202
$14 - c$	−377

49. WRITE Describe how you determine whether a function is quadratic and if it has a maximum or minimum value?

50. CREATE Give an example of a quadratic function with a

a. maximum of 8

b. minimum of −4

c. vertex of (−2, 6)

Solving Quadratic Equations by Graphing

Explore Roots of Quadratic Equations

Online Activity Use graphing technology to complete the Explore.

INQUIRY How can you use the graph of a quadratic function to find the solutions of its related equation?

Learn Solving Quadratic Equations by Graphing

A **quadratic equation** is an equation that includes a quadratic expression.

Key Concept • Standard Form of a Quadratic Equation

The **standard form of a quadratic equation** is $ax^2 + bx + c = 0$, where $a \neq 0$ and a, b, and c are integers.

One method for finding the roots of a quadratic equation is to find the zeros of a related quadratic function. You can identify the solutions or roots of an equation by finding the x-intercepts of the graph of a related function. Often, exact roots cannot be found be graphing. You can estimate the solutions by finding the integers between where the zeros are located on the graph of the related function.

Example 1 One Real Solution

Solve $10 - x^2 = 4x + 14$ by graphing.

Solve the equation for 0. $0 = x^2 +$ ___ $x +$ ___

Find the axis of symmetry. $x = -\frac{b}{2a} = -\frac{\quad}{2(\;)} =$ ___

Make a table of values, plot the points, and connect them with a curve.

x	y
−4	___
−3	___
−2	___
−1	___
0	___

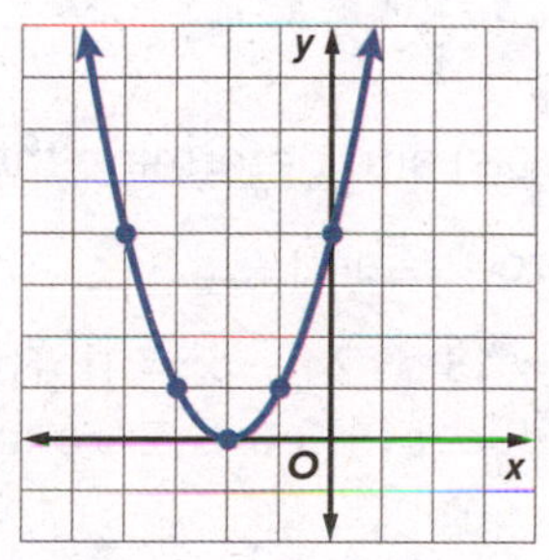

The zero of the function is ___.
Therefore, the solution of the equation is ___ or $\{x \mid x =$ ___$\}$.

Check

Solve $x^2 + 7x = 31x - 144$ by graphing. $x =$ ___

Today's Standards
A.CED.2, F.IF.4
MP4, MP5

Today's Vocabulary
quadratic equation
standard form of a quadratic equation

Think About It!
How can you determine the number of solutions of a quadratic equation?

Study Tip:
Solutions of Quadratic Equations A quadratic equation can have one real solution, two real solutions, or no real solutions.

Think About It!
How can you find the solution of the equation from the table?

Your Notes

Example 2 Two Real Solutions

NUMBER THEORY Use a quadratic equation to find two real numbers with a sum of 24 and a product of 119.

UNDERSTAND What do you know?

Let x represent one of the numbers. Then ____ $- x$ will represent the other number. So $x(24 - x) =$ ____.

What do you need to find?
x and $24 - x$

PLAN AND SOLVE

Step 1 Solve the equation for 0.

$x(24 - x) = 143$ Original equation

$24x - x^2 = 143$ Distributive Property

$0 = x^2 - 24x + 143$ Subtract $24x - x^2$ from each side.

Step 2 Find the axis of symmetry.

$x = -\frac{b}{2a}$ Equation of the axis of symmetry

$x = -\frac{\quad}{2(\quad)}$ $a = 1, b = -24$

$x =$ ____ Simplify.

Step 3 Make a table of values and graph the function.

x	y
14	
13	
12	
11	
10	

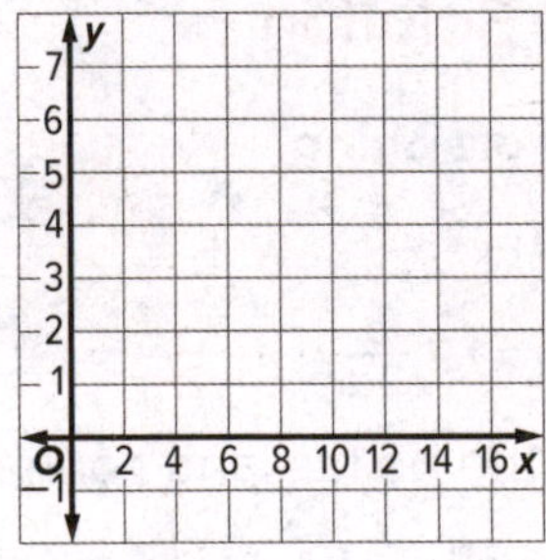

Steps 4 and 5 Find the zero(s) and determine the solution.

The zeros of the function are ____ and ____.

$x = 11$ or $x = 13$, so $24 - x = 13$ or $24 - x = 11$. Thus, the two numbers with a sum of 24 and a product of 119 are ____ and ____.

Check

NUMBER THEORY Use a quadratic equation to find two real numbers with a sum of -43 and a product of 306. ____ and ____

Go Online You can complete an Extra Example online.

Go Online You can watch a video to see how to solve quadratic equations by graphing on a graphing calculator.

Think About It!
Explain why 9 and 15 cannot be solutions, even though their sum is 24.

Example 3 Estimate Roots

Solve $-x^2 + 4x + 7 = 0$ by graphing. If the exact roots cannot be found, state the consecutive integers between which the roots are located.

Find the axis of symmetry. $x = -\frac{b}{2a} = -\frac{\quad}{2(\quad)} = \_\_$

Make a table of values, plot the points, and connect them with a curve.

x	y
−2	___
−1	___
0	___
1	___
2	___
3	___
4	___
5	___

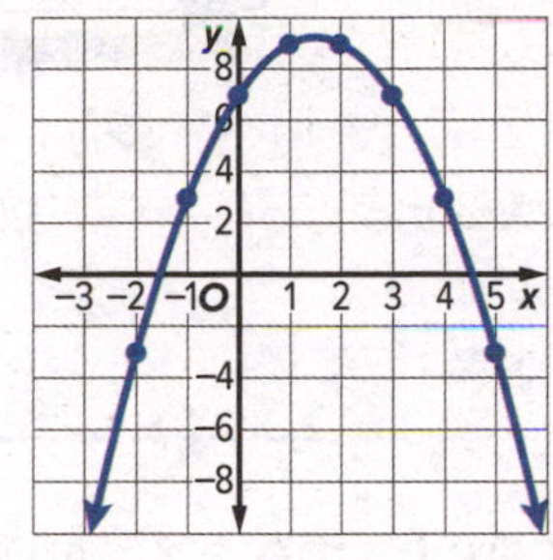

The x-intercepts of the graph indicate that one solution is between ___ and ___, and the other solution is between ___ and ___.

Check

Use a graph to find all of the solutions of $x^2 + 9x - 5 = 0$. Select all of the pairs of consecutive integers between which the roots are located.

Example 4 Solve by Using a Table

Use a table to solve $-x^2 + 5x - 1 = 0$.

Steps 1 and 2 Enter the function and view the table.

Enter $-x^2 + 5x - 1$ in the **Y=** list. Use the **TABLE** window to find where the sign of **Y1** changes. The sign changes between $x = 0$ and $x =$ ___.

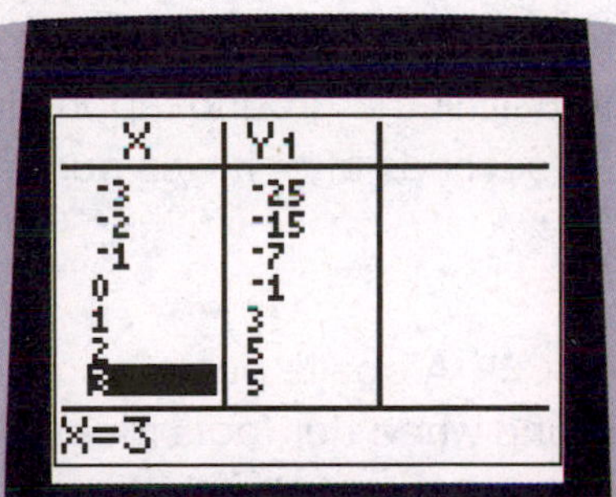

X	Y1
-3	-25
-2	-15
-1	-7
0	-1
1	3
2	5
3	5

X=3

Steps 3 and 4 Edit the table settings and find a more accurate location.

Use **TBLSET** to change **ΔTbl** to 0.1 and look again for the sign change. Repeat this for 0.1 and 0.001 to get a more accurate location of one zero.

X	Y1
.206	-.0124
.207	-.0078
.208	-.0033
.209	.00132
.21	.0059
.211	.01048
.212	.01506

Y1=.001319

One zero is located at approximately $x =$ ______

(continued on the next page)

Go Online You can complete an Extra Example online.

Talk About It

How can you estimate the solutions of the equation from the table? Explain your reasoning.

Watch Out!

Graphing Calculator If you cannot see the graph of the function on your graphing calculator, you may need to adjust the viewing window. Having the proper viewing window will also make it easier to see the zeros.

Think About It!

How can you check your solutions?

Steps 5 and 6 Repeat the process and determine the solutions of the equation.

The zeros of the function are at approximately 0.209 and 4.791, so the solutions to the equation are approximately ______ and ______.

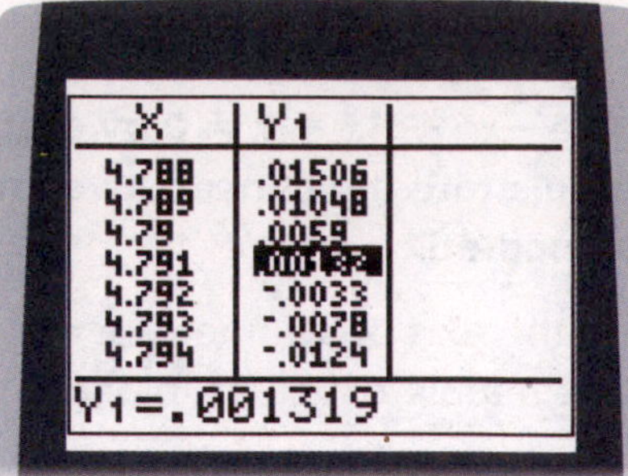

Check

Use a table to find all of the solutions of $-x^2 - 3x + 8 = 0$.

______ and ______

Example 5 Solve by Using a Calculator

FOOTBALL A kicker punts a football. If the ball is 1.5 feet above the ground when his foot meets the ball, how long will it take the ball to hit the ground? Use the formula $h(t) = -16t^2 + 50t + h_0$, where t is the time in seconds and h_0 is the initial height.

Think About It!

Why did you only find the positive zero?

We know that h_0 is the initial height, so $h_0 = 1.5$. We need to find t when $h(t)$ is 0. Use a graphing calculator to graph the related function $h(t) = -16t^2 + 50t +$ ___

Step 1 Enter the function in the Y =list, and press graph.

Step 2 Use the zero feature in the CALC menu to find the positive zero.

Step 3 Find the left bound.

Step 4 Find the right bound.

Step 5 Find and interpret the solution.

The zero is approximately ____. Thus, the ball hit the ground approximately ____ seconds after it was punted.

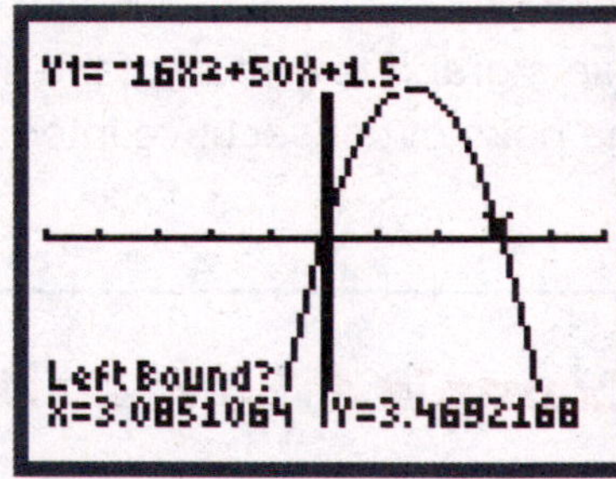

Check

SOCCER A goalie punts a soccer ball. If the ball is 1 foot above the ground when her foots meets the ball, find how long it will take, to the nearest hundredth of a second, for the ball to hit the ground. Use the formula $h(t) = -16t^2 + 35t + h_0$, where t is the time in seconds and h_0 is the initial height.

_____ seconds

Go Online You can complete an Extra Example online.

Name ______________________ Period ____________ Date ______________

Practice

Go Online You can complete your homework online.

Example 1

Use the related graph of each equation to determine its solutions.

1. $x^2 + 2x + 3 = 0$

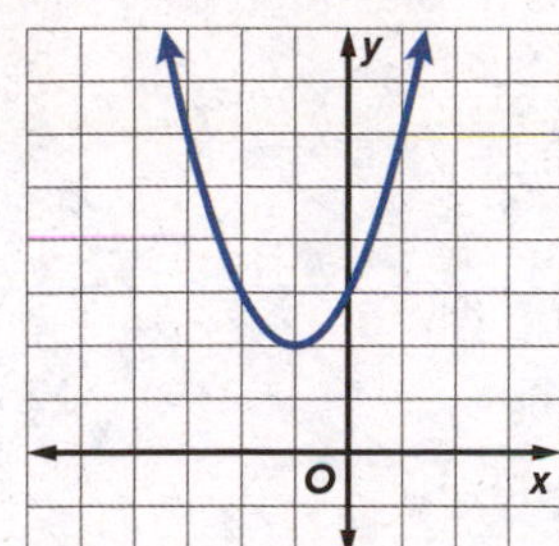

2. $x^2 - 3x - 10 = 0$

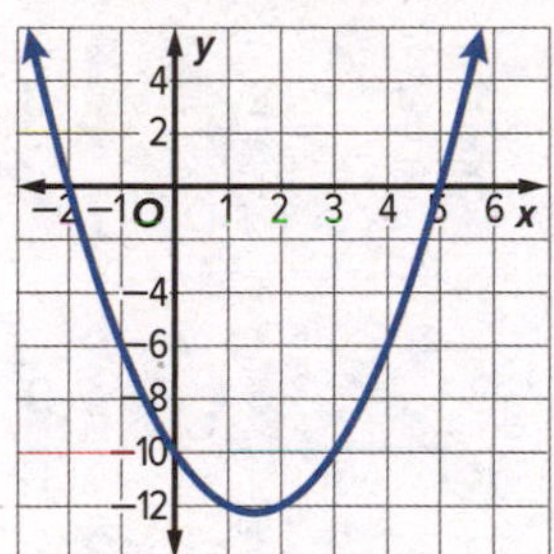

3. $-x^2 - 8x - 16 =$

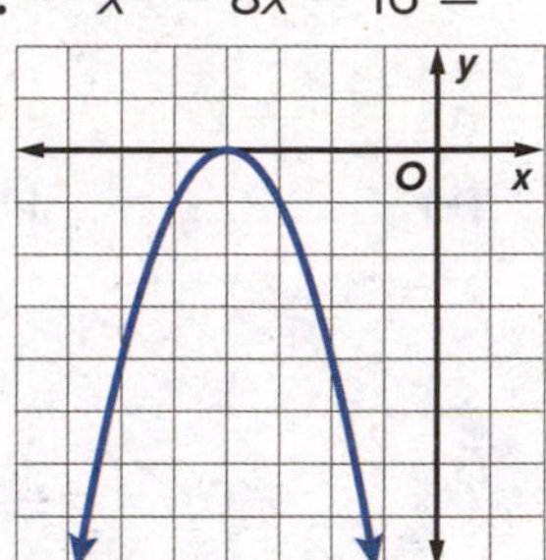

Solve each equation by graphing.

4. $x^2 - 10x + 21 = 0$

5. $4x^2 + 4x + 1 = 0$

6. $x^2 + x - 6 = 0$

7. $x^2 + 2x - 3 = 0$

8. $-x^2 - 6x - 9 = 0$

9. $x^2 - 6x + 5 = 0$

10. $x^2 + 2x + 3 = 0$

11. $x^2 - 3x - 10 = 0$

12. $-x^2 - 8x - 16 = 0$

Example 2

13. REASONING Use a quadratic equation to find two real numbers with a sum of 2 and a product of −24.

14. REASONING Use a quadratic equation to find two real numbers with a sum of −15 and a product of −54.

Example 3

Solve each equation by graphing. If the exact roots cannot be found, state the consecutive integers between which the roots are located.

15. $x^2 - 4x + 2 = 0$

16. $x^2 + 6x + 6 = 0$

17. $x^2 + 4x + 2 = 0$

18. $-x^2 - 4x = 0$

19. $-x^2 + 36 = 0$

20. $x^2 - 6x + 4 = 0$

21. $x^2 + 5x + 3 = 0$

22. $x^2 - 7 = 0$

23. $-x^2 - 4x - 6 = 0$

Example 4

Use the tables to determine the location of the zeros of each quadratic function.

24.

x	−7	−6	−5	−4	−3	−2	−1	−0
$f(x)$	−8	−1	4	4	−1	−8	− 22	−48

25.

x	−2	−1	0	1	2	3	4	5
$f(x)$	32	14	2	−3	−3	2	14	32

26.

x	−6	−3	0	3	6	9	12	15
$f(x)$	−6	−1	3	5	3	−1	−6	−14

USE TOOLS **Use a table to solve each equation. If the exact roots cannot be found, approximate the roots to the nearest hundredth.**

27. $-x^2 + 2x + 4 = 0$

28. $2x^2 - 12x + 17 = 0$

29. $-\frac{1}{2}x^2 + x + \frac{5}{2} = 0$

30. $x^2 - 2x - 2 = 0$

31. $-3x^2 + 3 = 0$

32. $x^2 - 3x + 2 = 0$

Example 5

MODELING **Use the formula $h(t) = -16t^2 + v_0t + h_0$, where $h(t)$ is the height of an object in feet, v_0 is the object's initial velocity in feet per second, t is the time in seconds, and h_0 is the initial height in feet from which the object is launched. Round to the nearest tenth, if necessary.**

33. USE TOOLS Melah throws a baseball with an initial upward velocity of 32 feet per second. The baseball is released from Melah's hand at a height of 4 feet. Use a graphing calculator to determine how long it will take the ball to hit the ground.

34. USE TOOLS A punter kicks a football with an initial upward velocity of 60 feet per second. The ball is 2 feet above the ground when his foot meets the ball. Use a graphing calculator to determine how long will it take the ball to hit the ground.

Mixed Exercises

Solve each equation by graphing. If the exact roots cannot be found, state the consecutive integers between which the roots are located.

35. $4x^2 - 15 = -4x$

36. $-35 = -3x - 2x^2$

37. $-3x^2 + 11x + 9 = 1$

38. $13 - 4x^2 = -3x$

39. $-0.5x^2 + 18 = -6x + 33$

40. $0.5x^2 + 0.75 = 0.25x$

41. $2x^2 + x = 11$

42. $3x^2 + 8x = 0$

43. $-0.1x^2 + 0.5x + 10 = 0$

Name ______________________ Period __________ Date __________

Use the related graph of each equation to determine its solutions.

44. $x^2 + 4x = 0$

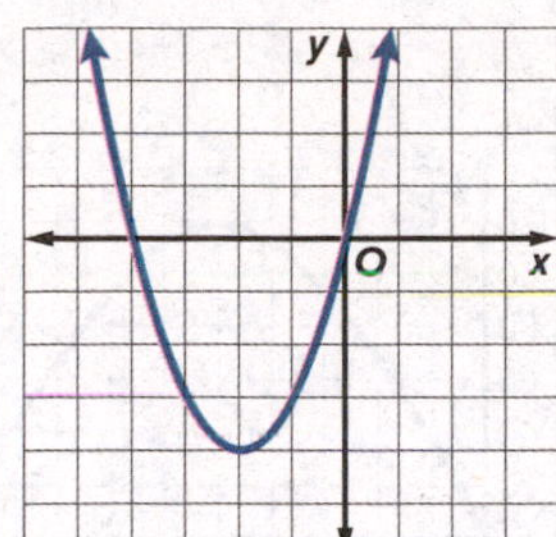

45. $-2x^2 - 4x - 5 = 0$

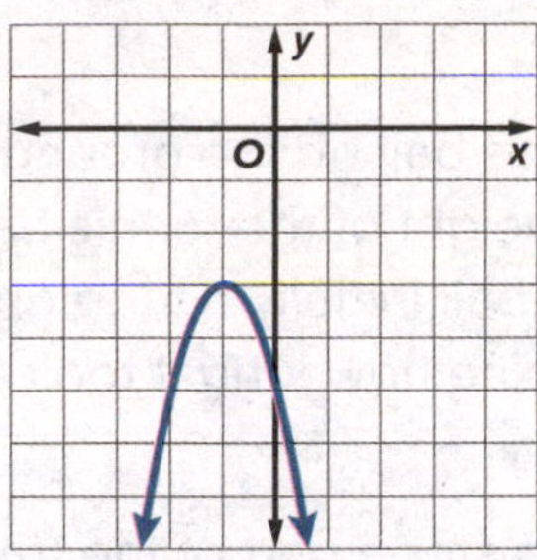

46. $0.5x^2 - 2x + 2 = 0$

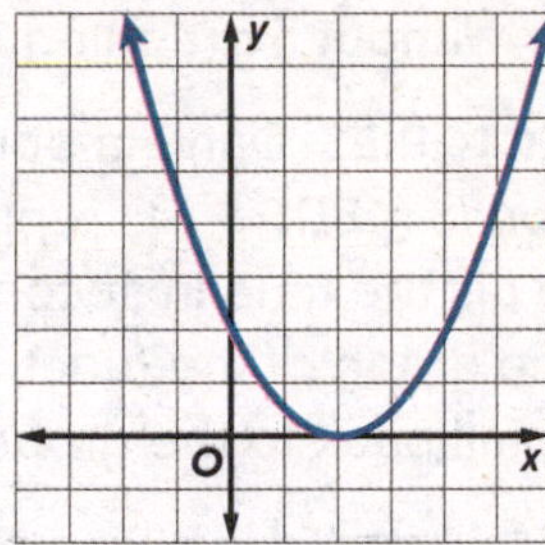

47. $-0.25x^2 - x - 1 = 0$

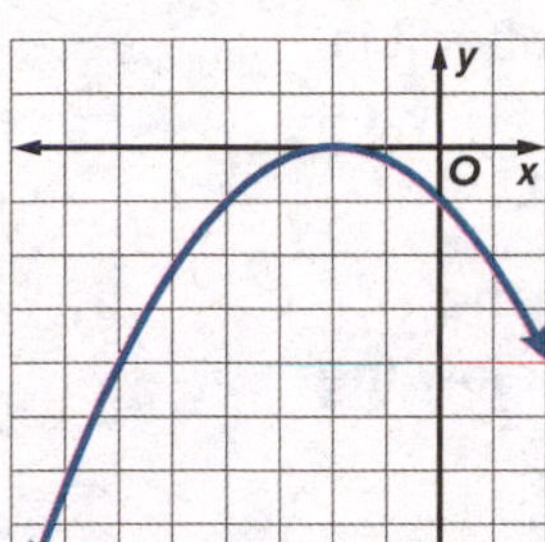

48. $x^2 - 6x + 11 = 0$

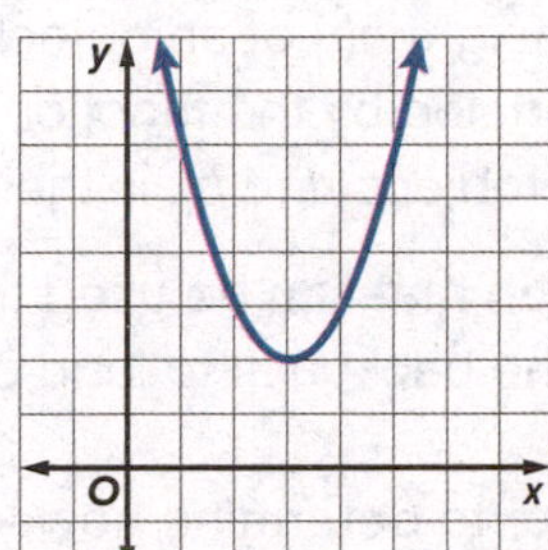

49. $-0.5x^2 + 0.5x + 6 = 0$

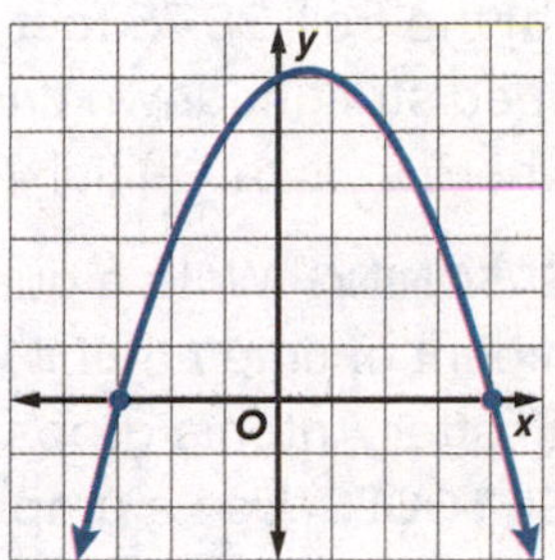

REGULARITY Use a quadratic equation to find two real numbers that satisfy each situation, or show that no such numbers exist.

50. Their sum is 4, and their product is −117.

51. Their sum is 12, and their product is −85.

52. Their sum is −13, and their product is 42.

53. Their sum is −8, and their product is −209.

54. **BRIDGES** In 1895, a brick arch railway bridge was built on North Avenue in Baltimore, Maryland. The arch is described by the equation $h = 9 - \frac{1}{50}x^2$, where h is the height in yards and x is the distance in yards from the center of the bridge. Graph this equation and describe, to the nearest yard, where the bridge touches the ground.

55. **RADIO TELESCOPES** The cross-section of a large radio telescope is a parabola. The dish is set into the ground. The equation that describes the cross-section is $d = \frac{2}{75}x^2 - \frac{4}{3}x - \frac{32}{3}$, where d gives the depth of the dish below ground and x is the distance from the control center, both in meters. If the dish does not extend above the ground level, what is the diameter of the dish? Solve by graphing.

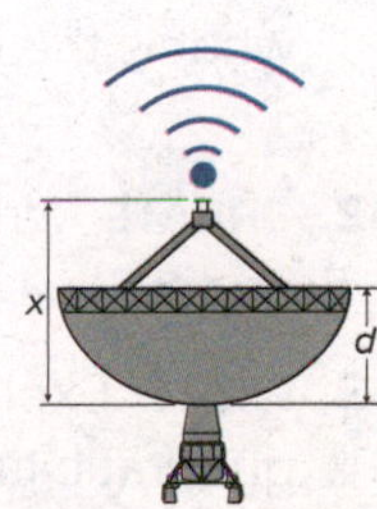

56. **VOLCANOES** A volcanic eruption blasts a boulder upward with an initial velocity of 240 feet per second. The height of the boulder in feet can be modeled by the function $h(t) = -16t^2 + v_0t$. How long will it take the boulder to hit the ground if it lands at the same elevation from which it was ejected? (Hint: This can be solved with or without a graphing calculator).

57. **TRAJECTORIES** Daniela bounced a tennis ball on the ground. The function $h = 80t - 6t^2$ represents the height of the tennis ball in feet, where t is the time in seconds after the ball initially hit the ground. Use the graph of the function to determine how long it took for the ball to fall back to the ground.

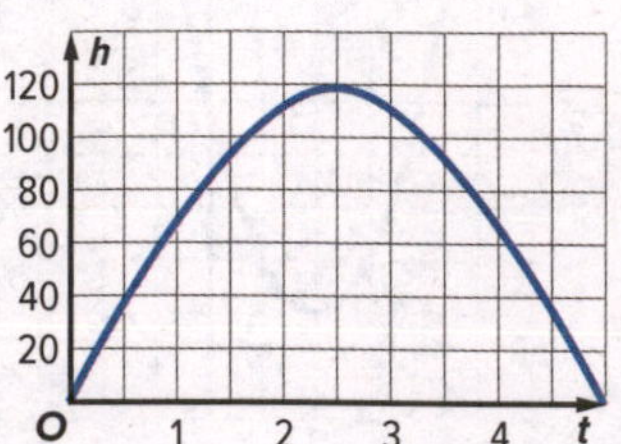

58. **HIKING** Antonia is hiking and reaches a steep part of the trail that runs along the edge of a cliff. In order to descend more safely, he drops his heavy backpack over the edge of the cliff so that it will land on a lower part of the trail, 38.75 feet below. The height $h(t)$ of an object t seconds after it is dropped straight down can also be modeled by the function $h(t) = -16t^2 + v_0t + h_0$, where v_0 is the initial velocity of the object, and h_0 is the initial height.

a. **REASONING** Write a quadratic function that can be used to determine the amount of time *t* that it will take for the backpack to land on the trail below the cliff after Antonia drops it.

b. **USE TOOLS** Use a graphing calculator to determine how long until the backpack will hit the ground. Round to the nearest tenth.

59. **FIND THE ERROR** Hakeem and Nandi were asked to find the location of the roots of the quadratic function represented by the table. Is either of them correct? Explain.

x	−4	−2	0	2	4	6	8	10
f(*x*)	52	26	8	−2	−4	2	16	38

Hakeem

The roots are between 4 and 6 because f(x) stops decreasing and begins to increase between x − 4 and x − 6.

Nandi

The roots are between −2 and 0 because x changes signs at that location.

60. **PERSEVERE** Find the value of a positive integer *k* such that $f(x) = x^2 - 2kx + 55$ has roots at $k + 3$ and $k - 3$.

61. **ANALYZE** If a quadratic function has a minimum at (−6, −14) and a root at $x = -17$, what is the other root? Explain your reasoning.

62. **CREATE** Write a quadratic function with a maximum at (3, 125) and roots at −2 and 8.

63. **WRITE** Explain how to solve a quadratic equation by graphing its related quadratic function.

Complex Numbers

Today's Standards
N.CN.1, N.CN.2
MP3, MP7, MP8

Today's Vocabulary
imaginary unit *i*
pure imaginary number
complex number
complex conjugates
rationalizing the denominator

Explore Factoring Prime Polynomials

Online Activity Use guiding exercises to complete the Explore.

INQUIRY Can you factor a prime polynomial?

Learn Pure Imaginary Numbers

In your math studies so far, you have worked with real numbers. However, some equations such as $y = x^2 + x + 1$ do not have real solutions. This led mathematicians to define imaginary numbers. The **imaginary unit *i*** is the principal square root of −1. Thus, $i = \sqrt{-1}$ and $i^2 = -1$.

Numbers of the form $6i$, $-2i$, and $i\sqrt{3}$ are called pure imaginary numbers. A **pure imaginary number** is a number of the form bi, where b is a real number and $i = \sqrt{-1}$ For any positive real number $\sqrt{-b^2} = \sqrt{b^2}\sqrt{-1}$ or bi.

The Commutative and Associative Properties of Multiplication hold true for pure imaginary numbers. The first few powers of i are shown.

$i^1 = i$	$i^2 = -1$	$i^3 = i^2 \cdot i$ or $-i$

Go Online You may want to complete the Concept Check to check your understanding.

Example 1 Square Roots of Negative Numbers

Simplify $\sqrt{-294}$.

$\sqrt{-294} = \sqrt{-1 \cdot 7^2 \cdot 6}$ Prime Factorization

$= \sqrt{}\sqrt{7^2}\sqrt{}$ Factor out the imaginary unit.

$= i \cdot$ ____ $\cdot \sqrt{6}$ or $7i$____ Simplify.

Study Tip:
Square Factors When factoring an expression under a radical, look for perfect square factors.

Check

Simplify $\sqrt{-75}$. ____

A $i\sqrt{75}$

B $3i\sqrt{5}$

C $5i\sqrt{3}$

D $-3\sqrt{5}$

Go Online You can complete an Extra Example online.

Your Notes

Talk About It

How can an expression with two imaginary expressions, $\sqrt{-10}$ and $\sqrt{-15}$, have a product that is real?

Think About It!

Compare and contrast the methods.

Example 2 Products of Pure Imaginary Numbers

Simplify $\sqrt{-10}\,\sqrt{-15}$.

$\sqrt{-10}\,\sqrt{-15} = i\sqrt{10}\,i\sqrt{15}$	$i = \sqrt{-1}$
$= i^2 \cdot \sqrt{150}$	Multiply.
$= -1 \cdot \sqrt{25} \cdot \sqrt{6}$	Simplify.
$= \underline{\quad\quad}\sqrt{6}$	Multiply.

Check

Simplify $\sqrt{-16} \cdot \sqrt{-25}$.

$\underline{\quad\quad\quad}$

Example 3 Equation with Pure Imaginary Solutions

Solve $x^2 + 81 = 0$.

$x^2 + 81 = 0$	Original equation
$x^2 = \underline{\quad\quad}$	Subtract 81 from each side.
$x = \pm\underline{\quad\quad\quad}$	Square Root Property
$x = \pm\underline{\quad\quad}$	Simplify.

ALTERNATE METHOD

$x^2 + 81 = 0$	Original equation
$x^2 + \underline{\quad}^2 = 0$	$81 = 9^2$
$x^2 - (-\underline{\quad})^2 = 0$	Rewrite in the difference of squares pattern.
$(x + \underline{\quad\quad})(x - \underline{\quad\quad}) = 0$	Difference of squares: $\sqrt{-9^2} = \sqrt{-81} = 9i$
$(x + \underline{\quad\quad}) = 0$ or $(x - \underline{\quad\quad}) = 0$	Zero Product Property
$x = -\underline{\quad\quad}$ or $x = \underline{\quad\quad}$	Simplify.

Check

Solve $3x^2 + 27 = 0$.

$x = \underline{\quad\quad}$ and $x = \underline{\quad\quad}$

Go Online You can complete an Extra Example online.

Learn Complex Numbers

Key Concept • Complex Numbers

A **complex number** is any number that can be written in the form $a + bi$, where a and b are real numbers and $\boldsymbol{i}$ is the imaginary unit. a is called the real part, and b is called the imaginary part. One example of a complex number is $5 + 2i$. Another example is $1 - 3i$, because it can be written as $1 + -3i$.

> **Think About It!**
> Compare and contrast the subsets of the complex number system using the Venn diagram above.

The Venn Diagram shows the set of complex numbers. Notice that all of the real numbers are part of the set of complex numbers.

Complex Numbers ($a + bi$)

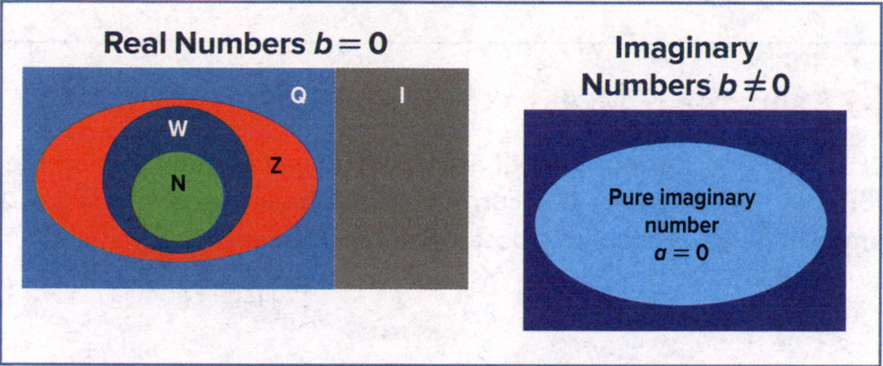

The Commutative and Associative Properties of Multiplication and Addition and the Distributive Property hold true for complex numbers. To add or subtract complex numbers, combine like terms. That is, combine the real parts, and combine the imaginary parts.

Two complex numbers of the form $a + bi$ and $a - bi$ are called **complex conjugates**. The product of complex conjugates is always a real number.

A radical expression is in simplest form if no radicands contain fractions and no radicals appear in the denominator of a fraction. Similarly, a complex number is in simplest form if no imaginary numbers appear in the denominator of a fraction. You can use complex conjugates to simplify a fraction with a complex number in the denominator. This process is called **rationalizing the denominator**.

Example 4 Equate Complex Numbers

Find the values of x and y that make $5x - 7 + (y + 4)i = 13 + 11i$ true.

Use equations relating the real and imaginary parts to solve for x and y.

$5x - 7 = $ ___	Real parts
$5x = $ ___	Add 13 to each side.
$x = $ ___	Divide each side by 5.
$y + 4 = $ ___	Real parts
$y = $ ___	Add 13 to each side.

Go Online You can complete an Extra Example online.

Example 5 Add or Subtract Complex Numbers

Go Online You can learn how to add or subtract complex numbers by watching the video online.

Simplify $(8 + 3i) - (4 - 10i)$.

$(8 + 3i) - (4 - 10i) = (8 - \_\_\_) + [3 - (\_\_\_)]i$ — Commutative and Associative Properties

$= \_\_\_ + 13i$ — Simplify.

Check

Simplify $(-5 + 5i) - (-3 + 8i)$.

$\_\_\_ + \_\_\_ i$

Example 6 Multiply Complex Numbers

ELECTRICITY **The voltage V of an AC circuit can be found using the formula $V = CI$, where C is current and I is impedance. If $C = 3 + 2j$ amps and $I = 7 - 5j$ ohms, determine the voltage.**

$V = CI$ — Voltage Formula

$= (3 + 2j)(7 - 5j)$ — $C = 3 + 2j$ and $I = 7 - 5j$

$= 3(\_\_\_) + 3(\_\_\_) + 2j(\_\_\_) = 2j(\_\_\_)$ — FOIL Method

$= \_\_\_ - 15j + \_\_\_ - 10j^2$ — Multiply.

$= 21 - \_\_\_ - 10(\_\_\_)$ — $j^2 = -1$

$= \_\_\_ - j$ — Add.

The voltage is ___ volts.

Example 7 Divide Complex Numbers

Simplify $\frac{5i}{3 + 2i}$.

Rationalize the denominator to simplify the fraction.

$\frac{5i}{3 + 2i} = \frac{5i}{3 + 2i} \cdot \frac{3 - 2i}{3 - 2i}$ — $3 + 2i$ and $3 - 2i$ are complex conjugates.

$= \frac{15i - 10i^2}{9 - 4i^2}$ — Multiply the numerator and denominator.

$= \frac{15i - 10(-1)}{9 - 4(-1)}$ — $i^2 = -1$

$= \frac{15i + 10}{13}$ — Simplify.

$= \frac{10}{13} + \frac{15}{13}i$ — $a + bi$ form

Check

Simplify $\frac{2i}{-4 + 3i}$ ___

Go Online You can complete an Extra Example online.

Name ______________________ Period ____________ Date ____________

Practice

Go Online You can complete your homework online.

Example 1

Simplify.

1. $\sqrt{-48}$
2. $\sqrt{-63}$
3. $\sqrt{-72}$
4. $\sqrt{-24}$
5. $\sqrt{-84}$
6. $\sqrt{-99}$

Example 2

Simplify.

7. $\sqrt{-23} \cdot \sqrt{-46}$
8. $\sqrt{-6} \cdot \sqrt{-3}$
9. $\sqrt{-5} \cdot \sqrt{-10}$
10. $(3i)(-2i)(5i)$
11. i^{11}
12. $4i(-6i)^2$

Example 3

Solve each equation.

13. $5x^2 + 45 = 0$
14. $4x^2 + 24 = 0$
15. $-9x^2 = 9$
16. $7x^2 + 84 = 0$
17. $5x^2 + 125 = 0$
18. $8x^2 + 96 = 0$

Example 4

Find the values of *x* and *y* that make each equation true.

19. $9 + 12i = 3x + 4yi$
20. $x + 1 + 2yi = 3 - 6i$
21. $2x + 7 + (3 - y)i = -4 + 6i$
22. $5 + y + (3x - 7)i = 9 - 3i$
23. $20 - 12i = 5x + (4y)i$
24. $x - 16i = 3 - (2y)i$

Example 5

Simplify.

25. $(6 + i) + (4 - 5i)$
26. $(8 + 3i) - (6 - 2i)$
27. $(5 - i) - (3 - 2i)$
28. $(-4 + 2i) + (6 - 3i)$
29. $(6 - 3i) + (4 - 2i)$
30. $(-11 + 4i) - (1 - 5i)$

Example 6

Simplify.

31. $(2 + i)(3 - i)$
32. $(5 - 2i)(4 - i)$
33. $(4 - 2i)(1 - 2i)$

34. **ELECTRICITY** Using the formula $V = CI$, find the voltage V in a circuit when the current $C = 3 - j$ amps and the impedance $I = 3 + 2j$ ohms.

Example 7

Simplify.

35. $\frac{5}{3 + i}$
36. $\frac{7 - 13i}{2i}$
37. $\frac{6 - 5i}{3i}$

Mixed Exercises

STRUCTURE Simplify.

38. $(1 + i)(2 + 3i)(4 - 3i)$

39. $\frac{4 - i\sqrt{2}}{4 + i\sqrt{2}}$

40. $\frac{2 - i\sqrt{3}}{2 + i\sqrt{3}}$

41. Find the sum of $ix^2 - (4 + 5i)x + 7$ and $3x^2 + (2 + 6i)x - 8i$.

42. Simplify $[(2 + i)x^2 - ix + 5 + i] - [(-3 + 4i)x^2 + (5 - 5i)x - 6]$.

ELECTRICITY Use the formula $V = CI$, where V is the voltage, C is the current, and I is the impedance.

43. The current in a circuit is $2 + 4j$ amps, and the impedance is $3 - j$ ohms. What is the voltage?

44. The voltage in a circuit is $24 - 8j$ volts, and the impedance is $4 - 2j$ ohms. What is the current?

45. **CIRCUITS** The impedance in one part of a series circuit is $1 + 3j$ ohms and the impedance in another part of the circuit is $7 - 5j$ ohms. Add these complex numbers to find the total impedance in the circuit.

46. **ELECTRICAL ENGINEERING** Alternating current (AC) in an electrical circuit can be described by complex numbers. In any electrical circuit, Z, the impedance in the circuit, is related to the voltage V and the current I by the formula $Z = \frac{V}{I}$. The standard electrical voltage in Europe is 220 volts, so use $V = 220$.

a. Find the impedance in a standard European circuit if the current is $22 - 11i$ amps.

b. Find the current in a standard European circuit if the impedance is $10 - 5i$ ohms.

c. Find the impedance in a standard European circuit if the current is $20i$ amps.

47. **FIND THE ERROR** Jose and Zoe are simplifying $(2i)(3i)(4i)$. Is either of them correct? Explain your reasoning.

Jose	Zoe
$24i^3 = -24$	$24i^3 = -24i$

48. **PERSEVERE** Simplify $(1 + 2i)^3$.

49. **ANALYZE** Determine whether the following statement is *always*, *sometimes*, or *never* true. Explain your reasoning.

Every complex number has both a real part and an imaginary part.

50. **CREATE** Write two complex numbers with a product of 20.

51. **WRITE** Explain how complex numbers are related to quadratic equations.

Solve Quadratic Equations by Factoring

Explore Finding the Solutions of Quadratic Equations by Factoring

Online Activity Use graphing technology to complete the Explore.

INQUIRY How can you use factoring to solve a quadratic equation?

The **factored form** of a quadratic equation is $0 = a(x - p)(x - q)$, where $a \neq 0$. In this equation, p and q represent the x-intercepts of the graph of the related function. For example, $0 = x^2 - 2x - 3$ can be written in the factored form $0 = (x - 3)(x + 1)$ and its related graph has x-intercepts of -1 and 3.

Learn Solving Quadratic Equations by Factoring

Key Concept • Factoring by Using the Distributive Property

Symbols: $ax + bx = x(a + b)$

Example: $20 + 15 = 5(4 + 3)$

Key Concept • Factoring Trinomials

Symbols: $x^2 + bx + c = (x + m)(x + p)$ when $m + p = b$ and $mp = c$

Example: $x^2 - 8x + 15 = (x - 5)(x - 3)$, because $-5 + (-3) = -8$ and $-5(-3) = 15$

Key Concept • Zero Product Property

Words: For any real numbers a and b, if $ab = 0$, then either $a = 0$, $b = 0$, or both a and $b = 0$.

Example: If $(x - 2)(x + 4) = 0$, then $x - 2 = 0$, $x + 4 = 0$, or $x - 2 = 0$ and $x + 4 = 0$.

Example 1 Use the Distributive Property

Solve $12x^2 - 2x = x$ by factoring. Check your solution.

$12x^2 - 2x = x$	Original equation
$12x^2 - \_\_\_x = 0$	Subtract x from each side.
$3x(\_\_\_) - 3x(\_\_\_) = 0$	Factor the GCF.
$\_\_\_(4x - 1) = 0$	Distributive Property
$3x = 0$ and $4x - 1 = 0$	Zero Product Property.
$x = \_\_\_$ and $x = \_\_\_$	Solve.

Go Online You can complete an Extra Example online.

Today's Standards
N.CN.7, N.CN.8, F.IF.8a
MP1, MP7

Today's Vocabulary
factored form
difference of squares
perfect square trinomials

Think About It!
The equation $x^2 - 2x - 3 = 0$ could be solved by factoring, where $x^2 - 2x - 3 = (x - 3)(x + 1)$. How are the factors of the equation related to the roots, or zeros, of the related function $f(x) = x^2 - 2x - 3$?

Go Online You can watch a video to see how to use algebra tiles to factor a polynomial using the Distributive Property online.

Your Notes 

Think About It!

Choose two integers and write an equation in standard form with these roots. How would the equation change if the signs of the two roots were switched?

Math History Minute

English mathematician and astronomer **Thomas Harriot (1560–1621)** was one of the first, if not the first, to consider the imaginary roots of equations. Harriot advanced the notation system for algebra and studied negative and imaginary numbers.

Example 2 Factor a Trinomial

Solve $x^2 + 4x - 46 = 71$ by factoring. Check your solution.

$x^2 + 4x - 46 = 71$	Original equation
$x^2 + 4x - \_\_\_ = 0$	Subtract 71 from each side.
$(x + \_\_\_)(x - \_\_\_) = 0$	Factor the trinomial.
$x + 13 = 0$ or $x - 9 = 0$	Zero Product Property
$x = \_\_\_ \quad x = \_\_\_$	Solve.

Example 3 Solve an Equation by Factoring

ACCELERATION **The equation $d = vt + \frac{1}{2}at^2$ represents the displacement d of a car traveling at an initial velocity v where the acceleration a is constant over a given time t. Find how long it takes a car to accelerate from 30 mph to 45 mph if the car moved 605 feet and accelerated slowly at a rate of 2 feet per second squared.**

Understand

What do you know?

$d = \_\_\_$ ft, $v = \_\_\_$ mph, and $a = \_\_\_$ ft/v^2.

What do you need to find? ___

Plan and Solve

Step 1 Convert so that the units are the same.

$$v = 30 \frac{\text{mi}}{\text{hr}} \times \frac{\_\_\_ \text{ ft}}{\text{mi}} \times \frac{1 \text{ hr}}{\_\_\_ \text{ s}} = \_\_\_ \frac{\text{ft}}{\text{s}}$$

Step 2 Substitute the known values in the equation.

$d = vt + \frac{1}{2}at^2$	Original equation
$\_\_\_ = \_\_\_ + \frac{1}{2}(\_\_\_)t^2$	$d = 605$, $v = 44$, and $a = 2$

Step 3 Solve the equation for t.

$605 = 44t + \frac{1}{2}(2)t^2$	Equation for displacement
$0 = t^2 - 44t - 605$	Subtract 605 from each side.
$0 = (t + \_\_\_)(t - \_\_\_)$	Factor.
$0 = t + 55$ or $0 = t - 11$	Zero Product Property
$t = -55 \; t = 11$	Solve.

Step 4 Interpret answers in the context of the situation.

Because time cannot be negative, $t = \_\_\_$ is the only viable solution.

So, it took the car ___ seconds to accelerate to 45 mph.

 **Go Online** You can complete an Extra Example online.

Check

SALES A clothing store is analyzing their market to determine the profitability of their new dress design. If $P(x) = -16x^2 + 1712x - 44{,}640$ represents the store's profit when x is the price of each dress, find the price range the store should charge to make the dress profitable. ____

A. between \$11.25 and \$15.50

B. between \$45 and \$62

C. between \$50 and \$54

D. between \$180 and \$248

Example 4 Factor a Trinomial Where a is Not 1

Solve $3x^2 + 5x + 15 = 17$ by factoring. Check your solution.

$3x^2 + 5x + 15 = 17$	Original equation
$3x^2 + 5x - 2 = 0$	Subtract 17 from each side.
$(3x - 1)(x + 2) = 0$	Factor the trinomial.
$(3x - 1) = 0$ or $x + 2 = 0$	Zero Product Property
$x = \frac{1}{3}$ $x = -2$	Solve.

Check

Solve $4x^2 + 12x - 27 = 13$ by factoring. Check your solution.

$x =$ ____, $x =$ ____.

Learn Solving Quadratic Equations by Factoring Special Products

Key Concept • Factoring Differences of Squares

Words: To factor $a^2 - b^2$, find the square roots of a^2 and b^2. Then apply the pattern.

Example: $a^2 - b^2 = (a + b)(a - b)$

Key Concept • Factoring Perfect Squares

Words: To factor $a^2 + 2ab + b^2$, find the square roots of a^2 and b^2. Then apply the pattern.

Example: $a^2 + 2ab + b^2 = (a + b)^2$

Not all quadratic equations have solutions that are real numbers. In some cases, the solutions are complex numbers of the form $a + bi$, where $b \neq 0$. For example, you know that the solution of $x^2 = 4$ must be complex because there is no real number for which its square is -4. If you take the square root of each side, $x = 2i$ and $-2i$.

Think About It!

Explain how to determine which values should be chose for m and p when factoring a polynomial of the form $ax^2 + bx + c$.

Talk About It

Is $5 + 3i$ in simplest form? Explain your reasoning.

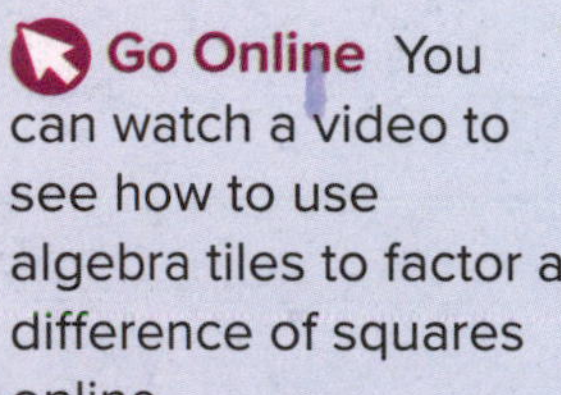

Go Online You can watch a video to see how to use algebra tiles to factor a difference of squares online.

Example 5 Factor a Difference of Squares

Solve $81 = x^2$ by factoring. Check your solution.

$81 = x^2$	Original equation
$81 - x^2 = 0$	Subtract x^2 from each side.
$\_\_^2 - \_\_^2 = 0$	Write in the form $a^2 - b^2$.
$(\_\_ + \_\_)(\_\_ - \_\_) = 0$	Factor the difference of squares.
$9 + x = 0$ or $9 - x = 0$	Zero Product Property
$x = \_\_$ $\quad x = \_\_$	Solve.

Check

Solve $x^2 = 529$ by factoring. Check your solution.

$x = \_\_, \_\_$

Think About It!

Why does this equation have one solution instead of two?

Example 6 Factor a Perfect Square Trinomial

Solve $16y^2 - 22y + 23 = 26y - 13$ by factoring. Check your solution.

$16y^2 - 22y + 23 = 26y - 13$	Original equation
$16y^2 - \_\_y + 23 = -13$	Subtract $26y$ from each side.
$16y^2 - 48y + \_\_ = 0$	Add 13 to each side.
$(\_\_)^2 - 2(\_\_)(\_\_) + \_\_^2 = 0$	Factor the perfect square trinomial.
$(\_\_ - \_\_)^2 = 0$	Simplify.
$y = \_\_$	Take the square root of each side and solve.

Check

Solve $16x^2 - 22x + 15 = 10x - 1$ by factoring. Check your solution.

$x = \_\_$

Think About It!

Explain why both $(-12i)^2$ and $(12i)^2$ equal -144.

Example 7 Complex Solutions

Solve $x^2 = -144$ by factoring. Check your solution.

$x^2 = -144$	Original equation
$x^2 + 144 = 0$	Add 144 to each side.
$x^2 - (\_\_^2) = 0$	$144 = -(12^2)$
$(x + \_\_)(x - \_\_) = 0$	Factor the difference of squares.
$x + 12i = 0$ or $x - 12i = 0$	Zero Product Property
$x = \_\_$ $\quad x = \_\_$	Solve.

Watch Out!

Complex Numbers Remember i^2 equals -1, not 1.

Go Online You can complete an Extra Example online.

Name ______________________ Period __________ Date __________

Practice

Go Online You can complete your homework online.

Examples 1 and 2

Solve each equation by factoring. Check your solution.

1. $6x^2 - 2x = 0$

2. $x^2 = 7x$

3. $20x^2 = -25x$

4. $x^2 + x - 30 = 0$

5. $x^2 + 14x + 33 = 0$

6. $x^2 - 3x = 10$

Example 3

7. GEOMETRY The length of a rectangle is 2 feet more than its width. Find the dimensions of the rectangle if its area is 63 square feet.

8. PHOTOGRAPHY The length and width of a 6-inch by 8-inch photograph are reduced by the same amount to make a new photograph whose area is half that of the original. By how many inches will the dimensions of the photograph have to be reduced?

Example 4

Solve each equation by factoring. Check your solution.

9. $2x^2 - x - 3 = 0$

10. $6x^2 - 5x - 4 = 0$

11. $5x^2 + 28x - 12 = 0$

12. $12x^2 - 8x + 1 = 0$

13. $2x^2 - 11x - 40 = 0$

14. $3x^2 + 2x = 21$

Example 5

Solve each equation by factoring. Check your solution.

15. $x^2 = 64$

16. $x^2 - 100 = 0$

17. $289 = x^2$

18. $x^2 + 14 = 50$

19. $x^2 - 169 = 0$

20. $124 = x^2 + 3$

Example 6

Solve each equation by factoring. Check your solution.

21. $4x^2 - 28x + 49 = 0$

22. $9x^2 + 6x = -1$

23. $16x^2 - 24x + 13 = 4$

24. $81x^2 + 36x = -4$

25. $25x^2 + 80x + 64 = 0$

26. $9x^2 + 60x + 95 = -5$

Example 7

Solve each equation by factoring. Check your solution.

27. $x^2 + 12 = -13$

28. $x^2 + 100 = 0$

29. $x^2 = -225$

30. $x^2 + 4 = 0$

31. $36x^2 = -25$

32. $64x^2 = -49$

Mixed Exercises

STRUCTURE Solve each equation by factoring. Check your solution.

33. $10x^2 + 25x = 15$

34. $27x^2 + 5 = 48x$

35. $x^2 + 81 = 0$

36. $45x^2 - 3x = 2x$

37. $80x^2 = -16$

38. $16x^2 + 8x = -1$

39. **MODELING** The area in square inches of the drawing *Maisons prés de la mer* by Claude Monet can be approximated by the equation $y = x^2 - 23x + 130$. Factor the equation to find the two roots, which are equal to the approximate length and width of the drawing.

40. **ANIMATION** A computer graphics animator would like to make a realistic simulation of a tossed ball. The animator wants the ball to follow the parabolic trajectory represented by the quadratic equation $f(x) = -0.2(x + 5)(x - 5)$.

a. What are the solutions of $f(x) = 0$?

b. Write $f(x)$ in standard form.

c. If the animator changes the equation to $f(x) = -0.2x^2 + 20$, what are the solutions of $f(x) = 0$?

REASONING

41. Find two consecutive even positive integers whose product is 624.

42. Find two consecutive odd positive integers whose product is 323.

43. **FIND THE ERROR** Jade and Mateo are solving $-12x^2 + 5x + 2 = 0$. Is either of them correct? Explain your reasoning.

Jade	Mateo
$-12x^2 + 5x + 2 = 0$	$-12x^2 + 5x + 2 = 0$
$-12x^2 + 8x - 3x + 2 = 0$	$-12x^2 + 8x - 3x + 2 = 0$
$4x(-3x + 2) - (3x + 2) = 0$	$4x(-3x + 2) - (3x + 2) = 0$
$(4x - 1)(3x + 2) = 0$	$(4x + 1)(-3x + 2) = 0$
$x = \frac{1}{4}$ or $\frac{2}{3}$	$x = -\frac{1}{4}$ or $\frac{2}{3}$

44. **PERSEVERE** The rule for factoring a difference of cubes is shown below. Use this rule to factor $40x^5 - 135x^2y^2$.

$$a^3 - b^3 = (a - b)(a^2 + ab + b^2)$$

45. **CREATE** Choose two integers. Then write an equation in standard form with those roots. How would the equation change if the signs of the two roots were switched?

46. **ANALYZE** Determine whether the following statement is *sometimes*, *always*, or *never* true. Explain your reasoning.

In a quadratic equation in standard form where a, b, and c are integers, If b is odd, then the quadratic cannot be a perfect square trinomial.

47. **WRITE** Explain how to factor a trinomial in standard form with $a > 1$.

Lesson 3-5

Solving Quadratic Equations by Completing the Square

Learn Solving Quadratic Equations by Using the Square Root Property

You can use square roots to solve equations like $x^2 - 49 = 0$. Remember that 7 and −7 are both square roots of 49 because $7^2 = 49$ and $(-7)^2 = 49$. Therefore, the solution set of $x^2 - 49 = 0$ is $\{-7, 7\}$. This can be written as $\{\pm 7\}$.

Key Concept • Square Root Property

Words: To solve a quadratic equation in the form $x^2 = n$, take the square root of each side.

Symbols: For any number $n \geq 0$, if $x^2 = n$, then $x = \pm n$.

Example: $x^2 = 121$, $x = \pm\sqrt{121}$ or ± 11.

Not all quadratic equations have solutions that are whole numbers. Roots that are irrational numbers may be written as exact answers in radical form or as approximate answers in decimal form when a calculator is used. Sometimes solutions of quadratic equations are not real numbers. Solutions that are complex numbers can be written in the form $a + bi$, where $b \neq 0$.

Example 1 Solve a Quadratic Equation with Rational Roots

Solve $x^2 - 4x + 4 = 25$ by using the Square Root Property.

$x^2 - 4x + 4 = 25$	Original equation
$(x - 2)^2 = 25$	Factor.
$x - 2 = \pm\sqrt{25}$	Square Root Property
$x - 2 = \pm$ ____	$25 = 5(5)$ or $-5(-5)$
$x = 2 \pm 5$	Add 2 to each side.
$x = 2 + 5$ or $x = 2 -$ ____	Write as two equations.
$x =$ ____ $x = -3$	Simplify.

The solution set is $\{x|x =$ ____, ____$\}$.

Check

Solve $x^2 - 38x + 361 = 576$ by using the Square Root Property.

$x =$ ____ and ____

Go Online You can complete an Extra Example online.

Today's Standards
N.CN.7, F.IF.8a
MP1, MP7

Today's Vocabulary
completing the square
vertex form
projectile motion problems

Think About It!
How can you determine whether an equation of the form $x^2 = n$ will have an answer that is a whole number?

Study Tip:
When using the Square Root Property, remember to include the ± before the radical.

Your Notes

Watch Out!

Perfect Squares The constant, 192, on the right side of the equation is not a perfect square. This means that the roots will be irrational numbers.

Example 2 Solve a Quadratic Equation with Irrational Roots

Solve $x^2 + 24x + 144 = 192$ by using the Square Root Property.

$x^2 + 24x + 144 = 192$	Original equation
$(x + 12)^2 = 192$	Factor.
$x + 12 = \pm\sqrt{192}$	Square Root Property.
$x + 12 = \pm 8\sqrt{3}$	$\sqrt{192} = 8\sqrt{3}$
$x =$ ____ $\pm 8\sqrt{3}$	Subtract 12 from each side.
$x = -12 + 8\sqrt{3}$ or ____ $- 8\sqrt{3}$	Write as two equations.
$x \approx$ ____ $x \approx$ ________	Use a calculator.

The exact solutions are $-12 - 8\sqrt{3}$ and $-12 - 8\sqrt{3}$. The approximate solutions are -25.86 and 1.86.

Example 3 Solve a Quadratic Equation with Complex Solutions

Solve $2x^2 - 92x + 1058 = -72$ by using the Square Root Property.

$2x^2 - 92x + 1058 = -72$	Original equation
$x^2 - 46x + 529 =$ ____	Divide each side by 2.
$(x -$ ____$)^2 = -36$	Factor.
$x - 23 = \pm\sqrt{-36}$	Square Root Property
$x - 23 = \pm$ ____	$\sqrt{-36} = 6i$
$x =$ ____ $\pm 6i$	Add 23 to each side.
$x = 23 \pm 6i$ or ____ $- 6i$	Write as two equations.

The solutions are $23 + 6i$ and $23 - 6i$.

Think About It!

Can you solve a quadratic equation by completing the square if the coefficient of the x^2-term is not 1? Justify your argument.

Explore Using Algebra Tiles to Complete the Square

Online Activity Use algebra tiles to complete the Explore.

INQUIRY How does forming a square to create a perfect square trinomial help you solve quadratic equations?

Go Online You can complete an Extra Example online.

Learn Solving Quadratic Equations by Completing the Square

Key Concept • Completing the Square

Words: To complete the square for any quadratic expression of the form $x^2 + bx$, follow the steps below.

Step 1 Find one half of b, the coefficient of x.
Step 2 Square the result in Step 1.
Step 3 Add the result of Step 2 to $x^2 + bx$.

Symbols: $x^2 + bx + \left(\frac{b}{2}\right)^2 = \left(x + \frac{b}{2}\right)^2$

Example 4 Complete the Square

Find the value of c that makes $x^2 - 7x + c$ a perfect square. Then write the expression as a perfect square trinomial.

Step 1 Find one half of −7.

$\frac{-7}{2} =$ ______

Step 2 Square the result from Step 1.

$(-3.5)^2 =$ ______

Step 3 Add the result from Step 2 to $x^2 - 7x$.

____

The expression $x^2 - 7x + 12.25$ can be written as ________.

Example 5 Solve by Completing the Square

Solve $x^2 + 18x - 4 = 0$ by completing the square.

$x^2 + 18x - 4 = 0$	Original equation
$x^2 + 18x = 4$	Add 4 to each side.
$x^2 + 18x +$ ____ $= 4 +$ ____	Add $\left(\frac{b}{2}\right)^2$ to each side.
$(x + 9)^2 =$ ____	Factor.
$x + 9 = \pm\sqrt{85}$	Square Root Property
$x = -9 \pm \sqrt{85}$	Subtract 9 from each side.
$x = -9 + \sqrt{85}$ or $-$ ____ $-\sqrt{85}$	Write as two equations.
$x \approx$ ____ ____________	Simplify.

The solution set is $\{x \mid x = -9 - \sqrt{85}, -9 + \sqrt{85}\}$.

Go Online to see Example 6.

Go Online You can complete an Extra Example online.

Talk About It

If a and b are real numbers, can the value of c ever be negative? Explain your reasoning.

Think About It!

Why do we first add 4 to each side?

Example 7 Solve When a is Not 1

Solve $4x^2 - 12x - 27 = 0$ by completing the square.

$4x^2 - 12x - 27 = 0$	Original equation
$x^2 - \_\_\_x - \frac{27}{4} = 0$	Divide each side by 4.
$x^2 - 3x = \_\_\_$	Add $\frac{27}{4}$ to each side.
$x^2 - 3x + \_\_\_ = \frac{27}{4} + \_\_\_$	Add $\left(\frac{b}{2}\right)^2$ or $\frac{9}{4}$ to each side.
$\left(x - \quad\right)^2 = \_\_\_$	Factor
$x - \frac{3}{2} = \pm\_\_\_$	Square Root Property
$x = \_\_\_ \pm 3$	Add $\frac{3}{2}$ to each side.
$x = \frac{3}{2} + 3$ or $x = \frac{3}{2}\_\_\_$	Write as two equations.
$x = \_\_\_ \quad x = \_\_\_$	Simplify.

The solution set is $\left\{x \mid x = -\frac{3}{2}, \frac{9}{2}\right\}$.

Check

Solve $6x^2 - 21x + 9 = 0$ by completing the square.

$x = \_\_\_, \_\_\_$

Think About It!

Compare and contrast the solutions of this equation and the ones in the previous example. Explain.

Example 8 Solve Equations with Imaginary Solutions

Solve $3x^2 - 72x + 465 = 0$ by completing the square.

$3x^2 - 72x + 465 = 0$	Original equation
$x^2 - \_\_\_x + \_\_\_ = 0$	Divide each side by 3.
$x^2 - 24x = \_\_\_$	Subtract 155 from each side.
$x^2 - 24x + \_\_\_ = -155 + \_\_\_$	Add $\left(\frac{b}{2}\right)^2$ to each side.
$(x - \_\_\_)^2 = \_\_\_$	Factor.
$x - 12 = \pm\sqrt{-11}$	Square Root Property
$x - 12 = \pm i\sqrt{11}$	$\sqrt{-1} =$ or i
$x = \_\_\_ \pm \_\_\_\sqrt{11}$	Add 12 to each side.
$x = 12 + i\sqrt{11}$ or $12 - i\sqrt{11}$	Write as two equations.

The solution set is $\{x \mid x = 12 + i\sqrt{11}, 12 - i\sqrt{11}\}$.

Go Online You can complete an Extra Example online.

Learn Quadratic Functions in Vertex Form

When a function is given in standard form, $y = ax^2 + bx + c$, you can complete the square to write it in vertex form.

Key Concept • Vertex Form of a Quadratic Function

Words: The vertex form of a quadratic function is $y = a(x - h)^2 + k$.

	Standard Form	Vertex Form
Symbols:	$y = ax^2 + bx + c$	$y = a(x - h)^2 + k$ The vertex is (h, k).
Example:	$y = 2x^2 + 12x + 16$	$y = 2(x + 3)^2 - 2$ The vertex is $(-3, -2)$.

After completing the square and writing a quadratic function in vertex form, you can analyze key features of the function. The vertex is (h, k) and $x = h$ is the equation of the axis of symmetry. The shape of the parabola and the direction that it opens are determined by a. The value of k is a minimum value if $a > 0$ or a maximum value if $a < 0$.

The path that an object travels when influenced by gravity is called a *trajectory*, and trajectories can be modeled by quadratic functions. The formula relating the height of the object $h(t)$ and time t is shown.

$$h(t) = -\frac{1}{2}gt^2 + vt + h_0$$

The acceleration due to gravity g is 9.8 meters per second squared or 32 feet per second squared. Problems that involve objects being thrown or dropped are called **projectile motion problems**.

Think About It!

What is the minimum value of $y = 2(x - 3)^2 - 1$? How do you know that this value is a minimum?

Example 9 Write Functions in Vertex Form

Write the $y = -x^2 - 12x - 9$ in vertex form.

$y = -x^2 - 12x - 9$	Original function
$y = (-x^2 - 12x) - 9$	Group $ax^2 + bx$.
$y = -(x^2 + 12x) - 9$	Factor out −1.
$y = -(x^2 + 12x + \_\_\_) - 9 - (\_\_\_)(\_\_\_)$	Complete the square.
$y = \_\_\_(x + \_\_\_)^2 + \_\_\_$	Simplify.

Watch Out!

The coefficient of the x^2-term must be 1 before you can complete the square.

Check

Write each function in vertex form.

a. $y = x^2 + 8x - 3$

$y = (x \_\_\_)^2 \_\_\_$

b. $y = -3x^2 - 6x - 5$

$y = \_\_\_(x \_\_\_)^2 \_\_\_$

Go Online You can complete an Extra Example online.

 Think About It!

How would your equation for the axis of symmetry change if the vertex form of the equation was $y = 3(x + 2)^2 - 7$? Justify your argument.

Example 10 Determine the Vertex and Axis of Symmetry

Consider $y = 3x^2 - 12x + 5$.

Part A Write the function in vertex form.

$y = 3x^2 - 12x + 5$	Original equation
$y = (3x^2 - 12x) + 5$	Group $ax^2 + bx$.
$y = 3(x^2 - 4x) + 5$	Factor.
$y = 3(x^2 - 4x + \_\_\_) + 5 - \_\_\_(\_\_\_)$	Complete the square.
$y = \_\_\_(x - \_\_\_)^2 - \_\_\_$	Simplify.

Part B Find the axis of symmetry.

The axis of symmetry is $x = h$ or $x = \_\_\_$.

Part C Find the vertex, and determine if it is a maximum or minimum.

The vertex is (h, k) or $(\_\_\_, \_\_\_)$. Because $a > 0$, this is a ______.

 Think About It!

If the firework reaches a height of 241 feet after 3 seconds, what is the height of the firework after 5 seconds? Justify your answer.

Example 11 Model with a Quadratic Function

FIREWORKS **If the firework is launched 1 foot off the ground at a velocity of 128 feet per second, write a function for the situation. Then find and interpret the axis of symmetry and vertex.**

Step 1 Write the function.

$h(t) = -\frac{1}{2}gt^2 + vt + h_0$	Function for projectile motion
$h(t) = -\frac{1}{2}(32)t^2 + 128t + 1$	$g = 32\,\frac{ft}{s^2}$, $v = 128\,\frac{ft}{s}$, $h_0 = 1$ ft
$h(t) = \_\_\_t^2 + \_\_\_t + \_\_\_$	Simplify.

Step 2 Rewrite the function in vertex form.

$h(t) = (-16t^2 + 128t) + 1$	Group $ax^2 + bx$.
$h(t) = -16(t^2 - 8t) + 1$	Factor.
$h(t) = -16(t^2 - 8t + 16) + 1 - 16(-16)$	Complete the square.
$h(t) = \_\_\_(t - \_\_\_)^2 + \_\_\_$	Simplify.

Step 3 Find and interpret the axis of symmetry.

Because the axis of symmetry divides the function into two equal halves, the firework will be at the same height after ___ seconds as it is after ___ seconds.

Step 4 Find and interpret the vertex.

The vertex is the maximum value of the function because $a < 1$. So the firework reached a maximum height of ___ feet after ___ seconds.

Study Tip:

Vertex When you interpret the vertex of a function, it is important to also consider the value of a when the function is in vertex or standard form. The value of a will tell you whether the vertex is a maximum or minimum.

Go Online You can complete an Extra Example online.

Name ______________________ Period __________ Date __________

Practice

Go Online You can complete your homework online.

Example 1

Solve each equation by using the Square Root Property.

1. $x^2 - 18x + 81 = 49$

2. $x^2 + 20x + 100 = 64$

3. $9x^2 - 12x + 4 = 4$

4. $4x^2 + 4x + 1 = 16$

5. $4x^2 - 28x + 49 = 64$

6. $16x^2 + 24x + 9 = 81$

Example 2

Solve each equation by using the Square Root Property.

7. $36x^2 + 12x + 1 = 18$

8. $25x^2 + 40x + 16 = 28$

9. $25x^2 + 20x + 4 = 75$

10. $36x^2 + 48x + 16 = 12$

11. $25x^2 - 30x + 9 = 96$

12. $4x^2 - 20x + 25 = 32$

Example 3

Solve each equation by using the Square Root Property.

13. $2x^2 - 20x + 50 = -128$

14. $2x^2 - 24x + 72 = -162$

15. $2x^2 + 28x + 98 = -200$

16. $x^2 - 8x + 16 = -36$

17. $3x^2 + 24x + 48 = -108$

18. $3x^2 - 24x + 48 = -363$

Example 4

Find the value of *c* that makes each trinomial a perfect square. Then write the trinomial as a perfect square trinomial.

19. $x^2 + 10x + c$

20. $x^2 - 14x + c$

21. $x^2 + 24x + c$

22. $x^2 + 5x + c$

23. $x^2 - 9x + c$

24. $x^2 - x + c$

Example 5

Solve each equation by completing the square.

25. $x^2 - 13x + 36 = 0$

26. $x^2 + x - 6 = 0$

27. $x^2 - 4x - 13 = 0$

28. $x^2 + 3x - 6 = 0$

29. $x^2 - x - 3 = 0$

30. $x^2 - 8x - 65 = 0$

Example 6

31. **REASONING** When the dimensions of a cube are reduced by 4 inches on each side, the surface area of the new cube is 864 square inches. What were the dimensions of the original cube?

32. **MODELING** The area in square inches of the drawing *Foliage* by Paul Cézanne can be approximated by the equation $y = x^2 - 40x + 396$. Complete the square and find the two roots, which are equal to the approximate length and width of the drawing.

Example 7

Solve each equation by completing the square.

33. $2x^2 - 8x - 24 = 0$

34. $2x^2 - 3x + 1 = 0$

36. $2x^2 - 13x - 7 = 0$

37. $25x^2 + 40x - 9 = 0$

38. $2x^2 + 7x - 4 = 0$

39. $3x^2 + 2x - 1 = 0$

Example 8

Solve each equation by completing the square.

40. $x^2 - 4x + 12 = 0$

41. $2x^2 - 3x + 5 = 0$

42. $2x^2 + 5x + 7 = 0$

43. $x^2 - 2x + 3 = 0$

44. $x^2 = -24$

45. $x^2 - 2x + 4 = 0$

Examples 9 and 10

Write each function in vertex form. Find the axis of symmetry. Then find the vertex, and determine if it is a *maximum* or *minimum*.

46. $y = x^2 + 2x - 5$

47. $y = x^2 + 6x + 1$

48. $y = -x^2 + 4x + 2$

49. $y = -x^2 - 8x - 5$

50. $y = 2x^2 + 4x + 3$

51. $y = 3x^2 + 6x - 1$

Example 11

52. **REASONING** The height of a firework at an amusement park celebration can be modeled by a quadratic function. Suppose the firework is launched 2 feet off the ground at a velocity of 96 feet per second. Hint: Use $h(t) = -\frac{1}{2}gt^2 + vt + h_0$, where $g = 32\frac{\text{ft}}{\text{s}^2}$.

a. Write a function to represent this situation.

b. Rewrite the function in vertex form.

c. Find the axis of symmetry and the vertex and interpret their meaning in the context of the situation.

53. **MODELING** Malik is participating in a diving championship. For one of his dives, he jumps off the platform and down into the pool. His height above the water during the dive can be modeled by a quadratic function. The diving board is 27 meters above the water and Cecil jump with a velocity of 4.18 meters per second. Hint: Use $h(t) = -\frac{1}{2}gt^2 + vt + h_0$, where $g = 9.8\frac{\text{m}}{\text{s}^2}$.

a. Write a function in vertex form to represent this situation.

b. Find the axis of symmetry and the vertex and interpret their meaning in the context of the situation.

Name ______________________ Period __________ Date __________

Mixed Exercises

PRECISION Solve each equation. Round to the nearest hundredth, if necessary.

54. $4x^2 - 28x + 49 = 5$

55. $9x^2 + 30x + 25 = 11$

56. $x^2 + x + \frac{1}{3} = \frac{2}{3}$

57. $x^2 + 1.2x + 0.56 = 0.91$

Find the value of *c* that makes each trinomial a perfect square. Then write the trinomial as a perfect square.

58. $x^2 + 0.7x + c$

59. $x^2 - 3.2x + c$

60. $x^2 - 1.8x + c$

61. FREE FALL A rock falls from the top of a cliff that is 25.8 meters high. Use the formula $h(t) = -\frac{1}{2}gt^2 + vt + h_0$, where $g = 9.8\frac{\text{m}}{\text{s}^2}$, to write a quadratic function that models the situation. Determine to the nearest tenth of a second the amount of time it takes the rock to strike the ground. Explain your reasoning.

62. REACTION TIME Liana was eating lunch when she saw her friend Jori approach. The room was crowded and Jason had to lift his tray to avoid obstacles. Suddenly, a glass on Jori's lunch tray tipped and fell off the tray. Liana lunged forward and managed to catch the glass just before it hit the ground. The height *h*, in feet, of the glass *t* seconds after it was dropped is given by $h = -16t^2 + 4.5$. Liana caught the glass when it was six inches off the ground. How long was the glass in the air before Liana caught it?

63. INVESTMENTS The amount of money *A* in an account in which *P* dollars are invested for 2 years is given by the formula $A = P(1 + r)^2$, where *r* is the interest rate compounded annually. If an investment of \$800 in the account grows to \$882 in two years, at what interest rate was it invested, to the nearest percent?

64. INVESTMENTS Niyati invested \$1000 in a savings account with interest compounded annually. After two years the balance in the account is \$1210. Use the compound interest formula $A = P(1 + r)^t$ to find the annual interest rate, to the nearest percent.

Write each function in vertex form. Then find the vertex.

65. $y = x^2 - 10x + 28$

66. $y = x^2 + 16x + 65$

67. $y = x^2 - 20x + 104$

68. $y = x^2 - 8x + 17$

69. AUDITORIUM SEATING The seats in an auditorium are arranged in a square grid pattern. There are 45 rows and 45 columns of chairs. For a special concert, organizers decide to increase seating by adding *n* rows and *n* columns to make a square pattern of seating 45 + *n* seats on a side.

a. How many seats are there after the expansion?

b. What is *n* if organizers wish to add 1000 seats?

c. If organizers do add 1000 seats, what is the seating capacity of the auditorium?

70. DECK DESIGN The Ray burns current deck is 12 feet by 12 feet. They decide they would like to expand their deck and maintain its square shape. How much larger will each side need to be for the deck to have an area of 200 square feet?

71. COMPLETING THE SQUARE Saura needs to solve the equation $x^2 - 12x = 40$. What must she do to each side of the equation to complete the square?

72. VOLUME A piece of sheet metal has a length that is three times its width w. It is used to make a box with an open top by cutting out 2-inch by 2-inch squares from each corner, then folding up the sides.

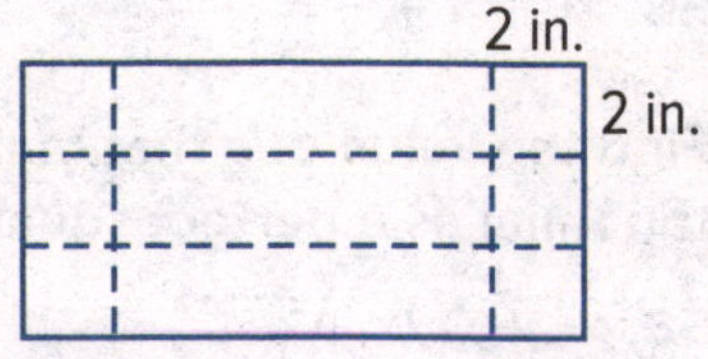

a. Write a quadratic function that represents the volume, $V(w)$, of the box, in square inches.

b. ARGUMENTS Tevari states that because all of the terms of the expression for the volume are even, 2 can be factored out of the right side of the function and then divided out of each side to give $V(w) = 3w^2 - 16w + 16$. Is he correct? Explain why or why not.

73. GEOMETRY If the length of one side of a square is increased by 4 centimeters and the length of an adjacent side is decreased by 8 centimeters, the area of the figure is decreased by 20%. Find the length of each side of the square to the nearest tenth.

74. FIND THE ERROR Alonso and Aika are solving $x^2 + 8x - 20 = 0$ by completing the square. Is either of them correct? Explain your reasoning.

Alonso	Aika
$x^2 + 8x - 20 = 0$	$x^2 + 8x - 20 = 0$
$x^2 + 8x = 20$	$x^2 + 8x = 20$
$x^2 + 8x + 16 = 20 + 16$	$x^2 + 8x + 16 = 20$
$(x + 4)^2 = 36$	$(x + 4)^2 = 20$
$x + 4 = \pm 6$	$x + 4 = \pm\sqrt{20}$
$x = -4 \pm 6$	$x = -4 \pm \sqrt{20}$

75. PERSEVERE Solve $x^2 + bx + c = 0$ by completing the square. Your answer will be an expression for x in terms of b and c.

76. ANALYZE Without solving, determine how many unique solutions there are for each equation. Are they rational, real, or complex? Justify your reasoning.

a. $(x + 2)^2 = 16$ **b.** $(x - 2)^2 = 16$ **c.** $-(x - 2)^2 = 16$

d. $36 - (x - 2)^2 = 16$ **e.** $16(x + 2)^2 = 0$ **f.** $(x + 4)^2 = (x + 6)^2$

77. CREATE Write a perfect square trinomial equation in which the linear coefficient is negative and the constant term is a fraction. Then solve the equation.

78. WRITE Explain what is means to complete the square. Describe each step.

Lesson 3-6

Using the Quadratic Formula and the Discriminant

Explore The Discriminant

Online Activity Use graphing technology to complete the Explore.

INQUIRY How does the discriminant of a quadratic equation relate to its roots?

Learn Using the Quadratic Formula

Key Concept • Quadratic Formula

Words: The solutions of a quadratic equation of the form $ax^2 + bx + c = 0$, where $a \neq 0$, are given by the following formula.

$$x = \frac{-b \pm \sqrt{b^2 - 4ac}}{2a}$$

Example: $2x^2 + 6x + 3 \rightarrow x = \frac{-6 + \sqrt{6^2 \pm 4(2)(3)}}{2(2)}$

Example 1 Real Roots, *c* is Positive

CONTEST **At the annual World Championship Punkin Chunkin contest in Bridgeville, Delaware, pumpkins are launched hundreds of yards. The path of a pumpkin can be modeled by the quadratic function $h = -4.9t^2 + 11.7t + 42$, where *h* is the height and *t* is the number of seconds after launch.**

Part A Use the Quadratic Formula to solve $0 = -4.9t^2 + 11.7t + 42$.

$t = \frac{-b \pm \sqrt{b^2 - 4ac}}{2a}$ — Quadratic Formula

$= \frac{-\_\_\_ \pm \sqrt{(11.7)^2 - 4(\_\_\_)(42)}}{2(\_\_\_)}$ — $a = -4.9$, $b = 11.7$, $c = 42$

$= \frac{-11.7 \pm \sqrt{136.89 + \_\_\_}}{\_\_\_}$ — Square and multiply.

$= \frac{-11.7 \pm \sqrt{\_\_\_}}{-9.8}$ — Add.

$= \frac{-11.7 \pm \sqrt{960.09}}{-9.8}$ or $\frac{-11.7 - \sqrt{960.09}}{-9.8}$ — Multiply by $\frac{-1}{-1}$.

The approximate solutions are _____ seconds and _____ seconds.

Part B Interpret the roots.

The negative root does not make sense in this context because the pumpkin launches at 0 seconds. The pumpkin lands after _____ seconds.

Go Online You can complete an Extra Example online.

Today's Standards
N.CN.7, N.CN.8, A.SSE.1b
MP1, MP4

Today's Vocabulary
discriminant

Think About It!
Why are the roots not at 0 and 4.4 seconds, when the pumpkin is launched and when it lands?

Your Notes

Check

DIVING A diver jumps from a diving board that is 10 feet high, and she wants to figure out how far from the board she is before she hits the water. Her arc can be modeled by the function $y = -4.9x^2 + 2.5 + 10$, where y is her height in meters and x is her distance from the diving board in meters.

Part A Solve $0 = -4.9x^2 + 2.5 + 10$.

______________, ______________

Part B Interpret the roots.

Erin hits the water at approximately ______ meters from the board.

Example 2 Real Roots, c is Negative

Solve $x^2 - 4x - 17 = 0$ by using the Quadratic Formula.

$$x = \frac{-b \pm \sqrt{b^2 - 4ac}}{2a}$$ Quadratic Formula

$$= \frac{-4 \pm \sqrt{(4)^2 - 4(1)(-17)}}{2(1)}$$ $a = 1, b = 4, c = -17$

$$= \frac{-4 \pm \sqrt{84}}{2}$$ Simplify.

$$= \frac{-4 \pm \sqrt{4}\sqrt{21}}{2}$$ Product Property of Square Roots

$$= \frac{-4 \pm 2\sqrt{21}}{2}$$ $\sqrt{4} = 2$

$$= -2 \pm \sqrt{21}$$ Divide the numerator and denominator by 2.

Check

Solve $3x^2 - 5x - 1 = 0$ by using the Quadratic Formula.

____

Example 3 Complex Roots

Solve $5x^2 - 8x - 11 = 0$ by using the Quadratic Formula.

$$x = \frac{-b \pm \sqrt{b^2 - 4ac}}{2a}$$ Quadratic Formula

$$= \frac{-8 \pm \sqrt{(8)^2 - 2(5)(11)}}{2(5)}$$ $a = 5, b = 8, c = 11$

$$= \frac{-8 \pm \sqrt{-156}}{10}$$ Simplify.

$$= \frac{-8 \pm \sqrt{-1}\sqrt{4}\sqrt{39}}{10}$$ Product Property of Square Roots

$$= \frac{-8 \pm 2i\sqrt{39}}{10}$$ Write as a complex number.

$$= \frac{-4 \pm i\sqrt{39}}{5}$$ Divide the numerator and denominator by 2.

Go Online You can complete an Extra Example online.

Check

Solve $9x^2 - 3x + 18 = 0$ by using the Quadratic Formula.

______

Learn Using the Discriminant

In the Quadratic Formula, the **discriminant** is the expression under the radical sign, $b^2 - 4ac$.

Key Concept • Discriminant

$b^2 - 4ac > 0$; $b^2 - 4ac$ is a perfect square

Type and Number of Roots

2 real, rational roots

Graph of Related Functions

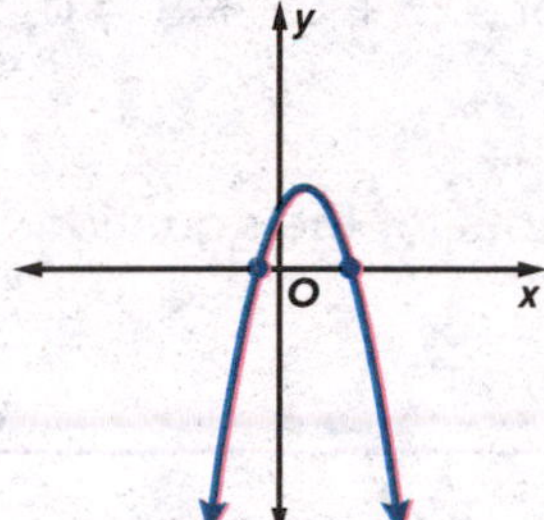

$b^2 - 4ac > 0$; $b^2 - 4ac$ is a not perfect square.

Type and Number of Roots

2 real, rational roots

Graph of Related Functions

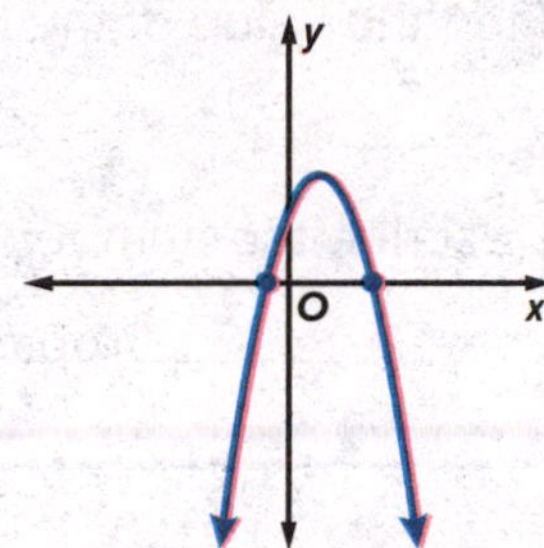

$b^2 - 4ac = 0$

Type and Number of Roots

1 real, rational root

Graph of Related Functions

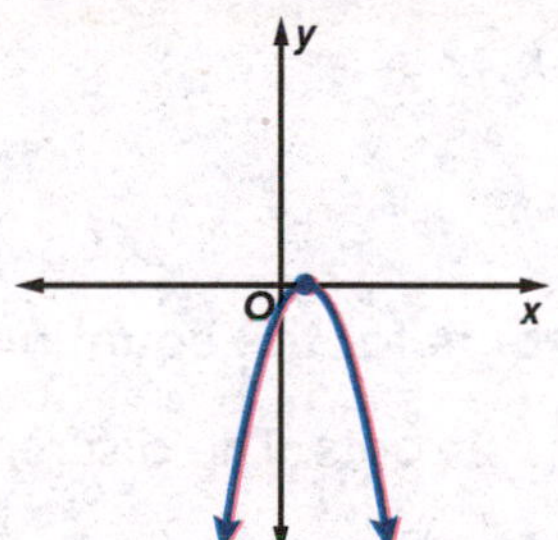

$b^2 - 4ac < 0$

Type and Number of Roots

2 complex roots

Graph of Related Functions

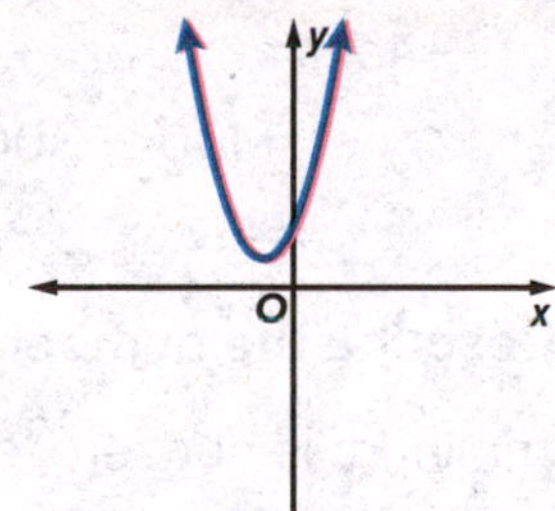

Talk About It

Why are the roots of a quadratic equation complex if the discriminant is negative?

Pause and Reflect

Did you struggle with anything in this lesson? If so, how did you deal with it?

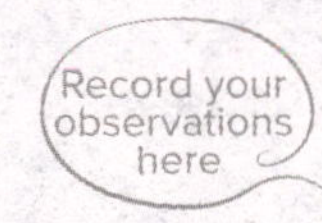

 **Go Online** You can complete an Extra Example online.

Think About It!

Is it possible for a quadratic equation to have zero real or complex roots?

Example 4 The Discriminant, Real Roots

Examine $2x^2 - 10x + 7 = 0$.

Part A Find the value of the discriminant for $2x^2 - 10x + 7 = 0$.

$a =$ ____ $b =$ ____ $c =$ ____

$b^2 - 4ac = (\_\_\_)^2 - 4(\_\_\_)(\_\_\_)$

$= 100 - 56$

$=$ ____

Part B Describe the number and type of roots for the equation.

The discriminant is nonzero, so there are ____ roots. The discriminant is positive and not a perfect square, so the roots are ________.

Check

Examine $2x^2 + 8x + 8 = 0$.

Part A Find the value of the discriminant for $2x^2 + 8x + 8 = 0$.

$b^2 - 4ac =$ ____

Part B Describe the number and type of roots for the equation.

There is/are ________ root(s).

Example 5 The Discriminant, Complex Roots

Examine $-5x^2 + 10x - 15 = 0$.

Part A Find the value of the discriminant for $-5x^2 + 10x - 15 = 0$.

$a =$ ____ $b =$ ____ $c =$ ____

$b^2 - 4ac = (\_\_\_)^2 - 4(\_\_\_)(\_\_\_)$

$= 100 - 300$

$=$ ____

Part B Describe the number and type of roots for the equation.

The discriminant is nonzero, so there are ____ roots. The discriminant is negative, so the roots are ________.

Check

Examine $10x^2 - 4x + 7 = 0$.

Part A Find the value of the discriminant for $10x^2 - 4x + 7 = 0$.

$b^2 - 4ac =$ ______

Part B Describe the number and type of roots for the equation.

There is/are ________ root(s).

Go Online You can complete an Extra Example online.

Go Online to practice what you've learned in Lessons 3-2 and 3-4 through 3-6.

Name ______________________ Period __________ Date __________

Practice

Go Online You can complete your homework online.

Example 1

1. **FOOTBALL** A quarterback throws a football to a receiver. The path of a football can be modeled by the quadratic function $h = -16t^2 + 45t + 4$, where h is the height in feet and t is the number of seconds after the football is thrown. If ball is overthrown and the receiver does not touch the ball, how long will it take the football to hit the ground?

2. **FOUNTAINS** The path of a particle of water from a water fountain can be modeled by the quadratic function $h = -16t^2 + 60t + 1.5$, where h is the height in feet and t is the number of seconds after the water is projected into the air. How long will a particle of water be in the air?

3. **VOLLEYBALL** Micah hits a volleyball in the air. The path of a volleyball can be modeled by the quadratic function $h = -16t^2 + 20.5t + 4$, where h is the height in feet and t is the number of seconds after the volleyball is hit into the air. How long will it take the volleyball to hit the ground?

Example 2

Solve each equation by using the Quadratic Formula.

4. $x^2 + 2x - 35 = 0$

5. $4x^2 + 19x - 5 = 0$

6. $2x^2 - x - 15 = 0$

7. $3x^2 + 5x = 2$

8. $2x^2 + x - 15 = 0$

9. $8x^2 + 6x - 9 = 0$

10. $x^2 - x - 30 = 0$

11. $16x^2 - 24x - 27 = 0$

12. $10x^2 - 13x - 3 = 0$

13. $5x^2 + 10x - 40 = 0$

Example 3

Solve each equation by using the Quadratic Formula.

14. $x^2 - 6x + 21 = 0$

15. $x^2 + 25 = 0$

16. $3x^2 + 36 = 0$

17. $8x^2 - 4x + 1 = 0$

18. $2x^2 + 2x + 3 = 0$

19. $x^2 - 14x + 53 = 0$

20. $4x^2 + 2x + 9 = 0$

21. $3x^2 - 6x + 11 = 0$

22. $2x^2 + 4x + 7 = 0$

23. $-6x^2 + 4x - 3 = 0$

Examples 4 and 5

Find the value of the discriminant for each quadratic equation. Then describe the number and type of roots for the equation.

24. $x^2 - 8x + 16 = 0$

25. $x^2 - 11x - 26 = 0$

26. $3x^2 - 2x = 0$

27. $20x^2 + 7x - 3 = 0$

28. $5x^2 - 6 = 0$

29. $x^2 - 6 = 0$

30. $x^2 + 8x + 13 = 0$

31. $5x^2 - x - 1 = 0$

32. $x^2 - 2x - 17 = 0$

33. $x^2 + 49 = 0$

34. $x^2 - x + 1 = 0$

35. $2x^2 - 3x = -2$

Mixed Exercises

REGULARITY **Describe the discriminant of the related equation of each graph. Then determine the type and number of roots.**

36.

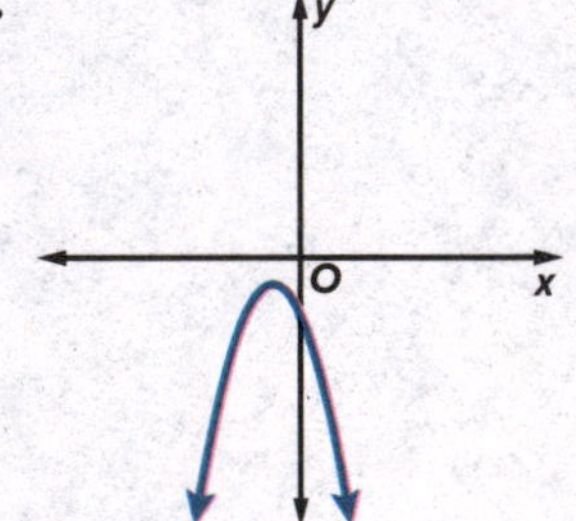

37.

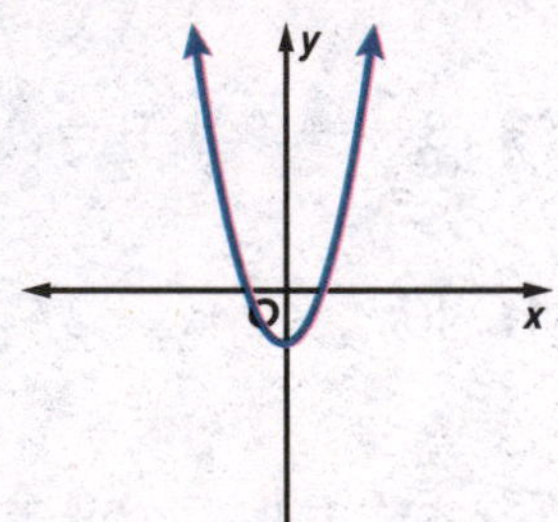

38.

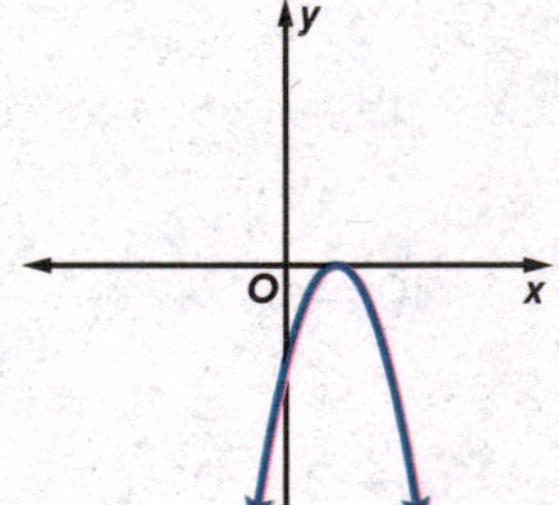

Solve each equation by using the Quadratic Formula.

39. $4x^2 - 4x + 17 = 0$

40. $8x - 1 = 4x^2$

41. $7x^2 - 5x = 0$

42. $x^2 + 10x + 24 = 0$

43. $x^2 - 11x + 24 = 0$

44. $14x^2 + 9x + 1 = 0$

45. $3x^2 - 16x + 16 = 0$

46. $r^2 - \frac{3r}{5} + \frac{2}{25} = 0$

47. $2x^2 + 10x + 11 = 0$

Name ______________________ Period ____________ Date ____________

48. **ARGUMENTS** Besides using the Quadratic Formula, describe another way Exercise 41 could be solved.

49. **PARACHUTING** Ignoring wind resistance, the distance $d(t)$ in feet that a parachutist falls in t seconds can be estimated using the formula $d(t) = 16t^2$. If a parachutist jumps from an airplane and falls for 1100 feet before opening her parachute, how many seconds pass before she opens the parachute?

50. **MODELING** The height $h(t)$ in feet of an object t seconds after it is propelled up from the ground with an initial velocity of 60 feet per second is modeled by the equation $h(t) = -16t^2 + 60t$. At what times will the object be at a height of 56 feet?

51. **STOPPING DISTANCE** The formula $d = 0.05s^2 + 1.1s$ estimates the minimum stopping distance d in feet for a car traveling s miles per hour. If a car stops in 200 feet, what is the fastest it could have been traveling when the driver applied the brakes?

52. **SPORTS** In 1990, American Randy Barnes set the world record for the shot put. His throw can be described by the equation $y = -16x^2 + 368x$. Use the Quadratic Formula to find how far his throw was to the nearest foot.

53. **REASONING** A rectangular box has a square base and a height that is one more than 3 times the length of a side of the base. If the sides of the base are each increased by 2 inches and the height is increased by 3 inches, the volume of the box increases by 531 cubic inches. What are the dimensions of the original box?

$$V_{new} = V_{original} + 531 \text{ in}^3$$

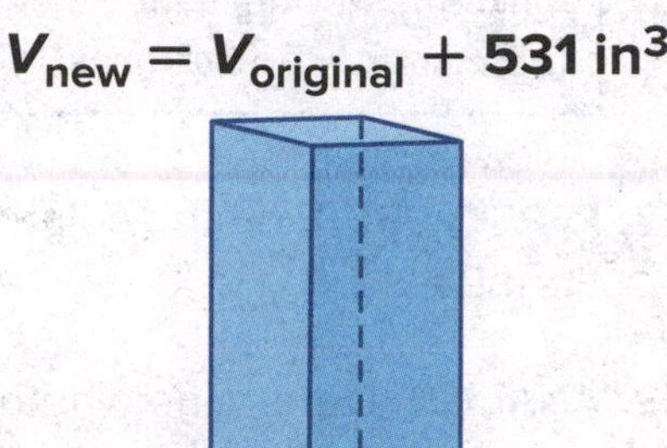

54. **REGULARITY** Construct graphs of the function $f(x) = x^2 + nx + n$, using three different values of n. Explain how to find the values of n for which the graph of $f(x)$ will not intersect the x-axis. Then find the solution set.

55. **PRECISION** A carnival game has players hit a pad with a large rubber mallet. This fires a ball up a 20-foot vertical chute toward a target at the top. A prize is awarded if the ball hits the target. Explain how to find the initial velocity (in feet per second) for which the ball will fail to hit the target. Assume the height of the ball can be modeled by the function $h(t) = -16t^2 + vt$, where v is the initial velocity.

56. **STRUCTURE** The quadratic equation $7x^2 + bx + 5 = 0$ has two complex roots. What are the possible values of b? Show your work.

57. **MODELING** Give an example of a quadratic function $f(x)$ that has the following properties.

I. The discriminant of f is zero.

II. There is no real solution when $f(x) = 10$.

Sketch the graph of $x = f(x)$.

58. **ARGUMENTS** Raoul claims that the sum of the roots of a quadratic equation is always equal to $-\frac{b}{a}$. Do you agree or disagree? Explain your reasoning.

59. STRUCTURE Let $f(x) = 3x^2 - kx + m$ where k and m are real numbers.

a. Find the roots of $f(x)$.

b. For what values of k and m does $f(x)$ have complex roots?

60. WHICH ONE DOESN'T BELONG? Use the discriminant to determine which of these equations is different from the others. Explain your reasoning.

$x^2 - 3x - 40 = 0$	$12x^2 - x - 6 = 0$	$12x^2 + 2x - 4 = 0$	$7x^2 + 6x + 2 = 0$

61. FIND THE ERROR Tama and Jonathan are determining the number of solutions of $3x^2 - 5x = 7$. Is either of them correct? Explain your reasoning.

Tama

$3x^2 - 5x = 7$

$b^2 - 4ac = (-5)^2 - 4(3)(7)$

$= -59$

Since the discriminant is negative, there are no real solutions.

Jonathan

$3x^2 - 5x = 7$

$3x^2 - 5x - 7 = 0$

$b^2 - 4ac = (-5)^2 - 4(3)(-7)$

$= 109$

Since the discriminant is positve, there are two real roots.

62. PERSEVERE Find the solutions of $4ix^2 - 4ix + 5i = 0$ by using the Quadratic Formula.

63. ANALYZE Determine whether each statement is *sometimes*, *always*, or *never* true. Explain your reasoning.

a. In a quadratic equation written in standard form, if a and c have different signs, then the solutions will be real.

b. If the discriminant of a quadratic equation is greater than 1, the two roots are real irrational numbers.

64. CREATE Sketch the corresponding graph and state the number and type of roots for each of the following.

a. $b^2 - 4ac$

b. A quadratic function in which $f(x)$ never equals zero.

c. A quadratic function in which $f(a) = 0$ and $f(b) = 0$; $a \neq b$.

d. The discriminant is less than zero.

e. a and b are both solutions and can be represented as fractions.

65. PERSEVERE Find the value(s) of m in the quadratic equation $x^2 + x + m + 1 = 0$ such that it has one solution.

66. WRITE Describe three different ways to solve $x^2 - 2x - 15 = 0$. Which method do you prefer, and why?

Quadratic Inequalities

Today's Standards
A.CED.1, A.CED.3
MP1, MP4

Today's Vocabulary
quadratic inequality

Explore Graphing Quadratic Inequalities

Online Activity Use graphing technology to complete the Explore.

INQUIRY How can you represent a quadratic inequality graphically?

Learn Using the Quadratic Formula

You can graph quadratic inequalities in two variables by using the same techniques used to graph linear inequalities in two variables. A **quadratic inequality** is an inequality that includes a quadratic expression.

Key Concept • Square Root Property

Step 1 Graph the related function.
Step 2 Test a point not on the parabola.
Step 3 Shade accordingly.

Think About It!
How do you know whether to make the parabola solid or dashed?

Example 1 Graph a Quadratic Inequality (< or ≤)

Graph $y \leq x^2 - 2x + 8$.

Step 1 Graph the related function.

Because the inequality is less than or equal to, the parabola should be solid.

Step 2 Test a point not on the parabola.

$y \leq x^2 - 2x + 8$	Original inequality
$0 \leq (0)^2 - 2(0) + 8$	$(x, y) = (0, 0)$
___ ≤ ___	True

Shade the region that contains the point.

Step 3 Shade accordingly.

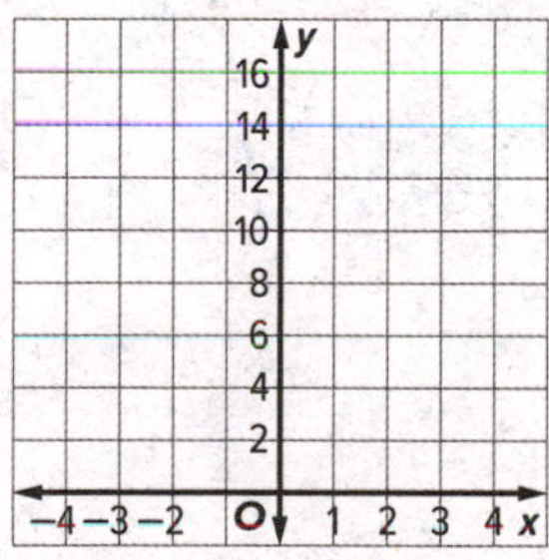

Study Tip:
(0, 0) If (0, 0) is not a point on the parabola, then it is often the easiest point to test when determining which part of the graph to shade.

Go Online You can complete an Extra Example online.

Your Notes

Example 2 Graph a Quadratic Inequality (> or ≥)

Graph $y > -5x^2 + 10x$.

Step 1 Graph the related function.

Because the inequality is greater than, the parabola should be dashed.

Step 2 Test a point not on the parabola.

$y > -5x^2 + 10x$	Original inequality
$0 > -5(1)^2 + 10(1)$	$(x, y) = (1, 1)$
___ > ___	True

So, (1, 0) is not a solution of the inequality.

Step 3 Shade accordingly.

Because (1, 0) is not a solution of the inequality, shade the region that does not contain the point.

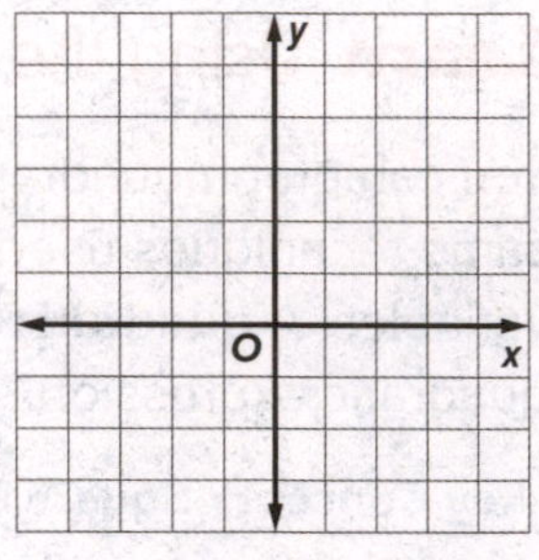

Learn Solving Quadratic Inequalities

Key Concept • Solving Quadratic Inequalities

$ax^2 + bx + c < 0$

Graph $y = ax^2 + bx + c$ and identify the x-values for which the graph lies *below* the x-axis.

For ≤, include the x-intercepts in the solution.

$a > 0$

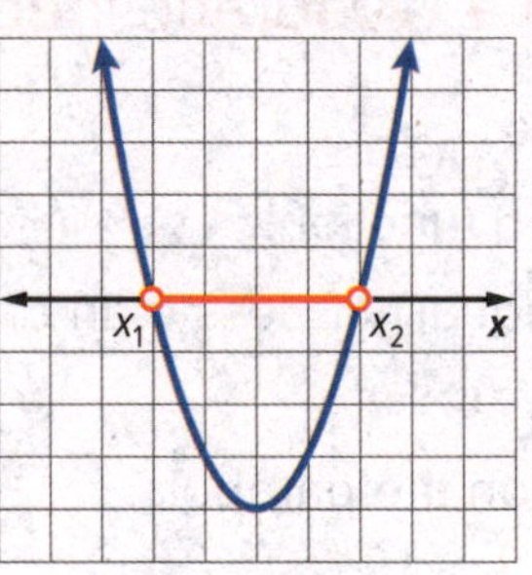

$\{x \mid x_1 < x < x_2\}$

$a < 0$

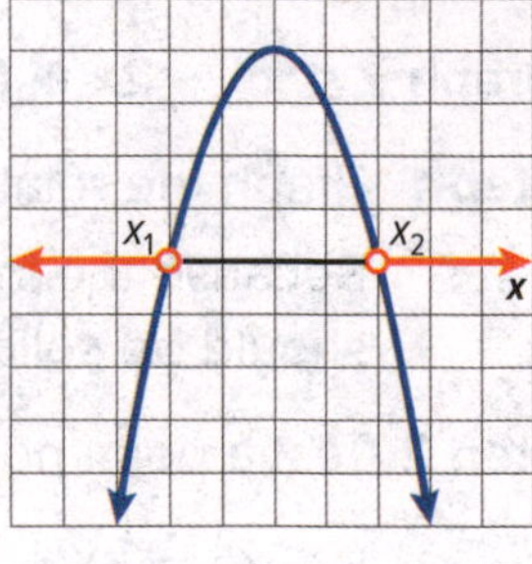

$\{x \mid x_1 < x < x_2\}$

$ax^2 + bx + c > 0$

Graph $y = ax^2 + bx + c$ and identify the x-values for which the graph lies *above* the x-axis.

For ≥, include the x-intercepts in the solution.

$a > 0$

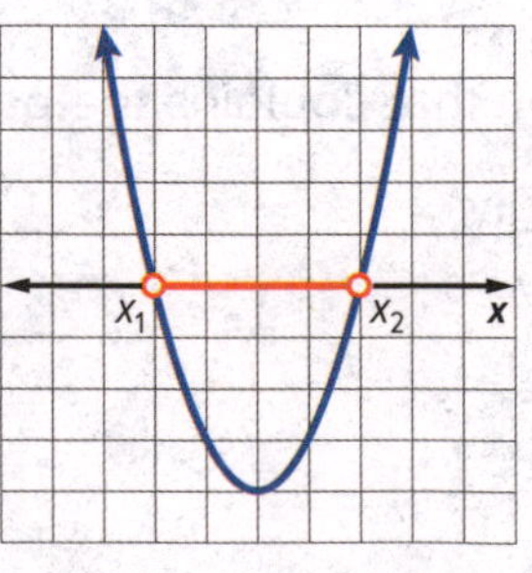

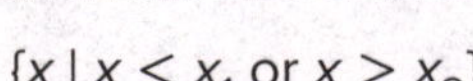
$\{x \mid x < x_1 \text{ or } x > x_2\}$

$a < 0$

$\{x \mid x_1 < x < x_2\}$

Go Online You can complete an Extra Example online.

Example 3 Solve a Quadratic Inequality ($<$ or $\leq$) by Graphing

Solve $x^2 + 2x - 6 < 0$ by graphing.

Because the quadratic expression is less than 0, the solution consists of x-values for which the graph of the related function lies *below* the x-axis. Begin by finding the zeros of the related function.

$x^2 + 2x - 6 = 0$	Related equation
$(x - \_\_\_\_)(x + \_\_\_\_) = 0$	Factor.
$x = \_\_\_\_$ or $x = \_\_\_\_$	Zero Product Property

Sketch the graph of a parabola that has x-intercepts at 2 or -3. The graph should open up because $a > 0$.

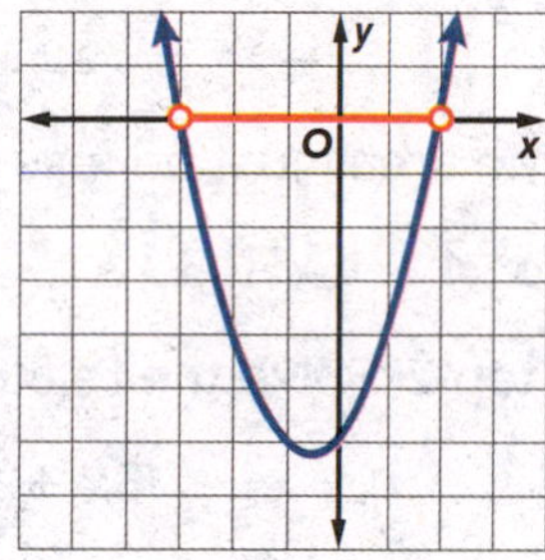

The graph lies below the x-axis between ____ and ____. Thus, the solution set is $\{x \mid \_\_\_\_ < x < \_\_\_\_\}$ or in interval notation (________).

Example 4 Solve a Quadratic Inequality ($>$ or $\geq$) by Graphing

Solve $x^2 - 3x - 4 \geq 0$ by graphing.

Because the quadratic expression is greater than or equal to 0, the solution consists of x-values for which the graph of the related function lies *on* and *above* the x-axis. Begin by finding the zeros of the related function.

$x^2 - 3x - 4 = 0$	Related equation
$(x - \_\_\_\_)(x + \_\_\_\_) = 0$	Factor.
$x = \_\_\_\_$ or $x = \_\_\_\_$	Zero Product Property

Sketch the graph of a parabola that has x-intercepts at –1 or 4. The graph should open up because $a > 0$.

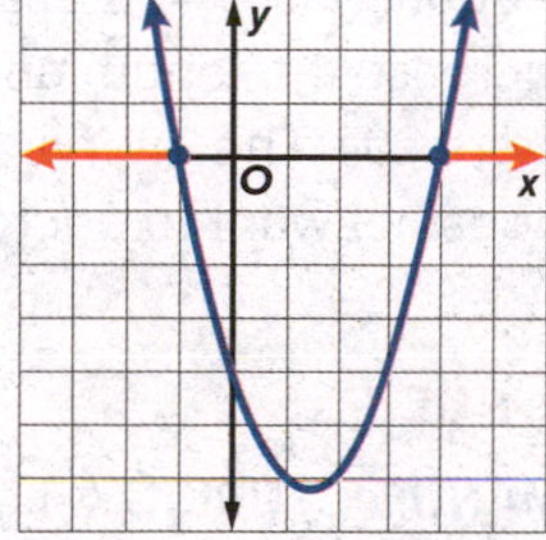

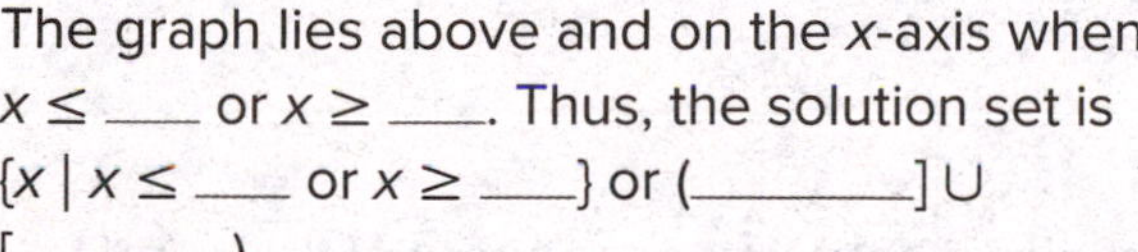

The graph lies above and on the x-axis when $x \leq \_\_\_\_$ or $x \geq \_\_\_\_$. Thus, the solution set is $\{x \mid x \leq \_\_\_\_$ or $x \geq \_\_\_\_\}$ or (________] ∪ [____, ____).

Check

Solve $-\frac{1}{4}x^2 + x + 1 > 0$ by graphing and write the solution set.

$\{x \mid \_\_\_\_\_\_\_\_ < x < \_\_\_\_\_\_\_\_\}$

Go Online You can complete an Extra Example online.

Think About It!

How could you check your solution?

Talk About It

For a quadratic inequality of the form $ax^2 + bx + c > 0$ where $a < 0$, if the related equation has no real roots, what is the solution set? Explain your reasoning.

Example 5 Solve a Quadratic Inequality Algebraically

GARDENING Marcus is planning a garden. He has enough soil to cover 104 square feet, and wants the dimensions of the garden to be at least 5 feet by 10 feet. If he wants to increase the length and width by the same number of feet, by what value can he increase the dimensions of the garden without needing to buy more soil? Create a quadratic inequality and solve it algebraically.

Step 1 Determine the quadratic inequality.

$A = \ell w$	Area formula
$= (x + 10)(x + 5)$	$\ell = x + 10$; $w + 5$
$= x^2 + \_\_\_\_ + 50$	FOIL and Simplify.

The area must be less than or equal to 104 square feet,

so $x^2 + 15x + 50 \leq \_\_\_\_$

Step 2 Solve the related equation.

$x^2 + 15x + 50 = 104$	Related equation
$x^2 + 15x \_\_\_\_ = 0$	Subtract 104 from each side.
$(x \_\_\_\_)(x \_\_\_\_) = 0$	Factor.
$x = -18$ or $x = 3$	Zero Product Property

Steps 3 and 4 Plot the solutions on a number line and test a value from each interval.

Use dots because −18 and 3 are solutions of the original inequality.

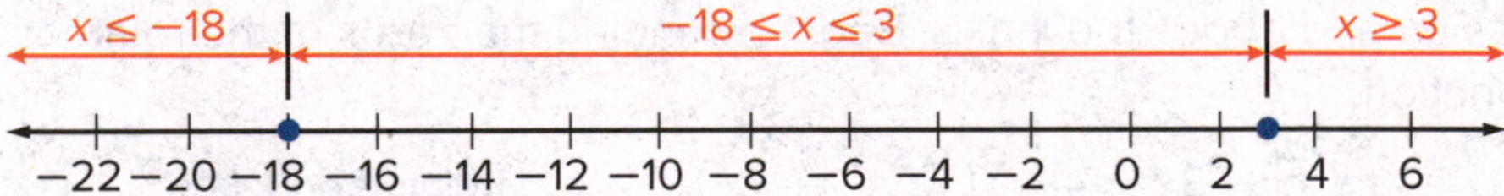

Test a value from each interval to see if it satisfies the original inequality.

Test $x = 20$, $x = 0$, and $x = 5$. The only value that satisfies the original inequality is $x = \_\_\_\_$, so the solution set is [−18, ____]. So, Marcus can increase the length and width up to ____ feet without needing the buy more soil. The interval $-18 \leq x \leq 0$ is not relevant because Marcus does not want to decrease the length and width or leave it as is.

Check

MANUFACTURING An electronics manufacturer can model their profits in dollars P when they sell x video players by using the function $P(x) = -0.1x^2 + 75x - 1000$. How many video players can they sell so they make \$7500 or less?

The company will make \$7500 or less if they make ____ video players or fewer and/or ____ video players or more.

Go Online You can complete an Extra Example online.

Name ____________ Period ________ Date ________

Practice

Go Online You can complete your homework online.

Example 1

Graph each inequality.

1. $y \leq x^2 + 6x + 4$

2. $y < -x^2 + 4x - 6$

3. $y \leq x^2 - 4$

4. $y \leq x^2 + 4$

5. $y < 2x^2 - 4x - 2$

6. $-x^2 + 12x - 36 > y$

Example 2

Graph each inequality.

7. $y > x^2 + 6x + 7$

8. $y > x^2 - 8x + 17$

9. $y \geq x^2 + 2x + 2$

10. $y \geq 2x^2 + 4x$

11. $y > -2x^2 - 4x + 2$

12. $y \geq x^2 - 4x + 4$

Examples 3 and 4

Solve each inequality by graphing.

13. $x^2 - 6x + 9 \leq 0$

14. $-x^2 - 4x + 32 \geq 0$

15. $\frac{3}{4}x^2 + \frac{3}{4}x - 10 > 5$

16. $x^2 - x - 6 \leq 0$

17. $x^2 + 8x + 16 \geq 0$

18. $x^2 - 2x - 24 \leq 0$

Example 5

19. FENCING Vanessa has 180 feet of fencing that she intends to use to build a rectangular play area for her dog. She wants the play area to enclose at least 1800 square feet. What are the possible widths of the play area?

20. BUSINESS A bicycle maker sold 300 bicycles last year at a profit of \$300 each. The maker wants to increase the profit margin this year, but predicts that each \$20 increase in profit will reduce the number of bicycles sold by 10. How many \$20 increases in profit can the maker add in and expect to make a total profit of at least \$100,000?

Mixed Exercises

Solve each quadratic inequality by using a graph, a table, or algebraically.

21. $-2x^2 + 12x < -15$

22. $5x^2 + x + 3 \geq 0$

23. $11 \leq 4x^2 + 7x$

24. $x^2 - 4x \leq -7$

25. $-3x^2 + 10x < 5$

26. $-1 \geq -x^2 - 5x$

27. $x^2 + 2x + 1 > 0$

28. $x^2 - 3x + 2 \leq 0$

29. $x^2 + 10x + 7 \geq 0$

30. $x^2 - 5x > 14$

31. $-x^2 - 15 \leq 8x$

32. $9x \leq 12x^2$

33. $4x^2 + 4x + 1 > 0$

34. $5x^2 + 10 \geq 27x$

35. $9x^2 + 31x + 12 \leq 0$

36. REASONING Consider the equation $ax^2 + bx + c = 0$. Assume that the discriminant is zero and that a is positive. What are the solutions of the inequality $ax^2 + bx + c \leq 0$?

Write a quadratic inequality for each graph.

37.

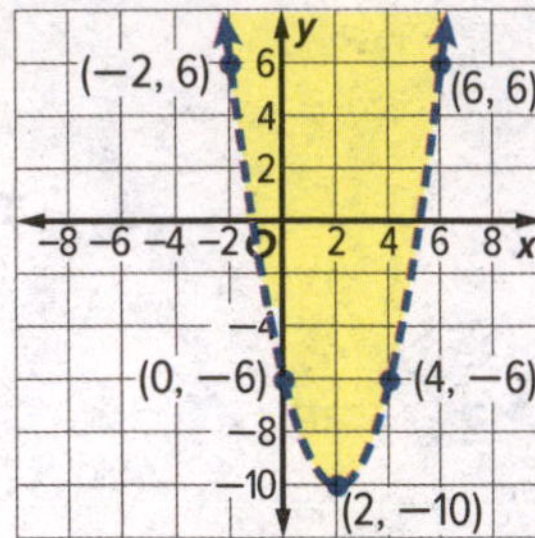

38.

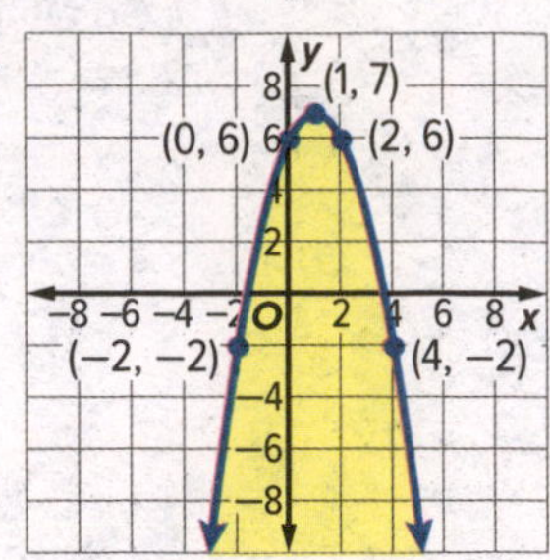

39.

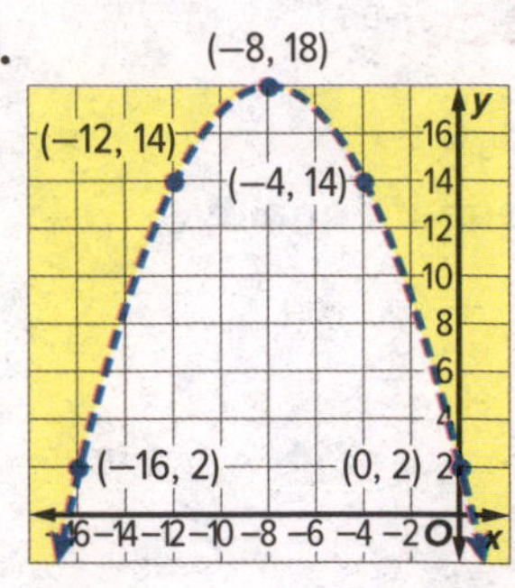

40. **DAMS** The Hoover Dam is a concrete arch dam designed to hold the water of Lake Mead. At its center, the dam's height is approximately 725 feet, and the dam varies from 45 to 660 feet thick. The dark line on this sketch of the cross section of the dam is a parabola.

Cross-Section of Hoover Dam

Lake Mead
Height
Dam
Thickness

a. Write an equation for the Hoover Dam parabola. Let the height be the y-value of the parabola and the thickness be the x-value of the parabola. (Hint: the equation will be in the form: $y = k(x - \text{maximum thickness}) + \text{maximum height}$.)

b. Using your equation, graph the parabola of the Hoover Dam for $45 \leq x \leq 660$.

c. Estimate to the nearest foot the thickness of the dam when the height is 200 feet.

41. **ARGUMENTS** Are the boundaries of the solution set of $x^2 + 4x - 12 \leq 0$ twice the value of the boundaries of $\frac{1}{2}x^2 + 2x - 6 \leq 0$? Explain.

42. **FIND THE ERROR** Don and Diego used a graph to solve the quadratic inequality $x^2 - 2x - 8 > 0$. Is either of them correct? Explain your reasoning.

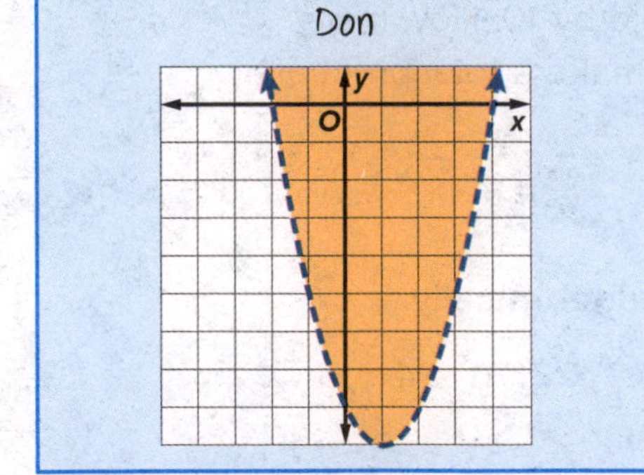

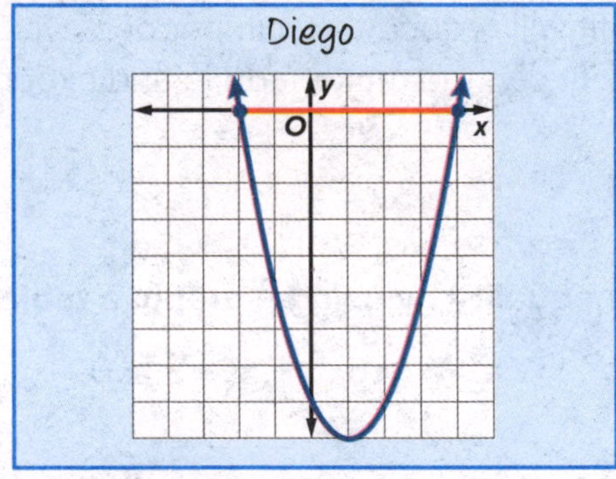

43. **CREATE** Write a quadratic inequality for each condition.

a. The solution set is all real numbers.

b. The solution set is the empty set.

44. **ANALYZE** Determine if the following statement is *sometimes*, *always*, or *never* true. Explain your reasoning.

The intersection of $y \leq -ax^2 + c$ and $y \geq ax^2 - c$ is the empty set.

45. **PERSEVERE** Graph the intersection of the graphs of $y \leq -x^2 + 4$ and $y \geq x^2 - 4$.

46. **WRITE** How are the techniques used when solving quadratic inequalities and linear inequalities similar? How are they different?

Solving Linear-Nonlinear Systems

Explore Linear-Quadratic Systems

Online Activity Use graphing technology to complete the Explore.

INQUIRY How many solutions can a linear-quadratic system of equations have?

Learn Solving Linear-Quadratic Systems

A quadratic equation can be solved by using a system of equations. For example, if $ax^2 + bx + c = mx + k$, each side of the equation can be written as a related function: $f(x) = ax^2 + bx + c$ and $g(x) = mx + k$ Because $ax^2 + bx + c = mx + k$ we can set each related function equal to the same variable y, so $y = f(x)$ and $y = g(x)$.

Example 1 Solve a Linear-Quadratic System by Using Substitution

Solve the system of equations.

$$x = 2y^2 + 3y + 1 \quad (1)$$
$$-x + y = -1 \quad (2)$$

Step 1 Solve Equation (2) for x.

$-x + y = -1$	Equation (2)
$-x =$ ____ -1	Subtract y from each side.
$x = y$ ____	Divide each side by -1.

Step 2 Substitute for x in Equation (1). Then solve for y.

$x = 2y^2 + 3y + 1$	Equation (1)
$y + 1 = 2y^2 + 3y + 1$	$x = y + 1$
____ $= 2y^2 + 2y$	Simplify.
$0 =$ ____$(y + 1)$	Factor out $2y$.
$y =$ ____ or $y =$ ____	Zero Product Property

Step 3 Substitute the y-values and solve for x.

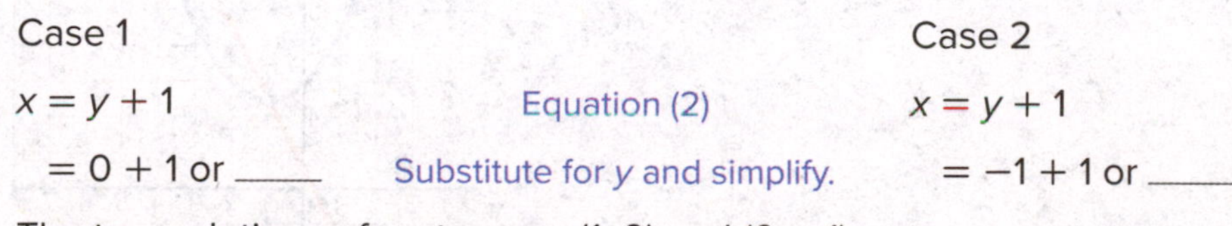

Case 1		Case 2
$x = y + 1$	Equation (2)	$x = y + 1$
$= 0 + 1$ or ____	Substitute for y and simplify.	$= -1 + 1$ or ____

The two solutions of system are (1, 0) and (0, −1).

Go Online You can complete an Extra Example online.

Today's Standards
A.REI.11
MP1, MP4

Today's Vocabulary
quadratic relations

Think About It!
A system of linear equations can have infinitely many solutions. Can a linear-quadratic system have infinitely many solutions? Explain.

Study Tip:
Algebra and Graphing Even when solving a system algebraically, it can be useful to graph the equations to ensure that you have the correct number of solutions.

Your Notes 

Go Online You can learn how to solve a system of linear and quadratic equations by watching the video online.

Example 2 Solve a Linear-Quadratic System by Using Elimination

Solve the system of equations.

$x^2 = y + 5$ (1)

$-x + y = 7$ (2)

Step 1 Solve so that the *y*s are on the same side of each equation.

$-x + y = 7$ Equation (2)

$-x =$ ____ $+ 7$ Subtract *y* from each side.

Step 2 Add the equations

$x^2 = y + 5$

$(+)\ -x = -y + 7$

$x^2 -$ ____ $=$ ____

Step 3 Solve for the remaining variable.

$x^2 - x = 12$ Sum of Equations (1) and (2)

$x^2 - x -$ ____ $=$ ____ Subtract 12 from each side.

$(x -$ ____$)(x +$ ____$) = 0$ Factor.

$x =$ ____ or $x =$ ____ Zero Product Property

Step 4 Solve for the other variable.

$-x + y = 7$	Equation (2)	$-x + y = 7$
$-4 + y = 7$	Substitute *x*.	$-(-3) + y = 7$
$y =$ ____	Simplify.	$y =$ ____

Use substitution to show that the two solutions are (4, 11) and (−3, 4).

Example 3 Use a System to Solve a Quadratic Equation

Use a system of equations to solve $x^2 - 2x + 6 = 4x + 1$.

Step 1 Create a system of equations.

$y = x^2 - 2x + 6$ (1)

$y = 4x + 1$ (2)

Step 2 Graph the system.

The functions appear to intersect at (1, 5) and (5, 21), so the solutions of $x^2 - 2x + 6 = 4x + 1$ are $x = 1$ and $x = 5$.

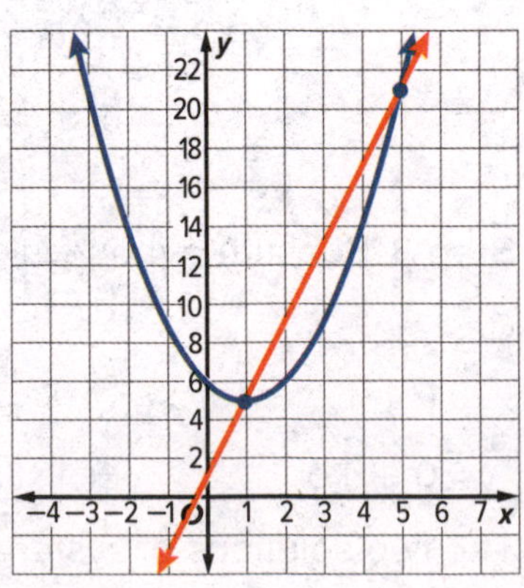

Go Online You can complete an Extra Example online.

Check

Use a system of equations to solve $2x + 11 = x^2 + x - 1$.

(____, ____) (____, ____)

Example 4 Solve a Linear-Quadratic System by Graphing

PRODUCTION A software developer determines that they can model their profit P in hundreds of thousands of dollars given the price x in dollars with the function $P = -0.1x^2 + 4x$. Create a linear-quadratic system and solve it graphically to determine the price for which the company will earn \$4.2 million.

Step 1 Create a linear-quadratic system.

The first equation is the given profit model $P =$ ________.

The line that represents a profit of \$4.2 million is $P =$ ____.

So, the linear-quadratic system is:

$P =$ ________ (1)

$P = 42$ (2)

Step 2 Graph the system.

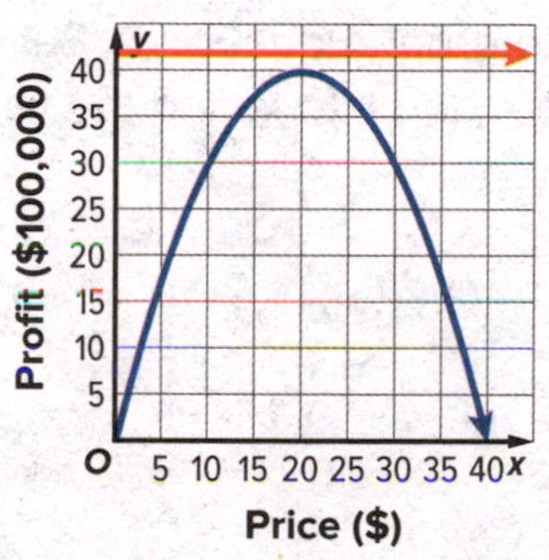

Step 3 Determine the solutions.

The graphs of the functions do not intersect at any point, so the system has ____ solutions.

Check

MOUNTAINS Engineers want to build a foot bridge with steps across a steep valley. They can model the valley with the equation $y = 0.05x^2 - 4x + 80$, where y is the height above the lowest point in the valley in feet and x is the distance from where they plan to start the bridge. If they start the bridge 80 feet above ground and want it to go down an inch for every foot to the right, then at what points will the bridge start and end?

Think About It!

What does the solution set of the system mean in the context of the situation?

Study Tip:

P is measured in hundreds of thousands of dollars, so the value of 42 on the y-axis indicates a profit of \$4.2 million.

Go Online

You can learn how to solve a system of linear and quadratic equations by using a graphing calculator by watching the video online.

Learn Solving Quadratic-Quadratic Systems

Equations of parabolas with vertical axes of symmetry have the parent function $y = x^2$ and can be written in the form $y = a(x - h)^2 + k$. Equations of parabolas with horizontal axes of symmetry are of the form $x = a(y - k)^2 + h$ and are not functions. These are often referred to as **quadratic relations**. The parent function for graphs of quadratic relations that are not functions is $x = y^2$.

If a system contains two quadratic relations, it may have anywhere from zero to four solutions. Just as with linear-quadratic systems, you can solve quadratic-quadratic systems by using graphical or algebraic methods.

> **Think About It!**
> Is $x = \frac{1}{5}(y - 6)^2 + \frac{6}{5}$ a function? Explain your reasoning.

Example 5 Solve a Quadratic-Quadratic System Graphically

Solve the system of equations by graphing.

$y = x^2$ (1)

$x = \frac{1}{5}(y - 6)^2 + \frac{6}{5}$ (2)

Step 1 Graph Equation 1.
Equation (1) has a vertex at ____ and goes through the points (−2, ____), (−1, ____) (1, ____) and (2, ____).

Step 2 Graph Equation 2.
You can use a table of values to graph Equation 2. Because the expression on the right is set equal to x, find the value of x for several values of y.

y	$x = \frac{1}{5}(y - 6)^2 + \frac{6}{5}$	x
3	$x = \frac{1}{5}(3 - 6)^2 + \frac{6}{5}$	
4	$x = \frac{1}{5}(4 - 6)^2 + \frac{6}{5}$	
5	$x = \frac{1}{5}(5 - 6)^2 + \frac{6}{5}$	$\frac{7}{5}$
6	$x = \frac{1}{5}(6 - 6)^2 + \frac{6}{5}$	$\frac{6}{7}$
7	$x = \frac{1}{5}(7 - 6^2 + \frac{6}{5}$	$\frac{7}{5}$
8	$x = \frac{1}{5}(8 - 6)^2 + \frac{6}{5}$	
9	$x = \frac{1}{5}(9 - 6)^2 + \frac{6}{5}$	3

> **Think About It!**
> How could you check your solutions?

Step 3 Graph and solve the system.
To solve the system, graph both relations on the same coordinate plane and see where they intersect.

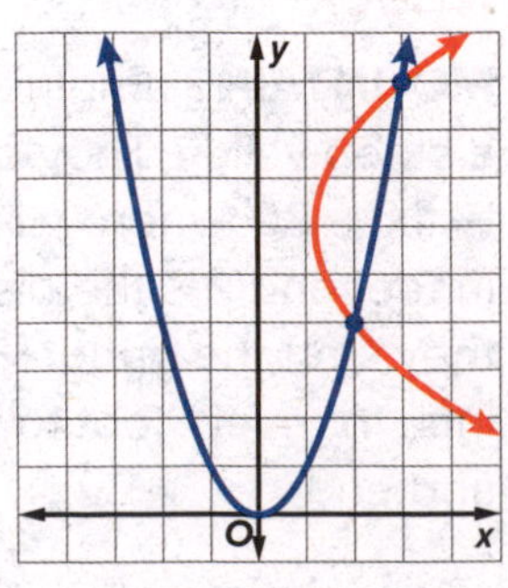

The relations intersect at ____ and ____, so those are the solutions of the system.

Check

Solve the system of equations.

$y = -x^2 + 5x - 6$

$3y = x^2 - x - 6$

(____, ____) (____, ____)

Example 6 Solve a Quadratic-Quadratic Systems Algebraically

Solve the system of equations.

$\mathbf{2x^2 - y = 4}$ (1)

$\mathbf{y = -\frac{1}{2}x^2 + 6}$ (2)

$2x^2 - y = 4$	Equation (1)
$2x^2 - (-\frac{1}{2}x^2 + 6) = 4$	Substitution
$2x^2 + \frac{1}{2}x^2 -$ ____ $= 4$	Distributive Property
$\frac{5}{2}x^2 -$ ____ $= 0$	Simplify.
$5x^2 - 20 = 0$	Multiply each side by 2.
$x^2 -$ ____ $= 0$	Divide each side by 5.
$(x + 2)(x - 2) = 0$	Difference of Two Squares
$x = \pm$____	Zero Product Property

Substitute –2 and 2 into one of the original equations and solve for y.

Case 1

$y = \frac{1}{2}x^2 + 6$	Equation (2)
$y = \frac{1}{2}($____$)^2 + 6$	Substitute for x.
= ____	Simplify.

Case 2

$y = \frac{1}{2}x^2 + 6$

$y = \frac{1}{2}($____$)^2 + 6$

= ____

The solutions are (2, 8) and (−2,8).

Check

Solve the system of equations.

$x = \frac{1}{18}y^2$

$y^2 = -18x + 72$

(____, ____) (____, ____)

Go Online You can complete an Extra Example online.

Example 7 Use a System to Solve a Quadratic Equation

Use a system of equations to solve $2x^2 - 3x + 4 = 11 - 4x^2$.

Step 1 Create a system of equations.

The related equations of each side of $2x^2 - 3x + 4 = 11 - 4x^2$ are:

$y = 2x^2 - 3x + 4$ (1)

$y = 11 - 4x^2$ (2)

Step 2 Graph and solve the system.

Graph the first equation.

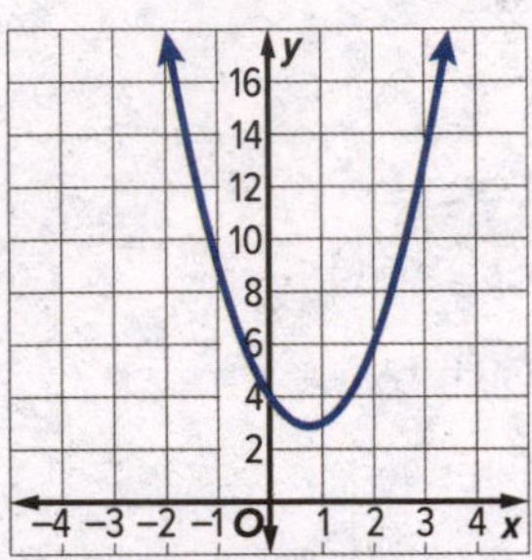

Then graph the second equation on the same coordinate plane.

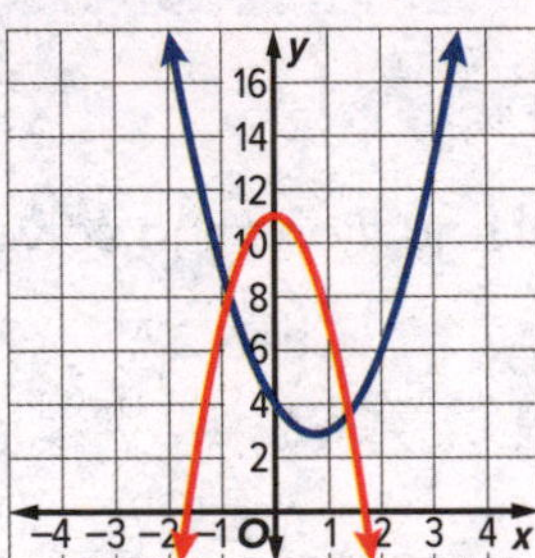

The functions appear to intersect at $\left(-\frac{1}{2}, \_\_\_\_\right)$ and (1, ____),

so the solutions of $2x^2 - 3x + 4 = 11 - 4x^2$ are and ____.

Check

Use a system of equations to solve $-x^2 + 3x + 14 = -\frac{1}{4}x^2 + 5$.

System Solutions: (____, ____) (____, ____)

Equation Solutions: ____, ____

Go Online You can complete an Extra Example online.

Name ____________________ Period __________ Date __________

Practice

Go Online You can complete your homework online.

Examples 1 and 2

Solve each system of equations by using substitution or elimination.

1. $y = x^2 - 5$
$y = x - 3$

2. $y = x - 2$
$y = x^2 - 2$

3. $y = x + 3$
$y = 2x^2$

4. $y = 3x$
$x = y^2$

5. $y = -2x + 2$
$y^2 = 2x$

6. $y = 2 - x$
$y = x^2 - 4x + 2$

7. $x - y + 1 = 0$
$y^2 = 4x$

8. $y = x - 1$
$y = x^2$

9. $y = x$
$y = -2x^2 + 4$

Example 3

Create and graph a system of equations to solve each quadratic equation.

10. $x^2 + 3x + 3 = -2x - 3$

11. $x^2 + 3x + 5 = 2x + 7$

12. $2x^2 + 4x - 3 = 9x$

13. $4x^2 - 6x - 3 = -3x - 2$

14. $3x^2 - 4x + 2 = 2 - 2x$

15. $x^2 - 4x + 5 = 2x + 12$

Example 4

16. BUSINESS An entrepreneur determines that the profit from sales of a specific item in thousands of dollars can be modeled by $P = 4x^2 + 10x$, where x is the selling price of the item in dollars.

- **a.** Create a linear-quadratic system to determine the price for which the company will reach its goal.
- **b.** USE TOOLS Use a graphing calculator to solve the system in **part a** graphically. Round to the nearest hundredth, if necessary.
- **c.** Find and interpret the solution in the context of the situation?

17. MANUFACTURING A manufacturer determines that the profit P from sales of a specific item in thousands of dollars can be modeled by $P = 2x^2 + 30x$, where x is the selling price of the item in dollars.

- **a.** Create a linear-quadratic system to determine the price for which the company will earn $50,000.
- **b.** Solve the system in **part a** graphically to determine the price for which the company will earn $50,000. Round to the nearest hundredth, if necessary.
- **c.** What does the solution set of the system mean in the context of the situation?

Example 5

Solve each system of equations by graphing.

18. $y = x^2$
$x = y^2$

19. $y = \frac{1}{2}x^2$
$x = y^2 + 2y + 1$

20. $y = -2x^2$
$y = 6x^2$

21. $x = (y - 2)^2$
$y = x^2 + 2$

22. $x = \frac{1}{2}y^2 + 1$
$y = \frac{1}{2}(x - 1)^2$

23. $x = \frac{1}{4}(y - 1)^2 + 1$
$y = \frac{1}{4}(x - 1)^2 + 1$

Example 6

Solve each system of equations algebraically.

24. $2x^2 - y = 8$
$y = x^2 + 8$

25. $x^2 - y = 4$
$y = 2x^2$

26. $x = \frac{1}{4}y^2$
$y^2 = -4x + 18$

27. $x = \frac{1}{2}y^2$
$y^2 = -4x + 12$

28. $2y = x^2$
$y = x^2 - 8$

29. $y = x^2 + 3x - 5$
$2y = x^2 + 9x - 6$

Example 7

Create and graph a system of equations to solve each quadratic equation.

30. $2x^2 + 5x + 3 = 2 - 2x^2$

31. $3x^2 - x + 2 = x^2 + 8$

32. $-3x^2 + 3x + 5 = 9 - 4x^2$

33. $2x^2 + 4x + 10 = x^2 + 6$

34. $4x^2 + 2x + 7 = 3x^2 + 6$

35. $5x^2 - 5x - 7 = 3x^2 - 4$

Mixed Exercises

Use the related graphs of each system of equations to determine the solutions.

36. $y = \frac{1}{4}x^2 + \frac{1}{2}x - 2$
$y = -\frac{1}{4}x^2 - \frac{1}{2}x + 2$

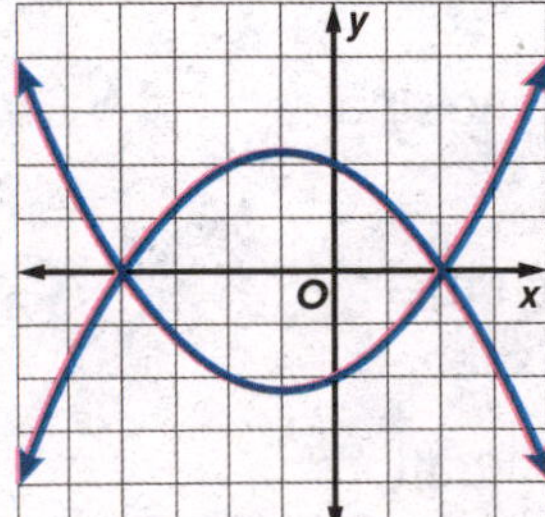

37. $y = x^2 + 4x - 1$
$y = -2x^2 - 8x - 13$

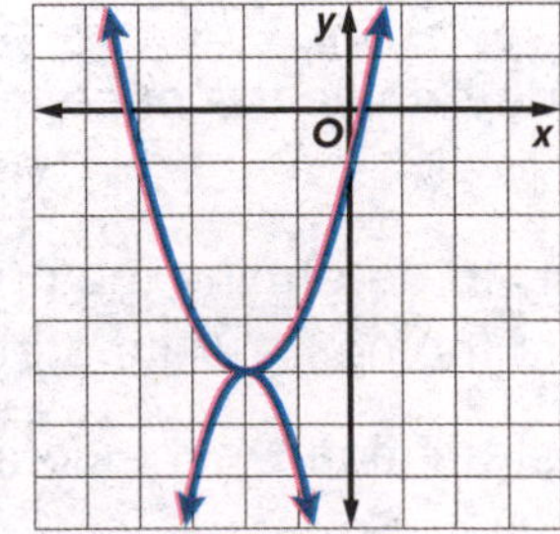

38. $y = 2x^2 - 4x + 6$
$y = -\frac{1}{2}x^2 - 2x + 1$

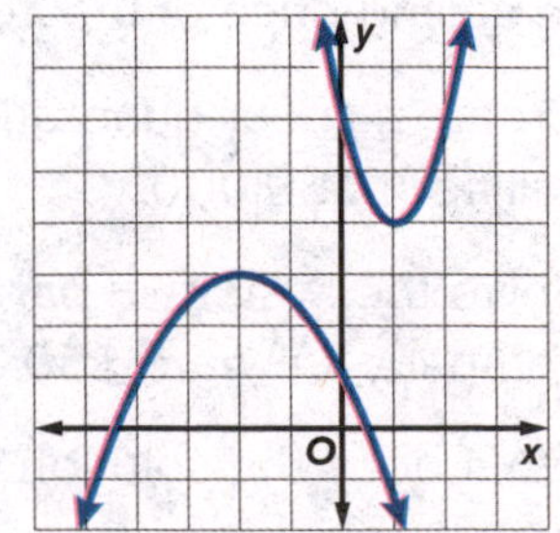

Name ______________________ Period ________ Date ________

Solve each system of equations by graphing, substitution, or elimination.

39. $y = x^2 + 9x + 8$
$y = 7x + 8$

40. $y = x^2 + 7x + 12$
$y = x + 7$

41. $y = x + 3$
$y = 2x^2 - x - 1$

42. $y = \left(\frac{1}{2}x\right)^2$
$4x = y^2$

43. $y = 2x^2$
$x = y^2 - 2y + 1$

44. $y = -8x^2$
$y = 4x^2 + 1$

45. $2x^2 - y = 2$
$y = -x^2 + 4$

46. $x^2 - y = -4$
$y = 4x^2 - 2$

47. $y = x^2$
$y^2 = -3x + 5$

48. $y = -x - 3$
$y = x^2 - 5$

49. $y = -x$
$y^2 = 2x$

50. $y = 3x - 4$
$y = x^2 + 9x + 20$

51. $x - 2 = (y - 2)^2$
$y = x^2 + 5$

52. $3x - 1 = \frac{1}{8}y^2$
$y = x^2 + 5x - 4$

53. $x = (y + 2)^2$
$y = (x + 2)^2$

54. $x = \frac{1}{4}y^2$
$y^2 = -8x + 6$

55. $4y + 3 = x^2$
$y = x^2 - 24$

56. $y = x^2 + x + 5$
$y = 2x^2 + 3x + 2$

Solve each system of equations by graphing, substitution, or elimination.

57. $2x^2 + x - 1 = -10x + 12$

58. $3x^2 - 5x - 2 = -16 - 8x$

59. $x^2 + 3x + 2 = x + 5$

60. $x^2 - 2x - 3 = -\frac{1}{3}x^2 + \frac{2}{3}x + \frac{23}{3}$

61. $3x^2 + 4x + 1 = -x^2 - 2x - 1$

62. $2x^2 - 6x + 4 = -x^2 + 3x - 2$

63. $2x^2 + 6x + 5 = x^2 - 4$

64. $4x^2 + 2x + 7 = 3x^2 + 6$

65. $5x^2 - 5x - 7 = 3x^2 - 4$

66. $x^2 + 4x + 4 = x + 4$

67. $x^2 + 5x + 12 = -4x - 6$

68. $2x^2 - x - 6 = -3x - 2$

69. **SALES** Two companies sell playing cards. Company ABC determines they can model the profit P of their company in thousands of dollars given the price x in dollars with the function $P = 3x^2 - 10x$. Company XYZ models their profit with the function $P = -x^2 + 5x$.

a. Create a quadratic-quadratic system and solve it graphically to determine the price for which both companies will earn the same profit.

b. **REASONING** Why is there only one solution in the context of the situation?

70. **TOOLS** Two companies manufacture drill bits. Company A determines they can model the profit P of their company in thousands of dollars given the price x in dollars with the function $P = 2x^2 - 5x$. Company B models their profit with the function $P = -x^2 + 8x$. Create a quadratic-quadratic system and solve it graphically to determine the price for which both companies will earn the same profit.

71. PACKAGING A manufacturer is making 2 different packages, measured in inches, as shown in the figure. The manufacturer wants the surface area of the 2 packages to be the same.

a. Create a quadratic equation that can be used to find the value of x, when the surface area of the packages is the same.

b. Solve the qu4zdratic equation using any method learned in this lesson.

c. Find and interpret the solution in the context of the situation. Explain.

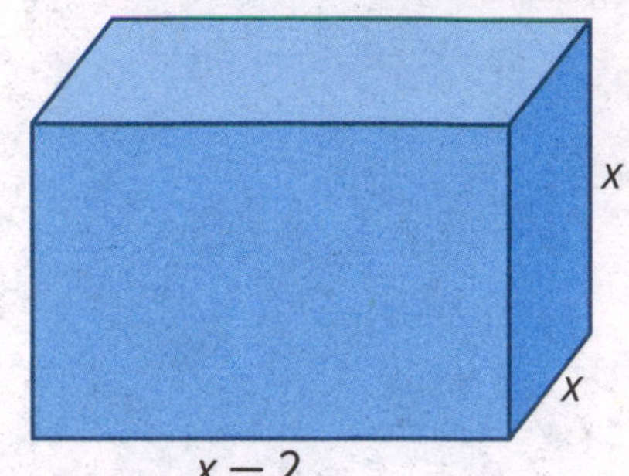

72. REGULARITY Describe the method for solving a linear-quadratic by substitution.

73. VOLLEYBALL The function $h(t) = -16t^2 + vt + h_0$ models the height of the volleyball where v represents initial velocity and h_0 represents initial height. A player bumps a volleyball when it is 3 feet from the ground with an initial velocity of 25 feet per second.

a. If the volleyball net is approximately 7 feet 4 inches, will the volleyball clear the net?

b. If the player on the other side of the net misses the ball, how long will it take for the ball to hit the floor?

c. What assumptions you make?

74. PERSEVERE Describe 3 linear-quadratic systems of equations. One with no solution, one with 1 solution, and one with 2 solutions.

75. ANALYZE Determine whether the statement is *true* or *false*. If false, give a counterexample.

A system of two quadratics has 0, 1, 2, 3, or 4 points in its solution.

76. CREATE Write a system of two quadratics in which there is one solution.

77. WRITE Describe a real-life situation that can be modeled by a system with a quadratic function and a linear function.

78. FIND THE ERROR Danny and Carol are solving the system $y = x^2 + 3x - 9$ and $-4x + y = 3$. Is either of them correct? Explain your reasoning.

Danny

$-4x + (x^2 + 3x - 9) = 3$

$x^2 - x - 9 = 3$

$x^2 - x - 12 = 0$

$(x + 3)(x - 4) = 0$

$x = -3$ or $x = 4$

Carol

$x^2 + 3x - 9 = -4x + 3$

$x^2 + 7x - 12 = 0$

$x \approx -8.42$ or $x \approx 1.42$

Review

Essential Question

What characteristics of quadratic functions are important when analyzing real-world situations that are modeled by quadratic functions?

Module Summary

Lessons 3-1 and 3-2

Graphs of Quadratic Functions

- When the coefficient on the x^2-term is positive, the parabola opens up. When it is negative, the parabola opens down.
- The average rate of change for a parabola over the interval $[b, a]$ is $\frac{f(b) - f(a)}{b - a}$.
- The solutions of an equation are the x-intercepts of the graph of a related function.

Lesson 3-3

Complex Numbers

- The imaginary unit i is the principal square root of -1. Thus, $i = \sqrt{-1}$ and $i^2 = -1$.
- Two complex numbers of the form $a + bi$ and $a - bi$ are called complex conjugates.

Lesson 3-4 through 3-6

Solving Quadratic Equations

- For any real numbers a and b, if $ab = 0$, then either $a = 0$, $b = 0$, or both a and $b = 0$.
- You can solve a quadratic equation by graphing, by factoring, by completing the square, or by using the quadratic formula.
- To solve a quadratic equation of the form $x^2 = n$, take the square root of each side.
- The solutions of a quadratic equation of the form $ax^2 + bx + c = 0$, where $a \neq 0$, are given by the formula $x = \frac{-b \pm \sqrt{b^2 - 4ac}}{2a}$.

Lesson 3-7

Quadratic Inequalities

- To graph a quadratic inequality, graph the related function, test a point not on the parabola and shade accordingly.
- For $ax^2 + bx + c < 0$, graph $y = ax^2 + bx + c$ and identify the x-values for which the graph lies *below* the x-axis. For $\leq$, include the x-intercepts in the solution.
- For $ax^2 + bx + c > 0$, graph $y = ax^2 + bx + c$ and identify the x-values for which the graph lies *above* the x-axis. For $\geq$, include the x-intercepts in the solution.

Lesson 3-8

Systems Involving Quadratic Equations

- You can use the substitution method or the elimination method to solve a system that includes a quadratic equation.
- If a system contains two quadratic relations, it may have anywhere from zero to four solutions.

Study Organizer

 **Foldables**

Use your Foldable to review this module. Working with a partner can be helpful. Ask for clarification of concepts as needed.

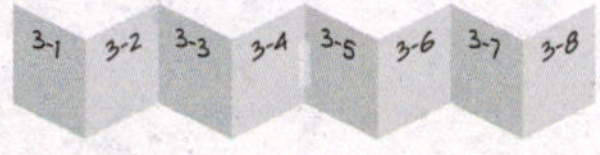

Name ______________________ Period __________ Date __________

Test Practice

1. MULTIPLE CHOICE Which is the graph of $f(x) = -x^2 - 2x + 3$? (Lesson 3-1)

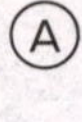

Ⓐ
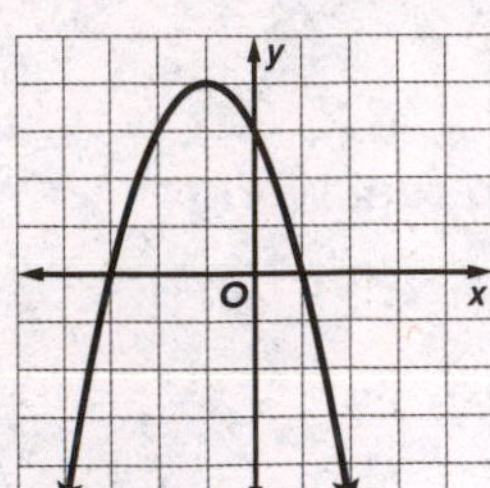

Ⓑ
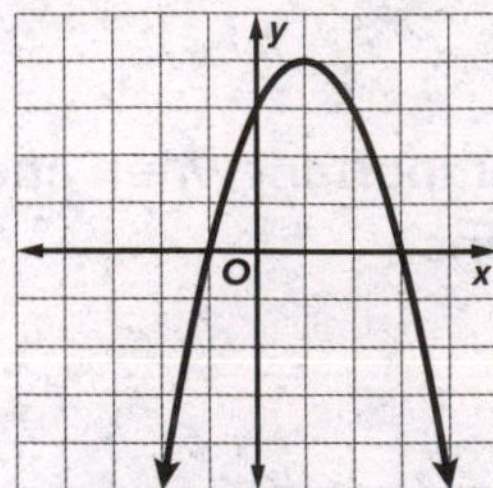

Ⓒ
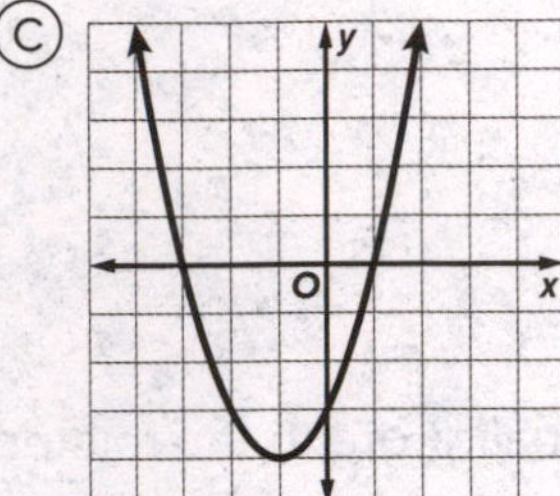

Ⓓ
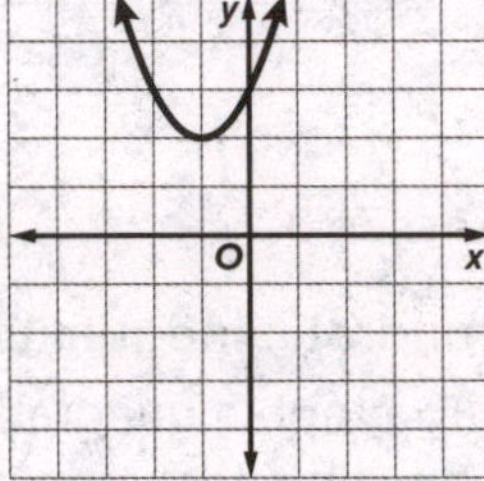

2. OPEN RESPONSE At a concert, a T-shirt cannon launches a T-shirt upward. The height of the T-shirt in feet a given number of seconds after the launch is shown in the table.

Time (s)	Height (ft)
1	74
2	116
3	126
4	104
5	50

Find and interpret the average rate of change in the height between 1 and 3 seconds after launch. (Lesson 3-1)

3. OPEN RESPONSE Use a quadratic equation to find two real numbers with a sum of 31 and a product of 210. (Lesson 3-2)

4. MULTI-SELECT The graph of $f(x) = x^2 - x - 6$ is shown.

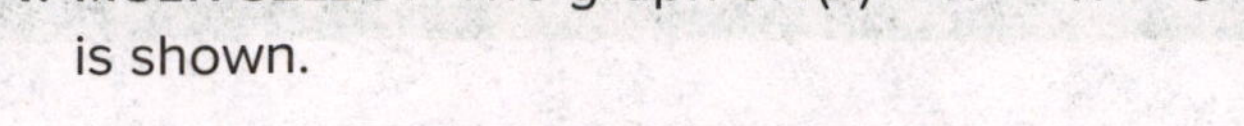

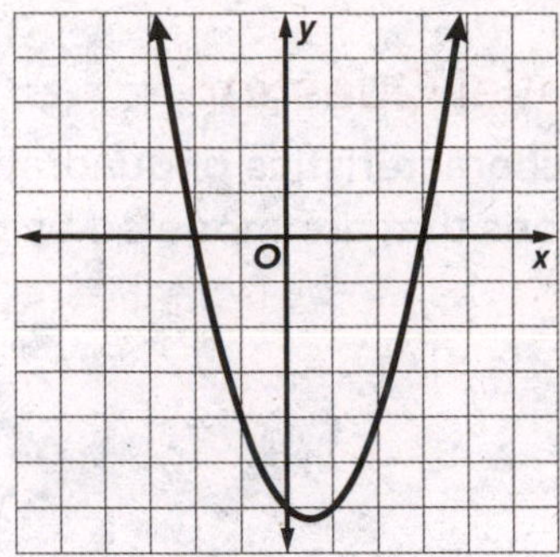

Find the solutions of $x^2 - x - 6 = 0$. Select all that apply. (Lesson 3-2)

Ⓐ -6

Ⓑ -3

Ⓒ -2

Ⓓ 2

Ⓔ 3

Ⓕ 6

5. MULTIPLE CHOICE Simplify $\sqrt{-9} \cdot \sqrt{-49}$. (Lesson 3-3)

Ⓐ $-21i$

Ⓑ $21i$

Ⓒ -21

Ⓓ 21

6. OPEN RESPONSE What is the voltage V of an electronic circuit with a current C of $3 + j$ and an impedance I of $5 - 2j$? Use the formula $V = CI$. (Lesson 3-3)

Name ______________________ Period ____________ Date ____________

7. OPEN RESPONSE Solve $4x^2 - 64 = 8x - 4$ by factoring. (Lesson 3-4)

8. MULTIPLE CHOICE A rectangular lawn has a width of 30 feet and a length of 45 feet. A diagram of the lawn is shown.

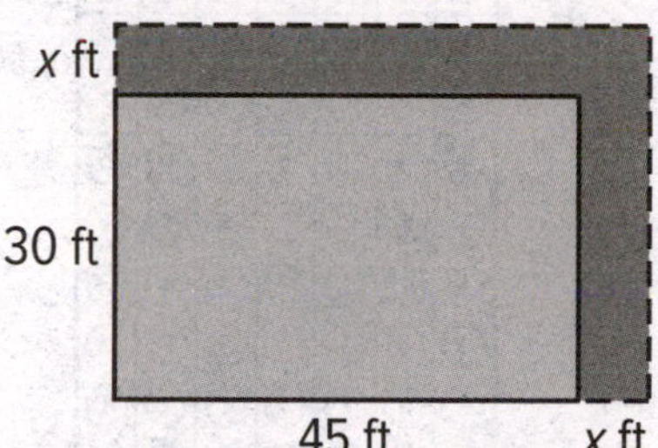

A landscape designer wants to increase the length and width of the lawn by the same amount so that the total area will be 2200 square feet. By how many feet should the designer increase the length and width of the lawn? (Lesson 3-4)

Ⓐ 10 feet

Ⓑ 19 feet

Ⓒ 28 feet

Ⓓ 29 feet

9. MULTIPLE CHOICE Solve $x^2 + 24x + 150 = 0$ by completing the square. (Lesson 3-5)

Ⓐ $12 \pm \sqrt{6}$

Ⓑ $12 \pm i\sqrt{6}$

Ⓒ $-12 \pm \sqrt{6}$

Ⓓ $-12 \pm i\sqrt{6}$

10. OPEN RESPONSE Use the square root property to solve $x^2 - 16 = 0$. (Lesson 3-5)

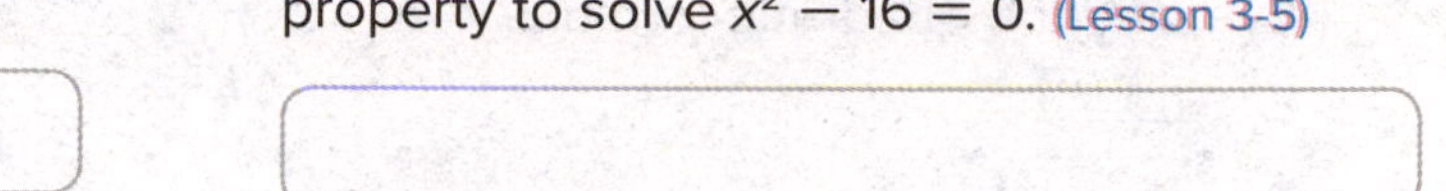

11. MULTI-SELECT Use the square root property to find the solutions of $x^2 + 10x + 25 = 81$. Select all that apply. (Lesson 3-5)

Ⓐ -14

Ⓑ -9

Ⓒ -4

Ⓓ 4

Ⓔ 9

Ⓕ 14

12. GRIDDED RESPONSE The height of a firework shell, in meters, t seconds after launch can be modeled by the function $f(t) = -4.9t^2 + 80t$. To the nearest tenth of a second, how many seconds does it take to first reach a height of 300 meters? (Lesson 3-6)

Name ____________________ Period ________ Date ________

13. MULTIPLE CHOICE Solve $4x^2 - 6x - 5 = 0$ by using the quadratic formula. (Lesson 3-6)

Ⓐ $\frac{3 \pm \sqrt{11}}{4}$

Ⓑ $\frac{-3 \pm \sqrt{29}}{4}$

Ⓒ $\frac{3 \pm \sqrt{29}}{4}$

Ⓓ $\frac{-3 \pm \sqrt{11}}{4}$

14. MULTIPLE CHOICE The graph of $y = x^2 - 4x + 3$ is shown. Select the values for which $x^2 - 4x + 3 < 0$. (Lesson 3-7)

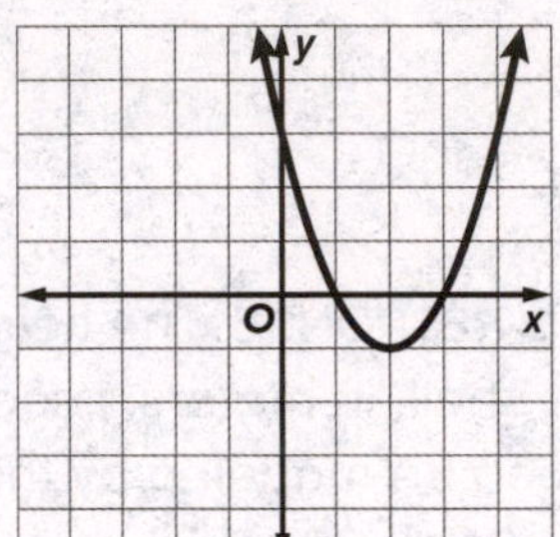

Ⓐ $x < 1, x < 3$

Ⓑ $x < 1, x > 3$

Ⓒ $x > 1, x < 3$

Ⓓ $x > 1, x > 3$

15. OPEN RESPONSE Solve the system of equations. Write the answers as ordered pairs. (Lesson 3-8)

$$\begin{cases} x^2 + y^2 = 25 \\ y = x^2 - 5 \end{cases}$$

16. GRIDDED RESPONSE How many solutions does this system of equations have? (Lesson 3-8)

$$\begin{cases} y = (x - 4)^2 - 3 \\ x = y^2 \end{cases}$$

17. TABLE ITEM Identify if each point is a solution to the first equation only, second equation only, both or neither. (Lesson 3-8)

(1) $y = x^2 - 2x - 1$

(2) $y = x + 3$

Point	First	Second	Both	Neither
(–4, 1)				
(–3, 0)				
(–1, 2)				
(1, 0)				
(1, 4)				
(4, 7)				

Module 4

Polynomials and Polynomial Functions

Essential Question

How does an understanding of polynomials and polynomial functions help us understand and interpret real-world events?

A.APR.1; A.APR.5, A.APR.6; F.IF.4; F.IF.7c
Mathematical Practices: MP1, MP2, MP3, MP4, MP5, MP6, MP7, MP8

What will you learn?

Place a checkmark (✓) in each row that corresponds with how much you already know about each topic **before** starting this module.

KEY
(thumbs down) — I don't know. (thumbs sideways) — I've heard of it. (thumbs up) — I know it!

	Before			After		
	(thumbs down)	(thumbs sideways)	(thumbs up)	(thumbs down)	(thumbs sideways)	(thumbs up)
graph power functions						
graph polynomial functions						
use the location principle to find zeros of a function						
identify extrema and turning points of graphs functions						
add and subtract polynomials						
multiply polynomials						
divide polynomials using long division						
divide polynomials using synthetic division						
expand powers of binomials						

Foldables Make this Foldable to help you organize your notes about polynomials and polynomial functions. Begin with one sheet of $8\frac{1}{2}$" by 14" paper.

1. **Fold** a 2" tab along the bottom of a long side.
2. **Fold** along the width into thirds.
3. **Staple** the outer edges of the tab.
4. **Label** the tabs *Polynomials, Polynomial Functions,* and *Polynomial Graphs*.

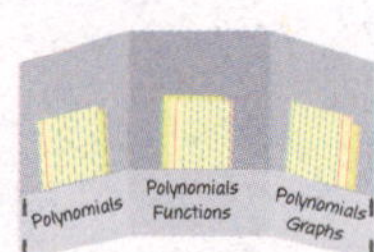

What Vocabulary Will You Learn?

Check the box next to each vocabulary term that you may already know.

- ☐ binomial
- ☐ degree
- ☐ degree of a polynomial
- ☐ FOIL method
- ☐ leading coefficient
- ☐ monomial function
- ☐ Pascal's triangle
- ☐ polynomial
- ☐ polynomial function
- ☐ power function
- ☐ quartic function
- ☐ quintic function
- ☐ standard form of a polynomial
- ☐ synthetic division
- ☐ trinomial
- ☐ turning point

Are You Ready?

Complete the Quick Review to see if you are ready to start this module. Then complete the Quick Check.

Quick Review

Example 1

Rewrite $2xy - 3 - z$ as a sum.

$2xy - 3 - z$	Original expression
$= 2xy + (-3) + (-z)$	Rewrite using addition.

Example 2

Use the Distributive Property to rewrite $-3(a + b - c)$.

$-3(a + b - c)$	Original expression
$= -3(a) + (-3)(b) + (-3)(-c)$	Distributive Property
$= -3a - 3b + 3c$	Simplify.

Quick Check

Rewrite each difference as a sum.

1. $-5 - 13$

2. $5 - 3y$

3. $5mr - 7mp$

4. $3x^2y - 14xy^2$

Use the Distributive Property to rewrite each expression without parenthesis.

5. $-4(a + 5)$

6. $-1(3b^2 + 2b - 1)$

7. $-\frac{1}{2}(2m - 5)$

8. $-\frac{3}{4}(3z + 5)$

How Did You Do?

Which exercises did you answer correctly in the Quick Check? Shade those exercise numbers below.

① ② ③ ④ ⑤ ⑥ ⑦ ⑧

Polynomial Functions

Explore Power Functions

Online Activity Use graphing technology to complete the Explore.

INQUIRY How do the coefficient and degree of a function of the form $f(x) = ax^n$ affect its end behavior?

Learn Graphing Power Functions

A **power function** is any function of the form $f(x) = ax^n$ where a and n are nonzero real numbers. For a power function, a is the **leading coefficient** and n is the **degree**, which is the value of the exponent. A power function with positive integer n is called a **monomial function**.

Key Concept • End Behavior of a Monomial Function

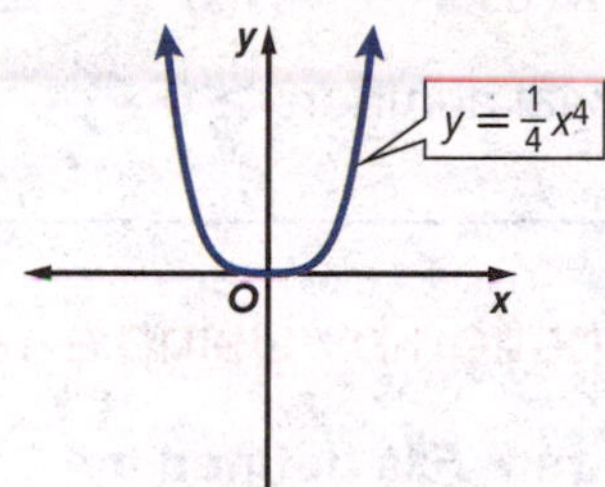

Degree: even
Leading Coefficient: positive
End Behavior:

As $x \to -\infty$, $f(x) \to \infty$
As $x \to \infty$, $f(x) \to \infty$

Domain: all real numbers
Range: all real numbers ≥ 0

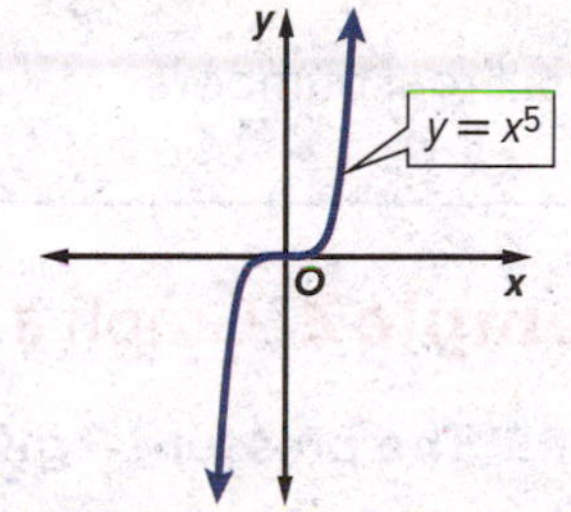

Degree: odd
Leading Coefficient: positive
End Behavior:

As $x \to -\infty$, $f(x) \to -\infty$
As $x \to \infty$, $f(x) \to \infty$

Domain: all real numbers
Range: all real numbers

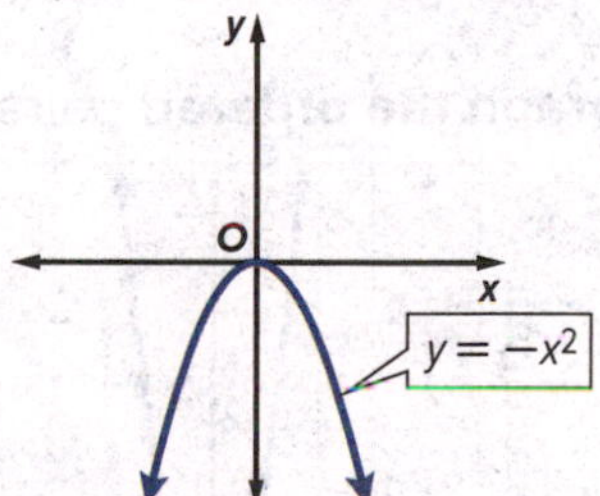

Degree: even
Leading Coefficient: negative
End Behavior:

As $x \to -\infty$, $f(x) \to -\infty$
As $x \to \infty$, $f(x) \to -\infty$

Domain: all real numbers
Range: all real numbers ≤ 0

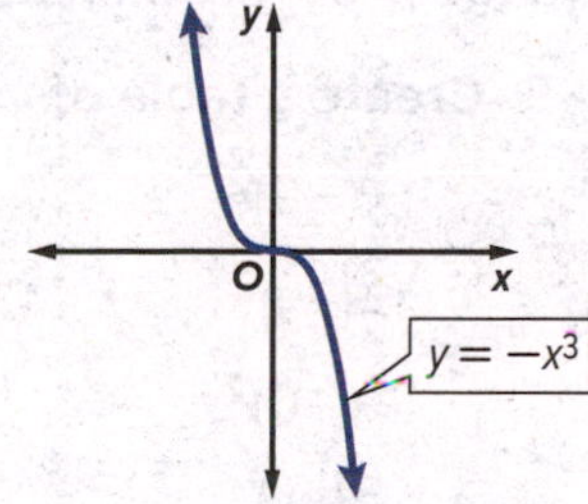

Degree: odd
Leading Coefficient: negative
End Behavior:

As $x \to -\infty$, $f(x) \to \infty$
As $x \to \infty$, $f(x) \to -\infty$

Domain: all real numbers
Range: all real numbers

Today's Standards
F.IF.4, F.IF.7c
MP1, MP6

Today's Vocabulary
- power function
- degree
- monomial function
- polynomial
- standard form of a polynomial
- degree of a polynomial
- leading coefficient
- polynomial function
- quartic function
- quintic function

Talk About It
Is $f(x) = \sqrt{x}$ power function? a monomial function? Explain your reasoning.

Your Notes

> **Go Online** You can watch a video to see how to graph power functions on a TI-84.

> **Think About It!** Interpret the domain and range given the context of the situation.

Key Concept • Zeros of Even and Odd Degree Functions

Odd-degree functions will always have at least one real zero. Even-degree functions may have any number of real zeros or no real zeros at all.

Example 1 End Behavior and Degree of Monomial Functions

Describe the end behavior of $f(x) = -2x^3$ using the leading coefficient and degree, and state the domain and range.

leading coefficient: ______, which is ________

degree: ______, which is ______

end behavior: Because the leading coefficient is negative and the degree is odd, the end behavior is that as $x \to -\infty$, $f(x) \to$ ______ and as $x \to \infty$, $f(x) \to$ ______.

domain: ______________ range: ______________

Check

Describe the end behavior, domain, and range of $f(x) = -10x^6$.

end behavior: As $x \to -\infty$, $f(x) \to$ ______ and as $x \to \infty$, $f(x) \to$ ______.

domain: all real numbers range: all real numbers ≥ 0

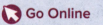

Example 2 Graph a Power Function by Using a Table

PRESSURE The pressure P given the flow rate F is defined by $P(F) = \frac{3}{2}F^2$. Graph the function $P(F)$, and state the domain and range.

Step 1 Find a and n.

For $P(F) = \frac{3}{2}F^2$, $a =$ ______, and $n =$ ______.

Step 2 State the domain and range.

Because a is positive and n is even, the domain is ____________ and the range is all real numbers ______.

Steps 3–5 Create a table of values and graph the ordered pairs.

-2	$\frac{3}{2}(-2)^2$	
-1	$\frac{3}{2}(-1)^2$	1.5
0	$\frac{3}{2}(-0)^2$	
1	$\frac{3}{2}(1)^2$	
2	$\frac{3}{2}(2)^2$	6

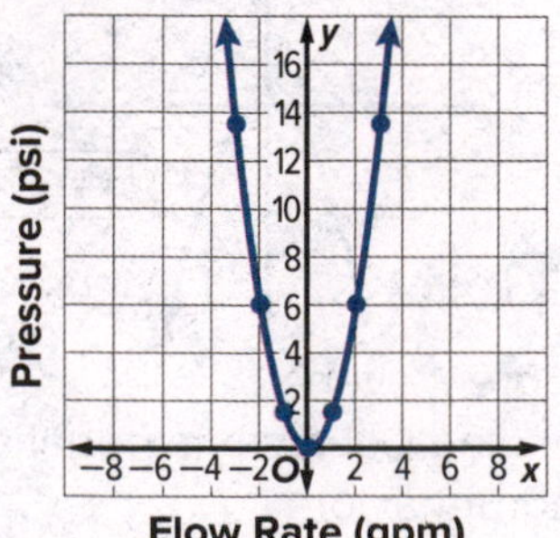

Go Online You can complete an Extra Example online.

Explore Polynomial Functions

Online Activity Use graphing technology to complete the Explore.

> **INQUIRY** How is the degree of a function related to the number of times its graph intersects the x-axis?

Learn Graphing Polynomial Functions

A **polynomial in one variable** is an expression of the form $a_n x^n + a_{n-1}x^{n-1} + \ldots a_2x^2 + a_1x + a_0$, where $a_n \neq 0$, a_{n-1}, a_1, and a_0 are real numbers, and n is a nonnegative integer. Because the terms are written in order from greatest to least degree, this polynomial is written in **standard form**. The **degree of the polynomial** is n and the leading coefficient is a_n.

A **polynomial function** is a continuous function that can be described by a polynomial equation in one variable. You have learned about constant, linear, quadratic, and cubic functions. A **quartic function** is a fourth-degree function. A **quintic function** is a fifth-degree function. The general shapes of the graphs of several polynomial functions show the maximum number of times the graphs of each function may intersect the x-axis. The degree tells you the maximum number of times that the graph of a polynomial function intersects the x-axis.

Example 3 Degrees and Leading Coefficients

State the degree and leading coefficient of each polynomial in one variable. If it is not a polynomial in one variable, explain why.

a. $2x^4 - 3x^3 - 4x^2 - 5x + 6a$ degree: __ leading coefficient: __

b. $7x^3 - 2$ degree: __ leading coefficient: __

c. $4x^2 - 2xy + 8y^2$ This is not a polynomial in one variable. There are two variables, x and y.

d. $x^5 + 12x^4 - 3x^3 + 2x^2 + 8x + 4$ degree: __ leading coefficient: __

Check

Select the degree and leading coefficient of $11x^3 + 5x^2 - 7x - \frac{6}{x}$. __

A. degree: 3, leading coefficient: 11

B. degree: 11, leading coefficient: 3

C. This is not a polynomial in one variable. There are two variables, x and y.

D. This is not a polynomial in one variable. The term $\frac{6}{x}$ has the variable with an exponent less than 0.

Go Online You can complete an Extra Example online.

Go Online
You can learn how to graph a polynomial function by watching the video online.

Think About It!
If a polynomial function has a leading coefficient of 4, can you determine its end behavior? Explain your reasoning.

Think About It!
Jamison says the leading coefficient of $4x^2 - 3 + 2x^3 - x$ is 4. Do you agree or disagree? Justify your reasoning.

Watch Out!
Leading Coefficients
If the term with the greatest degree has no coefficient shown, as in part d, the leading coefficient is 1.

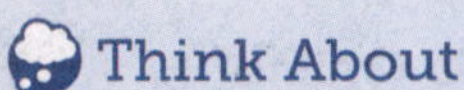

Think About It!

What values of x make sense in the context of the situation? Justify your reasoning.

Study Tip:

Labels Notice that the x-axis is measuring the percent of the radius, not the actual length of the radius.

Example 4 Evaluate and Graph a Polynomial Function

SUN The density of the Sun, in grams per centimeter cubed, expressed as a percent of the distance from the core of the Sun to its surface can be modeled by the function $f(x) = 519x^4 - 1630x^3 + 1844x^2 + 155$, where x represents the percent as a decimal. At the core, $x = 0$, and at the surface $x = 1$.

Part A Find the core density of the Sun at a radius 60% of the way to the surface.

Because we need to find the core density at a radius 60% of the way to the surface, $x = 0.6$. So, replace x with 0.6 and simplify.

$f(x) = 519x^4 - 1630x^3 + 1844x^2 + 155$

$= 519(\_\_\_)^4 - 1630(\_\_\_)^3 + 1844(\_\_\_)^2 + 155$

$= 67.2624 - 352.08 + 663.84 - 533.4 + 155$

$= \_\_\_\_\_ \frac{g}{cm^3}$

Part B Sketch a graph of the function.

Substitute values of x to create a table of values. Then plot the points, and connect them with a smooth curve.

x	$f(x)$
0.1	82.9619
0.2	
0.3	
0.4	3.4064
0.5	
0.7	1.7819
0.8	
0.9	

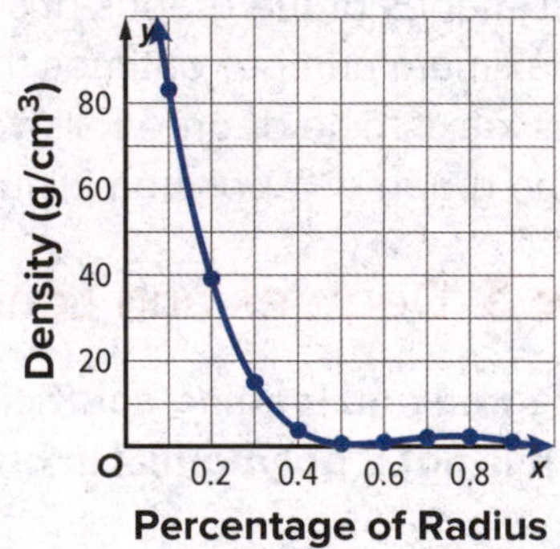

Check

CARDIOLOGY To help predict heart attacks, doctors can inject a concentration of dye in a vein near the heart to measure the cardiac output in patients. In a normal heart, the change in the concentration of dye can be modeled by $f(x) = -0.006x^4 + 0.140x^3 - 0.053x^2 + 1.79x$, where x is the time in seconds.

Part A Find the concentration of dye after 5 seconds.

$f(5) = \_\_\_\_\_$

Go Online You can complete an Extra Example online.

Part B Select the graph of the concentration of dye over 10 seconds. ____

A.

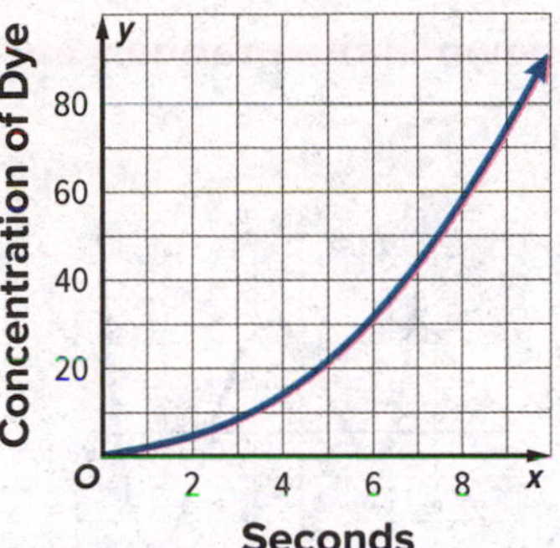

B.

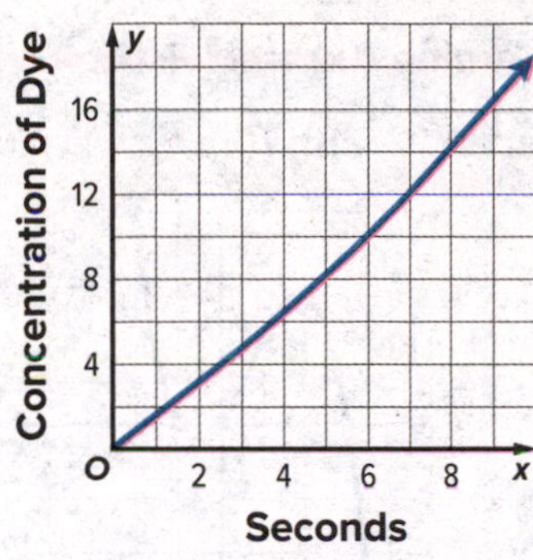

C.

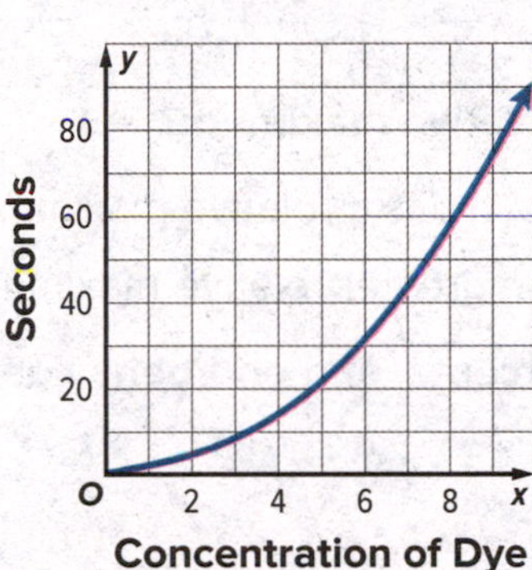

D.

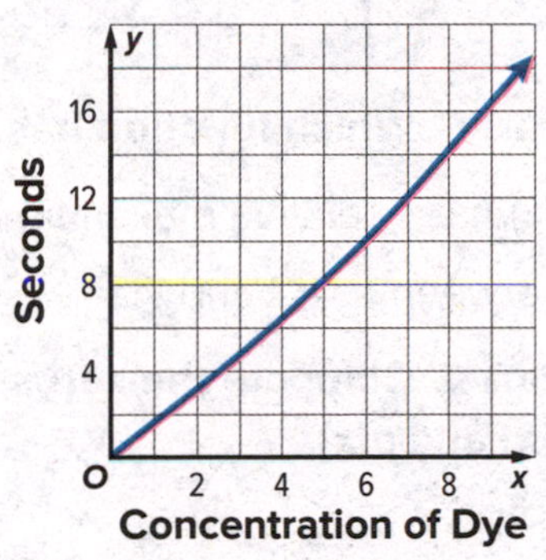

Example 5 Zeros of a Polynomial Function

Use the graph to state the number of real zeros of the function.

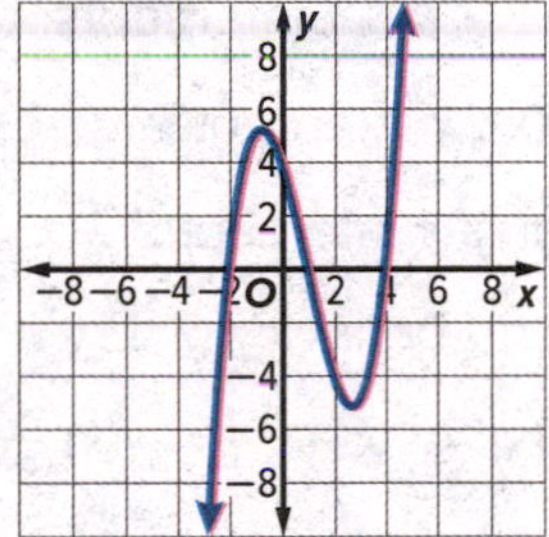

The real zeros occur at $x = -2$, 1, and 4, so there are ________ real zeros.

Study Tip:

Zeros The real zeros occur at values of x where $f(x) = 0$, or where the function intersects the x-axis. Recall that odd functions have at least one real zero and even functions have any number of real zeros. So, the minimum number of times that an odd function intersects the x-axis is 1, and the minimum number of times that an even function intersects the x-axis is 0.

Check

Use the graph to state the number of real zeros of the function.

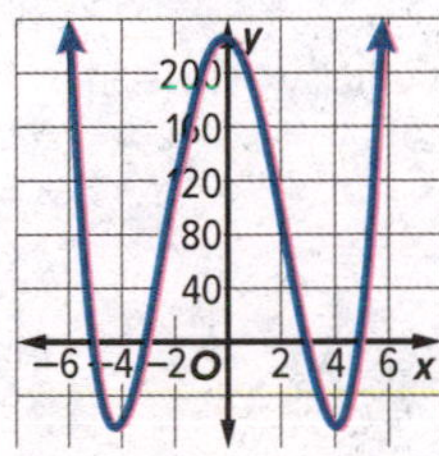

The function has _____ real zero(s).

Go Online You can complete an Extra Example online.

Example 6 Compare Polynomial Functions

Examine $f(x) = x^3 + 2x^2 - 3x$ and $g(x)$ shown in the graphs.

Part A Graph $f(x)$.

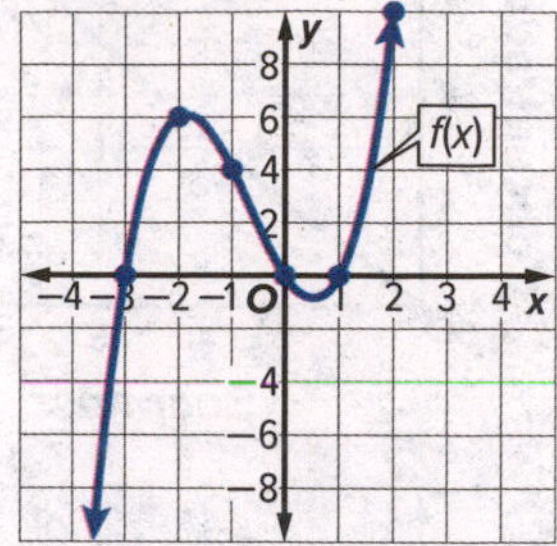

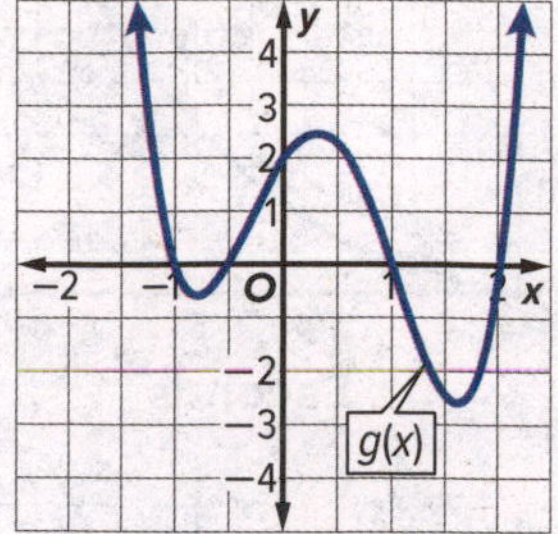

Part B Which function has the greater relative maximum?

$f(x)$ has a relative maximum at $y = 6$, and $g(x)$ has a relative maximum between $y = 2$ and $y = 3$. So, _____ has the greater relative maximum.

Part C Compare the zeros, x- and y-intercepts, and end behavior of $f(x)$ and $g(x)$.

zeros:

$f(x)$: _____, _____, _____

$g(x)$: The graph appears to intersect the x-axis at _____, _____, _____, _____

intercepts:

$f(x)$: x-intercepts: _____, _____, _____; y-intercept: 0

$g(x)$: x-intercepts: _____, _____, _____, _____; y-intercept: 2

end behavior:

$f(x)$: As $x \to -\infty$, $f(x) \to$ _____, and as $x \to \infty$, $f(x) \to$ _____

$g(x)$: As $x \to -\infty$, $g(x) \to$ _____, and as $x \to \infty$, $g(x) \to$ _____

Think About It!

Find the domain and range of $f(x)$. Does $g(x)$ have the same domain and range? Explain.

Study Tip:

Zeros The zeros of a polynomial function are the x-coordinates of the points at which the graph intersects the x-axis.

Pause and Reflect

Did you struggle with anything in this lesson? If so, how did you deal with it?

Go Online You can complete an Extra Example online.

Name ________________ Period ________ Date ________

Practice

Go Online You can complete your homework online.

Example 1

Describe the end behavior of each function using the leading coefficient and degree, and state the domain and range.

1. $f(x) = 3x^4$

2. $f(x) = -2x^3$

3. $f(x) = -\frac{1}{2}x^5$

4. $f(x) = \frac{3}{4}x^6$

Example 2

5. **MODELING** The parabolic reflector inside a flashlight can be modeled by the function $f(x) = \frac{4}{3}x^2$. Graph the function $f(x)$, and state the domain and range.

6. **MODELING** The amount of money earned on an initial deposit a after t years at interest rate r can be represented by $y = ax^t$, where x represents the growth rate, $1 + r$.

a. Consider a 15-year certificate of deposit (CD) with growth rate x. Write an equation that represents the amount of money y if $15,000 is deposited in the CD and comes to maturity.

b. Graph the function, and state the domain and range.

Example 3

State the degree and leading coefficient of each polynomial in one variable. If it is not a polynomial in one variable, explain why.

7. $a + 8$

8. $(2x - 1)(4x^2 + 3)$

9. $-5x^5 + 3x^3 - 8$

10. $18 - 3y + 5y^2 - y^5 + 7y^6$

11. $u^3 + 4u^2t^2 + t^4$

12. $2r - r^2 + \frac{1}{r^2}$

Example 4

13. **PENTAGONAL NUMBERS** The nth pentagonal number is given by the function $f(n) = \frac{n(3n - 1)}{2}$.

Part A What is the seventh pentagonal number?

Part B Graph the function.

14. **DRILLING** The volume of a drill bit can be estimated by the formula for a cone, $V = \frac{1}{3}\pi hr^2$, where h is the height of the bit and r is its radius. Substituting $\frac{\sqrt{3}}{3}r$ for h, the volume of the drill bit can be estimated by $V = \frac{\sqrt{3}}{9}\pi hr^3$.

Part A What is the volume of a drill bit with a radius of 3 centimeters?

Part B Graph the function.

15. **TRIANGLES** Dylan drew n dots on a piece of paper making sure that no line contained 3 of the dots. The number of triangles that can be made using the dots as vertices is equal to $f(n) = \frac{1}{6}(n^3 - 3n^2 + 2n)$.

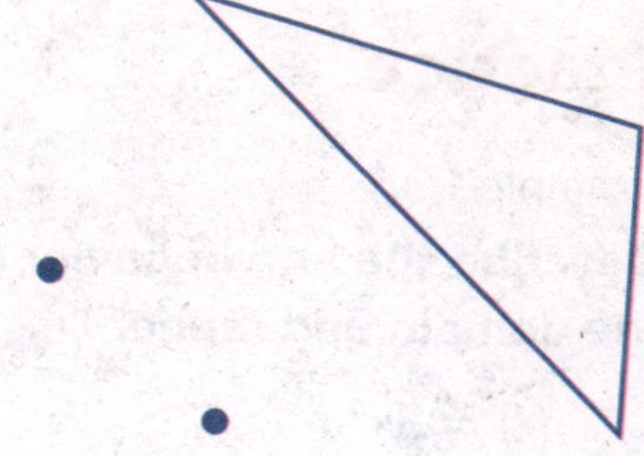

Part A If Dylan drew 15 dots, how many triangles can be made?

Part B Graph the function.

16. **MACHINE EFFICIENCY** A company uses the function $f(x) = x^3 + 3x^2 - 18x - 40$ to model the change in efficiency of a machine based on its position x.

Part A **REASONING** What is the efficiency for position 3? Explain the meaning of this value.

Part B Graph the function.

Example 5

Use the graph to state the number of real zeros of the function.

17.

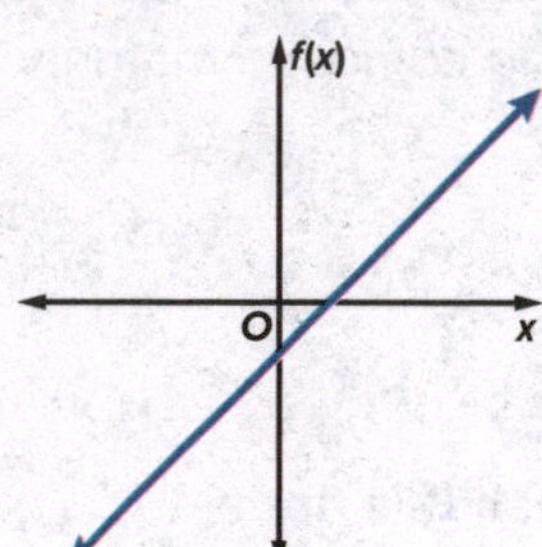

18.

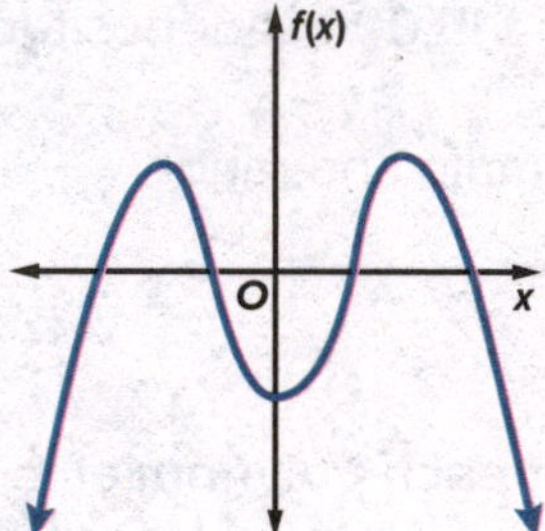

19.

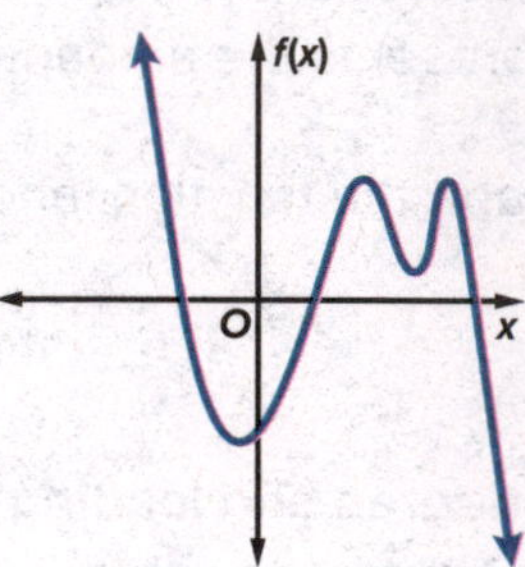

20.

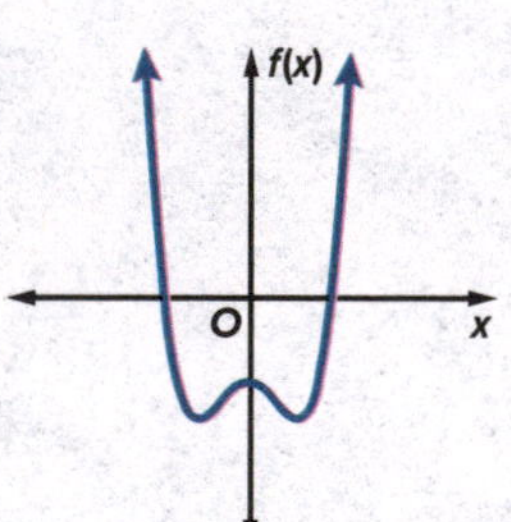

21.

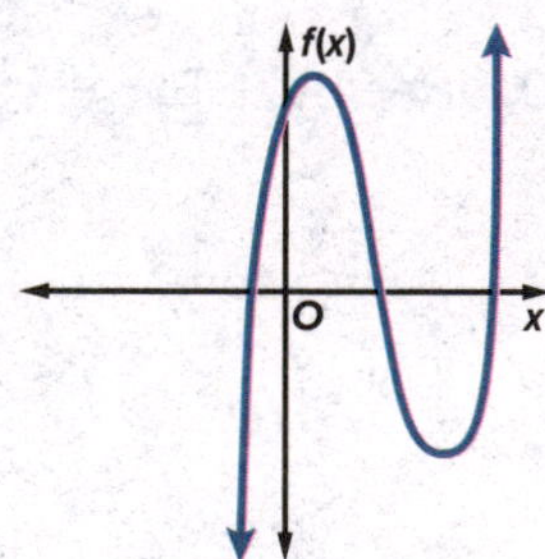

22.

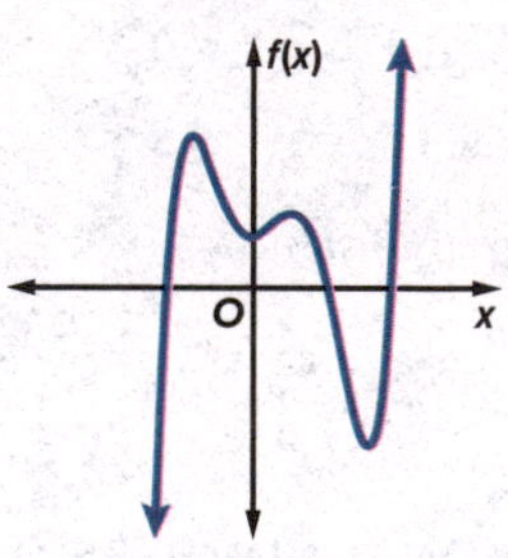

Example 6

23. **MODELING** Examine $f(x)$ and $g(x)$ shown in the equation and graph.

$$f(x) = x^3 - 2x^2 - 4x + 1$$

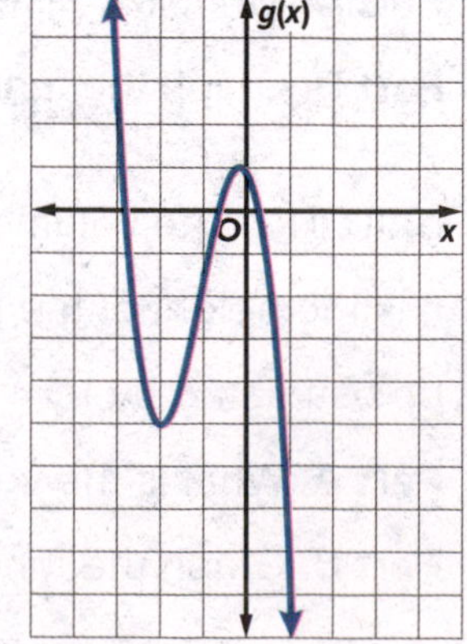

Part A Which function has the greater relative maximum?

Part B Compare the zeros, x- and y-intercepts, and end behavior of $f(x)$ and $g(x)$.

24. **MODELING** Examine $f(x)$ and $g(x)$ shown in the graph and table.

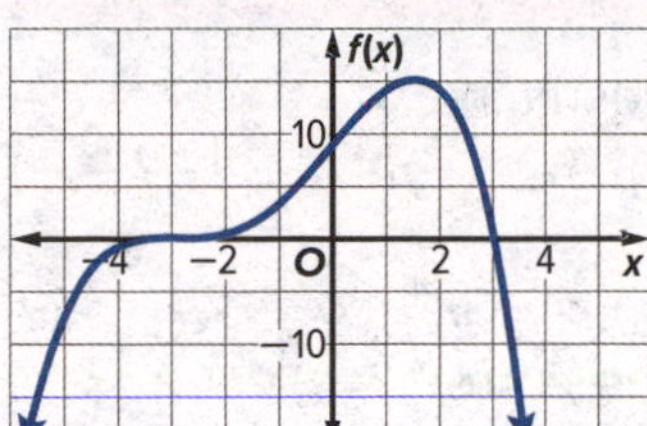

x	−5	−3	0	1.5	3
$g(x)$	7.5	0	−9	−15	0

Part A Which function has the greater relative maximum?

Part B Compare the zeros, x- and y-intercepts, and end behavior of $f(x)$ and $g(x)$.

Mixed Exercises

Describe the end behavior of the graph of each function.

25. $f(x) = -5x^4 + 3x^2$

26. $g(x) = 2x^5 + 6x^4$

27. $h(x) = -4x^7 + 8x^6 - 4x$

28. $f(x) = 6x - 7x^2$

29. $g(x) = 8x^4 + 5x^5$

30. $h(x) = 9x^6 - 5x^7 + 3x^2$

State the degree and leading coefficient of each polynomial in one variable. If it is not a polynomial in one variable, explain why.

31. $-6x^6 - 4x^5 + 13xy$

32. $3a^7 - 4a^4 + \frac{3}{a}$

33. $8x^5 - 12x^6 + 14x^3 - 9$

34. $-12 - 8x^2 + 5x - 21x^7$

35. $15x - 4x^3 + 3x^2 - 5x^4$

36. $13b^3 - 9b + 3b^5 - 18$

37. $(d + 5)(3d - 4)$

38. $(5 - 2y)(4 + 3y)$

39. $6x^5 - 5x^4 + 2x^9 - 3x^2$

40. $7x^4 + 3x^7 - 2x^8 + 7$

41. **GRAPHS** Kendra graphed the polynomial $f(x)$ shown. From this graph, describe the end behavior, degree, and sign of the leading coefficient.

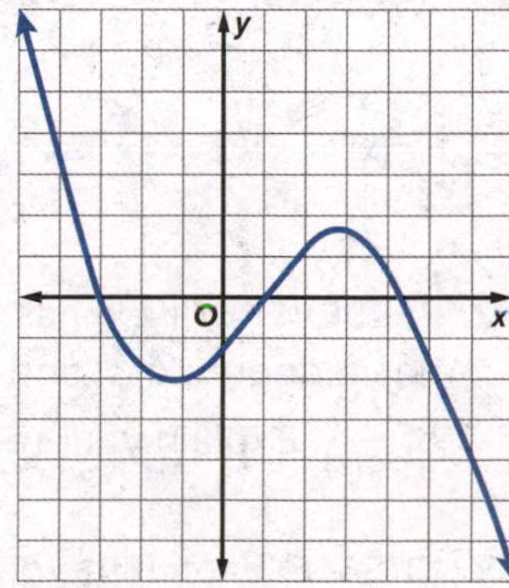

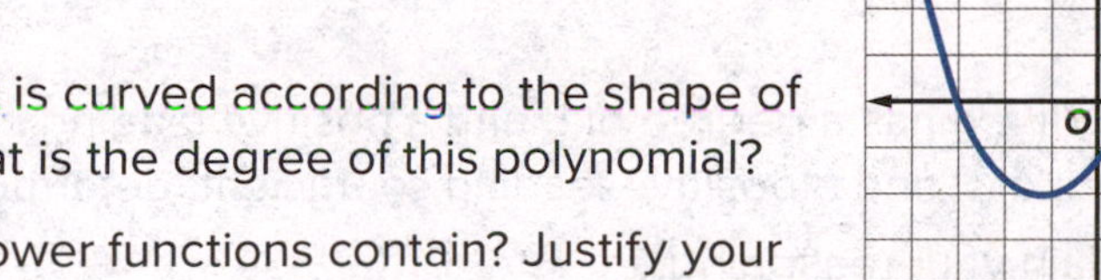

42. **MANUFACTURING** A metal sheet is curved according to the shape of the graph of $f(x) = x^4 - 9x^2$. What is the degree of this polynomial?

43. **REASONING** What point do all power functions contain? Justify your answer algebraically.

44. ARGUMENTS Explain why a polynomial function with an odd degree must have at least one real zero.

45. REASONING If $f(x) = ax^3 - bx^2 + x$, determine $f(1 - x)$. Express the result in standard form. How does the end behavior of $f(1 - x)$ compare to $f(x)$?

46. ARGUMENTS Yuan states that the end behaviors of the functions $g(x) = -3x^4 + 15x^3 - 12x^2 + 3x + 20$ and $h(x) = -3x^4 - 16x - 1$ are the same. Is she correct? Explain your reasoning.

47. STRUCTURE Consider the function $f(x) = -(3 - x)(4 - x)^2$. Identify the degree of the polynomial and any zeros.

48. MODELING A box has a square base with sides of 10 centimeters and a height of 4 centimeters. For a new box, the height is increased by twice the same amount as the lengths of the sides of the base are decreased. Graph the function. What new dimensions will produce a box with the greatest volume? Describe your solution process.

49. ARGUMENTS Draw a graph representing the relationship between the length of an edge of a cube and the volume of the cube. Why does this graph appear not to have symmetry?

50. FIND THE ERROR Shenequa and Virginia are determining the number of real zeros of the graph at the right. Is either of them correct? Explain your reasoning.

Shenequa

There are 7 real zeros because the graph intersects the x-axis 7 times.

Virginia

There are 8 real zeros because the graph intersects the x-axis 7 times, and there is a double zero.

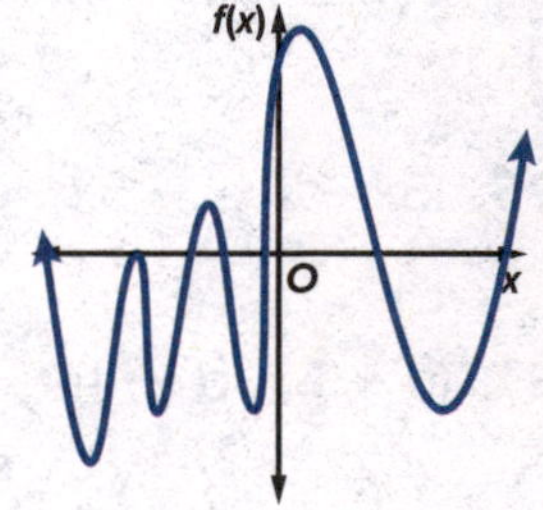

51. PERSEVERE Which function below has the potential for more real zeros? Find the degree of each function.

$g(x) = x^4 + x^3 - 13x^2 + x + 4$

x	−24	−18	−12	−6	0	6	12	18	24
$f(x)$	−8	−1	3	−2	4	7	−1	−8	5

52. PERSEVERE If $f(x)$ has a degree of 5 and a positive leading coefficient and $g(x)$ has a degree of 3 and a positive leading coefficient, determine the end behavior of $\frac{f(x)}{g(x)}$. Explain your reasoning.

53. CREATE Sketch the graph of an even-degree polynomial with 7 real zeros, one of them a double zero.

Analyzing Graphs of Polynomial Functions

Today's Standards
F.IF.4, F.IF.7c
MP4, MP5

Today's Vocabulary
turning point

Learn The Location Principle

If the value of $f(x)$ changes signs from one value of x to the next, then there is a zero between those two x-values. This is called the Location Principle.

Key Concept • Location Principle

Suppose $y = f(x)$ represents a polynomial function, and a and b are two real numbers such that $f(a) < 0$ and $f(b) < 0$. Then the function has at least one real zero between a and b.

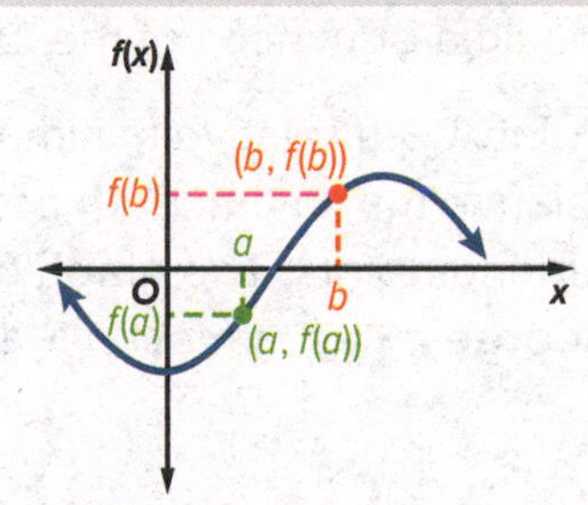

Think About It!
Not all real zeros can be found by using the Location Principle. Provide an example where $f(a) > 0$ and $f(b) > 0$, but there is a zero between $x = a$ and $x = b$.

Example 1 Locate Zeros of a Function

Determine the consecutive integer values of x between which each real zero of $f(x) = x^4 - 2x^3 - x^2 + 1$ is located. Then draw the graph.

Step 1 Make a table.

Because $f(x)$ is a fourth-degree polynomial, it will have as many as _____ real zeros or none at all.

x	−2	−1	0	1	2	3	4
$f(x)$		3		−1	−3		

Using the Location Principle, there are zeros between $x = 0$ and $x = 1$ and between $x = 2$ and $x = 3$.

Step 2 Sketch the graph

Use the table to sketch the graph and find the locations of the zeros.

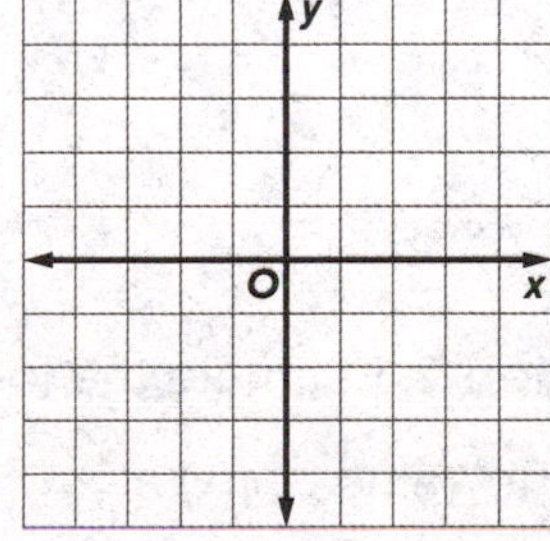

Check

Using the **zero** feature on a graphing calculator, the zeros are located at $x \approx 0.7213$ and $x \approx 2.3486$, which confirms the estimates.

Think About It!
How can you adjust the table on your graphing calculator to give a more precise interval for the value of each zero?

Go Online You can complete an Extra Example online.

Your Notes 

Study Tip:

Odd Functions Some odd functions, such as $f(x) = x^3$, have no turning points.

 **Talk About It**

Determine whether the following statement is *sometimes*, *always*, or *never* true. Justify your reasoning.

For any continuous polynomial function, the y-coordinate of a turning point is also either a relative maximum or relative minimum.

Check

Graph $f(x) = 2x^4 + x^3 - 3x^2 - 2$ and determine the consecutive integer values of x between which each real zero of is located.

$x =$ _____ and $x =$ _____

$x =$ _____ and $x =$ _____

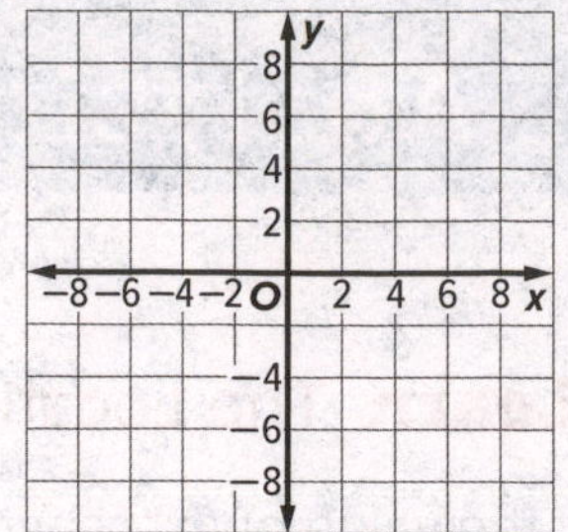

Learn Extrema and Turning Points

A **turning point** is a change in direction of a graph. The turning points occur at relative maxima or minima of the function.

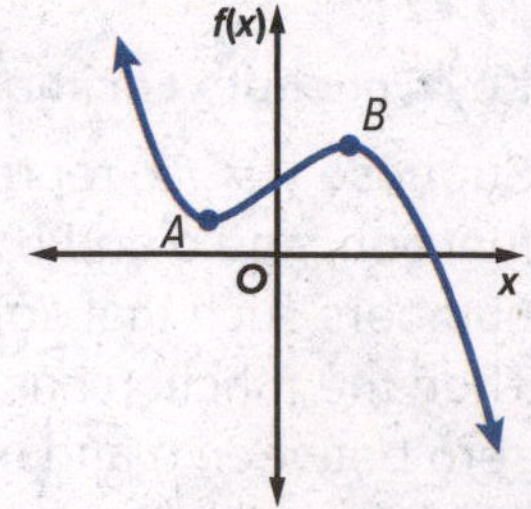

Point A is a relative minimum, and point B is a relative maximum. Both points A and B are turning points. The graph of a polynomial of degree n has at most $n - 1$ turning points.

Example 2 Identify Extrema and Turning Points

Use a table to graph $f(x) = x^3 + x^2 - 5x - 2$. Estimate the x-coordinates at which the relative maxima and relative minima occur.

Step 1 Make a table of values and graph the function.

x	y
−4	−30
−3	
−2	4
−1	3
0	
1	
2	0
3	

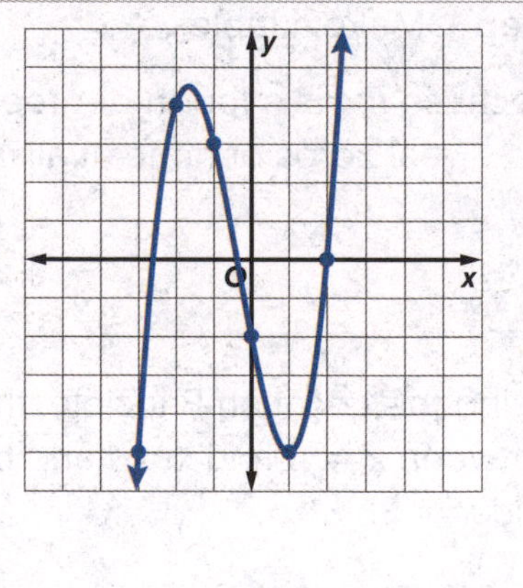

Step 2 Estimate the locations of the turning points.

The value of $f(x)$ at $x = -2$ is greater than the surrounding points indicating a turning point *near* $x =$ _____.

The value of $f(x)$ at $x = 1$ is less than the surrounding points indicating a turning point near $x =$ _____.

 **Go Online** You can complete an Extra Example online.

Check

Use a table of values of $f(x) = -x^4 - x^3 + 5x^2 + x - 3$ to estimate the x-coordinates at which the relative maxima and relative minima occur.

x	$f(x)$
−3	
−2	
−1	
0	
1	
2	
3	

The relative maxima occur near $x =$ ____ and $x =$ ____.

The relative minimum occurs near $x =$ ____.

Example 3 Analyze a Polynomial Function

PILOTS **The total number of certified pilots in the United States is approximated by $f(x) = 0.0000903x^4 - 0.0166x^3 + 0.762x^2 + 6.317x + 7.708$, where x is the number of years after 1930 and $f(x)$ is the number of pilots in thousands. Graph the function and describe its key features over its relevant domain.**

Step 1 Make a table of values and graph the function.

x	y
0	7.708
10	
20	320.496
30	507.961
40	
50	
60	714.616
70	
80	589.356
90	

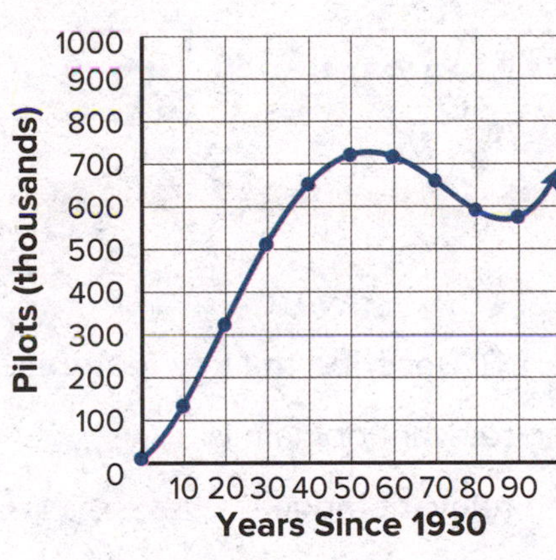

Step 2 Describe the key features.

Domain and Range

The domain and range of the function is all real numbers. Because the function models years after 1930, the relevant domain and range are $\{x \mid x \geq$ ____$\}$ and $\{f(x) \mid f(x) \geq$ ____$\}$.

(continued on the next page)

Study Tip:

Turning Points When graphing with a calculator, keep in mind that a polynomial of degree n has at most $n - 1$ turning points. This will help you to determine whether your viewing window is allowing you to see all of the extrema of the graph.

Go Online

You can learn how to graph and analyze a polynomial function on a graphing calculator by watching the video online.

Think About It!

What trends in the number of pilots does the graph suggest?

Think About It!

It is reasonable that the trend will continue indefinitely? Explain

Study Tip:

Assumptions Determining the end behavior for the graph of a polynomial that models data assumes that the trend continues and there are no other turning points.

Turning Points

There is a relative ________ between 1980 and 1990 and a relative ________ between 2010 and 2020 in the relevant domain.

End Behavior

As $x \to \infty$, $f(x) \to$ ____.

Intercepts

In the relevant domain, the y-intercept is at (0, ________). There is ____ x-intercept, or zero, because the function begins at a value greater than 0 and as As $x \to \infty$, $f(x) \to \infty$.

Symmetry The graph of the function ________ have symmetry.

Check

COINS The number of quarters produced by the United States Mint can be approximated by the function $f(x) = 16.4x^3 - 149.5x^2 - 148.9x + 3215.4$, where x is the number of years since 2005 and $f(x)$ is the total number of quarters produced in millions. Use the graph of the function to complete the table and describe its key features.

Part A Complete the table.

x	Quarters (millions)
0	
2	
4	
6	
8	
10	

Part B Describe the key features.

The relevant domain is ________.

The relevant range is ________________.

There is a relative maximum between ________ and ________.

The y-intercept is ________.

The graph of the function ________ have symmetry.

It is ____________ to assume that the trend will continue indefinitely.

Go Online You can complete an Extra Example online.

Example 4 Use Polynomial Functions and Technology to Model

BACKPACKS **The table shows U.S. backpack sales in millions of dollars, according to the Travel Goods Association. Make a scatter plot and a curve of best fit to show the trend over time. Then determine the backpack sales in 2015.**

Year	Sales (million $)	Year	Sales (million $)
2000	1140	2008	1246
2001	1144	2009	1235
2002	1113	2010	1419
2003	1134	2011	1773
2004	1164	2012	1930
2005	1180	2013	2255
2006	1364	2014	2779
2007	1436		

Step 1 Enter the data.

Let the year 2000 be represented by 0. Enter the years since 2000 in List 1. Enter the backpack sales in List 2.

Step 2 Graph the scatter plot.

Change the viewing so that all data are visible.

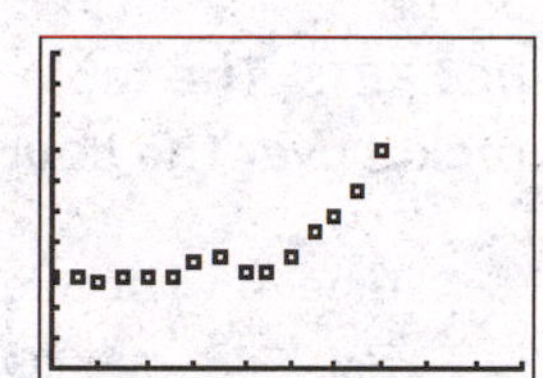

Step 3 Determine the polynomial function of best fit.

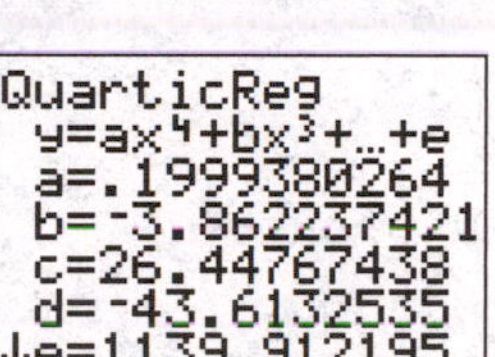

To determine the model that best fits the data, perform linear, quadratic, cubic, and quartic regressions, and compare the coefficients of determination, r^2. The polynomial with a coefficient of determination closest to 1 will fit the data best.

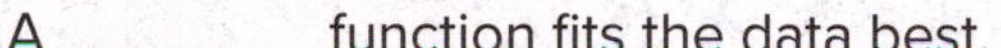

A ________ function fits the data best.

The regression equation with coefficients rounded to the nearest tenths is:

$$y \approx \_\_\_ x^4 - \_\_\_ x^3 + \_\_\_ x^2 - \_\_\_ x + \_\_\_.$$

Step 4 Graph and evaluate the regression function.

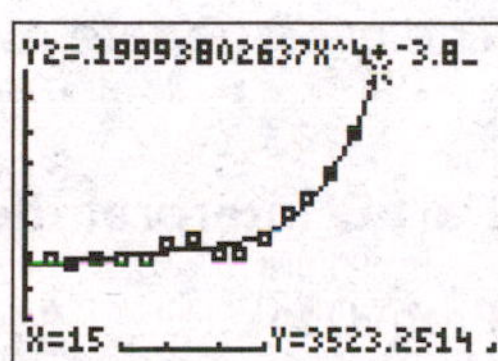

Assuming that the trend continues, the graph of the function can be used to predict backpack sales for a specific year. To determine the total sales in 2015, find the value of the function for $x =$ ____.

In 2015, there were about ________ billion in backpack sales.

Think About It!

Explain the approximation that is made when using the model to determine the backpack sales in a specific year.

Math History Minute:

By the age of 20, Italian mathematician Maria Gaetana Agnesi (1718–1799) had started working on her book *Analytical Institutions,* which was published in 1748. Early chapters included problems on maxima, minima, and turning points. Also described was a cubic curve called the "witch of Agnesi," which was translated incorrectly from the original Italian.

Check

TREES To estimate the amount of lumber that can be harvested from a tree, foresters measure the diameter of each tree. Determine the polynomial function of best fit, where x represents the diameter of a tree in inches and y is the estimated volume measured in board feet. Then estimate the volume of a tree with a diameter of 35 inches.

Diam (in.)	17	19	20	23	25	28	32	38	39	41
Vol (100s of board ft)	19	25	32	57	71	113	123	252	259	294

The polynomial function of best fit is $y =$ ______ $x^4 +$ ______ $x^3 -$ ______ $x^2 +$ ______ $x -$ ______.

The estimated volume of a 35-inch diameter tree to the nearest board foot is ______ or ______ of 100s board ft.

Example 5 Find Average Rate of Change

ROCKETS **The table shows the expected g-force on the Ares-V rocket over the course of its 200-second launch.**

Time (s)	Acceleration (Gs)	Time (s)	Acceleration (Gs)
0	1.34	120	1.46
20	1.26	140	1.93
40	1.12	160	2.47
60	1.01	180	2.84
80	1	200	2.2
100	1.15		

Think About It!

Does the average rate of change from 0 to 200 seconds accurately describe the acceleration 0of the launch? Justify your reasoning.

Part A Find the average rate of change.

Estimate: The change in the y-values is about 0.9, and the change in the x-values is 200. So, the rate of change is about $\frac{0.9}{200}$ or ______.

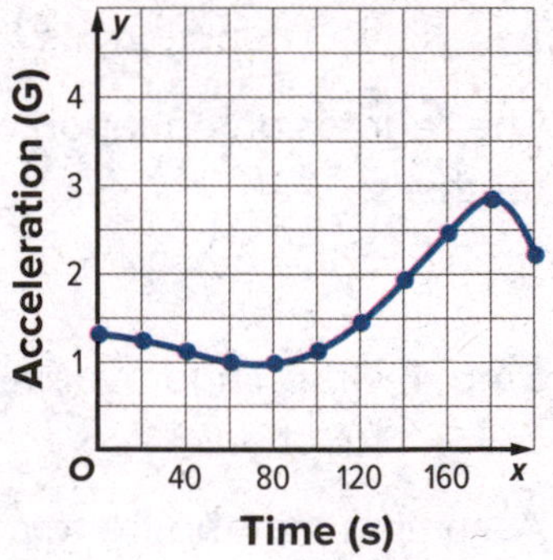

y
Acceleration (G)
4
3
2
1
O
40
80
120
160
x
Time (s)

Algebraically:

The average rate of change is $\frac{f(\quad) - f(\quad)}{200 - 0}$ or ______.

Part B Interpret the results.

From 0 to ______ seconds, the average rate of change in acceleration was an increase of ______ Gs per ______.

Go Online You can complete an Extra Example online.

Name ______________________ Period __________ Date __________

Practice

Go Online You can complete your homework online.

Examples 1 and 2

For each function, complete each of the following.

a. Graph each function by making a table of values.

b. Determine the consecutive integer values of *x* between which each real zero is located.

c. Estimate the *x*-coordinates at which the relative maxima and minima occur.

d. Estimate the location of the turning points.

1. $f(x) = x^3 + 3x^2$

2. $f(x) = -x^3 + 2x^2 - 4$

3. $f(x) = x^3 + 4x^2 - 5x$

4. $f(x) = x^3 - 5x^2 + 3x + 1$

5. $f(x) = -2x^3 + 12x^2 - 8x$

6. $f(x) = 2x^3 - 4x^2 - 3x + 4$

7. $f(x) = x^4 + 2x - 1$

8. $f(x) = x^4 + 8x^2 - 12$

Example 3

9. **BUSINESS** A banker models the expected value of a company in millions of dollars by using the formula $v = n^3 - 3n^2$, where n is the number of years in business. Graph the function and describe its key features over its relevant domain.

10. **REVENUE** The revenue for a start-up company can be approximated by the function $f(x) = -300x^4 + 3250x^3 - 11708x^2 + 23750x - 10{,}000$, where x is the number of years the company has been in business and $f(x)$ is the company's revenue. Graph the function and describe its key features over its relevant domain.

11. **HEIGHT** A plant's growth is modeled by the function $f(x) = 1.5x^3 - 20x^2 + 85x - 84$, where x is the number of weeks since the seed was planted and $f(x)$ is the height of the plant. Graph the function and describe its key features over its relevant domain.

12. **SALARY** Minimum wage in the U.S. since 1940 is modeled by the function $f(x) = 0.006x^3 + 0.056x^2 + 0.267x + 0.314$, where x is the number of years since 1940 and $f(x)$ is the minimum wage. Graph the function and describe its key features over its relevant domain.

Example 4

13. **SALES** The table shows U.S. car sales in millions of cars. Make a scatter plot and a curve of best fit to show the trend over time. Then determine the car sales in 2017. Assume 2008 is year 0 and round equation coefficients to the thousandths place.

Year	Cars (in millions)	Year	Cars (in millions)	Year	Cars (in millions)
2008	7.659	2011	6.769	2014	6.089
2009	7.761	2012	5.400	2015	7.243
2010	7.562	2013	5.635	2016	7.780

14. **POPULATION** The table shows the population in Cincinnati, Ohio in 10-year increments since 1960. Make a scatter plot and a curve of best fit to show the trend over time. Then determine the population of Cincinnati in 2020.

Year	Population	Year	Population
1960	502,550	1990	364,553
1970	452,524	2000	331,258
1980	385,457	2010	296,943

15. **VOLUNTEERS** The table shows average volunteer hours per month for a local non-profit. Make a scatter plot and a curve of best fit to show the trend over time. Then determine the volunteer hours for October.

Month	Average Volunteer Hours	Month	Average Volunteer Hours
Jan	48	Apr	75
Feb	60	May	100
Mar	72	Jun	110

16. **FARMS** The table shows the number of U.S. farms during certain years, according to the USDA Census of Agriculture. Make a scatter plot and a curve of best fit to show the trend over time. Then determine the number of U.S. farms in 2025.

Year	Number of Farms	Year	Number of Farms
1982	2,480,000	2002	2,130,000
1987	2,340,000	2007	2,200,000
1992	2,180,000	2012	2,110,000
1997	2,220,000		

Example 5

17. **SALARY** The table shows a salesman's salary. Find the average rate of change. Interpret the results in context of this situation.

Year	Salary	Year	Salary
2012	$45,000	2015	$55,500
2013	$49,000	2016	$73,000
2014	$47,500	2017	$67,500

18. **HAY** The table the number of square bales of hay a farmer produces. Find the average rate of change. Interpret the results in context of this situation.

Year	Number of Farms	Year	Number of Farms
2010	53,500	2013	43,500
2011	52,000	2014	47,000
2012	49,000	2015	41,500

Name ______________________ Period ____________ Date ______________

Mixed Exercises

For each function, complete each of the following.

a. Graph each function by making a table of values.

b. Determine the consecutive integer values of *x* between which each real zero is located.

c. Estimate the *x*-coordinates at which the relative maxima and minima occur.

d. Estimate the location of the turning points.

19. $f(x) = x^3 - 3x^2 + 1$

20. $f(x) = x^3 - 3x + 1$

21. $f(x) = 2x^3 + 9x^2 + 12x + 2$

22. $f(x) = 2x^3 - 3x^2 + 2$

23. $f(x) = x^4 - 2x^2 - 2$

24. $f(x) = 0.5x^4 - 4x^2 + 4$

Use a graphing calculator to estimate the *x*-coordinates at which the maxima and minima of each function occur. Round to the nearest hundredth.

25. $f(x) = x^3 + 3x^2 - 6x - 6$

26. $f(x) = -2x^3 + 4x^2 - 5x + 8$

27. $f(x) = -2x^4 + 5x^3 - 4x^2 + 3x - 7$

28. $f(x) = x^5 - 4x^3 + 3x^2 - 8x - 6$

For each function,

a. determine the zeros, *x*- and *y*-intercepts, and turning points,

b. determine the axis of symmetry, and

c. determine the intervals for which it is increasing, decreasing, or constant.

29. $y = x^4 - 8x^2 + 16$

30. $y = x^5 - 3x^3 + 2x - 4$

31. $y = -2x^4 + 4x^3 - 5x$

32. $y = \begin{cases} x^2 & \text{if } x \leq -4 \\ 5 & \text{if } -4 < x \leq 0 \\ x^3 & \text{if } x > 0 \end{cases}$

33. STRUCTURE Sketch the graph of a 3rd degree polynomial function that has a relative minimum at $x = -3$, passes through the origin, and has a relative maximum at $x = 2$. Describe the end behavior of the graph. Based on the sketch, determine whether the leading coefficient is negative or positive.

34. A canister has the shape of a cylinder with spherical caps on either end. The volume of the canister in cubic millimeters is modeled by the function $V(x) = \pi(x^3 + 3x^2) + \frac{4}{3}\pi x^3$ where x represents the radius of the canister in millimeters.

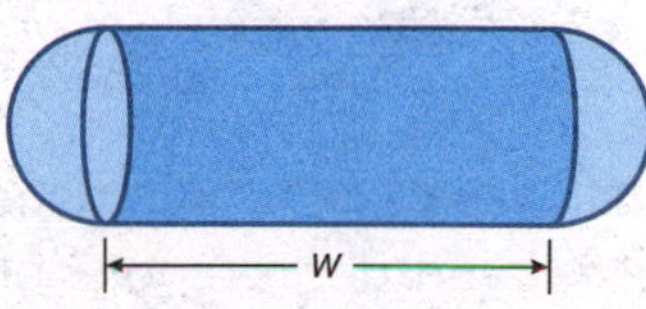

a. MODELING Find an expression for the width of the cylindrical portion of the canister w in terms of the radius x. Interpret the expression in the context of the problem. Hint: the volume of a sphere is $\frac{4}{3}\pi r^3$.

b. USE TOOLS Use a graphing calculator to sketch the model that represents the volume of the canister. Label axes appropriately.

c. REASONING What is the domain of the model? Explain any restrictions that apply.

35. **ARGUMENTS** What type of polynomial function best models the data in the graph? Explain your reasoning.

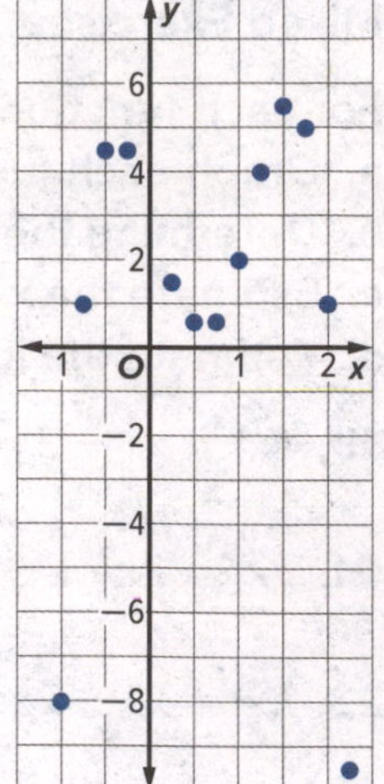

36. **FORECASTING** The table shows the number of babies a doctor has delivered each year for the last 8 years. Use a scatter plot and a curve of best fit to determine the number of babies the doctor can expect to deliver in year 10 of her practice.

Year	Babies Delivered	Year	Babies Delivered
1	60	5	168
2	90	6	144
3	192	7	106
4	96	8	97

37. **ANALYZE** Explain why the leading coefficient and the degree are the only determining factors in the end behavior of a polynomial function.

38. **ANALYZE** The table below shows the values of a cubic function. Could there be a zero between $x = 2$ and $x = 3$? Explain your reasoning.

x	−2	−1	0	1	2	3
$g(x)$	4	−2	−1	1	−2	−2

39. **CREATE** Sketch the graph of an odd degree polynomial function with 6 turning points and 2 double roots.

40. **ANALYZE** Determine whether the following statement is sometimes, always, or never true. Explain your reasoning.

For any continuous polynomial function, the y-coordinate of a turning point is also either a relative maximum or relative minimum.

41. **PERSEVERE** A function is said to be even if for every x in the domain of f, $f(x) = f(-x)$. Is every even-degree polynomial function also an even function? Explain.

42. **PERSEVERE** A function is said to be odd if for every x in the domain, $-f(x) = f(-x)$. Is every odd-degree polynomial function also an odd function? Explain.

43. **WRITE** How can you use the characteristics of a polynomial function to sketch its graph?

44. **WRITE** Explain how to find the average rate of change from a graph.

Operations with Polynomials

Learn Adding and Subtracting Polynomials

A **polynomial** is a monomial or the sum of two or more monomials. A **binomial** is the sum of two monomials, and a **trinomial** is the sum of three monomials. The **degree of a polynomial** is the greatest degree of any term in the polynomial.

Polynomials can be added or subtracted by performing the operations indicated and combining like terms. You can subtract a polynomial by adding its additive inverse.

The sum or difference of polynomials will have the same variables and exponents as the original polynomials, but possibly different coefficients. Thus, the sum or difference of two polynomials is also a polynomial.

A set is **closed** if and only if an operation on any two elements of the set produces another element of the same set. Because adding or subtracting polynomials results in a polynomial, the set of polynomials is closed under the operations of addition and subtraction.

Today's Standards
A.APR.1
MP2, MP8

Today's Vocabulary
binomial
trinomial

Think About It!
Identify the like terms in $8x^5 + 3x^2 - 10$ and $4x^3 - 7x^2 + 5$.

Example 1 Identify Polynomials

Determine whether each expression is a polynomial. If it is a polynomial, state the degree of the polynomial.

a. $x^6 + \sqrt[3]{x} - 4$

This expression is _____ a polynomial because _____ is not a monomial.

b. $5a^4b + 3a^2b^7 - 9$

This expression _____ a polynomial because each term is a _____________. The degree of the first term is 4 + 1 or 5, the degree of the second term is 2 + 7 or 9, and the degree of the third term is 0. So, the degree of the polynomial is _____.

c. $\frac{2}{3}x^{-5} - 6x^{-3} - x$

The expression is _____ a polynomial because x^{-5} and x^{-3} are not _____________.

Study Tip:
Degree 0 and 1 Remember that constant terms have a degree of 0 and variable term with no exponent indicated has a degree of 1.

Go Online You can learn how to add and subtract polynomials by watching the video online.

Check

State the degree of each polynomial.

a. $x^7 + 6x^5 - \frac{1}{3}$ _____

b. $3c^7d^2 + 5cd - 9$ _____

c. p^{10} _____

d. 25 _____

Go Online You can complete an Extra Example online.

Your Notes

Talk About It

Notice that the terms in the sum have the same variables and exponents as the terms of the original expressions: x^3, x^2, x and a constant. Will this always be the case? Explain.

Think About It!

Why is it helpful to insert placeholders for the $0x^3$ and $0x^5$ terms? Why were placeholders not included for the x^2-term in either polynomial?

Study Tip:

Additive Inverse Distributing −1 to each term in the polynomial being subtracted is the same as finding and adding its additive inverse.

Example 2 Add Polynomials

Find $(6x^3 + 7x^2 - 2x + 5) + (x^3 - 4x^2 - 8x + 1)$.

Method 1 Add horizontally.

Group and combine like terms.

$$(6x^3 + 7x^2 - 2x + 5) + (x^3 - 4x^2 - 8x + 1) = (6x^3 + x^3) + (7x^2 - 4x^2) + (-2x - 8x) + (5 + 1)$$

$$= \_\_x^3 + \_\_x^2 - \_\_x + \_\_$$

Method 2 Add vertically.

Align like terms vertically and add.

$$\begin{array}{r} 6x^3 + 7x^2 - 2x + 5 \\ (+)x^3 - 4x^2 - 8x + 1 \\ \hline = \quad x^3 + \quad x^2 - \quad x + \end{array}$$

Check

Find $(2x^3 + 9x^2 + 6x - 3) + (4x^3 - 7x^2 + 5x)$.

☐x^3 + ☐x^2 + ☐x + ☐

Example 3 Subtract Polynomials

Find $(2x^5 + 11x^4 + 7x - 8) - (5x^4 + 9x^3 - 3x + 4)$.

Method 1 Subtract horizontally.

Group and combine like terms.

$$(2x^5 + 11x^4 + 7x - 8) - (5x^4 + 9x^3 - 3x + 4) = 2x^5 + 11x^4 + 7x - 8 - 5x^4 - 9x^3 + 3x - 4$$

$$= 2x^5 + (11x^4 - 5x^4) + (-9x^3) + (7x + 3x) + (-8 + 4)$$

$$= \_\_x^5 + \_\_x^4 - \_\_x^3 + \_\_x \_\_$$

Method 2 Add vertically.

Align like terms vertically and subtract by adding the additive inverse.

$$\begin{array}{r} 2x^5 + 11x^4 + 0x^3 + 7x - 8 \\ (-)0x^5 + 5x^4 + 9x^3 - 3x + 4 \\ \hline = \quad x^5 + \quad x^4 - \quad x^3 + \quad x - \end{array}$$

Check

Find $(8x^2 - 3x + 1) - (5x^3 + 2x^2 - 6x - 9)$.

☐x^3 + ☐x^2 + ☐x + ☐

Go Online You can complete an Extra Example online.

Explore Multiplying Polynomials

Online Activity Use a table to complete the Explore.

> **INQUIRY** How is using a table to multiply polynomials related to the Distributive Property?

Learn Multiplying Polynomials

Polynomials can be multiplied by using the Distributive Property to multiply each term in one polynomial by each term in the other. When polynomials are multiplied, the product is also a polynomial. Therefore, the set of polynomials is closed under the multiplication. This is similar to the system of integers, which is also closed under multiplication. To multiply two binomials, you can use a shortcut called the FOIL method.

Key Concept • FOIL Method

Words: Find the sum of the products of ***F*** the *First* terms, ***O*** the *Outer* terms, ***I*** the *Inner* terms, and ***L*** the *last* terms.

Symbols:

F L I O

Product of First Terms | Product of Outer Terms | Product of Inner Terms | Product of Last Terms

$$(2x + 4)(x - 3) = (2x)(x) + (2x)(-3) + (4)(x) + (4)(-3)$$
$$= 2x^2 - 6x + 4x - 12$$
$$= 2x^2 - 2x - 12$$

Example 4 Simplify by Using the Distributive Property

Find $2x(4x^3 + 5x^2 - x - 7)$.

$$2x(4x^3 + 5x^2 - x - 7) = 2x(4x^3) + 2x(\_\_\_) + 2x(-x) + 2x(\_\_\_)$$
$$= \_\_\_x^4 + 10x^3 - \_\_\_x^2 - 14x$$

Think About It!

Why are the exponents added when you multiply the monomials?

Example 5 Multiply Binomials.

Find $(3a + 5)(a - 7)(4a + 1)$.

Step 1 Multiply any two binomials.

$(3a + 5)(a - 7) = 3a(\_) + 3a(\_\_\_) + 5(a) + 5(-7)$ FOIL Method

$= 3a^2 - 21a + \_\_a - \_\_\_$ Multiply.

$= 3a^2 - \_\_\_a - 35$ Combine like terms.

(continued on the next page)

Go Online You can complete an Extra Example online.

Step 2 Multiply the result by the remaining binomial.

$(3a^2 - 16a - 35)(4a + 1)$

$= 3a^2(4a + 1) + (\_\_\_\_)(4a + 1) + (\_\_\_\_)(4a + 1)$

$= \_\_\_\_ + 3a^2 - 64a^2 - 16a - 140a - 35$

$= 12a^3 - \_\_\_\_ - 156a \_\_\_\_$

Go Online for an example of how to multiply two trinomials.

Check

Find $(-2r - 3)(5r - 1)(r + 4)$.

$\square r^3 + \square r^2 + \square r + \square$

Think About It! What does x represent in the polynomial expression for the volume of the cake?

Example 6 Write and Simplify a Polynomial Expression

BAKING **Alo is baking a three-tier cake. Each tier will have $\frac{1}{2}$ the volume of the previous tier. The dimensions of the first tier are $4x - 3$, $2x + 1$, and x. Find the total volume of the cake.**

Step 1 Find the volume of tier 1.

$V = \text{length} \cdot \text{width} \cdot \text{height} = (4x - 3)(2x + 1)x$

Simplify the expression by using the Distributive Property.

$(4x - 3)(2x + 1)x = [4x(2x + 1) - 3(2x + 1)]x$

$= (8x^2 + 4x - 6x - 3)x$

$= (8x^2 - 2x - 3)x$

$= 8x^3 - 2x^2 - 3x$

The volume of tier 1 is $\_\_x^3 - \_\_x^2 - \_\_x$.

Step 2 Find the volume of tier 2.

The volume of the second tier is half the volume of tier 1.

$\frac{1}{2}(8x^3 - 2x^2 - 3x)$ or $4x^3 - x^2 - \_\_\_\_$

Step 3 Find the volume of tier 3.

The volume of the third tier is half the volume of tier 2.

$\frac{1}{2}(4x^3 - x^2 - 1.5x)$ or $\_\_\_\_x^3 - \_\_\_\_x^2 - \_\_\_\_x$

Step 4 Find the total volume.

Add the polynomial expressions for the volume of each tier to find the total volume of the cake.

$(8x^3 - 2x^2 - 3x) + (4x^3 - x^2 - 1.5x) + (2x^3 - 0.5x^2 - 0.75x)$

The volume of the cake can be represented by:

$\_\_\_\_x^3 - \_\_\_\_x^2 - \_\_\_\_x$

Problem-Solving Tip:

Solve a Simpler Problem Some complicated problems can be more easily solved by breaking them into several simpler problems. In this case, finding the volume of each tier individually simplifies the situation and makes finding total volume easier.

Go Online You can complete an Extra Example online.

Name ________________ Period ________ Date ________

Practice

Go Online You can complete your homework online.

Example 1

Determine whether each expression is a polynomial. If it is a polynomial, state the degree of the polynomial.

1. $2x^2 - 3x + 5$

2. $a^3 - 11$

3. $\frac{5np}{n^2} - \frac{2g}{h}$

4. $\sqrt{m - 7}$

Examples 2 and 3

Add or subtract.

5. $(6a^2 + 5a + 10) - (4a^2 + 6a + 12)$

6. $(7b^2 + 6b - 7) - (4b^2 - 2)$

7. $(g + 5) + (2g + 7)$

8. $(5d + 5) - (d + 1)$

9. $(x^2 - 3x - 3) + (2x^2 + 7x - 2)$

10. $(-2f^2 - 3f - 5) + (-2f^2 - 3f + 8)$

11. $(2x - 3) - (5x - 6)$

12. $(x^2 + 2x - 5) - (3x^2 - 4x + 7)$

Examples 4, 5 and 6

Multiply.

13. $3p(np - z)$

14. $4x(2x^2 + y)$

15. $-5(2c^2 - d^2)$

16. $x^2(2x + 9)$

17. $(a - 5)^2$

18. $(2x - 3)(3x - 5)$

19. $(x - y)(x^2 + 2xy + y^2)$

20. $(a + b)(a^3 - 3ab - b^2)$

21. $(x - y)(x + y)(2x + y)$

22. $(a + b)(2a + 3b)(2x - y)$

23. $(r - 2t)(r + 2t)$

24. $(3y + 4)(2y - 3)$

25. $(x^3 - 3x^2 + 1)(2x^2 - x + 2)$

26. $(4x^5 + x^3 - 7x^2 + 2)(3x - 1)$

Example 7

27. **CONSTRUCTION** A rectangular deck is built around a square pool. The pool has side length s. The length of the deck is 5 units longer than twice the side length of the pool. The width of the deck is 3 units longer than the side length of the pool. What is the area of the deck in terms of s?

28. **VOLUME** The volume of a rectangular prism is given by the product of its length, width, and height. A rectangular prism has a length of b^2 units, a width of a units, and a height of $ab + c$ units. What is the volume of the rectangular prism? Express your answer in simplified form.

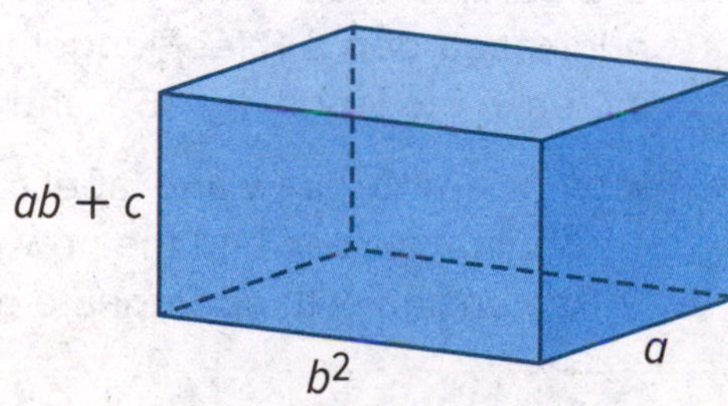

29. **SAIL BOATS** Tamara is making a sail for her sailboat. The base of her triangular sail is $2x + 1$ and the height is $4x + 6$.

a. Find the area of the sail.

b. If Tamara wants a different fabric on each side of her sail, write a polynomial to represent the total amount of fabric she will need to make the sail.

Mixed Exercises

Simplify.

30. $4(a^2 + 5a - 6) - 3(2a^3 + 4a - 5)$

31. $5c(2c^2 - 3c + 4) + 2c(7c - 8)$

32. $5xy(2x - y) + 6y^2(x^2 + 6)$

33. $3ab(4a - 5b) + 4b^2(2a^2 + 1)$

34. $\frac{1}{4}g^2(8g + 12h - 16gh^2)$

35. $\frac{1}{3}n^3(6n - 9p + 18np^4)$

36. $x^{-2}(x^4 - 3x^3 + x^{-1})$

37. $a^{-3}b^2(ba^3 + b^{-1}a^2 + b^{-2}a)$

38. $(g^3 - h)(g^3 + h)$

39. $(n^2 - 7)(2n^3 + 4)$

40. $(2x - 2y)^3$

41. $(4n - 5)^3$

42. $(3z - 2)^3$

43. $\frac{1}{4}(16x - 12y) + \frac{1}{3}(9x + 3y)$

44. **PRECISION** Use the polynomials $f(x) = -6x^3 + 2x^2 + 4$ and $g(x) = x^4 - 6x^3 - 2x$ to evaluate and simplify the given expression. Determine the degree of the resulting polynomial. Show your work.

a. $f(x) + g(x)$

b. $g(x) - f(x)$

45. **STRUCTURE** Use the polynomials $f(x) = 3x^2 - 1$, $g(x) = x + 2$, and $h(x) = -x^2 - x$ to evaluate and simplify the given expressions. Determine the degree of the resulting polynomial.

a. $f(x)g(x)$

b. $h(x)f(x)$

c. $[f(x)]^2$

46. **GARDENING** Inez wants to increase the size of her rectangular garden. The original garden is 8 feet longer than it is wide. For the new garden, she will increase the length by 25% and increase the width by 5 feet.

a. **MODELING** Draw and label a diagram with two rectangles representing the original garden and the new garden. Define a variable and label each dimension with appropriate expressions.

b. **STRUCTURE** Every foot of the perimeter of the original garden was lined with 7 stones. Write and simplify an expression to represent how many more stones Inez needs for the new garden.

c. **STRUCTURE** Write and simplify an expression for the increase in area of the garden. Find how many square feet the garden's area increased, if the original width of the garden was 10 feet.

47. **REASONING** Copy and complete the table showing closure for the sets shown by writing *yes* or writing *no* and providing a counterexample. You can assume that since division by zero is undefined, it does not affect closure.

	Addition and Subtraction	Multiplication	Division
Integers			
Rational Numbers			
Polynomials			

48. **STRUCTURE** The polynomial $2x^2 + 3x + 1$ can be represented by the tiles shown in the figure at the right. These tiles can be arranged to form the rectangle shown. Notice that the area of the rectangle is $2x^2 + 3x + 1$ units^2.

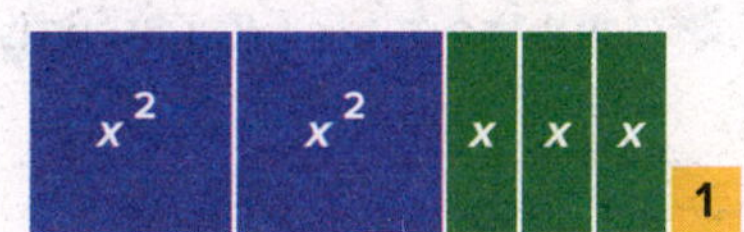

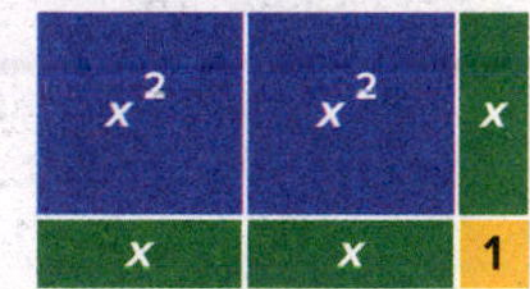

a. Find the length and width of the rectangle.

b. Explain how to find the perimeter of the rectangle. Then find the perimeter.

c. Select a value for x and substitute that value into each of the expressions above. For your value of x, state the length, width, perimeter, and area of the rectangle. Discuss any restrictions on your choice of x.

49. **BANKING** Terryl invests \$1500 in two mutual funds. The first year, one fund grows 3.8% and the other grows 6%. Write a polynomial to represent the amount Terryl's \$1500 grows to in that year if x represents the amount he invested in the fund with the lesser growth rate.

50. **PACKAGING** The area of the base of a rectangular crate measures $2x^2 + 4x - 3$ square units. The height of the crate measures x units. Write a polynomial expression to represent the volume of the crate.

51. **GEOMETRY** Consider a trapezoid that has one base that measures five feet greater than its height. The other base is one foot less than twice its height. Let x represent the height.

a. Write an expression for the area of the trapezoid.

b. Write an expression for the area of the trapezoid if its height is changed to $(x + 4)$ feet.

52. URBAN DEVELOPMENT The diagram represents the base area of a circular memorial in a town center. A sidewalk that is 12 feet wide with an area of 384π square feet surrounds the smaller circle.

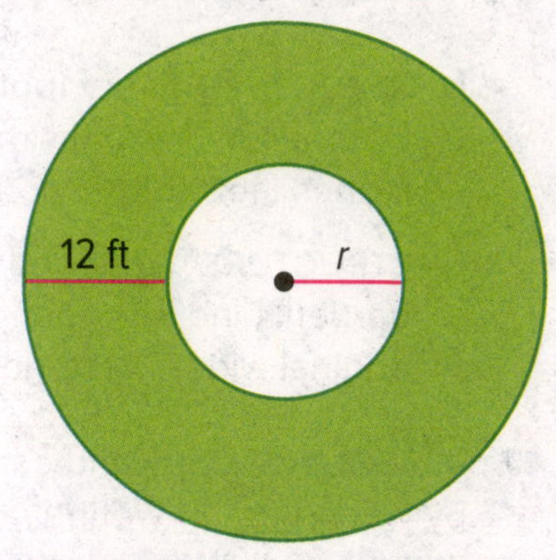

a. Find the radius of the smaller and larger circles. Show your work.

b. A nearby town wants to use the same design concept, but use two squares rather than two circles. Draw and label a diagram with two squares to represent a sidewalk with the same uniform width and area as the circular sidewalk.

c. If s represents the side length of the smaller square, write an expression for the area of the sidewalk that surrounds the smaller square.

53. ANALYZE Given $f(x)$ and $g(x)$ are polynomials, is the product always a polynomial? Explain why or why not.

54. PERSEVERE Use your result from Exercise 53 to make conjectures about the product of a polynomial with m terms and a polynomial with n terms. Justify your conjecture.

a. How many times are two terms multiplied?

b. What is the least number of terms in the simplified product?

55. FIND THE ERROR Isabella found the product of $3x^2 - 4x + 1$ and $x^2 + 5x + 6$ using vertical alignment. Is her answer correct? Explain your reasoning.

Isabella's Work

$$\begin{array}{rrrrr} & & 3x^2 & -\ 4x & +\ 1 \\ & & x^2 & +\ 5x & +\ 6 \\ \hline & & 18x^2 & -\ 24x & +\ 6 \\ & 15x^3 & -\ 20x^2 & +\ 5x & \\ 3x^4 & -\ 4x^3 & +\ x^2 & & \\ \hline 3x^4 & +\ 11x^3 & -\ x^2 & -\ 19x & +\ 6 \end{array}$$

56. WRITE Explain how to determine whether the expression $2x^2 - 5x^3 + 7x^4 - 9$ is a polynomial.

57. CREATE Write an expression where two binomials are multiplied and have a product of $9 - 4b^2$.

Dividing Polynomials

Today's Standards
A.APR.6
MP3, MP8

Today's Vocabulary
synthetic division

Explore Using Algebra Tiles to Divide Polynomials

Online Activity Use algebra tiles to complete the Explore.

INQUIRY How can you use a model to divide polynomials?

Learn Dividing Polynomials by Using Long Division

To divide a polynomial by a monomial, find the quotient of each term of the polynomial and the monomial.

$$\frac{6x^2 - 15x}{3x} = \frac{6x^2}{3x} - \frac{15x}{3x} = 2x - 5$$

You can divide a polynomial by a polynomial with more than one term by using a process similar to long division of real numbers. This process is known as the Division Algorithm. The resulting quotient may be a polynomial or a polynomial with a remainder.

Key Concept • Division Algorithm

Words: If $f(x)$ and $g(x)$ are two polynomials in which $g(x) \neq 0$ and the degree of $g(x)$ is less than the degree of $f(x)$, then there exists a unique quotient $q(x)$ and a unique remainder $r(x)$ such that $f(x) = q(x)g(x) + r(x)$, where the remainder is zero or the degree of $r(x)$ is less than the degree of $g(x)$.

Symbols: $\frac{f(x)}{g(x)} = q(x) \rightarrow f(x) = q(x)g(x)$

$$\frac{f(x)}{g(x)} = q(x) + \frac{r(x)}{g(x)} \rightarrow f(x) = q(x)g(x) + r(x)$$

Example: $\frac{2x^2 - 5x - 3}{x - 3} = 2x + 1 \rightarrow$

$$2x^2 - 5x - 3 = (x - 3)(2x + 1)$$
$$= 2x^2 - 5x - 3$$

$$\frac{x^2 - 4x - 1}{x + 1} = x - 5 + \frac{4}{x + 1} \rightarrow$$

$$x^2 - 4x - 1 = (x - 5)(x + 1) + 4$$
$$= x^2 - 5x - 5 + 4$$
$$= x^2 - 5x - 1$$

Go Online You can complete an Extra Example online.

Talk About It

Is the following statement *always*, *sometimes*, or *never* true? Justify your argument.

If a quadratic polynomial is divided by a binomial with a remainder of 0, the binomial is a factor of the polynomial.

Study Tip:

In algebra, *unique* means *only one*. So, there is only one quotient and remainder that will satisfy the Division Algorithm for each polynomial.

Your Notes

Think About It!

How can you check the solution?

Watch Out!

Signs Remember that you are subtracting throughout the process of long division. Carefully label the signs of the coefficients to avoid a sign error.

Go Online

You can learn how to divide polynomials by using long division by watching the video online.

Example 1 Divide a Polynomial by a Monomial

Find $(24a^4b^3 + 18a^2b^2 - 30ab^3)(6ab)^{-1}$.

$(24a^4b^3 + 18a^2b^2 - 30ab^3)(6ab)^{-1}$

$= \dfrac{24a^4b^3 + 18a^2b^2 - 30ab^3}{\_\_\_\_\_\_}$ Write a fraction.

$= \dfrac{24a^4b^3}{6ab} + \dfrac{18a^2b^2}{6ab} - \dfrac{30ab^3}{6ab}$ Sum of Quotients

$= \dfrac{24}{6}a^{4-1}b^{3-1} + \dfrac{18}{6}a^{2-1}b^{2-1} - \dfrac{30}{6}a^{1-1}b^{3-1}$ Divide.

$= \_\_\_\_\_ + 3ab - \_\_\_\_\_$ Simplify.

Check

Find $(9x^9y^5 + 21x^4y^4 - 12x^3y^2) \div (3x^2y^2)$. __________

Example 2 Divide a Polynomial by a Binomial

Find $(x^2 - 5x - 36) \div (x + 4)$.

```
              x − 9
x + 4 ) x² − 5x − 36
    (−) x² +  x
        ____x − 36
    (−)−9x − 36
```

The quotient is $x - $ ___ and the remainder is ___.

Check

Find $\dfrac{x^2 + 6x - 112}{x - 8}$. ______

Example 3 Find a Quotient with a Remainder

Find $\dfrac{3z^3 - 14z^2 - 7z + 3}{z - 5}$.

```
              3z² + z − 2
z − 5 ) 3z³ − 14z² − 7z + 3
    (−)3z³ −   z²
               z² − 7z
          (−)z² _____
                 −2z + ____
            (−) −2z + 10
```

 **Go Online** You can complete an Extra Example online.

The quotient is $3z^2 + z - 2$ and the remainder is ____.

Therefore, $\frac{3z^3 - 14z^2 - 7z + 3}{z - 5} = \_\_z^2 + z - 2 - \frac{\quad}{z - 5}$

Check

Find the quotient of $(-4x^3 + 5x^2 - 2x - 9)(x - 2)^{-1}$.

____

Learn Dividing Polynomials by Using Synthetic Division

Synthetic division is an alternate method used to divide a polynomial by a binomial of degree 1. You may find this to be a quicker, simpler method.

Key Concept • Synthetic Division

Step 1 After writing a polynomial in standard form, write the coefficients of the dividend. If the dividend is missing a term, use 0 as a placeholder. Write the constant a of the divisor $x - a$ in the box. Bring the first coefficient down.

Step 2 Multiply the number just written in the bottom row by a, and write the product under the next coefficient.

Step 3 Add the product and the coefficient above it.

Step 4 Repeat **Steps 2** and **3** until you reach a sum in the last column.

Step 5 Write the quotient. The numbers along the bottom row are the coefficients of the quotient. The power of the first term is one less than the degree of the dividend. The final number is the remainder.

Example 4 Use Synthetic Division

Find $(3x^3 - 2x^2 - 53x - 60) \div (x + 3)$.

Step 1 Write the coefficients of the dividend and write the constant a in the box. Bring the first coefficient, 3, down.
Because $x + 3 = x - (-3)$, $a = -3$.

Step 2 Multiply by a and write the product.
The product of the coefficient and a is $3 \cdot (-3) = -9$.

Step 3 Add the product and the coefficient.

Step 4 Repeat **Steps 2** and **3** until you reach a sum in the last column.

Step 5 Write the quotient.

___	3	−2	−53	−60
		−9	33	60
	___	___	___	___

(continued on the next page)

Go Online You can complete an Extra Example online.

Think About It!
What is another method you could use to check your answer?

Because the degree of the dividend is 3 and the degree of the divisor is 1, the degree of the quotient is 2. The final sum in the synthetic division is 0, so the remainder is 0.

The quotient is ______________.

Check

Find the quotient of $(4x^3 - 8x^2 - 5x + 20) \div (x - 2)$.

____

> **Watch Out!**
>
> **Missing terms** Add placeholders for terms that are missing from the polynomial. In this case, there are 0 x^3-terms.

Example 5 Divisor with Coefficient Other Than 1

Find $\frac{4x^4 - 37x^2 + 4x + 9}{2x - 1}$.

To use synthetic division, the lead coefficient of the divisor must be ___.

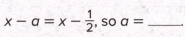

$\frac{(4x^4 - 37x^2 + 4x + 9) \div \quad}{(2x - 1) \div \quad}$ Divide the numerator and denominator by 2.

$= \frac{2x^4 - \quad x^2 + \quad x + \frac{9}{2}}{x - \quad}$ Simplify the numerator and denominator.

$x - a = x - \frac{1}{2}$, so $a =$ _____.

Complete the synthetic division.

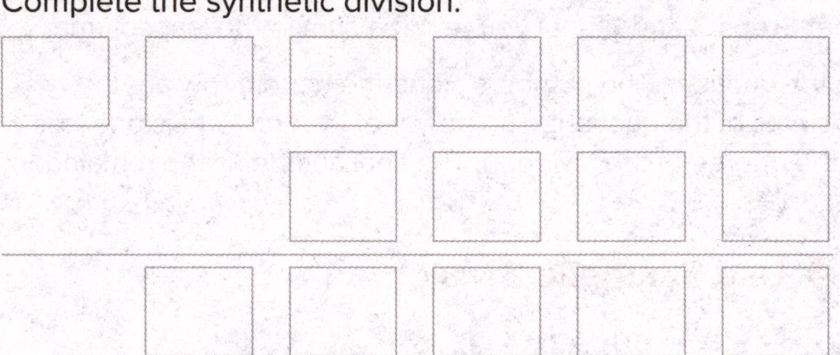

The resulting expression is $2x^3 + x^2 - 18x - 7 + \frac{1}{x - \frac{1}{2}}$. Simplify the fraction.

$\frac{1}{x - \frac{1}{2}} = \frac{(1)2}{\left(x - \frac{1}{2}\right) \cdot 2}$ Multiply the numerator and denominator by 2.

$=$ _____ Simplify.

The solution is $2x^3 + x^2 - 18x - 7 + \frac{2}{2x - 1}$

You can check your answer by using long division.

Check

Find $(4x^4 + 3x^3 - 12x^2 - x + 6)(4x + 3)^{-1}$

____

Go Online You can complete an Extra Example online.

Name ______________________ Period ________ Date ________

Practice

Go Online You can complete your homework online.

Examples 1–3

Simplify using long division.

1. $\frac{10c + 6}{2}$

2. $\frac{12x + 20}{4}$

3. $\frac{15y^3 + 6y^2 + 3y}{3y}$

4. $\frac{12x^3 - 4x - 8}{4x}$

5. $(15q^6 + 5q^2)(5q4)^{-1}$

6. $(4f^5 - 6f^4 + 12f^3 - 8f^2)(4f^2)^{-1}$

7. $(6j^2k - 9jk^2) \div 3jk$

8. $(4a^2h^2 - 8a^3h + 3a^4) \div (2a^2)$

9. $(n^2 + 7n + 10) \div (n + 5)$

10. $(d^2 + 4d + 3) \div (d + 1)$

11. $(2t^2 + 13t + 15) \div (t + 5)$

12. $(6y^2 + y - 2)(2y - 1)^{-1}$

13. $(4g^2 - 9) \div (2g + 3)$

14. $(2x^2 - 5x - 4) \div (x - 3)$

Examples 4 and 5

Simplify using synthetic division.

15. $\frac{u^3 + 5u - 12}{u - 3}$

16. $\frac{6x^3 + 5x^2 + 9}{2x + 3}$

17. $(3v^2 - 7v - 10)(v - 4)^{-1}$

18. $(3t^4 + 4t^3 - 32t^2 - 5t - 20)(t + 4)^{-1}$

19. $\frac{y^3 - y^3 - 6}{y + 2}$

20. $\frac{2x^3 - x^2 - 19x + 15}{x - 3}$

21. $(4p^3 - 3p^2 + 2p) \div (p - 1)$

22. $(3c^4 + 6c^3 - 2c + 4)(c + 2)^{-1}$

Mixed Exercises

Simplify.

23. $(12x^3 - 16x^2y + 3xy^2 + 9y^2)(2x^{-3}y)^{-1}$

24. $(30a^2 - 11a + 15)(5a - 6)^{-1}$

25. $(m^2 + m - 6) \div (m + 4)$

26. $(a^3 - 6a^2 + 10a - 3) \div (a - 3)$

27. $(2x^3 - 7x^2 + 7x - 2) \div (x - 2)$

28. $(x^3 + 2x^2 - 34x + 9) \div (x + 7)$

29. $(x^3 + 8) \div (x + 2)$

30. $(6x^3 + x^2 + x) \div (2x + 1)$

31. **GEOMETRY** The area of a rectangle is $x^3 + 8x^2 + 13x - 12$ square units. The width of the rectangle is $x + 4$ units. What is the length of the rectangle?

32. **QUOTIENTS AND REMAINDERS** For homework yesterday, Jordan divided the polynomial $p(x)$ by $(x^2 + x - 4)$. Today his work is smudged and he cannot read $p(x)$. The only parts of his work he can read are the quotient $x - 1$ and the remainder $x + 4$. What is $p(-2)$?

33. **PRECISION** Jada used long division to divide $x^4 + x^3 + x^2 + x + 1$ by $x + 2$. Her work is shown below with three numbers missing. What are A, B, and C?

$$\begin{array}{r}
x^3 - x^2 + 3x - 5 \\
x + 2 \overline{) x^4 + x^3 + x^2 + x + 1} \\
\underline{(-)\ x^4 - 2x^3} \qquad\qquad\quad \\
-x^3 + A \qquad\qquad \\
\underline{(-)\ -x^3 + 2x^2} \qquad\qquad \\
3x^2 + x \qquad \\
\underline{(-)\ 3x^2 + B} \qquad \\
-5x + 1 \\
\underline{(-)\ -5x + 10} \\
C
\end{array}$$

34. **AVERAGES** Shelby has a list of $n + 1$ numbers and she needs to find their average. Two of the numbers are n^3 and 2. Each of the other $n - 1$ numbers are all equal to 1. Find the average of these numbers.

35. **VOLUME** The volume of one cylindrical column of a building is $\pi(x^3 + 32x^2 - 304x + 640)$. If the height of the column is $x + 40$ feet, find the area of the base of the column in terms of x and π.

Name ______________________ Period __________ Date __________

Simplify.

36. $(x^4 - y^4) \div (x - y)$

37. $(28c^3d^2 - 21cd^2) \div (14cd)$

38. $a^3b^2 - a^2b + 2b)(-ab)^{-1}$

39. $\dfrac{n^3 + 3n^2 - 5n - 4}{n + 4}$

40. $\dfrac{p^3 + 2p^2 - 7p - 21}{p + 3}$

41. $\dfrac{3z^5 + 5z^4 + z + 5}{z + 2}$

42. **REASONING** Rewrite $\dfrac{6x^4 + 2x^3 - 16x^2 + 24x + 32}{2x + 4}$ as $q(x) + \dfrac{r(x)}{d(x)}$ using long division. What does the remainder indicate in this problem?

43. **ARGUMENTS** Maria spilled water on her homework. She says that she does not have enough information to recreate the problem. Do you agree? Justify your answer.

$$\begin{array}{r} 3x - \square \\ \square \overline{)\, 9x^2 + \square} \\ \underline{9x^2 + 3x} \\ -3x + 5 \end{array}$$

44. Rewrite $\dfrac{x^5 + 2x^2 + x - 2}{2x + 3}$ as $q(x) + \dfrac{r(x)}{d(x)}$ using long division.

a. **ARGUMENTS** George rewrote the rational expression as: $\frac{1}{4}x^4 - \frac{2}{3}x^3 + \frac{5}{6}x^2 - \frac{7}{8}x + \frac{28}{42} - \dfrac{\frac{95}{102}}{2x + 3}$. Without using paper and pencil, his friend told him that he had made a mistake. Do you agree? If so, what mistake did George make?

b. **REGULARITY** How can you use a pattern to tell if the leading coefficient of a quotient is wrong?

c. **STRUCTURE** Simplify $\dfrac{x^4 + 2x^2 + x - 2}{2x + 4}$.

45. **REGULARITY** Given $\dfrac{f(x)}{d(x)} = q(x) + \dfrac{r(x)}{d(x)}$, suppose that you know $q(x) + \dfrac{r(x)}{d(x)}$. Is it possible to determine $f(x)$? Use an example to illustrate your answer.

46. **MODELING** Mateo has a square garden. A new garden will have the same width and a length that is 3 feet more than twice the width of the original garden.

a. Define a variable and label each side of the diagrams with an expression for its length.

b. Write a ratio to represent the percent increase in the area of the garden. Use polynomial division to rewrite the expression.

c. Use your expression from **part b** to determine the percent of increase in area if the original garden was a 12-foot square. Check your answer.

47. STRUCTURE When a polynomial is divided by $4x - 6$, the quotient is $2x^2 + x + 1$ and the remainder is -4. What is the dividend, $f(x)$? Explain.

48. STRUCTURE Determine the constant c in $\frac{3x^5 + 4x^3 - 6x^2 - 15x + c}{3x^2 - 5}$ such that the denominator is a factor of the numerator.

49. REGULARITY Mariella makes the following claims about the degrees of the polynomials in $\frac{f(x)}{d(x)} = q(x) + \frac{r(x)}{d(x)}$. Do you agree with each claim? Justify your answers and provide examples.

a. The degree of $d(x)$ must be less than the degree of $f(x)$.

b. The degree of $r(x)$ must be at least 1 less than the degree of $d(x)$.

c. The degree of $q(x)$ must be the degree of $f(x)$ minus the degree of $d(x)$.

50. FIND THE ERROR Tomo and Jamal are dividing $2x^3 - 4x^2 + 3x - 1$ by $x - 3$. Look at their claims about the remainder. Is either of them correct? Explain your reasoning.

Sharon claims that the raminder is 26.	Tomo argues that the remainder is −100.

51. PERSEVERE If a polynomial is divided by a binomial and the remainder is 0, what does this tell you about the relationship between the binomial and the polynomial?

52. ANALYZE Review any of the division exercises in this lesson. What is the relationship between the degrees of the dividend, the divisor, and the quotient?

53. CREATE Write a quotient of two polynomials for which the remainder is 3.

54. WRITE Compare and contrast dividing polynomials using long division and using synthetic division.

55. PERSEVERE Mr. Collins has his class working with bases and polynomials. He wrote on the board that the number 1111 in base B has the value $B^3 + B^2 + B + 1$. The class was then given the following questions to answer.

a. The number 11 in base B has the value $B + 1$. What is 1111 (in base B) divided by 11 (in base B)?

b. The number 111 in base B has the value $B^2 + B + 1$. What is 1111 (in base B) divided by 111 (in base B)?

Powers of Binomials

Today's Standards
A.APR.5
MP4, MP7

Today's Vocabulary
Pascal's triangle

Explore Expanding Binomials

Online Activity Use interactive tool to complete the Explore.

INQUIRY How can you use Pascal's Triangle to write expansions of binomials?

Learn Powers of Binomials

Key Concept • Binomial Expansion

In the binomial expansion of $(a + b)^n$,

- there are $n + 1$ terms.
- n is the exponent of a in the first term and b in the last term.
- in successive terms, the exponent of a decreases by 1, and the exponent of b increases by 1.
- the sum of the exponents in each term is n.
- the coefficients are symmetric.

Think About It!
Both ${}_nC_0$ and ${}_nC_n$ equal 1. What does this mean for the terms of a binomial expansion? How does this relate to Pascal's triangle?

Pascal's triangle is a triangle of numbers in which a row represents the coefficients of an expanded binomial $(a + b)^n$. Each row begins and ends with 1. Each coefficient can be found by adding the two coefficients above it in the previous row.

Key Concept • Binomial Theorem

If n is a natural number, then $(a + b)^n =$

$${}_nC_0a^nb^0 + {}_nC_1a^{n-1}b^1 + {}_nC_2a^{n-2}b^2 + {}_nC_3a^{n-3}b^3 + \ldots + {}_nC_na^0b^n$$

OR

$$1a^nb^0 + \frac{n!}{1!(n-1)!}a^{n-1}b^1 + \frac{n!}{2!(n-2)!}a^{n-2}b^2 + \frac{n!}{3!(n-3)!}a^{n-3}b^3 + \ldots + 1a^0b^n$$

Study Tip
Combinations Recall that ${}_nC_r$ refers to the number of ways to choose r objects from n distinct objects. In the Binomial Theorem, n is the exponent of $(a + b)^n$, and r is the exponent of b in each term. To calculate the coefficients, remember that $n!$ represents n factorial. This is the product of all counting numbers beginning with n and counting backward to 1. For example, $3! = 3 \cdot 2 \cdot 1$

Example 1 Use Pascal's Triangle

Use Pascal's Triangle to expand $(x + y)^7$.

1
1 1
1 2 1
1 3 3 1
1 4 6 4 1
1 5 10 10 5 1
___ ___ ___ ___ ___ ___ ___
___ ___ ___ ___ ___ ___ ___ ___

$(x + y)^7 = x^7 + 7x^6y + 21x^5y^2 + 35x^4y^3 + 35x^3y^4 + 21x^2y^5 + 7xy^6 + y^7$

Your Notes

Talk About It

Describe a shortcut you could use to write out rows of Pascal's triangle instead of adding to find every number in a row. Explain your reasoning.

Study Tip:

Assumptions To use the Binomial Theorem, we assumed that the teams had an equal chance of winning and losing. Although teams are not always evenly matched and may benefit from a home field advantage, assuming there is an equal chance of either event occurring allows us to reasonably estimate the probability of an outcome.

Check

Write the expansion of $(c + d)^4$. ______________________

Example 2 Coefficients Other Than 1

BASEBALL **In 2016, the Chicago Cubs won the world series for the first time in 108 years. During the regular season, the Cubs played the Atlanta Braves 6 times, winning 3 games and losing 3 games. If the Cubs were as likely to win as to lose, find the probability of this outcome by expanding $(w + l)^6$.**

$(w + l)^6$

$= {}_6C_0w^6 + {}_6C_1w^5l +$ ______ $+ {}_6C_3w^3l^3 + {}_6C_4w^2l^4 +$ ______ $+ {}_6C_6l^6$

$= w^6 +$ ______ $+ \frac{6!}{2!4!}w^4l^2 +$ ______ $+ \frac{6!}{4!2!}w^2l^4 + \frac{6!}{5!}wl^5 + l^6$

$=$ ____ $+ 6w^5l + 15w^4l^2 + 20w^3l^3 + 15w^2l^4 +$ ____ $+ l^6$

By adding the coefficients, you can determine that there were 64 combinations of wins and losses that could have occurred.

______ represents the number of combinations of 3 wins and 3 losses. Therefore, there was a $\frac{\quad}{\quad}$ or about a ____% chance of the Cubs winning 3 games and losing 3 games against the Braves.

Check

GAME SHOW A group of 8 contestants are selected from the audience of a television game show. If there are an equal number of men and women in the audience, find the probability of the contestants being 5 women and 3 men by expanding $(w + m)^8$. Round to the nearest percent if necessary. ____%

Example 3 Coefficients Other Than 1

Expand $(2c - 6d)^4$.

$(2c - 6d)^4$

$=$ ______ $+ {}_4C_1(2c)^3(-6d) +$ __________ $+ {}_4C_3(2c)(-6d)^3 +$
${}_4C_4(-6d)^4$

$= 16c^4 +$ __________ $+ \frac{4!}{2!2!}(4c^2)(36d^2) + \frac{4!}{3!}(2c)(-216d^3) +$ __________

$= 16c^4 - 192c^3d +$ ________ $-$ ________ $+ 1296d^4$

 **Go Online** You can complete an Extra Example online.

Name ______ Period ______ Date ______

Practice

Go Online You can complete your homework online.

Examples 1 and 3

Expand each binomial.

1. $(x - y)^3$

2. $(a + b)^4$

3. $(g - h)^4$

4. $(m + 1)^4$

5. $(r + 4)^3$

6. $(a - 5)^4$

7. $(y - 7)^3$

8. $(d + 2)^5$

9. $(x - 1)^4$

10. $(2a + b)^4$

11. $(c - 4d)^3$

12. $(2a + 3)^3$

Example 2

13. BAND A school band went to 4 competitions during the year, receiving a superior rating 2 times and not receiving a superior rating 2 times. If the band is as likely to receive a superior rating as to not receive a superior rating, find the probability of this outcome by expanding $(s + n)^4$. Round to the nearest percent if necessary.

14. BASKETBALL Hector shot 8 free throws at practice, making 4 free throws and missing 4 free throws. If it is as likely to make a free throw as to miss a free throw, find the probability of this outcome by expanding $(m + n)^8$. Round to the nearest percent if necessary.

Mixed Exercises

Expand each binomial.

15. $\left(x + \frac{1}{2}\right)^5$

16. $\left(x - \frac{1}{3}\right)^4$

17. $\left(2b + \frac{1}{4}\right)^5$

18. $\left(3c + \frac{1}{3}\right)^5$

19. BOWLING Vince went bowling. After 12 rolls, he bowled 6 strikes and bowled 6 that were not strikes. If it is as likely bowl a strike as to not bowl a strike, find the probability of this outcome by expanding $(s + n)^{12}$. Round to the nearest percent if necessary.

20. CHOIR A group of 4 choir members are selected at random to perform solos. If there are an equal number of boys and girls in the choir, find the probability of the choir members selected being 3 boys and 1 girl by expanding $(b + g)^4$. Round to the nearest percent if necessary.

21. **USE A SOURCE** Research the number of judges on the Supreme Court. For most rulings, a majority is needed. How many combinations of votes are possible for a majority to be reached?

22. **REGULARITY** Each row of Pascal's triangle is like a palindrome. That is, the numbers read the same left to right as they do right to left. Explain why this is the case.

23. **VOLUME** The length of each side of a cube is $x + y$ units. Find the volume of the cube by expanding $(x + y)^3$ using the Binomial Theorem.

24. **REASONING** A test consists of 10 questions, with five answer choices for each question. Matthew forgets to study and must guess on every question. In how many ways can he get 8 or more correct answers on the test? Show your work using Pascal's Triangle.

25. **PRECISION** Use Pascal's Triangle to find the fourth term in the expansion of $(2x + 7)^6$. Why is it the same as the fourth term in the expansion of $(7 + 2x)^6$?

26. **STRUCTURE** Find the term containing x^3y^5 in the expansion of $(2x + 5y)^8$. Show your work and explain your reasoning.

27. **MODELING** A company that makes circuit boards uses a robotic welder in the creation process. Some of these are produced accurately, and others are not. Use the Binomial Theorem to find out how many ways exactly 5 of 7 circuit boards would be produced accurately.

28. **USE TOOLS** A manufacturing process is known to produce a defect in 1 out of 200 chairs. If a sample of 20 chairs is selected, how many different ways can no more than 2 of the chairs be defective?

29. **STRUCTURE** Find the term in $(a + b)^{12}$ where the exponent of a is 5.

30. **STRUCTURE** Shanna's dog had 4 puppies. How many ways are there of having 3 of one gender and 1 of another? Use Pascal's Triangle to help solve this problem.

31. **USE TOOLS** If we classify each day in a particular city as "sunny" or "cloudy," how many ways are there in a 7-day period of having more sunny days than cloudy days? Use the Binomial Theorem to answer this question.

32. **PERSEVERE** Find the sixth term of the expansion of $(\sqrt{a} + \sqrt{b})^{12}$.

33. **ANALYZE** Explain how the terms of $(x + y)^n$ and $(x - y)^n$ are the same and how they are different.

34. **ANALYZE** Determine whether the following statement is true or false. Explain your reasoning.

    The eighth and twelfth terms of $(x + y)^{20}$ have the same coefficients.

35. **CREATE** Write a power of a binomial for which the second term of the expansion is $6x^4y$.

36. **WRITE** Explain how to write out the terms of Pascal's triangle.

Review

 Essential Question

How does an understanding of polynomials and polynomial functions help us understand and interpret real-world events?

Module Summary

Lessons 4-1 and 4-2

Polynomial Functions and Their Graphs

- A power function has the form of the form $f(x) = ax^n$, where a is the leading coefficient and n is the degree.
- Odd-degree functions will always have at least one real zero.
- Even-degree functions may have any number of real zeros or no real zeros at all.
- A polynomial function is a continuous function that can be described by a polynomial equation.
- The degree of a polynomial function tells the maximum number of times that the graph of a polynomial function intersects the x-axis.
- If the value of $f(x)$ changes signs from one value of x to the next, then there is a zero between those two x-values.
- A turning point is a change in direction of a graph. The turning points occur at relative maxima or minima of the function.

Lessons 4-3 and 4-4

Operations with Polynomials

- Polynomials can be added or subtracted by performing the operations indicated and combining like terms.
- To subtract a polynomial, add its additive inverse.
- Polynomials can be multiplied by using the Distributive Property to multiply each term in one polynomial by each term in the other.
- The set of polynomials is closed under the operations of addition, subtraction, and multiplication.
- To multiply two binomials, you can use a shortcut called the FOIL method.
- You can divide a polynomial by a polynomial with more than one term by using a process similar to long division of real numbers.
- Synthetic division is an alternate method used to divide a polynomial by a binomial of degree 1.

Lesson 4-5

Powers of Binomials

- Pascal's triangle is a triangle of numbers in which a row represents the coefficients of an expanded binomial $(a + b)^n$. Each row begins and ends with 1. Each coefficient can be found by adding the two coefficients above it in the previous row.
- If n is a natural number, then $(a + b)^n = {}_nC_0a^nb^0 + {}_nC_1a^{n-1}b^1 + {}_nC_2a^{n-2}b^2 + {}_nC_3a^{n-3}b^3 + \ldots + {}_nC^na^0b^n$.

Study Organizer

 Foldables

Use your Foldable to review this module. Working with a partner can be helpful. Ask for clarification of concepts as needed.

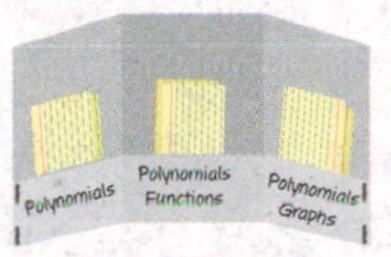

Name ______________________ Period ____________ Date ____________

Test Practice

1. MULTIPLE CHOICE The weight of an ideal cut round diamond can be modeled by $f(d) = 0.0071d^3 - 0.090d^2 + 0.48d$, where d is the diameter of the diamond. Find the domain and range of the function in the context of the situation. (Lesson 4-1)

Ⓐ The domain and range are both all real numbers.

Ⓑ The domain is $\{d \mid d \geq 0\}$, and the range is $\{f(d) \mid f(d) \geq 0\}$.

Ⓒ {The domain is $\{d \mid d \geq 0\}$, and the range is all real numbers.

Ⓓ The domain is all real numbers, and the range is $\{f(d) \mid f(d) \geq 0\}$.

2. OPEN RESPONSE Use the function $f(x) = 13 - 2x^2 + 6x - 9x^3$ to answer the following questions. (Lesson 4-1)

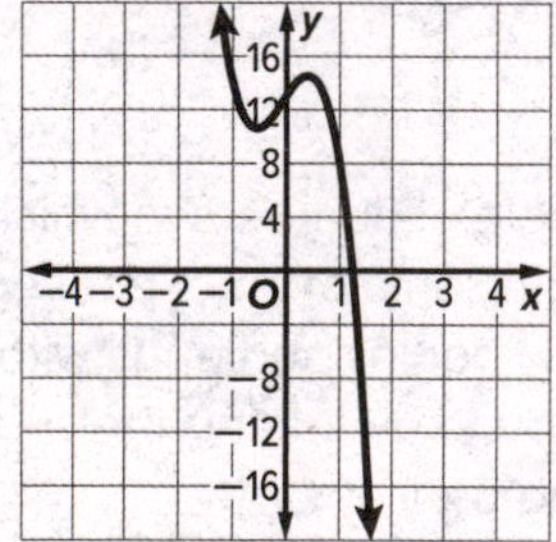

a) What is the degree?

b) What is the leading coefficient?

c) What is the number of real zeroes?

3. MULTIPLE CHOICE The revenue of a certain business can be modeled using $f(x) = -0.01(x^4 - 11x^3 + 4x^2 - 5x + 7)$, where x is the number of years since the business was started and $f(x)$ is the revenue in hundred-thousands of dollars. Which graph represents the function? (Lesson 4-1)

Ⓐ 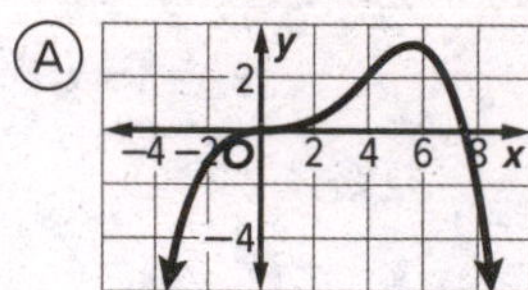

Ⓑ 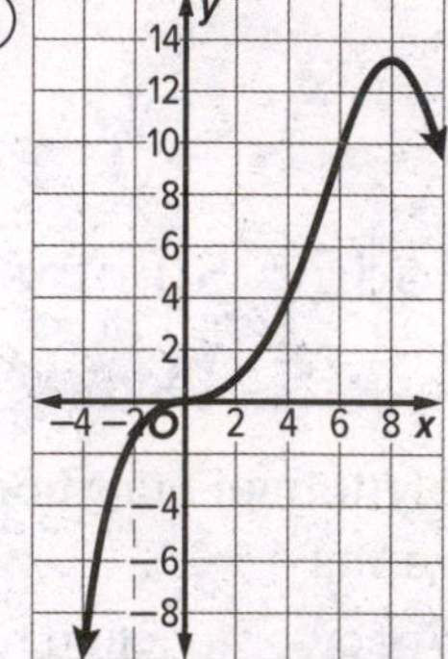

Ⓒ 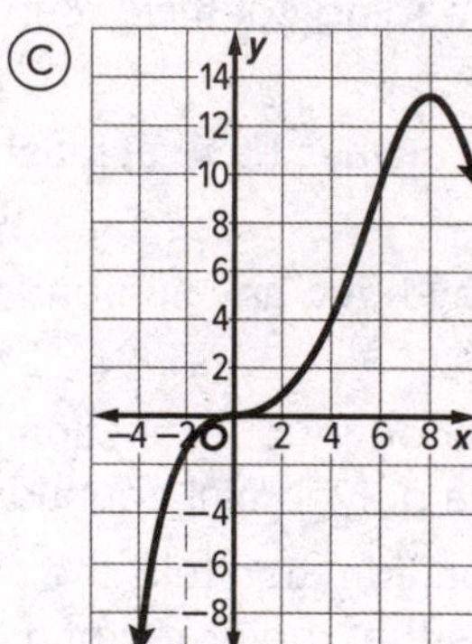

Ⓓ 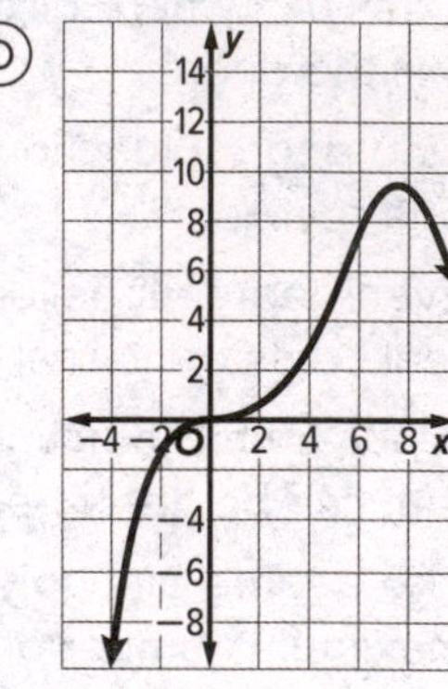

4. MULTI-SELECT Select all intervals in which a real zero is located for the function $f(x) = x^4 - 2x^3 + 3x^2 - 5$. (Lesson 4-2)

☐ $x = -2$ and $x = -1$

☐ $x = -1$ and $x = 0$

☐ $x = 0$ and $x = 1$

☐ $x = 1$ and $x = 2$

☐ $x = 2$ and $x = 3$

☐ $x = 3$ and $x = 4$

5. OPEN RESPONSE Describe the end behavior for $g(x) = -2x^4 - 6x^3 + 11x - 18$ as $x \to \infty$. (Lesson 4-2)

Name ______________________ Period ____________ Date ____________

6. **OPEN RESPONSE** Marshall claims that there is only one real zero in the function $f(x) = 4x^3 + 7x^2 - 5x + 3$. Use the table to determine whether you agree with Marshall. Then name the interval(s) in which the zero(s) is/are located. (Lesson 4-2)

x	$f(x)$
−3	−27
−2	9
1	11
0	3
1	9
2	53

7. **MULTIPLE CHOICE** Helen started a business several years ago. The table shows her profits, in millions of dollars, for the first 7 years. Select the polynomial function of best fit that could be used to model Helen's profits. (Lesson 4-2)

x	$f(x)$
1	1.425
2	1.46
3	1.5
4	1.53
5	1.56
6	1.58
7	1.58

Ⓐ $f(x) = 0.001\,(-3.49x^2 + 54.37x + 1370)$

Ⓑ $f(x) = 0.0001\,(-3.299x^3 + 88.09x^2 + 382.65x + 13{,}850)$

Ⓒ $f(x) = 0.00001(9.686x^4 - 205.83x^3 + 1122x^2 + 1471x + 140{,}100)$

Ⓓ $f(x) = 0.0001\,(-x^4 + 12x^3 - 77x^2 + 600x + 13{,}650)$

8. **OPEN RESPONSE** What is the difference? $(7x^4 - 3x^3 + 5x^2 + 8x - 11) - (3x^4 - 9x^3 - 4x^2 + 12x + 4)$ (Lesson 4-3)

9. **TABLE ITEM** Indicate whether each expression is a polynomial or not a polynomial. (Lesson 4-3)

Expression	Polynomial	Not a Polynomial
$x^2 + 7$		
$6x^4 + 3\sqrt{x}$		
$\frac{1}{2}x^4 + 8x^3 - 12$		
$3x^6 - 5x^3 + 2x^2 - 4x$		
$3d^2f + 7d^3f^4 - 9d^7f^2 - 11df^5$		

10. **MULTIPLE CHOICE** Enrique is designing a flag for a new school club. A blue square has been placed as part of the design and the rest of the flag will be red and yellow striped. (Lesson 4-3)

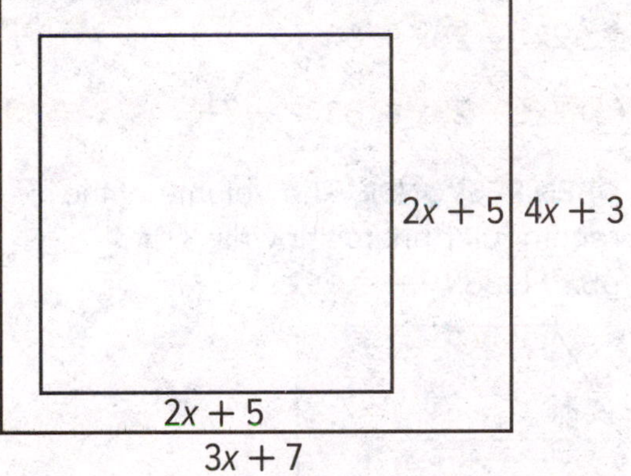

Which expression can be used to represent the area of the flag that will not be blue?

Ⓐ $16x^2 + 57x + 46$

Ⓑ $8x^2 + 35x + 16$

Ⓒ $8x^2 + 17x + 4$

Ⓓ $8x^2 + 17x - 4$

Name ______________________ Period __________ Date __________

11. GRIDDED RESPONSE Use synthetic division to determine the quotient.
$(5x^4 + 12x^3 - 64x^2 - 95x + 132) \div (x - 3)$
What is the coefficient of x^2 in the quotient? (Lesson 4-4)

12. MULTIPLE CHOICE Use synthetic division to determine the quotient. (Lesson 4-4)

$$\frac{6x^3 - 71x^2 + 139x + 130}{3x + 2}$$

Ⓐ $2x^2 - 25x + 63 + \frac{8}{3}$

Ⓑ $2x^2 - 25x + 63 + \frac{8}{3x + 2}$

Ⓒ $2x^2 - 25x + 63 + \frac{4}{3}$

Ⓓ $2x^2 - 25x + 63 + \frac{4}{3x + 2}$

13. OPEN RESPONSE The volume of the rectangular prism shown is $45x^3 + 83x^2 + x - 12$.

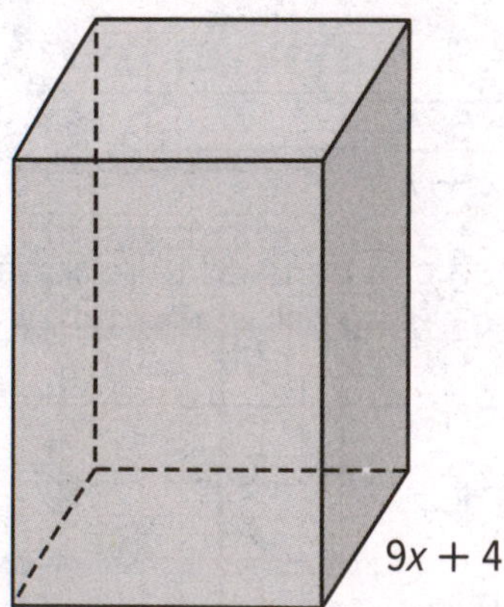

What is the area of the base? (Lesson 4-4)

14. MULTIPLE CHOICE Which of the following is the expansion of $(2h + f)^4$? (Lesson 4-5)

Ⓐ $2h^4 + 4h^3f + 6h^2f^2 + 4hf^3 + f^4$

Ⓑ $16h^4 + 32h^3f + 24h^2f^2 + 32hf^3 + 16f^4$

Ⓒ $16h^4 + 32h^3f + 32h^2f^2 + 8hf^3 + f^4$

Ⓓ $16h^4 + 32h^3f + 24h^2f^2 + 8hf^3 + f^4$

15. GRIDDED RESPONSE The first shelf on Hannah's bookshelf holds an equal number of fiction and nonfiction books. If Hannah selects 5 books randomly, what is the probability that 4 of the books will be fiction and 1 will be nonfiction?

Round your answer to the nearest tenth of a percent. (Lesson 4-5)

16. MULTI-SELECT Select all of the following that would be a coefficient of a term in the binomial expansion of $(x + y)^7$. (Lesson 4-5)

☐ 1
☐ 3
☐ 7
☐ 14
☐ 21
☐ 28
☐ 30
☐ 35

Module 5

Polynomial Equations

Essential Question

What methods are useful for solving polynomial equations and finding zeros of polynomial functions?

N.CN.9; A.APR.2; A.APR.3; A.APR.4; A.CED.1; A.REI.11; F.IF.7c
Mathematical Practices: MP1, MP2, MP3, MP4, MP5, MP6, MP7, MP8

What will you learn?

Place a checkmark (✓) in each row that corresponds with how much you already know about each topic **before** starting this module.

KEY

— I don't know. — I've heard of it. — I know it!

	Before			After		
	I don't know.	I've heard of it.	I know it!	I don't know.	I've heard of it.	I know it!
solve polynomial functions by graphing						
solve polynomial equations by factoring						
solve polynomial equations in quadratic form						
prove polynomial identities						
apply the Remainder Theorem						
use the Factor Theorem to determine whether a binomial is a factor of a polynomial						
use the Fundamental Theorem of Algebra						
find zeros of polynomial functions						

Foldables Make this Foldable to help you organize your notes about polynomial equations. Begin with three sheets of notebook paper.

1. **Fold** each sheet of paper in half from top to bottom.
2. **Cut** along the fold. Staple the six half-sheets together to form a booklet.
3. **Cut** tabs into the margin. The top tab is 2 lines deep, the next tab is 6 lines deep, and so on.
4. **Label** each tab except the first with a lesson number. Use the first tab as a cover page decorating it with a graph from lesson 1.

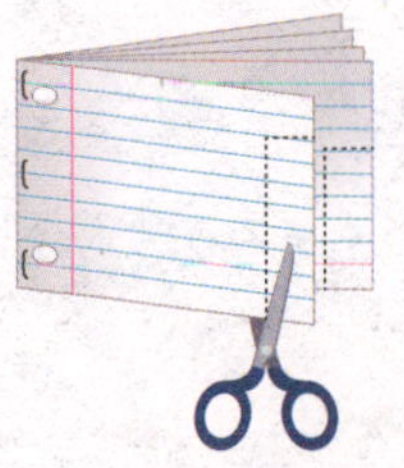

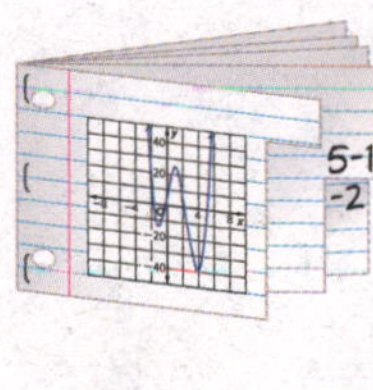

What Vocabulary Will You Learn?

Check the box next to each vocabulary term that you may already know.

☐ depressed polynomial	☐ polynomial identity	☐ synthetic substitution
☐ identity	☐ prime polynomial	
☐ multiplicity	☐ quadratic form	

Are You Ready?

Complete the Quick Review to see if you are ready to start this module. Then complete the Quick Check.

Quick Review

Example 1

Use the Distributive Property to multiply $(x^2 - 2x - 4)(x + 5)$.

$(x^2 - 2x - 4)(x + 5)$

$= x^2(x + 5) - 2x(x + 5) - 4(x + 5)$ — Distributive Property

$= x^2(x) + x^2(5) + (-2x)(x) + (-2x)(5) + (-4)(x) + (-4)(5)$ — Distributive Property

$= x^3 + 5x^2 - 2x^2 - 10x - 4x - 20$ — Multiply.

$= x^3 + 3x^2 - 14x - 20$ — Combine like terms.

Example 2

Solve $2x^2 + 8x + 1 = 0$.

$x = \frac{-b \pm \sqrt{b^2 - 4ac}}{2a}$ — Quadratic Formula

$= \frac{-8 \pm \sqrt{8^2 - 4(2)(1)}}{2(2)}$ — $a = 2, b = 8, c = 1$

$= \frac{-8 \pm \sqrt{56}}{4}$ — Simplify.

$= -2 \pm \frac{\sqrt{14}}{2}$ — $\sqrt{56} = \sqrt{4 \cdot 14}$ or $2\sqrt{14}$

The exact solutions are $-2 \pm \frac{\sqrt{14}}{2}$ and $-2 \pm \frac{\sqrt{14}}{2}$. The approximate solutions are -0.13 and -3.87.

Quick Check

Use the Distributive Property to multiply each set of polynomials.

1. $(6x^2 - x + 2)(4x + 2)$
2. $(x^2 - 2x + 7)(7x - 3)$
3. $(7x^2 - 6x - 6)(2x - 4)$
4. $(x^2 + 6x - 4)(2x - 4)$

Solve each equation.

5. $x^2 + 2x - 8 = 0$
6. $2x^2 + 7x + 3 = 0$
7. $6x^2 + 5x - 4 = 0$
8. $4x^2 - 2x - 1 = 0$

How Did You Do?

Which exercises did you answer correctly in the Quick Check? Shade those exercise numbers below.

① ② ③ ④ ⑤ ⑥ ⑦ ⑧

Solving Polynomial Functions by Graphing

Today's Standards
A.CED.1; A.REI.11
MP2, MP5

Explore Solutions of Polynomial Equations

Online Activity Use graphing technology to complete the Explore.

INQUIRY How can you solve a polynomial equation by using the graph of a related polynomial function?

Think About It!

How can you use the structure of the related function to determine the number of real solutions of the equation?

Learn Solving Polynomial Equations by Graphing

A related function is found by solving the equation for 0 and then replacing 0 with $f(x)$. The values of x for which $f(x) = 0$ are the real zeros of the function f. The real zeros of the function are the x-intercepts of its graph. The real solutions or real roots are the same as the real zeros or x-intercepts of its related function.

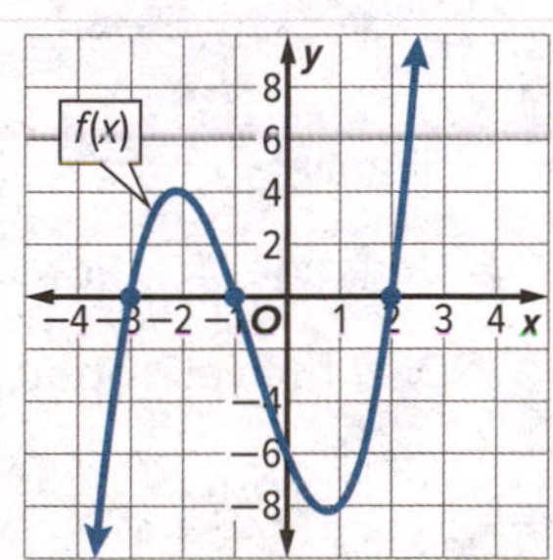

$x^3 + 2x^2 - 4x = x + 6$
- −3, −1, and 2 are solutions.
- −3, −1, and 2 are roots.

$f(x) = x^3 + 2x^2 - 5x - 6$
- −3, −1, and 2 are zeros.
- −3, −1, and 2 are x-intercepts.

Example 1 Solve a Polynomial Equation by Graphing

Use a graphing calculator to solve $x^4 + 3x^2 - 5 = -4x^3$ by graphing.

Step 1 Find a related function. Write the equation with 0 on the right.

$x^4 + 3x^2 - 5 = -4x^3$ Original equation

$x^4 + 3x^2 - 5$ ______ $= -4x^3$ ______ Add $4x^3$ to each side.

$x^4 + 4x^3 + 3x^2 - 5 =$ ___ Simplify.

The related function is $f(x) =$ ______________.

Step 2 Graph the related function.

Enter the equation in the **Y** = list and graph the function.

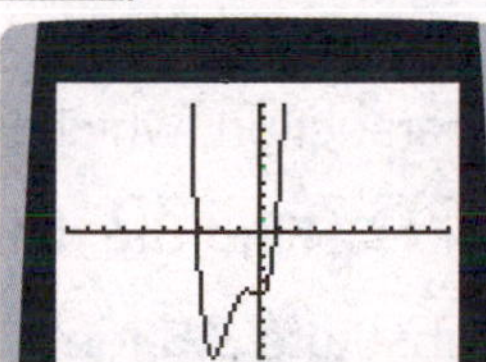

Step 3 Find the zeros.

Use the **zero** feature from the **CALC** menu.
The real zeros are about ______ and ______.

Step 4 Use a table.

You can use the **TABLE** feature to verify where the zeros lie.

Talk About It!

Explain how you could use the table feature to more accurately estimate the zeros of the related function. What are the limitations of the table feature?

Your Notes

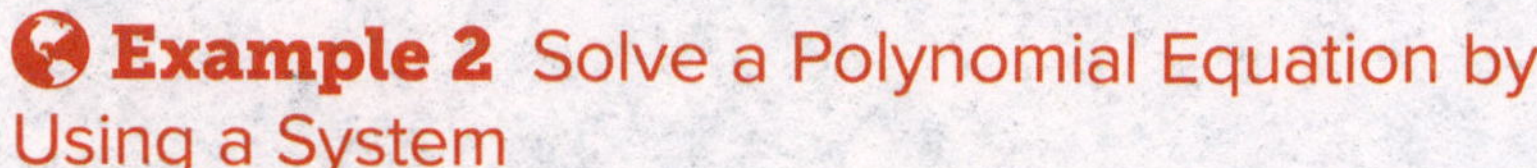

Example 2 Solve a Polynomial Equation by Using a System

ANIMALS **For an exhibit with six or fewer Emperor penguins, the pool must have a depth of at least 4 feet and a volume of at least 1620 gallons, or about 217 ft^3, per bird. If a zoo has five Emperor penguins, what should the dimensions of the pool shown at the right be to meet the minimum requirements?**

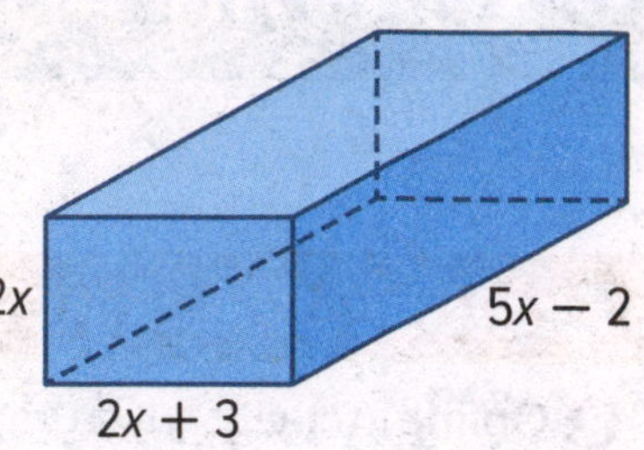

Part A Write a polynomial equation.

Use the formula for the volume of a rectangular prism, $V = \ell wh$, to write a polynomial equation that represents the volume of the pool. Let h represent the depth of the pool.

Since the minimum required volume for the pool is ____ ft^3 per penguin, or _____ $\cdot$ 5 = _____ ft^3, the equation that represents the volume of the pool is $(2x + 3)(5x - 2)2x =$ _____. Simplify the equation.

$(2x + 3)(5x - 2)2x = 1085$	Volume of pool
$[2x(5x) + 2x(-2) + 3(5x) + 3(-2)]2x = 1085$	FOIL
$(\_\_\_x^2 - 4x + 15x - \_\_\_)2x = 1085$	Simplify.
$(10x^2 + \_\_\_x - 6)2x = 1085$	Combine like terms.
______________ $= 1085$	Distributive Property

So, the volume of the pool is ________________________.

Part B Write and solve a system of equations.

Set each side equal to y to create a system of equations.

$y = 20x^3 + 22x^2 - 12x$	First equation
$y = 1085$	Second equation

Enter the equations in the **Y** = list and graph.

Use the **intersect** feature from the **CALC** menu to find the coordinates of the point of intersection.

The real solution is the x-coordinate of the intersection, which is _____.

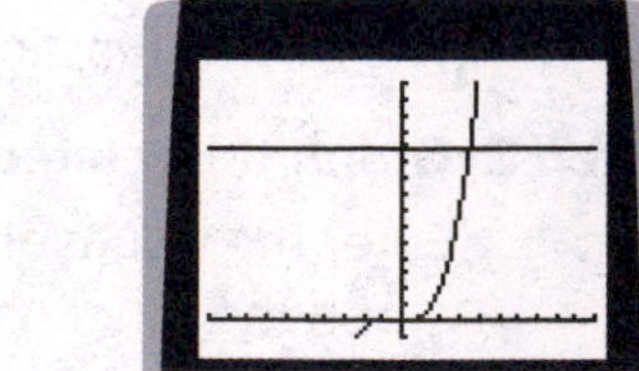

Part C Find the dimensions.

Substitute 3.5 feet for x in the length, width, and depth of the pool.

Length: $2x + 3 =$ _____ ft   Width: $5x - 2 =$ _____ ft

Depth: $2x =$ _____ ft

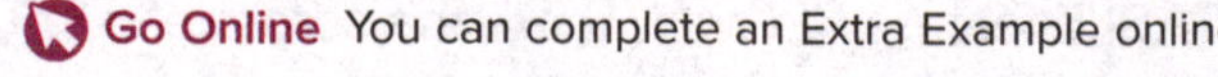

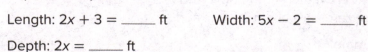

Go Online You can complete an Extra Example online.

Think About It!

Is your solution reasonable? Justify your conclusion.

Name ______________________ Period __________ Date __________

Practice

Go Online You can complete your homework online.

Example 1

Use a graphing calculator to solve each equation by graphing. Round to the nearest hundredth.

1. $\frac{2}{3}x^3 + x^2 - 5x = -9$

2. $x^3 - 9x^2 + 27x = 20$

3. $x^3 + 1 = 4x^2$

4. $x^6 - 15 = 5x^4 - x^2$

5. $\frac{1}{2}x^5 = \frac{1}{5}x^2 - 2$

6. $x^8 = -x^7 + 3$

Example 2

7. **SHIPPING** A shipping company will ship a package for $7.50 when the volume is no more than 15,000 cm^3. Grace needs to ship a package that is $3x - 5$ cm long, $2x$ cm wide, and $x + 20$ cm tall.

a. Write a polynomial equation to represent the situation.

b. Write and solve a system of equations.

c. What should the dimensions of the package be to meet the maximum volume?

8. **GARDEN** A rectangular garden is 12 feet across and 16 feet long. It is surrounded by a border of mulch that is a uniform width, x. The maximum area for the garden, plus border, is 285 ft^2.

a. Write a polynomial equation to represent the situation.

b. Write and solve a system of equations.

c. What are the dimensions of the garden plus border?

9. **PACKAGING** A soup manufacturer is creating new cylindrical packaging. The height of the cylinder is to be 3 units longer than the radius of the can. The cylinder is to have a volume of 628 in. Use 3.14 for π.

a. Write a polynomial equation to support the model.

b. Write and solve a system of equations.

c. What is the radius and height of the new packaging?

Mixed Exercises

Use a graphing calculator to solve each equation by graphing. Round to the nearest hundredth.

10. $x^4 + 2x^3 = 7$

11. $x^4 - 15x^2 = -24$

12. $x^3 - 6x^2 + 4x = -6$

13. $x^4 - 15x^2 + x + 65 = 0$

14. **BALLOON** Treyvon is standing 9 yards from the base of a hill that has a slope of $\frac{3}{4}$. He throws a water balloon from a height of 2 yards. Its path is modeled by $h(x) = -0.1x^2 + 0.8x + 2$, where h is the height of the balloon and x is the distance the balloon travels.

a. Write a polynomial equation to represent the situation.

b. How far from Treyvon will the balloon hit the hill?

15. **REASONING** Explain why the x-coordinates of the points of intersection of $f(x) = x^3 + x^2 - 14x - 4$ and $g(x) = x^3 - 3x^2 - 6x + 28$ represent the solutions to $x^3 + x^2 - 14x - 4 = x^3 - 3x^2 - 6x + 28$. Then use the graphs to solve the equation.

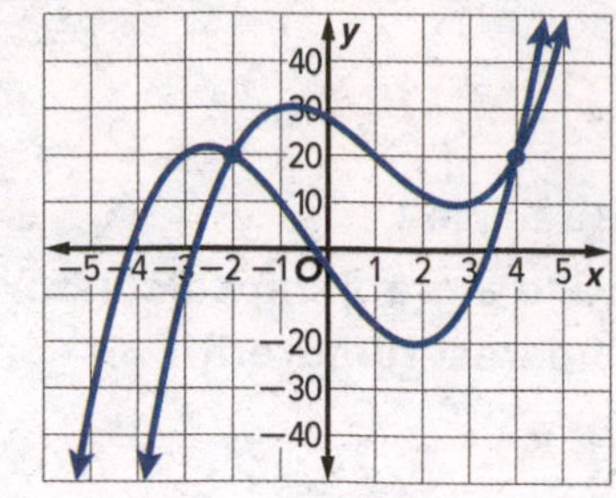

16. **REGULARITY** Explain two different methods for solving the equation $2x^3 - 3x^2 + 7x + 29 = x^3 + 2x^2 + 19x - 7$. Solve the equation using each method and verify that the results are the same.

17. **USE TOOLS** A company models its profit in dollars using the function $P(x) = 70{,}000(x - x^4)$ on the domain $(0, 1)$ where x is the price at which they sell their product in dollars. Use a graphing calculator to sketch a graph and find the price at which their product should be sold to make a profit of \$20,000. Describe your solution process.

18. The height of a passenger car for two roller coasters can be modeled by the functions $f(x) = \frac{1}{20}(x^3 - 60x^2 + 900x)$ and $g(x) = \frac{1}{12{,}000}(x^5 - 144x^4 + 7384x^3 - 158{,}400x^2 + 1{,}210{,}000x)$ where x is time in seconds for the first 35 seconds of the ride.

   a. **PRECISION** If the two roller coasters start at the same time, then what equation would determine the times when the passenger cars of each roller coaster are at the same height?

   b. **USE TOOLS** Use a graphing calculator to sketch a graph of $f(x)$ and $g(x)$ and solve the equation from **part a**. Interpret the solution in the context of the situation.

   c. **MODELING** Write an equation to determine the times for which the passenger car modeled by $f(x)$ was at a height of 150 feet. Use a graphing calculator to solve the equation. Interpret the solution in the context of the situation.

19. **WRITE** Why is it that a function with an even degree can have zero real solutions, but a function with an odd degree must have at least one real solution?

20. **CREATE** Write a polynomial equation and solve it by graphing a related function and finding its zeros.

21. **ANALYZE** Determine whether the following statement is *sometimes*, *always*, or *never* true. Explain.

    If a system of equations has more than one solution, then the positive solution is the only viable solution.

22. **PERSEVERE** Two students kick a soccer ball into the air. The first student kicks the ball from the ground with an initial velocity of 32 feet per second. The polynomial $f(x) = -16x^2 + 32x$ models the arc of this kick, where x represents time in seconds. The second student kicks the ball from a platform 6 feet off the ground with an initial velocity of 27 feet per second. The polynomial $f(x) = -16x^2 + 27x + 6$ models the arc of this kick. After how many seconds will both balls be at the same height in the air?

23. **WHICH ONE DOESN'T BELONG?** Which polynomial doesn't belong? Explain.

    $x - 17 = 18x^3 + 3x^2$ $\quad$ $x^2 = 4x^4 + 3x^2 - 8$ $\quad$ $5x^2 = -2x - 11$ $\quad$ $-4 = 2x^5 - x^2$

Solving Polynomial Equations Algebraically

Learn Solving Polynomial Equations by Factoring

Like quadratics, polynomials of higher degrees can be factored. A polynomial that cannot be written as a product of two polynomials with integral coefficients is called a **prime polynomial**.

Key Concept • Sum and Difference of Cubes

Factoring Technique	General Case
Sum of Two Cubes	$a^3 + b^3 = (a + b)(a^2 - ab + b^2)$
Difference of Two Cubes	$a^3 - b^3 = (a - b)(a^2 + ab - b^2)$

Learn Factoring Techniques

When factoring a polynomial, always look for a common factor first to simplify the expression. Then, determine whether the resulting polynomial factors can be factored using one or more methods.

Key Concept • Factoring Techniques

Number of Terms	Factoring Technique	General Case
any number	Greatest Common Factor	$2a^4b^3 + 6ab = 2ab(a^3b^2 + 6)$
two	Difference of Two Squares	$a^2 - b^2 = (a + b)(a - b)$
	Sum of Two Cubes	$a^3 + b^3 = (a + b)(a^2 - ab + b^2)$
	Difference of Two Cubes	$a^3 - b^3 = (a - b)(a^2 + ab + b^2)$
three	Perfect Square Trinomials	$a^2 + 2ab + b^2 = (a + b)^2$ $a^2 - 2ab + b^2 = (a - b)^2$
	General Trinomials	$acx^2 + (ad + bc)x + bd$ $= (ax + b)(cx + d)$
four or more	Grouping	$ax + bx + ay + by$ $= x(a + b) + y(a + b)$ $= (a + b)(x + y)$

Today's Standards
A.CED.1
MP 1, MP 7

Today's Vocabulary
prime polynomial
quadratic form

Think About It!
Mateo says that you could use the sum of two cubes to factor $x^{15} + y^{15}$? Is he correct? Why or why not?

Think About It!
How can you check that an expression has been factored correctly?

Your Notes

Study Tip

Grouping When grouping 6 or more terms, group the terms that have the *most* common values.

Think About It!

When factoring by grouping, what must be true about the expressions inside parentheses after factoring out a GCF from each group?

Example 1 Factor Sums and Differences of Cubes

Factor each polynomial. If the polynomial cannot be factored, write *prime*.

a. $8x^3 + 125y^{12}$

The GCF of the terms is 1, but $8x^3$ and $125y^{12}$ are both perfect cubes. Factor the sum of two cubes.

$8x^3 + 125y^{12}$

$= (2x)^3 + (\_\_\_\_)^3$ — $(2x)^3 = 8x^3$; $(5y^4)^3 = 125y^{12}$

$= (2x + 5y^4)[(2x)^2 - (2x)(5y^4) + (5y^4)^2]$ — Sum of two cubes

$= (2x + 5y^4)(\_\_\_\_ - 10xy^4 + \_\_\_\_)$ — Simplify.

b. $54x^5 - 128x^2y^3$

$54x^5 - 128x^2y^3 = 2x^2(27x^3 - 64y^3)$ — Factor out the GCF.

$2x^2(27x^3 - 64y^3)$

$= 2x^2[(\_\_\_\_)^3 - (\_\_\_\_)^3]$ — $(3x)^3 = 27x^3$; $(4y)^3 = 64y^3$

$= 2x^2(3x - 4y)[(3x)^2 + 3x(4y) + (4y)^2]$ — Difference of two cubes

$= 2x^2(3x + 4y)(9x^2 + \_\_\_\_ + \_\_\_\_)$ — Simplify.

Example 2 Factor by Grouping

Factor $14ax^2 + 16by - 20cy + 28bx^2 - 35cx^2 - 8ay$. If the polynomial cannot be factored, write *prime*.

$14ax^2 + 16by - 20cy + 28bx^2 - 35cx^2 - 8ay$ — Original expression

$= (14ax^2 + 28bx^2 - 35cx^2) + (-8ay + 16by - 20cy)$ — Group to find a GCF.

$= \_\_\_\_(2a + 4b - 5c) - \_\_\_\_(2a - 4b + 5c)$ — Factor out the GCF.

$= (7x^2 - 4y)(\_\_\_\_ + \_\_\_\_ - \_\_\_\_)$ — Distributive Property

Example 3 Combine Cubes and Squares

Factor $64x^6 - y^6$. If the polynomial cannot be factored, write *prime*.

This polynomial could be considered the difference of two squares or the difference of two cubes. The difference of two squares should always be done before the difference of two cubes.

$64x^6 - y^6$ — Original expression

$= (\_\_\_\_)^2 - (\_\_\_\_)^2$ — $(8x^3)^2 = 64x^6$; $(y^3)^2 = y^6$

$= (8x^3 + y^3)(8x^3 - y^3)$ — Difference of squares

$= [(\_\_\_\_)^3 + y^3)][(\_\_\_\_)^3 - y^3)]$ — $(2x)^3 = 8x^3$

$= (2x \_\_\_\_)(4x^2 \_\_\_\_ + y^2)(2x \_\_\_\_)(4x^2 \_\_\_\_ + y^2)$ — Sum and difference of cubes

 **Go Online** You can complete an Extra Example online.

Example 4 Solve a Polynomial Equation by Factoring

Solve $4x^3 + 12x^2 - 9x - 27 = 0$.

$4x^3 + 12x^2 - 9x - 27 = 0$	Original equation
$(4x^3 + 12x^2) + (-9x - 27) = 0$	Group to find a GCF.
____ $(x + 3) -$ ____ $(x + 3) = 0$	Factor out the GCFs.
$(4x^2 - 9)(x + 3) = 0$	Distributive Property
(____ + ____)$(2x - 3)(x + 3) = 0$	Difference of squares
$2x + 3 = 0$ or $2x - 3 = 0$ or $x + 3 = 0$	Zero Product Property

$x =$ ____ $x =$ ____ $x =$ ____

The solutions of the equation are ____, ____, and ____.

Check

Solve $x^3 + 4x^2 - 25x - 100 = 0$.
$x =$ ____, ____, and ____

Example 5 Write and Solve a Polynomial Equation by Factoring

GEOMETRY **In the figure, the small cube is one fourth the length of the larger cube. If the volume of the figure is 1701 cubic centimeters, what are the dimensions of the cubes?**

$(4x)^3 - x^3 = 1701$	Volume of figure
____ $x^3 - x^3 = 1701$	$(4x)^3 = 64x^3$
____ $x^3 = 1701$	Subtract.
$x^3 =$ ____	Divide each side by 63.
$x^3 - 27 = 0$	Subtract 27 from each side.
$(x - 3)($ ________ $) = 0$	Difference of cubes.

$x =$ ____ or $x = \frac{-3 + 3i\sqrt{3}}{2}$

Since ____ is the only real solution, the lengths of the cubes are ____ cm and ____ cm.

Think About It!

The following expressions can be written in quadratic form. What do you notice about the terms with variables in the original expressions?

$2x^{10} + x^5 + 9$

$12x^6 - 20x^3 + 6$

$15x^2 + 9x^4 - 1$

Learn Solving Polynomial Equations in Quadratic Form

Some polynomials in x can be rewritten in **quadratic form**, $au^2 + bu + c$, where u is an algebraic expression in x.

Key Concept • Quadratic Form

An expression in quadratic form can be written as $au^2 + bu + c$ for any numbers a, b, and c, $a \neq 0$, where u is some expression in x. The expression $au^2 + bu + c$ is called the quadratic form of the original expression.

Go Online You can complete an Extra Example online.

Example 6 Write Expressions in Quadratic Form

Write each expression in quadratic form, if possible.

a. $\mathbf{4x^{20} + 6x^{10} + 15}$

Examine the terms with variables to choose the expression equal to u.

$4x^{20} + 6x^{10} + 15 = (\_\_\_\_)^2 + \_\_\_\_(2x^{10}) + \_\_\_\_$ $\quad (2x^{10})^2 = 4x^{20}$

b. $\mathbf{18x^4 + 180x^8 - 28}$

If the polynomial is not already in standard form, rewrite it. Then examine the terms with variables to choose the expression equal to u.

$18x^4 + 180x^8 - 28 = 180x^8 + 18x^4 - 28$ $\quad$ Standard form of a polynomial

$= \_\_\_\_(6x^4)^2 + \_\_\_\_(6x^4) - \_\_\_\_$ $\quad (6x^4)^2 = 36x^8$

c. $\mathbf{9x^6 - 4x^2 - 12}$

Because x^6 ____ $(x^2)^2$, the expression ______ be written in quadratic form.

Check

What is the quadratic form of $10x^4 + 100x^8 - 9$?

____

Example 7 Solve Equations in Quadratic Form

Solve $\mathbf{8x^4 + 10x^2 - 12 = 0}$**.**

$8x^4 + 10x^2 - 12 = 0$	Original equation
$\_\_\_\_(2x^2)^2 + \_\_\_\_(2x^2) - 12 = 0$	$2(2x^2)^2 = 8x^4$
$2u^2 + 5u - 12 = 0$	Let $u = 2x^2$.
$(\_\_\_\_ - \_\_\_\_)(u + 4) = 0$	Factor.
$u = \_\_\_\_$ or $u = \_\_\_\_$	Zero Product Property
$\_\_\_\_ = \frac{3}{2}$ or $\_\_\_\_ = -4$	Replace u with $2x^2$.
$x^2 = \frac{3}{4}$ or $x^2 = -2$	Divide each side by 2.
$x = \pm \_\_\_$ or $x = \pm\sqrt{\ \ }\, i$	Take the square root of each side.

The solutions are $\frac{\sqrt{3}}{2}, -\frac{\sqrt{3}}{2}, \sqrt{2}i$, and $-\sqrt{2}i$.

Check

What are the solutions of $16x^4 + 24x^2 - 40 = 0$?

$x =$ ________________

Go Online You can complete an Extra Example online.

Talk About It!

Describe how the exponent of the expression equal to u relates to the exponents of the terms with variables.

Name ______________________ Period __________ Date __________

Practice

Go Online You can complete your homework online.

Examples 1-3

Factor completely. If the polynomial is not factorable, write *prime*.

1. $8c^3 - 27d^3$

2. $64x^4 + xy^3$

3. $a^8 - a^2b^6$

4. $x^6y^3 + y^9$

5. $18x^6 + 5y^6$

6. $w^3 - 2y^3$

7. $gx^2 - 3hx^2 - 6fy^2 - gy^2 + 6fx^2 + 3hy^2$

8. $12ax^2 - 20cy^2 - 18bx^2 - 10ay^2 + 15by^2 + 24cx^2$

9. $a^3x^2 - 16a^3x + 64a^3 - b^3x^2 + 16b^3x - 64b^3$

10. $8x^5 - 25y^3 + 80x^4 - x^2y^3 + 200x^3 - 10xy^3$

Example 4

Solve each equation.

11. $a^3 - 9a^2 + 14a = 0$

12. $x^3 = 3x^2$

13. $t^4 - 3t^3 - 40t^2 = 0$

14. $b^3 - 8b^2 + 16b = 0$

Example 5

15. **VOLUME** A standard shipping box measures x inches high. The width is 3.5 inches more than the height, and the length is 3 inches less than the height. The volume of the box is 561 cubic inches.

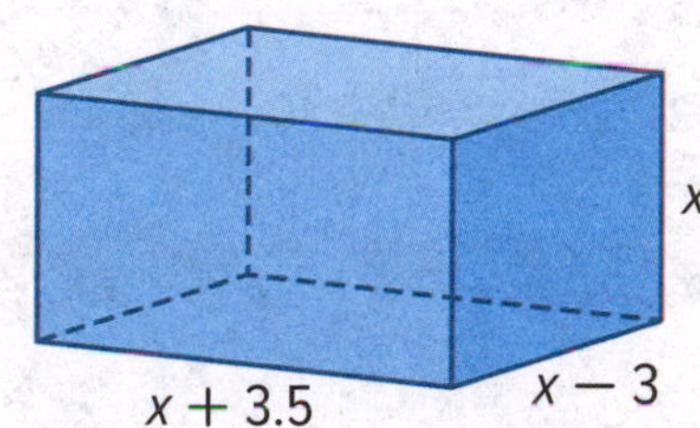

a. Write an equation that represents the volume of the shipping box.

b. What are the dimensions of the shipping box?

16. **PACKAGING** A small box is placed inside a larger box. The dimensions of the small box are $x + 1$ by $x + 2$ by $x - 1$. The dimensions of the larger box are $2x$ by $x + 4$ by $x + 2$.

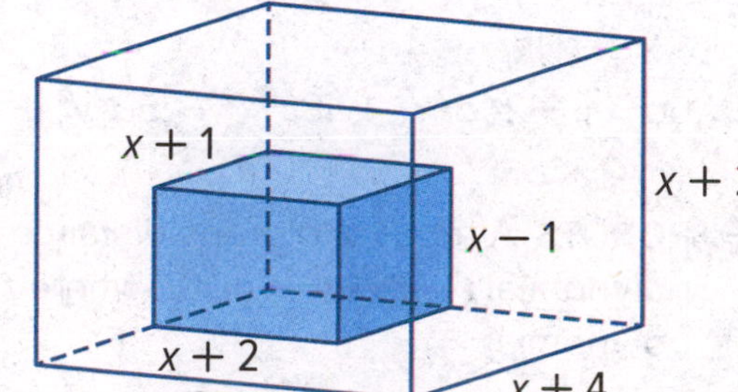

a. Write an expression for the volume of the space inside the larger box but outside the smaller box.

b. Find x if the volume of the space inside the larger box but outside the smaller box is equal to $33x + 162$ cubic units.

c. What is the volume of the smaller box?

d. What is the volume of the larger box?

Example 6

Write each expression in quadratic form, if possible.

17. $x^4 + 12x^2 - 8$

18. $-15x^4 + 18x^2 - 4$

19. $8x^6 + 6x^3 + 7$

20. $5x^6 - 2x^2 + 8$

21. $9x^8 - 21x^4 + 12$

22. $16x^{10} + 2x^5 + 6$

Example 7

Solve each equation.

23. $x^4 + 6x^2 + 5 = 0$

24. $x^4 - 3x^2 - 10 = 0$

25. $4x^4 - 14x^2 + 12 = 0$

26. $9x^4 - 27x^2 + 20 = 0$

27. $4x^4 - 5x^2 - 6 = 0$

28. $24x^4 + 14x^2 - 3 = 0$

Mixed Exercise

Factor completely. If the polynomial is not factorable, write *prime*.

29. $x^4 - 625$

30. $x^6 - 64$

31. $x^5 - 16x$

32. $8x^5y^2 - 27x^2y^5$

33. $6x^5 - 11x^4 - 10x^3 - 54x^3 + 99x^2 + 90x$

34. $20x^6 - 7x^5 - 6x^4 - 500x^4 + 175x^3 + 150x^2$

35. $x^6 - 4x^4 - 8x^4 + 32x^2 + 16x^2 - 64$

36. $y^9 - y^6 - 2y^6 + 2y^3 + y^3 - 1$

37. $15ax - 10bx + 5cx + 12ay - 8by + 4cy + 15az - 10bz + 5cz$

38. $6a^2x^2 - 24b^2x^2 + 18c^2x^2 - 5a^2y^3 + 20b^2y^3 - 15c^2y^3 + 2a^2z^2 - 8b^2z^2 + 6c^2z^2$

39. **ROBOTS** A robot explorer's distance from its starting location is given by the polynomial $t^5 - 29t^3 + 100t$, where t is time measured in hours. Factor this polynomial.

40. **CODES** Marisol has been trying to figure out the secret code for a lock. She determines that the numbers in the secret code are solutions of the polynomial equation $x^4 - 68x^3 + 1557x^2 - 13770x + 37800 = 0$. Marisol found that $x^4 - 68x^3 + 1557x^2 - 13770x + 37800 = (x - 5)(x - 12)(x - 21)(x - 30)$. What are the numbers in the secret code?

Name ______________________ Period ________ Date ________

Solve each equation.

41. $x^4 + x^2 - 90 = 0$

42. $x^4 - 16x^2 - 720 = 0$

43. $x^4 - 7x^2 - 44 = 0$

44. $x^4 + 6x^2 - 91 = 0$

45. $x^3 + 216 = 0$

46. $64x^3 + 1 = 0$

Write each expression in quadratic form, if possible.

47. $5x^4 + 2x^2 - 8$

48. $3y^8 - 4y^2 + 3$

49. $100a^6 + a^3$

50. $x^8 + 4x^4 + 9$

51. $12x^4 - 7x^2$

52. $6b^5 + 3b^3 - 1$

53. $m^6 + 5m^3 - 10$

54. $16x^{10} + 2x^5 + 7$

55. $8x^6 - 2x^3 - 1$

56. $4x^7 + 2x^5 + 9$

Solve each equation.

57. $8x^4 + 10x^2 - 3 = 0$

58. $6x^4 - 5x^2 - 4 = 0$

59. $20x^4 - 53x^2 + 18 = 0$

60. $18x^4 + 43x^2 - 5 = 0$

61. $8x^4 - 18x^2 + 4 = 0$

62. $3x^4 - 22x^2 - 45 = 0$

63. $x^6 + 7x^3 - 8 = 0$

64. $x^6 - 26x^3 - 27 = 0$

65. $8x^6 + 999x^3 = 125$

66. $4x^4 - 4x^2 - x^2 + 1 = 0$

67. $x^6 - 9x^4 - x^2 + 9 = 0$

68. $x^4 + 8x^2 + 15 = 0$

Factor completely. If the polynomial is not factorable, write *prime*.

69. $21x^3 - 18x^2y + 24xy^2$

70. $8j^3k - 4jk^3 - 7$

71. $a^2 + 7a - 18$

72. $2ak - 6a + k - 3$

73. $b^2 + 8b + 7$

74. $z^2 - 8z - 10$

75. $4f^2 - 64$

76. $d^2 - 12d + 36$

77. $9x^2 + 25$

78. $y^2 + 18y + 81$

79. $7x^2 - 14x$

80. $19x^3 - 38x^2$

81. $n^3 - 125$

82. $m^4 - 1$

83. **STRUCTURE** Find the solutions of $(a + 3)^4 - 2(a + 3)^2 - 8 = 0$. Show your work.

84. **STRUCTURE** If the equation $ax^2 + bx + c = 0$ has solutions $x = m$ and $x = n$, what are the solutions to $ax^4 + bx^2 + c = 0$. Explain your reasoning.

85. **REASONING** A rectangular box has dimensions of x inches, $(x + 5)$ inches, and $(x - 2)$ inches. If the volume of the box is $30x$ cubic inches, explain how to find the dimensions of the box. Show your work.

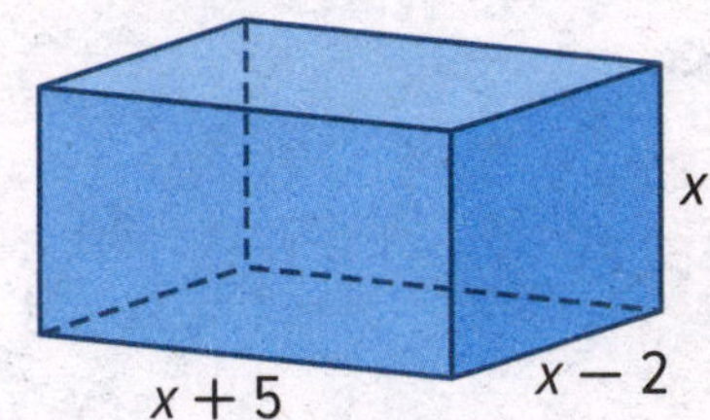

86. **STRUCTURE** The combined volume of a cube and a cylinder is 1,000 cubic inches. If the height of the cylinder is twice the radius and the side of the cube is four times the radius, find the radius of the cylinder to the nearest tenth of an inch.

87. **PERSEVERE** Factor $36x^{2n} + 12x^n + 1$.

88. **PERSEVERE** Solve $6x - 11\sqrt{3x} + 12 = 0$.

89. **ANALYZE** Find a counterexample to the statement $a^2 + b^2 = (a + b)^2$.

90. **CREATE** The cubic form of an equation is $ax^3 + bx^2 + cx + d = 0$. Write an equation with degree 6 that can be written in cubic form.

91. **WRITE** Explain how the graph of a polynomial function can help you factor the polynomial.

Proving Polynomial Identities

Explore Polynomial Identities

Online Activity Use graphing technology to complete the Explore.

INQUIRY How can you prove that two polynomial expressions form a polynomial identity?

Learn Polynomial Identities

An **identity** is an equation that is satisfied by any numbers that replace the variables. Thus, a **polynomial identity** is a polynomial equation that is true for any values that are substituted for the variables.

Key Concept • Verifying Identities by Transforming One Side

Step 1 Simplify one side of an equation until the two sides of the equation are the same.

Step 2 Transform that expression into the form of the simpler side.

Example 1 Transform One Side

Prove that $x^3 - y^3 = (x - y)(x^2 + xy + y^2)$.

$x^3 - y^3 = (x - y)(x^2 + xy + y^2)$	Original equation
$x^3 - y^3 = x(x^2) + x(xy) + x(y^2) - y(x^2) - y(xy) - y(y^2)$	Distributive Property
$x^3 - y^3 = \_\_ + \_\_ + xy^2 - \_\_ - \_\_ - y^3$	Simplify.
$x^3 - y^3 = x^3 + x^2y - x^2y + xy^2 - xy^2 - y^3$	Commutative Property
$x^3 - y^3 = \_\_ - \_\_$	Simplify.

Because the expression on the right can be simplified to be the same as the expression on the left, this proves the polynomial identity.

Go Online You can complete an Extra Example online.

Today's Standards
A.APR.4
MP6, MP8

Today's Vocabulary
identity
polynomial identity

Study Tip:

Transforming One Side It is often easier to work with the more complicated side of an equation. Look at each side and determine which requires more steps to be simplified. For example, it is often easier to work on the side that involves the square or cube of an algebraic expression.

Talk About It

If you multiplied each side of the equation by a variable z, would the result still be a polynomial identity? Explain your reasoning.

Your Notes

Math History Minute:

Former quarterback **Frank Ryan (1936–)** earned his Ph.D. in mathematics about six months after he led the Cleveland Browns to the NFL championship game of 1964, where they won 27-0. During part of his academic career, Ryan studied prime numbers, including Opperman's Conjecture that there is a prime number between n^2 and $n^2 + n$, where n is an integer. This work could eventually lead to a polynomial identity that could be used to identify prime numbers.

Example 2 Use Polynomial Identities

TRIANGLES Pedro claims that you can always create three lengths that form a right triangle by using the following method: take two positive integers x and y where $x > y$. Two legs of a right triangle are defined as $x^2 - y^2$ and $2xy$. The hypotenuse is defined as $x^2 + y^2$. Is Pedro correct? Explain your reasoning in the context of polynomial identities.

To determine whether Pedro is correct, we can use information about right triangles and the expressions involving x and y to try to construct a polynomial identity. If $x^2 - y^2$ and $2xy$ are the legs of the triangle, and $x^2 + y^2$ is the hypotenuse, then it should be true that $(x^2 - y^2)^2 + (2xy)^2 = (x^2 + y^2)^2$.

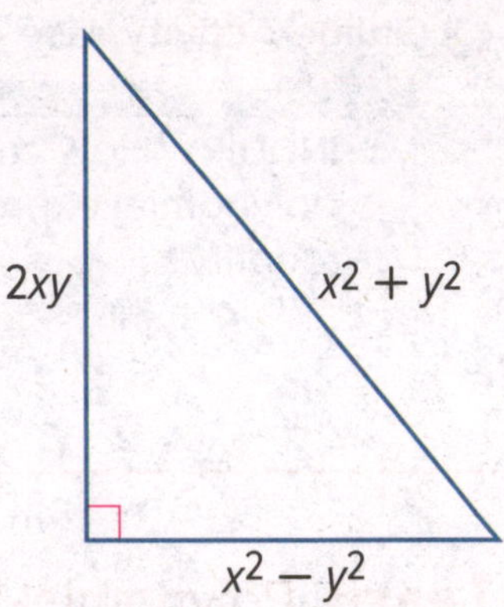

If this is an identity, you can simplify the expressions for the sides to be the same expression.

$(x^2 - y^2)^2 + (2xy)^2 = (x^2 + y^2)^2$ Original equation

$x^4 - 2x^2y^2 + y^4 + 4x^2y^2 = x^4 + 2x^2y^2 + y^4$ Square each term.

$x^4 + 2x^2y^2 + y^4 = x^4 + 2x^2y^2 + y^4$ True

Because the identity is ______, this proves that Pedro is correct. His process for creating the sides of a right triangle will always work.

Check

Write in the missing equations and explanations to prove that $x^4 - y^4 = (x - y)(x + y)(x^2 + y^2)$.

$x^4 - y^4 = (x - y)(x + y)(x^2 + y^2)$ Original equation

______

______

$x^4 - y^4 = x^4 - y^4$ Subtract.

 **Go Online** You can complete an Extra Example online.

Name ______________________ Period __________ Date __________

Practice

Go Online You can complete your homework online.

Example 1

Prove each polynomial identity.

1. $(x - y)^2 = x^2 - 2xy + y^2$

2. $(x + 5)^2 = x^2 + 10x + 25$

3. $4(x - 7)^2 = 4x^2 - 56x + 196$

4. $(2x^2 + y^2)^2 = (2x^2 - y^2)^2 + (2xy)^2$

Example 2

5. **SQUARES** Aponi claims that you can find the area of a square using the following method: take two positive integers x and y, where $x > y$. The side length of the square is defined by the expression $3x + y$. The area of the square is defined by the expression $9x^2 + 6xy + y^2$. Is Aponi correct? Explain your reasoning in the context of polynomial identities.

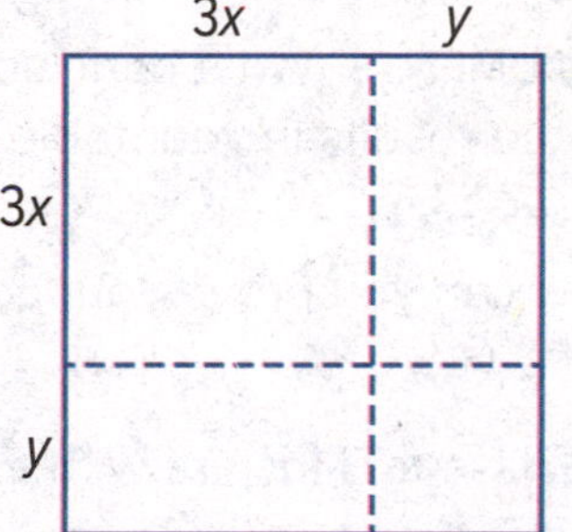

6. **MODELING** Julio claims that you can find the area of an irregular figures using the following method: take two positive integers x and y, where $x > y$. The side lengths of the irregular figure is defined by the expression $2x + y$ and $2x - y$. The area of the irregular figure is defined by the expression $4x^2 - y^2$. Is Julio correct? Explain your reasoning in the context of polynomial identities.

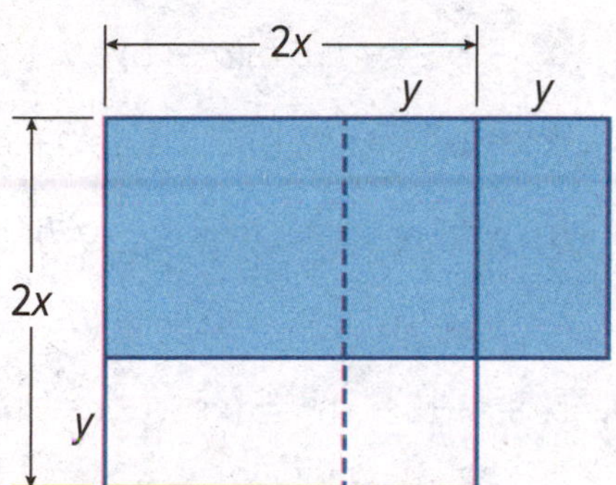

Mixed Exercises

Transform each equation to determine if it is an identity. Write *identity* or *not an identity.*

7. $(x + 3)^2(x^3 + 3x^2 + 3x + 1) = (x^2 + 6x + 9)(x + 1)^3$

8. $(x + 2)(x + 1)^2 = (x^2 + 3x + 2)(x + 1)$

9. $(x + 3)(x - 1)^2 = (x^2 - 2x - 3)(x - 1)$

10. $(x + 2)^2(x^3 - 3x^2 + 3x - 1) = (x^2 + 4x + 4)(x - 1)^3$

11. **REASONING** A textile designer is creating a tapestry in the shape of a right triangle, as shown. The length of the hypotenuse is defined by the expression $(x^2 + 25)$ inches, where x is a positive integer. The designer wants the length of the shorter leg of the triangular tapestry to be 50 inches less than the hypotenuse. The designer also wants the length of the longer leg of the triangular tapestry to be $10x$ inches. Can the textile designer create such a tapestry? Explain your reasoning in the context of polynomial identities.

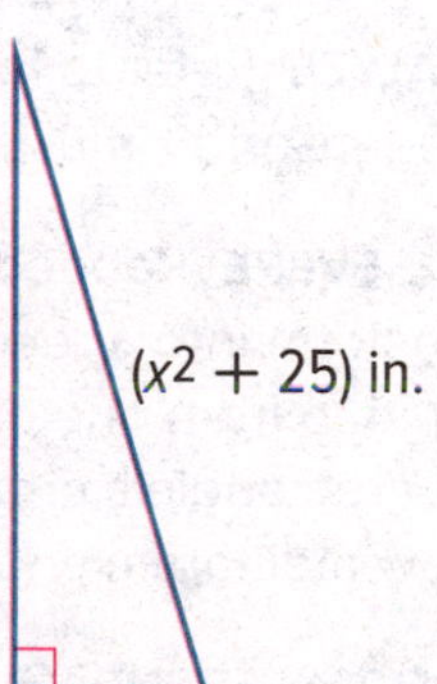

12. **STRUCTURE** Transform one side of the equation $(a + b)^2 = a^2 - 2ab + b^2$ to determine if it is a polynomial identity. Write *identity* or *not an identity*.

13. **TECHNOLOGY** Use the following equation to complete each part.

$(x-2)^2(x^3+9x^2+27x+27) = (x^2-4x+4)(x+3)^3$

a. Complete the columns for the left and right sides of the equation.

x	Left side	Right side
0		
1		
2		
3		
4		

b. **ARGUMENTS** What conclusion can you make about the equation, based on the results in your table? Explain.

c. How can you prove your conclusion from **part b**?

USE TOOLS **Use a TI-Inspire with a computer algebra system (CAS) to prove each identity.**

14. $a^2 - b^2 = (a+b)(a-b)$

15. $x^3 + y^3 = (x+y)(x^2 - xy + y^2)$

16. $p^4 - q^4 = (p-q)(p+q)(p^2+q^2)$

17. $a^5 - b^5 = (a-b)(a^4 + a^3b + a^2b^2 + ab^3 + b^4)$

18. $g^6 + h^6 = (g^2+h^2)(g^4 - g^2h^2 + h^4)$

19. $a^5 + b^5 = (a+b)(a^4 - a^3b + a^2b^2 - ab^3 + b^4)$

20. $u^6 - w^6 = (u+w)(u-w)(u^2+uw+w^2)(u^2-uw+w^2)$

21. $(x+1)^2(x-4)^3 = (x^2-3x-4)(x^3-7x^2+8x+16)$

22. **WRITE** Explain the meaning of polynomial identity and summarize the method for proving an equation is a polynomial identity.

23. **CREATE** Write and solve a system of equations using the identity, $(x^2-y^2)^2 + (2xy)^2 = (x^2+y^2)^2$, to find the values of x and y that make a 3, 4, 5 Pythagorean triple.

24. **ANALYZE** Refer to Example 2. Notice that Pedro says x and y must be positive integers and x must be greater than y. Explain why these restrictions are necessary.

25. **PERSEVERE** Rebecca has a square garden with side length a that she wants to transform into a rectangle. Rebecca speculates that if she subtracts the same length b from one dimension of the garden and adds it to the other dimension the new rectangle's area will be smaller than the original garden in the amount of b^2. Draw a diagram and show algebraically that Rebecca is correct.

26. **FIND THE ERROR** George is proving the identity $a^3 + b^3 = (a+b)(a^2 - ab + b^2)$ by simplifying the right side. His work is shown. Find George's error.

$$(a+b)(a^2-ab+b^2)$$
$$= a^3 - a^2b + ab^2 - a^2b - ab^2 + b^3$$
$$= a^3 - 2a^2b + b^3$$

The Remainder and Factor Theorems

Today's Standards
A.APR.2
MP3, MP4

Today's Vocabulary
synthetic substitution
depressed polynomial

Explore Remainders

Online Activity Use the interactive tool to complete the Explore.

INQUIRY How are the divisor and quotient of a polynomial related to its factors when the remainder is zero?

Learn The Remainder Theorem

Polynomial division can be used to find the value of a function. From the Division Algorithm, we know that $\frac{f(x)}{g(x)} = q(x) + \frac{r(x)}{g(x)}$ and that $f(x) = q(x)\,g(x) + r(x)$. Suppose we were to call the dividend $p(x)$ and the divisor $x - a$. Then the Division Algorithm would be $\frac{p(x)}{x-a} = q(x) + \frac{r}{x-a}$ and $p(x) = q(x)\,(x - a) + r$, where a is a constant and r is the remainder. Since any polynomial can be written in this form, evaluating $p(x)$ at a gives the following.

$p(x) = q(x)(x - a) + r$	Polynomial function $p(x)$
$p(a) = q(a)(a - a) + r$	Substitute a for x.
$p(a) = q(a)(0) + r$	$a - a = 0$
$p(a) = r$	$q(a)(0) = 0$

This shows how the Remainder Theorem can be used to evaluate a polynomial at $p(a)$.

Key Concept • Remainder Theorem

Words: For a polynomial $p(x)$ and a number a, the remainder upon division by $x - a$ is $p(a)$.

Example: Evaluate $p(x) = x^2 - 4x + 7$ when $x = 5$.

Synthetic division

$$\begin{array}{r|rrr} 5 & 1 & -4 & 7 \\ & & 5 & 5 \\ \hline & 1 & 1 & | \; 12 \end{array}$$

$p(5) = 12$

Direct substitution

$p(x) = x^2 - 4x + 7$

$p(5) = 5^2 - 4(5) + 7$

$p(5) = 12$

Applying the Remainder Theorem to evaluate a function is called **synthetic substitution**. You may find that synthetic substitution is a more convenient way to evaluate a polynomial function, especially when the degree of the function is greater than 2.

Your Notes

Study Tip:

Missing terms Remember to include zeros as placeholders for any missing terms in the polynomial.

Example 1 Synthetic Substitution

Use synthetic substitution to find $f(x) = -2x^4 + 3x^2 - 15x + 9$.

By the Remainder Theorem, $f(-3)$ is the remainder of $\frac{f(x)}{x-(-3)}$.

−3	−2	0	3	−15	9
		6	−18	45	−90
	−2	____	____	____	____

The remainder is −81. Therefore, $f(-3) =$ ____.

Use direct substitution to check.

$f(x) = -2x^4 + 3x^2 - 15x + 9$ — Original function

$f(-3) = -2(-3)^4 + 3(-3)^2 - 15(-3) + 9$ — Substitute −3 for x.

$= 162 + 27 + 45 + 9$ or 81 — True

Check

Use synthetic substitution to evaluate $f(x) = -6x^3 + 52x^2 - 27x - 31$.

$f(8) =$ ____

Example 2 Apply the Remainder Theorem

EGG PRODUCTION **The total production of eggs in billions in the United States can be modeled by the function $f(x) = 0.007x^3 - 0.149x^2 + 1.534x + 84.755$, where x is the number of years since 2000. Predict the total production of eggs in 2025.**

Since 2025 − 2000 = 25, use synthetic substitution to determine $f(25)$.

25	0.007	−0.149	1.534	84.755
		0.175	0.65	54.6
	0.007	____	____	____

In 2025, approximately ________ billion eggs will be produced in the United States.

Think About It!

How could you use the function and synthetic substitution to estimate the number of eggs produced in 1990?

Check

KITTENS The ideal weight of a kitten in pounds is modeled by the function $f(x) = 0.009x^2 + 0.127x + 0.377$, where x is the age of the kitten in weeks. Determine the ideal weight of a 9-week-old kitten. Round to the nearest tenth.

____ pounds

Think About It!

What assumptions did you make to solve this problem?

Go Online You can complete an Extra Example online.

Learn The Factor Theorem

When a binomial evenly divides a polynomial, the binomial is a factor of the polynomial. The quotient of this division is called a depressed polynomial. The **depressed polynomial** has a degree that is one less than the original polynomial.

A special case of the Remainder Theorem is called the Factor Theorem.

Key Concept • Factor Theorem

Words: The binomial $x - a$ is a factor of the polynomial $p(x)$ if and only if $p(a) = 0$.

Examples:

$$\underbrace{x^3 - x^2 - 30x + 72}_{\text{dividend}} = \underbrace{(x^2 - 7x + 12)}_{\text{quotient}} \cdot \underbrace{(x + 6)}_{\text{divisor}} + \underbrace{0}_{\text{remainder}}$$

$x + 6$ is a factor of $x^3 - x^2 - 30x + 72$.

Go Online You may want to complete the Concept Check to check your understanding.

Pause and Reflect

Did you struggle with anything in this lesson? If so, how did you deal with it?

Record your observations here

Study Tip:

Factoring Some depressed polynomials may not be factorable. In that case, the only factors are the divisor and the depressed polynomial.

Talk About It

Suppose you were asked to determine whether $3x + 4$ is a factor of $3x^3 - 2x^2 - 8x$. Describe the steps necessary to find a solution.

Example 3 Use the Factor Theorem

Show that $x + 8$ is a factor of $2x^3 + 15x^2 - 9x - 24$. Then find the remaining factors of the polynomial.

−8	2	15	−11	−24
		−16	8	24
	2	____	____	____

Because the remainder is 0, $x + 8$ _____ a factor of the polynomial by the Factor Theorem. So $2x^3 + 15x^2 - 9x - 24$ can be factored as $(x + 8)(2x^2 - x - 3)$. The depressed polynomial is _____________.

Check to see if this polynomial can be factored.

$2x^2 - x - 3 = (\_\_\_\_\_\_)(x + 1)$ Factor the trinomial.

Therefore, $2x^3 + 15x^2 - 9x - 24 = (x + 8)(2x - 3)(\_\_\_\_\_\_)$.

Check

Select all of the factors of $3x^3 + 10x^2 - 27x - 10$. _______

A. $x - 2$

B. $x + 5$

C. $x + 9$

D. $x - 10$

E. $3x + 1$

F. $3x - 10$

Pause and Reflect

Did you struggle with anything in this lesson? If so, how did you deal with it?

Go Online You can complete an Extra Example online.

Name ______________________ Period __________ Date __________

Practice

Go Online You can complete your homework online.

Example 1

Use synthetic substitution to find $f(-5)$ and $f(2)$ for each function.

1. $f(x) = x^3 + 2x^2 - 3x + 1$

2. $f(x) = x^2 - 8x + 6$

3. $f(x) = 3x^4 + x^3 - 2x^2 + x + 12$

4. $f(x) = 2x^3 - 8x^2 - 2x + 5$

5. $f(x) = x^3 - 5x + 2$

6. $f(x) = x^5 + 8x^3 + 2x - 15$

7. $f(x) = x^6 - 4x^4 + 3x^2 - 10$

8. $f(x) = x^4 - 6 - 8$

Example 2

9. **FOOTBALL** The number of yards a running back carries the football can be modeled by the polynomial $f(x) = x^4 - 8x - 11$, where x is the number of carries. Predict the number of yards the running back carries the football after 3 carries.

10. **POOL** The number of gallons of water in a swimming pool as it is being filled with water can be modeled by the polynomial $f(x) = x^3 + x^2 - 14x - 24$, where x is the number of minutes since the swimming pool started being filled. Predict the number of gallons of water in the swimming pool after 6 minutes.

11. **SANDBOX** The volume, in cubic feet, of a sandbox can be modeled by the polynomial $v(x) = x^3 - 5x^2 - 86x + 360$, where x is the size of the sandbox, as shown in the table. What is the volume of a medium-sized sandbox?

Size	x
Small	1
Medium	2
Large	3

12. **PROFIT** The profit, in thousands, of Clyde's Corporation can be modeled by the polynomial $P(y) = y^4 - 4y^3 + 2y^2 + 10y - 200$, where y is the number of years after the business was started. Predict the profit of Clyde's Corporation after 10 years.

Example 3

Given a polynomial and one of its factors, find the remaining factors of the polynomial.

13. $x^3 - 3x + 2$; $x + 2$

14. $x^4 + 2x^3 - 8x - 16$; $x + 2$

15. $x^3 - x^2 - 10x - 8$; $x + 2$

16. $x^3 - x^2 - 5x - 3$; $x - 3$

17. $2x^3 + 17x^2 + 23x - 42$; $x - 1$

18. $2x^3 + 7x^2 - 53x - 28$; $x - 4$

19. $x^4 + 2x^3 + 2x^2 - 2x - 3$; $x - 1$

20. $x^3 + 2x^2 - x - 2$; $x + 2$

Mixed Exercises

Use synthetic substitution to find $f(2)$ and $f(-1)$ for each function.

21. $f(x) = x^2 + 6x + 5$

22. $f(x) = x^2 - x + 1$

23. $f(x) = x^2 - 2x - 2$

24. $f(x) = x^3 + 2x^2 + 5$

25. $f(x) = x^3 - x^2 - 2x + 3$

26. $f(x) = x^3 + 6x^2 + x - 4$

27. $f(x) = x^3 - 3x^2 + x - 2$

28. $f(x) = x^3 - 5x^2 - x + 6$

29. $f(x) = x^4 + 2x^2 - 9$

30. $f(x) = x^4 - 3x^3 + 2x^2 - 2x + 6$

31. $f(x) = x^5 - 7x^3 - 4x + 10$

32. $f(x) = x^6 - 2x^5 + x^4 + x^3 - 9x^2 - 20$

Given a polynomial and one of its factors, find the remaining factors of the polynomial.

33. $x^3 + 2x^2 - x - 2$; $x + 1$

34. $x^3 + x^2 - 5x + 3$; $x - 1$

35. $x^3 + 3x^2 - 4x - 12$; $x + 3$

36. $x^3 - 6x^2 + 11x - 6$; $x - 3$

37. $x^3 + 2x^2 - 33x - 90$; $x + 5$

38. $x^3 - 6x^2 + 32$; $x - 4$

39. $x^3 - x^2 - 10x - 8$; $x + 2$

40. $x^3 - 19x + 30$; $x - 2$

41. $2x^3 + x^2 - 2x - 1$; $x + 1$

42. $2x^3 + x^2 - 5x + 2$; $x + 2$

43. $3x^3 + 4x^2 - 5x - 2$; $3x + 1$

44. $3x^2 + x^2 + x - 2$; $3x - 2$

45. $6x^3 - 25x^2 + 2x + 8$; $2x + 1$

46. $16x^5 - 32x^4 - 81x + 162$; $2x - 3$

47. REASONING Branford evaluates the polynomial $p(x) = x^3 - 5x^2 + 3x + 5$ for a factor using synthetic substitution. Some of his work is shown below. Find the value of a and b.

a	1	−5	3	5
		11	66	759
	1	6	69	***b***

Name ________________ Period ________ Date ________

48. MODELING A ball tossed into the air follows a parabolic trajectory. Its height after t seconds is given by a polynomial of degree two with leading coefficient -16. Using synthetic substitution, Norman found that the polynomial evaluates to 0 for the values $t = 0$ and $t = 4$. What is the polynomial that describes the ball's height as a function of t?

49. EXPONENTIALS The exponential function $y = e^x$ is a special function that you will learn about later. It is not a polynomial function. However, for small values of x, the value of e^x is very closely approximated by the polynomial function $f(x) = \frac{1}{6}x^3 + \frac{1}{2}x^2 + x + 1$. Use synthetic substitution to determine $f(0.1)$. Show your work.

REASONING Find values of k so that each remainder is 3.

50. $(x^2 - x + k) \div (x - 1)$

51. $(x^2 + kx - 17) \div (x - 2)$

52. $(x^2 + 5x + 7) \div (x + k)$

53. $(x^3 + 4x^2 + x + k) \div (x + 2)$

54. STRUCTURE If $f(-8) = 0$ and $f(x) = x^3 - x^2 - 58x + 112$, find all the factors of $f(x)$ and use them to graph the function. Explain your reasoning.

55. REASONING If $P(1) = 0$ and $P(x) = 10x^3 + kx^2 - 16x + 3$, find all the factors of $P(x)$ and use them to graph the function. Explain your reasoning.

56. STRUCTURE The graph of a polynomial function $f(x)$ is shown. What are the factors of the function? What is the related equation? Show your work.

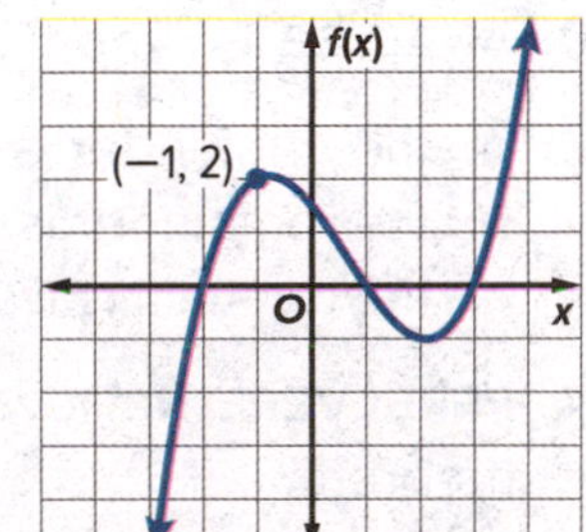

57. ARGUMENTS Divide the polynomial function $f(x) = 4x^3 - 10x + 8$ by the factor $(x + 5)$. Then state and confirm the Remainder Theorem for this particular polynomial function and factor.

58. REASONING The volume of a box with a square base is $V(x) = 2x^3 + 15x^2 + 36x + 27$. If the height of the box is $(2x + 3)$, what are the sides of the base in terms of x?

59. STRUCTURE The graph of a polynomial function $g(x)$ is shown. What are the factors of the function? What is the related equation of least degree to match the graph?

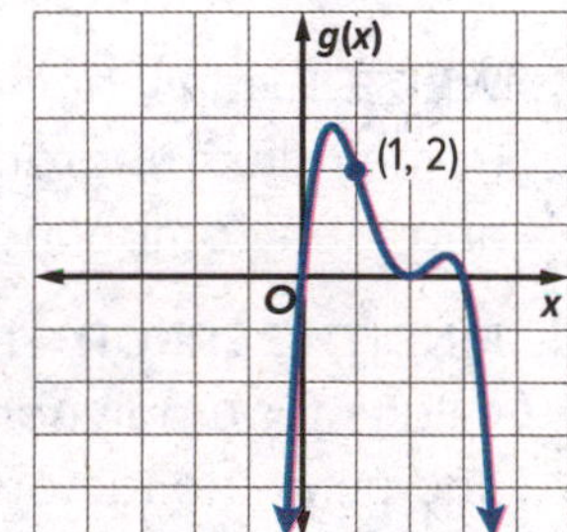

60. REGULARITY The polynomial function $P(x)$ is symmetric in the y-axis and contains the point $(2, -5)$. What is the remainder when $P(x)$ is divided by $(x + 2)$? Explain your reasoning.

61. STRUCTURE Verify the Remainder Theorem for the polynomial $x^2 + 3x + 5$ and the factor $(x - \sqrt{3})$ by first using synthetic division.

62. MODELING If $(x + 6)$ is a factor of $kx^3 + 15x^2 + 13x - 30$, determine the value of k, factor the polynomial and confirm the result graphically.

63. PRECISION When the function $P(x) = 2x^4 + 3x^3 - 24x^2 - 13x + 12$ is divided by $x^2 - 2x - 3$, the remainder is zero. Explain how you can find the zeros of $P(x)$. Determine the zeros and use them to sketch a graph of the function.

64. STRUCTURE The points $(-1, 4)$, $(5, 10)$, $(3, 0)$, and $(0, 0)$ are on the graph of a 4th degree polynomial function $P(x)$. Give two possible equations for $P(x)$. Show your work.

65. MODELING For a cubic function $P(x)$, if $P(-2) = -12$, $P(1) = -15$, $P(2) = 0$, and $P\left(-\frac{3}{2}\right) = 0$, write the equation for $P(x)$. Explain your answer.

66. STRUCTURE For a cubic function $P(x)$, $P(2) = -90$, $P(-8) = 0$, and $P(5) = 0$.

a. Write two possible equations for $P(x)$. Explain your answer.

b. Graph your equations from **part a**. What three points do these graphs have in common?

c. If $P(4) = 60$, write the equation for $P(x)$.

67. CREATE Write a polynomial function that has a double zero of 1 and a double zero of -5. Graph the function.

PERSEVERE Find the solutions of each polynomial equation.

68. $(x^2 - 4)^2 - (x^2 - 4) - 2 = 0$

69. $(x^2 + 3)^2 - 7(x^2 + 3) + 12 = 0$

70. ANALYZE Polynomial $f(x)$ is divided by $x - c$. What can you conclude if:

a. the remainder is 0?

b. the remainder is 1?

c. the quotient is 1, and the remainder is 0?

71. PERSEVERE Review the definition for the Factor Theorem. Provide a proof of the theorem.

72. CREATE Write a cubic function that has a remainder of 8 for $f(2)$ and a remainder of -5 for $f(3)$.

73. PERSEVERE Show that the quartic function $f(x) = ax^4 + bx^3 + cx^2 + dx + e$ will always have a rational zero when the numbers 1, -2, 3, 4, and -6 are randomly assigned to replace a through e, and all of the numbers are used.

74. WRITE Explain how the zeros of a function can be located by using the Remainder Theorem and making a table of values for different input values and then comparing the remainders.

75. FIND THE ERROR The table shows the x-values and their corresponding $P(x)$ values for a polynomial function. Tyrone and Nia used the Factor Theorem to find all of the factors of $P(x)$. Is either of them correct? Explain your reasoning.

x	-3	-1	0	1	2	4
$p(x)$	-18	0	6	2	0	122

Tyrone	**Nia**
$(x + 1)$ and $(x - 2)$	$(x - 6)$

Roots and Zeros

Today's Standards
N.CN.9, A.APR.3, F.IF.7c
MP1, MP7

Today's Vocabulary
multiplicity

Explore Roots of Quadratic Polynomials

Online Activity Use graphing technology to complete the Explore.

INQUIRY Is the Fundamental Theorem of Algebra true for quadratic polynomials?

Learn Fundamental Theorem of Algebra

The zero of a function $f(x)$ is any value c such that $f(c) = 0$.

Key Concept • Zeros, Factors, Roots, and Intercepts

Words: Let $P(x) = a_nx^n + \ldots + a_1x + a_0$ be a polynomial function. Then the following statements are equivalent.

- c is a zero of $P(x)$.
- c is a root or solution of $P(x) = 0$.
- $x - c$ is a factor of $a_nx^n + \ldots + a_1x + a_0$.

If c is a real number, then $(c, 0)$ is an x-intercept of the graph of $P(x)$.

Example: Consider the polynomial function $P(x) = x^2 + 3x - 18$.

The zeroes of $P(x) = x^2 + 3x - 18$ are -6 and 3.

The roots of $x^2 + 3x - 18 = 0$ are -6 and 3.

The factors of $x^2 + 3x - 18$ are $(x + 6)$ and $(x - 3)$.

The x-intercepts of $P(x) = x^2 + 3x - 18$ are $(-6, 0)$ and $(3, 0)$.

Key Concept • Fundamental Theorem of Algebra

Every polynomial equation with degree greater than zero has at least one root in the set of complex numbers.

Key Concept • Corollary to the Fundamental Theorem of Algebra

Words: A polynomial equation of degree n has exactly n roots in the set of complex numbers, including repeated roots.

Examples:

$2x^3 - 5x + 2$	$-x^4 + 2x^3 - 2x$	$x^5 - 6x^3 + x^2 - 1$
3 roots	4 roots	5 roots

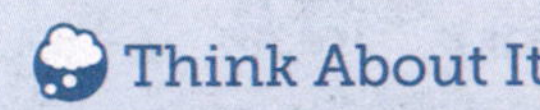

Think About It!
What is the multiplicity of the zero 1 for $p(x) = x - 15$? Explain your reasoning.

Repeated roots can also be called roots of multiplicity m where m is an integer greater than 1. **Multiplicity** is the number of times a number is a zero for a given polynomial. For example, $f(x) = x^3 = x \cdot x \cdot x$ has a zero at $x = 0$ with multiplicity 3, because x is a factor three times. However, the graph of the function still only intersects the x-axis once at the origin.

Your Notes

Study Tip:

Repeated Roots If you factor a polynomial and a factor is raised to a power greater than 1, then there is a repeated root. The power to which the factor is raised indicates the multiplicity of the root. To be sure that you do not miss a repeated root, it can help to write out each factor. For example, you would write x^2 as $x \cdot x$ as a reminder that x^2 indicates a root of multiplicity 2.

Key Concept • Descartes' Rule of Signs

Let $P(x) = a_n x^n + \ldots + a_1 x + a_0$ be a polynomial function with real coefficients. Then the number of positive real zeros of $P(x)$ is the same as the number of changes in sign of the coefficients of the terms, or is less than this by an even number, and the number of negative real zeros of $P(x)$ is the same as the number of changes in sign of the coefficients of the terms of $P(-x)$, or is less than this by an even number.

Example 1 Determine Number and Type of Roots

Solve $x^4 + 49x^2 = 0$. State the number and type of roots.

$x^4 + 49x^2 = 0$		Original equation
$x^2(x^2 + 49) = 0$		Factor.
$\_\_\_ = 0$ or	$\_\_\_\_\_ = 0$	Zero Product Property
$x = \_\_\_$	$x^2 = -49$	Subtract 49 from each side.
	$x = \pm\sqrt{\quad}$	Square Root Property
	$x = \pm\_\_\_$	Simplify.

The polynomial has degree 4, so there are four roots in the set of complex numbers. Because x^2 is a factor, $x = 0$ is a root with multiplicity 2, also called a double root. The equation has one real repeated root, ____, and two imaginary roots, ____.

Example 2 Find Numbers of Positive and Negative Zeros

State the possible number of positive real zeros, negative real zeros, and imaginary zeros of $f(x) = x^5 - 2x^4 - x^3 + 6x^2 - 5x + 10$.

Because $f(x)$ has degree ____, it has ____ zeros, either real or imaginary. Use Descartes' Rule of Signs to determine the possible number and types of *real* zeros.

Part A Find the possible number of positive real zeros.

Count the number of changes in sign for the coefficients of $f(x)$.

$$f(x) = x^5 - 2x^4 - x^3 + 6x^2 - 5x + 10$$

yes (+ to −), no (− to −), yes (− to +), yes (+ to −), yes (− to +)

There are ____ sign changes, so there are ____, ____, or ____ positive real zeros.

Part B Find the possible number of negative real zeros.

Count the number of changes in sign for the coefficients of $f(-x)$.

$$f(-x) = (-x)^5 - 2(-x)^4 - (-x)^3 + 6(-x)^2 - 5(-x) + 10$$
$$= -x^5 - 2x^4 + x^3 + 6x^2 + 5x + 10$$

no (− to −), yes (− to +), no (+ to +), no (+ to +), no (+ to +)

There is ____ sign change, so there is ____ negative real zero.

Go Online You can complete an Extra Example online.

Part C Find the possible number of imaginary zeros.

Number of Positive Real Zeros	Number of Negative Real Zeros	Number of Imaginary Zeros	Total Number of Zeros
4	1	0	$4 + 1 + 0 = 5$
___	1	2	$2 + 1 + 2 = 5$
0	1	___	$0 + 1 +$ ___ $= 5$

Talk About It!

If a polynomial has degree n and no real zeros, then how many imaginary zeros does it have? Explain your reasoning.

Check

State the possible number of positive real zeros, negative real zeros, and imaginary zeros of $f(x) = 3x^7 - x^6 + 2x^5 + x^4 - 3x^3 + 13x^2 + x$. Write the rows in ascending order of positive real zeros.

Number of Positive Real Zeros	Number of Negative Real Zeros	Number of Imaginary Zeros

Learn Finding Zeros of Polynomial Functions

Key Concept • Complex Conjugates Theorem

Words: Let a and b be real numbers, and $b \neq 0$. If $a + bi$ is a zero of a polynomial function with real coefficients, then $a - bi$ is also a zero of the function.

Examples: If $1 + 2i$ is a zero of $f(x) = x^3 - x^2 + 3x + 5$, then $1 - 2i$ is also a zero of the function.

When you are given all of the zeros of a polynomial function and asked to determine the function, use the zeros to write the factors and multiply them together. The result will be the polynomial function.

Example 3 Use Synthetic Substitution to Find Zeros

Find all of the zeros of $f(x) = x^3 + x^2 - 7x - 1$ and use them to sketch a rough graph.

Part A Find all of the zeros.

Step 1 Determine the total number of zeros.

Since $f(x)$ has degree 3, the function has ___ zeros.

Step 2 Determine the type of zeros.

Examine the number of sign changes for $f(x)$ and $f(-x)$.

$f(x) = x^3 + x^2 - 7x - 15$ — no, yes, no

$f(-x) = -x^3 + x^2 + 7x - 15$ — yes, no, yes

(continued on the next page)

Because there is ___ sign change for the coefficients of $f(x)$, the function has ___ positive real zero. Because there are ___ sign changes for the coefficients of $f(-x)$, $f(x)$ has ___ or ___ negative real zeros. Thus, $f(x)$ has 3 real zeros, or 1 real zero and 2 imaginary zeros.

Step 3 Determine the real zeros.

List some possible values, and then use synthetic substitution to evaluate $f(x)$ for real values of x.

x	1	1	−7	−15
−1	1	0	−7	−8
0	1	1	−7	−15
1	1	2	−5	−20
2	1	3	−1	−17
3	1	4	5	0
4	1	5	13	37

___ is a zero of the function, and the depressed polynomial is $x^2 + 4x + 5$. Since it is quadratic, use the Quadratic Formula. The zeros of $f(x) = x^2 + 4x + 5$ are ______ and ______.

The function has zeros at 3, $-2 - i$ and $-2 + i$.

Part B Sketch a rough graph.

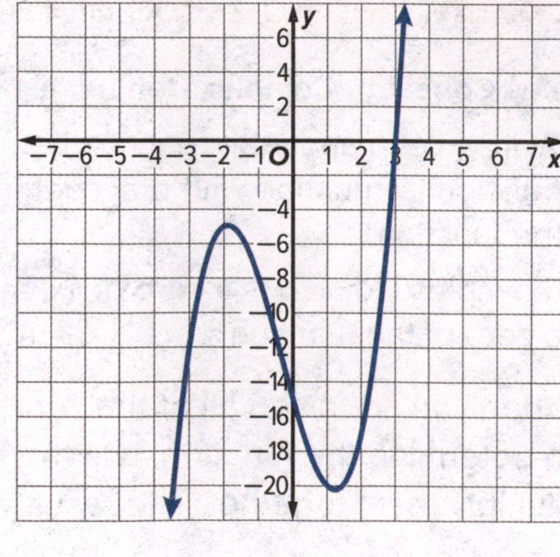

The function has one real zero at $x = 3$, so the function goes through (3, 0) and does not cross the x-axis at any other place.

Because the degree is odd and the leading coefficient is positive, the end behavior is that as $x \to -\infty$, $f(x) \to$ ___ and as $x \to \infty$, $f(x) \to$ ___

Check

Determine all of the zeros of $f(x) = x^4 - x^3 - 16x^2 - 4x - 80$, and use them to sketch a rough graph.

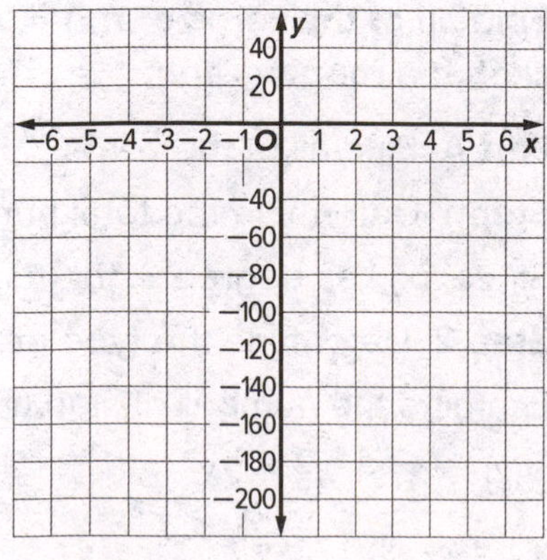

Real Zeros: ___, ___

Imaginary Zeros: ___, ___

Go Online You can complete an Extra Example online.

Example 4 Use a Graph to Write a Polynomial Function

Write a polynomial that could be represented by the graph.

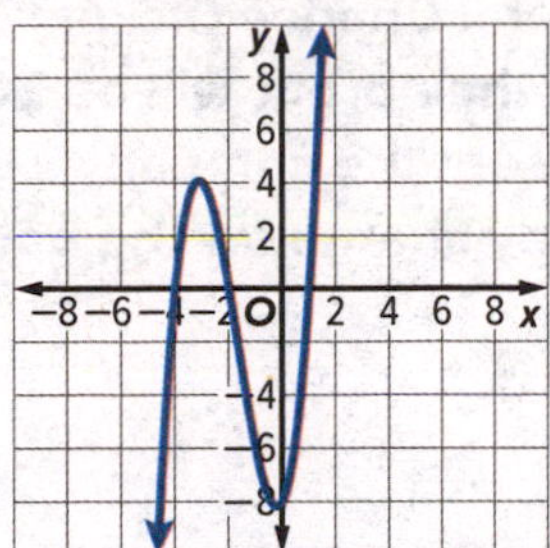

The graph crosses the x-axis ____ times, so it is at least of degree ____.

It crosses the x-axis at $x =$ ____, $x =$ ____, and $x =$ ____, so its factors are ______, ______, and ______.

To determine the polynomial, find the product of the factors.

$y = (x + 4)(x + 2)(x - 1)$ Set the product of the factors equal to y.

$= (\_\_\_\_\_\_\_\_\_\_)(x - 1)$ FOIL

$= \_\_\_\_\_\_\_\_\_\_\_\_\_\_$ Multiply.

The polynomial is $y =$ ______________.

Check

Write a polynomial that could be represented by the graph. ____

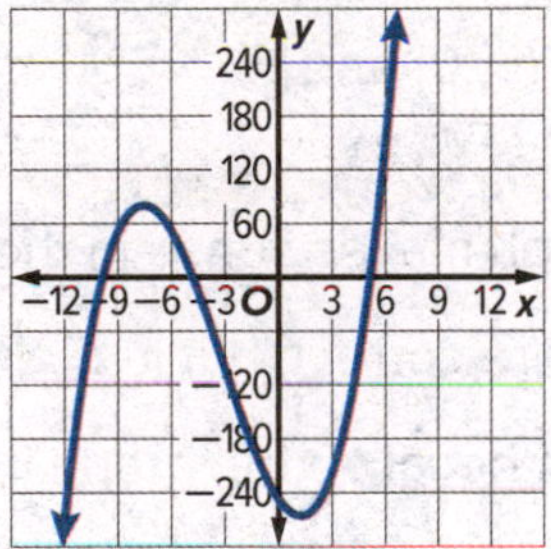

A. $y = x^3 - 6x^2 - 24x + 64$

B. $y = x^2 + 4x - 32$

C. $y = x^3 + 6x^2 - 24x - 64$

D. $y = x^3 - 64$

Go Online You can complete an Extra Example online.

Example 5 Use Zeros to Graph a Polynomial Function

PROFIT MARGIN **A book publisher wants to release a special hardcover version of several Charles Dickens books. They know that if they charge $5 or $40, their profit will be $0. Graph a polynomial function that could represent the company's profit in thousands of dollars given the price they charge for the book.**

Understand

What do you know?

Let x represent the price that the publisher ______, and let y represent the ______. Then $y = 0$ when $x =$ ____ or $x =$ ____.

What do you need to find?

A ______________ equation that relates x and y.

Plan and Solve

Step 1 Write the zeros as factors.

Then $y = 0$ when $x = 5$ or $x = 40$, then ______ and ______ are factors.

Step 2 Multiply the factors.

$(x - 5)(x - 40) =$ ______________

Step 3 Graph the polynomial.

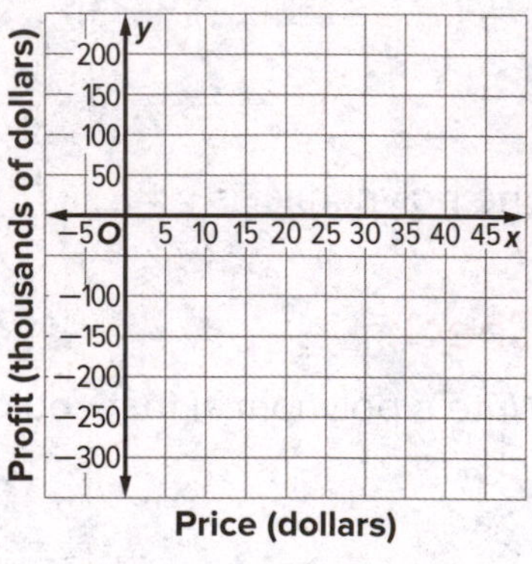

The function has zeros at (5, 0) and (40, 0).

Step 4 Make sure the graph makes sense in the context of the situation.

The zeros of the function are correct, but it ____________ make sense in the context of the situation because the graph indicates that the company would produce more profit by charging less than $______ or more than $______.

Step 5 Make any adjustments to the polynomial and graph.

The graph should be ____________, so multiply the polynomial by _____.

$y = -(x^2 - 45x + 200)$

$y =$ ________________

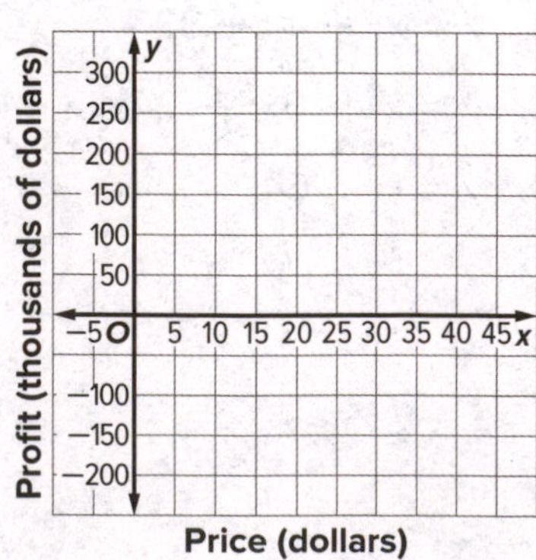

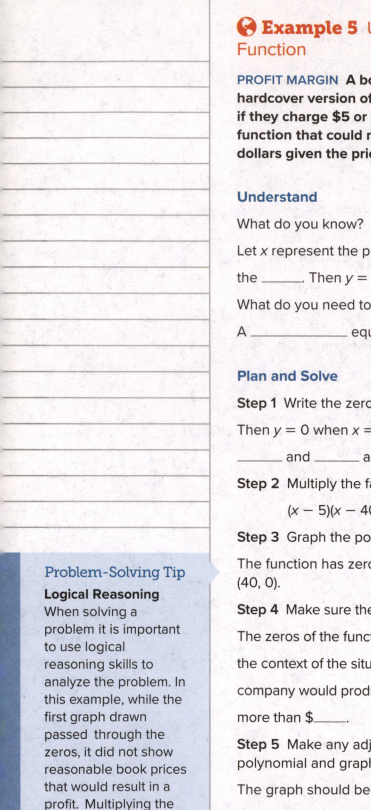

Problem-Solving Tip

Logical Reasoning When solving a problem it is important to use logical reasoning skills to analyze the problem. In this example, while the first graph drawn passed through the zeros, it did not show reasonable book prices that would result in a profit. Multiplying the polynomial by −1 produced a graph that made sense in the context of the situation.

Go Online You can complete an Extra Example online.

Name ______________________ Period ____________ Date ______________

Practice

Go Online You can complete your homework online.

Example 1

Solve each equation. State the number and type of roots.

1. $5x + 12 = 0$

2. $x^2 - 4x + 40 = 0$

3. $x^5 + 4x^3 = 0$

4. $x^4 - 625 = 0$

5. $4x^2 - 4x - 1 = 0$

6. $x^5 - 81x = 0$

Example 2

State the possible number of positive real zeros, negative real zeros, and imaginary zeros of each function.

7. $g(x) = 3x^3 - 4x^2 - 17x + 6$

8. $h(x) = 4x^3 - 12x^2 - x + 3$

9. $f(x) = x^3 - 8x^2 + 2x - 4$

10. $p(x) = x^3 - x^2 + 4x - 6$

11. $q(x) = x^4 + 7x^2 + 3x - 9$

12. $f(x) = x^4 - x^3 - 5x^2 + 6x + 1$

Example 3

Find all of the zeros of each function and use them to sketch a rough graph.

13. $h(x) = x^3 - 5x^2 + 5x + 3$

14. $g(x) = x^3 - 6x^2 + 13x - 10$

15. $h(x) = x^3 + 4x^2 + x - 6$

16. $q(x) = x^3 + 3x^2 - 6x - 8$

17. $g(x) = x^4 - 3x^3 - 5x^2 + 3x + 4$

18. $f(x) = x^4 - 21x^2 + 80$

Example 4

Write a polynomial that could be represented by each graph.

19.

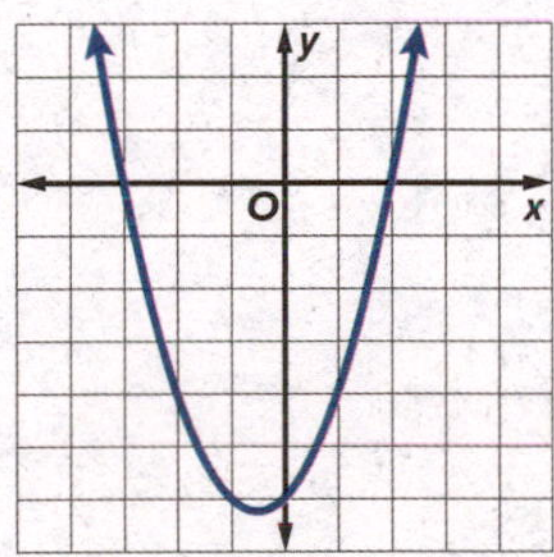

20.

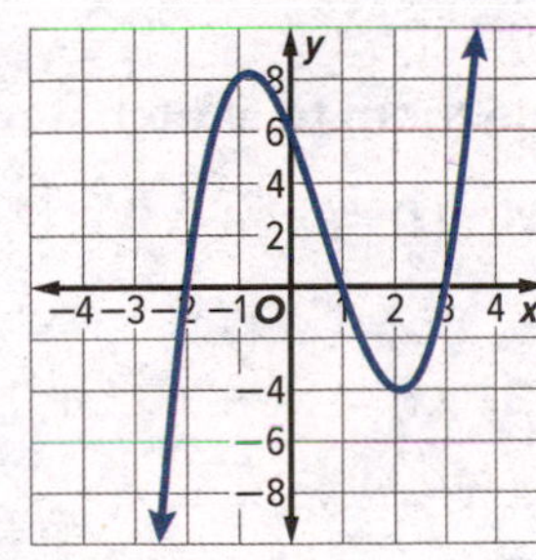

21.

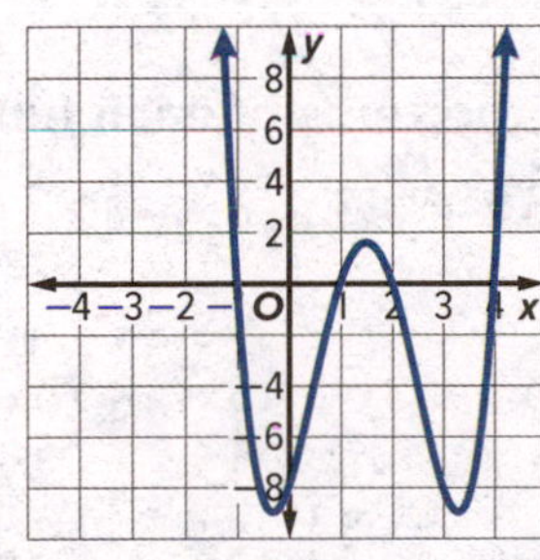

Example 5

22. **FISH** Some fish jump out of the water. When a fish is out of the water, its location is above sea level. When a fish dives back into the water, its location is below sea level. A biologist can use polynomial functions to model the location of fish compared to see level. A biologist noticed that a fish is at sea level at −3, −2, −1, 1, 2, and 3 minutes from noon. Graph a polynomial function that could represent the location of the fish compared to sea level y, in centimeters, x seconds from noon.

23. **REVENUE** After introducing a new product, a company's revenue is modeled by a polynomial function. At 2 and 7 years since 2010, the company's revenue was $0. Graph a polynomial function that could represent the amount of revenue, $R(x)$, in thousands of dollars, x years since 2010.

Mixed Exercises

Solve each equation. State the number and type of roots.

24. $2x^2 + x - 6 = 0$

25. $4x^2 + 1 = 0$

26. $x^3 + 1 = 0$

27. $2x^2 - 5x + 14 = 0$

28. $-3x^2 - 5x + 8 = 0$

29. $8x^3 - 27 = 0$

30. $16x^4 - 625 = 0$

31. $x^3 - 6x^2 + 7x = 0$

32. $x^5 - 8x^3 + 16x = 0$

33. $x^5 + 2x^3 + x = 0$

State the possible number of positive real zeros, negative real zeros, and imaginary zeros of each function.

34. $f(x) = x^4 - 5x^3 + 2x^2 + 5x + 7$

35. $f(x) = 2x^3 - 7x^2 - 2x + 12$

36. $f(x) = -3x^5 + 5x^4 + 4x^2 - 8$

37. $f(x) = x^4 - 2x^2 - 5x + 19$

38. $f(x) = 4x^6 - 5x^4 - x^2 + 24$

39. $f(x) = -x^5 + 14x^3 + 18x - 36$

Find all of the zeros of each function and use them to sketch a rough graph.

40. $f(x) = x^3 + 7x^2 + 4x - 12$

41. $f(x) = x^3 + x^2 - 17x + 15$

42. $f(x) = x^4 - 3x^3 - 3x^2 - 75x - 700$

43. $f(x) = x^4 + 6x^3 + 73x^2 + 384x + 576$

44. $f(x) = x^4 - 8x^3 + 20x^2 - 32x + 64$

45. $f(x) = x^5 - 8x^3 - 9x$

Name _______________ Period _______ Date _______

Write a polynomial function of least degree with integral coefficients that have the given zeros.

46. 5, −2, −1

47. −4, −3, 5

48. −1, −1, $2i$

49. −3, 1, $-3i$

50. 0, −5, $3 + i$

51. −2, −3, $4 - 3i$

Sketch the graph of each function using its zeros.

52. $f(x) = x^3 - 5x^2 - 2x + 24$

53. $f(x) = 4x^3 + 2x^2 - 4x - 2$

54. $f(x) = x^4 - 6x^3 + 7x^2 + 6x - 8$

55. $f(x) = x^4 - 6x^3 + 9x^2 + 4x - 12$

56. **TABLES** Li Pang made a table of values for the polynomial $p(x)$. Name three roots of $p(x)$.

x	$p(x)$
−4	−3
−3	−1
−2	0
−1	2
0	0
1	4
2	0
3	2
4	5

57. **REASONING** Ryan is an electrical engineer. He often solves polynomial equations to work out various properties of the circuits he builds. For one circuit, he must find the roots of a polynomial $p(x)$. He finds that $p(2 - 3i) = 0$. Give two different roots of $p(x)$.

58. **USE A SOURCE** Research "eigenvalues of a matrix" and how it relates to the roots of a polynomial function. Use what you learned to find the other 3 roots of the polynomial was $x^4 + 6x^2 + 25$, if one of the roots is $1 + 2i$. Explain.

59. **QUADRILATERALS** Shayna plotted the four vertices of a quadrilateral in the complex plane and then encoded the points in a polynomial $p(x)$ by making them the roots of $p(x)$. Let $p(x)$ is $x^4 - 9x^3 + 27x^2 + 23x - 150$.

a. The polynomial $p(x)$ has one positive real root, and it is an integer. Find the integer.

b. Find the negative real root(s) of $p(x)$.

c. Find the complex roots of $p(x)$.

60. Write and examine a polynomial function.

a. Write a fourth-degree polynomial $P(x)$ where no coefficient is zero, that is $a_n \neq 0$ for any n.

b. Find $P(-2)$ in two different ways.

c. Determine whether $x + 1$ is a factor of $P(x)$.

d. Explain what information Descartes' Rule of Signs provides about $P(x)$.

e. Explain how to find, then list, all of the possible rational zeros of $P(x)$.

f. Explain how to find, then state, the rational zeros of $P(x)$.

61. **MODELING** Determine all of the zeros of $P(x) = x^3 - x^2 - 15x - 9$ and construct a graph of the function.

62. **USE TOOLS** Sketch the graph of two functions of different degree that only have zeros −3, 1, and 2.

63. ARGUMENTS Explain why the graph of $P(x) = -4(x + 2)(x - 3)^3$ crosses the x-axis at $x = 3$, while the graph of $R(x) = 2(x - 1)(x - 3)^4$ does not cross the x-axis at $x = 3$.

64. Write and examine a polynomial function.

a. STRUCTURE Write a polynomial function of least degree with integral coefficients and zeros that include $-1 - 4i$ and $\frac{2}{3} + \frac{1}{3}i$. Explain your reasoning.

b. PRECISION Use your answer from **part a** to write another polynomial function with integral coefficients having the same degree and zeros. Explain your reasoning.

c. USE TOOLS Are you able to sketch these graphs based on the zeros? Explain your reasoning. Use a calculator to graph the functions from **parts a** and **b**.

65. REGULARITY Use the zeros to draw the graph of $P(x) = x^3 - 7x^2 + 7x + 15$ by hand. Discuss the accuracy of your graph, and what could be done to improve the accuracy.

66. Let the polynomial function $f(x)$ have real coefficients, be of degree 5, and have zeros $4 + 3i$, $2 - 7i$, and $6 + bi$ where b is some real number constant.

a. STATE YOUR ASSUMPTION What can be determined about the constant b? Explain your reasoning.

b. MODELING Using your answer from **part a**, write a possible related equation for $f(x)$.

67. CREATE Sketch the graph of a polynomial function with:

a. 3 real, 2 imaginary zeros **b.** 4 real zeros **c.** 2 imaginary zeros

68. PERSEVERE Write an equation in factored form of a polynomial function of degree 5 with 2 imaginary zeros, 1 nonintegral zero, and 2 irrational zeros. Explain.

69. WHICH ONE DOESN'T BELONG? Determine which equation is not like the others. Explain your reasoning.

$r^4 + 1 = 0$	$r^3 + 1 = 0$	$r^2 - 1 = 0$	$r^3 - 8 = 0$

70. ANALYZE Provide a counterexample for each statement.

a. All polynomial functions of degree greater than 2 have at least 1 negative real root.

b. All polynomial functions of degree greater than 2 have at least 1 positive real root.

71. WRITE Explain to a friend how you would use Descartes' Rule of Signs to determine the number of possible positive real roots and the number of possible negative roots of the polynomial function $f(x) = x^4 - 2x^3 + 6x^2 + 5x - 12$.

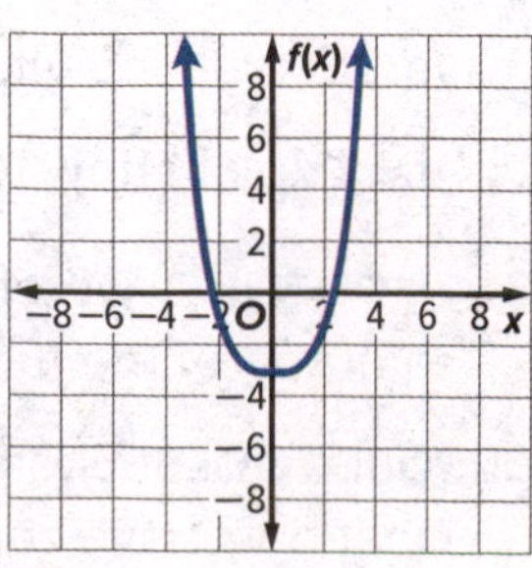

72. FIND THE ERROR The graph shows a polynomial function. Brianne says the function is a 4th degree polynomial. Cassandrea says the function is a 2nd degree polynomial. Is either of them correct? Explain your reasoning.

Review

 Essential Question

What methods are useful for solving polynomial equations and finding zeros of polynomial functions?

Module Summary

Lessons 5-1 and 5-2

Solving Polynomial Equations

- Polynomial equations can be solved by graphing or can be solved algebraically.
- $a^3 + b^3 = (a + b)(a^2 - ab + b^2)$
- $a^3 - b^3 = (a - b)(a^2 + ab - b^2)$
- When factoring a polynomial, look for a common factor to simplify the expression.
- An expression in quadratic form can be written as $au^2 + bu + c$ for any numbers a, b, and c, $a \neq 0$, where u is some expression in x.

Lesson 5-3

Polynomial Identities

- An identity is an equation that is satisfied by any numbers that replace the variables.
- A polynomial identity is a polynomial equation that is true for any values that are substituted for the variables.
- To verify an identify, simplify one side of an equation until the two sides of the equation are the same. Then, transform that expression into the form of the simpler side.

Lesson 5-4

The Remainder and Factor Theorems

- Remainder Theorem: For a polynomial $p(x)$ and a number a, the remainder upon division by $x - a$ is $p(a)$.
- Factor Theorem: The binomial $x - a$ is a factor of the polynomial $p(x)$ if and only if $p(a) = 0$.

Lesson 5-5

Roots and Zeros

- Let $P(x) = a_nx^n + ... + a_1x + a_0$ be a polynomial function. Then the following statements are equivalent.
  - c is a zero of $P(x)$.
  - c is a root or solution of $P(x)=0$.
  - $x - c$ is a factor of $a_nx^n + ... + a_1x + a_0$.
- If c is a real number, then $(c, 0)$ is an x-intercept of the graph of $P(x)$.
- A polynomial equation of degree n has exactly n roots in the set of complex numbers, including repeated roots.
- The number of positive real zeros of $P(x)$ is the same as the number of changes in sign of the coefficients of the terms, or is less than this by an even number, and the number of negative real zeros of $P(x)$ is the same as the number of changes in sign of the coefficients of the terms of $P(-x)$, or is less than this by an even number.
- If $a + bi$ is a zero of a polynomial function with real coefficients, then $a - bi$ is also a zero of the function.

Study Organizer

Use your Foldable to review this module. Working with a partner can be helpful. Ask for clarification of concepts as needed.

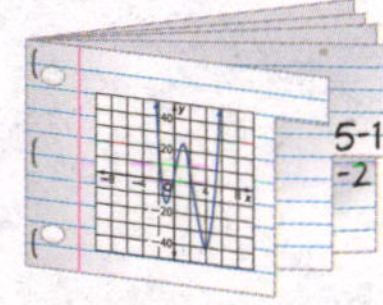

Name ______________________ Period ____________ Date ____________

Test Practice

1. MULTIPLE CHOICE Which function can be used to solve $x^3 - x = 2x^2 - 2$ by graphing? (Lesson 5-1)

Ⓐ $f(x) = x^3 - 2x^2 - x + 2$

Ⓑ $f(x) = x - 2$

Ⓒ $f(x) = x^3 + 2x^2 - x - 2$

Ⓓ $f(x) = 2x^5 - 4x^3 + 2x$

2. OPEN RESPONSE The graph of $f(x) = x^4 - 4x^2 + x + 1$ is shown.

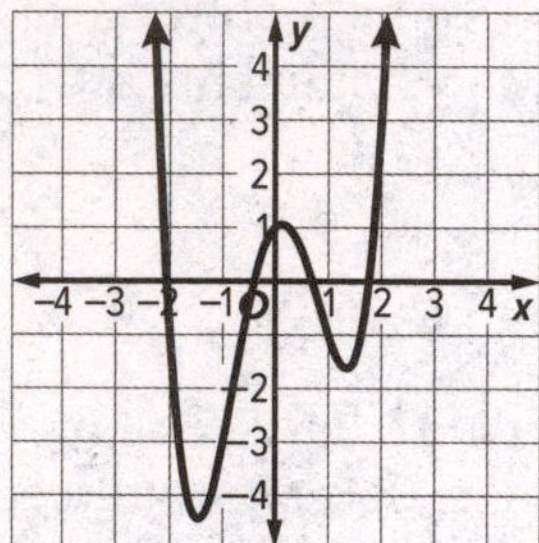

How many real solutions does the function have? (Lesson 5-1)

3. MULTI-SELECT Use a graphing calculator to solve $x^3 - 10x + 4 = 4 - x$. Select all of the solutions. (Lesson 5-1)

Ⓐ −3

Ⓑ 0

Ⓒ 1

Ⓓ 3

Ⓔ 4

Ⓕ 7

4. GRIDDED RESPONSE A jewelry box is 3 inches by 4 inches by 2 inches. If increasing the length of each edge by x inches doubles the volume of the jewelry box, what is the value of x? Round your answer to the nearest hundredth if necessary. (Lesson 5-1)

−	−	−	−	−	−	−
	/	/	/	/	/	
.	.	.	.	.	.	.
0	0	0	0	0	0	0
1	1	1	1	1	1	1
2	2	2	2	2	2	2
3	3	3	3	3	3	3
4	4	4	4	4	4	4
5	5	5	5	5	5	5
6	6	6	6	6	6	6
7	7	7	7	7	7	7
8	8	8	8	8	8	8
9	9	9	9	9	9	9

5. MULTI-SELECT Find the solutions of $x^3 - 9x = 8x^2$. Select all that apply. (Lesson 5-2)

Ⓐ −9

Ⓑ −1

Ⓒ 0

Ⓓ 1

Ⓔ 3

Ⓕ 9

Ⓖ 12

6. MULTIPLE CHOICE Which of the following is not a real solution to the equation $x^3 + 4x^2 - 4x - 16 = 0$? (Lesson 5-2)

Ⓐ −4

Ⓑ −2

Ⓒ 2

Ⓓ 4

Name ______________________ Period __________ Date __________

7. MULTI-SELECT Find the solutions of $x^4 - x^2 - 2 = 0$. Select all that apply. (Lesson 5-2)

Ⓐ $\pm\sqrt{2}$

Ⓑ $\pm i$

Ⓒ ± 1

Ⓓ ± 2

Ⓔ $\pm i\sqrt{2}$

8. OPEN RESPONSE Marco is making two rectangular table tops. The dimensions of both are shown. If both designs have the same area, what is the value of x? (Lesson 5-2)

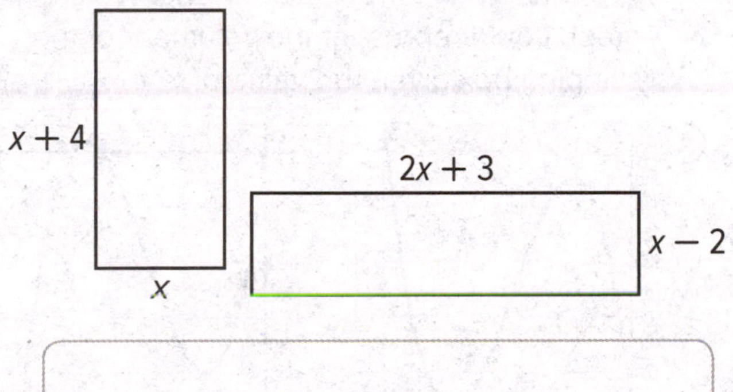

9. MULTI-SELECT Select all of the choices that are steps in the proof that $x^3 + y^3 = (x + y)(x^2 - xy + y^2)$. (Lesson 5-3)

Ⓐ $x^3 + y^3 = x(x^2) - x(xy) + x(y^2) + y(x^2) - y(xy) + y(y^2)$

Ⓑ $x^3 + y^3 = x^3 - x^2y + xy^2 + xy^2 - x^2y + y^3$

Ⓒ $x^3 + y^3 = x^3 - (x^2y + xy^2) + (x^2y - xy^2) + y^3$

Ⓓ $x^3 + y^3 = x^3 - x^2y + x^2y + xy^2 - xy^2 + y^3$

Ⓔ $x^3 + y^3 = x^3 - x^3y^3 + x^3y^3 + y^3$

Ⓕ $x^3 + y^3 = x^3 + y^3$

10. MULTIPLE CHOICE Which of the following is an equivalent expression to $(x + y)^3$? (Lesson 5-3)

Ⓐ $x^3 + y^3 + 3xy(x - y)$

Ⓑ $x^3 + y^3 + 3xy(x + y)$

Ⓒ $x^3 + y^3 + xy(x + y)$

Ⓓ $x^3 + y^3 + xy(x - y)$

11. MULTIPLE CHOICE Which of the following is an equivalent expression to $4xy$? (Lesson 5-3)

Ⓐ $(x + y)^2 - (x + y)^2$

Ⓑ $(x + y)^2 - (x - y)^2$

Ⓒ $2(x + y)^2 - (x + y)^2$

Ⓓ $(x + y)^2 - 2(x - y)^2$

12. GRIDDED RESPONSE What is the remainder when $f(x) = x^4 + x^3 - 2x^2 + 5x - 4$ is divided by $x + 3$? (Lesson 5-4)

13. MULTI-SELECT If $x - 1$ is a factor of $x^3 - 6x^2 + 11x - 6$, find the remaining factors of the polynomial. Select all that apply. (Lesson 5-4)

Ⓐ $x^2 - 5x + 6$

Ⓑ $x - 3$

Ⓒ $x + 2$

Ⓓ $x - 4$

14. MULTIPLE CHOICE The average price of gasoline, in dollars, from 2010 to 2016 can be modeled by the function $f(x) = 0.03x^3 - 0.4x^2 + 1.18x + 2.75$, where x represents the years since 2010. Which option below uses synthetic substitution to estimate the price of gasoline in 2011? (Lesson 5-4)

Ⓐ
$$\begin{array}{r|rrrr} 1 & 0.03 & -0.4 & 1.18 & 2.75 \\ & & 0.03 & -0.37 & 0.81 \\ \hline & 0.03 & -0.37 & 0.81 & 3.56 \end{array}$$

Ⓑ
$$\begin{array}{r|rrrr} -1 & 0.03 & -0.4 & 1.18 & 2.75 \\ & & -0.03 & 0.43 & -1.61 \\ \hline & 0.03 & -0.43 & 1.61 & 1.14 \end{array}$$

Ⓒ
$$\begin{array}{r|rrrr} 1 & 0.03 & -0.4 & 1.18 & 2.75 \\ & & 0.03 & -0.43 & 1.61 \\ \hline & 0.03 & -0.43 & 1.61 & 1.14 \end{array}$$

Ⓓ
$$\begin{array}{r|rrrr} -1 & 0.03 & -0.4 & 1.18 & 2.75 \\ & & -0.03 & 0.37 & -0.81 \\ \hline & 0.03 & -0.37 & 0.81 & 3.56 \end{array}$$

15. TABLE ITEM Identify if each value of x is a real root, an imaginary root or not a root in the equation $x^4 + 3x^2 - 4 = 0$. (Lesson 5-5)

x	Real Root	Imaginary Root	Not a Root
-2			
-1			
1			
2			
$-2i$			
$-i$			
i			
$2i$			

16. TABLE ITEM What are the possible numbers of positive real roots and negative real roots of $p(x) = x^5 - 2x^4 + 3x^3 - 4x^2 + 1$? Select all that apply. (Lesson 5-5)

Number of Real Roots	Positive	Negative
0		
1		
2		
3		
4		
5		

17. MULTIPLE CHOICE A template for a shipping box is made by cutting a square with side length x inches from each corner of a rectangular piece of cardboard that is 12 inches wide and 14 inches long. Which graph could represent the volume V of the shipping box given the value of x? (Lesson 5-5)

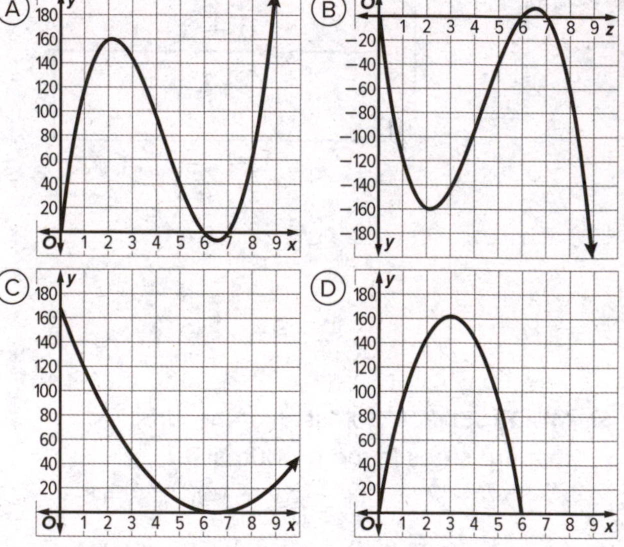

18. MULTIPLE CHOICE Consider the function $p(x) = x^5 - 3x^4 + 3x^3 - x^2$. Which of the following is a root of the function with multiplicity 3? (Lesson 5-5)

Ⓐ -1

Ⓑ 0

Ⓒ 1

Ⓓ 2

Module 6

Inverse and Radical Functions

Essential Question

How can the inverse of a function be used to help interpret a real-world event or solve a problem?

A.SSE.2, A.REI.2, F.IF.5, F.IF.7b; F.BF.1b, F.BF.3; F.BF.4a

Mathematical Practices: MP1, MP2, MP3, MP4, MP5, MP6, MP7, MP8

What will you learn?

Place a checkmark (✓) in each row that corresponds with how much you already know about each topic **before** starting this module.

KEY

— I don't know. — I've heard of it. — I know it!

	Before			After		
	I don't know.	I've heard of it.	I know it!	I don't know.	I've heard of it.	I know it!
perform operations on functions						
combine functions using a composition of functions						
verify mathematically two relations or functions are inverses						
write expressions with rational exponents						
graph square root functions						
graph cube root functions						
perform operations with radical expressions						
solve radical equations by graphing						
solve radical equations algebraically						

Foldables Make this Foldable to help you organize your notes about inverse and radical functions. Begin with three sheets of notebook paper.

1. **Stack** three sheets of notebook paper so that each is one inch higher than the previous
2. **Align** the bottom of all the sheets.
3. **Fold** the papers and crease well. Open the papers and staple them. Label the pages with lesson titles.

Solving Radical Equations
Operations with Radical Expressions
Graphing Radical Functions
nth Roots and Rational Exponents
Inverse Relations and Functions
Operations on Functions

What Vocabulary Will You Learn?

Check the box next to each vocabulary term that you may already know.

- ☐ composition of functions
- ☐ conjugates
- ☐ cube root function
- ☐ exponential form
- ☐ index
- ☐ inverse functions
- ☐ inverse relations
- ☐ like radical expressions
- ☐ principal root
- ☐ radical equation
- ☐ radical form
- ☐ radical function
- ☐ radicand
- ☐ rational exponent
- ☐ square root function
- ☐ square root inequality

Are You Ready?

Complete the Quick Review to see if you are ready to start this module. Then complete the Quick Check.

Quick Review

Example 1

Use the related graph of $0 = 3x^2 - 4x + 1$ to determine its roots. If exact roots cannot be found, state the consecutive integers between which the roots are located.

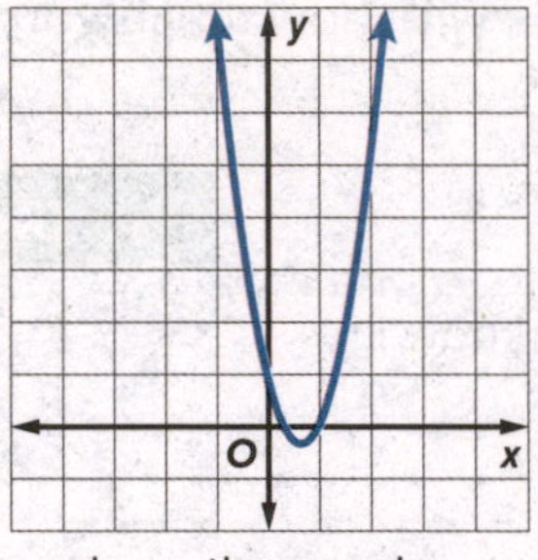

The roots are the x-coordinates where the graph crosses the x-axis.

The graph crosses the x-axis between 0 and 1 and at 1.

Example 2

Simplify $(3x^4 + 4x^3 + x^2 + 9x - 6) \div (x + 2)$ by using synthetic division.

$x - r = x + 2$, so $r = -2$

−2	3	4	1	9	−6
	↓	−6	4	−10	2
	3	−2	5	−1	−4

The result is $3x^3 - 2x^2 + 5x - 1 - \frac{4}{x + 2}$.

Quick Check

Use the related graph of each equation to determine its roots. If exact roots cannot be found, state the consecutive integers between which the roots are located.

1. $x^2 - 4x + 1 = 0$
2. $2x^2 + x - 6 = 0$
3. $3x^2 - 3x - 1 = 0$
4. $2x^2 - 9x + 4 = 0$

Simplify each expression by using synthetic division.

5. $(5x^2 - 22x - 15) \div (x - 5)$
6. $(3x^2 + 14x - 12) \div (x + 4)$
7. $(2x^3 + 7x^2 - 36x + 36) \div (x - 6)$
8. $(3x^4 - 13x^3 + 17x^2 - 18x + 15) \div (x - 3)$

How Did You Do?

Which exercises did you answer correctly in the Quick Check? Shade those exercise numbers below.

① ② ③ ④ ⑤ ⑥ ⑦ ⑧

Operations on Functions

Today's Standards
F.BF.1b
MP1, MP4, MP7

Today's Vocabulary
composition of functions

Explore Adding Functions

Online Activity Use graphing technology to complete the Explore.

INQUIRY Do you think that the graph of $f(x) + g(x)$ will be more or less steep than the graphs of $f(x)$ and $g(x)$?

Learn Operations on Functions

Key Concept • Operations on Functions

Operation	Definition	Example
		Let $f(x) = 3x$ and $g(x) = 2x - 4$
Addition	$(f + g)(x) = f(x) + g(x)$	$(f + g)(x) = 3x + (2x - 4)$ $= 5x - 4$
Subtraction	$(f - g)(x) = f(x) - g(x)$	$(f + g)(x) = 3x - (2x - 4)$ $= x + 4$
Multiplication	$(fg)(x) = f(x)g(x)$	$(fg)(x) = 3x(2x - 4)$ $= 6x^2 - 12x$
Division	$\left(\frac{f}{g}\right)(x) = \frac{f(x)}{g(x)}$, $g(x) \neq 0$	$\left(\frac{f}{g}\right)(x) = \frac{3x}{2x - 4}$, $x \neq 2$

To graph the sum or difference of functions, graph each function separately. Then add or subtract the corresponding functional values.

Example 1 Add and Subtract Functions

Given $f(x) = x^2 + 3x + 1$ and $g(x) = 2x^2 - 5$, find each function.

a. $(f + g)(x)$

$(f + g)(x) = f(x) + $ ____ — Addition of functions

$= (-x^2 + 3x + 1) + (2x^2 - 5)$ — $f(x) = -x^2 + 3x + 1$ and $g(x) = 2x^2 - 5$

$= -x^2 + 3x + 1 + 2x^2 - 5$ — Add.

$= x^2 + $ ____ $x - $ ____ — Simplify.

(continued on the next page)

Go Online You can complete an Extra Example online.

Study Tip:

Degree If the degree of $f(x)$ is m and the degree of $g(x)$ is n, then the degrees of $(f + g)(x)$ and $(f - g)(x)$ can be at most m or n, whichever is greater.

Your Notes

b. $(f - g)(x)$

$(f - g)(x) = f(x) - \_\_\_\_$	Subtraction of functions
$= (-\_\_\_\_\_\_\_\_) - (2x^2 - 5)$	$f(x) = -x^2 + 3x + 1$ and $g(x) = 2x^2 - 5$
$= -x^2 + 3x + 1 - 2x^2 + 5$	Subtract.
$= -3x^2 + \_\_\_x + \_\_\_$	Simplify.

Example 2 Multiply and Divide Functions

Given $f(x) = 4x^2 - 2x + 3$ and $g(x) = -x + 5$, find each function.

a. $(f \cdot g)(x)$

$(f \cdot g)(x) = f(x) \cdot g(x)$	Multiplication of functions
$= (4x^2 - 2x + 3)(\_\_\_\_\_\_)$	$f(x) = 4x^2 - 2x + 3$ and $g(x) = -x + 5$
$= -4x^3 + \_\_\_x^2 + \_\_\_x^2 - 10x - \_\_\_x + 15$	Distributive Property
$= -4x^3 + \_\_\_x^2 - \_\_\_x + 15$	Simplify.

b. $\left(\frac{f}{g}\right)(x)$

$\left(\frac{f}{g}\right)(x) = \frac{f(x)}{\_\_\_\_}$	Division of functions
$= \frac{\_\_\_\_\_\_}{-x + 5}, x \neq \_\_\_\_$	$f(x) = 4x^2 - 2x + 3$ and $g(x) = -x + 5$
$= \frac{\_\_\_\_\_\_}{x - 5}, x \neq \_\_\_\_$	Simplify the denominator.

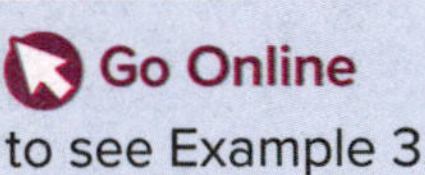

to see Example 3.

Check

Given $f(x) = -x^2 + 1$ and $g(x) = x + 1$, find each function.

$(f \cdot g)(x) = \_\_\_\_\_\_\_\_\_\_$ $\left(\frac{f}{g}\right)(x) = \_\_\_\_\_\_$

Learn Compositions of Functions

Key Concept • Composition of Functions

Suppose f and g are functions such that the range of g is a subset of the domain of f. Then the composition function $f \circ g$ can be described by $[f \circ g](x) = f[g(x)]$.

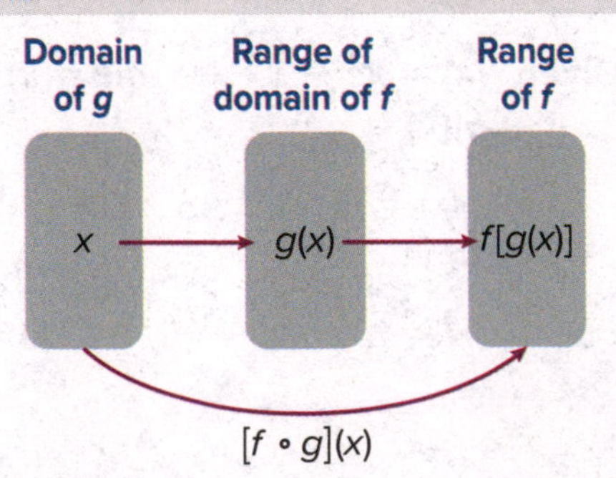

 **Go Online** You can complete an Extra Example online.

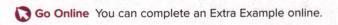

Example 4 Compose Functions by Using Ordered Pairs

Given f and g, find $[f \circ g](x)$ and $[g \circ f](x)$. State the domain and range for each.

$f = \{(1, 12), (10, 11), (0, 13), (9, 7)\}$ $g = \{(4, 1), (5, 0), (13, 9), (12, 10)\}$

Part A Find $[f \circ g](x)$ and $[g \circ f](x)$.

To find $f \circ g$ evaluate $g(x)$ first then use the range to evaluate $f(x)$.

$f[g(4)] = f(1)$ or ____ $g(4) =$ ____

$f[g(5)] = f(0)$ or ____ $g(5) =$ ____

$f[g(13)] = f(9)$ or ____ $g(13) =$ ____

$f[g(12)] = f(10)$ or ____ $g(12) =$ ____

To find $g \circ f$ evaluate $f(x)$ first then use the range to evaluate $g(x)$.

$g[f(1)] = g(12)$ or ____ $f(1) =$ ____

$g[f(10)] = g(11)$ $f(10) =$ ____

$g[f(0)] = g(13)$ or ____ ____ = ____

$g[f(9)] = g(7)$ $f(9) = 7$

Because 11 and 7 are not in the domain of g, $g \circ f$ is undefined for $x = 11$ and $x = 7$. So, $g \circ f = \{(1, 10), (0, 9)\}$.

Part B State the domain and range.

$[f \circ g](x)$: The domain is the x-coordinates of the composed function, so $D = \{$____, 5, ____, 13$\}$. The range is the y-coordinates of the composed function, so $R = \{7, 11,$ ____, ____$\}$.

$[g \circ f](x)$: The domain is the x-coordinates of the composed function, so $D = \{$____$\}$. The range is the y-coordinates of the composed function, so $R = \{9, 10\}$.

Example 5 Compose Functions

Given $f(x) = 2x - 5$ and $g(x) = 3x$, find $[f \circ g](x)$ and $[g \circ f](x)$. State the domain and range for each.

Part A Find $[f \circ g](x)$ and $[g \circ f](x)$.

$[f \circ g](x) = f[g(x)]$	Composition of functions	$[g \circ f](x) = g[f(x)]$
____________	Substitute.	$= g(2x - 5)$
$= 2(3x) - 5$	Substitute again.	____________
$= 6x - 5$	Simplify.	$= 6x - 15$

Part B State the domain and range.

Because $[f \circ g](x)$ and $[g \circ f](x)$ are both linear functions with nonzero slopes, $D = \{$________________$\}$ and $R = \{$all real numbers$\}$ for both functions.

Go Online You can complete an Extra Example online.

Study Tip:

Domain and Range To ensure you have the right domain and range, it can help to graph $[f \circ g](x)$ and $[g \circ f](x)$.

Check

Given $f(x) = -x + 1$ and $g(x) = 2x^3 - x$, find $[f \circ g](x)$ and $[g \circ f](x)$. State the domain and range for each.

$[f \circ g](x) =$ ________

$[g \circ f](x) =$ ________________

Domain of $[f \circ g](x)$: ____________

Range of $[f \circ g](x)$: ____________

Domain of $[g \circ f](x)$: ____________

Range of $[g \circ f](x)$: ____________

Example 6 Use Composition of Functions

BOX OFFICE A movie theater charges $8.50 for each of the x tickets sold. The manager wants to determine how much the movie theater gets to keep of the ticket sales if they have to give the studios 75% of the money earned on ticket sales $t(x)$. If the amount they keep of each ticket sale is $k(x)$, which composition represents the total amount of money the theater gets to keep?

Step 1 Determine the functions

Because the theater earns $8.50 per ticket sold, $t(x) =$ ______, where x is the number of tickets sold.

Because the theater gives the studio 75% of their earnings, the amount the theater keeps is 25%. So, $k(x) =$ ______ where x is the earnings.

Step 2 Determine the order of the composition.

The options are $[t \circ k](x)$ and $[k \circ t](x)$. Notice that in $t(x)$, x is the number of tickets sold and $t(x)$ is earnings. In $k(x)$, x is earnings and $k(x)$ is the amount the theater keeps. These units can guide the solution. Because we want the total amount the theater earns on ticket sales first, and then to take 25% of that amount, $t(x)$ should be evaluated first, and then $k(x)$. So, the composition is ___[(___(x)] = [___ ∘ ___](x), where x is the number of tickets sold.

Step 3 Simplify the function.

$[k \circ t](x) = k[(t(x)]$	Composition of functions
$= k[$________$x]$	$t(x) = 8.50x$
$=$ ________x	$k(x) = 0.25x$
	Simplify.

Watch Out!

Order Remember that, for two functions $f(x)$ and $g(x)$, $[f \circ g](x)$ is not always equal to $[g \circ f](x)$. So, given that the studios take their cut after the tickets have been sold, how does that affect the order of $t(x)$ and $k(x)$?

Go Online You can complete an Extra Example online.

Name ______ Period ______ Date ______

Practice

Go Online You can complete your homework online.

Examples 1 and 2

Find $(f + g)(x)$, $(f - g)(x)$, $(f \cdot g)(x)$, and $\left(\frac{f}{g}\right)(x)$ for each $f(x)$ and $g(x)$.

1. $f(x) = 2x$

$g(x) = -4x + 5$

2. $f(x) = x - 1$

$g(x) = 5x - 2$

3. $f(x) = x^2$

$g(x) = -x + 1$

4. $f(x) = 3x$

$g(x) = -2x + 6$

5. $f(x) = x - 2$

$g(x) = 2x - 7$

6. $f(x) = x^2$

$g(x) = x - 5$

7. $f(x) = -x^2 + 6$

$g(x) = 2x^2 + 3x - 5$

8. $f(x) = 3x^2 - 4$

$g(x) = x^2 - 8x + 4$

Example 3

9. GARDEN Aliyah is planning a rectangular garden and wants to know the amount of space in her backyard the garden will occupy. The length of the garden is represented by the function $L(x) = 2x + 1$ and the width of the garden is represented by the function $W(x) = x - 2$. What function represents the area of the garden, $A(x)$?

10. VOLUME The volume of a rectangular prism is represented by the function $V(x) = 24x^3 + 60x^2$. The area of the base of the rectangular prism is represented by the function $A(x) = 6x^2 + 15x$. What function represents the height of the rectangular prism, $H(x)$?

11. BASEBALL A coach is ordering boxes of baseballs for their upcoming season. Each box of baseballs costs \$72. There is a one-time shipping fee of \$50. The baseball company is offering one free box of baseballs for every 5 boxes of ordered.

a. Write a function $C(x)$ that represents the total cost of the boxes of baseballs, where x is the number of boxes of baseball ordered. (Assume at least 5 boxes and less than 10 boxes of baseballs are purchased.)

b. Write a function $N(x)$ that represents the number of boxes of baseballs the coach will pay for. (Assume at least 5 boxes and less than 10 boxes of baseballs are purchased.)

c. Find $\left(\frac{C}{N}\right)(x)$ and explain what this function represents. (Assume at least 5 boxes of baseballs are purchased.)

d. If the coach orders 5 boxes of baseballs, what is the average cost per box of baseballs?

12. MODELING The total cost of producing x photo greeting cards is given by the function $f(x) = 0.8x + 25$. Write a function showing $\left(\frac{f}{g}\right)(x)$, where $g(x) = x$. What does this new function model?

Examples 4 and 5

For each pair of functions, find $f \circ g$ and $g \circ f$, if they exist. State the domain and range for each.

13. $f = \{(-8, -4), (0, 4), (2, 6), (-6, -2)\}$
$g = \{(4, -4), (-2, -1), (-4, 0), (6, -5)\}$

14. $f = \{(-7, 0), (4, 5), (8, 12), (-3, 6)\}$
$g = \{(6, 8), (-12, -5), (0, 5), (5, 1)\}$

15. $f = \{(5, 13), (-4, -2), (-8, -11), (3, 1)\}$
$g = \{(-8, 2), (-4, 1), (3, -3), (5, 7)\}$

16. $f = \{(-4, -14), (0, -6), (-6, -18), (2, -2)\}$
$g = \{(-6, 1), (-18, 13), (-14, 9), (-2, -3)\}$

Find $[f \circ g](x)$ and $[g \circ f](x)$, if they exist. State the domain and range for each.

17. $f(x) = 2x$
$g(x) = x + 5$

18. $f(x) = -3x$
$g(x) = -x + 8$

19. $f(x) = x + 5$
$g(x) = 3x - 7$

20. $f(x) = x - 4$
$g(x) = x^2 - 10$

21. $f(x) = x^2 + 6x - 2$
$g(x) = x - 6$

22. $f(x) = 2x^2 - x + 1$
$g(x) = 4x + 3$

Example 6

23. COST Mr. Rivera wants to purchase a riding lawn mower, which is on sale for 15% off the original price of $3000. The sales tax is 6.5%. Write two functions representing the price after the discount $p(x)$ and the price after sales tax $t(x)$. Write a composition of functions that represents the price of the riding lawn mower. How much will Mr. Rivera pay for the riding lawn mower?

24. SALE Mrs. Sanchez wants to purchase a camper, which is on sale for 10% off the original price of $85,000. At the same time, the manufacturer is offering a $2500 rebate on all new campers. Will the final price be lower if the discount is applied before the rebate or if the rebate is applied before the discount?

25. LAVA The temperature of lava has been measured at up to 2000°F. A freshly ejected lava rock immediately begins to cool down. The temperature of the lava rock in degrees Fahrenheit as a function of time is given by $T(t)$. Let $C(F)$ be the function that gives degrees Celsius as a function of degrees Fahrenheit. What function gives the temperature of the lava rock in degrees Celsius as a function of time?

26. ENGINEERING A group of engineers is designing a staple gun. One team determines that the speed of impact s of the staple (in feet per second) as a function of the handle length ℓ (in inches) is given by $s(\ell) = 40 + 3\ell$. A second team determines that the number of sheets N that can be stapled as a function of the impact speed is given by $N(s) = \frac{s - 10}{3}$. What function gives N as a function of ℓ?

Mixed Exercises

Let $f(x) = 3$ and $g(x) = \frac{5}{x}$.

27. Find $(f + g)(x)$.

28. Find $(f - g)(x)$.

29. Find $(f \cdot g)(x)$.

30. Find $\left(\frac{f}{g}\right)(x)$.

Name ______________________ Period ____________ Date ____________

For each pair of functions, find $f \circ g$ and $g \circ f$ if they exist.

31. $f = \{(0, 0), (4, -2)\}$
$g = \{(0, 4), (-2, 0), (5, 0)\}$

32. $f = \{(0, -3), (1, 2), (2, 2)\}$
$g = \{(-3, 1), (2, 0)\}$

33. $f = \{(-4, 3), (-1, 1), (2, 2)\}$
$g = \{(1, -4), (2, -1), (3, -1)\}$

34. $f = \{(6, 6), (-3, -3), (1, 3)\}$
$g = \{(-3, 6), (3, 6), (6, -3)\}$

Find $[g \circ h](x)$ and $[h \circ g](x)$ if they exist.

35. $g(x) = 2x$
$h(x) = x + 2$

36. $g(x) = -3x$
$h(x) = 4x - 1$

37. $g(x) = x - 6$
$h(x) = x + 6$

38. $g(x) = x - 3$
$h(x) = x^2$

39. $g(x) = 5x$
$h(x) = x^2 + x - 1$

40. $g(x) = x + 2$
$h(x) = 2x^2 - 3$

If $f(x) = 3x$, $g(x) = x + 4$, and $h(x) = x^2 - 1$, find each value.

41. $f[g(1)]$

42. $g[h(0)]$

43. $g[f(-1)]$

44. $h[f(5)]$

45. $g[h(-3)]$

46. $h[f(10)]$

47. $f[h(8)]$

48. $[f \circ (h \circ g)](1)$

49. $[f \circ (g \circ h)](-2)$

50. $h[f(-6)]$

51. $f[h(0)]$

52. $f[g(7)]$

53. $f[h(-2)]$

54. $[g \circ (f \circ h)](-1)$

55. $[h \circ (f \circ g)](3)$

56. **AREA** Valeria wants to know the area of a figure made by joining an equilateral triangle and square along an edge. The function $f(s) = \frac{\sqrt{3}}{4}s^2$ gives the area of an equilateral triangle with side s. The function $g(s) =$ gives the area of a square with side s. What function $h(s)$ gives the area of the figure as a function of its side length s?

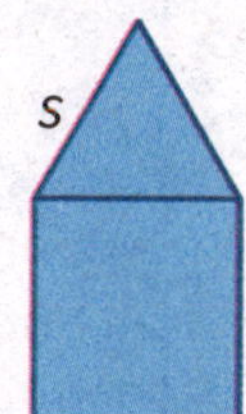

57. **PRICING** A computer company adjusts the pricing of, and discounts to, its newest model, in an effort to remain competitive. The function $P(t)$ gives the sale price of the new model as a function of time. The function $D(t)$ gives the value of a special discount offered to valued customers. How much would valued customers have to pay for their newest model computer?

58. **MODELING** Hannah and Terryl went on a one-hour hot air balloon ride. Let $T(A)$ be the outside air temperature as a function of altitude and let $A(t)$ be the altitude of the balloon as a function of time.

a. What function describes the air temperature Hannah and Terryl felt at different times during their trip?

b. Sketch a graph of the function you wrote for **part a** based on the table for $T(A)$ and the graph of $A(t)$.

Altitude (km)	Temperature (°F)
0	60
1	55
2	53
3	50
4	45
5	43
6	40

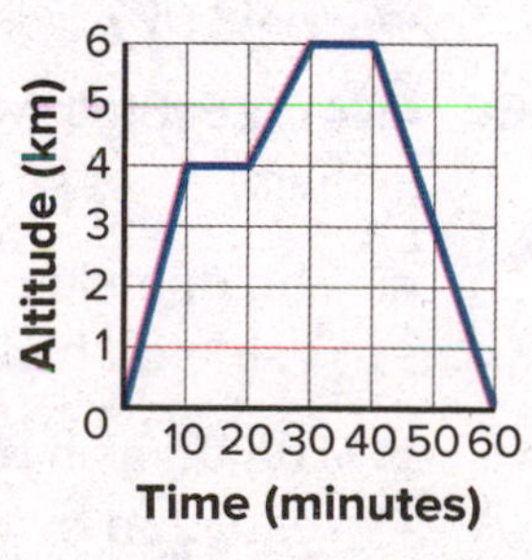

59. **REASONING** The National Center for Education Statistics reports data showing that since 2006, college enrollment for men (in thousands) can be modeled by $f(x) = 389x + 7500$, where x represents the number of years since 2006. Similarly, enrollment for women can be modeled by $g(x) = 480x + 10{,}075$. Write a function for $(f + g)(x)$ and interpret what it represents.

60. **STRUCTURE** Jasper is raising money for a local charity by making and selling cupcakes. The cost of making x cupcakes can be represented by $C(x) = 0.625x$, and his revenue from selling x cupcakes can be represented by $R(x) = 3.45x$. Explain what these functions must mean about Jasper's cupcakes. Then write a function that represents his profit. Explain your reasoning.

61. **STRUCTURE** The table shows various values of functions $f(x)$, $g(x)$, and $h(x)$.

x	−1	0	1	2	3	4
$f(x)$	7	−2	0	2	4	1
$g(x)$	−3	−4	−5	0	1	1
$h(x)$	0	4	1	1	5	5

Use the table to find the following values:

$(f + g)(-1)$ $\quad$ $(h - g)(0)$ $\quad$ $(f \cdot h)(4)$

$\left(\frac{f}{g}\right)(3)$ $\quad$ $\left(\frac{g}{h}\right)(2)$ $\quad$ $\left(\frac{g}{f}\right)(1)$

62. **STRUCTURE** If $(f + g)(3) = 5$ and $(f \cdot g)(3) = 6$, find $f(3)$ and $g(3)$. Explain.

63. **CREATE** Write two functions $f(x)$ and $g(x)$ such that $(f \circ g)(4) = 0$.

64. **FIND THE ERROR** Chris and Tobias are finding $(f \circ g)(x)$, where $f(x) = x^2 + 2x - 8$ and $g(x) = x^2 + 8$. Is either of them correct? Explain your reasoning.

Chris

$$\begin{aligned}(f \circ g)(x) &= f[g(x)]\\ &= (x^2+8)^2 + 2x - 8\\ &= x^4 + 16x^2 + 64 + 2x - 8\\ &= x^4 + 16x^2 + 2x + 58\end{aligned}$$

Tobias

$$\begin{aligned}(f \circ g)(x) &= f[g(x)]\\ &= (x^2+8)^2 + 2(x^2+8) - 8\\ &= x^4 + 16x^2 + 64 + 2x^2 + 16 - 8\\ &= x^4 + 18x^2 + 72\end{aligned}$$

65. **PERSEVERE** Given $f(x) = \sqrt{x^3}$ and $g(x) = \sqrt{x^6}$, determine each domain.

a. $g(x) \cdot g(x)$ $\quad$ **b.** $f(x) \cdot f(x)$

66. **ANALYZE** State whether each statement is *sometimes*, *always*, or *never* true. Explain.

a. The domain of two functions $f(x)$ and $g(x)$ that are composed $g[f(x)]$ is restricted by the domain of $f(x)$.

b. The domain of two functions $f(x)$ and $g(x)$ that are composed $g[f(x)]$ is restricted by the domain of $g(x)$.

67. **WRITE** In the real world, why would you perform a composition of functions?

Inverse Relations and Functions

Today's Standards
F.IF.5, F.BF.4a
MP2, MP6

Today's Vocabulary
inverse relations
inverse functions

Explore Graphs of Inverse Functions

Online Activity Use graphing technology to complete the Explore.

INQUIRY For what values of n will $f(x) = x^n$ have an inverse that is also a function?

Learn Inverse Relations and Functions and Restricted Domains

Two functions f and g are **inverse functions** if and only if both of their compositions are the identity function.

Key Concepts • Inverse Functions

Words: If f and f^{-1} are inverses, then $f(a) = b$ if and only if $f^{-1}(b) = a$.

Example: Let $f(x) = x - 5$ and represent its inverse as $f^{-1}(x) = x + 5$.

Evaluate $f(7)$.	Evaluate $f^{-1}(2)$.
$f(x) = x - 5$	$f^{-1}(x) = x + 5$
$f(7) = 7 - 5$ or 2	$f^{-1}(2) = 2 + 5$ or 7

Because $f(x)$ and $f^{-1}(x)$ are inverses, $f(7) = 2$ and $f^{-1}(2) = 7$.

If a function fails the horizontal line test, you can restrict the domain of the function to make the inverse a function. Choose a portion of the domain on which the function is one-to-one. There may be more than one possible domain.

Think About It!
Write a function that does not pass the horizontal line test.

Example 1 Find an Inverse Relation

GEOMETRY The vertices △*ABC* of can be represented by the relation {(2, 4), (−3, 2), (4, 1)}. Find the inverse of the relation. Graph both the original relation and its inverse.

Step 1 Graph the relation.
Graph the ordered pairs and connect the points to form a triangle.

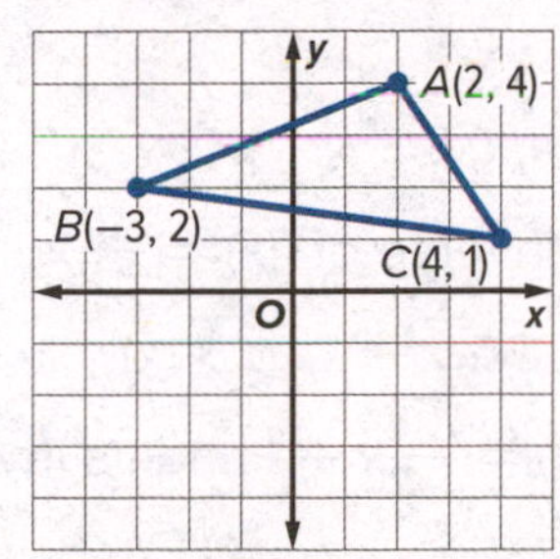

(continued on the next page)

Go Online You can complete an Extra Example online.

Your Notes

Think About It!

Describe the graph of the inverse relation.

Study Tip:

Inverses If $f^{-1}(x)$ is the inverse of $f(x)$, the graph of $f^{-1}(x)$ will be a reflection of the graph of $f(x)$ in the line $y = x$.

Go Online

You can learn how to graph a relation and its inverse on a graphing calculator by watching the video online.

Step 2 Find the inverse. To find the inverse, exchange the coordinates of the orderedpairs.

{(4, ____), (2, ____), (1, ____)}

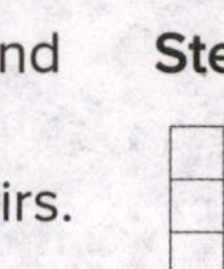

Step 3 Graph the inverse.

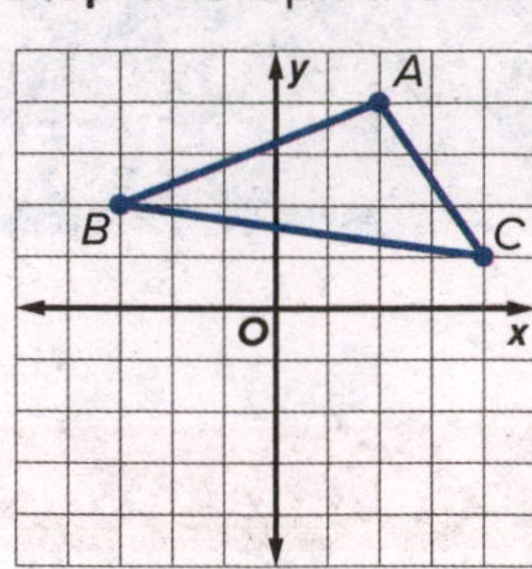

Example 2 Inverse Functions

Find the inverse of $f(x) = 3x + 2$. Then graph the function and its inverse.

Step 1 Rewrite the function.

Rewrite the function as an equation relating x and y.

$\_\_\_ = 3x + 2$

Step 2 Exchange x and y.

Exchange x and y in the equation.

$\_\_\_ = 3y + 2$

Step 3 Solve for y.

$$x = 3y + 2$$

$$x \_\_\_ = 3y$$

$$\frac{x-2}{\_\_\_} = y$$

Step 4 Replace y with $f^{-1}(x)$.

Replace y with $f^{-1}(x)$ in the equation.

$y = \frac{x-2}{3}$ $\_\_\_\_ = \frac{x-2}{3}$

The inverse of $f(x) = 3x + 2$ is $f^{-1}(x) = \frac{x-2}{3}$.

Step 5 Graph $f(x)$ and $f^{-1}(x)$.

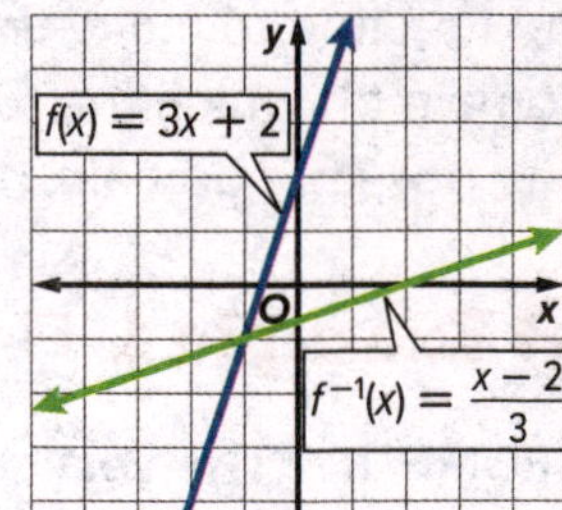

Check

Examine $f(x) = -\frac{1}{2}x + 1$.

Part A Find the inverse of $f(x) = -\frac{1}{2}x + 1$.

$f^{-1}(x) = \_\_\_\_x + \_\_\_\_$

Part B Graph $f(x) = -\frac{1}{2}x + 1$ and its inverse.

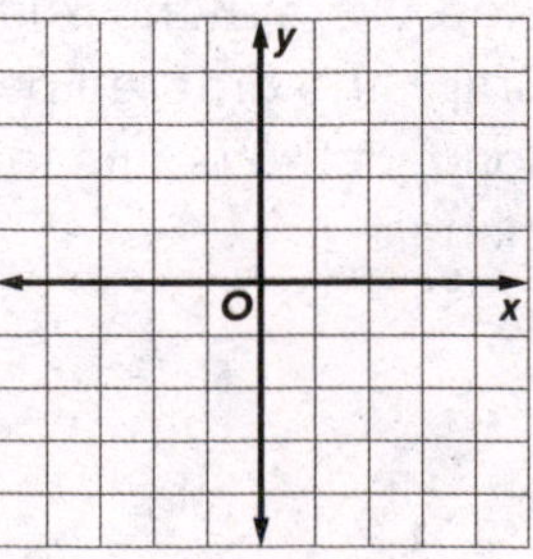

Go Online You can complete an Extra Example online.

Example 3 Inverses with Restricted Domains

Examine $f(x) = x^2 + 2x + 4$.

Part A Find the inverse of $f(x)$.

$f(x) = x^2 + 2x + 4$	Original function
$\_\_\_ = x^2 + 2x + 4$	Replace $f^{-1}(x)$ with y.
$\_\_\_ = \_\_\_^2 + 2\_\_\_ + 4$	Exchange x and y.
$x\,\_\_\_ = y^2 + 2y$	Subtract 4 from each side.
$x - 4 + 1 = y^2 + 2y + 1$	Complete the square.
$x - 3 = (\_\_\_\_\_)^2$	Simplify.
$\_\_\_\sqrt{x-3} = y + 1$	Take the square root of each side.
$\_\_\_ \pm \sqrt{x-3} = y$	Subtract 1 from each side.
$f^{-1}(x) = -1 \pm \sqrt{x-3}$	Replace y with $f^{-1}(x)$.

Part B If necessary, restrict the domain of the inverse so that it is a function.

Because $f(x)$ fails the horizontal line test, $f^{-1}(x)$ is not a function. Find the restricted domain of $f(x)$ so that $f^{-1}(x)$ will be a function. Look for a portion of the graph that is one-to-one. If the domain of $f(x)$ is restricted to $(-\infty, \_\_\_]$, then the inverse is $f^{-1}(x) = -1 + \sqrt{x-3}$.

If the domain of $f(x)$ is restricted to $[\_\_\_, \infty)$, then the inverse is $f^{-1}(x) = -1 - \sqrt{x-3}$.

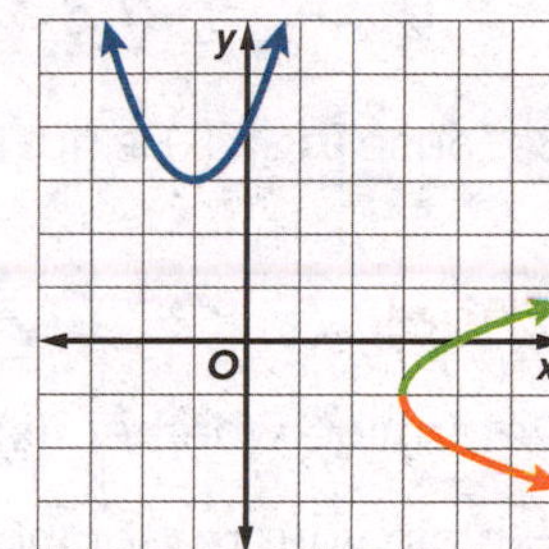

Example 4 Interpret Inverse Functions

TEMPERATURE A formula for converting a temperature in degrees Fahrenheit to degrees Celsius is $T(x) = \frac{5}{9}(x - 32)$.

Part A Find the inverse of $T(x)$, and describe its meaning.

$T(x) = \frac{5}{9}(x - 32)$	Original function
$\_\_\_ = \frac{5}{9}(x - 32)$	Replace $T(x)$ with y.
$\_\_\_ = \frac{5}{9}(\quad - 32)$	Exchange x and y.
$\frac{9x}{5} = \_\_\_\_\_$	Multiply each side by $\frac{9}{5}$.
$\frac{9x}{5}\,\_\_\_\_ = y$	Add 32 to each side.
$T^{-1}(x) = \_\_\_\_\_$	Replace y with $T^{-1}(x)$.

$T^{-1}(x) =$ can be used to convert a temperature in degrees Celsius to degrees Fahrenheit.

Go Online You can complete an Extra Example online.

Watch Out!

f^{-1} is read *f inverse* or *the inverse of f*. Note that -1 is not an exponent.

Go Online to see Part B of the example on interpreting inverse functions.

Think About It!

Find the domain of $T(x)$ and its inverse. Explain your reasoning.

Think About It!

If $j(x)$ and $k(x)$ are inverses, find $[k \circ j](x)$.

Watch Out!

Compositions of Functions Be sure to check both $[f \circ g](x)$ and $[g \circ f](x)$ to verify that functions are inverses. By definition, both compositions must result in the identity function.

Go Online to see **part a** of the example on verifying inverse functions.

Talk About It

Find the domain of the inverse, and describe its meaning in the context of the situation.

Study Tip:

Inverse Functions V and r are inverse functions because $V(r) = V$ and $r(V) = r$.

Learn Verifying Inverses

Key Concept • Inverse Functions

Words: Two functions f and g are inverse functions if and only if both of their compositions are the identity function.

Symbols: $f(x)$ and $g(x)$ are inverses if and only if $[f \circ g](x) = x$ and $[g \circ f](x) = x$.

Example 5 Use Compositions to Verify Inverses

Determine whether the functions are inverse functions.

b. $h(x) = \sqrt{x + 13}$ **and** $k(x) = (x - 13)^2$

Find $[h \circ k](x)$.

$$[h \circ k](x) = h[k(x)]$$
$$= h[\underline{\qquad\qquad}]$$
$$= \sqrt{(x - 13)^2 \qquad\qquad}$$
$$= \sqrt{x^2 - 26x \qquad\qquad + 13}$$
$$= \sqrt{x^2 \qquad\qquad + 182}$$

Because $[h \circ k](x)$ is not the identity function, $h(x)$ and $k(x)$ are ____ inverses.

Check

Determine whether $f(x) = \frac{x}{9} + \frac{4}{3}$ and $g(x) = 9x + 12$ are inverses.

Explain your reasoning. ______________________________

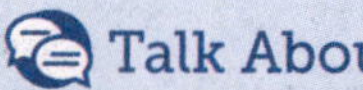

Example 6 Verify Inverse Functions

GEOMETRY **The formula for the volume of a cylinder with a height of 5 inches is $V = 5\pi r^2$. Determine whether $r = \sqrt{\frac{V}{5\pi}}$ is the inverse of the original function.**

$V = 5\pi r^2$	$r = \sqrt{\frac{V}{5\pi}}$
$= 5\pi(\qquad)^2$	$= \sqrt{\frac{\qquad}{5\pi}}$
$= 5\pi\left(\frac{V}{5\pi}\right)$	$= \sqrt{r^2}$
$= \underline{\qquad}$	$= \underline{\qquad}$

$r = \sqrt{\frac{V}{5\pi}}$ is the inverse of $V = 5\pi r^2$.

Go Online You can complete an Extra Example online.

Name ______________________ Period ________ Date ________

Practice

Go Online You can complete your homework online.

Example 1

1. **GEOMETRY** The vertices of $\triangle MNP$ can be represented by the relation {(−8, 6), (6, −2), (4, −6)}. Find the inverse of the relation. Graph both the original relation and its inverse.

2. **GEOMETRY** The vertices of $\triangle XYZ$ can be represented by the relation {(7, 7), (4, 9), (3, −7)}. Find the inverse of the relation. Graph both the original relation and its inverse.

3. **GEOMETRY** The vertices of trapezoid *QRST* can be represented by the relation {(8, −1), (−8, −1), (−2, −8), (2, −8)}. Find the inverse of the relation. Graph both the original relation and its inverse.

4. **GEOMETRY** The vertices of quadrilateral *FGHJ* can be represented by the relation {(4, 3), (−4, −4), (−3, −5), (5, 2)}. Find the inverse of the relation. Graph both the original relation and its inverse.

Examples 2 and 3

Find the inverse of each function. Then graph the function and its inverse. If necessary, restrict the domain of the inverse so that it is a function.

5. $f(x) = x + 2$

6. $g(x) = 5x$

7. $f(x) = -2x + 1$

8. $h(x) = \frac{x - 4}{3}$

9. $f(x) = -\frac{5}{3}x - 8$

10. $g(x) = x + 4$

11. $f(x) = 4x$

12. $f(x) = -8x + 9$

13. $f(x) = 5x^2$

14. $h(x) = x^2 + 4$

Example 4

15. **MODELING** The function $f(x) = 0.8x$ gives the discounted price for any original price x. Determine the inverse for this function. Then interpret what the function and its inverse mean in the context of this situation. What is the discount percentage?

16. **MODELING** An artificial pond has two inlet pipes and one outlet pipe. If all the pipes are working, the pond has at least 120 cubic meters of water. Each inlet pipe brings in 30 cubic meters of water per hour and the outlet pipe drains away 20 cubic meters per hour. The relationship between the volume of water in cubic meters $V(h)$ and the time in hours h is given by $V(h) = (2 \cdot 30 - 20)h + 120$. Determine the inverse for this function. Then interpret what the inverse means in the context of the situation.

Examples 5 and 6

Determine whether each pair of functions are inverse functions. Write *yes* or *no*.

17. $f(x) = x - 1$

$g(x) = 1 - x$

18. $f(x) = 2x + 3$

$g(x) = \frac{1}{2}(x - 3)$

19. $f(x) = 5x - 5$

$g(x) = \frac{1}{5}x + 1$

20. $f(x) = 2x$

$g(x) = \frac{1}{2}x$

21. $h(x) = 6x - 2$

$g(x) = \frac{1}{6}x + 3$

22. $f(x) = 8x - 10$

$g(x) = \frac{1}{8}x + \frac{5}{4}$

23. **GEOMETRY** The formula for the volume of a right circular cone with a height of 2 feet is $V = \frac{2}{3}\pi r^2$. Is $r = \sqrt{\frac{3v}{2\pi}}$ the inverse of the original function?

24. **GEOMETRY** The formula for the area of a trapezoid is $A = \frac{h}{2}(a + b)$. Is $h = 2A - (a + b)$ the inverse of the original function?

Mixed Exercises

The inverse of each relation is given. Find the original relation.

25. $\{(3, 1), (4, -3), (8, -3)\}$

26. $\{(-7, 1), (0, 5), (5, -1)\}$

27. $\{(-10, -2), (-7, 6), (-4, -2), (-4, 0)\}$

28. $\{(0, -9), (5, -3), (6, 6), (8, -3)\}$

29. $\{(-4, 12), (0, 7), (9, -1), (10, -5)\}$

30. $\{(-4, 1), (-4, 3), (0, -8), (8, -9)\}$

Find the inverse of each function. Then graph the function and its inverse. If necessary, restrict the domain of the inverse so that it is a function.

31. $y = 4$

32. $f(x) = 3x$

33. $f(x) = x + 2$

34. $g(x) = 2x - 1$

35. $h(x) = \frac{1}{4}x$

36. $y = \frac{2}{3}x + 2$

37. $f(x) = \frac{1}{2}x^2 - 1$

38. $f(x) = (x + 1)^2 + 3$

Determine whether each pair of functions are inverse functions. Write *yes* or *no*.

39. $f(x) = \frac{1}{2}x + 5$

$g(x) = 2x - 10$

40. $f(x) = \frac{x + 10}{8}$

$g(x) = 8x - 10$

Name ______________________ Period ____________ Date ____________

41. $f(x) = 4x^2$

$g(x) = \frac{1}{2}\sqrt{x}$

42. $f(x) = \frac{1}{3}x^2 + 1$

$g(x) = \sqrt{3x - 3}$

43. $f(x) = x^2 - 9$

$g(x) = x + 3$

44. $f(x) = \frac{2}{3}x^3$

$g(x) = \sqrt{\frac{2}{3}x}$

45. $f(x) = (x + 6)^2$

$g(x) = \sqrt{x} - 6$

46. $f(x) = 2\sqrt{x - 5}$

$g(x) = \frac{1}{4}x^2 - 5$

Use the horizontal line test to determine whether the inverse of each function is also a function.

47. $f(x) = 2x^2$

48. $f(x) = x^3 - 8$

49. $g(x) = x^4 - 6x^2 + 1$

50. $h(x) = 2x^4 - x - 2$

51. $g(x) = x^5 + x^2 - 4x$

52. $h(x) = x^3 + x^2 - 6x + 12$

53. VOLUME Jason wants to make a spherical water cooler that can hold half a cubic meter of water. He knows that $V = \frac{4}{3}\pi r^3$, but he needs to know how to find r given V. Find this inverse function.

54. EXERCISE Alex began a new exercise routine. To gain the maximum benefit from his exercise, Alex calculated his maximum target heart rate using the function $f(x) = 0.85(220 - x)$, where x represents his age. Find the inverse of this function.

55. ROCKETS The altitude of a rocket in feet as a function of time is given by $f(t) = 49t^2$, where $t \geq 0$. Find the inverse of this function and determine the times when the rocket will be 10, 100, and 1000 feet high. Round your answers to the nearest hundredth of a second.

56. The function graphed in the figure is its own inverse. Extend the graph for values of x between -7 and 2.

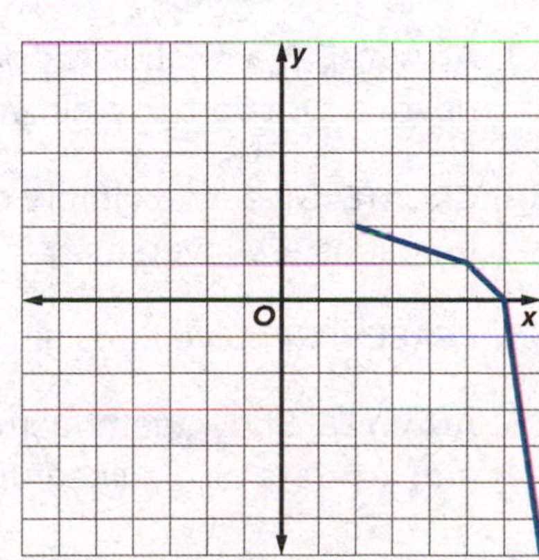

57. PLANETS The approximate distance of a planet from the Sun is

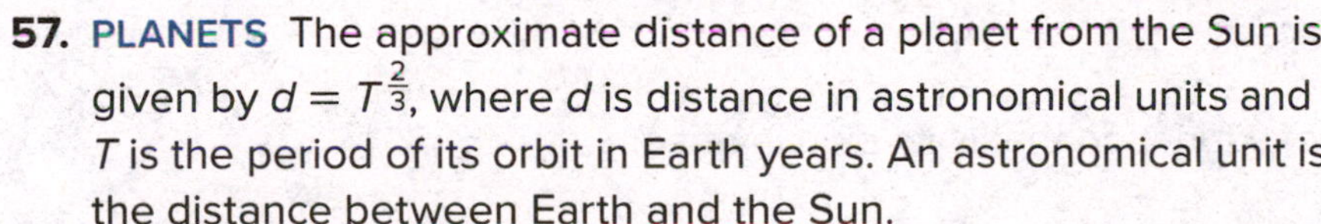

given by $d = T^{\frac{2}{3}}$, where d is distance in astronomical units and T is the period of its orbit in Earth years. An astronomical unit is the distance between Earth and the Sun.

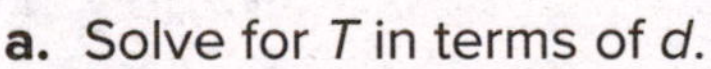

a. Solve for T in terms of d.

b. Pluto is about 39.44 times as far from the Sun as Earth. About how many years does it take Pluto to orbit the Sun?

58. a. MODELING The diagram shows an open box made from a sheet of metal with squares of side length x removed from each corner. Write and graph the function $V(x)$ which gives the volume of the open box. Explain how the domain of this function must be restricted to make sense within the context of this scenario.

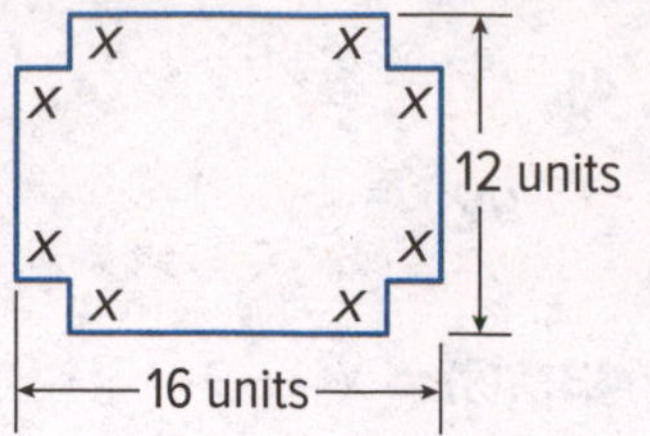

b. REASONING Does restricting the domain to $0 \leq x \leq 6$ in **part a** allow for the inverse to also be a function? How do you know?

59. ARGUMENTS Consider a real-world example in which an object is thrown upward with an initial velocity of v_0. Its height above the ground can be expressed as a function of time using $h(t) = v_0t - 16t^2$. Explain why this real-world function cannot have an inverse function and what restrictions would need to be placed on it to ensure that an inverse function exists.

60. STRUCTURE Show that $f(x) = 4x^3$ and $g(x) = \sqrt[3]{\frac{x}{4}}$ are inverses of each other.

61. REGULARITY Graph the function $f(x) = -\frac{3}{4}x + 5$, its inverse, and $y = x$. Write the equation of the inverse. Compare the slopes and y-intercepts. Can you come to a conclusion regarding the relationship between the slope and y-intercept of a linear function and its inverse?

62. Explore the relationship between $(f + g)^{-1}(x)$ and $f^{-1}(x) + g^{-1}(x)$.

x	0	1	2	3
$f(x)$	0	3	1	4
$g(x)$	1	0	4	3

a. STRUCTURE Suppose that functions $f(x)$, $g(x)$, and $(f + g)(x)$ all have inverse functions on the domain [0, 3]. Consider the following table of values. Calculate the following values.

$f^{-1}(3) + g^{-1}(3) =$ $\qquad$ $f^{-1}(1) + g^{-1}(1) =$

b. STRUCTURE Find $(f + g)(1)$. Use this to find $(f + g)^{-1}(3)$. Find $(f + g)(0)$. Use this to find $(f + g)^{-1}(1)$.

c. ARGUMENTS Jonathan claims that $(f + g)^{-1}(x) = f^{-1}(x) + g^{-1}(x)$ and $(f + g)^{-1}(x) = f^{-1}(x) + g^{-1}(x)$. Use **part b** to explain why he cannot be correct.

d. PRECISION Consider the functions $f(x) = 2x + 1$ and $g(x) = 2x - 1$. Find $(f + g)^{-1}(x)$ and $f^{-1}(x) + g^{-1}(x)$. Are they the same?

63. ANALYZE If a relation is not a function, then its inverse is *sometimes*, *always*, or *never* a function. Explain your reasoning.

64. CREATE Give an example of a function and its inverse. Verify that the two functions are inverses.

65. PERSEVERE Give an example of a function that is its own inverse.

66. ANALYZE Show that the inverse of a linear function $y = mx + b$, where $m \neq 0$ and $x \neq b$, is also a linear function.

67. WRITE Suppose you have a composition of two functions that are inverses. When you put in a value of 5 for x, why is the result always 5?

nth Roots and Rational Exponents

Today's Standards
A.SSE.2
MP2, MP6, MP7

Today's Vocabulary
index
radicand
principal root
exponential form
radical form
rational exponent

Explore Inverses of Power Functions

Online Activity Use a calculator to complete the Explore.

INQUIRY What conjectures can you make about $f(x) = x^n$ and $g(x) = \sqrt[n]{x}$ for all odd positive values of n?

Learn nth Roots

Finding the square root of a number and squaring a number are inverse operations. To find the square root of a, you must find a number with a square of a. The inverse of raising a number to the nth power is finding the ***n*th root** of a number. The symbol $\sqrt[n]{}$ indicates an nth root.

For any real numbers a and b and any positive integer n, if $a^n = b$, then a is an nth root of b. For example, because $(-2)^6 = 64$, -2 is a sixth root of 64 and 2 is a principal root.

An example of an nth root is $\sqrt[n]{36}$, which is read as *the nth root of 36*. In this example, n is the **index** and 36 is the **radicand**, or the expression under the radical symbol.

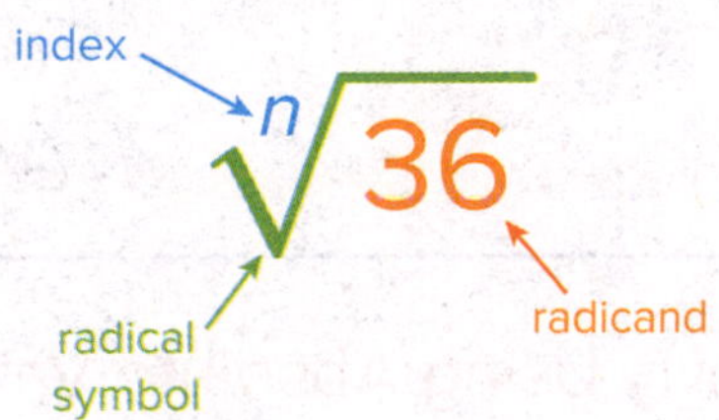

Some numbers have more than one real nth root. For example, 16 has two square roots, 4 and -4, since 4^2 and $(-4)^2$ both equal 16. When there is more than one real root and n is even, the nonnegative root is called the **principal root**.

Suppose n is an integer greater than 1, a is a real number, and a is an nth root of b.

a	n is even.	n is odd.
$a > 0$	1 unique positive and 1 unique negative real root: $\pm\sqrt[n]{a}$	1 unique positive and 0 negative real root: $\sqrt[n]{a}$
$a < 0$	0 real roots	0 positive and 1 negative real root: $\sqrt[n]{a}$
$a = 0$	1 real root: $\sqrt[n]{0} = 0$	1 real root: $\sqrt[n]{0} = 0$

Think About It!

Lorena says he can tell that $\sqrt[3]{-64}$ will have a real root without graphing. Do you agree or disagree? Explain your reasoning.

Math History Minute:

Christoff Rudolff (1499–1543) wrote the first German algebra textbook. It is believed that he introduced the radical symbol $\sqrt{}$ in 1525 in his book *Die Coss*. Some feel that this symbol was used because it resembled a small *r*, the first letter in the Latin word *radix* or root.

Your Notes

> **Watch Out!**
> **Principal Roots** Because $5^2 = 25$, 25 has two square roots, 5 and -5. However, the value of $\sqrt{25}$ is 5 only. To indicate both square roots and not just the principal square root, the expression must be written as $\pm\sqrt{25}$.

> **Talk About It**
> Compare the simplified expressions in the previous example with the ones in this example. Explain why the simplified expressions in this example require absolute value bars when the simplified expressions in the previous example did not.

Example 1 Find Roots

Simplify.

a. $\pm\sqrt{25x^4}$

$$\pm\sqrt{25x^4} = \pm\sqrt{(\quad)^2}$$
$$= \pm \_\_\_\_$$

b. $-\sqrt{(y^2+7)^{12}}$

$$-\sqrt{(y^2+7)^{12}} = -\sqrt{[(y^2+7)^6]}$$
$$= (y^2+7)$$

c. $\sqrt[3]{343a^{18}b^6}$

$$\sqrt[3]{343a^{18}b^6} = \sqrt[3]{(7a\ \ b\ \ )}$$
$$= 7a\ \ b$$

d. $\sqrt{-289c^8d^4}$

There are no real roots of $\sqrt{-289}$. However, there are two imaginary roots, $17i$ and $-17i$. Because we are only finding the principal square root, use $17i$.

$$\sqrt{-289c^8d^4} = \sqrt{\quad} \cdot \sqrt{289c^8d^4}$$
$$= \_\_ \cdot \sqrt{289c^8d^4}$$
$$= \quad ic\ \ d$$

Check

Write the simplified form of each expression.

$\pm\sqrt{196x^4}$ $\qquad$ $-\sqrt{196x^4}$

$\sqrt{-196x^4}$ $\qquad$ $\sqrt[3]{2744x^6y^6}$

Example 2 Simplify Using Absolute Value

Simplify.

a. $\sqrt[4]{81x^4}$

$$\sqrt[4]{81x^4} = \sqrt[4]{(3x)^4}$$
$$= \_\_|\_\_|$$

Since x could be negative, you must use the absolute value of x to ensure that the principal square root is nonnegative.

b. $\sqrt[8]{256(y^2-2)^{24}}$

$$\sqrt[8]{256(y^2-2)^{24}} = \sqrt[8]{\quad} \cdot \sqrt[8]{(y^2-2)^{24}}$$
$$= \_\_|(y^2-2)\ \ |$$

Since $(y^2-2)^3$ could be negative, you must use the absolute value of $(y^2-2)^3$ to ensure that the principal square root is nonnegative.

Go Online You can complete an Extra Example online.

Learn Rational Exponents

For any real number b and a positive integer n, $b^{\frac{1}{n}} = \sqrt[n]{b}$, except where $b < 0$ and n is even. When $b < 0$ and n is even, a complex root may exist.

Examples: $125^{\frac{1}{3}} = \sqrt[3]{125}$ or 5 $\quad (-49)^{\frac{1}{2}} = \sqrt{-49}$ or $7i$

The expression $b^{\frac{1}{n}}$ has a **rational exponent**. The rules for exponents also apply to rational exponents.

For any nonzero number b and any integers x and y, with $y > 1$, $b^{\frac{x}{y}} = \sqrt[y]{b^x} = \left(\sqrt[y]{b}\right)^x$, except when $b < 0$ and y is even. When $b < 0$ and y is even, a complex root may exist.

Examples: $125^{\frac{2}{3}} = \left(\sqrt[3]{125}\right)^2 = 5^2$ or 25

$(-49)^{\frac{3}{2}} = (\sqrt{-49})^3 = (7i)^3$ or $-343i$

Key Concept • Simplest Form of Expressions with Rational Exponents

An expression with rational exponents is in simplest form when all of the following conditions are met.

- It has no negative exponents.
- It has no exponents that are not positive integers in the denominator.
- It is not a complex fraction.
- The index of any remaining radical is the least number possible.

Example 3 Radical and Exponential Forms

Simplify.

a. Write $x^{\frac{4}{3}}$ in radical form.

$x^{\frac{4}{3}} = \sqrt{x}$

b. Write $\sqrt[5]{x^2}$ in exponential form.

$\sqrt[5]{x^2} = x$

Think About It!

Write two equivalent expressions, one in radical form and one in exponential form.

Example 4 Use Rational Exponents

FINANCIAL LITERACY The expression $c(1 + r)^t$ can be used to estimate the future cost of an item due to inflation, where c represents the current cost of the item, r represents the annual rate of inflation, and t represents the time in years. Write the expression in radical form for the future cost of an item 3 months from now if the annual rate of inflation is 4.7%.

$c(1 + r)^t = c(1 + 0.047)^{\frac{1}{4}}$ $\quad r = 0.047, t = \frac{1}{4}$

$= c(\underline{\qquad\qquad})^{\frac{1}{4}}$ $\quad$ Add.

$= c\sqrt{0.047}$ $\quad b^{\frac{1}{n}} = \sqrt[n]{b}$

Think About It!

Why did you set t equal to $\frac{1}{4}$?

 Go Online You can complete an Extra Example online.

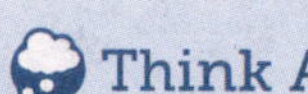

Think About It!

How can you tell if $x^{\frac{y}{z}}$ will simplify to an integer?

Go Online to see more examples of evaluating expressions with rational exponents.

Watch Out!

Exponents Recall that when you multiply powers, the exponents are added, and when you raise a power to a power, the exponents are multiplied.

Think About It!

How would the expression in **part c** change if the exponents were $\frac{1}{3}$ and $-\frac{3}{4}$?

Go Online You can complete an Extra Example online.

Example 5 Evaluate Expressions with Rational Exponents

Evaluate $32^{-\frac{2}{5}}$.

$32^{-\frac{2}{5}} = \frac{1}{32^{\frac{2}{5}}}$ $\quad b^{-n} = \frac{1}{b^n}$

$= \frac{1}{(2\ \ )^{\frac{2}{5}}}$ $\quad 32 = 2^5$

$= \frac{1}{2^{\ \frac{2}{5}}}$ $\quad$ Power of a Power

$= \frac{1}{2}$ or $\frac{1}{4}$ $\quad$ Multiply the exponents.

Check

Evaluate each expression.

$512^{\frac{1}{3}}$ ______ $\quad 16^{\frac{5}{4}}$ ______ $\quad 128^{-\frac{2}{7}}$ ______

Example 6 Simplify Expressions with Rational Exponents

Simplify each expression.

a. $64^{-\frac{1}{6}}$

$64^{-\frac{1}{6}} = \frac{1}{64^{\frac{1}{6}}}$ $\quad b^{-n} = \frac{1}{b^n}$

$= \frac{1}{(2^6)^{\frac{1}{6}}}$ $\quad 64 = 2^6$

$= \frac{1}{2^{6\cdot\frac{1}{6}}}$ or $\frac{1}{2}$ $\quad$ Power of a Power

b. $y^{-\frac{2}{3}}$

$y^{-\frac{2}{3}} = \frac{\ }{y^{\frac{2}{3}}}$ $\quad b^{-n} = \frac{1}{b^n}$

$= \frac{1}{y^{\frac{2}{3}}} \cdot \frac{y}{y}$ $\quad \frac{y^{\frac{1}{3}}}{y^{\frac{1}{3}}} = 1$

$= \frac{y^{\frac{1}{3}}}{y^{\frac{3}{3}}}$ or $\frac{y}{y}$ $\quad y^{\frac{2}{3}} \cdot y^{\frac{1}{3}} = y^{\frac{2}{3}+\frac{1}{3}}$

c. $z^{-\frac{1}{3}} \cdot z^{\frac{3}{4}}$

$z^{-\frac{1}{3}} \cdot z^{\frac{3}{4}} = z^{-\frac{1}{3}+\frac{3}{4}}$ $\quad$ Add powers.

$= z^{-\ \ +\frac{9}{12}}$ or z $\quad -\frac{1}{3} = \frac{4}{12}, \frac{3}{4} = \frac{9}{12}$

Check

Write each expression in simplified form.

$x^{-\frac{4}{5}}$ $\quad x^{\frac{4}{5}} \cdot x^{\frac{5}{4}}$

$x^{-\frac{4}{5}} \cdot x^{\frac{5}{4}}$ $\quad x^{\frac{4}{5}} \cdot x^{-\frac{5}{4}}$

Name ______________________ Period ________ Date ________

Practice

Go Online You can complete your homework online.

Examples 1 and 2

Simplify.

1. $\pm\sqrt{121x^4y^{16}}$
2. $\pm\sqrt{225a^{16}b^{36}}$
3. $\pm\sqrt{49x^4}$
4. $-\sqrt{16c^4d^2}$
5. $-\sqrt{81a^{16}b^{20}c^{12}}$
6. $-\sqrt{400x^{32}y^{40}}$
7. $-\sqrt{(x+15)^4}$
8. $\sqrt{(x^2+6)^{16}}$
9. $\sqrt{(a^2+4a)^{12}}$
10. $\sqrt[6]{x^{18}}$
11. $\sqrt[4]{a^{12}}$
12. $\sqrt[3]{12}$

Examples 3 and 4

Write each expression in radical form, or write each radical in exponential form.

13. $8^{\frac{1}{5}}$
14. $4^{\frac{2}{7}}$
15. $a^{\frac{3}{4}}$
16. $(x^3)^{\frac{3}{2}}$
17. $\sqrt{17}$
18. $\sqrt[4]{63}$
19. $\sqrt[3]{5xy^2}$
20. $\sqrt[4]{625x^2}$

21. **ORBITING** The distance in millions of miles a planet is from the Sun in terms of t, the number of Earth days it takes for the planet to orbit the Sun, can be modeled by the expression $\sqrt[3]{6t^2}$. Write the expression in exponential form.

22. **DEPRECIATION RATE** The depreciation rate is calculated by the expression $1-\left(\frac{T}{P}\right)^{\frac{1}{n}}$, where n is the age of the item in years, T is the resale price in dollars, and P is the original price in dollars. Write the expression in radical form for a car originally purchased for $52,425 that has depreciated over an eight-year period.

Example 5

Evaluate each expression.

23. $27^{\frac{1}{3}}$
24. $256^{\frac{1}{4}}$
25. $16^{-\frac{1}{2}}$
26. $81^{-\frac{1}{4}}$

Example 6

Simplify each expression.

27. $x^{\frac{1}{3}} \cdot x^{\frac{2}{5}}$
28. $a^{\frac{4}{9}} \cdot a^{\frac{1}{4}}$
29. $b^{-\frac{3}{4}}$
30. $y^{-\frac{4}{5}}$

Mixed Exercises

Simplify.

31. $\sqrt[3]{8a^6b^{12}}$

32. $\sqrt[6]{d^{24}x^{36}}$

33. $\sqrt[3]{27b^{18}c^{12}}$

34. $-\sqrt{(2x+1)^6}$

35. $\sqrt{-(x+2)^8}$

36. $\sqrt[3]{-(y-9)^9}$

37. $\sqrt[4]{81(x+4)^4}$

38. $\sqrt[3]{(4x-7)^{24}}$

39. $\sqrt[3]{(y^3+5)^{18}}$

40. $\sqrt[4]{256(5x-2)^{12}}$

41. $\sqrt[8]{x^{16}y^8}$

42. $\sqrt[5]{32a^{15}b^{10}}$

43. $\sqrt{196c^6d^4}$

44. $\sqrt{-64y^8z^6}$

45. $\sqrt[3]{-27a^{15}b^9}$

46. $\sqrt[4]{-16x^{16}y^8}$

47. $\sqrt{400x^{16}y^6}$

48. $\sqrt[3]{8c^3d^{12}}$

49. $\sqrt[3]{64(x+y)^6}$

50. $\sqrt[5]{-(y-z)^{15}}$

51. $a^{\frac{7}{4}} \cdot a^{\frac{5}{4}}$

52. $x^{\frac{2}{3}} \cdot x^{\frac{8}{3}}$

53. $\left(b^{\frac{3}{4}}\right)^{\frac{1}{3}}$

54. $\left(y^{-\frac{3}{5}}\right)^{-\frac{1}{4}}$

55. $d^{-\frac{5}{6}}$

56. $w^{-\frac{7}{8}}$

57. **PENDULUMS** Mr. Topalian's physics class is experimenting with pendulums. The class learned the formula $T = 2\pi\sqrt{\frac{L}{g}}$ which relates the time T that it takes for a pendulum to swing back and forth based on gravity g, equal to 32 feet per second squared, and the length of the pendulum L in feet.

a. One group in the class made a 2-foot long pendulum. Use the formula to determine how long it will take for their pendulum to swing back and forth.

b. Another group decided they wanted to make a pendulum that took about 1.76 seconds to go back and forth. Approximately how long should their pendulum be?

Name ________________ Period ________ Date ________

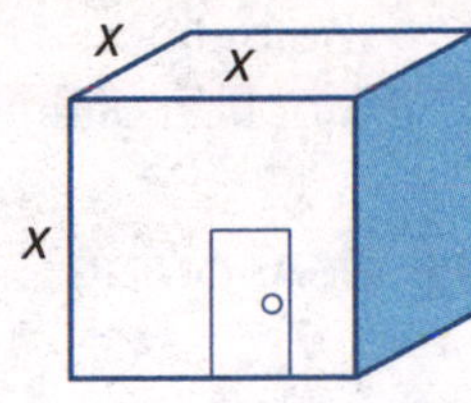

58. CUBES Cathy is building a shed in the shape of a cube. She wants the volume of the space to be 1728 cubic feet. What should be the dimensions of the shed?

59. MARKUPS A wholesaler manufactures a part for D dollars. The wholesaler sells the part to a dealer for a P percent markup. The dealer sells the part to a retailer at an additional P percent markup. The retailer in turn sells the part to its customers marking up the price yet another P percent. Write the price that customers see in exponential form. If the customer buys the part for $80 and the original cost to make the part was $29.15, what is the markup?

Simplify.

60. $\dfrac{f^{-\frac{1}{4}}}{4f^{\frac{1}{2}} \cdot f^{-\frac{1}{3}}}$

61. $\dfrac{c^{\frac{2}{3}}}{c^{\frac{1}{6}}}$

62. $\dfrac{z^{\frac{4}{5}}}{z^{\frac{1}{2}}}$

63. $\sqrt[8]{36h^4j^4}$

64. $\dfrac{ab}{\sqrt{c}}$

65. $\dfrac{xy}{\sqrt[3]{z}}$

66. CUBES A cube has side length s. What side length of the square base will cause its area to have the same numerical value as the volume of the cube? Write your answer using rational exponents.

67. WATER TOWER A water tower in a small town is 218 feet high and holds half a million gallons. The town is considering replacing its water tower. Civil engineers of the town insist that their new tower be a sphere. If the new tank will hold 10 times as much water as the old tank, how many times longer should the radius of the new tank be compared to the old tank?

Write your answer using rational exponents.

68. INTEREST Jada opened a bank account that accumulated interest at the rate of 1% compounded annually. Her money accumulated interest in that account for 8 years. She then took all of her money out of that account and placed it into another account that paid 5% interest compounded annually. After 4 years, she took all of her money out of that account. What single interest rate when compounded annually would give her the same outcome for those 12 years? Round your answer to the nearest hundredth of a percent.

69. CELLS The number of cells in a cell culture grows exponentially. The number of cells in the culture as a function of time is given by the expression $N\left(\frac{6}{5}\right)^t$, where t is measured in hours and N is the initial size of the culture.

a. After 3 hours, there were 1728 cells in the culture. What is N?

b. How many cells were in the culture after 20 minutes? Express your answer in simplest form.

c. How many cells were in the culture after 2.5 hours? Express your answer in simplest form.

70. **BALLOONS** A spherical balloon is being inflated faster and faster. The volume of the balloon as a function of time is $9\pi t^2$. What is the radius of the balloon as a function of time? Write your answer using rational exponents.

71. **REASONING** Simplify $\sqrt[b]{m^{3b}}$, where $b > 0$. Explain your reasoning.

72. **REGULARITY** There are no real *n*th roots of a number *w*. What can you conclude about the index and the number *w*?

73. **ARGUMENTS** Determine the values of x for which $\sqrt{x^2} \neq x$. Explain your answer.

74. **STATE YOUR ASSUMPTION** Do you think raising a constant to an *n*th power and then taking its *n*th root is commutative? Explain your reasoning using the law of exponents to prove or disprove your assumption.

75. **STRUCTURE** Which of the following functions are equivalent? Justify your answer.

$f(x) = \sqrt[3]{x^9}$ $\quad g(x) = \sqrt{x^6}$ $\quad r(x) = (\sqrt[3]{x})^9$ $\quad s(x) = (\sqrt{x})^6$

76. **FIND THE ERROR** Destiny and Kimi are simplifying $\sqrt[4]{16x^4y^8}$. Is either of them correct? Explain your reasoning.

Destiny	**Kimi**
$\sqrt[4]{16x^4y^8} = \sqrt[4]{(2xy^2)^4}$	$\sqrt[4]{16x^4y^8} = \sqrt[4]{(2xy^2)^4}$
$= 2\lvert xy^2\rvert$	$= 2y^2\lvert x\rvert$

77. **PERSEVERE** Under what conditions is $\sqrt{x^2 + y^2} = x + y$ true?

78. **ANALYZE** Determine whether the statement $\sqrt[4]{(-x)^4} = x$ is *sometimes*, *always*, or *never* true.

79. **PERSEVERE** For what real values of x is $\sqrt[3]{x} > x$?

80. **WRITE** Explain when and why absolute value symbols are needed when taking an *n*th root.

81. **PERSEVERE** Write an equivalent expression for $\sqrt[3]{2x} \cdot \sqrt[3]{8y}$. Simplify the radical.

82. **CREATE** Find two different expressions that equal 2 in the form $x^{\frac{1}{a}}$.

83. **WRITE** Explain how it might be easier to simplify an expression using rational exponents rather than using radicals.

Graphing Radical Functions

Explore Power Functions

Online Activity Use graphing technology to complete the Explore.

INQUIRY How does adding, subtracting, or multiplying a constant to a function affect the graph of the function?

Today's Standards
F.IF.7b, F.BF.3
MP1, MP3, MP5

Today's Vocabulary
radical function
square root function
square root inequality
cube root function

Learn Graphing Square Root Functions

A **radical function** is a function that contains radicals with variables in the radicand. One type of radical function is a **square root function**, which is a function that contains the square root of a variable expression.

Key Concept • Parent Function of Square Root Functions

The parent function of the square root functions is $f(x) = \sqrt{x}$.

Domain:	$\{x \mid x \geq 0\}$
Range:	$\{f(x) \mid f(x) \geq 0\}$
Intercepts:	$x = 0, f(x) = 0$
End behavior:	As $x \to 0, f(x) \to 0$, as $x \to \infty, f(x) \to \infty$.
Increasing/ decreasing:	increasing when $x > 0$
Positive/ negative:	positive for $x > 0$
Symmetry:	no symmetry

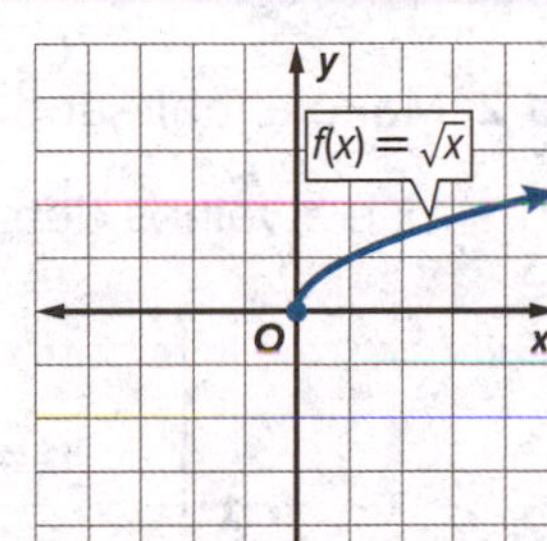

Think About It!
Why is the domain limited to $x \geq 0$ for the parent of the square root function?

Learn Transformations of Square Root Functions

A square root function can be written in the form $g(x) = a\sqrt{x - h} + k$. Each constant in the equation affects the parent graph.

- The value of $|a|$ stretches or compresses (dilates) the parent graph.
- When the value of a is negative, the graph is reflected in the x-axis.
- The value of h shifts (translates) the parent graph left or right.
- The value of k shifts (translates) the parent graph up or down.

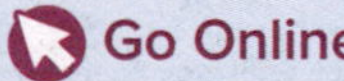

Go Online
You may want to complete the Concept Check to check your understanding.

Your Notes

Go Online You can learn how to graph radical functions by watching the video online.

Think About It!
How are the values of h and k related to the domain and range in this example?

Example 1 Identify Domain and Range Algebraically

Identify the domain and range of $f(x) = \sqrt{2x - 6} + 1$.

The domain is restricted to values for which the radicand is nonnegative.

$2x - 6$ ____ 0	Write an inequality using the radicand.
$2x \geq 6$	Add 6 to each side.
$x \geq$ ____	Divide each side by 2.

The domain is $\{x \mid x \geq 3\}$.

Find $f($____$)$ to determine the lower limit of the range.

$f(3) = \sqrt{2(\ \ ) - 6} + 1$ or 1

The range is $\{f(x) \mid f(x) \geq$ ____$\}$.

Example 2 Graph a Transformed Square Root Function

Graph $g(x) = -3\sqrt{x + 1} + 2$, and identify the domain and range. Then describe how it is related to the graph of the parent function.

Step 1 Determine the minimum domain value.

$x + 1 \geq 0$	Write an inequality using the radicand.
$x \geq$ ____	Simplify.

Step 2 Make a table and graph.

Use x-values determined from **Step 1** to make a table.

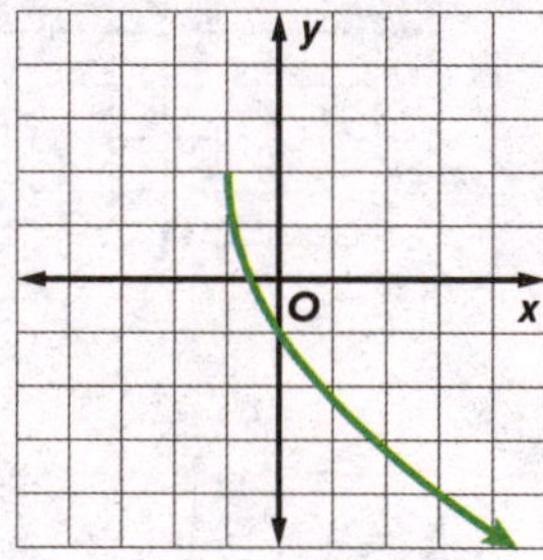

The domain is $\{x \mid x \geq$ ____$\}$ and the range is $\{g(x) \mid g(x) \leq$ ____$\}$.

Step 3 Compare $g(x)$ to the parent function.

The maximum point is at $(-1,$ ____$)$.

Because $f(x) = \sqrt{x}$, $g(x) = a\sqrt{x - h} + k$ where $a = -3$, $h = -1$, and $k = 2$.

$a < 0$ and $|a| > 1$, so the graph of $f(x) = \sqrt{x}$ is reflected across the ____-axis and stretched vertically by a factor of $|a|$, or ____.

$h < 0$, so the graph is then translated ____ $|h|$ units, or ____ unit.

$k > 0$, so the graph is then translated ____ k units, or ____ units.

 **Go Online** You can complete an Extra Example online.

Example 3 Analyze the Graph of a Square Root Function

BLOOD DONATION When blood is donated, medical professionals use a centrifuge to separate it. The centrifuge spins the blood, causing it to separate into three components, which are red cells, platelets, and plasma. In order to efficiently separate the blood, the centrifuge must spin at a specified rate, measured in rotations per minute (RPM), for the required gravitation force, or g-force, exerted on the blood. For a centrifuge with a radius of 7.8 centimeters, the RPM setting of the centrifuge is determined by the product of 104.23 and the square root of the g-force required.

Part A Write and graph the function.

Complete the table to write the function.

Words	The RPM setting of the centrifuge	is	the product of 104.23	and the square root of the g-force required.
Variables	Let g represent the force and r represent the RPM setting.			
Function	___	=	$104.23 \cdot$	$\sqrt{g}$

Make a table to graph the function.

g	r
0	0
400	2085
800	2948
1200	3611
1600	4422

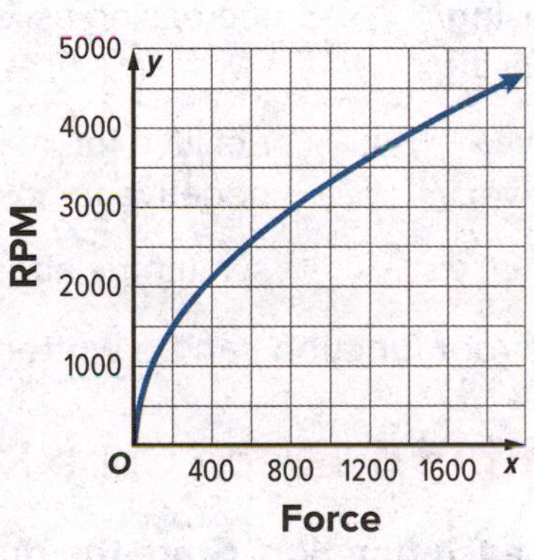

Part B Describe key features of the function.

Domain: $\{g \mid g \geq 0\}$ Range: ______

x-intercept: 0 y-intercept: 0

Increasing/Decreasing: ______

Positive/Negative: positive for $g > 0$

End Behavior: As $g \to \infty$, $r \to \infty$.

Think About It!

What does the domain and range mean in the context of the situation?

Go Online You can complete an Extra Example online.

Example 4 Graph a Square Root Inequality

Graph $y < \sqrt{2x + 5}$.

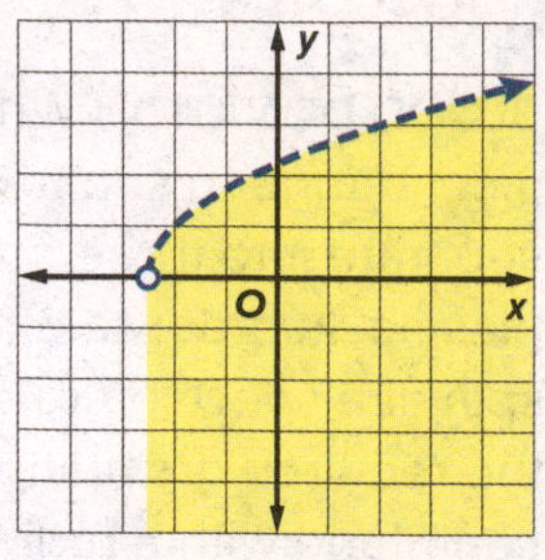

Step 1 Graph.

Graph the boundary $y = \sqrt{2x + 5}$, using a ______ line because the inequality is $<$.

Step 2 Shade.

The domain is $\{x \mid x \geq 2.5\}$. Shade the region ______ the boundary and within the domain.

Watch Out!

Test Point When selecting a test point, make sure the point is within the domain of the related function.

Learn Graphing Cube Root Functions

A **cube root function** is a radical function that contains the cube root of a variable expression.

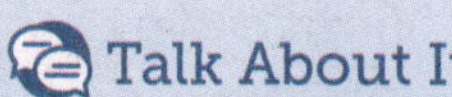

Talk About It

Describe how the domain and range differ for a radical function with an odd index and a radical function with an even index.

Key Concept • Parent Function of Square Root Functions

The parent function of the cube root functions is $f(x) = \sqrt[3]{x}$.

Domain:	all real numbers
Range:	all real numbers
Intercepts:	$x = 0, f(x) = 0$
End behavior:	As $x \to -\infty, f(x) \to -\infty$, as $x \to \infty, f(x) \to \infty$.
Increasing/ decreasing:	increasing as $x \to \infty$
Positive/ negative:	positive for $x > 0$ negative for $x < 0$
Symmetry:	symmetric about the origin

A cube root function can be written in the form $g(x) = a\sqrt[3]{x - h} + k$.

Example 5 Graph Cube Root Functions

Graph each function. State the domain and range.

a. $g(x) = \frac{1}{3}\sqrt[3]{x}$

In $g(x) = a\sqrt[3]{x - h} + k$, $a =$ ______, $h =$ ______, and $k =$ ______. So the function is centered at the origin and vertically compressed.

x	$g(x)$
−2	≈ -0.42
−1	$-0.\overline{33}$
0	0
1	$0.\overline{33}$
2	≈ 0.42

The domain is ______________, and the range is all real numbers.

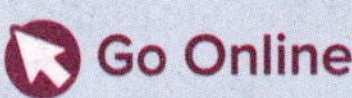

Go Online

You can learn how to graph radical functions on a graphing calculator by watching the video online.

b. $p(x) = \sqrt[3]{x + 5}$

In $p(x) = \sqrt[3]{x - h} + k$, $a = 1$, $h = -5$, and $k = 0$. So the function is translated __________ from the parent graph.

The domain is all real numbers, and the range is all real numbers.

x	y
−7	
−6	
−5	
−4	
−3	

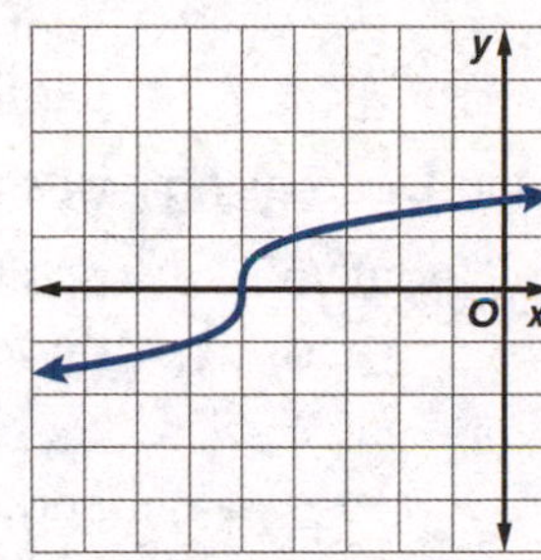

c. $q(x) = \sqrt[3]{4 - x} + 1$

The function can be written as $q(x) = \sqrt[3]{-(x - 4)} + 1$. So the function is reflected and translated 4 units right and 1 unit up from the parent graph.

x	y
2	≈ 2.26
3	2
4	1
5	0
6	≈ −0.26

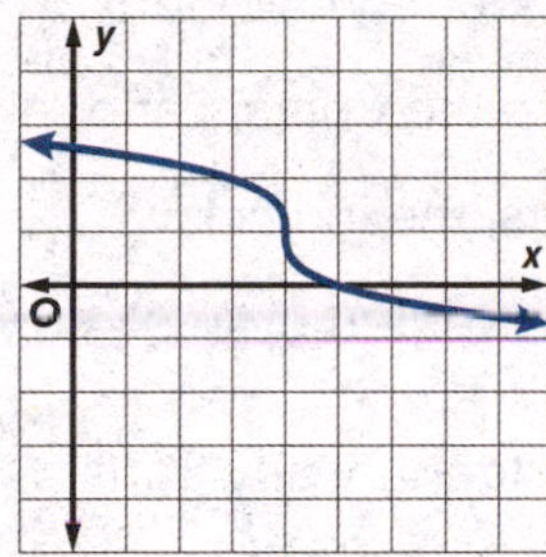

The domain is all real numbers, and the range is all real numbers.

Example 6 Compare Radical Functions

Examine $p(x) = -2\sqrt[3]{x - 6}$ and $q(x)$ shown in the graph.

Part A Graph $p(x)$.

Make a table of values for $p(x)$.
Then, graph the function.

x	y
0	≈ 3.63
2	≈ 3.17
4	≈ 2.52
6	0
8	≈ −2.52
10	≈ −3.18

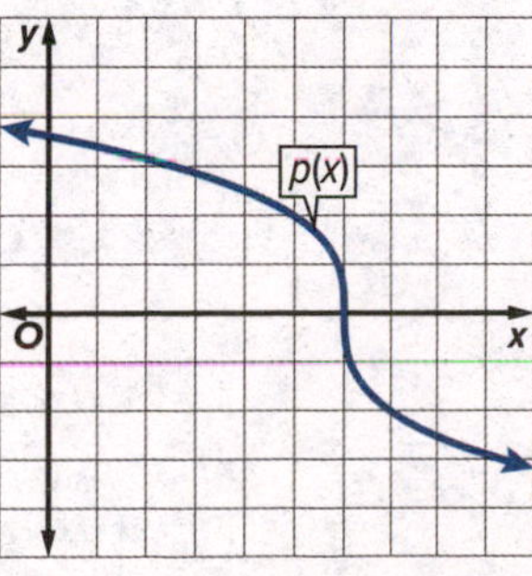

(continued on the next page)

Study Tip:

Tables When making a table of values for a radical function, first determine h. Then make a table using values that are greater than and less than h.

Think About It!

Describe the end behavior of the function in part c, $y = \sqrt[3]{4 - x} + 1$.

Think About It!

Determine whether the indexes of $p(x)$ and $q(x)$ are even or odd. Justify your response.

Part B **Compare key features.**

	$p(x)$:	$q(x)$:
Domain and Range	D: all real numbers, R: all real numbers	D: $\{x \mid x \geq 6\}$, R: $\{q(x) \mid q(x) \leq 0\}$
Intercepts	x-intercept: 6; y-intercept: 3.63	x-intercept: 6; y-intercept: none
Increasing/Decreasing	decreasing as $x \to \infty$	decreasing as $x \to \infty$
Positive/Negative	positive for $x < 6$; negative for $x > 6$	negative for $x > 6$
End Behavior	As $x \to \infty$, $p(x) \to \infty$, and as $x \to -\infty$, $p(x) \to -\infty$.	As $x \to 6$, $q(x) \to 0$, and as $x \to \infty$, $q(x) \to -\infty$.

Example 7 Write a Radical Function

Write a radical function for the graph of $g(x)$.

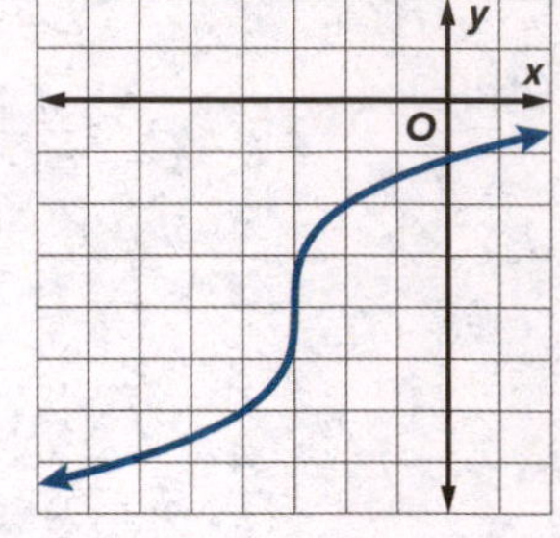

Step 1 Identify the index.

Because the domain and range for $g(x)$ is all real numbers, the index is ____. This function can be represented by $g(x) = a\sqrt[3]{x - h} + k$.

Step 2 Identify any transformations.

The function has been translated 3 units left and 4 units down.

Therefore, $h =$ ____ and $k =$ ____.

To find the value of a, use a point as well as the values of h and k.

$g(x) = a\sqrt[3]{x - h} + k$ Cube root function

____ $= a\sqrt[3]{\_\_\_\_ - (-3)} + (-4)$ $h = -3$, $k = -4$, $(x, g(x)) = (-2, -2)$

$-2 = a \cdot$ ____ $- 4$ Simplify.

$a =$ ____   Simplify.

Step 3 Write the function.

The graph is represented by $g(x) =$ ____ $\sqrt[3]{x + \_\_\_\_}$ $-$ ____.

> **Think About It!**
> Write a cube root function for a graph that has been reflected in the x-axis and translated 7 units right and 4 units down from the parent function.

Go Online You can complete an Extra Example online.

Name ______________________ Period ____________ Date ______________

Practice

Go Online You can complete your homework online.

Example 1

Identify the domain and range of each function.

1. $y = \sqrt{x - 9}$

2. $y = \sqrt{x + 7}$

3. $y = -\sqrt{6x}$

4. $y = 5\sqrt{x + 2} - 1$

5. $y = \sqrt{3x - 4}$

6. $y = -\sqrt{x - 2} + 2$

Example 2

Graph each function. State the domain and range of each function. Then describe how it is related to the graph of the parent function.

7. $y = \sqrt{2x}$

8. $y = -\sqrt{3x}$

9. $y = \sqrt{2x}$

10. $y = \sqrt{x + 3}$

11. $y = -\sqrt{2x - 5}$

12. $y = \sqrt{x + 4} - 2$

Example 3

13. SQUARES Cathy is building a square picture frame. The side length of the picture frame is given by the square root of the space the picture frame will occupy.

a. Write and graph a function, where x is the space the picture frame will occupy and y is the side length of the picture frame.

b. Describe the key features of the function.

14. REFLEXES Rachel and Ashley are testing one another's reflexes. Rachel drops a ruler from a given height so that it falls between Ashley's thumb and index finger. Ashley tries to catch the ruler before it falls through her hand. The time, in seconds, required to catch the ruler is given by the product of $\frac{1}{4}$ and the square root of the distance, in inches.

a. Write and graph a function, where d is the distance, in inches, and t is the time, in seconds.

b. Describe the key features of the function.

c. Graph the parent function on the same coordinate grid. How does the function you wrote in **part a** compare to the parent function?

15. DISTANCE Malik is standing at the side of a road watching a cyclist. The distance, in feet, between Malik and the cyclist as a function of time is given by the square root of the sum of 9 and the product of 36 and the time squared.

a. Write and graph a function, where t is the time, in seconds, and d is the distance, in feet.

b. Describe the key features of the function.

Example 4

Graph each inequality.

16. $y < \sqrt{x - 5}$

17. $y > \sqrt{x + 6}$

18. $y \geq -4\sqrt{x + 3}$

19. $y \leq -2\sqrt{x - 6}$

20. $y > 2\sqrt{x + 7} - 5$

21. $y \geq 4\sqrt{x - 2} - 12$

Example 5

Graph each function. State the domain and range of each function.

22. $f(x) = \sqrt[3]{x + 1}$

23. $f(x) = 3\sqrt[3]{x - 2}$

24. $f(x) = \sqrt[3]{x + 7} - 1$

25. $f(x) = -\sqrt[3]{x - 2} + 9$

Example 6

26. Examine $p(x) = -3\sqrt{x + 2}$ and $q(x)$ shown in the graph.

a. Graph $p(x)$.

b. Compare the key features of the functions.

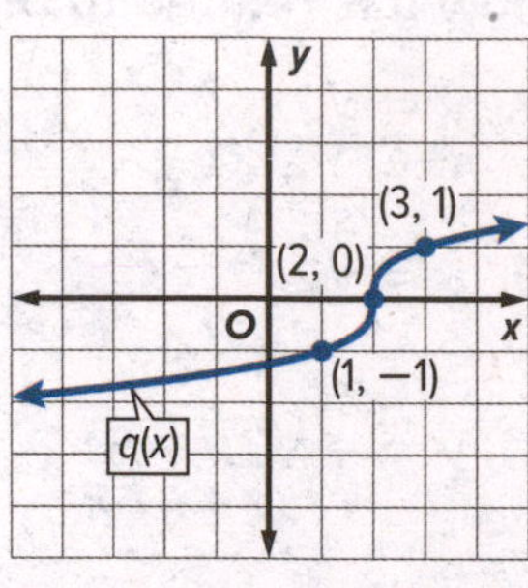

27. Examine $p(x) = \sqrt[3]{x - 2}$ and $q(x)$ shown in the graph.

a. Graph $p(x)$.

b. Compare the key features of the functions.

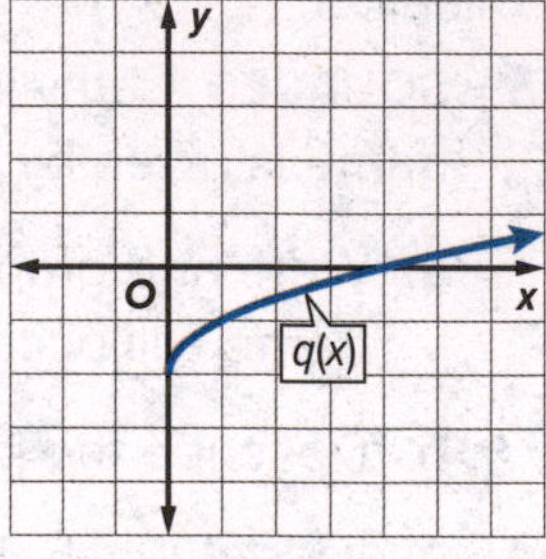

28. Examine $p(x) = \sqrt{x - 2} + 5$ and $q(x)$ shown in the graph.

a. Graph $p(x)$.

b. Compare the key features of the functions.

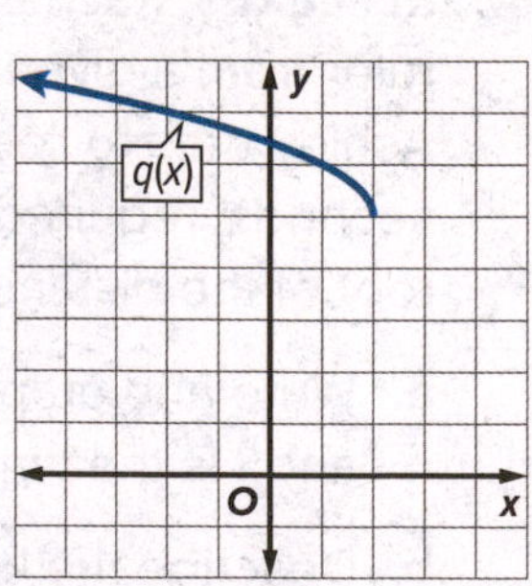

Example 7

Write a radical function for each graph.

29.

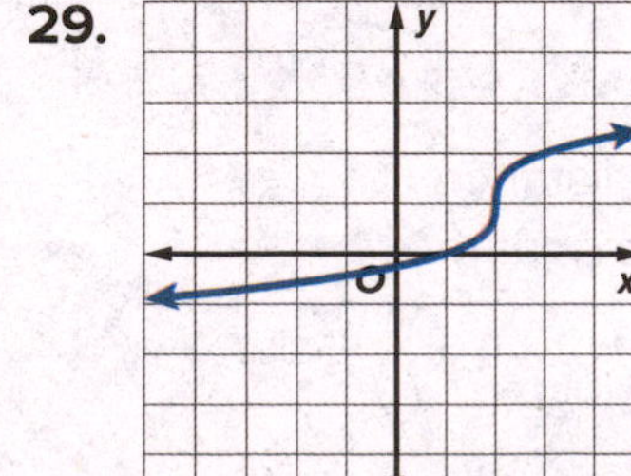

30.

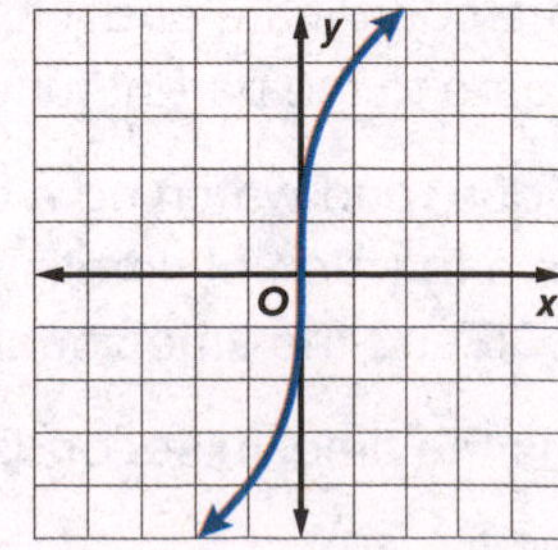

31.

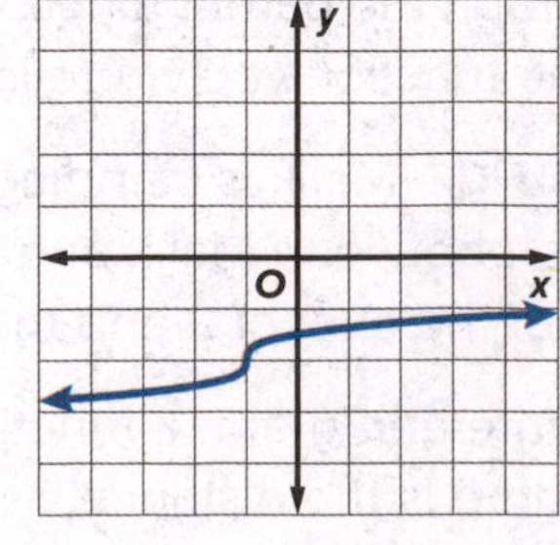

Name ______________________ Period __________ Date __________

Mixed Exercises

Identify the domain and range of each function.

32. $y = \sqrt{4x - 8} - 5$

33. $y = \sqrt{2x - 3} + 7$

34. $y = -\sqrt{6x + 7} - 1$

Graph each function. State the domain and range of each function. Then describe how it is related to the graph of the parent function.

35. $f(x) = 2\sqrt{x - 5} - 6$

36. $f(x) = \frac{3}{4}\sqrt{x + 12} + 3$

37. $f(x) = -\frac{1}{5}\sqrt{x - 1} - 4$

38. $f(x) = -3\sqrt{x + 7} + 9$

Graph each inequality.

39. $y \le 6 - 3\sqrt{x - 4}$

40. $y < \sqrt{4x - 12} + 8$

Graph each function. State the domain and range of each function.

41. $f(x) = -\frac{1}{3}\sqrt[3]{x + 2} - 3$

42. $f(x) = -\frac{1}{2}\sqrt[3]{2x - 1} + 3$

Write a radical function for each graph.

43.

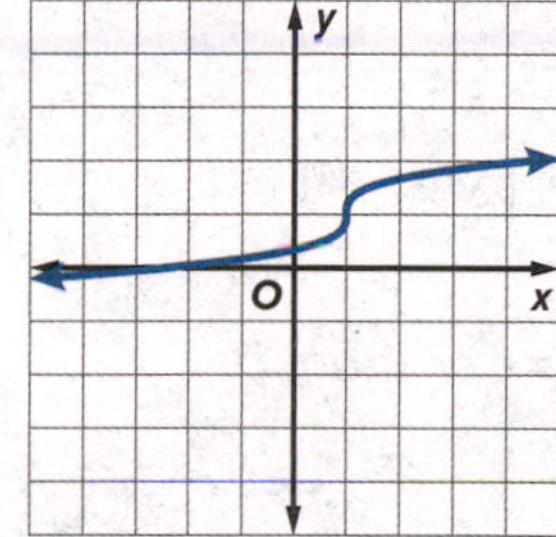

44.

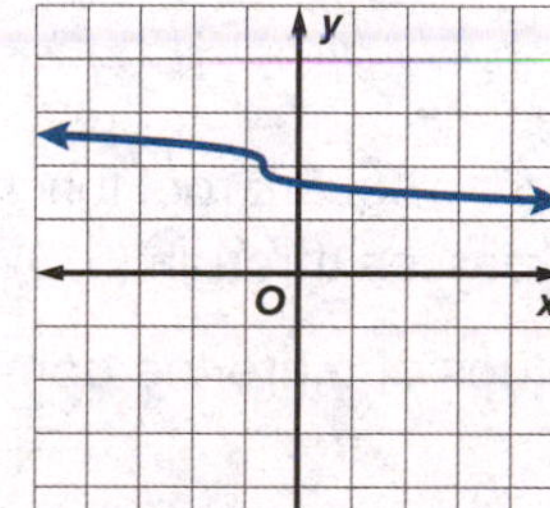

45. TUNING Two notes are an octave apart if the frequency of the higher note is x times the frequency of the lower note. Casey is experimenting with an instrument that has 4 notes tuned so that the frequency of each successive note increases by the same factor and the first and last note are an octave apart. The formula $y = \sqrt[3]{x}$ represents the factor the frequency increases by from note to note. Identify the domain and range of the function. Describe the key features of the graph.

46. STRUCTURE Consider the function $f(x) = -\sqrt{3 - x} + \frac{13}{2}$ and the function $g(x)$ whose graph is shown.

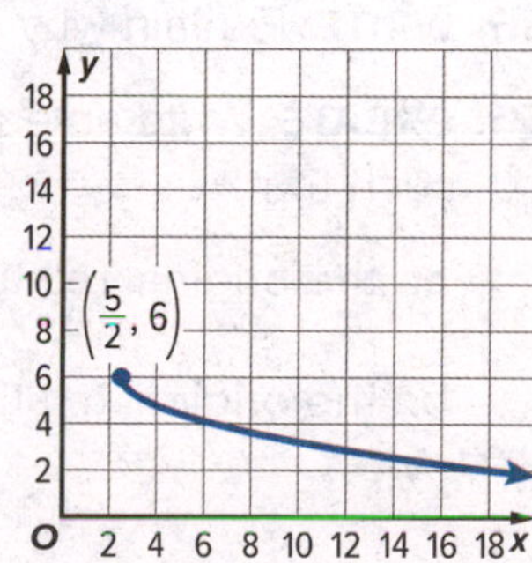

a. Determine which function has the greater maximum value. Explain your reasoning.

b. Compare the domains of the two functions.

c. Compare the rates of change of the two functions.

47. HEMISPHERE The length of the radius of a hemisphere can be found using the formula $r = \sqrt[3]{\frac{3V}{2\pi}}$, where V is the volume of the hemisphere. Graph the function. State the key features of the graph.

48. A silo is in the shape of a right circular cone sitting on the ground, as shown. The cost per square foot to apply an environmentally-friendly UV protective paint to the surface of the silo not on the ground is $1.25. Suppose the radius is $r = 60$ feet. The surface to be painted can be described by the following function of height, h: $S(h) = 60\pi\sqrt{3600 + h^2}$. Let $f = h^2$ in this formula to define the new function $S(f) = 60\pi\sqrt{3600 + f}$.

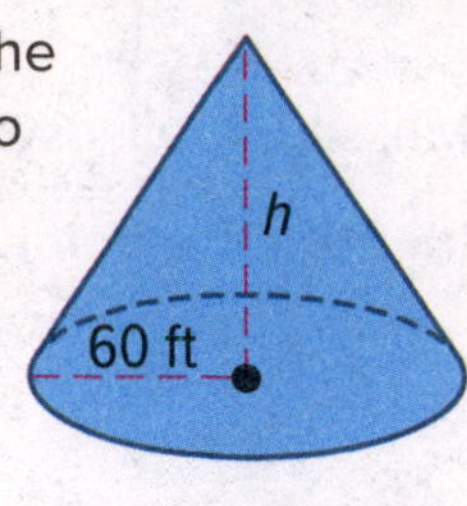

a. **USE TOOLS** Graph $S(f)$ and determine its domain in this context.

b. **MODELING** Construct a function of f that describes the cost of applying N coats of this paint to the surface of the silo. Explain your reasoning.

c. **REASONING** Determine the range of the cost that will be incurred by applying either 2 or 3 coats of this paint to the entire surface of the silo if the height can vary between 100 feet and 150 feet. Express your answer as an inequality where the endpoints are rounded to the nearest dollar. Explain your reasoning.

49. **MODELING** Pita produces the following graph for the inequality $f(x) > \sqrt{-x + 2} - 3$. Graph its inverse on the same coordinate plane along with the line of symmetry. Give the inequality that defines the graph of the inverse. Are there any restrictions that must be placed on the domain of the inverse?

50. **PERSEVERE** Write an equation for a square root function with a domain of $\{x \mid x \geq -4\}$, a range of $\{y \mid y \leq 6\}$, and that passes through (5, 3).

51. **ANALYZE** For what positive values of a are the domain and range of $f(x) = \sqrt[a]{x}$ the set of real numbers?

52. **CREATE** Write a square root function for which the domain is $\{x \mid x \geq 8\}$ and the range is $\{y \mid y \leq 14\}$.

53. **WRITE** Explain why there are limitations on the domain and range of square root functions.

54. **ANALYZE** Compare the graph with the provided square root function. Which function has a greater y-intercept? x-intercept?

55. **WRITE** Explain why $y = \pm\sqrt{x}$ is not a function.

56. **CREATE** Write an equation of a relation that contains a radical and its inverse such that:

a. the original relation is a function, and its inverse is not a function.

b. the original relation is not a function, and its inverse is a function.

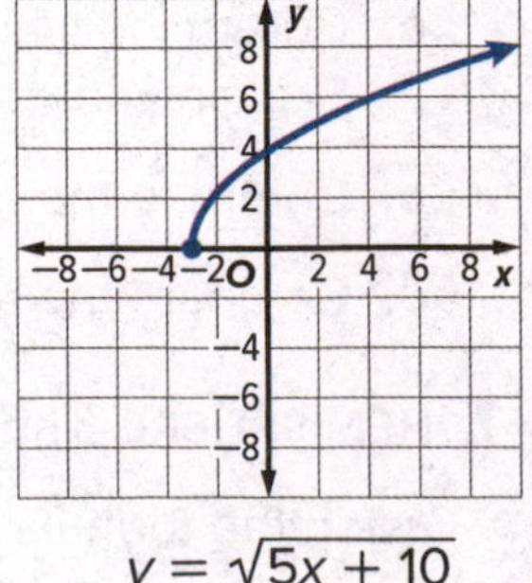

$y = \sqrt{5x + 10}$

Operations with Radical Expressions

Learn Properties of Radicals

Key Concept • Product Property of Radicals

Words: For any real numbers a and b and any integer $n > 1$,

$\sqrt[n]{ab} = \sqrt[n]{a} \cdot \sqrt[n]{b}$, if n is even and $a, b \geq 0$ or if n is odd.

Examples: $\sqrt{12} \cdot \sqrt{3} = \sqrt{36}$ or 6 and $\sqrt[3]{4} \cdot \sqrt[3]{16} = \sqrt[3]{64}$ or 4

Key Concept • Quotient Property of Radicals

Words: For any real numbers a and $b \neq 0$ and any integer

$n > 1$, $\sqrt[n]{\frac{a}{b}} = \frac{\sqrt[n]{a}}{\sqrt[n]{b}}$, if all roots are defined.

Examples: $\sqrt{\frac{x^4}{25}} = \frac{\sqrt{x^4}}{\sqrt{25}} = \frac{x^2}{5}$ or $\frac{1}{5}x^2$ and $\sqrt[3]{\frac{27}{8}} = \frac{\sqrt[3]{27}}{\sqrt[3]{8}} = \frac{3}{2}$

Learn Simplifying Radical Expressions

Key Concept • Simplest Form of Radical Expressions

A radical expression is in simplest form when the following conditions are met.

- The index n is as small as possible.
- The radicand contains no factors (other than 1) that are nth powers of an integer or polynomial.
- The radicand contains no fractions.
- No radicals appear in the denominator.

Today's Standards
A.SSE.2
MP4, MP7

Today's Vocabulary
like radical expressions
conjugates

Example 1 Simplify Expressions with the Product Property

Simplify each expression

a. $\sqrt[3]{-27a^6b^{14}}$

$= \sqrt[3]{(\quad)^3 \cdot (\quad)^3 \cdot (\quad)^3 \cdot b^2}$ — Factor into cubes.

$= \sqrt[3]{(-3)^3} \cdot \sqrt[3]{(a^2)^3} \cdot \sqrt[3]{(b^4)^3} \cdot \sqrt[3]{b^2}$ — Product Property of Radicals

$= \quad a \quad b \sqrt[3]{b}$ — Simplify.

b. $\sqrt{75x^{12}y^7}$

$= \sqrt{\quad^2 \cdot 3 \cdot (x\quad)^2 \cdot (y\quad)^2 \cdot y}$ — Factor into squares.

$= \sqrt{5^2} \cdot \sqrt{3} \cdot \sqrt{(x^6)^2} \cdot \sqrt{(y^3)^2} \cdot \sqrt{y}$ — Product Property of Radicals

$= \quad x \quad y \sqrt{\quad}$ — Simplify.

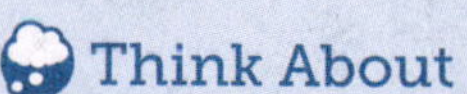

Think About It!

Why are absolute value symbols not necessary around y^3 in **part b** even though it is an odd power and the result of finding the even root of an even power?

Go Online You can complete an Extra Example online.

Your Notes

Check

Write the simplified form of the expressions.

a. $\sqrt[4]{4x^5y^{20}}$ ______

b. $\sqrt{60a^3b^{22}}$ ______

Example 2 Simplify Expressions with the Quotient Property

Simplify each expression.

a. $\sqrt[3]{\frac{24a^6}{125}}$

$\sqrt[3]{\frac{24a^6}{125}} = \frac{\sqrt[3]{\quad}}{\sqrt[3]{\quad}}$ Quotient Property of Radicals

$= \frac{\sqrt[3]{2\ \cdot\ \ \cdot (a\ )^3}}{\sqrt[3]{5}}$ Factor into cubes.

$= \frac{\sqrt[3]{2^3} \cdot \sqrt[3]{3} \cdot \sqrt[4]{(a^2)^3}}{\sqrt[3]{5^3}}$ Product Property of Radicals

$= \frac{\ \ \sqrt[3]{3}}{\quad}$ Simplify.

b. $\sqrt[4]{\frac{80y^{14}}{256z^4}}$

$\sqrt[4]{\frac{80y^{14}}{256z^4}} = \frac{\sqrt[4]{80y^{14}}}{\sqrt[4]{256z^4}}$ Quotient Property of Radicals

$= \frac{\sqrt[4]{2^4 \cdot 5 \cdot (y^3)^4 \cdot y^2}}{\sqrt[4]{\quad}}$ Factor into fourth powers.

$= \frac{\sqrt[4]{2^4} \cdot \sqrt[4]{5} \cdot \sqrt[4]{(y^3)^4} \cdot \sqrt[4]{y^2}}{\sqrt[4]{4^4} \cdot \sqrt[4]{z^4}}$ Product Property of Radicals

$= \frac{2|\quad|\sqrt[4]{5y^2}}{\quad}$ Simplify radicals.

$= \frac{|y^3|\sqrt[4]{5y^2}}{2z}$ Simplify.

Think About It!

Fudo says that you cannot combine $\sqrt[3]{40}$ and $6\sqrt[3]{5}$ because they do not have the same radicand. Is he correct? Why or why not?

Check

Write the simplified form of $\sqrt{\frac{9x^8y^{13}}{25x^2}}$. ______

Learn Adding and Subtracting Radical Expressions

Radicals can be added and subtracted in the same manner as monomials. In order to add or subtract, the radicals must be like terms. Radicals are **like radical expressions** if *both* the index and the radicand are the same.

Go Online You can complete an Extra Example online.

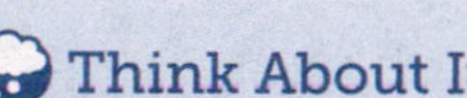

Learn Multiplying Radical Expressions

Radicals with the same index can be multiplied by using the Product Property of Radicals. If the radicals have coefficients before the radical symbol, multiply the coefficients. Then, multiply the radicands of each expression. To multiply radical expressions with more than one term, you can use the Distributive Property or FOIL method.

Example 3 Add and Subtract Radicals

Simplify $6\sqrt{45x} + \sqrt{12} - 3\sqrt{20x}$.

$$= 6\sqrt{\quad \cdot 5x} + \sqrt{\quad \cdot 3} - 3\sqrt{\quad \cdot 5x}$$

$$= 6(\sqrt{3^2} \cdot \sqrt{5x}) + (\sqrt{2^2} \cdot \sqrt{3}) - 3(\sqrt{2^2} \cdot \sqrt{5x})$$

$$= 6(\underline{\quad}\sqrt{\quad}) + (2\sqrt{3}) - 3(\underline{\quad}\sqrt{\quad})$$

$$= \underline{\quad}\sqrt{5x} + 2\sqrt{3} - \underline{\quad}\sqrt{5x}$$

$$= \underline{\quad}\sqrt{5x} + 2\sqrt{3}$$

Check

Write the simplified form of $\sqrt{18x} - 5\sqrt{28} - 3\sqrt{98x} + 3\sqrt{7x}$.

____

Example 4 Multiply Radicals

Simplify $4\sqrt[5]{-16x^2y^6} \cdot 3\sqrt[5]{10x^4y^4}$.

$$= 4 \cdot \underline{\quad} \cdot \sqrt[5]{-10x^2y^6 \cdot 16x^4y^4}$$

$$= \underline{\quad} \cdot \sqrt[5]{-1 \cdot 2 \cdot 5 \cdot x^2y^6 \cdot \quad 4 \cdot x^4y^4}$$

$$= 12 \cdot \sqrt[5]{-1 \cdot 2 \quad \cdot 5 \cdot x \quad \cdot x \cdot y}$$

$$= 12 \cdot \sqrt[5]{-1} \cdot \sqrt[5]{2^5} \cdot \sqrt[5]{5} \cdot \sqrt[5]{x^5} \cdot \sqrt[5]{x} \cdot \sqrt[5]{y^{10}}$$

$$= 12 \cdot (-1) \cdot 2 \cdot \quad \cdot y \quad \cdot \sqrt[5]{\quad} \cdot \sqrt[5]{\quad}$$

$$-12xy^2\sqrt[5]{\quad}$$

Check

Write the simplified form of $5\sqrt[5]{-9x^3y^5} \times 3\sqrt[5]{27x^4y^5}$.

____

Think About It!

Complete the statement to write a general method for multiplying radicals with coefficients.

For any real numbers a, b, c, and d and any integer $n > 1$, $c\sqrt{a} \cdot d\sqrt{b} =$

Think About It!

In the example, $\sqrt[5]{-1}$ simplifies to -1 because 5 is an odd root. What would happen if the example used an even root?

Study Tip:

Negative Radicands If a radicand has a negative constant, it may be helpful to use -1 as a factor. Then you can simply the nth root of -1, which will be -1 if n is odd and i if n is even.

Go Online You can complete an Extra Example online.

Watch Out!

Simplest Form Do not forget to check that your result is in simplest form. Make sure that none of the individual radicals can be further simplified or combined.

Example 5 Use the Distributive Property to Multiply Radicals

SPORTS A sports pennant has the dimensions shown. Find the area, in square inches.

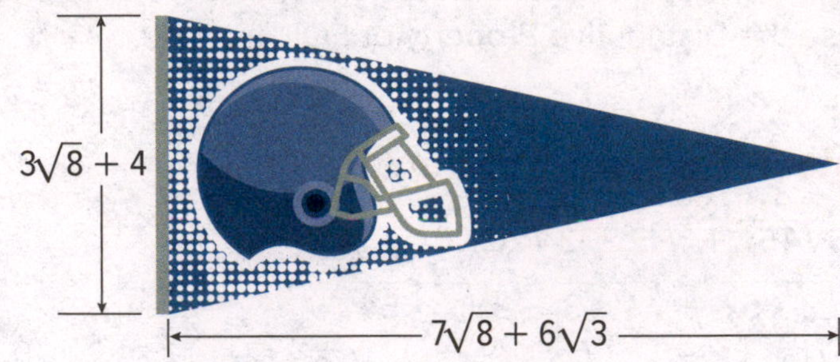

Area $= \frac{1}{2} \cdot$ base $\cdot$ height $\frac{1}{2}(3\sqrt{8} + 4)(\_\_\_\_ + \_\_\_\_)$.

$= \frac{1}{2} \cdot [3\sqrt{8} \cdot 7\sqrt{8} + 3\sqrt{8} \cdot 6\sqrt{3} + 4 \cdot 7\sqrt{8} + 4 \cdot 6\sqrt{3}]$

$= \frac{1}{2} \cdot [21\sqrt{8^2} + 18\sqrt{24} + 28\sqrt{8} + 24\sqrt{3}]$

$= \frac{1}{2} \cdot [21\sqrt{8^2} + 18\sqrt{2^2 \cdot 6} + 28\sqrt{2^2 \cdot 2} + 24\sqrt{3}]$

$= \frac{1}{2} \cdot [21\sqrt{8^2} + 18 \cdot \sqrt{2^2} \cdot \sqrt{6} + 28 \cdot \sqrt{2^2} \cdot \sqrt{2} + 24\sqrt{3}]$

$= \frac{1}{2} \cdot [\_\_\_\_ + \_\_\_\_\sqrt{6} + \_\_\_\_\sqrt{2} + \_\_\_\_\sqrt{3}]$

$= \_\_\_\_ + 18\sqrt{6} + \_\_\_\_\sqrt{2} + 12\sqrt{3}$

The area is $84 + 18\sqrt{6} + 28\sqrt{2} + 12\sqrt{3}$ in^2, or about ____ in^2.

Check

POOLS A rectangular pool safety cover has a length of $7\sqrt{10} - 4$ feet and a width of $6\sqrt{10} + 8\sqrt{5}$ feet. Which expression represents the area of the pool cover in simplest form? ____

A. $420 + 280\sqrt{2} + 24\sqrt{10} + 32\sqrt{5}$ ft^2

B. $42\sqrt{100} + 280\sqrt{2} - 24\sqrt{10} - 32\sqrt{5}$ ft^2

C. $420 + 280\sqrt{2} - 24\sqrt{10} - 32\sqrt{5}$ ft^2

D. $420 + 56\sqrt{50} - 24\sqrt{10} - 32\sqrt{5}$ ft^2

Learn Rationalizing the Denominator

If the denominator is:	Multiply the numerator and denominator by:	Examples
$\sqrt{b}$	$\sqrt{b}$	$\frac{4}{\sqrt{7}} = \frac{4}{\sqrt{7}} \cdot \frac{\sqrt{7}}{\sqrt{7}}$ or $\frac{4\sqrt{7}}{7}$
$\sqrt[n]{b^x}$	$\sqrt[n]{b^{n-x}}$	$\frac{3}{\sqrt[5]{2}} = \frac{3}{\sqrt[5]{2}} \cdot \frac{\sqrt[5]{2^4}}{\sqrt[5]{2^4}}$ or $\frac{3\sqrt[5]{16}}{2}$

Learn Using Conjugates

Binomials of the form $a\sqrt{b} + c\sqrt{d}$ and $a\sqrt{b} - c\sqrt{d}$, where a, b, c, and d are rational numbers, are called **conjugates** of each other. Multiplying the numerator and denominator by the conjugate of the denominator will eliminate the radical from the denominator of the expression.

Example 6 Rationalize the Denominator

Simplify $\sqrt[3]{\frac{250a^6}{7a}}$.

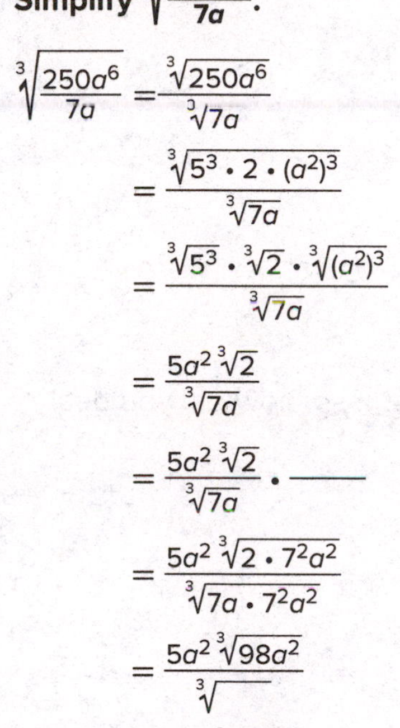

$\sqrt[3]{\frac{250a^6}{7a}} = \frac{\sqrt[3]{250a^6}}{\sqrt[3]{7a}}$ Quotient Property of Radicals

$= \frac{\sqrt[3]{5^3 \cdot 2 \cdot (a^2)^3}}{\sqrt[3]{7a}}$ Factor into cubes.

$= \frac{\sqrt[3]{5^3} \cdot \sqrt[3]{2} \cdot \sqrt[3]{(a^2)^3}}{\sqrt[3]{7a}}$ Product Property of Radicals

$= \frac{5a^2\sqrt[3]{2}}{\sqrt[3]{7a}}$ Simplify.

$= \frac{5a^2\sqrt[3]{2}}{\sqrt[3]{7a}} \cdot \underline{\qquad}$ Rationalize the denominator.

$= \frac{5a^2\sqrt[3]{2 \cdot 7^2a^2}}{\sqrt[3]{7a \cdot 7^2a^2}}$ Product Property of Radicals

$= \frac{5a^2\sqrt[3]{98a^2}}{\sqrt[3]{\qquad}}$ Multiply.

$= \frac{5a^2\sqrt[3]{98a^2}}{\qquad}$ $\sqrt[3]{7^3a^3} = 7a$

$= \frac{5a\sqrt[3]{98a^2}}{7}$ Simplify.

Go Online You can complete an Extra Example online.

Think About It!

Why is the product of $\sqrt[n]{b^x}$ and $\sqrt[n]{b^{n-x}}$ an exact root?

Think About It!

How does multiplying conjugates relate to the difference of squares identity that can be used when multiplying binomials?

Watch Out!

Rationalizing the Denominator When determining the quantity to multiply by when rationalizing the denominator, make sure you raise the entire term under the radical to the power of $n - x$.

Check

Write the simplified form of $\sqrt{\frac{20b}{3b^5}}$.

______

Example 7 Use Conjugates to Rationalize the Denominator

Simplify $\frac{4x}{2\sqrt{7}-5}$.

$\frac{4x}{2\sqrt{7}-5} = \frac{4x}{2\sqrt{7}-5} \cdot \frac{\quad}{\quad}$ — $2\sqrt{7}+5$ is the conjugate of $2\sqrt{7}-5$.

$= \frac{4x(\quad) + \quad(5)}{(2\sqrt{7})^2 + (\quad) - (\quad) - 5(5)}$ — Multiply.

$= \frac{8x\sqrt{7}+20x}{\quad + 10\sqrt{7} - 10\sqrt{7} - \quad}$ — Simplify.

$= \frac{8x\sqrt{7}+20x}{\quad}$ — Subtract

Check

Write the simplified form of $\frac{6x}{4\sqrt{5}-4}$.

______

Pause and Reflect

Did you struggle with anything in this lesson? If so, how did you deal with it?

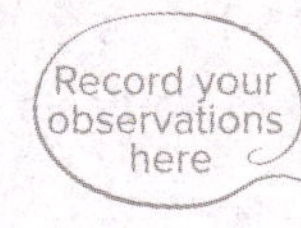

Go Online You can complete an Extra Example online.

Name ______ Period ______ Date ______

Practice

Go Online You can complete your homework online.

Examples 1 and 2

Simplify.

1. $\sqrt{72a^8b^5}$
2. $\sqrt{9a^{15}b^3}$
3. $\sqrt{24a^{16}b^8c}$
4. $\sqrt{18a^6b^3c^5}$
5. $\sqrt[4]{64a^4b^4}$
6. $\sqrt[3]{-8d^2f^5}$
7. $\sqrt{\frac{25}{36}r^2t}$
8. $\sqrt{\frac{192k^4}{64}}$
9. $\sqrt[5]{\frac{3072h^8}{243f^5}}$
10. $\sqrt[3]{\frac{432n^{12}}{64q^6}}$

Example 3

Simplify.

11. $\sqrt{2} + \sqrt{8} + \sqrt{50}$
12. $\sqrt{12} - 2\sqrt{3} + \sqrt{108}$
13. $8\sqrt{5} - \sqrt{45} - \sqrt{80}$
14. $2\sqrt{48} - \sqrt{75} - \sqrt{12}$
15. $\sqrt{28x} - \sqrt{14} + \sqrt{63x}$
16. $\sqrt{135} + 5\sqrt{10d} - 3\sqrt{60}$

Examples 4 and 5

Simplify.

17. $3\sqrt{5y} \cdot 8\sqrt{10yz}$
18. $2\sqrt{32a^3b^5} \cdot \sqrt{8a^7b^2}$
19. $6\sqrt{3ab} \cdot 4\sqrt{24ab^3}$
20. $5\sqrt{x^8y^3} \cdot 5\sqrt{2x^5y^4}$
21. $5\sqrt{2x} \cdot 3\sqrt{7x^2y^3}$
22. $3\sqrt{a^5b^7} \cdot 2\sqrt{5a^7b^3}$
23. $(7\sqrt{2} - 3\sqrt{3})(4\sqrt{6} + 3\sqrt{12})$
24. $(8\sqrt{5} - 6\sqrt{3})(8\sqrt{5} + 6\sqrt{3})$
25. $(12\sqrt{10} - 6\sqrt{5})(12\sqrt{10} + 6\sqrt{5})$
26. $(6\sqrt{3} + 5\sqrt{2})(2\sqrt{6} + 3\sqrt{8})$

27. **TRAMPOLINE** There are two trampoline runways at a gymnastics practice facility. Based on measurements using the Pythagorean Theorem, the runways are $\sqrt{3}$ meters wide; one is $6\sqrt{3}$ meters long and the other is $5\sqrt{2}$ meters long. What is the total area of the trampoline runways?

28. **DISTANCE** Jayla walks 5 blocks north, then 8 blocks east to get to the library. Each block is $5\sqrt{10}$ yards long. If Jayla could walk in a straight line to the library instead, how far would the walk be, in yards?

Examples 6 and 7

Simplify.

29. $\dfrac{\sqrt{5a^5}}{\sqrt{b^{13}}}$

30. $\dfrac{\sqrt{7x}}{\sqrt{10x^3}}$

31. $\dfrac{3\sqrt{6x^2}}{3\sqrt{5y}}$

32. $\sqrt[4]{\dfrac{7x^3}{4b^2}}$

33. $\dfrac{6}{\sqrt{3} - \sqrt{2}}$

34. $\dfrac{\sqrt{2}}{\sqrt{5} - \sqrt{3}}$

35. $\dfrac{9 - 2\sqrt{3}}{\sqrt{3} + 6}$

36. $\dfrac{2\sqrt{2} + 2\sqrt{5}}{\sqrt{5} + \sqrt{2}}$

37. $\dfrac{3\sqrt{7}}{\sqrt{5} - 1}$

38. $\dfrac{7x}{3 - \sqrt{2}}$

Mixed Exercises

Simplify.

39. $\sqrt[3]{16y^4z^{12}}$

40. $\sqrt[3]{-54x^6y^{11}}$

41. $\sqrt[4]{162a^6b^{13}c}$

42. $\sqrt[4]{48a^9b^3c^{16}}$

43. $\sqrt[4]{\dfrac{12x^3y^2}{5a^2b}}$

44. $\dfrac{\sqrt[3]{36xy^2}}{\sqrt[3]{10xz}}$

45. $\dfrac{x + 1}{\sqrt{x - 1}}$

46. $\dfrac{x - 2}{\sqrt{x^2 - 4}}$

47. $\dfrac{\sqrt{x}}{\sqrt{x^2 - 1}}$

48. $\sqrt[n]{\dfrac{2n^2}{8^{2n}}}$

49. $3\sqrt{24x} - 2\sqrt{54x} + \sqrt{48}$

50. $5\sqrt{18c} + 3\sqrt{72c} + 6\sqrt{76}$

51. $10\sqrt{175a} - 4\sqrt{112a} - 2\sqrt{63a}$

52. $7\sqrt{204y} + 4\sqrt{459y} - 8\sqrt{140y}$

53. CUBES McKenzie has a rectangular box with dimensions 20 inches by 35 inches by 40 inches. She would like to replace it with a box in the shape of a cube but with the same volume. What should the length of a side of the cube be? Express your answer as a radical expression in simplest form.

54. INSTRUMENTS Traditionally, musical instruments are tuned so that the note A is 440 Hertz. With each note higher on the instrument, the frequency of the pitch increases by a factor of $\sqrt[12]{2}$. What is the ratio of the frequencies of two notes that are 6 steps apart on the instrument? What is the ratio of the frequencies of two notes that are 9 steps apart on the instrument? Express your answers in simplest form.

Name ______________________ Period __________ Date __________

55. **PHYSICS** The speed of a wave traveling over a string is given by $\frac{\sqrt{t}}{\sqrt{u}}$, where t is the tension of the string and u is the density. Rewrite the expression in simplest form by rationalizing the denominator.

56. **LIGHTS** Suppose a light has a brightness intensity of I_1 when it is at a distance of d_1 and a brightness intensity of I_2 when it is at a distance of d_2. These quantities are related by the equation $\frac{d_2}{d_1} = \sqrt{\frac{I_1}{I_2}}$. Suppose $I_1 = 50$ units and $I_2 = 24$ units. What would $\frac{d_2}{d_1}$ be? Express your answer in simplest form.

57. **RACING** John is Jay's younger brother. They like to race and, after many races, they found that the fairest race was to run slightly different distances. They both start at the same place and run straight for 0.2 miles. Then they head for different finishes. In the figure, John and Jay's finishing paths are marked. This time, they tied. Both of them finished the race in exactly 4 minutes.

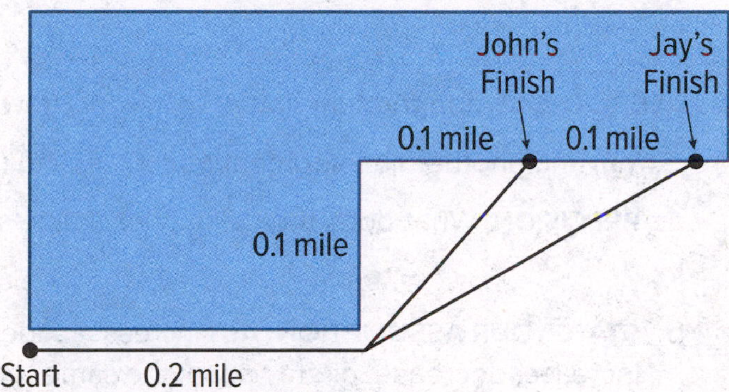

a. If John and Jay continued at their average paces during the race, exactly how many minutes would it take them each to run a mile? Express your answer as a radical expression in simplest form.

b. Exactly how many times as fast did John run as Jay? Express your answer as a radical expression in simplest form.

58. **STRUCTURE** Write, in simplest form, the ratio of the sides of the two cubes described.

a. The volumes of the two cubes are $270x$ cubic inches and $32x^2$ cubic inches.

b. The surface areas of the two cubes are $6x^4$ square feet and $6(x + 1)$ square feet.

59. **a.** **REASONING** Rewrite each of the following expressions as a single expression in the form ax^m for appropriate choices of a and m. Show your work.

i. $\sqrt{x}(\sqrt{x} + \sqrt{4x})$

ii. $\sqrt{x}(\sqrt{x} + \sqrt{4x} + \sqrt{9x})$

iii. $\sqrt{x}(\sqrt{x} + \sqrt{4x} + \sqrt{9x} + \sqrt{16x})$

b. **REGULARITY** More generally, simplify $\sqrt{x}(\sqrt{x} + \sqrt{4x} + \cdots + \sqrt{n^2x})$ for any positive integer n. Use the fact that $1 + 2 + \cdots + n = \frac{n(n+1)}{2}$.

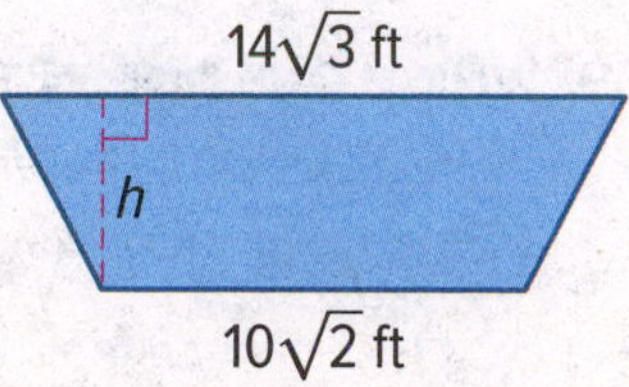

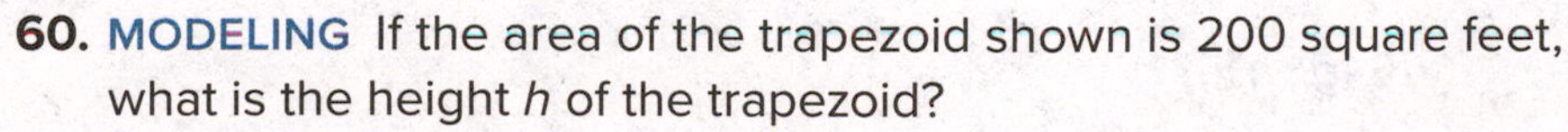

60. **MODELING** If the area of the trapezoid shown is 200 square feet, what is the height h of the trapezoid?

61. A spherical paperweight with a volume of 72π cubic centimeters is to be packaged in a gift box that is a cube. There must be at least 2 centimeters of packing material around the paperweight to protect it during shipping. The formula for the volume of a sphere is $V = \frac{4}{3}\pi r^3$.

a. **STRUCTURE** Write an expression for the minimum length of a side of the gift box. Show your work.

b. **ARGUMENTS** The shipper wants to use a box with a volume of 384 cubic centimeters that they already have in inventory. Is this box suitable?

62. **USE TOOLS** Graph the function $f(t) = \frac{100}{\sqrt{t-1}}$. Draw a line segment from $(2, f(2))$ to $(3, f(3))$ and another line segment from $(2, f(2))$ to $(5, f(5))$.

a. **PRECISION** What does the slope of each line segment represent?

b. **STATE YOUR ASSUMPTION** As t increases, does the slope between two points increase, decrease, or stay about the same? What does this mean? Explain your reasoning.

63. **FIND THE ERROR** Twyla and Brandon are simplifying $4\sqrt{32} + 6\sqrt{18}$. Is either of them correct? Explain your reasoning.

Twyla	Brandon
$4\sqrt{32} + 6\sqrt{18}$	$4\sqrt{32} + 6\sqrt{18}$
$= 4\sqrt{4^2 \cdot 2} + 6\sqrt{3^2 \cdot 2}$	$= 4\sqrt{16 \cdot 2} + 6\sqrt{9 \cdot 2}$
$= 16\sqrt{2} + 18\sqrt{2}$	$= 64\sqrt{2} + 54\sqrt{2}$
$= 34\sqrt{2}$	$= 118\sqrt{2}$

64. **PERSEVERE** Show that $\frac{-1 - i\sqrt{3}}{2}$ is a cube root of 1.

65. **ANALYZE** For what values of a is $\sqrt{a} \cdot \sqrt{-a}$ a real number? Explain.

66. **PERSEVERE** Find four combinations of whole numbers that satisfy $\sqrt[a]{256} = b$.

67. **CREATE** Find a number other than 1 that has a positive whole number for a square root, cube root, and fourth root.

68. **WRITE** Explain why absolute values may be unnecessary when an nth root of an even power results in an odd power.

69. **WHICH ONE DOESN'T BELONG?** Determine which of the radical expressions doesn't belong. Explain your reasoning.

$\sqrt[8]{256g^4h^{16}}$ $\quad$ $\sqrt[4]{16g^8h^2}$ $\quad$ $\sqrt[6]{64g^{12}h^3}$

Solving Radical Equations

Explore Solutions of Radical Equations

Online Activity Use graphing technology to complete the Explore.

INQUIRY When will a radical equation have a solution? When will it have no solution?

Today's Standards
A.REI.2
MP3, MP5, MP8

Today's Vocabulary
radical equation

Learn Solving Radical Equations Algebraically

Key Concept • Solving Radical Equations

Step 1 Isolate the radical on one side of the equation.

Step 2 To eliminate the radical, raise each side of the equation to a power equal to the index of the radical.

Step 3 Solve the resulting polynomial equation. Check your results.

Example 1 Solve a Square Root Equation

Solve $\sqrt{3x-5}+2=6$.

$\sqrt{3x-5}+2=6$	Original equation
$\sqrt{3x-5}=$ ____	Subtract 2 from each side.
$3x-5=$ ____	Square each side to eliminate the radical.
$3x=$ ____	Add 5 to each side.
$x=$ ____	Divide each side by 3.

Think About It!
How could you change the equation so that there is no solution?

Example 2 Solve a Cube Root Equation

Solve $4(2x+6)^{\frac{1}{3}}-9=3$.

$4(2x+6)^{\frac{1}{3}}-9=3$	Original equation
$4(2x+6)^{\frac{1}{3}}=$ ____	Add 9 to each side.
$(2x+6)^{\frac{1}{3}}=$ ____	Divide each side by 4.
$2x+6=$ ____	Cube each side.
$2x=$ ____	Subtract 6 from each side.
$x=\frac{21}{2}$	Divide each side by 2.

Go Online
You can learn how to solve radical equations by watching the video online.

(continued on the next page)

Your Notes

Check

$4(2x + 6)^{\frac{1}{3}} - 9 = 3$ — Original equation

$4\left(2 \cdot \quad + 6\right)^{\frac{1}{3}} - 9 \stackrel{?}{=} 3$ — Replace x with $\frac{21}{2}$.

$4(\_\_\_)^{\frac{1}{3}} - 9 \stackrel{?}{=} 3$ — Simplify.

$4(\_\_) - 9 \stackrel{?}{=} 3$ — The cube root of 27 is 3.

$\_\_ = 3$ — True

Example 3 Identify Extraneous Solutions

Solve $\sqrt{x + 21} = 3 - \sqrt{x}$.

$\sqrt{x + 21} = 3 - \sqrt{x}$ — Original equation

$x + 21 = \_\_ - \_\_\sqrt{x} + \_\_$ — Square each side.

$\_\_\_ = -6\sqrt{x}$ — Isolate the radical.

$\_\_\_ = \sqrt{x}$ — Divide each side by −6.

$\_\_\_ = x$ — Square each side.

Talk About It

In this example, could you tell that 4 was an extraneous solution before checking the result? Explain your reasoning.

Check

$\sqrt{x + 21} = 3 - \sqrt{x}$ — Original equation

$\sqrt{\quad + 21} \stackrel{?}{=} 3 - \sqrt{\quad}$ — Replace x with 4.

$\sqrt{25} \stackrel{?}{=} 3 - 2$ — Simplify.

$\_\_ \neq \_\_$ — False

The result does ____ satisfy the original equation, so it is an ________ solution. Therefore, there is ______________

Example 4 Solving a Radical Equation

Solve $\frac{2}{3}(11x + 14)^{\frac{1}{6}} + 8 = 10$.

$\frac{2}{3}(11x + 14)^{\frac{1}{6}} + 8 = 10$ — Original equation

$\frac{2}{3}(11x + 14)^{\frac{1}{6}} = 2$ — Subtract 8 from each side.

$(11x + 14)^{\frac{1}{6}} = 3$ — Multiply each side by $\frac{3}{2}$.

$11x + 14 = 729$ — Raise each side to the sixth power.

$11x = 715$ — Subtract 14 from each side.

$x = 65$ — Divide each side by 11.

The value of 65 _____ make the equation true.

Go Online You can complete an Extra Example online.

Learn Solving Radical Equations by Graphing and Using a System

To solve a radical equation using the graph of a related function, solve the equation for 0 and then replacce 0 with $f(x)$.

Equation: $\sqrt{2x+5}+1=4$

Related Function: $f(x)=\sqrt{2x+5}-3$ or $y=\sqrt{2x+5}-3$

The values of x for which $f(x)=0$ are the zeros of the function and occur at the x-intercepts of its graph. The solutions or roots of an equation are the zeros or x-intercepts of its related function.

You can also solve a radical equation by writing and solving a system of equations based on the equation. Set the expressions on each side of the equation equal to y to create the system of equations.

Equation: $\sqrt{2x+5}+1=4$

System of Equations: $y=\sqrt{2x+5}+1$ $\quad y=4$

The x-coordinate of the intersection of the system of equations is the value of x where the two equations are equal. Thus, the x-coordinate of the point of intersection is the solution of the radical equation.

> **Think About It!**
> What would the graph of the related function of a radical equation with no solution look like?

> **Watch Out!**
> **Misleading Graphs** Although the TI-84 may show what appears to be a discontinuity in the graphs of radical functions with odd roots, these functions are in fact continuous for all real numbers.

Example 5 Solve a Radical Equation by Graphing

Use a graphing calculator to solve $2\sqrt[3]{3x-4}+10=9$ by graphing.

Step 1 Find a related function: Rewrite equation with 0 on right side

$2\sqrt[3]{3x-4}+10=9$ — Original equation

$2\sqrt[3]{3x-4}+\_\_\_=\_\_\_$ — Subtract 9 from each side.

Replacing 0 with $f(x)$ gives the related function $f(x)=2\sqrt[3]{3x-4}+1$.

Step 2 Graph the related function: $f(x)=2\sqrt[3]{3x-4}+1$

Enter the equation in the **Y** = list and graph.

Step 3 Use a table.

You can use the **TABLE** feature to find the interval where the zero lies.

The function changes sign between $x=1$ and $x=2$ which indicates that there is a zero between ___ and ___.

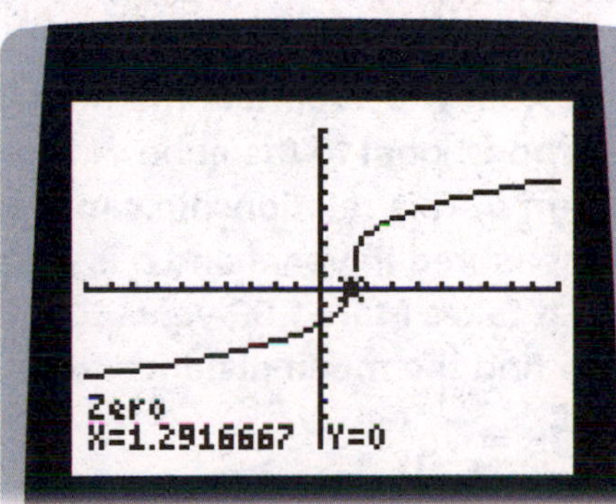

[−10, 10] scl: 1 by [−10, 10] scl: 1

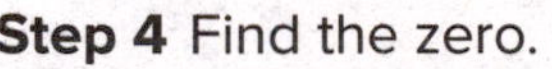

Step 4 Find the zero.

Use the **zero** feature from the **CALC** menu to find the zero of the function.

The zero is about ___. This is between 1 and 2, which is consistent with the interval we found using the table.

Go Online You can complete an Extra Example online.

Think About It!

How can you use the table feature on your calculator to find the intersection?

Use a Source

Research the time it takes another planet to orbit the Sun. Write and solve a radical equation to find that planet's mean distance from the Sun.

Example 6 Solve a Radical Equation by Using a System

Use a graphing calculator to solve $\sqrt{x+6} - 5 = -\sqrt{2x} + 1$ by using a system of equations.

Step 1 Write a system.

Set each side of $\sqrt{x+6} - 5 = -\sqrt{2x} + 1$ equal to y to create a system of equations.

$y = \sqrt{x+6} - 5$ First equation

$y =$ __________ Second equation

Step 2 Graph the system.

Enter the equations in the **Y** = list and graph in the standard viewing window.

Step 3 Find the intersection.

Use the **intersect** feature from the **CALC** menu to find the coordinates of the point of intersection.

The solution is the ___-coordinate of the __________, which is about _____.

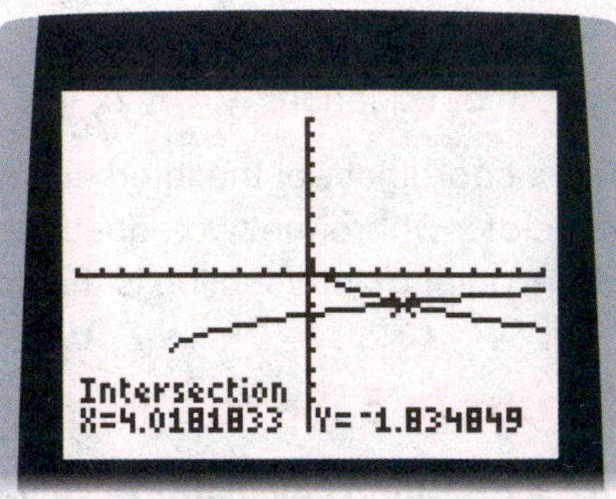

[−10, 10] scl: 1 by [−10, 10] scl: 1

Check

Use a graphing calculator to solve $-4(\sqrt[3]{x} - 2) = \sqrt[4]{x-3} - 6$ by using a system of equations. Round to the nearest hundredth if necessary.

$x \approx$ _____

Example 7 Confirm Solutions by Using Technology

SPACE **The square of the time it takes a planet to orbit the Sun T is proportional to the cube of the planet's mean distance from the Sun a. This relationship can also be written as $T = \sqrt{a^3}$, where T is measured in years and a is measured in astronomical units (AU). If it takes Mars 1.88 years to orbit the Sun, use a graphing calculator to find the mean distance from Mars to the Sun.**

$1.88 = \sqrt{a^3}$ $T = 1.88$

________ $= a^3$ Square each side.

________ $\approx a$ Take the cube root of each side.

So, the mean distance from Mars to the Sun is about ________ AU. Use a graphing calculator to confirm this solution by graphing.

 **Go Online** You can complete an Extra Example online.

Name ____________ Period ________ Date ________

Practice

Go Online You can complete your homework online.

Example 1

Solve each equation.

1. $\sqrt{x} = 5$
2. $\sqrt{x} + 3 = 7$
3. $5\sqrt{j} = 1$
4. $\sqrt{b - 5} = 4$
5. $\sqrt{3n + 1} = 5$
6. $2 + \sqrt{3p + 7} = 6$
7. $\sqrt{k - 4} - 1 = 5$
8. $5 = \sqrt{2g - 7}$

Example 2

Solve each equation.

9. $\sqrt[3]{x + 1} = 2$
10. $\sqrt[3]{2w} = 4$
11. $\sqrt[3]{3r - 6} = 3$
12. $(2d + 3)^{\frac{1}{3}} = 2$
13. $(t - 3)^{\frac{1}{3}} = 2$
14. $4 - (1 - 7u)^{\frac{1}{3}} = 0$
15. $\sqrt[3]{2v - 7} = -2$
16. $4(5n - 1)^{\frac{1}{3}} - 1 = 0$

Examples 3 and 4

Solve each equation. Identify any extraneous solutions.

17. $\sqrt{x - 15} = 3 - \sqrt{x}$
18. $(6q + 1)^{\frac{1}{4}} + 2 = 5$
19. $(3x + 7)^{\frac{1}{4}} - 3 = 1$
20. $(3y - 2)^{\frac{1}{5}} + 5 = 6$
21. $(4z - 1)^{\frac{1}{5}} - 1 = 2$
22. $\sqrt{x - 10} = 1 - \sqrt{x}$
23. $\sqrt[6]{y + 2} + 9 = 14$
24. $(2x - 1)^{\frac{1}{4}} - 2 = 1$

Example 5

Use a graphing calculator to solve each equation by graphing.

25. $\sqrt{x - 7} + 2 = 8$
26. $5 + \sqrt{3m + 9} = 10$
27. $\sqrt[3]{5b - 4} = 2$
28. $\sqrt[3]{2v + 3} = -2$

Example 6

Use a graphing calculator to solve each equation by using a system of equations.

29. $2\left(\sqrt[3]{2k - 3}\right) = \left(\sqrt[4]{k + 14}\right)$
30. $3\left(\sqrt[3]{d - 5}\right) = \left(\sqrt[4]{3d + 2}\right)$
31. $\sqrt{2x + 7} = 5 - \sqrt{3x}$
32. $\sqrt{n + 8} = \sqrt{4n - 9}$

Example 7

33. **GEOMETRY** Haruo's formula states that the area of a triangle whose sides have lengths a, b, and c is $A = \sqrt{s(s-a)(s-b)(s-c)}$ where s is the semiperimeter of the triangle. If the area of the triangle is 270 cm^2, the semiperimeter is 45 cm, a is 15 cm, and c is 39 cm, what is the length of side b?

34. **TWINE** The largest ball of twine was started in 1953 by Frank Stroeber and in 4 years had a volume of approximately 268 ft^3. What was the radius of the ball of twine at that time? Round your answer to the nearest tenth.

Mixed Exercises

Solve each equation. Identify any extraneous solutions.

35. $\sqrt{x+6} = 5 - \sqrt{x+1}$

36. $\sqrt{x-3} = \sqrt{x+4} - 1$

37. $6 + \sqrt{4x+8} = 9$

38. $\sqrt{7a-2} = \sqrt{a+3}$

39. $\sqrt{x-5} - \sqrt{x} = -2$

40. $\sqrt{b-6} + \sqrt{b} = 3$

41. $(5n-6)^{\frac{1}{3}} + 3 = 4$

42. $(5p-7)^{\frac{1}{3}} + 3 = 5$

43. $2(x-10)^{\frac{1}{3}} + 4 = 0$

44. $3(x+5)^{\frac{1}{3}} - 6 = 0$

45. $\sqrt[3]{5x+10} - 5 = 0$

46. $\sqrt[3]{4n-8} = 0$

47. $\frac{1}{7}(14a)^{\frac{1}{3}} = 1$

48. $\frac{1}{4}(32b)^{\frac{1}{3}} = 1$

49. $\sqrt{x-3} = 3 - x$

50. $\sqrt{x-2} = 22 - x$

51. $\sqrt{x+30} = x$

52. $\sqrt{x+22} = x + 2$

53. **SIGNS** A sign painter must spend $8n^{\frac{2}{3}} + 400$ to make n signs. How many signs can the painter make for \$1200?

54. **LATERAL AREA** The lateral area of a cone with base radius r and height h is given by the formula $L = \pi r\sqrt{r^2 + h^2}$. A cone has a lateral area of 65π square units and a base radius of 5 units. What is the height of the cone?

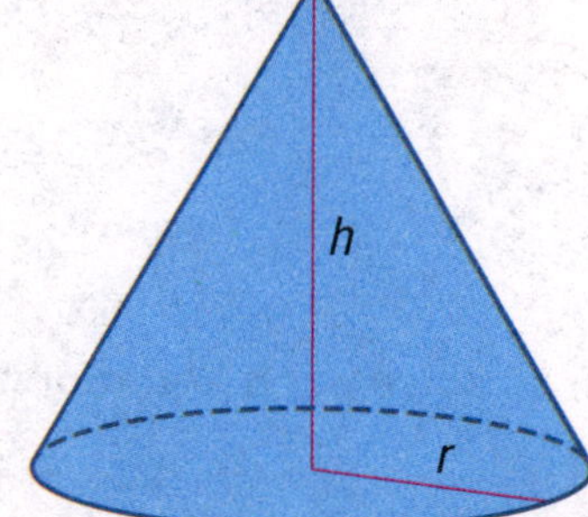

55. **TETHERS** A tether of length y secures a 25-foot pole to the ground. The distance from the tether to the pole along the ground is represented by x. The length of $x + y$ is 50. By the Pythagorean Theorem, the distance $y = \sqrt{x^2 + 25^2}$. What is the distance, x?

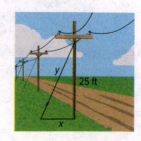

Name _______________ Period _______ Date _______

56. **RANGE** NASA's Near-Earth Asteroid Tracking System tracks more than 300 asteroids. An asteroid is passing near Earth. If Earth is located at the origin of a coordinate plane, the path that the asteroid will trace out is given by $y = \frac{17}{x}$, $x > 0$. One unit corresponds to one million miles. Caleb learns that he will be able to see the asteroid with his telescope when the asteroid is within $\frac{145}{12}$ million miles of Earth.

   a. Write an expression that gives the distance of the asteroid from Earth as a function of x.

   b. For what values of x will the asteroid be in range of Caleb's telescope?

Use a graphing calculator to solve each equation.

57. $2(\sqrt{x} - 5) = (\sqrt[4]{x} + 3)$

58. $3(\sqrt[3]{2d} + 1) = (\sqrt[4]{8d} - 2)$

59. $\sqrt{x + 4} = 3 - \sqrt{7x}$

60. $\sqrt{n + 12} = \sqrt{5n - 15}$

61. **DRIVING** The formula $s = \sqrt{30fd}$ where s is the speed of the car, f is the coefficient of friction, and d is the length of the skid marks in feet, can be used to determine the speed of a car when it begins to skid to a stop. If the speed limit is 25 mph and the coefficient of friction is 0.6, what is the longest the skid marks can be if the driver is driving the speed limit?

62. **PYRAMID** The side length of a square pyramid is given by the formula, $s = \sqrt{\frac{3V}{h}}$, where V is the volume of the pyramid and h is the height. If the side length is 5 m and the height is 21 m, what is the volume of the pyramid?

63. **SLEDS** Jorge works for the A-Glide Sled Company. This company estimates its monthly profit for the sale of x sleds, in hundreds of dollars, is given by the expression $\sqrt{3x + 19}$. Tia works for a competing sled manufacturer, SnowFun. Tia's company estimates that its monthly profit for the sale of x sleds, in hundreds of dollars, is given by the expression $3 + \sqrt{2x}$. Minh has been offered a job at both companies and decides he will work for the company that has the greatest monthly profit. Before he makes his decision, however, he asks Jorge and Tia the average number of sleds sold each month by each of their companies.

   a. Why is the number of sleds sold important to Minh?

   b. Assume both companies make the same number of sleds in a certain month. Determine a number of sleds that would make Minh want to work for SnowFun, and give the profit, to the nearest dollar, earned by each company during that month.

64. **REASONING** If you want the radical equation $\sqrt{a} = x + 2$ to have an extraneous solution of $x = -5$, what could you choose to replace a in the equation? Explain your answer, and find any true solutions to your equation.

65. **REASONING** If you want the radical equation $\sqrt{x + 7} = \sqrt{x - 5} + c$ to have an extraneous solution of $x = 9$, what number could you choose to replace c in the equation? Explain your answer, and find any true solutions to your equation.

66. **MODELING** Explain how to find the solutions to $\sqrt[4]{10x + 11} - \sqrt{x + 2} = 0$ graphically and confirm your results algebraically. What are the solutions? Construct the graph.

67. **STRUCTURE** Explain how to find the solutions to $\sqrt{x-5} - \sqrt[4]{x+7} = 0$, both algebraically and graphically. Describe how to find any extraneous solutions. Illustrate your answer.

68. **USE TOOLS** The surface area of a sphere is 20 cm^2 greater than the surface area of a cube. Find functions to represent the radius of the sphere and the side length of the cube, in terms of the surface area of the cube. Describe how a graphing calculator can be used to find the surface area of each object, if the radius of the sphere equals the side length of cube? Sketch the graph. Find the surface area of the cube and the sphere.

69. **ARGUMENTS** Explain how we know that the equation $\sqrt{x-5} + 1 = \sqrt{(2-x)}$ has no solutions without having to actually solve it. Confirm this by graphing the two sides of the equation.

70. **PRECISION** Solve the equation and graph the two sides of the equation to confirm your answer.

a. $\sqrt{x-1} + 1 = \sqrt{x-2}$

b. $\sqrt{x-1} + 1 = \sqrt{x+2}$

71. **WHICH ONE DOESN'T BELONG?** Which equation does not have a solution?

$\sqrt{x-1} + 3 = 4$	$\sqrt{x+1} + 3 = 4$	$\sqrt{x-2} + 7 = 10$	$\sqrt{x+2} - 7 = -10$

72. **PERSEVERE** Lola is working to solve $(x+5)^{\frac{1}{4}} = -4$. She said that she could tell there was no real solution without even working the problem. Is Lola correct? Explain your reasoning.

73. **ANALYZE** Determine whether $\frac{\sqrt{(x^2)^2}}{-x} = x$ is *sometimes*, *always*, or *never* true when x is a real number. Explain your reasoning.

74. **CREATE** Select a whole number. Now work backward to write two radical equations that have that whole number as solutions. Write one square root equation and one cube root equation. You may need to experiment until you find a whole number you can easily use.

75. **WRITE** Explain the relationship between the index of the root of a variable in an equation and the power to which you raise each side of the equation to solve the equation.

76. **CREATE** Write an equation that can be solved by raising each side of the equation to the given power.

a. $\frac{3}{2}$ power **b.** $\frac{5}{4}$ power **c.** $\frac{7}{8}$ power

77. **PERSEVERE** Solve $7^{3x-1} = 49^{x+1}$ for x. (Hint: $b^x = b^y$ if and only if $x = y$.)

ANALYZE **Determine whether the following statements are *sometimes*, *always*, or *never* true for $x^{\frac{1}{n}} = a$. Explain your reasoning.**

78. If n is odd, there will be extraneous solutions.

79. If n is even, there will be extraneous solutions.

Module 6 • Inverses and Radical Functions

Review

 Essential Question

How can the inverse of a function be used to help interpret a real-world event or solve a problem?

Module Summary

Lesson 6-1

Function Operations

- $(f + g)(x) = f(x) + g(x)$
- $(f - g)(x) = f(x) - g(x)$
- $(fg)(x) = f(x)g(x)$
- $\left(\frac{f}{g}\right)(x) = \frac{f(x)}{g(x)}, g(x) \neq 0$
- $[f \circ g](x) = f[g(x)]$.

Lesson 6-2

Functions and Their Inverses

- If f and f^{-1} are inverses, then $f(a) = b$ if and only if $f^{-1}(b) = a$.
- $f(x)$ and $g(x)$ are inverses if and only if $[f \circ g](x) = x$ and $[g \circ f](x) = x$.

Lesson 6-3

Rational Exponents

- For any real numbers a and b and any positive integer n, if $a^n = b$, then a is an nth root of b.
- When there is more than one real root and n is even, the nonnegative root is called the principal root.
- An expression with rational exponents is in simplest form when it has no negative exponents, it has no exponents that are not positive integers in the denominator, it is not a complex fraction, and the index of any remaining radical is the least number possible.

Lesson 6-4

Radical Functions

- The parent function of the square root functions is $f(x) = \sqrt{x}$. The parent function of the cube root functions is $f(x) = \sqrt[3]{x}$.
- A square root function can be written in the form $g(x) = a\sqrt{x - h} + k$. A cube root function can be written in the form $g(x) = a\sqrt[3]{x - h} + k$.

Lessons 6-5 and 6-6

Radical Expressions and Equations

- For any real numbers a and b and any integer $n > 1$, $\sqrt[n]{ab} = \sqrt[n]{a} \cdot \sqrt[n]{b}$, if n is even and $a, b \geq 0$ or if n is odd.
- For any real numbers a and $b \neq 0$ and any integer $n > 1$, $\sqrt[n]{\frac{a}{b}} = \frac{\sqrt[n]{a}}{\sqrt[n]{b}}$, if all roots are defined.
- $a\sqrt{b} + c\sqrt{d}$ and $a\sqrt{b} - c\sqrt{d}$ are conjugates of each other.
- To solve a radical equation, isolate the radical on one side of the equation. Raise each side of the equation to a power equal to the index of the radical. Solve the resulting polynomial equation. Check your results.

Study Organizer

Foldables

Use your Foldable to review this module. Working with a partner can be helpful. Ask for clarification of concepts as needed.

Solving Radical Equations
Operations with Radical Expressions
Graphing Radical Functions
nth Roots and Rational Exponents
Inverse Relations and Functions
Operations on Functions

Name ______________________ Period ____________ Date ____________

Test Practice

1. MULTIPLE CHOICE Given $f(x) = 4x^3 - 5x^2 + 8$ and $g(x) = 2x^3 - 9x^2 - 7x$, find $(f - g)(x)$. (Lesson 6-1)

Ⓐ $(f - g)(x) = 2x^3 - 14x^2 + x$

Ⓑ $(f - g)(x) = 2x^3 + 4x^2 + 15x$

Ⓒ $(f - g)(x) = 2x^3 - 14x^2 - 7x + 8$

Ⓓ $(f - g)(x) = 2x^3 + 4x^2 + 7x + 8$

2. OPEN RESPONSE Given $f(x) = 2x^3 + 7x^2 - 7x - 30$ and $g(x) = x - 2$ find $\left(\frac{f}{g}\right)(x)$. (Lesson 6-1)

3. TABLE ITEM Maria creates a new math game using the composition of functions. She hands each player a card with an ordered pair and the person must determine which composition was used to create the ordered pair.

For the first round of the game, she uses the following functions:

$f = \{(-1, 8), (2, -4), (5, -2), (7, 5)\}$

$g = \{(8, -2), (-4, 7), (5, -1), (2, -5)\}$

Determine which composition was used for each player.

Anna: $(-1, -2)$ ___

Brenden: $(5, -5)$ ___

Carlos: $(-4, 5)$ ___

Ana: $(2, 7)$ ___

(Lesson 6-1)

Player	$[f \cdot g](x)$	$[g \cdot f](x)$	Neither
Anna			
Brenden			
Carlos			
Ana			

4. OPEN RESPONSE Given $f(x) = 3x - 7$ and $g(x) = 4x + 5$, what is the domain and range of $[f \circ g](x)$? Explain your reasoning (Lesson 6-1)

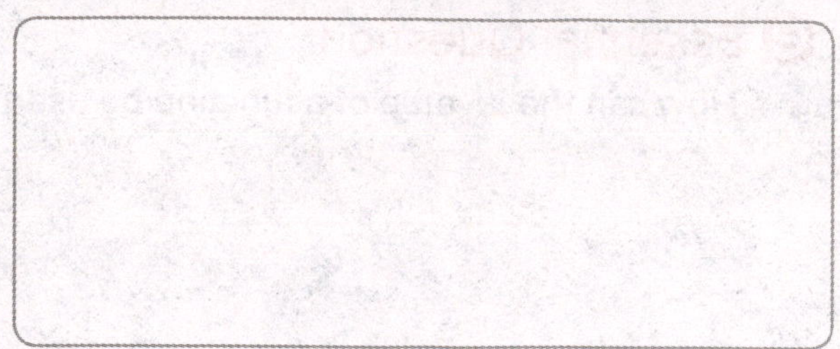

5. MULTIPLE CHOICE The graph shows $f(x)$. Which of the following shows $f^{-1}(x)$? (Lesson 6-2)

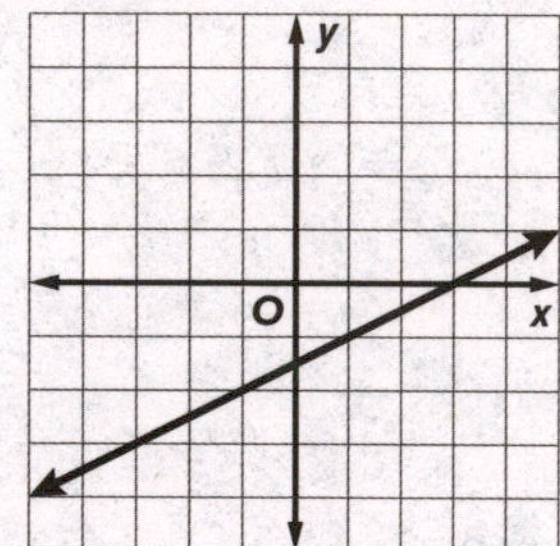

Ⓐ $f^{-1}(x) = 2x + 3$

Ⓑ $f^{-1}(x) = 3x + 2$

Ⓒ $f^{-1}(x) = x + 4$

Ⓓ $f^{-1}(x) = 4x$

6. MULTIPLE CHOICE Given $f(x) = 3x + 12$ and $g(x) = \frac{1}{3x} + 4$, determine whether $f(x)$ and $g(x)$ are inverses. Explain your reasoning. (Lesson 6-2)

Ⓐ Yes; $[f \circ g](x) = x$ and $[g \circ f](x) = x$

Ⓑ Yes; $[f \circ g](x) = x + 24$ and $[g \circ f](x) = x + 8$

Ⓒ No; $[f \circ g](x) = x + 24$ and $[g \circ f](x) = x + 8$

Ⓓ No; $[f \circ g](x) = x$ and $[g \circ f](x) = x$

Name ______________________ Period __________ Date __________

7. MULTI-SELECT The graph shows parallelogram *ABCD*.

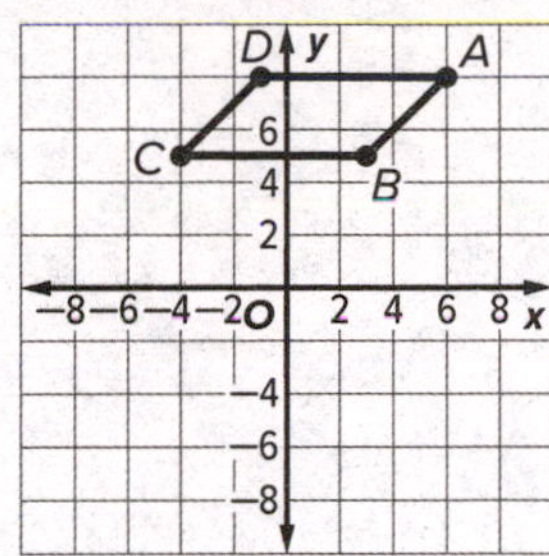

Select ALL of the coordinates that are vertices of the inverse of parallelogram *ABCD*. (Lesson 6-2)

- ☐ (8, 6)
- ☐ (1, 8)
- ☐ (5, 3)
- ☐ (−4, 5)
- ☐ (8, −1)
- ☐ (5, −4)
- ☐ (−3, 5)

8. GRIDDED RESPONSE Evaluate the expression: $256^{\frac{3}{8}} + 100{,}000^{-\frac{2}{5}}$ (Lesson 6-3)

9. MULTIPLE CHOICE Which of the following is the simplified form of $\sqrt[3]{729(x-7)^6}$? (Lesson 6-3)

Ⓐ $27(x-7)^3$

Ⓑ $27(x-7)^2$

Ⓒ $9(x-7)^3$

Ⓓ $9(x-7)^2$

10. MULTIPLE CHOICE The lung volume for mammals can be modeled using the expression $170x^{\frac{4}{5}}$, where x is the mass of the mammal. How can this expression be rewritten using radicals? (Lesson 6-3)

Ⓐ $170\sqrt[5]{x^4}$

Ⓑ $170\sqrt[4]{x^5}$

Ⓒ $\sqrt[5]{170x^4}$

Ⓓ $\sqrt[4]{170x^5}$

11. OPEN RESPONSE Determine the values of a and b. (Lesson 6-4)

$x^{\frac{2}{3}} \cdot x^{-\frac{1}{4}} = x^{\frac{a}{b}}$

12. MULTIPLE CHOICE Which of the following is the graph of $g(x) = -\sqrt{x+6} - 2$? (Lesson 6-4)

Ⓐ

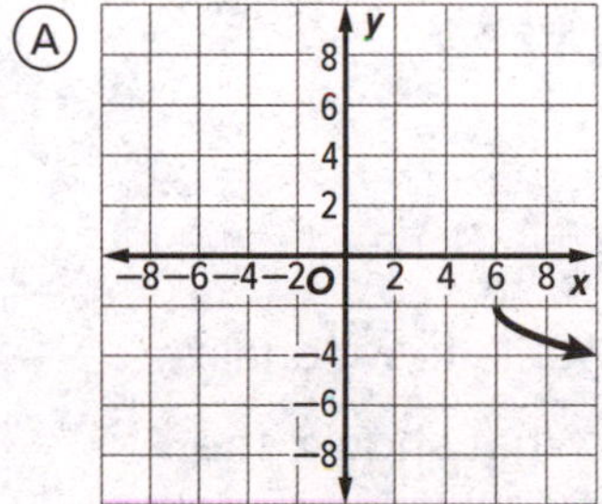

Ⓑ

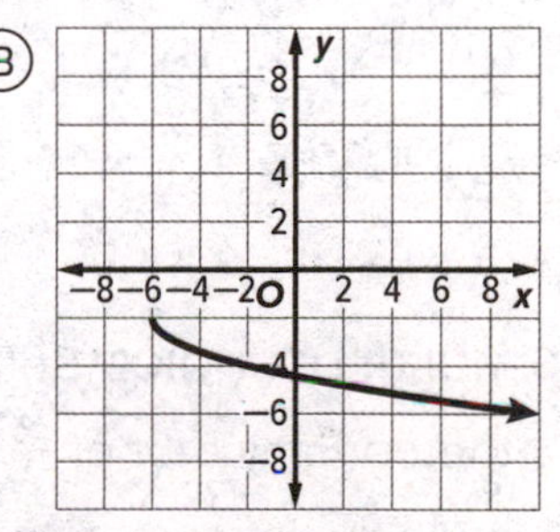

Ⓒ

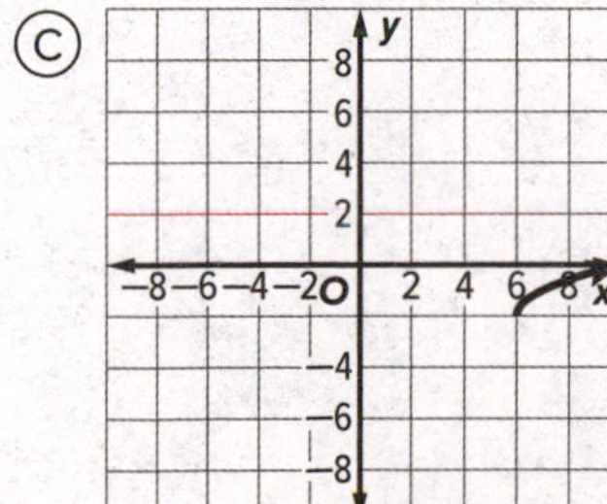

Ⓓ

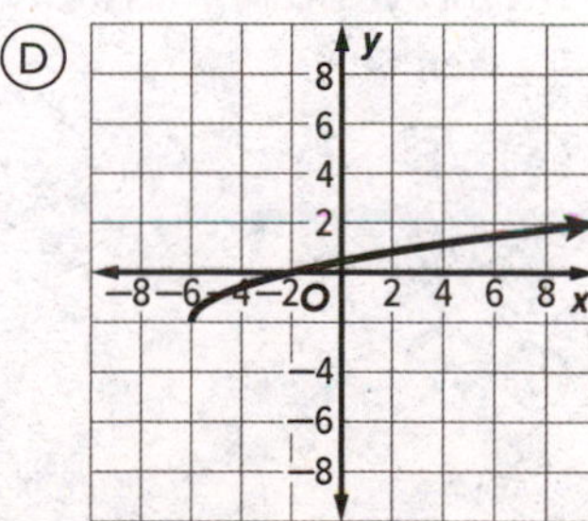

Name ______________________ Period ____________ Date ____________

13. MULTIPLE CHOICE Which function is shown on the graph? (Lesson 6-4)

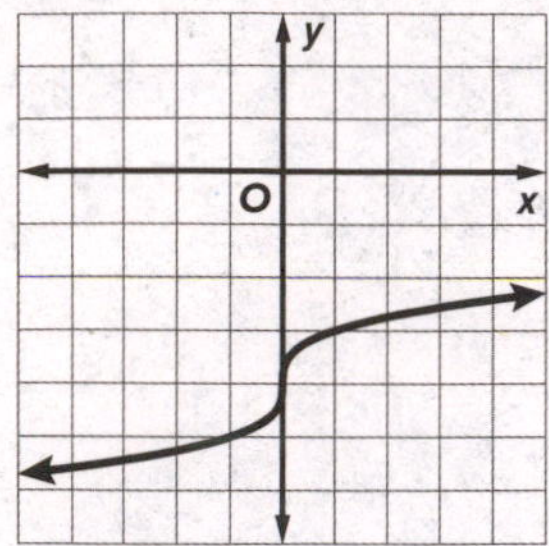

(A) $g(x) = (x + 4)^{\frac{1}{3}}$

(B) $g(x) = (x - 4)^{\frac{1}{3}}$

(C) $g(x) = x^{\frac{1}{3}} - 4$

(D) $g(x) = x^{\frac{1}{3}} + 4$

14. OPEN RESPONSE Determine the sum. $7\sqrt{12} + 2\sqrt{48} - 4\sqrt{75}$ (Lesson 6-5)

15. MULTIPLE CHOICE Heather drew a rectangle and labeled the length as $3\sqrt[4]{162x^4y^7}$ and the width as $2\sqrt[4]{40x^3y^5}$. Which is the simplified form of the area of the rectangle? (Lesson 6-5)

(A) $36\sqrt[3]{5x^{12}y^{35}}$

(B) $36xy^3\sqrt[4]{5x^3}$

(C) $36xy^3\sqrt[4]{5x^3y}$

(D) $36\sqrt[4]{5y^{12}}$

16. MULTIPLE CHOICE Sofia wants to rationalize the denominator of $\frac{7x^4y^5}{\sqrt[3]{8}}$. What should she multiply the numerator and denominator by? (Lesson 6-5)

(A) $\sqrt[3]{8}$

(B) $\sqrt{8}$

(C) x^4

(D) y^5

17. GRIDDED RESPONSE Solve the equation $3(6x - 8)^{\frac{1}{4}} + 3 = 9$. (Lesson 6-6)

18. MULTIPLE CHOICE Which of the following is/are the solution(s) for the equation $\sqrt{3x + 7} = x - 1$? Select all that apply. (Lesson 6-6)

(A) 6

(B) 3

(C) 2 and 3

(D) 6 and −1

19. GRIDDED RESPONSE The distance a pilot can see to the horizon depends on the altitude of the plane and can be modeled by the equation $d = 1.23\sqrt{a}$, where d is the distance in miles and a is the altitude in feet above sea level. How many miles to the horizon can a pilot flying a plane at an altitude of 30,000 feet see? Round your answer to the nearest mile. (Lesson 6-6)

Module 1

Module 1 Opener

1. −15 **3.** 10 **5.** $b = \frac{a}{3} - 3$ **7.** $x = \frac{4}{3}y + \frac{8}{3}$

Lesson 1-1

1. D = {all real numbers}; R = {all real numbers}; Codomain = all real numbers; onto
3. D = all real numbers, $R = \{y \mid y \geq 0\}$, Codomain = all real numbers; not onto
5. D = {1, 2, 3, 4, 5, 6, 7}; R = {56, 52, 44, 41, 43, 46, 53}; one-to-one
7. onto **9.** both
11. continuous; D = {all real numbers}, R = {all real numbers}
13. discrete; D = {1, 2, 3, 4, 5, 6}, R = {3, 4, 5, 6}
15. continuous; D = all positive real numbers, $R = \{y \mid y \geq 0\}$
17. $D = \{x \mid x \in \mathbb{R}\}$ or $(-\infty, \infty)$; $R = \{y \mid y \leq 0\}$ or $(-\infty, 0]$
19. $D = \{x \mid x \leq 1 \text{ or } x \geq 1\}$ or $(-\infty, -1] \cup [1, \infty)$; $R = \{y \mid y \in \mathbb{R}\}$ or $[-\infty, \infty)$
21. $D = \{x \mid x \leq -2 \text{ or } x \geq 1\}$ or $(-\infty, -2] \cup [1, \infty)$; $R = \{y \mid y \geq -2\}$ or $[-2, \infty)$
23. $D = \{x \mid x \in \mathbb{R}\}$ or $(-\infty, \infty)$; $R = \{y \mid y \geq -4\}$ or $[-4, \infty)$; neither one-to-one nor onto; continuous
25. $D = \{x \mid x \in \mathbb{R}\}$ or $(-\infty, \infty)$; $R = \{y \mid y \in \mathbb{R}\}$ or $[-\infty, \infty)$; both; continuous
27. $D = \{x \mid x \in \mathbb{R}\}$ or $(-\infty, \infty)$; $R = \{y \mid y \in \mathbb{R}\}$ or $[-\infty, \infty)$; onto; continuous
29. $D = \{w \mid 0 \leq w \leq 15\}$; $R = \{4 \leq L \leq 11.5\}$; one-to-one; continuous
31. neither one-to-one nor onto; discrete
33. $D = \{n \mid 0 \leq n \leq \infty\}$; $R = \{T(n) \mid 0 \leq n \leq \infty\}$; both (within the restrictions of the domain and range); continuous
35.

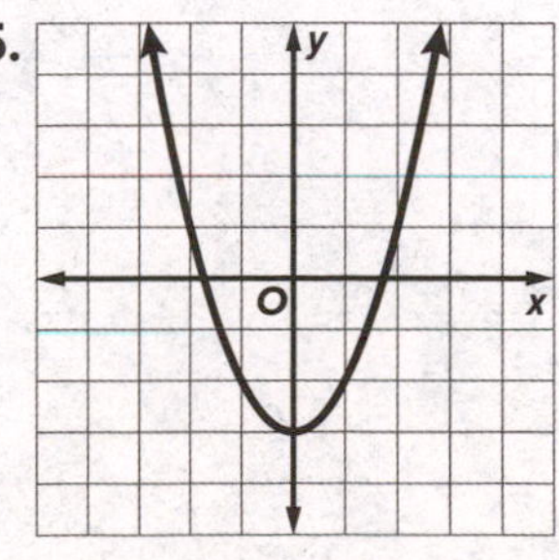

37. $D = \{x \mid x \neq 0\}$ or $(-\infty, 0) \cup (0, \infty)$; $R = \{y \mid y \neq 0\}$ or $(-\infty, 0) \cup (0, \infty)$; neither; continuous
39. Sample answer: The vertical line test is used to determine whether a relation is a function. If no vertical line intersects a graph in more than one point, the graph represents a function. The horizontal line test is used to determine whether a function is one-to-one. If no horizontal line intersects the graph more than once, then the function is one-to one. The horizontal line test can also be used to determine whether a function is onto. If every horizontal line intersects the graph at least once, then the function is onto.

Lesson 1-2

1. Yes; it can be written in $y = mx + b$ form.
3. Yes; it can be written in $y = mx +$ form.
5. nonlinear **7.** nonlinear **9.** The number of inches and corresponding number of feet is a linear function because when graphed, a line contains all of the points shown in the table.
11. *x*-int: 12; *y*-int: −18 **13.** *x*-int: 6; *y*-int: −18
15. *x*-int: 0, 4; *y*-int: 0 **17a.** *x*-int: 4; *y*-int: 20
17b. The *x*-intercept represents the number of days until Ava will run out of money. The *y*-intercept represents the total amount Ava had in her lunch account at the beginning of the week. **19.** point symmetry
21. point symmetry **23.** neither **25.** No; *x* is in a denominator. The equation is neither even nor odd. **27.** Yes; it can be written in $y = mx + b$ form. The equation is even.
29. No; there is an x^2 term. The equation is even. **31.** linear; *x*-int: $\frac{10}{3}$; *y*-int: $\frac{30}{7}$; point symmetry **33.** nonlinear; *x*-int: −3, −2, −1, 1, 2; *y*-int: 12; neither point nor line symmetry
35. line symmetry; $x = 0.4$
37a. $2x + 2y + 10 = 500$
37b. Yes; it can be written in $y = mx + b$ form.

37c. point symmetry;

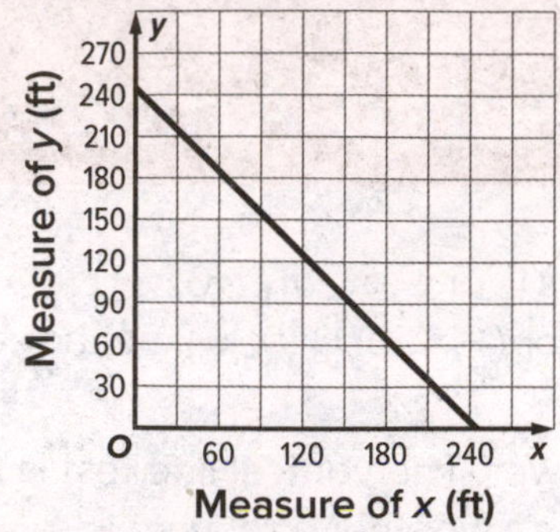

39. Odd; $f(-r) = -f(r)$

41. No; Sample answer: $f(x) = x^3 + 2x - 5$

43. Sample answer: Never; the graph of $x = a$ is a vertical line, so it is not a function.

Lesson 1-3

1. rel. max. at (−2, −2) rel. min. at (−1, −3)

3. rel. max. at (0, −2), min. at (−1, −3) and (1, −3)

5. The relative maxima occur at $x = -3.7$ and $x = 4.5$, and the relative minimum occurs at $x = 0$. The relative maxima at $x = -3.7$ and $x = 4.5$ represents the top of two hills. The relative minimum at $x = 0$ represents a valley between the hills.

7. As $x \to -\infty, y \to -\infty$ and as $x \to \infty, y \to -\infty$.

9. As $x \to -\infty, y \to \infty$ and as $x \to \infty, y \to -\infty$.

11a. $t = 1.5$; The fish reaches its maximum height 1.5 seconds after it is thrown.

11b. as $t \to -\infty, h(t) \to -\infty$ and as $t \to \infty$, $h(t) \to -\infty$; Because the height of the fish cannot be negative, the fish will hit the surface of the water if it is not caught by the dolphin. Because the fish begins at a height of 64 feet at 0 seconds, the time cannot be negative.

13. rel. max. at $x = 2.7$, rel. min. at $x = -1.2$; As $x \to -\infty, f(x) \to \infty$ and as $x \to \infty, f(x) \to -\infty$.

15. rel. max. at $x = -2$, rel. min. at $x = -1$; As $x \to -\infty, f(x) \to \infty$ and as $x \to \infty, f(x) \to \infty$.

17. no rel. max, min: $x = 0$; As $x \to -\infty, f(x) \to \infty$ and as $x \to \infty, f(x) \to \infty$.

19. Sample Answer:

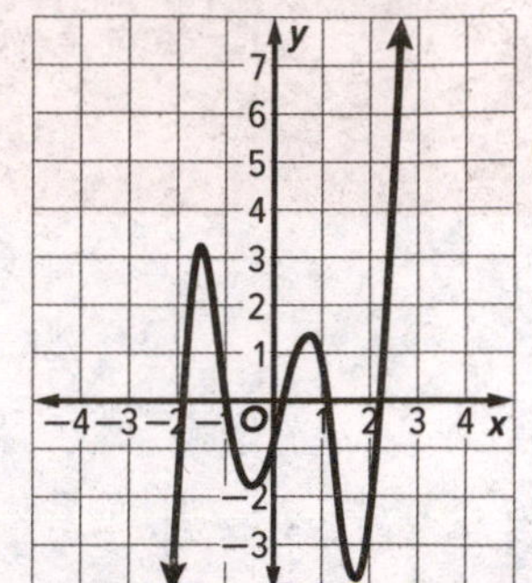

21. As $x \to -\infty, y \to -\infty$ and as $x \to \infty, y \to \infty$.

23. no relative max or min

25. rel. max: $x = -1.87$; rel. min: $x = 1.52$

27. The dynamic pressure would approach ∞.

29. as $r \to +\infty, V \to +\infty$

31. Sample answer: The end behavior of a graph describes the output values the input values approach negative and positive infinity. It can be determined by examining the graph.

33. As the concentration of the catalyst is increased, the reaction rate approaches 0.5.

Lesson 1-4

1.

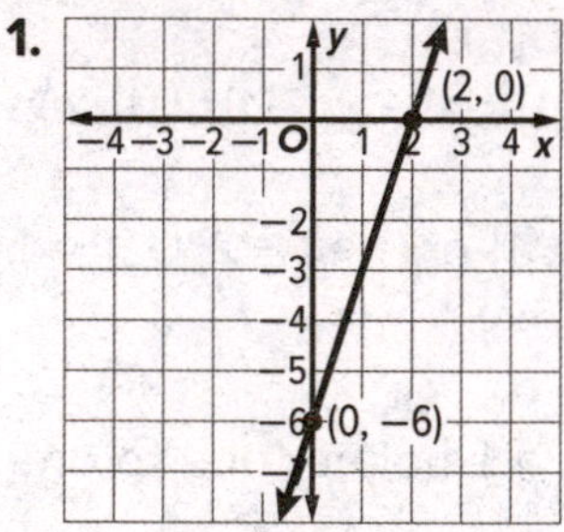

3.

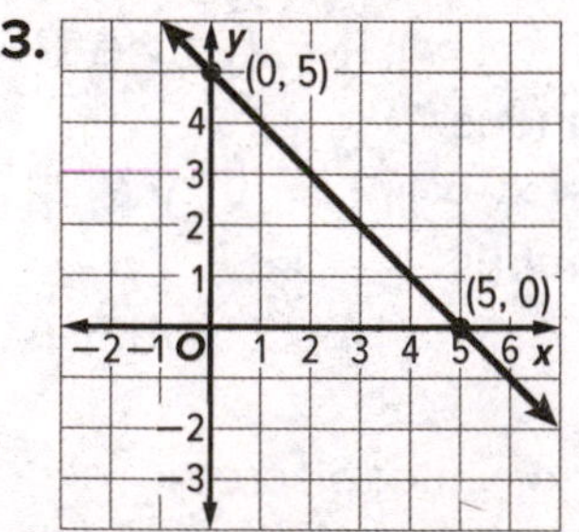

5.

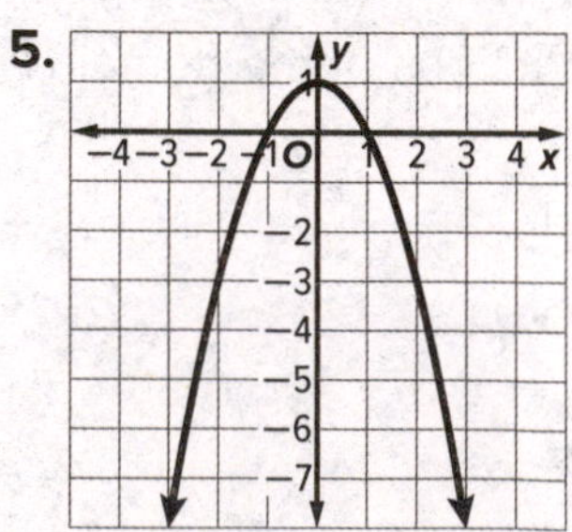

7. **Pelican's Height**

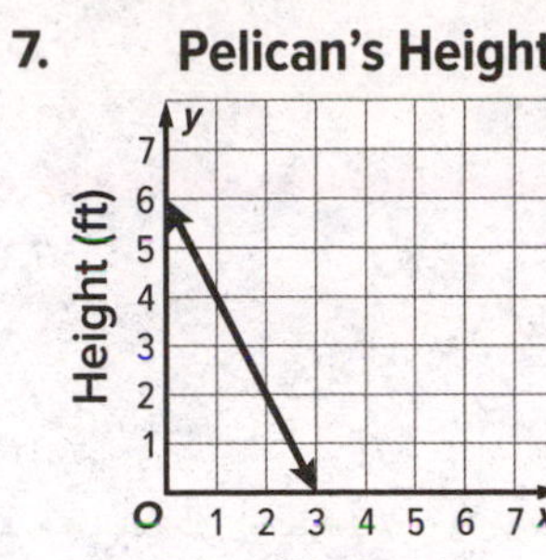

9. The x-intercept of $f(x)$ is 2, and the x-intercept of $g(x)$ is $-\frac{2}{3}$. The x-intercept of $f(x)$ is greater than the x-intercept of $g(x)$. So, $f(x)$ intersects the x-axis at a point farther to the right than $g(x)$. The y-intercept of $f(x)$ is -1, and the y-intercept of $g(x)$ is 2. The y-intercept of $g(x)$ is greater than the y-intercept of $f(x)$. So, $g(x)$ intersects the y-axis at a higher point than $f(x)$. The slope of $f(x)$ is $\frac{1}{2}$ and the slope of $g(x)$ is 3. Each function is increasing, but the slope of $g(x)$ is greater than the slope of $f(x)$. So, $g(x)$ increases faster than $f(x)$. **11.** Both x-intercepts of $f(x)$ are less than the x-intercept of $g(x)$. The graph of $f(x)$ intersects the x-axis more times than $g(x)$. The y-intercept of $g(x)$ is less than the y-intercept of $f(x)$. So, $f(x)$ intersects the y-axis at a higher point than $g(x)$. Neither function has a relative minimum or relative maximum. $f(x)$ has a minimum at $(-2, -4)$. The two functions have the opposite end behaviors as $x \to -\infty$. The two functions have the same end behavior as $x \to \infty$.

13.

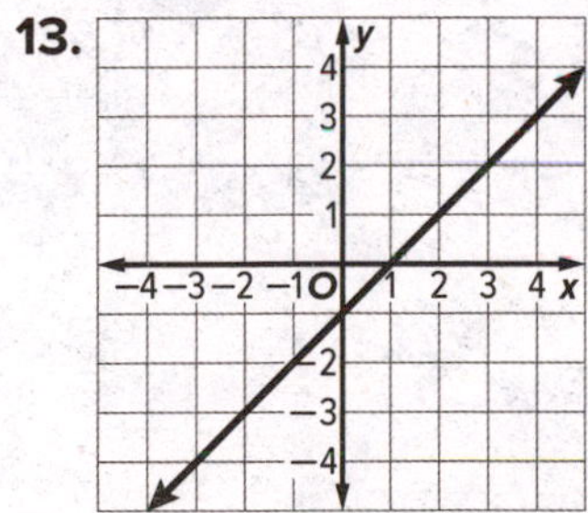

15. The x-intercept of $f(x)$ is $\frac{2}{3}$, and the x-intercept of $g(x)$ is $\frac{3}{8}$. The x-intercept of $f(x)$ is greater than the x-intercept of $g(x)$. So, $f(x)$ intersects the x-axis at a point farther to the right than $g(x)$. The y-intercept of $f(x)$ and $g(x)$ is $\frac{1}{2}$. So, $f(x)$ and $g(x)$ intersect the y-axis at the same point. The slope of $f(x)$ is $\frac{3}{4}$ and the slope of $g(x)$ is $-\frac{4}{3}$. Each function is decreasing, but the slope of $g(x)$ is less than the slope of $f(x)$. So, $g(x)$ decreases faster than $f(x)$.

17.

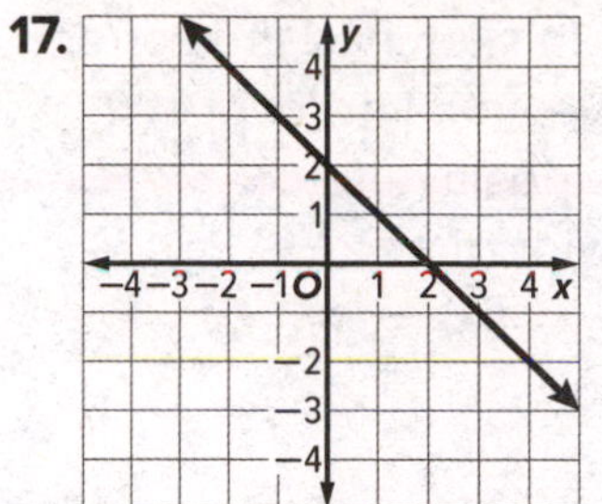

19. **Monica's Walk**

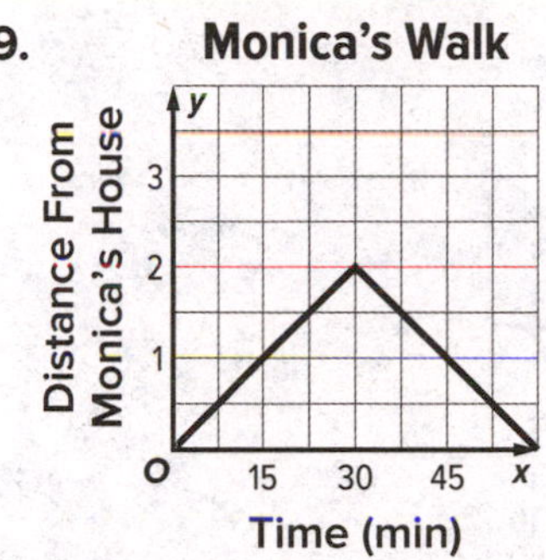

21a. linear; Sample answer: It is linear because it makes no stops along the way, and it descends at a steady pace, which indicates a constant rate of change, or slope.

21b. **Ski Lift Height**

23. Sample answer: The function is continuous. The function has a y-intercept at -3. The function has a maximum at $(-3, 1)$. The function has a minimum at $(1, -4)$. As $x \to -\infty$, $f(x) \to -\infty$ and as $x \to +\infty$, $f(x) \to +\infty$.

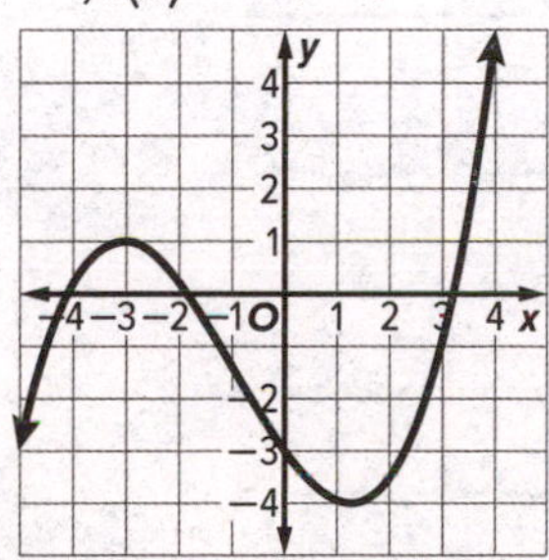

25. Always; Sample answer: A linear function cannot cross the x-axis more than once. So, if a function has more than one x-intercept, it is a nonlinear function.

27. Both Linda and Rubio sketched the correct graph. Both graphs have an x-intercept at 2, a y-intercept at -9, are positive for $x > 2$, and have an end behavior of as $x \to -\infty$, $f(x) \to -\infty$ and as $x \to \infty$, $f(x) \to \infty$.

Lesson 1-5

1.

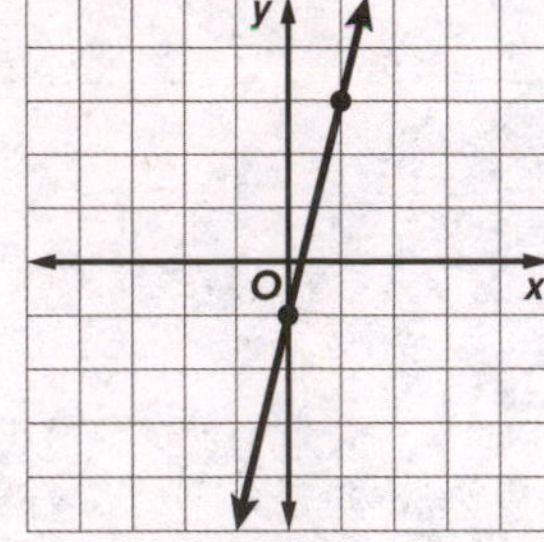

3.

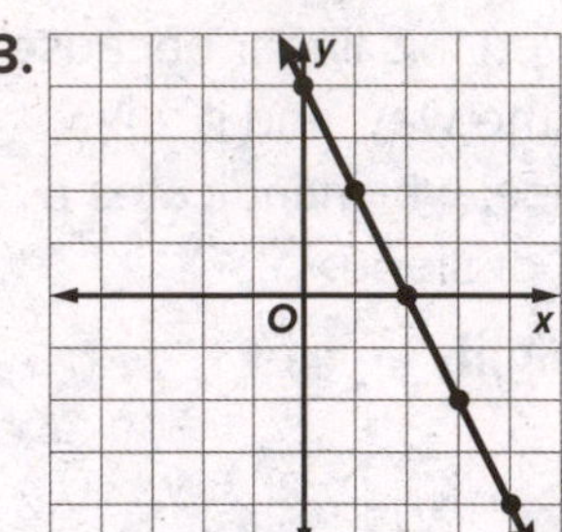

5.

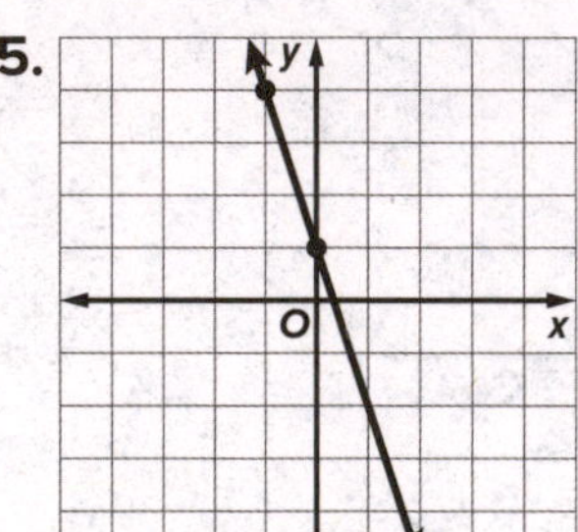

7.

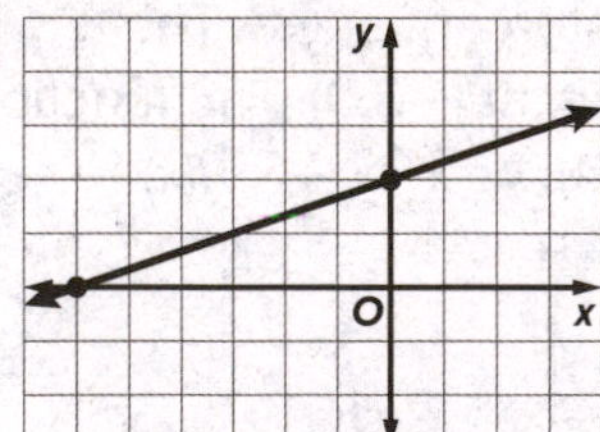

9.

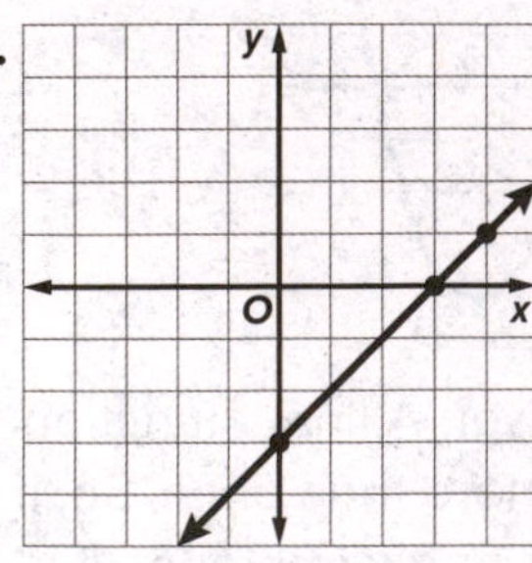

11.

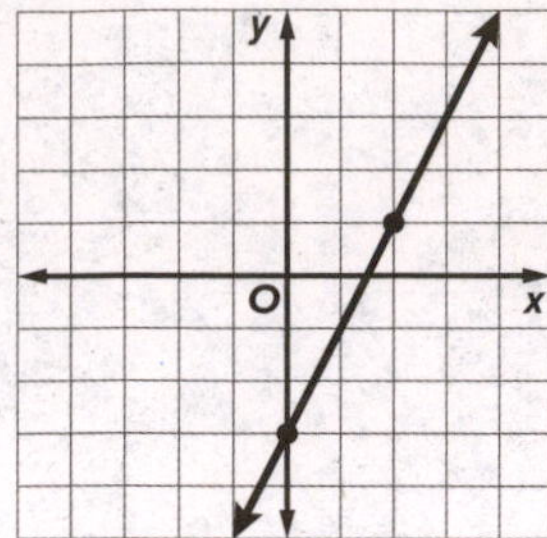

13.

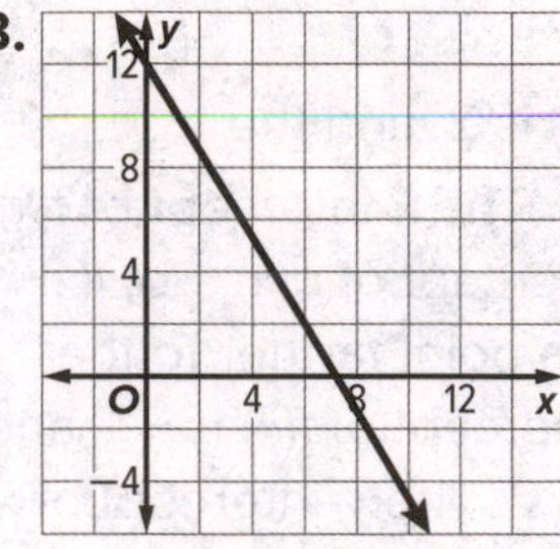

15.

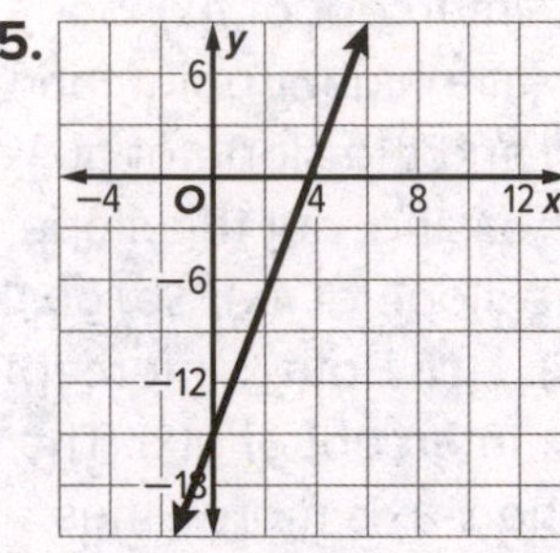

17.

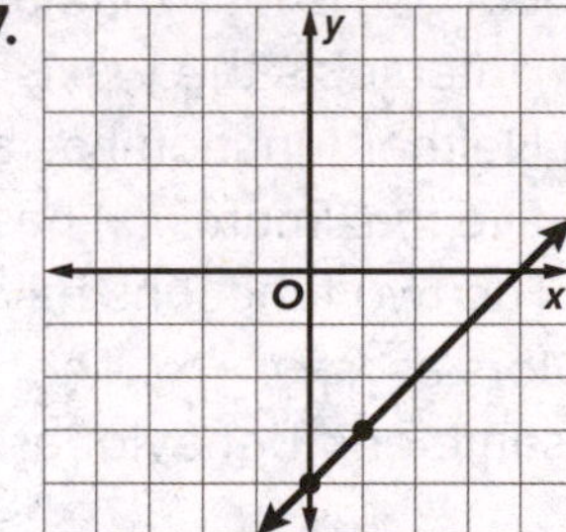

19.

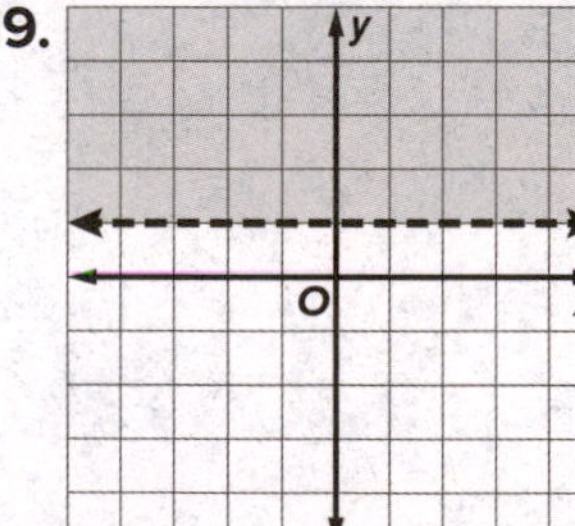

21.

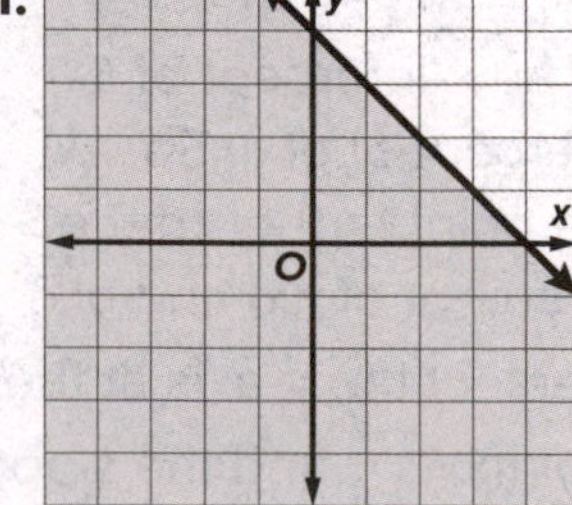

23.

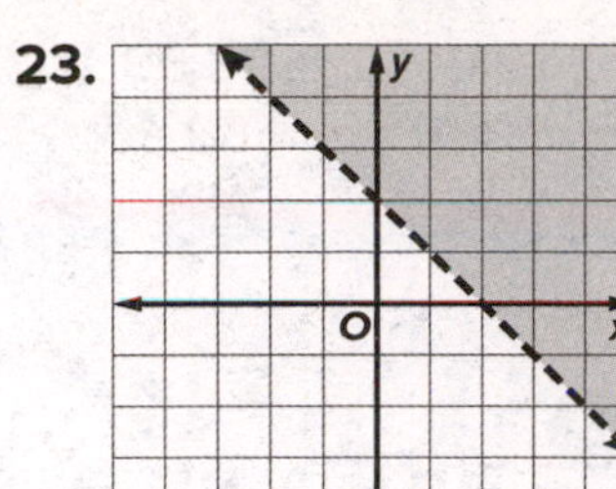

25.

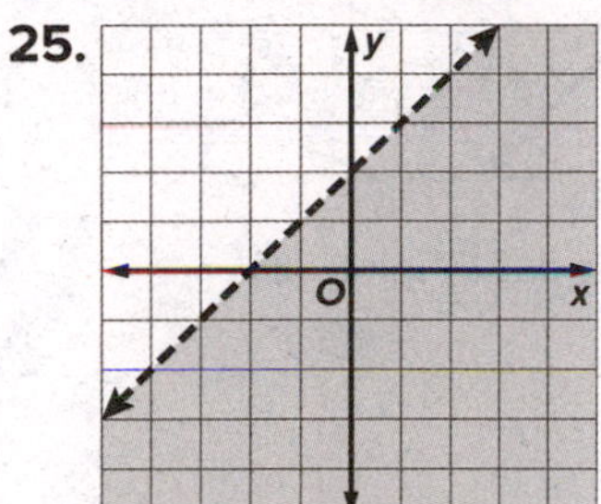

27.

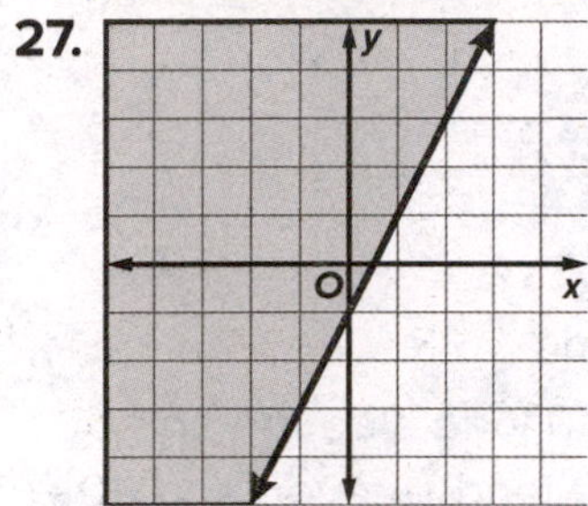

29.

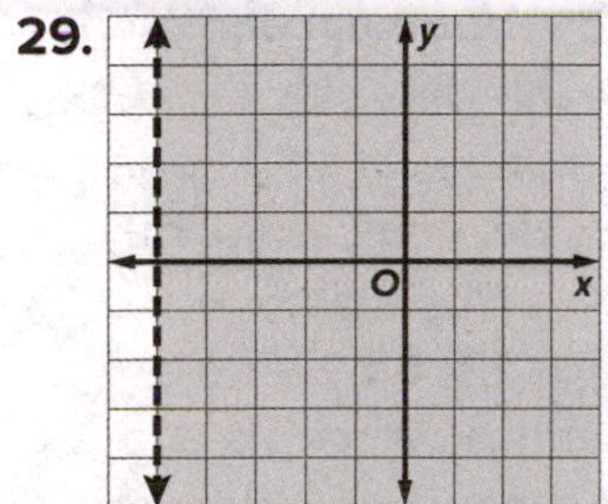

31a. $x + y \geq 400$

31b.

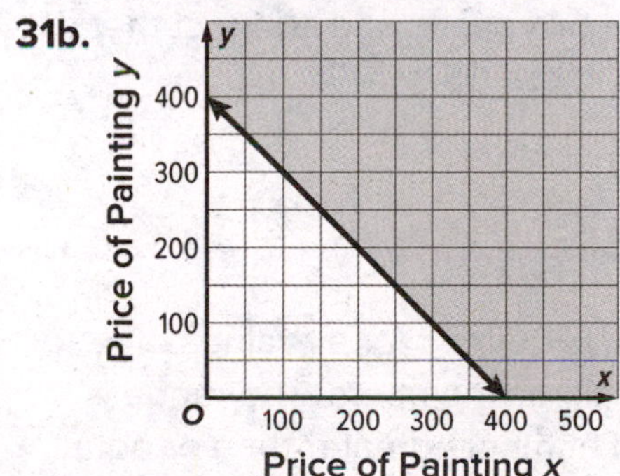

33.

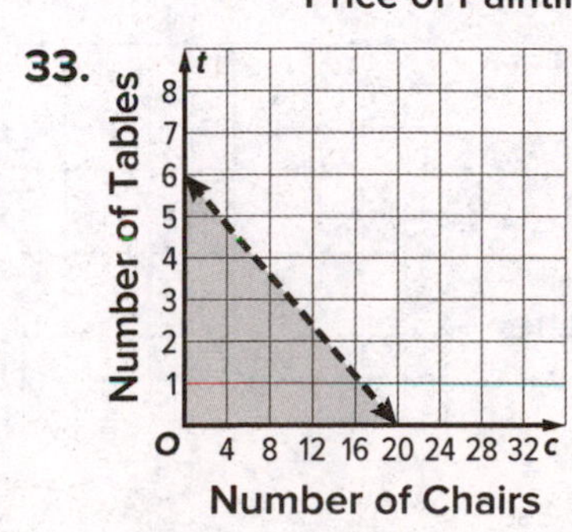

35.

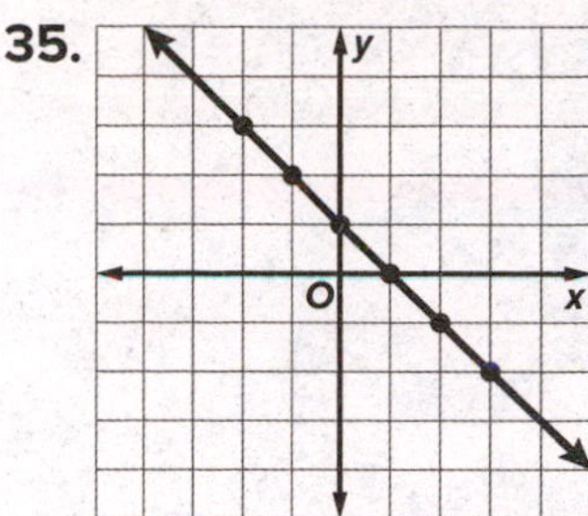

37.

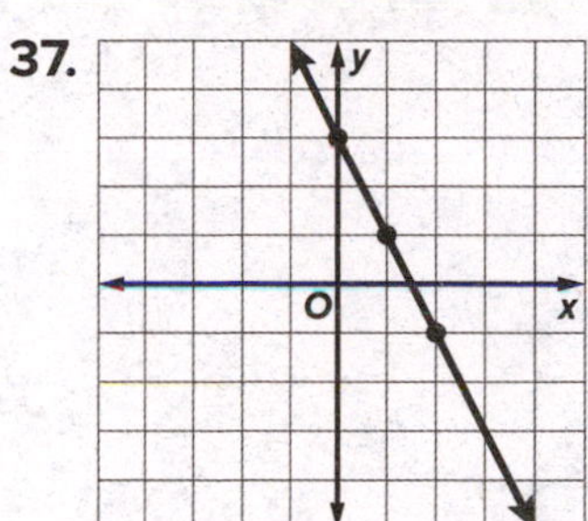

39.

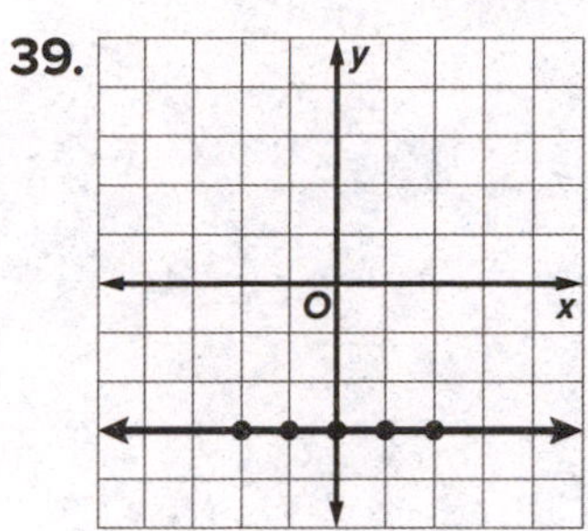

41.

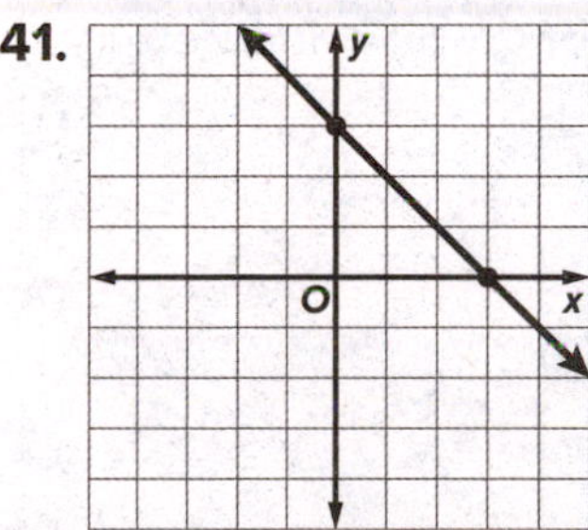

43.

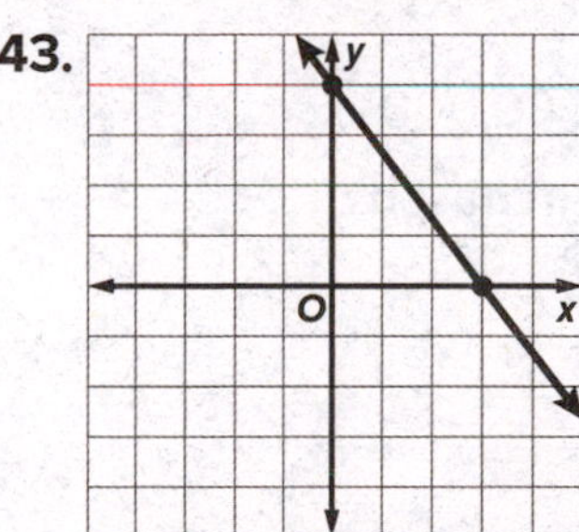

45.

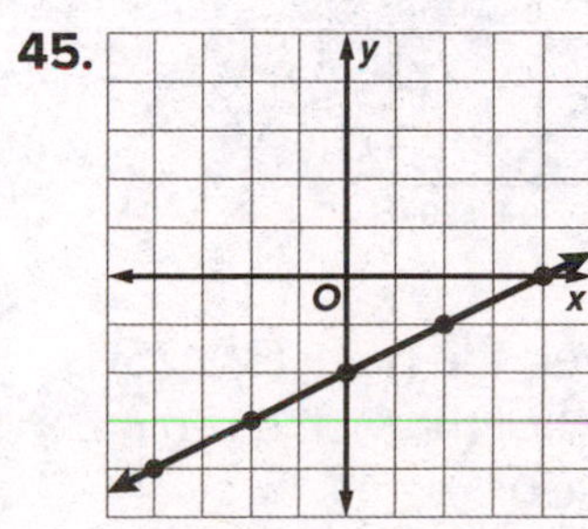

Selected Answers

47.

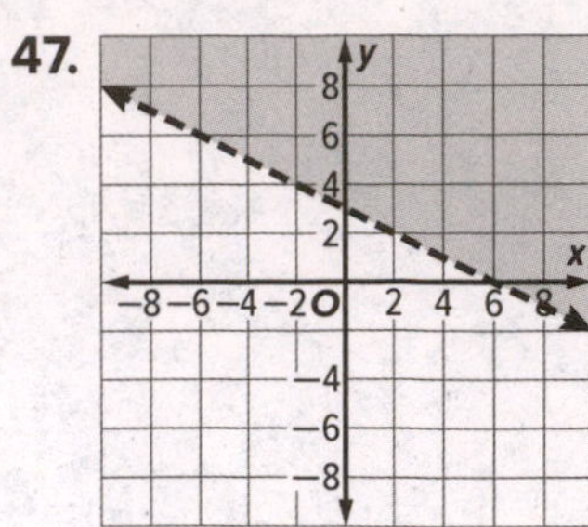

49.

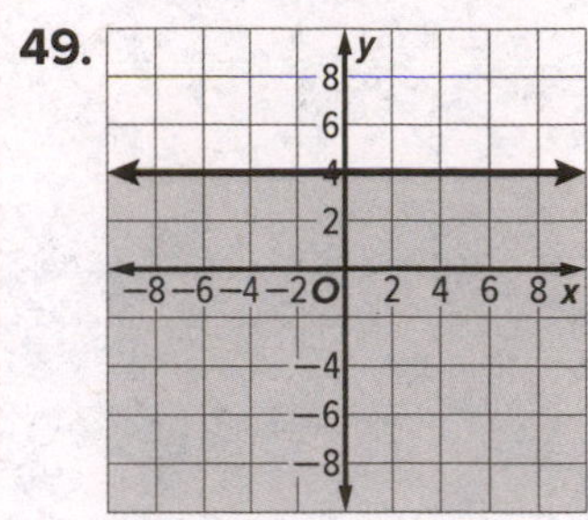

51.

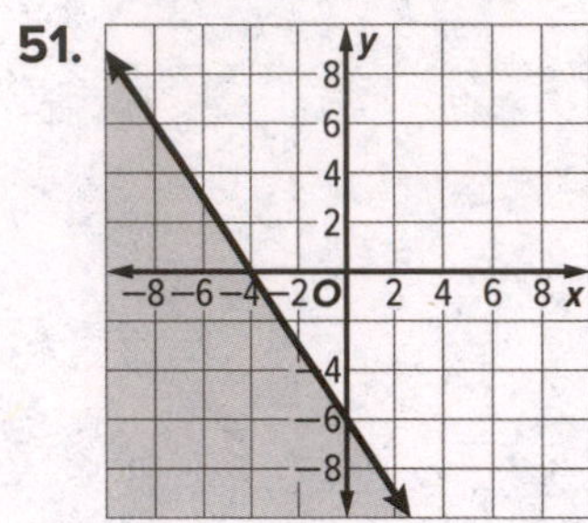

53. x-int = 2, y-int = −6; graph is increasing;

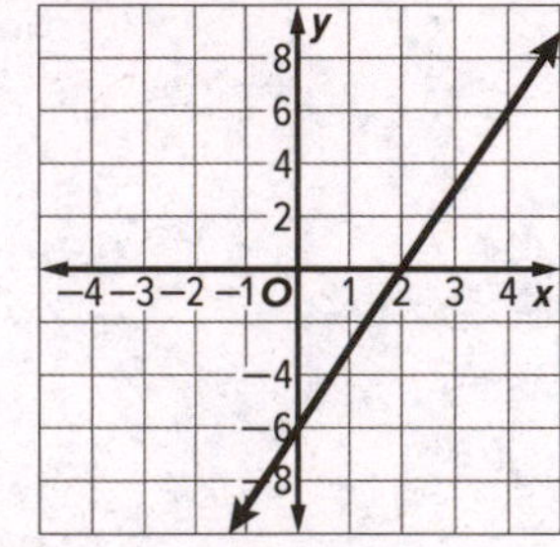

55a. $1000d + 1200n \leq 80{,}000$

55b. **Computers Purchased**

Notebooks

Desktops

55c. Yes; Sample answer: the point (50, 25) is on the line, which is part of the viable region. **59a.** $300s + 150a = 1800$

57b. Sample answer: $s = \$2.00$, $a = \$8.00$; $s = \$3.00$, $a = \$6.00$; $s = \$4.60$, $a = \$2.80$; $s = \$6.00$, $a = \$0.00$

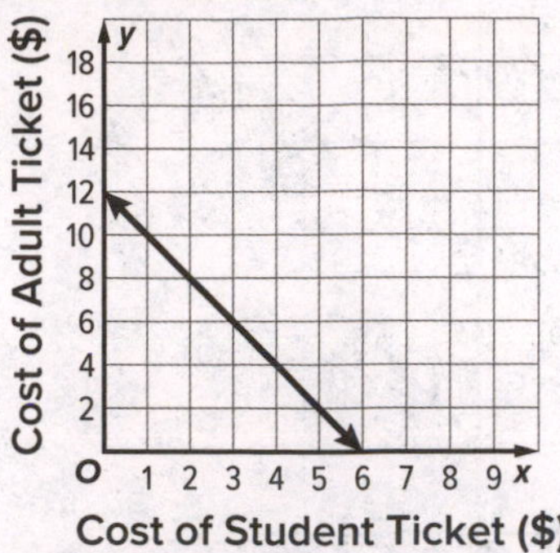

59a. $7\ell + 4s \geq 280$;

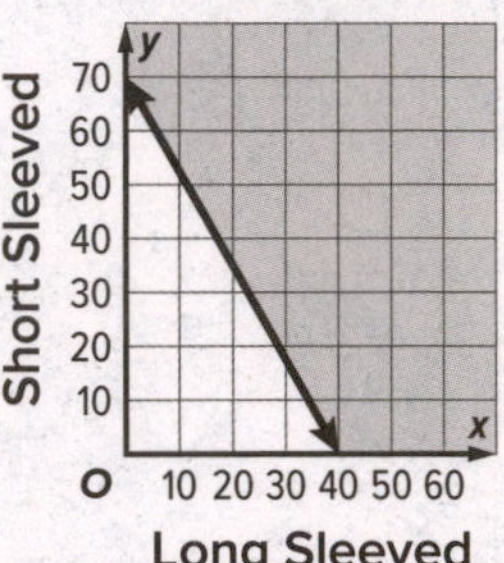

59b. Sample answer: 30 long-sleeved and 50 short-sleeved shirts; 60 long-sleeved and 40 short-sleeved shirts. **59c.** Domain and range values must be positive integers since you cannot buy a negative number of shirts or a portion of a shirt. **59d.** No, you cannot buy −10 long-sleeved shirts. **61.** Paulo; $x - y \geq 2$ can be written as $y \leq x - 2$. **63.** Sample answer: If given the x- and y-intercepts of a linear function, I already know two points on the graph. To graph the equation, I only need to graph those two points and connect them with a straight line. **65.** $y = \frac{1}{4}x + 5$

Lesson 1-6

1. The function is defined for all values of x, so the domain is all real numbers. The range is −1 and all real numbers greater than or equal to 0 and less than or equal to 6, which is also represented as $\{f(x) \mid f(x) = -1 \text{ or } 0 \leq f(x) \leq 6\}$. The y-intercept is 0, and the x-intercept is 0. The function is increasing when $0 \leq x \leq 3$.

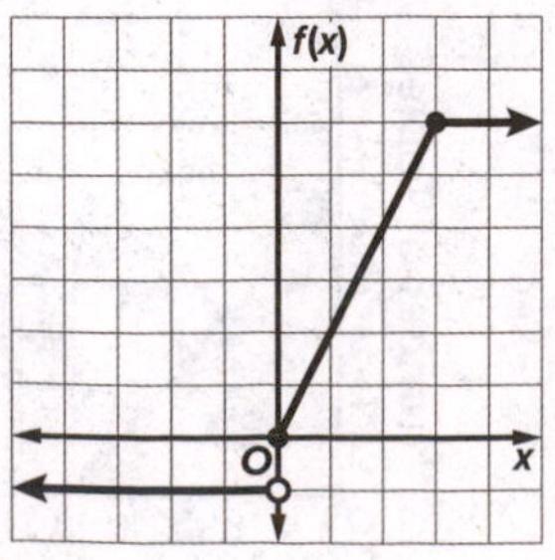

3. The function is defined for all values of x, so the domain is all real numbers. The range is 2 and all real numbers less than 0, which is also represented as $\{f(x) \mid f(x) = 0 \text{ or } f(x) < 0\}$. The y-intercept is 2, and there is no x-intercept. The function is decreasing when $x < 0$.

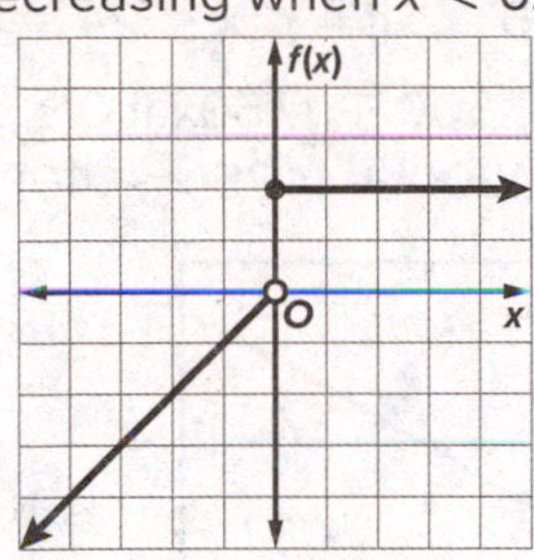

5a. $f(x) = \begin{cases} 48x & \text{if } 0 < x \leq 3 \\ 45x & \text{if } 3 < x \leq 8 \\ 42x & \text{if } 8 < x \leq 19 \\ 38x & \text{if } x > 19 \end{cases}$

5b. \$225; \$798

7. D = {all real numbers}; R = {all integers}

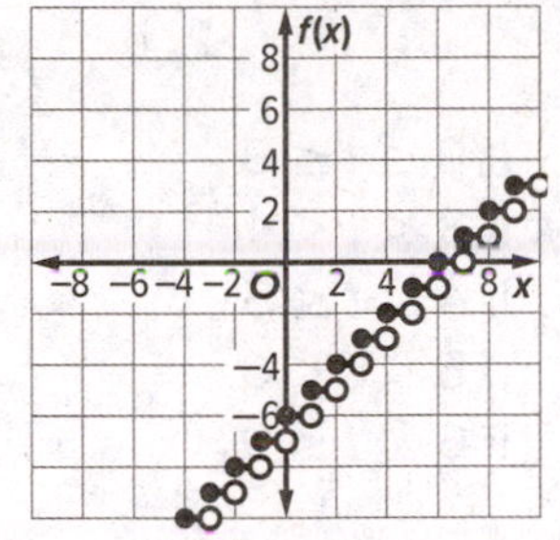

9. D = {all real numbers}; R = {all integers}

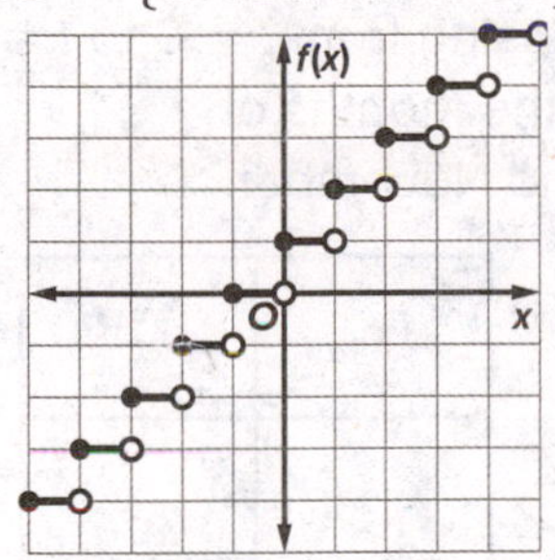

11. D = $\{x \mid 0 < x \leq 8\}$; R $\{y = 5.00, 10.00, 15.00, 20.00\}$

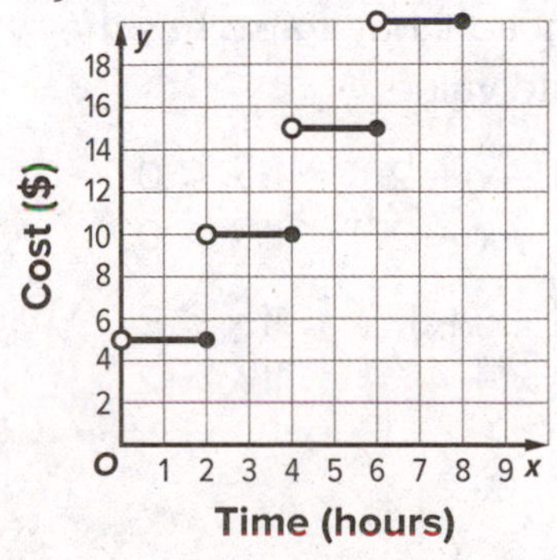

13. D = {all real numbers}; R = $\{f(x) \mid f(x) \geq 0\}$

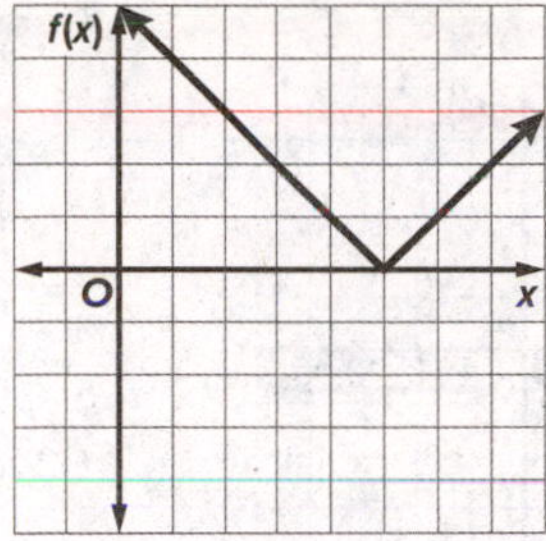

15. D = {all real numbers}; R = $\{h(x) \mid h(x) \geq -8\}$

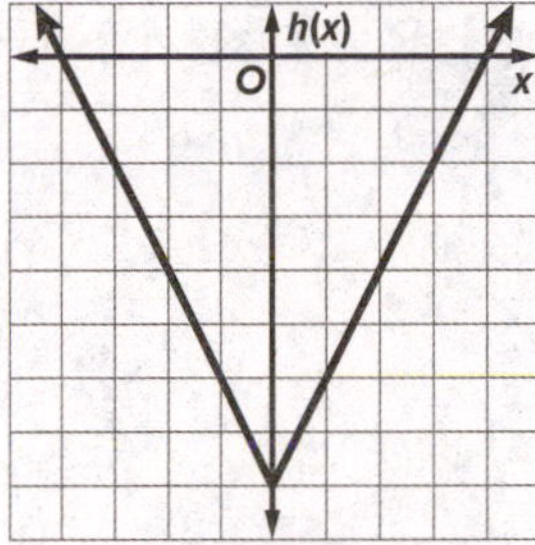

17. D = {all real numbers}; R = $\{f(x) \mid f(x) \geq 6\}$

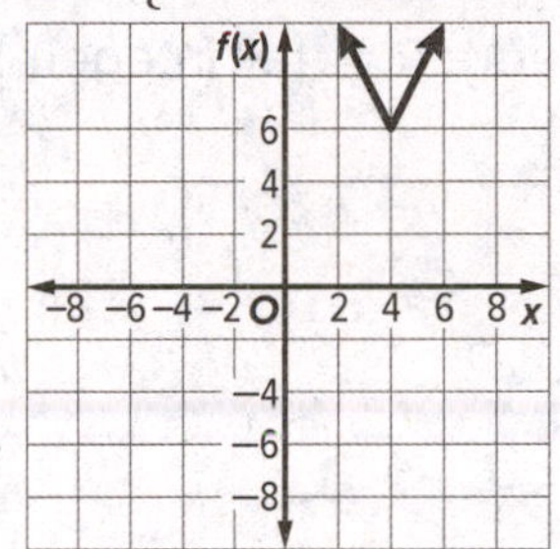

19. D = {all real numbers}; R = $\{g(x) \mid g(x) \geq 0\}$

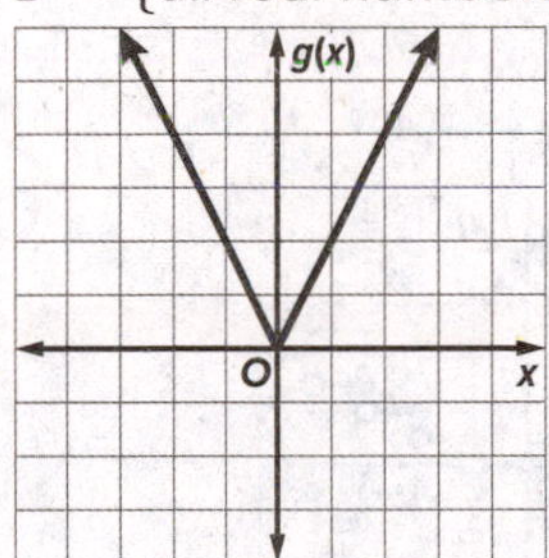

21. D = $\{x \mid x \leq -4 \text{ or } 0 < x\}$; R = $\{f(x) \mid f(x) \geq 12, f(x) = 8, \text{ or } 0 < f(x) \leq 3\}$

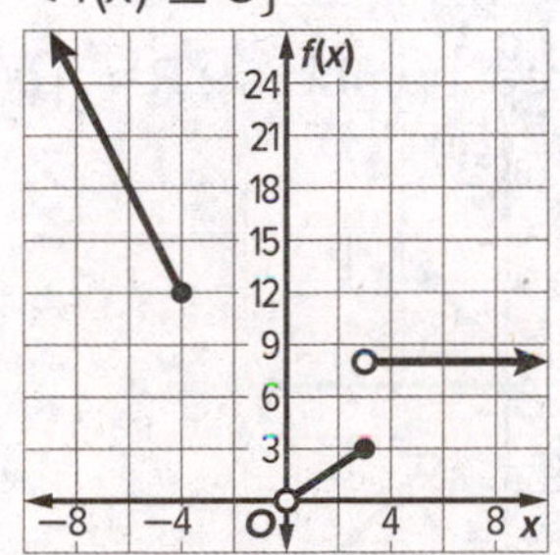

23. D = {all real numbers}; R = $\{g(x) \mid g(x) < -10$ or $-6 \leq g(x) \leq 2\}$

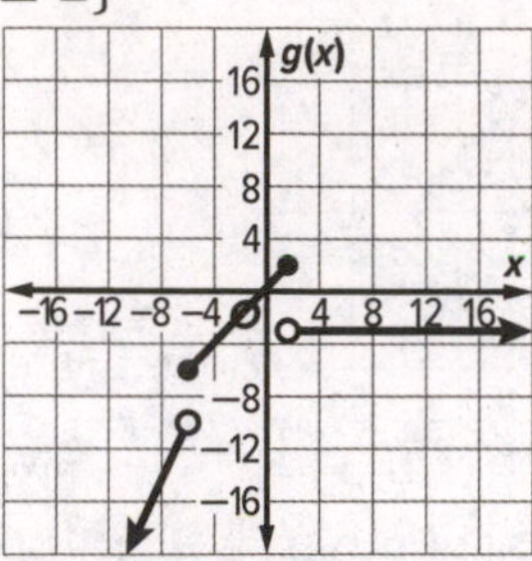

25. D = {all real numbers}; R = $\{f(x) \mid f(x) > -3\}$

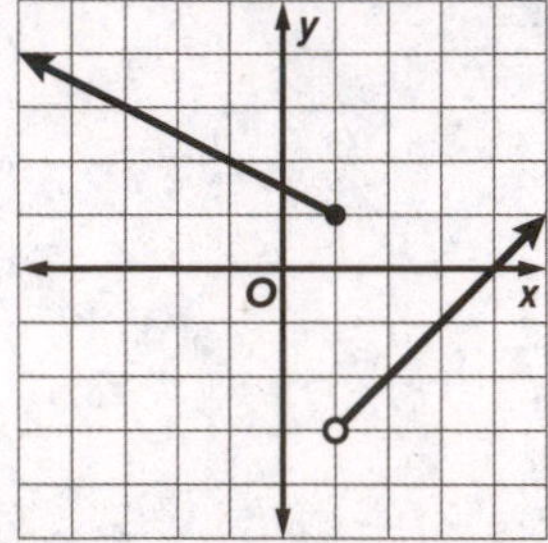

27. D = {all real numbers}; R = {all integers}

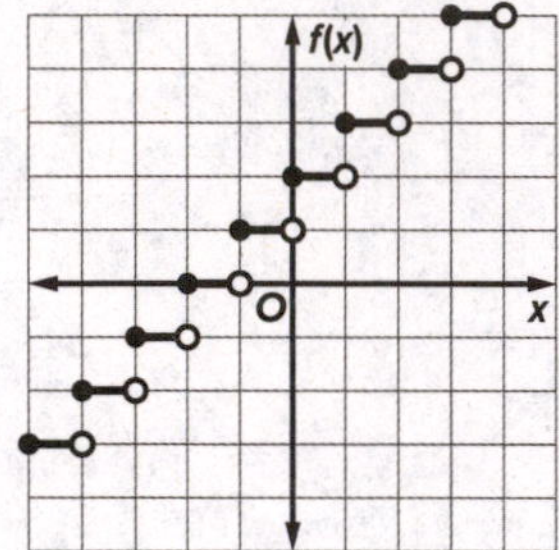

29. D = {all real numbers};
R = {all whole numbers}

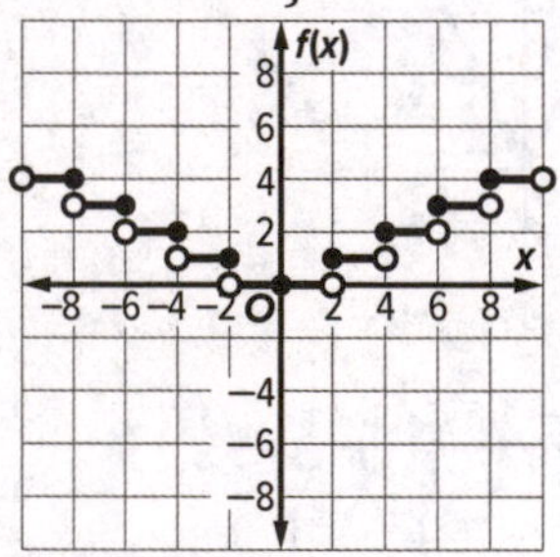

31. D = {all real numbers}; R = $\{g(x) \mid g(x) \leq 4\}$

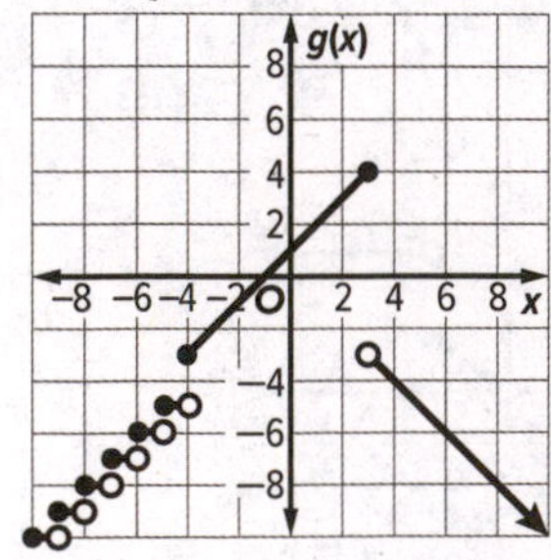

33. D = {all real numbers}; R = $\{y \mid y \geq 2\}$

35. $C(x) = \begin{cases} 5 & \text{if } 0 \leq x \leq 1 \\ 7.5 & \text{if } 1 < x \leq 2 \\ 10 & \text{if } 2 < x \leq 3 \\ 12.5 & \text{if } 3 < x \leq 4 \\ 15 & \text{if } 4 < x \leq 24 \end{cases}$

37a. $C(x) = \begin{cases} 500 + 17.50x \text{ if } 0 \leq x \leq 40 \\ 1200 + 14.75(x - 40) \text{ if } x \geq 41 \end{cases}$

37b.

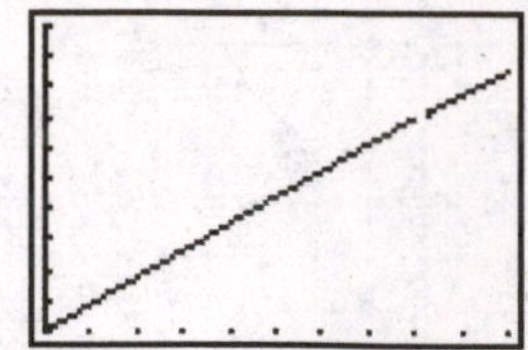

[0, 50] scl: 5 by [500, 1500] scl: 100

37c. Because it costs \$1200 for 40 guests to attend, use the first expression in the function $C(x)$. Solve the equation $500 + 17.50x = 900$ to obtain about 22.9. Because there cannot be a fraction of a guest, at most 22 guests can be invited to the reunion.

39a. $R(t) = \begin{cases} \frac{20}{3}t + 30 & \text{if } 0 \leq t \leq 3 \\ 60 & \text{if } 3 < t < 4 \\ 80 & \text{if } 4 \leq t \leq 5 \\ 60 & \text{if } 5 < t < 6 \\ -\frac{50}{3} + 160 & \text{if } 6 \leq t \leq 9 \end{cases}$

Range = [10, 60] ∪ {80}

39b. The graph is increasing from $t = 0$ to $t = 3$. This corresponds to the months of September, October, and November.

41. Because the absolute value takes negative f(x)-values and makes them positive, the graph retains the step-like nature of the greatest integer function, but it also has the "v" shape of the absolute value.

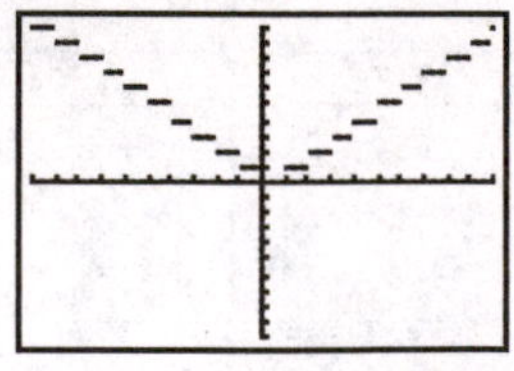

[−10, 10] scl: 1 by [−10, 10] scl: 1

43. $f(x) = \begin{cases} -x + 2 & \text{if } x \leq 0 \\ -x - 2 & \text{if } x > 0 \end{cases}$

45. $f(x) = \begin{cases} \frac{1}{2}x + 1 & \text{if } x < 2 \\ x - 4 & \text{if } x > 2 \end{cases}$

47. D = $\{t \mid 0 < t \leq 6\}$; R $\{d = 2.00, 4.00, 6.00, 8.00, 10.00, 12.00\}$

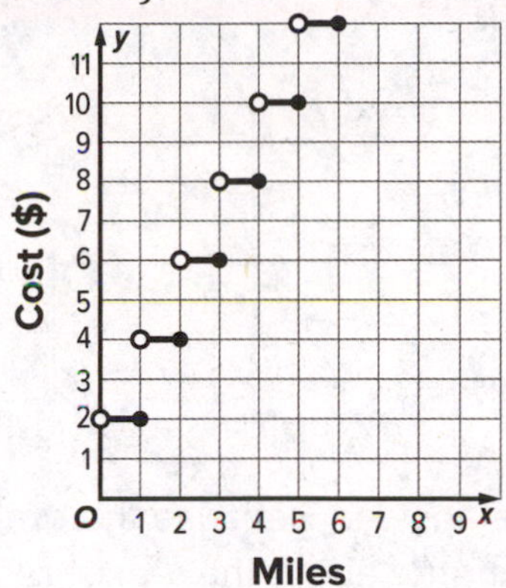

49. Sample answer: $|y| = x$ **51.** Sample answer: 8.6; The greatest integer function asks for the greatest integer less than or equal to the given value; thus 8 is the greatest integer. If we were to round this value to the nearest integer, we would round up to 9. **53.** Sample answer: Piecewise functions can be used to represent the cost of items when purchased in quantities, such as a dozen eggs.

Lesson 1-7

1. translation of the graph of $y = x^2$ up 4 units
3. translation of the graph of $y = x$ down 1 unit
5. translation of the graph of $y = x^2$ right 5 units
7. $y = x^2 - 2$ **9.** $y = x + 1$ **11.** $y = |x + 3| + 1$
13. compressed horizontally and reflected in the y-axis **15.** stretched vertically and reflected in the x-axis **17.** compressed vertically and reflected in the x-axis
19. stretched horizontally and reflected in the y-axis **21.** reflected in the x-axis, stretched vertically, and translated down 4 units
23. compressed vertically and translated down 2 units **25.** reflected in the x-axis, compressed vertically, and translated left 3 units **27.** stretched horizontally by a factor of 0.5; The absolute value function shows the ball bouncing off the edge of the pool table and the stretch shows the wide angle.
29. compressed vertically by a factor of 0.75 and translated up 25; there is a $25 fixed cost, plus $0.75 per mile, regardless of direction
31. $y = 2|x + 2| + 5$ **33.** $y = -|x| - 3$
35. $y = -(x - 4)^2$

37. translation of $y = |x|$ down 2 units

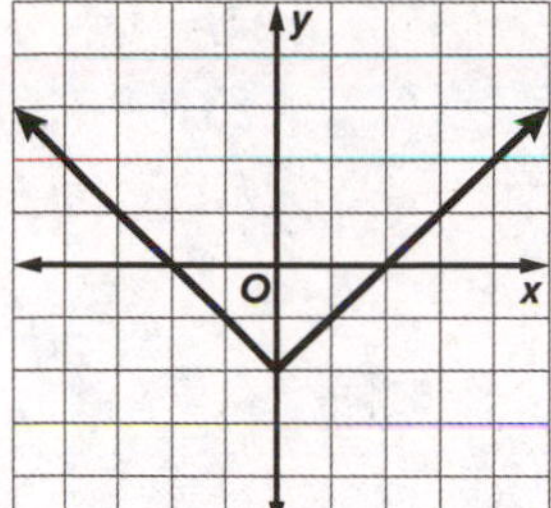

39. reflection of $y = x$ in the x-axis

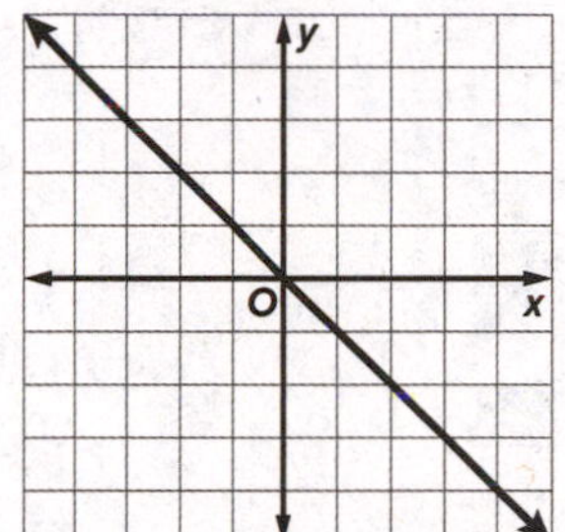

41. vertical stretch of $y = x$

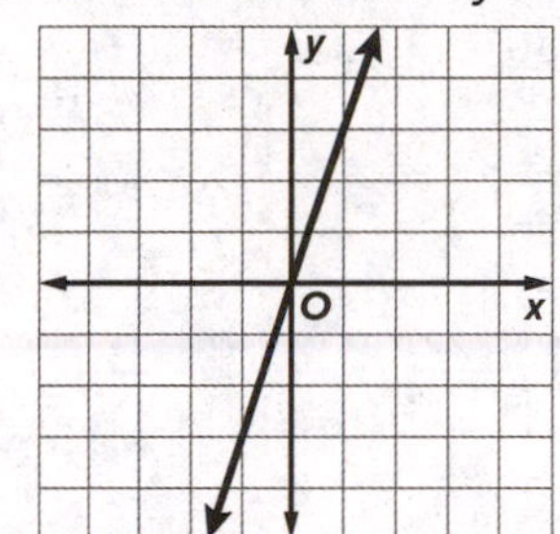

43. translation of $y = x^2$ down 4 units
45. horizontal compression of the graph of $y = x^2$
47. translation of $y = |x|$ right 8 units

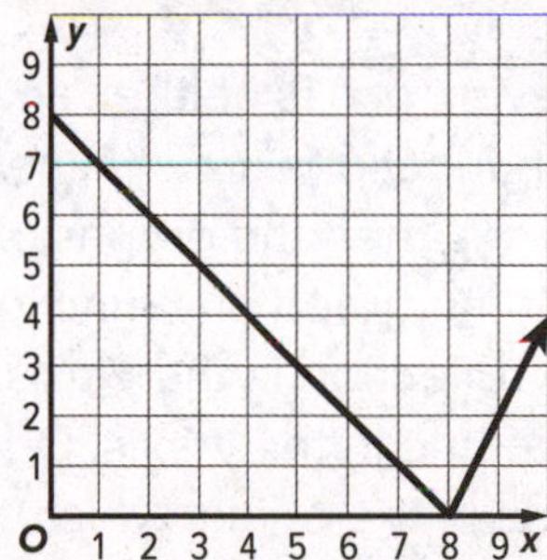

49. stretched vertically by a factor of 4
51. Maria stretched the function vertically by a factor of 10. **53a.** quadratic **53b.** x-axis
53c. right 25 units and up 81 units
53d. $y = -(x - 25)^2 + 81$

55a. 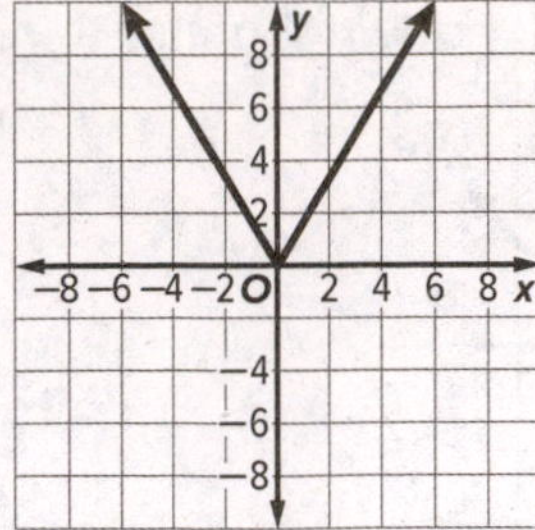

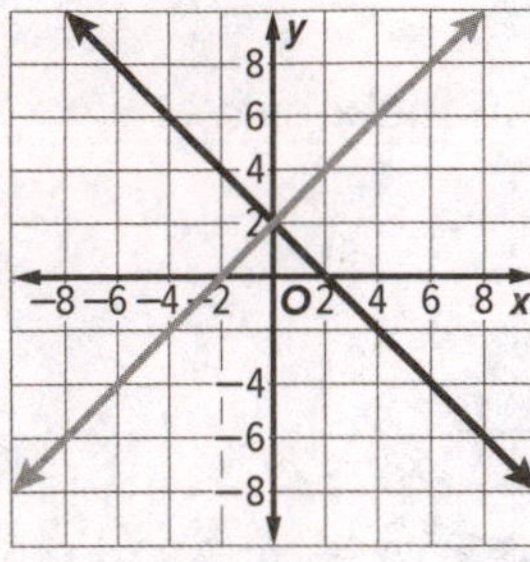

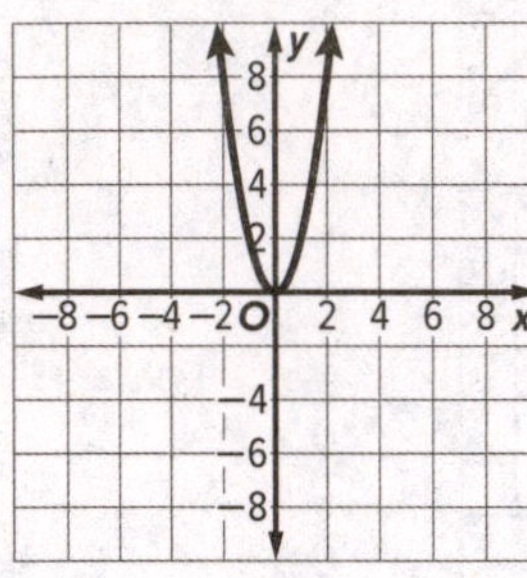

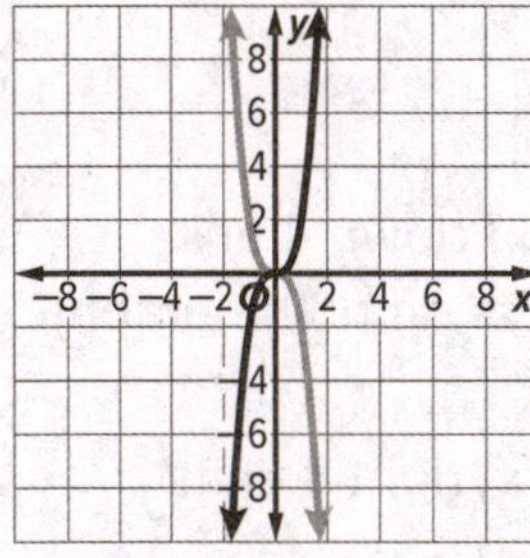

55b. *f*(*x*) and *h*(*x*) are even, *g*(*x*) is neither, and *k*(*x*) is odd. **55c.** Even functions are symmetric in the *y*-axis. If $f(-x) = f(x)$, then the graphs of *f*(-*x*) and *f*(*x*) coincide. If the graph of a function coincides with its own reflection in the *y*-axis, then the graph is symmetric in the *y*-axis. Odd functions are symmetric in the origin, which means that the graph of an odd function coincides with its rotation of 180° about the origin. A rotation of 180° is equivalent to reflection in two perpendicular lines. $f(-x)$ is a reflection in the *y*-axis and $-f(x)$ is a reflection in the *x*-axis. Thus if the graphs of $f(-x)$ and $-f(x)$ coincide, *f*(*x*) is symmetric about the origin.

57. Sample answer: The graph in Quadrant II has been reflected in the *x*-axis and moved right 10 units.

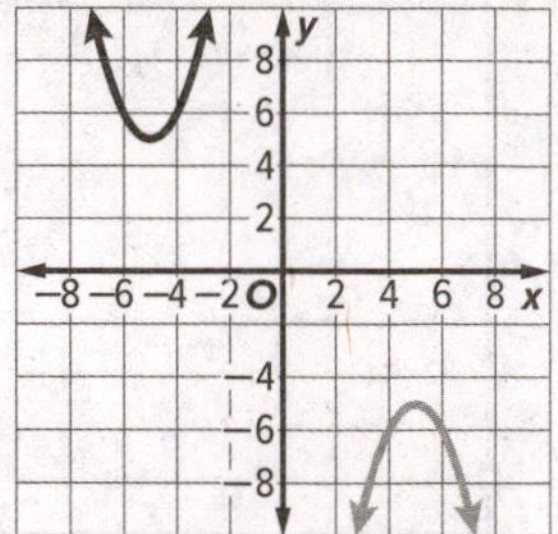

59. Sample answer: Because the graph of *g*(*x*) is symmetric about the *y*-axis, reflecting in the *y*-axis results in a graph that appears the same. It is not true for all quadratic functions. When the axis of symmetry of the parabola is not along the *y*-axis, the graph and the graph reflected in the *y*-axis will be different.

Module 1 Review

1. C **3.** A, B **5.** B **7.** Sample answer: The end behavior does not make sense because time and height cannot be negative. **9.** D **11.** A **13.** Sample answer: The graph of the parent function $f(x) = x^2$ has been stretched vertically by the 3, translated 2 units to the right, and translated up 9 units. **15.** −13

Module 2

Module 2 Opener

1. 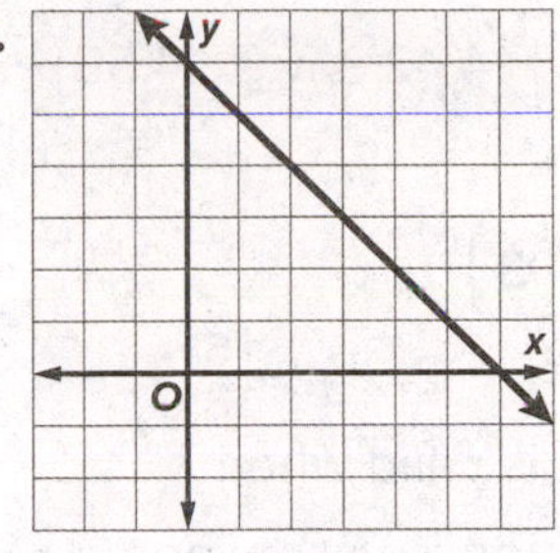

3. 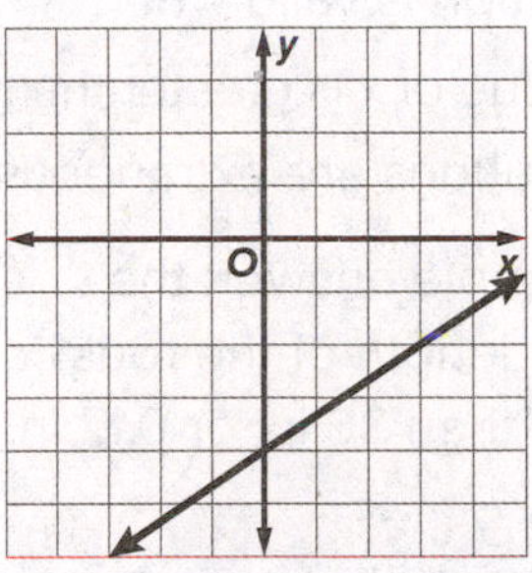

5. 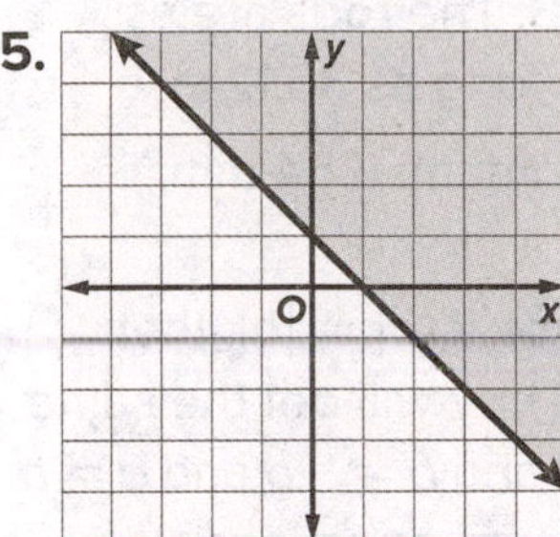

7. 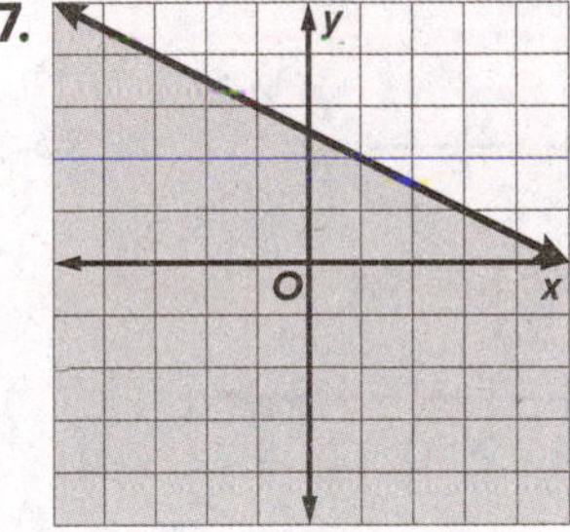

Lesson 2-1

1. −17 **3.** $\frac{1}{4}$ **5.** $\frac{4}{5}$ **7.** 5 **9.** $\frac{3}{7}$

11. g = green fees per person; $6(2) + 4g = 76$; \$16

13a. $321 = 4n + 1$ **13b.** 80 dominoes

15. $x = 4y + 48$ **17.** $h = \frac{A - 2\pi r^2}{2\pi r}$

19. $d = \frac{3c - 1}{2}$ **21.** $I = \frac{2(E - U)}{W^2}$

23. $f(x) = 2x + 12$ The solution is −6.

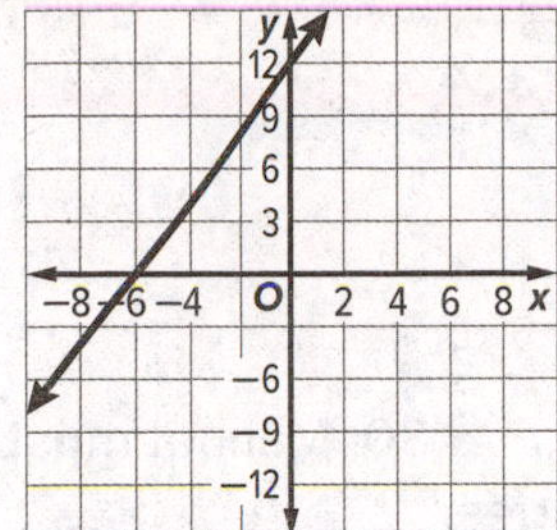

25. $f(x) = \frac{1}{2}x - 6$ The solution is 12.

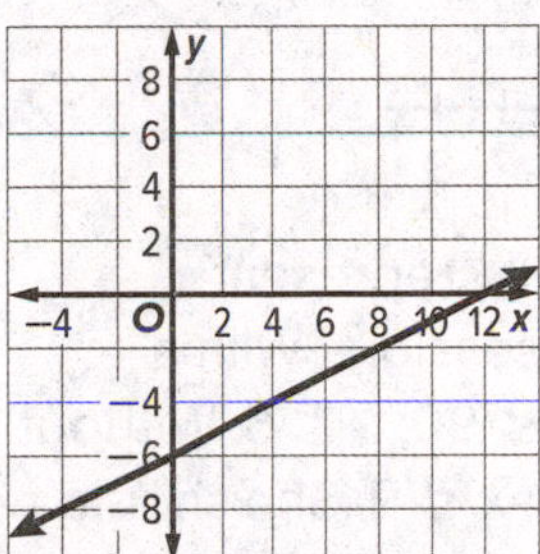

27. $f(x) = -3x - 2$ The solution is $x = -\frac{2}{3}$.

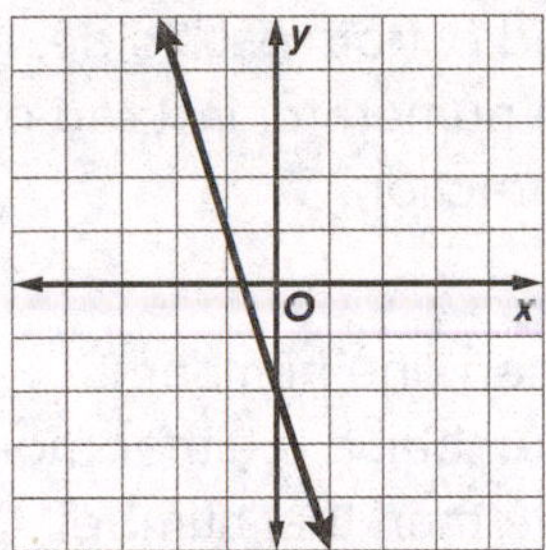

29a. $p = 500 - 24d$

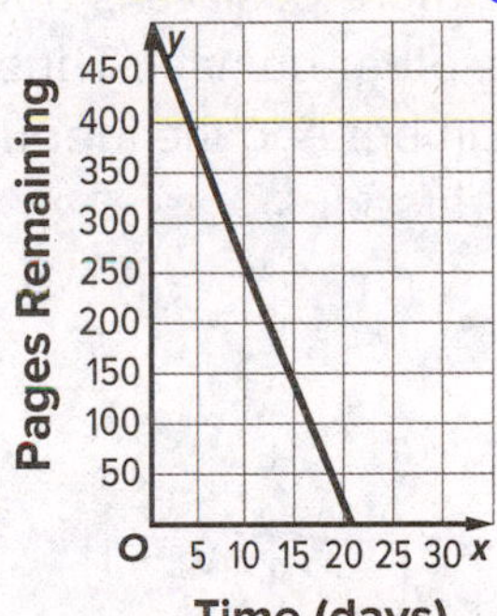

29b. Sample answer: The graph appears to intersect the x-axis at about 20. This means that Mario will finish the novel in about 20 days.

29c. Sample answer: $d \approx 20.83$. So, Mario completed the book on the 21st day, when he had fewer than 24 pages remaining.

31. $\{z \mid z \leq -8\}$

−9 −8 −7 −6 −5 −4 −3 −2 −1

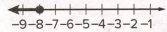

33. $\{n \mid n < 2\}$

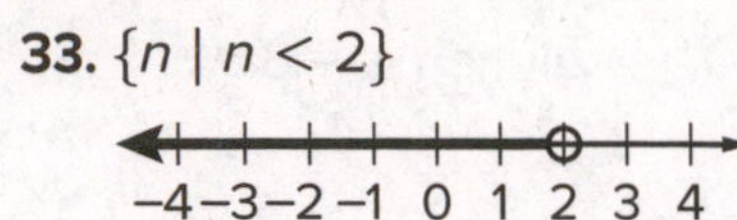

35. $\{m \mid m \leq 4\}$

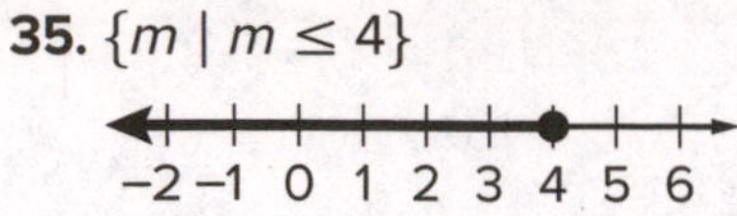

37. $15P + 300 \geq 1500$; $P \geq 80$; Manuel must translate at least 80 pages.

39. $\frac{22}{5}$ **41.** 5

43. $\{x \mid x \leq 6\}$

0 1 2 3 4 5 6 7 8

45. Sample answer: Let x represent the number of skating session. With a membership: $6x + 60 \leq 90$; $x \leq 5$. Without a membership: $10x \leq 90$; $x \leq 9$. She should not buy a membership.

47. Jade; Sample answer: in the last step, when Steven subtracted b_1 from each side, he mistakenly put b_1 in the numerator instead of subtracting it from the fraction.

49. $y_1 = y_2 - \sqrt{d^2 - (x_2 - x_1)^2}$

51. Sample answer: When one number is greater than another number, it is either more positive or less negative than that number. When these numbers are multiplied by a negative value, their roles are reversed. That is, the number that was more positive is now more negative than the other number. Thus, it is now *less than* that number and the inequality symbol needs to be reversed.

Lesson 2-2

1. $\{11\}$ **3.** $\{3, 4\}$ **5.** $\{-8\}$ **7.** $\{-2, -1\}$

9. $|x - 87.4| \leq 1.5$; or $85.9 \leq x \leq 88.9$

11. 13 or 21 **13.** $\{x \mid -2 \leq x \leq 0\}$

−4 −3 −2 −1 0 1 2 3 4

15. ∅

−4 −3 −2 −1 0 1 2 3 4

17. $\{x \mid -1.8 < x < 3.4\}$

−3 −2 −1 0 1 2 3 4 5 6

19. $\left\{x \mid x < -1 \text{ or } x > \frac{1}{3}\right\}$

-1 $-\frac{2}{3}$ $-\frac{1}{3}$ 0 $\frac{1}{3}$ $\frac{2}{3}$ 1

21. $|v - 14.5| \leq 0.08$; $\{v \mid 14.42 \leq v \leq 14.58\}$

23. $\left\{-\frac{4}{5}\right\}$

25. $\left\{y \mid y \leq -7\frac{2}{3} \text{ or } y \geq -3\right\}$

27. $|4x + 7| = 2x + 3$; $x = -2$, $x = -\frac{5}{3}$; The absolute value equation is valid when $2x + 3 \geq 0$, so the equation is valid when $x \geq -\frac{3}{2}$. Since neither value of x is greater than or equal to $-\frac{3}{2}$, both solutions are extraneous.

29a. $|x - 36| = 0.12$; Sample answer: the equation shows that the length of the rods, x, could be 0.12 in. greater than 36 in. or 0.12 in. less than 36 in.

29b. $x = 36.12$, $x = 35.88$; The rods are as short as 35.88 in. and as long as 36.12 in.

31. $|x - 6.5| = 0.04$; maximum: 6.54 mm, minimum: 6.46 mm

33. Yuki is correct because if $|a| = |b|$, then either $a = b$ or $a = -b$. They will get the same answers because $a = -b$ and $b = -a$ and $a = b$ and $-a = -b$ are equivalent equations.

35. $\left\{p \mid -\frac{9}{4} < p < \frac{5}{4}\right\}$

−3 −2 −1 0 1 2 3

37. $\left\{w \mid w \leq -\frac{23}{2} \text{ or } w \geq \frac{7}{2}\right\}$

−16 −14 −12 −10 −8 −6 −4 −2 0 2 4

39a. $|m - 28| > 3$

39b. $\{m \mid m < 25 \text{ or } m > 31\}$; in the other 5% of his trips, his mpg was either less than 25 mpg or greater than 31 mpg

41. Roberto is correct. Sample answer: the solution set for each inequality is all real numbers; for any value of c (positive, negative, or zero), each inequality will be true.

43. Each of these has a non-empty solution set except for $x > 5$ and $x < 1$. There are no values of x that are simultaneously greater than 5 and less than 1.

45. The 4 potential solutions are:

1. $(2x - 1) \geq 0$ and $(5 - x) \geq 0$
2. $(2x - 1) \geq 0$ and $(5 - x) < 0$
3. $(2x - 1) < 0$ and $(5 - x) \geq 0$
4. $(2x - 1) < 0$ and $(5 - x) < 0$

The resulting equations corresponding to these cases are:

1. $2x - 1 + 3 = 5 - x : x = 1$
2. $2x - 1 + 3 = x - 5 : x = -7$
3. $1 - 2x + 3 = 5 - x : x = -1$
4. $1 - 2x + 3 = x - 5 : x = 3$

The solutions from case 1 and case 3 work. The others are extraneous. The solution set is $\{-1, 1\}$.

47. Always; if $|x| < 3$, then x is between -3 or 3. Adding 3 to the absolute value of any of the numbers in this set will produce a positive number.

49. Sample answer: $\left|x - \frac{a+b}{2}\right| \leq b - \frac{a+b}{2}$

Lesson 2-3

1. $7x + 5y = -35$; $A = 7$, $B = 5$, $C = -35$

3. $3x - 10y = -5$; $A = 3$, $B = -10$, $C = -5$

5. $3x - y = 4$; $A = 3$, $B = -1$, $C = 4$

7. $9x - 8y = 2$; $A = 9$, $B = -8$, $C = 2$

9. $2x + 31y = 78$; $A = 2$, $B = 31$, $C = 78$

11. $y = 2x - 3$; $m = 2$, $b = -3$

13. $y = -\frac{1}{2}x$; $m = -\frac{1}{2}x$, $b = 2$

15. $y = -\frac{2}{5}x$; $m = -\frac{2}{5}x$, $b = 8$

17. $y = -6x - 16$; $m = -6$, $b = -16$

19. There were 83 shirts collected before noon. There were 20 shirts collected each hour after noon.

21a. Let x represent the number of hours the plumber spends working at a job site, and y represent the total cost for the services.

21b. $y = 40x + 60$

21c. \$260

23. $y + 3 = -5(x + 8)$

25. $y + 8 = -\frac{2}{3}(x - 6)$

27. $y + 4 = 3x$

29. $y + 3 = -8(x - 2)$ or $y - 5 = -8(x - 1)$

31. $y + 2 = -\frac{3}{2}(x + 1)$ or $y - 1 = -\frac{3}{2}(x + 3)$

33a. Let x be the number of years after 1995. Let y represent the number of millions of automobiles purchased by Americans.

33b. $y - 17.35 = 0.008(x - 5)$

33c. The rate at which the number of new autos purchased by Americans is constant.

35. $2x + y = -4$; $A = 2$, $B = 1$, $C = -4$

37. $y = \frac{1}{2}(x + 4)$

39. $y = -7x - 191$

41. $y - 6 = \frac{3}{2}(x - 1)$ or $y + 3 = \frac{3}{2}(x + 5)$

43. $y = 30x + 350$

45a. Sample answer: Two points are given, so the point-slope form can be used. However (0, 7) is also the y-intercept, so the slope-intercept form can also be used.

45b. Sample answer: the slope is $\frac{7-1}{0-3} = -2$. Using the slope-intercept form, the equation is $y = -2x + 7$. Using the point-slope form, we get $(y - 1) = -2(x - 3)$. However, solving this equation for y give $y = -2x + 7$.

47a. Sample answer: Both functions are linear and decreasing.

47b. Joe: y-int $= 585$, Alisha: y-int $= 450$. Sample answer: The book Joe is reading has 585 pages and the book Alisha is reading has 450 pages.

47c. Joe: $y = 585 - 65x \rightarrow 65x + y = 585$, Alisha: $y = 450 - 50x \rightarrow 50x + y = 450$

47d. Both will finish reading their books in 9 days. Sample answer: The books will be finished when the pages remaining is 0. $585 - 65x = 0$ when $x = 9$ and $450 - 50x = 0$ when $x = 9$. This is the x-intercept for each function.

47e. Joe by 15 pages per day. The number of pages in the table for Joe are 585, then 520, then 455, etc., so he is reading 65 pages per day. The graph of Alisha's remaining pages decreases by 50 pages for each day. $65 - 50 = 15$.

49. Sample answer: $y = 2(x - 3)$

51. No; Sample answer: You can choose points on the graph and show on a coordinate plane that they do not fall on a single line. For instance, the points (0, 2), (1, 10), (2, 24), and (3, 49) do not lie on a straight line.

53. Sample answer: Depending on what information is given and what the problem is, it might be easier to represent a linear equation in one form over another. For example, if you are given the slope and the *y*-intercept, you could represent the equation in slope-intercept form. If you are given a point and the slope, you could represent the equation in point-slope form. If you are trying to graph an equation using the *x*- and *y*-intercepts, you could represent the equation in standard form.

Lesson 2-4

1. 1; consistent and independent

3. 1; consistent and independent

5. infinitely many; consistent and dependent

7. (2, 1)

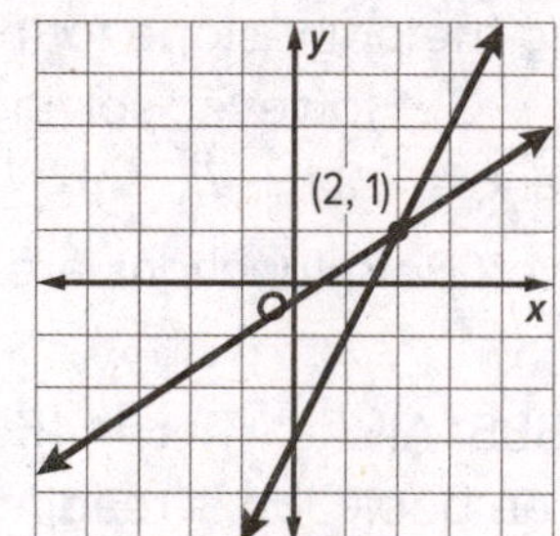

9. (3, −3)

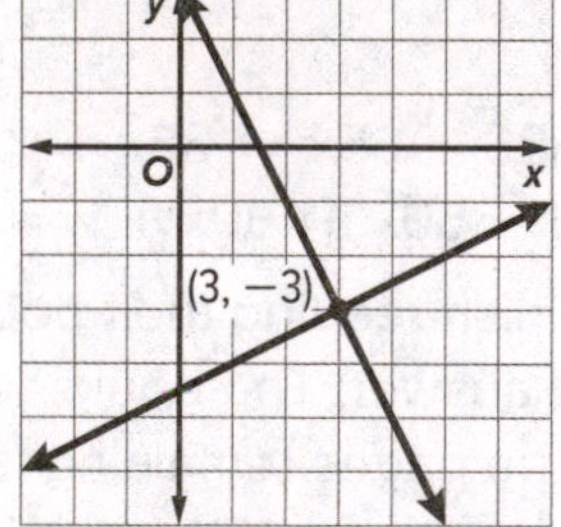

11. no solution

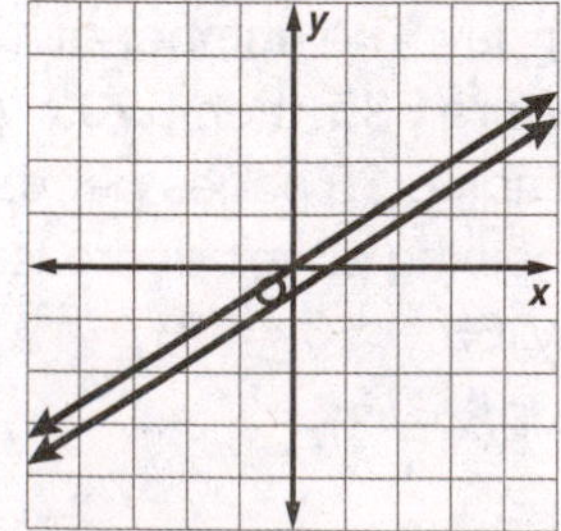

13a. $5x + 17y = 315$, $6x + 18y = 342$

13b. socks: 12, shorts: 15

15. (2.07, −0.39)

17. (15.03, 10.98)

19. (2, 1)

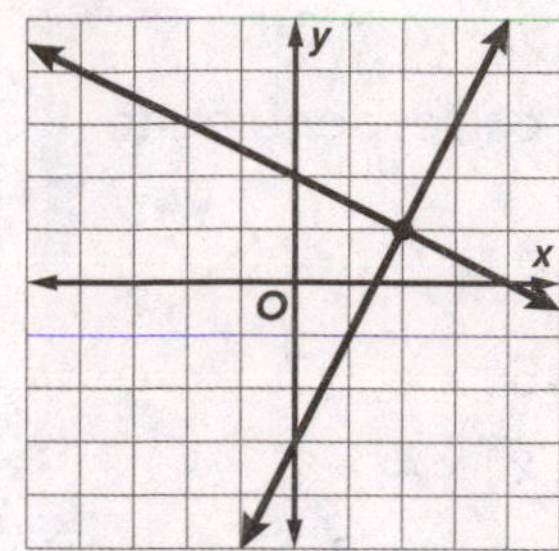

21. (3, 4)

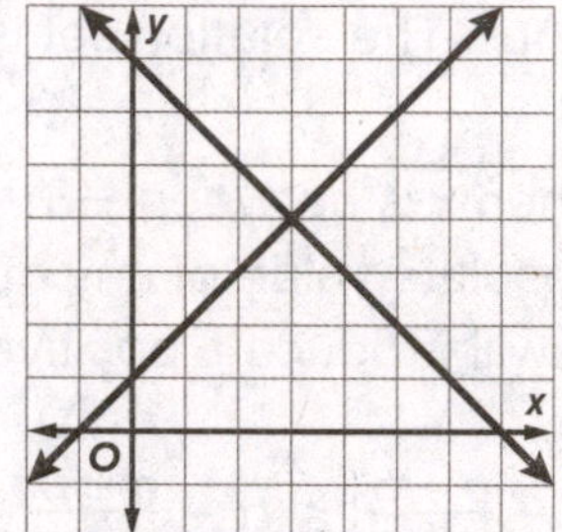

23a. $200x + 100y = 400$; $40x + 10y = 60$

23b. (1, 2)

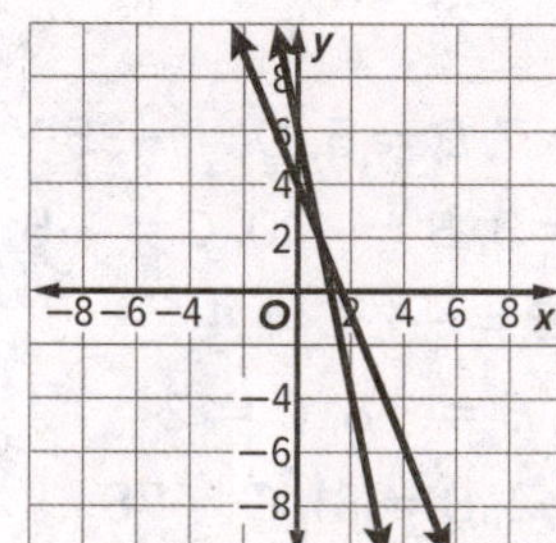

23c. Sample answer: The *x*-value represents the cost of a child ticket, \$1. The *y*-value represents the cost of an adult ticket, \$2.

25. Perpendicular lines have opposite, reciprocal slopes, and intersect to form a right angle. So, perpendicular lines are independent because it has exactly one solution.

27. Never; Sample answer: Lines cannot intersect at exactly two distinct points. Lines intersect once (one solution), coincide (infinite solutions), or never intersect (no solution).

29. $y = -\frac{1}{2}x + 11$ and $y = 4x + 2$; Sample answer: The other three systems have a solution of (−2, −10), but the system $y = -\frac{1}{2}x + 11$ and $y = 4x + 2$ has a solution of (2, 10).

Lesson 2-5

1. (3, −3) **3.** (2, 1) **5.** no solution
7a. Cassandra: $3x + 14y = 203$;
Alberto: $11x + 11y = 220$; $x = 7$, $y = 13$
7b. The cost of each small pie is $7. The cost of each large pie is $13.
7c. Sample answer: By substituting the solution into each equation in the system, you can verify that it is correct. $3(7) + 14(13) = 203$, and $11(7) + 11(13) = 220$.
9. (−2, −5) **11.** (−1, 3) **13.** (3, 5) **15.** (−2, 3)
17. (1, 6) **19.** (6, −5) **21.** 4, 8
23. adult ticket $8; student ticket $6.
25. Gloria is correct.; Sample answer: Syreeta subtracted 26 from 17 instead of 17 from 26 and got $3x = -9$ instead of $3x = 9$. She proceeded to get a value of −11 for y. She would have found her error if she had substituted the solution into the original equations.
27. Sample answer: It is more helpful to use substitution when one of the variables has a coefficient of 1 or if a coefficient can easily be reduced to 1.

Lesson 2-6

1.

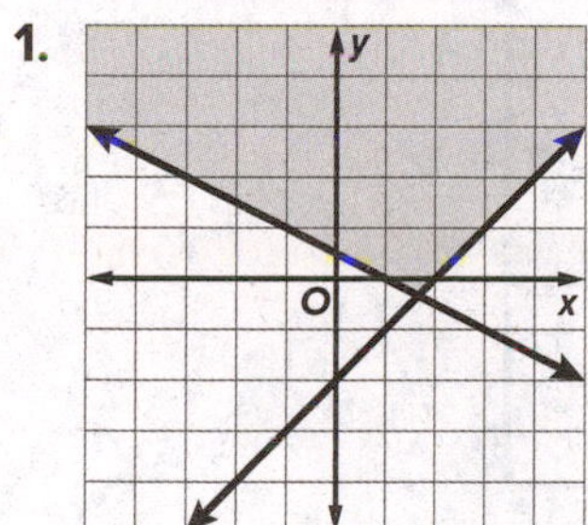

3.

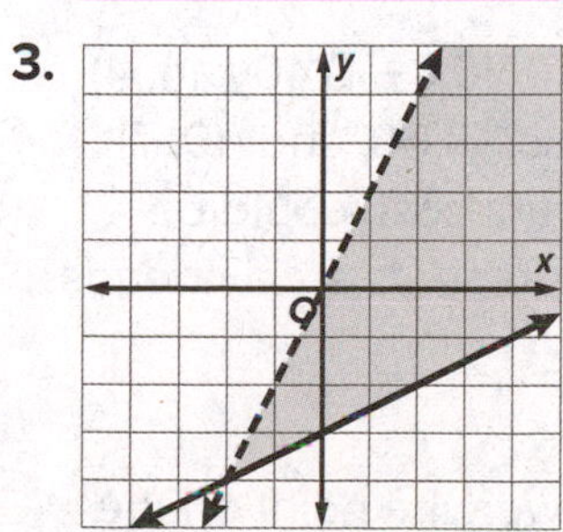

5.

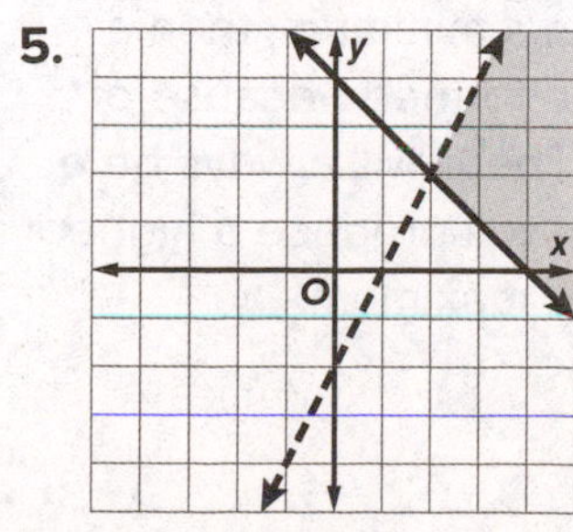

7.

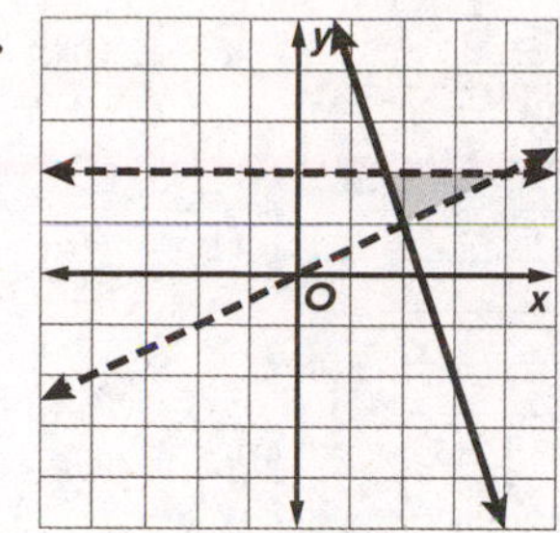

9.

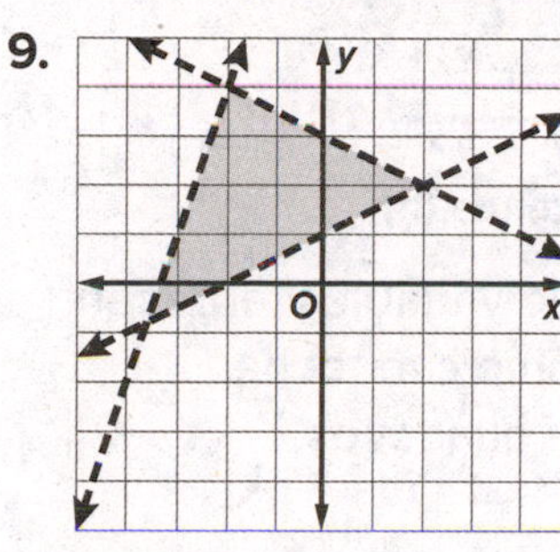

11.

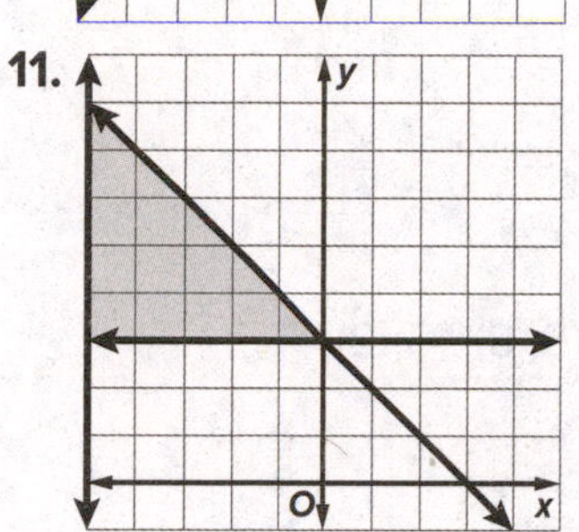

13a. $800 \geq x + y$; $3400 \leq 4x + 7y$
13b. Quadrant 1

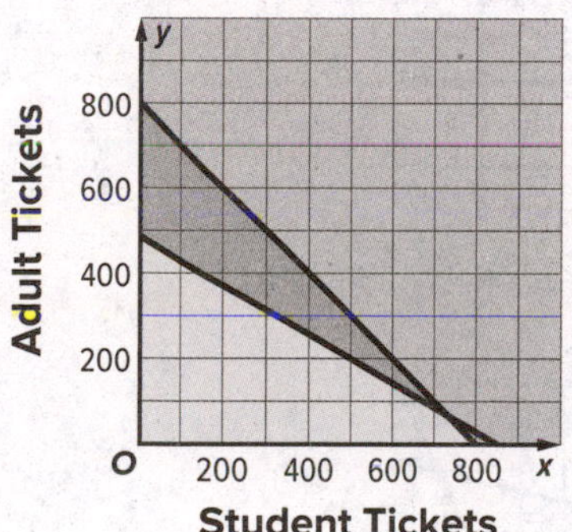

13c. No; they would only make $3300.

15.

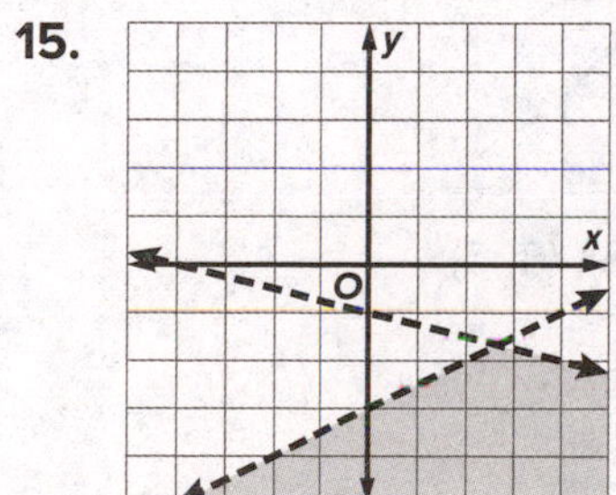

17. no solution

19a. $x \geq \frac{1}{2}, x \leq 2, x + y \leq 6$

Sheila's Day

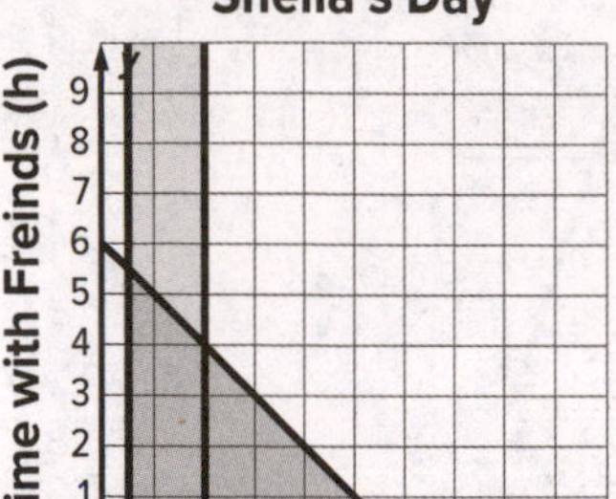

Time Running Errands (h)

19b. Sample answer: The variables represent measures of time, and time cannot be represented in negative quantities.

21. 75 units^2 **23.** true

Lesson 2-7

1. vertices: (1, 2), (1, 4), (5, 8), (5, 2); max: 11; min: −5

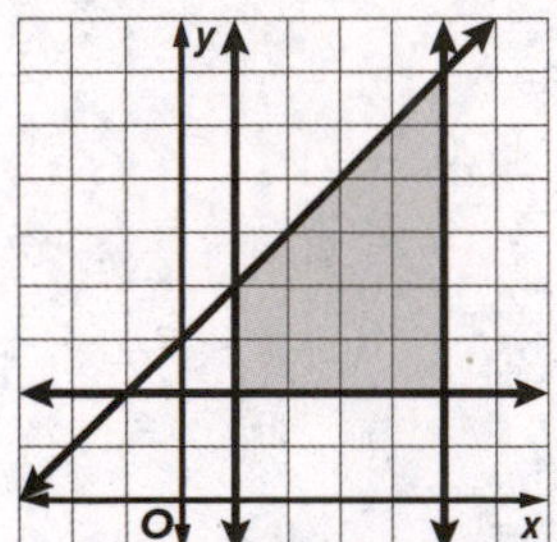

3. vertices: (0, 2), (4, 3), $\left(\frac{7}{3}, -\frac{1}{3}\right)$; max: 25; min: 6

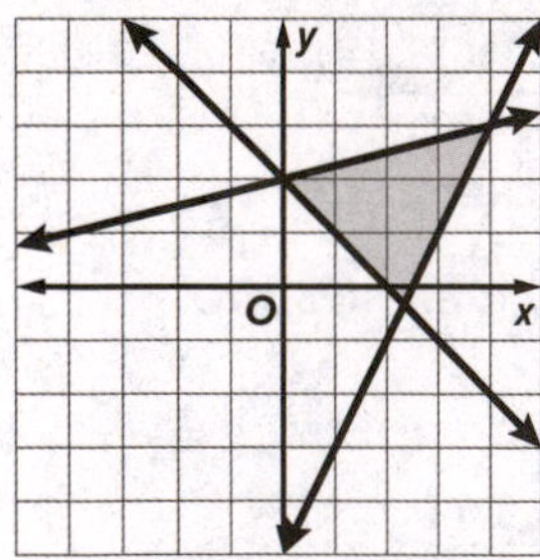

5. vertices: (1, −1), (1, 6), (8, 6); max: 2; min: −5

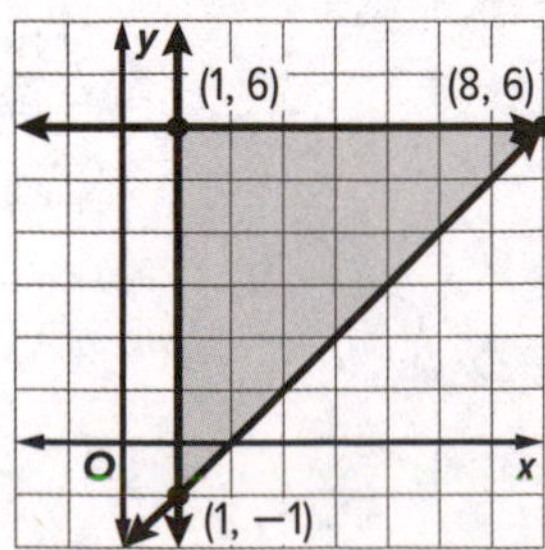

7. vertex: (−1, 7); max: 13; no min.

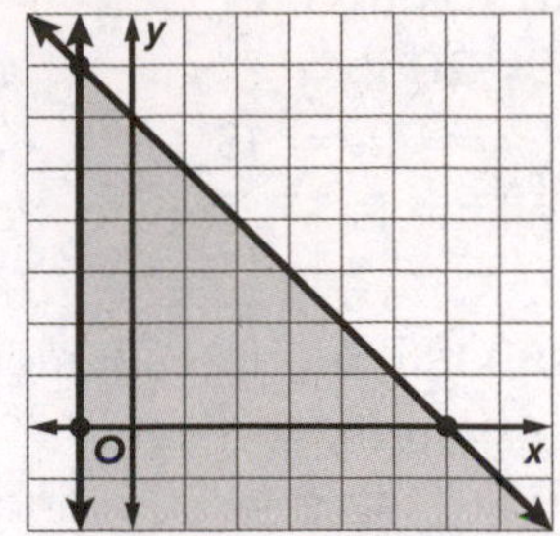

9. vertices: (−2, 0); $\left(-\frac{7}{5}, \frac{9}{5}\right)$; max: $-\frac{34}{4}$; no min.

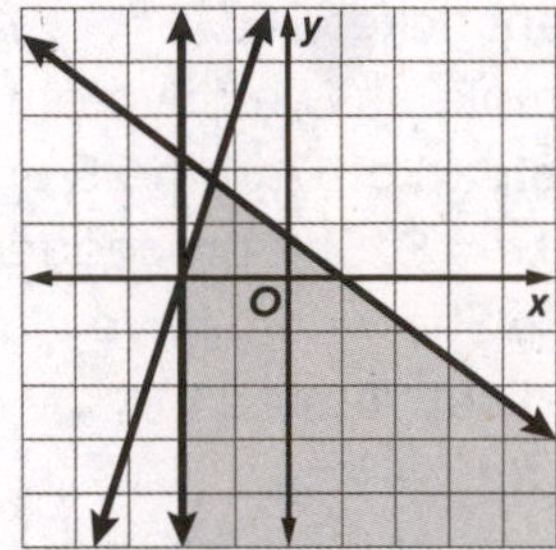

11a. Let x represent clay beads and y represent glass beads.; $0 \leq x \leq 10$; $y \geq 4$; $4y \leq 2x + 8$ $C = 0.20x + 0.40y$; The total cost equals 0.20 times the number of clay beads plus 0.40 times the number of glass beads.

11b. (4, 4), (10, 4), and (10, 7)

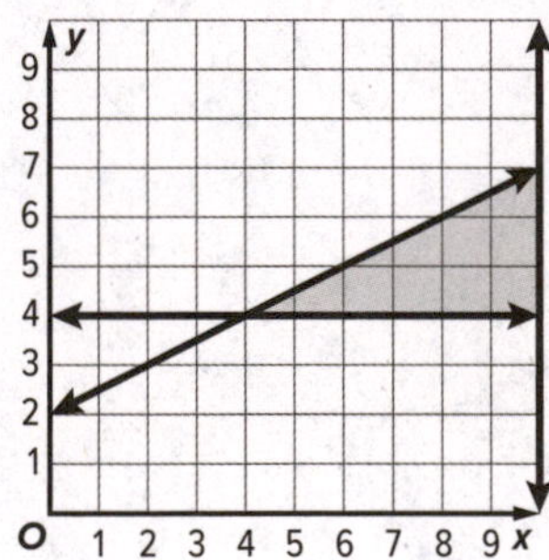

11c. Substitute into $C = 0.20x + 0.40y$: (4, 4) yields \$2.40, (10, 4) yields \$3.60, and (10, 7) yields \$4.80. The minimum cost would be \$2.40 at (4, 4), which represents 4 clay beads and 4 glass beads.

13. (5, 2)

15. Always; Sample answer: if a point on the unbounded region forms a minimum, then a maximum cannot also be formed because of the unbounded region. There will always be a value in the solution that will produce a higher value than any projected maximum.

17. Sample answer: Even though the region is bounded, multiple maximums occur at A and B and all of the points on the boundary of the feasible region containing both A and B. This happened because that boundary of the region has the same slope as the function.

Lesson 2-8

1. (4, −3, −1) **3.** infinitely many solutions
5. no solution **7.** (5, −5, −20)
9. (−3, 2, 1) **11.** (2, −1, 3)
13. ball: \$8; bat: \$5.40; base: \$1.40
15. 3 oz of apples, 7 oz of raisins, 6 oz of peanuts
17. 9, 6, 3 **19.** (1, −6, 2)
21. 56 miles
23. No; Sample answer: Let x = cost of 1 raft, y = cost of 1 chlorine filter, and z = cost of 1 large lounge chair. $x + 2y = 220$, $y + 2z = 245$, $x + 4z = 315$; Solve the first equation for y and the third for z to get $y = \frac{1}{2}(220 - x) = 110 - \frac{1}{2}x$, $z = \frac{1}{4}(315 - x) = \frac{315}{4} - \frac{1}{4}x$. Substitute to find $x = 22.50$, $y = 98.75$ and $z = 73.125$. The cost of buying one each, before sales tax, is \$194.38. If the sales tax is 6%, the total is \$206.04, which exceeds \$200.
25. Sample answer:
$a + b = (rx + ty + vz) + (rx - ty + vz)$
Replace a with $rx + ty + vz$, and b with $rx - ty + vz$

$a + b = 2rx + 2vz$	Simplify.
$a + (-a) = 2rx + 2vz$	Replace b with $-a$.
$0 = 2rx + 2vz$	Simplify.
$0 = rx + vz$	Divide each side by 2.
$rx + ty + vz = a$	Given
$ty + (rx + vz) = a$	Commutative and Associative Properties of Addition
$ty + 0 = a$	Substitution
$ty = a$	Simplify.

27. Sample answer:

$$3x + 4y + z = -17$$
$$2x - 5y - 3z = -18$$
$$-x + 3y + 8z = 47$$
$$3x + 4y + z = -17$$
$$3(-5) + 4(-2) + 6 = -17$$
$$-15 + (-8) + 6 = -17$$
$$-17 = -17 \checkmark$$
$$2x - 5y - 3z = -18$$
$$2(-5) - 5(-2) - 3(6) = -18$$
$$-10 + 10 - 18 = -18$$
$$-18 = -18 \checkmark$$
$$-x + 3y + 8z = 47$$
$$-(-5) + 3(-2) + 8(6) = 47$$
$$5 - 6 + 48 = 47$$
$$47 = 47 \checkmark$$

Lesson 2-9

1. $\{-1, 9\}$

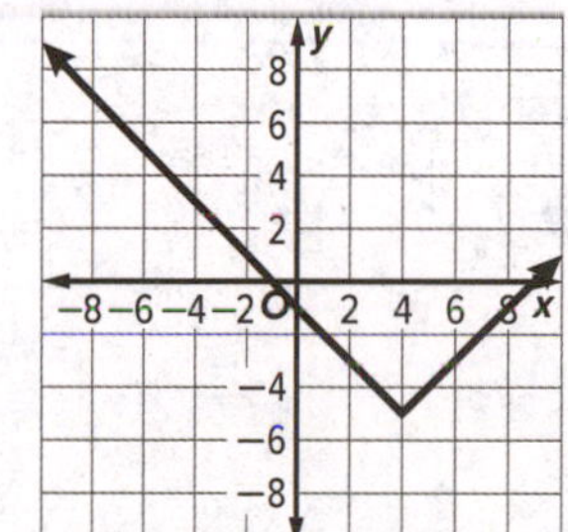

3. $\left\{-\frac{1}{2}\right\}$

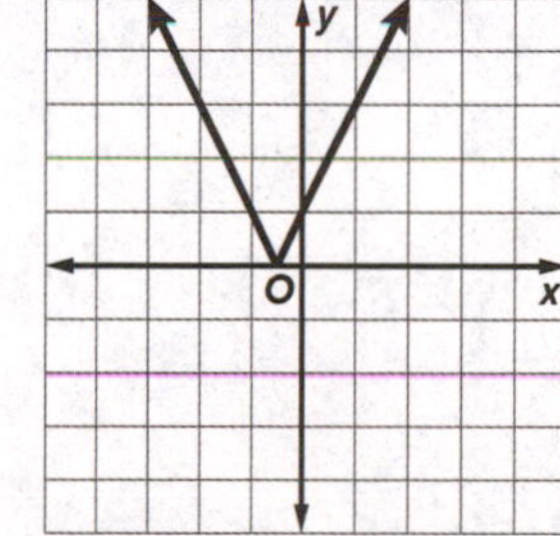

5. $\left\{\frac{1}{3}\right\}$

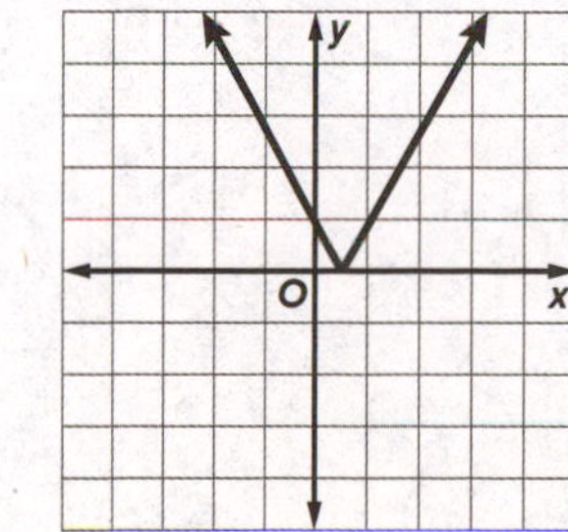

Selected Answers

7. $\{-7, 9\}$

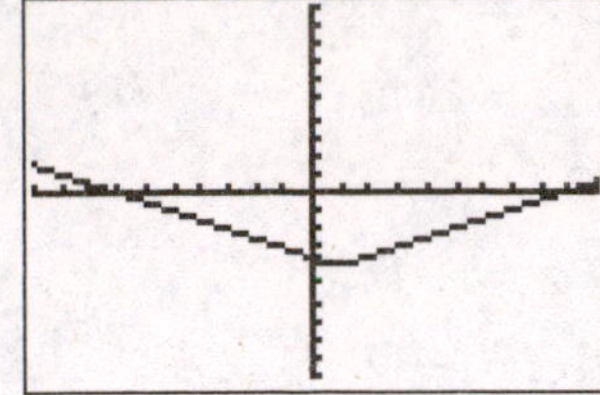

$[-10, 10]$ scl: 1 by $[-10, 10]$ scl: 1

9. $\{-10, 14\}$

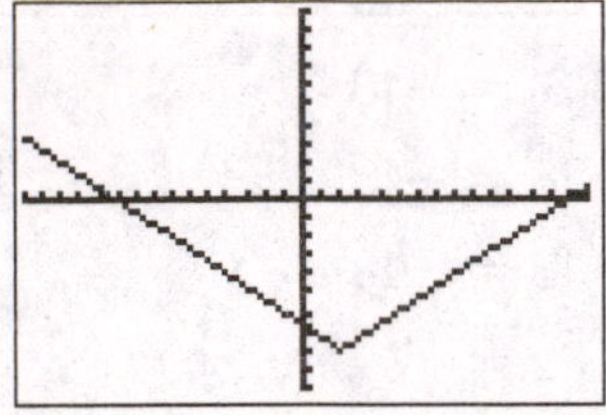

$[-15, 15]$ scl: 1 by $[-10, 10]$ scl: 1

11. $\{-56, 44\}$

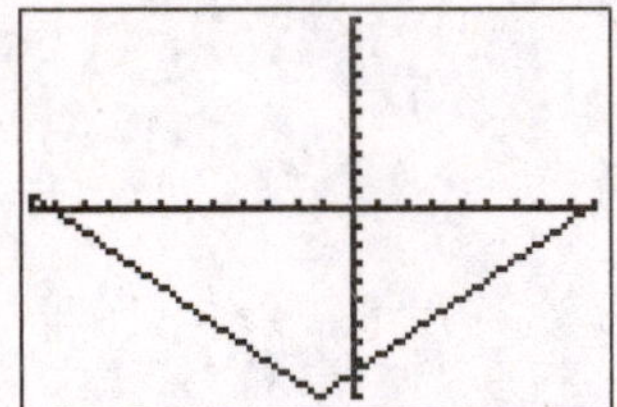

$[-60, 45]$ scl: 1 by $[-10, 10]$ scl: 1

13. $\{-12, 16\}$ 15. $\varnothing$ 17. $\{-2, -1\}$

19. $\{x \mid 1 \leq x \leq 5\}$; $[1, 5]$

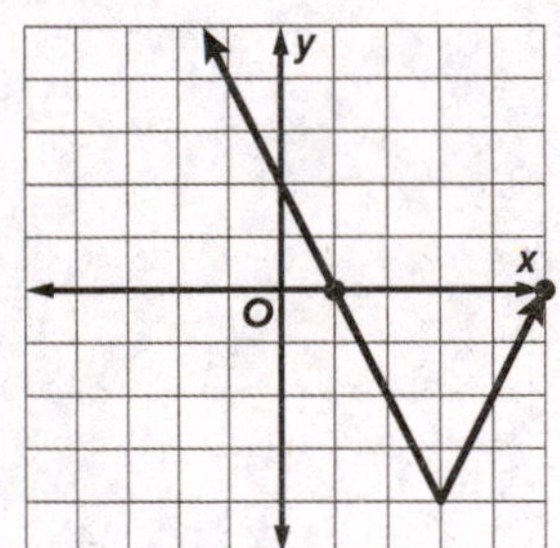

21. $\left\{x \mid x \leq -\frac{3}{2} \text{ or } x \geq \frac{5}{2}\right\}$; $\left[-\infty, -\frac{3}{2}\right]$; or $\left[\frac{5}{2}, \infty\right]$

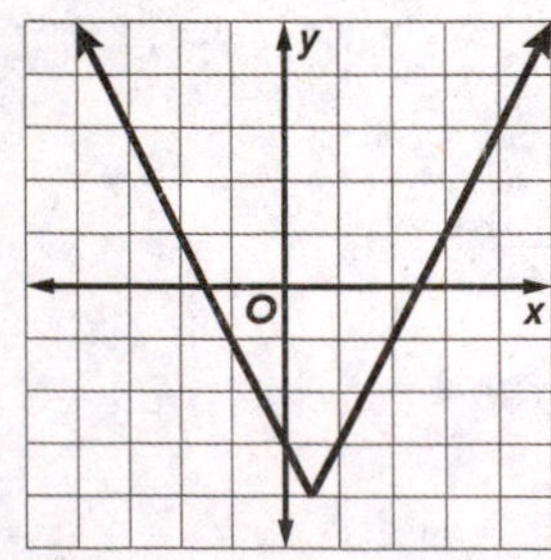

23. $\{x \mid -6 < x < 2\}$; $(-6, 2)$

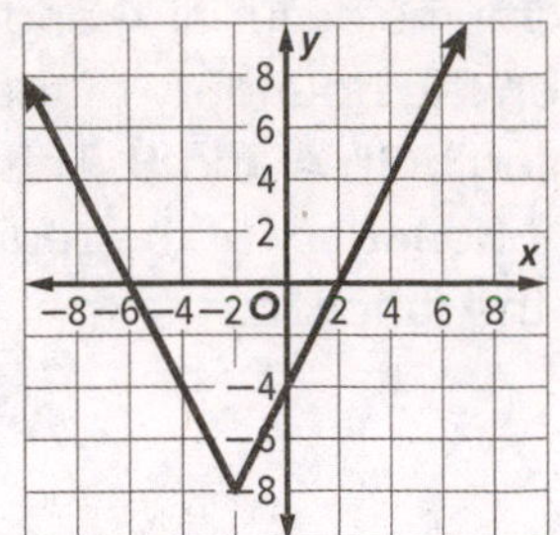

25. $\{x \mid x < -20 \text{ or } x > 12\}$; $(-\infty, -20)$ or $(-12, \infty)$

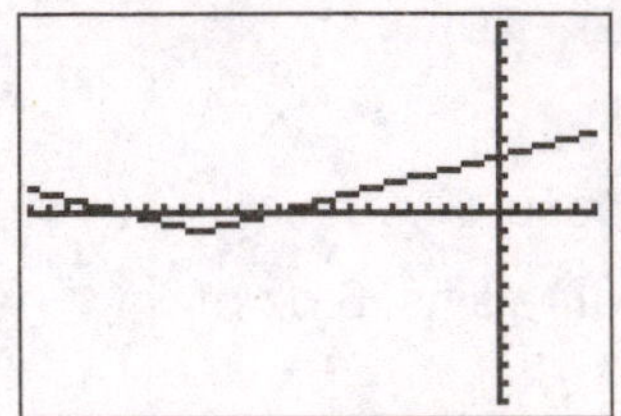

$[-25, 5]$ scl: 2 by $[-10, 10]$ scl: 1

27. $\left\{x \mid -\frac{1}{3} < x < 1\right\}$; $\left(-\frac{1}{3}, 1\right)$

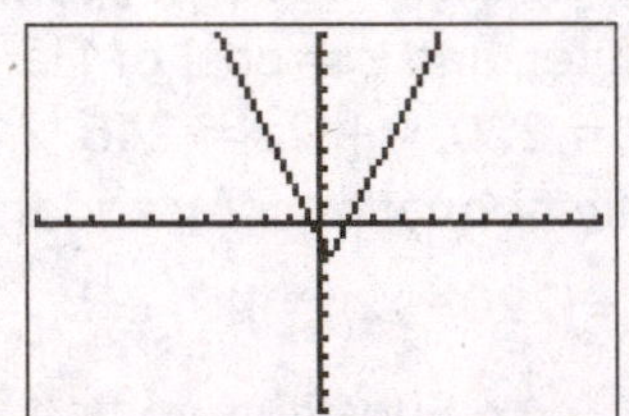

$[-10, 10]$ scl: 1 by $[-10, 10]$ scl: 1

29. $\varnothing$

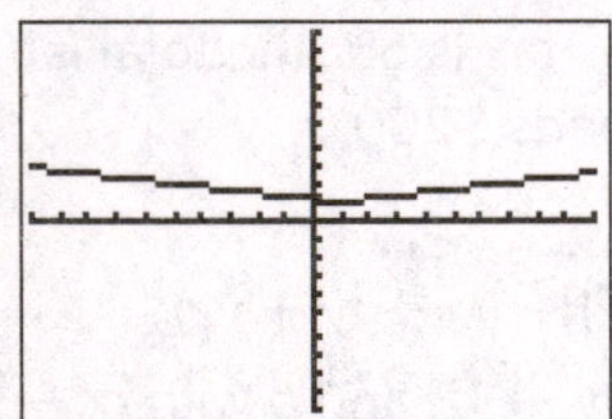

$[-10, 10]$ scl: 1 by $[-10, 10]$ scl: 1

31. $\{0.5, 1.5\}$

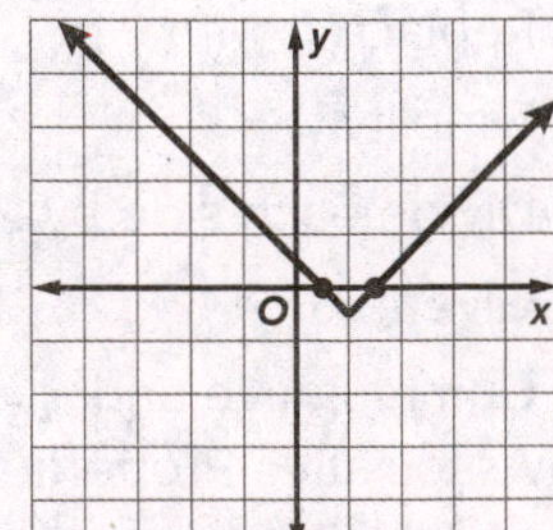

33. ∅

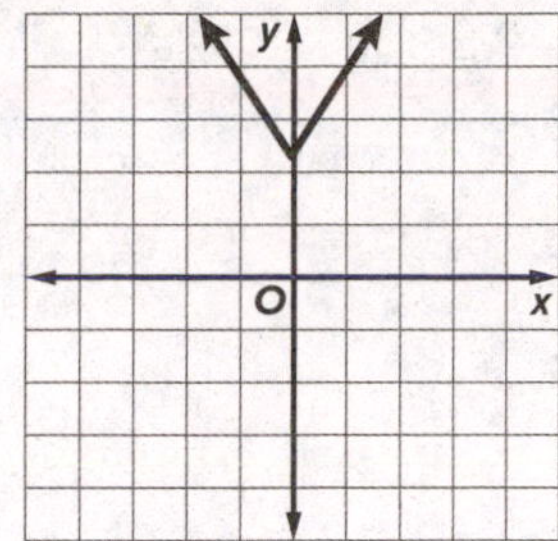

35. $\{x \mid 2 \le x \le 4\}$; [2, 4]

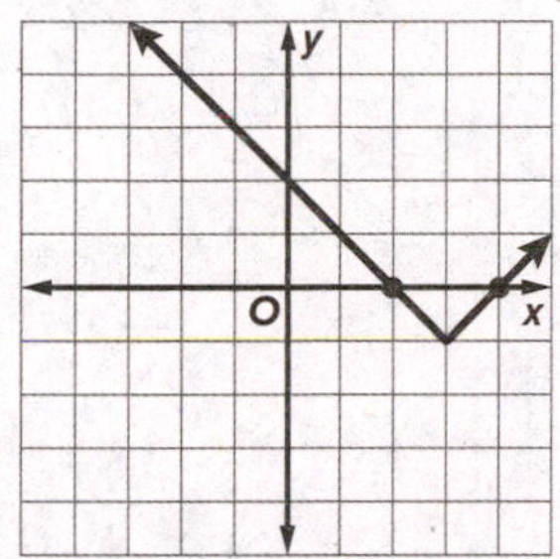

37. $\left\{x \mid x < -10\frac{4}{5} \text{ or } x > 7\frac{1}{5}\right\}$; $\left(-\infty, -10\frac{4}{5}\right)$ or $\left(7\frac{1}{5}, \infty\right)$

39. $\{-85, 95\}$

41. $|x - 63.5| \le 3.5$; $\{x \mid 60 < x < 67\}$: The range of comfortable temperatures for sleeping is at least 60° and no more than 67°.

43. $|x + 2| > 6$

45. Sample answer: The process by which the equation or inequality is set to zero to represent $f(x)$ and making a table of values is the same. However, the graph of an absolute value equation is restricted to having either 0, 1, or 2 solutions; whereas the absolute value inequalities can have infinitely many solutions.

47. Sample answer: $|x - 10| = 1$

Module 2 Review

1. 4 **3.** 77°F **5.** $y = 1.25x - 2.5$

7. A **9.** (0.5, 0.75) **11.** B

13. A, D, G **15.** (−3, 4, 1)

Module 3

Module 3 Opener

1. 22 **3.** − 21 **5.** $(x-3)(x-7)$
7. $(2x+3)(x-5)$

Lesson 3-1

1. D = {all real numbers}, R = $\{y \mid y \geq -1\}$

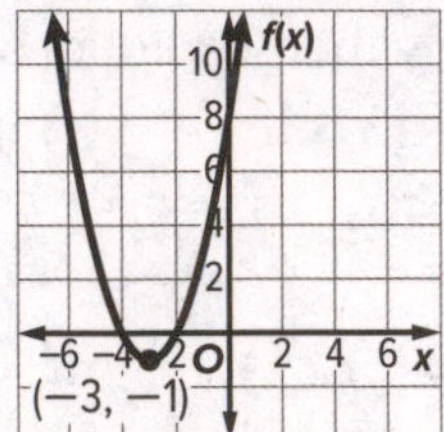

3. D = {all real numbers}, R = $\{y \mid y \geq 1\}$

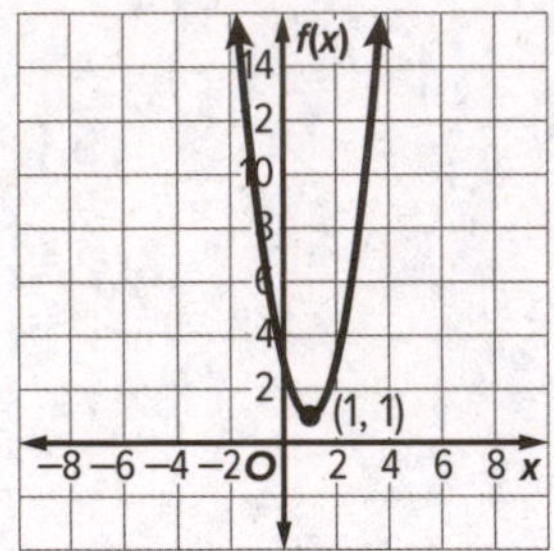

5. D = {all real numbers}, R = $\{y \mid y \geq 0\}$

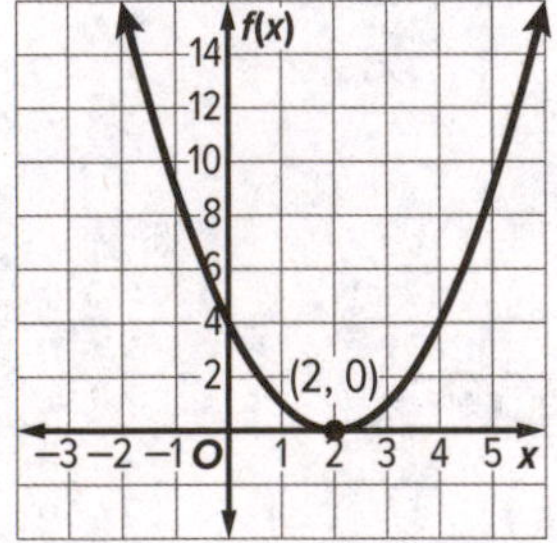

7. $g(x)$; Sample answer: Its vertex is a maximum point at (1, 3), which is 4 units above the vertex of $f(x)$ which is (1, −1).

9. $f(x)$; Sample answer: Its vertex is a minimum point at (5, −20), which is 10 units below the vertex of $g(x)$ which is (5, −10).

11a. \$100 per permit

11b. D = $\{x \mid x \geq 0\}$, R = $\{y \mid 0 \leq y \leq 40{,}000\}$

13. −10 **15.** −3 **17.** 0 **19.** 2 **21.** 3 **23.** 0

25a. $\approx \frac{12.5}{5} \approx 2.5$; $\frac{55.35 - 42.97}{5} = 2.476$

25b. Sample answer: From 2011–2016, the number of people in the U.S. who consumed between 8 and 11 bags of potato chips annually increased by 2.476 million people per year.

27a. y-int = −9; axis of symmetry: $x = 1.5$; x-coordinate of vertex = 1.5

27b.

x	$f(x)$
0	9
1	−13
1.5	−13.5
2	−13
3	−9

27c.

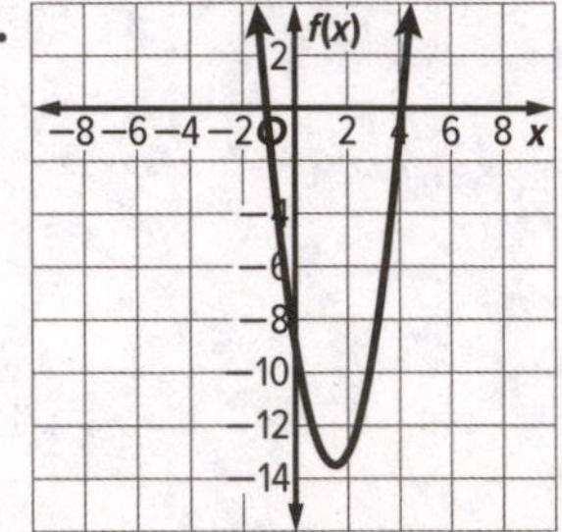

29a. y-int = 0; axis of symmetry: $x = \frac{5}{8}$; x-coordinate of vertex = $\frac{5}{8}$

29b.

x	$f(x)$
$-\frac{3}{4}$	−6
$\frac{1}{4}$	1
$\frac{5}{8}$	1.5625
1	1
2	−6

29c.

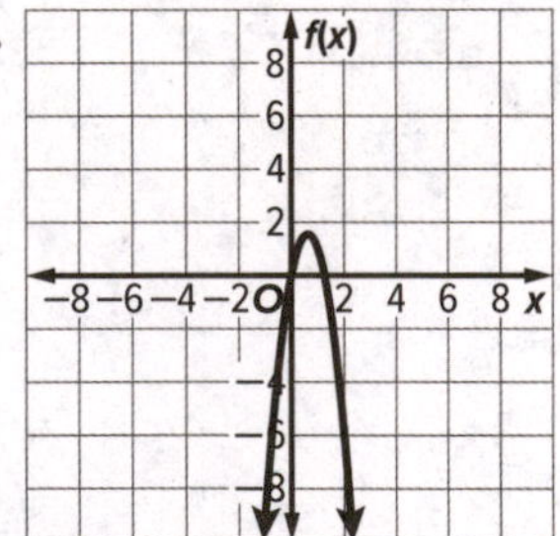

31a. y-int = 4; axis of symmetry: $x = -6$; x-coordinate of vertex = −6

31b.

x	$f(x)$
−10	−1
−8	−4
−6	−5
−4	−4
−2	−1

31c.

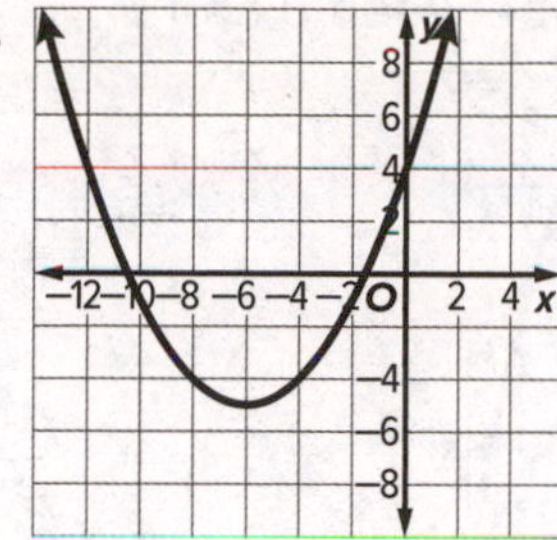

33.

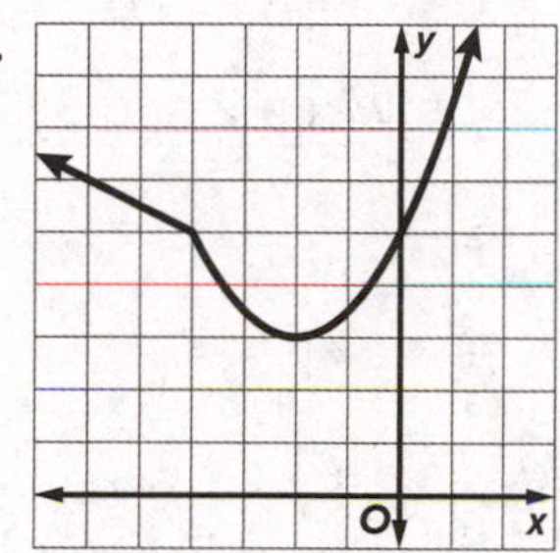

D = {all real numbers}, R = {y| $y \geq 3$}

35. min ≈ −1.19 **37.** min ≈ −13.36

39. max ≈ −11.92 **41.** $13.75

43. 20 ft; 1 second

45. Graph $f(x)$ on the same coordinate plane and compare; $g(x)$ has the greater maximum value.

47. Sample answer: Always; the coordinates of a quadratic function are symmetrical, so x-coordinates equidistant from the vertex will have the same y-coordinate.

49. Sample answer: A function is quadratic if it has no other terms than a quadratic term, linear term, and constant term. The function has a maximum if the coefficient of the quadratic term is negative and has a minimum if the coefficient of the quadratic term is positive.

Lesson 3-2

1. no real solution **3.** −4

5. $-\frac{1}{2}$

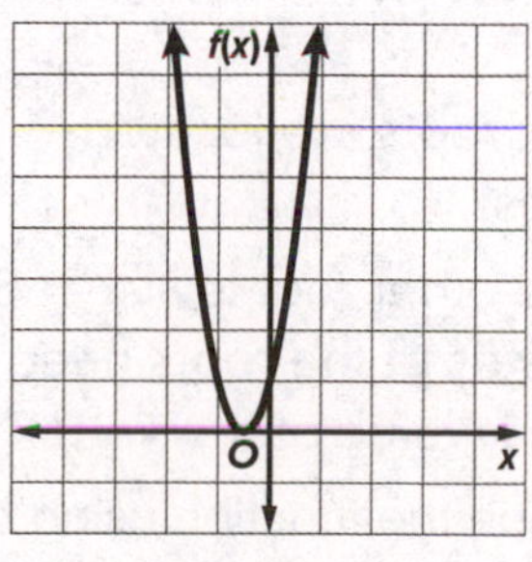

7. −3, 1

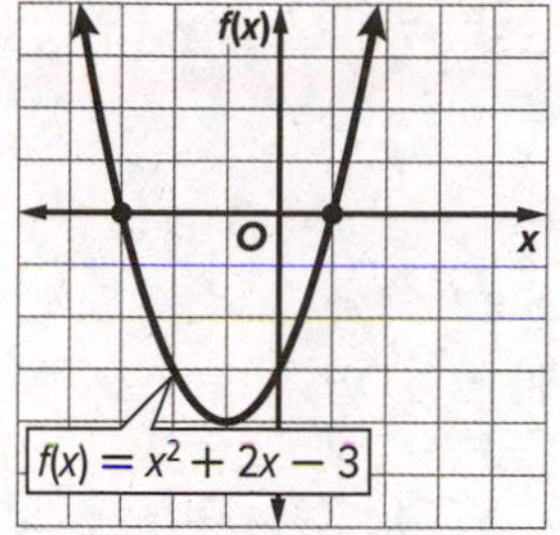

9. 1, 5

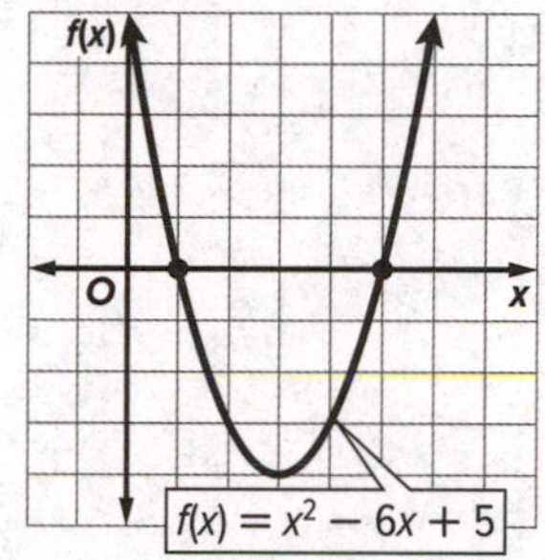

11. −2, 5

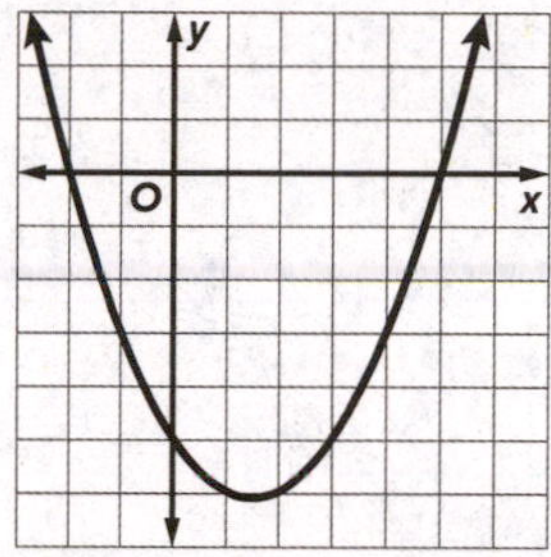

13. 6 and −4

15. between 0 and 1; between 3 and 4

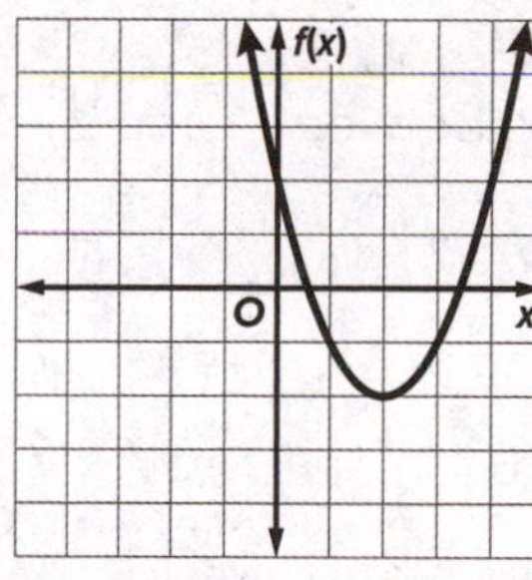

17. between −1 and 0; between −4 and −3

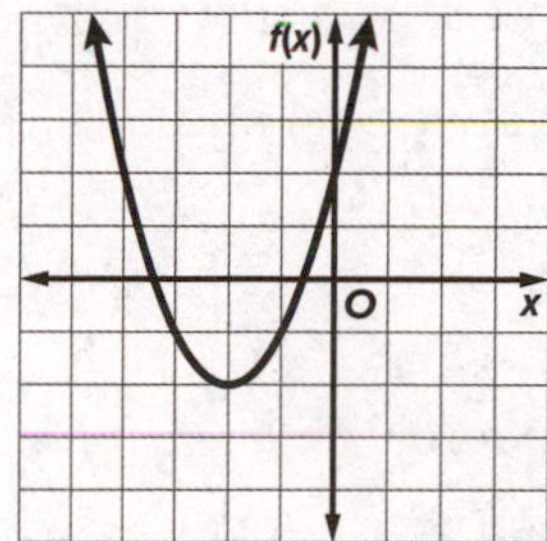

19. $-6, 6$

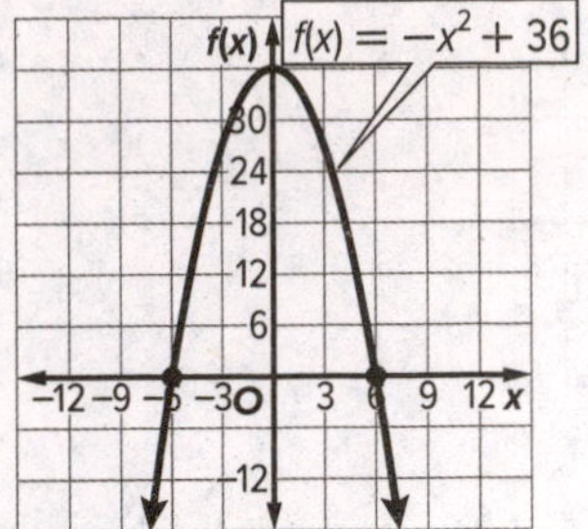

21. between -1 and 0; between -5 and -4

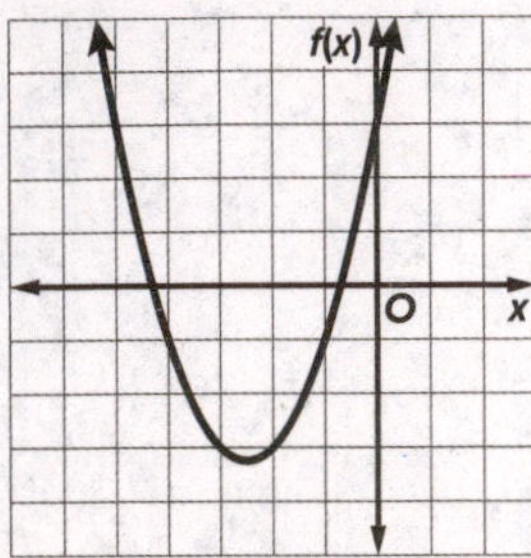

23. no real solution

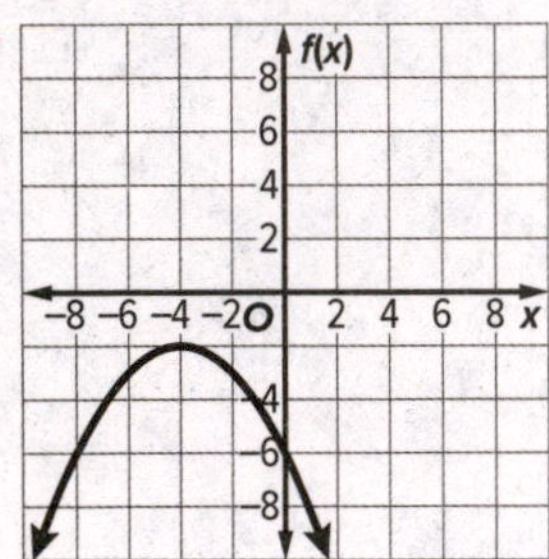

25. between 0 and 1; between 2 and 3

27. $\approx 3.24, \approx -1.24$ **29.** $\approx -1.45, \approx 3.45$

31. $-1, 1$ **33.** 2.1 seconds

35. between -3 and -2, between 1 and 2

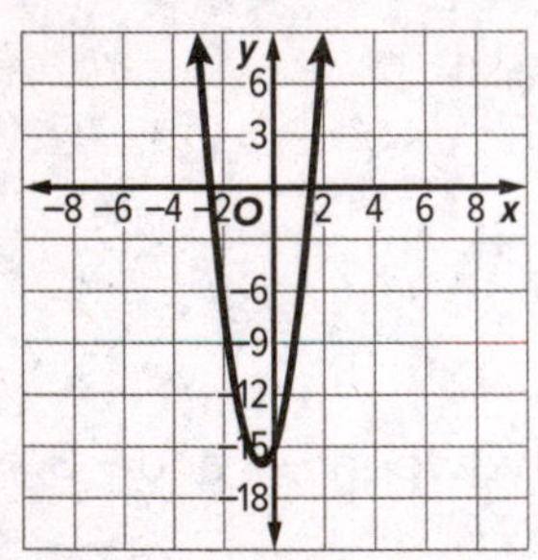

37. between -1 and 0, between 4 and 5

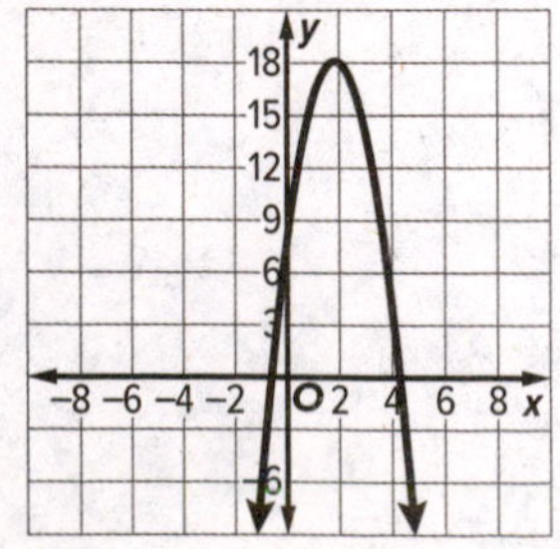

39. between 3 and 4, between 8 and 9

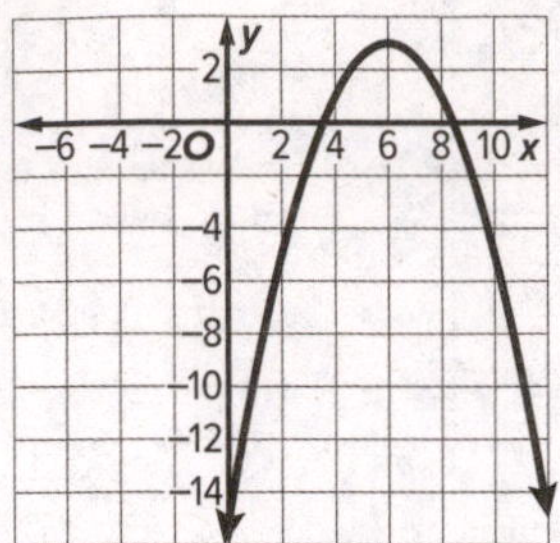

41. between -3 and -2; between 2 and 3

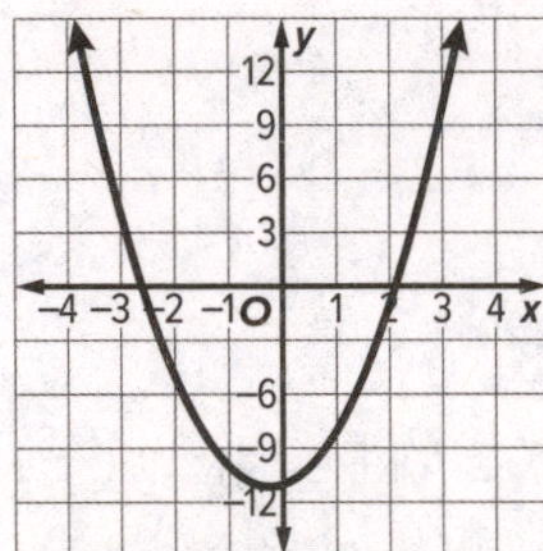

43. between -8 and -7; between 12 and 13

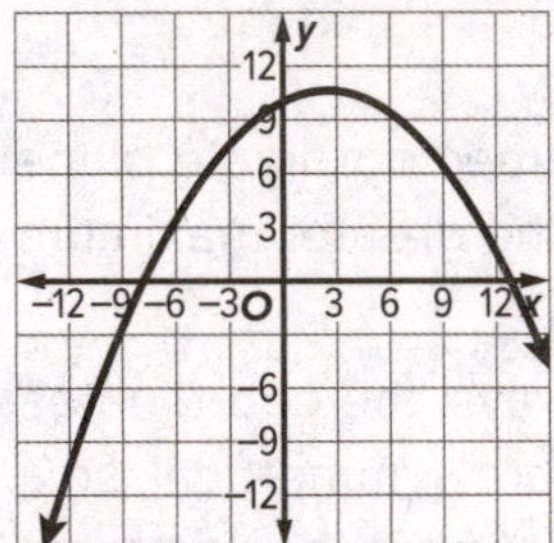

45. no real solution **47.** -2 **49.** $-3, 4$

51. about -5 and 17 **53.** 11 and -19

55. 64 m

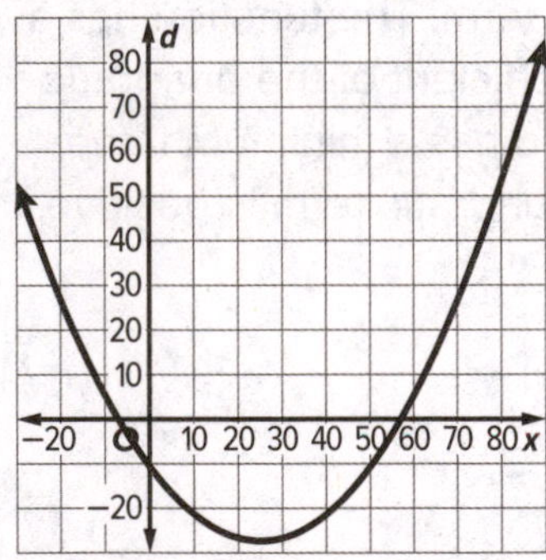

57. 5 seconds

59. Sample answer: No; roots are located where $f(x)$ changes signs.

61. Sample answer: The other root is at $x = 5$ because the x-coordinates of the roots need to be equidistant from the x-value of the vertex.

63. Sample answer: Graph the function using the axis of symmetry. Determine where the graph intersects the x-axis. The x-coordinates of those points are solutions of the quadratic equation.

Lesson 3-3

1. $4i\sqrt{3}$ **3.** $6i\sqrt{2}$ **5.** $2i\sqrt{21}$ **7.** $-23\sqrt{2}$
9. $-5\sqrt{2}$ **11.** $-i$ **13.** $\pm 3i$ **15.** $\pm i$ **17.** $\pm 5i$
19. 3, 3 **21.** $-\frac{11}{2}, -3$ **23.** 4, −3 **25.** $10 - 4i$
27. $2 + i$ **29.** $10 - 5i$ **31.** $7 + i$ **33.** $-10i$
35. $\frac{3}{2} - \frac{1}{2}i$ **37.** $-\frac{5}{3} - 2i$ **39.** $\frac{7}{9} - \frac{4i\sqrt{2}}{9}$
41. $(3 + i)x^2 + (-2 + i)x - 8i + 7$
43. $10 + 10j$ volts **45.** $8 - 2j$ ohms
47. Sue; $i^3 = -i$, not −1.
49. Sample answer: Always; the value of 5 can be represented by $5 + 0i$, and the value of $3i$ can be represented by $0 + 3i$.
51. Some quadratic equations have complex solutions and cannot be solved using only the real numbers.

Lesson 3-4

1. $\left\{0, \frac{1}{3}\right\}$ **3.** $\left\{0, -\frac{5}{4}\right\}$ **5.** −11, −3 **7.** 7 ft by 9 ft
9. $\left\{\frac{3}{2}, -1\right\}$ **11.** $\left\{\frac{2}{5}, -6\right\}$ **13.** $\left\{8, -\frac{5}{2}\right\}$
15. {−8, 8} **17.** {−17, 17} **19.** {−13, 13} **21.** $\left\{\frac{7}{2}\right\}$
23. $\left\{\frac{3}{4}\right\}$ **25.** $\left\{-\frac{8}{5}\right\}$ **27.** $\{5i, -5i\}$
29. $\{25i, -25i\}$ **33.** $\left\{\frac{5}{6}i, -\frac{5}{6}i\right\}$ **33.** $\left\{-3, \frac{1}{2}\right\}$
35. $\{9i, -9i\}$ **37.** $\left\{\frac{1}{5}i, -\frac{1}{5}i\right\}$
39. 10 inches by 13 inches
41. 24, 26
43. Sample answer: Morgan; Gwen did not have like terms in the parentheses in the third line.
45. Sample answer: 3 and 6 → $x^2 - 9x + 18 = 0$. −3 and −6 → $x^2 + 9x + 18 = 0$. The linear term changes sign.
47. Sample answer: Standard form is $ax^2 + bx + c$. Multiply a and c. Then find a pair of integers, g and h, that multiply to equal ac and add to equal b. Then write the quadratic expression, substituting the middle term, bx, with $gx + hx$. The expression is now $ax^2 + gx + hx + c$. Then factor the GCF from the first two terms and factor the GCF from the second two terms. So, the expression becomes $\text{GCF}(x - q) + \text{GCF}_2(x - q)$. Simplify to get $(\text{GCF} + \text{GCF}_2)(x - q)$ or $(x - p)(x - q)$.

Lesson 3-5

1. {2, 16} **3.** $\left\{0, \frac{4}{3}\right\}$ **5.** $\left\{\frac{15}{2}, -\frac{1}{2}\right\}$
7. $\left\{\frac{-1 \pm 3\sqrt{2}}{6}\right\}$ **9.** $\left\{\frac{-2 \pm 5\sqrt{3}}{5}\right\}$ **11.** $\left\{\frac{3 \pm 4\sqrt{6}}{5}\right\}$
13. $x = 8 \pm 8i$ **15.** $x = -7 \pm 10i$
17. $x = -4 \pm 6i$ **19.** 25; $(x + 5)^2$
21. 144; $(x + 12)^2$ **23.** $\frac{81}{4}$; $\left(x - \frac{9}{2}\right)^2$
25. 4, 9 **27.** $2 \pm \sqrt{17}$ **29.** $\frac{1 \pm \sqrt{13}}{2}$
31. 16 in. by 16 in. by 16 in.
33. 6, −2 **35.** $-\frac{1}{2}, 7$ **37.** $-4, \frac{1}{2}$
39. $\{2 \pm 2i\sqrt{2}\}$ **41.** $\left\{\frac{-5 \pm i\sqrt{31}}{4}\right\}$
43. $x = \pm 2i\sqrt{6}$
45. $y = (x + 1)^2 - 6$; $x = -1$; $(h, k) = (-1, -6)$; minimum
47. $y = -(x - 2)^2 + 6$; $x = 2$; $(h, k) = (2, 6)$; maximum
49. $y = 2(x + 1)^2 + 1$; $x = -1$; $(h, k) = (-1, 1)$; minimum
51a. $h(t) = -16t^2 + 96t + 2$
51b. $h(t) = -16(t - 3)^2 + 146$
51c. axis of symmetry is $t = 3$; because the axis of symmetry divides the function into two equal halves, the firework will be at the same height after 1 second as it is after 5 seconds. The vertex is (3, 146). This is the maximum value of the function because $a < 0$. So the firework reached a maximum height of 146 feet after 3 seconds.
53. {2.38, 4.62} **55.** {−1.26, 0.26}
57. 0.1225; $(x + 0.35)^2$ **59.** $\frac{81}{100}$; $\left(x - \frac{9}{10}\right)^2$
61. 0.5 second **63.** 10%
65. $y = (x + 8)^2 + 1$; (−8, 1)
67. $y = (x - 4)^2 + 1$; (4, 1) **69.** about 2.14 feet
71a. $V(w) = 2(w - 4)(3w - 4) = 6w^2 - 32w$
71b. Disagree; sample answer: Timothy may have been thinking of the case where a function is set equal to 0 to solve for the independent variable. In that case, a common factor can be factored out and then both sides divided by that factor because any number divided by 0 is still 0. In this case, however, if he divides both sides by 2, he will have $\frac{V(w)}{2}$ on the left side, not $V(w)$.

Selected Answers

73. Alsonso; Aida did not add 16 to each side; she added it only to the left side.

75a. 2; rational; 16 is a perfect square, so $x + 2$ and x are rational.

75b. 2; rational; 16 is a perfect square, so $x - 2$ and x are rational.

75c. 2; complex; if the opposite of a square is positive, the square is negative. The square root of a negative number is complex.

75d. 2; real; the square must equal 20. Since that is positive but not a perfect square, the solutions will be real but not rational.

75e. 1; rational; the expression must be equal to 0 and only -2 makes the expression equal to 0.

75f. 1; rational; the expressions $(x + 4)$ and $(x + 6)$ must either be equal or opposites. No value makes them equal, -5 makes them opposites. The only solution is -5.

77. Completing the square allows you to rewrite one side of a quadratic equation in the form of a perfect square. Once in this form, the equation can be solved by using the Square Root Property.

Lesson 3-6

1. 2.9 s **3.** 1.5 s **5.** $\frac{1}{4}, -5$ **7.** $-2, \frac{1}{3}$ **9.** $-\frac{3}{2}, \frac{3}{4}$

11. $-\frac{3}{4}, \frac{9}{4}$ **13.** $-4, 2$ **15.** $\pm 5i$ **17.** $\frac{1 \pm i}{4}$

19. $7 \pm 2i$ **21.** $\frac{3 \pm 2i\sqrt{6}}{3}$ **23.** $\frac{2 \pm i\sqrt{14}}{6}$

25. 225; 2 rational roots; $-2, 13$

27. 289; 2 rational roots; $-\frac{3}{5}, \frac{1}{4}$

29. 24; 2 irrational roots; $\pm\sqrt{6}$

31. 21; 2 irrational roots; $\frac{1 \pm \sqrt{21}}{10}$

33. -196; 2 complex roots; $\pm 7i$

35. -7; 2 complex roots; $\frac{3 \pm i\sqrt{7}}{4}$

37. $b^2 - 4ac > 0$
2 real rational or irrational roots

39. $\frac{1 \pm 4i}{2}$ **41.** $0, \frac{5}{7}$ **43.** 3, 8 **45.** $4, \frac{4}{3}$

47. $\frac{-5 \pm \sqrt{3}}{2}$ **49.** about 8.3 seconds

51. about 53.2 mi/h **53.** 5 in. by 5 in. by 16 in.

55. Set $h(t) = 20$; use the quadratic formula: $t = \frac{v \pm \sqrt{v^2 - 4(16)(20)}}{32}$. The ball fails to hit the target if the solutions are complex, when $v^2 - 1280 < 0$. If the initial velocity is less than approximately 35.8 feet per second, the ball will not hit the target.

57. Sample answer: $f(x) = -x^2$

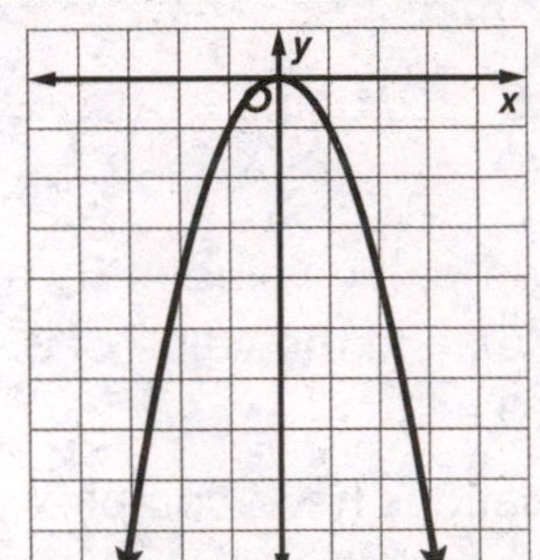

59a. $3x^2 - kx + m = 0$; Using the Quadratic Formula, $x = \frac{k \pm \sqrt{k^2 - 12m}}{6}$.

59b. Using the discriminant, $f(x)$ has complex roots for all values of k and m such that $k^2 - 12m < 0$ or $k^2 < 12m$.

61. Jonathan; you must first write the equation in the form $ax^2 + bx + c = 0$ to determine the values of a, b, and c. Therefore, the value of c is -7, not 7.

63a. Sample answer: Always; when a and c are opposite signs, then ac will always be negative and $-4ac$ will always be positive. Because b^2 will also always be positive, then $b^2 - 4ac$ represents the addition of two positive values, which will never be negative. Hence, the discriminant can never be negative and the solutions can never be imaginary.

63b. Sample answer: Sometimes; the roots will only be irrational if $b^2 - 4ac$ is not a perfect square.

65. -0.75

Lesson 3-7

1.

3. 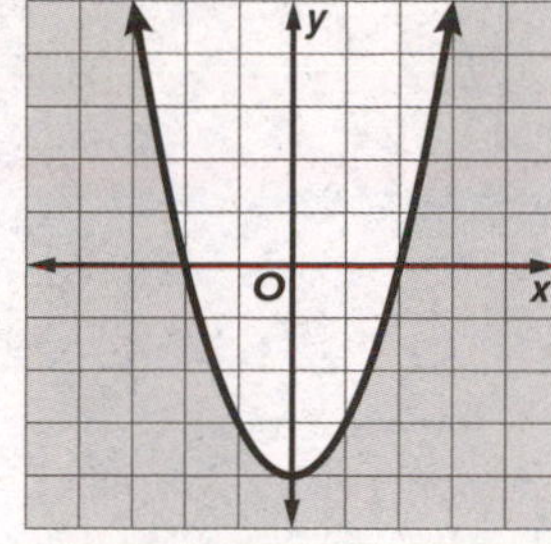

5. 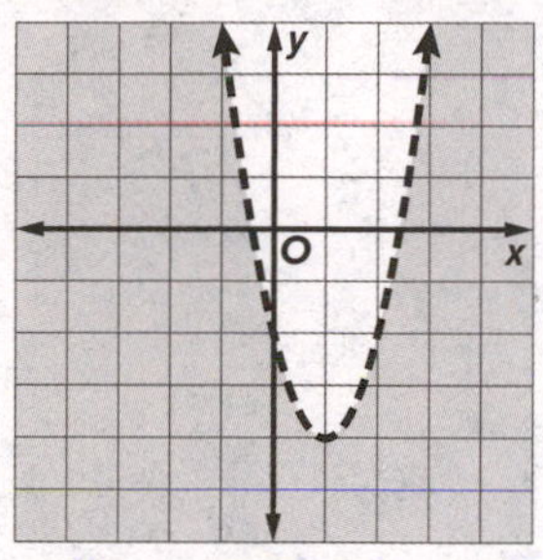

7. 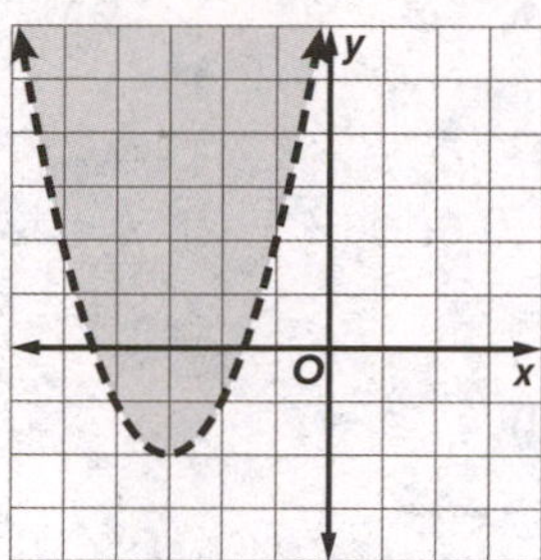

9. 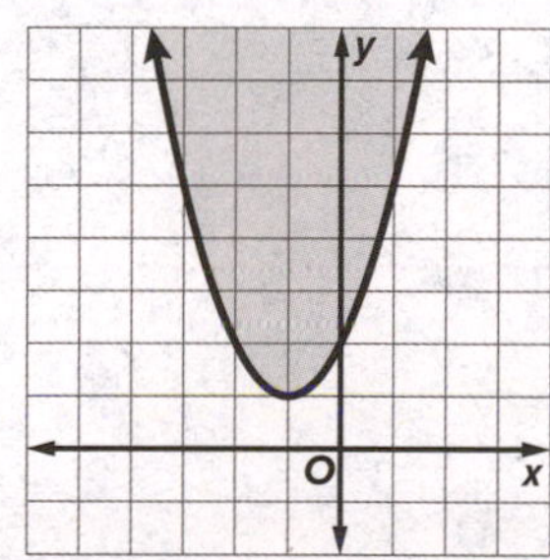

11. 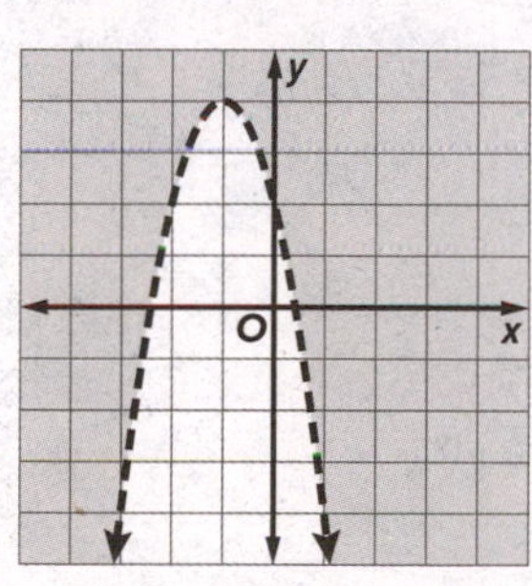

13. $\{x \mid x = 3\}$

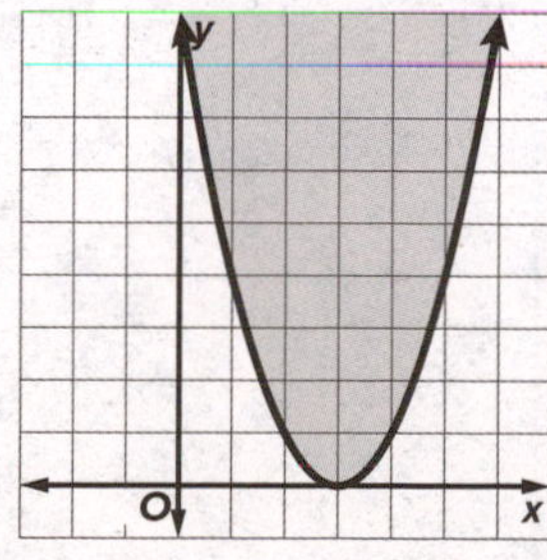

15. $\{x \mid x < -5 \text{ or } x > 4\}$

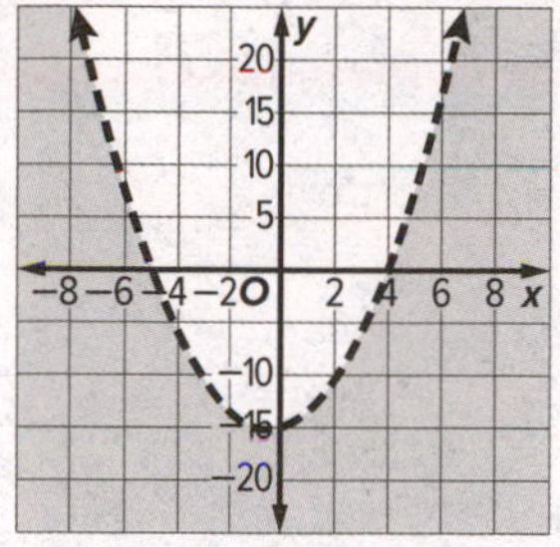

17. {all real numbers}

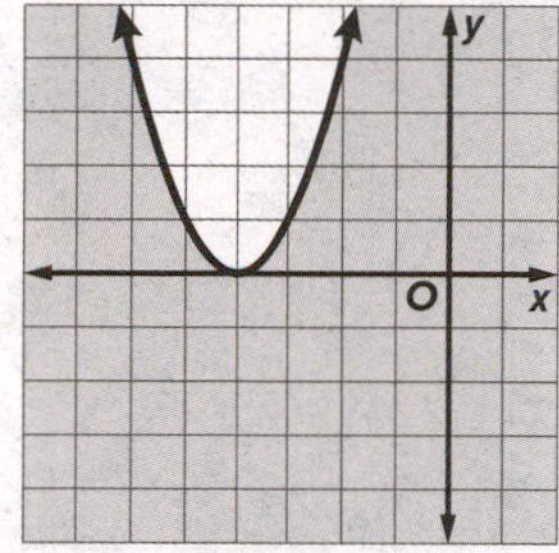

19. 30 ft to 60 ft **21.** $\{x \mid x < -1.06 \text{ or } x > 7.06\}$

23. $\{x \mid x \leq -2.75 \text{ or } x \geq 1\}$

25. $\{x \mid x < 0.61 \text{ or } x > 2.72\}$

27. {all real numbers}

29. $\{x \mid x \leq -9.24 \text{ or } x \geq -0.76\}$

31. $\{x \mid -5 \leq x \leq -3\}$

33. $\left\{x \mid x \neq -\frac{1}{2}\right\}$ **35.** $\left\{x \mid -3 \leq x \leq -\frac{4}{9}\right\}$

37. $y > x^2 - 4x - 6$ **39.** $y > -0.25x^2 - 4x + 2$

41. No; the graphs of the inequalities intersect the x-axis at the same points.

43a. Sample answer: $x^2 + 2x + 1 \geq 0$

43b. Sample answer: $x^2 - 4x + 6 < 0$

45. 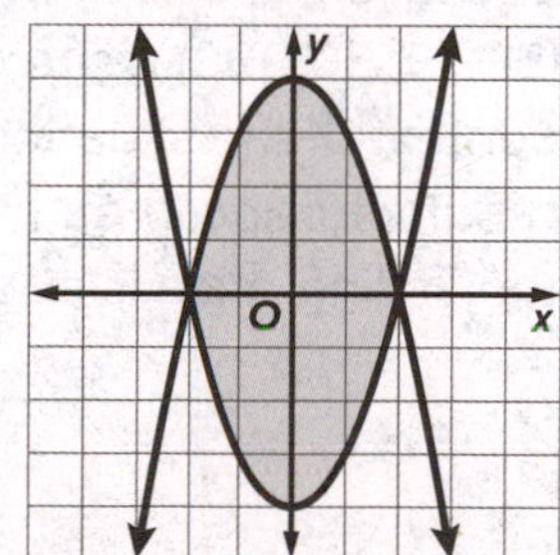

Lesson 3-8

1. $(2, -1), (-1, -4)$ **3.** $(-1, 2), (1.5, 4.5)$

5. $(2, -2), \left(\frac{1}{2}, 1\right)$ **7.** $(1, 2)$

9. $\left(\frac{-1 + \sqrt{33}}{4}, \frac{-1 + \sqrt{33}}{4}\right), \left(\frac{-1 - \sqrt{33}}{4}, \frac{-1 - \sqrt{33}}{4}\right)$

11. (−2, 3) and (1, 9)

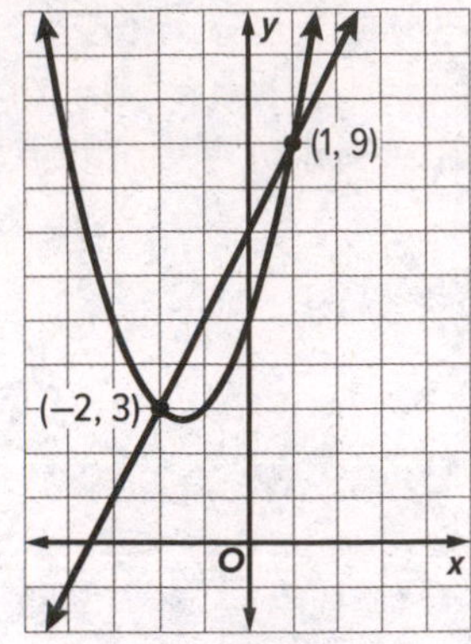

13. $\left(-\frac{1}{4}, -\frac{5}{4}\right)$ and (1, −5)

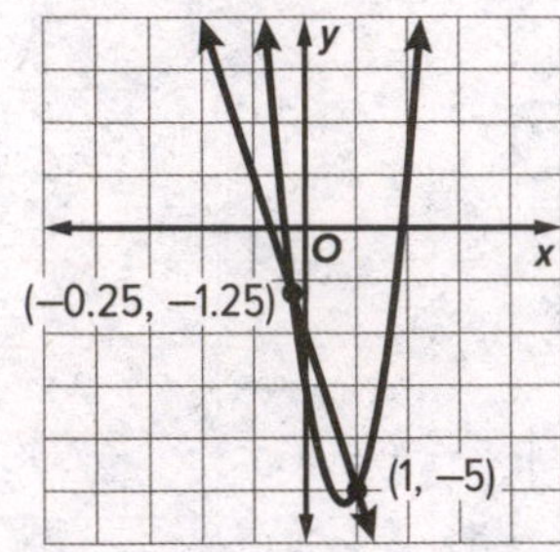

15. (−1, 10) and (7, 26)

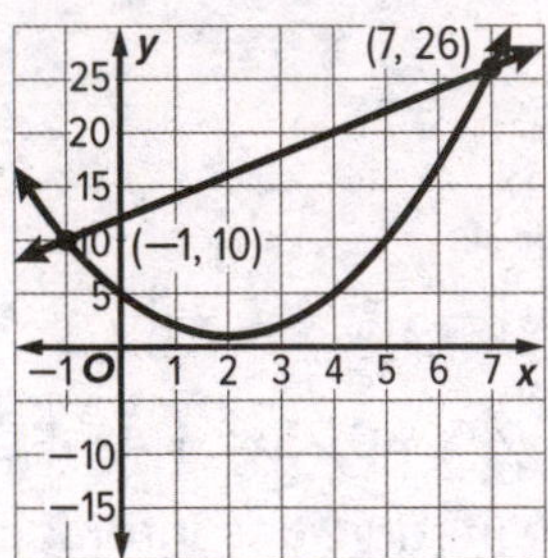

17a. $P = 2x^2 + 30x$ and $P = 50{,}000$

17b. $x \approx -165.79$, $x \approx \$150.79$

17c. Sample answer: Because the selling price cannot be negative, (150.79, 50,000) is the only viable solution in the context of the situation. This means that the manufacturer can earn a $50,000 profit when the selling price is about $150.79 per item.

19. no solution

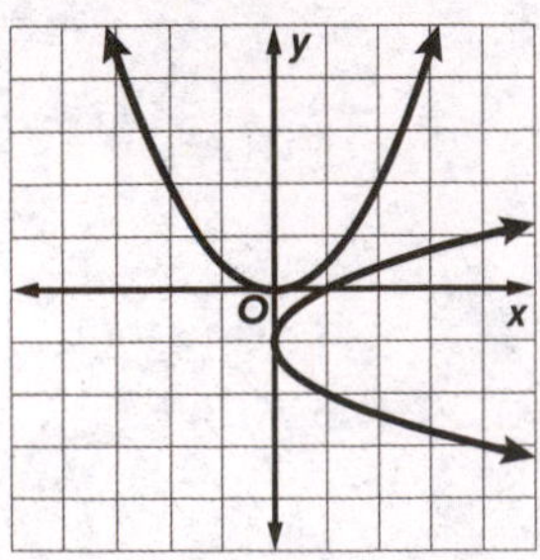

21. (0, 2) and (1, 3)

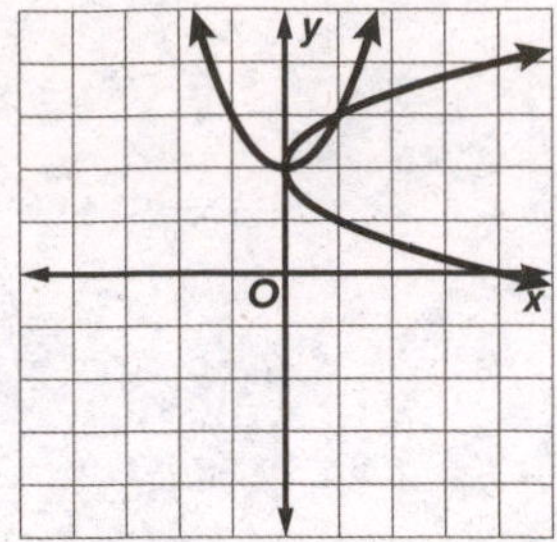

23. (1, 1) and (5, 5)

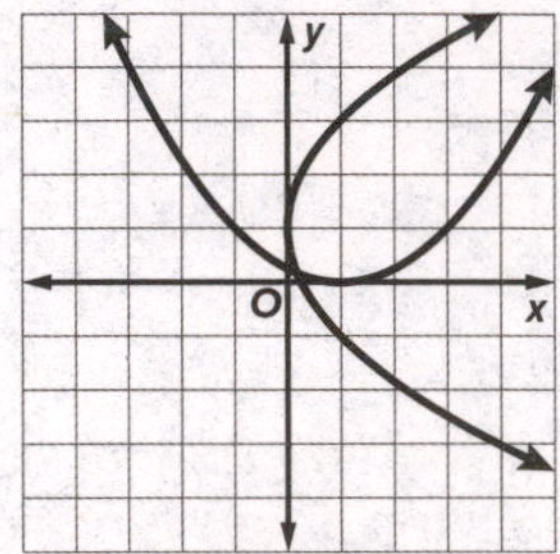

25. no solution **27.** (2, 2) and (2, −2)

29. (−1, −7) and (4, 23)

31. $\left(-\frac{3}{2}, 10\frac{1}{4}\right)$ and (2, 12)

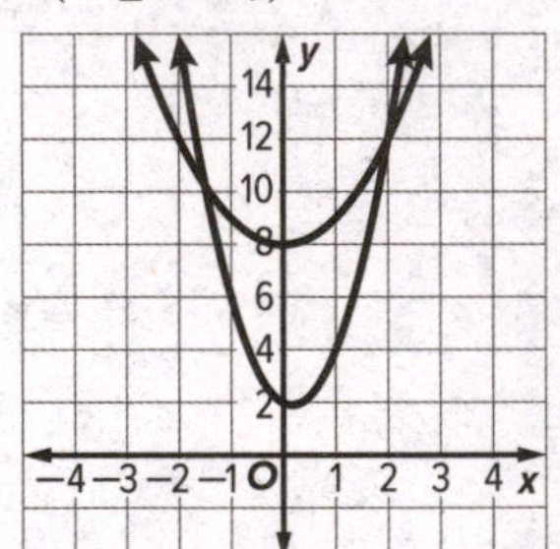

33. (−2, 10)

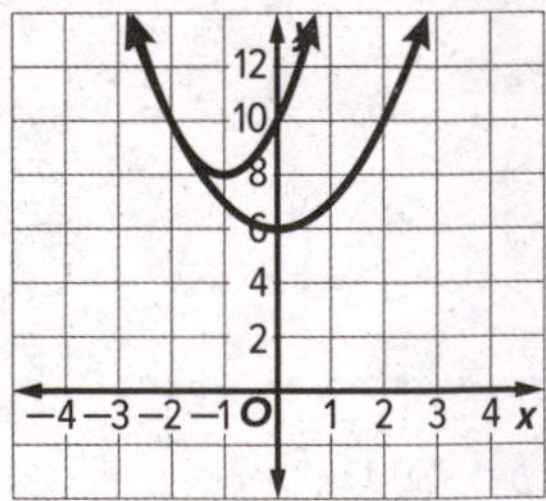

35. $\left(-\frac{1}{2}, -\frac{13}{4}\right)$ and (3, 23)

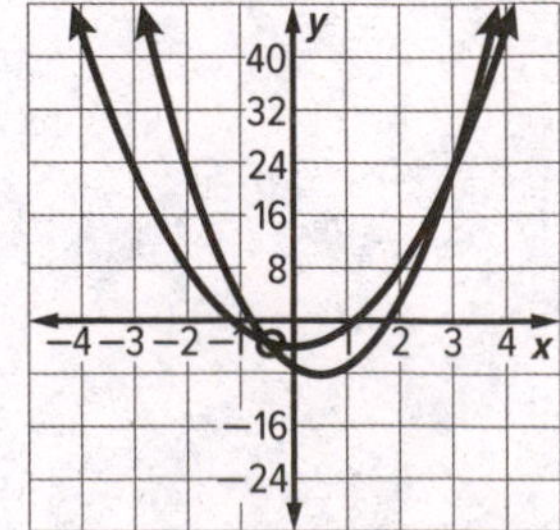

37. $(-2, -5)$ **39.** $(-2, -6), (0, 8)$
41. $(-1, 2), (2,5)$ **43.** $(0.42, 0.352)$ and $(1, 2)$
45. $(-1.4, 2)$ and $(1.4, 2)$
47. $(-1.8, 3.2)$ and $(1.1, 1.3)$
49. $(2, -2), (0, 0)$ **51.** no solution
53. no solution **55.** $(-\sqrt{31}, 7)$ and $(\sqrt{31}, 7)$
57. $\left(-6\frac{1}{2}, 77\right)$ and $(1, 2)$ **59.** $(-3, 2)$ and $(1, 6)$
61. $\left(-\frac{1}{2}, -\frac{1}{4}\right)$ and $(-1, 0)$ **63.** $(-3, 5)$
65. $\left(-\frac{1}{2}, -\frac{13}{4}\right)$ and $(3, 23)$
67. $(-6, 18)$ and $(-3, 6)$ **69a.** \$3.75
69b. Sample answer: The second point of intersection for both companies occurs at (0, 0), which would mean that the companies are giving their product away for free and making no profit. This solution does not make sense in the context of the situation.
71a. $6x^2 + 8x = 16x^2 - 16x$ **71b.** $x = 0, 3$
71c. Sample answer: Because the side length cannot be zero, (3, 78) is the only viable solution in the context of the situation. This means that the surface area of the packages is 78 in^2.
73a. yes
73b. about 1.7 seconds
73c. Sample answer: I had to assume that the student bumping the ball was far enough away from the net that she wouldn't hit it and that she hit the ball with a vertical velocity. I also assumed that the volleyball would not touch anything before hitting the ground.
75. true
77. Sample answer: Company profits can be modeled by a quadratic equation and a horizontal line can be added to the model to determine specific price points or quantities of items that maximize profit for the company.

Module 3 Review

1. A **3.** 10 and 21 **5.** C **7.** $x = -3, x = 5$
9. D **11.** A, D **13.** C
15. $(-3, 4)$ $(0, -5)$ $(3, 4)$
17.

Point	First	Second	Both	Neither
(−4, 1)				X
(−3, 0)		X		
(−1, 2)			X	
(1, 0)				X
(1, 4)		X		
(4, 7)			X	

Module 4

Module 4 Opener

1. $-5 + (-13)$ **3.** $5mr + (-7mp)$
5. $-4a - 20$ **7.** $-m + \frac{5}{2}$

Lesson 4-1

1. degree = 4; As $x \to -\infty$, $f(x) \to \infty$ and as $x \to \infty$ and $f(x) \to \infty$; D = $(-\infty, \infty)$, R = $[0, \infty)$

3. degree = 5; As $x \to -\infty$, $f(x) \to \infty$ and as $x \to \infty$ and $f(x) \to -\infty$; D = $(-\infty, \infty)$, R = $(-\infty, \infty)$

5. The domain is all real numbers and the range is all real numbers ≥ 0.

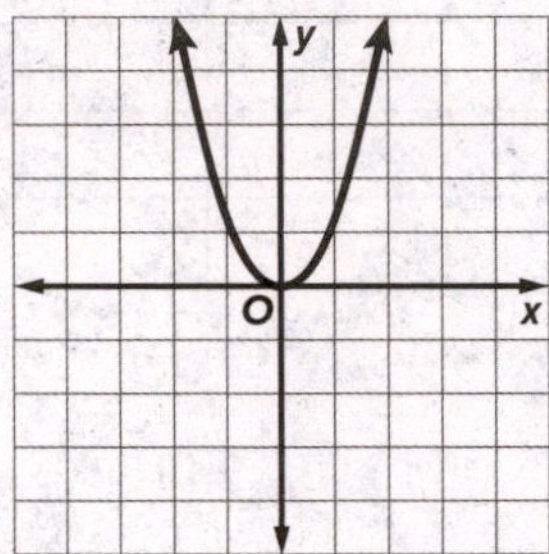

7. degree = 1, leading coefficient = 1

9. degree = 5, leading coefficient = −5

11. not in one variable because there are two variables, *u* and *t*

13a. 70

13b.

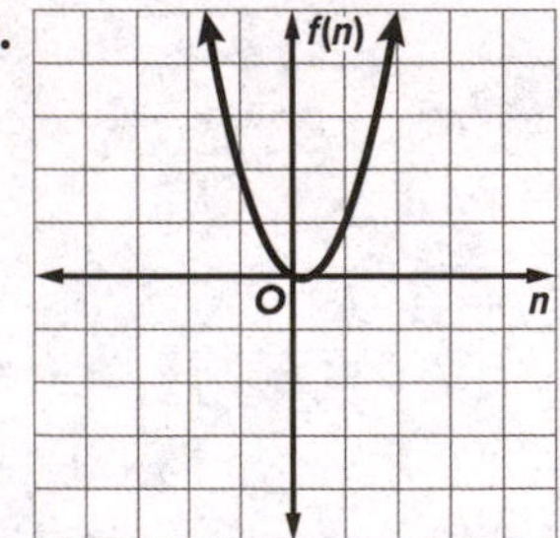

15a. 455

15b.

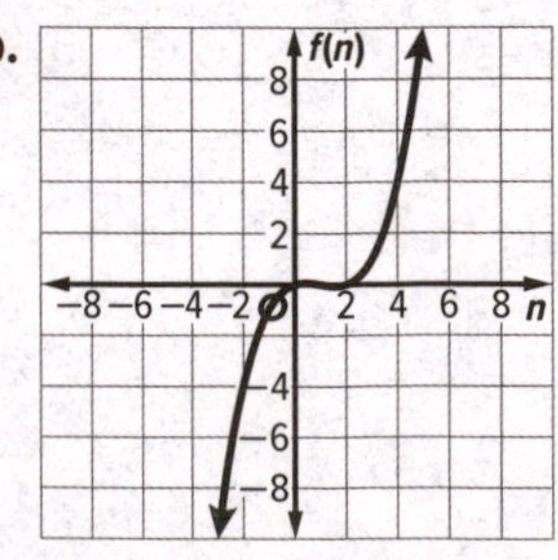

17. 1 **19.** 3 **21.** 3 **23a.** $f(x)$

23b. zeros: $f(x)$: −1.5, 0.25, 3.25; $g(x)$: −2.75, −0.5, 0.25

x−intercepts: $f(x)$: −1.5, 0.25, 3.25; $g(x)$: −2.75, −0.5, 0.25 y−intercept: $f(x)$: 1; $g(x)$: 1 end behavior: $f(x)$: As $x \to -\infty$, $f(x) \to -\infty$, and as $x \to \infty$, $f(x) \to \infty$; $g(x)$: As $x \to -\infty$, $g(x) \to \infty$, and as $x \to \infty$,
$g(x) \to -\infty$

25. As $x \to -\infty$, $f(x) \to -\infty$ and as $x \to \infty$, $f(x) \to -\infty$.

27. As $x \to -\infty$, $h(x) \to \infty$ and as $x \to \infty$, $h(x) \to -\infty$.

29. As $x \to -\infty$, $g(x) \to -\infty$ and as $x \to \infty$, $g(x) \to \infty$.

31. not in one variable because there are two variables, *x* and *y*

33. degree = 6, leading coefficient = −12

35. degree = 4, leading coefficient = −5

37. degree = 2, leading coefficient = 3

39. degree = 9, leading coefficient = 2

41. As $x \to \infty$, $f(x) \to -\infty$, and as $x \to -\infty$, $f(x) \to \infty$; degree = 3; the leading coefficient is negative

43. (0, 0); If you replace *x* with zero in a power function, the value of the function is always zero: $f(0) = a(0)^n = a(0) = 0$.

45. $f(1 - x) = a(1 - x)^3 - b(1 - x)^2 + (1 - x)$. So, $f(1 - x) = -ax^3 + (3a - b)x^2 +$ $(-3a + 2b - 1)x + (a - b + 1)$. The function $f(1 - x)$ has the opposite leading coefficient, representing a reflection in the *y*-axis. So, it has the opposite end behavior.

47. The function in standard form is $f(x) = x^3 - 11x^2 + 40x - 48$, so the degree is 3. Because the factored form of $f(x)$ is given, the zeros are 3 and 4.

49. Sample answer: The graph of the function over all real numbers is symmetric with respect to the origin, but in the context of the situation it only makes sense to graph the function in the first quadrant because lengths and volumes cannot be negative.

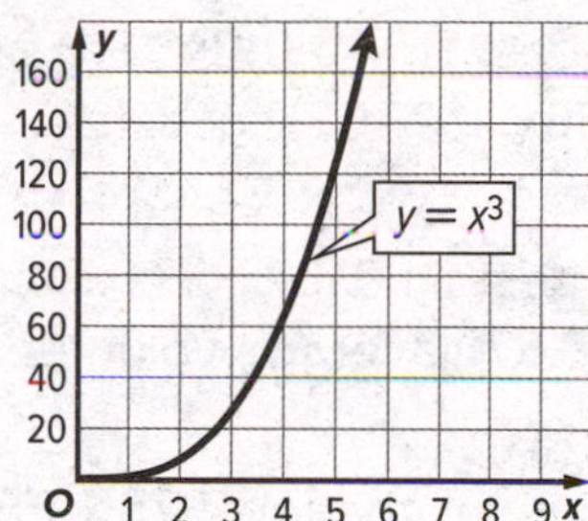

51. $f(x)$; $f(x)$ has potential for 5 or more real zeros and a degree of 5 or more. $g(x)$ has potential for 4 real zeros and a degree of 4.

53. Sample answer:

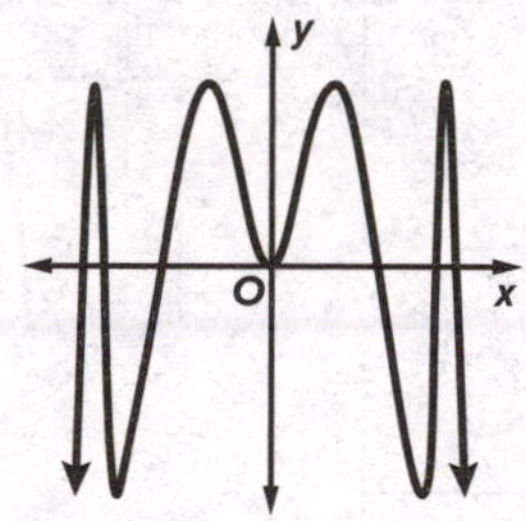

Lesson 4-2

1a.

x	$f(x)$
−4	−16
−3	0
−2	4
−1	2
0	0
1	4
2	20
3	54
4	112

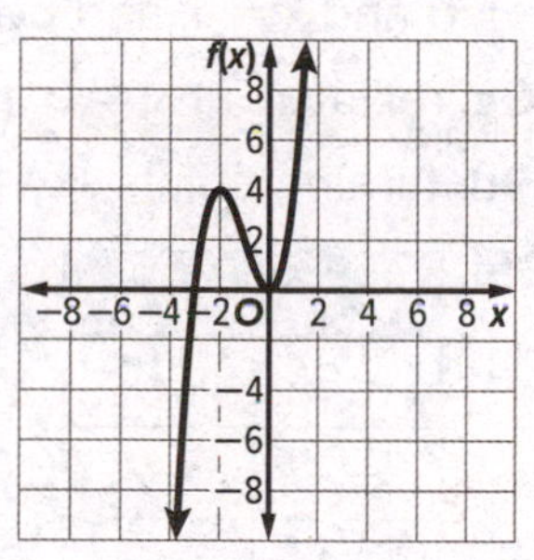

1b. zeros at $x = 0$ and at $x = -3$

1c. rel. max: $x = -2$; rel. min: $x = 0$

1d. turning points at $x = -2$ and $x = 0$

3a.

x	$f(x)$
−6	−42
−5	0
−4	20
−3	24
−2	18
−1	8
0	0
1	0
2	14
3	48

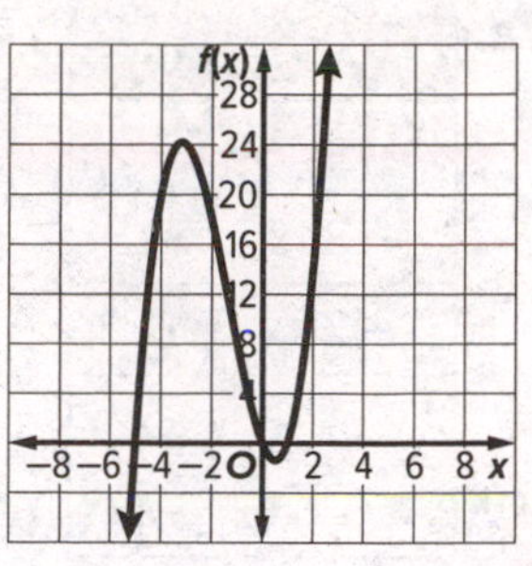

3b. zeros at $x = -5$, $x = 0$, and $x = 1$

3c. rel. max: $x = -3$; rel. min: between $x = 0$ and $x = 1$

3d. turning points at $x = -3$ and between $x = 0$ and $x = 1$

5a.

x	$f(x)$
−1	22
0	0
1	2
2	16
3	30
4	32
5	10
6	−48
7	−154

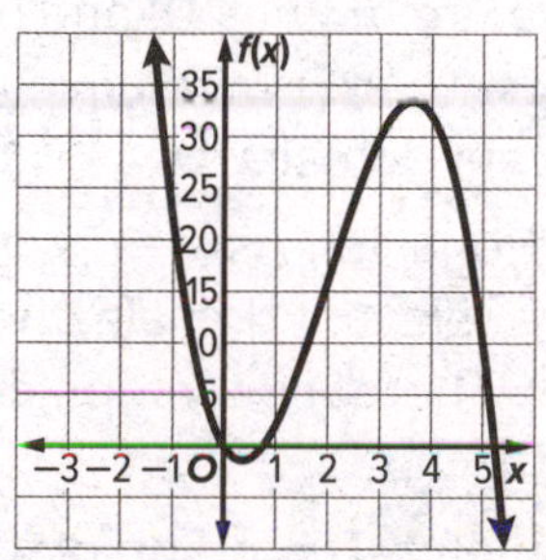

5b. zeros at $x = 0$, between $x = 0$ and $x = 1$, and between $x = 5$ and $x = 6$

5c. rel. min: between $x = 0$ and $x = 1$; rel. max: near $x = 4$

5d. turning points between $x = 0$ and $x = 1$ and near $x = 4$

7a.

x	$f(x)$
−4	247
−3	74
−2	11
−1	−2
0	−1
1	2
2	19
3	86
4	263

7b. zeros between $x = -2$ and $x = -1$ and between $x = 0$ and $x = 1$

7c. rel. min: near $x = -1$; no rel. max

7d. turning points near $x = -1$

9. Domain and Range: The domain and range of the function is all real numbers. Because the function models years, the relevant domain and range are $\{n \mid n \geq 0\}$ and $\{v \mid v \geq 0\}$. Turning Points: There is a relative minimum $n = 2$ in the relevant domain.

End Behavior: As $x \to \infty$, $f(x) \to \infty$. Intercepts: In the relevant domain, the v-intercept is at (0, 0). There n-intercept, or zero, is at about (3.1, 0).

Symmetry: The graph of the function has symmetry at $x = 2$.

11.

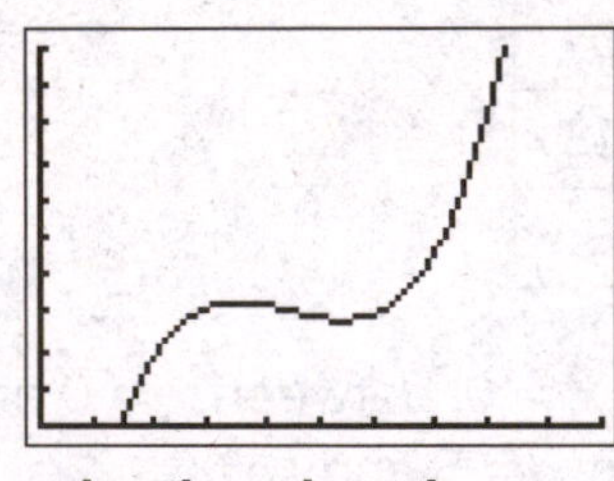

[0, 10] scl: 1 [0, 100] scl: 10

Domain and Range: The domain and range of the function is all real numbers. Because the function models weeks of growth, the relevant domain and range are $\{x \mid x \geq 0\}$ and $\{y \mid y \geq 0\}$. Turning Points: There is a relative maximum between $x = 1$ and $x = 2$ and between $x = 2$ and $x = 3$ and a relative minimum between $x = 6$ and $x = 7$ in the relevant domain.

End Behavior: As $x \to \infty$, $f(x) \to \infty$.

Intercepts: In the relevant domain, there is a y-intercept at (0, 0). There are two x-intercepts, or zeros, at about (1.6, 0) and (2.4, 0).

Symmetry: The graph does not have symmetry in the relevant domain.

13. Curve of best fit: $-0.012x^4 + 0.217x^3 - 1.116x^2 + 1.486x + 7.552$; car sales in 2017: 5.951 million

15. Curve of best fit: $0.167x^3 - 0.5x^2 + 10.905x + 48.571$; average volunteer hours for October: 28

17. average rate of change: 3750; From 2012 to 2017, the salesman's average rate of change in salary was an increase of $3750 per year.

19a.

x	$f(x)$
−2	−19
−1	−3
0	1
1	−1
2	−3
3	1
4	17

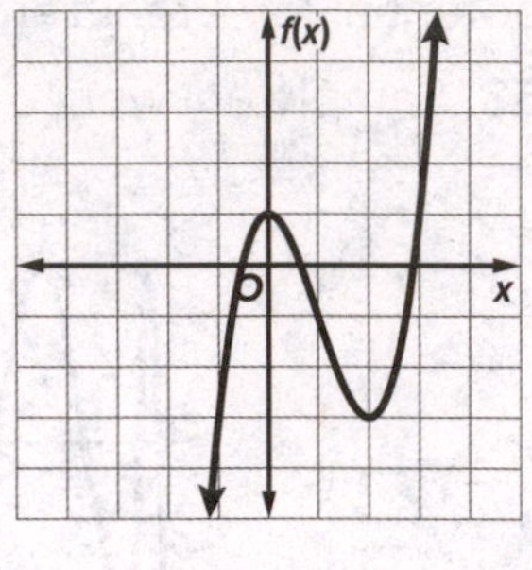

19b. zeros between $x = -1$ and $x = 0$, between $x = 0$ and $x = 1$, and between $x = 2$ and $x = 3$

19c. rel. max. at $x = 0$, rel. min. at $x = 2$

19d. turning points at $x = 0$ and at $x = 2$

21a.

x	$f(x)$
−3	−7
−2	−2
−1	−3
0	2
1	25

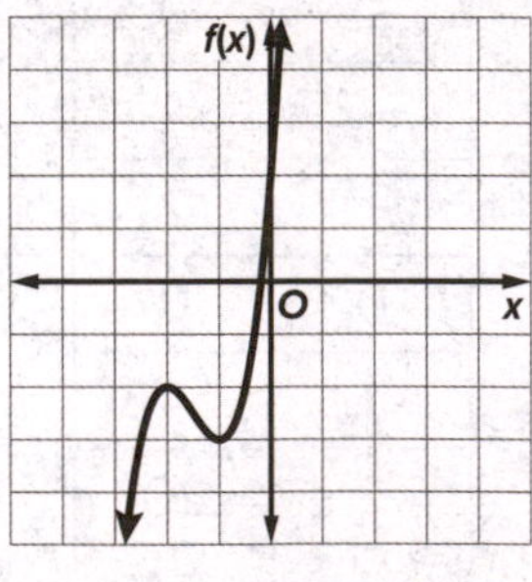

21b. zero between $x = -1$ and $x = 0$

21c. rel. max. at $x = -2$, rel. min. at $x = -1$

21d. turning points at $x = -2$ and at $x = -1$

23a.

x	$f(x)$
−3	61
−2	6
−1	−3
0	−2
1	−3
2	6
3	61

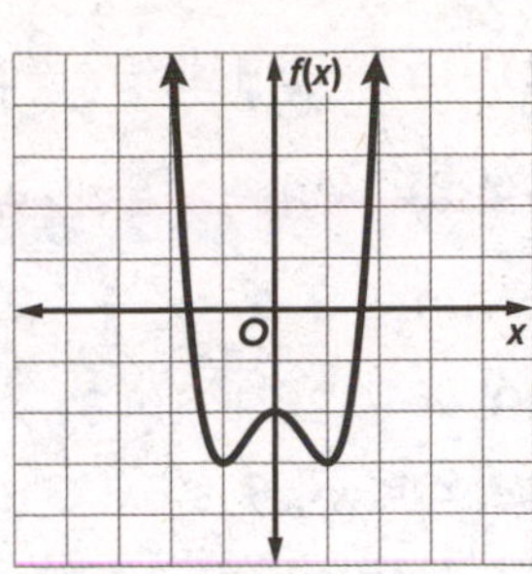

23b. zeros between $x = -2$ and $x = -1$, and between $x = 1$ and $x = 2$

23c. rel. max. at $x = 0$, min. at $x = -1$, and $x = 1$

23d. turning points at $x = 0$, $x = -1$, and $x = 1$

25. rel. max: $x \approx -2.73$; rel. min: $x \approx 0.73$

27. rel. max: $x \approx 1.34$; no rel. min

29a. zeros: $x = \pm 2$; x-intercepts: ± 2; y-intercept: 16; turning points: $x = -2, 0, 2$

29b. $x = 0$

29c. decreasing: $x < -2$ and $0 < x < 2$; increasing: $-2 < x < 0$ and $2 < x$

31a. zeros: $x \approx -1$ and 0; x-intercept: ≈ -1 and 0; y-intercept: 0; turning point: $x \approx -0.5$

31b. no axis of symmetry

31c. decreasing: $x \geq -0.5$; increasing: $x \leq -0.5$

33. Sample answer: $f(x) \to -\infty$ as $x \to +\infty$ and $f(x) \to +\infty$ as $x \to -\infty$; the leading coefficient is negative.

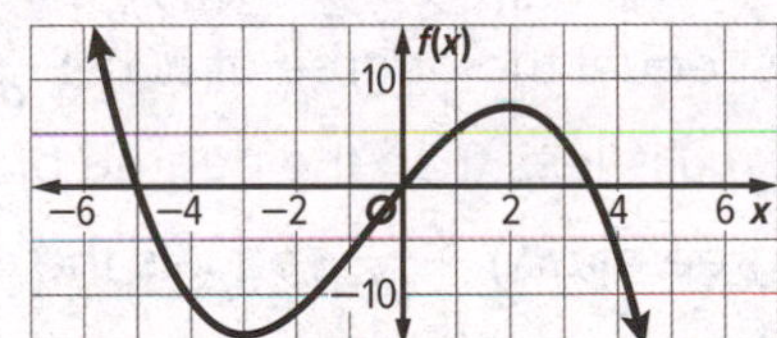

35. The type of polynomial function that should be used to model the graph is a function with an even degree with a negative leading coefficient. This is based on the fact that the graph is reflected in the x-axis and as $x \to -\infty$, $f(x) \to -\infty$ and as $x \to \infty$, $f(x) \to -\infty$.

37. As the x-values approach large positive or negative numbers, the term with the largest degree becomes more and more dominant in determining the value of $f(x)$.

39. Sample answer:

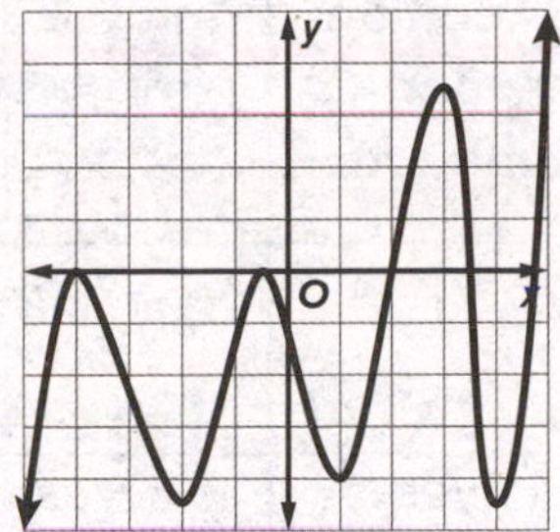

41. Sample answer: No; $f(x) = x^2 + x$ is an even degree, but $f(1) \neq f(-1)$.

43. Sample answer: From the degree, you can determine whether the graph is even or odd and the maximum number of zeros and turning points for the graph. You can create a table of values to help you find the approximate locations of turning points and zeros. The leading coefficient can be used to determine the end behavior of the graph, and, along with the degree, the shape of the graph.

Lesson 4-3

1. yes; 2 **3.** no **5.** $2a^2 - a - 2$ **7.** $3g + 12$
9. $3x^2 + 4x - 5$ **11.** $-3x + 3$ **13.** $3np^2 - 3pz$
15. $-10c^2 + 5d^2$ **17.** $a^2 - 10a + 25$
19. $x^3 + x^2y - xy^2 - y^3$
21. $2x^3 + x^2y - 2xy^2 - y^3$ **23.** $r^2 - 4t^2$
25. $2x^5 - 7x^4 + 5x^3 - 4x^2 - x + 2$
27. $s^2 + 11s + 15$ **29a.** $4x^2 + 8x + 3$
29b. $8x^2 + 16x + 6$ **31.** $10c^3 - c^2 + 4c$
33. $12a^2b + 8a^2b^2 - 15ab^2 + 4b^2$
35. $2n^4 - 3n^3p + 6n^4p^4$ **37.** $b^3 + \frac{b}{a} + \frac{1}{a^2}$
39. $2n^5 - 14n^3 + 4n^2 - 28$
41. $64n^3 - 240n^2 + 300n - 125$ **43.** $7x - 2y$
45a. $f(x)g(x) = (3x^2 - 1)(x + 2) = 3x^3 + 6x^2 - x - 2$; 3rd degree
45b. $h(x)f(x) = (-x^2 - x)(3x^2 - 1) = -3x^4 + x^2 - 3x^3 + x$; 4th degree
45c. $[f(x)]^2 = (3x^2 - 1)^2 = 9x^4 - 6x^2 + 1$; 4th degree

47.

	Addition and Subtraction	Multiplication	Division
Integers	yes	yes	No; $3 \div 2 = 1.5$
Rational Numbers	yes	yes	yes
Polynomials	yes	yes	No; $\frac{3}{x^2} = 3x^{-2}$

49. $-0.022x + 1590$

51a. $A = 0.5x[(x + 5) + (2x - 1)]$ or $(1.5x^2 + 2x)$ ft²

51b. $A = 1.5x^2 + 14x + 32$ ft²

53. Yes; sample answer: For $f(x)$ and $g(x)$ to be polynomials, they must have real coefficients and whole-number exponents. Real numbers and whole numbers are closed under addition and multiplication. So, when $f(x)$ and $g(x)$ are multiplied, the coefficients of each term are multiplied, yielding new real coefficients, and the exponents of each term are added, producing new whole number exponents. By the definition of polynomials, the product of polynomials is a polynomial because the coefficients are real and the exponents are whole numbers.

55. yes; Isabella correctly aligned like terms after multiplying each term in the first polynomial by each term in the second polynomial. She then correctly added like terms.

57. Sample answer: $(3 - 2b)(3 + 2b)$

Lesson 4-4

1. $5c + 3$ **3.** $5y^2 + 2y + 1$ **5.** $3q^2 + \frac{1}{q^2}$

7. $2j - 3k$ **9.** $n + 2$ **11.** $2t + 3$ **13.** $2g - 3$

15. $u^2 + 3u + 14 + \frac{30}{u - 3}$ **17.** $3v + 5 + \frac{10}{v - 4}$

19. $y^2 - 3y + 6 - \frac{18}{y + 2}$

21. $4q^2 + p + 3 + \frac{3}{p - 1}$

23. $\frac{6x^2}{y} - 8x^5 + \frac{3}{2}x^4y + \frac{9}{2}x^3y$

25. $m - 3 + \frac{6}{m + 4}$ **27.** $2x^2 - 3x + 1$

29. $x^2 - 2x + 4$ **31.** $x^2 + 4x - 3$ units

33. A is x^2; B is $6x$; C is 11. **35.** $\pi(x^2 - 8x + 16)$

37. $4c^2d - 3d^2$ **39.** $n^2 - n - 1$

41. $3z^4 - z^3 + 2z^2 - 4z + 9 - \frac{13}{z + 2}$

43. No; Because $3x$ times the divisor is $9x^2 + 3x$, the divisor must be $3x + 1$. The second and third terms of the dividend must be $0x + 5$ because the first difference is $-3x + 5$.

45. Yes; the divisor is $d(x)$, so $f(x) = d(x) \cdot q(x) + r(x)$. Sample answer: For example, if $q(x) + \frac{r(x)}{d(x)} = x - 2 + \frac{3}{x - 1}$, then the divisor is $x - 1$ and $f(x) = (x - 1)(x - 2) + 3$, or $x^2 - 3x + 5$.

47. $8x^3 - 8x^2 - 2x - 10$; I multiplied the divisor and the quotient and added the remainder: $(2x^2 + x + 1)(4x - 6) + (-4) = 8x^3 - 8x^2 - 2x - 10$.

49a. No; the degrees of $f(x)$ and $d(x)$ may be equal. For example, $\frac{3x^2 + 6}{x^2} = 3 + \frac{6}{x^2}$.

49b. Yes; if the degree of $r(x)$ is greater than or equal to the degree of $d(x)$, then the expression $\frac{r(x)}{d(x)}$ may be simplified by division. For example, if $\frac{r(x)}{d(x)} = \frac{8x + 1}{x}$, then $8x + 1$ may be divided by x to get $8 + \frac{1}{x}$.

49c. Yes; because $\frac{f(x)}{d(x)} = q(x) + \frac{r(x)}{d(x)}$, the degree of $\frac{f(x)}{d(x)}$ must equal the degree of $q(x) + \frac{r(x)}{d(x)}$. The degree of $r(x)$ is less than the degree of $d(x)$, so the degree of $q(x) + \frac{r(x)}{d(x)}$ equals the degree of $q(x)$. This means the degree of $\frac{f(x)}{d(x)}$ equals the degree of $q(x)$, and the degree of $\frac{f(x)}{d(x)}$ is the degree of $f(x)$ minus the degree of $d(x)$. For example, in $\frac{2x^3 - 1}{x^2 + 3} = 2x + \frac{-6x - 1}{x^2 + 3}$, the degree of $q(x)$ is the degree of $f(x)$ minus the degree of $d(x)$.

51. The binomial is a factor of the polynomial.

53. Sample answer: $\frac{x^2 + 5x + 9}{x + 2}$

55a. $B^2 + 1$

55b. $B + \frac{1}{B^2 + B + 1}$

Lesson 4-5

1. $x^3 - 3x^2y + 3xy^2 - y^3$

3. $g^4 - 4g^3h + 6g^2h^2 - 4gh^3 + h^4$

5. $r^3 + 12r^2 + 48r + 64$

7. $y^3 - 21y^2 + 147y - 343$

9. $x^4 - 4x^3 + 6x^2 - 4x + 1$

11. $c^3 - 12c^2d + 48cd^2 - 64d^3$ **13.** 38%

15. $x^5 + \frac{5}{2}x^4 + \frac{5}{2}x^3 + \frac{5}{4}x^2 + \frac{5}{16}x + \frac{1}{32}$

17. $32b^5 + 20b^4 + 5b^3 + \frac{5}{8}b^2 + \frac{5}{128}b + \frac{1}{1024}$

19. 23%

21. There are 9 judges on the Supreme Court. The majority could be 5, 6, 7, 8, or 9 votes. So, there are ${}_9C_5 + {}_9C_6 + {}_9C_7 + {}_9C_8 + {}_9C_9 = 256$ combinations.

23. $x^3 + 3x^2y + 3xy^2 + y^3$

25. The coefficient from Pascal's Triangle will be 20. The term itself is $(2x)^3(7)^3$, so the full term is $(20)(2x)^3(7)^3$, or $54{,}880x^3$. This is the same as the fourth term in the expansion of $(7 + 2x)^6$ because the fourth term is the middle term in the 6th row of Pascal's Triangle. So, the coefficient of the triangle will still be 20.

27. If A stands for "accurately" and N stands for "not accurately," then the number of ways for the robot to produce 5 of 7 circuit boards accurately is given by the coefficient of A^5N^2 in the expansion of $(A + N)^7$. Using the Binomial Theorem, the coefficient of A^5N^2 is ${}_7C_5$, or 21 ways.

29. $792a^5b^7$

31. If S stands for "sunny" and C stands for "cloudy," then the total number of ways of having more sunny days than cloudy days is the sum of the coefficients of S^4C^3, S^5C^2, S^6C, and S^7. According to the Binomial Theorem, these coefficients are $7C^4$, $7C^5$, $7C^6$, and $7C^7$. So the total is $35 + 21 + 7 + 1 = 64$.

33. Sample answer: While they have the same terms, the signs for $(x + y)^n$ will all be positive, while the signs for $(x - y)^n$ will alternate.

35. Sample answer: $\left(x + \frac{6}{5}y\right)^5$

Module 4 Review

1. B **3.** B **5.** $g(x) \to -\infty$ **7.** C

9.

Expression	Polynomial	Not a Polynomial
$x^2 + 7$	X	
$6x^4 + 3\sqrt{x}$		X
$\frac{1}{2}x^4 + 8x^3 - 12$	X	
$3x^6 - 5x^3 + 2x^2 - 4x$		X
$3d^2f + 7d^3f^4 - 9d^7f^2 - 11df^5$	X	

11. 27 **13.** $5x^2 + 7x - 3$ **15.** 15.6

Selected Answers

Module 5

Module 5 Opener

1. $24x^3 + 8x^2 + 6x + 4$
3. $14x^3 - 40x^2 + 12x + 24$
5. $-4, 2$ **7.** $-\frac{4}{3}, \frac{1}{2}$

Lesson 5-1

1. -4.12 **3.** $-0.47, 0.54, 3.94$ 5. -1.27
7a. $6x^3 + 110x^2 - 200x = 15{,}000$
7b. $y = 6x^3 + 110x^2 - 200x$, $y = 15{,}000$; $x = 10$ cm
7c. 25 cm by 20 cm by 30 cm
9a. $\pi x^3 + 3\pi x^2 = 628$
9b. $y = \pi x^3 + 3\pi x^2$, $y = 628$; $x = 5$
9c. radius = 5 in., height = 8 in.
11. $-3.63, -1.35, 1.35, 3.63$ **13.** no solution
15. The x-coordinate of a point of intersection is a value for which $f(x) = g(x)$. When $f(x) = g(x)$ the equation $x^3 + x^2 - 14x - 4 = x^3 - 3x^2 - 6x + 28$ is true. Therefore, x-values represent solutions to the equation. According to the graphs, the solutions are $x = -2$ and $x = 4$.
17. \$0.29, 0.88; sample answer: graph $f(x) = 70{,}000(x - x^4)$ and $f(x) = 20{,}000$ and find the x-values of the points of intersections.

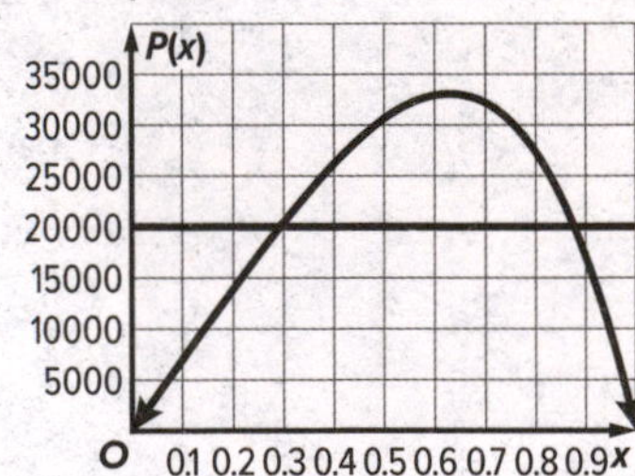

19. Sample answer: A function with an even degree reverses direction, so both ends extend in the same direction. That means that if the function opens up and the vertex is above the x-axis or if the function opens down and the vertex is below the x-axis, there are no real solutions. A function with an odd degree does not reverse direction, so the ends extend in opposite directions. Therefore, it must cross the x-axis at least once.

21. sometimes; sample answer: The positive solution is often correct when a negative value doesn't make sense, such as for distance or time; however, sometimes a negative solution is reasonable, such as for temperature or position problems. Also, sometimes there are two positive solutions and one may be unreasonable.

23. $5x^2 = -2x - 11$; it is the only one that has no real solutions.

Lesson 5-2

1. $(2c - 3d)(4c^2 + 6cd + 9d^2)$
3. $a^2(a - b)(a^2 + ab + b^2)(a + b)(a^2 - ab + b^2)$
5. prime **7.** $(x + y)(x - y)(6f + g - 3h)$
9. $(a - b)(a^2 + ab + b^2)(x - 8)^2$ **11.** $0, 7, 2$
13. $0, -5, 8$ **15a.** $x(x + 3.5)(x - 3) = 561$
15b. 8.5 in., 5.5 in., and 12 in.
17. $(x^2)^2 + 12(x^2) - 8$ **19.** $2(2x^3)^2 + 3(2x^3) + 7$
21. $(3x^4)^2 - 7(3x^4) + 12$ **23.** $\pm i\sqrt{5}, \pm I$
25. $\pm\sqrt{2}, \pm\frac{\sqrt{6}}{2}$ **27.** $\pm\sqrt{2}, \pm i\frac{\sqrt{3}}{2}$
29. $(x^2 + 25)(x + 5)(x - 5)$
31. $x(x + 2)(x - 2)(x^2 + 4)$
33. $x(x + 3)(x - 3)(3x + 2)(2x - 5)$
35. $(x + 2)^3(x - 2)^3$
37. $(5x + 4y + 5z)(3a - 2b + c)$
39. $t(t - 2)(t - 5)(t + 2)(t + 5)$
41. $3, -3, \pm i\sqrt{10}$ **43.** $\pm\sqrt{11}, \pm 2i$
45. $-6, 3 \pm 3i\sqrt{3}$ **47.** $5(x^2)^2 + 2(x^2) - 8$
49. $100(a^3)^2 + a^3$ **51.** $12(x^2)^2 - 7(x^2)$
53. $(m^3)^2 + 5(m^3) - 10$ **55.** $2(2x^3)^2 - 2x^3 - 1$
57. $\pm\frac{1}{2}, \pm i\frac{\sqrt{6}}{2}$ **59.** $\pm\frac{3}{2}, \pm\frac{\sqrt{10}}{5}$
61. $\pm\frac{1}{2}, \pm\sqrt{2}$ **63.** $1, -2, \frac{-1 \pm i\sqrt{3}}{2}, 1 \pm i\sqrt{3}$
65. $-5, \frac{1}{2}, \frac{-1 \pm i\sqrt{3}}{2}, \frac{5 \pm 5i\sqrt{3}}{2}$ **67.** $\pm 3, \pm 1, \pm I$
69. $3x(7x^2 - 6xy + 8y^2)$ **71.** $(a + 9)(a - 2)$
73. $(b + 7)(b + 1)$ **75.** $4(f + 4)(f - 4)$
77. prime **79.** $7x(x - 2)$
81. $(n - 5)(n^2 + 5n + 25)$

83. The solutions are $a = -1, -5, -3 + i\sqrt{2}, -3 - i\sqrt{2}$; Use the substitution $u = (a + 3)^2$ and factor to $(u - 4)(u + 2) = 0$. Substitute for u to get $(a + 3)^2 = 4$ and $(a + 3)^2 = -2$.

85. Volume equals the product of length, width, and height. An equation to represent the volume is $x^3 + 3x^2 - 10x = 30x$. The solutions of the equation are $x = -8, 0, 5$. Therefore, $x = 5$ and the dimensions of the box are 5 inches, 10 inches, and 3 inches.

87. $(6x^n + 1)^2$

89. Sample answer: $a = 1, b = -1$

91. Sample answer: The factors can be determined by the x-intercepts of the graph. An x-intercept of 5 represents a factor of $(x - 5)$.

Lesson 5-3

1. $(x - y)^2 = x^2 - 2xy + y^2$ (Original equation)
$x^2 - 2xy + y^2 = x^2 - 2xy + y^2$ (Distributive Property)

3. $4(x - 7)^2 = 4x^2 - 56x + 196$ (Original equation)
$4(x^2 - 14x + 49) = 4x^2 - 56x + 196$ (Distributive Property)
$4x^2 - 56x + 196 = 4x^2 - 56x + 196$ (Distributive Property)

5. $(3x + y)^2 = 9x^2 + 6xy + y^2$ (Original equation)
$9x^2 + 6xy + y^2 = 9x^2 + 6xy + y^2$ (Square the left side.)
$9x^2 + 6xy + y^2 = 9x^2 + 6xy + y^2$ (True)
Because the identity is true, this proves that Amber is correct. Her process for finding the area of a square will always work.

7. identity **9.** not an identity

11. $(x^2 + 25 - 50)^2 + (10x)^2 = (x^2 + 25)^2$ (Original equation)
$(x^2 - 25)^2 + (10x)^2 = (x^2 + 25)^2$ (Simplify in side parentheses.)
$x^4 - 50x^2 + 625 + 100x^2 = x^4 + 50x^2 + 625$ (Square each term.)
$x^4 + 50x^2 + 625 = x^4 + 50x^2 + 625$ (Combine like terms.)
$x^4 + 50x^2 + 625 = x^4 + 50x^2 + 625$ (True)
Because the identity is true, this proves that the textile designer can make the triangular tapestry. The textile designer's process for finding the side lengths of the triangular tapestry will always work.

13a.

x	Left side	Right side
0	108	108
1	64	64
2	0	0
3	216	216
4	1372	1372

13b. The equation may be a polynomial identity because the left side of the equation equals the right side of the equation for each x-value in the table.

13c. Sample answer: transform one side of the equation to determine if it is a polynomial identity.

15. Sample Answer:

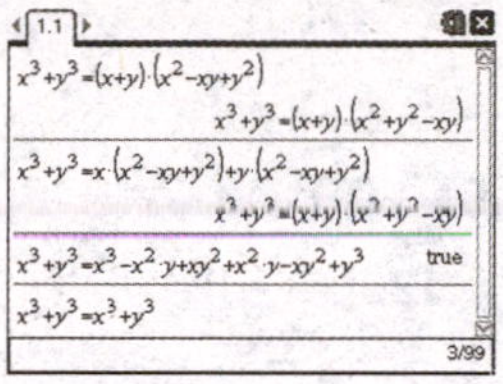

17. Sample Answer:

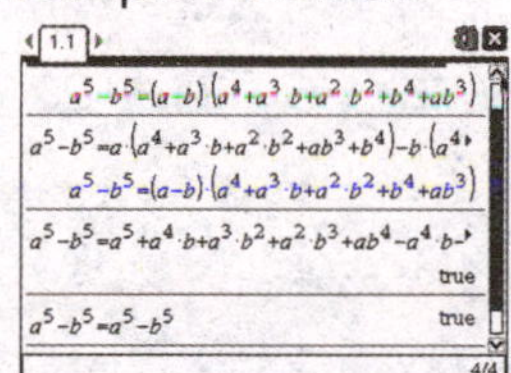

19. Sample Answer:

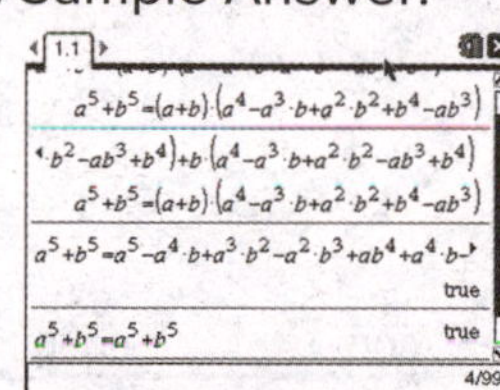

21. Sample Answer:

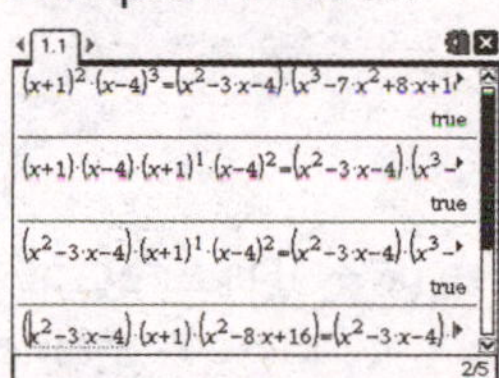

23. $x^2 - y^2 = 3, 2xy = 4, x^2 + y^2 = 5; x = 2, y = 1$

25. Sample diagram:

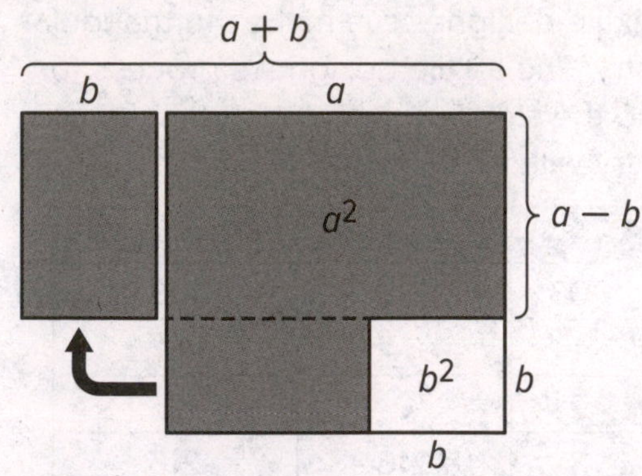

Sample algebraic answer:

$a^2 - (a + b)(a - b) = b^2$ (Original equation)
$a^2 - (a^2 - ab + ab - b^2) = b^2$ (Use the FOIL Method.)
$a^2 - a^2 + ab - ab + b^2 = b^2$ (Distribute −1.)
$b^2 = b^2$ (Combine like terms.)
$b^2 = b^2$ (True)

Lesson 5-4

1. −59; 11 **3.** 1707; 62 **5.** −98; 0 **7.** 13,190; 2
9. 46 **11.** 176 cubic feet **13.** $(x - 1)^2$
15. $x - 4, x + 1$ **17.** $x + 6, 2x + 7$
19. $x + 1, x^2 + 2x + 3$ **21.** 21, 0 **23.** −2, 1
25. 3, 3 **27.** −4, −7 **29.** 15, −6 **31.** −22, 20
33. $x - 1, x + 2$ **35.** $x - 2, x + 2$
37. $x + 3, x - 6$ **39.** $x + 1, x - 4$
41. $2x + 1, x - 1$ **43.** $x - 1, x + 2$
45. $x - 4, 3x - 2$ **47.** 11; 764
49.

0.1	$\frac{1}{6}$	$\frac{1}{2}$	1	1
		$\frac{1}{60}$	$\frac{31}{600}$	$\frac{631}{6000}$
	$\frac{1}{6}$	$\frac{31}{60}$	$\frac{631}{600}$	$\frac{6631}{6000}$

$1\frac{631}{6000}$

51. 8 **53.** −3

55. By the Factor Theorem, $(x - 1)$ is a factor. Use synthetic division with $x = 1$. The remainder is $k - 3$. For $(x - 1)$ to be a factor, $k - 3 = 0$, so $k = 3$. The quotient is $10x^2 + 13x - 3$, which factors as $(5x - 1)(2x + 3)$. $P(x) = (x - 1)(5x - 1)(2x + 3)$. The cubic has a positive leading coefficient and zeros at −1.5, 0.2, and 1.

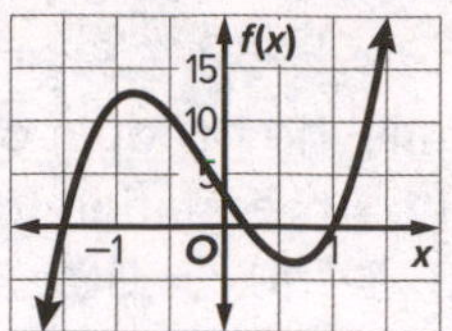

57. For $f(x) = 4x^3 - 10x + 8$, the remainder on division by $(x + 5)$ is −442. This means that $f(-5) = -442$; $4(-5)^3 - 10(-5) + 8 = -500 + 50 + 8 = -442$.

59. The factors are (x), $(x - 2)$, and $(x - 3)$. The graph intersects but does not cross the x-axis at $x = 2$, so, that factor must be $(x - 2)^2$. The polynomial function is $g(x) = k(x)(x - 2)^2(x - 3)$, then $g(1) = -2k$. If $-2k = 2$, then $k = -1$. That means that $g(x) = -x^4 + 7x^3 - 16x^2 + 12x$.

61.

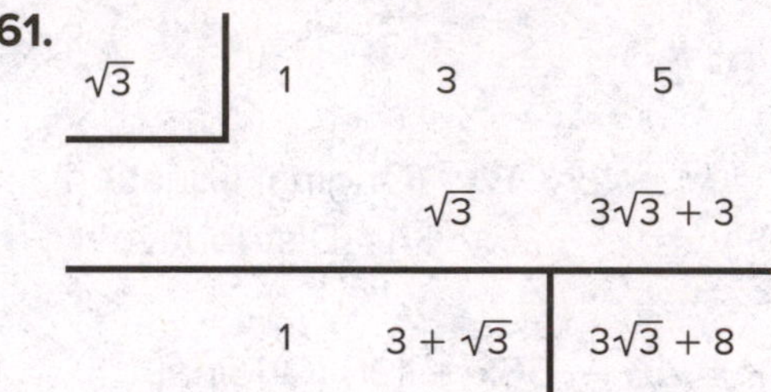

$(\sqrt{3})^2 + 3\sqrt{3} + 5 = 3 + 3\sqrt{3} + 5 = 3\sqrt{3} + 8$

63. Since $x^2 - 2x - 3 = (x + 1)(x - 3)$, both $x = -1$ and $x = 3$ are zeros of $P(x)$. Use synthetic division with each zero consecutively to find the other factor, $2x^2 + 7x - 4$, which factors to $(2x - 1)(x + 4)$. Once all four factors are known, the graph can be constructed.

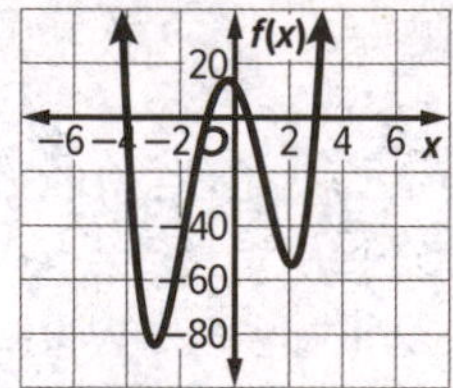

65. $P(x) = (2x + 3)(x - 2)(2x + 1)$; By the Factor Theorem, $P(x) = (2x + 3)(x - 2)(ax + b)$. Use $P(-2) = -12$ and $P(1) = -15$ to substitute for x and get a system of equations for a and b. Solve the system of equations to get $a = 2$ and $b = 1$.

67. $f(x) = 0.1(x - 1)^2(x + 5)^2$

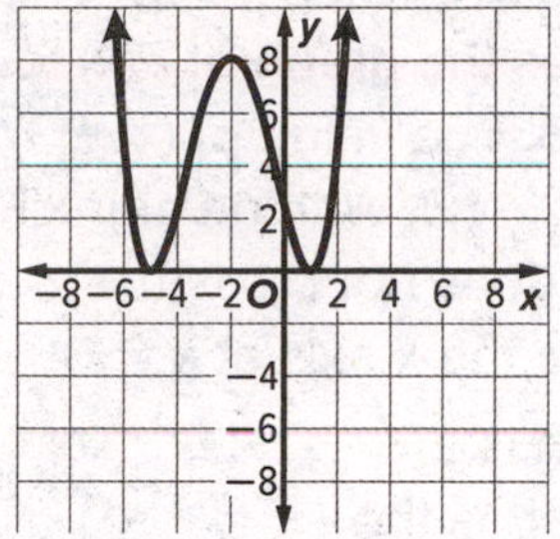

69. −1, 0, 1

71. If $x - a$ is a factor of $f(x)$, then $f(a)$ has a factor of $(a - a)$ or 0. Since a factor of $f(a)$ is 0, $f(a) = 0$. Now assume that $f(a) = 0$. If $f(a) = 0$, then the Remainder Theorem states that the remainder is 0 when $f(x)$ is divided by $x - a$. This means that $x - a$ is a factor of $f(x)$. This proves the Factor Theorem.

73. Sample answer: When $x = 1$, $f(1)$ is the sum of all of the coefficients and constants in $f(x)$, in this case, a, b, c, d, and e. The sum of a, b, c, d, and e is 0, so however the coefficients are arranged, $f(1)$ will always equal 0, and $f(x)$ will have a rational root.

75. Tyrone; Sample answer: By the Factor Theorem, $(x - r)$ is a factor when $P(r) = 0$. $P(r) = 0$ when $x = -1$ and $x = 2$.

Lesson 5-5

1. $-\frac{12}{5}$; 1 real

3. 0, 0, 0, $2i$, $-2i$; 3 real, 2 imaginary

5. $\frac{1 \pm \sqrt{2}}{2}$; 2 real **7.** 2 or 0; 1; 2 or 0

9. 3 or 1; 0; 2 or 0 **11.** 1; 1; 2

13. 3, $1 + \sqrt{2}$, $1 - \sqrt{2}$

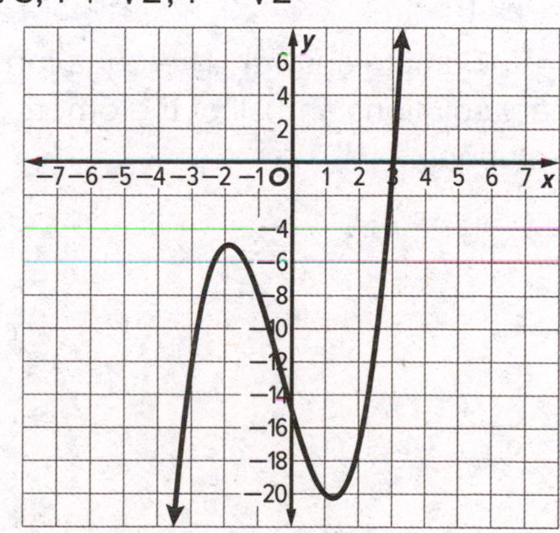

15. 1, −2, −3

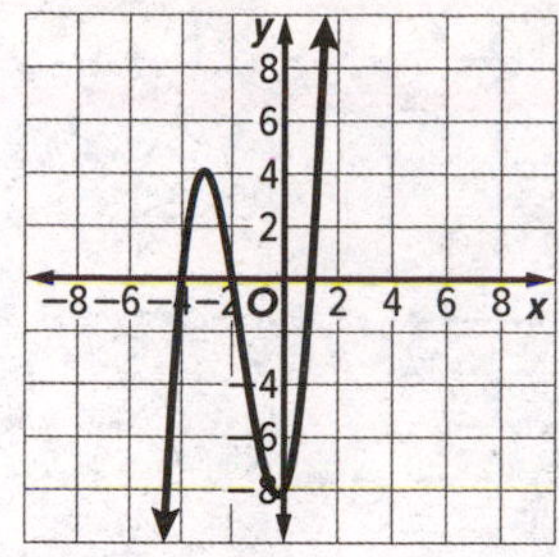

17. −1, −1, 1, 4

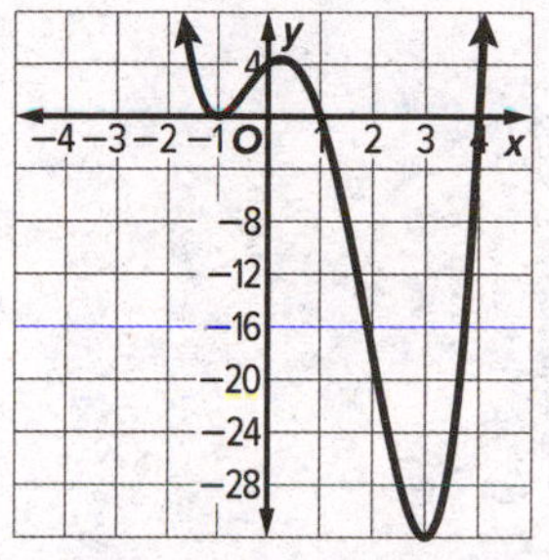

19. $y = x^2 + x - 6$

21. $y = x^4 - 6x^3 + 7x^2 + 6x - 8$

23. Sample Answer:

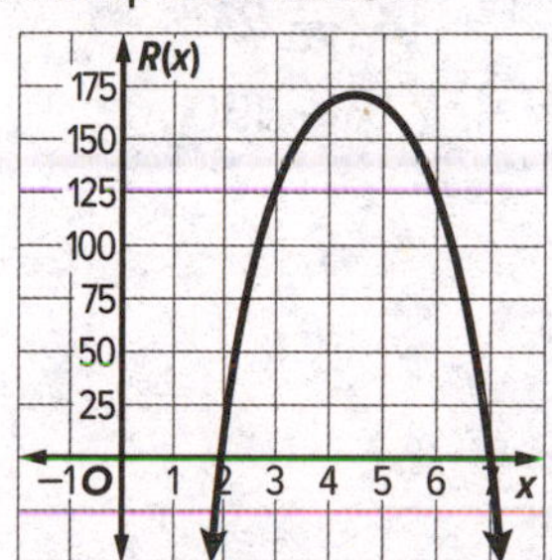

25. $-\frac{1}{2}i$, $\frac{1}{2}i$; 2 imaginary

27. $\frac{5 \pm i\sqrt{87}}{4}$; 2 imaginary

29. $\frac{3}{2}$, $\frac{-3 \pm 3i\sqrt{3}}{4}$; 1 real, 2 imaginary

31. 0, $3 + \sqrt{2}$, $3 - \sqrt{2}$; 3 real

33. 0, $-i$, $-i$, i, i; 1 real, 4 imaginary

35. 0 or 2; 1; 0 or 2

37. 0 or 2; 0 or 2; 0, 2, or 4

39. 0 or 2; 1; 2 or 4

41. −5, 1, 3

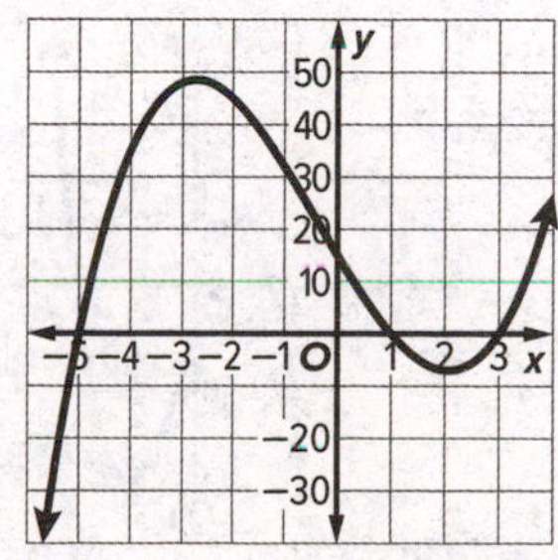

43. $-3, -3, -8i, 8i$

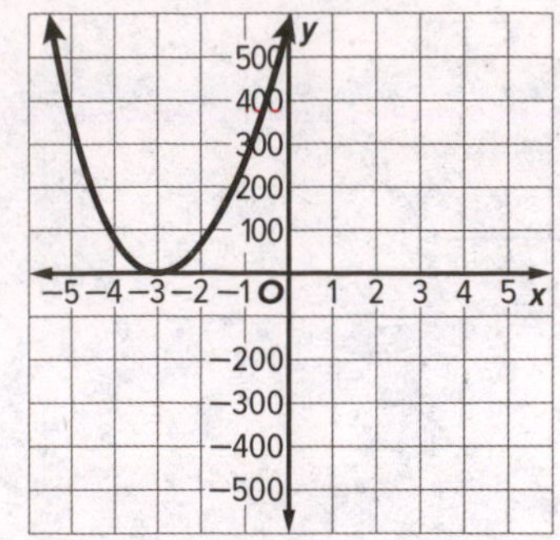

45. $-3, 0, 3, -i, i$

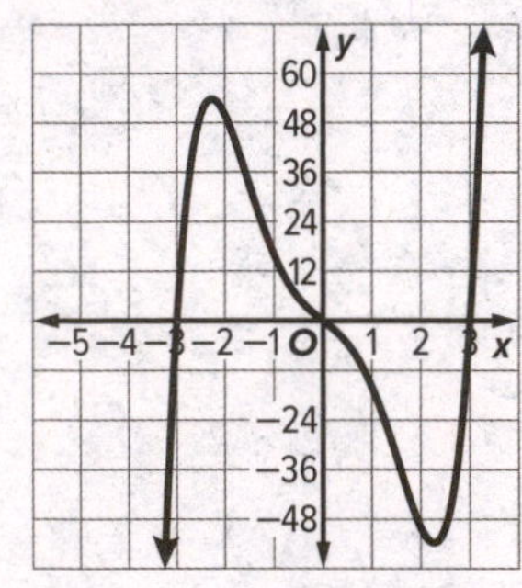

47. $f(x) = x^3 + 2x^2 - 23x - 60$

49. $f(x) = x^4 + 2x^3 + 6x^2 + 18x - 27$

51. $f(x) = x^4 - 3x^3 - 9x^2 + 77x + 150$

53.

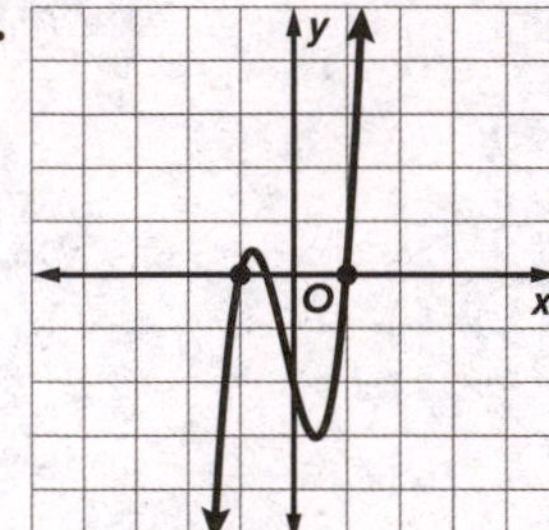

55.

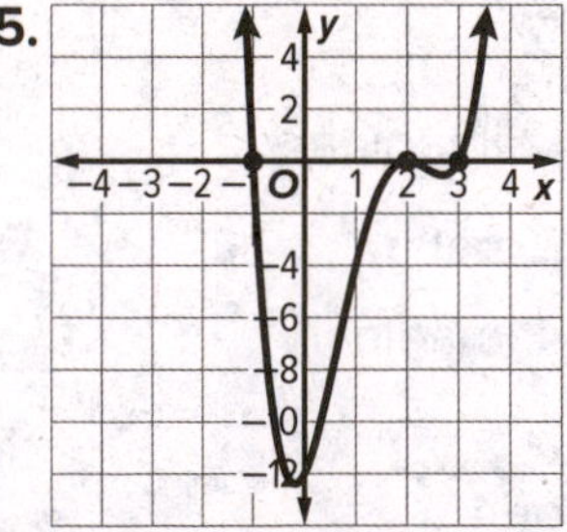

57. $2 - 3i$ and $2 + 3i$ **59a.** 3 **59b.** -2

59c. $4 + 3i$ and $4 - 3i$

61. Test factors of 9 such as 1, -1, 3, -3, etc. Because -3 is a zero, $(x + 3)$ is a factor. The other factor is $x^2 - 4x - 3$. The zeros are -3, $2 + \sqrt{7}$, and $2 - \sqrt{7}$.

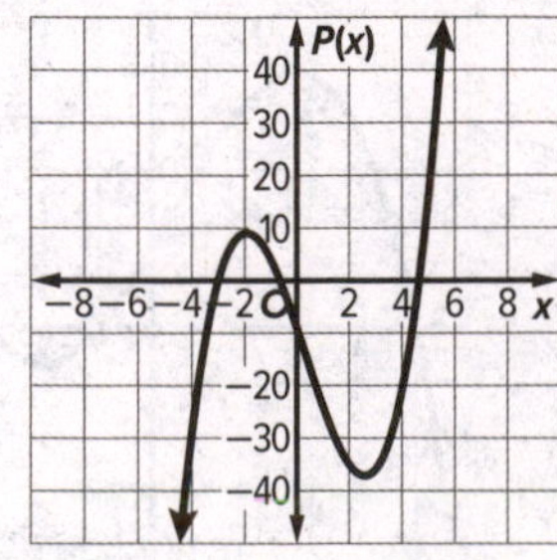

63. The value of $(x - 3)^3$ is negative when $x < 3$ and positive when $x > 3$. This sign change causes the graph of $P(x)$ to cross the x-axis at $x = 3$. The value of $(x - 3)^4$ is positive when $x < 3$ or $x > 3$. With no sign change, the graph of $R(x)$ does not cross the x-axis at $x = 3$; it is tangent to the x-axis at $x = 3$.

65. The graph is accurate as far as the location of the zeros, but does not consider any vertical dilation. It could be improved by finding more points between the roots.

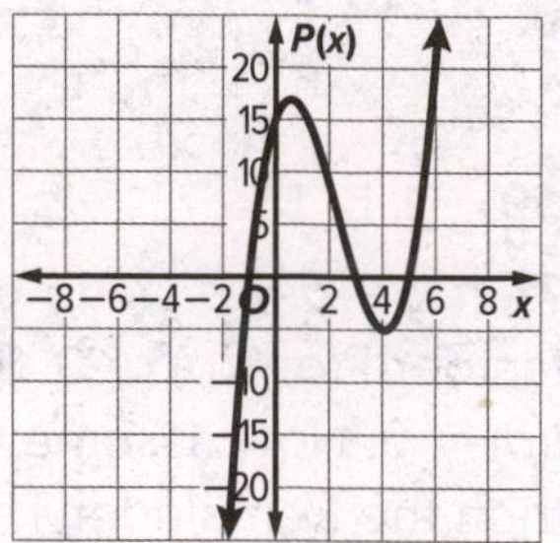

67a.

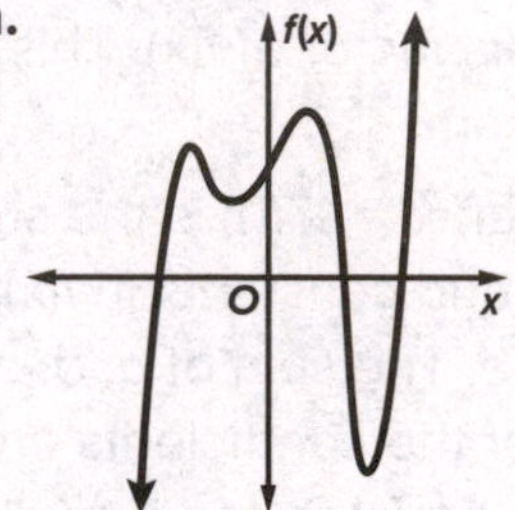

67b.

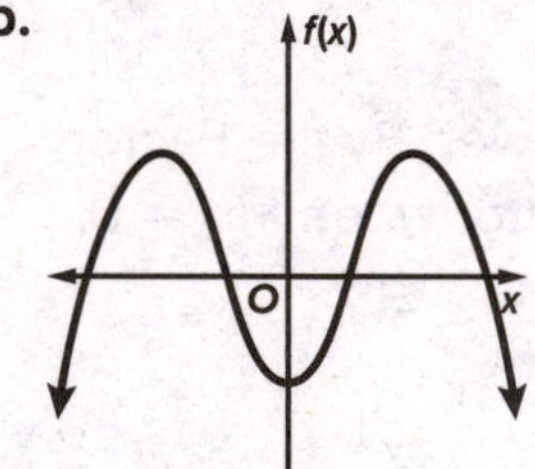

67c.

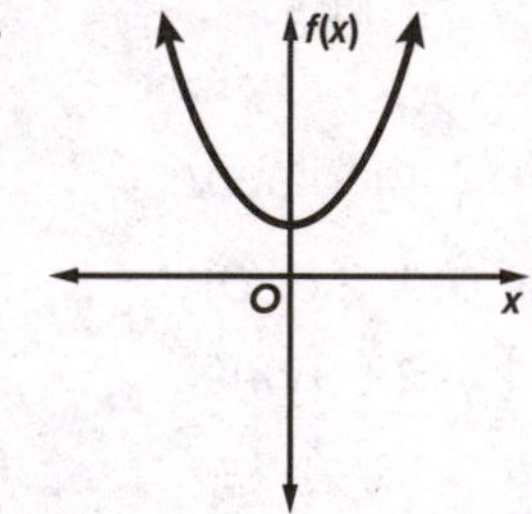

69. $r^4 + 1 = 0$; Sample answer: The equation has imaginary solutions and all of the others have real solutions.

71. Sample answer: To determine the number of positive real roots, determine how many time the signs change in the polynomial as you move from left to right. In this function there are 3 changes in sign. Therefore, there may be 3 or 1 positive real roots. To determine the number of negative real roots, I would first evaluate the polynomial for $-x$. All of the terms with an odd-degree variable would change signs. Then I would again count the number of sign changes as I move from left to right. There would be only one change. Therefore there may be 1 negative root.

Module 5 Review

1. A **3.** A, B, D **5.** B, C, F **7.** A, B
9. A, B, D, F **11.** B **13.** B, D
15.

x	Real Root	Imaginary Root	Not a Root
-2			X
-1	X		
1	X		
2			X
$-2i$		X	
$-i$			X
i			X
$2i$		X	

17. A

Selected Answers

Module 6

Module 6 Opener

1. between 0 and 1, and between 3 and 4

3. between −1 and 0, and between 1 and 2

5. $5x + 3$ **7.** $2x^2 + 5x - 6$

Lesson 6-1

1. $(f + g)(x) = -2x + 5$; $(f - g)(x) = 6x - 5$; $(f \cdot g)(x) = -8x^2 + 10x$; $\left(\frac{f}{g}\right)(x) = \frac{2x}{-4x + 5}, x \neq \frac{5}{4}$

3. $(f + g)(x) = x^2 - x + 1$; $(f - g)(x) = x^2 + x - 1$; $(f \cdot g)(x) = -x^3 + x^2$; $\left(\frac{f}{g}\right)(x) = \frac{x^2}{x + 1}, x \neq 1$

5. $(f + g)(x) = 3x - 9$; $(f - g)(x) = -x + 5$; $(f \cdot g)(x) = 2x^2 - 11x + 14$; $\left(\frac{f}{g}\right)(x) = \frac{x - 2}{2x - 7}, x \neq \frac{7}{2}$

7. $(f + g)(x) = x^2 + 3x + 1$; $(f - g)(x) = -3x^2 - 3x + 11$; $(f \cdot g)(x) = -2x^4 - 3x^3 + 17x^2 + 18x - 30$; $\left(\frac{f}{g}\right)(x) = \frac{-x^2 + 6}{2x^2 + 3x - 5}, x \neq 1 \text{ or } -\frac{5}{2}$

9. $A(x) = 2x^2 - 3x - 2$ **11a.** $C(x) = 72x - 22$

11b. $N(x) = x$

11c. $\left(\frac{C}{N}\right)(x) = \frac{72x - 22}{x}, x \neq 0$; This function represents the average cost per box of baseballs when at least 5 boxes of baseballs are purchased.

11d. $67.60

13. $f \circ g = \{(-4, 4)\}$, D = {−4}, R = {4}; $g \circ f = \{(-8, 0), (0, -4), (2, -5), (-6, -1)\}$, D = {−6, 0, 2}, R = {−5, −4, −1, 0}

15. $f \circ g$ is undefined, D = ø, R = ø; $g \circ f$ is undefined, D = ø, R = ø

17. $[f \circ g](x) = 2x + 10$, D = {all real numbers}, R = {all even numbers}; $[g \circ f](x) = 2x + 5$, D = {all real numbers}, R = {all odd numbers}

19. $[f \circ g](x) = 3x - 2$; $[g \circ f](x) = 3x + 8$

21. $[f \circ g](x) = x^2 - 6x - 2$, R = $\{y \mid y \geq -11\}$; $[g \circ f](x) = x^2 + 6x - 8$, R = $\{y \mid y \geq -17\}$

23. $p(x) = x - 0.15x$; $t(x) = x + 0.065x$; $t[p(x)]$; $2715.75 **25.** $C[T(t)]$ **27.** $\frac{3x^3 + 5}{x}, x \neq 0$

29. $15x, x \neq 0$

31. {(0, −2), (−2, 0), (5, 0)}; {(0, 4), (4, 0)}

33. {(1, 3), (2, 1), 3, 1)}; {(−4, −1), (−1, −4), (2, −1)}

35. $2x + 4$; $2x + 2$ **37.** x; x

39. $5x^2 + 5x - 5$; $25x^2 + 5x - 1$ **41.** 15 **43.** 1

45. 12 **47.** 189 **49.** 21 **51.** −3 **53.** 9

55. 440 **57.** $(P - D)(t)$

59. $(f + g)(x) = 869x + 17{,}575$. This function represents the enrollment of both men and women in college since 2006.

61. $(f + g)(-1) = 4$; $(h - g)(0) = 8$; $(f \cdot h)(4) = 5$; $\left(\frac{f}{g}\right)(3) = 4$; $\left(\frac{g}{h}\right)(2) = 0$; $\left(\frac{g}{f}\right)(1)$ = undefined

63. Sample answer: $f(x) = x - 9$, $g(x) = x + 5$

65a. D = {all real numbers}

65b. D = $\{x \mid x \geq 0\}$

67. Sample answer: Many situations in the real world involve complex calculations in which multiple functions are used. In order to solve some problems, a composition of those functions may need to be used. For example, the product of a manufacturing plant may have to go through several processes in a particular order, in which each process is described by a function. By finding the composition, only one calculation must be made to find the solution to the problem.

Lesson 6-2

1. {(6, −8), (−2, 6), (−3, 7)}

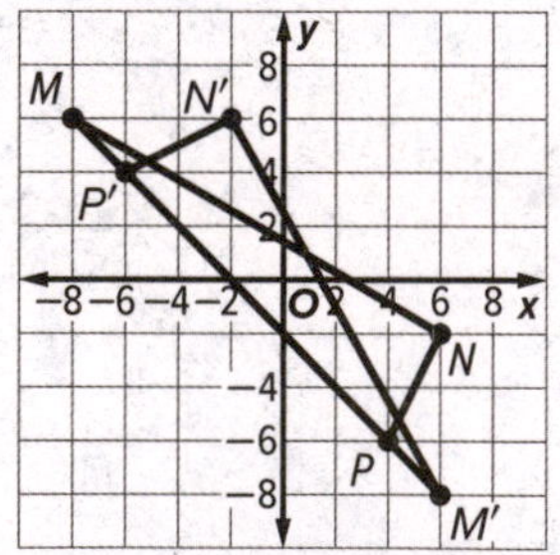

3. {(−1, 8), (−1, −8), (−8, −2), (−8, 2)}

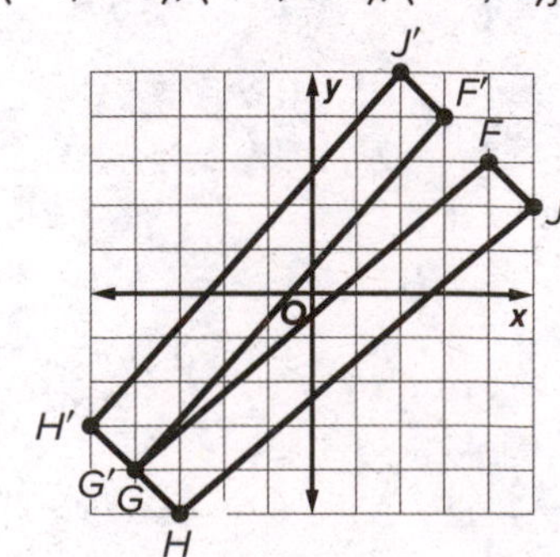

5.

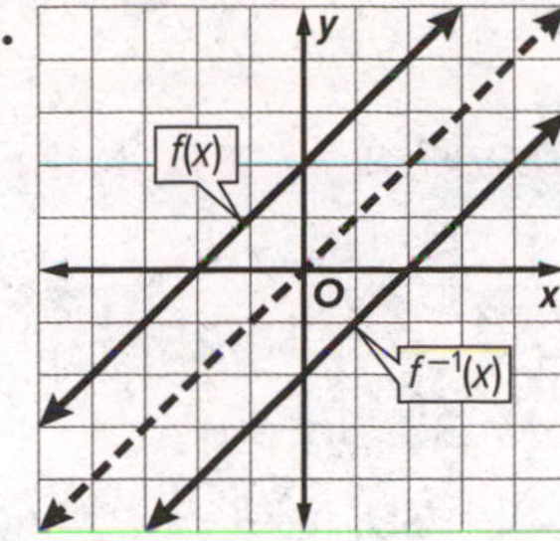

7.

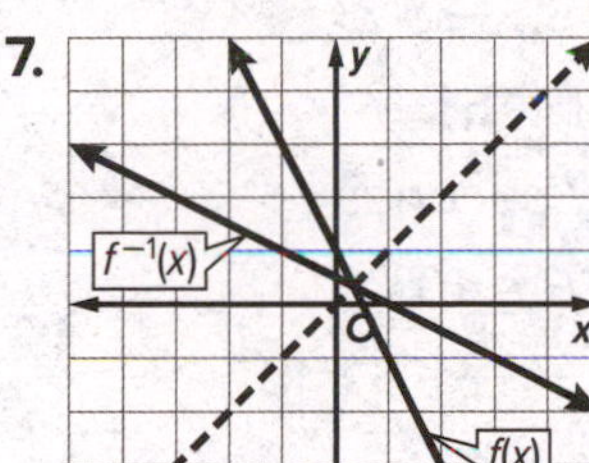

9.

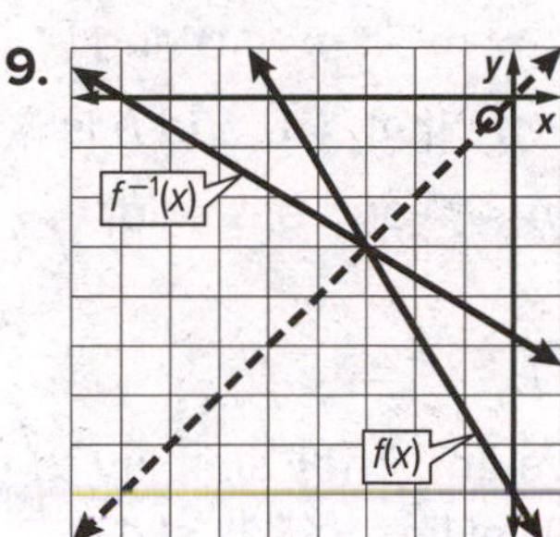

11.

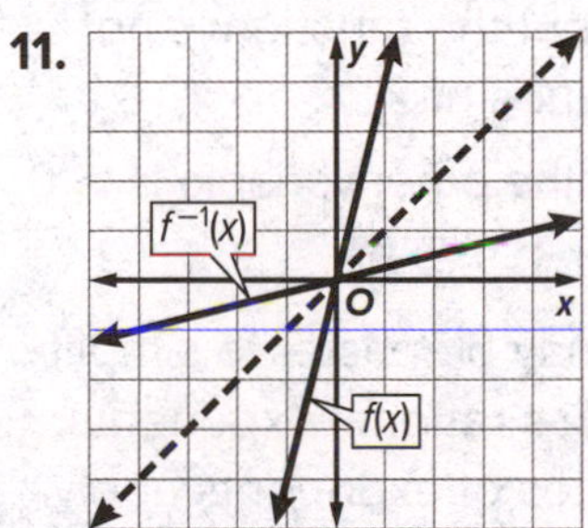

13. If the domain of $f(x)$ is restricted to $(-\infty, 0]$, then the inverse is $f^{-1}(x) = \sqrt{\frac{1}{5}x}$.
If the domain of $f(x)$ is restricted to $[0, \infty)$, then the inverse is $f^{-1}(x) = -\sqrt{\frac{1}{5}x}$.

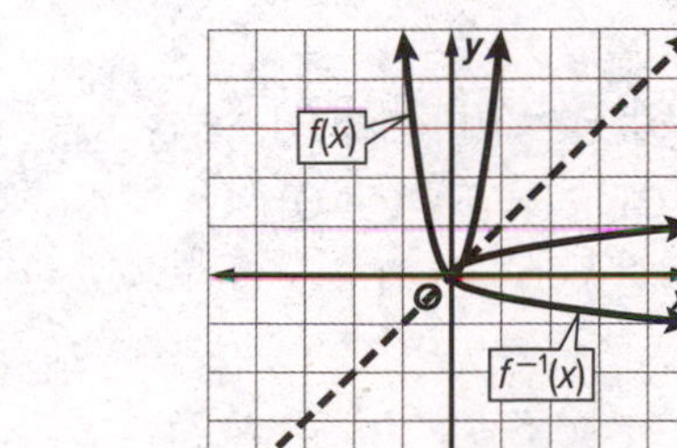

15. $f^{-1}(x) = 1.25x$. The function gives the discount price for any original price. The inverse function gives the original price for any discount price. The discount percentage is 20%.

17. no **19.** yes **21.** no **23.** yes

25. $\{(1, 3), (-3, 4), (-3, 8)\}$

27. $\{(-2, -10), (6, -7), (-2, -4), (0, -4)\}$

29. $\{(12, -4), (7, 0), (-1, 9), (-5, 10)\}$

31. $x = 4$

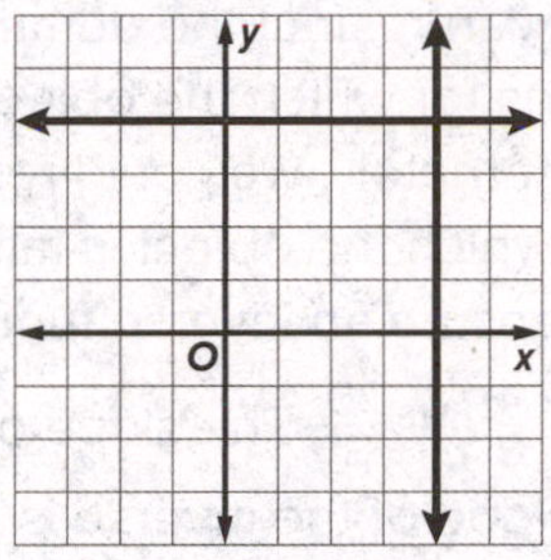

33. $f^{-1}(x) = x - 2$

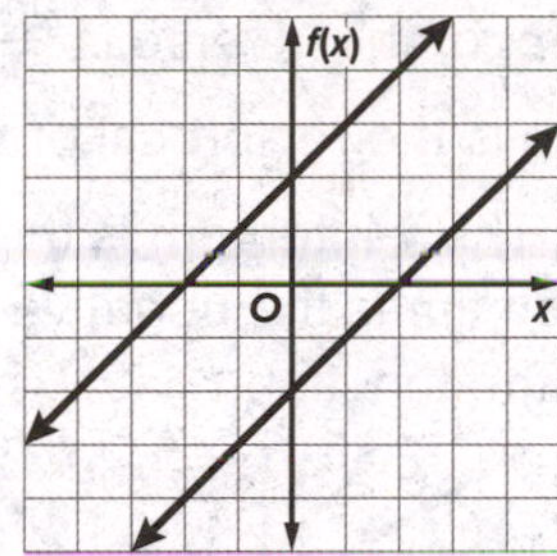

35. $h^{-1}(x) = 4x$

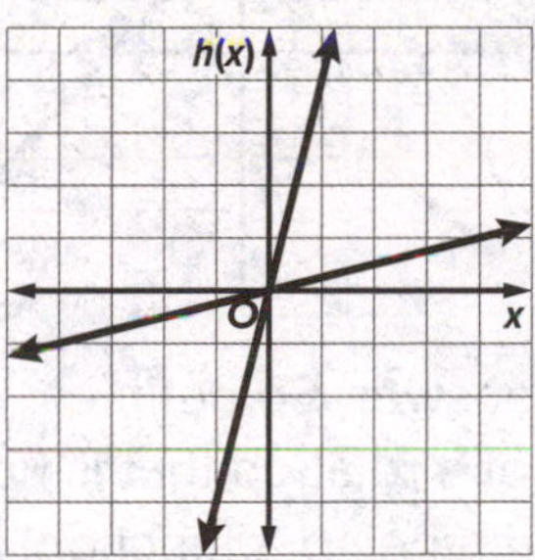

37. $f^{-1}(x) = \pm\sqrt{2x + 2}$
If the domain of $f(x)$ is restricted to $(-\infty, 0]$, then the inverse is $f^{-1}(x) = \sqrt{2x + 2}$. If the domain of $f(x)$ is restricted to $[0, \infty)$, then the inverse is $f^{-1}(x) = -\sqrt{2x + 2}$.

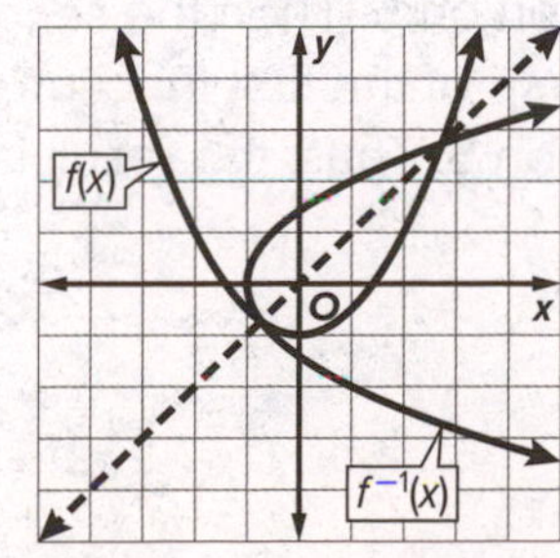

39. yes **41.** yes **43.** no **45.** yes **47.** no **49.** no **51.** no **53.** $r = \sqrt[3]{\frac{3V}{4\pi}}$

55. $f^{-1}(t)\ \frac{\sqrt{t}}{7} =$; 10 ft at 0.45 s, 100 ft at 1.43 s, 1000 ft at 4.52 s

57a. $T = d^{1.5}$ **57b.** 248 yr

59. Because the object is both going up and coming down, there will be two heights for most values of *t*, one for the way up, and one for the way down. Because of this, no inverse function can exist without a restriction on the domain. We can restrict the domain to only those *t* values for which the object is travelling upwards. Alternately, we could restrict it to only *t* values for which the object is falling. Either way would ensure an inverse function.

61. $f^{-1}(x) = -\frac{4}{3}x + \frac{20}{3}$. The slope of the function is $-\frac{3}{4}$. The slope of the inverse is $-\frac{4}{3}$. The *y*-intercept of the function is 5 and the *y*-intercept of the inverse is $\frac{20}{3}$. The slope of the inverse is the reciprocal of the slope of the function. The *y*-intercept is the *y*-intercept of the function times the negative reciprocal of the slope of the function.

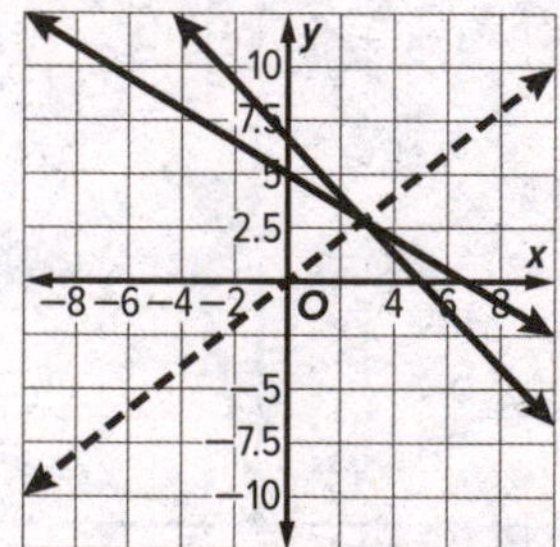

63. Sample answer: Sometimes; $y = \pm\sqrt{x}$ is an example of a relation that is not a function, with an inverse being a function. A circle is an example of a relation that is not a function with an inverse not being a function.

65. Sample answer: $f(x) = x$ and $f^{-1}(x) = x$ or $f(x) = -x$ and $f^{-1}(x) = -x$

67. Sample answer: One of the functions carries out an operation on 5. Then the second function that is an inverse of the first function reverses the operation on 5. Thus, the result is 5.

Lesson 6-3

1. $\pm 11x^2y^8$ **3.** $\pm 7x^2$ **5.** $-9a^8b^{10}c^6$ **7.** $(x + 15)^2$ **9.** $(a^2 + 4a)^6$ **11.** $|a^3|$ **13.** $\sqrt[5]{8}$ **15.** $\sqrt[4]{a^3}$ **17.** $17^{\frac{1}{2}}$ **19.** $5^{\frac{1}{3}}x^{\frac{1}{3}}y^{\frac{2}{3}}$ **21.** $6^{\frac{1}{3}}t^{\frac{2}{3}}$ **23.** 3 **25.** $\frac{1}{4}$ **27.** $x^{\frac{11}{15}}$ **29.** $\frac{b^{\frac{1}{4}}}{b}$ **31.** $2a^2b^4$ **33.** $3b^6c^4$ **35.** $i(x + 2)^4$ **37.** $3|(x + 4)|$ **39.** $(y^3 + 5)^6$ **41.** $x^2|y|$ **43.** $14|c^3|d^2$ **45.** $-3a^5b^3$ **47.** $20x^8|y^3|$ **49.** $4(x + y)^2$ **51.** a^3 **53.** $b^{\frac{1}{4}}$ **55.** $\frac{d^{\frac{1}{6}}}{d}$ **57a.** 1.57 seconds **57b.** 2.5 feet **59.** $D(1 + P)^3$; 40% **61.** $c^{\frac{1}{2}}$ **63.** $6^{\frac{1}{4}}h^{\frac{1}{2}}j^{\frac{1}{2}}$ **65.** $\frac{xy\sqrt[3]{z^2}}{z}$ **67.** $10^{\frac{1}{3}}$

69a. 1000 **69b.** $200 \cdot 150^{\frac{1}{3}}$ **69c.** $288 \cdot 30^{\frac{1}{2}}$

71. There are four cases to consider. If $m > 0$ and b is even, then $\sqrt[b]{m^{3b}} = m^3$. If $m < 0$ and b is even, then $\sqrt[b]{m^{3b}} = -m^3$. If $m > 0$ and b is odd, then $\sqrt[b]{m^{3b}} = m^3$. If $m < 0$ and b is odd, then $\sqrt[b]{m^{3b}} = m^3$.

73. $x < 0$; If $x < 0$, then $\sqrt{x^2} = -x$.

75. $f(x)$ and $r(x)$ are equivalent. They simplify to x^3. $g(x)$ is different and simplifies to $|x^3|$. $s(x)$ is almost the same as x^3, but the function is not defined for negative values of x.

77. when x or $y = 0$ and the other variable is ≥ 0

79. $0 < x < 1$, $x < -1$ **81.** $2\sqrt[3]{2xy}$

83. Sample answer: It may be easier to simplify an expression when it has rational exponents because all the properties of exponents apply. We do not have as many properties dealing directly with radicals. However, we can convert all radicals to rational exponents, and then use the properties of exponents to simplify.

Lesson 6-4

1. $D = \{x \mid x \geq 9\}$; $R = \{y \mid y \geq 0\}$

3. $D = \{x \mid x \geq 0\}$; $R = \{y \mid y \leq 0\}$

5. $D = \left\{x \mid x \geq \frac{4}{3}\right\}$; $R = \{y \mid y \geq 0\}$

7. D = $\{x \mid x \geq 0\}$; R = $\{y \mid y \geq 0\}$
compressed horizontally by a factor of 2

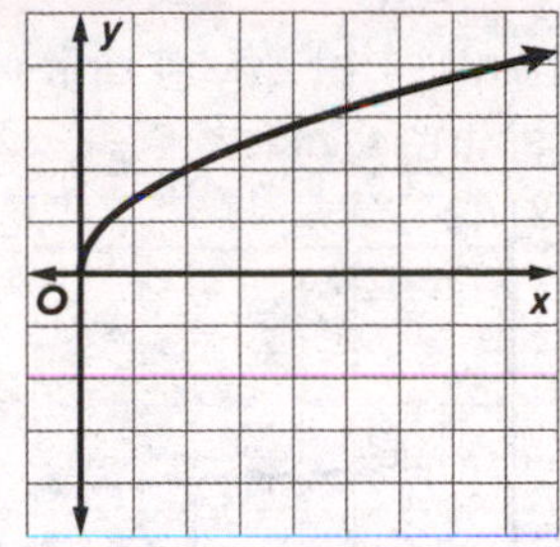

9. D = $\{x \mid x \geq 0\}$; R = $\{y \mid y \geq 0\}$
stretched vertically by a factor of 2

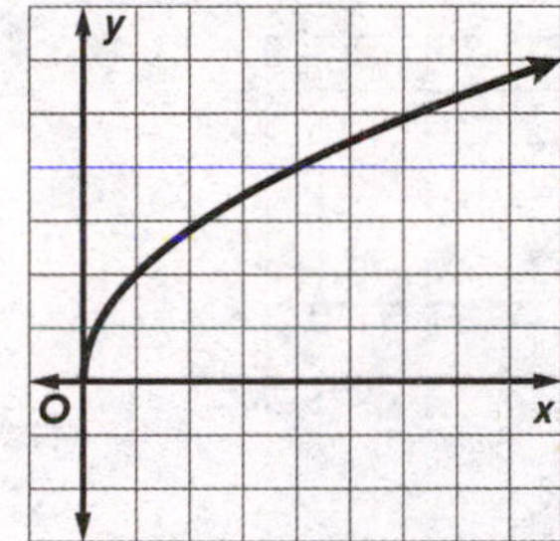

11. D = $\{x \mid x \geq 2.5\}$; R = $\{y \mid y \leq 0\}$
compressed horizontally by a factor of 2, translated 2.5 units right, and reflected across the x-axis

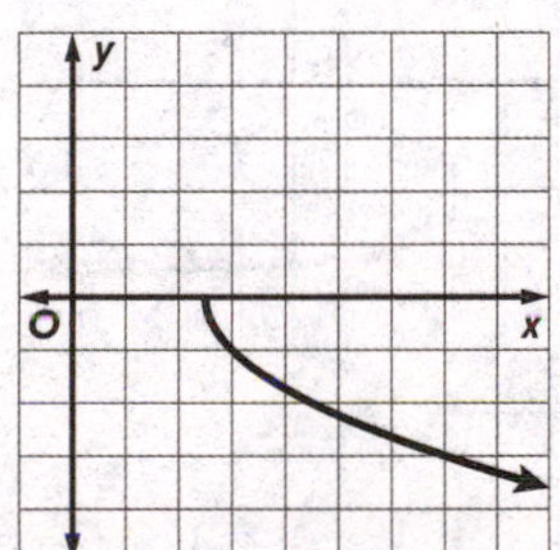

13a. $y = \sqrt{x}$

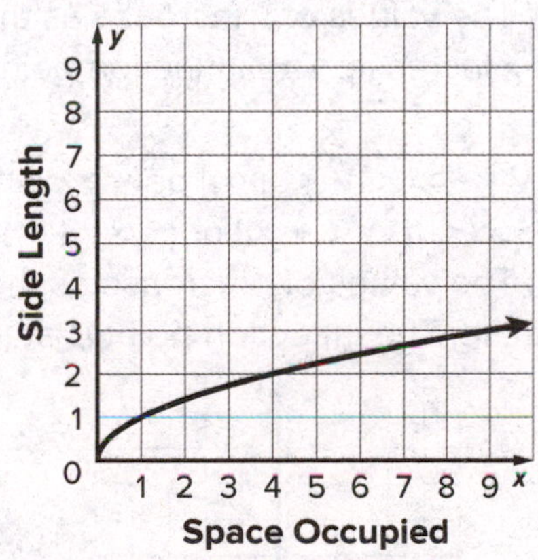

13b. D = $\{x \mid x \geq 0\}$; R = $\{y \mid y \geq 0\}$; increasing as $x \longrightarrow \infty$; positive for $x > 0$; As $x \longrightarrow \infty$, $y \longrightarrow \infty$.

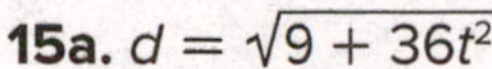

15a. $d = \sqrt{9 + 36t^2}$

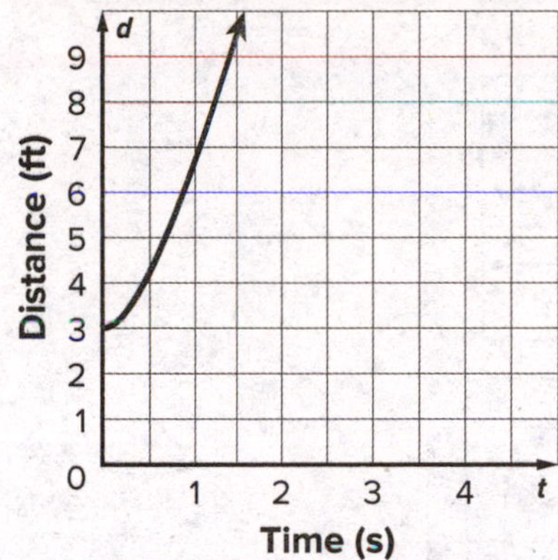

15b. D = $\{t \mid t \geq 0\}$; R = $\{d \mid d \geq 3\}$; increasing as $x \longrightarrow \infty$; positive for $x > 0$; As $x \longrightarrow \infty$, $y \longrightarrow \infty$.

17.

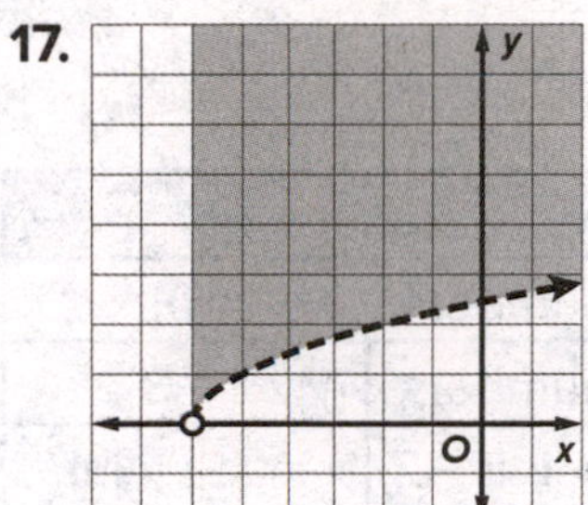

19.

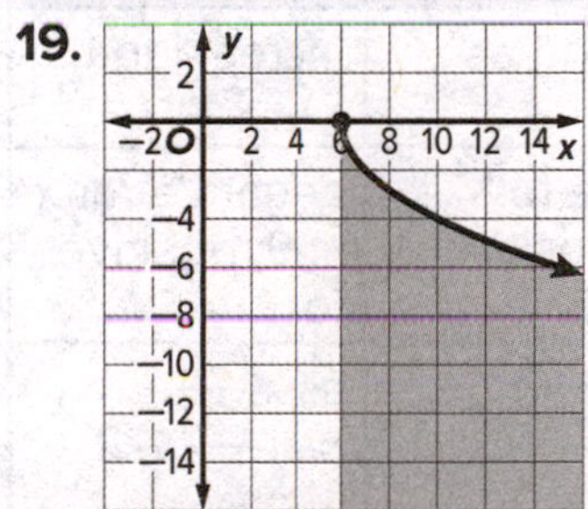

21.

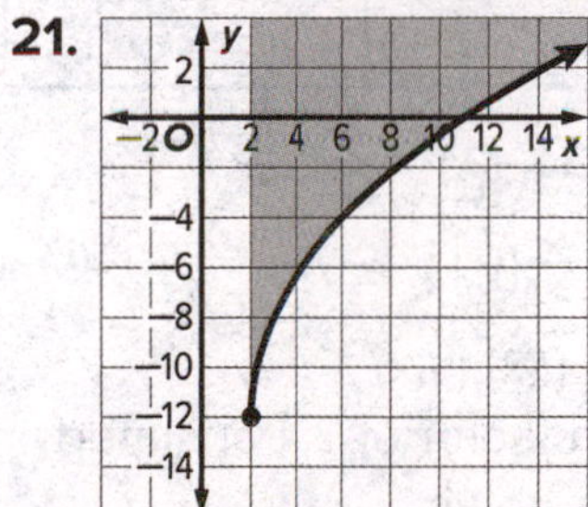

23. D = $(-\infty, +\infty)$; R = $(-\infty, +\infty)$

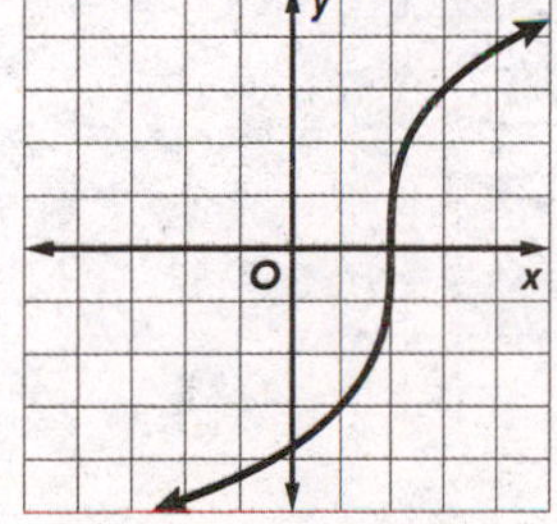

25. $D = (-\infty, +\infty)$; $R = (-\infty, +\infty)$

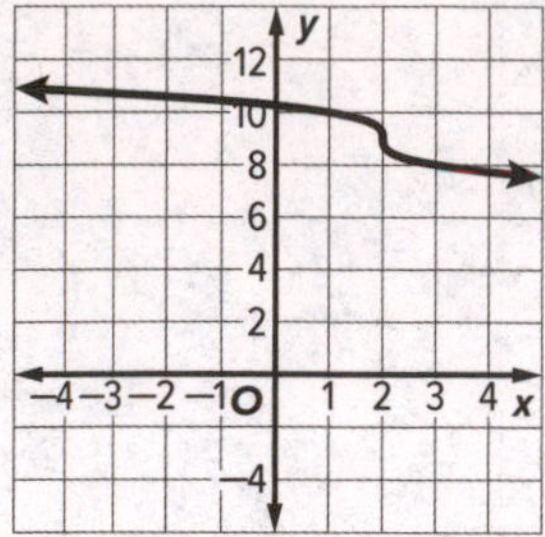

27a.

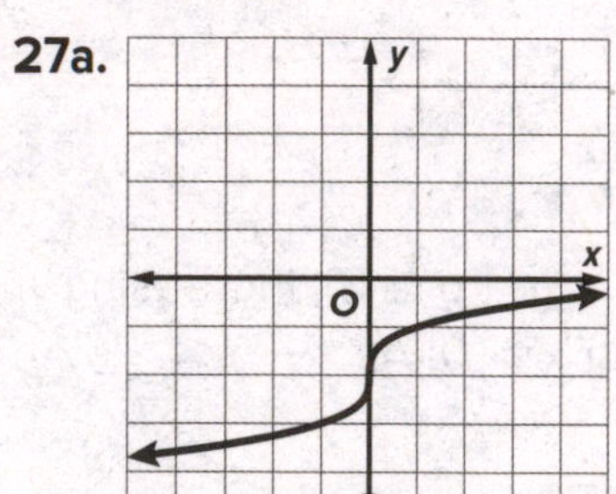

27b.

	$p(x) = \sqrt[3]{x} - 2$	$q(x)$
Domain	all real numbers	$\{x \mid x \geq 0\}$
Range	all real numbers	$\{y \mid y \leq -3\}$
Intercepts	x-int: 8; y-int: −2	x-int: 9; y-int: −3
Increasing/ Decreasing	increasing as $x \to \infty$	increasing as $x \to \infty$
Positive/ Negative	negative for $x < 8$; positive for $x > 8$	negative for $x < 9$; positive for $x > 9$
End Behavior	as $x \to -\infty$, $p(x) \to -\infty$ as $x \to \infty$, $p(x) \to \infty$	as $x \to -\infty$, $p(x) \to -2$ as $x \to \infty$, $p(x) \to \infty$

29. $f(x) = \sqrt[3]{x - 2} + 1$ **31.** $f(x) = \frac{1}{2}\sqrt[3]{x + 1} - 2$

33. $D = \left\{x \mid x \geq \frac{3}{2}\right\}$; $R = \{y \mid y \geq 7\}$

35. $D = \{x \mid x \geq 5\}$; $R = \{f(x) \mid f(x) \geq -6\}$ stretched vertically by a factor of 2, translated 5 units right and 6 units down

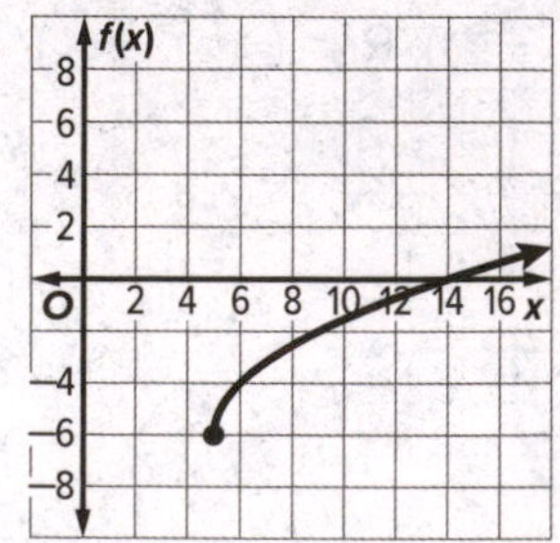

37. $D = \{x \mid x \geq 1\}$; $R = \{f(x) \mid f(x) \geq -4\}$ compressed vertically by a factor of $\frac{1}{5}$, translated 1 unit right and 4 units down, reflected across the x-axis

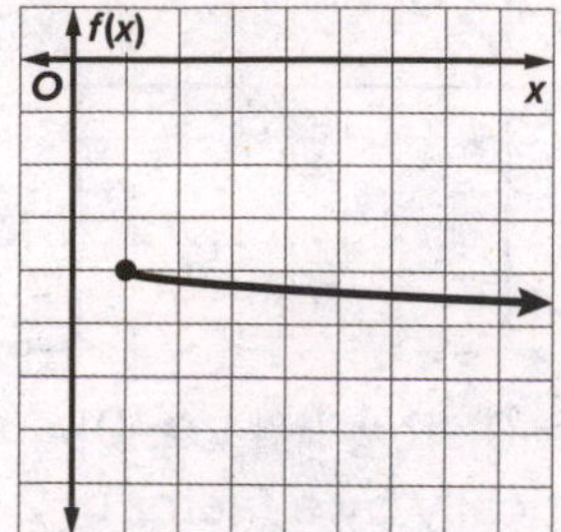

39.

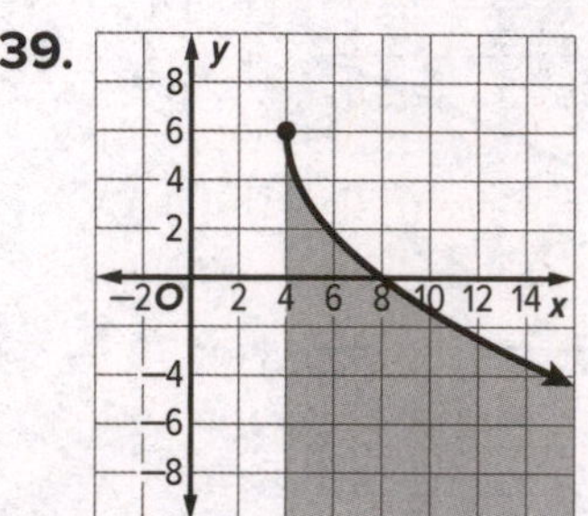

41. $D = (-\infty, +\infty)$; $R = (-\infty, +\infty)$

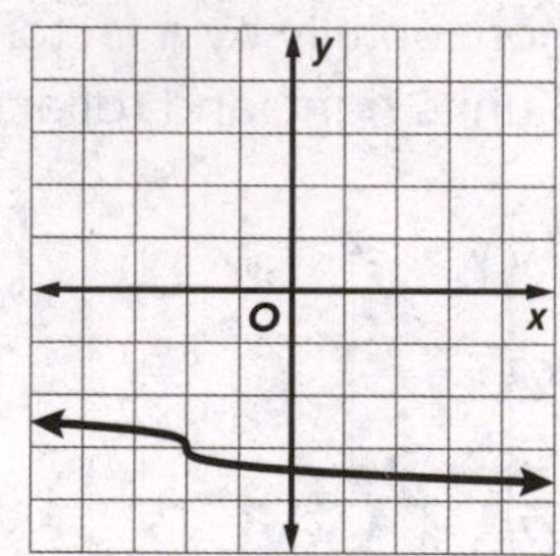

43. $f(x) = \frac{2}{3}\sqrt[3]{x - 1} + 1$

45. $D = \{x \mid -\infty < x < +\infty\}$ or $(-\infty, +\infty)$; $R = \{f(x) \mid -\infty < f(x) < +\infty\}$ or $(-\infty, +\infty)$; End behavior: The values of y increase as the values of x increase. The inflection point is at (0, 0).

47. $D = \{V \mid -\infty < V < +\infty\}$ or $(-\infty, +\infty)$; $R = \{r(V) \mid -\infty < r(V) < +\infty\}$ or $(-\infty, +\infty)$; End behavior: The values of r increase as the values of V increase. The inflection point is at (0, 0).

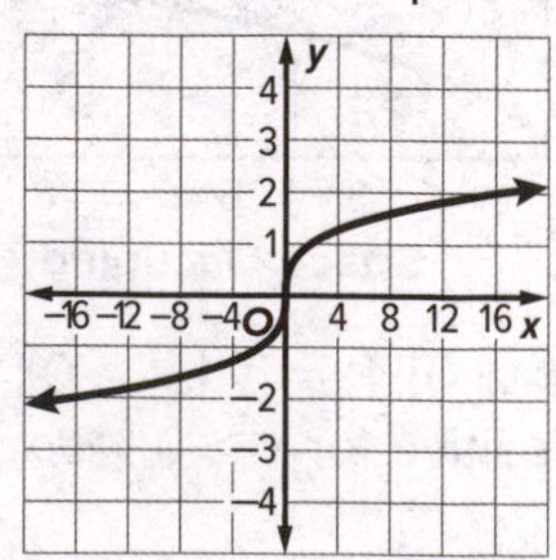

49. The inverse inequality is $f^{-1}(x) > -(x + 3)^2 + 2$. The domain of the inverse is restricted to $x > -3$.

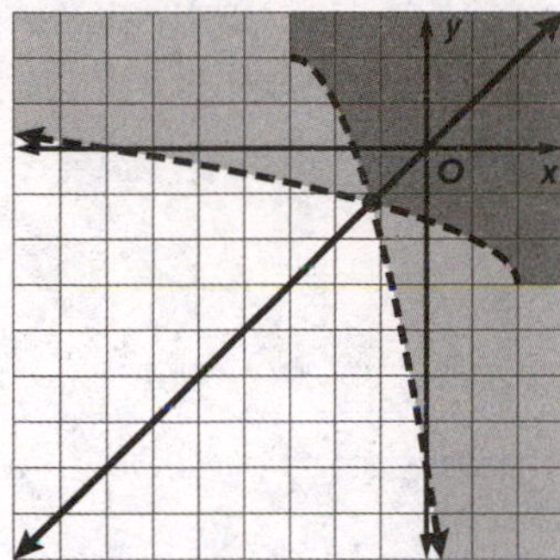

51. all positive odd numbers

53. Sample answer: The domain is limited because square roots of negative numbers are imaginary. The range is limited due to the limitation of the domain.

55. To be a function, for every x-value there must be exactly one y-value. For every x in this equation there are two y-values, one that is negative and one that is positive. Also, the graph of $y = \pm\sqrt{x}$ does not pass the vertical line test.

Lesson 6-5

1. $6a^4b^2\sqrt{2b}$ **3.** $2a^8b^4\sqrt{6cb}$ **5.** $2|ab|\sqrt{4}$

7. $\frac{5}{6}|r|\sqrt{t}$ **9.** $\frac{4h\sqrt[5]{3h^3}}{3f}$ **11.** $8\sqrt{2}$ **13.** $\sqrt{5}$

15. $5\sqrt{7x} - \sqrt{14}$ **17.** $120y\sqrt{2z}$ **19.** $144ab^2\sqrt{2}$

21. $15xy\sqrt{14xy}$

23. $56\sqrt{3} + 42\sqrt{6} - 36\sqrt{2} - 54$ **25.** 1260

27. $18 + 5\sqrt{6}m^2$ **29.** $\frac{a^2\sqrt{5ab}}{b^7}$ **31.** $\frac{\sqrt[3]{150x^2y^2}}{5y}$

33. $6\sqrt{3} + 6\sqrt{2}$ **35.** $\frac{20 - 7\sqrt{3}}{11}$ **37.** $\frac{3\sqrt{7} + 3\sqrt{35}}{4}$

39. $2yz^4\sqrt[3]{2y}$ **41.** $3|a|b^3\sqrt[4]{2a^2bc}$ **43.** $\frac{\sqrt[4]{1500a^2b^3x^3y^2}}{5|a|b}$

45. $\frac{(x + 1)(\sqrt{x} + 1)}{x - 1}$ or $\frac{x\sqrt{x} + \sqrt{x} + x + 1}{x - 1}$ **47.** $\frac{\sqrt{x^3 - x}}{x^2 - 1}$

49. $4\sqrt{3}$ **51.** $28\sqrt{7a}$ **53.** $103\sqrt{28}$ in. **55.** $\frac{\sqrt{tu}}{u}$

57a. John: $\frac{0.8 - 4\sqrt{0.02}}{0.02}$ or $40 - 20\sqrt{2}$ min;

Jay: $\frac{0.8 - 4\sqrt{0.05}}{-0.01}$ or $40\sqrt{5} - 80$ min

57b. $2 - \sqrt{2} + \sqrt{5} + \frac{\sqrt{10}}{2}$

59a.

i. $3x$; $(\sqrt{x} \cdot x) + (\sqrt{x} \cdot \sqrt{4x}) = (\sqrt{x^2} + \sqrt{4x^2}) = x + 2x = 3x$

ii. $6x$; $(\sqrt{x} \cdot \sqrt{x}) + (\sqrt{x} \cdot \sqrt{4x}) + (\sqrt{x} + \sqrt{9x}) = \left(\sqrt{x^2} + \sqrt{4x^2} + \sqrt{9x^2}\right) = x + 2x + 3x = 6x$

iii. $10x$; $(\sqrt{x} \cdot \sqrt{x}) + (\sqrt{x} \cdot \sqrt{4x}) + (\sqrt{x} \cdot \sqrt{9x}) + (\sqrt{x} \cdot \sqrt{16x}) = \left(\sqrt{x^2} + \sqrt{4x^2} + \sqrt{9x^2} + \sqrt{16x^2}\right) = x + 2x + 3x + 4x = 10x$

59b. $(\sqrt{x} \cdot \sqrt{x}) + (\sqrt{x} \cdot \sqrt{4x}) + \ldots + (\sqrt{x} + \sqrt{n^2x}) = x + 2x + \ldots + nx = (1 + 2 + \ldots + n)x = \left(\frac{n(n + 1)}{2}\right)x$

61a. $6\sqrt[3]{2} + 1$; $r = \sqrt[3]{\frac{3}{4\pi} \cdot 72\pi} = \sqrt[3]{54} = 3\sqrt[3]{2}$; $S = 3\sqrt[3]{2} + 2(2)$

61b. No; a box with a volume of 384 cm^3 has a side that is $\sqrt[3]{384}$, or about 7.27 cm; $s = 3\sqrt[3]{2} + 4 \approx 7.78$ is the least possible value for a side of the gift box.

63. Twyla; Ben's mistakes were multiplying the 4 by 16 instead of 4 and multiplying the 6 by 9 instead of 3.

65. Sample answer: 0 is the only possible value for a since $\sqrt{a}$ is defined for $a \geq 0$, and $\sqrt{-a}$ is defined for $a \leq 0$.

67. Sample answer: 4096

69. $\sqrt[8]{256g^4h^{16}}$ because the other two simplify to $2g^2\sqrt{h}$

Lesson 6-6

1. 25 **3.** $\frac{1}{25}$ **5.** 8 **7.** 40 **9.** 7 **11.** 11 **13.** 11

15. $-\frac{1}{2}$ **17.** 16 (extraneous solution) **19.** 83

21. 61 **23.** 15,623 **25.** 43 **27.** 2.4 **29.** 5

31. 1.23 **33.** 36 cm **35.** 3 **37.** $\frac{1}{4}$ **39.** $\frac{81}{16}$

41. $\frac{7}{5}$ **43.** 2 **45.** 23 **47.** 24.5

49. 3, 4 (extraneous solution)

51. 6, −5 (extraneous solution)

53. 1000 **55.** 18.75 ft **57.** 5.74 **59.** 0.13

61. 34.7 feet

63a. Student responses should indicate that the monthly profit for each company depends on the number of sleds sold; one company may have a greater profit for a given number of sleds, but the other company may have the greater profit for a different number of sleds.

63b. Student responses may vary but must be between 2 and 50. For a response of $x = 10$ sleds, the A-Glide Company would earn a profit of $\sqrt{3(10) + 19} = 7$ hundred dollars, or $700, while SnowFun would earn a profit of $3 + \sqrt{2(10)} \approx 7.47$ hundred dollars, or $747.

65. When $x = 9$, the value of the left side is $\sqrt{16} = 4$. The solution $x = 9$ will be extraneous if the right side of the equation is equal to -4. Since $\sqrt{4} = 2$, the value of c should be -6. The equation $\sqrt{x + 7} = \sqrt{x - 5} - 6$ has no solutions.

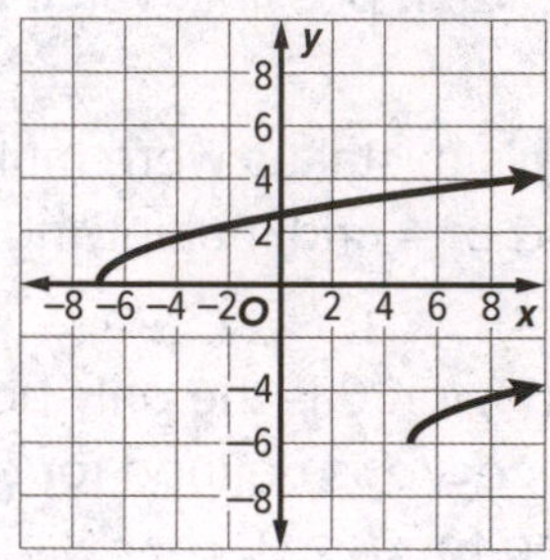

67. Algebraically: Isolate the radicals and raise each side to 4th power. The solutions are $x = 9$ and $x = 2$, but $x = 2$ is an extraneous solution. Graphically: Graphing $f(x) = \sqrt{x - 5}$ and $g(x) = \sqrt[4]{x + 7}$ will show the true solution. Square the original equation to get $x - 5 = \sqrt{x + 7}$. The extraneous solution occurs when $5 - x = \sqrt{x + 7}$. Change $f(x)$ to $f(x) = \sqrt{5 - x}$, and the graph shows the solution at $x = 2$.

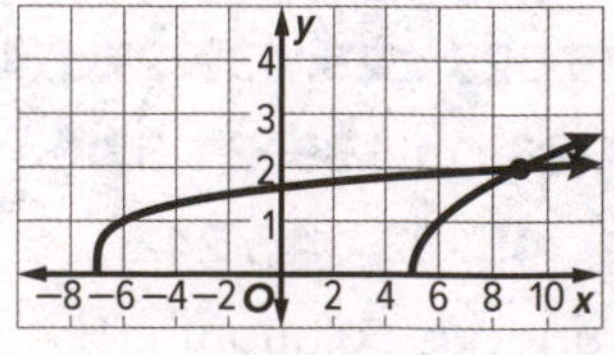

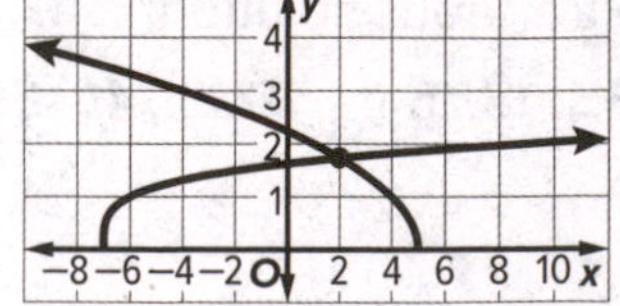

69. The domain of the left-hand side is $x \geq 5$. The domain of the right-hand side is $x \leq 2$. These two domains do not overlap, so no real x-value could simultaneously satisfy both sides of the equation. The graph confirms this.

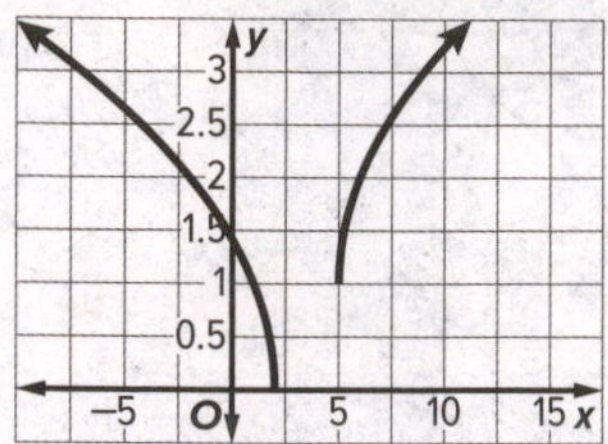

71. $\sqrt{x + 2} - 7 = -10$

73. never;

$\frac{\sqrt{(x^2)^2}}{-x} = x$

$\frac{x^2}{-x} = x$

$x^2 = (x)(-x)$

$x^2 \neq -x^2$

75. They are the same number.

77. 3

79. Sometimes; sample answer: when the radicand is negative, then there will be extraneous roots.

Module 6 Review

1. D

3.

Player	$[f \circ g](x)$	$[g \circ f](x)$	Neither
Anna		X	
Brenden			X
Carlos	X		
Deanna		X	

5. A **7.** A, C, E, F **9.** D **11.** $a = 5, b = 12$

13. C **15.** B **17.** 4 **19.** 213

Glossary

English	Español

A

absolute value (Lesson 2–2) The distance a number is from zero on the number line.

valor absoluto La distancia que un número es de cero en la línea numérica.

absolute value function (Lesson 1–6) A function written as $f(x) = |x|$, in which $f(x) \geq 0$ for all values of x.

función del valor absoluto Una función que se escribe $f(x) = |x|$, donde $f(x) \geq 0$, para todos los valores de x.

algebraic notation (Lesson 1–1) Mathematical notation that describes a set by using algebraic expressions.

notación algebraica Notación matemática que describe un conjunto usando expresiones algebraicas.

amplitude (Lesson 11–4) For functions of the form $y = a \sin b\theta$ or $y = a \cos b\theta$, the amplitude is $|a|$.

amplitud Para funciones de la forma $y = a$ sen $b\theta$ o $y = a \cos b\theta$, la amplitud es $|a|$.

asymptote (Lesson 7–1) A line that a graph approaches.

asíntota Una línea que se aproxima a un gráfico.

average rate of change (Lesson 3–1) The change in the value of the dependent variable divided by the change in the value of the independent variable.

tasa media de cambio El cambio en el valor de la variable dependiente dividido por el cambio en el valor de la variable independiente.

axis of symmetry (Lesson 3–1) The line about which a graph is symmetric.

eje de simetría Una línea sobre la cual un gráfica es simétrico.

B

bias (Lesson 10–1) An error that results in a misrepresentation of a population.

sesgo Un error que resulta en una tergiversación de una población.

binomial (Lesson 4–3) The sum of two monomials.

binomio La suma de dos monomios.

boundary (Lesson 1–5) The edge of the graph of an inequality that separates the coordinate plane into regions.

frontera El borde de la gráfica de una desigualdad que separa el plano de coordenadas en regiones.

bounded (Lesson 2–6) When the graph of a system of constraints is a polygonal region.

acotada Cuando la gráfica de un sistema de restricciones es una región poligonal.

C

central angle of a circle (Lesson 11–1) An angle with a vertex at the center of a circle and sides that are radii.

ángulo central de un círculo Un ángulo con un vértice en el centro de un círculo y los lados que son radios.

circular function (Lesson 11–3) A function that describes a point on a circle as the function of an angle defined in radians.

función circular Función que describe un punto en un círculo como la función de un ángulo definido en radianes.

closed (Lesson 4–3) If for any members in a set, the result of an operation is also in the set.

cerrado Si para cualquier número en el conjunto, el resultado de la operación es también en el conjunto.

closed half-plane (Lesson 1–5) The solution of a linear inequality that includes the boundary line.

semi-plano cerrado La solución de una desigualdad linear que incluye la línea de limite.

codomain (Lesson 1–1) The set of all the *y*-values that could possibly result from the evaluation of the function.

codominar El conjunto de todos los valores y que podrían resultar de la evaluación de la función.

coefficient of determination (Lesson 7–5) An indicator of how well a function fits a set of data.

coeficiente de determinación Un indicador de lo bien que una función se ajusta a un conjunto de datos.

cofunction identities (Lesson 12–1) Identities that show the relationships between sine and cosine, tangent and cotangent, and secant and cosecant.

identidades de cofunción Identidades que muestran las relaciones entre seno y coseno, tangente y cotangente, y secante y cosecante.

combined variation (Lesson 9–5) When one quantity varies directly and/or inversely as two or more other quantities.

variación combinada Cuando una cantidad varía directamente y / o inversamente como dos o más cantidades.

common logarithms (Lesson 8–3) Logarithms of base 10.

logaritmos comunes Logaritmos de base 10.

common ratio (Lesson 7–4) The ratio of consecutive terms of a geometric sequence.

razón común El razón de términos consecutivos de una secuencia geométrica.

completing the square (Lesson 3–5) A process used to turn a quadratic expression into a perfect square trinomial.

completar el cuadrado Un proceso usado para hacer una expresión cuadrática en un trinomio cuadrado perfecto.

complex conjugates (Lesson 3–3) Two complex numbers of the form $a + bi$ and $a - bi$.

conjugados complejos Dos números complejos de la forma $a + bi$ y $a - bi$.

complex fraction (Lesson 9–1) A rational expression with a numerator and/or denominator that is also a rational expression.

fracción compleja Una expresión racional con un numerador y / o denominador que también es una expresión racional.

complex number (Lesson 3–3) Any number that can be written in the form $a + bi$, where a and b are real numbers and i is the imaginary unit.

número complejo Cualquier número que se puede escribir en la forma $a + bi$, donde a y b son números reales e i es la unidad imaginaria.

composition of functions (Lesson 6–1) An operation that uses the results of one function to evaluate a second function.

composición de funciones Operación que utiliza los resultados de una función para evaluar una segunda función.

compound interest (Lesson 7–2) Interest calculated on the principal and on the accumulated interest from previous periods.

interés compuesto Intereses calculados sobre el principal y sobre el interés acumulado de períodos anteriores.

confidence interval (Lesson 10–5) An estimate of the population parameter stated as a range with a specific degree of certainty.

intervalo de confianza Una estimación del parámetro de población se indica como un rango con un grado específico de certeza.

conjugates (Lesson 6–5) Two expressions, each with two terms, in which the second terms are opposites.

conjugados Dos expresiones, cada una con dos términos, en la que los segundos términos son opuestos.

consistent (Lesson 2–4) A system of equations with at least one ordered pair that satisfies both equations.

consistente Una sistema de ecuaciones para el cual existe al menos un par ordenado que satisfice ambas ecuaciones.

constant function (Lesson 1–7) The function $f(x) = a$, where a is any number.

función constante La función $f(x) = a$, donde a es cualquier número.

constant of variation (Lesson 9–5) The constant in a variation function.

constante de variación La constante en una función de variación.

constraint (Lesson 1–5) A condition that a solution must satisfy.

restricción Una condición que una solución debe satisfacer.

continuous function (Lesson 1–1) A function that can be graphed with a line or a smooth curve.

función continua Una función que se puede representar gráficamente con una línea o una curva lisa.

continuous random variable (Lesson 10–4) The numerical outcome of a random event that can take on any value.

variable aleatoria continua El resultado numérico de un evento aleatorio que puede tomar cualquier valor.

convenience sample (Lesson 10–1) Members that are readily available or easy to reach are selected.

muestra conveniente Se seleccionan los miembros que están fácilmente disponibles o de fácil acceso.

correlation coefficient (Lesson 7–5) A measure that shows how well data are modeled by a regression function.

coeficiente de correlación Una medida que muestra cómo los datos son modelados por una función de regresión.

cosecant (Lesson 11–2) The ratio of the length of a hypotenuse to the length of the leg opposite the angle.

cosecante Relación entre la longitud de la hipotenusa y la longitud de la pierna opuesta al ángulo.

cosine (Lesson 11–2) The ratio of the length of the leg adjacent to an angle to the length of the hypotenuse.

coseno Relación entre la longitud de la pierna adyacente a un ángulo y la longitud de la hipotenusa.

cotangent (Lesson 11–2) The ratio of the length of the leg adjacent to an angle to the length of the leg opposite the angle.

cotangente La relación entre la longitud de la pata adyacente a un ángulo y la longitud de la pata opuesta al ángulo.

coterminal angles (Lesson 11–1) Angles in standard position that have the same terminal side.

ángulos coterminales Ángulos en posición estándar que tienen el mismo lado terminal.

critical values (Lesson 10–5) The z-values corresponding to the most common degrees of certainty.

valores críticos Los valores z correspondientes a los grados de certeza más comunes.

cube root function (Lesson 6–4) A radical function that contains the cube root of a variable expression.

función de la raíz del cubo Función radical que contiene la raíz cúbica de una expresión variable.

cycle (Lesson 11–3) One complete pattern of a periodic function.

ciclo Un patron completo de una función periódica.

D

decay factor (Lesson 7–1) The base of an exponential expression or $1 - r$.

degree (Lesson 4–1) The value of the exponent in a power function.

degree of a polynomial (Lesson 4–1) The greatest degree of any term in the polynomial.

dependent (Lesson 2–4) A consistent system of equations with an infinite number of solutions.

depressed polynomial (Lesson 5–4) A polynomial resulting from division with a degree one less than the original polynomial.

descriptive statistics (Lesson 10–3) The branch of statistics that focuses on collecting, summarizing, and displaying data.

difference of squares (Lesson 3–4) A binomial in which the first and last terms are perfect squares.

dilation (Lesson 1–7) A transformation that stretches or compresses the graph of a function.

direct variation (Lesson 9–5) When one quantity is equal to a constant times another quantity.

discontinuous function (Lesson 1–1) A function that is not continuous.

discrete function (Lesson 1–1) A function in which the points on the graph are not connected.

discrete random variable (Lesson 10–4) The numerical outcome of a random event that is finite and can be counted.

discriminant (Lesson 3–6) In the Quadratic Formula, the expression under the radical sign that provides information about the roots of the quadratic equation.

distribution (Lesson 10–3) A graph or table that shows the theoretical frequency of each possible data value.

domain (Lesson 1–1) The set of x-values to be evaluated by a function.

factor de decaimiento La base de una expresión exponencial o $1 - r$.

grado Valor del exponente en una función de potencia.

grado de un polinomio El grado mayor de cualquier término del polinomio.

dependiente Una sistema consistente de ecuaciones con un número infinito de soluciones.

polinomio reducido Un polinomio resultante de la división con un grado uno menos que el polinomio original.

estadística descriptiva Rama de la estadística cuyo enfoque es la recopilación, resumen y demostración de los datos.

diferencia de cuadrados Un binomio en el que los términos primero y último son cuadrados perfectos.

homotecia Una transformación que estira o comprime el gráfico de una función.

variación directa Cuando una cantidad es igual a una constante multiplicada por otra cantidad.

función discontinua Una función que no es continua.

función discreta Una función en la que los puntos del gráfico no están conectados.

variable aleatoria discreta El resultado numérico de un evento aleatorio que es finito y puede ser contado.

discriminante En la Fórmula cuadrática, la expresión bajo el signo radical que proporciona información sobre las raíces de la ecuación cuadrática.

distribución Un gráfico o una table que muestra la frecuencia teórica de cada valor de datos posible.

dominio El conjunto de valores x para ser evaluados por una función.

E

e (Lesson 7–3) An irrational number that approximately equals 2.7182818....

e Un número irracional que es aproximadamente igual a 2.7182818 ....

elimination (Lesson 2–5) A method that involves eliminating a variable by combining the individual equations within a system of equations.

eliminación Un método que consiste en eliminar una variable combinando las ecuaciones individuales dentro de un sistema de ecuaciones.

empty set (Lesson 2–2) The set that contains no elements, symbolized by { } or ∅.

conjunto vacio El conjunto que no contiene elementos, simbolizado por { } o ∅.

end behavior (Lesson 1–3) The behavior of a graph at the positive and negative extremes in its domain.

comportamiento del fin El comportamiento de un gráfico en los extremos positivo y negativo en su dominio.

equation (Lesson 2–1) A mathematical statement that contains two expressions and an equals sign, =.

ecuación Un enunciado matemático que contiene dos expresiones y un signo igual, =.

even functions (Lesson 1–2) Functions that are symmetric in the *y*-axis.

incluso funciones Funciones que son simétricas en el eje *y*.

excluded values (Lesson 9–2) Values for which a function is not defined.

valores excluidos Valores para los que no se ha definido una función.

exponential decay (Lesson 7–1) Change that occurs when an initial amount decreases by the same percent over a given period of time.

desintegración exponencial Cambio que ocurre cuando una cantidad inicial disminuye en el mismo porcentaje durante un período de tiempo dado.

experiment (Lesson 10–1) A sample is divided into two groups. The experimental group undergoes a change, while there is no change to the control group. The effects on the groups are then compared.

experimento Una muestra se divide en dos grupos. El grupo experimental experimenta un cambio, mientras que no hay cambio en el grupo de control. A continuación se comparan los efectos sobre los grupos.

experimental probability (Lesson 10–2) Probability calculated by using data from an actual experiment.

probabilidad experimental Probabilidad calculada utilizando datos de un experimento real.

explicit formula (Lesson 7–4) A formula that allows you to find any term a_n of a sequence by using a formula written in terms of n.

fórmula explícita Una fórmula que le permite encontrar cualquier término a_n de una secuencia usando una fórmula escrita en términos de n.

exponential equation (Lesson 7–2) An equation in which the independent variable is an exponent.

ecuación exponencial Una ecuación en la que la variable independiente es un exponente.

exponential form (Lesson 6–3) When an expression is in the form x^n.

forma exponencial Cuando una expresión está en la forma x^n.

exponential function (Lesson 7–1) A function in which the independent variable is an exponent.

función exponencial Una función en la que la variable independiente es el exponente.

exponential growth (Lesson 7–1) Change that occurs when an initial amount increases by the same percent over a given period of time.

crecimiento exponencial Cambio que ocurre cuando una cantidad inicial aumenta por el mismo porcentaje durante un período de tiempo dado.

exponential inequality (Lesson 7–2) An inequality in which the independent variable is an exponent.

desigualdad exponencial Una desigualdad en la que la variable independiente es un exponente.

extraneous solution (Lesson 2–2) A solution of a simplified form of an equation that does not satisfy the original equation.

solución extraña Una solución de una forma simplificada de una ecuación que no satisface la ecuación original.

extrema (Lesson 1–3) Points that are the locations of relatively high or low function values.

extrema Puntos que son las ubicaciones de valores de función relativamente alta o baja.

F

factored form (Lesson 3–4) A form of quadratic equation, $0 = a(x - p)(x - q)$, where $a \neq 0$, in which p and q are the x-intercepts of the graph of the related function.

forma factorizada Una forma de ecuación cuadrática, $0 = a(x - p)(x - q)$, donde $a \neq 0$, en la que p y q son las intercepciones x de la gráfica de la función relacionada.

family of graphs (Lesson 1–7) Graphs and equations of graphs that have at least one characteristic in common.

familia de gráficas Gráficas y ecuaciones de gráficas que tienen al menos una característica común.

feasible region (Lesson 2–6) The intersection of the graphs in a system of constraints.

región factible La intersección de los gráficos en un sistema de restricciones.

finite sequence (Lesson 7–4) A sequence that contains a limited number of terms.

secuencia finita Una secuencia que contiene un número limitado de términos.

frequency (Lesson 11–4) The number of cycles in a given unit of time.

frecuencia El número de ciclos en una unidad del tiempo dada.

G

geometric means (Lesson 7–4) The terms between two nonconsecutive terms of a geometric sequence.

medios geométricos Los términos entre dos términos no consecutivos de una secuencia geométrica.

geometric sequence (Lesson 7–4) A pattern of numbers that begins with a nonzero term and each term after is found by multiplying the previous term by a nonzero constant r.

secuencia geométrica Un patrón de números que comienza con un término distinto de cero y cada término después se encuentra multiplicando el término anterior por una constante no nula r.

geometric series (Lesson 7–4) The indicated sum of the terms in a geometric sequence.

series geométricas La suma indicada de los términos en una secuencia geométrica.

greatest integer function (Lesson 1–6) A step function in which $f(x)$ is the greatest integer less than or equal to x.

función más grande del número entero Una función del paso en que $f(x)$ es el número más grande menos que o igual a x.

growth factor (Lesson 7–1) The base of an exponential expression or $1 + r$.

factor de crecimiento La base de una expresión exponencial o $1 + r$.

H

horizontal asymptote (Lesson 9–2) A horizontal line that a graph approaches.

asíntota horizontal Una línea horizontal que se aproxima a un gráfico.

hyperbola (Lesson 9–2) The graph of a reciprocal function.

hipérbola La gráfica de una función recíproca.

I

identity (Lesson 5–3) An equation that is true for every value of the variable.

identidad Una ecuación que es verdad para cada valor de la variable.

identity function (Lesson 1–7) The function $f(x) = x$.

función identidad La función $f(x) = x$.

imaginary unit *i* (Lesson 3–3) The principal square root of -1.

unidad imaginaria *i* La raíz cuadrada principal de -1.

inconsistent (Lesson 2–4) A system of equations with no ordered pair that satisfies both equations.

inconsistente Una sistema de ecuaciones para el cual no existe par ordenado alguno que satisfaga ambas ecuaciones.

independent (Lesson 2–4) A consistent system of equations with exactly one solution.

independiente Un sistema consistente de ecuaciones con exactamente una solución.

index (Lesson 6–3) In *n*th roots, the value that indicates to what root the value under the radicand is being taken.

índice En enésimas raíces, el valor que indica a qué raíz está el valor bajo la radicand.

inequality (Lesson 2–1) An open sentence that contains $<, >, \leq, \geq$, or $\neq$.

desigualdad Una oración abierta que contiene uno o más de $<, >, \leq, \geq$, o $\neq$.

inferential statistics (Lesson 10–5) When the data from a sample is used to make inferences about the corresponding population.

estadísticas inferencial Cuando los datos de una muestra se utilizan para hacer inferencias sobre la población correspondiente.

infinite sequence (Lesson 7–4) A sequence that continues without end.

secuencia infinita Una secuencia que continúa sin fin.

initial side (Lesson 11–1) The part of an angle that is fixed on the x-axis.

lado inicial La parte de un ángulo que se fija en el eje x.

intercept (Lesson 1–2) A point at which the graph of a function intersects an axis.

interceptar Un punto en el que la gráfica de una función corta un eje.

interval notation (Lesson 1–1) Mathematical notation that describes a set by using endpoints with parentheses or brackets.

notación de intervalo Notación matemática que describe un conjunto utilizando puntos finales con paréntesis o soportes.

inverse functions (Lesson 6–2) Two functions, one of which contains points of the form (a, b) while the other contains points of the form (b, a).

funciones inversas Dos funciones, una de las cuales contiene puntos de la forma (a, b) mientras que la otra contiene puntos de la forma (b, a).

inverse relations (Lesson 6–2) Two relations, one of which contains points of the form (a, b) while the other contains points of the form (b, a).

relaciones inversas Dos relaciones, una de las cuales contiene puntos de la forma (a, b) mientras que la otra contiene puntos de la forma (b, a).

inverse trigonometric functions (Lesson 11–7) Arcsine, Arccosine, and Arctangent.

funciones trigonométricas inversas Arcsine, Arccosine y Arctangent.

inverse variation (Lesson 9–5) When the product of two quantities is equal to a constant k.

variación inversa Cuando el producto de dos cantidades es igual a una constante k.

J

joint variation (Lesson 9–5) When one quantity varies directly as the product of two or more other quantities.

variación conjunta Cuando una cantidad varía directamente como el producto de dos o más cantidades.

L

leading coefficient (Lesson 4–1) The coefficient of the first term when a polynomial is in standard form.

coeficiente líder El coeficiente del primer término cuando un polinomio está en forma estándar.

like radical expressions (Lesson 6–5) Radicals in which both the index and the radicand are the same.

expresiones radicales semejantes Radicales en los que tanto el índice como el radicand son iguales.

line of reflection (Lesson 1–7) A line that divides a figure in such a way that one side of the figure looks like the mirror image of another side.

línea de reflexión Una línea que divide una figura de tal manera que un lado de la figura se ve como la imagen especular de otro lado.

line of symmetry (Lesson 1–2) An imaginary line that separates a figure into two congruent parts.

línea de simetría Una línea imaginaria que separa una figura en dos partes congruentes.

line symmetry (Lesson 1–2) Each half of a figure matches the other half exactly.

simetría de línea Cada mitad de una figura coincide exactamente con la otra mitad.

linear equation (Lesson 1–2) An equation that can be written in the form $Ax + By = C$ with a graph that is a straight line.

ecuación lineal Una ecuación que puede escribirse de la forma $Ax + By = C$ con un gráfico que es una línea recta.

linear function (Lesson 1–2) A function in which no independent variable is raised to a power greater than 1.

función lineal Una función en la que ninguna variable independiente se eleva a una potencia mayor que 1.

linear inequality (Lesson 1–5) A half-plane with a boundary that is a straight line.

desigualdad lineal Un medio plano con un límite que es una línea recta.

linear programming (Lesson 2–7) The process of finding the maximum or minimum values of a function for a region defined by a system of inequalities.

programación lineal El proceso de encontrar los valores máximos o mínimos de una función para una región definida por un sistema de desigualdades.

logarithm (Lesson 8–1) In the function $x = b^y$, y is called the logarithm, base b, of x.

logaritmo En la función $x = b^y$, y se denomina logaritmo, base b, de x.

logarithmic equation (Lesson 8–2) An equation that contains one or more logarithms.

ecuación logarítmica Una ecuación que contiene uno o más logaritmos.

logarithmic function (Lesson 8–1) A function of the form $f(x) =$ log base b of x, where $b > 0$ and $b \neq 1$.

función logarítmica Una función de la forma $f(x) =$ base log b de x, donde $b > 0$ y $b \neq 1$.

M

maximum (Lesson 1–3) The highest point on the graph of a curve.

máximo El punto más alto en la gráfica de una curva.

maximum error of the estimate (Lesson 10–5) The maximum difference between the estimate of the population mean and its actual value.

error máximo de la estimación La diferencia máxima entre la estimación de la media de la población y su valor real.

midline (Lesson 11–4) The line about which the graph of a function oscillates.

linea media La línea sobre la cual oscila la gráfica de una función periódica.

minimum (Lesson 1–3) The lowest point on the graph of a curve.

mínimo El punto más bajo en la gráfica de una curva.

mixture problems (Lesson 9–6) Problems that involve creating a mixture of two or more kinds of things and then determining some quantity of the resulting mixture.

problemas de mezcla Problemas que implican crear una mezcla de dos o más tipos de cosas y luego determinar una cierta cantidad de la mezcla resultante.

monomial function (Lesson 4–1) A function of the form $f(x) = ax^n$, for which a is a nonzero real number and n is a positive integer.

función monomial Una función de la forma $f(x) = ax^n$, para la cual a es un número real no nulo y n es un entero positivo.

multiplicity (Lesson 5–5) The number of times a number is a zero for a given polynomial.

multiplicidad El número de veces que un número es cero para un polinomio dado.

N

natural base exponential function (Lesson 8–4) An exponential function with base e, written as $y = e^x$.

función exponencial de base natural An exponential function with base e, written as $y = e^x$.

natural logarithm (Lesson 8–4) The inverse of the natural base exponential function, most often abbreviated as ln x.

logaritmo natural La inversa de la función exponencial de base natural, más a menudo abreviada como ln x.

negatively skewed distribution (Lesson 10–3) A distribution that typically has a median greater than the mean and less data on the left side of the graph.

distribución negativamente sesgada Una distribución que típicamente tiene una mediana mayor que la media y menos datos en el lado izquierdo del gráfico.

nonlinear function (Lesson 1–2) A function that has a graph with points that cannot all lie on the same line.

función no lineal Una función en la que un conjunto de puntos no puede estar en la misma línea.

normal distribution (Lesson 10–4) A continuous, symmetric, bell-shaped distribution of a random variable.

distribución normal Distribución con forma de campana, simétrica y continua de una variable aleatoria.

***n*th root** (Lesson 6–3) If $a^n = b$ for a positive integer n, then a is the nth root of b.

raíz enésima Si $a^n = b$ para cualquier entero positive n, entonces a se llama una raíz enésima de b.

O

oblique asymptote (Lesson 9–4) An asymptote that is neither horizontal nor vertical.

asíntota oblicua Una asíntota que no es ni horizontal ni vertical.

observational study (Lesson 10–1) Members of a sample are measured or observed without being affected by the study.

estudio de observación Los miembros de una muestra son medidos o observados sin ser afectados por el estudio.

odd functions (Lesson 1–2) Functions that are symmetric in the origin.

funciones extrañas Funciones que son simétricas en el origen.

one-to-one function (Lesson 1–1) A function for which each element of the range is paired with exactly one element of the domain.

función biunívoca Función para la cual cada elemento del rango está emparejado con exactamente un elemento del dominio.

onto function (Lesson 1–1) A function for which the codomain is the same as the range.

sobre la función Función para la cual el codomain es el mismo que el rango.

open half-plane (Lesson 1–5) The solution of a linear inequality that does not include the boundary line.

medio plano abierto La solución de una desigualdad linear que no incluye la línea de limite.

optimization (Lesson 2–7) The process of seeking the optimal price or amount that is desired to minimize costs or maximize profits.

optimización El proceso de buscar el precio óptimo o la cantidad que se desea minimizar los costos o maximizar los beneficios.

ordered triple (Lesson 2–8) Three numbers given in a specific order used to locate points in space.

triple ordenado Tres números dados en un orden específico usado para localizar puntos en el espacio.

oscillation (Lesson 11–4) How much the graph of a function varies between its extreme values as it approaches positive or negative infinity.

oscilación Cuánto la gráfica de una función varía entre sus valores extremos cuando se acerca al infinito positivo o negativo.

outcome (Lesson 10–4) The result of a single event.

resultado El resultado de un solo evento.

outlier (Lesson 10–3) A value that is more than 1.5 times the interquartile range above the third quartile or below the first quartile.

parte aislada Un valor que es más de 1,5 veces el rango intercuartílico por encima del tercer cuartil o por debajo del primer cuartil.

P

parabola (Lesson 1–2) The graph of a quadratic function.

parábola La gráfica de una función cuadrática.

parameter (Lesson 10–1) A measure that describes a characteristic of a population.

parámetro Una medida que describe una característica de una población.

parent function (Lesson 1–6) The simplest of functions in a family.

función basica La función más fundamental de un familia de funciones.

Pascal's triangle (Lesson 4–5) A triangle of numbers in which a row represents the coefficients of an expanded binomial $(a + b)^n$.

triángulo de Pascal Un triángulo de números en el que una fila representa los coeficientes de un binomio expandido $(a + b)^n$.

percent rate of change (Lesson 7–1) The percent of increase per time period.

por ciento tasa de cambio El porcentaje de aumento por período de tiempo.

perfect square trinomials (Lesson 3–4) Squares of binomials.

trinomio cuadrado perfecto Cuadrados de los binomios.

period (Lesson 11–3) The horizontal length of one cycle.

periodo La longitud horizontal de un ciclo.

periodic function (Lesson 11–3) A function with *y*-values that repeat at regular intervals.

función periódica Una función con *y*-valores aquella repetición con regularidad.

phase shift (Lesson 11–6) A horizontal translation of the graph of a trigonometric function.

cambio de fase Una traducción horizontal de la gráfica de una función trigonométrica.

piecewise-defined function (Lesson 1–6) A function defined by at least two subfunctions, each of which is defined differently depending on the interval of the domain.

función definida por piezas Una función definida por al menos dos subfunciones, cada una de las cuales se define de manera diferente dependiendo del intervalo del dominio.

point discontinuity (Lesson 9–4) An area that appears to be a hole in a graph.

discontinuidad de punto Un área que parece ser un agujero en un gráfico.

point of symmetry (Lesson 1–2) The point about which a graph is rotated.

punto de simetría El punto sobre el que se gira un gráfico.

point symmetry (Lesson 1–2) A figure or graph has this when a figure is rotated 180° about a point and maps exactly onto the other part.

simetría de punto Una figura o gráfica tiene esto cuando una figura se gira 180 ° alrededor de un punto y se mapea exactamente sobre la otra parte.

polynomial (Lesson 4–1) A monomial or the sum of two or more monomials.

polinomio Un monomio o la suma de dos o más monomios.

polynomial function (Lesson 4–1) A continuous function that can be described by a polynomial equation in one variable.

función polinómica Función continua que puede describirse mediante una ecuación polinómica en una variable.

polynomial identity (Lesson 5–3) A polynomial equation that is true for any values that are substituted for the variables.

identidad polinomial Una ecuación polinómica que es verdadera para cualquier valor que se sustituya por las variables.

population (Lesson 10–1) All of the members of a group of interest about which data will be collected.

población Todos los miembros de un grupo de interés sobre cuáles datos serán recopilados.

population proportion (Lesson 10–5) The number of members in the population with a particular characteristic divided by the total number of members in the population.

proporción de la población El número de miembros en la población con una característica particular dividida por el número total de miembros en la población.

positively skewed distribution (Lesson 10–3) A distribution that typically has a mean greater than the median.

distribución positivamente sesgada Una distribución que típicamente tiene una media mayor que la mediana.

power function (Lesson 4–1) A function of the form $f(x) = ax^n$, where a and n are nonzero real numbers.

función de potencia Una ecuación polinomial que es verdadera para una función de la forma $f(x) = ax^n$, donde a y n son números reales no nulos.

prime polynomial (Lesson 5–2) A polynomial that cannot be written as a product of two polynomials with integer coefficients.

polinomio primo Un polinomio que no puede escribirse como producto de dos polinomios con coeficientes enteros.

principal root (Lesson 6–3) The nonnegative root of a number.

raíz principal La raíz no negativa de un número.

principal values (Lesson 11–7) The values in the restricted domains of trigonometric functions.

valores principales Valores de los dominios restringidos de las functiones trigonométricas.

probability (Lesson 10–2) The number of outcomes in which a specified event occurs to the total number of trials.

probabilidad El número de resultados en los que se produce un evento especificado al número total de ensayos.

probability distribution (Lesson 10–4) A function that maps the sample space to the probabilities of the outcomes in the sample space for a particular random variable.

distribución de probabilidad Una función que mapea el espacio de muestra a las probabilidades de los resultados en el espacio de muestra para una variable aleatoria particular.

probability model (Lesson 10–2) A mathematical representation of a random event that consists of the sample space and the probability of each outcome.

modelo de probabilidad Una representación matemática de un evento aleatorio que consiste en el espacio muestral y la probabilidad de cada resultado.

projectile motion problems (Lesson 3–5) Problems that involve objects being thrown or dropped.

problemas de movimiento del proyectil Problemas que involucran objetos que se lanzan o caen.

pure imaginary number (Lesson 3–3) A number of the form bi, where b is a real number and i is the imaginary unit.

número imaginario puro Un número de la forma bi, donde b es un número real e i es la unidad imaginaria.

Pythagorean identities (Lesson 12–1) Identities that express the Pythagorean Theorem in terms of the trigonometric functions.

identidades pitagóricas Identidades que expresan el Teorema de Pitágoras en términos de las funciones trigonométricas.

Q

quadrantal angle (Lesson 11–2) An angle in standard position with a terminal side that coincides with one of the axes.

ángulo de cuadrante Un ángulo en posición estándar con un lado terminal que coincide con uno de los ejes.

quadratic equation (Lesson 3–2) An equation that includes a quadratic expression.

ecuación cuadrática Una ecuación que incluye una expresión cuadrática.

quadratic form (Lesson 5–2) A form of polynomial equation, $au^2 + bu + c$, where u is an algebraic expression in x.

forma cuadrática Una forma de ecuación polinomial, $au^2 + bu + c$, donde u es una expresión algebraica en x.

quadratic function (Lesson 3–1) A function with a graph that is a parabola.

función cuadrática Una función con una gráfica que es una parábola.

quadratic inequality (Lesson 3–7) An inequality that includes a quadratic expression.

desigualdad cuadrática Una desigualdad que incluye una expresión cuadrática.

quadratic relations (Lesson 3–8) Equations of parabolas with horizontal axes of symmetry that are not functions.

relaciones cuadráticas Ecuaciones de parábolas con ejes horizontales de simetría que no son funciones.

quartic function (Lesson 4–1) A fourth-degree function.

función cuartica Una función de cuarto grado.

quintic function (Lesson 4–1) A fifth-degree function.

función quíntica Una función de quinto grado.

R

radian (Lesson 11–1) A unit of angular measurement equal to $\frac{180°}{\pi}$ or about 57.296°.

radián Una unidad de medida angular igual o $\frac{180°}{\pi}$ alrededor de 57.296°.

radical equation (Lesson 6–6) An equation with a variable in a radicand.

ecuación radical Una ecuación con una variable en un radicand.

radical form (Lesson 6–3) When an expression contains a radical symbol.

forma radical Cuando una expresión contiene un símbolo radical.

radical function (Lesson 6–4) A function that contains radicals with variables in the radicand.

función radical Función que contiene radicales con variables en el radicand.

radicand (Lesson 6–3) The expression under a radical sign.

radicando La expresión debajo del signo radical.

range (Lesson 1–1) The set of y-values that actually result from the evaluation of the function.

rango El conjunto de valores y que realmente resultan de la evaluación de la función.

rate of change (Lesson 3–1) How a quantity is changing with respect to a change in another quantity.

tasa de cambio Cómo cambia una cantidad con respecto a un cambio en otra cantidad.

rational equation (Lesson 9–6) An equation that contains at least one rational expression.

ecuación racional Una ecuación que contiene al menos una expresión racional.

rational exponent (Lesson 6–3) An exponent that is expressed as a fraction.

exponente racional Un exponente que se expresa como una fracción.

rational expression (Lesson 9–1) A ratio of two polynomial expressions.

expresión racional Una relación de dos expresiones polinomiales.

rational function (Lesson 9–4) An equation of the form $f(x) = \frac{a(x)}{b(x)}$, where $a(x)$ and $b(x)$ are polynomial expressions and $b(x) \neq 0$.

función racional Una ecuación de la forma $f(x) = \frac{a(x)}{b(x)}$, donde $a(x)$ y $b(x)$ son expresiones polinomiales y $b(x) \neq 0$.

rational inequality (Lesson 9–6) An inequality that contains at least one rational expression.

desigualdad racional Una desigualdad que contiene al menos una expresión racional.

rationalizing the denominator (Lesson 3–3) A method used to eliminate radicals from the denominator of a fraction or fractions from a radicand.

racionalizando el denominador Método utilizado para eliminar radicales del denominador de una fracción o fracciones de una radicand.

reciprocal function (Lesson 9–2) An equation of the form $f(x) = \frac{n}{b(x)}$, where n is a real number and $b(x)$ is a linear expression that cannot equal 0.

función recíproca Una ecuación de la forma $f(x) = \frac{n}{b(x)}$, donde n es un número real y $b(x)$ es una expresión lineal que no puede ser igual a 0.

reciprocal trigonometric functions (Lesson 11–5) Trigonometric functions that are reciprocals of each other.

funciones trigonométricas recíprocas Funciones trigonométricas que son reciprocales entre sí.

recursive formula (Lesson 7–4) A formula that gives the value of the first term in the sequence and then defines the next term by using the preceding term.

fórmula recursiva Una fórmula que da el valor del primer término en la secuencia y luego define el siguiente término usando el término anterior.

reference angle (Lesson 11–2) The acute angle formed by the terminal side of an angle and the x-axis.

ángulo de referencia El ángulo agudo formado por el lado terminal de un ángulo en posición estándar y el eje x.

reflection (Lesson 1–7) A transformation in which a figure, line, or curve is flipped across a line.

reflexión Una transformación en la que una figura, línea o curva se voltea a través de una línea.

regression function (Lesson 7–5) A function generated by an algorithm to find a line or curve that fits a set of data.

función de regresión Función generada por un algoritmo para encontrar una línea o curva que se ajuste a un conjunto de datos.

relative maximum (Lesson 1–3) A point on the graph of a function where no other nearby points have a greater y-coordinate.

máximo relativo Un punto en la gráfica de una función donde ningún otro punto cercano tiene una coordenada y mayor.

relative minimum (Lesson 1–3) A point on the graph of a function where no other nearby points have a lesser y-coordinate.

mínimo relativo Un punto en la gráfica de una función donde ningún otro punto cercano tiene una coordenada y menor.

root (Lesson 2–1) A solution of an equation.

raíz Una solución de una ecuación.

S

sample (Lesson 10–1) A subset of a population.

muestra Un subconjunto de una población.

sample space (Lesson 10–4) The set of all possible outcomes.

espacio muestral El conjunto de todos los resultados posibles.

sampling error (Lesson 10–5) The variation between samples taken from the same population.

error de muestreo La variación entre muestras tomadas de la misma población.

secant (Lesson 11–2) The ratio of the length of the hypotenuse to the length of the leg adjacent to the angle.

secante Relación entre la longitud de la hipotenusa y la longitud de la pierna adyacente al ángulo.

self-selected sample (Lesson 10–1) Members volunteer to be included in the sample.

muestra auto-seleccionada Los miembros se ofrecen como voluntarios para ser incluidos en la muestra.

sequence (Lesson 7–4) A list of numbers in a specific order.

secuencia Una lista de números en un orden específico.

series (Lesson 7–4) The indicated sum of the terms in a sequence.

serie La suma indicada de los términos en una secuencia.

set-builder notation (Lesson 1–1) Mathematical notation that describes a set by stating the properties that its members must satisfy.

notación de construción de conjuntos Notación matemática que describe un conjunto al declarar las propiedades que sus miembros deben satisfacer.

sigma notation (Lesson 7–4) A notation that uses the Greek uppercase letter S to indicate that a sum should be found.

notación de sigma Una notación que utiliza la letra mayúscula griega S para indicar que debe encontrarse una suma.

simple random sample (Lesson 10–1) Each member of the population has an equal chance of being selected as part of the sample.

muestra aleatoria simple Cada miembro de la población tiene la misma posibilidad de ser seleccionado como parte de la muestra.

simulation (Lesson 10–2) The use of a probability model to imitate a process or situation so it can be studied.

simulación El uso de un modelo de probabilidad para imitar un proceso o situación para que pueda ser estudiado.

sine (Lesson 10–2) The ratio of the length of the leg opposite an angle to the length of the hypotenuse.

seno La relación entre la longitud de la pierna opuesta a un ángulo y la longitud de la hipotenusa.

sinusoidal function (Lesson 11–4) A function that can be produced by translating, reflecting, or dilating the sine function.

función sinusoidal Función que puede producirse traduciendo, reflejando o dilatando la función sinusoidal.

solution (Lesson 2–1) A value that makes an equation true.

solución Un valor que hace que una ecuación sea verdadera.

square root function (Lesson 6–4) A radical function that contains the square root of a variable expression.

función raíz cuadrada Función radical que contiene la raíz cuadrada de una expresión variable.

square root inequality (Lesson 6–4) An inequality that contains the square root of a variable expression.

square root inequality Una desigualdad que contiene la raíz cuadrada de una expresión variable.

standard deviation (Lesson 10–3) A measure that shows how data deviate from the mean.

desviación estándar Una medida que muestra cómo los datos se desvían de la media.

standard error of the mean (Lesson 10–5) The standard deviation of the distribution of sample means taken from a population.

error estandar de la media La desviación estándar de la distribución de los medios de muestra se toma de una población.

standard form of a linear equation (Lesson 2–3) Any linear equation can be written in this form, $Ax + By = C$, where $A \geq 0$, A and B are not both 0, and A, B, and C are integers with a greatest common factor of 1.

forma estándar de una ecuación lineal Cualquier ecuación lineal se puede escribir de esta forma, $Ax + By = C$, donde $A \geq 0$, A y B no son ambos 0, y A, B y C son enteros con el mayor factor común de 1.

standard form of a polynomial (Lesson 4–1) The terms of a polynomial written in order from greatest to least degree.

forma estándar de un polinomio Un polinomio que se escribe con los términos en orden del grado más grande a menos grado.

standard form of a quadratic equation (Lesson 3–2) A quadratic equation can be written in the form $ax^2 + bx + c = 0$, where $a \neq 0$ and a, b, and c are integers.

forma estándar de una ecuación cuadrática Una ecuación cuadrática puede escribirse en la forma $ax^2 + bx + c = 0$, donde $a \neq 0$ y a, b, y c son enteros.

standard normal distribution (Lesson 10–4) A normal distribution with a mean of 0 and a standard deviation of 1.

distribución normal estándar Distribución normal con una media de 0 y una desviación estándar de 1.

standard position (Lesson 11–1) An angle positioned so that the vertex is at the origin and the initial side is on the positive x-axis.

posición estándar Un ángulo colocado de manera que el vértice está en el origen y el lado inicial está en el eje x positivo.

statistic (Lesson 10–1) A measure that describes a characteristic of a sample.

estadística Una medida que describe una característica de una muestra.

statistics (Lesson 10–1) An area of mathematics that deals with collecting, analyzing, and interpreting data.

estadísticas El proceso de recolección, análisis e interpretación de datos.

step function (Lesson 1–6) A type of piecewise-linear function with a graph that is a series of horizontal line segments.

función escalonada Un tipo de función lineal por piezas con un gráfico que es una serie de segmentos de línea horizontal.

stratified sample (Lesson 10–1) The population is first divided into similar, nonoverlapping groups. Then members are randomly selected from each group.

muestra estratificada La población se divide primero en grupos similares, sin superposición. A continuación, los miembros se seleccionan aleatoriamente de cada grupo.

substitution (Lesson 2–5) A process of solving a system of equations in which one equation is solved for one variable in terms of the other.

sustitución Un proceso de resolución de un sistema de ecuaciones en el que una ecuación se resuelve para una variable en términos de la otra.

survey (Lesson 10–1) Data are collected from responses given by members of a group regarding their characteristics, behaviors, or opinions.

encuesta Los datos se recogen de las respuestas dadas por los miembros de un grupo con respecto a sus características, comportamientos u opiniones.

symmetric distribution (Lesson 10–3) A distribution in which the mean and median are approximately equal.

distribución simétrica Un distribución en la que la media y la mediana son aproximadamente iguales.

symmetry (Lesson 1–2) A figure has this if there exists a rigid motion—reflection, translation, rotation, or glide reflection—that maps the figure onto itself.

simetría Una figura tiene esto si existe una reflexión-reflexión, una traducción, una rotación o una reflexión de deslizamiento rígida-que mapea la figura sobre sí misma.

synthetic division (Lesson 4–4) An alternate method used to divide a polynomial by a binomial of degree 1.

división sintética Un método alternativo utilizado para dividir un polinomio por un binomio de grado 1.

synthetic substitution (Lesson 5–4) The process of using synthetic division to find a value of a polynomial function.

sustitución sintética El proceso de utilizar la división sintética para encontrar un valor de una función polynomial.

systematic sample (Lesson 10–1) Members are selected according to a specified interval from a random starting point.

muestra sistemática Los miembros se seleccionan de acuerdo con un intervalo especificado desde un punto de partida aleatorio.

system of equations (Lesson 2–4) A set of two or more equations with the same variables.

sistema de ecuaciones Un conjunto de dos o más ecuaciones con las mismas variables.

system of inequalities (Lesson 2–6) A set of two or more inequalities with the same variables.

sistema de desigualdades Un conjunto de dos o más desigualdades con las mismas variables.

T

tangent (Lesson 11–2) The ratio of the length of the leg opposite an angle to the length of the leg adjacent to the angle.

tangente La relación entre la longitud de la pata opuesta a un ángulo y la longitud de la pata adyacente al ángulo.

terminal side (Lesson 11–1) The part of an angle that rotates about the center.

lado terminal La parte de un ángulo que gira alrededor de un centro.

term of a sequence (Lesson 7–4) A number in a sequence.

término de una sucesión Un número en una secuencia.

theoretical probability (Lesson 10–2) Probability based on what is expected to happen.

probabilidad teórica Probabilidad basada en lo que se espera que suceda.

transformation (Lesson 1–7) The movement of a graph on the coordinate plane.

transformación El movimiento de un gráfico en el plano de coordenadas.

translation (Lesson 1–7) A transformation in which a figure is slid from one position to another without being turned.

translación El movimiento de un gráfico en el plano de coordenadas.

trigonometric equation (Lesson 12–5) An equation that includes at least one trigonometric function.

ecuación trigonométrica Una ecuación que incluye al menos una función trigonométrica.

trigonometric function (Lesson 11–2) A function that relates the measure of one nonright angle of a right triangle to the ratios of the lengths of any two sides of the triangle.

función trigonométrica Función que relaciona la medida de un ángulo no recto de un triángulo rectángulo con las relaciones de las longitudes de cualquiera de los dos lados del triángulo.

trigonometric identity (Lesson 12–1) An equation involving trigonometric functions that is true for all values for which every expression in the equation is defined.

identidad trigonométrica Una ecuación que implica funciones trigonométricas que es verdadera para todos los valores para los cuales se define cada expresión en la ecuación.

trigonometric ratio (Lesson 11–2) A ratio of the lengths of two sides of a right triangle.

relación trigonométrica Una relación de las longitudes de dos lados de un triángulo rectángulo.

trigonometry (Lesson 11–2) The study of the relationships between the sides and angles of triangles.

trigonometría El estudio de las relaciones entre los lados y los ángulos de los triángulos.

trinomial (Lesson 4–3) The sum of three monomials.

trinomio La suma de tres monomios.

turning point (Lesson 4–2) A change in direction of a graph.

punto de retorno Un cambio en la dirección de un gráfico.

U

unbounded (Lesson 2–6) When the graph of a system of constraints is open.

no acotado Cuando la gráfica de un sistema de restricciones está abierta.

uniform motion problems (Lesson 9–6) Problems that use the formula $d = rt$, where d is the distance, r is the rate, and t is the time.

problemas de movimiento uniforme Problemas que utilizan la fórmula $d = rt$, donde d es la distancia, r es la velocidad y t es el tiempo.

unit circle (Lesson 11–3) A circle with a radius of 1 unit centered at the origin on the coordinate plane.

círculo unitario Un círculo con un radio de 1 unidad centrado en el origen en el plano de coordenadas.

variance (Lesson 10–3) The square of the standard deviation.

varianza El cuadrado de la desviación estándar.

vertex (Lesson 3–1) Either the lowest point or the highest point on a parabola.

vértice El punto más bajo o el punto más alto de una parábola.

vertex form (Lesson 3–5) A quadratic function written in the form $f(x) = a(x - h)^2 + k$.

forma de vértice Una función cuadrática escribirse de la forma $f(x) = a(x - h)^2 + k$.

vertical asymptote (Lesson 9–2) A vertical line that a graph approaches.

asíntota vertical Una línea vertical que se aproxima a un gráfico.

vertical shift (Lesson 11–6) A vertical translation of the graph of a trigonometric function.

cambio vertical Una traducción vertical de la gráfica de una función trigonométrica.

work problems (Lesson 9–6) Problems that involve two people working at different rates who are trying to complete a single job.

problemas de trabajo Problemas que involucran a dos personas trabajando a diferentes ritmos que están tratando de completar un solo trabajo.

X

***x*-intercept** (Lesson 1–2) The x-coordinate of a point where a graph crosses the x-axis.

intercepción *x* La coordenada x de un punto donde la gráfica corte al eje de x.

Y

***y*-intercept** (Lesson 1–2) The y-coordinate of a point where a graph crosses the y-axis.

intercepción *y* La coordenada y de un punto donde la gráfica corte al eje de y.

Z

zero (Lesson 2–1) The x-intercept of the graph of a function; the value of x for which $f(x) = 0$.

cero La intercepción x de la gráfica de una función; el punto x para los que $f(x) = 0$.

***z*-value** (Lesson 10–4) The number of standard deviations that a given data value is from the mean.

valor *z* El número de variaciones estándar que separa un valor dado de la media.

Index

Q

R

S

T

Standard Normal Cumulative Probability Table

Cumulative probabilities for negative z-values are shown in the following table.

z	0.00	0.01	0.02	0.03	0.04	0.05	0.06	0.07	0.08	0.09
−3.4	0.0003	0.0003	0.0003	0.0003	0.0003	0.0003	0.0003	0.0003	0.0003	0.0002
−3.3	0.0005	0.0005	0.0005	0.0004	0.0004	0.0004	0.0004	0.0004	0.0004	0.0003
−3.2	0.0007	0.0007	0.0006	0.0006	0.0006	0.0006	0.0006	0.0005	0.0005	0.0005
−3.1	0.0010	0.0009	0.0009	0.0009	0.0008	0.0008	0.0008	0.0008	0.0007	0.0007
−3.0	0.0013	0.0013	0.0013	0.0012	0.0012	0.0011	0.0011	0.0011	0.0010	0.0010
−2.9	0.0019	0.0018	0.0018	0.0017	0.0016	0.0016	0.0015	0.0015	0.0014	0.0014
−2.8	0.0026	0.0025	0.0024	0.0023	0.0023	0.0022	0.0021	0.0021	0.0020	0.0019
−2.7	0.0035	0.0034	0.0033	0.0032	0.0031	0.0030	0.0029	0.0028	0.0027	0.0026
−2.6	0.0047	0.0045	0.0044	0.0043	0.0041	0.0040	0.0039	0.0038	0.0037	0.0036
−2.5	0.0062	0.0060	0.0059	0.0057	0.0055	0.0054	0.0052	0.0051	0.0049	0.0048
−2.4	0.0082	0.0080	0.0078	0.0075	0.0073	0.0071	0.0069	0.0068	0.0066	0.0064
−2.3	0.0107	0.0104	0.0102	0.0099	0.0096	0.0094	0.0091	0.0089	0.0087	0.0084
−2.2	0.0139	0.0136	0.0132	0.0129	0.0125	0.0122	0.0119	0.0116	0.0113	0.0110
−2.1	0.0179	0.0174	0.0170	0.0166	0.0162	0.0158	0.0154	0.0150	0.0146	0.0143
−2.0	0.0228	0.0222	0.0217	0.0212	0.0207	0.0202	0.0197	0.0192	0.0188	0.0183
−1.9	0.0287	0.0281	0.0274	0.0268	0.0262	0.0256	0.0250	0.0244	0.0239	0.0233
−1.8	0.0359	0.0351	0.0344	0.0336	0.0329	0.0322	0.0314	0.0307	0.0301	0.0294
−1.7	0.0446	0.0436	0.0427	0.0418	0.0409	0.0401	0.0392	0.0384	0.0375	0.0367
−1.6	0.0548	0.0537	0.0526	0.0516	0.0505	0.0495	0.0485	0.0475	0.0465	0.0455
−1.5	0.0668	0.0655	0.0643	0.0630	0.0618	0.0606	0.0594	0.0582	0.0571	0.0559
−1.4	0.0808	0.0793	0.0778	0.0764	0.0749	0.0735	0.0721	0.0708	0.0694	0.0681
−1.3	0.0968	0.0951	0.0934	0.0918	0.0901	0.0885	0.0869	0.0853	0.0838	0.0823
−1.2	0.1151	0.1131	0.1112	0.1093	0.1075	0.1056	0.1038	0.1020	0.1003	0.0985
−1.1	0.1357	0.1335	0.1314	0.1292	0.1271	0.1251	0.1230	0.1210	0.1190	0.1170
−1.0	0.1587	0.1562	0.1539	0.1515	0.1492	0.1469	0.1446	0.1423	0.1401	0.1379
−0.9	0.1841	0.1814	0.1788	0.1762	0.1736	0.1711	0.1685	0.1660	0.1635	0.1611
−0.8	0.2119	0.2090	0.2061	0.2033	0.2005	0.1977	0.1949	0.1922	0.1894	0.1867
−0.7	0.2420	0.2389	0.2358	0.2327	0.2296	0.2266	0.2236	0.2206	0.2177	0.2148
−0.6	0.2743	0.2709	0.2676	0.2643	0.2611	0.2578	0.2546	0.2514	0.2483	0.2451
−0.5	0.3085	0.3050	0.3015	0.2981	0.2946	0.2912	0.2877	0.2843	0.2810	0.2776
−0.4	0.3446	0.3409	0.3372	0.3336	0.3300	0.3264	0.3228	0.3192	0.3156	0.3121
−0.3	0.3821	0.3783	0.3745	0.3707	0.3669	0.3632	0.3594	0.3557	0.3520	0.3483
−0.2	0.4207	0.4168	0.4129	0.4090	0.4052	0.4013	0.3974	0.3936	0.3897	0.3859
−0.1	0.4602	0.4562	0.4522	0.4483	0.4443	0.4404	0.4364	0.4325	0.4286	0.4247
0.0	0.5000	0.4960	0.4920	0.4880	0.4840	0.4801	0.4761	0.4721	0.4681	0.4641

Standard Normal Cumulative Probability Table

Cumulative probabilities for positive z-values are shown in the following table.

z	0.00	0.01	0.02	0.03	0.04	0.05	0.06	0.07	0.08	0.
0.0	0.5000	0.5040	0.5080	0.5120	0.5160	0.5199	0.5239	0.5279	0.5319	0.5
0.1	0.5398	0.5438	0.5478	0.5517	0.5557	0.5596	0.5636	0.5675	0.5714	0.5
0.2	0.5793	0.5832	0.5871	0.5910	0.5948	0.5987	0.6026	0.6064	0.6103	0.6
0.3	0.6179	0.6217	0.6255	0.6293	0.6331	0.6368	0.6406	0.6443	0.6480	0.6
0.4	0.6554	0.6591	0.6628	0.6664	0.6700	0.6736	0.6772	0.6808	0.6844	0.6
0.5	0.6915	0.6950	0.6985	0.7019	0.7054	0.7088	0.7123	0.7157	0.7190	0.7
0.6	0.7257	0.7291	0.7324	0.7357	0.7389	0.7422	0.7454	0.7486	0.7517	0.7
0.7	0.7580	0.7611	0.7642	0.7673	0.7704	0.7734	0.7764	0.7794	0.7823	0.7
0.8	0.7881	0.7910	0.7939	0.7967	0.7995	0.8023	0.8051	0.8078	0.8106	0.8
0.9	0.8159	0.8186	0.8212	0.8238	0.8264	0.8289	0.8315	0.8340	0.8365	0.8
1.0	0.8413	0.8438	0.8461	0.8485	0.8508	0.8531	0.8554	0.8577	0.8599	0.8
1.1	0.8643	0.8665	0.8686	0.8708	0.8729	0.8749	0.8770	0.8790	0.8810	0.8
1.2	0.8849	0.8869	0.8888	0.8907	0.8925	0.8944	0.8962	0.8980	0.8997	0.9
1.3	0.9032	0.9049	0.9066	0.9082	0.9099	0.9115	0.9131	0.9147	0.9162	0.9
1.4	0.9192	0.9207	0.9222	0.9236	0.9251	0.9265	0.9279	0.9292	0.9306	0.9
1.5	0.9332	0.9345	0.9357	0.9370	0.9382	0.9394	0.9406	0.9418	0.9429	0.9
1.6	0.9452	0.9463	0.9474	0.9484	0.9495	0.9505	0.9515	0.9525	0.9535	0.9
1.7	0.9554	0.9564	0.9573	0.9582	0.9591	0.9599	0.9608	0.9616	0.9625	0.9
1.8	0.9641	0.9649	0.9656	0.9664	0.9671	0.9678	0.9686	0.9693	0.9699	0.9
1.9	0.9713	0.9719	0.9726	0.9732	0.9738	0.9744	0.9750	0.9756	0.9761	0.9
2.0	0.9772	0.9778	0.9783	0.9788	0.9793	0.9798	0.9803	0.9808	0.9812	0.9
2.1	0.9821	0.9826	0.9830	0.9834	0.9838	0.9842	0.9846	0.9850	0.9854	0.9
2.2	0.9861	0.9864	0.9868	0.9871	0.9875	0.9878	0.9881	0.9884	0.9887	0.9
2.3	0.9893	0.9896	0.9898	0.9901	0.9904	0.9906	0.9909	0.9911	0.9913	0.9
2.4	0.9918	0.9920	0.9922	0.9925	0.9927	0.9929	0.9931	0.9932	0.9934	0.9
2.5	0.9938	0.9940	0.9941	0.9943	0.9945	0.9946	0.9948	0.9949	0.9951	0.9
2.6	0.9953	0.9955	0.9956	0.9957	0.9959	0.9960	0.9961	0.9962	0.9963	0.9
2.7	0.9965	0.9966	0.9967	0.9968	0.9969	0.9970	0.9971	0.9972	0.9973	0.9
2.8	0.9974	0.9975	0.9976	0.9977	0.9977	0.9978	0.9979	0.9979	0.9980	0.9
2.9	0.9981	0.9982	0.9982	0.9983	0.9984	0.9984	0.9985	0.9985	0.9986	0.9
3.0	0.9987	0.9987	0.9987	0.9988	0.9988	0.9989	0.9989	0.9989	0.9990	0.9
3.1	0.9990	0.9991	0.9991	0.9991	0.9992	0.9992	0.9992	0.9992	0.9993	0.9
3.2	0.9993	0.9993	0.9994	0.9994	0.9994	0.9994	0.9994	0.9995	0.9995	0.9
3.3	0.9995	0.9995	0.9995	0.9996	0.9996	0.9996	0.9996	0.9996	0.9996	0.9
3.4	0.9997	0.9997	0.9997	0.9997	0.9997	0.9997	0.9997	0.9997	0.9997	0.9